# Delaware-English / English-Delaware Dictionary

Munsee Delaware, an Eastern Algonquian language, is spoken by a small and steadily declining number of individuals. The Delaware-speaking peoples originally lived in the area of what is now New York City, adjacent regions of New York State, New Jersey, Pennsylvania, and Delaware. Today, a small number of speakers of the closely related Unami Delaware language are located in Oklahoma, and, of the three sites where Munsee Delaware was the predominant Delaware language spoken in Canada, only Moraviantown, Ontario, has surviving speakers.

Based on linguistic research carried out with Delaware speakers at Moraviantown, this is the first modern dictionary of Munsee Delaware. Each of the 7,100 entries in the Delaware-English section includes information on the word's grammatical category and gives examples of different inflected forms where appropriate. Also included are sample sentences used by Delaware speakers, grammatical and usage notes, cross-references, and indications of words borrowed from Dutch and English. The English-Delaware section functions as an index to the Delaware-English section, and is based on the major vocabulary.

JOHN O'MEARA is an associate professor in the Native Language Instructor's Program, Faculty of Education, Lakehead University.

JOHN O'MEARA

# Delaware-English / English-Delaware Dictionary

UNIVERSITY OF TORONTO PRESS
Toronto Buffalo London

Toronto Buffalo London
www.utppublishing.com
Printed in the U.S.A.

Reprinted in paperback 2014

ISBN 978-0-8020-0670-7 (cloth)
ISBN 978-1-4426-2710-9 (paper)

Printed on acid-free paper

**Library and Archives Canada Cataloguing in Publication**

O'Meara, John, 1954–
Delaware-English, English-Delaware dictionary / John O'Meara.

ISBN 978-0-8020-0670-7 (bound). – ISBN 978-1-4426-2710-9 (pbk.)

1. Delaware language – Dictionaries – English. 2. English language – Dictionaries – Delaware. I. Title

PM1033.O54 1996 497'.3 C959-32374-0

All royalties from the sale of this work are paid to the Delaware Language Development and Training Fund, Delaware Nation Council.

Financial support of this publication has been provided by the Government of Ontario through the Ministry of Education and Training.

University of Toronto Press acknowledges the financial assistance to its publishing program of the Canada Council for the Arts and the Ontario Arts Council.

University of Toronto Press acknowledges the financial support for its publishing activities of the Government of Canada through the Canada Book Fund.

# Contents

# Preface

What follows is a dictionary of Ontario Delaware, the aboriginal language spoken at Moraviantown, Ontario, approximately fifty miles southwest of London, Ontario. The history of the Delaware-speaking peoples is long and complex; over the past three hundred or so years they have migrated from their original homeland in the area of Manhattan Island to a variety of locations in the United States and Canada. A summary of Delaware history may be found in Goddard (1978). The language of the Delawares at Moraviantown is frequently referred to by linguists as Munsee or Munsee Delaware, while Delawares residing at Moraviantown refer to it simply as Delaware. Here we follow the practice of Moraviantown residents and use the term Delaware, or, when more precision is required, Ontario Delaware. Ontario Delaware is distinct from the closely related Unami Delaware language, which is still spoken by probably no more than five individuals in Oklahoma. Goddard (1974a) contains a discussion of names for Delaware groups.

This dictionary is hardly the final word in Delaware lexicography. It reflects material which I collected during the 1980s and the 1990s. Inevitably there are some Delaware words which did not make their way into the dictionary simply because I did not happen to hear them. As well there are many cases in which speakers were uncertain about the Delaware equivalent of an English word, or about Delaware terms which I had obtained from other sources.

Ontario Delaware is spoken by a small and steadily declining number of individuals, all at or from Moraviantown. There may be no more than five or ten speakers of Ontario Delaware, as well as perhaps ten or fifteen individuals who understand Delaware to varying degrees. Most speakers known to me are in their seventies or eighties. Although there were speakers of Ontario Delaware at Six Nations and Munceytown, Ontario, as recently as the 1970s, the decline of the language has meant that Moraviantown is now the last location where it is spoken. The language was also spoken in other locations in the United States during the late nineteenth and early twentieth centuries, as is reflected in the material collected by Truman Michelson (1912) in Kansas and by J.N.B. Hewitt (1896) at Cattaraugus, New York.

Several publications by Ives Goddard have greatly improved my understanding of Delaware, notably Goddard (1979) and Goddard (1982). These important works have enabled me to focus on other aspects of Delaware. I have also examined a variety of existing publications and manuscripts which contain Delaware words. These include Brinton (1888), Brinton and Anthony (1888), Harrington (1908), Prince (1900, 1902), Speck (1946), Speck and Moses (1945), and Wampum and Hogg (1887).

This dictionary will, I hope, be of interest to multiple audiences: Delawares who wish to know something of their tribal language, students of Algonquian languages, and more generally anyone who wishes to find information about words and their usage in this interesting language. The structure of the dictionary reflects my desire to accommodate different users in several respects, most notably the choice of orthography and the information included in dictionary entries. Both of these are discussed in more detail below.

## Acknowledgments

A number of Delaware speakers have helped me to learn about their language, and this is reflected in the contents of this dictionary. During 1980 and 1981 I worked primarily with the late Mrs. Emily Johnson (deceased 1985), and during 1984 and 1985 primarily with the late Mrs. Ethel Peters (deceased 1988) and Mrs. Beulah Timothy. Since 1992 I have worked extensively with Mrs. Timothy. Lesser amounts of time were spent working with Mr. Enoch Jacobs (deceased 1981), Mrs. Mattie Huff, Mrs. Nellie Noah (deceased 1992), Mr. Peter Noah (deceased 1988), and Mrs. Rebecca Snake (deceased 1983). I am extremely grateful to all of these individuals, but particularly to Mrs. Timothy for her assistance with the detailed work of collecting and reviewing dictionary material from 1993 to 1995.

My original research on Delaware was supported by the Canadian Ethnology Service of the National Museum of Man (now the National Museum of Civilization) under Personal Service Contracts 1630-0-132 and 1630-4M-030. Work on the dictionary itself from 1993 to 1995 has been supported by the Ontario Training and Adjustment Board, an agency of the Ontario Ministry of Education and Training, in conjunction with myself and the Delaware Nation Council, Moravian of the Thames Band, at Moraviantown, Ontario. I wish to thank these organizations for their assistance, which has been essential to the completion of this undertaking. I am grateful to Chief Philip Snake and the council for their support of this project, and to Dianne Snake for her help during this project and more generally in my previous work on Delaware. I am also grateful to former Chief Richard Snake and the late Chief John Peters, and former council members for their support of my work at Moraviantown.

# Guide to Using the Dictionary

## Linguistic Variation

This dictionary no doubt underrepresents the total amount of linguistic variation in Delaware as spoken by the last few generations of Delaware speakers, particularly given that the bulk of my information comes primarily from a small number of speakers with more or less incidental information obtained from others. Phonological variation is a significant phenomenon in Delaware. Some of this variation is directly reflected within entries for verbs, where, as noted in the section on grammatical forms, we give alternative pronunciations for certain inflected forms. Preverbs, prenouns, particles, and some verb endings are also subject to variation. Final long vowels may be shortened, reduced to *-u*, and in some cases deleted. For example, the particle meaning 'have to, must' may be realized as *áskii*, reduplicated *ayásku*, or *ásk*, while the preverb meaning 'because' may be realized as *éeli-* or *éel-*.

No attempt is made to normalize these variants and whatever variants were collected are listed separately and cross-referenced, with *See* references.

The following represents my understanding of the parameters of phonological variation in Delaware. The variants with reduced or deleted vowels represent an informal style. Entries for these variants include the designation *informal*, in italics. Although variant forms can be placed on a scale of formality, it is my experience that some speakers invariably (or primarily) use either the more or less formal variants. In dictionary entries I have not attempted to categorize individual speakers along this parameter.

## Dictionary Entries

In this section I explain first the structure of dictionary entries in the Delaware-English section, and then in the English-Delaware section. In preparing the layout of dictionary entries I have been influenced by studying several dictionaries of languages related to Delaware. These include Baraga (1878), Frantz and Russell (1989), Leavitt and Francis (1984), Nichols and Nyholm (1979), Piggott and Grafstein (1983), and Rhodes (1985).

### *Delaware-English*

In the Delaware-English section, Delaware words and sentences are written in bold type. English translations are written in plain type, with optional supplementary information (in parentheses) presented in italics following the main translation. Italic type is also used for English introductions to inflected forms of Delaware words within each entry, for example '*ind 3rd singular,*' as well as in a few other places for information in English. Word-classes (parts of speech) are written in small capital letters. A complete list of word-classes is found in the next section.

The following alphabetic order is used for Delaware headwords in the Delaware-English section:

*aa, a, b, ch, d, ee, e, f, g, h, ii, i, j, k, l, m, n, oo, o, p, r, s, sh, t, u, v, w, x, y, z, zh.*

Each dictionary entry consists at a minimum of a headword, in bold type, followed by an abbreviation for word-class (part of speech), a gloss or translation, and a variety of relevant grammatical (inflected) forms. A complete list of abbreviations used in dictionary entries may be found on page 2. A typical example is as follows.

**aapíikwus** NA mouse. *pl* **aapíikwsak**. *dimin* **aapíikwshush**. *obv* **aapíikwsal**.

**Headwords.** Each dictionary entry begins with a headword. The headword, presented in boldface type, is a complete Delaware word, with the exception of preverbs and prenouns, which must always be followed by a verb or a noun, respectively.

Nouns come in two main types, animate and inanimate. Animate nouns have the word-class abbreviation *na* and inanimate nouns have the word-class abbreviation *ni*. Both are usually presented in the singular form, as in the following examples.

**pámbiil** NA book, paper, letter. **Xúwiipambíilak.** 'Old books.' *pl* **pambíilak**. *poss* **mbambíilum**. *loc* **pambíilung**. *dim* **pambíilush**. *From Dutch.*

**áhpapoon** NI chair. *pl* **ahpapóonal**. *poss* **ndáhpapoon**. *loc* **ahpapóonung**. *dim* **ahpapóonush**.

Nouns which are always plural are presented with a plural suffix following the noun stem. The suffix is usually *-ak* for animate nouns and *-al* for inanimate nouns.

**koonjcháashak** NA checkers. *usually plural. pl* **koonjcháashak**. *obv* **koonjcháashal**.

**machiixáskwal** NI weeds. *usually plural. loc* **machiixáskwung**. *See* **matáskwal**.

Certain nouns are described by Algonquianists as dependent, that is, they are always possessed. This is especially true of nouns which refer to body parts and kinship terms. Dependent nouns may be animate or inanimate (word-class abbreviations: *nad*, *nid*) and must occur with a person prefix which refers to the possessor. Dependent nouns appear with the first-person prefix, written *n-*, *ni-*, *no-*, *nu-*, or *m-*, before the noun stem, set in plain type and disregarded in the alphabetic order. Note also in the first example below that the equals sign ('=') is used as a hyphen in Delaware words to indicate that a word has been broken at the end of a line; wherever possible words are broken syllabically.

ni**hkáxkwan** NID my shin. *pl* **nihkáxkwanal**. *3rd poss* **wihkáxkwan**. *loc* **nihkáxkwa=nung**.

n**íimatus** NAD my brother. *pl* **niimatúsak**. *3rd poss* **wiimatúsal**. *See* n**íimat**.

If the noun stem begins with the consonants *n* or *l*, by general rules of Delaware phonology the prefix is not pronounced and is not written.

**náxk** NID my hand, my arm. *pl* **náxkal**. *3rd poss* **wŭnáxk**. *loc* **náxkung**. *dimin* **náxkush**.

The headwords for verb entries are also complete words. All headwords for verb entries are presented in the independent indicative, the class of verbal inflection used to make main clause constructions for declarative statements and questions.

The complexities of verbal inflection in Delaware require different treatments of transitive and intransitive verbs. There are two types of transitive verbs, transitive animate (word-class abbreviation *vta*) and transitive inanimate (word-class abbreviation *vti*). Transitive animate verbs have a grammatically animate object, and transitive inanimate verbs have a grammatically inanimate object. Transitive animate verbs are entered in the independent indicative absolute form with a third-person subject ('s/he…') and a third-person animate indefinite object ('someone, something animate'; Goddard (1979: 40-1) contains more information on the absolute construction). The headword for most transitive animate entries consists of the verb stem followed by the suffix *-eew*.

**alumshíiheew** VTA send s.o. away. *ind 1st sg* **ndalŭmushíihaaw**, **ndalŭmushíiha**. *ind 3rd sg* **wtalŭmushiiháawal**. *ind inv* **ndalŭmushíihukw**. *ind I-you* **ktalŭ=mushíihul**. *conj 3rd* **alumshíihaat**. *imp* **alúmshiih**. *ptcple* **eelŭmushíihaat**.

Transitive inanimate verbs are cited in the independent indicative absolute form with a third-person animate subject and a third-person inanimate indefinite object ('something'). There are four different subtypes of transitive inanimate verbs, which are largely determined by the form of the verb stem. The word-class abbreviations for transitive inanimate classes are *vti1a*, *vti1b*, *vti2*, and *vti3*. The headword for class *vti1a*, *vti1b*, and those *vti3* verbs that end in a consonant consists of the basic verb stem without any suffix. The headword for class *vti2* and the single *vti3* verb stem that ends in a vowel consists of the basic verb stem followed by the suffix *-w*.

**akíindam** VTI1A read s.t., count s.t. *ind 1st sg* **ndakíindamun**. *ind 3rd sg* **wtakíin=damun**. *conj 1st sg* **akíindamaan**. *conj 3rd* **akíindang**. *imp* **akíindah**. *ptcple* **eekíindang**.

**cháskŭnum** VTI1B touch s.t. lightly *(with the hands)*. *ind 1st sg* **njaskŭnúmun**. *ind 3rd sg* **wchaskŭnúmun**. *conj 1st sg* **chaskŭ=númaan**. *conj 3rd* **cháskŭnung**. *imp* **cháskŭnih**. *ptcple* **chéeskŭnung**.

**kóxptoow** VTI2 tie s.t. up. *ind 1st sg* **ngóxp=toon**. *ind 3rd sg* **kóxptoon**. *conj 1st sg* **koxptáwaan**. *conj 3rd* **kóxptaakw**. *imp* **kóxptool**. *ptcple* **kéexptaakw**.

**míichuw** VTI3 eat s.t. **Kwíila- kwéek -míichŭwak.** 'They didn't have anything to eat.' *ind 1st sg* **nŭmíichiin**. *ind 3rd sg* **míichiin**. *conj 1st sg* **míichŭyaan**. *conj 3rd* **míichiit**. *imp* **míichiil**. *ptcple* **míichiit**.

Intransitive verbs are divided into two types, animate intransitive (word-class abbreviation *vai*) and inanimate intransitive (word-class abbreviation *vii*). Animate intransitive verbs have an animate subject, while Inanimate intransitive verbs have an inanimate subject. Animate intransitive verbs are cited in the third-person independent indicative, that is, the form that means 's/he…' The headword for animate intransitive stems that end in a vowel consists of the stem followed by the third-person suffix *-w*. The headword for animate intransitive stems that end in a consonant consists of the bare stem.

**eewaxkhíikeew** VAI stir things. *ind 1st sg* **ndeewaxkhíike, ndeewaxkhíikeem**. *conj 3rd* **eewaxkhíikeet**. *imp* **eewaxkhíikeel**. *ptcple* **eewaxkhíikeet**.

**kshusiitéexiin** VAI have hot feet. *ind 1st sg* **ngush'siitéexiin, ngush'siitéexi**. *conj 3rd* **kshusiitéexiing**. *ptcple* **keesh'siitéexiing**.

Similarly, inanimate intransitive verbs are cited in the third-person independent indicative form that means 'it…' The headword for inanimate intransitive stems that end in a vowel consists of the stem followed by the third-person suffix *-w*. The headword for inanimate intransitive stems that end in a consonant consists of the bare stem.

**chpwéew** VII be pointed. *conj 3rd* **chpwéek**. *ptcple* **chéepweek**.

**wŭliipóokwat** VII taste good. *conj 3rd* **wŭliipóokwahk**. *ptcple* **weeliipóo=kwahk**.

The headword for animate intransitive verbs which require a plural subject consists of the verb stem followed by the third-person plural suffix *-wak* if the verb stem ends in a vowel, or *-ook* if the verb stem ends in a consonant.

**psakwapúwak** VAI sit close together. *usually plural. ind 1st pl* **mbusakwapíhna**. *conj 3rd* **psakwapíhtiit**. *imp* **psákwapiikw**. *ptcple* **peesakwapíhtiit**. *See* **psakoh=kwéepŭwak**.

**takwiixíinook** VAI lie close together. *usually plural. ind 1st pl* **ndakwiixiinóhna**. *conj 3rd* **takwiixiinóhtiit**. *imp* **takwíixiikw**. *ptcple* **teekwiixiinóhtiit**.

The headword for inanimate intransitive verbs which require a plural subject consists of the verb stem followed by the third-person plural suffix *-wal* if the verb stem ends in a vowel, or *-ool* if the verb stem ends in a consonant.

**amangéewal** VII be big. *usually plural. conj 3rd* **amángeek**. *ptcple* **meemangéekiil**.

**nxúnool** VII be three of them, be three in number. *usually plural. conj 3rd* **nxúng**. *ptcple* **neexúngiil**.

A small number of intransitive verbs are classified as *vai-s* or *vii-s*. Most intransitive verbs that end in the long vowels *-aa* or *-ii* shift the stem-final vowel to *-ee* and *-u*, respectively, when independent indicative third-person suffixes of the form *-w* are added. Verbs classified as *vai-s* or *vii-s* do not undergo this shift and are considered 'stable,' hence the distinction in the word-class abbreviation.

**máachiiw** VAI-S go home. *ind 1st sg* **nŭ=máachi, nŭmáachiim**. *emphatic plural* **maachooltúwak**. *conj 3rd* **máachiit**. *imp* **máachiil**. *ptcple* **máachiit**.

**páasiiw** VII-S swell up. *conj 3rd* **páasiik**. *ptcple* **páasiik**.

Certain transitive animate verbs occur with two objects. Verbs of this type are sometimes referred to as double-object or ditransitive verbs. The word-class abbreviation *vtao* reflects the presence of this secondary object.

**akwíimeew** VTAO blame s.o. for s.t. *ind 1st sg* **ndakwíimaan**. *ind 3rd sg* **wtakwíi=maan**. *ind inv* **ndakwíimkwun**. *ind I-you* **ktakwiimóolun**. *conj 3rd* **akwíimaat**. *imp* **akwíim**. *ptcple* **eekwíimaat**.

Similarly, some animate intransitive verbs may also occur with a grammatical object which may be either animate or inanimate. These verbs have the word-class abbreviation *vaio*.

**mŭnéew** VAIO drink s.t. *ind 1st sg* **nŭmúneen**. *ind 3rd sg* **múneen**. *conj 3rd* **mŭnéet**. *imp* **mŭnéel**. *ptcple* **méeneet**.

A small number of verbs have the structural characteristics of transitive inanimate verbs but do not require a grammatical object. Verbs of this type are sometimes referred to as objectless transitive inanimate verbs. There are objectless transitive inanimate verbs corresponding to the *vti1a*, *vti1b*, and *vti2* verb classes discussed above. Syntactically they can be analysed as a special class of animate intransitive verb. They are distinguished with the word-class abbreviations *voti1a*, *voti1b*, or *voti2*.

**wŭleelúndam** VOTI1A be glad, be happy. *ind 1st sg* **nooleelúndam**. *conj 3rd* **wŭlee=lúndang**. *ptcple* **weeleelúndang**.

**psúm** VOTI1B have something in one's eye. *ind 1st sg* **mbúsum**. *conj 3rd* **psúng**. *ptcple* **péesung**.

**kshiilawéhtoow** VOTI2 show off. *ind 1st sg* **ngushiilawéhto**. *conj 3rd* **kshiilawéh=taakw**. *imp* **kshiilawéhtool**. *ptcple* **keeshiilawéhtaakw**.

Prenouns (word-class abbreviation *pn*) and preverbs (word-class abbreviation *pv*) do not occur as separate words. They are added before nouns or verbs, respectively, to form a type of compound stem. Prenouns and preverbs may usually occur with a wide variety of nouns or verbs, and thus we do not attempt to list every possible combination. Entries for prenouns and preverbs contain examples which illustrate their use, as in the following entries. In headwords and example sentences prenouns and preverbs are followed by hyphens to indicate that they are not complete words.

**piilii-** PN clean. **Píilii-waapasáanay.** 'A clean sheet.'; **Píilii-pàkíinjuw.** 'A clean plate.'

**nihtaa-** PV skillfully, know how to *(do something)*. **Wŭníhtaa- wéemi kwéek -saakíhtoon.** 'He watches everything.'; **Níhtaa-pŭmutóonheew.** 'He's a good preacher.'*ptcple* **néhtaa-**.

Particles (word-class abbreviation *pc*) are independent words that are invariant in shape. They do not occur with prefixes or suffixes.

**láapii** PC again. **Kwáy láapii máw-aláwiil.** 'Now go and hunt again.'; **Láapii oolíix=toon.** 'He fixed it again.'

Pronouns (word-class abbreviation *pr*) include personal pronouns, demonstrative pronouns, and interrogative pronouns.

**awéen** PR who, someone, a person. **Awéen éet há ná kwáy?** 'Who could that be now?'; **Awéeniil há wiichéewe?** 'Who's he going with?' *pl* **awéeniik**. *obv* **awéeniil**.

**Word Classes.** There are three main types of words in Delaware: noun, verb, and particle. Each Delaware entry in the dictionary is assigned to a word-class. Nouns and verbs are further subdivided according to a variety of syntactical and morphological criteria. Particles are words that do not occur with prefixes or suffixes that indicate person, number, or other inflectional categories. The various word-classes distinguished in the dictionary have been exemplified in the previous section, and are summarized below.

**Noun Classes**

| | |
|---|---|
| na | animate noun |
| ni | inanimate noun |
| nad | animate noun which is obligatorily possessed |
| nid | inanimate noun which is obligatorily possessed |

**Verb Classes**

| | |
|---|---|
| vai | intransitive verb with animate subject |
| vai-s | animate verb with animate subject and stable stem-final vowel |
| vii | intransitive verb with inanimate subject |
| vii-s | inanimate verb with animate subject and stable stem-final vowel |
| vta | transitive verb with animate subject |
| vti1a | transitive verb with inanimate object, Class 1a |
| vti1b | transitive verb with inanimate object, Class 1b |
| vti2 | transitive verb with inanimate object, Class 2 |
| vti3 | transitive verb with inanimate object, Class 3 |
| vtao | transitive verb with two objects |
| vaio | intransitive verb with animate subject and animate or inanimate object |
| voti | intransitive verb with animate subject and morphological characteristics of transitive inanimate verb |

**Other Word-classes**

| | |
|---|---|
| pc | particle |
| pr | pronoun |
| pv | preverb |
| pn | prenoun |

**Translations.** Each Delaware entry has an English translation. The translation is intended as a relatively concrete English equivalent of the Delaware term. Material within a translation may be separated by commas to indicate closely related English variants. A semicolon is used to separate elements of the translation which indicate significantly different aspects of the meaning of the Delaware term. Inevitably there is some subjectivity involved in deciding which elements of the translation are sufficiently distinct that they need to be differentiated. The translation of each term may be followed by italicized material in parentheses; this material indicates some further restriction or qualification of the basic meaning of the Delaware entry.

In the English translations certain abbreviations and conventional phrases are employed. The abbreviation 's.t.' is used for 'something'; 's.o.' is used for 'someone.' These abbreviations are used to refer to the objects of transitive verbs, where 's.t.' refers to an inanimate object, and 's.o.' refers to an animate object. As well, the phrase 's.t. animate' is used to refer to non-human entities which are classified in Delaware as animate. In this respect 's.o.' and 's.t. animate' are entirely equivalent in meaning when they are used in the translations of Delaware terms. Although 's.t. animate' is usually reserved for cases where the subject or object would not be perceived as living, both refer to animate subjects or objects.

The term 'people' is used in the translation of certain intransitive verbs to refer to an unspecified animate object. Similarly, the term 'things' is used in the translation of certain intransitive verbs to refer to an unspecified inanimate object.

**Examples.** Example sentences or words are given to help illustrate the meaning or use of dictionary entries. Most entries for particles, preverbs, and prenouns contain an example. Examples have also been included for other types of words when they illustrate some aspect of the meaning or use of the word that may not be apparent from the translation.

**éet** PC maybe. **Píht éet katá-sóokŭlaan.** 'Maybe it's going to rain.'; **Nún éet há.** 'That must be it.'

**Grammatical Forms.** Most entries for verbs and nouns include forms which show the headword marked for various inflectional categories. Although Delaware inflectional marking is quite regular I have included more information about inflected forms than might be considered normal for a dictionary. This is primarily because of the complex but regular variations in shape that Delaware words are subject to when prefixes and suffixes are added. The inclusion of inflected forms is intended to facilitate understanding of the details of the various forms.

Entries for verbs and preverbs use the following abbreviations: *ind* independent; *conj* conjunct; *imp* imperative; *ptcple* participle; *inv* inverse; *1st* first-person; *3rd* third-person; *sg* singular; *pl* plural. Entries for nouns use the following abbreviations: *pl* plural; *loc* locative; *poss* possessive; *obv* obviative; *dimin* diminutive; *3rd* third-person.

Entries for inanimate intransitive verbs include the third-person conjunct form (the form that means '(that) it...') and the participle ('the thing that...'), where collected.

Entries for animate intransitive verbs also include independent indicative forms for first-person singular ('I...'), conjunct third person ('(that) s/he...'), the imperative ('you...'), where collected, and the participle ('the one who...'), as well as the independent form for emphatic plural subject, where collected. Some animate intransitive verbs list two alternative forms for the first-person singular.

Entries for transitive inanimate verbs include forms for independent first-person subject and third-person object ('I...it'), independent third-person subject and third-person object ('he...it'), conjunct first-person subject and third-person object, conjunct third-person subject and third-person object, the imperative ('you...it'), and the participle ('the thing that...s/he').

Entries for transitive animate verbs include two alternative forms for independent first-person subject and third-person object ('I...him/her'), independent third-person subject and third-person object ('s/he...him/her'), independent inverse with third-person subject and first-person object ('s/he...me'), independent I-You form with first-person subject and second-person object ('I...you'), conjunct third-person subject and third-person object, conjunct third-person subject and third-person object, imperative ('you...him/her'), and the participle with third-person subject and object ('the one who...s/he').

Entries for nouns usually include, where available, forms for plural, possessive (first-person singular, 'my...'), locative, and diminutive. Entries for dependent (obligatorily possessed) nouns include the form for a third-person singular possessor ('his/her...'). Animate nouns include the form for obviative inflection.

Entries for preverbs include the participle form, where collected.

A few comments about the inflected forms listed with entries are in order. All inflected forms listed were obtained from Delaware speakers, sometimes in textual or volunteered material, but primarily through elicitation. In some cases expected inflected forms are not listed, for several reasons: some possible forms were rejected as being semantically or pragmatically implausible (for example, imperative forms of certain verbs), oversight on the author's part, or uncertainty on the part of Delaware speakers about particular inflected forms. Participles are perhaps the most significant inflected forms of verbs, since they may reveal information about the underlying forms of certain verb stems not available from other inflected forms. Participles of verbs undergo the form of verbal ablaut referred to by Algonquianists as initial change: if the first syllable contains an underlying *a* or *u*, the vowel shifts to long *ee* in the participial form. In some cases my consultants were uncertain about participles and in such instances the participle is not listed.

**Cross-references.** Cross-references are sometimes given to other words in the dictionary. Usually cross-references are to alternative forms of the same word, or to entries which share the same or a similar meaning. Cross-references begin with the word *See* in italic type.

**nànakíixsuw** VAI stutter. *ind 1st sg* **nàna=kíixsi**, **nànakíixsiim**. *conj 3rd* **nànakíix=siit**. *imp* **nànakíixsiil**. *ptcple* **nànakíix=siit**. *See* **nahnakúweew**.

**Loanwords.** Where a word is known to be borrowed from English, the English word which is the source of the borrowing is listed where possible. Dutch loanwords are identified as being from Dutch, but the source word is not indicated. For the identification of Dutch loanwords I have been greatly assisted by Goddard (1974b), which contains a list of most Dutch loanwords in Delaware; I have added a few words of Dutch origin not mentioned in this article.

**sóochul** NA soldier. *pl* **sóochŭlak**. *dimin* **shóochŭlush**. *obv* **sóochŭlal**. *From English* soldier.

**Reduplication.** For Delaware entries I have listed, where available, reduplicated forms which are based upon the headword. Reduplication in Delaware usually involves the prefixing of material copied from the first syllable of the uninflected word stem, sometimes in association with fixed elements. Reduplicated stems may make reference to concepts such as plurality, intensity, the frequency of an action, and others. In some cases the main entry is itself a reduplicated form; no special mention is made of these stems. Several different patterns of reduplication may be noted in entries, but no attempt is made here to comprehensively list all possible patterns of reduplication.

**shiipíhleew** VII stretch, spread, spread out.

*conj 3rd* **shiipíhlaak**. *ptcple* **shiipíhlaak**. *intensive reduplication* **shihshiipíhleew**.

**Grammatical Notes.** Information about grammatical details of an entry may be noted in italics immediately following the English gloss. For example, if a verb occurs only with a plural subject or object, it is noted here.

**takwámbtoow** VTI2 tie s.t. together. *object usually plural*. *ind 1st sg* **ndakwamb=tóonal**. *ind 3rd sg* **wtakwambtóonal**. *conj 1st sg* **takwambtáwaan**. *conj 3rd* **takwámbtaakw**. *imp* **takwámbtool**. *ptcple* **teekwámbtaakw**.

**Usage Notes.** For some entries, general remarks are included about some feature of the entry which is worth noting. These occur in italics, toward the end of the entry.

**kŭnoopáhksun** NI button shoe. *pl* **kŭnoo=pahksúnal**. *poss* **ngunoopáhksun**. *loc* **kŭnoopahksúnung**. *dimin* **kŭnoopahk=shúnush**. *fancy shoe worn especially by women*.

*English-Delaware*

The English-Delaware section contains, at a minimum, a headword which is an English term, the part of speech of the English term, the complete English translation of a Delaware word, and the Delaware word and its grammatical category (part of speech). English glosses are presented in bold and italic type. Delaware words and sentences are presented in plain type.

**broom** N chiikhíikan NI.

All of the example sentences and grammatical comments found in the Delaware-English section also occur in the English-Delaware section. The English translation precedes the Delaware sentence, which is set off in single quotation marks.

**pass by** VI lóowiiw VAI-S **I passed by there.** 'Náh mbúmu-lóowi.'

Subentries within an entry are separated by semicolons.

**mirror** N pehpŭnáwus NA; **look in a mirror** pehpŭnáwsuw VAI.

As with many dictionaries of aboriginal languages, the English-Delaware section is intended primarily as an index to the Delaware-English section, where more complete information about each Delaware word, particularly grammatical forms, may be found.

## Spelling and Pronunciation

The writing system used in this dictionary is intended to enable speakers of Delaware and non-native speakers to read and write Delaware. This type of system was adopted because of the interest of individuals at Moraviantown in learning to write Delaware. This writing system is based on the linguistic transcription system used in Goddard (1979). It substitutes English-based characters or sequences of characters for several symbols commonly used in phonetic transcription systems. Linguists will also recognize that the writing system used in the dictionary is not strictly phonemic in that it overdifferentiates by incorporating the effect of the rule of progressive voicing assimilation found in nasal-obstruent clusters. Nonetheless the benefits of the transparency found in this system outweigh any possible drawbacks which might be perceived by those linguists who insist that writing systems be phonemic in character. I merely observe that a writing system is conceptually distinct from a transcription system.

**Sounds and Letters.** In this section we outline the sounds of Delaware and how they are represented in this dictionary, as well as a variety of spelling conventions.

**Consonants.** The consonant letters used in writing Delaware are as follows: *b, ch, d, f, g, h, k, j, l, m, n, p, r, s, sh, v, w, x, y, z, zh*. Although *ch, sh,* and *zh* are written with two letters, each represents a single Delaware sound. The letters *f, v,* and *r* occur only in English loanwords. Examples of each of these sounds and approximate English equivalents are given in this section.

In the consonant chart, some consonants are organized into pairs consisting of a 'strong' consonant and a corresponding 'weak' consonant. The weak member of each pair occurs only after the sounds *m* or *n* (in other words, in a phonemic transcription, the 'weak' consonants would not be necessary, and would be written as the corresponding 'strong' sounds).

| | | | | | |
|---|---|---|---|---|---|
| **stops and affricates** | | | | | |
| strong | p | t | ch | k | |
| weak | b | d | j | g | |
| **fricatives** | | | | | |
| strong | f | s | sh | x | |
| weak | v | z | zh | | |
| **nasal** | m | n | | | |
| **others** | w | y, l, r | | | h |

Here we give examples of each Delaware consonant at the beginning, middle, and end of a word, with the exception that the weak consonants do not occur at the beginning of a word. An English equivalent is given for each Delaware sound, with the exception of the Delaware sound *x,* which has no English equivalent. It is similar to the German pronunciation of the last sound of the name 'Ba*ch*.'

| Sound | Delaware Examples | Translation | English Equivalent |
|---|---|---|---|
| **b** | am**b**iilaméekwaan | 'needle' | **b**oy |
| | wíim**b** | 'heartwood, spine' | |
| **ch** | **ch**iikhíikan | 'broom' | **ch**urch |
| | pee**ch**íikwsuw | 's/he crawls here' | |
| | íiyaa**ch** | 'still, yet' | |
| **d** | tún**d**eew | 'fire' | **d**ay |
| | páyun**d** | 'dipper' | |
| **f** | **f**éeliin | 'there is a fair' | **f**ather |
| | nù**f**óoti | 'I vote' | |
| **g** | mbíin**g** | 'in the water' | **g**ame |
| | wíin**g**an | 'it tastes good' | |
| **h** | **h**óosus | 'kettle' | **h**air |
| | á**h**teew | 'it is there' | |
| | píinti**h** | 'put it on!' | |
| **j** | piin**j**íikeew | 's/he comes inside' | **J**ohn |

| Sound | Delaware Examples | Translation | English Equivalent |
|---|---|---|---|
| | píi**nj** | 'pin' | |
| **k** | **k**óoshkoosh | 'pig' | **k**id |
| | tŭmahíi**k**an | 'ax' | |
| | wchápih**k** | 'medicine' | |
| **l** | **l**ŭmátapuw | 's/he sits' | **l**and |
| | píi**l**suw | 's/he is clean' | |
| | áh**l** | 'put him/her down!' | |
| **m** | **m**éenaxk | 'fence' | **m**an |
| | pŭ**m**úy | 'grease' | |
| | xwáskwii**m** | 'corn' | |
| **n** | **n**éewaaw | 'I see him/her' | **n**ame |
| | kpú**n**awaaw | 'you look at him/her' | |
| | któo**n** | 'your mouth' | |
| **p** | **p**ayaxkhíikan | 'gun' | **p**en |
| | a**p**úw | 's/he is there' | |
| | shkú**p** | 'shovel, playing card' | |
| **r** | f**r**áyteew | 'it is Friday' | **r**ain |
| **s** | **s**óokŭlaan | 'be raining' | **s**ing |
| | aaháa**s**uw | 'crow' | |
| | axkóoku**s** | 'bug, insect' | |
| **sh** | **sh**káakwus | 'skunk' | **sh**ip |
| | paxk**sh**íikan | 'knife' | |
| | chŭlóochŭloo**sh** | 'cricket' | |
| **t** | **t**héew | 'it's cold' | **t**ime |
| | áh**t**ool | 'put it down!' | |
| | níhkaa**t** | 'my leg' | |
| **v** | n**v**óotuw | 's/he votes' | **v**ery |
| **w** | **w**ŭyóos | 'meat' | **w**in |
| | a**w**éen | 'who, someone' | |
| | pée**w** | 's/he is coming' | |
| **x** | **x**ám | 'feed him/her!' | (German Ba**ch**) |
| | á**x**kook | 'snake' | |
| | takwá**x** | 'turtle' | |
| **y** | **y**áanee | 'often' | **y**es |
| | awée**y**ayus | 'animal' | |
| | chíipa**y** | 'ghost, corpse' | |
| **z** | akíin**z**uw | 's/he is reading' | **z**oom |
| | nxán**z** | 'my older brother' | |
| **zh** | apán**zh**uy | 'timber' | mea**s**ure |
| | shíikaan**zh** | 'very' | |

**Vowels.** Delaware vowels may be long or short. Long vowels are written double, but still count as one sound. The vowel letters used in writing Delaware are long *ii*, *ee*, *oo*, *aa*, and short *i*, *e*, *o*, *a*, and *u*. The letter *u* is used to represent the vowel schwa, which is usually represented by the phonetic symbol ə. In the following table, we give examples of each Delaware vowel at the beginning, middle, and end of a word, where available.

| Sound | Delaware Examples | Translation | English Equivalent |
|---|---|---|---|
| **ii** | **ii**yéeskwa | 'before' | **lea**n |
| | ks**íi**t | 'your foot' | |
| | awás**ii** | 'on the other side' | |
| **i** | **i**halóhkeew | 's/he used to work' | b**i**t |
| | xw**í**hk | 'liver' | |
| | ngwút**i** | 'one' | |
| **oo** | **oo**téenay | 'town' | b**o**ne |
| | k**óo**n | 'snow' | |
| **o** | **ó**xkweew | 'woman' | p**u**t |
| | nŭm**ó**xkamun | 'I found it' | |
| | mbaskwiipáht**o** | 'I get up in a hurry' | |
| **ee** | **ee**mhwáanus | 'spoon' | b**e**d |
| | m**ée**ngweew | 'Oneida Indian' | |
| | ngúm**ee** | 'always' | |
| **e** | **e**hkwtóonheew | 's/he stops talking' | b**e**t |
| | m**é**hch | 'now' | |
| | ndalóhk**e** | 'I'm working' | |
| **aa** | **áa**nay | 'road' | **o**dd |
| | piimŭnáht**aa**n | 'string' | |
| | wéen**aa** | 'almost' | |
| **a** | **á**hpapoon | 'chair' | b**u**t |
| | m**á**xkw | 'bear' | |
| | wíixk**a** | 'ever' | |
| **u** | **ú**w | 's/he says' | nos**e**s |
| | k**ú**k | 'your mother' | |
| | láawat**u** | 'long ago' | |

**Accents and Apostrophes.** Accents are included as an aid to pronunciation, although stress is usually predictable, except in some reduplicated syllables and loanwords. Each word form in the dictionary bears an indication of the main stress in the word, which is marked with the acute accent: *kóoshkoosh* 'pig.' Long vowels have accents marked only on the first vowel letter. Secondary stress is marked in certain words only, with a grave accent. Secondary stress is also usually predictable, and is only marked under two conditions: (a) when a syllable is unpredictably stressed, as frequently happens in loanwords or reduplicated syllables: *kòkómush* 'cucumber'; or (b) when the operation of pronunciation rules obscures the environment for secondary stress: *mùnháawal* 's/he gives him/her a drink.'

The breve accent is used to indicate a weak variety of the short vowel *u* which occurs before the consonants *m*, *n*, *l*, *w*, or *y* in an unstressed syllable. The vowel written as *ŭ* is pronounced very short or may be deleted entirely.

| | |
|---|---|
| ndal**ŭ**móoxwe | 'I walk away' |
| p**ŭ**níhleew | 's/he fell down' |
| k**ŭ**lúksuw | 's/he is laughing' |
| xwáal**ŭ**wees | 'wolf' |
| p**ŭ**níhleew | 's/he fell down' |
| míich**ŭ**yaan | 'what I ate' |

The apostrophe is used in Delaware words for two purposes. First, it distinguishes the single consonant *sh* (pronounced like English '*sh*ip') from the sequence of consonants *s'h*, as in the Delaware words *shíiwang* 'salt' and *ngwus'hámun* 'I measured it.' Similarly, it also distinguishes the single consonant *zh* (pronounced like English 'mea*s*ure') from the sequence of consonants *z'h*, as in the Delaware words *apánzhuy* 'timber' and *ndanz'hámun* 'I scoop it up.' Second, it is also used to help break up certain sequences of letters which might be confusing to read, although they are not actually ambiguous: *nzhíich'shal* 'my toes,' *ngwash'shúmun* 'I cut it into chunks.'

**Specific Pronunciation Rules.** The vowel written here with the letter *u* is subject to several rules of pronunciation whose effects are not indicated in the writing system. The letter *u* is pronounced like English *i* in *bit* when it is has either primary or secondary stress and is followed by one of the following letters: *t*, *s*, *ch*, *sh*, *l*, or *n*, except when preceded by *b*, *p*, *g*, *k*, *x*, *m*, or *w*. This rule does not apply in the final syllable of a word, except in words of less than three syllables. In each of the following words, *u* (in boldface type) is pronounced like *i:*

| | |
|---|---|
| ksh**ú**teew | 'it is hot' |
| nz**u**luskóonzhe | 'I have many children' |
| tŭm**u**shíikeew | 's/he cuts the grass' |
| as**ú**nal | 'stones' |
| **u**spíhleew | 'fly up' |
| ms**ú**chee | 'hardly at all' |

When followed by *y*, *u* is always pronounced like *i*:

| | |
|---|---|
| mb**ú**y | 'water' |

As well, when followed by the letter *w*, *u* is pronounced like short *o*, as in the following words.

| | |
|---|---|
| máxks**u**w | 's/he is red' |
| waaps**u**wíhleew | 'goose' |

# Abbreviations

Word Classes (Delaware)

Noun Classes

| | |
|---|---|
| na | animate noun |
| ni | inanimate noun |
| nad | animate noun which is obligatorily possessed |
| nid | inanimate noun which is obligatorily possessed |

Verb Classes

| | |
|---|---|
| vai | intransitive verb with animate subject |
| vai-s | animate verb with animate subject and stable stem-final vowel |
| vii | intransitive verb with inanimate subject |
| vii-s | inanimate verb with animate subject and stable stem-final vowel |
| vta | transitive verb with animate subject |
| vti 1a | transitive verb with inanimate object, Class 1a |
| vti 1b | transitive verb with inanimate object, Class 1b |
| vti2 | transitive verb with inanimate object, Class 2 |
| vti3 | transitive verb with inanimate object, Class 3 |
| vtao | transitive verb with two objects |
| vaio | transitive verb with animate subject and animate or inanimate object |
| voti | intransitive verb with animate subject and morphological characteristics of transitive inanimate verb |

Other Word Classes

| | |
|---|---|
| pc | particle |
| pr | pronoun |
| pv | preverb |
| pn | prenoun |

Word Classes (English)

| | |
|---|---|
| adj | adjective |
| adv | adverb |
| n | noun |
| vi | intransitive verb |
| vt | transitive verb |
| cj | conjunction |
| ij | interjection |
| prep | preposition |

Other Abbreviations

| | |
|---|---|
| conj | conjunct |
| dimin | diminutive |
| imp | imperative |
| ind | independent |
| indef | indefinite |
| inv | inverse |
| loc | locative |

| | |
|---|---|
| obv | obviative |
| pl | plural |
| poss | possessive |
| ptcple | participle |
| s.o. | someone |
| s.t. | something |
| s.t. animate | something animate |
| sg | singular |
| 1st | first |
| 3rd | third |

# ENGLISH-DELAWARE DICTIONARY

# AA

**áa** PC should, would, can, could. **Kiilóona áa kaatapíhna.** 'We (inclusive) should hide.'; **Písh áa móxa kŭ=wíingu-wiicheewŭlóhmwa.** 'I'd really like to go with you (pl).'

**aachŭmohkéewak** VAI hold a council. *usually plural. ind 1st pl* **ndaachŭ=mohkáhna**. *indef subject* **aachŭ=móhkaan**. *conj 3rd pl* **aachŭmoh=káhtiit**. *imp* **aachŭmóhkaakw**. *ptcpl* **aachŭmohkáhtiit**.

**áahaas** NA crow. *pl* **aaháasak**. *dimin* **aaháashush**. *obv* **aaháasal**. *See* **aaháasuw**.

**aaháasuw** NA crow. *pl* **aaháasŭwak**. *dimin* **aaháashoosh**. *obv* **aaháa=sŭwal**. *See* **áahaas**.

**aakawáxun** VII be protected from the wind, be away from the wind. *conj 3rd sg* **aakawáxung**. *ptcpl* **aaka=wáxung**.

**aakongweepíisuw** VAI wear a hat. *ind 1st sg* **ndaakongweepíisi**, **ndaakon=gweepíisiim**. *conj 3rd sg* **aakon=gweepíisiit**. *imp* **aakongweepíisiil**. *ptcpl* **aakongweepíisiit**.

**aakongwéepuy** NI hat. *pl* **aakongwée=pŭyal**. *poss* **ndaakongwéepuy**. *dimin* **aakongwéepiish**.

**áakshun** NA ox. *pl* **aakshúnak**. *loc* **aakshúnung**. *dimin* **aakshúnush**. *obv* **aakshúnal**. *From English* oxen.

**aalaanjkwéexiin** VAI lie on one's stomach. *ind 1st sg* **ndaalaanjkwéexiin**, **ndaalaanjkwéexi**. *conj 3rd sg* **aa=laanjkwéexiing**. *imp* **aalaanjkwée=xiil**. *ptcpl* **aalaanjkwéexiing**.

**aalaaptóoneew** VAI be unable to speak. *ind 1st sg* **ndaalaaptóone**, **ndaa=laaptóoneem**. *conj 3rd sg* **aalaap=tóoneet**. *ptcpl* **aalaaptóoneet**.

**áalful** NA Oliver. *obv* **aalfúlal**. *From English* Oliver.

**aali-** PV unable, unable to, be unable to *(do something).* **Áali-hulŭníixsuw.** 'He is unable to speak Delaware.' *ptcpl* **áali-**. *See* **aalu-**.

**aalooláaheew** VAIO throw s.t. upside down. *ind 1st sg* **ndaalooláaheen**. *ind 3rd sg* **wtaalooláaheen**. *conj 3rd sg* **aalooláaheet**. *imp* **aalooláaheel**. *ptcpl* **aalooláaheet**.

**aaloolíixtoow** VTI2 put s.t. upside down. *ind 1st sg* **ndaaloolíixtoon**. *ind 3rd sg* **wtaaloolíixtoon**. *conj 1st sg* **aa=looliixtáwaan**. *conj 3rd sg* **aaloolíix=taakw**. *imp* **aaloolíixtool**. *ptcpl* **aaloolíixtaakw**.

**aaloolíixŭmeew** VTA put s.o. upside down. *ind 1st sg* **ndaaloolíixŭmaaw**, **ndaaloolíixŭma**. *ind 3rd sg* **wtaa=looliixŭmáawal**. *ind inv* **ndaaloolíi=xŭmukw**. *ind I-you* **ktaaloolíixŭmul**. *conj 3rd sg* **aaloolíixŭmaat**. *imp* **aaloolíixum**. *ptcpl* **aaloolíixŭmaat**.

**aaloolíhleew** VAI flip over. *ind 1st sg* **ndaaloolíhla**, **ndaaloolíhlaam**. *conj 3rd sg* **aaloolíhlaat**. *ptcpl* **aaloolíh=laat**.

**aaloolíhleew** VII flip over. *conj 3rd sg* **aaloolíhlaak**. *ptcpl* **aaloolíhlaak**.

**aaloolihtéexiin** VAI fall upside down. *ind 1st sg* **ndaaloolihtéexiin**, **ndaa=loolihtéexi**. *conj 3rd sg* **aaloolihtée=xiing**. *ptcpl* **aaloolihtéexiing**.

**aaloolihtéextoow** VTI2 hit and turn s.t. upside down, hit and invert s.t. *ind 1st sg* **ndaaloolihtéextoon**. *ind 3rd sg* **wtaaloolihtéextoon**. *conj 1st sg* **aa=loolihteextáwaan**. *conj 3rd sg* **aa=loolihtéextaakw**. *imp* **aaloolihtéex=tool**. *ptcpl* **aaloolihtéextaakw**.

**aaloolihtéexŭmeew** VTA hit and turn s.o. upside down, hit and invert s.o. *ind 1st sg* **ndaaloolihtéexŭmaaw**, **ndaa=loolihtéexŭma**. *ind 3rd sg* **wtaaloo=lihteexŭmáawal**. *ind inv* **ndaaloo=lihtéexŭmukw**. *ind I-you* **ktaaloo=lihtéexŭmul**. *conj 3rd sg* **aaloolih=**

**téexŭmaat**. *imp* **aaloolihtéexum**. *ptcpl* **aaloolihtéexŭmaat**.

**aaloolihtéexun** VII fall upside down. *conj 3rd sg* **aaloolihtéexung**. *ptcpl* **aaloolihtéexung**.

**aalóolŭneew** VTA put s.o. upside down *(using the hands)*. *ind 1st sg* **ndaa=lóolŭnaaw**, **ndaalóolŭna**. *ind 3rd sg* **wtaaloolŭnáawal**. *ind inv* **ndaalóo=lŭnukw**. *ind I-you* **ktaalóolŭnul**. *conj 3rd sg* **aalóolŭnaat**. *imp* **aalóolun**. *ptcpl* **aalóolŭnaat**.

**aalóolŭnum** VTI1B put s.t. upside down *(using the hands)*. *ind 1st sg* **ndaa=loolŭnúmun**. *ind 3rd sg* **wtaaloolŭ=númun**. *conj 1st sg* **aaloolŭnúmaan**. *conj 3rd sg* **aalóolŭnung**. *imp* **aalóo=lŭnih**. *ptcpl* **aalóolŭnung**.

**aalu-** PV unable, be unable, be unable to *(do something)*. *informal*. **Ndáalu-míitsi.** 'I can't eat.'; **Ndáalu-kawíim.** 'I couldn't sleep.' *ptcpl* **áalu-**. *See* **aali-**.

**aalŭmuníikan** NI calendar. *pl* **aalŭ=muníikanal**. *poss* **ndaalŭmuníikan**. *From English* almanac.

**áalund** PC some. **Áalund awéen.** 'Some people.'

**áalunj** NA orange. *pl* **aalúnjak**. *poss* **ndaalúnjum**. *loc* **aalúnjung**. *dimin* **aalúnjush**. *obv* **aalúnjal**. *From English* orange.

**aalŭwásktuw** VAI be constipated, be unable to defecate. *ind 1st sg* **ndaalŭ=wáskti**, **ndaalŭwásktiim**. *conj 3rd sg* **aalŭwásktiit**. *ptcpl* **aalŭwásktiit**. *See* **pwaawásktuw**.

**aalŭwíisheew** VAI be unable to urinate. *ind 1st sg* **ndaalŭwíishe**, **ndaalŭ=wíisheem**. *conj 3rd sg* **aalŭwíisheet**. *ptcpl* **aalŭwíisheet**.

**aalŭwíhleew** VAI be unable to work, be unable to move, be unable to run, be out of order. *conj 3rd sg* **aalŭwíhlaat**. *ptcpl* **aalŭwíhlaat**.

**aalŭwíhleew** VII be unable to work, be unable to move, be unable to run, be out of order. *conj 3rd sg* **aalŭwíhlaak**. *ptcpl* **aalŭwíhlaak**.

**aalŭwúlaan** VII be unable to rain. *conj 3rd sg* **aalŭwúlaang**. *ptcpl* **aalŭwúl=aang**.

**aamáaheew** VAIO tip something over, tip something backwards, knock something over, knock something over backwards. *ind 1st sg* **ndaamáaheen**. *ind 3rd sg* **wtaamáaheen**. *conj 3rd sg* **aamáaheet**. *imp* **aamáaheel**. *ptcpl* **aamáaheet**.

**aamáhkhweew** VTA knock s.t. animate over *(of wood, using a tool or instrument)*. *ind 1st sg* **ndaamáhkhwaaw**, **ndaamáhkhwa**. *ind 3rd sg* **wtaa=mahkhwáawal**. *ind inv* **ndaamáhk=hookw**. *ind I-you* **ktaamáhkhool**. *conj 3rd sg* **aamáhkhwaat**. *imp* **aamáhkhwaw**. *ptcpl* **aamáhkhwaat**.

**aamáhkhwam** VTI1A knock s.t. over *(of wood, using a tool or instrument)*. *ind 1st sg* **ndaamahkhwámun**. *ind 3rd sg* **wtaamahkhwámun**. *conj 1st sg* **aamahkhwámaan**. *conj 3rd sg* **aamáhkhwang**. *imp* **aamáhkhwah**. *ptcpl* **aamáhkhwang**.

**áaman** NI rope, piece of rope. *pl* **áama=nal**. *poss* **ndáaman**. *dimin* **áamanush**.

**aamaniikéexiin** VAI have a tooth knocked out. *ind 1st sg* **ndaamaniikéexiin**, **ndaamaniikéexi**. *conj 3rd sg* **aama=niikéexiing**. *ptcpl* **aamaniikéexiing**.

**aamaniikéexŭmeew** VTA knock s.o.'s tooth out. *ind 1st sg* **ndaamaniikée=xŭmaaw**, **ndaamaniikéexŭma**. *ind 3rd sg* **wtaamaniikeexŭmáawal**. *ind inv* **ndaamaniikéexŭmukw**. *ind I-you* **ktaamaniikéexŭmul**. *conj 3rd sg* **aamaniikéexŭmaat**. *imp* **aamanii=kéexum**. *ptcpl* **aamaniikéexŭmaat**.

**áamapuw** VAI sit back. *ind 1st sg* **ndáa=mapi**, **ndáamapiim**. *conj 3rd sg* **áa=mapiit**. *imp* **áamapiil**. *ptcpl* **áamapiit**.

**aamchéepuw** VAI lean back while sitting.

*ind 1st sg* **ndaamchéepi**, **ndaam=chéepiim**. *conj 3rd sg* **aamchéepiit**. *imp* **aamchéepiil**. *ptcpl* **aamchéepiit**.

**aamchéexiin** VAI lean back. *ind 1st sg* **ndaamchéexiin**, **ndaamchéexi**. *conj 3rd sg* **aamchéexiing**. *imp* **aamchée=xiil**. *ptcpl* **aamchéexiing**.

**aamháhkweew** VAI chop down a tree. *ind 1st sg* **ndaamháhkwe**, **ndaam=háhkweem**. *conj 3rd sg* **aamháh=kweet**. *imp* **aamháhkweel**. *ptcpl* **aamháhkweet**.

**aamíhkam** VTI1A knock s.t. over, tip s.t. over *(using the foot or body)*. *ind 1st sg* **ndaamíhkamun**. *ind 3rd sg* **wtaa=míhkamun**. *conj 1st sg* **aamíhka=maan**. *conj 3rd sg* **aamíhkang**. *imp* **aamíhkah**. *ptcpl* **aamíhkang**.

**aamíhkaweew** VTA knock s.o. over, tip s.o. over *(using the foot or body)*. *ind 1st sg* **ndaamíhkawaaw**, **ndaamíh=kawa**. *ind 3rd sg* **wtaamihkawáa=wal**. *ind inv* **ndaamíhkaakw**. *ind I-you* **ktaamíhkool**. *conj 3rd sg* **aa=míhkawaat**. *imp* **aamíhkaw**. *ptcpl* **aamíhkawaat**.

**aamíhleew** VAI fall over, be knocked down, be knocked over. *ind 1st sg* **ndaamíhla**, **ndaamíhlaam**. *conj 3rd sg* **aamíhlaat**. *ptcpl* **aamíhlaat**.

**aamíhleew** VII fall over, be knocked down, be knocked over. *conj 3rd sg* **aamíhlaak**. *ptcpl* **aamíhlaak**.

**aamihtéeham** VTI1A hit s.t. and knock it over, hit s.t. and make it fall backwards. *ind 1st sg* **ndaamihtéehŭmun**. *ind 3rd sg* **wtaamihtéehŭmun**. *conj 1st sg* **aamihtéehŭmaan**. *conj 3rd sg* **aamihtéehang**. *imp* **aamihtéehih**. *ptcpl* **aamihtéehang**.

**aamihtéeheew** VTA hit s.o. and knock them over, hit s.o. and make them fall backwards. *ind 1st sg* **ndaamihtée=haaw**, **ndaamihtéeha**. *ind 3rd sg* **wtaamihteeháawal**. *ind inv* **ndaa=mihtéehookw**. *ind I-you* **ktaamih=téehool**. *conj 3rd sg* **aamihtéehaat**. *imp* **aamíhteeh**. *ptcpl* **aamihtéehaat**.

**aamihtéexiin** VAI fall backwards. *ind 1st sg* **ndaamihtéexiin**, **ndaamihtéexi**. *conj 3rd sg* **aamihtéexiing**. *ptcpl* **aamihtéexiing**.

**aamihtéextoow** VTI2 make s.t. fall backwards. *ind 1st sg* **ndaamihtéextoon**. *ind 3rd sg* **wtaamihtéextoon**. *conj 1st sg* **aamihteextáwaan**. *conj 3rd sg* **aamihtéextaakw**. *imp* **aamihtéex=tool**. *ptcpl* **aamihtéextaakw**.

**aamihtéexŭmeew** VTA make s.o. fall backwards. *ind 1st sg* **ndaamihtée=xŭmaaw**, **ndaamihtéexŭma**. *ind 3rd sg* **wtaamihteexŭmáawal**. *ind inv* **ndaamihtéexŭmukw**. *ind I-you* **ktaamihtéexŭmul**. *conj 3rd sg* **aa=mihtéexŭmaat**. *imp* **aamihtéexum**. *ptcpl* **aamihtéexŭmaat**.

**aamihtéexun** VII fall backwards. *conj 3rd sg* **aamihtéexung**. *ptcpl* **aamih=téexung**.

**aamootŭyéhleew** VAI fall on one's behind *(especially when squatting down)*. *ind 1st sg* **ndaamootŭyéhla**, **ndaamootŭyéhlaam**. *conj 3rd sg* **aamootŭyéhlaat**. *ptcpl* **aamootŭ=yéhlaat**.

**áamsheew** VTA cut and knock over s.t. animate. *ind 1st sg* **ndáamshaaw**, **ndáamsha**. *ind 3rd sg* **wtaamsháa=wal**. *ind inv* **ndáamshookw**. *ind I-you* **ktáamshool**. *conj 3rd sg* **áamshaat**. *imp* **áamush**. *ptcpl* **áamshaat**.

**áamshum** VTI1B cut and knock s.t. over. *ind 1st sg* **ndaamshúmun**. *ind 3rd sg* **wtaamshúmun**. *conj 1st sg* **aam=shúmaan**. *conj 3rd sg* **áamshung**. *imp* **áamshih**. *ptcpl* **áamshung**.

**áamŭlam** VTI1A knock s.t. down, knock s.t. over *(with a stick, with a car, with a bicycle, with a gunshot)*. *ind 1st sg* **ndaamŭlámun**. *ind 3rd sg* **wtaamŭ=lámun**. *conj 1st sg* **aamŭlámaan**. *conj 3rd sg* **áamŭlang**. *imp* **áamŭlah**.

*ptcpl* **áamŭlang**.

**aamŭláweew** VTA knock s.o. down, knock s.o. over *(with a stick, with a car, with a bicycle, with a gunshot)*. *ind 1st sg* **ndaamŭláwaaw, ndaamŭ=láwa**. *ind 3rd sg* **wtaamŭlawáawal**. *ind inv* **ndáamŭlaakw**. *ind I-you* **ktáamŭlool**. *conj 3rd sg* **aamŭláw=aat**. *imp* **áamŭlaw**. *ptcpl* **aamŭláw=aat**.

**áamŭneew** VTA knock s.o. over, push s.o. over, bend s.o. over, tilt s.o. over *(using the hands)*. *ind 1st sg* **ndáamŭ=naaw, ndáamŭna**. *ind 3rd sg* **wtaa=mŭnáawal**. *ind inv* **ndáamŭnukw**. *ind I-you* **ktáamŭnul**. *conj 3rd sg* **áamŭnaat**. *imp* **áamun**. *ptcpl* **áamŭnaat**.

**áamŭnum** VTI1B knock s.t. over, push s.t. over, bend s.t. over, tilt s.t. over *(using the hands)*. *ind 1st sg* **ndaa=mŭnúmun**. *ind 3rd sg* **wtaamŭnúm=un**. *conj 1st sg* **aamŭnúmaan**. *conj 3rd sg* **áamŭnung**. *imp* **áamŭnih**. *ptcpl* **áamŭnung**.

**áamweew** NA bee. *pl* **aamwéewak**. *dimin* **aamwéesh**. *obv* **aamwéewal**.

**áamwiiw** VAI-S get up from lying down. *ind 1st sg* **ndáamwi, ndáamwiim**. *conj 3rd sg* **áamwiit**. *imp* **áamwiil**. *ptcpl* **áamwiit**.

**aamwiipáhtoow** VAI get up quickly from lying down. *ind 1st sg* **ndaa=mwiipáhto**. *conj 1st sg* **aamwiipáh=tawaan**. *conj 3rd sg* **aamwiipáh=taakw**. *imp* **aamwiipáhtool**. *ptcpl* **aamwiipáhtaakw**.

**aamwiiwáakan** NI Resurrection.

**aamwihkíimeew** VTA talk to s.o. to get them up from lying down, holler at s.o. to get them up from lying down. *ind 1st sg* **ndaamwihkíimaaw, ndaa=mwihkíima**. *ind 3rd sg* **wtaamwih=kiimáawal**. *ind inv* **ndaamwihkíi=mukw**. *ind I-you* **ktaamwihkíimul**. *conj 3rd sg* **aamwihkíimaat**. *imp* **aamwíhkiim**. *ptcpl* **aamwihkíimaat**.

**aamwihkshíhkaweew** VTA make s.o. get up from lying down. *ind 1st sg* **ndaamwihkshíhkawaaw, ndaa=mwihkshíhkawa**. *ind 3rd sg* **wtaa=mwihkshihkawáawal**. *ind inv* **ndaa=mwihkshíhkaakw**. *ind I-you* **ktaa=mwihkshíhkool**. *conj 3rd sg* **aa=mwihkshíhkawaat**. *imp* **aamwih=kshíhkaw**. *ptcpl* **aamwihkshíhka=waat**.

**aamwíhkŭneew** VTA get s.o. into sitting position, raise s.o., raise s.o. in bed *(from lying down)*. *ind 1st sg* **ndaa=mwíhkŭnaaw, ndaamwíhkŭna**. *ind 3rd sg* **wtaamwihkŭnáawal**. *ind inv* **ndaamwíhkŭnukw**. *ind I-you* **ktaa=mwíhkŭnul**. *conj 3rd sg* **aamwíhkŭ=naat**. *imp* **aamwíhkun**. *ptcpl* **aamwíhkŭnaat**.

**aamwihtéeheew** VTA hit s.o. and make them get up from lying down. *ind 1st sg* **ndaamwihtéehaaw, ndaamwih=téeha**. *ind 3rd sg* **wtaamwihteeháa=wal**. *ind inv* **ndaamwihtéehookw**. *ind I-you* **ktaamwihtéehool**. *conj 3rd sg* **aamwihtéehaat**. *imp* **aamwíhteeh**. *ptcpl* **aamwihtéehaat**.

**áamxookw** VAI be blown over by the wind *(s.t. animate)*. *ind 1st sg* **ndáa=mxookw**. *conj 3rd sg* **aamxóokwuk**. *ptcpl* **aamxóokwuk**.

**áamxun** VII be blown over by the wind. *conj 3rd sg* **aámxung**. *ptcpl* **áam=xung**.

**áanay** NI road. *pl* **áanayal**. *loc* **áaneeng**.

**aanayaapasíhkan** NI plantain. *pl* **aana=yaapasíhkanal**. *medicine used for infections, applied in a poultice.*

**aandáakchehl** VAI jump to a new location. *ind 1st sg* **ndaandáakchehl**. *conj 3rd sg* **aandaakchéhluk**. *imp* **aandaakchéhlih**. *ptcpl* **aandaak=chéhluk**.

**áandakuw** VAI change one's clothes. *ind 1st sg* **ndáandakwi, ndáandakwiim**.

*conj 3rd sg* **áandakwiit**. *imp* **áanda=kwiil**. *ptcpl* **áandakwiit**.

**aandapíhleew** VAI change seats, sit somewhere else. *ind 1st sg* **ndaan=dapíhla**, **ndaandapíhlaam**. *conj 3rd sg* **aandapíhlaat**. *imp* **aandapíhlaal**. *ptcpl* **aandapíhlaat**.

**áandapuw** VAI change one's place while sitting. *ind 1st sg* **ndáandapi**, **ndáan=dapiim**. *conj 3rd sg* **áandapiit**. *imp* **áandapiil**. *ptcpl* **áandapiit**.

**aandhéembteew** VAI change one's shirt. *ind 1st sg* **ndaandhéembta**, **ndaand=héembtaam**. *conj 3rd sg* **aandhéemb=taat**. *imp* **aandhéembtaal**. *ptcpl* **aandhéembtaat**.

**aandihtéeham** VTI1A hit s.t. again. *ind 1st sg* **ndaandihtéehŭmun**. *ind 3rd sg* **wtaandihtéehŭmun**. *conj 1st sg* **aandihtéehŭmaan**. *conj 3rd sg* **aan=dihtéehang**. *imp* **aandihtéehah**. *ptcpl* **aandihtéehang**.

**aandihtéeheew** VTA hit s.o. anew, hit s.o. another time. *ind 1st sg* **ndaandih=téehaaw**, **ndaandihtéeha**. *ind 3rd sg* **wtaandihteeháawal**. *ind inv* **ndaan=dihtéehookw**. *ind I-you* **ktaandih=téehool**. *conj 3rd sg* **aandihtéehaat**. *imp* **aandíhteeh**. *ptcpl* **aandihtée=haat**.

**aandóoxwaleew** VTA move s.o. from one place to another. *ind 1st sg* **ndaandóoxwalaaw**, **ndaandóoxwa=la**. *ind 3rd sg* **wtaandooxwaláawal**. *ind inv* **ndaandóoxwalukw**. *ind I-you* **ktaandóoxwalul**. *conj 3rd sg* **aan=dóoxwalaat**. *imp* **aandóoxwal**. *ptcpl* **aandóoxwalaat**.

**aandóoxwatoow** VTI2 move s.t. from one place to another. *ind 1st sg* **ndaan=dóoxwatoon**. *ind 3rd sg* **wtaandóo=xwatoon**. *conj 1st sg* **aandooxwa=táwaan**. *conj 3rd sg* **aandóoxwa=taakw**. *imp* **aandóoxwatool**. *ptcpl* **aandóoxwataakw**.

**aandóoxweew** VAI move on, go from one place to another. *ind 1st sg* **ndaan=dóoxwe**, **ndaandóoxweem**. *conj 3rd sg* **aandóoxweet**. *imp* **aandóoxweel**. *ptcpl* **aandóoxweet**.

**aandshiilúndam** VOTI1A marry and add on to one's family, take on relatives. *ind 1st sg* **ndaandshiilúndam**. *conj 3rd sg* **aandshiilúndang**. *imp* **aand=shiilúndah**. *ptcpl* **aandshiilúndang**.

**aaníhkhwam** VTI1A add on to s.t., extend s.t. *ind 1st sg* **ndaanihkhwám=un**. *ind 3rd sg* **wtaanihkhwámun**. *conj 1st sg* **aanihkhwámaan**. *conj 3rd sg* **aaníhkhwang**. *imp* **aaníhk=hwah**. *ptcpl* **aaníhkhwang**.

**aaníhkhweew** VTA add on to s.t. animate, extend s.t. animate. *ind 1st sg* **ndaa=níhkhwaaw**, **ndaaníhkhwa**. *ind 3rd sg* **wtaanihkhwáawal**. *ind inv* **ndaa=níhkhookw**. *ind I-you* **ktaaníhkhool**. *conj 3rd sg* **aaníhkhwaat**. *imp* **aaníhkhwaw**. *ptcpl* **aaníhkhwaat**.

**aanihkwaachíimuw** VAI add on to a story; interpret. *ind 1st sg* **ndaanih=kwaachíimwi**, **ndaanihkwaachíi=mwiim**. *conj 3rd sg* **aanihkwaachíi=mwiit**. *imp* **aanihkwaachíimwiil**. *ptcpl* **aanihkwaachíimwiit**.

**aanihkwíiheew** VTA add on to s.t. animate; lengthen s.t. animate, make s.t. animate longer. *ind 1st sg* **ndaanih=kwíihaaw**, **ndaanihkwíiha**. *ind 3rd sg* **wtaanihkwiiháawal**. *conj 3rd sg* **aanihkwíihaat**. *imp* **aaníhkwiih**. *ptcpl* **aanihkwíihaat**.

**aanihkwíhtoow** VTI2 add on to s.t.; lengthen s.t., make s.t. longer. *ind 1st sg* **ndaanihkwíhtoon**. *ind 3rd sg* **wtaanihkwíhtoon**. *conj 1st sg* **aa=nihkwíhtawaan**. *conj 3rd sg* **aanih=kwíhtaakw**. *imp* **aanihkwíhtool**. *ptcpl* **aanihkwíhtaakw**.

**áanjii-katúm** VAI have a birthday. *ind 1st sg* **ndáanjii-katúm**. *conj 3rd sg* **áanjii-katúng**. *ptcpl* **áanjii-katúng**.

**aanjiikáapaleew** VTA transplant s.t. animate. *ind 1st sg* **ndaanjiikáapalaaw, ndaanjiikáapala**. *ind 3rd sg* **wtaan=jiikaapaláawal**. *ind inv* **ndaanjii=káapalukw**. *ind I-you* **ktaanjiikáa=palul**. *conj 3rd sg* **aanjiikáapalaat**. *imp* **aanjiikáapal**. *ptcpl* **aanjiikáa=palaat**.

**aanjiikáapatoow** VTI2 transplant s.t. *ind 1st sg* **ndaanjiikáapatoon**. *ind 3rd sg* **wtaanjiikáapatoon**. *conj 1st sg* **aan=jiikaapatáwaan**. *conj 3rd sg* **aanjii=káapataakw**. *imp* **aanjiikáapatool**. *ptcpl* **aanjiikáapataakw**.

**aanjíisheew** VAI urinate in a new place. *ind 1st sg* **ndaanjíishe, ndaanjíi=sheem**. *conj 3rd sg* **aanjíisheet**. *imp* **aanjíisheel**. *ptcpl* **aanjíisheet**.

**aanjíhkam** VTI1A try s.t. on *(of clothing)*. *ind 1st sg* **ndaanjíhkamun**. *ind 3rd sg* **wtaanjíhkamun**. *conj 1st sg* **aan=jíhkamaan**. *conj 3rd sg* **aanjíhkang**. *imp* **aanjíhkah**. *ptcpl* **aanjíhkang**.

**aanjíhleew** VAI change; take a turn for the worse, have one's medical condition worsen. *ind 1st sg* **ndaanjíhla, ndaanjíhlaam**. *conj 3rd sg* **aanjíh=laat**. *ptcpl* **aanjíhlaat**.

**aanjíhtoow** VTI2 change s.t., alter s.t., make s.t. over. *ind 1st sg* **ndaanjíh=toon**. *ind 3rd sg* **wtaanjíhtoon**. *conj 1st sg* **aanjíhtawaan**. *conj 3rd sg* **aanjíhtaakw**. *imp* **aanjíhtool**. *ptcpl* **aanjíhtaakw**.

**aapáachiiw** VAI-S return home. *ind 1st sg* **ndaapáachi, ndaapáachiim**. *conj 3rd sg* **aapáachiit**. *imp* **aapáachiil**. *ptcpl* **aapáachiit**.

**aapaachíhleew** VAI go home, drive home, fly home, pedal home. *ind 1st sg* **ndaapaachíhla, ndaapaachíhlaam**. *conj 3rd sg* **aapaachíhlaat**. *imp* **aapaachíhlaal**. *ptcpl* **aapaachíhlaat**.

**aapaalŭwéhleew** VAI take off, run with one's tail up. **Wíixkwii ndaapaalŭ=wéhla.** 'I just took off all of a sudden.'; **Ndaapaalŭwéhla ootéeneeng ndá.** 'I'm running off into town.' *ind 1st sg* **ndaapaalŭwéhla, ndaapaalŭ=wéhlaam**. *conj 3rd sg* **aapaalŭwéh=laat**. *imp* **aapaalŭwéhlaal**. *ptcpl* **aapaalŭwéhlaat**.

**aapahkíiheew** VAI come back from planting. *ind 1st sg* **ndaapahkíihe, ndaa=pahkíiheem**. *conj 3rd sg* **aapahkíi=heet**. *imp* **aapahkíiheel**. *ptcpl* **aapahkíiheet**.

**aapakíingweew** VAI open one's eyes. *ind 1st sg* **ndaapakíingwe, ndaapa=kíingweem**. *conj 3rd sg* **aapakíin=gweet**. *imp* **aapakíingweel**. *ptcpl* **aapakíingweet**.

**aapakiingwéexiin** VAI have one's eyes open. *ind 1st sg* **ndaapakiingwée=xiin, ndaapakiingwéexi**. *conj 3rd sg* **aapakiingwéexiing**. *ptcpl* **aapakiin=gwéexiing**.

**aapaláwiiw** VAI-S come back from hunting. *ind 1st sg* **ndaapaláwi, ndaapa=láwiim**. *conj 3rd sg* **aapaláwiit**. *ptcpl* **aapaláwiit**.

**aapalóhkeew** VAI come back from working. *ind 1st sg* **ndaapalóhke, ndaa=palóhkeem**. *conj 3rd sg* **aapalóh=keet**. *ptcpl* **aapalóhkeet**.

**aapamíhleew** VAI fall backwards. *ind 1st sg* **ndaapamíhla, ndaapamíhlaam**. *conj 3rd sg* **aapamíhlaat**. *ptcpl* **aapamíhlaat**.

**aapanáxeew** VAI come back from cutting wood. *ind 1st sg* **ndaapanáxe, ndaa=panáxeem**. *conj 3rd sg* **aapanáxeet**. *imp* **aapanáxeel**. *ptcpl* **aapanáxeet**.

**aapchii-** PN to death, dead, permanently, for good. **Áapchii-kihtóxkwees.** 'Woman who died of old age.' *See* **aaptii-**.

**aapchii-** PV to death, dead, permanently, for good. **Piilkúshak áapchii-atúsŭ=wak.** 'The peaches are really overripe.' *ptcpl* **áapchii-**. *See* **aapchu-**.

**áapchii-kihtoxkwéesuw** VAI be a woman who died of old age. *ind 1st sg* **ndáa=**

**pchii-kihtoxkwéesi**, **ndáapchii-kihtoxkwéesiim**. *conj 3rd sg* **áapchii-kihtoxkwéesiit**. *ptcpl* **áapchii-kihtoxkwéesiit**.

**aapchíikun** VII go to seed, be overgrown. *conj 3rd sg* **aapchíikung**. *ptcpl* **aapchíikung**.

**aapchíikuw** VAI go to seed, be overgrown *(of plants)*. *conj 3rd sg* **aapchíikiit**. *ptcpl* **aapchíikiit**.

**aapchíilateew** VAI choke. *ind 1st sg* **ndaapchíilata**, **ndaapchíilataam**. *conj 3rd sg* **aapchíilataat**. *ptcpl* **aapchíilataat**.

**aapchíinaleew** VTA drive s.o. to death, work s.o. to death, work s.o. very hard. *ind 1st sg* **ndaapchíinalaaw**, **ndaapchíinala**. *ind 3rd sg* **wtaap=chiinaláawal**. *ind inv* **ndaapchíina=lukw**. *ind I-you* **ktaapchíinalul**. *conj 3rd sg* **aapchíinalaat**. *imp* **aapchíinal**. *ptcpl* **aapchíinalaat**.

**aapchiinalúkwsuw** VAI be driven to one's death, be tormented to death. *ind 1st sg* **ndaapchiinalúkwsi**, **ndaapchii=nalúkwsiim**. *conj 3rd sg* **aapchiina=lúkwsiit**. *ptcpl* **aapchiinalúkwsiit**.

**aapchíisŭmuw** VAI drink oneself to death. *ind 1st sg* **ndaapchíisŭmwi**, **ndaapchíisŭmwiim**. *conj 3rd sg* **aap=chíisŭmwiit**. *ptcpl* **aapchíisŭmwiit**.

**aapchíixiin** VAI lean *(against something)*. *ind 1st sg* **ndaapchíixiin**, **ndaap=chíixi**. *conj 3rd sg* **aapchíixiing**. *imp* **aapchíixiil**. *ptcpl* **aapchíixiing**.

**aapchíixtoow** VTI2 lean s.t. *(against something)*. *ind 1st sg* **ndaapchíix=toon**. *ind 3rd sg* **wtaapchíixtoon**. *conj 1st sg* **aapchiixtáwaan**. *conj 3rd sg* **aapchíixtaakw**. *imp* **aapchíixtool**. *ptcpl* **aapchíixtaakw**.

**aapchíixŭmeew** VTA lean s.o., lean s.t. animate *(against something)*. *ind 1st sg* **ndaapchíixŭmaaw**, **ndaapchíi=xŭma**. *ind 3rd sg* **wtaapchiixŭmáa=wal**. *ind inv* **ndaapchíixŭmukw**. *ind I-you* **ktaapchíixŭmul**. *conj 3rd sg* **aapchíixŭmaat**. *imp* **aapchíixum**. *ptcpl* **aapchíixŭmaat**.

**aapchíixun** VII lean *(against something)*. *conj 3rd sg* **aapchíixung**. *ptcpl* **aapchíixung**.

**aapchíhleew** VAI have whooping cough. *ind 1st sg* **ndaapchíhla**, **ndaapchíh=laam**. *conj 3rd sg* **aapchíhlaat**. *ptcpl* **aapchíhlaat**. *See* **àhaapchíhleew**.

**aapchu-** PV to death, dead, permanently, for good. *informal*. **Ndáapchu-aníhtoon.** 'I lost it for good.'; **Áapchu-mohkwíixiin.** 'He bled to death.' *ptcpl* **áapchu-**. *See* **aapchii-**.

**aapeekíhleew** VAI turn *(s.t. animate, of something sheet-like)*. *usually of pieces of paper*. *ind 1st sg* **ndaapee=kíhla**, **ndaapeekíhlaam**. *conj 3rd sg* **aapeekíhlaat**. *ptcpl* **aapeekíhlaat**.

**aapéeksuw** VAI turn *(s.t. animate, of something sheet-like)*. *usually of pieces of paper*. *conj 3rd sg* **aapée=ksiit**. *ptcpl* **aapéeksiit**.

**aapéekŭneew** VTA turn s.t. animate over, open s.t. animate up *(of something sheet-like)*. *usually of pieces of paper*. *ind 1st sg* **ndaapéekŭnaaw**, **ndaa=péekŭna**. *ind 3rd sg* **wtaapeekŭnáa=wal**. *ind inv* **ndaapéekŭnukw**. *ind I-you* **ktaapéekŭnul**. *conj 3rd sg* **aapéekŭnaat**. *imp* **aapéekun**. *ptcpl* **aapéekŭnaat**.

**aapeekŭnáasuw** VAI be turned *(of something sheet-like)*. *usually of pieces of paper*. *conj 3rd sg* **aapeekŭnáasiit**. *ptcpl* **aapeekŭnáasiit**.

**aapéekxookw** VAI be turned by the wind, be blown by the wind *(s.t. animate, of something sheet-like)*. *usually of pieces of paper*. *conj 3rd sg* **aapeek=xóokwuk**. *ptcpl* **aapeekxóokwuk**.

**aapíikwam** VTI1A put a hem on s.t. *ind 1st sg* **ndaapíikwamun**. *ind 3rd sg* **wtaapíikwamun**. *conj 1st sg* **aapíi=kwamaan**. *conj 3rd sg* **aapíikwang**.

*imp* **aapíikwah**. *ptcpl* **aapíikwang**.

**aapíikwus** NA mouse. *pl* **aapíikwsak**. *dimin* **aapíikwshush**. *obv* **aapíikwsal**.

**aapiilúnjeew** VAI open one's hand. *ind 1st sg* **ndaapiilúnje**, **ndaapiilún=jeem**. *conj 3rd sg* **aapiilúnjeet**. *ptcpl* **aapiilúnjeet**. *See* **aapŭlúnjeew**.

**aapiilunjéexiin** VAI have one's hands open, have one's hands wide open. *ind 1st sg* **ndaapiilunjéexiin**, **ndaa=piilunjéexi**. *conj 3rd sg* **aapiilunjée=xiing**. *ptcpl* **aapiilunjéexiing**. *See* **aapŭlunjéexiin**.

**aapi-** PV return from *(doing something)*. **Ndáapi-kwtawŭníike.** 'I came back from the funeral.' *ptcpl* **áapi-**. *See* **aap-**, **aapu-**.

**aapíhleew** VAI open up *(as a flower)*, come open. *ind 1st sg* **ndaapíhla**, **ndaapíhlaam**. *conj 3rd sg* **aapíhlaat**. *ptcpl* **aapíhlaat**.

**aapíhleew** VII open up, come open *(as a shoe with sole flapping)*. *conj 3rd sg* **aapíhlaak**. *ptcpl* **aapíhlaak**.

**áapkeew** VAI come back from dancing, return from dancing. *ind 1st sg* **ndáapka**, **ndáapkaam**. *conj 3rd sg* **áapkaat**. *imp* **áapkaal**. *ptcpl* **áapkaat**.

**aapoochíixiin** VAI be on inside out; be upside down. *ind 1st sg* **ndaapoo=chíixiin**, **ndaapoochíixi**. *conj 3rd sg* **aapoochíixiing**. *ptcpl* **aapoochíi=xiing**.

**aapoochíixtoow** VTI2 put s.t. on wrong side out; put s.t. upside down. *ind 1st sg* **ndaapoochíixtoon**. *ind 3rd sg* **wtaapoochíixtoon**. *conj 1st sg* **aa=poochiixtáwaan**. *conj 3rd sg* **aapoo=chíixtaakw**. *imp* **aapoochíixtool**. *ptcpl* **aapoochíixtaakw**.

**aapoochíixŭmeew** VTA put s.t. animate on wrong side out, put s.t. animate on inside out; put s.o. upside down. *ind 1st sg* **ndaapoochíixŭmaaw**, **ndaa=poochíixŭma**. *ind 3rd sg* **wtaapoo=chiixŭmáawal**. *ind inv* **ndaapoochíi=xŭmukw**. *ind I-you* **ktaapoochíixŭ=mul**. *conj 3rd sg* **aapoochíixŭmaat**. *imp* **aapoochíixum**. *ptcpl* **aapoochíi=xŭmaat**.

**aapoochíixun** VII be on inside out; be upside down. *conj 3rd sg* **aapoochíi=xung**. *ptcpl* **aapoochíixung**.

**aapoochíhkam** VTI1A have s.t. on inside out, put s.t. on inside out *(of clothing)*. *ind 1st sg* **ndaapoochíhkamun**. *ind 3rd sg* **wtaapoochíhkamun**. *conj 1st sg* **aapoochíhkamaan**. *conj 3rd sg* **aapoochíhkang**. *imp* **aapoochíhkah**. *ptcpl* **aapoochíhkang**.

**aapoochíhkaweew** VTA have s.t. animate on inside out *(of clothing)*. *ind 1st sg* **ndaapoochíhkawaaw**, **ndaapoo=chíhkawa**. *ind 3rd sg* **wtaapoochih=kawáawal**. *ind inv* **ndaapoochíh=kaakw**. *ind I-you* **ktaapoochíhkool**. *conj 3rd sg* **aapoochíhkawaat**. *imp* **aapoochíhkaw**. *ptcpl* **aapoochíh=kawaat**.

**aapoochkwàláaheew** VAIO throw s.t. upside down. *ind 1st sg* **ndaapooch=kwàláaheen**. *ind 3rd sg* **wtaapooch=kwàláaheen**. *conj 3rd sg* **aapooch=kwàláaheet**. *imp* **aapoochkwàláa=heel**. *ptcpl* **aapoochkwàláaheet**.

**aapoochkwàlaapéhlaleew** VTA hang s.o. upside down, hang s.t. animate upside down. *ind 1st sg* **ndaapoochkwàlaa=péhlalaaw**, **ndaapoochkwàlaapéh=lala**. *ind 3rd sg* **wtaapoochkwàlaa=pehlaláawal**. *ind inv* **ndaapooch=kwàlaapéhlalukw**. *ind I-you* **ktaa=poochkwàlaapéhlalul**. *conj 3rd sg* **aapoochkwàlaapéhlalaat**. *imp* **aa=poochkwàlaapéhlal**. *ptcpl* **aapooch=kwàlaapéhlalaat**.

**aapoochkwàlaapéhlatoow** VTI2 hang s.t. upside down. *ind 1st sg* **ndaa=poochkwàlaapéhlatoon**. *ind 3rd sg* **wtaapoochkwàlaapéhlatoon**. *conj 1st sg* **aapoochkwàlaapehlatáwaan**. *conj 3rd sg* **aapoochkwàlaapéhla=**

**taakw**. *imp* **aapoochkwàlaapéhla=tool**. *ptcpl* **aapoochkwàlaapéhla=taakw**.

**aapoochkwàlaapéhleew** VAI hang upside down *(s.t. animate)*. *ind 1st sg* **ndaapoochkwàlaapéhla**, **ndaa=poochkwàlaapéhlaam**. *conj 3rd sg* **aapoochkwàlaapéhlaat**. *imp* **aa=poochkwàlaapéhlaal**. *ptcpl* **aa=poochkwàlaapéhlaat**.

**aapoochkwàlaapéhleew** VII hang upside down. *conj 3rd sg* **aapoochkwàlaa=péhlaak**. *ptcpl* **aapoochkwàlaa=péhlaak**.

**aapoochkwàlhóosuw** VAI do a somersault. *ind 1st sg* **ndaapoochkwàl=hóosi**, **ndaapoochkwàlhóosiim**. *conj 3rd sg* **aapoochkwàlhóosiit**. *imp* **aa=poochkwàlhóosiil***ptcpl* **aapooch=kwalhóosiit**.

**aapoochkwàlíixiin** VAI lie upside down. *ind 1st sg* **ndaapoochkwàlíixiin**, **ndaapoochkwàlíixi**. *conj 3rd sg* **aa=poochkwàlíixiing**. *ptcpl* **aapooch=kwàlíixiing**.

**aapoochkwàlíixtoow** VTI2 turn s.t. inside out, turn s.t. upside down. *ind 1st sg* **ndaapoochkwàlíixtoon**. *ind 3rd sg* **wtaapoochkwàlíixtoon**. *conj 1st sg* **aapoochkwàliixtáwaan**. *conj 3rd sg* **aapoochkwàlíixtaakw**. *imp* **aa=poochkwàlíixtool**. *ptcpl* **aapooch=kwàlíixtaakw**.

**aapoochkwàlíixŭmeew** VTA turn s.o. upside down. *ind 1st sg* **ndaapooch=kwàlíixŭmaaw**, **ndaapoochkwàlíi=xŭma**. *ind 3rd sg* **wtaapoochkwàlii=xŭmáawal**. *ind inv* **ndaapoochkwàl=íixŭmukw**. *ind I-you* **ktaapooch=kwàlíixŭmul**. *conj 3rd sg* **aapooch=kwàlíixŭmaat**. *imp* **aapoochkwàl=íixum**. *ptcpl* **aapoochkwàlíixŭmaat**.

**aapoochkwàlíixun** VII lie upside down. *conj 3rd sg* **aapoochkwàlíixung**. *ptcpl* **aapoochkwàlíixung**.

**aapoochkwàlíhleew** VAI fall upside down. *ind 1st sg* **ndaapoochkwàlíh=la**, **ndaapoochkwàlíhlaam**. *conj 3rd sg* **aapoochkwàlíhlaat**. *imp* **aa=poochkwàlíhlaal**. *ptcpl* **aapooch=kwàlíhlaat**.

**aapoochkwàlihtéexiin** VAI lie upside down, come to rest in an upside down position. *ind 1st sg* **ndaapoochkwàl=ihtéexiin**, **ndaapoochkwàlihtéexi**. *conj 3rd sg* **aapoochkwàlihtéexiing**. *ptcpl* **aapoochkwàlihtéexiing**.

**aapoochkwàlihtéexun** VII lie upside down, come to rest in an upside down position. *conj 3rd sg* **aapoochkwàl=ihtéexung**. *ptcpl* **aapoochkwàlih=téexung**.

**aapoochkwálŭneew** VTA hold s.o. upside down *(using the hands)*. *ind 1st sg* **ndaapoochkwálŭnaaw**, **ndaa=poochkwálŭna**. *ind 3rd sg* **wtaa=poochkwàlŭnáawal**. *ind inv* **ndaa=poochkwálŭnukw**. *ind I-you* **ktaa=poochkwálŭnul**. *conj 3rd sg* **aa=poochkwálŭnaat**. *imp* **aapooch=kwálun**. *ptcpl* **aapoochkwálŭnaat**.

**aapoochkwálŭnum** VTI1B hold s.t. upside down *(using the hands)*. *ind 1st sg* **ndaapoochkwàlŭnúmun**. *ind 3rd sg* **wtaapoochkwàlŭnúmun**. *conj 1st sg* **aapoochkwàlŭnúmaan**. *conj 3rd sg* **aapoochkwálŭnung**. *imp* **aa=poochkwálŭnih**. *ptcpl* **aapooch=kwálŭnung**.

**aapoochkwíhleew** VAI lie upside down, turn upside down, fall upside down. *ind 1st sg* **ndaapoochkwíhla**, **ndaa=poochkwíhlaam**. *conj 3rd sg* **aa=poochkwíhlaat**. *imp* **aapoochkwíh=laal**. *ptcpl* **aapoochkwíhlaat**.

**aapoosktóoneew** VAI have thick lips. *ind 1st sg* **ndaapoosktóona**, **ndaapoos=któonaam**. *conj 3rd sg* **aapoosktóo=naat**. *ptcpl* **aapoosktóonaat**.

**aapootawéeheew** VAIO wear s.t. inside out. *ind 1st sg* **ndaapootawéeheen**. *ind 3rd sg* **wtaapootawéeheen**. *conj*

*3rd sg* **aapootawéeheet**. *imp* **aapoo=taweéheel**. *ptcpl* **aapootawéeheet**.

**aapóotŭneew** VTA turn s.t. animate inside out *(using the hands)*. *ind 1st sg* **ndaapóotŭnaaw, ndaapóotŭna**. *ind 3rd sg* **wtaapootŭnáawal**. *ind inv* **ndaapóotŭnukw**. *ind I-you* **ktaa=póotŭnul**. *conj 3rd sg* **aapóotŭnaat**. *imp* **aapóotun**. *ptcpl* **aapóotŭnaat**.

**aapóotŭnum** VTI 1B turn s.t. inside out *(using the hands)*. *ind 1st sg* **ndaa=pootŭnúmun**. *ind 3rd sg* **wtaapoo=tŭnúmun**. *conj 1st sg* **aapootŭnúm=aan**. *conj 3rd sg* **aapóotŭnung**. *imp* **aapóotŭnih**. *ptcpl* **aapóotŭnung**.

**aapsúpaleew** VTA drown s.o. *ind 1st sg* **ndaapsúpalaaw, ndaapsúpala**. *ind 3rd sg* **wtaapsupaláawal**. *ind inv* **ndaapsúpalukw**. *ind I-you* **ktaap=súpalul**. *conj 3rd sg* **aapsúpalaat**. *imp* **aapsúpal**. *ptcpl* **aapsúpalaat**.

**aapsúpeew** VAI drown. *ind 1st sg* **ndaap=súpe, ndaapsúpeem**. *conj 3rd sg* **aapsúpeet**. *ptcpl* **aapsúpeet**. *See* **aaptúpeew**.

**aaptáchuw** VAI freeze to death. *ind 1st sg* **ndaaptáchi, ndaaptáchiim**. *conj 3rd sg* **aaptáchiit**. *ptcpl* **aaptáchiit**.

**aaptahpáaheew** VTA scare s.o. to death. *ind 1st sg* **ndaaptahpáahaaw, ndaa=ptahpáaha**. *ind 3rd sg* **wtaaptah=paaháawal**. *ind inv* **ndaaptahpáa=hukw**. *ind I-you* **ktaaptahpáahul**. *conj 3rd sg* **aaptahpáahaat**. *imp* **aaptáhpaah**. *ptcpl* **aaptahpáahaat**.

**aaptalóhkeew** VAI work oneself to death. **Mawí-aaptalóhkeew.** 'He went to prison for life.' *ind 1st sg* **ndaaptal=óhke, ndaaptalóhkeem**. *conj 3rd sg* **aaptalóhkeet**. *ptcpl* **aaptalóhkeet**.

**aaptàwéendam** VOTI 1A die in pain. *ind 1st sg* **ndaaptàwéendam**. *conj 3rd sg* **aaptàwéendang**. *ptcpl* **aaptàwéen=dang**.

**aapteelúndam** VOTI 1A grieve oneself to death, die of grief, be grieving. *ind 1st sg* **ndaapteelúndam**. *conj 3rd sg* **aapteelúndang**. *ptcpl* **aapteelún=dang**.

**aaptii-** PN to death. **Áaptii-kihtóxkwees.** 'Woman who died of old age.' *See* **aapchii-**.

**aaptihlóosuw** VAI be a man who died of old age. **Péexoot ndaaptihlóosi.** 'I'm just about dying of old age.' *ind 1st sg* **ndaaptihlóosi, ndaaptihlóosiim**. *conj 3rd sg* **aaptihlóosiit**. *ptcpl* **aaptihlóosiit**.

**aaptihtéexiin** VAI fall to one's death. *ind 1st sg* **ndaaptihtéexiin, ndaaptih=téexi**. *conj 3rd sg* **aaptihtéexiing**. *ptcpl* **aaptihtéexiing**.

**aaptoonáakan** NI voice *(especially of the Lord)*; rule. *pl* **aaptoonáakanal**.

**aaptoonáaleew** VTA speak with s.o. *(especially on the telephone)*. *ind 1st sg* **ndaaptoonáalaaw, ndaaptoonáala**. *ind 3rd sg* **wtaaptoonaaláawal**. *ind inv* **ndaaptoonáalukw**. *ind I-you* **ktaaptoonáalul**. *conj 3rd sg* **aaptoo=náalaat**. *imp* **aaptóonaal**. *ptcpl* **aaptoonáalaat**.

**aaptóoneew** VAI speak *(especially in public)*; speak at a meeting, speak at a gathering. **Kwáy méhch aaptóone.** 'Now he's speaking (as of a baby starting to talk)' *ind 1st sg* **ndaap=tóona, ndaaptóonaam**. *conj 3rd sg* **aaptóonaat**. *imp* **aaptóonaal**. *ptcpl* **aaptóonaat**. *See* **aaptóoneew**.

**aaptóoneew** VAI speak *(especially in public)*; speak at a meeting, speak at a gathering. *ind 1st sg* **ndaaptóone, ndaaptóoneem**. *conj 3rd sg* **aaptóo=neet**. *imp* **aaptóoneel**. *ptcpl* **aaptóo=neet**. *See* **aaptóoneew**.

**aaptóngwaam** VAI die in one's sleep, die while sleeping. *ind 1st sg* **ndaap=tóngwaam**. *conj 3rd sg* **aaptón=gwaang**. *ptcpl* **aaptóngwaang**.

**aaptulóosuw** VAI overeat to the point of being sick. *ind 1st sg* **ndaaptulóosi**,

**ndaaptulóosiim**. *conj 3rd sg* **aaptul=óosiit**. *ptcpl* **aaptulóosiit**.

**aaptúpeew** VAI drown. *ind 1st sg* **ndaa=ptúpe**, **ndaaptúpeem**. *conj 3rd sg* **aaptúpeet**. *ptcpl* **aaptúpeet**. *See* **aapsúpeew**.

**aaptupéhleew** VAI bleed to death. *ind 1st sg* **ndaaptupéhla**, **ndaaptup=éhlaam**. *conj 3rd sg* **aaptupéhlaat**. *ptcpl* **aaptupéhlaat**.

**aaptúsuw** VAI be overheated, be overcome with heat, faint from the heat. *ind 1st sg* **ndaaptúsi**, **ndaaptúsiim**. *conj 3rd sg* **aaptúsiit**. *ptcpl* **aaptúsiit**.

**aapu-** PV return from *(doing something)*. *informal*. **Áapu-manáxe.** 'He comes back from cutting wood.' *ptcpl* **áapu-**. *See* **aap-**, **aapi-**.

**áapul** NA apple; Apple *(man's name)*. **Aapŭláya.** 'The late Apple.' *obv* **áapŭlal**. *From Dutch.*

**aapŭlúnjeew** VAI open one's hand. *ind 1st sg* **ndaapŭlúnja**, **ndaapŭlún=jaam**. *conj 3rd sg* **aapŭlúnjaat**. *imp* **aapŭlúnjaal**. *ptcpl* **aapŭlúnjaat**. *See* **aapiilúnjeew**.

**aapŭlunjéexiin** VAI have one's hands open, have one's hands wide open. *ind 1st sg* **ndaapŭlunjéexiin**, **ndaa=pŭlunjéexi**. *conj 3rd sg* **aapŭlunjée=xiing**. *ptcpl* **aapŭlunjéexiing**. *See* **aapiilunjéexiin**.

**aapŭlúsh'heew** VAI work in an apple orchard. *ind 1st sg* **ndaapŭlúsh'he**, **ndaapŭlúsh'heem**. *conj 3rd sg* **aapŭlúsh'heet**. *imp* **aapŭlúsh'heel**. *ptcpl* **aapŭlúsh'heet**.

**áapŭlush** NA apple. *pl* **aapŭlúshak**. *poss* **ndaapŭlúshum**. *obv* **aapŭlúshal**. *From Dutch.*

**aapŭlúshahkw** NA apple tree. *pl* **aapŭ=lusháhkwak**. *poss* **ndaapŭlusháh=kwum**. *loc* **aapŭlusháhkwung**. *dimin* **aapŭlusháhkwush**. *obv* **aapŭlusháhkwal**.

**áapŭneew** VTA open s.t. animate, take the lid off s.t. animate *(as the cover of a pail)*. *ind 1st sg* **ndáapŭnaaw**, **ndáapŭna**. *ind 3rd sg* **wtaapŭnáa=wal**. *ind inv* **ndáapŭnukw**. *ind I-you* **ktáapŭnul**. *conj 3rd sg* **áapŭnaat**. *imp* **áapun**. *ptcpl* **áapŭnaat**.

**áapŭnum** VTI1B open s.t., lift s.t. off *(as the cover of a box or coffin)*. *ind 1st sg* **ndaapŭnúmun**. *ind 3rd sg* **wtaa=pŭnúmun**. *conj 1st sg* **aapŭnúmaan**. *conj 3rd sg* **áapŭnung**. *imp* **áapŭnih**. *ptcpl* **áapŭnung**.

**aapŭwáawatuw** VII be cheap, be inexpensive. *conj 3rd sg* **aapŭwáawatiik**. *ptcpl* **aapŭwáawatiik**.

**aapŭwáawatuw** VAI be cheap, be inexpensive *(s.t. animate)*. *conj 3rd sg* **aa=pŭwáawatiit**. *ptcpl* **aapŭwáawatiit**.

**aapŭwahpáasuw** VAI scare easily, be easy to scare. *ind 1st sg* **ndaapŭ=wahpáasi**, **ndaapŭwahpáasiim**. *conj 3rd sg* **aapŭwahpáasiit**. *ptcpl* **aa=pŭwahpáasiit**. *intensive reduplication* **ayaapŭwahpáasuw**.

**aapŭwalóhkeew** VAI get an easy job, have an easy job. *ind 1st sg* **ndaa=pŭwalóhke**, **ndaapŭwalóhkeem**. *conj 3rd sg* **aapŭwalóhkeet**. *ptcpl* **aapŭwalóhkeet**.

**aapŭwalóhkeew** VAIO get s.t. cheap, pay a little for s.t. *ind 1st sg* **ndaapŭwal=óhkeen**. *ind 3rd sg* **wtaapŭwalóh=keen**. *conj 3rd sg* **aapŭwalóhkeet**. *imp* **aapŭwalóhkeel**. *ptcpl* **aapŭwal=óhkeet**.

**áapŭwat** VII be easy *(to do)*. *conj 3rd sg* **áapŭwahk**. *ptcpl* **áapŭwahk**.

**aapŭwéelŭmeew** VTA find s.o. easy *(to do something with)*. **Ndaapŭwéelŭ=maaw ndakehkíimaan.** 'I find him easy to teach.'; **Ndaapŭwéelŭmaaw nŭmeelawusóomaan.** 'I find him easy to play with.' *ind 1st sg* **ndaa=pŭwéelŭmaaw**, **ndaapŭwéelŭma**. *ind 3rd sg* **wtaapŭweelŭmáawal**. *ind inv* **ndaapŭwéelŭmukw**. *ind I-you*

**ktaapŭwéelŭmul**. *conj 3rd sg* **aapŭ=wéelŭmaat**. *ptcpl* **aapŭwéelŭmaat**.

**aapŭweelúndam** VTI1A find s.t. easy to do, think s.t. easy to do. **Ndaapŭ=weelúndamun ootéeneeng ndáan.** 'I don't think anything of going to town.'; **Ndaapŭweelúndamun nŭmáw-kawí.** 'I find it easy to go to sleep.' *ind 1st sg* **ndaapŭweelún=damun**. *ind 3rd sg* **wtaapŭweelún=damun**. *conj 1st sg* **aapŭweelún=damaan**. *conj 3rd sg* **aapŭweelún=dang**. *ptcpl* **aapŭweelúndang**.

**aapŭwíiheew** VTA get s.t. animate cheaply, buy s.t. animate cheaply. *ind 1st sg* **ndaapŭwíihaaw**, **ndaapŭwíiha**. *ind 3rd sg* **wtaapŭwiiháawal**. *ind inv* **ndaapŭwíihukw**. *ind I-you* **ktaapŭ=wíihul**. *conj 3rd sg* **aapŭwíihaat**. *imp* **áapŭwiih**. *ptcpl* **aapŭwíihaat**.

**aapŭwíixiin** VAI be easy to do, be easy *(to read, to understand)*. *conj 3rd sg* **aapŭwíixiing**. *ptcpl* **aapŭwíixiing**.

**aapŭwíixtoow** VTI2 make it easy for someone to do s.t., fix s.t. so it would be easy *(to do something)*. *ind 1st sg* **ndaapŭwíixtoon**. *ind 3rd sg* **wtaapŭ=wíixtoon**. *conj 1st sg* **aapŭwiixtáw=aan**. *conj 3rd sg* **aapŭwíixtaakw**. *imp* **aapŭwíixtool**. *ptcpl* **aapŭwíixtaakw**.

**aapŭwíixŭmeew** VTA make s.t. animate so that it would be easy, fix s.t. animate so that it would be easy *(for someone to do something)*. **Ndaapŭwíixŭ=maaw eeheeshandéekan wéenj-káng-tawúnak.** 'I made it so that the window would be easy for me to open.' *ind 1st sg* **ndaapŭwíixŭmaaw**, **ndaapŭwíixŭma**. *ind 3rd sg* **wtaa=pŭwiixŭmáawal**. *conj 3rd sg* **aapŭ=wíixŭmaat**. *imp* **aapŭwíixum**. *ptcpl* **aapŭwíixŭmaat**.

**aapŭwíixun** VII be easy *(to do)*. *conj 3rd sg* **aapŭwíixung**. *ptcpl* **aapŭwíixung**.

**aapŭwíhtoow** VTI2 get s.t. cheaply, buy s.t. cheaply. **Kángu-uch lúkih -aapŭwíhtawan.** 'Get it as cheaply as you can.' *ind 1st sg* **ndaapŭwíhtoon**. *ind 3rd sg* **wtaapŭwíhtoon**. *conj 1st sg* **aapŭwíhtawaan**. *conj 3rd sg* **aapŭwíhtaakw**. *imp* **aapŭwíhtool**. *ptcpl* **aapŭwíhtaakw**.

**aapŭwu-** PV early; easily. *informal.* **Ndáapŭwu-áamwi.** 'I got up early.'; **Ayáapŭwu-maxkchàlíingweew.** 'He blushes easily' *ptcpl* **áapŭwu-**. *intensive reduplication* **ayáapŭwu-**. *See* **aapwi-**, **aapwu-**.

**áapwi** PC early; easily. **Áapwi mbáam.** 'I came early.'; **Áapwi aapalóhkeew.** 'He's coming back from working soon.'

**aapwi-** PV early; easily. **Ndáapwi-pá.** 'I came early.' *ptcpl* **áapwi-**. *See* **aapŭwu-**, **aapwu-**.

**áapwu** PC early; easily. *informal.* **Áapwu há kíi káwi?** 'Did you go to sleep early?'; **Áapwu nŭmawalóhke.** 'I went to work early.' *See* **áapwi**.

**aapwu-** PV early; easily. *informal.* **Áapwu- nóohum -wiinamálsuw, lumtiisíineew.** 'My grandmother was sick early on, she had rheumatism.'; **Ktáapwu-lpákw.** 'You cry easily.' *ptcpl* **áapwu-**. *See* **aapŭwu-**, **aapwi-**.

**aapxéexiin** VAI listen, listen intently. *ind 1st sg* **ndaapxéexiin**, **ndaapxéexi**. *conj 3rd sg* **aapxéexiing**. *imp* **aapxée=xiil**. *ptcpl* **aapxéexiing**, **aapxéexiit**.

**naasíituy** NID my behind, my backside, my ass. *3rd poss* **waasíituy**. *loc* **naasíitiing**.

**aashóokeew** VAI walk in the water. *ind 1st sg* **ndaashóoke**, **ndaashóokeem**. *conj 3rd sg* **aashóokeet**. *imp* **aashóo=keel**. *ptcpl* **aashóokeet**.

**áashtee** PC instead, next, then. **Áashtee-uch yéelak ndá.** 'I'll go there instead.'; **Áashtee-uch yóon ndawée=heen.** 'I'll use this instead, I'll wear this instead.'

**aashtéhleew** VAI run across. *ind 1st sg*

ndaashtéhla, ndaashtéhlaam. *conj 3rd sg* **aashtéhlaat**. *imp* **aashtéhlaal**. *ptcpl* **aashtéhlaat**.

**aashtehtéeheew** VTA crucify s.o., put s.o. on the cross. *ind 1st sg* **ndaashteh=téehaaw, ndaashtehtéeha**. *ind 3rd sg* **wtaashtehteeháawal**. *ind inv* **ndaa=shtehtéehookw**. *ind I-you* **ktaash=tehtéehool**. *conj 3rd sg* **aashtehtée=haat**. *imp* **aashtéhteeh**. *ptcpl* **aash=tehtéehaat**.

**aashtehteehíikan** NI cross. *pl* **aashteh=teehíikanal**. *poss* **ndaashtehteehíi=kan**. *loc* **aashtehteehíikanung**. *dimin* **aashtehteehíikanush**.

**aashŭwaakchóoxwee** VAI walk across the water. *ind 1st sg* **ndaashŭwaak=chóoxwe, ndaashŭwaakchóoxweem**. *conj 3rd sg* **aashŭwaakchóoxweet**. *imp* **aashŭwaakchóoxweel**. *ptcpl* **aashŭwaakchóoxweet**.

**aashŭwahéembteew** VAI change one's shirt. *ind 1st sg* **ndaashŭwahéembta, ndaashŭwahéembtaam**. *conj 3rd sg* **aashŭwahéembtaat**. *imp* **aashŭ=wahéembtaal**. *ptcpl* **aashŭwah=éembtaat**.

**aashŭwahksúneew** VAI trade shoes, change one's shoes. *ind 1st sg* **ndaa=shŭwahksúna, ndaashŭwahksún=aam**. *conj 3rd sg* **aashŭwahksúnaat**. *imp* **aashŭwahksúnaal**. *ptcpl* **aashŭ=wahksúnaat**.

**aashŭwahpapoonéewak** VAI trade chairs, change chairs. *usually plural. ind 1st pl* **ndaashŭwahpapoonáhna**. *conj 3rd pl* **aashŭwahpapoonáhtiit**. *imp* **aashŭwahpapóonaakw**. *ptcpl* **aashŭwahpapoonáhtiit**.

**aashŭwahpapóonheew** VAI trade chairs, change chairs. *ind 1st sg* **ndaashŭ=wahpapóonhe, ndaashŭwahpa=póonheem**. *conj 3rd sg* **aashŭwah=papóonheet**. *imp* **aashŭwah=papóonheel**. *ptcpl* **aashŭwahpa=póonheet**.

**aashŭwahtakíhleew** VAI run across *(the road)*. *ind 1st sg* **ndaashŭwahta=kíhla, ndaashŭwahtakíhlaam**. *conj 3rd sg* **aashŭwahtakíhlaat**. *imp* **aashŭwahtakíhlaal**. *ptcpl* **aashŭ=wahtakíhlaat**.

**aashŭwákuw** VAI change one's clothes. *ind 1st sg* **ndaashŭwákwi, ndaa=shŭwákwiim**. *conj 3rd sg* **aashŭ=wákwiit**. *imp* **aashŭwákwiil**. *ptcpl* **aashŭwákwiit**.

**aashŭwalóoleew** VTA trade with s.o. *ind 1st sg* **ndaashŭwalóolaaw, ndaa=shŭwalóola**. *ind 3rd sg* **wtaashŭwal=ooláawal**. *ind inv* **ndaashŭwalóol=ukw**. *ind I-you* **ktaashŭwalóolul**. *conj 3rd sg* **aashŭwalóolaat**. *imp* **aashŭwálool**. *ptcpl* **aashŭwalóolaat**.

**aashŭwámbtoow** VTI2 tie s.t. across. *ind 1st sg* **ndaashŭwámbtoon**. *ind 3rd sg* **wtaashŭwámbtoon**. *conj 1st sg* **aashŭwambtáwaan**. *conj 3rd sg* **aashŭwámbtaakw**. *imp* **aashŭ=wámbtool**. *ptcpl* **aashŭwámbtaakw**.

**aashŭwashíikaneew** VAI change one's socks. *ind 1st sg* **ndaashŭwashíikana, ndaashŭwashíikanaam**. *conj 3rd sg* **aashŭwashíikanaat**. *imp* **aashŭ=washíikanaal**. *ptcpl* **aashŭwashíi=kanaat**.

**aashŭwatéexun** VII be a crossroads; the Four Corners *(main intersection near band office at Moraviantown, Ontario)*. **Aashŭwatéexun numáw-níipawi.** 'I'm going to the Four Corners.' *conj 3rd sg* **aashŭwatéexung**. *ptcpl* **aashŭwatéexung**.

**aashŭwiikéewak** VAI trade houses. *usually plural. ind 1st pl* **ndaashŭwii=kéhna**. *conj 3rd pl* **aashŭwiikéhtiit**. *imp* **aashŭwíikeekw**.*ptcpl* **aashŭwii=kéhtiit**.

**aashŭwíikwsuw** VAI crawl across. *ind 1st sg* **ndaashŭwíikwsi, ndaashŭ=wíikwsiim**. *conj 3rd sg* **aashŭwíi=kwsiit**. *imp* **aashŭwíikwsiil**. *ptcpl*

**aashŭwíikwsiit**.

**aashŭwiináxkeew** VAI reach across. *ind 1st sg* **ndaashŭwiináxke**, **ndaashŭ=wiináxkeem**. *conj 3rd sg* **aashŭwii=náxkeet**. *imp* **aashŭwiináxkeel**. *ptcpl* **aashŭwiináxkeet**.

**aashŭwiipáhtoow** VTI2 take s.t. across in a hurry. *ind 1st sg* **ndaashŭwii=páhtoon**. *ind 3rd sg* **wtaashŭwii=páhtoon**. *conj 1st sg* **aashŭwiipáh=tawaan**. *conj 3rd sg* **aashŭwiipáh=taakw**. *imp* **aashŭwiipáhtool**. *ptcpl* **aashŭwiipáhtaakw**.

**aashŭwíipheew** VTA take s.o. across in a hurry. *ind 1st sg* **ndaashŭwíiphaaw**, **ndaashŭwíipha**. *ind 3rd sg* **wtaa=shŭwiipháawal**. *ind inv* **ndaashŭ=wíiphukw**. *ind I-you* **ktaashŭwíip=hul**. *conj 3rd sg* **aashŭwíiphaat**. *imp* **aashŭwíipah**. *ptcpl* **aashŭwíiphaat**.

**aashŭwiipŭlóokeew** VAI change one's pants. *ind 1st sg* **ndaashŭwiipŭlóoke**, **ndaashŭwiipŭlóokeem**. *conj 3rd sg* **aashŭwiipŭlóokeet**. *imp* **aashŭwii=pŭlóokeel**. *ptcpl* **aashŭwiipŭlóokeet**.

**aashŭwiixkéexiin** VAI cross one's legs. *ind 1st sg* **ndaashŭwiixkéexiin**, **ndaashŭwiixkéexi**. *conj 3rd sg* **aa=shŭwiixkéexiing**. *imp* **aashŭwiix=kéexiil**. *ptcpl* **aashŭwiixkéexiing**.

**aashŭwíixtoow** VTI2 cross s.t. *ind 1st sg* **ndaashŭwíixtoon**. *ind 3rd sg* **wtaa=shŭwíixtoon**. *conj 1st sg* **aashŭwiix=táwaan**. *conj 3rd sg* **aashŭwíixtaakw**. *imp* **aashŭwíixtool**. *ptcpl* **aashŭ=wíixtaakw**.

**aashŭwíhleew** VAI go across, drive across, pedal across, fly across. *ind 1st sg* **ndaashŭwíhla**, **ndaashŭwíhlaam**. *conj 3rd sg* **aashŭwíhlaat**. *imp* **aa=shŭwíhlaal**. *ptcpl* **aashŭwíhlaat**.

**aashŭwóoxweew** VAI walk across. *ind 1st sg* **ndaashŭwóoxwe**, **ndaashŭwóo=xweem**. *conj 3rd sg* **aashŭwóoxweet**. *imp* **aashŭwóoxweel**. *ptcpl* **aashŭ=wóoxweet**.

**aashŭwuchéhleew** VAI drive across. *ind 1st sg* **ndaashŭwuchéhla**, **ndaashŭ=wuchéhlaam**. *conj 3rd sg* **aashŭ=wuchéhlaat**. *imp* **aashŭwuchéhlaal**. *ptcpl* **aashŭwuchéhlaat**.

**aashŭwukaatéexiin** VAI have one's legs crossed. *ind 1st sg* **ndaashŭwukaa=téexiin**, **ndaashŭwukaatéexi**. *conj 3rd sg* **aashŭwukaatéexiing**. *ptcpl* **aashŭwukaatéexiing**. *moderative reduplication* **aayaashŭwukaatéexiin**.

**aashŭwúneew** VTA exchange s.t. animate, return s.t. animate, give s.t. animate back *(after borrowing it)*. *ind 1st sg* **ndaashŭwúnaaw**, **ndaashŭ=wúna**. *ind 3rd sg* **wtaashŭwunáa=wal**. *ind inv* **ndaashŭwúnukw**. *ind I-you* **ktaashŭwúnul**. *conj 3rd sg* **aashŭwúnaat**. *imp* **áashŭwun**. *ptcpl* **aashŭwúnaat**.

**aashŭwúnum** VTI1B exchange s.t., give s.t. back, return s.t. *(after borrowing it)*. *ind 1st sg* **ndaashŭwúnŭmun**. *ind 3rd sg* **wtaashŭwúnŭmun**. *conj 1st sg* **aashŭwúnŭmaan**. *conj 3rd sg* **aashŭwúnung**. *imp* **aashŭwúnih**. *ptcpl* **aashŭwúnung**.

**naawíikan** NID my back. *3rd poss* **waawíikan**. *loc* **naawíikanung**. *See* nŭ**waawíikan**.

**áawiis** PC late. **Áawiis péew.** 'He came late.'

**aayáaxkwu** PC later, eventually. **Aayáaxkwu náh ndá.** 'I went later.'; **Aayáaxkwu-ch ktalŭmusíhna.** 'We'll be leaving eventually.'

**aayaláwii** PC peacefully, quietly, contentedly. **Aayaláwii laalŭmátapuw.** 'He's sitting quietly.'; **Aayaláwii meelawúsŭwak.** 'They're playing quietly.' *See* **naláwii**.

**áayee** PC emphatic. **Ootéeneeng áa kwáy ktáhna kwáy kíishkwihk áayee má ngíish-pumúsiin.** 'Let's go to town today while I'm able to walk.'; **Áayee má kŭwíichŭmi.** 'Please help me.'

# A

**ách** PC even. **Ách máh pasíi.** 'Not even half of it.'; **Ách nú kóotum eewée=heet kwuníi-shkwúnayeew wtéeng.** 'Even the coat he was wearing had a long tail behind.' *See* **áhch**.

**achahkwalihkéeshuw** VAI take short steps *(dimin). ind 1st sg* **njachah=kwalihkáashi**, **njachahkwalihkáa=shiim**. *conj 3rd sg* **achahkwalih=káashiit**. *imp* **achahkwalihkáashiil**. *ptcpl* **cheechahkwalihkáashiit**.

**achahkwalihkehléeshuw** VAI take short steps *(dimin). ind 1st sg* **njachah=kwalihkehláashi**, **njachahkwalih=kehláashiim**. *conj 3rd sg* **achahkwa=lihkehláashiit**. *imp* **achahkwalih=kehláashiil**. *ptcpl* **cheechahkwalih=kehláashiit**.

**achahkwkaacheeyéeshuw** VII have short legs *(dimin). conj 3rd sg* **achahkwkaacheeyáashiik**.

**achahkwŭnaxkéeshuw** VAI have short arms *(dimin). ind 1st sg* **njachahkwŭ=naxkáashi**, **njachahkwŭnaxkáa=shiim**. *conj 3rd sg* **achahkwŭnax=káashiit**.

**achangiixshíishuw** VAI talk in a low voice, talk in a soft voice *(dimin). ind 1st sg* **njachangiixshíishi**, **njachan=giixshíishiim**. *conj 3rd sg* **achan=giixshíishiit**. *imp* **achangiixshíishiil**. *ptcpl* **cheechangiixshíishiit**.

**achangkaachéeshuw** VAI have small legs *(dimin). ind 1st sg* **njachang=kaacháashi**, **njachangkaacháa=shiim**. *conj 3rd sg* **achangkaacháa=shiit**. *ptcpl* **cheechangkaacháashiit**.

**acheexáakwsuw** VAI be balky, be stubborn. *ind 1st sg* **njacheexáakwsi**, **njacheexáakwsiim**. *conj 3rd sg* **acheexáakwsiit**.

**achiichkwalehtéexiin** VAI fall forward. *ind 1st sg* **njachiichkwalehtéexiin**, **njachiichkwalehtéexi**. *conj 3rd sg* **achiichkwalehtéexiing**. *imp* **achii=chkwalehtéexiil**. *ptcpl* **cheechiich=kwalehtéexiing**, **cheechiichkwal=ehtéexiit**.

**achiichkwalíhleew** VAI fall head first. *ind 1st sg* **njachiichkwalíhla**, **njachiich=kwalíhlaam**. *conj 3rd sg* **achiich=kwalíhlaat**. *ptcpl* **cheechiichkwal=íhlaat**.

**achíikaweew** VTA crowd s.o. out. *ind 1st sg* **ndachíikawaaw**, **ndachíikawa**. *ind 3rd sg* **wtachiikawáawal**. *ind inv* **ndachíikaakw**. *ind I-you* **ktachíi=kool**. *conj 3rd sg* **achíikawaat**. *imp* **achíikaw**.

**achiingíiwsuw** VAI disobey, refuse to listen, be stubborn. *ind 1st sg* **njachiin=gíiwsi**, **njachiingíiwsiim**. *conj 3rd sg* **achiingíiwsiit**. *ptcpl* **cheechiin=gíiwsiit**.

**achiipahksúneew** VAI have bad shoes. *ind 1st sg* **njachiipahksúna**, **njach=iipahksúnaam**. *conj 3rd sg* **achii=pahksúnaat**. *ptcpl* **cheechiipahk=súnaat**.

**achiipíilatoow** VAI eat like a pig. *ind 1st sg* **njachiipíilato**, **njachiipíilatoom**. *conj 3rd sg* **achiipíilataakw**. *ptcpl* **cheechiipíilataakw**.

**achiipi-** PV frightful, terrible. **Njachíipi-liitéeha.** 'I think bad thoughts.' *ptcpl* **cheechíipi-**. *See* **chiipii-**, **chiipu-**, **achiipu-**.

**achíipsuw** VAI be shy, be 'backwards.' *ind 1st sg* **njachíipsi**, **njachíipsiim**. *conj 3rd sg* **achíipsiit**. *ptcpl* **chee=chíipsiit**.

**achiipu-** PV frightful, terrible. *informal.*

**Áalund awéen achíipu-ashiilón=gwane.** 'Some people have bad underarm perspiration' *ptcpl* **cheechíipu-**. *See* **chiipii-**, **chiipu-**, **achiipi-**.

**achíipŭnum** VOTI1B make faces, act up, act out of the ordinary. *ind 1st sg* **njachíipunum**. *conj 3rd sg* **achíipŭ=nung**. *ptcpl* **cheechíipŭnung**.

**achihtawohkwéexiin** VAI have one's head hanging down. *ind 1st sg* **njachihtawohkwéexiin**, **njachihta=wohkwéexi**. *conj 3rd sg* **achihtawoh=kwéexiing**. *ptcpl* **cheechihtawoh=kwéexiing**.

**àhaapchíhleew** VAI have whooping cough. *ind 1st sg* **ndahaapchíhla**, **ndahaapchíhlaam**. *conj 3rd sg* **àhaapchíhlaat**. *See* **aapchíhleew**.

**àhahtéhtoow** VTI2 nod s.t. *(of one's head)*. *ind 1st sg* **ndahahtéhtoon**. *ind 3rd sg* **wtahahtéhtoon**. *conj 1st sg* **àhahtéhtawaan**. *conj 3rd sg* **àhah=téhtaakw**. *imp* **àhahtéhtool**. *ptcpl* **àhahtéhtaakw**.

**áhch** PC even. **Áhch-uch wáak née=waaw.** 'I'll see him anyway.'; **Áhch máh náh éewu.** 'He didn't even go there.' *See* **ách**.

**ahkachíhteew** VII be shade. **Éenda-ahkachíhteek lŭmátapuw.** 'He's sitting in the shade.'; **Pŭmíichii wiikwáhmung talí ahkachíhteew.** 'It's shady by the house.' *conj 3rd sg* **ahkachíhteek**.

**ahkachihtéexiin** VAI be in the shade *(s.t. animate)*. **Ahkachihtéexiin apúw.** 'He's sitting in the shade.' *ind 1st sg* **ndahkachihtéexiin**, **ndahkachih=téexi**. *conj 3rd sg* **ahkachihtéexiing**. *ptcpl* **ahkachihtéexiing**.

**ahkachihtéexun** VII be in the shade. **Éenda-ahkchihtéexung laalŭmáta=puw.** 'He's sitting where there's shade.' *conj 3rd sg* **ahkachihtéexung**. *ptcpl* **ahkachihtéexung**.

**ahkchíikŭloos** NA umbrella. *pl* **ahkchii=kŭlóosak**. *poss* **ndahkchiikŭlóosum**. *loc* **ahkchiikŭlóosung**. *dimin* **ahk=chiikŭlóoshush**. *obv* **ahkchiikŭ=lóosal**.

**ahkiiháakan** NI field. *pl* **ahkiiháa=kanal**. *poss* **ndahkiiháakan**. *loc* **ahkiiháakanung**. *dimin* **ahkiiháa=kanush**.

**ahkíiheew** VAI be planting. *ind 1st sg* **ndahkíihe**, **ndahkíiheem**. *conj 3rd sg* **ahkíiheet**. *imp* **ahkíiheel**. *ptcpl* **ehkíiheet**.

**ahkíiheew** VAIO plant s.t. **Ptukwii=míinzhuy ndahkíihe.** 'I planted a walnut tree.' *ind 1st sg* **ndahkíiheen**. *ind 3rd sg* **wtahkíiheen**. *conj 3rd sg* **ahkíiheet**. *imp* **ahkíiheel**. *ptcpl* **ehkíiheet**.

**áhkuy** NI land, earth. *pl* **áhkŭyal**. *poss* **ndáhkŭyum**. *loc* **áhkiing**.

**ahkŭyáalakw** NI root cellar. *pl* **ahkŭ=yáalakwal**. *poss* **ndahkŭyáalakwum**. *loc* **ahkŭyáalakwung**.

**ahkŭyóowuw** VII have dirt on it, be sandy. *conj 3rd sg* **ahkŭyóowiik**. *ptcpl* **ehkŭyóowiik**.

**ahkwíhleew** VII recede, go down *(of the water level)*. *conj 3rd sg* **ahkwíhlaak**. *ptcpl* **ahkwíhlaak**.

**ahkwŭléeneew** VTA turn s.t. animate down *(of lights or sources of heat)*. *ind 1st sg* **ndahkwŭléenaaw**, **ndah=kwŭléena**. *ind 3rd sg* **wtahkwŭlee=náawal**. *conj 3rd sg* **ahkwŭléenaat**. *imp* **áhkwŭleen**. *See* **áhkwŭneew**.

**ahkwŭléenum** VTI1B turn s.t. down *(of lights or sources of heat)*. *ind 1st sg* **ndahkwŭléenŭmun**. *ind 3rd sg* **wtahkwŭléenŭmun**. *conj 1st sg* **ah=kwŭléenŭmaan**. *conj 3rd sg* **ahkwŭ=léenung**. *imp* **ahkwŭléenih**. *See* **áhkwŭnung**.

**áhkwŭneew** VTA turn s.t. animate down *(of lights or sources of heat)*. *ind 1st sg* **ndáhkwŭnaaw**, **ndáhkwŭna**. *ind 3rd sg* **wtahkwŭnáawal**. *conj 3rd sg*

**áhkwŭnaat**. *imp* **áhkwun**. *ptcpl* **áhkwŭnaat**. *See* **ahkwŭléeneew**.

**áhkwŭnum** VTI 1B turn s.t. down *(of lights or sources of heat)*. *ind 1st sg* **ndahkwŭnúmun**. *ind 3rd sg* **wtah=kwŭnúmun**. *conj 1st sg* **ahkwŭ=númaan**. *conj 3rd sg* **áhkwŭnung**. *imp* **áhkwŭnih**. *ptcpl* **áhkwŭnung**. *See* **ahkwŭléenung**.

**áhleew** VTA put s.o. down, put s.t. animate down. *ind 1st sg* **ndáhlaaw**, **ndáhla**. *ind 3rd sg* **wtahláawal**. *ind inv* **ndáhlukw**. *ind I-you* **ktáhlul**. *conj 3rd sg* **áhlaat**. *imp* **áhl**. *ptcpl* **éhlaat**.

**áhlap** NA flax plant, wild hemp. *pl* **áhlapak**. *See* **áhlapiis**.

**áhlapiis** NA flax plant, wild hemp. *pl* **ahlapíisak**. *See* **áhlap**.

**ahpalíhkeew** VAIO step upon s.t., step upon s.o. *ind 1st sg* **ndahpalíhkeen**. *ind 3rd sg* **wtahpalíhkeen**. *conj 3rd sg* **ahpalíhkeet**. *imp* **ahpalíhkeel**. *ptcpl* **ehpalíhkeet**.

**ahpalihkéhleew** VAIO step upon s.t. *ind 1st sg* **ndahpalihkéhlaan**. *ind 3rd sg* **wtahpalihkéhlaan**. *conj 3rd sg* **ahpalihkéhlaat**. *imp* **ahpalihkéh=laal**. *ptcpl* **ehpalihkéhlaat**.

**áhpapoon** NI chair. *pl* **ahpapóonal**. *poss* **ndáhpapoon**. *loc* **ahpapóo=nung**. *dimin* **ahpapóonush**.

**áhpapuw** VAIO sit upon something. *ind 1st sg* **ndáhpapiin**. *ind 3rd sg* **wtáhpapiin**. *conj 3rd sg* **áhpapiit**. *imp* **áhpapiil**. *ptcpl* **éhpapiit**.

**ahpawéeheew** VOTI use s.t. with something else. *ind 1st sg* **ndahpawée=heen**. *ind 3rd sg* **wtahpawéeheen**. *conj 3rd sg* **ahpawéeheet**. *imp* **ahpawéeheel**. *ptcpl* **ehpawéeheet**.

**ahpcháawan** NI diaper, napkin. *pl* **ahp=cháawanal**. *poss* **ndahpcháawan**. *loc* **ahpcháawanung**. *dimin* **ahp=cháawanush**.

**ahpchaawanáhŭmeew** VAI wear a diaper. *ind 1st sg* **ndahpchaawanáhŭma**, **ndahpchaawanáhŭmaam**. *conj 3rd sg* **ahpchaawanáhŭmaat**. *imp* **ahp=chaawanáhŭmaal**. *ptcpl* **ehpchaa=wanáhŭmaat**.

**ahpchéhkaweew** VTA step upon s.o. *ind 1st sg* **ndahpchéhkawaaw**, **ndahp=chéhkawa**. *ind 3rd sg* **wtahpcheh=kawáawal**. *ind inv* **ndahpchéhkaakw**. *ind I-you* **ktahpchéhkool**. *conj 3rd sg* **ahpchéhkawaat**. *imp* **ahpchéhkaw**. *ptcpl* **ehpchéhkawaat**.

**ahpiikwáaleew** VTA sew something onto s.t. animate. *ind 1st sg* **ndahpiikwáa=laaw**, **ndahpiikwáala**. *ind 3rd sg* **wtahpiikwaaláawal**. *conj 3rd sg* **ahpiikwáalaat**. *imp* **ahpíikwaal**. *ptcpl* **ehpiikwáalaat**.

**ahpíikwam** VTI 1A sew something onto s.t. *ind 1st sg* **ndahpíikwamun**. *ind 3rd sg* **wtahpíikwamun**. *conj 1st sg* **ahpíikwamaan**. *conj 3rd sg* **ahpíi=kwang**. *imp* **ahpíikwah**. *ptcpl* **ehpíikwang**.

**ahpíhkam** VTI 1A step upon s.t., fall upon s.t., sit upon s.t. *ind 1st sg* **ndahpíhkamun**. *ind 3rd sg* **wtah=píhkamun**. *conj 1st sg* **ahpíhka=maan**. *conj 3rd sg* **ahpíhkang**. *imp* **ahpíhkah**. *ptcpl* **ehpíhkang**.

**ahpíhkaweew** VTA step upon s.o., fall upon s.o., sit upon s.o. *ind 1st sg* **ndahpíhkawaaw**, **ndahpíhkawa**. *ind 3rd sg* **wtahpihkawáawal**. *ind inv* **ndahpíhkaakw**. *ind I-you* **ktahpíh=kool**. *conj 3rd sg* **ahpíhkawaat**. *imp* **ahpíhkaw**. *ptcpl* **ehpíhkawaat**.

**ahtáasuw** VII be placed, be put down. *conj 3rd sg* **ahtáasiik**. *ptcpl* **ehtáa=siik**.

**ahtamóombiil** NA car, automobile. *pl* **ahtamoombíilak**. *poss* **ndahta=moombíilum**. *loc* **ahtamoombíi=lung**. *dimin* **ahtamoombíilush**. *obv* **ahtamoombíilal**. *See* **káal**. *From English* automobile.

**ahtamoombiilhámeew** VAI drive a car, use an automobile. *ind 1st sg* **ndah=tamoombiilháma, ndahtamoom=biilhámaam**. *conj 3rd sg* **ahta=moombiilhámaat**. *imp* **ahtamoom=biilhámaal**.

**áhteew** VII be there. *conj 3rd sg* **áhteek**. *ptcpl* **éhteek**.

**ahteeháaleew** VTA turn s.t. animate down *(of lights or sources of heat)*. *ind 1st sg* **ndahteeháalaaw, ndah=teeháala**. *ind 3rd sg* **wtahteehaaláa=wal**. *ind inv* **ndahteeháalukw**. *ind I-you* **ktahteeháalul**. *conj 3rd sg* **ahteeháalaat**. *imp* **ahtéehaal**. *ptcpl* **ehteeháalaat**.

**ahtéeham** VTI1A put s.t. out *(of fires)*. *ind 1st sg* **ndahtéehŭmun**. *ind 3rd sg* **wtahtéehŭmun**. *conj 1st sg* **ahtée=hŭmaan**. *conj 3rd sg* **ahtéehang**. *imp* **ahtéehih**. *ptcpl* **ehtéehang**.

**ahteewohkwéepuw** VAI sit bent over, sit hunched over. *ind 1st sg* **ndahtee=wohkwéepi, ndahteewohkwéepiim**. *conj 3rd sg* **ahteewohkwéepiit**. *imp* **ahteewohkwéepiil**. *ptcpl* **ahteewoh=kwéepiit**.

**ahtéewuw** VAI be bending over. *ind 1st sg* **ndahtéewi, ndahtéewiim**. *conj 3rd sg* **ahtéewiit**. *imp* **ahtéewiil**. *ptcpl* **ahtéewiit**.

**ahtéexiin** VAI bend over, be hunched over, be bent over. *ind 1st sg* **ndah=téexiin, ndahtéexi**. *conj 3rd sg* **ahtéexiing**. *ptcpl* **ahtéexiing**.

**ahtéhleew** VAI bend over. *ind 1st sg* **ndahtéhla, ndahtéhlaam**. *conj 3rd sg* **ahtéhlaat**. *imp* **ahtéhlaal**. *ptcpl* **ahtéhlaat**. *intensive reduplication* **àhahtéhleew**.

**ahtéhleew** VII go out, be extinguished *(of fires)*. *conj 3rd sg* **ahtéhlaak**. *ptcpl* **ehtéhlaak**.

**ahtíikan** NI container. *pl* **ahtíikanal**. *poss* **ndahtíikan**. *loc* **ahtíikanung**. *dimin* **ahchíikanush**.

**ahtíikeew** VAI bet, play for money. *ind 1st sg* **ndahtíike, ndahtíikeem**. *conj 3rd sg* **ahtíikeet**. *imp* **ahtíikeel**. *ptcpl* **ehtíikeet**.

**áhtoow** VTI2 put s.t. down. *ind 1st sg* **ndáhtoon**. *ind 3rd sg* **wtáhtoon**. *conj 1st sg* **áhtawaan**. *conj 3rd sg* **áhtaakw**. *imp* **áhtool**. *ptcpl* **éhtaakw**.

**àhwáaleew** VTA love s.o. *ind 1st sg* **ndahwáalaaw, ndahwáala**. *ind 3rd sg* **wtahwaaláawal**. *ind inv* **ndah=wáalukw**. *ind I-you* **ktahwáalul**. *conj 3rd sg* **àhwáalaat**. *imp* **áhwaal**. *ptcpl* **ehwáalaat**.

**àhwaalkwúsuw** VAI be loved. *ind 1st sg* **ndahwaalkwúsi, ndahwaalkwúsiim**. *conj 3rd sg* **àhwaalkwúsiit**. *ptcpl* **ehwaalkwúsiit**.

**àhwaaltúwak** VAI love each other. *usually plural*. *ind 1st pl* **ndahwaal=tíhna**. *conj 3rd pl* **àhwaaltíhtiit**. *imp* **àhwáaltiikw**. *ptcpl* **ehwaaltíhtiit**.

**àhwaaltuwáakan** NI loving.

**àhwaangóomeew** VTA be closely related to s.o.; want to be related to s.o. *ind 1st sg* **ndahwaangóomaaw, ndah=waangóoma**. *ind 3rd sg* **wtahwaan=goomáawal**. *ind inv* **ndahwaangóo=mukw**. *ind I-you* **ktahwaangóomul**. *conj 3rd sg* **àhwaangóomaat**. *imp* **ahwáangoom**. *ptcpl* **ehwaangóo=maat**.

**àhwaapéenzuw** VAI be ind. *ind 1st sg* **ndahwaapéenzi, ndahwaapéenziim**. *conj 3rd sg* **àhwaapéenziit**. *imp* **àhwaapéenziil**. *ptcpl* **ehwaapéenziit**.

**àhwaapéewuw** VAI be ind, be smart, be alive; be strong *(especially a sick person who gets up because he or she is feeling better)*. *ind 1st sg* **ndahwaa=péewi, ndahwaapéewiim**. *conj 3rd sg* **àhwaapéewiit**. *imp* **àhwaapéewiil**. *ptcpl* **ehwaapéewiit**.

**àhwaatáasuw** VII be loved. *conj 3rd sg* **àhwaatáasiik**. *ptcpl* **ehwaatáasiik**.

**àhwáatam** VTI1A like s.t., be stingy

about s.t. *ind 1st sg* **ndahwáatamun**. *ind 3rd sg* **wtahwáatamun**. *conj 1st sg* **àhwáatamaan**. *conj 3rd sg* **àhwáatang**. *ptcpl* **ehwáatang**.

**àhwaawúngeew** VII be a steep hill. *conj 3rd sg* **àhwaawúngeek**. *ptcpl* **ehwaawúngeek**.

**àhwalákay** PC ouch! *considered impolite.*

**àhwalóhkeew** VAI work hard. *ind 1st sg* **ndahwalóhke**, **ndahwalóhkeem**. *conj 3rd sg* **àhwalóhkeet**. *imp* **àhwalóhkeel**. *ptcpl* **ehwalóhkeet**.

**àhwamálsuw** VAI be very sick. *ind 1st sg* **ndahwamálsi**, **ndahwamálsiim**. *conj 3rd sg* **àhwamálsiit**. *ptcpl* **ehwamálsiit**.

**áhwan** VII be strong *(of a sensation)*. *conj 3rd sg* **áhwang**. *ptcpl* **éhwang**.

**áhwat** VII be difficult, be hard. *conj 3rd sg* **áhwahk**. *ptcpl* **éhwahk**.

**áhweel** PC deliberately, on purpose. **Áhweel mbákamaaw.** 'I hit him on purpose.'; **Áhweel wtulŭnúmun.** 'He did it on purpose.'

**àhweelúndam** VOTI 1A come to a difficult decision. *ind 1st sg* **ndahwee=lúndam**. *conj 3rd sg* **àhweelúndang**. *ptcpl* **ehweelúndang**.

**àhweelúndam** VTI 1A find s.t. difficult, find s.t. difficult to do. *ind 1st sg* **ndahweelúndamun**. *ind 3rd sg* **wtahweelúndamun**. *conj 1st sg* **àh=weelúndamaan**. *conj 3rd sg* **àhwee=lúndang**. *ptcpl* **ehweelúndang**.

**àhwiimáakwat** VII smell strong, have a strong smell. *conj 3rd sg* **àhwiimáa=kwahk**. *ptcpl* **ehwiimáakwahk**.

**àhwiimáakwsuw** VAI smell strong, have a strong smell *(s.t. animate)*. *ind 1st sg* **ndahwiimáakwsi**, **ndahwiimáa=kwsiim**. *conj 3rd sg* **àhwiimáakw=siit**. *ptcpl* **ehwiimáakwsiit**.

**àhwiipóokwat** VII taste strong, be strong in taste. *conj 3rd sg* **àhwiipóokwahk**. *ptcpl* **ehwiipóokwahk**.

**àhwiipóokwsuw** VAI taste strong, be strong in taste *(s.t. animate)*. *ind 1st sg* **ndahwiipóokwsi**, **ndahwiipóo=kwsiim**. *conj 3rd sg* **àhwiipóokwsiit**. *ptcpl* **ehwiipóokwsiit**.

**àhwíisŭmuw** VAI take a strong drink *(including non-alcoholic beverages)*. *ind 1st sg* **ndahwíisŭmwi**, **ndahwíisŭ=mwiim**. *conj 3rd sg* **àhwíisŭmwiit**. *imp* **àhwíisŭmwiil**. *ptcpl* **ehwíisŭ=mwiit**. *intensive reduplication* **ayahwíisŭmuw**.

**ahwi-** PV very, intense, hard, difficult. **Áhwi-shŭwaháasuw.** 'It has a lot of salt on it.' *ptcpl* **éhwi-**. *See* **ahwu-**.

**àhwóoxweew** VAI have difficulty while walking, have difficulty in travelling, be hard for one to travel. *ind 1st sg* **ndahwóoxwe**, **ndahwóoxweem**. *conj 3rd sg* **àhwóoxweet**. *ptcpl* **ehwóo=xweet**.

**áhwsuw** VAI be shy *(of animals)*; be stingy. *ind 1st sg* **ndáhwsi**, **ndáhw=siim**. *conj 3rd sg* **áhwsiit**. *ptcpl* **éhwsiit**.

**ahwu-** PV very, intense, hard, difficult. *informal.* **Áhwu-líinam.** 'He has a hard time, he has bad luck.'; **Áhwu-wulíikuw.** 'He is getting enormously big.' *ptcpl* **éhwu-**. *See* **ahwi-**.

**akáameew** VII be wide. *conj 3rd sg* **akáameek**. *ptcpl* **eekáameek**. *See* **páaneew**.

**akáamsuw** VAI be wide *(s.t. animate)*. *ind 1st sg* **ndakáamsi**, **ndakáamsiim**. *conj 3rd sg* **akáamsiit**. *ptcpl* **eekáa=msiit**. *See* **páansuw**.

**akaanzhaaptóoneew** VAI brag, say great things *(especially when making a speech)*. *ind 1st sg* **ngakaanzhaap=tóone**, **ngakaanzhaaptóoneem**. *conj 3rd sg* **akaanzhaaptóoneet**. *imp* **akaanzhaaptóoneel**. *ptcpl* **kee=kaanzhaaptóoneet**.

**akaanzháhkuw** VII be a thunderstorm. *conj 3rd sg* **akaanzháhkwiik**.

**akaanzháhkweew** VII be a bad thunderstorm. *conj 3rd sg* **akaanzháhkweek**.
**akáawee** PC hurry up!; in a hurry. **Néeka akáawee alúmsuw.** 'He left in a hurry.' *See* **akáawii**.
**akaawéechpuw** VAI dress in a hurry. *ind 1st sg* **ngakaawéechpi**, **ngakaa=wéechpiim**. *conj 3rd sg* **akaawéech=piit**. *imp* **akaawéechpiil**. *ptcpl* **keekaawéechpiit**.
**akáawii** PC hurry up!; in a hurry. *See* **akáawee**.
**akaawíhlatoow** VOTI2 hurry, hurry up. **Kéeng- lúkih -akaawihlatáwaan.** 'I'm hurrying as fast as I can.' *ind 1st sg* **ngakaawíhlato**. *conj 3rd sg* **a=kaawíhlataakw**. *imp* **akaawíhlatool**. *ptcpl* **keekaawíhlataakw**.
**akawóngxwiin** VAI be sleepy. *ind 1st sg* **ngakawóngxwiin**, **ngakawóngxwi**. *conj 3rd sg* **akawóngxwiing**.
**akaxeelúnzuw** VAI be jealous, be envious. *ind 1st sg* **ngakxeelúnzi**, **ngak=xeelúnziim**. *conj 3rd sg* **akaxee=lúnziit**.
**akayihkíiheew** VTA tease s.o. *ind 1st sg* **ngakayihkíihaaw**, **ngakayihkíiha**. *ind 3rd sg* **kwakayihkiiháawal**. *ind inv* **ngakayihkíihukw**. *ind I-you* **kàkayihkíihul**. *conj 3rd sg* **akayih=kíihaat**. *imp* **akayíhkiih**.
**akayihkíihŭweew** VAI tease people. *ind 1st sg* **ngakayihkíihŭwe**, **ngakayih=kíihŭweem**. *conj 3rd sg* **akayihkíi=hŭweet**. *imp* **akayihkíihŭweel**.
**akayíhksuw** VAI tease. *ind 1st sg* **ngak=ayíhksi**, **ngakayíhksiim**. *conj 3rd sg* **akayíhksiit**.
**akeelxáksuw** VAI be ticklish. *ind 1st sg* **ngakeelxáksi**, **ngakeelxáksiim**. *conj 3rd sg* **akeelxáksiit**. *ptcpl* **keekeel=xáksiit**.
**akeelxákŭneew** VTA tickle s.o. *ind 1st sg* **ngakeelxákŭnaaw**, **ngakeelxákŭna**. *ind 3rd sg* **kwakeelxakŭnáawal**. *ind inv* **ngakeelxákŭnukw**. *ind I-you* **kàkeelxákŭnul**. *conj 3rd sg* **akeel=xákŭnaat**. *imp* **akeelxákun**. *ptcpl* **keekeelxákŭnaat**.
**akeenjíimuw** VAI make a noise like an animal, make a crowing noise. *ind 1st sg* **ngakeenjíimwi**, **ngakeenjíi=mwiim**. *conj 3rd sg* **akeenjíimwiit**. *imp* **akeenjíimwiil**. *ptcpl* **keekeenjíi=mwiit**. *See* **kunjíimuw**.
**akeepíingweew** VAI be blind. *ind 1st sg* **ngakeepíingwa**, **ngakeepíingwaam**. *conj 3rd sg* **akeepíingwaat**. *ptcpl* **keekeepíingwaat**.
**akeeptóoneew** VAI be unable to talk, be mute. *ind 1st sg* **ngakeeptóona**, **ngakeeptóonaam**. *conj 3rd sg* **a=keeptóonaat**. *ptcpl* **keekeeptóonaat**.
**akéepxweew** VAI be deaf. *ind 1st sg* **ngakéepxwa**, **ngakéepxwaam**. *conj 3rd sg* **akéepxwaat**. *ptcpl* **keekéep=xwaat**.
**akeexpéengweew** VAI have tears in one's eyes. *ind 1st sg* **ngakeexpéengwa**, **ngakeexpéengwaam**. *conj 3rd sg* **akeexpéengwaat**. *ptcpl* **keekeex=péengwaat**.
**akehkíimeew** VTA teach s.o. *ind 1st sg* **ndakehkíimaaw**, **ndakehkíima**. *ind 3rd sg* **wtakehkiimáawal**. *ind inv* **ndakehkíimukw**. *ind I-you* **ktakeh=kíimul**. *conj 3rd sg* **akehkíimaat**. *imp* **akéhkiim**. *ptcpl* **eekehkíimaat**.
**akehkíingeew** VAI teach people. *ind 1st sg* **ndakehkíinge**, **ndakehkíingeem**. *conj 3rd sg* **akehkíingeet**. *imp* **akehkíingeel**. *ptcpl* **eekehkíingeet**.
**akíimeew** VTA count s.t. animate, read s.t. animate. *ind 1st sg* **ndakíimaaw**, **ndakíima**. *ind 3rd sg* **wtakiimáawal**. *ind inv* **ndakíimukw**. *ind I-you* **ktakíimul**. *conj 3rd sg* **akíimaat**. *imp* **akíim**. *ptcpl* **eekíimaat**.
**akiinaníikeew** VAI have sharp teeth. *ind 1st sg* **ngakiinaníika**, **ngakiinaníi=kaam**. *conj 3rd sg* **akiinaníikaat**. *ptcpl* **keekiinaníikaat**.

**akíindam** VTI1A count s.t., read s.t., *ind 1st sg* **ndakíindamun**. *ind 3rd sg* **wtakíindamun**. *conj 1st sg* **akíinda=maan**. *conj 3rd sg* **akíindang**. *imp* **akíindah**. *ptcpl* **eekíindang**.

**akiindamáweew** VTAO read s.t. to s.o. *ind 1st sg* **ndakiindamáwaan**. *ind 3rd sg* **wtakiindamáwaan**. *ind inv* **ndakiindamáakwun**. *ind I-you* **ktakiindamóolun**. *conj 3rd sg* **akiin=damáwaat**. *imp* **akíindamaw**. *ptcpl* **eekiindamáwaat**.

**akíinŭweew** VAI boast. *ind 1st sg* **ngak=íinŭwe, ngakíinŭweem**. *conj 3rd sg* **akíinŭweet**.

**akíinzuw** VAI read, count. *ind 1st sg* **ndakíinzi, ndakíinziim**. *emphatic pl* **akiinz'hátŭwak**. *conj 3rd sg* **akíin=ziit**. *imp* **akíinziil**. *ptcpl* **eekíinziit**.

**akiinzŭwóoleew** VTA read to s.o. *ind 1st sg* **ndakiinzŭwóolaaw, ndakiinzŭ=wóola**. *ind 3rd sg* **wtakiinzŭwooláa=wal**. *ind inv* **ndakiinzŭwóolukw**. *ind I-you* **ktakiinzŭwóolul**. *conj 3rd sg* **akiinzŭwóolaat**. *imp* **akíinzŭwool**. *ptcpl* **eekiinzŭwóolaat**.

**akiiwóngxwiin** VAI wake after a bad dream, wake up screaming, have a nightmare. *ind 1st sg* **ngakiiwóng=xwiin, ngakiiwóngxwi**. *conj 3rd sg* **akiiwóngxwiing**. *ptcpl* **keekiiwóng=xwiing, keekiiwóngxwiit**.

**akóotay** NI slip, petticoat. *pl* **akóotayal**. *poss* **ndakóotay, nakóotay**. *dimin* **akóocheesh**.

**akúw** VAIO wear s.t. **Eekwŭyáaniil.** 'My clothing.'; **Eekwíichiil.** 'His/her clothing.' *ind 1st sg* **ndákwiin**. *ind 3rd sg* **wtákwiin**. *conj 3rd sg* **akwíit**. *imp* **akwíil**. *ptcpl* **éekwiit**.

**akulkúsuw** VAI laugh. *ind 1st sg* **ngak=ŭlúksi, ngakŭlúksiim**. *conj 3rd sg* **akulkúsiit**. *ptcpl* **keekŭlúksiit**.

**akulóoneew** VAI tell a lie. *ind 1st sg* **ngakŭlóona, ngakŭlóonaam**. *conj 3rd sg* **akulóonaat**. *ptcpl* **keekŭlóo=naat**. *See* **kŭlóoneew**.

**akúmahkw** NA cloud. *pl* **akumáhkwak**. *obv* **akumáhkwal**.

**akumáhkwat** VII be cloudy. *conj 3rd sg* **akumáhkwahk**. *ptcpl* **eekŭmáh=kwahk**.

**akuníimeew** VTA talk about s.o. *ind 1st sg* **ndakŭníimaaw, ndakŭníima**. *ind 3rd sg* **wtakŭniimáawal**. *ind inv* **ndakŭníimukw**. *ind I-you* **ktakŭníi=mul**. *conj 3rd sg* **akuníimaat**. *imp* **akúniim**. *ptcpl* **eekŭníimaat**.

**akuníingeew** VAI talk about things, talk about people. *ind 1st sg* **ndakŭníinge, ndakŭníingeem**. *conj 3rd sg* **akun=íingeet**. *imp* **akuníingeel**. *ptcpl* **eekŭníingeet**.

**akunóotam** VTI1A talk about s.t. *ind 1st sg* **ndakŭnóotŭmun**. *ind 3rd sg* **wtakŭnóotŭmun**. *conj 1st sg* **akun=óotŭmaan**. *conj 3rd sg* **akunóotang**. *imp* **akunóotah**. *ptcpl* **eekŭnóotang**.

**akushaaptóonheew** VAI speak quickly, talk fast. *ind 1st sg* **ngakshaaptóon=he, ngakshaaptóonheem**. *conj 3rd sg* **akushaaptóonheet**. *imp* **akush=aaptóonheel**.

**akushakíinzuw** VAI read quickly. *ind 1st sg* **ngakshakíinzi, ngakshakíinziim**. *conj 3rd sg* **akushakíinziit**. *imp* **a=kushakíinziil**. *ptcpl* **keekshakíinziit**.

**akushakuníimeew** VTA criticize s.o., abuse s.o. verbally, 'run s.o. down'. *ind 1st sg* **ngakshakŭníimaaw, ngakshakŭníima**. *ind 3rd sg* **kwak=shakŭniimáawal**. *ind inv* **ngakshak=ŭníimukw**. *ind I-you* **kàkshakŭníi=mul**. *conj 3rd sg* **akushakuníimaat**. *imp* **akushakúniim**. *ptcpl* **keekshak=ŭníimaat**.

**akúshameew** VTA bite s.o., bite s.o. hard. *ind 1st sg* **ngakshámaaw, ngak=sháma**. *ind 3rd sg* **kwakshamáawal**. *ind inv* **ngakshámukw**. *ind I-you* **kàkshámul**. *conj 3rd sg* **akúsha=maat**. *imp* **akúsham**. *ptcpl* **keek=**

**shámaat**.

**akushándam** VTI1A bite s.t., bite s.t. hard. *ind 1st sg* **ngakshándamun**. *ind 3rd sg* **kwakshándamun**. *conj 1st sg* **akushándamaan**. *conj 3rd sg* **akushándang**. *imp* **akushándah**. *ptcpl* **keekshándang**.

**akusheekhíikeew** VAI write quickly. *ind 1st sg* **ngaksheekhíike**, **ngaksheek=híikeem**. *conj 3rd sg* **akusheekhíi=keet**. *imp* **akusheekhíikeel**. *ptcpl* **keeksheekhíikeet**.

**akushíimeew** VTA criticize s.o., abuse s.o. verbally, 'run s.o. down.' *ind 1st sg* **ngakshíimaaw**, **ngakshíima**. *ind 3rd sg* **kwakshiimáawal**. *ind inv* **ngakshíimukw**. *ind I-you* **kàkshíi=mul**. *conj 3rd sg* **akushíimaat**. *imp* **akúshiim**. *ptcpl* **keekshíimaat**.

**akushíixsuw** VAI talk quickly. *ind 1st sg* **ngakshíixsi**, **ngakshíixsiim**. *conj 3rd sg* **akushíixsiit**. *imp* **akushíixsiil**. *ptcpl* **keekshíixsiit**.

**akushóoxweew** VAI walk quickly. *ind 1st sg* **ngakshóoxwe**, **ngakshóoxweem**. *conj 3rd sg* **akushóoxweet**. *imp* **a=kushóoxweel**. *ptcpl* **keekshóoxweet**.

**akutakóoxweew** VAI walk quickly. *ind 1st sg* **ngaktakóoxwe**, **ngaktakóo=xweem**. *conj 3rd sg* **akutakóoxweet**. *imp* **akutakóoxweel**. *ptcpl* **keektak=óoxweet**.

**akutaku-** PV quick, fast. **Ngaktáku-alúmsi.** 'I went away fast.' *ptcpl* **kaktáku-**.

**akutakúkeew** VAI do a fast dance. *ind 1st sg* **ngaktákka**, **ngaktákkaam**. *conj 3rd sg* **akutakúkaat**. *imp* **akut=akúkaal**. *See* **kàktákkeew**.

**akwaakwalihlóosus** NA rotten old man. *pl* **akwaakwalihlóosak**. *dimin* **a=kwaakwalihlóoshush**. *obv* **akwaa=kwalihlóosal**.

**akwaanalíhkeew** VAI take long steps. *ind 1st sg* **ngwakwaanalíhke**, **ngwakwaanalíhkeem**. *conj 3rd sg* **akwaanalíhkeet**. *imp* **akwaanalíh=keel**. *ptcpl* **kweekwaanalíhkeet**.

**akwaanamwíhleew** VAI have one's feet sinking into a substance *(of mud, of snow, of sand, of grain)*. *ind 1st sg* **ngwakwaanamwíhla**, **ngwakwaa=namwíhlaam**. *conj 3rd sg* **akwaana=mwíhlaat**. *ptcpl* **kweekwaana=mwíhlaat**.

**akwaananíikeew** VAI have long teeth. *ind 1st sg* **ngwakwaananíika**, **ngwakwaananíikaam**. *conj 3rd sg* **akwaananíikaat**. *ptcpl* **kweekwaa=naníikaat**.

**akwaanéewal** VII be long. *usually plural. conj 3rd pl* **akwáaneek**. *ptcpl* **kweekwaanéekiil**.

**akwaanéeshŭwal** VII be long *(dimin)*. *usually plural. conj 3rd pl* **akwaa=néeshiik**. *ptcpl* **kweekwaanee=shíikiil**.

**akwaaníikan** NA fishing net. *pl* **akwaa=níikanak**. *poss* **ndakwaaníikan**. *loc* **akwaaníikanung**. *dimin* **akwaaníi=kanush**. *obv* **akwaaníikanal**.

**akwaaníilaneew** VAI have long breasts; have long udders *(of a cow)*. *ind 1st sg* **ngwakwaaníilana**, **ngwakwaaníila=naam**. *conj 3rd sg* **akwaaníilanaat**. *ptcpl* **kweekwaaníilanaat**.

**akwaaníilŭnus** NA thimbleberry. *pl* **akwaaniilŭnúsak**. *obv* **akwaaniilŭ=núsal**.

**akwaaníixsuw** VAI take a long time to say one's words. *ind 1st sg* **ngwak=waaníixsi**, **ngwakwaaníixsiim**. *conj 3rd sg* **akwaaníixsiit**. *ptcpl* **kwee=kwaaníixsiit**.

**akwaaníhkasheew** VAI have long finger-nails. *ind 1st sg* **ngwakwaaníhkasha**, **ngwakwaaníhkashaam**. *conj 3rd sg* **akwaaníhkashaat**. *ptcpl* **kwee=kwaaníhkashaat**.

**akwaankáateew** VAI have long legs. *ind 1st sg* **ngwakwaankáata**, **ngwak=waankáataam**. *conj 3rd sg* **akwaan=**

káataat. *ptcpl* **kweekwaankáataat**.

**akwaankaatéeyeew** VII have long legs. *conj 3rd sg* **akwaankaatéeyeek**. *ptcpl* **kweekwaankaatéeyeek**.

**akwaansúwak** VAI be long *(s.t. animate)*. *usually plural. ind 1st pl* **ngwak=waansíhna**. *conj 3rd pl* **akwaansíh=tiit**. *ptcpl* **kweekwaansíhtiit**.

**akwáanŭmeew** VAI fish with a net. *ind 1st sg* **ndakwáanŭma**, **ndakwáanŭ=maam**. *conj 3rd sg* **akwáanŭmaat**. *imp* **akwáanŭmaal**. *ptcpl* **eekwáa=nŭmaat**.

**akwaanŭnáxkeew** VAI have long arms. *ind 1st sg* **ngwakwaanŭnáxka**, **ngwakwaanŭnáxkaam**. *conj 3rd sg* **akwaanŭnáxkaat**. *ptcpl* **kweekwaa=nŭnáxkaat**.

**akwaanŭnaxkéeyeew** VII have long sleeves. *especially of shirts or coats. conj 3rd sg* **akwaanŭnaxkéeyeek**. *ptcpl* **kweekwaanŭnaxkéeyeek**.

**akwáanxeew** VAI have long ears. *ind 1st sg* **ngwakwáanxa**, **ngwakwáan=xaam**. *conj 3rd sg* **akwáanxaat**. *ptcpl* **kweekwáanxaat**.

**akwáawu** PC either, any. **Akwáawu kwéekw ngatáatam.** 'I want anything.'; **Akwáawu táa ndá.** 'I can go anywhere.'

**akwanóopeew** VAI be soaking wet. *ind 1st sg* **ngwakwanóope**, **ngwakwan=óopeem**. *conj 3rd sg* **akwanóopeet**.

**akweechi-** PV try to (do), try and (do). **Ngwakwéechi-wŭlíixtoon.** 'I'm trying to fix it.' *See* **kwchi-**.

**akwéendameew** VAI gulp things down, be hungry for things. **Móxa ngwak=wéendama.** 'I'm really hungry for something.' *ind 1st sg* **ngwakwéen=dama**, **ngwakwéendamaam**. *conj 3rd sg* **akwéendamaat**. *imp* **akwée=ndamaal**. *ptcpl* **kweekwéendamaat**.

**akweetáaheew** VAI practice throwing. *ind 1st sg* **ngwakweetáahe**, **ngwak=weetáaheem**. *conj 3rd sg* **akweetáa=heet**. *imp* **akweetáaheel**.

**akweetaaméhleew** VAI practice running. *ind 1st sg* **ngwakweetaaméhla**, **ngwakweetaaméhlaam**. *conj 3rd sg* **akweetaaméhlaat**. *imp* **akweetaa=méhlaal**.

**akweetaláamuw** VAI practice singing. *ind 1st sg* **ngwakweetaláamwi**, **ngwakweetaláamwiim**. *conj 3rd sg* **akweetaláamwiit**. *imp* **akweetaláa=mwiil**.

**akweetaxkhíikeew** VAI practice shooting. *ind 1st sg* **ngwakweetaxkhíike**, **ngwakweetaxkhíikeem**. *conj 3rd sg* **akweetaxkhíikeet**. *imp* **akweetaxk=híikeel**.

**akwíimeew** VTAO blame s.o. for s.t. *ind 1st sg* **ndakwíimaan**. *ind 3rd sg* **wtakwíimaan**. *ind inv* **ndakwíim=kwun**. *ind I-you* **ktakwiimóolun**. *conj 3rd sg* **akwíimaat**. *imp* **akwíim**. *ptcpl* **eekwíimaat**.

**akwiipŭláawan** NI hoe. *pl* **akwiipŭláa=wanal**. *poss* **ndakwiipŭláawan**. *dimin* **akwiipŭláawanush**. *See* **takwiipŭláawan**.

**akwúneew** VTA buy s.o. clothes to wear, get s.o. clothes to wear, dress s.o. *ind 1st sg* **ndákwŭnaaw**, **ndákwŭna**. *ind 3rd sg* **wtakwŭnáawal**. *ind inv* **ndákwŭnukw**. *ind I-you* **ktákwŭnul**. *conj 3rd sg* **akwúnaat**. *imp* **akwún**. *ptcpl* **éekwŭnaat**.

**akwúnheew** VTA put bedcovers on s.o. *ind 1st sg* **ndakwŭnáhaaw**, **ndak=wŭnáha**. *ind 3rd sg* **wtakwŭnaháa=wal**. *ind inv* **ndakwŭnáhookw**. *ind I-you* **ktakwŭnáhool**. *conj 3rd sg* **akwúnhaat**. *imp* **akwúnah**. *ptcpl* **eekwŭnáhaat**.

**àkwúshtiin** NA Augustine. *obv* **àkwush=tíinal**. *From English* Augustine.

**alaamaawúnge** PC bottom of a hill.

**aláamatay** PC inside the stomach. **Alaamatáye.** 'Inside the stomach.'

**alaameenáxke** PC inside the fence.

**alaamháasuw** VII have a lining inside. *conj 3rd sg* **alaamháasiik**. *ptcpl* **eelaamháasiik**.

nd**alaamhákeeng** NID inside my body.

**alaamheembtáhŭmeew** VAI wear an undershirt. *ind 1st sg* **ndalaamheemb=táhŭma**, **ndalaamheembtáhŭmaam**. *conj 3rd sg* **alaamheembtáhŭmaat**. *imp* **alaamheembtáhŭmaal**. *ptcpl* **eelaamheembtáhŭmaat**.

**aláamii** PC inside. **Aláamii tiihíinjuw ndulóhkween.** 'I looked inside the cup.'

**alaamíikaan** NI inside a house. *pl* **alaamiikáanal**.

**alaamiikwáhmung** PC inside a house.

**alaamíixiin** VAI fall underneath something, lie underneath something. *ind 1st sg* **ndalaamíixiin**, **ndalaamíixi**. *conj 3rd sg* **alaamíixiing**. *imp* **alaa=míixiil**. *ptcpl* **eelaamíixiing**.

**alaamíixtoow** VTI2 put s.t. underneath something. *ind 1st sg* **ndalaamíix=toon**. *ind 3rd sg* **wtalaamíixtoon**. *conj 1st sg* **alaamiixtáwaan**. *conj 3rd sg* **alaamíixtaakw**. *imp* **alaamíixtool**. *ptcpl* **eelaamíixtaakw**.

**alaamíixŭmeew** VTA put s.o. underneath. *ind 1st sg* **ndalaamíixŭmaaw**, **ndal=aamíixŭma**. *ind 3rd sg* **wtalaamii=xŭmáawal**. *ind inv* **ndalaamíixŭ=mukw**. *ind I-you* **ktalaamíixŭmul**. *conj 3rd sg* **alaamíixŭmaat**. *imp* **alaamíixum**. *ptcpl* **eelaamíixŭmaat**.

**alaamíixun** VII fall underneath something, lie underneath something. *conj 3rd sg* **alaamíixung**. *ptcpl* **eelaa=míixung**.

**alaamihtéexiin** VAI fall underneath something. *ind 1st sg* **ndalaamihtée=xiin**, **ndalaamihtéexi**. *conj 3rd sg* **alaamihtéexiing**. *ptcpl* **eelaamihtée=xiing**.

**aláamsiit** PC sole of the foot.

**aláamŭlunj** PC palm of the hand.

**aláangweesh** NA star. *pl* **alaangwée=shak**. *obv* **alaangwéeshal**. *See* **aláangweew**.

**aláangweew** NA star. *pl* **alaangwéewak**. *dimin* **aláangweesh**. *obv* **alaangwée=wal**. *See* **aláangweesh**.

**aláawan** NI cane. *pl* **aláawanal**. *poss* **ndaláawan**. *loc* **aláawanung**. *dimin* **aláawanush**.

**alaawhúnzuw** VAI use a cane. *ind 1st sg* **ndalaawhúnzi**, **ndalaawhúnziim**. *conj 3rd sg* **alaawhúnziit**. *imp* **alaawhúnziil**. *ptcpl* **eelaawhúnziit**.

**alaawíiyayuw** VAI be slow-moving. *ind 1st sg* **ndalaawíiyayi**, **ndalaawíiya=yiim**. *conj 3rd sg* **alaawíiyayiit**. *ptcpl* **eelaawíiyayiit**.

**alaaxíimuw** VAI rest, take a rest. *ind 1st sg* **ndalaaxíimwi**, **ndalaaxíimwiim**. *conj 3rd sg* **alaaxíimwiit**. *imp* **alaa=xíimwiil**. *ptcpl* **eelaaxíimwiit**.

**alaaxiimŭwáakan** NI rest, resting *(especially after death)*.

**alaaxiimwahtéenamuw** VAI feel as if one would like to rest. *ind 1st sg* **ndalaaxiimwahtéenami**, **ndalaa=xiimwahtéenamiim**. *conj 3rd sg* **alaaxiimwahtéenamiit**. *ptcpl* **eelaaxiimwahtéenamiit**.

**aláham** VTI1A touch s.t., run into s.t., drive into s.t., make contact with s.t. forcefully, hit s.t. **Ná ndalhámun.** 'I ran into it.' *ind 1st sg* **ndalhámun**. *ind 3rd sg* **wtalhámun**. *conj 1st sg* **aláhŭmaan**. *conj 3rd sg* **aláhang**. *imp* **aláhih**. *ptcpl* **éelhang**.

**aláheew** VTA touch s.o., make contact with s.o., run into s.o., hit s.o. *ind 1st sg* **ndálhaaw**, **ndálha**. *ind 3rd sg* **wtalháawal**. *ind inv* **ndálhookw**. *ind I-you* **ktálhool**. *conj 3rd sg* **aláhaat**. *imp* **aláh**. *ptcpl* **éelhaat**.

**aláhookw** VAI be hit. *ind 1st sg* **ndál=hookw**. *conj 3rd sg* **alahóokwuk**. *ptcpl* **eelhóokwuk**.

**alakweelúndam** VOTI1A be sorry. *ind 1st sg* **ndalakweelúndam**. *conj 3rd sg*

**alakweelúndang**. *ptcpl* **eelakwee=lúndang**.

**alakweelúndam** VTI 1A be sorry about s.t. *ind 1st sg* **ndalakweelúndamun**. *ind 3rd sg* **wtalakweelúndamun**. *conj 1st sg* **alakweelúndamaan**. *conj 3rd sg* **alakweelúndang**. *ptcpl* **eela=kweelúndang**.

**alákwe** PC too bad *(that it happened)*.

**alán** PC emphatic. **Alán ná.** 'I don't care.'; **Alán áa máh há.** 'I'd better not.'

**aláw** PC it's no use. **Aláw há yú koon=jíimi.** 'There's no use in you calling me.'; **Aláw nŭmíitsi, máh ngatoo=pwíiwi.** 'There's no use in my eating, I'm not hungry.' *intensive reduplication* **áhalaw**.

**aláwiiw** VAI-S hunt. *ind 1st sg* **ndálawi**, **ndálawiim**. *conj 3rd sg* **aláwiit**. *imp* **aláwiil**. *ptcpl* **éelawiit**.

**alaxáaheew** VAIO throw s.t. and empty it out, empty s.t. out. *ind 1st sg* **ndal=xáaheen**. *ind 3rd sg* **wtalxáaheen**. *conj 3rd sg* **alaxáaheet**. *imp* **alaxáa=heel**. *ptcpl* **eelxáaheet**.

**aláxakw** NI decayed wood. *pl* **aláxa=kwal**. *poss* **ndalxákwum**. *loc* **aláxa=kwung**. *dimin* **aláxakwush**.

**aláxan** VII be empty. *conj 3rd sg* **aláx=ang**. *ptcpl* **éelxang**.

**alaxootéenayuw** VII be an empty town, be no one in town. *conj 3rd sg* **alax=ootéenayiik**. *ptcpl* **eelxootéenayiik**.

**aláxsuw** VAI be empty *(s.t. animate)*. *conj 3rd sg* **aláxsiit**. *ptcpl* **eelxúsiit**.

**aláxŭneew** VTA empty s.t. animate *(using the hands)*. *ind 1st sg* **ndalxún=aaw**, **ndalxúna**. *ind 3rd sg* **wtalxun=áawal**. *ind inv* **ndalxúnukw**. *ind I-you* **ktalxúnul**. *conj 3rd sg* **aláxŭnaat**. *imp* **aláxun**. *ptcpl* **eelxúnaat**.

**alaxúndeew** VII be an empty room. *conj 3rd sg* **alaxúndeek**. *ptcpl* **eelxúndeek**.

**aláxŭnum** VTI 1B empty s.t. *(using the hands)*. *ind 1st sg* **ndalxúnŭmun**. *ind 3rd sg* **wtalxúnŭmun**. *conj 1st sg* **alaxŭnúmaan**. *conj 3rd sg* **aláxŭ=nung**. *imp* **aláxŭnih**. *ptcpl* **eelxún=ung**.

**alíike** PC reluctantly. **Alíike salápwaan numíichiin.** 'I ate the fried bread reluctantly.'; **Alíike nŭmáw-maawéewi.** 'I went to church reluctantly.'

**aliimáakwat** VII smell rotten, have a rotten smell. *conj 3rd sg* **aliimáakwahk**. *ptcpl* **eeliimáakwahk**.

**aliimáakwsuw** VAI smell rotten, have a rotten smell *(s.t. animate)*. *ind 1st sg* **ndaliimáakwsi**, **ndaliimáakwsiim**. *conj 3rd sg* **aliimáakwsiit**. *ptcpl* **eeliimáakwsiit**.

**alíipheew** VTA grab s.o. *ind 1st sg* **ndal=íiphaaw**, **ndalíipha**. *ind 3rd sg* **wtal=iipháawal**. *ind inv* **ndalíiphukw**. *ind I-you* **ktalíiphul**. *conj 3rd sg* **alíip=haat**. *imp* **alíipah**. *ptcpl* **eelíiphaat**.

**aliipóokwat** VII taste rotten, have a rotten taste. *conj 3rd sg* **aliipóokwahk**. *ptcpl* **eeliipóokwahk**. *See* **aliipóo=kwan**.

**aliipóokwsuw** VAI taste rotten, have a rotten taste *(s.t. animate)*. *ind 1st sg* **ndaliipóokwsi**, **ndaliipóokwsiim**. *conj 3rd sg* **aliipóokwsiit**. *ptcpl* **eeliipóokwsiit**.

**àlífush** NA Olive *(woman's name)*. *obv* **àlífshal**. *From English* Olive.

**alíhkam** VTI 1A run into s.t., make physical contact with s.t. *ind 1st sg* **ndal=íhkamun**. *ind 3rd sg* **wtalíhkamun**. *conj 1st sg* **alíhkamaan**. *conj 3rd sg* **alíhkang**. *imp* **alíhkah**. *ptcpl* **eelíhkang**.

**nalíhkan** NAD my sister-in-law *(woman speaking)*. *pl* **nalíhkanak**. *3rd poss* **walíhkanal**.

**alíhkaweew** VTA run into s.o., make physical contact with s.o. *ind 1st sg* **ndalíhkawaaw**, **ndalíhkawa**. *ind 3rd sg* **wtalihkawáawal**. *ind inv* **ndal=íhkaakw**. *ind I-you* **ktalíhkool**. *conj*

*3rd sg* **alíhkawaat**. *imp* **alíhkaw**. *ptcpl* **eelíhkawaat**.

**alíhkeew** VAI take a step, put one's foot in something, put one's foot on something. **Ndalíhke móhkamiing, noo=sháaxihla.** 'I put my foot on the ice and I slipped.'; **Mbíing alíhkeew.** 'He put his foot in the water.' *ind 1st sg* **ndalíhke, ndalíhkeem**. *conj 3rd sg* **alíhkeet**. *imp* **alíhkeel**. *ptcpl* **eelíhkeet**.

**alihlóosus** NA rotten old man. *pl* **alih=lóosak**. *dimin* **alihlóoshush**. *obv* **alihlóosal**.

nd**aloohíikan** NID my pointing finger. *poss* **ndaloohíikanal**. *3rd poss* **wtal=oohíikan**. *loc* **ndaloohíikanung**. *See* nd**uloohíikan**.

**alóoleew** VTA hire s.o. *ind 1st sg* **ndal=óolaaw, ndalóola**. *ind 3rd sg* **wtal=ooláawal**. *ind inv* **ndalóolukw**. *ind I-you* **ktalóolul**. *conj 3rd sg* **alóolaat**. *imp* **alóol**. *ptcpl* **eelóolaat**.

**alóot** PC anyway. **Wáak-uch alóot nŭmíitsi.** 'I'll eat anyway.'; **Alóot nŭwíingu-néewukw.** 'He was glad to see me anyway.'

**alohkáakan** NA servant, worker. *pl* **alohkáakanak**. *poss* **ndalohkáakan**. *dimin* **alohkáakanush**. *obv* **alohkáa=kanal**.

**alóhkeew** VAI work. *ind 1st sg* **ndalóhke, ndalóhkeem**. *emphatic pl* **alohkhát=ŭwak**. *conj 3rd sg* **alóhkeet**. *imp* **alóhkeel**. *ptcpl* **eelóhkeet**.

**alohkehtáasuw** VII be worked at, be farmed, be worked *(of fields)*. *conj 3rd sg* **alohkehtáasiik**. *ptcpl* **eeloh=kehtáasiik**.

**alohkéhtam** VTI1A work at s.t. *ind 1st sg* **ndalohkéhtamun**. *ind 3rd sg* **wtalohkéhtamun**. *conj 1st sg* **aloh=kéhtamaan**. *conj 3rd sg* **alohkéhtang**. *imp* **alohkéhtah**. *ptcpl* **eelohkéhtang**.

**alohkéhtaweew** VTA work for s.o. *ind 1st sg* **ndalohkéhtawaaw, ndaloh=kéhtawa**. *ind 3rd sg* **wtalohkehta=wáawal**. *ind inv* **ndalohkéhtaakw**. *ind I-you* **ktalohkéhtool**. *conj 3rd sg* **alohkéhtawaat**. *imp* **alohkéhtaw**. *ptcpl* **eelohkéhtawaat**.

**alohtáameew** VTA talk back to s.o. *ind 1st sg* **ndalohtáamaaw, ndalohtáa=ma**. *ind 3rd sg* **wtalohtaamáawal**. *ind inv* **ndalohtáamukw**. *ind I-you* **ktalohtáamul**. *conj 3rd sg* **alohtáa=maat**. *imp* **alóhtaam**. *ptcpl* **eeloh=táamaat**.

**alóhtaweew** VTA talk back to s.o. *ind 1st sg* **ndalóhtawaaw, ndalóhtawa**. *ind 3rd sg* **wtalohtawáawal**. *ind inv* **ndalóhtaakw**. *ind I-you* **ktalóhtool**. *conj 3rd sg* **alóhtawaat**. *imp* **alóhtaw**. *ptcpl* **eelóhtawaat**.

**alu-** PV begin to. **Ndálu-xámaaw.** 'I'm starting to feed him.'; **Ndálu-wŭlamalúsi.** 'I'm starting to feel better.' *ptcpl* **éelu-**. *See* **alumu-**.

**alúl** VAI rot, be rotten *(s.t. animate)*. *conj 3rd sg* **alúluk**. *ptcpl* **éelŭluk**.

**alumáaheew** VAIO throw s.t., throw s.t. off. *ind 1st sg* **ndalŭmáaheen**. *ind 3rd sg* **wtalŭmáaheen**. *conj 3rd sg* **alumáaheet**. *imp* **alumáaheel**. *ptcpl* **eelŭmáaheet**.

**alumáakchehl** VAI jump away. *ind 1st sg* **ndalŭmáakchehl**. *conj 3rd sg* **alumaakchéhluk**. *imp* **alumaak=chéhlih**. *ptcpl* **eelŭmaakchéhluk**.

**alumáasŭleew** VAI shine going away *(s.t. animate, of lights)*. *conj 3rd sg* **alumáasŭleet**. *ptcpl* **eelŭmáasŭleet**.

**alumáasŭleew** VII shine going away *(of lights)*. *conj 3rd sg* **alumáasŭleek**. *ptcpl* **eelŭmáasŭleek**.

**alumáashŭweew** VAI swim away. *ind 1st sg* **ndalŭmáashŭwe, ndalŭmáa=shŭweem**. *conj 3rd sg* **alumáashŭ=weet**. *imp* **alumáashŭweel**. *ptcpl* **eelŭmáashŭweet**.

**alumáashŭwihl** VAI swim away, float away. *ind 1st sg* **ndalŭmáashŭwihl**.

*conj 3rd sg* **alumaashŭwíhluk**. *imp* **alumaashŭwíhlih**. *ptcpl* **eelŭmaa=shŭwíhluk**. *See* **alumaashŭwíhleew**.

**alumaashŭwíhleew** VAI swim away, float away. *ind 1st sg* **ndalŭmaashŭ=wíhla, ndalŭmaashŭwíhlaam**. *conj 3rd sg* **alumaashŭwíhlaat**. *imp* **alumaashŭwíhlaal**. *ptcpl* **eelŭmaa=shŭwíhlaat**. *See* **alumáashŭwihl**.

**alumáathookw** VAI float away. *ind 1st sg* **ndalŭmáathookw**. *conj 3rd sg* **alumaathóokwuk**. *ptcpl* **eelŭmaat=hóokwuk**.

**alumáathun** VII float away. *conj 3rd sg* **alumáathung**. *ptcpl* **eelŭmáathung**.

**alumahtakíhleew** VAI leave running, run away, start to run. *ind 1st sg* **ndalŭmahtakíhla, ndalŭmahtakíh=laam**. *conj 3rd sg* **alumahtakíhlaat**. *imp* **alumahtakíhlaal**. *ptcpl* **eelŭ=mahtakíhlaat**.

**alumakóosuw** VAI climb away, climb up. *ind 1st sg* **ndalŭmakóosi, ndalŭma=kóosiim**. *conj 3rd sg* **alumakóosiit**. *imp* **alumakóosiil**. *ptcpl* **eelŭma=kóosiit**.

**alumaláamuw** VAI start singing. *ind 1st sg* **ndalŭmaláamwi, ndalŭmaláa=mwiim**. *conj 3rd sg* **alumaláamwiit**. *imp* **alumaláamwiil**.*ptcpl* **eelŭmal=áamwiit**.

**alumasaníhleew** VAIO carry something away quickly. *ind 1st sg* **ndalŭma=saníhlaan**. *ind 3rd sg* **wtalŭmasan=íhlaan**. *conj 3rd sg* **alumasaníhlaat**. *imp* **alumasaníhlaal**. *ptcpl* **eelŭma=saníhlaat**.

**alumasánuw** VAIO carry s.t. away. *ind 1st sg* **ndalŭmásaniin**. *ind 3rd sg* **wtalŭmásaniin**. *conj 3rd sg* **aluma=sániit**. *imp* **alumasániil**. *ptcpl* **eelŭmásaniit**.

**alumatéexun** VII be the start of a road. *conj 3rd sg* **alumatéexung**. *ptcpl* **eelŭmatéexung**.

**alumchéhlaleew** VTA drive away with s.o. *ind 1st sg* **ndalŭmuchéhlalaaw, ndalŭmuchéhlala**. *ind 3rd sg* **wtal=ŭmuchehlaláawal**. *ind inv* **ndalŭ=muchéhlalukw**. *ind I-you* **ktalŭ=muchéhlalul**. *conj 3rd sg* **alum=chéhlalaat**. *imp* **alumchéhlal**. *ptcpl* **eelŭmuchéhlalaat**.

**alumchéhlatoow** VTI2 drive away with s.t. *ind 1st sg* **ndalŭmuchéhlatoon**. *ind 3rd sg* **wtalŭmuchéhlatoon**. *conj 1st sg* **alumchehlatáwaan**. *conj 3rd sg* **alumchéhlataakw**. *imp* **alum=chéhlatool**. *ptcpl* **eelŭmuchéhla=taakw**.

**alumchéhleew** VAI drive away. *ind 1st sg* **ndalŭmuchéhla, ndalŭmuchéh=laam**. *conj 3rd sg* **alumchéhlaat**. *imp* **alumchéhlaal**. *ptcpl* **eelŭmuchéh=laat**.

**aluméewaleew** VTA gather up and take away a load of s.t. animate. *ind 1st sg* **ndalŭméewalaaw, ndalŭméewala**. *ind 3rd sg* **wtalŭmeewaláawal**. *ind inv* **ndalŭméewalukw**. *ind I-you* **ktalŭméewalul**. *conj 3rd sg* **alumée=walaat**. *imp* **aluméewal**. *ptcpl* **eelŭ=méewalaat**.

**aluméewatoow** VTI2 gather up and take away a load of s.t. *ind 1st sg* **ndalŭ=méewatoon**. *ind 3rd sg* **wtalŭmée=watoon**. *conj 1st sg* **alumeewatáw=aan**. *conj 3rd sg* **aluméewataakw**. *imp* **aluméewatool**. *ptcpl* **eelŭmée=wataakw**.

**aluméewtam** VOTI1A go away crying. *ind 1st sg* **ndalŭméewtam**. *conj 3rd sg* **aluméewtang**. *ptcpl* **eelŭméew=tang**.

**alúmham** VOTI1A paddle away, row away. *ind 1st sg* **ndalŭmáham**. *conj 3rd sg* **alúmhang**. *imp* **alúmhah**. *ptcpl* **eelŭmáhang**.

**alumhéewaleew** VTA gather up and take away a load of s.t. animate. *ind 1st sg* **ndalŭmahéewalaaw, ndalŭmah=éewala**. *ind 3rd sg* **wtalŭmaheewa=**

láawal. *ind inv* **ndalŭmahéewalukw**. *ind I-you* **ktalŭmahéewalul**. *conj 3rd sg* **alumhéewalaat**. *imp* **alumhéewal**. *ptcpl* **eelŭmahéewalaat**.

**alumhéewasuw** VAI cart away a load *(of one's belongings)*. *ind 1st sg* **ndalŭ=mahéewasi, ndalŭmahéewasiim**. *conj 3rd sg* **alumhéewasiit**. *imp* **alumhéewasiil**. *ptcpl* **eelŭmahée=wasiit**.

**alumhéewatoow** VTI2 gather up and take away a load of s.t. *ind 1st sg* **ndalŭ=mahéewatoon**. *ind 3rd sg* **wtalŭ=mahéewatoon**. *conj 1st sg* **alumhee=watáwaan**. *conj 3rd sg* **alumhéewa=taakw**. *imp* **alumhéewatool**. *ptcpl* **eelŭmahéewataakw**.

**alumhóomeew** VAI ride away on horse-back. *ind 1st sg* **ndalŭmahóoma, ndalŭmahóomaam**. *conj 3rd sg* **alumhóomaat**. *imp* **alumhóomaal**. *ptcpl* **eelŭmahóomaat**.

**alumíikun** VII grow, be growing. *conj 3rd sg* **alumíikung**. *ptcpl* **eelŭmíi=kung**.

**alumíikuw** VAI grow, be growing *(s.t. animate)*. *ind 1st sg* **ndalŭmíiki, ndalŭmíikiim**. *conj 3rd sg* **alumíi=kiit**. *ptcpl* **eelŭmíikiit**.

**alumíikwsuw** VAI crawl away. *ind 1st sg* **ndalŭmíikwsi, ndalŭmíikwsiim**. *conj 3rd sg* **alumíikwsiit**. *imp* **alumíikw=siil**. *ptcpl* **eelŭmíikwsiit**.

**alumiinjkweeyáaheew** VAIO roll s.t. away. *ind 1st sg* **ndalŭmiinjkwee=yáaheen**. *ind 3rd sg* **wtalŭmiinj=kweeyáaheen**. *conj 3rd sg* **alumiinj=kweeyáaheet**. *imp* **alumiinjkwee=yáaheel**. *ptcpl* **eelŭmiinjkwee=yáaheet**.

**alumiinjkwéhleew** VAI roll away. *ind 1st sg* **ndalŭmiinjkwéhla, ndalŭ=miinjkwéhlaam**. *conj 3rd sg* **alum=iinjkwéhlaat**. *imp* **alumiinjkwéh=laal**. *ptcpl* **eelŭmiinjkwéhlaat**.

**alumiipáhtoow** VTI2 take s.t. away in a hurry. *ind 1st sg* **ndalŭmiipáhtoon**. *ind 3rd sg* **wtalŭmiipáhtoon**. *conj 1st sg* **alumiipáhtawaan**. *conj 3rd sg* **alumiipáhtaakw**. *imp* **alumiipáh=tool**. *ptcpl* **eelŭmiipáhtaakw**.

**alumíipheew** VTA take s.o. away in a hurry. *ind 1st sg* **ndalŭmíiphaaw, ndalŭmíipha**. *ind 3rd sg* **wtalŭmiip=háawal**. *ind inv* **ndalŭmíiphukw**. *ind I-you* **ktalŭmíiphul**. *conj 3rd sg* **alumíiphaat**. *imp* **alumíipah**. *ptcpl* **eelŭmíiphaat**.

**alumíhleew** VAI fly away, go away, pedal away. *ind 1st sg* **ndalŭmíhla, ndalŭ=míhlaam**. *conj 3rd sg* **alumíhlaat**. *imp* **alumíhlaal**. *ptcpl* **eelŭmíhlaat**. *intensive reduplication* **hàlŭmíhleew**.

**alumihtéeheew** VTA hit s.o. and send them away. *ind 1st sg* **ndalŭmihtée=haaw, ndalŭmihtéeha**. *ind 3rd sg* **wtalŭmihteeháawal**. *ind inv* **ndal=ŭmihtéehookw**. *ind I-you* **ktalŭmih=téehool**. *conj 3rd sg* **alumihtéehaat**. *imp* **alumíhteeh**. *ptcpl* **eelŭmih=téehaat**.

nd**álŭmoonz** NAD my dog, my horse; my close pet *(of dogs and horses)*. *pl* **ndalŭmóonzak**. *3rd poss* **wtalŭ=móonzal**.

**alumóonzuw** VAIO have s.o. for a pet, keep s.o. as a pet, make a pet out of s.o. **Wtalŭmoonzíinal pooshíishal.** 'He made a pet out of the cat.' *ind 1st sg* **ndalŭmóonziin**. *ind 3rd sg* **wtal=ŭmoonzíinal**. *conj 3rd sg* **alum=óonziit**. *imp* **alumóonziil**. *ptcpl* **eelŭmóonziit**. *See* **wtalŭmóonzuw**.

**alumóoxwaleew** VTA take s.o. along, re-move s.o. *ind 1st sg* **ndalŭmóoxwa=laaw, ndalŭmóoxwala**. *ind 3rd sg* **wtalŭmooxwaláawal**. *ind inv* **ndalŭ=móoxwalukw**. *ind I-you* **ktalŭmóo=xwalul**. *conj 3rd sg* **alumóoxwalaat**. *imp* **alumóoxwal**. *ptcpl* **eelŭmóo=xwalaat**.

**alumóoxwatoow** VTI2 take s.t. along,

remove s.t. *ind 1st sg* **ndalŭmóo=xwatoon**. *ind 3rd sg* **wtalŭmóoxwa=toon**. *conj 1st sg* **alumooxwatáwaan**. *conj 3rd sg* **alumóoxwataakw**. *imp* **alumóoxwatool**. *ptcpl* **eelŭmóo=xwataakw**.

**alúmshum** VTI 1A start cutting s.t. *ind 1st sg* **ndalŭmúshŭmun**. *ind 3rd sg* **wtalŭmúshŭmun**. *conj 1st sg* **alum=shúmaan**. *conj 3rd sg* **alúmshung**. *imp* **alúmshih**. *ptcpl* **eelŭmúshung**.

**alúmsuw** VAI leave, go off. *ind 1st sg* **ndalŭmúsi**, **ndalŭmúsiim**. *conj 3rd sg* **alúmsiit**. *imp* **alúmsiil**. *ptcpl* **eelŭmúsiit**.

**alúmsheew** VTA start cutting s.t. animate. *ind 1st sg* **ndalŭmúshaaw**, **ndalŭ=músha**. *ind 3rd sg* **wtalŭmusháawal**. *ind inv* **ndalŭmúshookw**. *ind I-you* **ktalŭmúshool**. *conj 3rd sg* **alúm=shaat**. *imp* **alúmush**. *ptcpl* **eelŭ=múshaat**.

**alumshíiheew** VTA send s.o. away. *ind 1st sg* **ndalŭmushíihaaw**, **ndalŭ=mushíiha**. *ind 3rd sg* **wtalŭmushii=háawal**. *ind inv* **ndalŭmushíihukw**. *ind I-you* **ktalŭmushíihul**. *conj 3rd sg* **alumshíihaat**. *imp* **alúmshiih**. *ptcpl* **eelŭmushíihaat**.

**alumshíikeew** VAI start cutting things. *ind 1st sg* **ndalŭmushíike**, **ndalŭ=mushíikeem**. *conj 3rd sg* **alumshíi=keet**. *imp* **alumshíikeel**. *ptcpl* **eelŭmushíikeet**.

**alumshíimuw** VAI run away, flee. *ind 1st sg* **ndalŭmushíimwi**, **ndalŭmush=íimwiim**. *conj 3rd sg* **alumshíimwiit**. *imp* **alumshíimwiil**. *ptcpl* **eelŭmush=íimwiit**.

**alumshíhkaweew** VTA send s.o. away. *ind 1st sg* **ndalŭmushíhkawaaw**, **ndalŭmushíhkawa**. *ind 3rd sg* **wtal=ŭmushihkawáawal**. *ind inv* **ndalŭ=mushíhkaakw**. *ind I-you* **ktalŭ=mushíhkool**. *conj 3rd sg* **alumshíh=kawaat**. *imp* **alumshíhkaw**. *ptcpl* **eelŭmushíhkawaat**.

**alumtóonheew** VAI start to speak. *ind 1st sg* **ndalŭmutóonhe**, **ndalŭ=mutóonheem**. *conj 3rd sg* **alum=tóonheet**. *imp* **alumtóonheel**. *ptcpl* **eelŭmutóonheet**.

**alumu-** PV begin to. **Alúmu-machíikŭ=nool.** 'They're starting to grow badly.'; **Alúmu-síhleew.** 'It (water level) is starting to go down.' *ptcpl* **éelŭmu-**. *See* **alu-**.

**alúmu-waaxéhleew** VII be the break of day, be clearing *(of the sky)*. *conj 3rd sg* **alúmu-waaxéhlaak**. *ptcpl* **éelŭmu-waaxéhlaak**.

**alúmŭlaan** VII begin raining. *conj 3rd sg* **alúmulaang**. *ptcpl* **eelŭmúlaang**.

**alumŭwáleew** VAIO carry s.t. away in a pack or bundle. *ind 1st sg* **ndalŭ=múwaleen**. *ind 3rd sg* **wtalumúwa=leen**. *conj 3rd sg* **alumŭwáleet**. *imp* **alumŭwáleel**. *ptcpl* **eelŭmúwaleet**.

**alumŭwaléhleew** VAI go away with things. *ind 1st sg* **ndalŭmuwaléhla**, **ndalŭmuwaléhlaam**. *conj 3rd sg* **alumŭwaléhlaat**. *imp* **alumŭwal=éhlaal**. *ptcpl* **eelŭmuwaléhlaat**.

**alumŭwaléhleew** VAIO carry s.t. away, carry s.t. away in a pack. *ind 1st sg* **ndalŭmuwaléhlaan**. *ind 3rd sg* **wtalŭmuwaléhlaan**. *conj 3rd sg* **alumŭwaléhlaat**. *imp* **alumŭwal=éhlaal**. *ptcpl* **eelŭmuwaléhlaat**.

**alúmxookw** VAI blow away in the wind, be blown away by the wind *(s.t. animate)*. *ind 1st sg* **ndalŭmáxookw**. *conj 3rd sg* **alumxóokwuk**. *ptcpl* **eelŭmaxóokwuk**.

**alúmxun** VII blow away in the wind, be blown away by the wind. *conj 3rd sg* **alúmxung**. *ptcpl* **eelŭmáxung**.

**alúneew** VTA touch s.o. *ind 1st sg* **ndálŭnaaw**, **ndálŭna**. *ind 3rd sg* **wtalŭnáawal**. *ind inv* **ndálŭnukw**. *ind I-you* **ktálŭnul**. *conj 3rd sg* **alúnaat**. *imp* **alún**. *ptcpl* **éelŭnaat**.

**alúnum** VTI1B touch s.t. *ind 1st sg* **ndalŭnúmun**. *ind 3rd sg* **wtalŭ=númun**. *conj 1st sg* **alúnŭmaan**. *conj 3rd sg* **alúnung**. *imp* **alúnih**. *ptcpl* **éelŭnung**.

**alút** VII rot, be rotten. *conj 3rd sg* **alíhk**. *ptcpl* **éelihk**.

**alutóoneew** VAI have trenchmouth. *ind 1st sg* **ndaltóona, ndaltóonaam**. *conj 3rd sg* **alutóonaat**. *ptcpl* **eeltóonaat**.

**aluwéelŭmeew** VTA prefer s.o. to someone else, think more of s.o. than of someone else, think s.o. better than someone else. *ind 1st sg* **ndalŭwée=lŭmaaw, ndalŭwéelŭma**. *ind 3rd sg* **wtalŭweelŭmáawal**. *ind inv* **ndalŭ=wéelŭmukw**. *ind I-you* **ktalŭwéelŭ=mul**. *conj 3rd sg* **aluwéelŭmaat**. *imp* **aluwéelum**. *ptcpl* **eelŭwéelŭmaat**.

**aluweelúndam** VTI1A prefer s.t. to s.t. else, think more of s.t. than of something else, think s.t. better than something else; want to do s.t. first. *ind 1st sg* **ndalŭweelúndamun**. *ind 3rd sg* **wtalŭweelúndamun**. *conj 1st sg* **aluweelúndamaan**. *conj 3rd sg* **aluweelúndang**. *imp* **aluweelúndah**. *ptcpl* **eelŭweelúndang**.

**aluweelunzíhtaweew** VTA think oneself better than s.o. *ind 1st sg* **ndalŭwee=lunzíhtawaaw, ndalŭweelunzíh=tawa**. *ind 3rd sg* **wtalŭweelunzihta=wáawal**. *ind inv* **ndalŭweelunzíh=taakw**. *ind I-you* **ktalŭweelunzíh=tool**. *conj 3rd sg* **aluweelunzíhta=waat**. *imp* **aluweelunzíhtaw**. *ptcpl* **eelŭweelunzíhtawaat**.

**aluweelúnzuw** VAIO think oneself better than s.o. else. *ind 1st sg* **ndalŭwee=lúnziin**. *ind 3rd sg* **wtalŭweelunzíi=nal**. *conj 3rd sg* **aluweelúnziit**. *ptcpl* **eelŭweelúnziit**.

**alúwii** PC more, more than, early. *See* **hálŭwii**.

**aluwii-** PV more, more than, early. **Alúwii-laawahkwéewŭnii.** 'Early afternoon.' *ptcpl* **éelŭwii-**.

**aluwíhkam** VTI1A overcome s.t. *ind 1st sg* **ndalŭwíhkamun**. *ind 3rd sg* **wtalŭwíhkamun**. *conj 1st sg* **aluw=íhkamaan**. *conj 3rd sg* **aluwíhkang**. *imp* **aluwíhkah**. *ptcpl* **eelŭwíhkang**.

**aluwíhkaweew** VTA overcome s.o., dominate s.o. *(especially one's spouse)*. *ind 1st sg* **ndalŭwíhkawaaw, ndalŭ=wíhkawa**. *ind 3rd sg* **wtalŭwihka=wáawal**. *ind inv* **ndalŭwíhkaakw**. *ind I-you* **ktalŭwíhkool**. *conj 3rd sg* **aluwíhkawaat**. *imp* **aluwíhkaw**. *ptcpl* **eelŭwíhkawaat**.

**aluwíhlateew** VAI be some left over, be left over *(of s.t. animate)*. *conj 3rd sg* **aluwíhlataat**. *ptcpl* **eelŭwíhlataat**.

**aluwíhlateew** VII be some left over, be left over. *conj 3rd sg* **aluwíhlataak**. *ptcpl* **eelŭwíhlataak**.

**aluwíhleew** VAI be left over, be some left over *(s.t. animate)*. **Aluwíhleew namées.** 'There's some fish left over.' *conj 3rd sg* **aluwíhlaat**. *ptcpl* **eelŭ=wíhlaat**.

**aluwíhleew** VII be left over, be some left over. *conj 3rd sg* **aluwíhlaak**. *ptcpl* **eelŭwíhlaak**.

**amáameew** VTA notify s.o. **Ndamáa=mkee.** 'I was notified.' *ind 1st sg* **ndamáamaaw, ndamáama**. *ind 3rd sg* **wtamaamáawal**. *ind inv* **ndam=áamukw**. *ind I-you* **ktamáamul**. *conj 3rd sg* **amáamaat**. *imp* **amáam**.

**amaashíiyayuw** VAI act strangely. *ind 1st sg* **nŭmamaashíiyayi, nŭmam=aashíiyayiim**. *conj 3rd sg* **amaashíi=yayiit**. *ptcpl* **meemaashíiyayiit**.

**amáashŭnum** VOTI1B act oddly, act strangely, make faces. *ind 1st sg* **nŭmamáashunum**. *conj 3rd sg* **amáashŭnung**. *ptcpl* **meemáa=shŭnung**. *moderative reduplication* **maamáashŭnum**.

**amachiikwáakeew** VAI sew badly. *ind 1st sg* **nŭmamachiikwáake**,

**nŭmamachiikwáakeem**. *conj 3rd sg* **amachiikwáakeet**. *ptcpl* **meema=chiikwáakeet**.

**amachu-** PV carelessly, bad. **Nŭmám=achu-wŭleekŭnúmun.** 'I fold it carelessly.' *ptcpl* **méemachu-**.

**amáchu-leew** VTA swear at s.o. **Nŭ=mámachu-lúkw, noondanóongsiin.** 'He swore at me and that's the reason I got mad.' *ind 1st sg* **nŭmámachu-láaw**, **nŭmámachu-lá**. *ind 3rd sg* **mámachu-láawal**. *ind inv* **nŭmám=achu-lúkw**. *ind I-you* **kŭmámachu-lúl**. *conj 3rd sg* **amáchu-láat**. *ptcpl* **méemachu-láat**. *See* **kŭlóoleew**.

**amakwŭnáxkeew** VAI have swollen hands. *ind 1st sg* **nŭmamakwun=áxka**, **nŭmamakwunáxkaam**. *conj 3rd sg* **amakwŭnáxkaat**. *ptcpl* **meemakwunáxkaat**.

**amámeew** VTA feel the sensation that s.o. makes, feel the sensation of s.o. *ind 1st sg* **ndámamaaw**, **ndámama**. *ind 3rd sg* **wtamamáawal**. *ind inv* **ndámamukw**. *ind I-you* **ktámamul**. *conj 3rd sg* **amámaat**. *ptcpl* **éema=maat**.

**amándam** VTI 1A feel s.t. as an ache, feel s.t. as a pain, feel s.t. as a soreness in one's body. *ind 1st sg* **ndamánda=mun**. *ind 3rd sg* **wtamándamun**. *conj 1st sg* **amándamaan**. *conj 3rd sg* **amándang**. *ptcpl* **eemándang**.

**amandamuwáakan** NI feeling, sensation, feeling in a sore body part.

**amangaalakíingweew** VAI have big eyes. *ind 1st sg* **nŭmamangaalakíingwe**, **nŭmamangaalakíingweem**. *conj 3rd sg* **amangaalakíingweet**. *ptcpl* **mee=mangaalakíingweet**.

**amangaalakiingwéexiin** VAI be big eyed *(after seeing something unusual)*; lie with one's eyes open *(especially if one cannot sleep)*. *ind 1st sg* **nŭmam=angaalakiingwéexiin**, **nŭmaman=gaalakiingwéexi**. *conj 3rd sg* **aman=gaalakiingwéexiing**. *ptcpl* **mee=mangaalakiingwéexiing**.

**amangaaptóoneew** VAI talk loudly. *ind 1st sg* **nŭmamangaaptóona**, **nŭ=mamangaaptóonaam**. *conj 3rd sg* **amangaaptóonaat**. *ptcpl* **meeman=gaaptóonaat**.

**amangaawangéeyayeew** VII be hilly, be mountainous. **Níi kíixkii nŭwíiki éenda-amangaawangéeyayeek.** 'I live near the mountains.' *conj 3rd sg* **amangaawangéeyayeek**.

**amangaawatóoheew** VAI charge a lot. **Kóosaa-amangaawatóohe.** 'You charge too much.' *ind 1st sg* **nŭmam=angaawatóohe**, **nŭmamangaawa=tóoheem**. *conj 3rd sg* **amangaawa=tóoheet**. *ptcpl* **meemangaawa=tóoheet**.

**amangaawatúwal** VII be expensive, cost a lot. *usually plural. conj 3rd pl* **amangáawatiik**. *ptcpl* **meemangaa=watíikiil**.

**amangaawúnge** PC mountain, hill.

**amangachii-** PN big. *usually plural only.* **Amángachii-kiikíipshak.** 'Big chickens.' *See* **xwachii-**.

**amangachiikáanal** NI big houses. *usually plural. See* **xwachíikaan**.

**amangahkíiheew** VAI plant many things, plant lots, plant a large amount. *ind 1st sg* **nŭmamangahkíihe**, **nŭmam=angahkíiheem**. *conj 3rd sg* **aman=gahkíiheet**. *imp* **amangahkíiheel**. *ptcpl* **meemangahkíiheet**.

**amangahksúneew** VAI have big shoes. *ind 1st sg* **nŭmamangahksúne**, **nŭmamangahksúneem**. *conj 3rd sg* **amangahksúneet**. *ptcpl* **meeman=gahksúneet**.

**amangaláamuw** VAI sing out loud. *ind 1st sg* **nŭmamangaláamwi**, **nŭmam=angaláamwiim**. *conj 3rd sg* **aman=galáamwiit**. *imp* **amangaláamwiil**. *ptcpl* **meemangaláamwiit**.

**amangapíikweew** VAI play loud music.

*ind 1st sg* **nŭmamangapíikwe**, **nŭmamangapíikweem**. *conj 3rd sg* **amangapíikweet**. *imp* **amangapíi=kweel**. *ptcpl* **meemangapíikweet**.

**amangásktuw** VAI defecate a large amount, go to the bathroom a lot. *ind 1st sg* **nŭmamangáskti**, **nŭmaman=gásktiim**. *conj 3rd sg* **amangásktiit**. *ptcpl* **meemangásktiit**. *See* **xwásk=tuw**.

**amangéewal** VII be big. *usually plural.* *conj 3rd pl* **amángeek**. *ptcpl* **mee=mangéekiil**.

**amangíilaneew** VAI have big breasts. *ind 1st sg* **nŭmamangíilana**, **nŭmaman=gíilanaam**. *conj 3rd sg* **amangíila=naat**. *ptcpl* **meemangíilanaat**.

**amangíisheew** VAI urinate a lot. *ind 1st sg* **nŭmamangíishe**, **nŭmamangíi=sheem**. *conj 3rd sg* **amangíisheet**. *imp* **amangíisheel**. *ptcpl* **meeman=gíisheet**.

**amangíixsuw** VAI talk in a loud voice, talk loudly. *ind 1st sg* **nŭmamangíi=xsi**, **nŭmamangíixsiim**. *conj 3rd sg* **amangíixsiit**. *ptcpl* **meemangíixsiit**.

**amangkáateew** VAI have big legs. *ind 1st sg* **nŭmamangkáata**, **nŭmam=angkáataam**. *conj 3rd sg* **amang=káataat**. *ptcpl* **meemangkáataat**. *See* **xwukáateew**.

**amangkíilook** VAI be big. *usually plural.* *ind 1st pl* **nŭmamangkiilóhna**. *conj 3rd pl* **amangkiilóhtiit**. *ptcpl* **mee=mangkiilóhtiit**.

**amangpeekíixun** VII be a big puddle. *conj 3rd sg* **amangpeekíixung**. *ptcpl* **meemangpeekíixung**.

**amangsíiteew** VAI have big feet. *ind 1st sg* **nŭmamangsíita**, **nŭmamangsíi=taam**. *conj 3rd sg* **amangsíitaat**. *ptcpl* **meemangsíitaat**. *See* **xwusíiteew**.

**amangshámuw** VII be a big pile *(as of hay)*. *conj 3rd sg* **amangshámwiik**. *ptcpl* **meemangshámwiik**.

**amangu-** PV big. **Amangu-pangéeyeew.** 'It's in big pieces.'; **Nŭmángu-ayúwa pehpaxkwŭléeshak.** 'I gathered a lot of flowers.' *ptcpl* **méemángu-**, **méengu-**.

**amángu-láatam** VOTI I A laugh a lot, laugh out loud. *ind 1st sg* **numam=ángu-láatam**. *conj 3rd sg* **amángu-láatang**. *ptcpl* **meemángu-láatang**. *See* **mángu-láatam**.

**amangŭnánŭweew** VAI have big cheeks. *ind 1st sg* **nŭmamamangŭnánuwe**, **nŭmamangŭnánŭweem**. *conj 3rd sg* **amangŭnánuweet**. *ptcpl* **meeman=gŭnánŭweet**.

**amangúndeew** VII have large rooms *(of buildings)*. *conj 3rd sg* **amangúndeek**. *ptcpl* **meemangúndeek**.

**amángŭweew** VAI make a lot of noise, make a big noise *(s.t. animate)*. *ind 1st sg* **nŭmamángŭwe**, **nŭmam=ángŭweem**. *conj 3rd sg* **amángŭweet**. *imp* **amángŭweel**. *ptcpl* **meemángŭ=weet**.

**amángŭweew** VII make a lot of noise, make a big noise. *conj 3rd sg* **amán=gŭweet**. *ptcpl* **meemángŭweek**.

**amángxeew** VAI have big ears. *ind 1st sg* **nŭmamángxa**, **nŭmamángxaam**. *conj 3rd sg* **amángxaat**. *ptcpl* **meemángxaat**.

**amataaptóoneew** VAI speak improperly, pronounce words incorrectly. *ind 1st sg* **nŭmamataaptóona**, **nŭmama=taaptóonaam**. *conj 3rd sg* **amataap=tóonaat**. *imp* **amataaptóonaal**. *ptcpl* **meemataaptóonaat**.

**amatakíinzuw** VAI read badly, be a poor reader. *ind 1st sg* **nŭmamatakíinzi**, **nŭmamatakíinziim**. *conj 3rd sg* **a=matakíinziit**. *ptcpl* **meematakíinziit**.

**amataláamuw** VAI sing badly. *ind 1st sg* **nŭmamataláamwi**, **nŭmam=ataláamwiim**. *conj 3rd sg* **amata=láamwiit**. *imp* **amataláamwiil**. *ptcpl* **meemataláamwiit**.

**amatalóhkeew** VAI be a bad worker; do

bad deeds. *ind 1st sg* **nŭmamatalóh=ke, nŭmamatalóhkeem**. *conj 3rd sg* **amatalóhkeet**. *imp* **amatalóhkeel**. *ptcpl* **meematalóhkeet**.

**amataníikeew** VAI have bad teeth. *ind 1st sg* **nŭmamataníika, nŭmama=taníikaam**. *conj 3rd sg* **amataníi=kaat**. *ptcpl* **meemataníikaat**.

**amatayáxkham** VOTI1A shoot badly, be a bad shot. *ind 1st sg* **numamatay=áxkham**. *conj 3rd sg* **amatayáxk=hang**. *ptcpl* **meematayáxkhang**.

**amateekhíikeew** VAI have messy writing. *ind 1st sg* **nŭmamateekhíike, nŭmamateekhíikeem**. *conj 3rd sg* **amateekhíikeet**. *ptcpl* **meemateek=híikeet**.

**amatóoxweew** VAI walk badly, have a hard time walking. *ind 1st sg* **nŭ=mamatóoxwe, nŭmamatóoxweem**. *conj 3rd sg* **amatóoxweet**. *ptcpl* **meematóoxweet**.

**amaxksheetóoneew** VAI have red lips. *ind 1st sg* **nŭmamaxksheetóone, nŭmamaxksheetóoneem**. *conj 3rd sg* **amaxksheetóoneet**. *ptcpl* **meemaxksheetóoneet**.

**amayakíiheew** VTA waste s.t. animate. *ind 1st sg* **nŭmamayakíihaaw, nŭmamayakíiha**. *ind 3rd sg* **màm=ayakiiháawal**. *ind inv* **nŭmamayak=íihukw**. *ind I-you* **kŭmamayakíihul**. *conj 3rd sg* **amayakíihaat**. *imp* **amáyakiih**. *ptcpl* **meemayakíihaat**.

**amayakíhtoow** VTI2 waste s.t. *ind 1st sg* **nŭmamayakíhtoon**. *ind 3rd sg* **màmayakíhtoon**. *conj 1st sg* **amay=akíhtawaan**. *conj 3rd sg* **amayakíh=taakw**. *imp* **amayakíhtool**. *ptcpl* **meemayakíhtaakw**.

**amayakúsuw** VAI be wasteful. *ind 1st sg* **nŭmamayáksi, nŭmamayáksiim**. *conj 3rd sg* **amayakúsiit**. *ptcpl* **meemayáksiit**.

**ámbee** PC also. **Ámbee níi.** 'Me too.'; **Ámbee-uch nŭwíite.** 'I'm going to go too.'

**ambiilaméekwaan** NA needle. *pl* **ambiilameekwáanak**. *poss* **ndam=biilaméekwaan**. *loc* **ambiilamee=kwáanung**. *dimin* **ambiilamee=kwáanush**. *obv* **ambiilameekwáa=nal**.

**ambíisoon** NI cradleboard. *pl* **ambii=sóonal**. *poss* **ndambíisoon**. *loc* **ambiisóonung**. *dimin* **ambiishóo=nush**.

**amehchkáxkwaneew** VAI have bare shins *(of a woman not wearing stockings)*. *ind 1st sg* **nŭmamehchkáxkwana, nŭmamehchkáxkwanaam**. *conj 3rd sg* **amehchkáxkwanaat**.

**amíimunz** NA child. *pl* **amiimúnzak**. *poss* **níichaan**. *dimin* **amiimún=zhush**. *obv* **amiimúnzal**.

**amiimúnzuw** VAI be a child. *ind 1st sg* **ndamiimúnzi, ndamiimúnziim**. *conj 3rd sg* **amiimúnziit**. *ptcpl* **eemii=múnziit**.

**amiimúnzhush** NA baby. *pl* **amii=múnzh'shak**. *obv* **amiimúnzhshal**.

**amiixanii-** PV ashamed. **Amíixanii-kŭlúksuw.** 'S/he laughs nervously.' *ptcpl* **meemíixanii-**. *See* **amiixu-**.

**amiixu-** PV ashamed. *informal*. **Amíixu-láatam.** 'S/he snickers.' *ptcpl* **meemíixu-**. *See* **amiixanii-**.

**amóxkw** NA beaver. *pl* **amóxkwak**. *dimin* **amóxkwush**. *obv* **amóxkwal**.

**amóxool** NA boat. *pl* **amoxóolak**. *poss* **ndámxool**. *loc* **amoxóolung**. *dimin* **amoxóolush**. *obv* **amoxóolal**.

**amóxool** NI boat. *pl* **amoxóolal**. *poss* **ndámxool**. *loc* **amoxóolung**. *dimin* **amoxóolush**.

**amoxóolham** VOTI1A sail a boat, use a boat. *ind 1st sg* **ndamxóolham**. *conj 3rd sg* **amoxóolhang**. *imp* **amox=óolhah**. *ptcpl* **eemxóolhang**. *See* **amoxoolhámeew**.

**amoxoolhámeew** VAI sail a boat, use a boat. *ind 1st sg* **ndamxoolháma**,

**ndamxoolhámaam**. *conj 3rd sg* **amoxoolhámaat**. *imp* **amoxool=hámaal**. *ptcpl* **eemxoolhámaat**. *See* **amoxóolham**.

**anáanzoon** NI sheet. *pl* **anaanzóonal**. *poss* **ndanáanzoon**. *loc* **anaanzóo=nung**. *dimin* **anaanzhóonush**.

**anaanzŭwahíikan** NI bedding material. *pl* **anaanzŭwahíikanal**. *poss* **ndan=aanzŭwahíikan**. *loc* **anaanzŭwahíi=kanung**.

**anáheew** VTA lose s.o., lose s.t. animate. *ind 1st sg* **ndánhaaw**, **ndánha**. *ind 3rd sg* **wtanháawal**. *ind inv* **ndánhookw**. *ind I-you* **ktánhool**. *conj 3rd sg* **anáhaat**. *ptcpl* **éenhaat**.

**anáhookw** VAI be lost. *ind 1st sg* **ndán=hookw**. *conj 3rd sg* **anahóokwuk**. *ptcpl* **eenhóokwuk**.

**áng** PC emphatic. **Mbahchíinawaa áng táas.** 'Sometimes I mistake him for someone else.'; **Ách áng wtayáalu-kihkŭlooláawal ngúkal.** 'He couldn't even talk to my mother.'

**aníiskakuw** VAI wear dirty clothes. *ind 1st sg* **nàníiskakwi**, **nàniiskákwiim**. *conj 3rd sg* **aníiskakwiit**. *imp* **aníis=kakwiil**. *ptcpl* **neeníiskakwiit**.

**aníiskii-paxkŭníikeew** VAI be a 'dirty' picker, pick only the most accessible fruits or berries, pick only the most accessible products. *ind 1st sg* **nàníiskii-paxkŭníike**, **nàníiskii-paxkŭníikeem**. *conj 3rd sg* **aníiskii-paxkŭníikeet**. *ptcpl* **neeníiskii-paxkŭníikeet**.

**aniiskiiktúkweew** VAI have dirty knees. *ind 1st sg* **nàniiskiiktúkwa**, **nàniis=kiiktúkwaam**. *conj 3rd sg* **aniiskiik=túkwaat**. *ptcpl* **neeniiskiiktúkwaat**.

**aniiskíhkasheew** VAI have dirty fingernails. *ind 1st sg* **nàniiskíhkasha**, **nàniiskihkáshaam**. *conj 3rd sg* **aniiskíhkashaat**. *ptcpl* **neeniiskíh=kashaat**.

**aniiskshíikeew** VAI cut things up and make a mess, make a mess while cutting. *ind 1st sg* **nàniiskshíike**, **nàn=iiskshíikeem**. *conj 3rd sg* **aniiskshíi=keet**. *ptcpl* **neeniiskshíikeet**.

**aniisku-** PV habitually, lots; dirty. **Aníisku-kawíiw.** 'He loves to sleep, he sleeps easily, he sleeps lots.'; **Aníisku-kshiixíinjŭwe.** 'He washes the dishes and leaves them dirty.' *ptcpl* **neeníisku-**.

**aniiskŭnáxkeew** VAI have dirty hands. *ind 1st sg* **nàniiskŭnáxka**, **nàniiskŭ=náxkaam**. *conj 3rd sg* **aniiskŭnáx=kaat**. *ptcpl* **neeniiskŭnáxkaat**.

**aníixan** NA shoelace. *pl* **aníixanak**. *poss* **ndaníixan**. *loc* **aníixanung**. *dimin* **aníixanush**. *obv* **aníixanal**.

**aníixan** NI shoelace. *pl* **aníixanal**. *poss* **ndaníixan**. *loc* **aníixanung**. *dimin* **aníixanush**.

**aníhteew** VII be lost. *conj 3rd sg* **aníh=taak**. *ptcpl* **eeníhtaak**.

**aníhtoow** VTI2 lose s.t. *ind 1st sg* **ndan=íhtoon**. *ind 3rd sg* **wtaníhtoon**. *conj 1st sg* **aníhtawaan**. *conj 3rd sg* **aníhtaakw**. *ptcpl* **eeníhtaakw**.

**anúshiik** PC thank you.

**ánz'ham** VTI1A scoop s.t. up *(using a tool or instrument)*. *ind 1st sg* **ndan=z'hámun**. *ind 3rd sg* **wtanz'hámun**. *conj 1st sg* **anz'hámaan**. *conj 3rd sg* **ánz'hang**. *imp* **ánz'hah**. *ptcpl* **éen=z'hang**.

**ánz'heew** VTA scoop s.t. animate up *(using a tool or instrument)*. *ind 1st sg* **ndánz'haaw**, **ndánz'ha**. *ind 3rd sg* **wtanz'háawal**. *ind inv* **ndánz'hookw**. *ind I-you* **ktánz'hool**. *conj 3rd sg* **ánz'haat**. *imp* **ánz'haw**. *ptcpl* **éenz'haat**.

**anz'híikan** NI scoop, dipper, something used to dip for water. *pl* **anz'híi=kanal**. *poss* **ndanz'híikan**. *loc* **anz'=híikanung**. *dimin* **anz'híikanush**. *See* **ehanz'híikan**.

**anz'híikeew** VAI scoop things up, dip

*(for water). ind 1st sg* **ndanz'híike, ndanz'híikeem**. *conj 3rd sg* **anz'híi=keet**. *imp* **anz'híikeel**. *ptcpl* **eenz'=híikeet**.

**anziikwáaleew** VTA scoop s.t. animate up *(with something held in the hand). ind 1st sg* **ndanziikwáalaaw, ndan=ziikwáala**. *ind 3rd sg* **wtanziikwaa=láawal**. *conj 3rd sg* **anziikwáalaat**. *imp* **anzíikwaal**. *ptcpl* **eenziikwáa=laat**.

**anzíikwam** VTI 1A scoop s.t. up *(with something held in the hand). ind 1st sg* **ndanzíikwamun**. *ind 3rd sg* **wtanzíikwamun**. *conj 1st sg* **anzíi=kwamaan**. *conj 3rd sg* **anzíikwang**. *imp* **anzíikwah**. *ptcpl* **eenzíikwang**.

**anziipáhtoow** VTI2 grab s.t. in a hurry, grab s.t. quickly, grab a handful of s.t. **Ánziipáhtool shúlpul ootéeneeng áatookw.** 'Grab the money and let's go to town.' *ind 1st sg* **ndanziipáh=toon**. *ind 3rd sg* **wtanziipáhtoon**. *conj 1st sg* **anziipáhtawaan**. *conj 3rd sg* **anziipáhtaakw**. *imp* **anziipáhtool**. *ptcpl* **eenziipáhtaakw**.

**anzíipheew** VTA grab a handful of s.t. animate. *ind 1st sg* **ndanzíiphaaw, ndanzíipha**. *ind 3rd sg* **wtanziip=háawal**. *ind inv* **ndanzíiphukw**. *ind I-you* **ktanzíiphul**. *conj 3rd sg* **anzíi=phaat**. *imp* **anzíipah**. *ptcpl* **eenzíip=haat**.

**ánzŭneew** VTA take a handful of s.t. animate, scoop s.t. animate up *(using the hands). ind 1st sg* **ndánzŭnaaw, ndánzŭna**. *ind 3rd sg* **wtanzŭnáa=wal**. *ind inv* **ndánzŭnukw**. *ind I-you* **ktánzŭnul**. *conj 3rd sg* **ánzŭnaat**. *imp* **ánzun**. *ptcpl* **éenzŭnaat**.

**anzŭníikeew** VAI scoop things, dip *(for water). ind 1st sg* **ndanzŭníike, ndanzŭníikeem**. *conj 3rd sg* **anzŭ=níikeet**. *imp* **anzŭníikeel**. *ptcpl* **eenzŭníikeet**.

**ánzŭnum** VOTI 1B scoop things, dip *(for water). ind 1st sg* **ndánzŭnum**. *conj 3rd sg* **ánzŭnung**. *imp* **ánzŭnih**. *ptcpl* **éenzŭnung**.

**ánzŭnum** VTI 1B take a handful of s.t., scoop s.t. up *(using the hands). ind 1st sg* **ndanzŭnúmun**. *ind 3rd sg* **wtanzŭnúmun**. *conj 1st sg* **anzŭ=númaan**. *conj 3rd sg* **ánzŭnung**. *imp* **ánzŭnih**. *ptcpl* **éenzŭnung**.

**apaamáakchehl** VAI jump here and there, jump about, jump around. *ind 1st sg* **mbapaamáakchehl**. *conj 3rd sg* **apaamaakchéhluk**. *imp* **apaa=maakchéhlih**. *ptcpl* **peepaamaak=chéhluk**.

**apaamaashóokeew** VAI wade here and there in the water, wade around in the water, wade across. *ind 1st sg* **mbap=aamaashóoke, mbapaamaashóo=keem**. *conj 3rd sg* **apaamaashóo=keet**. *imp* **apaamaashóokeel**. *ptcpl* **peepaamaashóokeet**.

**apaamáashŭweew** VAI swim here and there, swim about. *ind 1st sg* **mbap=aamáashŭwe, mbapaamáashŭ=weem**. *conj 3rd sg* **apaamáashŭ=weet**. *imp* **apaamáashŭweel**. *ptcpl* **peepaamáashŭweet**.

**apaamáashŭwihl** VAI swim here and there, swim about. *ind 1st sg* **mbap=aamáashŭwihl**. *conj 3rd sg* **apaa=maashŭwíhluk**. *imp* **apaamaashŭ=wíhlih**. *ptcpl* **peepaamaashŭwíhluk**. *See* **apaamaashŭwíhleew**.

**apaamaashŭwíhleew** VAI swim here and there, swim about. *ind 1st sg* **mbapaamaashŭwíhla, mbapaa=maashŭwíhlaam**. *conj 3rd sg* **apaa=maashŭwíhlaat**. *imp* **apaamaashŭ=wíhlaal**. *ptcpl* **peepaamaashŭwíh=laat**. *See* **apaamáashŭwihl**.

**apaamáathookw** VAI float here and there, float about, float around. *ind 1st sg* **mbapaamáathookw**. *conj 3rd sg* **apaamaathóokwuk**. *ptcpl* **peepaamaathóokwuk**.

**apaamáathun** VII float here and there, float about, float around. *conj 3rd sg* **apaamáathung**. *ptcpl* **peepaamáat=hung**.

**apaamahtakíhleew** VAI run here and there, run about, run around. *ind 1st sg* **mbapaamahtakíhla**, **mbapaa=mahtakíhlaam**. *conj 3rd sg* **apaa=mahtakíhlaat**. *imp* **apaamahtakíh=laal**. *ptcpl* **peepaamahtakíhlaat**.

**apaamasánuw** VAI carry something around. *ind 1st sg* **mbapaamasáni**, **mbapaamasániim**. *conj 3rd sg* **apaamasániit**. *imp* **apaamasániil**. *ptcpl* **peepaamasániit**.

**apaamchéhleew** VAI drive here and there, drive about, drive around. *ind 1st sg* **mbapaamchéhla**, **mbapaamchéh=laam**. *conj 3rd sg* **apaamchéhlaat**. *imp* **apaamchéhlaal**. *ptcpl* **pee=paamchéhlaat**.

**apaameekhíikeew** VAI make marks here and there, make streaks all over *(on paper)*. *ind 1st sg* **mbapaameek=híike**, **mbapaameekhíikeem**. *conj 3rd sg* **apaameekhíikeet**. *imp* **apaa=meekhíikeel**.

**apaaméewtam** VOTI 1 A go here and there crying, go about crying. *ind 1st sg* **mbapaaméewtam**. *conj 3rd sg* **apaaméewtang**.

**apáamham** VOTI 1 A paddle here and there, paddle about. *ind 1st sg* **mbapáamham**. *conj 3rd sg* **apáam=hang**. *imp* **apáamhah**.

**apaamiikwsíhleew** VAI waltz around, do a round dance. *ind 1st sg* **mbapaa=miikwsíhla**, **mbapaamiikwsíhlaam**. *conj 3rd sg* **apaamiikwsíhlaat**. *imp* **apaamiikwsíhlaal**.

**apaamíikwsuw** VAI crawl here and there, crawl about. *ind 1st sg* **mbapaa=míikwsi**, **mbapaamíikwsiim**. *conj 3rd sg* **apaamíikwsiit**. *imp* **apaa=míikwsiil**.

**apaamóhkweew** VAI look here and there, look about, look around. *ind 1st sg* **mbapaamóhkwe**, **mbapaamóh=kweem**. *conj 3rd sg* **apaamóhkweet**. *imp* **apaamóhkweel**. *See* **apaamoh=kwéhleew**.

**apaamohkwéhleew** VAI look here and there, look about, look around. *ind 1st sg* **mbapaamohkwéhla**, **mbap=aamohkwéhlaam**. *conj 3rd sg* **apaa=mohkwéhlaat**. *imp* **apaamohkwéh=laal**. *See* **apaamóhkweew**.

**apáamsuw** VAI walk here and there, walk about. *ind 1st sg* **mbapáamsi**, **mbapáamsiim**. *conj 3rd sg* **apáam=siit**. *imp* **apáamsiil**. *ptcpl* **peepáam=siit**.

**apáamu** PC about, approximately. **Nál náh nóonj-alúmsiin wíixkwii ndíit, "Ngwiilamúnal kwáchŭmung apáamu yú talí."** 'And as I left from there suddenly I thought, "I'll look for them outside around here."'; **Apáamu níish-katúne náh talalóh=keew.** 'He worked there about two years.'

**apaamu-** PV about, around, here and there. **Nxóo mbapáamu-kawíhla.** 'I fell about by myself.' *ptcpl* **peepáa=mu-**. *See* **papaa-**.

**apaamshíhkaweew** VTA chase s.o. around. *ind 1st sg* **mbapaamshíh=kawaaw**, **mbapaamshíhkawa**. *ind 3rd sg* **pàpaamshihkawáawal**. *ind inv* **mbapaamshíhkaakw**. *ind I-you* **kpapaashíhkool**. *conj 3rd sg* **apaam=shíhkawaat**. *imp* **apaamshíhkaw**. *ptcpl* **peepaamshíhkawaat**.

**apahahkáakan** NI roof. *pl* **apahahkáa=kanal**. *poss* **ndaphahkáakan**. *loc* **apahahkáakanung**. *dimin* **apahah=káakanush**. *See* **apaháakan**.

**apahahkáasuw** VII be covered in shingles *(of a house)*. *conj 3rd sg* **apah=ahkáasiik**. *ptcpl* **peephahkáasiik**.

**apaháhkeew** VAI put shingles on a roof. *ind 1st sg* **ndapháhke**, **ndapháh=**

keem. *conj 3rd sg* **apaháhkeet**. *imp* **apaháhkeel**. *ptcpl* **eepháhkeet**.
**apanzhíikaan** NI log house. *pl* **apan=zhiikáanal**. *loc* **apanzhiikáanung**. *dimin* **apanzhiikáanush**.
**apánzhuy** NI timber. *pl* **apánzhŭyal**. *loc* **apánzhiing**. *dimin* **apánzhiish**.
**apawáaheew** VAIO shake s.t. *ind 1st sg* **mbapawáaheen**. *ind 3rd sg* **pàpa=wáaheen**. *conj 3rd sg* **apawáaheet**. *imp* **apawáaheel**. *ptcpl* **peepawáa=heet**.
**apawíhleew** VAI shake back and forth, sway back and forth *(s.t. animate)*. *ind 1st sg* **mbapawíhla**, **mbapawíh=laam**. *conj 3rd sg* **apawíhlaat**. *ptcpl* **peepawíhlaat**. *See* **pawíhleew**.
**apawíhleew** VII shake back and forth, sway back and forth. *conj 3rd sg* **apawíhlaak**. *ptcpl* **peepawíhlaak**. *See* **pawíhleew**.
**apáwxookw** VAI be blown back and forth by the wind, be shaken by the wind. *ind 1st sg* **mbapawáxookw**. *conj 3rd sg* **apawxóokwuk**. *ptcpl* **peepawaxóokwuk**.
**apáwxun** VII be blown back and forth by the wind, be shaken by the wind. *conj 3rd sg* **apáwxung**. *ptcpl* **peepa=wáxung**.
**apíikw** NA flea. *pl* **apíikwak**. *poss* **ndapíikwum**. *dimin* **apíikwush**. *obv* **apíikwal**.
**apíikwan** NI musical instrument. *pl* **apíikwanal**. *poss* **ndapíikwan**. *loc* **apíikwanung**. *dimin* **apíikwanush**.
**apíikweew** VAI play a musical instrument. *ind 1st sg* **ndapíikwe**, **ndapíi=kweem**. *conj 3rd sg* **apíikweet**. *imp* **apíikweel**. *ptcpl* **eepíikweet**.
**apíilakuw** VAI wear clean clothes. *ind 1st sg* **mbapíilakwi**, **mbapíilakwiim**. *conj 3rd sg* **apíilakwiit**. *imp* **apíila=kwiil**. *ptcpl* **peepíilakwiit**.
**apiilaníikeew** VAI have clean teeth. *ind 1st sg* **mbapiilaníika**, **mbapiilaníi=kaam**. *conj 3rd sg* **apiilaníikaat**. *ptcpl* **peepiilaníikaat**.
**apiilíhkasheew** VAI have clean finger-nails. *ind 1st sg* **mbapiilíhkasha**, **mbapiilíhkashaam**. *conj 3rd sg* **apiilíhkashaat**. *ptcpl* **peepiilíh=kashaat**.
**apiimaníikeew** VAI have crooked teeth. *ind 1st sg* **mbapiimaníika**, **mbapii=maníikaam**. *conj 3rd sg* **apiimaníi=kaat**. *ptcpl* **peepiimaníikaat**.
**apíinay** NI bed. *pl* **apíinayal**. *poss* **ndapíinay**. *loc* **apíineeng**. *dimin* **apíineesh**.
**apiisŭlóoxweew** VAI walk limply, walk lethargically. *ind 1st sg* **mbapiisŭ=lóoxwe**, **mbapiisŭlóoxweem**. *conj 3rd sg* **apiisŭlóoxweet**. *imp* **apiisŭ=lóoxweel**. *ptcpl* **peepiisŭlóoxweet**.
**apiisŭlunáxkeew** VAI have wrinkled hands. *ind 1st sg* **mbapiisŭlunáxka**, **mbapiisŭlunáxkaam**. *conj 3rd sg* **apiisŭlunáxkaat**. *ptcpl* **peepiisŭlun=áxkaat**.
**ápih** PC might; future. **Ápih láapii mbáam.** 'I'll be back.'; **Ápih kóokhoos kpúndaakw.** 'The owl might hear you.'
**apóosuw** VAI roast, be roasting *(s.t. animate, of foods)*. *ind 1st sg* **ndapóosi**, **ndapóosiim**. *conj 3rd sg* **apóosiit**. *imp* **apóosiil**. *ptcpl* **eepóosiit**.
**apóosuw** VAIO roast s.t. *ind 1st sg* **ndapóosiin**. *ind 3rd sg* **wtapóosiin**. *conj 3rd sg* **apóosiit**. *imp* **apóosiil**. *ptcpl* **eepóosiit**.
**apúw** VAI be there, be here. **Ná éepiit.** 'There he is.' *ind 1st sg* **ndápi**, **ndáp=iim**. *conj 3rd sg* **apíit**. *ptcpl* **éepiit**. *intensive reduplication* **ayápuw**; *moderative reduplication* **áayapuw**.
**apwaalíiyayuw** VAI act shy. *ind 1st sg* **mbapwaalíiyayi**, **mbapwaalíiya=yiim**. *conj 3rd sg* **apwaalíiyayiit**. *ptcpl* **peepwaalíiyayiit**.
**apwáan** NI bread. *pl* **apwáanal**. *poss*

ndapwáanum. *loc* **apwáanung**. *dimin* **apwáanush**.

**apwáanheew** VAI make bread. *ind 1st sg* **ndapwáanhe, ndapwáanheem**. *conj 3rd sg* **apwáanheet**. *imp* **apwáan=heel**. *ptcpl* **eepwáanheet**.

**asahkóoxweew** VAI pace back and forth. *ind 1st sg* **nzasahkóoxwe, nzasah=kóoxweem**. *conj 3rd sg* **asahkóo=xweet**. *imp* **asahkóoxweel**. *ptcpl* **seesahkóoxweet**. *See* **sahkóoxweew**.

**asanakóonzhuy** NA elderberry. *pl* **asan=akóonzhŭyak**. *poss* **nzanakóonzhŭ=yum**. *obv* **asanakóonzhŭyal**.

**asíiskuw** NI mud. *loc* **asíiskoong**.

**asiiskŭwáapŭweew** VII be muddy water. *conj 3rd sg* **asiiskŭwáapŭweek**. *ptcpl* **eesiiskŭwáapŭweek**.

**asiiskŭwáham** VTI 1A pack mud onto s.t. *(as of houses)*; put plaster onto s.t. **Ndasiiskŭwáhŭmun wíikwahm.** 'I put mud/plaster on the house.' *ind 1st sg* **ndasiiskŭwáhŭmun**. *ind 3rd sg* **wtasiiskŭwáhŭmun**. *conj 1st sg* **asiiskŭwáhŭmaan**. *conj 3rd sg* **asiiskŭwáhang**. *imp* **asiiskŭwáhah**. *ptcpl* **eesiiskŭwáhang**.

**asiiskŭwahíikeew** VAI pack mud on things *(as between logs of a house)*; pack plaster on things. *ind 1st sg* **ndasiiskŭwahíike, ndasiiskŭwah=íikeem**. *conj 3rd sg* **asiiskŭwahíi=keet**. *imp* **asiiskŭwahíikeel**. *ptcpl* **eesiiskŭwahíikeet**.

**asiiskŭwáhksun** NI muddy shoe. *pl* **asiiskŭwahksúnal**. *poss* **ndasiiskŭ=wáhksun**.

**asiiskŭwahksúneew** VAI have muddy shoes. *ind 1st sg* **ndasiiskŭwahk=súna, ndasiiskŭwahksúnaam**. *conj 3rd sg* **asiiskŭwahksúnaat**. *ptcpl* **eesiiskŭwahksúnaat**.

**asiiskŭwáhoos** NA clay pot. *pl* **asiiskŭ=wahóosak**. *obv* **asiiskŭwahóosal**. *See* **asiiskŭwahóosus**.

**asiiskŭwahóosus** NA clay pot. *pl* **asiis=kŭwahóossak**. *obv* **asiiskŭwahóos=sal**. *See* **asiiskŭwáhoos**.

**asiiskŭwatéexun** VII be a muddy road. *conj 3rd sg* **asiiskŭwatéexung**. *ptcpl* **eesiiskŭwatéexung**.

**asíiskŭwii-éhakwiing** NI muddy clothes. *pl* **asíiskŭwii-ehakwíingiil**.

**ásk** PC have to, must. *informal*. **Ásk éet náh apúw.** 'He must be there.' *See* **áskii, ayáskii, ayásku**.

**áskameew** VTA eat s.t. animate raw. *ind 1st sg* **ndáskamaaw, ndáskama**. *ind 3rd sg* **wtaskamáawal**. *ind inv* **ndáskamukw**. *ind I-you* **ktáskamul**. *conj 3rd sg* **áskamaat**. *imp* **áskam**. *ptcpl* **éeskamaat**.

**askándam** VTI 1A eat s.t. raw. *ind 1st sg* **ndaskándamun**. *ind 3rd sg* **wtask=ándamun**. *conj 1st sg* **askándamaan**. *conj 3rd sg* **askándang**. *imp* **askán=dah**. *ptcpl* **eeskándang**.

**askaskwaalakíingweew** VAI have green eyes. *ind 1st sg* **ndaskaskwaalakíin=gwa, ndaskaskwaalakíingwaam**. *conj 3rd sg* **askaskwaalakíingwaat**. *ptcpl* **eeskaskwaalakíingwaat**.

**askaskwaapamúkwat** VII be green in colour, be green-coloured. *conj 3rd sg* **askaskwaapamúkwahk**. *ptcpl* **eeskaskwaapamúkwahk**.

**askaskwaapamúkwsuw** VAI be green in colour, be green-coloured *(s.t. animate)*. *ind 1st sg* **ndaskaskwaapa=múkwsi, ndaskaskwaapamúkw=siim**. *conj 3rd sg* **askaskwaapa=múkwsiit**. *ptcpl* **eeskaskwaapa=múkwsiit**.

**askaskwáhtakw** NI green thread. *pl* **askaskwáhtakwal**. *poss* **ndaskas=kwáhtakw**. *loc* **askaskwáhtakwung**. *dimin* **askaskwáhchakwush**.

**askaskwáxkook** NA green snake. *pl* **askaskwaxkóokak**. *loc* **askaskwax=kóokung**. *dimin* **askaskwaxkóo=**

**kush**. *obv* **askaskwaxkóokal**.

**askaskwcháseew** VTA dye s.o. green. *ind 1st sg* **ndaskaskwchásaaw**, **ndaskaskwchása**. *ind 3rd sg* **wtaskaskwchasáawal**. *ind inv* **ndaskaskwchásookw**. *ind I-you* **ktaskaskwchásool**. *conj 3rd sg* **askaskwchásaat**. *imp* **askáskwchas**. *ptcpl* **eeskaskwchásaat**.

**askaskwchásum** VTI1B dye s.t. green. *ind 1st sg* **ndaskaskwchásŭmun**. *ind 3rd sg* **wtaskaskwchásŭmun**. *conj 1st sg* **askaskwchásŭmaan**. *conj 3rd sg* **askaskwchásung**. *imp* **askaskw=chásih**. *ptcpl* **eeskaskwchásung**.

**askáskweew** VII be green. *conj 3rd sg* **askáskweek**. *ptcpl* **eeskáskweek**.

**askaskwii-** PV green. **Ndaskáskwii-shóohŭmun.** 'I painted it green' *ptcpl* **eeskáskwii-**.

**askaskwíhleew** VAI turn green *(s.t. animate)*. *ind 1st sg* **ndaskaskwíhla**, **ndaskaskwíhlaam**. *conj 3rd sg* **ask=askwíhlaat**. *ptcpl* **eeskaskwíhlaat**.

**askaskwíhleew** VII turn green. *conj 3rd sg* **askaskwíhlaak**. *ptcpl* **eeskask=wíhlaak**.

**askáskwsuw** VAI be green *(s.t. animate)*. *ind 1st sg* **ndaskáskwsi**, **ndaskásk=wsiim**. *conj 3rd sg* **askáskwsiit**. *ptcpl* **eeskáskwsiit**.

**askaskwŭléexiin** VAI be a greenish colour, have a green tinge to it *(s.t. animate)*. *ind 1st sg* **ndaskaskwŭléexiin**, **ndaskaskwŭléexi**. *conj 3rd sg* **ask=askwŭléexiing**. *ptcpl* **eeskaskwŭ=léexiing**.

**askaskwŭléexun** VII be a greenish colour, have a green tinge to it. *conj 3rd sg* **askaskwŭléexung**. *ptcpl* **eeskask=wŭléexung**.

**askatúpuw** VAI be undercooked *(s.t. animate)*. **Askatúpuw namées.** 'The fish is undercooked.' *conj 3rd sg* **askatúpwiit**. *ptcpl* **eeskatúpwiit**.

**askatúpuw** VII be undercooked. **Aska=túpuw wúyoos.** 'The meat is undercooked.' *conj 3rd sg* **askatúpwiik**. *ptcpl* **eeskatúpwiik**.

**askatúpuw** VAIO undercook s.t., cook s.t. raw, cook s.t. rare. *ind 1st sg* **ndaskatúpwiin**. *ind 3rd sg* **wtaska=túpwiin**. *conj 3rd sg* **askatúpwiit**. *imp* **askatúpwiil**. *ptcpl* **eeskatúpwiit**.

**askcháseew** VTA undercook s.t. animate, cook s.t. animate raw. *ind 1st sg* **ndaskchásaaw**, **ndaskchása**. *ind 3rd sg* **wtaskchasáawal**. *ind inv* **ndask=chásookw**. *ind I-you* **ktaskchásool**. *conj 3rd sg* **askchásaat**. *imp* **áskchas**. *ptcpl* **eeskchásaat**.

**askchásum** VTI1B undercook s.t., cook s.t. raw. *ind 1st sg* **ndaskchásŭmun**. *ind 3rd sg* **wtaskchásŭmun**. *conj 1st sg* **askchásŭmaan**. *conj 3rd sg* **askchásung**. *imp* **askchásih**. *ptcpl* **eeskchásung**.

**askchéepuw** VAI be undercooked. *ind 1st sg* **ndaskchéepwi**, **ndaskchéep=wiim**. *conj 3rd sg* **askchéepwiit**. *ptcpl* **eeskchéepwiit**.

**askéewakw** NI raw meat, unsalted meat. *pl* **askéewakwal**. *poss* **ndaskéewa=kwum**. *loc* **askéewakwung**. *dimin* **askéewakwush**.

**áskii** PC have to, must. **Áskii mbeeháa=wak.** 'I had to wait for them.'; **Áskii kùlámbtoon.** 'You had to tie it.' *See* **ásk**, **ayásku**.

**askii-** PN raw. **Áskii-wŭyóos.** 'Raw meat.'

**askiinóonzhuy** NA green onion. *pl* **ask=iinóonzhŭyak**. *obv* **askiinóonzhŭyal**.

**askíixaskwal** NI green grass. *usually plural*. *loc* **askiixáskwung**.

**askíhpun** NA raw potato. *pl* **askíhpŭ=nak**. *dimin* **askíhpŭnush**. *obv* **askíhpŭnal**.

**ásksuw** VAI be raw *(s.t. animate)*. *conj 3rd sg* **ásksiit**. *ptcpl* **éesksiit**.

**asku-** PV have to. *informal.* **Nún há nóonj-níhtaa-póxkapiin éel-ásku-naatkóoyayaan.** 'That's the reason why I was good at riding a horse, because I had to fetch the cows.'

**áskun** VII be raw, be unripe. *conj 3rd sg* **áskung**. *ptcpl* **éeskung**.

**áskxakw** NI green wood. *pl* **askxákwal**. *poss* **ndaskxákwum**. *loc* **askxák=wung**. *dimin* **askxákwush**.

**askxáskwiim** NI green corn. *pl* **askxas=kwíimal**. *poss* **ndaskxaskwíimum**. *loc* **askxaskwíimung**. *dimin* **askxas=kwíimush**.

**asún** NI stone, rock. *pl* **asúnal**. *poss* **ndásun**. *loc* **asúnung**. *dimin* **ashún=ush**.

**asunaamíinzhuy** NA hard maple tree. *pl* **asunaamíinzhŭyak**. *obv* **asunaa=míinzhŭyal**.

**asunahkéeyeew** VII be stony ground. *conj 3rd sg* **asunahkéeyeek**. *ptcpl* **eesŭnahkéeyeek**.

**asúnameekw** NA Stonefish *(family name)*. *pl* **asŭnaméekwak**. *obv* **asunaméekwal**.

**asuníikaan** NI stone house. *pl* **asŭnii=káanal**. *loc* **asuniikáanung**. *dimin* **asuniikáanush**.

**ashaaxkàníikeew** VAI have straight teeth. *ind 1st sg* **nzhashaaxkàníika**, **nzhashaaxkàníikaam**. *conj 3rd sg* **ashaaxkàníikaat**.

**ashaaxkùnáxkeew** VAI have one's hands straight out. *ind 1st sg* **nzhashaax=kùnáxka**, **nzhashaaxkùnáxkaam**. *conj 3rd sg* **ashaaxkùnáxkaat**.

**ashahkcheewaashŭwíhleew** VAI swim backwards. *ind 1st sg* **nzhashahk=cheewaashŭwíhla**, **nzhashahkchee=waashŭwíhlaam**. *conj 3rd sg* **ashahkcheewaashŭwíhlaat**. *imp* **ashahkcheewaashŭwíhlaal**. *ptcpl* **sheeshahkcheewaashŭwíhlaat**.

**ashahkcheewahtakíhleew** VAI run backwards. *ind 1st sg* **nzhashahkchee=wahtakíhla**, **nzhashahkcheewah=takíhlaam**. *conj 3rd sg* **ashahkchee=wahtakíhlaat**. *imp* **ashahkcheewah=takíhlaal**. *ptcpl* **sheeshahkcheewah=takíhlaat**.

**ashahkcheewíikwsuw** VAI crawl backwards. *ind 1st sg* **nzhashahkchee=wíikwsi**, **nzhashahkcheewíikwsiim**. *conj 3rd sg* **ashahkcheewíikwsiit**. *imp* **ashahkcheewíikwsiil**. *ptcpl* **sheeshahkcheewíikwsiit**.

**ashahkchéewxeew** VAI walk backwards. *ind 1st sg* **nzhashahkchéewxe**, **nzhashahkchéewxeem**. *conj 3rd sg* **ashahkchéewxeet**. *imp* **ashahk=chéewxeel**. *ptcpl* **sheeshahk=chéewxeet**.

**ashahkchéhleew** VAI drive backwards. *ind 1st sg* **nzhashahkchéhla**, **nzhashahkchéhlaam**. *conj 3rd sg* **ashahkchéhlaat**. *imp* **ashahkchéh=laal**. *ptcpl* **sheeshahkchéhlaat**.

**ashahwahtakíhleew** VAI run slowly. *ind 1st sg* **nzhashahwahtakíhla**, **nzhashahwahtakíhlaam**. *conj 3rd sg* **ashahwahtakíhlaat**. *imp* **ashahw=ahtakíhlaal**. *ptcpl* **sheeshàhwahta=kíhlaat**. *See* **chkawahchakih=léeshuw**.

**ashahwaashŭwíhleew** VAI swim slowly. *ind 1st sg* **nzhashahwaashŭwíhla**, **nzhashahwaashŭwíhlaam**. *conj 3rd sg* **ashahwaashŭwíhlaat**. *imp* **a=shahwaashŭwíhlaal**. *ptcpl* **shee=shàhwaashŭwíhlaat**. *See* **chkawaa=shŭwihléeshuw**.

**ashahwakíinzuw** VAI read slowly. *ind 1st sg* **nzhashahwakíinzi**, **nzhash=ahwakíinziim**. *conj 3rd sg* **ashahw=akíinziit**. *imp* **ashahwakíinziil**. *ptcpl* **sheeshàhwakíinziit**.

**ashahwchéhleew** VAI drive slowly. *ind 1st sg* **nzhashahwchéhla**, **nzhash=ahwchéhlaam**. *conj 3rd sg* **ashahw=**

**chéhlaat**. *imp* **ashahwchéhlaal**. *ptcpl* **sheeshahwchéhlaat**. *See* **chkaw=chehléeshuw**.

**ashahweekhíikeew** VAI write slowly. *ind 1st sg* **nzhashahweekhíike, nzhashahweekhíikeem**. *conj 3rd sg* **ashahweekhíikeet**. *imp* **ashahweek=híikeel**. *ptcpl* **sheeshàhweekhíikeet**.

**ashahwíikwsuw** VAI crawl slowly. *ind 1st sg* **nzhashahwíikwsi, nzhash=ahwíikwsiim**. *conj 3rd sg* **ashahwíi=kwsiit**. *imp* **ashahwíikwsiil**. *ptcpl* **sheeshàhwíikwsiit**.

**ashahwíikwsuw** VAI crawl slowly. *ind 1st sg* **nzhashahwíikwsi, nzhash=ahwíikwsiim**. *conj 3rd sg* **ashahw=íikwsiit**. *imp* **ashahwíikwsiil**. *ptcpl* **sheeshahwíikwsiit**. *See* **chkawiikw=shíishuw**.

**ashahwíixsuw** VAI talk slowly. *ind 1st sg* **nzhashahwíixsi, nzhashahwíixsiim**. *conj 3rd sg* **ashahwíixsiit**. *imp* **a=shahwíixsiil**. *ptcpl* **sheeshàhwíixsiit**.

**ashahwóoxweew** VAI walk slowly, be a slow walker. *ind 1st sg* **nzhashahw=óoxwe, nzhashahwóoxweem**. *conj 3rd sg* **ashahwóoxweet**. *imp* **ashah=wóoxweel**. *ptcpl* **sheeshahwóoxweet**.

**ashawéesheew** VTA cut s.t. animate and make it square, cut s.t. animate square. *ind 1st sg* **ndashawéeshaaw, ndash=awéesha**. *ind 3rd sg* **wtashawee=sháawal**. *ind inv* **ndashawéeshookw**. *ind I-you* **ktashawéeshool**. *conj 3rd sg* **ashawéeshaat**. *imp* **asháweesh**. *ptcpl* **eeshawéeshaat**.

**ashawéeshum** VTI1B cut s.t. and make it square, cut s.t. square. *ind 1st sg* **ndashawéeshŭmun**. *ind 3rd sg* **wtashawéeshŭmun**. *conj 1st sg* **ashawéeshŭmaan**. *conj 3rd sg* **ashawéeshung**. *imp* **ashawéeshih**. *ptcpl* **eeshawéeshung**.

**ashíikan** NI sock. *pl* **ashíikanal**. *poss* **ndashíikan**. *loc* **ashíikanung**. *dimin* **ashíikanush**.

**ashiikanáhtakw** NI yarn. *pl* **ashiika=náhtakwal**. *poss* **ndashiikanáhta=kwum**. *loc* **ashiikanáhtakwung**. *dimin* **ashiikanáhchakwush**.

**ashíikw** NA woodtick. *pl* **ashíikwak**. *loc* **ashíikwung**. *dimin* **ashíikwush**. *obv* **ashíikwal**.

**ashiilóngwaneew** VAI perspire from one's armpits. *ind 1st sg* **ndashii=lóngwana, ndashiilóngwanaam**. *conj 3rd sg* **ashiilóngwaneet**.

**ashóokuw** VAI be poor. *ind 1st sg* **ndashóoki, ndashóokiim**. *conj 3rd sg* **ashóokiit**. *ptcpl* **eeshóokiit**.

**natáy** NID my stomach. *poss* **natáy, ndáy**. *3rd poss* **watáy**.

**atíhteew** VII be ripe. **Shùkéhla eetih=téekiil ayíh.** 'Only pick the ripe ones.' *conj 3rd sg* **atíhteek**. *ptcpl* **eetíhteek**.

**ató** NA deer. *pl* **atóhak**. *dimin* **atóhush**. *obv* **atóhal**. *See* **atóh**.

**atóh** NA deer. *pl* **atóhwak**. *dimin* **atóhwush**. *obv* **atóhwal**. *See* **ató**.

**atúsuw** VAI be ripe *(s.t. animate)*. *conj 3rd sg* **atúsiit**. *ptcpl* **éetsiit**.

**awaakkáateew** VAI be bowlegged. *ind 1st sg* **nŭwawaakkáata, nŭwaw=aakkáataam**. *conj 3rd sg* **awaak=káataat**.

**awáaniiw** VAI-S be lost. *ind 1st sg* **ndawáani, ndawáaniim**. *conj 3rd sg* **awáaniit**. *ptcpl* **eewáaniit**.

**awáhleew** VAI land, land on the ground, alight. **Yéelak ndúlu-awáhla.** 'I landed over there.' *conj 3rd sg* **awáhlaat**. *ptcpl* **eewáhlaat**.

**awahlŭmahkwsúwak** VAI be far apart *(of trees)*. *usually plural. ind 1st pl* **nŭwawahlŭmahkwsíhna**. *conj 3rd pl* **awahlŭmahkwsíhtiit**.

**awahlŭmahtéewal** VII be far apart. *usually plural. conj 3rd pl* **awahlŭ=mahtéek**.

**awahlŭmohkwéepŭwak** VAI sit far apart. *usually plural. ind 1st pl* **nŭwawahlŭmohkweepíhna**. *conj 3rd pl* **awahlŭmohkweepíhtiit**. *imp* **awahlumohkwéepiikw**.
**awáhŭlaan** VII be fine rain, be misty rain. *conj 3rd sg* **awáhŭlaang**.
**awán** VII be fog. *conj 3rd sg* **awáng**. *ptcpl* **éewang**.
**awaníixun** VII be foggy, be misty. *conj 3rd sg* **awaníixung**.
**awánuw** VII be fog. *conj 3rd sg* **awániik**. *ptcpl* **éewaniik**.
**awasáaku** PC on the other side of the house. **Mbáksh awasáaku áhte.** 'The box is on the other side of the house.'
**awasáhkameew** PC heaven.
**awaseenáxke** PC the other side of the fence.
**awásii** PC the other side of something. **Yéelak awásii ndáhtoon.** 'I put it over there on the other side.'; **Awásii kpahóonung.** 'On the other side of the door.'
**awasiixkanáwe** PC the other side of the road.
**awásuw** VAI warm oneself. *ind 1st sg* **ndáwasi**, **ndáwasiim**. *conj 3rd sg* **awásiit**. *imp* **awásiil**. *ptcpl* **éewasiit**.
**awéeheew** VAIO use s.t., wear s.t. *ind 1st sg* **ndawéeheen**. *ind 3rd sg* **wtawée=heen**. *conj 3rd sg* **awéeheet**. *imp* **awéeheel**. *ptcpl* **eewéeheet**.
**awéen** PR who, someone, a person. **Awéen éet há ná kwáy?** 'Who could that be now?'; **Awéeniil há wiichée=we?** 'Who's he going with?' *pl* **awéeniik**. *obv* **awéeniil**.
**aweenáhkeew** NA foreigner. *pl* **awee=nahkéewak**. *obv* **aweenahkéewal**.
**awéendam** VOTI1A be in pain, suffer. *ind 1st sg* **ndawéendam**. *conj 3rd sg* **awéendang**. *ptcpl* **eewéendang**.
**aweendamuwáakan** NI extreme pain, suffering.
**awéeyayus** NA animal. *pl* **aweeyayúsak**. *dimin* **aweeyayúshush**. *obv* **aweeya=yúsal**.
**awehléeshoosh** NA bird. *pl* **awehlee=shóoshak**. *obv* **awehleeshóoshal**.
**awéhleew** NA hawk, large bird. *pl* **awehléewak**. *obv* **awehléewal**.
**awíi** PC ouch!
**awíilpiish** NA louse. *pl* **awiilpíishak**. *obv* **awiilpíishal**.
**awiilpíishuw** VAI be lousy. *ind 1st sg* **ndawiilpíishi**, **ndawiilpíishiim**. *conj 3rd sg* **awiilpíishiit**. *ptcpl* **eewiil=píishiit**.
**awiiníhtoow** VOTI2 make people mad. *ind 1st sg* **nuwawiiníhto**. *conj 1st sg* **awiiníhtawaan**. *conj 3rd sg* **awii=níhtaakw**.
**awulaaptóoneew** VAI talk well, say good things. *ind 1st sg* **nŭwawŭlaaptóone**, **nŭwawŭlaaptóoneem**. *conj 3rd sg* **awulaaptóoneet**. *ptcpl* **weewŭlaap=tóoneet**.
**awulaníikeew** VAI have good teeth. *ind 1st sg* **nŭwawŭlaníika**, **nŭwawŭ=laníikaam**. *conj 3rd sg* **awulaníi=kaat**. *ptcpl* **weewŭlaníikaat**.
**awuleekhíikeew** VAI write well, have good handwriting. *ind 1st sg* **nŭ=wawŭleekhíike**, **nŭwawŭleekhíi=keem**. *conj 3rd sg* **awuleekhíikeet**. *imp* **awuleekhíikeel**. *ptcpl* **weewŭ=leekhíikeet**.
**awulsútam** VOTI1A obey. *ind 1st sg* **nuwawulústam**. *conj 3rd sg* **awul=sútang**. *imp* **awulsútah**. *ptcpl* **weewŭlústang**.
**awúyee** PC might. **Awúyee nooshan=zhíhla.** 'I might slip.'; **Awúyee noosaamwíisŭmwi.** 'I might drink too much.'
**áx** PC indeed, emphatic. **Ktúlul áx**

**amiimúnzal katá-kxánuw.** 'I told you she was going to have a child.'

**áxkook** NA snake. *pl* **axkóokak**. *dimin* **axkóokush**. *obv* **axkóokal**.

**axkóokus** NA insect, bug. *pl* **axkóoksak**. *dimin* **axkóokshush**. *obv* **axkóoksal**.

**ayaapŭwanóongsuw** VAI get angry very easily. *ind 1st sg* **ndayaapŭwanóon= gsi**, **ndayaapŭwanóongsiim**. *conj 3rd sg* **ayaapŭwanóongsiit**. *ptcpl* **eeyaapŭwanóongsiit**.

**ayáhwachuw** VAI get cold easily. *ind 1st sg* **ndayáhwachi**, **ndayáhwachiim**. *conj 3rd sg* **ayáhwachiit**. *ptcpl* **eeyáhwachiit**.

**ayahwhiingwéexiin** VAI like to stare. *ind 1st sg* **ndayàhwhiingwéexiin**, **ndayàhwhiingwéexi**. *conj 3rd sg* **ayahwhiingwéexiing**. *ptcpl* **eeyàhw= hiingwéexiing**.

**ayapáawŭnii** PC in the morning. *See* **nayapáawŭnii**.

**ayapáayu** PC in the morning. **Mbúmŭ= naa ayapáayu níi nzháye-áamwi.** 'I got up first in the morning before he did.'

**ayáskii** PC have to, must. **Ayáskii nzhashahkamóolaaw.** 'I have to feed him by hand.' *See* **ásk**, **áskii**, **ayáskii**.

**ayásku** PC have to, must. *informal.* **Ayásku ndalŭmúsi.** 'I have to leave right away.'; **Ayásku ngúmee kwéek úw.** 'He always has to say something.' *See* **ásk**, **áskii**, **ayáskii**.

**áyshuk** NA Isaac. *obv* **àyshúkal**. *From English* Isaac.

**ayúm** VTI1B get s.t., buy s.t., keep s.t., have s.t. *ind 1st sg* **ndáyŭmun**. *ind 3rd sg* **wtáyŭmun**. *conj 1st sg* **ayúmaan**. *conj 3rd sg* **ayúng**. *imp* **ayíh**. *ptcpl* **éeyung**.

**ayúweew** VTA get s.o., buy s.o., keep s.o., have s.o. *ind 1st sg* **ndáyŭwaaw**, **ndáyŭwa**. *ind 3rd sg* **wtayŭwáawal**. *conj 3rd sg* **ayúwaat**. *imp* **ayúw**. *ptcpl* **éeyŭwaat**.

# B

**mbaakchóosum** NAD my former friend. *pl* **mbaakchóosŭmak**. *3rd poss* **paakchóosŭmal**.

**mbooshíishum** NAD my navel. **Wíhwiing sh'xeehíikeew, pooshíishŭmal anaháate.** 'He's nosy (because) he lost his umbilical cord.'; **Kpooshíi= shum ktánhaaw.** 'You're nosy ('you've lost your navel').' *3rd poss* **pooshíishŭmal**. *obv* **pooshíishŭmal**.

**mbwáam** NID my thigh. *pl* **mbwáamal**. *3rd poss* **pwáam**. *loc* **mbwáamung**. *dimin* **mbwáamush**.

# CH

**chaacháshkwshush** NA sleigh. *pl* **chaachashkwshúshak**. *poss* **njaa= chashkwshúshum**. *loc* **chaachashk= wshúshung**. *obv* **chaachashkw= shúshal**. *See* **táataskw**.

**cháachxiish** PC very little, not a lot. **Cháachxiish ngáwi.** 'I slept very little.'; **Cháachxiish ndalóhke.** 'I didn't work a lot.'

**chaachxupeekachúshuw** VII be shallow water. *conj 3rd sg* **chaachxupeeka= chúshiik**. *ptcpl* **chaachxupeeka= chúshiik**. *See* **taatxupéekat**.

**cháahuw** VAI chew tobacco. *ind 1st sg* **njáahi**, **njáahiim**. *conj 3rd sg* **cháa= hiit**. *imp* **cháahiil**. *ptcpl* **cháahiit**.

**chaangaaháaleew** VTA throw s.o. and make them cry. *ind 1st sg* **njaangaa=**

**háalaaw**, **njaangaaháala**. *ind 3rd sg* **wchaangaahaaláawal**. *ind inv* **njaangaaháalukw**. *ind I-you* **kchaangaaháalul**. *conj 3rd sg* **chaangaaháalaat**. *imp* **chaangáa=haal**. *ptcpl* **chaangaaháalaat**.

**chaangáaheew** VAIO throw s.o. and make them cry. *ind 1st sg* **njaangáa=heen**. *ind 3rd sg* **wchaangaahéenal**. *conj 3rd sg* **chaangáaheet**. *imp* **chaangáaheel**. *ptcpl* **chaangáaheet**.

**chaangii-** PV cry *(while doing something)*. **Njáangii-ngálaaw.** 'I was crying as I left him behind.'; **Cháangii-kshiixíinjŭweew.** 'She was crying as she washed the dishes.' *ptcpl* **cháan=gii-**. *See* **cháangu-**.

**chaangíimeew** VTA talk to s.o. and make them cry. *ind 1st sg* **njaangíimaaw**, **njaangíima**. *ind 3rd sg* **wchaangii=máawal**. *ind inv* **njaangíimukw**. *ind I-you* **kchaangíimul**. *conj 3rd sg* **chaangíimaat**. *imp* **cháangiim**. *ptcpl* **chaangíimaat**.

**chaangíhkaweew** VTA make s.o. cry *(using the foot or body)*; kick s.o. and make them cry. *ind 1st sg* **njaangíh=kawaaw**, **njaangíhkawa**. *ind 3rd sg* **wchaangihkawáawal**. *ind inv* **njaangíhkaakw**. *ind I-you* **kchaan=gíhkool**. *conj 3rd sg* **chaangíhka=waat**. *imp* **chaangíhkaw**. *ptcpl* **chaangíhkawaat**.

**chaangíhleew** VAI cry. *ind 1st sg* **njaan=gíhla**, **njaangíhlaam**. *conj 3rd sg* **chaangíhlaat**. *ptcpl* **chaangíhlaat**.

**chaangihtéeheew** VTA hit s.o. and make them cry. *ind 1st sg* **njaangihtée=haaw**, **njaangihtéeha**. *ind 3rd sg* **wchaangihteeháawal**. *ind inv* **njaa=ngihtéehookw**. *ind I-you* **kchaan=gihtéehool**. *conj 3rd sg* **chaangih=téehaat**. *imp* **chaangíhteeh**. *ptcpl* **chaangihtéehaat**.

**chaangihtéexŭmeew** VTA knock s.o. down and make them cry. *ind 1st sg* **njaangihtéexŭmaaw**, **njaangihtée=xŭma**. *ind 3rd sg* **wchaangihteexŭ=máawal**. *ind inv* **njaangihtéexŭ=mukw**. *ind I-you* **kchaangihtéexŭ=mul**. *conj 3rd sg* **chaangihtéexŭ=maat**. *imp* **chaangihtéexum**. *ptcpl* **chaangihtéexŭmaat**.

**chaangtoonháaleew** VTA talk to s.o. and make them cry. *ind 1st sg* **njaang=toonháalaaw**, **njaangtoonháala**. *ind 3rd sg* **wchaangtoonhaaláawal**. *ind inv* **njaangtoonháalukw**. *ind I-you* **kchaangtoonháalul**. *conj 3rd sg* **chaangtoonháalaat**. *imp* **chaang=tóonhaal**. *ptcpl* **chaangtoonháalaat**.

**chaangu-** PV cry *(while doing something)*. *informal*. **Njáangu-kundaa=háalaaw.** 'I was crying while I pushed him down.'; **Cháangu-alúmsuw.** 'He was crying as he left.' *ptcpl* **cháangu-**. *See* **chaangii-**.

**chàchanaandpéhleew** VAI be mixed up, be confused. *ind 1st sg* **njacha=naandpéhla**, **njachanaandpéhlaam**. *conj 3rd sg* **chàchanaandpéhlaat**. *ptcpl* **chàchanaandpéhlaat**.

**chàchpíikŭwak** VAI grow apart *(s.t. animate)*. *usually plural. ind 1st pl* **njachpiikíhna**. *conj 3rd pl* **chàch=piikíhtiit**.

**chàchpíikŭnool** VII grow apart. *usually plural. conj 3rd pl* **chàchpíikung**. *ptcpl* **chàchpiikúngiil**.

**chàchxuwaapŭwéhleew** VII make noise while moving *(of water)*. *conj 3rd sg* **chàchxuwaapŭwéhlaak**. *ptcpl* **chàchxuwaapŭwéhlaak**.

**chàchxúweew** VII make noise *(of water)*. **Ndáy chàchxúweew.** 'My belly is making noise.' *conj 3rd sg* **chàchxúweek**. *ptcpl* **chàchxúweek**.

**chahkhooshíishuw** VAI have a short dress on, wear a short dress. *ind 1st sg* **njahkhooshíishi**, **njahkhooshíi=shiim**. *conj 3rd sg* **chahkhooshíi=shiit**. *ptcpl* **chehkhooshíishiit**.

**chahkwaalóhkweew** VAI have short hair. *ind 1st sg* **njahkwaalóhkwa, njahkwaalóhkwaam**. *conj 3rd sg* **chahkwaalóhkwaat**. *ptcpl* **cheh=kwaalóhkwaat**.

**chahkwáamanush** NI short piece of rope, short piece of string. *pl* **chah=kwaamanúshal**. *poss* **njahkwaama=núshum**. *loc* **chahkwaamanúshung**.

**chahkwahkwshíishuw** VAI be short. *ind 1st sg* **njahkwahkwshíishi, njah=kwahkwshíishiim**. *conj 3rd sg* **chahkwahkwshíishiit**. *ptcpl* **cheh=kwahkwshíishiit**.

**chahkwaskwéeyeew** VII be short grass. *conj 3rd sg* **chahkwaskwéeyeek**. *ptcpl* **chehkwaskwéeyeek**.

**chahkweehundáxpoon** NI short table. *pl* **chahkweehundaxpóonal**.

**chahkweenjakwíiwanush** NI short dress. *pl* **chahkweenjakwiiwanúsh=al**. *poss* **njahkweenjakwiiwanúm=ush**.

**chahkwéeshuw** VII be short *(dimin)*. *conj 3rd sg* **chahkwéeshiik**. *ptcpl* **chehkwéeshiik**.

**chahkwii-** PN short. **Cháhkwii-aníixanal.** 'Short laces.'

**chahkwiixáskwal** NI short grass. *loc* **chahkwiixáskwung**. *usually plural.*

**chahkwiixáskwat** VII be short grass. *conj 3rd sg* **chahkwiixáskwahk**. *ptcpl* **chehkwiixáskwahk**.

**chahkwihchóoshuw** VTI2 make s.t. short, shorten s.t. *(diminutive) ind 1st sg* **njahkwihchóoshiin**. *ind 3rd sg* **wchahkwihchóoshiin**. *conj 3rd sg* **chahkwihchóoshiit**. *imp* **chahkwih=chóoshiil**. *ptcpl* **chehkwihchóoshiit**.

**cháhkwsheew** VTA cut s.t. animate short. **Njáhkwshaaw eeheeshun=déekan.** 'I cut the window (glass) short.' *ind 1st sg* **njáhkwshaaw, njáhkwsha**. *ind 3rd sg* **wchahkw=sháawal**. *conj 3rd sg* **cháhkwshaat**. *imp* **cháhkwush**. *ptcpl* **chéhkwshaat**.

**chahkwshaashíishuw** VII be cut short *(dimin)*. *conj 3rd sg* **chahkwshaa=shíishiik**. *ptcpl* **chehkwshaashíi=shiik**.

**chahkwshiichéeshuw** VAI have a short foot. *ind 1st sg* **njahkwshiicháashi, njahkwshiicháashiim**. *conj 3rd sg* **chahkwshiicháashiit**. *ptcpl* **chehk=wshiicháashiit**.

**cháhkwshum** VTI1B cut s.t. short. *ind 1st sg* **njahkwshúmun**. *ind 3rd sg* **wchahkwshúmun**. *conj 1st sg* **chahkwshúmaan**. *conj 3rd sg* **cháhkwshung**. *imp* **cháhkwshih**.

**chahkwŭnaxkéeshuw** VAI have a short arm *(dimin)*. *ind 1st sg* **njahkwŭ=naxkáashi, njahkwŭnaxkáashiim**. *conj 3rd sg* **chahkwŭnaxkáashiit**. *ptcpl* **chehkwŭnaxkáashiit**.

**chahkwŭnaxkéeyeew** VII have short sleeves. *conj 3rd sg* **chahkwŭnax=kéeyeek**. *ptcpl* **chehkwŭnaxkée=yeek**.

**chahkwŭnaxkeeyéeshuw** VII have short sleeves *(dimin)*. *conj 3rd sg* **chahkw=ŭnaxkeeyéeshiik**. *ptcpl* **chehkwŭ=naxkeeyéeshiik**.

**chàhwaandpéeheew** VTA hit s.o. on the head. *ind 1st sg* **njahwaandpéehaaw, njahwaandpéeha**. *ind 3rd sg* **wchahwaandpeeháawal**. *ind inv* **njahwaandpéehukw**. *ind I-you* **kchahwaandpéehul**. *conj 3rd sg* **chàhwaandpéehaat**. *imp* **chàhw=áandpeeh**. *ptcpl* **chàhwaandpéehaat**.

**chàhwíixiin** VAI fall and make a sharp noise when dropped *(s.t. animate)*. *ind 1st sg* **njahwíixiin, njahwíixi**. *conj 3rd sg* **chàhwíixiing**. *ptcpl* **chàhwíixiing**.

**chàhwíixtoow** VTI2 drop s.t. so that it makes a sharp noise. *ind 1st sg* **njahwíixtoon**. *ind 3rd sg* **wchahw=íixtoon**. *conj 1st sg* **chàhwiixtáwaan**. *conj 3rd sg* **chàhwíixtaakw**. *imp* **chàhwíixtool**.

**chàhwíixun** VII fall and make a sharp noise, make a sharp noise when dropped. *conj 3rd sg* **chàhwíixung**. *ptcpl* **chàhwíixung**.

**chàhwihtéeheew** VTA hit s.o. so that they make a sharp noise. *ind 1st sg* **njahwihtéehaaw**, **njahwihtéeha**. *ind 3rd sg* **wchahihteeháawal**. *ind inv* **njahwihtéehukw**. *ind I-you* **kchah=wihtéehul**. *conj 3rd sg* **chàhwihtée=haat**. *imp* **chàhwíhteeh**. *ptcpl* **chàhwihtéehaat**.

**chàhwihtéextoow** VTI2 drop s.t. so that it makes a sharp noise. *ind 1st sg* **njahwihtéextoon**. *ind 3rd sg* **wchahwihtéextoon**. *conj 1st sg* **chàhwihteextáwaan**. *conj 3rd sg* **chàhwihtéextaakw**. *imp* **chàhwih=téextool**. *ptcpl* **chàhwihtéextaakw**.

**chàhwihtéexŭmeew** VTA drop s.t. animate so that it makes a sharp noise. *ind 1st sg* **njahwihtéexŭmaaw**, **njahwihtéexŭma**. *ind 3rd sg* **wchahwihteexŭmáawal**. *ind inv* **njahwihtéexŭmukw**. *ind I-you* **kchahwihtéexŭmul**. *conj 3rd sg* **chàhwihtéexŭmaat**. *imp* **chàh=wihtéexum**. *ptcpl* **chàhwihtée=xŭmaat**.

**chanawéeheew** VAIO put s.t. on wrongly, put on the wrong one of s.t. *(of clothing)*. *ind 1st sg* **njanawéeheen**. *ind 3rd sg* **wchanawéeheen**. *conj 3rd sg* **chanawéeheet**. *imp* **chanawéeheel**. *ptcpl* **cheenawéeheet**.

**chanáxeew** VAI hear incorrectly. *ind 1st sg* **njánxa**, **njánxaam**. *conj 3rd sg* **chanáxaat**. *ptcpl* **chéenxaat**. *intensive reduplication* **chàchanáxeew**.

**chaneekhíikeew** VAI make a mistake in writing. *ind 1st sg* **njaneekhíike**, **njaneekhíikeem**. *conj 3rd sg* **chan=eekhíikeet**. *imp* **chaneekhíikeel**. *ptcpl* **cheeneekhíikeet**.

**chaneelúndam** VOTI1A be annoyed, be discouraged. *ind 1st sg* **njaneelún=dam**. *conj 3rd sg* **chaneelúndang**. *ptcpl* **cheeneelúndang**.

**chaneelúndam** VTI1A be annoyed about s.t. *ind 1st sg* **njaneelúndamun**. *ind 3rd sg* **wchaneelúndamun**. *conj 1st sg* **chaneelúndamaan**. *conj 3rd sg* **chaneelúndang**. *ptcpl* **cheeneelún=dang**.

**cháng-póoshiish** NA kitten. *pl* **cháng-pooshíishak**. *poss* **njáng-pooshíi=shum**. *obv* **cháng-pooshíishal**.

**changaalakaxoonéeshuw** VAI have a soft voice, have a high pitched voice *(dimin)*. *ind 1st sg* **njangaalakaxoo=náashi**, **njangaalakaxoonáashiim**. *conj 3rd sg* **changaalakaxoonáa=shiit**. *ptcpl* **cheengaalakaxoonáa=shiit**.

**changáhkwush** NA small tree *(dimin)*. *pl* **changáhkwshak**. *loc* **changáhk=wshung**. *obv* **changáhkwshal**.

**changáhwalush** NI little egg *(dimin)*. *pl* **changàhwalúshal**.

**changaméeshush** NA small fish. *pl* **changaméesh'shak**. *loc* **changa=méesh'shung**. *obv* **changamée=sh'shal**.

**changaxkóokush** NA small snake. *pl* **changaxkóokshak**. *obv* **changax=kóokshal**.

**changchaaléeshuw** VAI have a small nose *(dimin)*. *ind 1st sg* **njangchaa=láashi**, **njangchaaláashiim**. *conj 3rd sg* **changchaaláashiit**. *ptcpl* **cheeng=chaaláashiit**.

**changeelunzhíishuw** VAI act like a baby, feel babyish, don't want to act one's age *(especially of children)*. *ind 1st sg* **njangeelunzhíishi**, **njangeelunzhíi=shiim**. *conj 3rd sg* **changeelunzhíi=shiit**. *ptcpl* **cheengeelunzhíishiit**.

**changii-** PN small. **Chángii-páyush.** 'A little pie.' *See* **changu-**.

**changiikáanush** NI small house. *pl* **changiikáanshal**. *poss* **njangiikáa=nŭmush**. *loc* **changiikáanshung**.

**chángiish** PC some, a small amount, a little bit. **Chángiish shúkw tóhpun.** 'There's just a little frost.'; **Chángiish mbiiwándamun.** 'I left a little bit of the food.' *See* **changíiwiish**, **tángii**.

**changíiwiish** PC some, a small amount, a little bit. **Máhta níi nŭmunéewi changíiwiish shúkw nŭmúne.** 'I don't drink but I drink a little bit.' *See* **chángiish**.

**changíhchkwush** NA small tree. *pl* **changihchkwúshak**. *obv* **changih=chkwúshal**.

**changihchoonayéeshuw** VAI have a small beard, have a small mustache. *ind 1st sg* **njangihchoonayáashi**, **njangihchoonayáashiim**. *conj 3rd sg* **changihchoonayáashiit**. *ptcpl* **cheengihchoonayáashiit**.

**changihlóoshush** NA little old man. *pl* **changihlóoshak**. *obv* **changih=lóoshal**.

**changu-** PN small. *informal*. **Chángu-chaweenaxkŭníikanush.** 'A little gate.' *See* **changii-**.

**changu-** PV small. *informal*. **Chángu-pangeeyéeshuw.** 'It's in small pieces.' *ptcpl* **chéengu-**.

**changŭlunjáawanush** NI little finger. *pl* **changŭlunjaawanúshal**. *poss* **njangŭlunjáawanush**.

**changxúmwush** NA puppy. *pl* **chang=xúmwshak**. *obv* **changxúmwshal**.

**chaniikwáakeew** VAI sew at the wrong place. *ind 1st sg* **njaniikwáake**, **njaniikwáakeem**. *conj 3rd sg* **cha=niikwáakeet**. *imp* **chaniikwáakeel**. *ptcpl* **cheeniikwáakeet**.

**chaniikwáaleew** VTA make a mistake in sewing s.t. animate, sew s.t. animate wrongly, sew s.t. animate in the wrong place. *ind 1st sg* **njaniikwáalaaw**, **njaniikwáala**. *ind 3rd sg* **wchanii=kwaaláawal**. *ind inv* **njaniikwáa=lukw**. *ind I-you* **kchaniikwáalul**. *conj 3rd sg* **chaniikwáalaat**. *imp* **chaníikwaal**. *ptcpl* **cheeniikwáalaat**.

**chaníikwam** VTI1A make a mistake in sewing s.t., sew s.t. wrongly, sew s.t. in the wrong place. *ind 1st sg* **njan=íikwamun**. *ind 3rd sg* **wchaníikwa=mun**. *conj 1st sg* **chaníikwamaan**. *conj 3rd sg* **chaníikwang**. *imp* **chaníikwah**. *ptcpl* **cheeníikwang**.

**chaniilawéeheew** VTA annoy s.o. *ind 1st sg* **njaniilawéehaaw**, **njaniilawéeha**. *ind 3rd sg* **wchaniilaweeháawal**. *ind inv* **njaniilawéehukw**. *ind I-you* **kchaniilawéehul**. *conj 3rd sg* **chaniilawéehaat**. *imp* **chaníilaweeh**. *ptcpl* **cheeniilawéehaat**.

**chaníimeew** VTA disagree with s.o., find fault with s.o. *ind 1st sg* **njaníimaaw**, **njaníima**. *ind 3rd sg* **wchaniimáa=wal**. *ind inv* **njaníimukw**. *ind I-you* **kchaníimul**. *conj 3rd sg* **chaníimaat**. *ptcpl* **cheeníimaat**.

**chaníixtoow** VTI2 make a mistake in putting s.t. on, put s.t. on wrongly. *ind 1st sg* **njaníixtoon**. *ind 3rd sg* **wchaníixtoon**. *conj 1st sg* **chaniix=táwaan**. *conj 3rd sg* **chaníixtaakw**. *imp* **chaníixtool**. *ptcpl* **cheeníix=taakw**.

**chaníixŭmeew** VTA make a mistake in putting s.t. animate on, put s.t. animate on wrongly. *ind 1st sg* **njaníi=xŭmaaw**, **njaníixŭma**. *ind 3rd sg* **wchaniixŭmáawal**. *ind inv* **njaníi=xŭmukw**. *ind I-you* **kchaníixŭmul**. *conj 3rd sg* **chaníixŭmaat**. *imp* **chaníixum**. *ptcpl* **cheeníixŭmaat**.

**chaníhkam** VTI1A put s.t. on wrongly *(of clothing)*; put on the wrong one of s.t. *ind 1st sg* **njaníhkamun**. *ind 3rd sg* **wchaníhkamun**. *conj 1st sg* **cha=níhkamaan**. *conj 3rd sg* **chaníhkang**. *imp* **chaníhkah**. *ptcpl* **cheeníhkang**.

**chaníhkaweew** VTA put s.t. animate on wrongly *(of clothing)*; put on the wrong one of s.t. animate. *ind 1st sg* **njaníhkawaaw**, **njaníhkawa**. *ind 3rd* *sg* **wchanihkawáawal**. *ind inv* **njan=íhkaakw**. *ind I-you* **kchaníhkool**. *conj 3rd sg* **chaníhkawaat**. *imp* **chaníhkaw**. *ptcpl* **cheeníhkawaat**.

**chanohkwéepuw** VAI sit the wrong way. *ind 1st sg* **njanohkwéepi**, **njanoh=kwéepiim**. *conj 3rd sg* **chanohkwée=piit**. *imp* **chanohkwéepiil**. *ptcpl* **cheenohkwéepiit**.

**chanohkwéexiin** VAI face in the wrong direction, face the wrong way. *ind 1st sg* **njanohkwéexiin**, **njanohkwéexi**. *conj 3rd sg* **chanohkwéexiing**. *imp* **chanohkwéexiil**. *ptcpl* **cheenoh=kwéexiing**.

**chanohkwéextoow** VTI2 turn s.t. to face in the wrong direction, turn s.t. to face the wrong way. *ind 1st sg* **njan=ohkwéextoon**. *ind 3rd sg* **wchanoh=kwéextoon**. *conj 1st sg* **chanoh=kweextáwaan**. *conj 3rd sg* **chanoh=kwéextaakw**. *imp* **chanohkwéextool**. *ptcpl* **cheenohkwéextaakw**.

**chanohkwéexŭmeew** VTA turn s.o. to face in the wrong direction, turn s.o. to face the wrong way. *ind 1st sg* **njanohkwéexŭmaaw**, **njanohkwée=xŭma**. *ind 3rd sg* **wchanohkweexŭ=máawal**. *ind inv* **njanohkwéexŭ=mukw**. *ind I-you* **kchanohkwéexŭ=mul**. *conj 3rd sg* **chanohkwéexŭ=maat**. *imp* **chanohkwéexum**. *ptcpl* **cheenohkwéexŭmaat**.

**chanohkwéexun** VII face in the wrong direction, face the wrong way. *conj 3rd sg* **chanohkwéexung**. *ptcpl* **cheenohkwéexung**.

**chanu-** PV by mistake, in error. *informal*. **Kchánu-íin.** 'You said it wrong.' *ptcpl* **chéenu-**.

**chanústam** VTI1A misunderstand s.t., mishear s.t., hear s.t. erroneously, don't hear s.t. correctly. *ind 1st sg* **njansútamun**. *ind 3rd sg* **wchansút=amun**. *conj 1st sg* **chanustámaan**. *conj 3rd sg* **chanústang**. *ptcpl* **cheensútang**.

**chanustáweew** VTA misunderstand s.o., mishear s.o., hear s.o. erroneously, don't hear s.o. correctly. *ind 1st sg* **njansútawaaw**, **njansútawa**. *ind 3rd sg* **wchansutawáawal**. *ind inv* **njan=sútaakw**. *ind I-you* **kchansútool**. *conj 3rd sg* **chanustáwaat**. *ptcpl* **cheensútawaat**.

**chanutóonheew** VAI say the wrong thing. *ind 1st sg* **njantóonhe**, **njan=tóonheem**. *conj 3rd sg* **chanutóon=heet**. *imp* **chanutóonheel**. *ptcpl* **cheentóonheet**.

**cháskham** VTI1A brush up against s.t. *(using a tool or instrument)*. *ind 1st sg* **njaskhámun**. *ind 3rd sg* **wchask=hámun**. *conj 1st sg* **chaskhámaan**. *conj 3rd sg* **cháskhang**. *imp* **chásk=hah**. *ptcpl* **chéeskhang**.

**cháskheew** VTA brush up against s.o. *(using a tool or instrument)*. *ind 1st sg* **njáskhaaw**, **njáskha**. *ind 3rd sg* **wchaskháawal**. *ind inv* **njáskhookw**. *ind I-you* **kcháskhool**. *conj 3rd sg* **cháskhaat**. *imp* **cháskhaw**. *ptcpl* **chéeskhaat**.

**chaskíixiin** VAI brush up against something. *ind 1st sg* **njaskíixiin**, **njaskíi=xi**. *conj 3rd sg* **chaskíixiing**. *imp* **chaskíixiil**. *ptcpl* **cheeskíixiing**.

**chaskíixun** VII brush up against something. *conj 3rd sg* **chaskíixung**. *ptcpl* **cheeskíixung**.

**chaskíhkam** VTI1A brush up against s.t. *(using the foot or body)*. *ind 1st sg* **njaskíhkamun**. *ind 3rd sg* **wchas=kíhkamun**. *conj 1st sg* **chaskíhka=maan**. *conj 3rd sg* **chaskíhkang**. *imp* **chaskíhkah**. *ptcpl* **cheeskíhkang**.

**chaskíhkaweew** VTA brush up against s.o. *(using the foot or body)*. *ind 1st sg* **njaskíhkawaaw**, **njaskíhkawa**. *ind 3rd sg* **wchaskihkawáawal**. *ind inv* **njaskíhkaakw**. *ind I-you* **kchas=kíhkool**. *conj 3rd sg* **chaskíhkawaat**.

*imp* **chaskíhkaw**. *ptcpl* **cheeskíh=kawaat**.

**chaskihtéeheew** VTA almost hit s.o., 'nick' s.o. *ind 1st sg* **njaskihtéehaaw**, **njaskihtéeha**. *ind 3rd sg* **wchaskih=teeháawal**. *ind inv* **njaskihtéehukw**. *ind I-you* **kchaskihtéehul**. *conj 3rd sg* **chaskihtéehaat**. *imp* **chaskíhteeh**. *ptcpl* **cheeskihtéehaat**.

**chasksiitéexiin** VAI have one's feet brushing against a surface, have one's feet contacting a surface. *ind 1st sg* **njasksiitéexiin**, **njasksiitéexi**. *conj 3rd sg* **chasksiitéexiing**. *ptcpl* **chees=ksiitéexiing**.

**cháskŭneew** VTA touch s.o. lightly *(using the hands)*. *ind 1st sg* **njáskŭ=naaw**, **njáskŭna**. *ind 3rd sg* **wchas=kŭnáawal**. *ind inv* **njáskŭnukw**. *ind I-you* **kcháskŭnul**. *conj 3rd sg* **chás=kŭnaat**. *imp* **cháskun**. *ptcpl* **chées=kŭnaat**.

**cháskŭnum** VTI 1B touch s.t. lightly *(using the hands)*. *ind 1st sg* **njaskŭ=númun**. *ind 3rd sg* **wchaskŭnúmun**. *conj 1st sg* **chaskŭnúmaan**. *conj 3rd sg* **cháskŭnung**. *imp* **cháskŭnih**. *ptcpl* **chéeskŭnung**.

**chéehakwaak** NA skate. *pl* **cheeha=kwáakak**. *poss* **njeehakwáakum**. *loc* **cheehakwáakung**. *dimin* **cheeha=kwáakush**. *obv* **cheehakwáakal**.

**cheehakwáakuw** VAI skate, be skating. *ind 1st sg* **njeehakwáaki**, **njeeha=kwáakiim**. *emphatic pl* **cheeha=kwaakhátŭwak**. *conj 3rd sg* **chee=hakwáakiit**. *imp* **cheehakwáakiil**. *ptcpl* **cheehakwáakiit**.

**chéeliis** NA cherry. *pl* **cheelíisak**. *loc* **cheelíisung**. *dimin* **cheelíishush**. *obv* **cheelíisal**. *See* **chéliis**. *From English* cherries.

**cheelíis'heew** VAI pick cherries, work in a cherry orchard. *ind 1st sg* **njeelíis='he**, **njeelíis'heem**. *conj 3rd sg* **cheelíis'heet**. *imp* **cheelíis'heel**. *ptcpl* **cheelíis'heet**. *See* **chèlíis'heew**. *From English* cherries.

**cheemíhleew** VAI stagger. *ind 1st sg* **njeemíhla**, **njeemíhlaam**. *conj 3rd sg* **cheemíhlaat**. *ptcpl* **cheemíhlaat**. *moderative reduplication* **chaachee=míhleew**.

**chehchíipsiit** NA shy person, 'backwards' person. *pl* **chehchiipsíhtiit**.

**chehchpiinaakwsúwak** VAI look different. *usually plural*. *ind 1st pl* **njeh=chpiinaakwsíhna**. *conj 3rd pl* **cheh=chpiinaakwsíhtiit**. *ptcpl* **chehchpii=naakwsíhtiit**.

**chpíhleew** VII come apart. *conj 3rd sg* **chpíhlaak**. *ptcpl* **cheepíhlaak**. *intensive reduplication* **cehchpíhleew**.

**chékut** NI jacket, corset, vest. *pl* **chèk=útal**. *poss* **njekútum**. *loc* **chèkútung**. *dimin* **chèkútush**. *From English* jacket.

**chèkùthámeew** VAI wear a jacket. *ind 1st sg* **njèkùtháma**, **njèkùthámaam**. *conj 3rd sg* **chèkùthámaat**. *imp* **chèkùthámaal**. *ptcpl* **chèkùthámaat**.

**chéliis** NA cherry. *pl* **chèlíisak**. *poss* **njelíisum**. *loc* **chèlíisung**. *dimin* **chèlíishush**. *obv* **chèlíisal**. *See* **chéeliis**. *From English* cherries.

**chèlíis'heew** VAI pick cherries, work in a cherry orchard. *ind 1st sg* **njelíis'he**, **njelíis'heem**. *conj 3rd sg* **chèlíis'heet**. *imp* **chèlíis'heel**. *ptcpl* **chèlíis'heet**. *See* **cheelíis'heew**. *From English* cherries.

**chétum** NI Chatham, Ontario. **Chétum éew.** 'He's going to Chatham.' *From English* Chatham.

**chíi** PC don't. **Chíi wiichŭmáawu!** 'Don't help him!'; **Chíi kawíiwi!** 'Don't go to sleep!' *See* **chíile**.

**chíikham** VTI 1A sweep s.t. *ind 1st sg* **njiikhámun**. *ind 3rd sg* **wchiik=hámun**. *conj 1st sg* **chiikhámaan**. *conj 3rd sg* **chíikhang**. *imp* **chíikhah**. *ptcpl* **chíikhang**.

**chiikhíikan** NI broom. *pl* **chiikhíikanal**. *poss* **njiikhíikan**. *loc* **chiikhíika=nung**. *dimin* **chiikhíikanush**.

**chiikhíikeew** VAI sweep, sweep things. *ind 1st sg* **njiikhíike**, **njiikhíikeem**. *conj 3rd sg* **chiikhíikeet**. *imp* **chiikhíikeel**. *ptcpl* **chiikhíikeet**.

**chíikŭneew** VTA take away from s.o. *ind 1st sg* **njíikŭnaaw**, **njíikŭna**. *ind 3rd sg* **wchiikŭnáawal**. *ind inv* **njíikŭ=nukw**. *ind I-you* **kchíikŭnul**. *conj 3rd sg* **chíikŭnaat**. *imp* **chíikun**. *ptcpl* **chíikŭnaat**.

**chíikŭneew** VTAO take s.t. away from s.o. *ind 1st sg* **njíikŭnaan**. *ind 3rd sg* **wchíikŭnaan**. *ind inv* **njiikŭnúkwun**. *ind I-you* **kchiikŭnúlun**. *conj 3rd sg* **chíikŭnaat**. *imp* **chíikun**. *ptcpl* **chíikŭnaat**.

**chiikwaláleesh** NA sea shell, snail. *pl* **chiikwalaléeshak**. *obv* **chiikwalal=éeshal**. *rare*.

**chíikwameew** VTA eat s.t. animate bare, strip s.t. animate to the bone. *ind 1st sg* **njíikwamaaw**, **njíikwama**. *ind 3rd sg* **wchiikwamáawal**. *ind inv* **njíikwamukw**. *ind I-you* **kchíikwa=mul**. *conj 3rd sg* **chíikwamaat**. *imp* **chíikwam**. *ptcpl* **chíikwamaat**.

**chiikwándam** VTI 1A eat s.t. bare, strip s.t. to the bone. **Nehnayóongus wchiikwándamun miixáskwal.** 'The horse ate the grass to the ground.' *ind 1st sg* **njiikwándamun**. *ind 3rd sg* **wchiikwándamun**. *conj 1st sg* **chii=kwándamaan**. *conj 3rd sg* **chii=kwándang**. *imp* **chiikwándah**. *ptcpl* **chiikwándang**.

**chíikweew** VII be bare, be stripped bare. **Chíikweew kóhpii.** 'The forest is bare.' *conj 3rd sg* **chíikweek**. *ptcpl* **chíikweek**.

**chíikwsuw** VAI be bare, be stripped bare *(s.t. animate)*. **Chíikwsuw míhtukw.** 'The tree is bare.' *ind 1st sg* **njíikwsi**, **njíikwsiim**. *conj 3rd sg* **chíikwsiit**. *ptcpl* **chíikwsiit**.

**chíikwsheew** VTA cut s.t. animate close-ly *(as whiskers)*. *ind 1st sg* **njíikw=shaaw**, **njíikwsha**. *ind 3rd sg* **wchii=kwsháawal**. *ind inv* **njíikwshookw**. *ind I-you* **kchíikwshool**. *conj 3rd sg* **chíikwshaat**. *imp* **chíikwush**. *ptcpl* **chíikwshaat**.

**chíikwshum** VTI 1B cut s.t. closely. *ind 1st sg* **njiikwshúmun**. *ind 3rd sg* **wchiikwshúmun**. *conj 1st sg* **chiik=wshúmaan**. *conj 3rd sg* **chíikw=shung**. *imp* **chíikwshih**. *ptcpl* **chíi=kwshung**.

**chíile** PC don't. **Chíile náh áawu!** 'Don't go that way!'; **Chíilu níil wteehíimal miichíiwu!** 'Don't eat those strawberries!' *See* **chíi**.

**chiilíixiin** VAI have a sprain. *ind 1st sg* **njiilíixiin**, **njiilíixi**. *conj 3rd sg* **chiilíixiing**. *ptcpl* **chiilíixiing**.

**chiilíhleew** VAI have a sprain *(of body parts)*. **Njiilíhla nihkáxkwanal.** 'I sprained my ankles.' *ind 1st sg* **njiilíhla**, **njiilíhlaam**. *conj 3rd sg* **chiilíhlaat**. *ptcpl* **chiilíhlaat**.

**chíilŭneew** VTA sprain s.t. animate *(of body parts)*. *ind 1st sg* **njíilŭnaaw**, **njíilŭna**. *ind 3rd sg* **wchiilŭnáawal**. *ind inv* **njíilŭnukw**. *ind I-you* **kchíi=lŭnul**. *conj 3rd sg* **chíilŭnaat**. *ptcpl* **chíilŭnaat**.

**chiilŭnáxkeew** VAI have a sprained hand. *ind 1st sg* **njiilŭnáxka**, **njiilŭnáx=kaam**. *conj 3rd sg* **chiilŭnáxkaat**. *ptcpl* **chiilŭnáxkaat**.

**chiilŭnaxkéexiin** VAI have a sprained hand. *ind 1st sg* **njiilŭnaxkéexiin**, **njiilŭnaxkéexi**. *conj 3rd sg* **chiilŭ=naxkéexiing**. *ptcpl* **chiilŭnaxkée=xiing**.

**chíilŭnum** VTI 1B sprain s.t. *(of body parts)*. *ind 1st sg* **njiilŭnúmun**. *ind 3rd sg* **wchiilŭnúmun**. *conj 1st sg* **chiilŭnúmaan**. *conj 3rd sg* **chíilŭ=nung**. *ptcpl* **chíilŭnung**.

**chiingaalchásum** VTI1B put starch on s.t. *(of clothing)*. *ind 1st sg* **njiin=gaalchásŭmun**. *ind 3rd sg* **wchiin=gaalchásŭmun**. *conj 1st sg* **chiin=gaalchásŭmaan**. *conj 3rd sg* **chiin=gaalchásung**. *imp* **chiingaalchásih**. *ptcpl* **chiingaalchásung**.

**chiingáaleew** VII be stiff. *conj 3rd sg* **chiingáaleek**. *ptcpl* **chiingáaleek**.

**chiingaalkáateew** VAI have a stiff leg. *ind 1st sg* **njiingaalkáata**, **njiingaal=káataam**. *conj 3rd sg* **chiingaalkáa=taat**. *ptcpl* **chiingaalkáataat**.

**chiingaalsíikan** NI clothes iron. *pl* **chiingaalsíikanal**. *poss* **njiingaal=síikan**. *loc* **chiingaalsíikanung**. *dimin* **chiingaalshíikanush**. *See* **shaaxkùtsíikan**.

**chiingáalsuw** VAI be stiff *(s.t. animate)*. *ind 1st sg* **njiingáalsi**, **njiingáalsiim**. *conj 3rd sg* **chiingáalsiit**. *ptcpl* **chiingáalsiit**.

**chiingaalxóoneew** VAI have a stiff neck. *ind 1st sg* **njiingaalxóona**, **njiin=gaalxóonaam**. *conj 3rd sg* **chiin=gaalxóonaat**. *ptcpl* **chiingaal=xóonaat**.

**chiingaalxoonéexiin** VAI have a stiff neck. *ind 1st sg* **njiingaalxoonéexiin**, **njiingaalxoonéexi**. *conj 3rd sg* **chiingaalxoonéexiing**. *ptcpl* **chiin=gaalxoonéexiing**.

**chíingu** PC some time ago. **Chíingu ootéeneeng nóom.** 'I went to town some time ago.'; **Chíingu léepwaat ngihkŭlóolaaw.** 'I talked to the clever one recently.'

**chiipaalóhkweew** VAI have terrible looking hair. *ind 1st sg* **njiipaalóh=kwe**, **njiipaalóhkweem**. *conj 3rd sg* **chiipaalóhkweet**. *ptcpl* **chiipaalóh=kweet**.

**chiipáhkwsuw** VAI be in terrible shape, have a terrible figure, have a terrible shape, be in a bad shape. *ind 1st sg* **njiipáhkwsi**, **njiipáhkwsiim**. *conj 3rd sg* **chiipáhkwsiit**. *ptcpl* **chii=páhkwsiit**.

**chiipahtéenamuw** VAI have a bad thought, think bad thoughts, have bad feelings. *ind 1st sg* **njiipahtéenami**, **njiipahtéenamiim**. *conj 3rd sg* **chii=pahtéenamiit**. *ptcpl* **chiipahtée=namiit**.

**chíipaween** PR odd person, bad person, person who does bad things. *pl* **chii=pawéeniik**. *obv* **chiipawéeniil**.

**chíipay** NA ghost. *pl* **chíipayak**. *obv* **chíipayal**.

**chiipeelúndam** VAI be horrified about something, think something to be terrible. *ind 1st sg* **njiipeelúndam**. *conj 3rd sg* **chiipeelúndang**. *ptcpl* **chii=peelúndang**.

**chiipii-** PV frightful, terrible. **Chíipii-pehtáhkuw.** 'It is thundering loudly.' *ptcpl* **chíipii-**. *See* **chiipu-**, **achiipi-**, **achiipu-**.

**chiipiináakwat** VII look terrible, be terrible looking, have a frightful appearance. *conj 3rd sg* **chiipiináakwahk**. *ptcpl* **chiipiináakwahk**.

**chiipiináakwsuw** VAI look terrible, be terrible looking, have a frightful appearance. *ind 1st sg* **njiipiináakwsi**, **njiipiináakwsiim**. *conj 3rd sg* **chii=piináakwsiit**. *ptcpl* **chiipiináakwsiit**.

**chiipiingwéexiin** VAI make a face, have an unpleasant face. *ind 1st sg* **njii=piingwéexiin**, **njiipiingwéexi**. *conj 3rd sg* **chiipiingwéexiing**. *imp* **chii=piingwéexiil**. *ptcpl* **chiipiingwée=xiing**.

**chiipiitéeheew** VAI have evil thoughts, have bad thoughts *(as if without regret)*. *ind 1st sg* **njiipiitéeha**, **njii=piitéehaam**. *conj 3rd sg* **chiipiitée=haat**. *ptcpl* **chiipiitéehaat**.

**chiipihtáakwat** VII sound loud, sound terrible. *conj 3rd sg* **chiipihtáa=kwahk**. *ptcpl* **chiipihtáakwahk**.

**chiipihtáakwsuw** VAI sound loud, sound

terrible. *ind 1st sg* **njiipihtáakwsi**, **njiipihtáakwsiim**. *conj 3rd sg* **chii=pihtáakwsiit**. *ptcpl* **chiipihtáakwsiit**.

**chiipóngwaam** VAI have a bad dream. *ind 1st sg* **njiipóngwaam**. *conj 3rd sg* **chiipóngwaang**. *ptcpl* **chiipón=gwaang**.

**chiipsútam** VTI 1A find that s.t. sounds awful. *ind 1st sg* **njiipsútamun**. *ind 3rd sg* **chiipsútamun**. *conj 1st sg* **chiipsútamaan**. *conj 3rd sg* **chiip=sútang**. *ptcpl* **chiipsútang**.

**chiipsútaweew** VTA find that s.o. sounds awful. *ind 1st sg* **njiipsútawaaw**, **njiipsútawa**. *ind 3rd sg* **chiipsuta=wáawal**. *ind inv* **njiipsútaakw**. *ind I-you* **kchiipsútool**. *conj 3rd sg* **chiip=sútawaat**. *ptcpl* **chiipsútawaat**.

**chiiptóonheew** VAI talk terribly, talk badly, use foul language. *ind 1st sg* **njiiptóonhe**, **njiiptóonheem**. *conj 3rd sg* **chiiptóonheet**. *imp* **chiip=tóonheel**. *ptcpl* **chiiptóonheet**.

**chiipu-** PV frightful, terrible. *informal.* **Chíipu-léew.** 'Something terrible happened.' *ptcpl* **chíipu-**. *See* **chiipii-**, **achiipi-**, **achiipu-**.

**chiipŭlóosuw** VAI eat an awful lot, overeat. *considered impolite. ind 1st sg* **njiipŭlóosi**, **njiipŭlóosiim**. *conj 3rd sg* **chiipŭlóosiit**. *ptcpl* **chiipŭlóosiit**.

**chiishkóhkoosh** NA robin. *pl* **chiish=kohkóoshak**. *obv* **chiishkohkóoshal**.

**chiixakwíhleew** VAI slide down on something *(from roof, from snow pile)*; slide down *(of windows). ind 1st sg* **njiixakwíhla**, **njiixakwíhlaam**. *conj 3rd sg* **chiixakwíhlaat**. *ptcpl* **chiixakwíhlaat**.

**chiixakwíhleew** VII slide down *(of curtains). conj 3rd sg* **chiixakwíhlaak**. *ptcpl* **chiixakwíhlaak**.

**chíixham** VTI 1A comb s.t. *(of hair). ind 1st sg* **njiixhámun**. *ind 3rd sg* **wchiixhámun**. *conj 1st sg* **chiix=hámaan**. *conj 3rd sg* **chíixhang**. *imp* **chíixhah**. *ptcpl* **chíixhang**.

**chiixhámaweew** VTAO comb s.o.'s hair for them. *ind 1st sg* **njiixhámawaan**. *ind 3rd sg* **wchiixhámawaan**. *ind inv* **njiixhamáakwun**. *ind I-you* **kchiix=hamóolun**. *conj 3rd sg* **chiixháma=waat**. *imp* **chiixhámaw**. *ptcpl* **chiixhámawaat**.

**chiixíikan** NA comb. *pl* **chiixíikanak**. *poss* **njiixíikan**. *dimin* **chiixíikanush**. *obv* **chiixíikanal**.

**chiixiikwsíhleew** VAI slide downhill, slide down a hill. *ind 1st sg* **njii=xiikwsíhla**, **njiixiikwsíhlaam**. *conj 3rd sg* **chiixiikwsíhlaat**. *imp* **chii=xiikwsíhlaal**. *ptcpl* **chiixiikwsíhlaat**.

**chiixíikwsuw** VAI crawl down. *ind 1st sg* **njiixíikwsi**, **njiixíikwsiim**. *conj 3rd sg* **chiixíikwsiit**. *imp* **chiixíikwsiil**. *ptcpl* **chiixíikwsiit**. *intensive reduplication* **chihchiixíikwsuw**. *See* **niixíikwsuw**.

**chiixíhleew** VAI slide down. *ind 1st sg* **njiixíhla**, **njiixíhlaam**. *conj 3rd sg* **chiixíhlaat**. *imp* **chiixíhlaal**. *ptcpl* **chiixíhlaat**.

**chiixíhleew** VII go down, fall down, slide down *(of curtains, of pants). conj 3rd sg* **chiixíhlaak**. *ptcpl* **chii=xíhlaak**.

**chíixkw** NA 'wolf,' man who chases after women. *pl* **chíixkwak**. *obv* **chíixkwal**.

**chíixŭnum** VTI 1B pull s.t. down, lower s.t. *(using the hands). ind 1st sg* **njiixŭnúmun**. *ind 3rd sg* **wchiixŭ=númun**. *conj 1st sg* **chiixŭnúmaan**. *conj 3rd sg* **chíixŭnung**. *imp* **chíixŭnih**. *ptcpl* **chíixŭnung**.

**chihchpiináasuw** VAI 'make strange' *(of babies)*; be able to tell the difference between people. *ind 1st sg* **njihch=piináasi**, **njihchpiináasiim**. *conj 3rd sg* **chihchpiináasiit**. *ptcpl* **chihch=piináasiit**. *See* **chpiináasuw**.

**chihtamwúsuw** VAI be silent, keep quiet.

*ind 1st sg* **njihtamwúsi**, **njihta=mwúsiim**. *conj 3rd sg* **chihtamwús=iit**. *imp* **chihtamwúsiil**. *ptcpl* **chih=tamwúsiit**.

**chkáhaaw** NA Mohawk. *pl* **chkaháa=wak**. *obv* **chkaháawal**.

**chkawaashŭwihléeshuw** VAI swim slowly. *ind 1st sg* **njukawaashŭwih=láashi**, **njukawaashŭwihláashiim**. *conj 3rd sg* **chkawaashŭwih=láashiite**. *imp* **chkawaashŭwihláa=shiil**. *ptcpl* **cheekawaashŭwihláa=shiit**. *See* **ashahwaashŭwíhleew**.

**chkawahchakihléeshuw** VAI run slowly. *ind 1st sg* **njukawahchakihláashi**, **njukawahchakihláashiim**. *conj 3rd sg* **chkawahchakihláashiit**. *imp* **chkawahchakihláashiil**. *ptcpl* **chee=kawahchakihláashiit**. *See* **ashah=wahtakíhleew**.

**chkawchehléeshuw** VAI drive slowly (*dimin*). *ind 1st sg* **njukawucheh=láashi**, **njukawuchehláashiim**. *conj 3rd sg* **chkawchehláashiit**. *imp* **chkawchehláashiil**. *ptcpl* **cheeka=wuchehláashiit**. *moderative reduplication* **chaachkawchehláashuw**. *See* **ashahwchéhleew**.

**chkawiikwshíishuw** VAI crawl slowly. *ind 1st sg* **njukawiikwshíishi**, **njuk=awiikwshíishiim**. *conj 3rd sg* **chkawiikwshíishiit**. *imp* **chkaw=iikwshíishiil**. *ptcpl* **cheekawiikw=shíishiit**. *See* **ashahwíikwsuw**.

**chkáwiish** PC slowly. **Chkáwiish íil!** 'Say it slowly!'

**chkawooxwéeshuw** VAI walk slowly (*dimin*). *ind 1st sg* **njukawooxwée=shi**, **njukawooxwéeshiim**. *conj 3rd sg* **chkawooxwéeshiit**. *ptcpl* **cheeka=wooxwéeshiit**.

**chkawŭláanzhuw** VII rain steadily (*dimin*). *conj 3rd sg* **chkawŭláan=zhiik**. *ptcpl* **cheekawuláanzhiik**.

**chkwál** NA frog. *pl* **chkwálak**. *dimin* **chkwálush**. *obv* **chkwálal**.

**chóoskŭneew** VTA put s.o. on to boil. *ind 1st sg* **njóoskŭnaaw**, **njóoskŭna**. *ind 3rd sg* **wchooskŭnáawal**. *ind inv* **njóoskŭnukw**. *ind I-you* **kchóos=kŭnul**. *conj 3rd sg* **chóoskŭnaat**. *imp* **chóoskun**. *ptcpl* **chóoskŭnaat**.

**chooskŭnápwaan** NI boiled cornbread. *pl* **chooskŭnapwáanal**. *poss* **njoos=kŭnapwáanum**. *loc* **chooskŭnap=wáanung**. *dimin* **chooshkŭnap=wáanush**.

**chooskŭnapwáanush** NI dumpling. *pl* **chooskŭnapwáanshal**. *loc* **choos=kŭnapwáanshung**.

**chóoskŭnum** VTI 1B put s.t. on to boil. *ind 1st sg* **njooskŭnúmun**. *ind 3rd sg* **wchooskŭnúmun**. *conj 1st sg* **chooskŭnúmaan**. *conj 3rd sg* **chóos=kŭnung**. *imp* **chóoskŭnih**. *ptcpl* **chóoskŭnung**.

**chooxpwáaheew** VAIO throw s.o. in the water, throw s.t. in the water. *ind 1st sg* **njooxpwáaheen**. *ind 3rd sg* **wchooxpwáaheen**. *conj 3rd sg* **chooxpwáaheet**. *imp* **chooxpwáa=heel**. *ptcpl* **chooxpwáaheet**.

**chooxpwáakchehl** VAI jump in the water. *ind 1st sg* **njooxpwáakchehl**. *conj 3rd sg* **chooxpwaakchéhluk**. *imp* **chooxpwaakchéhlih**. *ptcpl* **chooxpwaakchéhluk**.

**chooxpwíhleew** VAI fall into water. *ind 1st sg* **njooxpwíhla**, **njooxpwíhlaam**. *conj 3rd sg* **chooxpwíhlaat**. *ptcpl* **chooxpwíhlaat**.

**chooxpwsiitéexiin** VAI have one's feet in the water, soak one's feet. *ind 1st sg* **njooxpwsiitéexiin**, **njooxpwsiitéexi**. *conj 3rd sg* **chooxpwsiitéexiing**. *imp* **chooxpwsiitéexiil**. *ptcpl* **chooxpw=siitéexiing**.

**chooxpwshíiheew** VTA chase s.o. into the water. *ind 1st sg* **njooxpwshíi=haaw**, **njooxpwshíiha**. *ind 3rd sg* **wchooxpwshiiháawal**. *ind inv* **njooxpwshíihukw**. *ind I-you*

**kchooxpwshíihul**. *conj 3rd sg* **chooxpwshíihaat**. *imp* **chóoxpw=shiih**. *ptcpl* **chooxpwshíihaat**.

**chooxpwshíhkaweew** VTA chase s.o. out of the water. *ind 1st sg* **njooxpw=shíhkawaaw**, **njooxpwshíhkawa**. *ind 3rd sg* **wchooxpwshihkawáawal**. *ind inv* **njooxpwshíhkaakw**. *ind I-you* **kchooxpwshíhkool**. *conj 3rd sg* **chooxpwshíhkawaat**. *imp* **chooxp=wshíhkaw**. *ptcpl* **chooxpwshíh=kawaat**.

**chóoxpwŭnum** VTI1A put s.t. in the water. *ind 1st sg* **njooxpwŭnúmun**. *ind 3rd sg* **wchooxpwŭnúmun**. *conj 1st sg* **chooxpwŭnúmaan**. *conj 3rd sg* **chóoxpwŭnung**. *imp* **chóoxpwŭnih**. *ptcpl* **chóoxpwŭnung**.

**chóoxpwŭneew** VTA put s.o. in the water. *ind 1st sg* **njóoxpwŭnaaw**, **njóoxpwŭna**. *ind 3rd sg* **wchoox=pwŭnáawal**. *ind inv* **njóoxpwŭnukw**. *ind I-you* **kchóoxpwŭnul**. *conj 3rd sg* **chóoxpwŭnaat**. *imp* **chóoxpwun**. *ptcpl* **chóoxpwŭnaat**.

**chpahéewaleew** VTA sort s.t. animate, sort s.t. animate out. *object usually plural. ind 1st sg* **njupheewaláawak**. *ind 3rd sg* **wchupheewaláawal**. *conj 3rd* **chpahéewalaat**. *imp* **chpahéewal**. *ptcpl* **cheephéewalaat**.

**chpahéewatoow** VTI2 sort s.t., sort s.t. out. *object usually plural. ind 1st sg* **njupheewatóonal**. *ind 3rd sg* **wchupheewatóonal**. *conj 1st sg* **chpaheewatáwaan**. *conj 3rd sg* **chpahéewataakw**. *imp* **chpahée=watool**. *ptcpl* **cheephéewataakw**.

**chpáhkhweew** VTA take s.t. animate apart, take s.o. apart *(using a tool or instrument). ind 1st sg* **njupáhk=hwaaw**, **njupáhkhwa**. *ind 3rd sg* **wchupahkhwáawal**. *ind inv* **njup=áhkhookw**. *ind I-you* **kchupáhkhool**. *conj 3rd sg* **chpáhkhwaat**. *imp* **chpáhkhwaw**. *ptcpl* **cheepáhk=hwaat**.

**chpáhkhwam** VTI1A take s.t. apart *(using a tool or instrument). ind 1st sg* **njupahkhwámun**. *ind 3rd sg* **wchupahkhwámun**. *conj 1st sg* **chpahkhwámaan**. *conj 3rd sg* **chpáhkhwang**. *imp* **chpáhkhwah**. *ptcpl* **cheepáhkhwang**.

**chpáhleew** VTA place s.o. apart, place s.t. animate apart. *object usually plural. ind 1st sg* **njupahláawak**. *ind 3rd sg* **wchupahláawal**. *conj 3rd sg* **chpáh=laat**. *imp* **chpáhl**. *ptcpl* **cheepáhlaat**.

**chpahtéewal** VII be apart. *usually plural. conj 3rd pl* **chpáhteek**. *ptcpl* **cheepahtéekiil**.

**chpáhtoow** VTI2 place s.t. apart, set s.t. aside. *object usually plural. ind 1st sg* **njupahtóonal**. *ind 3rd sg* **wchupah=tóonal**. *conj 1st sg* **chpáhtawaan**. *conj 3rd sg* **chpáhtaakw**. *imp* **chpáhtool**. *ptcpl* **cheepáhtaakw**.

**chpápŭwak** VAI be apart, be separated by birth or location. *usually plural. ind 1st pl* **njupapíhna**. *conj 3rd pl* **chpapíhtiit**. *ptcpl* **cheepapíhtiit**.

**chpiináasuw** VAI 'make strange' *(of babies)*; be able to tell the difference between people. *ind 1st sg* **njupiináasi**, **njupiináasiim**. *conj 3rd sg* **chpii=náasiit**. *ptcpl* **cheepiináasiit**. *See* **chihchpiináasuw**.

**chpíinam** VTI1A find that s.t. looks different, s.t. looks different to someone. *ind 1st sg* **njupíinamun**. *ind 3rd sg* **wchupíinamun**. *conj 1st sg* **chpíi=namaan**. *conj 3rd sg* **chpíinang**. *ptcpl* **cheepíinang**.

**chpíinaweew** VTA find that s.o. looks different. *ind 1st sg* **njupíinawaaw**, **njupíinawa**. *ind 3rd sg* **wchupiina=wáawal**. *ind inv* **njupíinaakw**. *ind I-you* **kchupíinool**. *conj 3rd sg* **chpíinawaat**. *ptcpl* **cheepíinawaat**.

**chpiixíinook** VAI be apart, be separated. *usually plural. ind 1st pl* **njupiixii=nóhna**. *conj 3rd pl* **chpiixiinóhtiit**. *ptcpl* **cheepiixiinóhtiit**.

**chpíixtoow** VTI2 separate s.t., sort s.o. *object usually plural. ind 1st sg* **njupiixtóonal**. *ind 3rd sg* **wchupiix=tóonal**. *conj 1st sg* **chpiixtáwaan**. *conj 3rd sg* **chpíixtaakw**. *imp* **chpíixtool**. *ptcpl* **cheepíixtaakw**.

**chpíixŭmeew** VTA separate s.o., sort s.o. *object usually plural. ind 1st sg* **njupiixŭmáawak**. *ind 3rd sg* **wchup=iixŭmáawal**. *ind inv* **njupiixŭmuk=óona**. *conj 3rd sg* **chpíixŭmaat**. *imp* **chpíixum**. *ptcpl* **cheepíixŭmaat**.

**chpíixŭnool** VII be apart, be separated. *usually plural. conj 3rd pl* **chpíixung**. *ptcpl* **cheepiixúngiil**.

**chpooxwéewak** VAI be separated from one's spouse, live apart. *usually plural. ind 1st pl* **njupooxwéhna**. *conj 3rd pl* **chpooxwéhtiit**. *imp* **chpóo=xweekw**. *ptcpl* **cheepooxwéhtiit**. *See* **machíilŭnuw**.

**chpúneew** VTA separate s.t. animate, sort s.t. animate *(using the hands). ind 1st sg* **njúpŭnaaw**, **njúpŭna**. *ind 3rd sg* **wchupŭnáawal**. *ind inv* **njúpŭnukw**. *ind I-you* **kchúpŭnul**. *conj 3rd sg* **chpúnaat**. *imp* **chpún**. *ptcpl* **chéepŭnaat**.

**chpúndeew** VII be a room, be a divided room, be different rooms, be another room *(in a dwelling). conj 3rd sg* **chpúndeek**. *ptcpl* **cheepúndeek**. *intensive reduplication* **chàchpúndeew**.

**chpúnum** VTI1B separate s.t., sort s.t. *(using the hands). ind 1st sg* **njupŭ=númun**. *ind 3rd sg* **wchupŭnúmun**. *conj 1st sg* **chpúnŭmaan**. *conj 3rd sg* **chpúnung**. *imp* **chpúnih**. *ptcpl* **chéepŭnung**.

**chpúsuw** VAI be apart, be isolated, be separated from other people. *ind 1st sg* **njúpsi**, **njúpsiim**. *conj 3rd sg* **chpúsiit**. *ptcpl* **chéepsiit**.

**chpwaakongwéepuy** NI pointed hat. *pl* **chpwaakongwéepŭyal**. *poss* **njup=waakongwéepuy**. *dimin* **chpwaa=kongwéepiish**.

**chpwaakongwéepŭyeew** VAI have a pointed hat. *ind 1st sg* **njupwaakon=gwéepŭya**, **njupwaakongwéepŭ=yaam**. *conj 3rd sg* **chpwaakongwée=pŭyaat**. *ptcpl* **cheepwaakongwée=pŭyaat**.

**chpwéew** VII be pointed. *conj 3rd sg* **chpwéek**. *ptcpl* **chéepweek**.

**chpwíikaan** NI house with a pointed roof. *pl* **chpwiikáanal**. *poss* **njup=wíikaan**. *loc* **chpwiikáanung**. *dimin* **chpwiikáanush**.

**chpwúsuw** VAI be pointed *(s.t. animate). ind 1st sg* **njúpwsi**, **njúpwsiim**. *conj 3rd sg* **chpwúsiit**. *ptcpl* **chéepwsiit**.

**chpwúsheew** VTA cut s.t. animate and make a point on it, cut a point on s.t. animate. *ind 1st sg* **njúpwshaaw**, **njúpwsha**. *ind 3rd sg* **wchupwsháa=wal**. *ind inv* **njúpwshookw**. *ind I-you* **kchúpwshool**. *conj 3rd sg* **chpwúsh=aat**. *imp* **chpwúsh**. *ptcpl* **chéepw=shaat**.

**chpwúshum** VTI1B cut s.t. and make a point on it, cut a point on s.t. *ind 1st sg* **njupwshúmun**. *ind 3rd sg* **wchupw=shúmun**. *conj 1st sg* **chpwúshŭ=maan**. *conj 3rd sg* **chpwúshung**. *imp* **chpwúshih**. *ptcpl* **chéepwshung**.

**chpwutoonéexiin** VAI purse one's lips, have one's mouth in a pout, have one's mouth sticking out pointed. *ind 1st sg* **njupwtoonéexiin**, **njupwtoo=néexi**. *conj 3rd sg* **chpwutoonée=xiing**. *ptcpl* **cheepwtoonéexiing**.

**chŭlóochŭloosh** NA cricket. *pl* **chŭloo=chŭlóoshak**. *poss* **njuloochŭlóo=shum**. *dimin* **chŭloochŭlóoshush**. *obv* **chŭloochŭlóoshal**.

**chŭmoochŭyéeshuw** VAI have a bobbed tail, have a cut-off tail *(dimin)*. *ind 1st sg* **njumoochŭyáashi**, **njumoochŭ=yáashiim**. *conj 3rd sg* **chŭmoochŭ=yáashiit**. *ptcpl* **cheemoochŭyáashiit**.

# D

**ndaangwsóxkweew** NAD my female cousin. *pl* **ndaangwsoxkwéewak**. *3rd poss* **wtaangwsoxkwéewal**.

**ndáangwus** NAD my male cousin. *pl* **ndáangwsak**. *3rd poss* **wtáangwsal**. *dimin* **ndáangwshush**.

**ndáanus** NAD my daughter. *pl* **ndáansak**. *3rd poss* **wtáansal**. *dimin* **ndáan=shush**.

**ndaatxóoxwiis** NAD my great-grandchild. *pl* **ndaatxooxwíisak**. *3rd poss* **wtaat=xooxwíisal**.

**ndawambíikan** NID my jaw. *3rd poss* **wtawambíikan**. *loc* **ndawambíi=kanung**.

**ndéeh** NAD my heart. *3rd poss* **wtéehal**. *loc* **ndéehung**.

**ndóolheew** NID my chest. *3rd poss* **wtóolheew**. *loc* **ndoolhéewung**.

**ndóon** NID my mouth. *3rd poss* **wtóon**. *loc* **ndóonung**.

**ndóhwan** NID my branch, my limb. *pl* **ndóhwanal**. *3rd poss* **wtóhwan**.

**ndúkuy** NAD my shoulder. *pl* **ndúkŭyak**. *3rd poss* **wtúkŭyal**. *loc* **ndúkiing**.

**ndúkuy** NID my shoulder. *pl* **ndúkŭyal**. *3rd poss* **wtúkuy**.

**ndúmb** NID my brain. *3rd poss* **wtúmb**.

# EE

**eeheesháapamukw** NA bottle, jar. *pl* **eeheeshaapamúkwak**. *poss* **ndee=heesháapamukw**. *loc* **eeheeshaapa=múkwung**. *dimin* **eeheeshaapamúk=wush**. *obv* **eeheeshaapamúkwal**. *See* **eeheeshaapamúkwahk**.

**eeheeshaapamúkwahk** NA bottle, jar. *pl* **eeheeshaapamukwáhkak**. *poss* **ndeeheeshaapamúkwahk**. *loc* **eeheeshaapamukwáhkung**. *dimin* **eeheeshaapamukwáhkush**. *obv* **eeheeshaapamukwáhkal**. *See* **eeheesháapamukw**.

**eeheeshándeek** NA window. *pl* **eehee=shandéekak**. *poss* **ndeeheeshán=deek**. *loc* **eeheeshandéekung**. *dimin* **eeheeshanjéekush**. *obv* **eeheeshan=déekal**. *See* **eeheeshandéekan**.

**eeheeshandéekan** NA window. *pl* **ee=heeshandéekanak**. *poss* **ndeehee=shandéekan**. *loc* **eeheeshandéeka=nung**. *dimin* **eeheeshanjéekanush**. *obv* **eeheeshandéekanal**. *See* **eehee=shándeek**.

**eehundáxpoon** NI table. *pl* **eehundax=póonal**. *poss* **ndeehundáxpoon**. *loc* **eehundaxpóonung**. *dimin* **eehun=jaxpóonush**. *See* **eehundáxpwiing**.

**eehundáxpwiing** VII table. *conj 3rd sg* **eehundáxpwiing** *pl* **eehundax=pwiingiil**. *See* **eehundáxpoon**.

**eekwawéeheew** VAIO wear s.t. under something else. *ind 1st sg* **ndeekwa=wéeheen**. *ind 3rd sg* **wteekwawée=heen**. *conj 3rd sg* **eekwawéeheet**. *imp* **eekwawéeheel**. *ptcpl* **eekwa=wéeheet**.

**éekwii** PC under. **Éekwii mbíng óonju-nihláawal.** 'He killed him from under the water.'; **Éekwii ndáhtoon.** 'I put it underneath.'

**eekwíixtoow** VTI2 put s.t. underneath something. *ind 1st sg* **ndeekwíixtoon**. *ind 3rd sg* **wteekwíixtoon**. *conj 1st sg* **eekwiixtáwaan**. *conj 3rd sg* **eekwíixtaakw**. *imp* **eekwíixtool**. *ptcpl* **eekwíixtaakw**.

**eekwíixŭmeew** VTA put s.o. underneath something. *ind 1st sg* **ndeekwíixŭ=**

maaw, **ndeekwíixŭma**. *ind 3rd sg* **wteekwiixŭmáawal**. *ind inv* **ndee=kwíixŭmukw**. *ind I-you* **kteekwíi=xŭmul**. *conj 3rd sg* **eekwíixŭmaat**. *imp* **eekwíixum**. *ptcpl* **eekwíixŭmaat**.

**eekwihtéexiin** VAI fall under something, fall underneath something. *ind 1st sg* **ndeekwihtéexiin, ndeekwihtéexi**. *conj 3rd sg* **eekwihtéexiing**. *ptcpl* **eekwihtéexiing**.

**eekwsháamuw** VAI sneeze. *ind 1st sg* **ndeekwsháamwi, ndeekwsháa=mwiim**. *conj 3rd sg* **eekwsháamwiit**. *imp* **eekwsháamwiil**. *ptcpl* **eekw=sháamwiit**. *intensive reduplication* **eeheekwsháamuw**.

**eel-** PV because, in a certain manner, in a certain direction. *followed by verb in conjunct order*. **Nál xéet ná kwáy éel- wchápihk -aluwíhkang.** 'Now it must be because he had overcome the medicine.'; **Kwáy éel-náatŭnat ngúmee-uch xwéelu kwéek kŭmóx=kam.** 'Because you picked him up you'll always find lots of things (to hunt).' *See* **eeli-**, **li-**, **lu-**.

**eelíikwus** NA ant. *pl* **eelíikwsak**. *dimin* **eelíikwshush**. *obv* **eelíikwsal**.

**eeli-** PV because, in a certain manner, in a certain direction. *followed by verb in conjunct order*. **Kwáta-nihláawal éeli- wáhwal -pwáhkhang.** 'She wanted to kill him because he had cracked the eggs.' *See* **eel-**, **li-**, **lu-**.

**eelkih-** PV certain amount, certain extent. *followed by verb in conjunct order*. **Peexŭwíhle éelkih-katá-alumsúy=aan.** 'It's getting close to when I want to leave.'; **Éelkih-miitsáhtiing.** 'It's time to eat.' *ptcpl* **éelkih-**.

**eelóngwaam** VAI oversleep, sleep late, sleep in. *ind 1st sg* **ndeelóngwaam**. *conj 3rd sg* **eelóngwaang**. *ptcpl* **eelóngwaang**.

**eemhwáanus** NA spoon. *pl* **eemhwáan=sak**. *poss* **ndeemhwáanus**. *loc* **eem=hwáansung**. *dimin* **eemhwáanshush**. *obv* **eemhwáansal**.

**éemul** NA tub. *pl* **éemŭlak**. *poss* **ndée=mŭlum**. *loc* **éemŭlung**. *dimin* **éemŭ=lush**. *obv* **éemŭlal**. *From Dutch.*

**eenda-** PV when. *followed by verb in conjunct order*. **Éenda- nzhiis -wuskii=lŭnuwíite, wihwiichéeweew ox=kwéessal.** 'When my uncle was a young man he used to go with a girl.'; **Sháa éenda-mihkwchéenungu sháa liitéehe, "Yóon éet kwáy."** 'Right away when he felt for it he thought right away, "Now this must be it."'

**eenda-** PV where. *followed by verb in conjunct order*. **Xwánzal wtuláawal, "Liindawáakan-uch náh kŭwéhla=laan éenda-wíhkweek shiipóoshush wéenj-uch -weewíhtawaan táa neekíhlayaan."** 'He told his older brother, "Hang the lantern at the end of the creek so I'll know where to stop."'; **Nál ngwúteel wíikŭwak tá kóhpii nzhíis éenda-làlóhkeet.** 'Then they lived together in the forest where my uncle worked.'

**éenda-maawéewiing** VII church. *conj 3rd sg* **éenda-maawéewiing**

**éenda-wsíhkaang** VII west *(where the sun sets)*. *conj 3rd sg* **éenda-wsíhkaang**

**eenglúshmaan** NA English person. *pl* **eenglushmáanak**. *obv* **eenglush=máanal**. *From English* Englishman.

**eenglushmaaníiwu-pehpŭmutóonhees** NA Anglican minister. *pl* **eenglush=maaníiwu-pehpŭmutoonhéesak**. *obv* **eenglushmaaníiwu-pehpŭmut=oonheésal**.

**eenháweew** VTA pay s.o. *ind 1st sg* **ndeenháwaaw, ndeenháwa**. *ind 3rd sg* **wteenhawáawal**. *ind inv* **ndéen=haakw**. *ind I-you* **ktéenhool**. *conj 3rd sg* **eenháwaat**. *imp* **éenhaw**. *ptcpl* **eenháwaat**.

**eenheelxáweew** VTA pay for s.o., pay to

s.o. *ind 1st sg* **ndeenheelxáwaaw**, **ndeenheelxáwa**. *ind 3rd sg* **wteen=heelxawáawal**. *ind inv* **ndeenhéel=xaakw**. *ind I-you* **kteenhéelxool**. *conj 3rd sg* **eenheelxáwaat**. *imp* **eenhéelxaw**. *ptcpl* **eenheelxáwaat**.

**eenheelxáweew** VTAO pay s.o. for s.t. *ind 1st sg* **ndeenheelxáwaan**. *ind 3rd sg* **wteenheelxáwaan**. *ind inv* **ndeenheelxáakwun**. *ind I-you* **kteenheelxóolun**. *conj 3rd sg* **een=heelxáwaat**. *imp* **eenhéelxaw**. *ptcpl* **eenheelxáwaat**.

**eenhíikeew** VAIO pay s.t. **Ndeenhíikeen keelŭnumáasŭyaan.** 'I paid what I owe.' *ind 1st sg* **ndeenhíikeen**. *ind 3rd sg* **wteenhíikeen**. *conj 3rd sg* **eenhíikeet**. *imp* **eenhíikeel**. *ptcpl* **eenhíikeet**.

**éeskwa** PC not yet. *followed by negative verb.* **Éeskwa létul nŭmushŭnáawi.** 'I didn't get a letter yet.'; **Éeskwa nŭmiitsíiwi.** 'I didn't eat yet.'

**éespan** NA raccoon. *pl* **éespanak**. *dimin* **eeshpánush**. *obv* **eespánal**.

**éesh** PC every. **Éesh tá lúkih.** 'Every once in a while.' *See* **héesh**.

**eeshatawáapuw** VAI look through. *ind 1st sg* **ndeeshatawáapi**, **ndeesha=tawáapiim**. *conj 3rd sg* **eeshatawáa=piit**. *imp* **eeshatawáapiil**. *ptcpl* **eeshatawáapiit**.

**eeshatawáapuw** VAIO look through something, see through something. *ind 1st sg* **ndeeshatawáapiin**. *ind 3rd sg* **wteeshatawáapiin**. *conj 3rd sg* **eeshatawáapiit**. *imp* **eeshatawáapiil**. *ptcpl* **eeshatawáapiit**.

**éeshiiw** VAI-S go through, pass through, get through. *ind 1st sg* **ndéeshi**, **ndéeshiim**. *conj 3rd sg* **éeshiit**. *imp* **éeshiil**. *ptcpl* **éeshiit**.

**éeshiiw** VAIO go through s.t., pass through s.t., get through s.t. **Ndéeshiin wtoo=téeneeng.** 'I went across his property.' *ind 1st sg* **ndéeshiin**. *ind 3rd sg* **wtéeshiin**. *conj 3rd sg* **éeshiit**. *imp* **éeshiil**. *ptcpl* **éeshiit**.

**eeshii-** PV through. **Ndéeshii-néewaaw.** 'I see through him (as of a window).' *ptcpl* **éeshii-**. *See* **eeshu-**.

**eeshíikwsuw** VAI crawl through *(a space)*. *ind 1st sg* **ndeeshíikwsi**, **ndeeshíikwsiim**. *conj 3rd sg* **eeshíi=kwsiit**. *imp* **eeshíikwsiil**. *ptcpl* **eeshíikwsiit**.

**eeshiipáhtoow** VTI2 take s.t. through in a hurry. *ind 1st sg* **ndeeshiipáhtoon**. *ind 3rd sg* **wteeshiipáhtoon**. *conj 1st sg* **eeshiipáhtawaan**. *conj 3rd sg* **eeshiipáhtaakw**. *imp* **eeshiipáhtool**. *ptcpl* **eeshiipáhtaakw**.

**eeshíipheew** VTA take s.o. through in a hurry. *ind 1st sg* **ndeeshíiphaaw**, **ndeeshíipha**. *ind 3rd sg* **wteeshiip=háawal**. *ind inv* **ndeeshíiphukw**. *ind I-you* **kteeshíiphul**. *conj 3rd sg* **eeshíiphaat**. *imp* **eeshíipah**. *ptcpl* **eeshíiphaat**.

**eeshíhleew** VAI go through, fall through. **Móhkamiing ndeeshíhla.** 'I went through the ice.' *ind 1st sg* **ndeeshíhla**, **ndeeshíhlaam**. *conj 3rd sg* **eeshíh=laat**. *imp* **eeshíhlaal**. *ptcpl* **eeshíh=laat**.

**eeshíhleew** VII go through, fall through. *conj 3rd sg* **eeshíhlaak**. *ptcpl* **eeshíh=laak**.

**eeshóoxwaleew** VTA take s.o. through something, take s.o. through an experience. *ind 1st sg* **ndeeshóoxwalaaw**, **ndeeshóoxwala**. *ind 3rd sg* **wtee=shooxwaláawal**. *ind inv* **ndeeshóo=xwalukw**. *ind I-you* **kteeshóoxwalul**. *conj 3rd sg* **eeshóoxwalaat**. *imp* **eeshóoxwal**. *ptcpl* **eeshóoxwalaat**.

**eeshooxwatáasuw** VII be put through *(of a motion at a meeting, of business)*. *conj 3rd sg* **eeshooxwatáasiik**. *ptcpl* **eeshooxwatáasiik**.

**eeshóoxwatoow** VTI2 take s.t. through something *(of a matter of business). ind 1st sg* **ndeeshóoxwatoon**. *ind 3rd sg* **wteeshóoxwatoon**. *conj 1st sg* **eeshooxwatáwaan**. *conj 3rd sg* **eeshóoxwataakw**. *imp* **eeshóoxwa=tool**. *ptcpl* **eeshóoxwataakw**.

**eeshóoxweew** VAIO go through s.t., experience s.t. *ind 1st sg* **ndeeshóo=xween**. *ind 3rd sg* **wteeshóoxween**. *conj 3rd sg* **eeshóoxweet**. *imp* **eeshóoxweel**. *ptcpl* **eeshóoxweet**.

**éeshpeew** VAI be soaked through *(s.t. animate). ind 1st sg* **ndéeshpe**, **ndéeshpeem**. *conj 3rd sg* **éeshpeet**. *ptcpl* **éeshpeet**.

**éeshpeew** VII be soaked through. *conj 3rd sg* **éeshpeek**. *ptcpl* **éeshpeek**.

**éesh'sheew** VTA cut through s.t. animate. *ind 1st sg* **ndéesh'shaaw**, **ndéesh'sha**. *ind 3rd sg* **wteesh'sháawal**. *ind inv* **ndéesh'shookw**. *ind I-you* **ktée=sh'shool**. *conj 3rd sg* **éesh'shaat**. *imp* **éeshush**. *ptcpl* **éesh'shaat**.

**eesh'shéesuw** VAI be a hole through something. **Eesh'shéesuw eehee=shandéekan.** 'The window has a hole in it.' *conj 3rd sg* **eesh'shéesiit**. *ptcpl* **eesh'shéesiit**.

**eesh'shéeyeew** VII be a hole through something. **Eesh'shéeyeew nŭmáh=ksun.** 'I've got a hole in my shoe.' *conj 3rd sg* **eesh'shéeyeek**. *ptcpl* **eesh'shéeyeek**.

**éesh'shum** VTI1B cut through s.t. *ind 1st sg* **ndeesh'shúmun**. *ind 3rd sg* **wtee=sh'shúmun**. *conj 1st sg* **eesh'shúm=aan**. *conj 3rd sg* **éesh'shung**. *imp* **éesh'shih**. *ptcpl* **éesh'shung**.

**eeshu-** PV through. *informal.* **Éeshu-laapamúkwat.** 'It can be seen through.' *ptcpl* **éeshu-**. *See* **eeshii-**.

**eeshŭláandeew** VII be the sun coming through. *conj 3rd sg* **eeshŭláandeek**. *ptcpl* **eeshŭláandeek**.

**éeshŭlam** VTI1A knock s.t. through *(with a stick). ind 1st sg* **ndeeshŭlámun**. *ind 3rd sg* **wteeshŭlámun**. *conj 1st sg* **eeshŭlámaan**. *conj 3rd sg* **éeshŭ=lang**. *imp* **éeshŭlah**. *ptcpl* **éeshŭlang**.

**éet** PC maybe. **Píht éet katá-sóokŭlaan.** 'Maybe it's going to rain.'; **Nún éet há.** 'That must be it.'

**éew** VAI go. **Yéelak áal!** 'Go away!'; **Yóh áal!** 'Come here!' *ind 1st sg* **ndá**, **ndáam**. *conj 3rd sg* **áat**. *imp* **áal**. *ptcpl* **éeyaat**.

**eewachíisŭmuw** VAI drink often, drink a lot. *ind 1st sg* **ndeewachíisŭmwi**, **ndeewachíisŭmwiim**. *conj 3rd sg* **eewachíisŭmwiit**. *imp* **eewachíisŭ=mwiil**. *ptcpl* **eewachíisŭmwiit**.

**eewachíisheew** VAI urinate often. *ind 1st sg* **ndeewachíishe**, **ndeewachíi=sheem**. *conj 3rd sg* **eewachíisheet**. *imp* **eewachíisheel**. *ptcpl* **eewachíi=sheet**.

**eewachu-** PV often. **Ndéewachu-míitsi.** 'I eat often.'; **Éewachu- ndaaktúl=ung -éew.** 'He goes to the doctor often.' *ptcpl* **éewachu-**. *See* **wŭyaku-**, **yáanee**.

**eewatahtakíhleew** VAI run often. *ind 1st sg* **ndeewatahtakíhla**, **ndeewatah=takíhlaam**. *conj 3rd sg* **eewatahta=kíhlaat**. *imp* **eewatahtakíhlaal**. *ptcpl* **eewatahtakíhlaat**.

**eewataláamuw** VAI sing often. *ind 1st sg* **ndeewataláamwi**, **ndeewataláa=mwiim**. *conj 3rd sg* **eewataláamwiit**. *imp* **eewataláamwiil**. *ptcpl* **eewatal=áamwiit**.

**éewatoow** VTI2 bring a load of s.t., go by with a load of s.t., haul a load of s.t. **Ndéewato miixáskwal.** 'I hauled a load of hay.' *ind 1st sg* **ndéewato**. *ind 1st sg* **ndéewatoon**. *ind 3rd sg* **wtéewatoon**. *conj 1st sg* **eewatáw=aan**. *conj 3rd sg* **éewataakw**. *imp* **éewatool**. *ptcpl* **éewataakw**.

**eewatóoxweew** VAI walk often. *ind 1st sg* **ndeewatóoxwe, ndeewatóoxweem**. *conj 3rd sg* **eewatóoxweet**. *imp* **eewatóoxweel**. *ptcpl* **eewatóoxweet**.

**eewaxkhíikan** NI stirring stick. *pl* **eewaxkhíikanal**. *poss* **ndeewaxk=híikan**. *loc* **eewaxkhíikanung**. *dimin* **eewaxkhíikanush**.

**eewaxkhíikeew** VAI stir things. *ind 1st sg* **ndeewaxkhíike, ndeewaxkhíikeem**. *conj 3rd sg* **eewaxkhíikeet**. *imp* **eewaxkhíikeel**. *ptcpl* **eewaxkhíikeet**.

**éeylii** PC both. **Éeylii nŭwiinamánda=mun nzíital.** 'Both my feet are sore.'; **Éeylii nehnayóongsak nŭmahla=wáawak.** 'I bought both horses.'

**eeyŭliinaakwsúwak** VAI look the same, look alike. *usually plural. ind 1st pl* **ndeeyŭliinaakwsíhna**. *conj 3rd pl* **eeyŭliinaakwsíhtiit**. *ptcpl* **eeyŭlii=naakwsíhtiit**.

# E

**échun** NA Indian agent. **Échŭnung ndá.** 'I'm going to the agent's.' *pl* **échŭnak**. *loc* **échŭnung**. *obv* **échŭnal**. *From English* agent.

**éflin** NA Evelyn. *obv* **eflínal**. *From English* Evelyn.

**eháashtee** PC one after the other, in turn, every other one. **Eháashtee miit=súwak.** 'They took turns eating'; **Eháashtee ndá.** 'I went from one place to another (and then back).'

**ehahpalíhkeeng** VII carpet, rug. *conj 3rd sg* **ehahpalíhkeeng** *pl* **ehahpa=lihkeengiil**. *'What one steps upon.'*

**eháhpapiing** NI cushion, saddle. *pl* **ehahpapíingiil**. *poss* **ndeháhpa=piing**. *'What one sits upon.'*

**ehahtíikeeng** VII container, trunk. *conj 3rd sg* **ehahtíikeeng** *pl* **ehahtii=kéengiil**.

**éhakwiing** VII clothing. *conj 3rd sg* **éhakwiing** *pl* **ehakwíingiil**. *'What one puts on.'*

**ehaláamakwiing** NI underclothes. *pl* **ehalamakwíingal**. *poss* **ndehalaa=makwíingum**.

**ehanz'híikan** NI well sweep. *pl* **ehanz'=híikanal**. *poss* **ndehanz'híikan**. *loc* **ehanz'híikanung**. *dimin* **ehanz'híi=kanush**. *stick with hook or nail at one end, used for raising water pails. See* **anz'híikan**.

**ehapíikwees** NA musician. *pl* **ehapii=kwéesak**. *obv* **ehapiikwéesal**.

**ehkoohaawatúwak** VAI be finished an activity. *usually plural. ind 1st pl* **ndehkoohaawatíhna**. *indef subject* **ehkoohháawatiin**. *conj 3rd pl* **ehkoo=haawatíhtiit**. *ptcpl* **ehkoohaawa=tíhtiit**.

**ehkwáawsuw** VAI die, be dead. *ind 1st sg* **ndehkwáawsi, ndehkwáawsiim**. *conj 3rd sg* **ehkwáawsiit**. *ptcpl* **eh=kwáawsiit**. *See* **maníhleew, éhkwi-pŭmáawsuw, éhkwu-pŭmáawsuw**.

**ehkwáhkwalus** NA black cap. *pl* **eh=kwahkalúsak**. *loc* **ehkwahkwalús=ung**. *dimin* **ehkwahkwalúshush**. *obv* **ehkwahkwalúsal**.

**ehkwalóoleew** VTA no longer require s.o.'s services. *ind 1st sg* **ndehkwa=lóolaaw, ndehkwalóola**. *ind 3rd sg* **wtehkwalooláawal**. *ind inv* **ndeh=kwalóolukw**. *ind I-you* **ktehkwalóo=lul**. *conj 3rd sg* **ehkwalóolaat**. *imp* **éhkwalool**. *ptcpl* **ehkwalóolaat**.

**ehkwanóongsuw** VAI be through being angry. *ind 1st sg* **ndehkwanóongsi, ndehkwanóongsiim**. *conj 3rd sg* **eh=kwanóongsiit**. *ptcpl* **ehkwanóongsiit**.

**ehkwchásuw** VAI stop burning *(s.t. animate). ind 1st sg* **ndehkwchási**. *conj*

*3rd sg* **ehkwchásiit**. *ptcpl* **ehkw=chásiit**.
**ehkwcháteew** VII stop burning. *conj 3rd sg* **ehkwcháteek**. *ptcpl* **ehkwcháteek**.
**ehkwíikun** VII stop growing. *conj 3rd sg* **ehkwíikung**. *ptcpl* **ehkwíikung**.
**ehkwíikuw** VAI stop growing *(s.t. animate)*. *ind 1st sg* **ndehkwíiki**, **ndeh=kwíikiim**. *conj 3rd sg* **ehkwíikiit**. *imp* **ehkwíikiil**. *ptcpl* **ehkwíikiit**.
**ehkwíisŭmuw** VAI stop drinking. **Kóolu-áa -ehkwíisŭmwi.** 'You should quit drinking.' *ind 1st sg* **ndehkwíisŭmwi**, **ndehkwíisŭmwiim**. *conj 3rd sg* **ehkwíisŭmwiit**. *imp* **ehkwíisŭmwiil**. *ptcpl* **ehkwíisŭmwiit**.
**ehkwíisheew** VAI stop urinating, cease urinating, quit urinating. *ind 1st sg* **ndehkwíishe**, **ndehkwíisheem**. *conj 3rd sg* **ehkwíisheet**. *imp* **ehkwíisheel**. *ptcpl* **ehkwíisheet**.
**ehkwi-** PV stop, cease. **Ndéhkwi-néewa.** 'I couldn't see him.' *ptcpl* **éhkwi-**. *See* **ehkwu-**.
**éhkwi-pŭmáawsuw** VAI die. *ind 1st sg* **ndéhkwi-pŭmáawsi**, **ndéhkwi-pŭmáawsiim**. *conj 3rd sg* **éhkwi-pŭmáawsiit**. *ptcpl* **éhkwi-pŭmáaw=siit**. *See* **maníhleew**, **ehkwáawsuw**, **éhkwu-pŭmáawsuw**.
**ehkwíhleew** VAI stop going, stop working *(s.t. animate)*. *conj 3rd sg* **ehkwíhlaat**. *ptcpl* **ehkwíhlaat**.
**ehkwíhleew** VII stop going, stop working *(of machines)*. *conj 3rd sg* **ehkwíhlaak**. *ptcpl* **ehkwíhlaak**.
**éhkwsuw** VAI stop burning, cease burning *(s.t. animate)*. *conj 3rd sg* **éhkwsiit**. *ptcpl* **éhkwsiit**.
**éhkwsheew** VTA stop cutting s.t. animate, cease cutting s.t. animate. *ind 1st sg* **ndéhkwshaaw**, **ndéhkwsha**. *ind 3rd sg* **wtehkwsháawal**. *ind inv* **ndéhkwshookw**. *ind I-you* **ktéhkw=shool**. *conj 3rd sg* **éhkwshaat**. *imp* **éhkwush**. *ptcpl* **éhkwshaat**.
**ehkwshíikeew** VAI stop cutting things, cease cutting things. *ind 1st sg* **ndehkwshíike**, **ndehkwshíikeem**. *conj 3rd sg* **ehkwshíikeet**. *imp* **ehkwshíikeel**. *ptcpl* **ehkwshíikeet**.
**éhkwshum** VTI1B stop cutting s.t., cease cutting s.t. *ind 1st sg* **ndehkwshúm=un**. *ind 3rd sg* **wtehkwshúmun**. *conj 1st sg* **ehkwshúmaan**. *conj 3rd sg* **éhkwshung**. *imp* **éhkwshih**. *ptcpl* **éhkwshung**.
**éhkwteew** VII stop burning, cease burning. *conj 3rd sg* **éhkwteek**. *ptcpl* **éhkwteek**.
**ehkwtóonheew** VAI stop talking, cease talking. *ind 1st sg* **ndehkwtóonhe**, **ndehkwtóonheem**. *conj 3rd sg* **ehkwtóonheet**. *imp* **ehkwtóonheel**. *ptcpl* **ehkwtóonheet**.
**ehkwu-** PV stop, cease. *informal.* **Éhkwu-léexeew.** 'He quit breathing.'; **Éhkwu-maawéewiin.** 'The service is over.' *ptcpl* **éhkwu-**. *See* **ehkwi-**.
**éhkwu-pŭmáawsuw** VAI die. *ind 1st sg* **ndéhkwu-pŭmáawsi**, **ndéhkwu-pŭmáawsiim**. *conj 3rd sg* **éhkwu-pŭmáawsiit**. *ptcpl* **éhkwu-pŭmáaw=siit**. *See* **maníhleew**, **éhkwáawsuw**, **éhkwi-pŭmáawsuw**.
**éhkwŭlaan** VII stop raining. *conj 3rd sg* **éhkwŭlaang**. *ptcpl* **éhkwŭlaang**.
**ehóhpwaang** VII tobacco, what one smokes. *conj 3rd sg* **ehóhpwaang**
**ehŭliingwáhteek** NI chimney pipe. *pl* **ehŭliingwahtéekal**. *poss* **ndehŭliin=gwahtéekum**. *loc* **ehŭliingwahtée=kung**. *dimin* **ehŭliingwahchéekush**.
**éhunda-kshiixíinjŭweeng** VII dishpan. *conj 3rd sg* **éhunda-kshiixíinjŭweeng** *pl* **ehunda-kshiixiinjuweengiil**.
**éhwiis** NA thimble. *pl* **èhwíisak**. *poss* **ndehwíisum**. *dimin* **èhwíishush**. *obv*

**èhwíisal**.

**élput** NA Albert *(man's name)*. *obv* **èlpútal**. *From English* Albert.

**émshun** NA Emerson *(man's name)*. *obv* **èmshúnal**. *From English* Emerson.

**éshŭlush** NA Ethel. *obv* **èshŭlúshal**. *From English* Ethel.

**étŭwat** NA Edward. *obv* **ètŭwátal**. *From English* Edward.

# F

**fáamŭl** NA farmer. *pl* **fáamŭlak**. *obv* **fáamŭlal**. *From English* farmer.

**fáamŭluw** VAI be a farmer, farm. *ind 1st sg* **nváamŭli**, **nváamŭliim**. *conj 3rd sg* **fáamŭliit**. *ptcpl* **fáamŭliit**. *From English* farmer.

**féeliin** VAI be a fair going on *(indef subject)*. *indef subject* **féeliin**. *conj 3rd sg* **féeliing**. *From English* fair.

**fíipii** NA Phoebe. *obv* **fiipíihal**. *From English* Phoebe.

**fráyteew** VII be Friday. **Nŭmáw-ootee=wáalaaw éenda-fraytéeke.** 'I'm going to visit him on Friday.' *conj 3rd sg* **fráyteek**. *From English* Friday.

# G

**ngúk** NAD my mother. **Ngúkaa.** 'Mother (vocative).'; **Ngúkaash.** 'Mother (vocative).' *pl* **ngúkak**. *3rd poss* **kwúkal**.

**ngúkush** NAD my maternal aunt, my mother's sister; my parallel aunt. *pl* **ngúkshak**. *3rd poss* **kwúkshal**.

**ngútko** NAD my knee. *pl* **ngutkóohak**. *3rd poss* **kwutkóohal**. *loc* **ngutkóo=hung**. *dimin* **nguchkóohush**.

**ngútkuw** NAD my knee. *pl* **ngutkúwak**. *3rd poss* **kwutkúwal**.

**ngwíisus** NAD my son. *pl* **ngwíissak**. *3rd poss* **kwíissal**.

# H

**háaw há** PC let's go. **Háaw há.** 'Let's go.'

**há** PC question marker, emphatic. **Nún há wtihúnda-alóhkeen.** 'This is where he used to work.'; **Ktíit há?** 'Do you think so?'

**hachíingi** PC anyway *(contrary to expectation)*. **Hachíingi náh ndá.** 'I went there anyways.'; **Hachíingi wtulŭnúmun.** 'He went ahead and did it.'

**nhákay** NAD my self *(in reflexive expressions)*. **Lóosaaw nhákay.** 'I burned myself.'; **Níhlii pàyaxkháawal hwákayal.** 'He shot himself.' *3rd poss* **hwákayal**.

**nhákay** NID my body. *3rd poss* **hwákay**. *loc* **nhákeeng**.

**hálŭmii** PC forever, everlasting. **Hálŭ=mii ndalŭmúsi.** 'I went away eventually.'

**hálŭwii** PC more. **Hálŭwii njachíipsi.** 'I speak badly.' *See* **alúwii**.

**hámul** NA hammer. *pl* **hámŭlak**. *poss* **ndahámŭlum**. *obv* **hámŭlal**. *From Dutch.*

**hánaas** NA Hanna. *dimin* **hànáashush**. *obv* **hànáasal**. *From English* Hanna.

**hàshawéesuw** VAI be square *(s.t. animate)*. *conj 3rd sg* **hàshawéesiit**.

**hàshawéeyeew** VII be square. *conj 3rd sg* **hàshawéeyeek**.

**hàshawuchéesuw** VAI have a square shape *(s.t. animate)*. *conj 3rd sg* **hàsh=awuchéesiit**. *ptcpl* **hàshawuchéesiit**.

**hàshawuchéeyeew** VII have a square shape. *conj 3rd sg* **hàshawuchée=yeek**. *ptcpl* **hàshawuchéeyeek**.

**heembtáhŭmeew** VAI wear a shirt. *ind 1st sg* **ndaheembtáhŭma, ndah=eembtáhŭmaam**. *conj 3rd sg* **heembtáhŭmaat**. *imp* **heembtáh=ŭmaal**.

**héembut** NI shirt. *pl* **héembtal**. *poss* **ndahéembut**. *loc* **héembtung**. *dimin* **héembchush**. *From Dutch.*

**héengchiis** NI handkerchief, shawl. *pl* **heengchíisal**. *poss* **ndahéengchiis**. *From English* handkerchief.

**héenŭliis** NA Henry. *obv* **heenŭlíisal**. *From English* Henry.

**héesh** PC every. **Héesh náh ayáan.** 'Everytime I go there.'; **Héesh wŭláakwiik nóox ndukw: "Naat=kóoyeel awasiixkanáwe."** 'Every evening my father told me: "Fetch the cows from the other side of the road."' *See* **éesh**.

**níhkaat** NID my leg. *pl* **nihkáatal**. *3rd poss* **wíhkaat**. *loc* **nihkáatung**. *dimin* **nihkáachush**.

**níhkash** NAD my fingernail. *pl* **níhka=shak**. *3rd poss* **wíhkashal**. *loc* **níhkashung**. *dimin* **níhkashush**.

**nihkáxkwan** NID my shin. *pl* **nihkáx=kwanal**. *3rd poss* **wihkáxkwan**. *loc* **nihkáxkwanung**.

**nihkíiwan** NID my nose. *3rd poss* **wihkíiwan**. *loc* **nihkíiwanung**.

**hóosus** NA kettle, pot. *pl* **hóossak**. *poss* **ndahóosus, ndáhoos, ndahóossum**. *loc* **hóossung**. *obv* **hóossal**.

**nihtángan** NID my back of neck. *3rd poss* **wihtángan**. *loc* **nihtánganung**.

**níhtawak** NID my ear. *pl* **nihtawákal**. *3rd poss* **wíhtawak**. *loc* **nihtawákung**.

**nihtóonay** NAD my beard, my whiskers. *pl* **nihtóonayak**. *3rd poss* **wihtóona=yal**. *See* **wihtóonay**.

**hulŭníixsuw** VAI speak Delaware, speak a native language. *ind 1st sg* **ndihŭ=luníixsi, ndihŭluníixsiim**. *conj 3rd sg* **hulŭníixsiit**. *imp* **hulŭníixsiil**. *ptcpl* **ìhŭluníixsiit**.

**hulŭniixsuwáakan** NI speaking an Indian language; the Delaware language.

**hwákees** NA bark. *pl* **hwakéesak**. *loc* **hwakéesung**. *obv* **hwakéesal**.

# II

**níil** NID my head. *3rd poss* **wíil**. *loc* **níilung**. *dimin* **níilush**. *See* **niilush=tíikan**.

**níilanuw** NID my tongue. *3rd poss* **wíilanuw**. *loc* **níilanoong**.

**níilaxk** NID my hair on head. *pl* **niiláxkal**. *3rd poss* **wíilaxk**. *loc* **niiláxkung**.

**iiláyush** NA Eli. *obv* **iiláyshal**. *From English* Eli.

**níilum** NAD my sister-in-law *(man speaking)*; my brother-in-law *(woman speaking)*. *pl* **níilŭmak**. *3rd poss* **wíilŭmal**.

**niilushtíikan** NID my head. *3rd poss* **wiilushtíikan**. *rare*. *See* **níil**.

**níimat** NAD my brother *(man speaking)*. *pl* **níimatak**. *3rd poss* **wíimatal**. *See* **níimatus**.

**níimatus** NAD my brother *(man speaking)*. *pl* **niimatúsak**. *3rd poss* **wiimatúsal**. *See* **níimat**.

**níip** NID my arrow. *pl* **níipal**. *3rd poss* **wíip**.

**níipiit** NID my tooth. *pl* **niipíital**. *3rd poss* **wíipiit**. *loc* **niipíitung**.

**íipŭleesh** NA Ephraim. *obv* **iipŭléeshal**. *From English* Ephraim.

**íisŭliin** VAI celebrate Easter, be Easter

*(indef subject)*. *indef subject* **íisŭliin**. *conj 3rd sg* **íisŭliing**. *See* **íishtaliin**. *From English* Easter.

**íishtaliin** VAI celebrate Easter, be Easter *(indef subject)*. *indef subject* **íishta=liin**. *conj 3rd sg* **íishtaliing**. *See* **íisŭliin**. *From English* Easter.

ndíit PC I think so. **Ktíit.** 'You think so.'; **Ktíit há?** 'Do you think so?' *See* **liitéeheew**.

**íiyaach** PC still, yet. **Íiyaach ndalóhke.** 'I'm still working.'; **Íiyaach kúsh'si.** 'You're still sweating.'

**iiyéeskwa** PC before. *followed by conjunct verb*. **Noolíixŭmaaw káal iiyéeskwa alúmsiikw.** 'I fixed the car before he left.'; **Nzháyee-kwchíhla=toon iiyéeskwa máhlamaan.** 'I tried it on before I bought it.'

# I

**ihkáaleew** VTA defend s.o. in a fight. *ind 1st sg* **ndihkáalaaw**, **ndihkáala**. *ind 3rd sg* **wtihkaaláawal**. *ind inv* **ndihkáalukw**. *ind I-you* **ktihkáalul**. *conj 3rd sg* **ihkáalaat**. *imp* **íhkaal**.

**ihkáameew** VTA take s.o.'s side in an argument, speak on s.o.'s behalf in an argument, defend s.o. *ind 1st sg* **ndihkáamaaw**, **ndihkáama**. *ind 3rd sg* **wtihkaamáawal**. *ind inv* **ndih=káamukw**. *ind I-you* **ktihkáamul**. *conj 3rd sg* **ihkáamaat**. *imp* **íhkaam**. *ptcpl* **ihkáamaat**.

**ihkpéesuw** VAI boil dry, boil down *(s.t. animate)*. *conj 3rd sg* **ihkpéesiit**. *ptcpl* **ihkpéesiit**.

**ihkpéesum** VTI1B boil s.t. down. *ind 1st sg* **ndihkpéesŭmun**. *ind 3rd sg* **wtihkpéesŭmun**. *conj 1st sg* **ihk=péesŭmaan**. *conj 3rd sg* **ihkpéesung**. *imp* **ihkpéesih**. *ptcpl* **ihkpéesung**.

**ihkpéeteew** VII boil dry, boil down. *conj 3rd sg* **ihkpéeteek**. *ptcpl* **ihkpéeteek**.

**ìhŭlutóonheew** VAI butt in, disrupt the conversation. *ind 1st sg* **ndihŭlut=óonhe**, **ndihŭlutóonheem**. *conj 3rd sg* **ìhŭlutóonheet**. *imp* **ìhŭlutóon=heel**. *ptcpl* **ìhulutóonheet**.

# J

njóos NAD my friend. **Njó.** 'My friend (vocative).' *pl* **njóosak**. *3rd poss* **wchóosal**.

# K

**káa** PC do reluctantly, I guess I'll do *(something)*. **Sháxkii káa nŭmáw-kawí.** 'I guess I'll go to bed.'; **Káa mbúmsi.** 'I'll walk (rather than riding).'

**kaachiipáhtoow** VTI2 hide s.t. in a hurry. *ind 1st sg* **ngaachiipáhtoon**. *ind 3rd sg* **kwaachiipáhtoon**. *conj 1st sg* **kaachiipáhtawaan**. *conj 3rd sg* **kaachiipáhtaakw**. *imp* **kaachii=páhtool**. *ptcpl* **kaachiipáhtaakw**.

**kaachíixiin** VAI hide, lie hidden, be hidden. *ind 1st sg* **ngaachíixiin**, **ngaa=chíixi**. *conj 3rd sg* **kaachíixiing**. *imp* **kaachíixiil**. *ptcpl* **kaachíixiing**.

**kaachíixtoow** VTI2 hide s.t., put s.t. away. *ind 1st sg* **ngaachíixtoon**. *ind 3rd sg* **kwaachíixtoon**. *conj 1st sg* **kaachiixtáwaan**. *conj 3rd sg* **kaa=chíixtaakw**. *imp* **kaachíixtool**. *ptcpl* **kaachíixtaakw**.

**kaachíixŭmeew** VTA hide s.o., put s.o. away. *ind 1st sg* **ngaachíixŭmaaw**, **ngaachíixŭma**. *ind 3rd sg* **kwaachii=xŭmáawal**. *ind inv* **ngaachíixŭmukw**. *ind I-you* **kkaachíixŭmul**. *conj 3rd sg* **kaachíixŭmaat**. *imp* **kaachíixum**.

*ptcpl* **kaachíixŭmaat**.

**kaachíixun** VII hide, lie hidden, be hidden. *conj 3rd sg* **kaachíixung**. *ptcpl* **kaachíixung**.

**kaachíipheew** VTA hide s.o. in a hurry. *ind 1st sg* **ngaachíiphaaw**, **ngaa=chíipha**. *ind 3rd sg* **kwaachiipháa=wal**. *ind inv* **ngaachíiphukw**. *ind I-you* **kaachíiphul**. *conj 3rd sg* **kaa=chíiphaat**. *imp* **kaachíipah**. *ptcpl* **kaachíiphaat**.

**kaaháapŭlush** NA dried apple. *pl* **kaa=haapŭlúshak**. *poss* **ngaahaapŭlúsh=um**. *loc* **kaahaapŭlúshung**. *dimin* **kaahaapŭlúshush**. *obv* **kaahaapŭ=lúshal**.

**kaahahkéeyeew** VII be dry ground. *conj 3rd sg* **kaahahkéeyeek**. *ptcpl* **kaahahkéeyeek**.

**kaaháhkwteew** NI corn soup. *pl* **kaa=hahkwtéewal**. *poss* **ngaahahkw=téehum**.

**káahapwaan** NI dried-out bread. *pl* **kaahapwáanal**. *poss* **ngaahapwáa=num**. *loc* **kaahapwáanung**. *dimin* **kaahapwáanush**.

**kaahiikwáaleew** VTA dry s.o. *(with a towel held in the hand)*. *ind 1st sg* **ngaahiikwáalaaw**, **ngaahiikwáala**. *ind 3rd sg* **kwaahiikwaaláawal**. *ind inv* **ngaahiikwáalukw**. *ind I-you* **kaahiikwáalul**. *conj 3rd sg* **kaahii=kwáalaat**. *imp* **kaahíikwaal**. *ptcpl* **kaahiikwáalaat**.

**káahkeew** VII be dry weather. *conj 3rd sg* **káahkeek**. *ptcpl* **káahkeek**.

**kaahsáasuw** VAI be dried *(by heat, s.t. animate)*. *conj 3rd sg* **kaahsáasiit**. *ptcpl* **kaahsáasiit**.

**kaahsáasuw** VII be dried *(by heat)*. *conj 3rd sg* **kaahsáasiik**. *ptcpl* **kaahsáa=siik**.

**káahseew** VTA dry s.t. animate out *(by heat)*. *ind 1st sg* **ngáahsaaw**, **ngáah=sa**. *ind 3rd sg* **kwaahsáawal**. *ind inv* **ngáahsookw**. *ind I-you* **káahsool**. *conj 3rd sg* **káahsaat**. *imp* **káahus**. *ptcpl* **káahsaat**.

**káahsum** VTI 1B dry s.t. out *(by heat)*. *ind 1st sg* **ngaahsúmun**. *ind 3rd sg* **kwaahsúmun**. *conj 1st sg* **kaah=súmaan**. *conj 3rd sg* **káahsung**. *imp* **káahsih**. *ptcpl* **káahsung**.

**káahsuw** VAI be dry, be dried out *(s.t. animate, by heat)*. *conj 3rd sg* **káahsiit**. *ptcpl* **káahsiit**.

**káahteew** VII be dry, be dried out *(by heat)*. *conj 3rd sg* **káahteek**. *ptcpl* **káahteek**.

**káahxakw** NI piece of dried wood. *pl* **kaahxákwal**. *poss* **ngaahxákwum**. *loc* **kaahxákwung**. *dimin* **kaahxák=wush**.

**kaakáapush** NA butterfly. *pl* **kaakáap=shak**. *poss* **ngaakáapshum**. *loc* **kaakáapshung**. *dimin* **kaakáap=shush**. *obv* **kaakáapshal**.

**kaakiimooxwéewuw** VAI try to be a witch. *ind 1st sg* **ngaakiimooxwéewi**, **ngaakiimooxwéewiim**. *conj 3rd sg* **kaakiimooxwéewiit**. *imp* **kaakii=mooxwéewiil**. *ptcpl* **kaakiimoo=xwéewiit**.

**kaakshaaméhleew** VAI run sort of quickly, run at half-speed. **Móxa kaak=shaaméhleew kíhkata-wéewsuw.** 'He was trotting by because he's nosy.' *ind 1st sg* **ngaakshaaméhla**, **ngaakshaaméhlaam**. *conj 3rd sg* **kaakshaaméhlaat**. *imp* **kaakshaa=méhlaal**. *ptcpl* **kaakshaaméhlaat**.

**kaakŭlóoleew** VTA swear at s.o. *ind 1st sg* **ngaakŭlóolaaw**, **ngaakŭlóola**. *ind 3rd sg* **kwaakulooláawal**. *ind inv* **ngaakŭlóolukw**. *ind I-you* **kaakŭ=lóolul**. *conj 3rd sg* **kaakŭlóolaat**. *imp* **káakŭlool**. *ptcpl* **kaakŭlóolaat**. *See* **kŭlóoleew**.

**kaakŭlóhkeew** VAI swear. *ind 1st sg* **ngaakŭlóhke**, **ngaakŭlóhkeem**. *conj 3rd sg* **kaakŭlóhkeet**. *imp* **kaakŭ=lóhkeel**. *ptcpl* **kaakŭlóhkeet**.

**kaakŭlúksuw** VAI smile. *ind 1st sg* **ngaakŭlúksi**, **ngaakŭlúksiim**. *conj 3rd sg* **kaakŭlúksiit**. *imp* **kaakŭ=lúksiil**. *ptcpl* **kaakulúksiit**.

**kaakŭluksuwiingwéexiin** VAI smile, have a smile on one's face. *ind 1st sg* **ngaakŭluksuwiingwéexiin**, **ngaa=kŭluksuwiingwéexi**. *conj 3rd sg* **kaakŭluksuwiingwéexiing**. *imp* **kaakŭluksuwiingwéexiil**. *ptcpl* **kaakŭluksuwiingwéexiing**.

**káal** NA car, train car. *pl* **káalak**. *poss* **ngáalum**. *loc* **káalung**. *dimin* **káa=lush**. *obv* **káalal**. *See* **ahtamóombiil**. *From English* car.

**káaleew** VTA put s.o. away, hide s.o., put s.t. animate away, hide s.t. animate. *ind 1st sg* **ngáalaaw**, **ngáala**. *ind 3rd sg* **kwaaláawal**. *ind inv* **ngáalukw**. *ind I-you* **káalul**. *conj 3rd sg* **káalaat**. *imp* **káal**. *ptcpl* **káalaat**.

**kaalhámeew** VAI drive a car, use a car. *ind 1st sg* **ngaalháma**, **ngaalhám=aam**. *conj 3rd sg* **kaalhámaat**. *imp* **kaalhámaal**. *ptcpl* **kaalhámaat**.

**káamung** PC the other side of the river.

**kaamŭnúwiing** PC over across the river.

**kaanjchéena** PC goodness!

**káanoos** NA coal oil. *poss* **ngaanóosum**. *obv* **kaanóosal**.

**kaanoosiilamóokan** NA oil can. *pl* **kaa=noosiilamóokanak**. *obv* **kaanoosii=lamóokanal**.

**káanzhŭweew** VII make noise, make a lot of noise. *conj 3rd sg* **káanzhŭ=week**. *ptcpl* **káanzhŭweek**.

**kaanzhaachíimuw** VAI tell a tall tale, tell an exciting story, brag. *ind 1st sg* **ngaanzhaachíimwi**, **ngaanzhaa=chíimwiim**. *conj 3rd sg* **kaanzhaa=chíimwiit**. *imp* **kaanzhaachíimwiil**. *ptcpl* **kaanzhaachíimwiit**. *intensive reduplication* **akaanzhaachíimuw**.

**kaanzhaachŭmóhkaweew** VTA tell s.o. a tall tale, tell s.o. an exciting story. *ind 1st sg* **ngaanzhaachŭmóhka=waaw**, **ngaanzhaachŭmóhkawa**. *ind 3rd sg* **kwaanzhaachŭmohkawáa=wal**. *ind inv* **ngaanzhaachŭmóh=kaakw**. *ind I-you* **kaanzhaachŭ=móhkool**. *conj 3rd sg* **kaanzhaachŭ=móhkawaat**. *imp* **kaanzhaachŭ=móhkaw**. *ptcpl* **kaanzhaachŭmóh=kawaat**.

**kaanzhaalóhkweew** VAI have long hair. *ind 1st sg* **ngaanzhaalóhkwa**, **ngaanzhaalóhkwaam**. *conj 3rd sg* **kaanzhaalóhkwaat**. *ptcpl* **kaan=zhaalóhkwaat**.

**kaanzhahkwíixun** VII be a flood, be a lot of water lying around. *conj 3rd sg* **kaanzhahkwíixung**. *ptcpl* **kaan=zhahkwíixung**.

**kaanzhaláamuw** VAI yell, holler. *ind 1st sg* **ngaanzhaláamwi**, **ngaanzhaláa=mwiim**. *conj 3rd sg* **kaanzhaláa=mwiit**. *imp* **kaanzhaláamwiil**. *ptcpl* **kaanzhaláamwiit**. *intensive reduplication* **akaanzhaláamuw**; *moderative reduplication* **kaakaanzhaláamuw**.

**kaanzhalaamwíhtaweew** VTA yell at s.o. *ind 1st sg* **ngaanzhalaamwíhtawaaw**, **ngaanzhalaamwíhtawa**. *ind 3rd sg* **kwaanzhalaamwihtawáawal**. *ind inv* **ngaanzhalaamwíhtaakw**. *ind I-you* **kaanzhalaamwíhtool**. *conj 3rd sg* **kaanzhalaamwíhtawaat**. *imp* **kaanzhalaamwíhtaw**. *ptcpl* **kaan=zhalaamwíhtawaat**. *intensive reduplication* **kwàkaanzhalaamwih=tawáawal**.

**kaanzháskweew** VII be a lot of weeds. *conj 3rd sg* **kaanzháskweek**. *ptcpl* **kaanzháskweek**.

**káanzhaween** PR important person. *pl* **kaanzhawéeniik**. *obv* **kaanzha=wéeniil**.

**kaanzhchéenaakw** PC goodness! **Kaanzhchéenaakw ndáalu-íin.** 'My goodness, I can't say it.'

**kaanzhéelham** VAI make a lot of tracks. *ind 1st sg* **ngaanzhéelham**. *conj 3rd* *sg* **kaanzhéelhang**. *imp* **kaanzhéel=hah**. *ptcpl* **kaanzhéelhang**.

**kaanzhéelŭmeew** VTA think a lot of s.o., think highly of s.o., have a high regard for s.o. *ind 1st sg* **ngaanzhée=lŭmaaw**, **ngaanzhéelŭma**. *ind 3rd sg* **kwaanzheelŭmáawal**. *ind inv* **ngaanzhéelŭmukw**. *ind I-you* **kaanzhéelŭmul**. *conj 3rd sg* **kaan=zhéelŭmaat**. *imp* **kaanzhéelum**. *ptcpl* **kaanzhéelŭmaat**.

**kaanzheelŭmúkwsuw** VAI be well thought of. *ind 1st sg* **ngaanzhee=lŭmúkwsi**, **ngaanzheelŭmúkwsiim**. *conj 3rd sg* **kaanzheelŭmúkwsiit**. *ptcpl* **kaanzheelŭmúkwsiit**.

**kaanzheelúndam** VOTI1A be surprised. *ind 1st sg* **ngaanzheelúndam**. *conj 3rd sg* **kaanzheelúndang**. *ptcpl* **kaanzheelúndang**.

**kaanzheelúndam** VTI1A think a lot of s.t., think highly of s.t., have a high regard for s.t. *ind 1st sg* **ngaanzhee=lúndamun**. *ind 3rd sg* **kwaanzhee=lúndamun**. *conj 1st sg* **kaanzhee=lúndamaan**. *conj 3rd sg* **kaanzhee=lúndang**. *imp* **kaanzheelúndah**. *ptcpl* **kaanzheelúndang**.

**kaanzh'háhkweew** VAI pound on wood a lot. *ind 1st sg* **ngaanzh'háhkwe**, **ngaanzh'háhkweem**. *conj 3rd sg* **kaanzh'háhkweet**. *imp* **kaanzh'=háhkweel**. *ptcpl* **kaanzh'háhkweet**.

**kaanzh'hiingwéexiin** VAI stare. *ind 1st sg* **ngaanzh'hiingwéexiin**, **ngaanzh'hiingwéexi**. *conj 3rd sg* **kaanzh'hiingwéexiing**. *imp* **kaan=zh'hiingwéexiil**. *ptcpl* **kaanzh'hiin=gwéexiing**, **kaanzh'hiingwéexit**.

**kaanzhiilawéeheew** VTA surprise s.o. *ind 1st sg* **ngaanzhiilawéehaaw**, **ngaanzhiilawéeha**. *ind 3rd sg* **kwaanzhiilaweeháawal**. *ind inv* **ngaanzhiilawéehukw**. *ind I-you* **kaanzhiilawéehul**. *conj 3rd sg* **kaanzhiilawéehaat**. *imp* **kaanzhíi=laweeh**. *ptcpl* **kaanzhiilawéehaat**.

**kaanzhiináakwat** VII look important. *conj 3rd sg* **kaanzhiináakwahk**. *ptcpl* **kaanzhiináakwahk**.

**kaanzhiináakwsuw** VAI look important *(s.t. animate)*. *ind 1st sg* **ngaanzhii=náakwsi**, **ngaanzhiináakwsiim**. *conj 3rd sg* **kaanzhiináakwsiit**. *ptcpl* **kaanzhiináakwsiit**.

**kaanzhiingwahtawásuw** VAI make a lot of smoke. *ind 1st sg* **ngaanzhiin=gwahtawási**, **ngaanzhiingwahta=wásiim**. *conj 3rd sg* **kaanzhiing=wahtawásiit**. *imp* **kaanzhiingwah=tawásiil**. *ptcpl* **kaanzhiingwahta=wásiit**.

**kaanzhiingwáhteew** VII be a lot of smoke *(from a chimney)*; be smoky. *conj 3rd sg* **kaanzhiingwáhteek**. *ptcpl* **kaanzhiingwáhteek**.

**kaanzhiingwahteeníikeew** VAI make a lot of smoke, make a lot of smoke with things. *ind 1st sg* **ngaanzhiin=gwahteeníike**, **ngaanzhiingwahtee=níikeem**. *conj 3rd sg* **kaanzhiin=gwahteeníikeet**. *imp* **kaanzhiin=gwahteeníikeel**. *ptcpl* **kaanzhiin=gwahteeníikeet**.

**kaanzhíixsuw** VAI talk a lot, brag. *ind 1st sg* **ngaanzhíixsi**, **ngaanzhíixsiim**. *conj 3rd sg* **kaanzhíixsiit**. *imp* **kaan=zhíixsiil**. *ptcpl* **kaanzhíixsiit**.

**kaanzhihtáakwat** VII be a great noise, be a big rumour, be a great report of an activity *(especially of a story that gets modified or exaggerated)*. *conj 3rd sg* **kaanzhihtáakwahk**. *ptcpl* **kaanzhihtáakwahk**.

**kaanzhihtáakwsuw** VAI make a great noise *(s.t. animate)*. *ind 1st sg* **ngaanzhihtáakwsi**, **ngaanzhihtáa=kwsiim**. *conj 3rd sg* **kaanzhihtáa=kwsiit**. *imp* **kaanzhihtáakwsiil**. *ptcpl* **kaanzhihtáakwsiit**.

**kaanzhihtóonayeew** VAI have a heavy beard. *ind 1st sg* **ngaanzhihtóonaya**, ngaanzhihtóonayaam. *conj 3rd sg* **kaanzhihtóonayaat**. *ptcpl* **kaanzh=ihtóonayaat**.

**kaanzhpéhleew** VAI be hemorrhaging. *ind 1st sg* **ngaanzhpéhla, ngaanzh=péhlaam**. *conj 3rd sg* **kaanzhpéh=laat**. *ptcpl* **kaanzhpéhlaat**. *intensive reduplication* **akaanzhpéhleew**.

**kaanzhtóonheew** VAI talk lots. *ind 1st sg* **ngaanzhtóonhe, ngaanzhtóon=heem**. *conj 3rd sg* **kaanzhtóonheet**. *imp* **kaanzhtóonheel**. *ptcpl* **kaanzh=tóonheet**.

**kaanzhu-** PV great, wonderful, amazing. **Káanzhu-léew.** 'Something wonderful happened.' *ptcpl* **káanzhu-**.

**káanzhŭweew** VAI make noise, make a lot of noise. *ind 1st sg* **ngáanzhŭwe, ngáanzhŭweem**. *conj 3rd sg* **káanzhŭweet**. *imp* **káanzhŭweel**. *ptcpl* **káanzhŭweet**.

**kaanzhŭwéhtoow** VTI2 make s.t. make noise *(especially when blowing a horn)*. *ind 1st sg* **ngaanzhŭwéhtoon**. *ind 3rd sg* **kwaanzhŭwéhtoon**. *conj 1st sg* **kaanzhuwéhtawaan**. *conj 3rd sg* **kaanzhŭwéhtaakw**. *imp* **kaan=zhŭwéhtool**. *ptcpl* **kaanzhŭwéh=taakw**.

**kaasahkhwíikan** NI tea towel. *pl* **kaasahkhwíikanal**. *poss* **ngaasahk=hwíikan**. *loc* **kaasahkhwíikanung**. *dimin* **kaashahkhwíikanush**.

**káasameew** VTA lick s.o., wipe s.t. animate with the mouth. *ind 1st sg* **ngáasamaaw, ngáasama**. *ind 3rd sg* **kwaasamáawal**. *ind inv* **ngáasa=mukw**. *ind I-you* **káasamul**. *conj 3rd sg* **káasamaat**. *imp* **káasam**. *ptcpl* **káasamaat**.

**kaasándam** VTI1A lick s.t., wipe s.t. with the mouth. *ind 1st sg* **ngaasán=damun**. *ind 3rd sg* **kwaasándamun**. *conj 1st sg* **kaasándamaan**. *conj 3rd sg* **kaasándang**. *imp* **kaasándah**. *ptcpl* **kaasándang**.

**kaaschéaleew** VAI wipe one's nose. *ind 1st sg* **ngaascháala, ngaascháalaam**. *conj 3rd sg* **kaascháalaat**. *imp* **kaascháalaal**. *ptcpl* **kaascháalaat**.

**kaaschásuw** VAI be faded *(s.t. animate, by sun or heat)*. *ind 1st sg* **ngaas=chási, ngaaschásiim**. *conj 3rd sg* **kaaschásiit**. *ptcpl* **kaaschásiit**.

**kaascháteew** VII be faded *(by sun or heat)*. *conj 3rd sg* **kaascháteek**. *ptcpl* **kaascháteek**.

**káas'heew** VTA wipe s.o. off, wipe s.t. animate off. *ind 1st sg* **ngáas'haaw, ngáas'ha**. *ind 3rd sg* **kwaas'háawal**. *ind inv* **ngáas'hookw**. *ind I-you* **káas'hool**. *conj 3rd sg* **káas'haat**. *imp* **káas'haw**. *ptcpl* **káas'haat**.

**káas'ham** VTI1A wipe s.t. off. *ind 1st sg* **ngaas'hámun**. *ind 3rd sg* **kwaas'=hámun**. *conj 1st sg* **kaas'hámaan**. *conj 3rd sg* **káas'hang**. *imp* **káas'hah**. *ptcpl* **káas'hang**.

**kaas'híikan** NI cloth for wiping. *pl* **kaas'híikanal**. *poss* **ngaas'híikan**. *loc* **kaas'híikanung**. *dimin* **kaash'híikanush**.

**kaasiikwáaleew** VTA wipe s.o. off. *ind 1st sg* **ngaasiikwáalaaw, ngaasii=kwáala**. *ind 3rd sg* **kwaasiikwaa=láawal**. *ind inv* **ngaasiikwáalukw**. *ind I-you* **kaasiikwáalul**. *conj 3rd sg* **kaasiikwáalaat**. *imp* **kaasíikwaal**. *ptcpl* **kaasiikwáalaat**.

**kaasíikwam** VTI1A wipe s.t. off. *ind 1st sg* **ngaasíikwamun**. *ind 3rd sg* **kwaasíikwamun**. *conj 1st sg* **kaa=síikwamaan**. *conj 3rd sg* **kaasíi=kwang**. *imp* **kaasíikwah**. *ptcpl* **kaasíikwang**.

**kaasíhleew** VAI be faded *(s.t. animate, of colours)*. *conj 3rd sg* **kaasíhlaat**. *ptcpl* **kaasíhlaat**.

**kaasíhleew** VII be faded *(of colours)*. *conj 3rd sg* **kaasíhlaak**. *ptcpl* **kaasíhlaak**.

**kaaspáteew** VII be faded from washing.

*conj 3rd sg* **kaaspáteek**. *ptcpl* **kaaspáteek**.
**kaaspátoow** VTI2 wash s.t. and make it fade, make s.t. fade by washing it. *ind 1st sg* **ngaaspátoon**. *ind 3rd sg* **kwaaspátoon**. *conj 1st sg* **kaaspát=awaan**. *conj 3rd sg* **kaaspátaakw**. *imp* **kaaspátool**. *ptcpl* **kaaspátaakw**.
**kaassiitéexiin** VAI wipe one's feet. *ind 1st sg* **ngaassiitéexiin**, **ngaassiitéexi**. *conj 3rd sg* **kaassiitéexiing**. *imp* **kaassiitéexiil**. *ptcpl* **kaassiitéexiing**, **kaassiitéexiit**.
**kaasxásuw** VAI be faded *(s.t. animate, by heat)*. *ind 1st sg* **ngaasxási**, **ngaasxásiim**. *conj 3rd sg* **kaasxásiit**. *ptcpl* **kaasxásiit**.
**kaasxáteew** VII be faded *(by heat)*. *conj 3rd sg* **kaasxáteek**. *ptcpl* **kaasxáteek**.
**kaatáhleew** VTA put s.t. animate away, put s.o. away, hide s.o. *ind 1st sg* **ngaatáhlaaw**, **ngaatáhla**. *ind 3rd sg* **kwaatahláawal**. *ind inv* **ngaatáh=lukw**. *ind I-you* **kaatáhlul**. *conj 3rd sg* **kaatáhlaat**. *imp* **káatahl**. *ptcpl* **kaatáhlaat**.
**kaatáhteew** VII be hidden, lie placed out of sight. *conj 3rd sg* **kaatáhteek**. *ptcpl* **kaatáhteek**.
**kaatáhtoow** VTI2 put s.t. away, hide s.t. *ind 1st sg* **ngaatáhtoon**. *ind 3rd sg* **kwaatáhtoon**. *conj 1st sg* **kaatáh=tawaan**. *conj 3rd sg* **kaatáhtaakw**. *imp* **kaatáhtool**. *ptcpl* **kaatáhtaakw**.
**kaatáhwheew** VAI hide eggs *(of chickens)*. *ind 1st sg* **ngaatáhwhe**, **ngaa=táhwheem**. *conj 3rd sg* **kaatáhwheet**. *imp* **kaatáhwheel**. *ptcpl* **kaatáhw=heet**.
**kaatakóosuw** VAI climb out of sight. *ind 1st sg* **ngaatakóosi**, **ngaatakóosiim**. *conj 3rd sg* **kaatakóosiit**. *imp* **kaatakóosiil**. *ptcpl* **kaatakóosiit**.
**kaatapóomeew** VTA hide from s.o. *ind 1st sg* **ngaatapóomaaw**, **ngaatapóo=ma**. *ind 3rd sg* **kwaatapoomáawal**. *ind inv* **ngaatapóomukw**. *ind I-you* **kaatapóomul**. *conj 3rd sg* **kaata=póomaat**. *imp* **káatapoom**. *ptcpl* **kaatapóomaat**.
**káatapuw** VAI hide, hide sitting down. *ind 1st sg* **ngáatapi**, **ngáatapiim**. *conj 3rd sg* **káatapiit**. *imp* **káatapiil**. *ptcpl* **káatapiit**.
**kaatasánuw** VAIO hide s.t. while carrying it. *ind 1st sg* **ngaatasániin**. *ind 3rd sg* **kwaatasániin**. *conj 3rd sg* **kaatasániit**. *imp* **kaatasániil**. *ptcpl* **kaatasániit**.
**kaateelawúsuw** VAI play hide-and-seek. *ind 1st sg* **ngaateelawúsi**, **ngaatee=lawúsiim**. *conj 3rd sg* **kaateela=wúsiit**. *imp* **kaateelawúsiil**. *ptcpl* **kaateelawúsiit**. *See* **kahkáatapuw**.
**káatoow** VTI2 put s.t. away, hide s.t. *ind 1st sg* **ngáatoon**. *ind 3rd sg* **kwáa=toon**. *conj 1st sg* **káatawaan**. *conj 3rd sg* **káataakw**. *imp* **káatool**. *ptcpl* **káataakw**.
**kaatohkwéepuw** VAI hide, hide sitting down. *ind 1st sg* **ngaatohkwéepi**, **ngaatohkwéepiim**. *conj 3rd sg* **kaatohkwéepiit**. *imp* **kaatohkwée=piil**. *ptcpl* **kaatohkwéepiit**.
**káatŭneew** VTA hide s.o. *(using the hands)*. *ind 1st sg* **ngáatŭnaaw**, **ngáatŭna**. *ind 3rd sg* **kwaatŭnáa=wal**. *ind inv* **ngáatŭnukw**. *ind I-you* **káatŭnul**. *conj 3rd sg* **káatŭnaat**. *imp* **káatun**. *ptcpl* **káatŭnaat**.
**káatŭnum** VTI1B hide s.t. *(using the hands)*. *ind 1st sg* **ngaatŭnúmun**. *ind 3rd sg* **kwaatŭnúmun**. *conj 1st sg* **kaatŭnúmaan**. *conj 3rd sg* **káa=tŭnung**. *imp* **káatŭnih**. *ptcpl* **káatŭnung**.
**kaatxákhweew** VAI cut cordwood. *ind 1st sg* **ngaatxákhwe**, **ngaatxák=hweem**. *conj 3rd sg* **kaatxákhweet**. *imp* **kaatxákhweel**. *ptcpl* **kaa=txákhweet**.
**káatxakw** NI cord wood. *pl* **kaatxák=**

**wal**. *poss* **ngaatxákwum**. *loc* **kaat=xákwung**. *dimin* **kaatxákwush**. *From English* cord.

**káawunzh** NA thistle. *pl* **kaawúnzhak**. *dimin* **kaawúnzhush**. *obv* **kaa=wúnzhal**.

**kaawúnzhahkw** NA thistle bush. *pl* **kaawunzháhkwak**. *obv* **kaawun=zháhkwal**.

**kaawunzhíhkeew** VII be a lot of thistles. *conj 3rd sg* **kaawunzhíhkeek**. *ptcpl* **kaawunzhíhkeek**.

**kaaxkamámeew** VTA have s.t. animate that feels rough. **Ngaaxkamámaaw ngútkuw.** 'My knee feels rough.' *ind 1st sg* **ngaaxkamámaaw**, **ngaaxka=máma**. *ind 3rd sg* **kwaaxkamam=áawal**. *conj 3rd sg* **kaaxkamámaat**. *ptcpl* **kaaxkamámaat**.

**kaaxkamámkwat** VII feel rough. *conj 3rd sg* **kaaxkamámkwahk**. *ptcpl* **kaaxkamámkwahk**.

**kaaxkamamkwúsuw** VAI feel rough (*s.t. animate*). *ind 1st sg* **ngaaxka=mamkwúsi**, **ngaaxkamamkwúsiim**. *conj 3rd sg* **kaaxkamamkwúsiit**. *ptcpl* **kaaxkamamkwúsiit**.

**kaaxkamándam** VTI1A have s.t. that feels rough. **Ngaaxkamándamun ngwundáakan.** 'My throat feels rough.' *ind 1st sg* **ngaaxkamán=damun**. *ind 3rd sg* **kwaaxkamán=damun**. *conj 1st sg* **kaaxkamán=damaan**. *conj 3rd sg* **kaaxkamán=dang**. *ptcpl* **kaaxkamándang**.

**káaxkasheew** VII be rough, be coarse. *conj 3rd sg* **káaxkasheek**. *ptcpl* **káaxkasheek**.

**kaaxkashii-** PN rough, coarse. **Káax=kashii-lohkhámun.** 'Coarse flour.'; **Káaxkashii-wshapakwíiwan.** 'Coarse cloth.'

**káaxkashii-chkwál** NA toad. *pl* **káax=kashii-chkwálak**. *loc* **káaxkashii-chkwálung**. *dimin* **káaxkashii-chkwálush**. *obv* **káaxkashii-chkwálal**.

**kaaxkashúsuw** VAI be rough, be coarse (*s.t. animate*). *ind 1st sg* **ngaaxka=shúsi**, **ngaaxkashúsiim**. *conj 3rd sg* **kaaxkashúsiit**. *ptcpl* **kaaxkashúsiit**.

**kaaxkiipóokwsuw** VAI taste rough (*s.t. animate*). *conj 3rd sg* **kaaxkii=póokwsiit**. *ptcpl* **kaaxkiipóokwsiit**.

**káaxksuw** VAI be rough (*s.t. animate*). *ind 1st sg* **ngáaxksi**, **ngáaxksiim**. *conj 3rd sg* **káaxksiit**. *ptcpl* **káaxksiit**.

**kaaxksheetóoneew** VAI have rough lips. *ind 1st sg* **ngaaxksheetóona**, **ngaax=ksheetóonaam**. *conj 3rd sg* **kaaxk=sheetóonaat**. *ptcpl* **kaaxkshee=tóonaat**.

**kaaxkŭnáxkeew** VAI have rough hands, have chapped hands. *ind 1st sg* **ngaaxkŭnáxka**, **ngaaxkŭnáxkaam**. *conj 3rd sg* **kaaxkŭnáxkaat**. *ptcpl* **kaaxkŭnáxkaat**.

**káaxkw** NA heron. *pl* **káaxkwak**. *obv* **káaxkwal**.

**kách** PC even. **Kách wáak?** 'What, again?'; **Nál kách apwáan noolíh=toon.** 'I've already made the bread.'

**kahkáatapuw** VAI play hide-and-seek. *ind 1st sg* **ngahkáatapi**, **ngahkáa=tapiim**. *conj 3rd sg* **kahkáatapiit**. *imp* **kahkáatapiil**. *ptcpl* **kahkáa=tapiit**. *See* **kaateelawúsuw**.

**kahkanaapamúkwat** VII be a plain colour, be plain coloured. *conj 3rd sg* **kahkanaapamúkwahk**. *ptcpl* **kahkanaapamúkwahk**.

**kahkanaapamúkwsuw** VAI be a plain colour, be plain coloured (*s.t. animate*). *ind 1st sg* **ngahkanaapa=múkwsi**, **ngahkanaapamúkwsiim**. *conj 3rd sg* **kahkanaapamúkwsiit**. *ptcpl* **kahkanaapamúkwsiit**.

**kahkanákuw** VAI dress plainly, be dressed plainly. *ind 1st sg* **ngahka=nákwi**, **ngahkanákwiim**. *conj 3rd sg* **kahkanákwiit**. *imp* **kahkanákwiil**. *ptcpl* **kahkanákwiit**.

**kahkanii-** PN plain, ordinary. **Káhkanii-kshíiteew.** 'Broth, plain soup.'
**kahkaniináakwat** VII be plain looking, have a plain appearance. *conj 3rd sg* **kahkaniináakwahk**. *ptcpl* **kahka=niináakwahk**.
**kahkaniináakwsuw** VAI be plain looking, have a plain appearance *(s.t. animate)*. *ind 1st sg* **ngahkaniináakwsi**, **ngahkaniináakwsiim**. *conj 3rd sg* **kahkaniináakwsiit**. *ptcpl* **kahkanii=náakwsiit**.
**kahkaniipóokwat** VII have a plain taste. *conj 3rd sg* **kahkaniipóokwahk**. *ptcpl* **kahkaniipóokwahk**.
**kahkaniipóokwsuw** VAI have a plain taste *(s.t. animate)*. *ind 1st sg* **ngah=kaniipóokwsi**, **ngahkaniipóokw=siim**. *conj 3rd sg* **kahkaniipóokwsiit**. *ptcpl* **kahkaniipóokwsiit**.
**káhkham** VTI1A scrape s.t. *(using a tool or instrument)*. *ind 1st sg* **ngahk=hámun**. *ind 3rd sg* **kwahkhámun**. *conj 1st sg* **kahkhámaan**. *conj 3rd sg* **káhkhang**. *imp* **káhkhah**. *ptcpl* **káhkhang**.
**káhkheew** VTA scrape s.o., scrape s.t. animate *(using a tool or instrument)*. *ind 1st sg* **ngáhkhaaw**, **ngáhkha**. *ind 3rd sg* **kwahkháawal**. *ind inv* **ngáhkhookw**. *ind I-you* **káhkhool**. *conj 3rd sg* **káhkhaat**. *imp* **káhkhaw**. *ptcpl* **káhkhaat**.
**kahkhíikan** NI scraper. *pl* **kahkhíika=nal**. *poss* **ngahkhíikan**. *loc* **kahk=híikanung**. *dimin* **kahkhíikanush**.
**kahkhíhpŭneew** VAI scrape potatoes. *ind 1st sg* **ngahkhíhpŭne**, **ngahk=híhpŭneem**. *conj 3rd sg* **kahkhíh=pŭneet**. *imp* **kahkhíhpŭneel**. *ptcpl* **kahkhíhpŭneet**.
**kahkíikwam** VTI1A scrape s.t. *ind 1st sg* **ngahkíikwamun**. *ind 3rd sg* **kwah=kíikwamun**. *conj 1st sg* **kahkíikwa=maan**. *conj 3rd sg* **kahkíikwang**. *imp* **kahkíikwah**. *ptcpl* **kahkíikwang**.
**kàkatíhkeew** VII have grooves *(usually of wooden objects)*. *conj 3rd sg* **kàkatíhkeek**. *ptcpl* **kàkatíhkeek**.
**kàkatihkíhtoow** VTI2 make grooves in s.t. *ind 1st sg* **ngakatihkíhtoon**. *ind 3rd sg* **kwakatihkíhtoon**. *conj 1st sg* **kàkatihkíhtawaan**. *conj 3rd sg* **kàkatihkíhtaakw**. *imp* **kàkatihkíh=tool**. *ptcpl* **kàkatihkíhtaakw**.
**kàkchúkamuw** VAI be in a group of people crowded close together, make one's way through the crowd. *ind 1st sg* **ngakchúkamwi**, **ngakchúka=mwiim**. *conj 3rd sg* **kàkchúkamwiit**. *imp* **kàkchúkamwiil**. *ptcpl* **kàk=chúkamwiit**.
**kàkpíixiin** VAI be in the way. *ind 1st sg* **ngakpíixiin**, **ngakpíixi**. *conj 3rd sg* **kàkpíixiing**. *ptcpl* **kàkpíixiing**.
**kàkpíixun** VII be in the way. *conj 3rd sg* **kàkpíixung**. *ptcpl* **kàkpíixung**. *See* **kpíixun**.
**kàktákkeew** VAI do a fast dance. *ind 1st sg* **ngaktákka**, **ngaktákkaam**. *conj 3rd sg* **kàktákkaat**. *imp* **kàktákkaal**. *ptcpl* **kàktákkaat**. *See* **akutakúkeew**.
**kàktóohŭweew** VII creak. *conj 3rd sg* **kàktóohŭweek**. *ptcpl* **kàktóohŭ=week**.
**kálul** NI collar. *pl* **kálŭlal**. *poss* **ngálŭlum**. *From English* collar.
**kamúkhweew** VTA soak s.o., soak s.t. animate. *ind 1st sg* **ngamkwáhaaw**, **ngamkwáha**. *ind 3rd sg* **kwam=kwaháawal**. *ind inv* **ngamkwáh=ookw**. *ind I-you* **kamkwáhool**. *conj 3rd sg* **kamúkhwaat**. *imp* **kamúkwah**. *ptcpl* **keemkwáhaat**.
**kamukhwáasuw** VAI soak in the water *(s.t. animate)*. *ind 1st sg* **ngamkwah=áasi**, **ngamkwaháasiim**. *conj 3rd sg* **kamukhwáasiit**. *imp* **kamukhwáa=siil**. *ptcpl* **keemkwaháasiit**.
**kamukhwáasuw** VII soak in the water. *conj 3rd sg* **kamukhwáasiik**. *ptcpl* **keemkwaháasiik**.

**kamúkhwam** VTI1A soak s.t. in the water. *ind 1st sg* **ngamkwáhŭmun**. *ind 3rd sg* **kwamkwáhŭmun**. *conj 1st sg* **kamukhwámaan**. *conj 3rd sg* **kamúkhwang**. *imp* **kamúkhwah**. *ptcpl* **keemkwáhang**.

**kamukwáaheew** VAIO throw s.t. in the water. *ind 1st sg* **ngamkwáaheen**. *ind 3rd sg* **kwamkwáaheen**. *conj 3rd sg* **kamukwáaheet**. *imp* **kamukwáa=heel**. *ptcpl* **keemkwáaheet**.

**kamukwáakchehl** VAI jump in the water. *ind 1st sg* **ngamkwáakchehl**. *conj 3rd sg* **kamukwaakchéhluk**. *imp* **kamukwaakchéhlih**. *ptcpl* **keemkwaakchéhluk**.

**kamukwchéhleew** VAI drive through the water. *ind 1st sg* **ngamkwuchéhla**, **ngamkwuchéhlaam**. *conj 3rd sg* **kamukwchéhlaat**. *imp* **kamukw=chéhlaal**. *ptcpl* **keemkwuchéhlaat**.

**kamukwíixiin** VAI lie immersed in the water, lie soaking in the water. *ind 1st sg* **ngamkwíixiin**, **ngamkwíixi**. *conj 3rd sg* **kamukwíixiing**. *imp* **kamuk=wíixiil**. *ptcpl* **keemkwíixiing**. *moderative reduplication* **kaakamu=kwíixiin**.

**kamukwíixtoow** VTI2 lay s.t. to soak in the water. *ind 1st sg* **ngamkwíixtoon**. *ind 3rd sg* **kwamkwíixtoon**. *conj 1st sg* **kamukwiixtáwaan**. *conj 3rd sg* **kamukwíixtaakw**. *imp* **kamukwíix=tool**.*ptcpl* **keemkwíixtaakw**.

**kamukwíixŭmeew** VTA lay s.o. to soak in the water. *ind 1st sg* **ngamkwíi=xŭmaaw**, **ngamkwíixŭma**. *ind 3rd sg* **kwamkwiixŭmáawal**. *ind inv* **ngamkwíixŭmukw**. *ind I-you* **kam=kwíixŭmul**. *conj 3rd sg* **kamukwíi=xŭmaat**. *imp* **kamukwíixum**. *ptcpl* **keemkwíixŭmaat**.

**kamukwíixun** VII lie immersed in the water, lie soaking in the water. *conj 3rd sg* **kamukwíixung**. *ptcpl* **keem=kwíixung**.

**kamukwíhleew** VAI fall in the water, get soaked, get immersed. *ind 1st sg* **ngamkwíhla**, **ngamkwíhlaam**. *conj 3rd sg* **kamukwíhlaat**. *ptcpl* **keem=kwíhlaat**.

**kamukwkáateew** VAI soak one's legs in the water, put one's legs in the water. *ind 1st sg* **ngamkwukáata**, **ngam=kwukáataam**. *conj 3rd sg* **kamukw=káataat**. *imp* **kamukwkáataal**. *ptcpl* **keemkwukáataat**.

**kamukwkaatéexiin** VAI have one's legs in the water. *ind 1st sg* **ngamkwuk=aatéexiin**, **ngamkwukaatéexi**. *conj 3rd sg* **kamukwkaatéexiing**. *imp* **kamukwkaatéexiil**. *ptcpl* **keem=kwukaatéexiit**.

**kamukwsíiteew** VAI soak one's feet in the water. *ind 1st sg* **ngamkwusíita**, **ngamkwusíitaam**. *conj 3rd sg* **kamukwsíitaat**. *imp* **kamukwsíitaal**. *ptcpl* **keemkwusíitaat**.

**kamukwsiitéexiin** VAI soak one's feet in the water, have one's feet in the water. *ind 1st sg* **ngamkwusiitéexiin**, **ngamkwusiitéexi**. *conj 3rd sg* **ka=mukwsiitéexiing**. *imp* **kamukwsii=téexiil**. *ptcpl* **keemkwusiitéexiit**.

**kamukwshíiheew** VTA chase s.o. into the water, drive s.o. into the water. *ind 1st sg* **ngamkwushíihaaw**, **ngamkwushíiha**. *ind 3rd sg* **kwam=kwushiiháawal**. *ind inv* **ngam=kwushíihukw**. *ind I-you* **kam=kwushíihul**. *conj 3rd sg* **kamukw=shíihaat**. *imp* **kamúkwshiih**. *ptcpl* **keemkwushíihaat**.

**kamúkwŭneew** VTA soak s.o. in water *(using the hands)*. *ind 1st sg* **ngam=kwúnaaw**, **ngamkwúna**. *ind 3rd sg* **kwamkwŭnáawal**. *ind inv* **ngam=kwúnukw**. *ind I-you* **kamkwúnul**. *conj 3rd sg* **kamúkwŭnaat**. *imp* **kamúkwun**. *ptcpl* **keemkwúnaat**.

**kamukwŭnáxkeew** VAI soak one's hand(s) in water, immerse one's hand(s) in water. *ind 1st sg* **ngam=kwunáxka**, **ngamkwunáxkaam**. *conj 3rd sg* **kamukwŭnáxkaat**. *imp* **kamukwŭnáxkaal**. *ptcpl* **keem=kwunáxkaat**.

**kamukwŭnaxkéexiin** VAI have one's hand(s) in water, soak one's hand(s) in water. *ind 1st sg* **ngamkwunax=kéexiin**, **ngamkwunaxkéexi**. *conj 3rd sg* **kamukwŭnaxkéexiing**. *imp* **kamukwŭnaxkéexiil**. *ptcpl* **keem=kwunaxkéexiit**.

**kamúkwŭnum** VTI1B soak s.t. in water *(using the hands)*. *ind 1st sg* **ngam=kwúnŭmun**. *ind 3rd sg* **kwam=kwúnŭmun**. *conj 1st sg* **kamukwŭ=númaan**. *conj 3rd sg* **kamúkwŭnung**. *imp* **kamúkwŭnih**. *ptcpl* **keem=kwúnung**.

**kang-** PV can do something *(that was previously impossible)*. *informal*. **Nál nú nóonj-káng- náh wáxkiich lŭmátapiin nehnayóongsung.** 'That's the reason why I was able to sit on top of the horse.' *ptcpl* **kéeng-**. *See* **kangu-**.

**kangu-** PV can do something *(that was previously impossible)*. *informal*. **Kángu- áa há nú -kíish-lúnŭmun?** 'Can you do it?'; **Kwángu- áa há nú -kíish-lúnŭmun?** 'Can he do it?' *ptcpl* **kéengu-**. *See* **kang-**.

**kapées** NA twin. *pl* **kapéesak**. *dimin* **kapéeshush**. *obv* **kapéesal**.

**kapéesŭwak** VAI be twins. *usually plural*. *ind 1st pl* **ngapeesíhna**. *conj 3rd pl* **kapeesíhtiit**. *ptcpl* **keepeesíhtiit**.

**kaskatéeneew** VTA hold s.o. tightly around the waist, have one's arms around s.t. animate. *ind 1st sg* **ngas=katéenaaw**, **ngaskatéena**. *ind 3rd sg* **kwaskateenáawal**. *ind inv* **ngaska=téenukw**. *ind I-you* **kaskatéenul**. *conj 3rd sg* **kaskatéenaat**. *imp* **káskateen**. *ptcpl* **keeskatéenaat**.

**kaskatéenum** VTI1B hold s.t. tightly, have one's arms around s.t. *ind 1st sg* **ngaskatéenŭmun**. *ind 3rd sg* **kwas=katéenŭmun**. *conj 1st sg* **kaskatée=nŭmaan**. *conj 3rd sg* **kaskatéenung**. *imp* **kaskatéenih**. *ptcpl* **keeskatée=nung**.

**káskham** VTI1A mark s.t. *(using a tool or instrument)*; make a mark on s.t. *(using a tool or instrument)*. *ind 1st sg* **ngaskhámun**. *ind 3rd sg* **kwask=hámun**. *conj 1st sg* **kaskhámaan**. *conj 3rd sg* **káskhang**. *imp* **káskhah**. *ptcpl* **kéeskhang**.

**káskheew** VTA put a mark on s.t. animate *(using a tool or instrument)*. *ind 1st sg* **ngáskhaaw**, **ngáskha**. *ind 3rd sg* **kwaskháawal**. *ind inv* **ngásk=hookw**. *ind I-you* **káskhool**. *conj 3rd sg* **káskhaat**. *imp* **káskhaw**. *ptcpl* **kéeskhaat**.

**káshayeem** NI green bean. *pl* **kàsha=yéemal**. *poss* **ngashayéemum**. *dimin* **kàshayéemush**.

**katáaleew** VTA want s.o. *ind 1st sg* **ngatáalaaw**, **ngatáala**. *ind 3rd sg* **kwàtaaláawal**. *ind inv* **ngatáalukw**. *ind I-you* **katáalul**. *conj 3rd sg* **katáalaat**. *ptcpl* **keetáalaat**.

**katáalkwat** VII be wanted, be needed. *conj 3rd sg* **katáalkwahk**. *ptcpl* **keetáalkwahk**.

**kataalkwúsuw** VAI be wanted, be needed *(s.t. animate)*. *ind 1st sg* **ngataal=kwúsi**, **ngataalkwúsiim**. *conj 3rd sg* **kataalkwúsiit**. *ptcpl* **keetaalkwúsiit**.

**katáatam** VTI1A want s.t., need s.t. *ind 1st sg* **ngatáatamun**. *ind 3rd sg* **kwàtáatamun**. *conj 1st sg* **katáata=maan**. *conj 3rd sg* **katáatang**. *ptcpl* **keetáatang**.

**kata-** PV want to, intend. **Katá-sóokŭ=laan.** 'It's going to rain.'; **Ngáta-kihkŭlóolaaw.** 'I want to talk to him.' *ptcpl* **kéeta-**.

**katá-waapéenzuw** VAI want a share of an inheritance *(especially someone* *who is not a member of the immediate family). ind 1st sg* **ngáta-waa=péenzi, ngáta-waapéenziim**. *conj 3rd sg* **katá-waapéenziit**. *ptcpl* **kéeta-waapéenziit**.

**katá-wéewsuw** VAI be nosy, want to know things. *ind 1st sg* **ngáta-wéewsi, ngáta-wéewsiim**. *conj 3rd sg* **katá-wéewsiit**. *ptcpl* **kéeta-wéewsiit**. *intensive reduplication* **kíhkata-wéewsuw**. *See* **kíhkata-wéewsuw**.

**kátoon** NI cotton batting. *pl* **kàtóonal**. *poss* **ngatóonum**. *dimin* **kàchóo=nush**. *From Dutch.*

**katoonáasuw** VAI want to fight, want to compete. *ind 1st sg* **ngatoonáasi, ngatoonáasiim**. *conj 3rd sg* **katoo=náasiit**. *ptcpl* **keetoonáasiit**.

**katóonaleew** VTA want to fight s.o., want to kill s.o., want to compete with s.o. *ind 1st sg* **ngatóonalaaw, ngatóonala**. *ind 3rd sg* **kwàtoona=láawal**. *ind inv* **ngatóonalukw**. *ind I-you* **katóonalul**. *conj 3rd sg* **katóo=nalaat**. *ptcpl* **keetóonalaat**.

**katóopuw** VAI be hungry; have the sole of one's shoe come off and flap around. *ind 1st sg* **ngatóopwi, ngat=óopwiim**. *conj 3rd sg* **katóopwiit**. *ptcpl* **keetóopwiit**. *moderative reduplication* **kaakatóopuw**.

**katóopweew** VTA be hungry for s.t. animate. *ind 1st sg* **ngatóopwaaw, ngatóopwa**. *ind 3rd sg* **kwàtoop=wáawal**. *conj 3rd sg* **katóopwaat**. *ptcpl* **keetóopwaat**.

**katóosŭmuw** VAI be thirsty. *ind 1st sg* **ngatóosŭmwi, ngatóosŭmwiim**. *conj 3rd sg* **katóosŭmwiit**. *ptcpl* **keetóo=sŭmwiit**.

**katóotam** VTI 1A be hungry for s.t. *ind 1st sg* **ngatóotamun**. *ind 3rd sg* **kwàtóotamun**. *conj 1st sg* **katóota=maan**. *conj 3rd sg* **katóotang**. *ptcpl* **keetóotang**.

**kátul** NA cutter *(type of carriage). pl* **kátŭlak**. *poss* **ngátŭlum**. *obv* **kátŭlal**. *From English* cutter.

**kàtŭláhŭmeew** VAI use a cutter. *ind 1st sg* **ngatŭláhŭma, ngatŭláhŭmaam**. *conj 3rd sg* **kàtŭláhumaat**. *imp* **kàtŭláhŭmaal**. *ptcpl* **kàtŭláhŭmaat**.

**katúm** VAI be so many years of age *(with number preverb).* **Naalanaaníhka txíi-katúm.** 'He is fifteen years old.' *conj 3rd sg* **katúng**.

**katún** VII be a year. **Kwáy kéetung.** 'This year.'; **Láapii katúnge.** 'Next year.' *conj 3rd sg* **katúng**. *ptcpl* **kéetung**.

**kawaaháaleew** VTA throw s.o. down. *ind 1st sg* **ngawaaháalaaw, ngawaa=háala**. *ind 3rd sg* **kwàwaahaaláawal**. *ind inv* **ngawaaháalukw**. *ind I-you* **kawaaháalul**. *conj 3rd sg* **kawaa=háalaat**. *imp* **kawáahaal**. *ptcpl* **keewaaháalaat**.

**kawáaheew** VAIO throw s.o. down, throw s.t. down. *ind 1st sg* **ngawáa=heen**. *ind 3rd sg* **kwawáaheen**. *conj 3rd sg* **kawáaheet**. *imp* **kawáaheel**. *ptcpl* **keewáaheet**.

**kawaháhkweew** VAI fell trees, knock trees down. *ind 1st sg* **ngawháhkwe, ngawháhkweem**. *conj 3rd sg* **ka=waháhkweet**. *imp* **kawaháhkweel**. *ptcpl* **keewháhkweet**.

**kawáxookw** VAI be knocked over by the wind, be blown over by the wind *(s.t. animate). ind 1st sg* **ngáwxookw**. *conj 3rd sg* **kawaxóokwuk**. *ptcpl* **keewxóokwuk**.

**kawáxun** VII be knocked over by the wind, be blown over by the wind. *conj 3rd sg* **kawáxung**. *ptcpl* **kéewxung**.

**kawíiw** VAI-S sleep. **Máamchiish ngáwi piiskéeke.** 'I slept very little last night.' *ind 1st sg* **ngáwi, ngáwiim**. *conj 3rd sg* **kawíit**. *imp* **kawíil**. *ptcpl* **kéewiit**.

**kawíhkam** VTI 1A knock s.t. down *(using the foot or body)*. *ind 1st sg* **ngawíh=kamun**. *ind 3rd sg* **kwàwíhkamun**. *conj 1st sg* **kawíhkamaan**. *conj 3rd sg* **kawíhkang**. *imp* **kawíhkah**. *ptcpl* **keewíhkang**.

**kawíhkaweew** VTA make s.o. fall down, knock s.o. down *(using the foot or body)*. *ind 1st sg* **ngawíhkawaaw**, **ngawíhkawa**. *ind 3rd sg* **kwàwihka=wáawal**. *ind inv* **ngawíhkaakw**. *ind I-you* **kawíhkool**. *conj 3rd sg* **kawíhkawaat**. *imp* **kawíhkaw**. *ptcpl* **keewíhkawaat**.

**kawíhleew** VAI fall down. *ind 1st sg* **ngawíhla**, **ngawíhlaam**. *conj 3rd sg* **kawíhlaat**. *ptcpl* **keewíhlaat**.

**kawihtéeham** VTI 1A hit s.t. and knock it down, knock s.t. down by hitting it. *ind 1st sg* **ngawihtéehŭmun**. *ind 3rd sg* **kwàwihtéehŭmun**. *conj 1st sg* **kawihtéehŭmaan**. *conj 3rd sg* **kawihtéehang**. *imp* **kawihtéehih**. *ptcpl* **keewihtéehang**.

**kawihtéeheew** VTA hit s.o. and knock them down. *ind 1st sg* **ngawihtée=haaw**, **ngawihtéeha**. *ind 3rd sg* **kwàwihteeháawal**. *ind inv* **ngawih=téehookw**. *ind I-you* **kàwihtéehool**. *conj 3rd sg* **kawihtéehaat**. *imp* **kawíhteeh**. *ptcpl* **keewihtéehaat**.

**kawóoheew** VAIO put s.o. to sleep. *ind 1st sg* **ngawóoheen**. *ind 3rd sg* **kwàwoohéenal**. *conj 3rd sg* **kawóo=heet**. *imp* **kawóoheel**. *ptcpl* **keewóo=heet**.

**kawúsheew** VTA cut s.t. animate down. *ind 1st sg* **ngáwshaaw**, **ngáwsha**. *ind 3rd sg* **kwàwsháawal**. *ind inv* **ngáw=shookw**. *ind I-you* **káwshool**. *conj 3rd sg* **kawúshaat**. *imp* **kawúsh**. *ptcpl* **kéewshaat**.

**kawushíhkaweew** VTA send s.o. to bed. *ind 1st sg* **ngawshíhkawaaw**, **ngaw=shíhkawa**. *ind 3rd sg* **kwàwshihka=wáawal**. *ind inv* **ngawshíhkaakw**. *ind I-you* **kawshíhkool**. *conj 3rd sg* **kawushíhkawaat**. *imp* **kawushíh=kaw**. *ptcpl* **keewshíhkawaat**.

**kawúshum** VTI 1B cut s.t. down. *ind 1st sg* **ngawshúmun**. *ind 3rd sg* **kwàw=shúmun**. *conj 1st sg* **kawúshŭmaan**. *conj 3rd sg* **kawúshung**. *imp* **kawúshih**. *ptcpl* **kéewshung**.

**kaxkaniikéexiin** VAI have a broken tooth. *ind 1st sg* **ngaxkaniikéexiin**, **ngaxkaniikéexi**. *conj 3rd sg* **kaxka=niikéexiing**. *ptcpl* **keexkaniikée=xiing**.

**kaxkcháaleew** VAI have a broken nose. *ind 1st sg* **ngaxkcháala**, **ngaxkcháa=laam**. *conj 3rd sg* **kaxkcháalaat**. *ptcpl* **keexkcháalaat**.

**kaxkchaaléeheew** VTA break s.o.'s nose. *ind 1st sg* **ngaxkchaaléehaaw**, **ngax=kchaaléeha**. *ind 3rd sg* **kwaxkchaa=leeháawal**. *ind inv* **ngaxkchaalée=hukw**. *ind I-you* **kaxkchaaléehul**. *conj 3rd sg* **kaxkchaaléehaat**. *imp* **kaxkcháaleeh**. *ptcpl* **keexkchaalée=haat**.

**kaxkchaaléexiin** VAI have one's nose broken, have a broken nose. *ind 1st sg* **ngaxkchaaléexiin**, **ngaxkchaa=léexi**. *conj 3rd sg* **kaxkchaaléexiing**. *ptcpl* **keexkchaaléexiing**.

**kaxkéeweew** VAI go across, take a short-cut. *ind 1st sg* **ngaxkéewe**, **ngaxkée=weem**. *conj 3rd sg* **kaxkéeweet**. *imp* **kaxkéeweel**. *ptcpl* **keexkéeweet**.

**káxkham** VTI 1A break s.t., run over s.t. *ind 1st sg* **ngaxkhámun**. *ind 3rd sg* **kwaxkhámun**. *conj 1st sg* **kaxk=hámaan**. *conj 3rd sg* **káxkhang**. *imp* **káxkhah**. *ptcpl* **kéexkhang**.

**káxkheew** VTA run over s.o. *(especially in a car)*. *ind 1st sg* **ngáxkhaaw**, **ngáxkha**. *ind 3rd sg* **kwaxkháawal**. *ind inv* **ngáxkhookw**. *ind I-you* **káxkhool**. *conj 3rd sg* **káxkhaat**. *imp* **káxkhaw**. *ptcpl* **kéexkhaat**.

**káxkhookw** VAI get run over, be broken

off *(s.t. animate)*. *ind 1st sg* **ngáxk=hookw**. *conj 3rd sg* **kaxkhóokwuk**. *ptcpl* **keexkhóokwuk**.

**kaxkíixiin** VAI be broken *(s.t. animate)*. *ind 1st sg* **ngaxkíixiin**, **ngaxkíixi**. *conj 3rd sg* **kaxkíixiing**. *ptcpl* **keexkíixiing**.

**kaxkíixtoow** VTI2 break s.t. *ind 1st sg* **ngaxkíixtoon**. *ind 3rd sg* **kwaxkíix=toon**. *conj 1st sg* **kaxkiixtáwaan**. *conj 3rd sg* **kaxkíixtaakw**. *imp* **kaxkíixtool**. *ptcpl* **keexkíixtaakw**.

**kaxkíixŭmeew** VTA break s.o. *ind 1st sg* **ngaxkíixŭmaaw**, **ngaxkíixŭma**. *ind 3rd sg* **kwaxkiixŭmáawal**. *ind inv* **ngaxkíixŭmukw**. *ind I-you* **kaxkíi=xŭmul**. *conj 3rd sg* **kaxkíixŭmaat**. *imp* **kaxkíixum**. *ptcpl* **keexkíixŭ=maat**.

**kaxkíixun** VII be broken. *conj 3rd sg* **kaxkíixung**. *ptcpl* **keexkíixung**.

**kaxkíhkam** VTI break s.t. *(using the foot or body)*; step on and break s.t. **Ngaxkíhkamun wíhkaat.** 'I stepped on his leg and broke it.' *ind 1st sg* **ngaxkíhkamun**. *ind 3rd sg* **kwax=kíhkamun**. *conj 1st sg* **kaxkíhka=maan**. *conj 3rd sg* **kaxkíhkang**. *imp* **kaxkíhkah**. *ptcpl* **keexkíhkang**.

**kaxkíhkaweew** VTA break s.t. animate *(using the foot or body)*; step on and break s.t. animate. *ind 1st sg* **ngax=kíhkawaaw**, **ngaxkíhkawa**. *ind 3rd sg* **kwaxkihkawáawal**. *ind inv* **ngaxkíhkaakw**. *ind I-you* **kaxkíh=kool**. *conj 3rd sg* **kaxkíhkawaat**. *imp* **kaxkíhkaw**. *ptcpl* **keexkíhkawaat**.

**kaxkíhleew** VAI be broken *(s.t. animate)*. *ind 1st sg* **ngaxkíhla**, **ngaxkíhlaam**. *conj 3rd sg* **kaxkíhlaat**. *ptcpl* **keexkíhlaat**.

**kaxkíhleew** VII be broken. *conj 3rd sg* **kaxkíhlaak**. *ptcpl* **keexkíhlaak**.

**kaxkihtéeham** VTI1A hit and break s.t. *ind 1st sg* **ngaxkihtéehŭmun**. *ind 3rd sg* **kwaxkihtéehŭmun**. *conj 1st sg* **kaxkihtéehŭmaan**. *conj 3rd sg* **kaxkihtéehang**. *imp* **kaxkihtéehih**. *ptcpl* **keexkihtéehang**.

**kaxkihtéeheew** VTA hit and break s.o. *ind 1st sg* **ngaxkihtéehaaw**, **ngax=kihtéeha**. *ind 3rd sg* **kwaxkihtee=háawal**. *ind inv* **ngaxkihtéehookw**. *ind I-you* **kaxkihtéehool**. *conj 3rd sg* **kaxkihtéehaat**. *imp* **kaxkíhteeh**. *ptcpl* **keexkihtéehaat**.

**kaxkkáateew** VAI have a broken leg. *ind 1st sg* **ngaxkkáata**, **ngaxkkáataam**. *conj 3rd sg* **kaxkkáataat**. *ptcpl* **keexkkáataat**.

**kaxkkaatéeheew** VTA break s.o.'s leg. *ind 1st sg* **ngaxkkaatéehaaw**, **ngaxkkaatéeha**. *ind 3rd sg* **kwaxk=kaateeháawal**. *ind inv* **ngaxkkaa=téehukw**. *ind I-you* **kaxkkaatéehul**. *conj 3rd sg* **kaxkkaatéehaat**. *imp* **kaxkkáateeh**. *ptcpl* **keexkkaa=téehaat**.

**kaxkkaatéhkaweew** VTA break s.o.'s leg *(using the foot or body)*; step on and break s.o.'s leg. *ind 1st sg* **ngaxk=kaatéhkawaaw**, **ngaxkkaatéhkawa**. *ind 3rd sg* **kwaxkkaatehkawáawal**. *ind inv* **ngaxkkaatéhkaakw**. *ind I-you* **kaxkkaatéhkool**. *conj 3rd sg* **kaxkkaatéhkawaat**. *imp* **kaxkkaa=téhkaw**. *ptcpl* **keexkkaatéhkawaat**.

**káxkŭneew** VTA break s.t. animate *(using the hands)*. *ind 1st sg* **ngáxkŭ=naaw**, **ngáxkŭna**. *ind 3rd sg* **kwax=kŭnáawal**. *ind inv* **ngáxkŭnukw**. *ind I-you* **káxkŭnul**. *conj 3rd sg* **káxkŭ=naat**. *imp* **káxkun**. *ptcpl* **kéexkŭnaat**.

**kaxkŭnáxkeew** VAI have a broken arm, have a broken hand. *ind 1st sg* **ngax=kŭnáxka**, **ngaxkŭnáxkaam**. *conj 3rd sg* **kaxkŭnáxkaat**. *ptcpl* **keexkŭnáx=kaat**.

**kaxkŭnaxkéeheew** VTA break s.o.'s arm, break s.o.'s hand. *ind 1st sg* **ngaxkŭ=naxkéehaaw**, **ngaxkŭnaxkéeha**. *ind 3rd sg* **kwaxkunaxkeeháawal**. *ind* *inv* **ngaxkŭnaxkéehukw**. *ind I-you* **kaxkunaxkéehul**. *conj 3rd sg* **kax=kŭnaxkéehaat**. *imp* **kaxkŭnáxkeeh**. *ptcpl* **keexkŭnaxkéehaat**.

**kaxkŭnaxkéexiin** VAI have a broken arm, have a broken hand. *ind 1st sg* **ngaxkŭnaxkéexiin**, **ngaxkŭnaxkée=xi**. *conj 3rd sg* **kaxkŭnaxkéexiing**. *ptcpl* **keexkŭnaxkéexiing**.

**kaxkŭnaxkéexŭmeew** VTA break s.o.'s arm, break s.o.'s hand. *ind 1st sg* **ngaxkŭnaxkéexŭmaaw**, **ngaxkŭ=naxkéexŭma**. *ind 3rd sg* **kwaxkŭ=naxkeexŭmáawal**. *ind inv* **ngaxkŭ=naxkéexŭmukw**. *ind I-you* **kaxkŭ=naxkéexŭmul**. *conj 3rd sg* **kaxkŭ=naxkéexŭmaat**. *imp* **kaxkŭnaxkée=xum**. *ptcpl* **keexkŭnaxkéexŭmaat**.

**káxkŭnum** VTI1B break s.t. *(using the hands)*. *ind 1st sg* **ngaxkŭnúmun**. *ind 3rd sg* **kwaxkŭnúmun**. *conj 1st sg* **kaxkŭnúmaan**. *conj 3rd sg* **káxkŭnung**. *imp* **káxkŭnih**. *ptcpl* **kéexkŭnung**.

**kaxkxoonéeheew** VTA break s.o.'s neck. *ind 1st sg* **ngaxkxoonéehaaw**, **ngax=kxoonéeha**. *ind 3rd sg* **kwaxkxoo=neeh//áawal**. *ind inv* **ngaxkxoonée=hukw**. *ind I-you* **kaxkxoonéehul**. *conj 3rd sg* **kaxkxoonéehaat**. *imp* **kaxkxóoneeh**. *ptcpl* **keexkxoo=néehaat**.

**kaxkxoonéeneew** VTA break s.o.'s neck *(using the hands)*. *ind 1st sg* **ngaxk=xoonéenaaw**, **ngaxkxoonéena**. *ind 3rd sg* **kwaxkxooneenáawal**. *ind inv* **ngaxkxoonéenukw**. *ind I-you* **kaxk=xoonéenul**. *conj 3rd sg* **kaxkxoo=néenaat**. *imp* **kaxkxóoneen**. *ptcpl* **keexkxoonéenaat**.

**kcháxkeew** VII be scratched, have a scratch. *conj 3rd sg* **kcháxkeek**. *ptcpl* **keecháxkeek**.

**kchaxkíingweew** VAI have a scratch on one's face. *ind 1st sg* **nguchaxkíin=gwa**, **nguchaxkíingwaam**. *conj 3rd sg* **kchaxkíingwaat**. *ptcpl* **keechíin=gwaat**.

**kchaxkíixiin** VAI be scratched, get scratched. *ind 1st sg* **nguchaxkíixiin**, **nguchaxkíixi**. *conj 3rd sg* **kchaxkíi=xiing**. *ptcpl* **keechaxkíixiing**.

**kchaxkíixiin** VAI be undone *(s.t. animate, of items of clothing)*. *ind 1st sg* **nguchaxkíixiin**, **nguchaxkíixi**. *conj 3rd sg* **kchaxkíixiing**. *ptcpl* **kee=chaxkíixiing**.

**kchaxkíixteew** VAI have an item of clothing undone *(especially fly of pants)*. *ind 1st sg* **nguchaxkíixta**, **nguchax=kíixtaam**. *conj 3rd sg* **kchaxkíixtaat**. *ptcpl* **keechaxkíixtaat**.

**kchaxkíixtoow** VTI2 leave s.t. undone, unhitch s.t. *ind 1st sg* **nguchaxkíix=toon**. *ind 3rd sg* **kwuchaxkíixtoon**. *conj 1st sg* **kchaxkiixtáwaan**. *conj 3rd sg* **kchaxkíixtaakw**. *imp* **kchax=kíixtool**. *ptcpl* **keechaxkíixtaakw**.

**kchaxkíixŭmeew** VTA leave s.o. undone, unhitch s.o. *ind 1st sg* **nguchaxkíi=xŭmaaw**, **nguchaxkíixŭma**. *ind 3rd sg* **kwuchaxkiixŭmáawal**. *ind inv* **nguchaxkíixŭmukw**. *ind I-you* **kùchaxkíixŭmul**. *conj 3rd sg* **kchax=kíixŭmaat**. *imp* **kchaxkíixum**. *ptcpl* **keechaxkíixŭmaat**.

**kchaxkíixun** VII be scratched, get scratched. *conj 3rd sg* **kchaxkíixung**. *ptcpl* **keechaxkíixung**.

**kchaxkíixun** VII be undone *(of items of clothing)*. *conj 3rd sg* **kchaxkíixung**. *ptcpl* **keechaxkíixung**.

**kcháxkihl** VAI come undone *(s.t. animate)*. *ind 1st sg* **nguchaxkihl**, **nguchaxkihl**. *conj 3rd sg* **kchax=kíhluk**. *ptcpl* **keechaxkíhluk**.

**kchaxkíhleew** VAI come undone *(s.t. animate)*. *ind 1st sg* **nguchaxkíhla**, **nguchaxkíhlaam**. *conj 3rd sg* **kchaxkíhlaat**. *ptcpl* **keechaxkíhlaat**.

**kcháxkŭneew** VTA unfasten s.o, unhook s.o., undo s.o. *ind 1st sg* **nguchaxkŭ=**

naaw, nguchaxkŭna. *ind 3rd sg* kwuchaxkŭnáawal. *ind inv* nguch=áxkŭnukw. *ind I-you* kùcháxkŭnul. *conj 3rd sg* kcháxkŭnaat. *imp* kcháxkun. *ptcpl* keecháxkŭnaat.

**kchaxkŭnaháasuw** VII be undone, be unhooked. *conj 3rd sg* **kchaxkŭnah=áasiik**. *ptcpl* **keechaxkŭnaháasiik**.

**kchaxkŭnáxkeew** VAI have a scratch on one's arm, have a scratch on one's hand. *ind 1st sg* **nguchaxkŭnáxka, nguchaxkŭnáxkaam**. *conj 3rd sg* **kchaxkŭnáxkaat**. *ptcpl* **keechaxkŭ=náxkaat**.

**kcháxkŭnum** VTI1B unfasten s.t., unhook s.t., undo s.t. *ind 1st sg* **nguch=axkunúmun**. *ind 3rd sg* **kwuchax=kŭnúmun**. *conj 1st sg* **kchaxkŭ=númaan**. *conj 3rd sg* **kcháxkŭnung**. *imp* **kcháxkŭnih**. *ptcpl* **keecháxkŭ=nung**.

**kchíiw** VAI-S come out, go out; go to the bathroom. **Wiikwáhmung nóonj-kchíim.** 'I came out of the house.' *ind 1st sg* **ngúchi, ngúchiim**. *emphatic pl* **kchooltúwak**. *conj 3rd sg* **kchíit**. *imp* **kchíil**. *ptcpl* **kéechiit**.

**kchiikwáaleew** VTA dig s.o out, pry s.o out, remove s.o. *(using a tool or instrument)*. *ind 1st sg* **nguchiikwáa=laaw, nguchiikwáala**. *ind 3rd sg* **kwuchiikwaaláawal**. *ind inv* **nguch=iikwáalukw**. *ind I-you* **kùchii=kwáalul**. *conj 3rd sg* **kchiikwáalaat**. *imp* **kchíikwaal**. *ptcpl* **keechii=kwáalaat**.

**kchiikwáatam** VTI1A dig s.t. out, pry s.t. out, remove s.t. *(using a tool or instrument)*. *ind 1st sg* **nguchiikwáa=tamun**. *ind 3rd sg* **kwuchiikwáa=tamun**. *conj 1st sg* **kchiikwáata=maan**. *conj 3rd sg* **kchiikwáatang**. *imp* **kchiikwáatah**. *ptcpl* **keechii=kwáatang**.

**kchíikwsuw** VAI crawl out. *ind 1st sg* **nguchíikwsi, nguchíikwsiim**. *conj 3rd sg* **kchíikwsiit**. *imp* **kchíikwsiil**. *ptcpl* **keechíikwsiit**.

**kchiinaxkéexiin** VAI stick one's hand out, have one's hand sticking out. *ind 1st sg* **nguchiinaxkéexiin, nguchii=naxkéexi**. *conj 3rd sg* **kchiinaxkée=xiing**. *imp* **kchiinaxkéexiil**. *ptcpl* **keechiinaxkéexiing**. *See* **ktunax=kéexiin**.

**kchiingwéexiin** VAI lie with one's face sticking out, lie with one's face showing, have one's face showing. *ind 1st sg* **nguchiingwéexiin, nguchiin=gwéexi**. *conj 3rd sg* **kchiingwée=xiing**. *imp* **kchiingwéexiil**. *ptcpl* **keechiingwéexiing**.

**kchiingwéhleew** VAI show one's face *(quickly)*. *ind 1st sg* **nguchiingwéhla, nguchiingwéhlaam**. *conj 3rd sg* **kchiingwéhlaat**. *imp* **kchiingwéh=laal**. *ptcpl* **keechiingwéhlaat**.

**kchiipáhtoow** VTI2 hurry out with s.t. *ind 1st sg* **nguchiipáhtoon**. *ind 3rd sg* **kwuchiipáhtoon**. *conj 1st sg* **kchiipáhtawaan**. *conj 3rd sg* **kchii=páhtaakw**. *imp* **kchiipáhtool**. *ptcpl* **keechiipáhtaakw**.

**kchiixkwéeneew** VTA choke s.o., strangle s.o. *ind 1st sg* **nguchiixkwée=naaw, nguchiixkwéena**. *ind 3rd sg* **kwuchiixkweenáawal**. *ind inv* **nguchiixkwéenukw**. *ind I-you* **kùch=iixkwéenul**. *conj 3rd sg* **kchiixkwée=naat**. *imp* **kchíixkween**. *ptcpl* **kee=chiixkwéenaat**.

**kchíhlaleew** VTA betray s.o., tell on s.o., betray s.o.'s confidence. *ind 1st sg* **nguchíhlalaaw, nguchíhlala**. *ind 3rd sg* **kwuchihlaláawal**. *ind inv* **nguch=íhlalukw**. *ind I-you* **kùchíhlalul**. *conj 3rd sg* **kchíhlalaat**. *imp* **kchíhlal**. *ptcpl* **keechíhlalaat**.

**kchíhlatoow** VTI2 tell about s.t., reveal s.t. **Kùchíhlatoon kwéek éeleek.** 'You told about what happened (and weren't supposed to).' *ind 1st sg* nguchíhlatoon. *ind 3rd sg* **kwuch=íhlatoon**. *conj 1st sg* **kchihlatáwaan**. *conj 3rd sg* **kchíhlataakw**. *imp* **kchíhlatool**. *ptcpl* **keechíhlataakw**.

**kchíhleew** VAI fall out, run out, come out. *ind 1st sg* **nguchíhla, nguchíh=laam**. *conj 3rd sg* **kchíhlaat**. *ptcpl* **keechíhlaat**.

**kchíhleew** VII fall out, run out, come out. *conj 3rd sg* **kchíhlaak**. *ptcpl* **keechíhlaak**.

**kchukaandpeexíinook** VAI have one's heads together. *usually plural. ind 1st pl* **nguchkaandpeexiinóhna**. *conj 3rd pl* **kchukaandpeexiinóhtiit**. *ptcpl* **keechkaandpeexiinóhtiit**.

**kchukaangwéewak** VAI lie close together. *usually plural. ind 1st pl* **nguchkaangwéhna**. *conj 3rd pl* **kchukaangwéhtiit**. *imp* **kchukáan=gweekw**. *ptcpl* **keechkaangwéhtiit**.

**kchukáhteew** VII be close together. *conj 3rd sg* **kchukáhteek**. *ptcpl* **keech=káhteek**.

**kchukapúwak** VAI sit close together. *usually plural. ind 1st pl* **nguchkap=íhna**. *conj 3rd pl* **kchukapíhtiit**. *imp* **kchúkapiikw**. *ptcpl* **keechkapíhtiit**. *See* **kchukohkwéepŭwak**.

**kchukiikaapawúwak** VAI stand close together. *usually plural. ind 1st pl* **nguchkiikaapawíhna**. *conj 3rd pl* **kchukiikaapawíhtiit**. *imp* **kchukii=káapawiikw**. *ptcpl* **keechkiikaapa=wíhtiit**.

**kchukíikŭwak** VAI grow close together. *usually plural. ind 1st pl* **nguchkii=kíhna**. *conj 3rd pl* **kchukiikíhtiit**. *ptcpl* **keechkiikíhtiit**.

**kchukohkwéepŭwak** VAI sit close together. *usually plural. ind 1st pl* **nguchkohkweepíhna**. *conj 3rd pl* **kchukohkweepíhtiit**. *imp* **kchukoh=kwéepiikw**. *ptcpl* **keechkohkwee=píhtiit**. *See* **kchukapúwak**.

**kchíipheew** VTA hurry out with s.o. *ind 1st sg* **nguchíiphaaw, nguchíipha**. *ind 3rd sg* **kwuchiipháawal**. *ind inv* **nguchíiphukw**. *ind I-you* **kùchíiphul**. *conj 3rd sg* **kchíiphaat**. *imp* **kchíipah**. *ptcpl* **keechíiphaat**.

**keekíingŭlush** NA gooseberry. *pl* **kee=kiingŭlúshak**. *poss* **ngeekiingŭlúsh=um**. *dimin* **keekiingŭlúshush**. *obv* **keekiingŭlúshal**.

**keenáamuw** VAI say grace. *ind 1st sg* **ngeenáamwi, ngeenáamwiim**. *conj 3rd sg* **keenáamwiit**. *imp* **keenáam=wiil**. *ptcpl* **keenáamwiit**.

**kéendŭwees** NA Christian Indian, Moravian convert. *pl* **keendŭwéesak**. *obv* **keendŭwéesal**. *used at Munceytown, Ontario for Delawares living at Moraviantown, Ontario.*

**kéenham** VTI 1A can s.t., put s.t. in cans. *ind 1st sg* **ngeenhámun**. *ind 3rd sg* **kweenhámun**. *conj 1st sg* **keen=hámaan**. *conj 3rd sg* **kéenhang**. *imp* **kéenhah**. *ptcpl* **kéenhang**. *From English* can.

**kéenheew** VTA can s.t. animate, put s.t. animate in cans. *ind 1st sg* **ngéen=haaw, ngéenha**. *ind 3rd sg* **kween=háawal**. *conj 3rd sg* **kéenhaat**. *imp* **kéenhaw**. *ptcpl* **kéenhaat**. *From English* can.

**keenhíikeew** VAI can things, put things in cans. *ind 1st sg* **ngeenhíike, ngeenhíikeem**. *conj 3rd sg* **keen=híikeet**. *imp* **keenhíikeel**. *ptcpl* **keenhíikeet**. *From English* can.

**kéenj** PC long ago. **Kéenj táa éenda-wŭlú-léek.** 'Back in the good old days.'; **Kéenj táa.** 'Long ago.'

**kéeptoon** NA a mute, a person who can't talk. *pl* **keeptóonak**. *obv* **keeptóonal**.

**kéesan** PC shoot! gosh! silly question! shame on you! *See* **kéesand**.

**kéesand** PC shoot! gosh! silly question! shame on you! *See* **kéesan**.

**keeslukíiwi-pehpŭmutóonhees** NA Catholic priest. *pl* **keeslukíiwi-**

**pehpŭmutoonhéesak**. *obv* **keeslukíiwi-pehpŭmutoonhéesal**.

**keeshéetsuw** VAI save, be thrifty. *ind 1st sg* **ngeeshéetsi**, **ngeeshéetsiim**. *conj 3rd sg* **keeshéetsiit**. *imp* **keeshéetsiil**. *ptcpl* **keeshéetsiit**.

**keeshéetsuw** VAIO save s.t. *(of money)*; be thrifty about s.t. **Ngeeshéetsiin ndahtamoombíilum.** 'I'm thrifty about my car.' *ind 1st sg* **ngeeshéet=siin**. *ind 3rd sg* **kweeshéetsiin**. *conj 3rd sg* **keeshéetsiit**. *imp* **keeshéetsiil**. *ptcpl* **keeshéetsiit**.

**keeshéewsuw** VAI be thrifty. *ind 1st sg* **ngeeshéewsi**, **ngeeshéewsiim**. *conj 3rd sg* **keeshéewsiit**. *imp* **keeshéew=siil**. *ptcpl* **keeshéewsiit**.

**keexéeli** PC several. **Keexéeli laapa=múkwat.** 'It is several different colours.'

**keexookwŭnáhkeew** VAI be gone for several days. *ind 1st sg* **ngeexoo=kwŭnáhke**, **ngeexookwŭnáhkeem**. *conj 3rd sg* **keexookwŭnáhkeet**. *ptcpl* **keexookwŭnáhkeet**.

**kéexu** PC amount. *informal*. **Kéexu póondakat?** 'How much does it weigh?'; **Kéexu ktúndxii-katúm?** 'How old are you?'

**kéexun** PC several times. **Kéexun áng páan nxóoxwe.** 'He came alone several times.'

**kehkaasiingweehíikan** NI towel. *pl* **kehkaasiingweehíikanal**. *poss* **ngehkaasiingweehíikan**. *loc* **keh=kaasiingweehíikanung**. *dimin* **keh=kaashiingweehíikanush**. *See* **keh=kaasíingweeng**, **kehkaasiingwée=hoon**.

**kehkaasiingwéehoon** NI towel. *pl* **keh=kaasiingweehóonal**. *poss* **ngeh=kaasiingwéehoon**. *loc* **kehkaasiin=gweehóonung**. *dimin* **kehkaashiin=gweehóonush**. *See* **kehkaasíin=gweeng**, **kehkaasiingweehíikan**.

**kehkaasíingweeng** VAI towel. *conj 3rd sg* **kehkaasíingweeng**. *pl* **kehkaa=siingwéengiil**. *See* **kehkaasiingwée=hoon**, **kehkaasiingweehíikan**.

**kehkéchiis** NA catcher. *pl* **kehkechíisak**. *dimin* **kehkechíishush**. *obv* **keh=kechíisal**. *baseball*. *From English* catcher.

**kehkshiixtíikan** NI washing machine. *pl* **kehkshiixtíikanal**. *poss* **ngehkshiix=tíikan**. *loc* **kehkshiixtíikanung**. *dimin* **kehkshiixchíikanush**. *See* **kehkshiixtíikeeng**.

**kehkshiixtíikeeng** VII washing machine. *conj 3rd sg* **kehkshiixtíikeeng** *pl* **kehkshiixtiikeengiil**. *See* **kehks=hiixtíikan**.

**kehkshúteek** NI stove. *pl* **kehkshutée=kal**. *poss* **ngehkshutéekum**. *loc* **kehkshutéekung**. *dimin* **kehk=shuchéekush**.

**kehkŭlúndang** NI bit for horse's bridle. *pl* **kehkŭlundángiil**.

**kéhla** PC really. **Wúlu kéhla máh wŭlamalusíiwu.** 'For sure he's not well.'; **Kéhla-uch mbeesíhna-uch náake.** 'We'll wait for a while.'

**kéhtaam** NI hazelnut. *pl* **kehtáamal**.

**kehtéexiin** VAI wait to take off, wait to leave, be ready for action. *ind 1st sg* **ngehtéexiin**, **ngehtéexi**. *conj 3rd sg* **kehtéexiing**. *imp* **kehtéexiil**. *ptcpl* **kehtéexiing**.

**kehtéexŭmeew** VTA get s.o. ready. *ind 1st sg* **ngehtéexŭmaaw**, **ngehtée=xŭma**. *ind 3rd sg* **kwehteexŭmáa=wal**. *ind inv* **ngehtéexŭmukw**. *ind I-you* **kehtéexŭmul**. *conj 3rd sg* **kehtéexŭmaat**. *imp* **kehtéexum**. *ptcpl* **kehtéexŭmaat**.

**kép** NI cap. *pl* **képal**. *poss* **ngépum**. *From English* cap.

**képuch** NI cabbage. *pl* **kepúchal**. *poss* **ngepúchum**. *dimin* **kepúchush**. *From English* cabbage.

**kíi** PR you. **Kíi áashtee.** 'It's your turn.'

**kiihíicheew** VII be sore, be tender, ache

*(of body parts). conj 3rd sg* **kiihíi=cheek**. *ptcpl* **kiihíicheek**.
**kiihiichiiktúkweew** VAI have an sore knee. *ind 1st sg* **ngiihiichiiktúkwa**, **ngiihiichiiktúkwaam**. *conj 3rd sg* **kiihiichiiktúkwaat**. *ptcpl* **kiihii=chiiktúkwaat**.
**kiihíimeew** VTA encourage s.o. *ind 1st sg* **ngiihíimaaw**, **ngiihíima**. *ind 3rd sg* **kwiihiimáawal**. *ind inv* **ngiihíi=mukw**. *ind I-you* **kiihíimul**. *conj 3rd sg* **kiihíimaat**. *imp* **kíihiim**. *ptcpl* **kiihíimaat**.
**kiihiitalíhkeew** VAI limp, be lame. *ind 1st sg* **ngiihiitalíhke**, **ngiihiitalíh=keem**. *conj 3rd sg* **kiihiitalíhkeet**. *ptcpl* **kiihiitalíhkeet**.
**kiihiitkáateew** VAI have a sore leg. *ind 1st sg* **ngiihiitkáata**, **ngiihiitkáa=taam**. *conj 3rd sg* **kiihiitkáataat**. *ptcpl* **kiihiitkáataat**.
**kiihiitsíiteew** VAI have a sore foot. *ind 1st sg* **ngiihiitsíita**, **ngiihiitsíitaam**. *conj 3rd sg* **kiihiitsíitaat**. *ptcpl* **kiihiitsíitaat**.
**kiihíitsuw** VAI be sore, be tender, ache *(s.t. animate). ind 1st sg* **ngiihíitsi**, **ngiihíitsiim**. *conj 3rd sg* **kiihíitsiit**. *ptcpl* **kiihíitsiit**.
**kiihiitŭnáxkeew** VAI have a sore arm, have a sore hand. *ind 1st sg* **ngiihii=tŭnáxka**, **ngiihiitŭnáxkaam**. *conj 3rd sg* **kiihiitŭnáxkaat**. *ptcpl* **kiihiitŭnáxkaat**.
**kíikeew** VAI be cured, be healed. *ind 1st sg* **ngíike**, **ngíikeem**. *conj 3rd sg* **kíikeet**. *ptcpl* **kíikeet**.
**kiikéeheew** VTA cure s.o., heal s.o. *ind 1st sg* **ngiikéehaaw**, **ngiikéeha**. *ind 3rd sg* **kwiikeeháawal**. *ind inv* **ngiikéehukw**. *ind I-you* **kiikéehul**. *conj 3rd sg* **kiikéehaat**. *imp* **kíikeeh**. *ptcpl* **kiikéehaat**.
**kiikéehŭweew** VAI cure people. *ind 1st sg* **ngiikéehŭwe**, **ngiikéehŭweem**. *conj 3rd sg* **kiikéehŭweet**. *imp* **kiikéehŭweel**. *ptcpl* **kiikéehŭweet**.
**kiikéhleew** VAI recover from an illness. *ind 1st sg* **ngiikéhla**, **ngiikéhlaam**. *conj 3rd sg* **kiikéhlaat**. *ptcpl* **kiikéh=laat**.
**kiikiipshíikaan** NI chicken house. *pl* **kiikiipshiikáanal**. *poss* **ngiikiip=shíikaan**. *loc* **kiikiipshiikáanung**. *dimin* **kiikiipshiikáanush**.
**kiikiipsúhchuy** NI chicken droppings, chicken excrement. *pl* **kiikiipshúch=ŭyal**.
**kiikiipshupéhleew** VAI have chicken pox. *ind 1st sg* **ngiikiipshupéhla**, **ngiikiipshupéhlaam**. *conj 3rd sg* **kiikiipshupéhlaat**. *ptcpl* **kiikiip=shupéhlaat**.
**kiikíipush** NA chicken. *pl* **kiikíipshak**. *poss* **ngiikíipshum**. *loc* **kiikíipshung**. *dimin* **kiikíipshush**. *obv* **kiikíipshal**. *From Dutch.*
**kiilóona** PR we *(inclusive).*
**kiilóowa** PR you *(pl).*
**kiimahtakíhleew** VAI run secretly, run in secret. *ind 1st sg* **ngiimahtakíhla**, **ngiimahtakíhlaam**. *conj 3rd sg* **kiimahtakíhlaat**. *imp* **kiimahta=kíhlaal**. *ptcpl* **kiimahtakíhlaat**.
**kíimii** PC secretly. **Kíimii mbiimóhkwe.** 'I sneaked a glance to the side.'
**kiimii-** PV secretly. **Kwíimii-wiichee=wáawal.** 'He's hovering around him.' *ptcpl* **kíimii-**.
**kiimíikwsuw** VAI sneak around crawl-ing, crawl secretly. *ind 1st sg* **ngii=míikwsi**, **ngiimíikwsiim**. *conj 3rd sg* **kiimíikwsiit**. *imp* **kiimíikwsiil**. *ptcpl* **kiimíikwsiit**.
**kiimóoxweew** NA witch. *pl* **kiimoo=xwéewak**. *obv* **kiimooxwéewal**.
**kíimŭneew** VTA rape s.o. in secret, feel s.o. secretly. *ind 1st sg* **ngíimŭnaaw**, **ngíimŭna**. *ind 3rd sg* **kwiimŭnáa=wal**. *ind inv* **ngíimŭnukw**. *ind I-you* **kíimŭnul**. *conj 3rd sg* **kíimŭnaat**. *imp* **kíimun**. *ptcpl* **kíimŭnaat**.

**kiinalóosuw** VAI have a sharp point, be sharp and pointed *(s.t. animate). conj 3rd sg* **kiinalóosiit**. *ptcpl* **kiinalóosiit**.

**kiinalóowŭyeew** VII have a sharp point, be sharp and pointed. *conj 3rd sg* **kiinalóowŭyeek**. *ptcpl* **kiinalóowŭ=yeek**.

**kiinanzhíikan** NI sharp knife. *pl* **kii=nanzhíikanal**. *poss* **ngiinanzhíikan**. *loc* **kiinanzhíikanung**. *dimin* **kiinanzhíikanush**.

**kíineew** VII be sharp. *conj 3rd sg* **kíineek**. *ptcpl* **kíineek**.

**kíinham** VTI1A sharpen s.t. *ind 1st sg* **ngiinhámun**. *ind 3rd sg* **kwiinhám=un**. *conj 1st sg* **kiinhámaan**. *conj 3rd sg* **kíinhang**. *imp* **kíinhah**. *ptcpl* **kíinhang**.

**kíinheew** VTA sharpen s.t. animate. *ind 1st sg* **ngíinhaaw**, **ngíinha**. *ind 3rd sg* **kwiinháawal**. *ind inv* **ngíinhookw**. *ind I-you* **kíinhool**. *conj 3rd sg* **kíinhaat**. *imp* **kíinhaw**. *ptcpl* **kíinhaat**.

**kiinhíikan** NI file, sharpening stone, grindstone. *pl* **kiinhíikanal**. *poss* **ngiinhíikan**. *loc* **kiinhíikanung**. *dimin* **kiinhíikanush**.

**kiinhóhkwus** NA pike fish. *pl* **kiin=hóhkwsak**. *obv* **kiinhóhkwsal**.

**kiinii-** PN sharp. **Kíinii-paxkshíikan.** 'A sharp knife.'; **Kíinii-tŭmahíikan.** 'A sharp axe.'

**kíinsuw** VAI be sharp *(s.t. animate). conj 3rd sg* **kíinsiit**. *ptcpl* **kíinsiit**.

**kíinshum** VTI1B cut s.t. and sharpen it, sharpen s.t. by cutting. *ind 1st sg* **ngiinshúmun**. *ind 3rd sg* **kwiin=shúmun**. *conj 1st sg* **kiinshúmaan**. *conj 3rd sg* **kíinshung**. *imp* **kíinshih**. *ptcpl* **kíinshung**.

**kíiskŭweew** VAI creak, squeak, make a creaking sound, make a squeaking sound *(s.t animate). ind 1st sg* **ngíiskŭwe**, **ngíiskŭweem**. *conj 3rd sg* **kíiskŭweet**. *ptcpl* **kíiskŭweet**. *intensive reduplication* **akíiskŭweew**, **kihkíiskŭweew**.

**kíiskŭweew** VII squeak, creak, make a creaking sound, make a squeaking sound. *conj 3rd sg* **kíiskŭweek**. *ptcpl* **kíiskŭweek**. *intensive reduplication* **akiiskŭwéew**, **kihkiiskŭwéew**.

**kiispáapŭweew** VAI drink one's fill, be full from drinking. *ind 1st sg* **ngiis=páapŭwe**, **ngiispáapŭweem**. *conj 3rd sg* **kiispáapŭweet**. *ptcpl* **kiis=páapŭweet**.

**kíispuw** VAI be full from eating. *ind 1st sg* **ngíispwi**, **ngíispwiim**. *conj 3rd sg* **kíispwiit**. *ptcpl* **kíispwiit**.

**kiispwulóosuw** VAI overeat, be full to the bursting point. *ind 1st sg* **ngiispwul=óosi**, **ngiispwulóosiim**. *conj 3rd sg* **kiispwulóosiit**. *ptcpl* **kiispwulóosiit**.

**kiish-** PV able to, be able to. **Kwáy máh há njíhnal kíish-mateelŭmíiwu.** 'Now you won't be able to abuse me anymore.'; **Kíish- áa -leekhíike.** 'You can write.' *ptcpl* **kíish-**.

**kiish-** PV completed action. **Ootéeneeng ndá kíish-eenhawíite.** 'I went to town after he paid me.' *ptcpl* **kíish-**.

**kiishaaméhleew** VAI finish running, be through running. *ind 1st sg* **ngiishaa=méhla**, **ngiishaaméhlaam**. *conj 3rd sg* **kiishaaméhlaat**. *imp* **kiishaa=méhlaal**. *ptcpl* **kiishaaméhlaat**.

**kiishaaptóoneew** VAI finish speaking, be finished speaking. *ind 1st sg* **ngiishaaptóone**, **ngiishaaptóoneem**. *conj 3rd sg* **kiishaaptóoneet**. *imp* **kiishaaptóoneel**. *ptcpl* **kiishaap=tóoneet**.

**kiishahkíiheew** VAI be finished planting. *ind 1st sg* **ngiishahkíihe**, **ngiishah=kíiheem**. *conj 3rd sg* **kiishahkíiheet**. *imp* **kiishahkíiheel**. *ptcpl* **kiishah=kíiheet**.

**kiisháhleew** VTA finish putting s.o. down, finish putting s.o. there. *ind 1st sg* **ngiisháhlaaw**, **ngiisháhla**. *ind 3rd sg*

**kwiishahláawal**. *ind inv* **ngiisháh=lukw**. *ind I-you* **kiisháhlul**. *conj 3rd sg* **kiisháhlaat**. *imp* **kíishahl**. *ptcpl* **kiisháhlaat**.

**kiisháhteew** VII be finished, be already placed there. *conj 3rd sg* **kiisháhteek**. *ptcpl* **kiisháhteek**.

**kiisháhtoow** VTI2 finish putting s.t. there. *ind 1st sg* **ngiisháhtoon**. *ind 3rd sg* **kwiisháhtoon**. *conj 1st sg* **kiisháhtawaan**. *conj 3rd sg* **kiisháh=taakw**. *imp* **kiisháhtool**. *ptcpl* **kii=sháhtaakw**.

**kiishakuníimeew** VTA judge s.o., finish talking about s.o. *ind 1st sg* **ngiisha=kuníimaaw**, **ngiishakuníima**. *ind 3rd sg* **kwiishakuniimáawal**. *ind inv* **ngiishakuníimukw**. *ind I-you* **kii=shakuníimul**. *conj 3rd sg* **kiisha=kuníimaat**. *imp* **kiishakúniim**. *ptcpl* **kiishakuníimaat**.

**kiishakunootáasuw** VII be finished being discussed. *conj 3rd sg* **kiisha=kunootáasiik**. *ptcpl* **kiishakunoo=táasiik**.

**kiishakunóotum** VTI1B finish talking about s.t. *ind 1st sg* **ngiishakunóo=tŭmun**. *ind 3rd sg* **kwiishakunóo=tŭmun**. *conj 1st sg* **kiishakunóo=tŭmaan**. *conj 3rd sg* **kiishakunóo=tung**. *imp* **kiishakunóotih**. *ptcpl* **kiishakunóotung**.

**kiishambíileew** VTA finish tying s.o., finish harnessing s.o. *ind 1st sg* **ngii=shambíilaaw**, **ngiishambíila**. *ind 3rd sg* **kwiishambiiláawal**. *ind inv* **ngii=shambíilukw**. *ind I-you* **kiishambíi=lul**. *conj 3rd sg* **kiishambíilaat**. *imp* **kiishámbiil**. *ptcpl* **kiishambíilaat**.

**kiishámbtoow** VTI2 finish tying s.t. up. *ind 1st sg* **ngiishámbtoon**. *ind 3rd sg* **kwiishámbtoon**. *conj 1st sg* **kii=shambtáwaan**. *conj 3rd sg* **kiishám=btaakw**. *imp* **kiishámbtool**. *ptcpl* **kiishámbtaakw**.

**kiishanáakwsuw** VAI finish one's chores, be finished one's chores, get through one's chores. *ind 1st sg* **ngiishanáa=kwsi**, **ngiishanáakwsiim**. *conj 3rd sg* **kiishanáakwsiit**. *imp* **kiishanáakw=siil**. *ptcpl* **kiishanáakwsiit**.

**kiishásktuw** VAI finish defecating, be finished defecating. *ind 1st sg* **ngiishásktí**, **ngiishásktiim**. *conj 3rd sg* **kiishásktiit**. *imp* **kiishásktiil**. *ptcpl* **kiishásktiit**.

**kiishaskŭneextíikeew** VAI finish packing up, be finished packing up. *ind 1st sg* **ngiishaskŭneextíike**, **ngii=shaskŭneextíikeem**. *conj 3rd sg* **kiishaskŭneextíikeet**. *imp* **kiishas=kŭneextíikeel**. *ptcpl* **kiishaskŭneex=tíikeet**.

**kiishatúpuw** VAI be done cooking, be finished cooking *(of cooks)*. *ind 1st sg* **ngiishatúpwi**, **ngiishatúpwiim**. *conj 3rd sg* **kiishatúpwiit**. *ptcpl* **kiishatúpwiit**.

**kiishéechpuw** VAI get dressed, get ready, be ready, be dressed. *ind 1st sg* **ngii=shéechpi**, **ngiishéechpiim**. *conj 3rd sg* **kiishéechpiit**. *imp* **kiishéech=piil**. *ptcpl* **kiishéechpiit**.

**kiisheelŭmúkweengw** VTA the Creator, He who created us. *conj order form only*. *conj 3rd sg* **kiisheelŭmúkw=eengw**. *ptcpl* **kiisheelŭmúkweengw**.

**kiisheelúndam** VOTI1A make up one's mind. *ind 1st sg* **ngiisheelúndam**. *conj 3rd sg* **kiisheelúndang**. *imp* **kii=sheelúndah**. *ptcpl* **kiisheelúndang**.

**kiishíiheew** VTA make s.t. animate, finish making s.t. animate, be finished making s.t. animate. *ind 1st sg* **ngiishíihaaw**, **ngiishíiha**. *ind 3rd sg* **kwiishiiháawal**. *ind inv* **ngiishíih=ukw**. *ind I-you* **kiishíihul**. *conj 3rd sg* **kiishíihaat**. *imp* **kíishiih**. *ptcpl* **kiishíihaat**.

**kiishíikheew** VAI finish building a house. *ind 1st sg* **ngiishíikhe**, **ngii=shíikheem**. *conj 3rd sg* **kiishíikheet**.

*imp* **kiishíikheel**. *ptcpl* **kiishíikheet**.

**kiishíikun** VII be grown, be through growing. *conj 3rd sg* **kiishíikung**. *ptcpl* **kiishíikung**.

**kiishíikŭneew** VTA raise s.o., be through with planting s.t. animate. *ind 1st sg* **ngiishíikŭnaaw**, **ngiishíikŭna**. *ind 3rd sg* **kwiishiikŭnáawal**. *ind inv* **ngiishíikŭnukw**. *ind 1-you* **kiishíi=kŭnul**. *conj 3rd sg* **kiishíikŭnaat**. *imp* **kiishíikun**. *ptcpl* **kiishíikŭnaat**.

**kiishíikŭnum** VTI1B raise s.t. *(of crops)*. *ind 1st sg* **ngiishiikŭnúmun**. *ind 3rd sg* **kwiishiikŭnúmun**. *conj 1st sg* **kiishiikŭnúmaan**. *conj 3rd sg* **kii=shíikŭnung**. *imp* **kiishíikŭnih**. *ptcpl* **kiishíikŭnung**.

**kiishíikuw** VAI be born. *ind 1st sg* **ngiishíiki**, **ngiishíikiim**. *conj 3rd sg* **kiishíikiit**. *ptcpl* **kiishíikiit**.

**kiishiikwáakeew** VAI finish sewing, finish sewing things. *ind 1st sg* **ngiishii=kwáake**, **ngiishiikwáakeem**. *conj 3rd sg* **kiishiikwáakeet**. *imp* **kiishii=kwáakeel**. *ptcpl* **kiishiikwáakeet**.

**kiishíimeew** VTA nominate s.o. for an office, nominate s.o. for a position. *ind 1st sg* **ngiishíimaaw**, **ngiishíima**. *ind 3rd sg* **kwiishiimáawal**. *ind inv* **ngiishíimukw**. *ind 1-you* **kiishíimul**. *conj 3rd sg* **kiishíimaat**. *imp* **kíishiim**. *ptcpl* **kiishíimaat**.

**kiishiitéeheew** VAI make up one's mind. *ind 1st sg* **ngiishiitéeha**, **ngiishiitée=haam**. *conj 3rd sg* **kiishiitéehaat**. *imp* **kiishiitéehaal**. *ptcpl* **kiishiitéehaat**.

**kiishíixiin** VAI be ready to use, be all set *(s.t. animate)*. *ind 1st sg* **ngiishíixiin**, **ngiishíixi**. *conj 3rd sg* **kiishíixiing**. *ptcpl* **kiishíixiing**.

**kiishiinjŭweextíikeew** VAI finish setting the table, be finished setting the table. *ind 1st sg* **ngiishiinjŭweextíike**, **ngii=shiinjŭweextíikeem**. *conj 3rd sg* **kii=shiinjŭweextíikeet**. *imp* **kiishiinjŭ=weextíikeel**. *ptcpl* **kiishiinjŭweex=tíikeet**.

**kiishíixtoow** VTI2 finish making s.t. *ind 1st sg* **ngiishíixtoon**. *ind 3rd sg* **kwiishíixtoon**. *conj 1st sg* **kiishiix=táwaan**. *conj 3rd sg* **kiishíixtaakw**. *imp* **kiishíixtool**. *ptcpl* **kiishíixtaakw**.

**kiishíixŭmeew** VTA get s.o. ready. *ind 1st sg* **ngiishíixŭmaaw**, **ngiishíixŭma**. *ind 3rd sg* **kwiishiixŭmáawal**. *ind inv* **ngiishíixŭmukw**. *ind 1-you* **kiishíi=xŭmul**. *conj 3rd sg* **kiishíixŭmaat**. *imp* **kiishíixum**. *ptcpl* **kiishíixŭmaat**.

**kiishíixun** VII be ready to use, be all set. **Kiishíixun ndapíinay.** 'My bed is made.' *conj 3rd sg* **kiishíixung**. *ptcpl* **kiishíixung**.

**kiishihtáawanuw** VII be ready-made. *conj 3rd sg* **kiishihtáawaniik**. *ptcpl* **kiishihtáawaniik**.

**kiishíhtoow** VTI2 make s.t., finish making s.t., be finished making s.t. **Méhch ngiishíhtoon.** 'I've finished making it.' *ind 1st sg* **ngiishíhtoon**. *ind 3rd sg* **kwiishíhtoon**. *conj 1st sg* **kiishíhtawaan**. *conj 3rd sg* **kiishíh=taakw**. *imp* **kiishíhtool**. *ptcpl* **kiishíhtaakw**.

**kíishkeew** VAI finish dancing, be finished dancing. *ind 1st sg* **ngíishka**, **ngíishkaam**. *conj 3rd sg* **kíishkaat**. *ptcpl* **kíishkaat**.

**kíishkwihk** PC today. **Kwáy kíishkwihk.** 'Today.'

**kiishkwŭnúwii** PC during the daytime. **Kiishkwŭnúwii ápih nátpwi.** 'I'll cook during the daytime.'

**kíishooxkw** NA sun. *pl* **kiishóoxkwak**. *obv* **kiishóoxkwal**. *See* **kíishŭwoxkw**.

**kíish'seew** VTA cook s.t. animate done, cook s.t. animate to completion. *ind 1st sg* **ngíish'saaw**, **ngíish'sa**. *ind 3rd sg* **kwiish'sáawal**. *ind inv* **ngíish'=sookw**. *ind 1-you* **kíish'sool**. *conj 3rd sg* **kíish'saat**. *imp* **kíishus**. *ptcpl* **kíish'saat**.

**kíish'sum** VTI1B cook s.t. done, cook s.t.

to completion. *ind 1st sg* **ngiish'=súmun**. *ind 3rd sg* **kwiish'súmun**. *conj 1st sg* **kiish'súmaan**. *conj 3rd sg* **kíish'sung**. *imp* **kíish'sih**. *ptcpl* **kíish'sung**.

**kíish'suw** VAI be done cooking, be finished cooking *(s.t. animate)*. *ind 1st sg* **ngíish'si**, **ngíish'siim**. *conj 3rd sg* **kíish'siit**. *ptcpl* **kíish'siit**.

**kíish'sheew** VTA finish cutting s.t. animate. *ind 1st sg* **ngíish'shaaw**, **ngíish'sha**. *ind 3rd sg* **kwiish'sháa=wal**. *ind inv* **ngíish'shookw**. *ind I-you* **kíish'shool**. *conj 3rd sg* **kíish'shaat**. *imp* **kíishush**. *ptcpl* **kíish'shaat**.

**kiish'shíikeew** VAI finish cutting things. *ind 1st sg* **ngiish'shíike**, **ngiish'shíi=keem**. *conj 3rd sg* **kiish'shíikeet**. *imp* **kiish'shíikeel**. *ptcpl* **kiish'shíikeet**.

**kíish'shum** VTI1B finish cutting s.t. *ind 1st sg* **ngiish'shúmun**. *ind 3rd sg* **kwiish'shúmun**. *conj 1st sg* **kiish'=shúmaan**. *conj 3rd sg* **kíish'shung**. *imp* **kíish'shih**. *ptcpl* **kíish'shung**.

**kíishteew** VII be done cooking, be finished cooking. *conj 3rd sg* **kíishteek**. *ptcpl* **kíishteek**.

**kiishtóonheew** VAI finish talking. *ind 1st sg* **ngiishtóonhe**, **ngiishtóonheem**. *conj 3rd sg* **kiishtóonheet**. *imp* **kiishtóonheel**. *ptcpl* **kiishtóonheet**.

**kiishŭwáapŭweew** VII be warm water. *conj 3rd sg* **kiishŭwáapŭweek**. *ptcpl* **kiishŭwáapŭweek**.

**kiishŭwaapŭwéesum** VTI1A heat s.t. up *(of water)*. *ind 1st sg* **ngiishŭwaapŭ=wéesŭmun**. *ind 3rd sg* **kwiishŭwaa=pŭwéesŭmun**. *conj 1st sg* **kiishŭ=waapŭwéesŭmaan**. *conj 3rd sg* **kii=shŭwaapŭwéesung**. *imp* **kiishŭwaa=pŭwéesih**. *ptcpl* **kiishŭwaapŭwée=sung**.

**kiishŭwálheew** VAI finish packing a load on one's back, be finished packing a load on one's back, be already packed. *ind 1st sg* **ngiishŭwálhe**, **ngiishŭwálheem**. *conj 3rd sg* **kii=shŭwálheet**. *imp* **kiishŭwálheel**. *ptcpl* **kiishŭwálheet**.

**kíishŭweew** VII be warm *(of temperatures)*. *conj 3rd sg* **kíishŭweek**. *ptcpl* **kíishŭweek**.

**kiishŭwii-** PN warm. **Kíishŭwii-wíikwahm.** 'Warm house.'

**kiishŭwíikaan** NI warm house. *pl* **kiishŭwiikáanal**.

**kiishŭwiikamíikat** VII be a warm room. *conj 3rd sg* **kiishŭwiikamíikahk**. *ptcpl* **kiishŭwiikamíikahk**.

**kiishŭwíikeew** VAI have a warm house. *ind 1st sg* **ngiishŭwíike**, **ngiishŭ=wíikeem**. *conj 3rd sg* **kiishŭwíikeet**. *ptcpl* **kiishŭwíikeet**.

**kiishŭwíhleew** VAI get warm. *ind 1st sg* **ngiishŭwíhla**, **ngiishŭwíhlaam**. *conj 3rd sg* **kiishŭwíhlaat**. *ptcpl* **kiishŭ=wíhlaat**.

**kiishŭwíhleew** VII get warm. *conj 3rd sg* **kiishŭwíhlaak**. *ptcpl* **kiishŭwíhlaak**.

**kíishŭwoxkw** NA sun. *pl* **kiishŭwóx=kwak**. *obv* **kiishŭwóxkwal**. *See* **kíishooxkw**.

**kiishŭwúndeew** VII be a warm room. *conj 3rd sg* **kiishŭwúndeek**. *ptcpl* **kiishŭwúndeek**.

**kiishŭwúpatoow** VTI2 heat s.t. up *(of water)*. *ind 1st sg* **ngiishŭwúpatoon**. *ind 3rd sg* **kwiishŭwúpatoon**. *conj 1st sg* **kiishŭwupatáwaan**. *conj 3rd sg* **kiishŭwúpataakw**. *imp* **kiishŭ=wúpatool**. *ptcpl* **kiishŭwúpataakw**.

**kiishŭwúpuy** NI warm water. *loc* **kiishŭwúpiing**.

**kiishŭwúseew** VTA heat s.o. up. *ind 1st sg* **ngiishŭwúsaaw**, **ngiishŭwúsa**. *ind 3rd sg* **kwiishŭwusáawal**. *ind inv* **ngiishŭwúsookw**. *ind I-you* **kiishŭ=wúsool**. *conj 3rd sg* **kiishŭwúsaat**. *imp* **kíishŭwus**. *ptcpl* **kiishŭwúsaat**.

**kiishŭwusíiteew** VAI have warm feet. *ind 1st sg* **ngiishŭwusíita**, **ngiishŭ=wusíitaam**. *conj 3rd sg* **kiishŭwus=**

íitaat. *ptcpl* **kiishŭwusíitaat**. *intensive reduplication* **akiishŭwusíiteew**.

**kiishŭwusiitéexiin** VAI have warm feet. *ind 1st sg* **ngiishŭwusiitéexiin, ngii=shŭwusiitéexi**. *conj 3rd sg* **kiishŭ=wusiitéexiing**. *ptcpl* **kiishŭwusii=téexiing**.

**kiishŭwúsum** VTI 1A heat s.t. up. *ind 1st sg* **ngiishŭwúsŭmun**. *ind 3rd sg* **kwiishŭwúsŭmun**. *conj 1st sg* **kii=shŭwúsŭmaan**. *conj 3rd sg* **kiishŭ=wúsung**. *imp* **kiishŭwúsih**. *ptcpl* **kiishŭwúsung**.

**kiiwaníindkweew** VAI be dizzy. *ind 1st sg* **ngiiwaníindkwe, ngiiwaníind=kweem**. *conj 3rd sg* **kiiwaníind=kweet**. *ptcpl* **kiiwaníindkweet**.

**kiiwaniindkwéhleew** VAI get dizzy all of a sudden. *ind 1st sg* **ngiiwaniind=kwéhla, ngiiwaniindkwéhlaam**. *conj 3rd sg* **kiiwaniindkwéhlaat**. *ptcpl* **kiiwaniindkwéhlaat**.

**kíixkii** PC near. **Kíixkii wiikwáhmung.** 'Near the house.'; **Níi kíixkii nŭwíiki eénda-amangaawungéeyayeek.** 'I lived near the mountains.' *See* **kíixku**.

**kiixkíhkaweew** VTA nudge s.o., kick s.o., poke s.o. *(to get his or her attention)*. *ind 1st sg* **ngiixkíhkawaaw, ngiix=kíhkawa**. *ind 3rd sg* **kwiixkihka=wáawal**. *ind inv* **ngiixkíhkaakw**. *ind I-you* **kiixkíhkool**. *conj 3rd sg* **kiixkíhkawaat**. *imp* **kiixkíhkaw**. *ptcpl* **kiixkíhkawaat**.

**kíixku** PC near. *informal*. **Kíixku peechíhle.** 'He flew close by.' *See* **kíixkii**.

**kíixkŭneew** VTA poke s.o., nudge s.o. *(to get his or her attention)*. *ind 1st sg* **ngíixkŭnaaw, ngíixkŭna**. *ind 3rd sg* **kwiixkŭnáawal**. *ind inv* **ngíixkŭ=nukw**. *ind I-you* **kíixkŭnul**. *conj 3rd sg* **kíixkŭnaat**. *imp* **kíixkun**. *ptcpl* **kíixkŭnaat**. *intensive reduplication* **kwihkiixkŭnáawal**.

**kihchi-** PV big, very. **Kíhchi-tóhpun.** 'There is a heavy frost.'; **Kíhchi-pahtamawéewak.** 'They're praying hard.' *ptcpl* **kéhchi-**. *intensive reduplication* **kihkihchu-**. *See* **kihchu-**, **kihkihchu-**.

**kihchu-** PV big, very. *informal*. **Kwíhchu-shoohŭmúnal.** 'They're painting them.'; **Kíhchu-kaatxak=hwátiin.** 'Everybody is cutting cordwood' *ptcpl* **kéhchu-**. *See* **kihchi-**, **kihkihchu-**.

**kihkáapeew** NA bachelor. *pl* **kihkaa=péewak**. *obv* **kihkaapéewal**.

**kihkaapéexkweew** NA unmarried adult woman. *pl* **kihkaapeexkwéewak**. *obv* **kihkaapeexkwéewal**.

**kihkaatéepuy** NI garter. *pl* **kihkaatée=pŭyal**. *poss* **ngihkaatéepŭyum**. *dimin* **kihkaachéepŭyush**.

**kíhkata-wéewsuw** VAI be nosy, want to know things. *ind 1st sg* **ngíhkata-wéewsi, ngíhkata-wéewsiim**. *conj 3rd sg* **kíhkata-wéewsiit**. *ptcpl* **kíhkata-wéewsiit**. *See* **katá-wéewsuw**.

**kíhkay** NA chief. *pl* **kíhkayak**. *poss* **ngíhkayum**. *obv* **kíhkayal**.

**kíhkayuw** VAI be chief, be the leader. *ind 1st sg* **ngíhkayi, ngíhkayiim**. *conj 3rd sg* **kíhkayiit**. *ptcpl* **kéhkayiit**.

**kíhkayuw** VAIO be older than s.o. *ind 1st sg* **ngíhkayiin**. *ind 3rd sg* **kwihka=yíinal**. *conj 3rd sg* **kíhkayiit**. *ptcpl* **kéhkayiit**.

**kihkayúmeew** VTA be older than s.o. *ind 1st sg* **ngihkayúmaaw, ngihkayúma**. *ind 3rd sg* **kwihkayumáawal**. *ind inv* **ngihkayúmukw**. *ind I-you* **kihka=yúmul**. *conj 3rd sg* **kihkayúmaat**. *ptcpl* **kehkayúmaat**.

**kihkayúmheew** VAIO make s.o. chief, make s.o. be the leader. *ind 1st sg* **ngihkayúmheen**. *ind 3rd sg* **kwih=kayumhéenal**. *conj 3rd sg* **kihka=yúmheet**. *imp* **kihkayúmheel**. *ptcpl* **kehkayúmheet**.

**kíhkees** NA old person. *pl* **kihkéesak**. *poss* **ngihkéesum**. *dimin* **kihkée=shush**. *obv* **kihkéesal**.
**kihkéesuw** VAI be old, get old. *ind 1st sg* **ngihkéesi**, **ngihkéesiim**. *conj 3rd sg* **kihkéesiit**.
**kihkeesŭwiináakwsuw** VAI look old, look like an elderly person. *ind 1st sg* **ngihkeesŭwiináakwsi**, **ngihkeesŭ=wiináakwsiim**. *conj 3rd sg* **kihkee=sŭwiináakwsiit**.
**kihkháasuw** VAI be marked *(s.t. animate)*. *ind 1st sg* **ngihkháasi**, **ngih=kháasiim**. *conj 3rd sg* **kihkháasiit**.
**kihkháasuw** VII be marked. *conj 3rd sg* **kihkháasiik**. *ptcpl* **kihkháasiik**.
**kíhkham** VTI IA mark s.t., make a sign on s.t., put one's name on clothes, mark the perimeters of s.t. *(using a tool or instrument)*. *ind 1st sg* **ngihk=hámun**. *ind 3rd sg* **kwihkhámun**. *conj 1st sg* **kihkhámaan**. *conj 3rd sg* **kíhkhang**. *imp* **kíhkhah**. *ptcpl* **kíhkhang**.
**kíhkheew** VTA mark s.t. animate, make a sign on s.t. animate, make a mark on s.t. animate *(using a tool or instrument)*. *ind 1st sg* **ngíhkhaaw**, **ngíhk=ha**. *ind 3rd sg* **kwihkháawal**. *ind inv* **ngíhkhookw**. *ind I-you* **kíhkhool**. *conj 3rd sg* **kíhkhaat**. *imp* **kíhkhaw**. *ptcpl* **kíhkhaat**.
**kihkiimalíhkeew** VAI tiptoe. *ind 1st sg* **ngihkiimalíhke**, **ngihkiimalíhkeem**. *conj 3rd sg* **kihkiimalíhkeet**. *imp* **kihkiimalíhkeel**. *ptcpl* **kihkiima=líhkeet**.
**kihkihchu-** PV very, intensely. *informal*. **Kihkíhchu-lpákshuw.** 'The little one was really crying.' *See* **kihchi-**, **kihchu-**.
**kihkoxkwéeneew** VTA hug s.o. around the neck. *ind 1st sg* **ngihkoxkwée=naaw**, **ngihkoxkwéena**. *ind 3rd sg* **kwihkoxkweenáawal**. *ind inv* **ngih=koxkwéenukw**. *ind I-you* **kihkox=kwéenul**. *conj 3rd sg* **kihkoxkwée=naat**. *imp* **kihkóxkween**. *ptcpl* **kihkoxkwéenaat**.
**kihkóxkweew** NA older single woman. *pl* **kihkoxkwéewak**. *obv* **kihkox=kwéewal**.
**kihkŭlóoleew** VTA talk to s.o. *ind 1st sg* **ngihkŭlóolaaw**, **ngihkŭlóola**. *ind 3rd sg* **kwihkŭlooláawal**. *ind inv* **ngih=kŭlóolukw**. *ind I-you* **kihkŭlóolul**. *conj 3rd sg* **kihkŭlóolaat**. *imp* **kíhkŭlool**. *ptcpl* **kihkŭlóolaat**.
**kihkŭwawéenuw** VAI be grown-up, be an adult. *ind 1st sg* **ngihkŭwawéeni**, **ngihkŭwawéeniim**. *conj 3rd sg* **kih=kŭwawéeniit**. *ptcpl* **kihkŭwawéeniit**.
**kihkŭwíilunuw** NA adult male, adult man. *pl* **kihkŭwiilŭnúwak**. *obv* **kihkŭwiilŭnúwal**. *See* **kíhkwu-lúnuw**.
**kihkŭwiináakwsuw** VAI look old, be old-looking, look older than one's age. *ind 1st sg* **ngihkŭwiináakwsi**, **ngih=kŭwiináakwsiim**. *conj 3rd sg* **kih=kŭwiináakwsiit**. *ptcpl* **kihkŭwii=náakwsiit**.
**kíhkwu-lúnuw** NA adult male, adult man. *pl* **kíhkwu-lúnŭwak**. *obv* **kíhkwu-lúnŭwal**. *See* **kihkuwíilŭnuw**.
**kíhkwu-óxkweew** NA adult woman. *pl* **kíhkwu-oxkwéewak**. *obv* **kíhkwu-oxkwéewal**.
**kihtaachíimuw** VAI tell a great story. *ind 1st sg* **ngihtaachíimwi**, **ngihtaachíi=mwiim**. *conj 3rd sg* **kihtaachíimwiit**. *imp* **kihtaachíimwiil**. *ptcpl* **kehtaa=chíimwiit**.
**kihtaaméhleew** VAI run fast. *ind 1st sg* **ngihtaaméhla**, **ngihtaaméhlaam**. *conj 3rd sg* **kihtaaméhlaat**. *imp* **kih=taaméhlaal**. *ptcpl* **kehtaaméhlaat**.
**kihtaaptóoneew** VAI make a speech. *ind 1st sg* **ngihtaaptóone**, **ngihtaaptóo=neem**. *conj 3rd sg* **kihtaaptóoneet**. *imp* **kihtaaptóoneew**. *ptcpl* **kehtaa=ptóoneet**.

**kihtahkwíixun** VII be high water. *conj 3rd sg* **kihtahkwíixung**. *ptcpl* **keh=tahkwíixung**.

**kihtamúneew** VAI be lazy. *ind 1st sg* **ngihtamúna, ngihtamúnaam**. *conj 3rd sg* **kihtamúnaat**. *ptcpl* **kehta=múnaat**.

**kihtanóongsuw** VAI be very angry, go into a rage. *ind 1st sg* **ngihtanóongsi, ngihtanóongsiim**. *conj 3rd sg* **kih=tanóongsiit**. *ptcpl* **kehtanóongsiit**.

**kihtapánzhuy** NI large piece of timber. *pl* **kihtapánzhŭyal**.

**kihtatáhkeew** VAI fight vigourously, have a big fight. *ind 1st sg* **ngihta=táhke, ngihtatáhkeem**. *conj 3rd sg* **kihtatáhkeet**. *imp* **kihtatáhkeel**. *ptcpl* **kehtatáhkeet**.

**kihtayapáayu** PC early in the morning.

**kihtéelook** VAI be a lot of people. *usually plural. ind 1st pl* **ngihteelóhna**. *indef subject* **kihtéelun**. *conj 3rd pl* **kihteelóhtiit**. *ptcpl* **kehteelóhtiit**.

**kihteelúndam** VOTI1A be in earnest, be serious *(about something)*; get up the nerve *(to do something)*. **Ngihtee=lúndam náh ndá.** 'I'm serious about going there.'; **Ngihteelúndam, ndúlaa máachiil.** 'I got up the nerve to tell him to go home.' *ind 1st sg* **ngihteelúndam**. *conj 3rd sg* **kihtee=lúndang**. *imp* **kihteelúndah**. *ptcpl* **kehteelúndang**.

**kihtootéenay** NI big town, city. *pl* **kihtootéenayal**. *loc* **kihtootéeneeng**.

**kihtootéenayuw** VAI have a lot of land. *ind 1st sg* **ngihtootéenayi, ngihtoo=téenayiim**. *conj 3rd sg* **kihtootéena=yiit**. *ptcpl* **kehtootéenayiit**. *See* **xwatootéenayuw**.

**kihtóxkwees** NA old woman. *pl* **kihtox=kwéesak**. *dimin* **kihchoxkwéeshush**. *obv* **kihtoxkwéesal**.

**kihtoxkwéesuw** VAI be an old woman, undergo menopause, undergo change of life. *ind 1st sg* **ngihtoxkwéesi, ngihtoxkwéesiim**. *conj 3rd sg* **kih=toxkwéesiit**. *ptcpl* **kehtoxkwéesiit**.

**kihtoxkweesŭwiináakwsuw** VAI look like an old woman. *ind 1st sg* **ngih=toxkweesŭwiináakwsi, ngihtox=kweesŭwiináakwsiim**. *conj 3rd sg* **kihtoxkweesŭwiináakwsiit**. *ptcpl* **kehtoxkweesŭwiináakwsiit**.

**kihtsíipuw** NI big river. *pl* **kihtsíipŭwal**. *loc* **kihtsíipoong**.

**kihtshámuw** VAI be piled high *(s.t. animate)*. *ind 1st sg* **ngihtshámwi, ngihtshámwiim**. *conj 3rd sg* **kiht=shámwiit**. *ptcpl* **kehtshámwiit**.

**kihtshámuw** VII be piled high. *conj 3rd sg* **kihtshámwiik**. *ptcpl* **kehtshám=wiik**.

**kihtshíimuw** VAI run away in a hurry. *ind 1st sg* **ngihtshíimwi, ngihtshíim=wiim**. *conj 3rd sg* **kihtshíimwiit**. *imp* **kihtshíimwiil**. *ptcpl* **kehtshíimwiit**.

**kíhtxun** VII be a strong wind *(especially of tornados)*. *conj 3rd sg* **kíhtxung**. *ptcpl* **kéhtxung**.

**kóokhoos** NA owl. *pl* **kookhóosak**. *poss* **ngookhóosum**. *loc* **kookhóosung**. *dimin* **kookhóoshush**. *obv* **kook=hóosal**.

**kóon** NA snow. *loc* **kóonung**. *dimin* **kóonush**. *obv* **kóonal**.

**koonahkéeyeew** VII be snowy ground, be snow on the ground. *conj 3rd sg* **koonahkéeyeek**. *ptcpl* **koonah=kéeyeek**.

**koonéelham** VAI make tracks in the snow. *ind 1st sg* **ngoonéelham**. *conj 3rd sg* **koonéelhang**. *ptcpl* **koonéelhang**.

**koonjcháashak** NA checkers. *usually plural. pl* **koonjcháashak**. *obv* **koonjcháashal**.

**koonjcháashuw** VAI play checkers. *ind 1st sg* **ngoonjcháashi, ngoonjcháa=shiim**. *conj 3rd sg* **koonjcháashiit**. *imp* **koonjcháashiil**. *ptcpl* **koonj=cháashiit**.

**koonóowuw** VAI be covered in snow,

have snow on oneself. **Wéemu táa ndúlu-koonóowiin.** 'I'm all covered in snow.' *ind 1st sg* **ngoonóowi, ngoonóowiim**. *conj 3rd sg* **koonóowiit**. *ptcpl* **koonóowiit**.

**kóonuw** VAI be snowy *(s.t. animate)*. *conj 3rd sg* **kóoniit**. *ptcpl* **kóoniit**.

**kóonuw** VII be snowy. *conj 3rd sg* **kóoniik**. *ptcpl* **kóoniik**.

**kóopmaan** NA storekeeper. *pl* **koop=máanak**. *obv* **koopmáanal**. *From Dutch.*

**koopmaanáhtakw** NI string. *pl* **koop=maanáhtakwal**. *poss* **ngoopmaa=náhtakwum**. *dimin* **koopmaanáh=chakwush**. *See* **koxptíikan**.

**koopmaaníikaan** NI store. *pl* **koop=maaniikáanal**. *loc* **koopmaaniikáa=nung**. *dimin* **koopmaaniikáanush**.

**kóoshkoosh** NA pig. *pl* **kooshkóoshak**. *poss* **ngooshkóoshum**. *loc* **koosh=kóoshung**. *dimin* **kooshkóoshush**. *obv* **kooshkóoshal**.

**kooshkooshóandup** NI pig's head. *pl* **kooshkooshóandpal**. *poss* **ngoosh=kooshóandpush**. *dimin* **kooshkoo=shóanjpush**.

**kooshkooshéewakw** NI pork. *pl* **koosh=kooshéewakwal**. *poss* **ngooshkoo=shéewakwum**. *loc* **kooshkooshée=wakwung**. *dimin* **kooshkooshéewa=kwush**.

**kóot** NI coat. *pl* **kóotal**. *poss* **ngóotum**. *loc* **kóotung**. *dimin* **kóochush**. *From English* coat.

**koothámeew** VAI wear a coat. *ind 1st sg* **ngootháma, ngoothámaam**. *conj 3rd sg* **koothámaat**. *imp* **koothámaal**. *ptcpl* **koothámaat**.

**kóowuy** NA cow. *pl* **kóoyak**. *poss* **ngóo=yum**. *dimin* **kóoyush**. *obv* **kóoyal**. *From Dutch.*

**kooxkáaweew** VAI upset, turn over in a boat, turn over in a car *(s.t. animate)*. *ind 1st sg* **ngooxkáawe, ngooxkáa=weem**. *conj 3rd sg* **kooxkáaweet**. *ptcpl* **kooxkáaweet**.

**kooxkáaweew** VII upset, turn over. *conj 3rd sg* **kooxkáaweek**. *ptcpl* **koox=káaweek**.

**kooxkáhleew** VII upset *(of boats)*. *conj 3rd sg* **kooxkáhlaak**. *ptcpl* **koox=káhlaak**.

**kóoychuy** NI cow droppings, cow excrement. *pl* **kooychúyal**.

**kooyéewakw** NI beef. *pl* **kooyéewa=kwal**. *poss* **ngooyéewakwum**. *loc* **kooyéewakwung**. *dimin* **kooyéewa=kwush**.

**kooyíikaan** NI cow shed, cow barn. *pl* **kooyiikáanal**. *poss* **ngooyiikáanum**. *loc* **kooyiikáanung**. *dimin* **kooyii=káanush**.

**kòhíikeew** VAI make a racket, make a non-oral sound. *ind 1st sg* **ngohíike, ngohíikeem**. *conj 3rd sg* **kòhíikeet**. *imp* **kóhíikeel**. *ptcpl* **kòhíikeet**.

**kóhla** PC mixed, mixed in *(with something)*. **Kíi kóhla kŭlunaapéewi.** 'You're part Indian.'; **Shŭwáapoow kóhla mbúy náh áhteew.** 'There's some water mixed in with the vinegar.'

**kohlawáaheew** VAIO mix s.t. in with something. *ind 1st sg* **ngohlawáa=heen**. *ind 3rd sg* **kohlawáaheen**. *conj 3rd sg* **kohlawáaheet**. *imp* **kohla=wáaheel**. *ptcpl* **kohlawáaheet**.

**kohlawíikun** VII grow mixed in with others. *conj 3rd sg* **kohlawíikung**. *ptcpl* **kohlawíikung**.

**kohlawíikuw** VAI grow mixed in with others. *ind 1st sg* **ngohlawíiki, ngohlawíikiim**. *conj 3rd sg* **kohlawíikiit**. *ptcpl* **kohlawíikiit**.

**kohlawíixiin** VAI be mixed in with others. *ind 1st sg* **ngohlawíixiin, ngohla=wíixi**. *conj 3rd sg* **kohlawíixiing**. *ptcpl* **kohlawíixiing**.

**kohlawíixtoow** VTI2 mix s.t. in with others. *ind 1st sg* **ngohlawíixtoon**. *ind 3rd sg* **kohlawíixtoon**. *conj 1st sg*

**kohlawiixtáwaan**. *conj 3rd sg* **kohlawíixtaakw**. *imp* **kohlawíixtool**. *ptcpl* **kohlawíixtaakw**.

**kohlawíixŭmeew** VTA mix s.o. in with others. *ind 1st sg* **ngohlawíixŭmaaw**, **ngohlawíixŭma**. *ind 3rd sg* **kohla=wiixŭmáawal**. *ind inv* **ngohlawíixŭ=mukw**. *ind I-you* **kohlawíixŭmul**. *conj 3rd sg* **kohlawíixŭmaat**. *imp* **kohlawíixum**. *ptcpl* **kohlawíi=xŭmaat**.

**kohlawíixun** VII be mixed in with others. *conj 3rd sg* **kohlawíixung**. *ptcpl* **kohlawíixung**.

**kohlawíhleew** VAI get mixed in *(with something)*. **Kohlawíhleew éenda-xwéelung.** 'He got mixed in with the crowd.' *ind 1st sg* **ngohlawíhla**, **ngohlawíhlaam**. *conj 3rd sg* **kohlawíhlaat**. *ptcpl* **kohlawíhlaat**.

**kohlawíhleew** VII get mixed in *(with something)*. *conj 3rd sg* **kohlawíh=laak**. *ptcpl* **kohlawíhlaak**.

**kohpaaháaleew** VTA throw s.o. off, unload s.o. *ind 1st sg* **ngohpaaháalaaw**, **ngohpaaháala**. *ind 3rd sg* **kohpaa=haaláawal**. *ind inv* **ngohpaaháa=lukw**. *ind I-you* **kohpaaháalul**. *conj 3rd sg* **kohpaaháalaat**. *imp* **kohpáahaal**. *ptcpl* **kohpaaháalaat**.

**kohpáaheew** VAIO throw s.t. off, unload s.t. *ind 1st sg* **ngohpáaheen**. *ind 3rd sg* **kohpáaheen**. *conj 3rd sg* **koh=páaheet**. *imp* **kohpáaheel**. *ptcpl* **kohpáaheet**.

**kohpakaalóhkweew** VAI have thick hair. *ind 1st sg* **ngohpakaalóhkwa**, **ngoh=pakaalóhkwaam**. *conj 3rd sg* **koh=pakaalóhkwaat**. *ptcpl* **kohpakaa=lóhkwaat**.

**kohpakaapéeksuw** VAI be thick *(of books or papers)*. *conj 3rd sg* **koh=pakaapéeksiit**. *ptcpl* **kohpakaa=péeksiit**.

**kohpakáhtakw** NI thick thread, yarn. *pl* **kohpakáhtakwal**. *poss* **ngohpakáh=takwum**. *loc* **kohpakáhtakwung**. *dimin* **kohpakáhchakwush**.

**kóhpakan** VII be thick. *conj 3rd sg* **kóhpakang**. *ptcpl* **kóhpakang**.

**kohpakii-** PN thick. **Kóhpakii-kehkaasiingwéehiin.** 'A thick towel.'

**kohpakiikaapawúwak** VAI stand in a bunch, be bunched up standing together. *usually plural*. *ind 1st pl* **ngoh=pakiikaapawíhna**. *conj 3rd pl* **koh=pakiikaapawíhtiit**. *imp* **kohpakii=káapawiikw**. *ptcpl* **kohpakiikaa=pawíhtiit**.

**kohpaku-** PV thick. *informal*. **Kóhpaku-pangéeyeew.** 'It's in thick pieces.' *ptcpl* **kóhpaku-**.

**kohpakúsuw** VAI be thick *(s.t. animate)*. *ind 1st sg* **ngohpakúsi**, **ngohpakús=iim**. *conj 3rd sg* **kohpakúsiit**. *ptcpl* **kohpakúsiit**.

**kohpakúsheew** VTA cut s.t. animate thickly. *ind 1st sg* **ngohpakúshaaw**, **ngohpakúsha**. *ind 3rd sg* **kohpa=kusháawal**. *ind inv* **ngohpakúsh=ookw**. *ind I-you* **kohpakúshool**. *conj 3rd sg* **kohpakúshaat**. *imp* **kóhpa=kush**. *ptcpl* **kohpakúshaat**.

**kohpakusháasuw** VAI be cut thick *(s.t. animate)*. *ind 1st sg* **ngohpakusháasi**, **ngohpakusháasiim**. *conj 3rd sg* **kohpakusháasiit**. *ptcpl* **kohpa=kusháasiit**.

**kohpakusháasuw** VII be cut thick. *conj 3rd sg* **kohpakusháasiik**. *ptcpl* **kohpakusháasiik**.

**kohpakúshum** VTI1B cut s.t. thickly. *ind 1st sg* **ngohpakúshŭmun**. *ind 3rd sg* **kohpakúshŭmun**. *conj 1st sg* **koh=pakúshŭmaan**. *conj 3rd sg* **kohpa=kúshung**. *imp* **kohpakúshih**. *ptcpl* **kohpakúshung**.

**kóhpii** PC forest, in the bush. **Wéemi talí wŭlatéexun kóhpii.** 'There are lots of good roads in the bush.'; **Kóhpii éewak.** 'They went in the bush.'

**kóhpiiw** VAI-S disembark, get out of a vehicle. *ind 1st sg* **ngóhpi**, **ngóhpiim**. *emphatic pl* **kohpooltúwak**. *conj 3rd sg* **kóhpiit**. *imp* **kóhpiil**. *ptcpl* **kóhpiit**.

**kóhpŭneew** VTA unload s.o., take s.o. out of the water, take s.o. out of a vehicle, remove s.o. **Ngohpŭnáawak óhpŭnak.** 'I took the potatoes off (the stove).' *ind 1st sg* **ngóhpŭnaaw**, **ngóhpŭna**. *ind 3rd sg* **kohpŭnáawal**. *ind inv* **ngóhpŭnukw**. *ind I-you* **kóhpŭnul**. *conj 3rd sg* **kóhpŭnaat**. *imp* **kóhpun**. *ptcpl* **kóhpŭnaat**.

**kóhpŭnum** VTI1B unload s.t., take s.t. out of the water, take s.t. out of a vehicle. *ind 1st sg* **ngohpŭnúmun**. *ind 3rd sg* **kohpŭnúmun**. *conj 1st sg* **kohpŭnúmaan**. *conj 3rd sg* **kóhpŭ=nung**. *imp* **kóhpŭnih**. *ptcpl* **kóhpŭnung**.

**kòhŭnáakwsuw** VAI make noise. *ind 1st sg* **ngohŭnáakwsi**, **ngohŭnáakwsiim**. *conj 3rd sg* **kòhŭnáakwsiit**. *imp* **kòhŭnáakwsiil**. *ptcpl* **kòhŭnáakw=siit**.

**kòkómush** NI cucumber. *pl* **kòkómshal**. *poss* **ngokómshum**. *loc* **kòkóm=shung**. *dimin* **kòkómshush**. *See* **kòmkómush**. *From Dutch.*

**kòmkómush** NI cucumber. *pl* **kòm=kómshal**. *poss* **ngomkómshum**. *loc* **kòmkómshung**. *dimin* **kòmkóm=shush**. *See* **kòkómush**. *From Dutch.*

**koxpíileew** VTA tie s.o. up. *ind 1st sg* **ngoxpíilaaw**, **ngoxpíila**. *ind 3rd sg* **koxpiiláawal**. *ind inv* **ngoxpíilukw**. *ind I-you* **koxpíilul**. *conj 3rd sg* **koxpíilaat**. *imp* **kóxpiil**. *ptcpl* **keexpíilaat**.

**koxpiilkwúsuw** VAI be tied up. *ind 1st sg* **ngoxpiilkwúsi**, **ngoxpiilkwúsiim**. *conj 3rd sg* **koxpiilkwúsiit**. *ptcpl* **keexpiilkwúsiit**.

**koxpíisuw** VAI be tied up. *ind 1st sg* **ngoxpíisi**, **ngoxpíisiim**. *conj 3rd sg* **koxpíisiit**. *ptcpl* **keexpíisiit**.

**koxptáasuw** VII be tied up. *conj 3rd sg* **koxptáasiik**. *ptcpl* **keexptáasiik**.

**koxptíikan** NI string. *pl* **koxptíikanal**. *poss* **ngoxptíikan**. *loc* **koxptíika=nung**. *dimin* **koxpchíikanush**. *See* **koopmaanáhtakw**.

**kóxptoow** VTI2 tie s.t. up. *ind 1st sg* **ngóxptoon**. *ind 3rd sg* **kóxptoon**. *conj 1st sg* **koxptáwaan**. *conj 3rd sg* **kóxptaakw**. *imp* **kóxptool**. *ptcpl* **kéexptaakw**.

**kpáaheew** VAIO slam s.t. shut *(of windows, of doors)*. *ind 1st sg* **ngupáa=heen**. *ind 3rd sg* **kwupáaheen**. *conj 3rd sg* **kpáaheet**. *imp* **kpáaheel**. *ptcpl* **keepáaheet**.

**kpáandpeew** VAI be empty headed, be stupid. *ind 1st sg* **ngupáandpa**, **ngupáandpaam**. *conj 3rd sg* **kpáandpaat**. *ptcpl* **keepáandpaat**.

**kpaandpeepíisuw** VAI have something wrapped around one's head, wrap one's head up. *ind 1st sg* **ngupaand=peepíisi**, **ngupaandpeepíisiim**. *conj 3rd sg* **kpaandpeepíisiit**. *ptcpl* **keepaandpeepíisiit**.

**kpaapehlatíikan** NI curtain. *pl* **kpaa=pehlatíikanal**. *poss* **ngupaapehlatíi=kan**. *loc* **kpaapehlatíikanung**. *dimin* **kpaapehlachíikanush**.

**kpaapéhleew** VII hang closed, be closed. *conj 3rd sg* **kpaapéhlaak**. *ptcpl* **keepaapéhlaak**.

**kpaasíitŭyeew** VAI have a tight backside, have a tight ass. *ind 1st sg* **ngupaasíitŭya**, **ngupaasíitŭyaam**. *conj 3rd sg* **kpaasíitŭyaat**. *ptcpl* **keepaasíitŭyaat**.

**kpaháasuw** VAI be in jail, be shut in, be shut out. *ind 1st sg* **ngupháasi**, **ngupháasiim**. *conj 3rd sg* **kpaháasiit**. *ptcpl* **keepháasiit**.

**kpaháasuw** VII be closed, be shut in, be shut out. *conj 3rd sg* **kpaháasiik**. *ptcpl* **keepháasiik**.

**kpáham** VTI 1A shut s.t. out, shut s.t. in, close s.t. *ind 1st sg* **nguphámun**. *ind 3rd sg* **kwuphámun**. *conj 1st sg* **kpáhŭmaan**. *conj 3rd sg* **kpáhang**. *imp* **kpáhih**. *ptcpl* **kéephang**.

**kpáheew** VTA shut s.o. out, shut s.o. in, close s.t. animate. *ind 1st sg* **ngúp=haaw**, **ngúpha**. *ind 3rd sg* **kwup=háawal**. *ind inv* **ngúphookw**. *ind I-you* **kúphool**. *conj 3rd sg* **kpáhaat**. *imp* **kpáh**. *ptcpl* **kéephaat**.

**kpahíikeew** VAI close things up, shut things in, shut things out. *ind 1st sg* **nguphíike**, **nguphíikeem**. *conj 3rd sg* **kpahíikeet**. *imp* **kpahíikeel**. *ptcpl* **keephíikeet**.

**kpáhoon** NI door. *pl* **kpahóonal**. *poss* **ngúphoon**. *loc* **kpahóonung**. *dimin* **kpahóonush**.

**kpahootíikaan** NI jail. *pl* **kpahootii=káanal**. *loc* **kpahootiikáanung**.

**kpáskham** VTI 1A bottle s.t., put s.t. in cans; block s.t. *ind 1st sg* **ngupask=hámun**. *ind 3rd sg* **kwupaskhámun**. *conj 1st sg* **kpaskhámaan**. *conj 3rd sg* **kpáskhang**. *imp* **kpáskhah**. *ptcpl* **keepáskhang**.

**kpáskheew** VTA can s.t. animate, put s.t. animate in cans; block s.o., plug s.t. animate, fill in the cracks of s.t. animate, winterize s.t. animate *(especially of windows)*. *ind 1st sg* **ngup=áskhaaw**, **ngupáskha**. *ind 3rd sg* **kwupaskháawal**. *ind inv* **ngupásk=hookw**. *ind I-you* **kupáskhool**. *conj 3rd sg* **kpáskhaat**. *imp* **kpáskhaw**. *ptcpl* **keepáskhaat**.

**kpaskhíikan** NI plug, cork. *pl* **kpask=híikanal**. *poss* **ngupaskhíikan**. *loc* **kpaskhíikanung**. *dimin* **kpashkhíi=kanush**.

**kpaskhíikeew** VAI plug things up, caulk things, fill in chinks. *ind 1st sg* **ngupaskhíike**, **ngupaskhíikeem**. *conj 3rd sg* **kpaskhíikeet**. *imp* **kpaskhíikeel**. *ptcpl* **keepaskhíikeet**.

**kpaskíhleew** VAI be constipated. *ind 1st sg* **ngupaskíhla**, **ngupaskíhlaam**. *conj 3rd sg* **kpaskíhlaat**. *ptcpl* **keepaskíhlaat**.

**kpaskŭníikan** NI plug, cork. *pl* **kpas=kŭníikanal**. *poss* **nkupaskŭníikan**. *obv* **kpaskuníikanush**.

**kpátun** VII be covered, have a lid; be frozen over. *conj 3rd sg* **kpátung**. *ptcpl* **kéepatung**.

**kpaxéeneew** VTA cover s.o.'s ears *(using the hands)*. *ind 1st sg* **ngupxéenaaw**, **ngupxéena**. *ind 3rd sg* **kwupxee=náawal**. *ind inv* **ngupxéenukw**. *ind I-you* **kupxéenul**. *conj 3rd sg* **kpaxée=naat**. *imp* **kpáxeen**. *ptcpl* **keepxée=naat**. *See* **kpoxwéeneew**.

**kpaxéexiin** VAI cover one's ears, have one's ears covered. *ind 1st sg* **ngup=xéexiin**, **ngupxéexi**. *conj 3rd sg* **kpaxéexiing**. *imp* **kpaxéexiil**. *ptcpl* **keepxéexiing**. *See* **kpoxwéexiin**.

**kpaxéexŭmeew** VTA cover s.o.'s ears. *ind 1st sg* **ngupxéexŭmaaw**, **ngup=xéexŭma**. *ind 3rd sg* **kwupxeexŭ=máawal**. *ind inv* **ngupxéexŭmukw**. *ind I-you* **kupxéexŭmul**. *conj 3rd sg* **kpaxéexŭmaat**. *imp* **kpaxéexum**. *ptcpl* **keepxéexŭmaat**.

**kpáxookw** VAI be blown shut by the wind, be shut in by the wind, be shut out by the wind. *ind 1st sg* **ngúp=xookw**. *conj 3rd sg* **kpaxóokwuk**. *ptcpl* **keepxóokwuk**.

**kpáxun** VII be blown shut by the wind, be shut in by the wind, be shut out by the wind. *conj 3rd sg* **kpáxung**. *ptcpl* **kéepxung**.

**kpiikáapawuw** VAI stand in the way. *ind 1st sg* **ngupiikáapawi**, **ngupiikáa=pawiim**. *conj 3rd sg* **kpiikáapawiit**. *imp* **kpiikáapawiil**. *ptcpl* **keepiikáa=pawiit**.

**kpiingwéeneew** VTA blindfold s.o. *indef subject* **kpiingwéenaaw**. *ind 1st sg* **ngupiingwéenaaw**, **ngupiingwéena**.

*ind 3rd sg* **kwupiingweenáawal**. *ind inv* **ngupiingwéenukw**. *ind I-you* **kupiingwéenul**. *conj 3rd sg* **kpiin=gwéenaat**. *imp* **kpíingween**. *ptcpl* **keepiingwéenaat**.

**kpiingwéexŭmeew** VTA put blinders on s.o. *(especially of horses)*. *ind 1st sg* **ngupiingwéexŭmaaw**, **ngupiin=gwéexŭma**. *ind 3rd sg* **kwupiin=gweexŭmáawal**. *ind inv* **ngupiin=gwéexŭmukw**. *ind I-you* **kupiin=gwéexŭmul**. *conj 3rd sg* **kpiingwée=xŭmaat**. *imp* **kpiingwéexum**. *ptcpl* **keepiingwéexŭmaat**.

**kpíitŭyeew** VAI be constipated. *ind 1st sg* **ngupíitŭya**, **ngupíitŭyaam**. *conj 3rd sg* **kpíitŭyaat**. *ptcpl* **keepíitŭyaat**.

**kpíixiin** VAI be in the way. *ind 1st sg* **ngupíixiin**, **ngupíixi**. *conj 3rd sg* **kpíixiing**. *ptcpl* **keepíixiing**.

**kpíixun** VII be in the way. *conj 3rd sg* **kpíixung**. *ptcpl* **keepíixung**. *See* **kàkpíixun**.

**kpíhleew** VII close. *conj 3rd sg* **kpíhlaak**. *ptcpl* **keepíhlaak**.

**kpoxwéeneew** VTA cover s.o.'s ears *(using the hands)*. *ind 1st sg* **ngupxwée=naaw**, **ngupxwéena**. *ind 3rd sg* **kwupxweenáawal**. *ind inv* **ngup=xwéenukw**. *ind I-you* **kupxwéenul**. *conj 3rd sg* **kpoxwéenaat**. *imp* **kpóxween**. *ptcpl* **keepxéenaat**. *See* **kpaxéeneew**.

**kpoxwéexiin** VAI cover one's ears, have one's ears covered. *ind 1st sg* **ngupxwéexiin**, **ngupxwéexi**. *conj 3rd sg* **kpoxwéexiing**. *ptcpl* **keepxéexiing**. *See* **kpaxéexiin**.

**kpúcheew** VAI be silly, be foolish. *ind 1st sg* **ngúpcha**, **ngúpchaam**. *conj 3rd sg* **kpúchaat**. *ptcpl* **kéepchaat**.

**kpucheewháasuw** VAI have fun, get into things in a playful way. *ind 1st sg* **ngupcheewháasi**, **ngupcheewháa=siim**. *conj 3rd sg* **kpucheewháasiit**. *ptcpl* **keepcheewháasiit**.

**kpucheewíineew** VAI be mentally ill. *ind 1st sg* **ngupcheewíine**, **ngupchee=wíineem**. *conj 3rd sg* **kpucheewíi=neet**. *ptcpl* **keepcheewíineet**.

**kpucheewíisŭmuw** VAI be crazy from drinking, be silly from drinking. *ind 1st sg* **ngupcheewíisŭmwi**, **ngup=cheewíisŭmwiim**. *conj 3rd sg* **kpucheewíisŭmwiit**. *ptcpl* **keepc=heewíisŭmwiit**.

**kpucheewtóonheew** VAI talk foolishly. *ind 1st sg* **ngupcheewtóonhe**, **ngup=cheewtóonheem**. *conj 3rd sg* **kpuch=eewtóonheet**. *imp* **kpucheewtóon=heel**. *ptcpl* **keepcheewtóonheet**. *moderative reduplication* **kaakpuch=eewtóonheew**.

**kpuchéhleew** VAI become silly, become crazy. *ind 1st sg* **ngupchéhla**, **ngup=chéhlaam**. *conj 3rd sg* **kpuchéhlaat**. *ptcpl* **keepchéhlaat**.

**kpútoon** NA a mute, person who can't talk. *pl* **kputóonak**. *obv* **kputóonal**.

**kputóoneew** VAI be mute, be unable to talk. *ind 1st sg* **nguptóona**, **ngup=tóonaam**. *conj 3rd sg* **kputóonaat**. *ptcpl* **keeptóonaat**.

**ksiilúnjeew** VAI wash one's hands. *ind 1st sg* **ngusiilúnje**, **ngusiilúnjeem**. *conj 3rd sg* **ksiilúnjeet**. *imp* **ksiilúnjeel**. *ptcpl* **keesiilúnjeet**.

**ksíingweew** VAI wash one's face. *ind 1st sg* **ngusíingwe**, **ngusíingweem**. *conj 3rd sg* **ksíingweet**. *imp* **ksíingweel**. *ptcpl* **keesíingweet**.

**ksiingwéeneew** VTA wash s.o.'s face. *ind 1st sg* **ngusiingwéenaaw**, **ngusiin=gwéena**. *ind 3rd sg* **kwusiingwee=náawal**. *ind inv* **ngusiingwéenukw**. *ind I-you* **kusiingwéenul**. *conj 3rd sg* **ksiingwéenaat**. *imp* **ksíingween**. *ptcpl* **keesiingwéenaat**.

**ksháaheew** VAIO throw s.t. hard. *ind 1st sg* **ngusháaheen**. *ind 3rd sg* **kwush=áaheen**. *conj 3rd sg* **ksháaheet**. *imp* **ksháaheel**. *ptcpl* **keesháaheet**. *inten-*

*sive reduplication* **kwaksháaheen**.

**kshaaptoonáaleew** VTA make a cutting remark to s.o., talk so as to injure s.o. *ind 1st sg* **ngushaaptoonáalaaw**, **ngushaaptoonáala**. *ind 3rd sg* **kwushaaptoonaaláawal**. *ind inv* **nngushaaptoonáalukw**. *ind I-you* **kushaaptoonáalul**. *conj 3rd sg* **kshaaptoonáalaat**. *imp* **kshaap=tóonaal**. *ptcpl* **keeshaaptoonáalaat**.

**kshaaptóoneew** VAI speak quickly, speak in a harsh tone, speak in a sharp tone, say harsh things, say sharp things. *ind 1st sg* **ngushaap=tóone**, **ngushaaptóoneem**. *conj 3rd sg* **kshaaptóoneet**. *imp* **kshaaptóo=neel**. *ptcpl* **keeshaaptóoneet**. *intensive reduplication* **akushaaptóoneew**.

**kshaashŭwíhleew** VAI swim quickly. *ind 1st sg* **ngushaashŭwíhla**, **ngushaa=shŭwíhlaam**. *conj 3rd sg* **kshaashŭ=wíhlaat**. *imp* **kshaashŭwíhlaal**. *ptcpl* **keeshaashŭwíhlaat**.

**kshahtakíhleew** VAI run fast. *ind 1st sg* **ngushahtakíhla**, **ngushahtakíh=laam**. *conj 3rd sg* **kshahtakíhlaat**. *imp* **kshahtakíhlaal**. *ptcpl* **keeshah=takíhlaat**.

**kshalaawhúnzuw** VAI go quickly using a cane. *ind 1st sg* **ngushalaawhúnzi**, **ngushalaawhúnziim**. *conj 3rd sg* **kshalaawhúnziit**. *imp* **kshalaaw=húnziil**. *ptcpl* **keeshalaawhúnziit**.

**kshalóhkeew** VAI work fast. *ind 1st sg* **ngushalóhke**, **ngushalóhkeem**. *conj 3rd sg* **kshalóhkeet**. *imp* **kshalóhkeel**. *ptcpl* **keeshalóhkeet**.

**kshámeew** VTA bite and injure s.o. *ind 1st sg* **ngúshamaaw**, **ngúshama**. *ind 3rd sg* **kwushamáawal**. *ind inv* **ngúshamukw**. *ind I-you* **kúshamul**. *conj 3rd sg* **kshámaat**. *imp* **ksham**. *ptcpl* **kéeshamaat**.

**kshamándam** VTI1A have s.t. hurt *(of one's feelings)*. **Néeka kwéek úw, móxa ngushamándamun.** 'He said something and really hurt my feelings.' *ind 1st sg* **ngushamándamun**. *ind 3rd sg* **kwushamándamun**. *conj 1st sg* **kshamándamaan**. *conj 3rd sg* **kshamándang**. *ptcpl* **keeshamán=dang**.

**kshándam** VTI1A bite s.t. and injure it. *ind 1st sg* **ngushándamun**. *ind 3rd sg* **kwushándamun**. *conj 1st sg* **kshándamaan**. *conj 3rd sg* **kshán=dang**. *imp* **kshándah**. *ptcpl* **kee=shándang**.

**ksháxun** VII be windy, be blowing *(of the wind)*. *conj 3rd sg* **ksháxung**. *ptcpl* **kéesh'xung**.

**kshéelŭmeew** VTA think s.o. to be smart, have a high opinion of s.o., think s.o. competent. *ind 1st sg* **ngushéelŭ=maaw**, **ngushéelŭma**. *ind 3rd sg* **kwusheelŭmáawal**. *ind inv* **ngush=éelŭmukw**. *ind I-you* **kushéelŭmul**. *conj 3rd sg* **kshéelŭmaat**. *imp* **kshéelum**. *ptcpl* **keeshéelŭmaat**.

**kshíikun** VII grow quickly. *conj 3rd sg* **kshíikung**. *ptcpl* **keeshíikung**.

**kshíikuw** VAI grow quickly *(s.t. animate)*. *ind 1st sg* **ngushíiki**, **ngushíikiim**. *conj 3rd sg* **kshíikiit**. *ptcpl* **keeshíi=kiit**.

**kshiikwsíhleew** VAI crawl quickly. *ind 1st sg* **ngushiikwsíhla**, **ngushiikw=síhlaam**. *conj 3rd sg* **kshiikwsíhlaat**. *imp* **kshiikwsíhlaal**. *ptcpl* **keeshii=kwsíhlaat**.

**kshíikwsuw** VAI crawl quickly. *ind 1st sg* **ngushíikwsi**, **ngushíikwsiim**. *conj 3rd sg* **kshíikwsiit**. *imp* **kshíikwsiil**. *ptcpl* **keeshíikwsiit**.

**kshíilaan** VII rain hard, rain heavily. *conj 3rd sg* **kshíilaang**. *ptcpl* **kee=shíilaang**.

**kshiilawéhtoow** VOTI2 show off. *ind 1st sg* **ngushiilawéhto**. *conj 3rd sg* **kshii=lawéhtaakw**. *imp* **kshiilawéhtool**. *ptcpl* **keeshiilawéhtaakw**.

**kshiipaalakíingweew** VAI scratch one's

eyes, have itchy eyes. *ind 1st sg* **ngushiipaalakíingwa**, **ngushiipaa=lakíingwaam**. *conj 3rd sg* **kshiipaa=lakíingwaat**. *imp* **kshiipaalakíin=gwaal**. *ptcpl* **keeshiipaalakíingwaat**.

**kshiipáandpeew** VAI scratch one's head, have an itchy head. *ind 1st sg* **ngush=iipáandpa**, **ngushiipáandpaam**. *conj 3rd sg* **kshiipáandpaat**. *imp* **kshii=páandpaal**. *ptcpl* **keeshiipáandpaat**.

**kshíipeew** VII be itchy. *conj 3rd sg* **kshíipeek**. *ptcpl* **keeshíipeek**.

**kshiipiingwáaleew** VTA scratch an itch on s.o.'s face for them. *ind 1st sg* **ngushiipiingwáalaaw**, **ngushiipiin=gwáala**. *ind 3rd sg* **kwushiipiin=gwaaláawal**. *ind inv* **ngushiipiin=gwáalukw**. *ind I-you* **kushiipiin=gwáalul**. *conj 3rd sg* **kshiipiingwáa=laat**. *imp* **kshiipíingwaal**. *ptcpl* **kee=shiipiingwáalaat**. *See* **kshiipiin=gwéeneew**.

**kshiipiingwéeneew** VTA scratch an itch on s.o.'s face for them. *ind 1st sg* **ngushiipiingwéenaaw**, **ngushiipiin=gwéena**. *ind 3rd sg* **kwushiipiin=gweenáawal**. *ind inv* **nkushiipiin=gwéenukw**. *ind I-you* **kushiipiin=gwéenul**. *conj 3rd sg* **kshiipiingwée=naat**. *imp* **kshiipíingween**. *ptcpl* **keeshiipiingwéenaat**. *See* **kshii=piingwáaleew**.

**kshiipíingweew** VAI scratch one's face, have an itchy face. *ind 1st sg* **ngush=iipíingwa**, **ngushiipíingwaam**. *conj 3rd sg* **kshiipíingweew**. *imp* **kshii=píingwaal**. *ptcpl* **keeshiipíingwaat**.

**kshiipkáateew** VAI scratch one's leg, have an itchy leg. *ind 1st sg* **ngush=iipkáata**, **ngushiipkáataam**. *conj 3rd sg* **kshiipkáataat**. *imp* **kshiip=káataal**. *ptcpl* **keeshiipkáataat**.

**kshiippóxkwaneew** VAI scratch one's back, have an itchy back. *ind 1st sg* **ngushiippóxkwana**, **ngushiippóx=kwanaam**. *conj 3rd sg* **kshiippóx=kwanaat**. *imp* **kshiippóxkwanaal**. *ptcpl* **keeshiippóxkwanaat**.

**kshiippoxkwanéeneew** VTA scratch s.o.'s back. *ind 1st sg* **ngushiippoxkwa=néenaaw**, **ngushiippoxkwanéena**. *ind 3rd sg* **kwushiippoxkwanee=náawal**. *ind inv* **ngushiippoxkwa=néenukw**. *ind I-you* **kushiippox=kwanéenul**. *conj 3rd sg* **kshiippox=kwanéenaat**. *imp* **kshiippóxkwa=neen**. *ptcpl* **keeshiippoxkwanéenaat**.

**kshiipsíiteew** VAI scratch one's feet, have itchy feet. *ind 1st sg* **ngushiipsíita**, **ngushiipsíitaam**. *conj 3rd sg* **kshiip=síitaat**. *imp* **kshiipsíitaal**. *ptcpl* **keeshiipsíitaat**.

**kshíipsuw** VAI be itchy, scratch oneself. *ind 1st sg* **ngushíipsi**, **ngushíipsiim**. *conj 3rd sg* **kshíipsiit**. *imp* **kshíipsiil**. *ptcpl* **keeshíipsiit**.

**kshíipŭneew** VTA scratch s.o.'s itch. *ind 1st sg* **ngushíipŭnaaw**, **ngushíipŭna**. *ind 3rd sg* **kwushiipŭnáawal**. *ind inv* **ngushíipŭnukw**. *ind I-you* **kushíi=pŭnul**. *conj 3rd sg* **kshíipŭnaat**. *imp* **kshíipun**. *ptcpl* **keeshíipŭnaat**.

**kshiipŭníikeew** VAI scratch an itch. *ind 1st sg* **ngushiipŭníike**, **ngushiipŭ=níikeem**. *conj 3rd sg* **kshiipŭníikeet**. *imp* **kshiipŭníikeel**. *ptcpl* **keeshiipŭ=níikeet**.

**kshíipŭnum** VTI 1B scratch s.t., scratch s.t. that is itchy. *ind 1st sg* **ngushii=pŭnúmun**. *ind 3rd sg* **kwushiipŭ=númun**. *conj 1st sg* **kshiipŭnúmaan**. *conj 3rd sg* **kshíipŭnung**. *imp* **kshíipŭnih**. *ptcpl* **keeshíipŭnung**.

**kshíiteew** NI soup. *poss* **ngushiitéehum**. *loc* **kshiitéehung**.

**kshiitéewheew** VAI make soup. *ind 1st sg* **ngushiitéewhe**, **ngushiitéewheem**. *conj 3rd sg* **kshiitéewheet**. *imp* **kshiitéewheel**. *ptcpl* **keeshiitéew=heet**.

**kshiixáapan** VII be the break of day, get to be daylight *(just before dawn)*.

*conj 3rd sg* **kshiixáapang**. *ptcpl* **kee=shiixáapang**.

**kshiixaníikeew** VAI brush one's teeth. *ind 1st sg* **ngushiixaníika, ngushiixaníi=kaam**. *conj 3rd sg* **kshiixaníikaat**. *imp* **kshiixaníikaal**. *ptcpl* **keeshiixa=níikaat**.

**kshiixhúnzuw** VAI wash oneself. *ind 1st sg* **ngushiixhúnzi, ngushiixhúnziim**. *conj 3rd sg* **kshiixhúnziit**. *imp* **kshiixhúnziil**. *ptcpl* **keeshiixhúnziit**.

**kshiixiiktúkweew** VAI wash one's knees. *ind 1st sg* **ngushiixiiktúkwa, ngushiixiiktúkwaam**. *conj 3rd sg* **kshiixiiktúkwaat**. *imp* **kshiixiiktúk=waal**. *ptcpl* **keeshiixiiktúkwaat**.

**kshiixiikwáhmeew** VAI scrub the floor. *ind 1st sg* **ngushiixiikwáhme, ngushiixiikwáhmeem**. *conj 3rd sg* **kshiixiikwáhmeet**. *imp* **kshiixii=kwáhmeel**. *ptcpl* **keeshiixiikwáh=meet**.

**kshiixiinjŭwáakan** NI dishcloth. *pl* **kshiixiinjŭwáakanal**. *poss* **ngushii=xiinjŭwáakan**. *loc* **kshiixiinjŭwáa=kanung**. *dimin* **kshiixiinjŭwáaka=nush**.

**kshiixíinjŭweew** VAI wash the dishes. *ind 1st sg* **ngushiixíinjŭwe, ngushiixíinjŭweem**. *conj 3rd sg* **kshiixíinjŭweet**. *imp* **kshiixíin=jŭweel**. *ptcpl* **keeshiixíinjŭweet**.

**kshiixíiskwaneew** VAI wash one's elbows. *ind 1st sg* **ngushiixíiskwana, ngushiixíiskwanaam**. *conj 3rd sg* **kshiixíiskwanaat**. *imp* **kshiixíis=kwanaal**. *ptcpl* **keeshiixíiskwanaat**.

**kshiixihtawákeew** VAI wash one's ears. *ind 1st sg* **ngushiixihtawáke, ngush=iixihtawákeem**. *conj 3rd sg* **kshiixih=tawákeet**. *imp* **kshiixihtawákeel**. *ptcpl* **keeshiixihtawákeet**.

**kshiixihtawakéeneew** VTA wash s.o.'s ears. *ind 1st sg* **ngushiixihtawakée=naaw, ngushiixihtawakéena**. *ind 3rd sg* **kwushiixihtawakeenáawal**. *ind inv* **ngushiixihtawakéenukw**. *ind I-you* **kushiixihtawakéenul**. *conj 3rd sg* **kshiixihtawakéenaat**. *imp* **kshii=xihtawákeen**. *ptcpl* **keeshiixihta=wakéenaat**.

**kshiixihtawakeeníikeew** VAI wash people's ears. *ind 1st sg* **ngushiixihta=wakeeníike, ngushiixihtawakee=níikeem**. *conj 3rd sg* **kshiixihtawak=eeníikeet**. *imp* **kshiixihtawakeeníi=keel**. *ptcpl* **keeshiixihtawakee=níikeet**.

**kshiixkáateew** VAI wash one's legs. *ind 1st sg* **ngushiixkáata, ngushiixkáa=taam**. *conj 3rd sg* **kshiixkáataat**. *imp* **kshiixkáataal**. *ptcpl* **keeshiixkáa=taat**.

**kshiixkaatéeneew** VTA wash s.o.'s legs. *ind 1st sg* **ngushiixkaatéenaaw, ngushiixkaatéena**. *ind 3rd sg* **kwushiixkaateenáawal**. *ind inv* **ngushiixkaatéenukw**. *ind I-you* **kushiixkaatéenul**. *conj 3rd sg* **kshiixkaatéenaat**. *imp* **kshiixkáa=teen**. *ptcpl* **keeshiixkaatéenaat**.

**kshiixóhkweew** VAI wash one's hair. *ind 1st sg* **ngushiixóhkwa, ngushiixóh=kwaam**. *conj 3rd sg* **kshiixóhkwaat**. *imp* **kshiixóhkwaal**. *ptcpl* **keeshii=xóhkwaat**. *See* **kshiixóhkweew**.

**kshiixóhkweew** VAI wash one's hair. *ind 1st sg* **ngushiixóhkwe, ngushiixóh=kweem**. *conj 3rd sg* **kshiixóhkweet**. *imp* **kshiixóhkweel**. *ptcpl* **keeshii=xóhkweet**. *See* **kshiixóhkweew**.

**kshiixpéhlaleew** VTA rinse s.t. animate, rinse s.t. animate out. *ind 1st sg* **ngushiixpéhlalaaw, ngushiixpéhla=la**. *ind 3rd sg* **kwushiixpehlaláawal**. *ind inv* **ngushiixpéhlalukw**. *ind I-you* **kushiixpéhlalul**. *conj 3rd sg* **kshiix=péhlalaat**. *imp* **kshiixpéhlal**. *ptcpl* **keeshiixpéhlalaat**.

**kshiixpehlatíikeew** VAI rinse, rinse things. *ind 1st sg* **ngushiixpehlatíike, ngushiixpehlatíikeem**. *conj 3rd sg* kshiixpehlatíikeet. *imp* **kshiixpeh=latíikeel**. *ptcpl* **keeshiixpehlatíikeet**.

**kshiixpéhlatoow** VTI2 rinse s.t., rinse s.t. out. *ind 1st sg* **ngushiixpéhlatoon**. *ind 3rd sg* **kwushiixpéhlatoon**. *conj 1st sg* **kshiixpehlatáwaan**. *conj 3rd sg* **kshiixpéhlataakw**. *imp* **kshiix=péhlatool**. *ptcpl* **keeshiixpéh=lataakw**.

**kshiixsíiteew** VAI wash one's feet. *ind 1st sg* **ngushiixsíita**, **ngushiixsíitaam**. *conj 3rd sg* **kshiixsíitaat**. *imp* **kshiixsíitaal**. *ptcpl* **keeshiixsíitaat**.

**kshiixsiitéeneew** VTA wash s.o.'s feet. *ind 1st sg* **ngushiixsiitéenaaw**, **ngushiixsiitéena**. *ind 3rd sg* **kwush=iixsiiteenáawal**. *ind inv* **ngushiixsii=téenukw**. *ind I-you* **kushiixsiitéenul**. *conj 3rd sg* **kshiixsiitéenaat**. *imp* **kshiixsíiteen**. *ptcpl* **keeshiixsii=téenaat**.

**kshíixsuw** VAI wash oneself. *ind 1st sg* **ngushíixsi**, **ngushíixsiim**. *conj 3rd sg* **kshíixsiit**. *imp* **kshíixsiil**. *ptcpl* **keeshíixsiit**.

**kshiixtáasuw** VII be washed. *conj 3rd sg* **kshiixtáasiik**. *ptcpl* **keeshiixtáasiik**.

**kshiixtíikeew** VAI wash things, do the washing. *ind 1st sg* **ngushiixtíike**, **ngushiixtíikeem**. *conj 3rd sg* **kshiix=tíikeet**. *imp* **kshiixtíikeel**. *ptcpl* **keeshiixtíikeet**.

**kshíixtoow** VTI2 injure s.t. *ind 1st sg* **ngushíixtoon**. *ind 3rd sg* **kwushíix=toon**. *conj 1st sg* **kshiixtáwaan**. *conj 3rd sg* **kshíixtaakw**. *imp* **kshíixtool**. *ptcpl* **keeshíixtaakw**.

**kshíixtoow** VTI2 wash s.t. *ind 1st sg* **ngushíixtoon**. *ind 3rd sg* **kwushíix=toon**. *conj 1st sg* **kshiixtáwaan**. *conj 3rd sg* **kshíixtaakw**. *imp* **kshíixtool**. *ptcpl* **keeshíixtaakw**.

**kshíixŭmeew** VTA wash s.o. **Ngushíi=xŭmaaw káalum.** 'I washed your car.' *ind 1st sg* **ngushíixŭmaaw**, **ngushíixŭma**. *ind 3rd sg* **kwushii=xŭmáawal**. *ind inv* **ngushíixŭmukw**. *ind I-you* **kushíixŭmul**. *conj 3rd sg* **kshíixŭmaat**. *imp* **kshíixum**. *ptcpl* **keeshíixŭmaat**.

**kshi-** PV fast, quickly. **Níi áa ngíish-kshí-kúndka.** 'I can dance fast.' *ptcpl* **kéeshi-**. *See* **kshu-**.

**kshíhkam** VTI1A injure s.t. *(using the foot or body)*; kick and injure s.t., sit on and injure s.t. *ind 1st sg* **ngushíh=kamun**. *ind 3rd sg* **kwushíhkamun**. *conj 1st sg* **kshíhkamaan**. *conj 3rd sg* **kshíhkang**. *imp* **kshíhkah**. *ptcpl* **keeshíhkang**.

**kshíhkaweew** VTA injure s.o. *(using the foot or body)*; kick and injure s.o., sit on and injure s.o. *ind 1st sg* **ngush=íhkawaaw**, **ngushíhkawa**. *ind 3rd sg* **kwushihkawáawal**. *ind inv* **ngush=íhkaakw**. *ind I-you* **kushíhkool**. *conj 3rd sg* **kshíhkawaat**. *imp* **kshíhkaw**. *ptcpl* **keeshíhkawaat**.

**kshíhleew** VAI run fast, run quickly, fly quickly, go quickly. *ind 1st sg* **ngushíhla**, **ngushíhlaam**. *conj 3rd sg* **kshíhlaat**. *imp* **kshíhlaal**. *ptcpl* **keeshíhlaat**.

**kshihleewiináakwsuw** VAI look like one could run fast, look smartly dressed, look frisky while going by. *ind 1st sg* **ngushihleewiináakwsi**, **ngushih=leewiináakwsiim**. *conj 3rd sg* **kshih=leewiináakwsiit**. *ptcpl* **keeshihlee=wiináakwsiit**.

**kshihtéeheew** VTA hit and injure s.o. *ind 1st sg* **ngushihtéehaaw**, **ngushih=téeha**. *ind 3rd sg* **kwushihteeháawal**. *ind inv* **ngushihtéehukw**. *ind I-you* **kushihtéehul**. *conj 3rd sg* **kshihtée=haat**. *imp* **kshíhteeh**. *ptcpl* **keeshih=téehaat**.

**kshihtéexiin** VAI be injured, get hurt, fall and get injured. *ind 1st sg* **ngushih=téexiin**, **ngushihtéexi**. *conj 3rd sg* **kshihtéexiing**. *ptcpl* **keeshihtée=xiing**.

**kshihtéextoow** VTI2 hit and injure s.t. **Ngushihtéextoon nzíit.** 'I injured my foot.' *ind 1st sg* **ngushihtéextoon**. *ind 3rd sg* **kwushihtéextoon**. *conj 1st sg* **kshihteextáwaan**. *conj 3rd sg* **kshihtéextaakw**. *imp* **kshihtéextool**. *ptcpl* **keeshihtéextaakw**.

**kshihtéexŭmeew** VTA hit and injure s.o., injuring s.o. by making them fall. *ind 1st sg* **ngushihtéexŭmaaw**, **ngushih=téexŭma**. *ind 3rd sg* **kwushihtee=xŭmáawal**. *ind inv* **ngushihtéexŭ=mukw**. *ind I-you* **kushihtéexŭmul**. *conj 3rd sg* **kshihtéexŭmaat**. *imp* **kshihtéexum**. *ptcpl* **keeshihtée=xŭmaat**.

**kshihtéexun** VII be injured, get hurt. **Kshihtéexun nzíit.** 'My foot got hurt.' *conj 3rd sg* **kshihtéexung**. *ptcpl* **keeshihtéexung**.

**kshóoxweew** VAI walk quickly. *ind 1st sg* **ngushóoxwe**, **ngushóoxweem**. *conj 3rd sg* **kshóoxweet**. *imp* **kshóo=xweel**. *ptcpl* **keeshóoxweet**.

**kshu-** PV fast, quickly. *informal*. **Kshú-kŭlákuw.** 'The time is going quick=ly.'; **Kshú-wíineew.** 'It's snowing a lot.' *ptcpl* **kéeshu-**. *intensive reduplication* **akúshu-**. *See* **kshi-**.

**kshuchéhleew** VAI drive fast, drive quickly. *ind 1st sg* **ngush'chéhla**, **ngush'=chéhlaam**. *conj 3rd sg* **kshuchéh=laat**. *imp* **kshuchéhlaal**. *ptcpl* **keesh'chéhlaat**.

**kshuláandeew** VII be a hot day. *conj 3rd sg* **kshuláandeek**. *ptcpl* **keeshŭ=láandeek**.

**kshúlaweew** VTA injure s.o. *(with an instrument)*. *ind 1st sg* **ngushŭláwaaw**, **ngushŭláwa**. *ind 3rd sg* **kwushŭlaw=áawal**. *ind inv* **ngúshŭlaakw**. *ind I-you* **kúshŭlool**. *conj 3rd sg* **kshúla=waat**. *imp* **kshúlaw**. *ptcpl* **keeshŭ=láwaat**.

**kshuléexiin** VAI have a fever. *ind 1st sg* **ngushŭléexiin**, **ngushŭléexi**. *conj 3rd sg* **kshuléexiing**. *ptcpl* **keeshŭ=léexiing**.

**kshúneew** VTA injure s.o. **Ngushŭ=núkwun.** 'It is tight on me.' *ind 1st sg* **ngúshŭnaaw**, **ngúshŭna**. *ind 3rd sg* **kwushŭnáawal**. *ind inv* **ngúshŭ=nukw**. *ind I-you* **kúshŭnul**. *conj 3rd sg* **kshúnaat**. *imp* **kshún**. *ptcpl* **kéeshŭnaat**.

**kshúnum** VTI1B injure s.t. *(using the hands)*. *ind 1st sg* **ngushŭnúmun**. *ind 3rd sg* **kwushŭnúmun**. *conj 1st sg* **kshúnŭmaan**. *conj 3rd sg* **kshún=ung**. *imp* **kshúnih**. *ptcpl* **kéeshŭnung**.

**kshupéeteew** VII be hot water. *conj 3rd sg* **kshupéeteek**. *ptcpl* **keeshpéeteek**.

**kshupéhleew** VII be rapidly moving water. *conj 3rd sg* **kshupéhlaak**. *ptcpl* **keeshpéhlaak**.

**kshúseew** VTA heat s.o. up, warm s.o. up. *ind 1st sg* **ngúsh'saaw**, **ngúsh'sa**. *ind 3rd sg* **kwush'sáawal**. *ind inv* **ngúsh'sookw**. *ind I-you* **kúsh'sool**. *conj 3rd sg* **kshúsaat**. *imp* **kshús**. *ptcpl* **kéesh'saat**.

**kshusiitéeneew** VTA wash s.o.'s feet. *ind 1st sg* **ngush'siitéenaaw**, **ngush'sii=téena**. *ind 3rd sg* **kwush'siiteenáa=wal**. *ind inv* **ngush'siitéenukw**. *ind I-you* **kush'siitéenul**. *conj 3rd sg* **kshusiitéenaat**. *imp* **kshusíiteen**. *ptcpl* **keesh'siitéenaat**.

**kshusiitéexiin** VAI have hot feet. *ind 1st sg* **ngush'siitéexiin**, **ngush'siitéexi**. *conj 3rd sg* **kshusiitéexiing**. *ptcpl* **keesh'siitéexiing**.

**kshúsum** VTI1B heat s.t. up, warm s.t. up. *ind 1st sg* **ngush'súmun**. *ind 3rd sg* **kwush'súmun**. *conj 1st sg* **kshúsŭmaan**. *conj 3rd sg* **kshúsung**. *imp* **kshúsih**. *ptcpl* **kéesh'sung**.

**kshúsuw** VAI be hot, be sweating. *ind 1st sg* **ngúsh'si**, **ngúsh'siim**. *conj 3rd sg* **kshúsiit**. *ptcpl* **kéesh'siit**.

**kshushíimuw** VAI run away quickly. *ind 1st sg* **ngush'shíimwi**, **ngush'shíi=**

mwiim. *conj 3rd sg* **kshushíimwiit**. *imp* **kshushíimwiil**. *ptcpl* **keesh'=shíimwiit**.

**kshushíhkaweew** VTA make s.o. go fast. *ind 1st sg* **ngush'shíhkawaaw**, **ngush'shíhkawa**. *ind 3rd sg* **kwush'shihkawáawal**. *ind inv* **ngush'shíhkaakw**. *ind I-you* **kush'=shíhkool**. *conj 3rd sg* **kshushíhka=waat**. *imp* **kshushíhkaw**. *ptcpl* **kesh'shíhkawaat**.

**kshúteew** VII be hot. *conj 3rd sg* **kshúteek**. *ptcpl* **kéeshteek**.

**kshuteewáapŭweew** VII be hot water. *conj 3rd sg* **kshuteewáapŭweek**. *ptcpl* **keeshteewáapŭweek**.

**kshuteewáhkameew** VII be a hot day. *conj 3rd sg* **kshuteewáhkameek**. *ptcpl* **keeshteewáhkameek**.

**kshuteewiikamíikat** VII be a hot room, be warm in the house. *conj 3rd sg* **kshuteewiikamíikahk**. *ptcpl* **keeshteewiikamíikahk**.

**kshuteewsiitéexiin** VAI have warm feet *(inside one's shoes)*. *ind 1st sg* **ngushteewsiitéexiin**, **ngushteew=siitéexi**. *conj 3rd sg* **kshuteewsiitée=xiing**. *ptcpl* **keeshteewsiitéexiing**.

**kshutéhleew** VAI get hot *(all of a sudden)*. *ind 1st sg* **ngushtéhla**, **ngushtéhlaam**. *conj 3rd sg* **kshutéhlaat**. *ptcpl* **keeshtéhlaat**.

**kshuwóoleew** VTA make s.o. go overboard *(romantically)*. *ind 1st sg* **ngushŭwóolaaw**, **ngushŭwóola**. *ind 3rd sg* **kwushŭwooláawal**. *ind inv* **ngushŭwóolukw**. *ind I-you* **kushŭ=wóolul**. *conj 3rd sg* **kshuwóolaat**. *imp* **kshúwool**. *ptcpl* **keeshŭwóolaat**.

**ktáaheew** VAIO throw something out. *ind 1st sg* **ngutáaheen**. *ind 3rd sg* **kwutáaheen**. *conj 3rd sg* **ktáaheet**. *imp* **ktáaheel**. *ptcpl* **keetáaheet**.

**ktáakchehl** VAI jump out. *ind 1st sg* **ngutáakchehl**. *conj 3rd sg* **ktaak=chéhluk**. *imp* **ktaakchéhlih**. *ptcpl* **keetaakchéhluk**.

**ktáam** VTI3 eat s.t. up. *ind 1st sg* **ngut=áamun**. *ind 3rd sg* **kwutáamun**. *conj 1st sg* **ktáamaan**. *conj 3rd sg* **ktáang**. *imp* **ktáh**. *ptcpl* **kéetaang**.

**ktaandpéexiin** VAI stick one's head out, have one's head sticking out. *ind 1st sg* **ngutaandpéexiin**, **ngutaandpée=xi**. *conj 3rd sg* **ktaandpéexiing**. *imp* **ktaandpéexiil**. *ptcpl* **keetaand=péexiing**.

**ktaapéhleew** VAI hang out *(s.t. animate)*. **Ktaapehléewak nŭwándŭmak.** 'My mitts are hanging out.' *conj 3rd sg* **ktaapéhlaat**. *ptcpl* **keetaapéhlaat**.

**ktaapéhleew** VII hang out. *conj 3rd sg* **ktaapéhlaak**. *ptcpl* **keetaapéhlaak**.

**ktáhkhweew** VTA pry s.o. out *(using a tool or instrument)*; bail s.o. out of jail. *ind 1st sg* **ngutáhkhwaaw**, **ngutáhkhwa**. *ind 3rd sg* **kwutahk=hwáawal**. *ind inv* **ngutáhkhookw**. *ind I-you* **kutáhkhool**. *conj 3rd sg* **ktáhkhwaat**. *imp* **ktáhkhwaw**. *ptcpl* **keetáhkhwaat**.

**ktáhkhwam** VTI1A pry s.t. out of wood *(using a tool or instrument)*. *ind 1st sg* **ngutahkhwámun**. *ind 3rd sg* **kwutahkhwámun**. *conj 1st sg* **ktahkhwámaan**. *conj 3rd sg* **ktáhk=hwang**. *imp* **ktáhkhwah**. *ptcpl* **kee=táhkhwang**.

**ktahóosuw** VAI have one's slip sticking out. *ind 1st sg* **nguthóosi**, **nguthóo=siim**. *conj 3rd sg* **ktahóosiit**. *ptcpl* **keethóosiit**.

**ktahtakíhleew** VAI run outside, run out. *ind 1st sg* **ngutahtakíhla**, **ngutahta=kíhlaam**. *conj 3rd sg* **ktahtakíhlaat**. *imp* **ktahtakíhlaal**. *ptcpl* **keetahta=kíhlaat**.

**ktakáawsuw** VAI lead a fast life. *ind 1st sg* **ngutakáawsi**, **ngutakáawsiim**. *conj 3rd sg* **ktakáawsiit**. *ptcpl* **keetakáawsiit**.

**ktakamálsuw** VAI feel 'smart,' feel

lively. *ind 1st sg* **ngutakamalúsi**, **ngutakamalúsiim**. *conj 3rd sg* **ktakamálsiit**. *ptcpl* **keetakamalúsiit**.

**ktákan** PR other, the other *(inanimate)*. *pl* **ktákaniil**.

**ktákan** PR other, the other *(animate)*. **Níi ngúk wunáxoo-kíhkayiin, nál há wá nzhíis, nál wáak ktákan oxkwéesus.** 'My mother was the oldest, then there was my uncle, and then another girl.' *pl* **ktákaniik**. *obv* **ktákaniil**.

**ktakíixiin** VAI start off fast, start off running *(especially when running in a race)*. *ind 1st sg* **ngutakíixiin**, **ngutakíixi**. *conj 3rd sg* **ktakíixiing**. *imp* **ktakíixiil**. *ptcpl* **keetakíixiing**, **keetakíixiit**.

**ktakíhlaleew** VTA surprise s.o., startle s.o., make s.o. jump. *ind 1st sg* **ngutakíhlalaaw**, **ngutakíhlala**. *ind 3rd sg* **kwutakihlaláawal**. *ind inv* **ngutakíhlalukw**. *ind I-you* **kutakíh=lalul**. *conj 3rd sg* **ktakíhlalaat**. *imp* **ktakíhlal**. *ptcpl* **keetakíhlalaat**.

**ktakíhleew** VAI be startled, be surprised, jump. *ind 1st sg* **ngutakíhla**, **ngut=akíhlaam**. *conj 3rd sg* **ktakíhlaat**. *ptcpl* **keetakíhlaat**.

**ktakŭléexiin** VAI be brightly coloured, wear bright colours *(s.t. animate)*. *ind 1st sg* **ngutakuléexiin**, **ngutakuléexi**. *conj 3rd sg* **ktakŭléexiing**. *imp* **ktakŭléexiil**. *ptcpl* **keetakuléexiing**. *See* **wŭluléexiin**.

**ktakŭléexun** VII be brightly coloured. *conj 3rd sg* **ktakŭléexung**. *ptcpl* **keetakuléexung**. *See* **wŭluléexun**.

**ktámuw** VAI stick out *(s.t. animate)*. **Uskwáande wúnj-ktámuw.** 'He's sticking out the door.' *ind 1st sg* **ngútamwi**, **ngútamwiim**. *conj 3rd sg* **ktámwiit**. *ptcpl* **kéetamwiit**.

**ktámuw** VII stick out. *conj 3rd sg* **ktámwiik**. *ptcpl* **kéetamwiik**.

**ktámweew** VTA eat s.t. animate up. **Ngihktámwa.** 'I ate him up long ago.' *ind 1st sg* **ngútamwaaw**, **ngútamwa**. *ind 3rd sg* **kwutamwáawal**. *conj 3rd sg* **ktámwaat**. *imp* **ktám**. *ptcpl* **kéetamwaat**.

**ktanaxkíhleew** VII be the sun coming up. **Éhunda-ktanaxkíhlaak.** 'East, where the sun comes up.' *conj 3rd sg* **ktanaxkíhlaak**. *ptcpl* **keetanax=kíhlaak**.

**ktaniikehtéexiin** VAI have a tooth knocked out. *ind 1st sg* **ngutaniikeh=téexiin**, **ngutaniikehtéexi**. *conj 3rd sg* **ktaniikehtéexiing**. *ptcpl* **keeta=niikehtéexiing**.

**ktáskaneew** VII stick out, stick out over the top. *conj 3rd sg* **ktáskaneek**. *ptcpl* **keetáskaneek**.

**ktáskaneew** VAI stick out, stick out over the top *(s.t. animate)*. **Kpooshíishum péech-ktáskaneew.** 'Your navel's sticking out.'; **Óhpŭnak wshaphóo=sung wúnj-ktaskanéewak.** 'The potatoes are sticking up out of the pail.' *conj 3rd sg* **ktáskaneet**. *ptcpl* **keetáskaneet**.

**kteekháasuw** VAI have one's picture taken. *ind 1st sg* **nguteekháasi**, **nguteekháasiim**. *conj 3rd sg* **kteekháasiit**. *imp* **kteekháasiil**. *ptcpl* **keeteekháasiit**.

**ktéekham** VTI 1A take a photograph of s.t., draw a picture of s.t., make a tracing of s.t. *ind 1st sg* **nguteek=hámun**. *ind 3rd sg* **kwuteekhámun**. *conj 1st sg* **kteekhámaan**. *conj 3rd sg* **ktéekhang**. *imp* **ktéekhah**. *ptcpl* **keetéekhang**.

**ktéekheew** VTA take a photograph of s.o., draw a picture of s.o., make a tracing of s.o. *ind 1st sg* **ngutéek=haaw**, **ngutéekha**. *ind 3rd sg* **kwut=eekháawal**. *ind inv* **ngutéekhookw**. *ind I-you* **kutéekhool**. *conj 3rd sg* **ktéekhaat**. *imp* **ktéekhaw**. *ptcpl* **keetéekhaat**.

**kteekhíikan** NI camera. *pl* **kteekhíika=nal**. *poss* **nguteekhíikan**. *loc* **kteek=híikanung**. *dimin* **kcheekhíikanush**.

**kteekhíikeew** VAI take photographs, make a drawing, draw things. *ind 1st sg* **nguteekhíike**, **nguteekhíikeem**. *conj 3rd sg* **kteekhíikeet**. *imp* **kteekhíikeel**. *ptcpl* **keeteekhíikeet**.

**ktiingwéexiin** VAI have one's eyes sticking out, look out, peek out. *ind 1st sg* **ngutiingwéexiin**, **ngutiingwéexi**. *conj 3rd sg* **ktiingwéexiing**. *imp* **ktiingwéexiil**. *ptcpl* **keetiingwée=xiing**, **keetiingwéexiit**.

**któoxweew** VAI go out. *ind 1st sg* **ngut=óoxwe**, **ngutóoxweem**. *conj 3rd sg* **któoxweet**. *imp* **któoxweel**. *ptcpl* **keetóoxweet**.

**któhkweew** VAI look out. *ind 1st sg* **ngutóhkwe**, **ngutóhkweem**. *conj 3rd sg* **któhkweet**. *imp* **któhkweel**. *ptcpl* **keetóhkweet**.

**ktohkwéeneew** VTA take the bridle off s.o. *ind 1st sg* **ngutohkwéenaaw**, **ngutohkwéena**. *ind 3rd sg* **kwut=ohkweenáawal**. *ind inv* **ngutoh=kwéenukw**. *ind I-you* **kutohkwéenul**. *conj 3rd sg* **ktohkwéenaat**. *imp* **któhkween**. *ptcpl* **keetohkwéenaat**.

**ktohkwéexiin** VAI look out, peek out. **Ktohkwéexiin wúnj-kpahóonung.** 'He was looking out from the door.' *ind 1st sg* **ngutohkwéexiin**, **ngutoh=kwéexi**. *conj 3rd sg* **ktohkwéexiing**. *imp* **ktohkwéexiil**. *ptcpl* **keetoh=kwéexiing**.

**ktohkwéhleew** VAI peek, peep out. *ind 1st sg* **ngutohkwéhla**, **ngutohkwéh=laam**. *conj 3rd sg* **ktohkwéhlaat**. *imp* **ktohkwéhlaal**. *ptcpl* **keetohkwéh=laat**. *intensive reduplication* **kàktoh=kwéhleew**.

**ktuchaaléexiin** VAI stick one's nose out, have one's nose sticking out. *ind 1st sg* **ngutchaaléexiin**, **ngutchaaléexi**. *conj 3rd sg* **ktuchaaléexiing**. *imp* **ktuchaaléexiil**. *ptcpl* **keetchaa=léexiing**, **keetchaaléexiit**.

**ktumaakáawsuw** VAI lead a pitiful life, lead a not very good life. *ind 1st sg* **ngutŭmaakáawsi**, **ngutŭmaakáaw=siim**. *conj 3rd sg* **ktumaakáawsiit**. *ptcpl* **keetŭmaakáawsiit**.

**ktumaakamálsuw** VAI feel poorly, feel low. *ind 1st sg* **ngutŭmaakamálsi**, **ngutŭmaakamálsiim**. *conj 3rd sg* **ktumaakamálsiit**. *ptcpl* **keetŭmaa=kamálsiit**.

**ktumaakéelŭmeew** VTA feel sorry for s.o. *ind 1st sg* **ngutŭmaakéelŭmaaw**, **ngutŭmaakéelŭma**. *ind 3rd sg* **kwutŭmaakeelŭmáawal**. *ind inv* **ngutŭmaakéelŭmukw**. *ind I-you* **kutumaakéelŭmul**. *conj 3rd sg* **ktumaakéelŭmaat**. *imp* **ktumaa=kéelum**. *ptcpl* **keetŭmaakéelŭmaat**.

**ktumaakeelúnzuw** VAI feel sorry for oneself. *ind 1st sg* **ngutŭmaakee=lúnzi**, **ngutŭmaakeelúnziim**. *conj 3rd sg* **ktumaakeelúnziit**. *ptcpl* **keetŭmaakeelúnziit**.

**ktumaakíixiin** VAI lie in a pitiful state, lie in a sickly state. *ind 1st sg* **ngutŭ=maakíixiin**, **ngutŭmaakíixi**. *conj 3rd sg* **ktumaakíixiing**. *ptcpl* **keetŭ=maakíixiing**.

**ktumáaksuw** VAI be poor, feel poorly, be pitiable. *ind 1st sg* **ngutŭmáaksi**, **ngutŭmáaksiim**. *conj 3rd sg* **ktum=áaksiit**. *ptcpl* **keetŭmáaksiit**. *moderative reduplication* **kaaktum=áaksuw**.

**ktúneew** VTA pull s.t. animate off, take s.t. animate off, take s.t. animate out *(using the hands)*. *ind 1st sg* **ngútŭ=naaw**, **ngútŭna**. *ind 3rd sg* **kwutŭ=náawal**. *ind inv* **ngútŭnukw**. *ind I-you* **kútŭnul**. *conj 3rd sg* **ktúnaat**. *imp* **ktún**. *ptcpl* **kéetŭnaat**.

**ktunahksúneew** VAI take off one's shoes. *ind 1st sg* **ngutŭnahksúna**, **ngutŭnahksúnaam**. *conj 3rd sg* ktunahksúnaat. *imp* **ktunahksún=aal**. *ptcpl* **keetŭnahksúnaat**.

**ktunashíikaneew** VAI take off one's socks. *ind 1st sg* **ngutŭnashíikana, ngutŭnashíikanaam**. *conj 3rd sg* **ktunashíikanaat**. *imp* **ktunashíika=naal**. *ptcpl* **keetŭnashíikanaat**.

**ktunaxkéexiin** VAI have one's arms out. *ind 1st sg* **ngutŭnaxkéexiin, ngutŭ=naxkéexi**. *conj 3rd sg* **ktunaxkée=xiing**. *imp* **ktunaxkéexiil**. *ptcpl* **kee=tŭnaxkéexiing**. *See* **kchiinaxkéexiin**.

**ktuneechpóoleew** VTA undress s.o. *ind 1st sg* **ngutŭneechpóolaaw, ngutŭ=neechpóola**. *ind 3rd sg* **kwutŭnee=chpooláawal**. *ind inv* **ngutŭneech=póolukw**. *ind I-you* **kutŭneechpóo=lul**. *conj 3rd sg* **ktuneechpóolaat**. *imp* **ktunéechpool**. *ptcpl* **keetŭnee=chpóolaat**.

**ktunéechpuw** VAI get undressed, take off one's clothes. *ind 1st sg* **ngutŭ=néechpi, ngutŭnéechpiim**. *conj 3rd sg* **ktunéechpiit**. *imp* **ktunéechpiil**. *ptcpl* **keetŭnéechpiit**.

**ktuniipŭlóokeew** VAI take off one's pants. *ind 1st sg* **ngutŭniipŭlóoka, ngutŭniipŭlóokaam**. *conj 3rd sg* **ktuniipŭlóokaat**. *imp* **ktunii=pŭlóokaal**. *ptcpl* **keetŭniipŭlóokaat**.

**ktúnum** VTI 1B pull s.t. off, take s.t. off, take s.t. out *(using the hands)*. *ind 1st sg* **ngutŭnúmun**. *ind 3rd sg* **kwutŭ=númun**. *conj 1st sg* **ktúnŭmaan**. *conj 3rd sg* **ktúnung**. *imp* **ktúnih**. *ptcpl* **kéetŭnung**.

**ktunŭmáweew** VTAO take s.o.'s clothes off for s.o., take s.t. out for s.o. *ind 1st sg* **ngutŭnúmawaan**. *ind 3rd sg* **kwutŭnúmawaan**. *ind inv* **ngutŭ=numáakwun**. *ind I-you* **kutŭnum=óolun**. *conj 3rd sg* **ktunŭmáwaat**. *imp* **ktúnŭmaw**. *ptcpl* **keetŭnúm=awaat**.

**ktunŭnaxkéexiin** VAI have one's arms out. *ind 1st sg* **ngutŭnunaxkéexiin, ngutŭnunaxkéexi**. *conj 3rd sg* **ktun=ŭnaxkéexiing**. *ptcpl* **keetŭnunax=kéexiing**.

**ktupéhleew** VII come out *(of water)*. *conj 3rd sg* **ktupéhlaak**. *ptcpl* **keetpéhlaak**.

**ktusiitéexiin** VAI stick one's feet out, have one's feet sticking out. *ind 1st sg* **ngutsiitéexiin, ngutsiitéexi**. *conj 3rd sg* **ktusiitéexiing**. *imp* **ktusiitéexiil**. *ptcpl* **keetsiitéexiing**.

**ktúsheew** VTA cut s.t. animate out. *ind 1st sg* **ngútshaaw, ngútsha**. *ind 3rd sg* **kwutsháawal**. *ind inv* **ngútshookw**. *ind I-you* **kútshool**. *conj 3rd sg* **ktúshaat**. *imp* **ktúsh**. *ptcpl* **kéet=shaat**.

**ktushíikeew** VAI cut out a pattern. *ind 1st sg* **ngutshíike, ngutshíikeem**. *conj 3rd sg* **ktushíikeet**. *imp* **ktush=íikeel**. *ptcpl* **keetshíikeet**.

**ktushíhkaweew** VTA send s.o. out. *ind 1st sg* **ngutshíhkawaaw, ngutshíh=kawa**. *ind 3rd sg* **kwutshihkawáa=wal**. *ind inv* **ngutshíhkaakw**. *ind I-you* **kutshíhkool**. *conj 3rd sg* **ktush=íhkawaat**. *imp* **ktushíhkaw**. *ptcpl* **keetshíhkawaat**.

**ktúshum** VTI 1B cut s.t. out of something. *ind 1st sg* **ngutshúmun**. *ind 3rd sg* **kwutshúmun**. *conj 1st sg* **ktúshŭmaan**. *conj 3rd sg* **ktúshung**. *imp* **ktúshih**. *ptcpl* **kéetshung**.

**kŭlaandpeepíisuw** VAI have something tied around one's head. *ind 1st sg* **ngulaandpeepíisi, ngulaandpee=píisiim**. *conj 3rd sg* **kŭlaandpeepíi=siit**. *imp* **kŭlaandpeepíisiil**. *ptcpl* **keelaandpeepíisiit**.

**kŭláchuw** VAI freeze *(s.t. animate)*. *ind 1st sg* **ngúlachi, ngúlachiim**. *conj 3rd sg* **kŭláchiit**. *ptcpl* **kéelachiit**.

**kŭláheew** VTA trap s.o., trap s.t. animate, knock a tree down on s.o. *ind 1st sg* **ngúlhaaw, ngúlha**. *ind 3rd sg* **kwulháawal**. *ind inv* **ngúlhookw**. *ind*

*I-you* **kúlhool**. *conj 3rd sg* **kŭláhaat**. *imp* **kŭláh**. *ptcpl* **kéelhaat**.

**kŭlahíikan** NI trap. *pl* **kŭlahíikanal**. *poss* **ngulhíikan**. *loc* **kŭlahíikanung**. *dimin* **kŭlahíikanush**.

**kŭlahíikeew** VAI trap things, be trapping. *ind 1st sg* **ngulhíike, ngulhíikeem**. *conj 3rd sg* **kŭlahíikeet**. *imp* **kŭlah=íikeel**. *ptcpl* **keelhíikeet**.

**kŭláhkhweew** VTA hook s.o. up, hook up s.t. animate *(as a belt)*; trap s.t. animate. *ind 1st sg* **nguláhkhwaaw, nguláhkhwa**. *ind 3rd sg* **kwulahk=hwáawal**. *ind inv* **nguláhkhookw**. *ind I-you* **kuláhkhool**. *conj 3rd sg* **kŭláhkhwaat**. *imp* **kŭláhkhwaw**. *ptcpl* **keeláhkhwaat**.

**kŭlahkhwáasuw** VII be buttoned, be hooked up. *conj 3rd sg* **kŭlahk=hwáasiik**. *ptcpl* **keelahkhwáasiik**.

**kŭláhkhwam** VTI1A button s.t. up, do s.t. up tightly; make a down payment on s.t. *ind 1st sg* **ngulahkhwámun**. *ind 3rd sg* **kwulahkhwámun**. *conj 1st sg* **kŭlahkhwámaan**. *conj 3rd sg* **kŭláhkhwang**. *imp* **kŭláhkhwah**. *ptcpl* **keeláhkhwang**.

**kŭlahkhwíikan** NI clothes pin. *pl* **kŭlahkhwíikanal**. *poss* **ngulahk=hwíikan**. *loc* **kŭlahkhwíikanung**. *dimin* **kŭlahkhwíikanush**.

**kŭlahkhwíikeew** VAI fasten things, button things, hook things up. *ind 1st sg* **ngulahkhwíike, ngulahkhwíikeem**. *conj 3rd sg* **kŭlahkhwíikeet**. *imp* **kŭlahkhwíikeel**. *ptcpl* **keelahk=hwíikeet**.

**kŭláhkweew** VAI be stuck, get stuck, be trapped. *ind 1st sg* **nguláhkwe, nguláhkweem**. *conj 3rd sg* **kŭláh=kweet**. *ptcpl* **keeláhkweet**.

**kŭláhkweew** VII be stuck, get stuck, be trapped. **Kŭláhkweew nŭmáhksun.** 'My shoe is stuck.' *conj 3rd sg* **kŭláhkweek**. *ptcpl* **keeláhkweek**.

**kŭláhookw** VAI be hit, be trapped, be hit by a car. *ind 1st sg* **ngúlhookw**. *conj 3rd sg* **kŭlahóokwuk**. *ptcpl* **keelhóo=kwuk**.

**kŭlák** NA clock, hour of the day. **Néew-kŭlák-uch kúnj kpá.** 'You will come at four o'clock.' *pl* **kŭlákak**. *poss* **ngúlakum**. *loc* **kŭlákung**. *dimin* **kŭlákush**. *obv* **kŭlákal**. *From English* clock.

**kŭlákuw** VII be a certain hour of the day *(with number preverb)*. **Wíimbat txú-kŭlakíike.** 'At ten o'clock.'; **Néew-kŭlakíike-uch kúnj kpá.** 'You'll come at four o'clock.' *conj 3rd sg* **kŭlákiik**.

**kŭlamahtéenamuw** VAI have a peaceful mind, have a calm mind. *ind 1st sg* **ngulamahtéenami, ngulamahtée=namiim**. *conj 3rd sg* **kŭlamahtée=namiit**. *ptcpl* **keelamahtéenamiit**.

**kŭlámapuw** VAI sit quietly, be quiet. *ind 1st sg* **ngulamápi, ngulamápiim**. *conj 3rd sg* **kŭlámapiit**. *imp* **kŭlám=apiil**. *ptcpl* **keelamápiit**.

**kŭlambíileew** VTA tie s.o. to something, tie s.o. securely to something. *ind 1st sg* **ngulambíilaaw, ngulambíila**. *ind 3rd sg* **kwulambiiláawal**. *ind inv* **ngulambíilukw**. *ind I-you* **kulambíi=lul**. *conj 3rd sg* **kŭlambíilaat**. *imp* **kŭlámbiil**. *ptcpl* **keelambíilaat**.

**kŭlambíisuw** VAI be tied up. *ind 1st sg* **ngulambíisi, ngulambíisiim**. *conj 3rd sg* **kŭlambíisiit**. *ptcpl* **keelam=bíisiit**.

**kŭlámbtoow** VTI2 tie s.t. to something, tie s.t. securely to something. *ind 1st sg* **ngulámbtoon**. *ind 3rd sg* **kwul=ámbtoon**. *conj 1st sg* **kŭlambtáw=aan**. *conj 3rd sg* **kŭlámbtaakw**. *imp* **kŭlámbtool**. *ptcpl* **keelámbtaakw**.

**kŭlameelúndam** VOTI1A have a calm mind. *ind 1st sg* **ngulameelúndam**. *conj 3rd sg* **kŭlameelúndang**. *imp* **kŭlameelúndah**. *ptcpl* **keelamee=lúndang**.

**kŭlámeew** VTA hold s.t. animate firmly *(in the mouth, with the mouth)*. *ind 1st sg* **ngúlamaaw**, **ngúlama**. *ind 3rd sg* **kwulamáawal**. *ind inv* **ngúl=amukw**. *ind I-you* **kúlamul**. *conj 3rd sg* **kŭlámaat**. *imp* **kŭlám**. *ptcpl* **kéelamaat**.

**kŭlamíixiin** VAI lie still, lie quietly. **Áxkook kŭlamíixiin.** 'The snake is still.' *ind 1st sg* **ngulamíixiin**, **ngul=amíixi**. *conj 3rd sg* **kŭlamíixiing**. *imp* **kŭlamíixiil**. *ptcpl* **keelamíixiing**.

**kŭlamíixun** VII lie still. *conj 3rd sg* **kŭlamíixung**. *ptcpl* **keelamíixung**.

**kŭlamóoleew** VTA fasten something onto s.o. *ind 1st sg* **ngulamóolaaw**, **ngulamóola**. *ind 3rd sg* **kwulamoo=láawal**. *ind inv* **ngulamóolukw**. *ind I-you* **kulamóolul**. *conj 3rd sg* **kŭ=lamóolaat**. *imp* **kŭlámool**. *ptcpl* **keelamóolaat**.

**kŭlamóotoow** VTI2 fasten s.t. onto something, stick s.t. onto something. **Kpahóonung ngulamóotoon.** 'I stuck it onto the door.' *ind 1st sg* **ngulamóotoon**. *ind 3rd sg* **kwulam=óotoon**. *conj 1st sg* **kŭlamóotawaan**. *conj 3rd sg* **kŭlamóotaakw**. *imp* **kŭlamóotool**. *ptcpl* **keelamóotaakw**.

**kŭlamohkwéepuw** VAI sit quietly. *ind 1st sg* **ngulamohkwéepi**, **ngulamoh=kwéepiim**. *conj 3rd sg* **kŭlamoh=kwéepiit**. *imp* **kŭlamohkwéepiil**. *ptcpl* **keelamohkwéepiit**.

**kŭlampéekat** VII be still water. *conj 3rd sg* **kŭlampéekahk**. *ptcpl* **keelamup=éekahk**.

**kŭlampéexun** VII be still water. *conj 3rd sg* **kŭlampéexung**. *ptcpl* **keelamup=éexung**.

**kŭlámuw** VAI be stuck onto something. *ind 1st sg* **ngúlamwi**, **ngúlamwiim**. *conj 3rd sg* **kŭlámwiit**. *imp* **kŭ=lámwiil**. *ptcpl* **kéelamwiit**.

**kŭlándam** VTI1A hold s.t. firmly *(in the mouth, with the mouth)*. *ind 1st sg* **ngulándamun**. *ind 3rd sg* **kwulán=damun**. *conj 1st sg* **kŭlándamaan**. *conj 3rd sg* **kŭlándang**. *imp* **kŭlán=dah**. *ptcpl* **keelándang**.

**kŭlasíiskŭweew** VAI be stuck in mud. *ind 1st sg* **ngulasíiskŭwe**, **ngulasíis=kŭweem**. *conj 3rd sg* **kŭlasíiskŭ=weet**. *ptcpl* **keelasíiskŭweet**.

**kulátun** VII freeze. *conj 3rd sg* **kŭlát=ung**. *ptcpl* **kéelatung**.

**kŭlatŭnahkéeyeew** VII be frozen ground. *conj 3rd sg* **kŭlatŭnahkéeyeek**. *ptcpl* **keelatunahkéeyeek**.

**kŭlaxéexiin** VAI listen. *ind 1st sg* **ngul=xéexiin**, **ngulxéexi**. *conj 3rd sg* **kŭ=laxéexiing**. *imp* **kŭlaxéexiil**. *ptcpl* **keelxéexiing**, **keelxéexiit**.

**kŭleelúndam** VTI1A keep s.t. in mind. *ind 1st sg* **nguleelúndamun**. *ind 3rd sg* **kwuleelúndamun**. *conj 1st sg* **kŭleelúndamaan**. *conj 3rd sg* **kŭlee=lúndang**. *imp* **kŭleelúndah**. *ptcpl* **keeleelúndang**.

**kŭléshii** NA Clara, Clarisse. *obv* **kŭleshíihal**. *From English* Clara.

**kŭliikwáaleew** VTA sew s.t. animate tightly, sew s.t. animate down, fasten s.t. animate down by sewing it. *ind 1st sg* **nguliikwáalaaw**, **nguliikwáa=la**. *ind 3rd sg* **kwuliikwaaláawal**. *ind inv* **nguliikwáalukw**. *ind I-you* **kulii=kwáalul**. *conj 3rd sg* **kŭliikwáalaat**. *imp* **kŭlíikwaal**. *ptcpl* **keeliikwáa=laat**.

**kŭliikwáasuw** VII be tightly sewn. *conj 3rd sg* **kŭliikwáasiik**. *ptcpl* **keelii=kwáasiik**.

**kŭlíikwam** VTI1A sew s.t. tightly, sew s.t. down, fasten s.t. down by sewing. *ind 1st sg* **ngulíikwamun**. *ind 3rd sg* **kwulíikwamun**. *conj 1st sg* **kŭlíi=kwamaan**. *conj 3rd sg* **kŭlíikwang**. *imp* **kŭlíikwah**. *ptcpl* **keelíikwang**.

**kŭlíhkam** VTI1A hold s.t. down *(using the foot or body)*; step on s.t. and hold it down, sit on s.t. and hold it down. *ind 1st sg* **ngulíhkamun**. *ind 3rd sg* **kwulíhkamun**. *conj 1st sg* **kŭlíhkamaan**. *conj 3rd sg* **kŭlíhkang**. *imp* **kŭlíhkah**. *ptcpl* **keelíhkang**.

**kŭlíhkaweew** VTA hold s.o. down *(using the foot or body)*; step on s.o. and hold them down, sit on s.o. and hold them down. *ind 1st sg* **ngulíhka=waaw, ngulíhkawa**. *ind 3rd sg* **kwul=ihkawáawal**. *ind inv* **ngulíhkaakw**. *ind I-you* **kulíhkool**. *conj 3rd sg* **kŭlíhkawaat**. *imp* **kŭlíhkaw**. *ptcpl* **keelíhkawaat**.

**kŭlóoleew** VTA swear at s.o. *ind 1st sg* **ngulóolaaw, ngulóola**. *ind 3rd sg* **kwulooláawal**. *ind inv* **ngulóolukw**. *ind I-you* **kulóolul**. *conj 3rd sg* **kŭlóolaat**. *imp* **kŭlóol**. *ptcpl* **keelóolaat**. *intensive reduplication* **kwàkŭlooláawal**. *See* **amáchu-léew, kaakŭlóoleew**.

**kŭlóoneew** VAI tell a lie. *ind 1st sg* **ngulóone, ngulóoneem**. *conj 3rd sg* **kŭlóoneet**. *imp* **kŭlóoneel**. *ptcpl* **keelóoneet**. *moderative reduplication* **kaakakulóoneew**.

**kŭloonéeheew** VTA tell s.o. a lie. *ind 1st sg* **nguloonéehaaw, nguloonéeha**. *ind 3rd sg* **kwulooneeháawal**. *ind inv* **nguloonéehukw**. *ind I-you* **kuloo=néehul**. *conj 3rd sg* **kŭloonéehaat**. *imp* **kŭlóoneeh**. *ptcpl* **keeloonéehaat**.

**kŭlooshliihíikaan** NI grocery store. *pl* **kŭlooshliihiikáanal**. *loc* **kŭlooshlii=hiikáanung**. *dimin* **kŭlooshliihii=káanush**. *From English* grocery.

**kŭlooshliihiiwáakanal** NI groceries. *usually plural. poss* **ngulooshliihii=wáakanal**. *dimin* **kŭlooshliihiiwaa=kanúshal**. *From English* grocery.

**kŭlooshlíilŭnuw** NA grocery peddler. *pl* **kŭlooshliilŭnúwak**. *obv* **kŭlooshlii=lŭnúwal**.

**kŭlukeelúndam** VOTI 1A feel in good humour, want to laugh. *ind 1st sg* **ngul=keelúndam**. *conj 3rd sg* **kŭlukée=lundang**. *ptcpl* **keelkeelúndang**.

**kŭlukíiheew** VTA make s.o. laugh. *ind 1st sg* **ngulkíihaaw, ngulkíiha**. *ind 3rd sg* **kwulkiiháawal**. *ind inv* **ngul=kíihukw**. *ind I-you* **kulkíihul**. *conj 3rd sg* **kŭlukíihaat**. *imp* **kŭlúkiih**. *ptcpl* **keelkíihaat**.

**kŭluksíhtaweew** VTA smile at s.o. *ind 1st sg* **ngulkusíhtawaaw, ngulkusíhta=wa**. *ind 3rd sg* **kwulkusihtawáawal**. *ind inv* **ngulkusíhtaakw**. *ind I-you* **kulkusíhtool**. *conj 3rd sg* **kŭluksíh=tawaat**. *imp* **kŭluksíhtaw**. *ptcpl* **keelkusíhtawaat**.

**kŭlúksuw** VAI laugh. *ind 1st sg* **ngulkúsi, ngulkúsiim**. *conj 3rd sg* **kŭlúksiit**. *imp* **kŭlúksiil**. *ptcpl* **keelkúsiit**.

**kŭlúneew** VTA hold s.o., hold on to s.o., hold on tightly to s.o., carry s.o. *(using the hands)*. *ind 1st sg* **ngúlŭnaaw, ngúlŭna**. *ind 3rd sg* **kwulŭnáawal**. *ind inv* **ngúlŭnukw**. *ind I-you* **kúlŭ=nul**. *conj 3rd sg* **kŭlúnaat**. *imp* **kŭlún**. *ptcpl* **kéelŭnaat**. *intensive reduplication* **kwàkeelŭnáawal**.

**kŭlúnum** VTI 1B hold s.t., hold onto s.t., hold on tightly to s.t., carry s.t. *(using the hands)*. *ind 1st sg* **ngulŭnúmun**. *ind 3rd sg* **kwulŭnúmun**. *conj 1st sg* **kŭlúnŭmaan**. *conj 3rd sg* **kŭlúnung**. *imp* **kŭlúnih**. *ptcpl* **kéelŭnung**. *intensive reduplication* **kwàkeelŭnúmun**.

**kŭlunŭmáasuw** VAIO owe s.t. to people. **Kŭlunŭmáasuw xwéelu shúlpul.** 'He owes a lot of money.' *ind 1st sg* **ngulŭnumáasiin**. *ind 3rd sg* **kwùlŭ=numáasiin**. *conj 3rd sg* **kŭlunŭmáa=siit**. *ptcpl* **keelŭnumáasiit**.

**kŭlunŭmáweew** VTA owe to s.o. *ind 1st sg* **ngulŭnúmawaaw, ngulŭnúmawa**. *ind 3rd sg* **kwulŭnumawáawal**. *ind inv* **ngulŭnúmaakw**. *ind I-you* **kulŭ=númool**. *conj 3rd sg* **kŭlunŭmáwaat**. *ptcpl* **keelŭnúmaat**.

**kŭlústam** VTI 1A listen to s.t. *ind 1st sg* **ngulsútamun**. *ind 3rd sg* **kwulsúta=mun**. *conj 1st sg* **kŭlustámaan**. *conj*

*3rd sg* **kŭlústang**. *imp* **kŭlústah**. *ptcpl* **keelsútang**.

**kŭlustáweew** VTA listen to s.o. *ind 1st sg* **ngulsútawaaw**, **ngulsútawa**. *ind 3rd sg* **kwulsutawáawal**. *ind inv* **ngulsútaakw**. *ind I-you* **kulsútool**. *conj 3rd sg* **kŭlustáwaat**. *imp* **kŭlústaw**. *ptcpl* **keelsútawaat**.

**kŭlúshmish** NI Christmas. *From English* Christmas.

**kŭlushmíshiin** VAI celebrate Christmas. *usually with indefinite subject only*. *indef subject* **kulushmíshiin**. *conj 3rd sg* **kŭlushmíshiing**. *From English* Christmas.

**kŭmóotkeew** VAI steal. *ind 1st sg* **ngumóotke**, **ngumóotkeem**. *conj 3rd sg* **kŭmóotkeet**. *imp* **kŭmóotkeel**. *ptcpl* **keemóotkeet**. *intensive reduplication* **kihkŭmóotkeew**.

**kŭmóotkeew** VAIO steal s.t. *ind 1st sg* **ngumóotkeen**. *ind 3rd sg* **kwum=óotkeen**. *conj 3rd sg* **kŭmóotkeet**. *imp* **kŭmóotkeel**. *ptcpl* **keemóotkeet**.

**kŭmóotŭmeew** VTAO steal s.t. from s.o. *ind 1st sg* **ngumóotŭmaan**. *ind 3rd sg* **kwumóotŭmaan**. *ind inv* **ngum=ootŭmáakwun**. *ind I-you* **kumootŭ=móolun**. *conj 3rd sg* **kŭmóotumaat**. *imp* **kŭmóotum**. *ptcpl* **keemóo=tŭmaat**.

**kundaaháaleew** VTA push s.o. down, shove s.o. down. *ind 1st sg* **ngun=daaháalaaw**, **ngundaaháala**. *ind 3rd sg* **kwundaahaaláawal**. *ind inv* **ngundaaháalukw**. *ind I-you* **kun=daaháalul**. *conj 3rd sg* **kundaahá=laat**. *imp* **kundáahaal**. *ptcpl* **keen=daaháalaat**.

**kundáaheew** VAIO push s.o., push s.t. over, shove s.o. over, shove s.t. over. *ind 1st sg* **ngundáaheen**. *ind 3rd sg* **kwundáaheen**. *conj 3rd sg* **kundáa=heet**. *imp* **kundáaheel**. *ptcpl* **keen=dáaheet**.

**kundakóosuw** VAI climb straight up. *ind 1st sg* **ngundakóosi**, **ngundakóo=siim**. *conj 3rd sg* **kundakóosiit**. *imp* **kundakóosiil**. *ptcpl* **keendakóosiit**.

**kundaláamuw** VAI start off singing *(especially in church)*; burst out crowing *(of roosters)*. *ind 1st sg* **ngunda=láamwi**, **ngundaláamwiim**. *conj 3rd sg* **kundaláamwiit**. *imp* **kundaláa=mwiil**. *ptcpl* **keendaláamwiit**.

**kundéelŭmeew** VTA condemn s.o., want s.o. to die; think s.o. incapable of doing something. *ind 1st sg* **ngundée=lŭmaaw**, **ngundéelŭma**. *ind 3rd sg* **kwundeelŭmáawal**. *ind inv* **ngun=déelŭmukw**. *ind I-you* **kundéelŭmul**. *conj 3rd sg* **kundéelŭmaat**. *imp* **kundéelum**. *ptcpl* **keendéelŭmaat**.

**kundeelŭmúkwsuw** VAI be condemned to die for evil deeds, die deservedly; be thought incapable. *ind 1st sg* **ngundeelŭmúkwsi**, **ngundeelŭ=múkwsiim**. *conj 3rd sg* **kundeelŭ=múkwsiit**. *ptcpl* **keendeelŭmúkwsiit**.

**kundeelŭmukwsuwáakan** NI condemnation; being thought incapable.

**kúndkeew** VAI dance, be dancing. *ind 1st sg* **ngúndka**, **ngúndkaam**. *emphatic pl* **kundkáhtŭwak**. *conj 3rd sg* **kúndkaat**. *imp* **kúndkaal**. *ptcpl* **kéendkaat**. *moderative reduplication* **kaakúndkeew**.

**kúndŭween** PC Sunday, week *(with number prefix)*. **Ngwút-kúndŭween.** 'One week.'; **Níish-kúndŭween.** 'Two weeks.'

**kúndŭween** VII be Sunday, be a week. **Keendŭwéenge ndáap-maawéewi.** 'I went to church last Sunday.'; **Kun=dŭwéenge nŭmáw-maawéewi.** 'I go to church on Sunday.' *conj 3rd sg* **kúndŭweeng**. *ptcpl* **kéendŭweeng**.

**kundŭweewíikaan** NI church. *pl* **kun=dŭweewiikáanal**. *poss* **ngundŭwee=wíikaan**. *loc* **kundŭweewiikáanung**.

**kundŭweewŭnáhkeew** VAI be gone for so many weeks. *usually with number* *preverb*. **Níish-kundŭweewŭnáh=keew.** 'He was gone for two weeks.'; **Kŭnéewu-kundŭweewŭnáhke.** 'You were gone for four weeks.' *conj 3rd sg* **kundŭweewŭnáhkeet**.

**kúnj** PC long ago, until, emphatic. **Néew-kŭlák-uch kúnj kpá.** 'You will come at four o'clock.'; **Kúnj wéeti péew.** 'He came a while ago.' *See* **kéenj**.

**kunjchaaháaleew** VTA push s.o., shove s.o. *ind 1st sg* **ngunjchaaháalaaw**, **ngunjchaaháala**. *ind 3rd sg* **kwunj=chaahaaláawal**. *ind inv* **ngunjchaa=háalukw**. *ind I-you* **kunjchaaháalul**. *conj 3rd sg* **kunjchaaháalaat**. *imp* **kunjcháahaal**. *ptcpl* **keenjchaa=háalaat**.

**kunjcháaheew** VAIO push s.t., shove s.t. *ind 1st sg* **ngunjcháaheen**. *ind 3rd sg* **kwunjcháaheen**. *conj 3rd sg* **kunj=cháaheet**. *imp* **kunjcháaheel**. *ptcpl* **keenjcháaheet**.

**kunjchahíikan** NI pole, something used for pushing. *pl* **kunjchahíikanal**. *poss* **ngunjchahíikan**. *loc* **kunjchahíi=kanung**. *dimin* **kunjchahíikanush**.

**kunjchíimeew** VTA urge s.o. on. *especially to horses. ind 1st sg* **ngunjchíi=maaw**, **ngunjchíima**. *ind 3rd sg* **kwunjchiimáawal**. *ind inv* **ngunj=chíimukw**. *ind I-you* **kunjchíimul**. *conj 3rd sg* **kunjchíimaat**. *imp* **kúnjchiim**. *ptcpl* **keenjchíimaat**.

**kunjchíhkam** VTI 1A push s.t. *(using the foot or body). ind 1st sg* **ngunjchíh=kamun**. *ind 3rd sg* **kwunjchíhka=mun**. *conj 1st sg* **kunjchíhkamaan**. *conj 3rd sg* **kunjchíhkang**. *imp* **kunjchíhkah**. *ptcpl* **keenjchíhkang**.

**kunjchíhkaweew** VTA push s.o. *(using the foot or body). ind 1st sg* **ngunj=chíhkawaaw**, **ngunjchíhkawa**. *ind 3rd sg* **kwunjchihkawáawal**. *ind inv* **ngunjchíhkaakw**. *ind I-you* **kunj=chíhkool**. *conj 3rd sg* **kunjchíhka=waat**. *imp* **kunjchíhkaw**. *ptcpl* **keenjchíhkawaat**.

**kunjchihtéeham** VTI 1A pound s.t. in, drive s.t. in. *ind 1st sg* **ngunjchihtée=hŭmun**. *ind 3rd sg* **kwunjchihtée=hŭmun**. *conj 1st sg* **kunjchihtéehŭ=maan**. *conj 3rd sg* **kunjchihtéehang**. *imp* **kunjchihtéehih**. *ptcpl* **keenj=chihtéehang**.

**kunjchihtéeheew** VTA pound s.t. animate in, drive s.t. animate in. *ind 1st sg* **ngunjchihtéehaaw**, **ngunjchih=téeha**. *ind 3rd sg* **kwunjchihteeháa=wal**. *ind inv* **ngunjchihtéehookw**. *ind I-you* **kunjchihtéehool**. *conj 3rd sg* **kunjchihtéehaat**. *imp* **kunjchíhteeh**. *ptcpl* **keenjchihtéehaat**.

**kunjchúneew** VTA push s.o., shove s.o. *(using the hands).* **Kwunjchunáawal chaachpùniikanúshal.** 'He pushed the baby buggy.' *ind 1st sg* **ngunj=chúnaaw**, **ngunjchúna**. *ind 3rd sg* **kwunjchunáawal**. *ind inv* **ngunj=chúnukw**. *ind I-you* **kunjchúnul**. *conj 3rd sg* **kunjchúnaat**. *imp* **kúnjchun**. *ptcpl* **keenjchúnaat**.

**kunjchuníikeew** VAI push things *(using the hands). ind 1st sg* **ngunjchuníike**, **ngunjchuníikeem**. *conj 3rd sg* **kunjchuníikeet**. *imp* **kunjchun=íikeel**. *ptcpl* **keenjchuníikeet**.

**kunjchúnum** VTI 1B push s.t., shove s.t. *(using the hands)*; move s.t. *(of motions at a meeting). ind 1st sg* **ngunj=chúnŭmun**. *ind 3rd sg* **kwunjchún=ŭmun**. *conj 1st sg* **kunjchúnŭmaan**. *conj 3rd sg* **kunjchúnung**. *imp* **kunjchúnih**. *ptcpl* **keenjchúnung**.

**kunjíimuw** VAI make a noise. *ind 1st sg* **ngunjíimwi**, **ngunjíimwiim**. *conj 3rd sg* **kunjíimwiit**. *imp* **kunjíimwiil**. *ptcpl* **keenjíimwiit**. *intensive reduplication* **akeenjíimuw**. *usually of animals.*

**kunjóoka** PC recently. **Kunjóoka Dianne néewaaw.** 'I saw Dianne recently.'; **Kunjóoka noolíixŭmaaw ngáalum.** 'I fixed my car recently.'

**kŭnóop** NA button. *pl* **kŭnóopak**. *poss* **ngunóopum**. *loc* **kŭnóopung**. *dimin* **kŭnóopush**. *obv* **kŭnóopal**. *From Dutch.*

**kŭnoopaalakíingweew** VAI have round ('button') eyes. *ind 1st sg* **ngunoo=paalakíingwe**, **ngunoopaalakíin=gweem**. *conj 3rd sg* **kŭnoopaala=kíingweet**. *ptcpl* **keenoopaala=kíingweet**.

**kŭnoopáalakw** NI button hole. *pl* **kŭnoopáalakwal**. *poss* **ngunoo=páalakwum**. *loc* **kŭnoopáalakwung**. *dimin* **kŭnoopáalakwush**.

**kŭnoopáhksun** NI button shoe. *pl* **kŭnoopahksúnal**. *poss* **ngunoopáh=ksun**. *loc* **kŭnoopahksúnung**. *dimin* **kŭnoopahkshúnush**. *fancy shoe worn especially by women.*

**kŭnoopháasuw** VAI have buttons *(s.t. animate). ind 1st sg* **ngunoopháasi**, **ngunoopháasiim**. *conj 3rd sg* **kŭ=noopháasiit**. *ptcpl* **keenoopháasiit**.

**kŭnoopháasuw** VII have buttons. *conj 3rd sg* **kŭnoopháasiik**. *ptcpl* **kee=noopháasiik**.

**kúsht** NI chest, trunk, small box, casket, coffin. *pl* **kúshtal**. *poss* **ngúshtum**. *loc* **kúshtung**. *dimin* **kúshchush**. *From Dutch.*

**kwáachund** PC goodness! **Nál ngúk úw, "Kwáachund, máh noolsutamóo=wun shúkw sháxkii-léew."** 'Then my mother said, "Goodness, I wouldn't have believed if it hadn't happened."'

**kwáakwalul** VAI be mouldy *(s.t. animate). ind 1st sg* **ngwáakwalul**, **ngwáakwalul**. *conj 3rd sg* **kwaa=kwalúluk**. *intensive reduplication* **akwáakwalul**.

**kwáakwalut** VII be mouldy. *conj 3rd sg* **kwáakwalihk**. *ptcpl* **kwáakwalihk**. *intensive reduplication* **akwáa=kwalut**.

**kwáalŭmuw** VAI have a car. *ind 1st sg* **nookáalŭmi**, **nookáalŭmiim**. *conj 3rd sg* **kwáalŭmiit**. *ptcpl* **weekáa=lŭmiit**.

**kwáalxeew** VII be smoky, smoke. *conj 3rd sg* **kwáalxeek**. *ptcpl* **kwáalxeek**.

**kwaalxeeníikeew** VAI make smoke. *ind 1st sg* **ngwaalxeeníike**, **ngwaalxee=níikeem**. *conj 3rd sg* **kwaalxeeníi=keet**. *imp* **kwaalxeeníikeel**. *ptcpl* **kwaalxeeníikeet**. *used as smudge for mosquitoes.*

**kwaalxéenŭmeew** VAI make smoke. *ind 1st sg* **ngwaalxéenŭma**, **ngwaalxée=nŭmaam**. *conj 3rd sg* **kwaalxéenŭ=maat**. *imp* **kwaalxéenŭmaal**. *ptcpl* **kwaalxéenŭmaat**.

**kwaalxéesuw** VAI make a lot of smoke, smoke, be smoking *(s.t. animate). ind 1st sg* **ngwaalxéesi**, **ngwaalxéesiim**. *conj 3rd sg* **kwaalxéesiit**. *ptcpl* **kwaalxéesiit**.

**kwaaxkwsóngwaam** VAI snore. *ind 1st sg* **ngwaaxkwsóngwaam**. *conj 3rd sg* **kwaaxkwsóngwaang**. *ptcpl* **kwaax=kwsóngwaang**.

**kwachŭmeenáxke** PC outside the fence.

**kwáchŭmung** PC outside. **Nál há yóol sheengiixúngiil, kwáchumung, wúlu náh ahtamóombil pehpŭmíhlaat.** 'So they were lying there, outside, just where the car tracks are.'

**kwàkwashíhleew** VAI fall out in chunks, be a chunk falling out, have a chip fall out, have a chunk fall out, break off. *ind 1st sg* **ngwakwashíhla**, **ngwakwashíhlaam**. *conj 3rd sg* **kwàkwashíhlaat**. *ptcpl* **kwàkwa=shíhlaat**.

**kwàkwashíhleew** VII fall out in chunks, be a chunk falling out, have a chip fall out, have a chunk fall out, break off. *conj 3rd sg* **kwàkwashíhlaak**. *ptcpl* **kwàkwashíhlaak**.

**kwàkwcheeníikeew** VAI grope around, feel around for things. *ind 1st sg*

**ngwakwcheeníike, ngwakwchee=níikeem**. *conj 3rd sg* **kwàkwchee=níikeet**. *imp* **kwàkwcheeníikeel**. *ptcpl* **kwàkwcheeníikeet**.

**kwàkwchúkhookw** VAI be moved back and forth, be shaken back and forth. *ind 1st sg* **ngwakwchúkhookw**. *conj 3rd sg* **kwàkwchukhóokwuk**. *ptcpl* **kwàkwchukhóokwuk**.

**kwàkwchukohkwéhleew** VAI shake one's head, move one's head back and forth. *ind 1st sg* **ngwakwchuk=ohkwéhla, ngwakwchukohkwéh=laam**. *conj 3rd sg* **kwàkwchukoh=kwéhlaat**. *imp* **kwàkwchukoh=kwéhlaal**. *ptcpl* **kwàkwchukoh=kwéhlaat**.

**kwàkwchúkuw** VAI move, stir. **Kwàkw=chúkuw. Pŭmáawsuw éet.** 'He's moving. Maybe he's alive.' *ind 1st sg* **ngwakwchúkwi, ngwakwchúkwiim**. *conj 3rd sg* **kwàkwchúkwiit**. *imp* **kwàkwchúkwiil**. *ptcpl* **kwàkw=chúkwiit**. *See* **kwchúkwiiw**.

**kwàkwchukwaaháaleew** VTA shake s.o. back and forth, move s.o. back and forth, wave s.o. back and forth, rock s.o. back and forth. *ind 1st sg* **ngwak=wchukwaaháalaaw, ngwakw=chukwaaháala**. *ind 3rd sg* **kwàkw=chukwaahaaláawal**. *ind inv* **ngwa=kwchukwaaháalukw**. *ind I-you* **kwàkwchukwaaháalul**. *conj 3rd sg* **kwàkwchukwaaháalaat**. *imp* **kwàkwchukwáahaal**. *ptcpl* **kwàkw=chukwaaháalaat**.

**kwàkwchukwáaheew** VAIO shake s.t. back and forth, move s.t. back and forth, wave s.t. back and forth, rock s.t. back and forth. *ind 1st sg* **ngwak=wchukwáaheen**. *ind 3rd sg* **kwàkw=chukwáaheen**. *conj 3rd sg* **kwàkw=chukwáaheet**. *imp* **kwàkwchuk=wáaheel**. *ptcpl* **kwàkwchukwáaheet**.

**kwàkwchukwaalŭwéhleew** VAI wag one's tail. *ind 1st sg* **ngwakwchuk=waalŭwéhla, ngwakwchukwaalŭ=wéhlaam**. *conj 3rd sg* **kwàkwchuk=waalŭwéhlaat**. *imp* **kwàkwchuk=waalŭwéhlaal**. *ptcpl* **kwàkwchuk=waalŭwéhlaat**.

**kwàkwchúkwapuw** VAI shift around while sitting, fidget. *ind 1st sg* **ngwakwchúkwapi, ngwakwchúk=wapiim**. *conj 3rd sg* **kwàkwchúk=wapiit**. *imp* **kwàkwchúkwapiil**. *ptcpl* **kwàkwchúkwapiit**.

**kwàkwchukwíixiin** VAI move about while lying down. *ind 1st sg* **ngwak=wchukwíixiin, ngwakwchukwíixi**. *conj 3rd sg* **kwàkwchukwíixiing**. *imp* **kwàkwchukwíixiil**. *ptcpl* **kwàkwchukwíixiing**.

**kwàkwchukwíhleew** VAI shake, move, be thrown about. *ind 1st sg* **ngwakw=chukwíhla, ngwakwchukwíhlaam**. *conj 3rd sg* **kwàkwchukwíhlaat**. *imp* **kwàkwchukwíhlaal**. *ptcpl* **kwàkw=chukwíhlaat**.

**kwàkwchukwíhleew** VII shake, move, be thrown about. *conj 3rd sg* **kwàkw=chukwíhlaak**. *ptcpl* **kwàkwchuk=wíhlaak**.

**kwàkwchúkxookw** VAI be blown back and forth by the wind. *ind 1st sg* **ngwakwchúkxookw, ngwakwchúk=xookw**. *conj 3rd sg* **kwàkwchuk=xóokwuk**. *ptcpl* **kwàkwchukxóo=kwuk**.

**kwàkwchúkxwun** VII be blown back and forth by the wind. *conj 3rd sg* **kwàkwchúkxwung**. *ptcpl* **kwàkw=chúkxwung**.

**kwàkwtakwŭníikee** VAI pick things up with one's fingers, use one's hands to pick things up. *ind 1st sg* **ngwakw=takwŭníike, ngwakwtakwŭníikeem**. *conj 3rd sg* **kwàkwtakwŭníikeet**. *imp* **kwàkwtakwŭníikeel**. *ptcpl* **kwàkwtakwŭníikeet**.

**kwàkwtákwŭnum** VTI1B pick s.t. up with one's fingers, use one's fingers to pick s.t. up. *ind 1st sg* **ngwakw=takwŭnúmun**. *ind 3rd sg* **kwàkw=takwŭnúmun**. *conj 1st sg* **kwàkw=takwŭnúmaan**. *conj 3rd sg* **kwàkw=takwúnung**. *imp* **kwàkwtákwŭnih**. *ptcpl* **kwàkwtákwŭnung**.

**kwàkwtuchéeneew** VTA feel s.o. *(using the hands)*. *ind 1st sg* **ngwakwtuch=éenaaw, ngwakwtuchéena**. *ind 3rd sg* **kwàkwtucheenáawal**. *ind inv* **ngwakwtuchéenukw**. *ind I-you* **kwakwtuchéenul**. *conj 3rd sg* **kwàkwtuchéenaat**. *imp* **kwàkw=túcheen**. *ptcpl* **kwàkwtuchéenaat**.

**kwàkwtuchéenum** VTI1B feel s.t. *(using the hands)*. *ind 1st sg* **ngwakwtuch=éenŭmun**. *ind 3rd sg* **kwàkwtuchée=nŭmun**. *conj 1st sg* **kwàkwtuch=éenŭmaan**. *conj 3rd sg* **kwàkwtuch=éenung**. *imp* **kwàkwtuchéenih**. *ptcpl* **kwàkwtuchéenung**.

**kwàkwtukohkwaandpéhleew** VAI shake one's head. *ind 1st sg* **ngwak=wtukohkwaandpéhla, ngwakwtuk=ohkwaandpéhlaam**. *conj 3rd sg* **kwàkwtukohkwaandpéhlaat**. *imp* **kwàkwtukohkwaandpéhlaal**. *ptcpl* **kwàkwtukohkwaandpéhlaat**.

**kwàkwtukohkwéhleew** VAI shake one's head. *ind 1st sg* **ngwakwtukoh=kwéhla, ngwakwtukohkwéhlaam**. *conj 3rd sg* **kwàkwtukohkwéhlaat**. *imp* **kwàkwtukohkwéhlaal**. *ptcpl* **kwàkwtukohkwéhlaat**.

**kwashámeew** VTA take a bite out of s.o. *ind 1st sg* **ngwáshamaaw, ngwásha=ma**. *ind 3rd sg* **kwàshamáawal**. *ind inv* **ngwáshamukw**. *ind I-you* **kwáshamul**. *conj 3rd sg* **kwashám=aat**. *imp* **kwashám**. *ptcpl* **kwée=shamaat**.

**kwashándam** VTI1A take a bite out of s.t. *ind 1st sg* **ngwashándamun**. *ind 3rd sg* **kwàshándamun**. *conj 1st sg* **kwashándamaan**. *conj 3rd sg* **kwashándang**. *imp* **kwashándah**. *ptcpl* **kweeshándang**.

**kwashaníikeew** VAI have a chipped tooth, have a chip off one's tooth. *ind 1st sg* **ngwashaníika, ngwashaníi=kaam**. *conj 3rd sg* **kwashaníikaat**. *ptcpl* **kweeshaníikaat**.

**kwashát** VII be chipped, have a chip missing, have a chunk missing. *conj 3rd sg* **kwasháhk**. *ptcpl* **kwéeshahk**.

**kwashíhleew** VII break off in chunks. *conj 3rd sg* **kwashíhlaak**. *ptcpl* **kweeshíhlaak**. *intensive reduplication* **akwashíhleew**.

**kwashihtéexiin** VAI crack, fall and crack, fall and get chipped *(s.t. animate)*. *conj 3rd sg* **kwashihtéexiing**. *ptcpl* **kweeshihtéexiing**.

**kwashihtéextoow** VTI2 drop and chip s.t. *ind 1st sg* **ngwashihtéextoon**. *ind 3rd sg* **kwàshihtéextoon**. *conj 1st sg* **kwashihteextáwaan**. *conj 3rd sg* **kwashihtéextaakw**. *imp* **kwashih=téextool**. *ptcpl* **kweeshihtéextaakw**.

**kwashihtéexŭmeew** VTA drop and chip s.t. animate. *ind 1st sg* **ngwashihtée=xŭmaaw, ngwashihtéexŭma**. *ind 3rd sg* **kwàshihteexŭmáawal**. *ind inv* **ngwashihtéexŭmukw**. *ind I-you* **kwàshihtéexŭmul**. *conj 3rd sg* **kwa=shihtéexŭmaat**. *imp* **kwashihtée=xum**. *ptcpl* **kweeshihtéexŭmaat**.

**kwashihtéexun** VII crack, fall and crack, fall and get chipped. *conj 3rd sg* **kwashihtéexung**. *ptcpl* **kweeshih=téexung**.

**kwashúneew** VTA break a piece off s.t. animate, break a chunk off s.t. animate *(using the hands)*. *ind 1st sg* **ngwáshŭnaaw, ngwáshŭna**. *ind 3rd sg* **kwàshŭnáawal**. *ind inv* **ngwásh=ŭnukw**. *ind I-you* **kwáshŭnul**. *conj 3rd sg* **kwashúnaat**. *imp* **kwashún**. *ptcpl* **kwéeshŭnaat**. *intensive reduplication* **kwàkwashunáawal**.

**kwashúnum** VTI1B break a piece off s.t., break a chunk off s.t. *(using the* *hands). ind 1st sg* **ngwashŭnúmun**. *ind 3rd sg* **kwàshŭnúmun**. *conj 1st sg* **kwashúnŭmaan**. *conj 3rd sg* **kwashúnung**. *imp* **kwashúnih**. *ptcpl* **kwéeshŭnung**. *intensive reduplication* **kwàkwashúnŭmun**.

**kwashúsuw** VAI be chipped, have a chip missing, have a chunk missing *(s.t. animate). ind 1st sg* **ngwásh'si**, **ngwásh'siim**. *conj 3rd sg* **kwa=shúsiit**. *ptcpl* **kwéesh'siit**.

**kwashúsheew** VTA cut a piece off s.t. animate. *ind 1st sg* **ngwásh'shaaw**, **ngwásh'sha**. *ind 3rd sg* **kwàsh'=sháawal**. *ind inv* **ngwásh'shookw**. *ind I-you* **kwásh'shool**. *conj 3rd sg* **kwashúshaat**. *imp* **kwashúsh**. *ptcpl* **kwéesh'shaat**.

**kwashúshum** VTI1B cut a piece off s.t. *ind 1st sg* **ngwash'shúmun**. *ind 3rd sg* **kwàsh'shúmun**. *conj 1st sg* **kwashúshŭmaan**. *conj 3rd sg* **kwashúshung**. *imp* **kwashúshih**. *ptcpl* **kwéesh'shung**.

**kwashutóoneew** VAI have a chipped spout *(s.t. animate). ind 1st sg* **ngwashtóona**, **ngwashtóonaam**. *conj 3rd sg* **kwashutóonaat**. *ptcpl* **kweeshtóonaat**.

**kwàtalákay** PC damn! *considered impolite.*

**kwaxkaashŭwíhleew** VAI swim across. *ind 1st sg* **ngwaxkaashŭwíhla**, **ngwaxkaashŭwíhlaam**. *conj 3rd sg* **kwaxkaashŭwíhlaat**. *imp* **kwaxkaa=shŭwíhlaal**. *ptcpl* **kweexkaashŭ=wíhlaat**.

**kwaxkakáham** VOTI1A cross in a boat. *ind 1st sg* **ngwaxkakáham**. *conj 3rd sg* **kwaxkakáhang**. *imp* **kwaxka=káhah**. *ptcpl* **kweexkakáhang**.

**kwáxkakeew** VAI go across the water. *ind 1st sg* **ngwáxkaka**, **ngwáxka=kaam**. *conj 3rd sg* **kwáxkakaat**. *imp* **kwáxkakaal**. *ptcpl* **kwéexkakaat**.

**kwaxkchéhleew** VAI drive back, drive across *(the river). ind 1st sg* **ngwax=kchéhla**, **ngwaxkchéhlaam**. *conj 3rd sg* **kwaxkchéhlaat**. *imp* **kwaxk=chéhlaal**. *ptcpl* **kweexkchéhlaat**.

**kwaxkeenháweew** VTA pay s.o. back. *ind 1st sg* **ngwaxkeenháwaaw**, **ngwaxkeenháwa**. *ind 3rd sg* **kwax=keenhawáawal**. *ind inv* **ngwaxkéen=haakw**. *ind I-you* **kwaxkéenhool**. *conj 3rd sg* **kwaxkeenháwaat**. *imp* **kwaxkéenhaw**. *ptcpl* **kweexkeen=háwaat**.

**kwaxkhámeew** VAI row across the water, paddle across the water. *ind 1st sg* **ngwaxkháma**, **ngwaxkhámaam**. *conj 3rd sg* **kwaxkhámaat**. *imp* **kwaxkhámaal**. *ptcpl* **kweexk=hámaat**.

**kwáxkiiw** VAI-S return, come back. **Méhch wáak mbéech-kwáxki.** 'I'm back.' *ind 1st sg* **ngwáxki**, **ngwáx=kiim**. *conj 3rd sg* **kwáxkiit**. *imp* **kwáxkiil**. *ptcpl* **kwéexkiit**.

**kwaxkíhleew** VAI fly back, go back. *ind 1st sg* **ngwaxkíhla**, **ngwaxkíhlaam**. *conj 3rd sg* **kwaxkíhlaat**. *imp* **kwax=kíhlaal**. *ptcpl* **kweexkíhlaat**.

**kwaxkihtéeheew** VTA retaliate by hitting s.o., hit s.o. in return. *ind 1st sg* **ngwaxkihtéehaaw**, **ngwaxkihtéeha**. *ind 3rd sg* **kwaxkihteeháawal**. *ind inv* **ngwaxkihtéehookw**. *ind I-you* **kwaxkihtéehool**. *conj 3rd sg* **kwax=kihtéehaat**. *imp* **kwaxkíhteeh**. *ptcpl* **kweexkihtéehaat**.

**kwaxkóoxwaleew** VTA return s.o., bring s.o. back. *ind 1st sg* **ngwaxkóoxwa=laaw**, **ngwaxkóoxwala**. *ind 3rd sg* **kwaxkooxwaláawal**. *ind inv* **ngwax=kóoxwalukw**. *ind I-you* **kwaxkóo=xwalul**. *conj 3rd sg* **kwaxkóoxwa=laat**. *imp* **kwaxkóoxwal**. *ptcpl* **kweexkóoxwalaat**.

**kwaxkóoxwatoow** VTI2 return s.t., bring s.t. back. *ind 1st sg* **ngwaxkóoxwa=toon**. *ind 3rd sg* **kwaxkóoxwatoon**.

*conj 1st sg* **kwaxkooxwatáwaan**. *conj 3rd sg* **kwaxkóoxwataakw**. *imp* **kwaxkóoxwatool**. *ptcpl* **kweexkóo=xwataakw**.

**kwaxku-** PV back, return. *informal*. **Ngwáxku-méekun.** 'I gave it back.' *ptcpl* **kwéexku-**.

**kwáxkŭneew** VTA turn s.t. animate back *(of clocks, with the hands)*; return s.o. *ind 1st sg* **ngwáxkŭnaaw**, **ngwáx=kŭna**. *ind 3rd sg* **kwaxkŭnáawal**. *ind inv* **ngwáxkŭnukw**. *ind I-you* **kwáx=kŭnul**. *conj 3rd sg* **kwáxkŭnaat**. *imp* **kwáxkun**. *ptcpl* **kwéexkŭnaat**.

**kwáxkŭnum** VTI 1B turn s.t. back *(using the hands)*; return s.t. *ind 1st sg* **ngwaxkŭnúmun**. *ind 3rd sg* **kwax=kŭnúmun**. *conj 1st sg* **kwaxkŭnúm=aan**. *conj 3rd sg* **kwáxkŭnung**. *imp* **kwáxkŭnih**. *ptcpl* **kwéexkŭnung**.

**kwaxkwíixiin** VAI rebound off something, bounce back and fall, fall back *(s.t. animate)*; be a foul ball *(baseball)*. *ind 1st sg* **ngwaxkwíixiin**, **ngwaxkwíixi**. *conj 3rd sg* **kwax=kwíixiing**. *ptcpl* **kweexkwíixiing**.

**kwaxkwíixŭmeew** VTA bounce s.t. animate *(off something)*. *ind 1st sg* **ngwaxkwíixŭmaaw**, **ngwax=kwíixŭma**. *ind 3rd sg* **kwaxkwiixŭ=máawal**. *ind inv* **ngwaxkwíixŭmukw**. *ind I-you* **kwaxkwíixŭmul**. *conj 3rd sg* **kwaxkwíixŭmaat**. *imp* **kwax=kwíixum**. *ptcpl* **kweexkwíixŭmaat**.

**kwaxkwíixun** VII bounce. *conj 3rd sg* **kwaxkwíixung**. *ptcpl* **kweex=kwíixung**.

**kwáy** PC now. **Kwáy sháawu kawíikw!** 'Go to sleep right away (you plural)!'; **Kwáy kíishkwihk ápih náh ndáan.** 'I'm going there today.'

**kwchiimáaleew** VTA smell s.o. *ind 1st sg* **ngwuchiimáalaaw**, **ngwuchiimáala**. *ind 3rd sg* **kwuchiimaaláawal**. *ind inv* **ngwuchiimáalukw**. *ind I-you* **kwuchiimáalul**. *conj 3rd sg* **kwchii=máalaat**. *imp* **kwchíimaal**. *ptcpl* **kweechiimáalaat**. *intensive reduplication* **kwàkwchiimaaláawal**.

**kwchiimáatam** VTI 1A smell s.t. *ind 1st sg* **ngwuchiimáatamun**. *ind 3rd sg* **kwuchiimáatamun**. *conj 1st sg* **kwchiimáatamaan**. *conj 3rd sg* **kwchiimáatang**. *imp* **kwchiimáatah**. *ptcpl* **kweechiimáatang**.

**kwchiimóoleew** VTA ask s.o. *ind 1st sg* **ngwuchiimóolaaw**, **ngwuchiimóola**. *ind 3rd sg* **kwuchiimooláawal**. *ind inv* **ngwuchiimóolukw**. *ind I-you* **kwuchiimóolul**. *conj 3rd sg* **kwchii=móolaat**. *imp* **kwchíimool**. *ptcpl* **kweechiimóolaat**.

**kwchiimóhkeew** VAI ask, ask people. *ind 1st sg* **ngwuchiimóhke**, **ngwuchii=móhkeem**. *conj 3rd sg* **kwchiimóh=keet**. *imp* **kwchiimóhkeel**. *ptcpl* **kweechiimóhkeet**.

**kwchiináhkeew** VAI wrestle. *ind 1st sg* **ngwuchiináhke**, **ngwuchiináhkeem**. *conj 3rd sg* **kwchiináhkeet**. *imp* **kwchiináhkeel**. *ptcpl* **kweechii=náhkeet**.

**kwchíinaleew** VTA wrestle s.o. *ind 1st sg* **ngwuchíinalaaw**, **ngwuchíinala**. *ind 3rd sg* **kwuchiinaláawal**. *ind inv* **ngwuchíinalukw**. *ind I-you* **kwuch=íinalul**. *conj 3rd sg* **kwchíinalaat**. *imp* **kwchíinal**. *ptcpl* **kweechíi=nalaat**.

**kwchi-** PV try to *(do)*; try and *(do)*. **Kwchí-wŭlíixtool!** 'Try to fix it!' *ptcpl* **kwéechi-**. *See* **akweechi-**, **kwàkweechi-**.

**kwchíhkam** VTI 1A try s.t. on *(of clothing)*. *ind 1st sg* **ngwuchíhkamun**. *ind 3rd sg* **kwuchíhkamun**. *conj 1st sg* **kwchíhkamaan**. *conj 3rd sg* **kwchíh=kang**. *imp* **kwchíhkah**. *ptcpl* **kwee=chíhkang**.

**kwchíhkaweew** VTA try s.t. animate on *(of clothing)*. *ind 1st sg* **ngwuchíh=kawaaw**, **ngwuchíhkawa**. *ind 3rd sg* kwuchihkawáawal. *ind inv* **ngwuch=íhkaakw**. *ind I-you* **kwuchíhkool**. *conj 3rd sg* **kwchíhkawaat**. *imp* **kwchíhkaw**. *ptcpl* **kweechíhkawaat**.

**kwchíhlaleew** VTA try s.t. animate out, test s.t. animate. *ind 1st sg* **ngwuchíh=lalaaw, ngwuchíhlala**. *ind 3rd sg* **kwuchihlaláawal**. *ind inv* **ngwuch=íhlalukw**. *ind I-you* **kwuchíhlalul**. *conj 3rd sg* **kwchíhlalaat**. *imp* **kwchíhlal**. *ptcpl* **kweechíhlalaat**.

**kwchíhlatoow** VTI2 try s.t. out, test s.t. *ind 1st sg* **ngwuchíhlatoon**. *ind 3rd sg* **kwuchíhlatoon**. *conj 1st sg* **kwchihlatáwaan**. *conj 3rd sg* **kwchíhlataakw**. *imp* **kwchíhlatool**. *ptcpl* **kweechíhlataakw**.

**kwchu-** PV try to *do*; try and *(do)*. *informal*. **Ngwúchu-msháatamun** 'I'm trying to think about it.'; **Kwchú-alúmsuw.** 'He tried to leave.' *ptcpl* **kwéechu-**. *See* **kwchi-**.

**kwchukwáaheew** VAIO shake s.t. *ind 1st sg* **ngwuchkwáaheen**. *ind 3rd sg* **kwùchkwáaheen**. *conj 3rd sg* **kwchukwáaheet**. *imp* **kwchukwáa=heel**. *ptcpl* **kweechkwáaheet**.

**kwchúkwiiw** VAI-S move. *ind 1st sg* **ngwúchkwi, ngwúchkwiim**. *conj 3rd sg* **kwchúkwiit**. *imp* **kwchúkwiil**. *ptcpl* **kwéechkwiit**. *See* **kwàkw=chúkuw**.

**kwchukwíhkam** VTI1A move s.t. *(using the foot or body)*. *ind 1st sg* **ngwuch=kwíhkamun**. *ind 3rd sg* **kwuch=kwíhkamun**. *conj 1st sg* **kwchuk=wíhkamaan**. *conj 3rd sg* **kwchuk=wíhkang**. *imp* **kwchukwíhkah**. *ptcpl* **kweechkwíhkang**.

**kwchukwíhkaweew** VTA move s.o. *(using the foot or body)*. *ind 1st sg* **ngwuchkwíhkawaaw, ngwuch=kwíhkawa**. *ind 3rd sg* **kwuchkwih=kawáawal**. *ind inv* **ngwuchkwíh=kaakw**. *ind I-you* **kwuchkwíhkool**. *conj 3rd sg* **kwchukwíhkawaat**. *imp* **kwchukwíhkaw**. *ptcpl* **kweech=kwíhkawaat**.

**kwchúkwihl** VAI move, stir, shake. *ind 1st sg* **ngwúchkwihl**. *conj 3rd sg* **kwchukwíhluk**. *ptcpl* **kweech=kwíhluk**.

**kwchukwíhleew** VAI move, stir, shake. *ind 1st sg* **ngwuchkwíhla, ngwuch=kwíhlaam**. *conj 3rd sg* **kwchukwíh=laat**. *ptcpl* **kweechkwíhlaat**.

**kwchúkwŭneew** VTA move s.o. *ind 1st sg* **ngwuchkwúnaaw, ngwuchkwúna**. *ind 3rd sg* **kwuchkwùnáawal**. *ind inv* **ngwuchkwúnukw**. *ind I-you* **kwuchkwúnul**. *conj 3rd sg* **kwchúk=wŭnaat**. *imp* **kwchúkwun**. *ptcpl* **kweechkwúnaat**.

**kwchúkwŭnum** VTI1 move s.t. *ind 1st sg* **ngwuchkwúnŭmun**. *ind 3rd sg* **kwuchkwúnŭmun**. *conj 1st sg* **kwchukwŭnúmaan**. *conj 3rd sg* **kwchúkwŭnung**. *imp* **kwchúkwŭ=nih**. *ptcpl* **kweechkwúnung**. *intensive reduplication* **kwàkwchukwŭ=númun**.

**kwéek** PR something, what, thing. **Wíhwiing- kwéek -úw.** 'He likes to talk'; **Kwéek ksí?** 'What did you say?'

**kwéekw** PR something, what, thing. **Xúwu-kwéekwiil awéehe.** 'He wears old things.'; **Kwéekw há kóonj-mataangóomi?** 'Why are you mad at me?' *pl* **kwéekwiil**.

**kweekwáanxaash** NA donkey. *pl* **kwee=kwaanxáashak**. *obv* **kweekwaan=xáashal**.

**kwehkwchiináhkees** NA wrestler. *pl* **kwehkwchiinahkéesak**. *obv* **kweh=kwchiinahkéesal**.

**kwehkwsáapiis** NA fortune teller. *pl* **kwehkwsaapíisak**. *obv* **kwehk=wsaapíisal**.

**kwehkwsahíikeet** VAI inchworm. *conj 3rd sg* **kwehkwsahíikeet** *pl* **kweh=kwsahiikéhtiit**.

**kwehkwundáasiik** NI pill. *pl* **kweh=kwundaasíikiil**.

**kwiila-** PV lacking. **Ngwíila- kwéek -lúnum.** 'I have nothing to do.'; **Ngwíila- kwéek -xamáawak.** 'I didn't have anything to feed them.' *ptcpl* **kwíila-**.

**kwíilam** VTI 1 A look for s.t., search for s.t. *(especially in vain)*. **Ápih ngwihkwíilamun.** 'I won't be able to find it.' *ind 1st sg* **ngwíilamun**. *ind 3rd sg* **kwíilamun**. *conj 1st sg* **kwíilamaan**. *conj 3rd sg* **kwíilang**. *imp* **kwíilah**. *ptcpl* **kwíilang**.

**kwíilaweew** VTA look for s.o., search for s.o. *(especially in vain)*. *ind 1st sg* **ngwíilawaaw**, **ngwíilawa**. *ind 3rd sg* **kwiilawáawal**. *ind inv* **ngwíilaakw**. *ind I-you* **kwíilool**. *conj 3rd sg* **kwíilawaat**. *imp* **kwíilaw**. *ptcpl* **kwíilawaat**.

**kwiilaweelúndam** VOTI 1 A be at a loss, don't know which way to turn, feel one has no place to go, not know where one will stay. *ind 1st sg* **ngwiilaweelúndam**. *conj 3rd sg* **kwiilaweelúndang**. *ptcpl* **kwiila=weelúndang**.

**kwiilaweelúnzuw** VAI feel oneself to be at a loss, feel desolate *(having no place to go or to live)*. *ind 1st sg* **ngwiilaweelúnzi**, **ngwiilaweelún=ziim**. *conj 3rd sg* **kwiilaweelúnziit**. *ptcpl* **kwiilaweelúnziit**.

**kwiilóomeew** VTA miss s.o. *ind 1st sg* **ngwiilóomaaw**, **ngwiilóoma**. *ind 3rd sg* **kwiiloomáawal**. *ind inv* **ngwiilóo=mukw**. *ind I-you* **kwiilóomul**. *conj 3rd sg* **kwiilóomaat**. *ptcpl* **kwiilóo=maat**.

**kwíiskweew** VII squeak, creak. *conj 3rd sg* **kwíiskweek**. *ptcpl* **kwíiskweek**.

**kwíiskwsuw** VAI squeak, creak *(s.t. animate)*. *ind 1st sg* **ngwíiskwsi**, **ngwíis=kwsiim**. *conj 3rd sg* **kwíiskwsiit**. *ptcpl* **kwíiskwsiit**.

**kwíissuw** VAI have a son. *ind 1st sg* **nookwíissi**, **nookwíissiim**. *conj 3rd sg* **kwíissiit**. *ptcpl* **weekwíissiit**.

**kwiishkwchéhleew** VAI drive quietly. **Móxa kwiishkwchéhle.** 'He drives quietly.' *ind 1st sg* **ngwiishkwchéhla**, **ngwiishkwchéhlaam**. *conj 3rd sg* **kwiishkwchéhlaat**. *imp* **kwiishk=wchéhlaal**. *ptcpl* **kwiishkwchéhlaat**.

**kwiishkwíhleew** VAI run quietly *(s.t. animate)*. *especially of vehicles*. *ind 1st sg* **ngwiishkwíhla**, **ngwiishkwíh=laam**. *conj 3rd sg* **kwiishkwíhlaat**. *ptcpl* **kwiishkwíhlaat**.

**kwiishkwíhleew** VII run quietly. *usually of motors*. *conj 3rd sg* **kwiishkwíh=laak**. *ptcpl* **kwiishkwíhlaak**.

**kwiishkwihtáakwat** VII run silently, whisper, run well. *conj 3rd sg* **kwii=shkwihtáakwahk**. *ptcpl* **kwiish=kwihtáakwahk**.

**kwiishkwihtáakwsuw** VAI run silently, whisper, run well. *ind 1st sg* **ngwii=shkwihtáakwsi**, **ngwiishkwihtáa=kwsiim**. *conj 3rd sg* **kwiishkwih=táakwsiit**. *ptcpl* **kwiishkwihtáa=kwsiit**.

**kwiishkwtóonheew** VAI whisper. *ind 1st sg* **ngwiishkwtóonhe**, **ngwiishk=wtóonheem**. *conj 3rd sg* **kwiishk=wtóonheet**. *imp* **kwiishkwtóonheel**. *ptcpl* **kwiishkwtóonheet**.

**kwíishkwŭweew** VAI make a soft sound, make a low sound, say in a soft voice, say in a low voice. *ind 1st sg* **ngwíish=kwŭwe**, **ngwíishkwŭweem**. *conj 3rd sg* **kwíishkwŭweet**. *imp* **kwíishkwŭ=weel**. *ptcpl* **kwíishkwŭweet**. *intensive reduplication* **kwihkwíish=kwŭweew**.

**kwíishkwŭweew** VII make a soft sound, make a low sound. *conj 3rd sg* **kwíishkwŭweek**. *ptcpl* **kwíish=kwŭweek**.

**kwíhleew** VTA swallow s.t. animate. *ind 1st sg* **ngwíhlaaw**, **ngwíhla**. *ind 3rd* *sg* **kwihláawal**. *ind inv* **ngwíhlukw**. *ind I-you* **kwíhlul**. *conj 3rd sg* **kwíh=laat**. *imp* **kwíhl**. *ptcpl* **kwéhlaat**.

**kwihlóotaweew** VTA attack s.o.; come up to s.o. *ind 1st sg* **ngwihlóota=waaw**, **ngwihlóotawa**. *ind 3rd sg* **kwihlootawáawal**. *ind inv* **ngwih=lóotaakw**. *ind I-you* **kwihlóotool**. *conj 3rd sg* **kwihlóotawaat**. *imp* **kwihlóotaw**. *ptcpl* **kwihlóotawaat**.

**kwíhtam** VTI1A be frightened of s.t., be nervous about s.t. *ind 1st sg* **ngwíh=tamun**. *ind 3rd sg* **kwíhtamun**. *conj 1st sg* **kwíhtamaan**. *conj 3rd sg* **kwíhtang**. *imp* **kwíhtah**.

**kwihtíhkeew** VAI advise people against a course of action. *ind 1st sg* **ngwih=tíhke**, **ngwihtíhkeem**. *conj 3rd sg* **kwihtíhkeet**. *imp* **kwihtíhkeel**.

**kwihtu-** PV be afraid. *informal.* **Ngwíhtu-míitsi.** 'I'm afraid to eat.'; **Kwíhtu-wíiteew.** 'He's afraid to go along.' *ptcpl* **kwéhtu-**.

**kwíhtŭleew** VTA advise s.o. against a course of action, advise s.o. against an intention. *ind 1st sg* **ngwíhtŭlaaw**, **ngwíhtŭla**. *ind 3rd sg* **kwihtŭláawal**. *ind inv* **ngwíhtŭlukw**. *ind I-you* **kwíhtŭlul**. *conj 3rd sg* **kwíhtŭlaat**. *imp* **kwíhtul**.

**kwsáham** VTI1A measure the dimensions of s.t. *ind 1st sg* **ngwus'hámun**. *ind 3rd sg* **kwus'hámun**. *conj 1st sg* **kwsáhŭmaan**. *conj 3rd sg* **kwsáhang**. *imp* **kwsáhih**. *ptcpl* **kwées'hang**.

**kwsáheew** VTA measure s.o. *ind 1st sg* **ngwús'haaw**, **ngwús'ha**. *ind 3rd sg* **kwus'háawal**. *ind inv* **ngwús'hookw**. *ind I-you* **kwús'hool**. *conj 3rd sg* **kwsáhaat**. *imp* **kwsáh**. *ptcpl* **kwées'haat**.

**kwsahíikeew** VAI measure things. *ind 1st sg* **ngwus'híike**, **ngwus'híikeem**. *conj 3rd sg* **kwsahíikeet**. *imp* **kwsah=íikeel**. *ptcpl* **kwees'híikeet**.

**kwsháhteew** NI tobacco. *poss* **ngwush=ahtéehum**.

**kwshahtéewheew** VAI work in a tobacco field, work picking tobacco. *ind 1st sg* **ngwushahtéewhe**, **ngwushah=téewheem**. *conj 3rd sg* **kwshahtéew=heet**. *imp* **kwshahtéewheel**. *ptcpl* **kweeshahtéewheet**.

**kwtákwteew** VAI go uphill. *ind 1st sg* **ngwutakwúte**, **ngwutakwúteem**. *conj 3rd sg* **kwtákwteet**. *imp* **kwtákwteel**. *ptcpl* **kweetakwúteet**.

**kwtámeew** VTA taste s.t. animate. *ind 1st sg* **ngwútamaaw**, **ngwútama**. *ind 3rd sg* **kwutamáawal**. *ind inv* **ngwútamukw**. *ind I-you* **kwútamul**. *conj 3rd sg* **kwtámaat**. *imp* **kwtám**. *ptcpl* **kwéetamaat**.

**kwtándam** VTI1A taste s.t. *ind 1st sg* **ngwutándamun**. *ind 3rd sg* **kwut=ándamun**. *conj 1st sg* **kwtándamaan**. *conj 3rd sg* **kwtándang**. *imp* **kwtándih**. *ptcpl* **kweetándang**.

**kwtawíhleew** VAI sink, sink down in the water. *ind 1st sg* **ngwutawíhla**, **ngwutawíhlaam**. *conj 3rd sg* **kwtawíhlaat**. *ptcpl* **kweetawíhlaat**.

**kwtawíhleew** VII sink, sink down in the water. *conj 3rd sg* **kwtawíhlaak**. *ptcpl* **kweetawíhlaak**.

**kwtáwŭnaaw** VTA have one's funeral. *indefinite subject only. indef subject* **kwtáwunaaw**. *conj 3rd sg* **kwtáwŭ=nund**. *ptcpl* **kweetawúnund**.

**kwtawŭnáasuw** VAI be buried. *ind 1st sg* **ngwutawunáasi**, **ngwutawunáa=siim**. *conj 3rd sg* **kwtawŭnáasiit**. *ptcpl* **kweetawunáasiit**.

**kwtawúndiin** VAI be a funeral going on. *indefinite subject only. indef subject* **kwtawúndiin**. *conj 3rd sg* **kwtaw=úndiing**.

**kwtawŭníikeew** VAI have one's funeral. *ind 1st sg* **ngwutawuníike**, **ngwuta=wuníikeem**. *conj 3rd sg* **kwtawŭ=níikeet**. *ptcpl* **kweetawuníikeet**.

**kwtáwŭnum** VTI1B sink s.t. *ind 1st sg*

**ngwutawúnŭmun**. *ind 3rd sg* **kwut=awúnŭmun**. *conj 1st sg* **kwtawŭ=númaan**. *conj 3rd sg* **kwtáwŭnung**. *imp* **kwtáwŭnih**. *ptcpl* **kweetawún=ung**.

**kwtucheeníikeew** VAI grope around for things, feel around for things. *ind 1st sg* **ngwutcheeníike**, **ngwutcheeníi=keem**. *conj 3rd sg* **kwtucheeníikeet**. *imp* **kwtucheeníikeel**. *ptcpl* **kweet=cheeníikeet**. *intensive reduplication* **kwàkwtucheeníikeew**.

**kwtúneew** VTA grope for s.o., feel for s.o. *(using the hands)*. *ind 1st sg* **ngwútŭnaaw**, **ngwútŭna**. *ind 3rd sg* **kwutŭnáawal**. *ind inv* **ngwútŭnukw**. *ind I-you* **kwútŭnul**. *conj 3rd sg* **kwtúnaat**. *imp* **kwtún**. *ptcpl* **kwéetŭnaat**.

**kwtúnum** VTI1B grope for s.t., feel for s.t. *(using the hands)*. *ind 1st sg* **ngwutŭnúmun**. *ind 3rd sg* **kwutŭ=númun**. *conj 1st sg* **kwtúnŭmaan**. *conj 3rd sg* **kwtúnung**. *imp* **kwtúnih**. *ptcpl* **kwéetŭnung**.

**kwúkuw** VAI have a mother. *ind 1st sg* **nóokki**, **nóokkiim**. *conj 3rd sg* **kwúkiit**. *ptcpl* **wéekkiit**.

**kwúkuw** VAIO have s.o. as a mother. **Nóokkiin.** 'She is my mother.'; **Ook=kíinal.** 'She is his mother.' *ind 1st sg* **nóokkiin**. *ind 3rd sg* **ookkíinal**. *conj 3rd sg* **kwúkiit**. *ptcpl* **wéekkiit**.

**kwŭlápeew** VII be dented. *conj 3rd sg* **kwŭlápeek**. *ptcpl* **kwéelapeek**.

**kwŭlápham** VTI1A dent s.t. *(using a tool or instrument)*. *ind 1st sg* **ngwula=páhŭmun**. *ind 3rd sg* **kwulapáhŭ=mun**. *conj 1st sg* **kwŭlaphámaan**. *conj 3rd sg* **kwŭláphang**. *imp* **kwŭ=láphah**. *ptcpl* **kweelapáhang**.

**kwŭlápheew** VTA dent s.t. animate *(using a tool or instrument)*. *ind 1st sg* **ngwulapáhaaw**, **ngwulapáha**. *ind 3rd sg* **kwulapaháawal**. *ind inv* **ngwula=páhookw**. *ind I-you* **kwulapáhool**. *conj 3rd sg* **kwŭláphaat**. *imp* **kwŭlápah**. *ptcpl* **kweelapáhaat**.

**kwŭlapíhkam** VTI1A dent s.t. *(using the foot or body)*; kick and dent s.t. *ind 1st sg* **ngwulapíhkamun**. *ind 3rd sg* **kwulapíhkamun**. *conj 1st sg* **kwŭ=lapíhkamaan**. *conj 3rd sg* **kwŭlap=íhkang**. *imp* **kwŭlapíhkah**. *ptcpl* **kweelapíhkang**.

**kwŭlapíhkaweew** VTA dent s.t. animate *(using the foot or body)*; kick and dent s.t. animate. *ind 1st sg* **ngwula=píhkawaaw**, **ngwulapíhkawa**. *ind 3rd sg* **kwulapihkawáawal**. *ind inv* **ngwulapíhkaakw**. *ind I-you* **kwula=píhkool**. *conj 3rd sg* **kwŭlapíhka=waat**. *imp* **kwŭlapíhkaw**. *ptcpl* **kweelapíhkawaat**.

**kwŭlapihtéeham** VTI1A hit and dent s.t. *(using a tool or instrument)*. *ind 1st sg* **ngwulapihtéehŭmun**. *ind 3rd sg* **kwulapihtéehŭmun**. *conj 1st sg* **kwŭlapihtéehŭmaan**. *conj 3rd sg* **kwŭlapihtéehang**. *imp* **kwŭlapih=téehih**. *ptcpl* **kweelapihtéehang**.

**kwŭlapihtéeheew** VTA hit and dent s.t. animate. *ind 1st sg* **ngwulapihtée=haaw**, **ngwulapihtéeha**. *ind 3rd sg* **kwulapihteeháawal**. *ind inv* **ngwul=apihtéehookw**. *ind I-you* **kwulapih=téehool**. *conj 3rd sg* **kwŭlapihtée=haat**. *imp* **kwŭlapíhteeh**. *ptcpl* **kweelapihtéehaat**.

**kwŭlapihtéextoow** VTI2 hit and dent s.t. *ind 1st sg* **ngwulapihtéextoon**. *ind 3rd sg* **kwulapihtéextoon**. *conj 1st sg* **kwŭlapihteextáwaan**. *conj 3rd sg* **kwŭlapihtéextaakw**. *imp* **kwŭlapih=téextool**. *ptcpl* **kweelapihtéextaakw**.

**kwŭlapihtéexŭmeew** VTA hit and dent s.o., hit and dent s.t. animate *(as the body of a car)*. *ind 1st sg* **ngwula=pihtéexŭmaaw**, **ngwulapihtéexŭma**. *ind 3rd sg* **kwulapihteexŭmáawal**. *ind inv* **ngwulapihtéexŭmukw**. *ind I-you* **kwulapihtéexŭmul**. *conj 3rd sg* kwŭlapihtéexŭmaat. *imp* **kwŭlap=ihtéexum**. *ptcpl* **kweelapihtée=xŭmaat**.

**kwŭlápsuw** VAI be dented *(s.t. animate)*. *ind 1st sg* **ngwulapúsi**, **ngwulapús=iim**. *conj 3rd sg* **kwŭlápsiit**. *ptcpl* **kweelapúsiit**.

**kwŭlápŭneew** VTA dent s.t. animate *(using the hands)*. *ind 1st sg* **ngwula=púnaaw**, **ngwulapúna**. *ind 3rd sg* **kwulapunáawal**. *ind inv* **ngwula=púnukw**. *ind I-you* **kwulapúnul**. *conj 3rd sg* **kwŭlápŭnaat**. *imp* **kwŭlápun**. *ptcpl* **kweelapúnaat**.

**kwŭlápŭnum** VTI 1A dent s.t. *(using the hands)*. *ind 1st sg* **ngwulapúnŭmun**. *ind 3rd sg* **kwulapúnŭmun**. *conj 1st sg* **kwŭlapŭnúmaan**. *conj 3rd sg* **kwŭlápŭnung**. *imp* **kwŭlápŭnih**. *ptcpl* **kweelapúnung**.

**kwŭlukhwámeew** VAI cluck, make a noise like a chicken. *ind 1st sg* **ngwulkwáhŭma**, **ngwulkwáhŭ=maam**. *conj 3rd sg* **kwŭlukhwám=aat**. *imp* **kwŭlukhwámaal**. *ptcpl* **kweelkwáhŭmaat**.

**kwŭlúkwat** VII have a bend in it. **Kwŭ=lúkwat áanay.** 'The road has a bend in it.' *conj 3rd sg* **kwŭlúkwahk**. *ptcpl* **kwéelkwahk**.

**kwŭlukwiitŭyéhleew** VAI be lame in the hip. *ind 1st sg* **ngwulkwiitŭyéhla**, **ngwulkwiitŭyéhlaam**. *conj 3rd sg* **kwŭlukwiitŭyéhlaat**. *ptcpl* **kweel=kwiitŭyéhlaat**.

**kwŭlukwíixiin** VAI be lame, have a sprain. *ind 1st sg* **ngwulkwíixiin**, **ngwulkwíixi**. *conj 3rd sg* **kwŭluk=wíixiing**. *ptcpl* **kweelkwíixiing**.

**kwŭlukwíixun** VII be lame, have a sprain. *conj 3rd sg* **kwŭlukwíixung**. *ptcpl* **kweelkwíixung**.

**kwŭlukwíhleew** VAI be lame, walk with a limp. *ind 1st sg* **ngwulkwíhla**, **ngwulkwíhlaam**. *conj 3rd sg* **kwŭ=lukwíhlaat**. *ptcpl* **kweelkwíhlaat**. *intensive reduplication* **kwàkwŭluk=wíhleew**.

**kwŭlúkwŭnum** VTI 1B damage s.t., make s.t. lame. **Ngwulkwúnŭmun nzíit.** 'I sprained my foot.' *ind 1st sg* **ngwul=kwúnŭmun**. *ind 3rd sg* **kwulkwúnŭ=mun**. *conj 1st sg* **kwŭlukwŭnúm=aan**. *conj 3rd sg* **kwŭlúkwŭnung**. *imp* **kwŭlúkwŭnih**. *ptcpl* **kweel=kwúnung**.

**kwŭlúp** PC also, emphatic. **Níi nú wúndakw ndá, kwŭlúp néeka yée=lak wúndakw éew.** 'I went that way, and also he went the other way.'; **Kwŭlúp liitéeheew wŭlóngwanuw.** 'He thinks he's a real angel ('He thinks he has wings').'

**kwŭlupáaheew** VAIO flip s.o., flip s.t. over. *ind 1st sg* **ngwulpáaheen**. *ind 3rd sg* **kwulpáaheen**. *conj 3rd sg* **kwŭlupáaheet**. *imp* **kwŭlupáaheel**. *ptcpl* **kweelpáaheet**.

**kwŭlúpapuw** VAI turn around while sitting. *ind 1st sg* **ngwulpápi**, **ngwul=pápiim**. *conj 3rd sg* **kwŭlúpapiit**. *imp* **kwŭlúpapiil**. *ptcpl* **kweelpápiit**.

**kwŭlupatéexiin** VAI turn over from one side to the other, turn over in bed. *ind 1st sg* **ngwulpatéexiin**, **ngwulpatée=xi**. *conj 3rd sg* **kwŭlupatéexiing**. *imp* **kwŭlupatéexiil**. *ptcpl* **kweelpatée=xiing**.

**kwŭlúpiiw** VAI-S turn around. *ind 1st sg* **ngwúlpi**, **ngwúlpiim**. *conj 3rd sg* **kwŭlúpiit**. *imp* **kwŭlúpiil**. *ptcpl* **kwéelpiit**.

**kwŭlupiikáapawuw** VAI turn around while standing. *ind 1st sg* **ngwulpii=káapawi**, **ngwulpiikáapawiim**. *conj 3rd sg* **kwŭlupiikáapawiit**. *imp* **kwŭlupiikáapawiil**. *ptcpl* **kweelpii=káapawiit**.

**kwŭlupíikwsuw** VAI turn around while crawling. *ind 1st sg* **ngwulpíikwsi**, **ngwulpíikwsiim**. *conj 3rd sg* **kwŭ=lupíikwsiit**. *imp* **kwŭlupíikwsiil**.

*ptcpl* **kweelpíikwsiit**.

**kwŭlupíixiin** VAI turn over while lying down. *ind 1st sg* **ngwulpíixiin, ngwulpíixi**. *conj 3rd sg* **kwŭlupíi=xiing**. *imp* **kwŭlupíixiil**. *ptcpl* **kweel=píixiing, kweelpíixiit**.

**kwŭlupíhkam** VTI1A turn s.t. over, turn s.t. around *(using the foot or body)*. *ind 1st sg* **ngwulpíhkamun**. *ind 3rd sg* **kwulpíhkamun**. *conj 1st sg* **kwŭlupíhkamaan**. *conj 3rd sg* **kwŭlupíhkang**. *imp* **kwŭlupíhkah**. *ptcpl* **kweelpíhkang**.

**kwŭlupíhkaweew** VTA turn s.o. over, turn s.o. around *(using the foot or body)*. *ind 1st sg* **ngwulpíhkawaaw, ngwulpíhkawa**. *ind 3rd sg* **kwulpih=kawáawal**. *ind inv* **ngwulpíhkaakw**. *ind I-you* **kwulpíhkool**. *conj 3rd sg* **kwŭlupíhkawaat**. *imp* **kwŭlupíh=kaw**. *ptcpl* **kweelpíhkawaat**.

**kwŭlupíhleew** VAI turn around, turn around while in motion, turn around while driving, flip over. *ind 1st sg* **ngwulpíhla, ngwulpíhlaam**. *conj 3rd sg* **kwŭlupíhlaat**. *imp* **kwŭlup=íhlaal**. *ptcpl* **kweelpíhlaat**.

**kwŭlupóhkweew** VAI turn one's head, look back. *ind 1st sg* **ngwulpóhkwe, ngwulpóhkweem**. *conj 3rd sg* **kwŭ=lupóhkweet**. *imp* **kwŭlupóhkweel**. *ptcpl* **kweelpóhkweet**.

**kwŭlúpŭneew** VTA turn s.o. over, turn s.o. around *(using the hands)*. *ind 1st sg* **ngwulpúnaaw, ngwulpúna**. *ind 3rd sg* **kwulpunáawal**. *ind inv* **ngwulpúnukw**. *ind I-you* **kwulpún=ul**. *conj 3rd sg* **kwŭlúpŭnaat**. *imp* **kwŭlúpun**. *ptcpl* **kweelpúnaat**.

**kwŭlúpŭnum** VTI1B turn s.t. over, turn s.t. around *(using the hands)*. *ind 1st sg* **ngwulpúnŭmun**. *ind 3rd sg* **kwulpúnŭmun**. *conj 1st sg* **kwŭlup=ŭnúmaan**. *conj 3rd sg* **kwŭlúpŭ=nung**. *imp* **kwŭlúpŭnih**. *ptcpl* **kweelpúnung**.

**kwŭnáalakat** VII be a deep hole. *conj 3rd sg* **kwŭnáalakahk**. *ptcpl* **kwee=náalakahk**.

**kwŭnáalheew** VAI make a big hole, make a deep hole. *ind 1st sg* **ngwun=áalhe, ngwunáalheem**. *conj 3rd sg* **kwŭnáalheet**. *imp* **kwŭnáalheel**. *ptcpl* **kweenáalheet**.

**kwŭnaalóhkweew** VAI have long hair. *ind 1st sg* **ngwunaalóhkwa, ngwun=aalóhkwaam**. *conj 3rd sg* **kwŭnaa=lóhkwaat**. *ptcpl* **kweenaalóhkwaat**.

**kwŭnáalŭweew** VAI have a long tail. *ind 1st sg* **ngwunáalŭwe, ngwunáalŭ=weem**. *conj 3rd sg* **kwŭnáalŭweet**. *ptcpl* **kweenáalŭweet**.

**kwŭnáameew** VAI be long, be in a long line *(s.t. animate)*. **Áxkook kwŭnáa=me.** 'The snake is long.' *ind 1st sg* **ngwunáame, ngwunáameem**. *conj 3rd sg* **kwŭnáameet**. *ptcpl* **kwee=náameet**.

**kwŭnáameew** VII be long, be in a long line. **Xwáskwiim kwŭnáame.** 'There is a long row of corn.' *conj 3rd sg* **kwŭnáameek**. *ptcpl* **kweenáameek**.

**kwŭnáandpeew** VAI have a long head. *ind 1st sg* **ngwunáandpa, ngwun=áandpaam**. *conj 3rd sg* **kwŭnáan=dpaat**. *ptcpl* **kweenáandpaat**.

**kwŭnaapéhleew** VII hang down a long way. *conj 3rd sg* **kwŭnaapéhlaak**. *ptcpl* **kweenaapéhlaak**.

**kwŭnáawsuw** VAI live a long life, live for a long time. **Táas áa kwùnáawsi.** 'Maybe you'll live a long life.' *ind 1st sg* **ngwunáawsi, ngwunáawsiim**. *conj 3rd sg* **kwŭnáawsiit**. *ptcpl* **kweenáawsiit**.

**kwŭnaawúngeew** VII be a mountain. **Ndúlu-pumúsi éenda-kwŭnaawún=geek.** 'I walked to the mountain.' *conj 3rd sg* **kwŭnaawúngeek**. *ptcpl* **kweenaawúngeek**.

**kwŭnahkachíhteew** VII give long shade. *conj 3rd sg* **kwŭnahkachíhteek**.

*ptcpl* **kweenahkachíhteek**.

**kwŭnahkachihtéexiin** VAI give long shade *(s.t. animate)*. *ind 1st sg* **ngwunahkachihtéexiin**, **ngwunah=kachihtéexi**. *conj 3rd sg* **kwŭnahka=chihtéexiing**. *ptcpl* **kweenahkachih=téexiing**. *especially of trees*.

**kwŭnahkachihtéexun** VII give long shade. *conj 3rd sg* **kwŭnahkachih=téexung**. *ptcpl* **kweenahkachih=téexung**.

**kwŭnáhkeew** VAI be away a long time. *ind 1st sg* **ngwunáhke**, **ngwunáh=keem**. *conj 3rd sg* **kwŭnáhkeet**. *ptcpl* **kweenáhkeet**.

**kwŭnáhkwat** VII be high, be tall. *conj 3rd sg* **kwŭnáhkwahk**. *ptcpl* **kwee=náhkwahk**.

**kwŭnáhkwsuw** VAI be long *(of something wood- or stick-like)*; be tall *(of a person)*. *ind 1st sg* **ngwunáhkwsi**, **ngwunáhkwsiim**. *conj 3rd sg* **kwŭ=náhkwsiit**. *ptcpl* **kweenáhkwsiit**.

**kwŭnahóosuw** VAI wear a long dress, have a long dress on. *ind 1st sg* **ngwunhóosi**, **ngwunhóosiim**. *conj 3rd sg* **kwŭnahóosiit**. *imp* **kwŭ=nahóosiil**. *ptcpl* **kweenhóosiit**.

**kwŭnáhtakat** VII be long *(of something string-like)*. *conj 3rd sg* **kwŭnáhta=kahk**. *ptcpl* **kweenáhtakahk**.

**kwŭnahtakúsuw** VAI be long *(s.t. animate, of something string-like)*. *conj 3rd sg* **kwŭnahtakúsiit**. *ptcpl* **kweenahtakúsiit**.

**kwŭnakóosuw** VAI climb up a long flight of stairs. *ind 1st sg* **ngwuna=kóosi**, **ngwunakóosiim**. *conj 3rd sg* **kwŭnakóosiit**. *imp* **kwŭnakóosiil**. *ptcpl* **kweenakóosiit**.

**kwŭnanzhíikan** NI long knife. *pl* **kwŭ=nanzhíikanal**. *poss* **ngwunanzhíi=kan**. *loc* **kwŭnanzhíikanung**. *dimin* **kwŭnanzhíikanush**.

**kwŭnasíiskŭwat** VII be deep mud. *conj 3rd sg* **kwŭnasíiskŭwahk**. *ptcpl* **kweenasíiskŭwahk**.

**kwŭnáskwat** VII be long grass. *conj 3rd sg* **kwŭnáskwahk**. *ptcpl* **kweenás=kwahk**.

**kwŭnaskwéeyeew** VII be long grass. *conj 3rd sg* **kwŭnaskwéeyeek**. *ptcpl* **kweenaskwéeyeek**.

**kwŭnawéesuw** VAI have long hair *(especially of non-humans)*. *conj 3rd sg* **kwŭnawéesiit**. *ptcpl* **kweenawéesiit**.

**kwŭnáxakw** NI long piece of wood. *pl* **kwŭnáxakwal**. *poss* **ngwunxák=wum**. *loc* **kwŭnáxakwung**. *dimin* **kwŭnáxakwush**.

**kwŭnáxeew** VAI have a long ear. *ind 1st sg* **ngwúnxa**, **ngwúnxaam**. *conj 3rd sg* **kwŭnáxaat**. *ptcpl* **kwéenxaat**. *See* **kwŭnihtawákeew**.

**kwŭnaxóoneew** VAI have a long neck. *ind 1st sg* **ngwunxóona**, **ngwunxóo=naam**. *conj 3rd sg* **kwŭnaxóonaat**. *ptcpl* **kweenxóonaat**.

**kwundáakan** NI throat. *poss* **ngwun=dáakan**. *loc* **kwŭndáakanung**. *dimin* **kwunjáakanush**.

**kwundaakaníineew** VAI have a sore throat. *ind 1st sg* **ngwundaakaníine**, **ngwundaakaníineem**. *conj 3rd sg* **kwundaakaníineet**. *ptcpl* **kween=daakaníineet**.

**kwundáasuw** VII be swallowed. *conj 3rd sg* **kwundáasiik**. *ptcpl* **kween=dáasiik**.

**kwúndam** VTI1A swallow s.t. *ind 1st sg* **ngwúndamun**. *ind 3rd sg* **kwún=damun**. *conj 1st sg* **kwúndamaan**. *conj 3rd sg* **kwúndang**. *imp* **kwún=dah**. *ptcpl* **kwéendang**.

**kwŭneelúndam** VTI1A think s.t. to be a long time. **Níi ngwuneelúndamun nál ápih wŭláakuw.** 'I think it's taking a long time for evening to come.'; **Níi ngwuneelúndamun nál-uch éhkwu-maawéewiin.** 'I think that it's a long time until the end of the service.' *ind 1st sg* **ngwuneelúndamun**.

*ind 3rd sg* **kwuneelúndamun**. *conj 1st sg* **kwŭneelúndamaan**. *conj 3rd sg* **kwŭneelúndang**. *ptcpl* **kwee=neelúndang**.

**kwŭnéew** VII be long. *conj 3rd sg* **kwŭnéek**. *ptcpl* **kwéeneek**.

**kwŭnii-** PN long. **Kwŭníi-kóot.** 'Over-coat'

**kwŭnii-** PV long. **Kwúnii-wiitaawsoo=máawal.** 'He lived with her for a long time.'; **Nóosaa-kwŭníi-ndupwíinak aapŭlúshak.** 'I cooked the apples too long.' *ptcpl* **kwéenii-**.

**kwŭníi-koothámeew** VAI wear a long coat, have a long coat on. *ind 1st sg* **ngwúnii-kooth//áma, ngwunii-koothámaam**. *conj 3rd sg* **kwŭníi-koothámaat**. *imp* **kwŭníi-koothám=aal**. *ptcpl* **kwéenii-koothámaat**.

**kwŭníi-shkwúnayeew** VAI wear some-thing that has a long tail. *usually of coats. ind 1st sg* **ngwúnii-shkwúna=ya, ngwúnii-shkwúnayaam**. *conj 3rd sg* **kwŭníi-shkwúnayaat**. *imp* **kwŭníi-shkwúnayaal**. *ptcpl* **kwéenii-shkwúnayaat**.

**kwŭníi-shkwúnayii-koothámeew** VAI wear a coat with a long tail. *ind 1st sg* **ngwúnii-shkwúnayii-kooth//áma, ngwúnii-shkwúnayii-koothámaam**. *conj 3rd sg* **kwŭníi-shkwúnayii-koothámaat**. *imp* **kwŭníi-shkwúna=yii-koothámaal**. *ptcpl* **kwéenii-shkwúnayii-koothámaat**.

**kwŭniináxkeew** VAI have a long arm, reach a long way. *ind 1st sg* **ngwun=iináxka, ngwuniináxkaam**. *conj 3rd sg* **kwŭniináxkaat**. *imp* **kwŭniináx=kaal**. *ptcpl* **kweeniináxkaat**. *See* **kwŭniináxkeew**.

**kwŭniináxkeew** VAI have a long arm, reach a long way. *ind 1st sg* **ngwun=iináxke, ngwuniináxkeem**. *conj 3rd sg* **kwŭniináxkeet**. *imp* **kwŭniináx=keel**. *ptcpl* **kweeniináxkeet**. *See* **kwŭniináxkeew**.

**kwŭníingweew** VAI have a long face. *ind 1st sg* **ngwuníingwa, ngwuníin=gwaam**. *conj 3rd sg* **kwŭníingwaat**. *ptcpl* **kweeníingwaat**.

**kwŭníinjuw** NI trough. *pl* **kwŭníinjŭ=wal**. *loc* **kwŭníinjoong**. *dimin* **kwŭníinjoosh**.

**kwŭnihtawákeew** VAI have a long ear. *ind 1st sg* **ngwunihtawáka, ngwun=ihtawákaam**. *conj 3rd sg* **kwŭnihta=wákaat**. *ptcpl* **kweenihtawákaat**. *See* **kwŭnáxeew**.

**kwŭnihtóonayeew** VAI have a long beard, have long whiskers. *ind 1st sg* **ngwunihtóonaya, ngwunihtóona=yaam**. *conj 3rd sg* **kwŭnihtóonayaat**. *ptcpl* **kweenihtóonayaat**.

**kwŭnoochéeyeew** VII have a long shape, have a long body. **Kéhla wáak chah=kwéeshuw, tàtùpháasuw, kwŭnoo=cheeyéeshuw.** 'And it was short, it was wrapped around in a bundle, and it was a rectangular little thing.' *conj 3rd sg* **kwŭnoochéeyeek**. *ptcpl* **kwee=noochéeyeek**. *See* **kwŭnuchéeyeew**.

**kwŭnóosuw** VAI be long *(s.t. animate)*. *ind 1st sg* **ngwunóosi, ngwunóosiim**. *conj 3rd sg* **kwŭnóosiit**. *ptcpl* **kwee=nóosiit**.

**kwŭnucháaleew** VAI have a long nose. *ind 1st sg* **ngwuncháala, ngwun=cháalaam**. *conj 3rd sg* **kwŭnucháa=laat**. *ptcpl* **kweencháalaat**.

**kwŭnuchéesuw** VAI be long in shape, have a long shape. *ind 1st sg* **ngwun=chéesi, ngwunchéesiim**. *conj 3rd sg* **kwŭnuchéesiit**. *ptcpl* **kweenchéesiit**.

**kwŭnuchéeyayeew** VII be long in shape, have a long shape. *conj 3rd sg* **kwŭ=nuchéeyayeek**. *ptcpl* **kweenchée=yayeek**.

**kwŭnuchéeyeew** VII have a long shape, have a long body. *conj 3rd sg* **kwŭ=nuchéeyeek**. *ptcpl* **kweenchéeyeek**.

*See* **kwŭnoochéeyeew**.
**kwŭnunaxkamáyal** NI long sleeves. *usually plural. poss* **ngwunŭnax=kamáyal**.
**kwŭnunaxkamáyeew** VII have long sleeves. *conj 3rd sg* **kwŭnunaxka=máyeek**. *ptcpl* **kweenŭnaxkamáy=eek**.
**kwŭnúpeew** VII be deep water. *conj 3rd sg* **kwŭnúpeek**. *ptcpl* **kwéenpeek**.
**kwŭnupéekat** VII be deep water. *conj 3rd sg* **kwŭnupéekahk**. *ptcpl* **kweenpéekahk**.
**kwŭnushéesuw** VAI be deep *(s.t. animate, of pockets). conj 3rd sg* **kwŭnushéesiit**. *ptcpl* **kweenshéesiit**.
**kwŭnushéeyeew** VII be deep *(of bodies of water). conj 3rd sg* **kwŭnush=éeyeek**. *ptcpl* **kweenshéeyeek**.
**kwŭnutoonéexiin** VAI be angry. *ind 1st sg* **ngwuntoonéexiin**, **ngwuntoo=néexi**. *conj 3rd sg* **kwŭnutoonée=xiing**. *ptcpl* **kweentoonéexiing**, **kweentoonéexiit**.
**kxahwéemwiish** NA screech owl. *pl* **kxahweemwíishak**. *obv* **kxahwee=mwíishal**.
**kxahwéexiin** VAI set *(as a chicken on eggs). ind 1st sg* **ngaxàhwéexiin**, **ngaxàhwéexi**. *conj 3rd sg* **kxàhwée=xiing**. *imp* **kxàhwéexiil**. *ptcpl* **keexàhwéexiing**.
**kxahwéexŭmeew** VTA set s.o. on eggs *(of chickens). ind 1st sg* **ngaxahwée=xŭmaaw**, **ngaxahwéexŭma**. *ind 3rd sg* **kwaxahweexŭmáawal**. *ind inv* **ngaxahwéexŭmukw**. *ind 1-you* **kax=ahwéexŭmul**. *conj 3rd sg* **kxahwée=xŭmaat**. *imp* **kxahwéexum**. *ptcpl* **keexàhwéexŭmaat**.
**kxánuw** VAIO have s.t., have s.t. animate. **Ngáxani shúlpul.** 'I have some money.'; **Níi ngáxaniin payaxkhíi=kan.** 'I've got the gun.' *ind 1st sg* **ngáxaniin**. *ind 3rd sg* **kwáxaniin**. *conj 3rd sg* **kxániit**. *ptcpl* **kéexaniit**.
**kxéelŭmeew** VTA be jealous of s.o.'s achievements, be jealous of s.o.'s possessions, be envious of s.o. *ind 1st sg* **ngaxéelŭmaaw**, **ngaxéelŭma**. *ind 3rd sg* **kwaxeelŭmáawal**. *ind inv* **ngaxéelŭmukw**. *ind 1-you* **kaxéelŭ=mul**. *conj 3rd sg* **kxéelŭmaat**. *imp* **kxéelum**. *ptcpl* **keexéelŭmaat**. *intensive reduplication* **kwàkxeelŭ=máawal**.
**kxeelúngeew** VAI be jealous of people, be envious of people. *ind 1st sg* **ngaxeelúnge**, **ngaxeelúngeem**. *conj 3rd sg* **kxeelúngeet**. *ptcpl* **keexee=lúngeet**. *intensive reduplication* **akaxeelúngeew**.
**kxupéexun** VII be water in a puddle. *conj 3rd sg* **kxupéexung**. *ptcpl* **keexpéexung**. *intensive reduplication* **kàkxupéexun**.
**kxúweew** VAI be afraid of people. *ind 1st sg* **ngwáxŭwe**, **ngwáxŭweem**. *conj 3rd sg* **kxúweet**. *ptcpl* **kwéexŭweet**.
**kxwéew** VTA be afraid of s.o., be wary of s.o. *ind 1st sg* **ngwáxaaw**, **ngwáxa**. *ind 3rd sg* **kwaxáawal**. *ind inv* **ngwáxookw**. *ind 1-you* **kwáxool**. *conj 3rd sg* **kxwáat**. *ptcpl* **kwéexaat**.
**kxwáatam** VTI 1A be afraid of s.t. *ind 1st sg* **ngwaxáatamun**. *ind 3rd sg* **kwàx=áatamun**. *conj 1st sg* **kxwáatamaan**. *conj 3rd sg* **kxwáatang**. *imp* **kxwáa=tah**. *ptcpl* **kweexáatang**.
**kxwaawiináakwat** VII look dangerous, look scary. *conj 3rd sg* **kxwaawii=náakwahk**. *ptcpl* **kweexaawii=náakwahk**.
**kxwaawiináakwsuw** VAI look dangerous, look scary. *ind 1st sg* **ngwaxaa=wiináakwsi**, **ngwaxaawiináakwsiim**. *conj 3rd sg* **kxwaawiináakwsiit**. *ptcpl* **kweexaawiináakwsiit**.
**kxwaawíixiin** VAI be in a frightening condition, be in a dangerous condi-

tion. *ind 1st sg* **ngwaxaawíixiin**, **ngwaxaawíixi**. *conj 3rd sg* **kxwaa=wíixiing**. *ptcpl* **kweexaawíixiing**.

**kxwaawíixun** VII be in a frightening condition, be in a dangerous condition. *conj 3rd sg* **kxwaawíixung**. *ptcpl* **kweexaawíixung**.

# L

**laachiimóoleew** VTA tell s.o. about something. *ind 1st sg* **ndulaachii=móolaaw**, **ndulaachiimóola**. *ind 3rd sg* **wtulaachiimooláawal**. *ind inv* **ndulaachiimóolukw**. *ind I-you* **ktulaachiimóolul**. *conj 3rd sg* **laa=chiimóolaat**. *imp* **laachíimool**. *ptcpl* **eelaachiimóolaat**.

**laachíimuw** VAI tell a story. *ind 1st sg* **ndulaachíimwi**, **ndulaachíimwiim**. *conj 3rd sg* **laachíimwiit**. *imp* **laachíimwiil**. *ptcpl* **eelaachíimwiit**.

**laachŭmóhkaweew** VTA tell s.o. a story. *ind 1st sg* **ndulaachŭmóhkawaaw**, **ndulaachŭmóhkawa**. *ind 3rd sg* **wtulaachŭmohkawáawal**. *ind inv* **ndulaachŭmóhkaakw**. *ind I-you* **ktulaachŭmóhkool**. *conj 3rd sg* **laachŭmóhkawaat**. *imp* **laachŭ=móhkaw**. *ptcpl* **eelaachŭmóh=kawaat**.

**láaheew** VAIO throw s.t., throw s.t. in a certain direction, throw s.t. in a certain manner. *ind 1st sg* **nduláaheen**. *ind 3rd sg* **wtuláaheen**. *conj 3rd sg* **láaheet**. *imp* **láaheel**. *ptcpl* **eeláaheet**.

**láakchehl** VAI jump in the water. *ind 1st sg* **nduláakchehl**. *conj 3rd sg* **laak=chéhluk**. *imp* **laakchéhlih**. *ptcpl* **eelaakchéhluk**.

**láakuw** VII be a certain kind of evening. **Thíi-láakuw.** 'It's a cold evening.' *conj 3rd sg* **láakwiik**. *ptcpl* **eeláa=kwiik**.

**laalakwíhleew** VAI slide down, slide off. *ind 1st sg* **laalakwíhla**, **laalakwíh=laam**. *conj 3rd sg* **laalakwíhlaat**. *imp* **laalakwíhlaal**. *ptcpl* **laalakwíhlaat**. *intensive reduplication* **lahlaakwíh=leew**.

**láalameew** VTA lick s.o., rub, nuzzle s.o. with mouth. *ind 1st sg* **láalamaaw**, **láalama**. *ind 3rd sg* **wŭlaalamáawal**. *ind inv* **láalamukw**. *ind I-you* **kŭláa=lamul**. *conj 3rd sg* **láalamaat**. *imp* **láalam**. *ptcpl* **láalamaat**.

**laalamúwees** NA nettle. *pl* **laalamuw=éesak**. *loc* **laalamuwéesung**. *dimin* **laalamuwéeshush**. *obv* **laalamuw=éesal**.

**laalándam** VTI1B lick s.t. *ind 1st sg* **laalándamun**. *ind 3rd sg* **wŭlaalán=damun**. *conj 1st sg* **laalándamaan**. *conj 3rd sg* **laalándang**. *imp* **laalándah**. *ptcpl* **laalándang**.

**láalham** VTI1A brush s.t., rub s.t. *(using a tool or instrument). ind 1st sg* **laal=hámun**. *ind 3rd sg* **wŭlaalhámun**. *conj 1st sg* **laalhámaan**. *conj 3rd sg* **láalhang**. *imp* **láalhah**. *ptcpl* **láalhang**.

**laalíixiin** VAI brush up against something. *ind 1st sg* **laalíixiin**, **laalíixi**. *conj 3rd sg* **laalíixiing**. *imp* **laalíixiil**. *ptcpl* **laalíixiing**, **laalíixiit**.

**laalíixun** VII brush up against something. *conj 3rd sg* **laalíixung**. *ptcpl* **laalíixung**.

**laalíhkam** VTI1A brush up against s.t. *(using the foot or body). ind 1st sg* **laalíhkamun**. *ind 3rd sg* **wŭlaalíh=kamun**. *conj 1st sg* **laalíhkamaan**. *conj 3rd sg* **laalíhkang**. *imp* **laalíh=kah**. *ptcpl* **laalíhkang**.

**laalíhkaweew** VTA brush up against s.o. *(using the foot or body). ind 1st sg* **laalíhkawaaw**, **laalíhkawa**. *ind 3rd sg* **wŭlaalihkawáawal**. *ind inv* **laalíhkaakw**. *ind I-you* **kŭlaalíhkool**. *conj 3rd sg* **laalíhkawaat**. *imp*

**laalíhkaw**. *ptcpl* **laalíhkawaat**.

**laalihtéeheew** VTA hit and graze s.o. with an object. *ind 1st sg* **laalihtée=haaw**, **laalihtéeha**. *ind 3rd sg* **wŭlaalihteeháawal**. *ind inv* **laalih=téehookw**. *ind I-you* **kŭlaalihtéehool**. *conj 3rd sg* **laalihtéehaat**. *imp* **laalíhteeh**. *ptcpl* **laalihtéehaat**.

**laalihtéexiin** VAI rub against something and fall, brush up against something and fall. *ind 1st sg* **laalihtéexiin**, **laalihtéexi**. *conj 3rd sg* **laalihtée=xiing**. *ptcpl* **laalihtéexiing**.

**laalihtéextoow** VTI2 contact and brush up against s.t. *ind 1st sg* **laalihtée=xtoon**. *ind 3rd sg* **wŭlaalihtéextoon**. *conj 1st sg* **laalihteextáwaan**. *conj 3rd sg* **laalihtéextaakw**. *imp* **laalih=téextool**. *ptcpl* **laalihtéextaakw**.

**laalihtéexŭmeew** VTA contact and brush up against s.o. *ind 1st sg* **laalihtée=xŭmaaw**, **laalihtéexŭma**. *ind 3rd sg* **wŭlaalihteexŭmáawal**. *ind inv* **laa=lihtéexŭmukw**. *ind I-you* **kŭlaalih=téexŭmul**. *conj 3rd sg* **laalihtéexŭ=maat**. *imp* **laalihtéexum**. *ptcpl* **laalihtéexŭmaat**.

**láalsheew** VTA cut s.t. animate smoothly, scrape s.t. animate smooth, cut s.t. animate lightly, trim s.t. animate. *ind 1st sg* **láalshaaw**, **láalsha**. *ind 3rd sg* **wŭlaalsháawal**. *ind inv* **láalshookw**. *ind I-you* **kŭláalshool**. *conj 3rd sg* **láalshaat**. *imp* **láalush**. *ptcpl* **láalshaat**.

**laalsháasuw** VAI be marked, be trimmed, be pruned *(of trees)*. *ind 1st sg* **laalsháasi**, **laalsháasiim**. *conj 3rd sg* **laalsháasiit**. *ptcpl* **laalsháasiit**.

**laalsháasuw** VII be trimmed. *conj 3rd sg* **laalsháasiik**. *ptcpl* **laalsháasiik**.

**láalshum** VTI1B cut s.t. smoothly, scrape s.t. smooth, cut s.t. lightly, trim s.t. *ind 1st sg* **laalshúmun**. *ind 3rd sg* **wŭlaalshúmun**. *conj 1st sg* **laal=shúmaan**. *conj 3rd sg* **láalshung**. *imp* **láalshih**. *ptcpl* **láalshung**.

**láalŭneew** VTA rub s.o., brush up against s.t. animate, pet s.o., caress s.o. *(using the hands)*. *ind 1st sg* **láalŭnaaw**, **láalŭna**. *ind 3rd sg* **wŭlaalŭnáawal**. *ind inv* **láalŭnukw**. *ind I-you* **kŭláa=lŭnul**. *conj 3rd sg* **láalŭnaat**. *imp* **láalun**. *ptcpl* **láalŭnaat**.

**láalŭnum** VTI1B rub s.t. *(using the hands)*; run one's hand over s.t. *ind 1st sg* **laalŭnúmun**. *ind 3rd sg* **wŭlaa=lŭnúmun**. *conj 1st sg* **laalŭnúmaan**. *conj 3rd sg* **láalŭnung**. *imp* **láalŭnih**. *ptcpl* **láalŭnung**.

**laalŭwéhleew** VAI go with one's tail in a certain direction, go with one's tail in a certain manner. *ind 1st sg* **ndulaa=lŭwéhla**, **ndulaalŭwéhlaam**. *conj 3rd sg* **laalŭwéhleet**. *imp* **laalŭwéhlaal**. *ptcpl* **eelaalŭwéhlaat**.

**laalxawalóhkeew** VAI do dangerous work, work regardless of the consequences or risks. *ind 1st sg* **laalxaw=alóhke**, **laalxawalóhkeem**. *conj 3rd sg* **laalxawalóhkaat**. *imp* **laalxawa=lóhkeel**. *ptcpl* **laalxawalóhkeet**.

**laalxawíixiin** VAI lie in a dangerous place. *ind 1st sg* **laalxawíixiin**, **laal=xawíixi**. *conj 3rd sg* **laalxawíixiing**. *imp* **laalxawíixiil**. *ptcpl* **laalxaw=íixiing**.

**laalxawíixtoow** VTI2 place s.t. recklessly, put s.t. in a dangerous spot, place s.t. regardless of the consequences or risks. *ind 1st sg* **laalxawíixtoon**. *ind 3rd sg* **wŭlaalxawíixtoon**. *conj 1st sg* **laalxawiixtáwaan**. *conj 3rd sg* **laal=xawíixtaakw**. *imp* **laalxawíixtool**. *ptcpl* **laalxawíixtaakw**.

**laalxawíixŭmeew** VTA place s.o. recklessly, place s.o. in a dangerous spot, place s.o. regardless of the consequences or risks. *ind 1st sg* **laalxaw=íixŭmaaw**, **laalxawíixŭma**. *ind 3rd sg* **wŭlaalxawiixŭmáawal**. *ind inv* **laalxawíixŭmukw**. *ind I-you* **kŭlaal=**

**xawíixŭmul**. *conj 3rd sg* **laalxawíi=xŭmaat**. *imp* **laalxawíixum**. *ptcpl* **laalxawíixŭmaat**.

**laalxawíixun** VII lie in a dangerous place. *conj 3rd sg* **laalxawíixung**. *ptcpl* **laalxawíixung**.

**laalxawíhleew** VAI drive recklessly, go regardless of the consequences or risks. *ind 1st sg* **laalxawíhla**, **laal=xawíhlaam**. *conj 3rd sg* **laalxawíh=laat**. *imp* **laalxawíhlaal**. *ptcpl* **laalxawíhlaat**.

**láameew** VAI be in a line in a certain manner, be a line in a certain direction *(s.t. animate)*. **Yéelak laamée=wak káalak.** 'The cars are in a line over there.'; **Xwáchu-áxkook wtul=áameen apánzhŭyung séhkeek wíikwahm.** 'A big snake was lying on the timbers the length of the house.' *ind 1st sg* **nduláame**, **ndul=áameem**. *conj 3rd sg* **láameet**. *ptcpl* **eeláameet**.

**láameew** VII be in a line in a certain manner, be in a line in a certain direction. **Yéelak láameew méenaxk.** 'The fence is in a line over there.' *conj 3rd sg* **láameek**. *ptcpl* **eeláameek**.

**laaméhleew** VAI run in a certain manner, run in a certain direction. **Kóhpii laaméhleew.** 'He's running towards the forest.' *ind 1st sg* **ndulaaméhla**, **ndulaaméhlaam**. *conj 3rd sg* **laa=méhlaat**. *imp* **laaméhlaal**. *ptcpl* **eelaaméhlaat**.

**láandeew** VII shine in a certain direction *(of the sun)*. *conj 3rd sg* **láandeek**. *ptcpl* **eeláandeek**.

**laangáhkwsuw** VAI have a slight build, be slim. *ind 1st sg* **laangáhkwsi**, **laangáhkwsiim**. *conj 3rd sg* **laan=gáhkwsiit**. *ptcpl* **laangáhkwsiit**.

**láangan** VII be light in weight. *conj 3rd sg* **láangang**. *ptcpl* **láangang**.

**laangánzhuw** VII be light in weight *(diminutive)*. *conj 3rd sg* **laangánzhiik**. *ptcpl* **laangánzhiik**.

**laangiináakwat** VII be lightweight looking, look light in weight. *conj 3rd sg* **laangiináakwahk**. *ptcpl* **laangiináa=kwahk**.

**laangiináakwsuw** VAI be lightweight looking, look light in weight *(s.t. animate)*. *ind 1st sg* **laangiináakwsi**, **laangiináakwsiim**. *conj 3rd sg* **laan=giináakwsiit**. *ptcpl* **laangiináakwsiit**.

**laangíhleew** VAI be relieved. *ind 1st sg* **laangíhla**, **laangíhlaam**. *conj 3rd sg* **laangíhlaat**. *ptcpl* **laangíhlaat**.

**laangóomeew** VTA be related to s.o. *ind 1st sg* **ndulaangóomaaw**, **ndulaan=góoma**. *ind 3rd sg* **wtulaangoomáa=wal**. *ind inv* **ndulaangóomukw**. *ind I-you* **ktulaangóomul**. *conj 3rd sg* **laangóomaat**. *ptcpl* **eelaangóomaat**.

**laangóondŭwak** VAI be related to each other. *usually plural*. *ind 1st pl* **ndul=aangoondíhna**. *conj 3rd sg* **laan=goondíhtiit**. *ptcpl* **eelaangoondíhtiit**.

**láangsuw** VAI be light in weight *(s.t. animate)*. *ind 1st sg* **láangsi**, **láangsiim**. *conj 3rd sg* **láangsiit**. *ptcpl* **láangsiit**.

**laanzhíhkan** VII be heavy in weight. *conj 3rd sg* **laanzhíhkang**. *ptcpl* **laanzhíhkang**.

**laanzhíhksuw** VAI be heavy in weight. *ind 1st sg* **laanzhíhksi**, **laanzhíhk=siim**. *conj 3rd sg* **laanzhíhksiit**. *ptcpl* **laanzhíhksiit**.

**laanzhihkŭwáleew** VAI carry a heavy load on one's back. *ind 1st sg* **laanzhihkŭwále**, **laanzhihkŭwál=eem**. *conj 3rd sg* **laanzhihkŭwáleet**. *imp* **laanzhihkŭwáleel**. *ptcpl* **laanzhihkŭwáleet**.

**laapaapéhlatoow** VTI2 hang s.t. over something. *ind 1st sg* **laapaapéhla=toon**. *ind 3rd sg* **wŭlaapaapéhla=toon**. *conj 1st sg* **laapaapehlatáw=aan**. *conj 3rd sg* **laapaapéhlataakw**. *imp* **laapaapéhlatool**. *ptcpl* **laapaa=péhlataakw**.

**laapaapéhleew** VAI hang over something *(s.t. animate)*. *conj 3rd sg* **laapaapéhlaat**. *ptcpl* **laapaapéhlaat**.

**laapaapéhleew** VII hang over something. *conj 3rd sg* **laapaapéhlaak**. *ptcpl* **laapaapéhlaak**.

**laapahkíiheew** VAI replant, put in new plants. *ind 1st sg* **laapahkíihe**, **laa=pahkíiheem**. *conj 3rd sg* **laapahkíi=heet**. *imp* **laapahkíiheel**. *ptcpl* **laa=pahkíiheet**.

**laapáhleew** VTA replace s.o., replace s.t. animate. *ind 1st sg* **laapáhlaaw**, **laa=páhla**. *ind 3rd sg* **wŭlaapahláawal**. *ind inv* **laapáhlukw**. *ind I-you* **kŭlaa=páhlul**. *conj 3rd sg* **laapáhlaat**. *imp* **láapahl**. *ptcpl* **laapáhlaat**.

**laapáhtaweew** VTAO replace s.t. for s.o. *ind 1st sg* **laapáhtawaan**. *ind 3rd sg* **wŭlaapáhtawaan**. *ind inv* **laapah=táakwun**. *ind I-you* **kŭlaapahtóolun**. *conj 3rd sg* **laapáhtawaat**. *imp* **laapáhtaw**. *ptcpl* **laapáhtawaat**.

**laapáhtoow** VTI2 replace s.t. *ind 1st sg* **laapáhtoon**. *ind 3rd sg* **wŭlaapáh=toon**. *conj 1st sg* **laapáhtawaan**. *conj 3rd sg* **laapáhtaakw**. *imp* **laapáhtool**. *ptcpl* **laapáhtaakw**.

**laapamúkwat** VII be coloured in a certain manner; be seen in a certain manner. **Éeshu-laapamúkwat.** 'It can be seen through.' *conj 3rd sg* **laapa=múkwahk**. *ptcpl* **eelaapamúkwahk**.

**laapamúkwsuw** VAI be coloured in a certain manner *(s.t. animate)*; be seen in a certain manner *(s.t. animate)*. *ind 1st sg* **ndulaapamúkwsi**, **ndulaapa=múkwsiim**. *conj 3rd sg* **laapamúk=wsiit**. *ptcpl* **eelaapamúkwsiit**.

**láapapuw** VAIO take s.o.'s place. *ind 1st sg* **láapapiin**. *ind 3rd sg* **wŭlaapa=píinal**. *conj 3rd sg* **láapapiit**. *imp* **láapapiil**. *ptcpl* **láapapiit**.

**laapéemeew** VTA find s.o. useful, find s.t. animate useful; be useful to s.o. **Ndulaapéemaaw.** 'He's useful to me.'; **Ndulaapéemukw.** 'I'm useful to him.' *ind 1st sg* **ndulaapéemaaw**, **ndulaapéema**. *ind 3rd sg* **wtulaa=peemáawal**. *ind inv* **ndulaapée=mukw**. *ind I-you* **ktulaapéemul**. *conj 3rd sg* **laapéemaat**. *ptcpl* **eelaa=péemaat**.

**laapéeneew** VTA lead s.o. in a certain direction with a string, lead s.o. in a certain manner with a string; lead s.o. in a certain direction by the reins, lead s.o. in a certain manner by the reins, put the reins on s.o. *(of horses)*. *ind 1st sg* **ndulaapéenaaw**, **ndulaa=péena**. *ind 3rd sg* **wtulaapeenáawal**. *ind inv* **ndulaapéenukw**. *ind I-you* **ktulaapéenul**. *conj 3rd sg* **laapée=naat**. *imp* **láapeen**. *ptcpl* **eelaa=péenaat**.

**laapéendam** VTI1A find s.t. useful; be useful to s.o. *ind 1st sg* **ndulaapéen=damun**. *ind 3rd sg* **wtulaapéenda=mun**. *conj 1st sg* **laapéendamaan**. *conj 3rd sg* **laapéendang**. *ptcpl* **eelaapéendang**.

**laapéenzuw** VAI make oneself useful, be useful. **Káta- xáa -laapéenzi.** 'You should make yourself useful.'; **Ira kwáy laapéenzuw éel-alúwi-xwukíiluk.** 'Ira's useful now that he's older.' *ind 1st sg* **ndulaapéenzi**, **ndulaapéenziim**. *conj 3rd sg* **laa=péenziit**. *imp* **laapéenziil**. *ptcpl* **eelaapéenziit**.

**laapéewuw** VAI have a certain characteristic *(of people)*; be a certain type of person. **Máh kwéek laapeewíiwu.** 'He's good for nothing.' *ind 1st sg* **ndulaapéewi**, **ndulaapéewiim**. *conj 3rd sg* **laapéewiit**. *ptcpl* **eelaa=péewiit**.

**laapeexíikan** NI plow. *pl* **laapeexíika=nal**. *poss* **laapeexíikan**. *loc* **laapee=xíikanung**. *dimin* **laapeexíikanush**.

**laapeexíikeew** VAI use a plow, plow things, be plowing. *ind 1st sg* **laa=**

**peexíike**, **laapeexíikeem**. *conj 3rd sg* **laapeexíikeet**. *imp* **laapeexíikeel**. *ptcpl* **laapeexíikeet**.

**laapéextoow** VTI2 plow s.t. *ind 1st sg* **laapéextoon**. *ind 3rd sg* **wŭlaapéex=toon**. *conj 1st sg* **laapeextáwaan**. *conj 3rd sg* **laapéextaakw**. *imp* **laapéextool**. *ptcpl* **laapéextaakw**.

**laapéhleew** VII hang in a certain direction, hang in a certain manner. *conj 3rd sg* **laapéhlaak**. *ptcpl* **eelaa=péhlaak**.

**láapham** VTI1A lace s.t. up, thread s.t. *ind 1st sg* **laaphámun**. *ind 3rd sg* **wŭlaaphámun**. *conj 1st sg* **laap=hámaan**. *conj 3rd sg* **láaphang**. *imp* **láaphah**. *ptcpl* **láaphang**.

**láapheew** VTA thread s.t. animate *(of needles)*. *ind 1st sg* **láaphaaw**, **láapha**. *ind 3rd sg* **wŭlaapháawal**. *ind inv* **láaphookw**. *ind I-you* **kŭláaphool**. *conj 3rd sg* **láaphaat**. *imp* **láaphaw**. *ptcpl* **láaphaat**.

**laaphíikeew** VAI sew things, be sewing; lace things, thread things. *ind 1st sg* **laaphíike**, **laaphíikeem**. *conj 3rd sg* **laaphíikeet**. *imp* **laaphíikeel**. *ptcpl* **laaphíikeet**.

**láapii** PC again. **Kwáy láapii máw-aláwiil.** 'Now go and hunt again.'; **Láapii oolíixtoon.** 'He fixed it again.'

**laapíilŭnuw** VAI get together again, reunite. *ind 1st sg* **laapíilŭni**, **laapíilŭ=niim**. *conj 3rd sg* **laapíilŭniit**. *imp* **laapíilŭniil**. *ptcpl* **laapíilŭniit**.

**laapiináxkeew** VAIO lead s.o. by the arm, take s.o. by the arm, be arm in arm with s.o. *ind 1st sg* **laapiináxkeen**. *ind 3rd sg* **wŭlaapiinaxkéenal**. *conj 3rd sg* **laapiináxkeet**. *ptcpl* **laapii=náxkeet**.

**laapiinaxkéeneew** VTA lead s.o. by the arm, take s.o. by the arm, be arm in arm with s.o. *ind 1st sg* **laapiinax=kéenaaw**, **laapiinaxkéena**. *ind 3rd sg* **wŭlaapiinaxkeenáawal**. *ind inv* **laapiinaxkéenukw**. *ind I-you* **kŭlaa=piinaxkéenul**. *conj 3rd sg* **laapii=naxkéenaat**. *imp* **laapiináxkeen**. *ptcpl* **laapiinaxkéenaat**.

**laapiinaxkeeniikéewak** VAI have one's arms linked. *usually plural*. *ind 1st pl* **laapiinaxkeeniikéhna**. *conj 3rd sg* **laapiinaxkeeniikéhtiit**. *imp* **laapii=naxkeeníikeekw**. *ptcpl* **laapiinax=keeniikéhtiit**.

**laapiinaxkéexiin** VAI have one's arms together, have one's arms intertwined. *ind 1st pl* **laapiinaxkeexiinóhna**. *conj 3rd sg* **laapiinaxkeexiinóhtiit**. *imp* **laapiinaxkéexiikw**. *ptcpl* **laapiinaxkeexiinóhtiit**.

**laapíixiin** VAI hang over something, be put over something. *ind 1st sg* **laa=píixiin**, **laapíixi**. *conj 3rd sg* **laapíi=xiing**. *imp* **laapíixiil**. *ptcpl* **laapíi=xiing**.

**laapíixsuw** VAI repeat, say something over. *ind 1st sg* **laapíixsi**, **laapíix=siim**. *conj 3rd sg* **laapíixsiit**. *imp* **laapíixsiil**. *ptcpl* **laapíixsiit**. *intensive reduplication* **lahlaapíixsuw**.

**laapíixtoow** VTI2 put s.t. over something, put s.t. on something, put s.t. around something. *ind 1st sg* **laa=píixtoon**. *ind 3rd sg* **wŭlaapíixtoon**. *conj 1st sg* **laapiixtáwaan**. *conj 3rd sg* **laapíixtaakw**. *imp* **laapíixtool**. *ptcpl* **laapíixtaakw**.

**laapíixŭmeew** VTA put s.o. over something, put s.o. on something, put s.o. around something. *ind 1st sg* **laapíi=xŭmaaw**, **laapíixŭma**. *ind 3rd sg* **wŭlaapiixŭmáawal**. *conj 3rd sg* **laapíixŭmaat**. *imp* **laapíixum**. *ptcpl* **laapíixŭmaat**.

**laapíixun** VII hang over something, be put over something. *conj 3rd sg* **laapíixung**. *ptcpl* **laapíixung**.

**laapsiitéhkaweew** VTA trip s.o. *ind 1st sg* **laapsiitéhkawaaw**, **laapsiitéh=kawa**. *ind 3rd sg* **wŭlaapsiitehka=**

**wáawal**. *ind inv* **laapsiitéhkaakw**. *ind I-you* **kŭlaapsiitéhkool**. *conj 3rd sg* **laapsiitéhkawaat**. *imp* **laapsii=téhkaw**. *ptcpl* **laapsiitéhkawaat**.

**laapsiitéhleew** VAI get one's foot snagged, have one's foot snagged. *ind 1st sg* **laapsiitéhla**, **laapsiitéhlaam**. *conj 3rd sg* **laapsiitéhlaat**. *ptcpl* **laapsii=téhlaat**.

**laapsheengwéeheew** VTA graze s.o.'s eye. *ind 1st sg* **laapsheengwéehaaw**, **laapsheengwéeha**. *ind 3rd sg* **wŭlaapsheengweeháawal**. *ind inv* **laapsheengwéehookw**. *ind I-you* **kŭlaapsheengwéehool**. *conj 3rd sg* **laapsheengwéehaat**. *imp* **laap=shéengweeh**. *ptcpl* **laapsheen=gwéehaat**.

**laapsheengwéeneew** VTA stick one's finger in s.o.'s eye. *ind 1st sg* **laap=sheengwéenaaw**, **laapsheengwéena**. *ind 3rd sg* **wŭlaapsheengweenáawal**. *ind inv* **laapsheengwéenukw**. *ind I-you* **kŭlaapsheengwéenul**. *conj 3rd sg* **laapsheengwéenaat**. *imp* **laap=shéengween**. *ptcpl* **laapsheen=gwéenaat**.

**laapsheengwéexiin** VAI be struck in the eye, brush against something which goes into the eye. *ind 1st sg* **laap=sheengwéexiin**, **laapsheengwéexi**. *conj 3rd sg* **laapsheengwéexiing**. *ptcpl* **laapsheengwéexiing**.

**laaptoonéepuy** NI horse's bridle. *pl* **laaptoonéepŭyal**.

**laapxóoneew** VAI wear a necklace. *ind 1st sg* **laapxóona**, **laapxóonaam**. *conj 3rd sg* **laapxóonaat**. *imp* **laap=xóonaal**. *ptcpl* **laapxóonaat**. *See* **laapxoonéexiin**.

**laapxoonéexiin** VAI wear a necklace. *ind 1st sg* **laapxoonéexiin**, **laapxoonée=xi**. *conj 3rd sg* **laapxoonéexiing**. *imp* **laapxoonéexiil**. *ptcpl* **laapxoonée=xiing**, **laapxoonéexiit**. *See* **laap=xóoneew**.

**laasŭléenum** VTI1A shine s.t. in a certain direction, shine s.t. in a certain manner *(of lights)*. *ind 1st sg* **ndulaasŭ=léenŭmun**. *ind 3rd sg* **wtulaasŭlée=nŭmun**. *conj 1st sg* **laasŭléenŭm=aan**. *conj 3rd sg* **laasŭléenung**. *imp* **laasŭléenih**. *ptcpl* **eelaasŭléenung**.

**laasŭléenŭmeew** VAI shine a light in a certain direction, shine a light in a certain manner. *ind 1st sg* **ndulaasŭ=léenŭma**, **ndulaasŭléenŭmaam**. *conj 3rd sg* **laasŭléenŭmaat**. *imp* **laasŭ=léenŭmaal**. *ptcpl* **eelaasŭléenŭmaat**.

**laasŭléenŭmeew** VAIO shine s.t. in a certain direction, shine s.t. in a certain manner *(of lights)*. **Yeelak ndulaa=sŭléenŭmaan waasŭleeníikan.** 'I shone the lantern over there.' *ind 1st sg* **ndulaasŭléenŭmaan**. *ind 3rd sg* **wtulaasŭléenŭmaan**. *conj 3rd sg* **laasuléenŭmaat**. *imp* **laasŭléenŭ=maal**. *ptcpl* **eelaasŭléenŭmaat**.

**laashíinam** VTI1A see s.t. briefly, see s.t. for a moment. *ind 1st sg* **laashíina=mun**. *ind 3rd sg* **wŭlaashíinamun**. *conj 1st sg* **laashíinamaan**. *conj 3rd sg* **laashíinang**. *ptcpl* **laashíinang**.

**laashíinaweew** VTA see s.o. briefly, see s.o. for a moment. *ind 1st sg* **laashíi=nawaaw**, **laashíinawa**. *ind 3rd sg* **wŭlaashiinawáawal**. *ind inv* **laashíi=naakw**. *ind I-you* **kŭlaashíinool**. *conj 3rd sg* **laashíinawaat**. *ptcpl* **laashíi=nawaat**.

**laashíhleew** VAI be a glimpse of someone seen while going by. **Éelkih-kshíhlaat shùkéhla laashíhleew.** 'He was going so fast that one only saw a glimpse of him.' *ind 1st sg* **laashíhla**, **laashíhlaam**. *conj 3rd sg* **laashíhlaat**. *ptcpl* **laashíhlaat**. *intensive reduplication* **lahlaashíhleew**.

**laashóokeew** VAI walk in the water. *ind 1st sg* **ndulaashóoke**, **ndulaashóo=keem**. *conj 3rd sg* **laashóokeet**. *imp* **laashóokeel**. *ptcpl* **eelaashóokeet**.

**láashu-lúnum** VTI1A touch s.t. briefly, touch s.t. for a moment. *ind 1st sg* **láashu-lúnŭmun**. *ind 3rd sg* **wŭláa=shu-lúnŭmun**. *conj 1st sg* **láashu-lúnŭmaan**. *conj 3rd sg* **láashu-lún=ung**. *ptcpl* **láashu-lúnung**.

**laashŭwíhleew** VAI swim in a certain direction, swim in a certain manner. *ind 1st sg* **ndulaashŭwíhla, ndulaashŭ=wíhlaam**. *conj 3rd sg* **laashŭwíhlaat**. *imp* **laashŭwíhlaal**. *ptcpl* **eelaashŭ=wíhlaat**.

**laawáandpe** PC forehead, top of head.

**laawaaxkaláwe** PC middle of the forehead.

**laawáhkweew** VII be noontime. *conj 3rd sg* **laawáhkweek**. *ptcpl* **laawáh=kweek**.

**laawahkwéewŭni** PC noontime. **Péexoot laawahkwéewŭni.** 'It's almost noon.'

**laawalóhkeew** VAI have an overwhelming amount of work to do. *ind 1st sg* **laawalóhke, laawalóhkeem**. *conj 3rd sg* **laawalóhkeet**. *ptcpl* **laawa=lóhkeet**.

**laawáskwe** PC in the middle of the high weeds. **Laawáskwe pŭmúsuw.** 'He's walking in the middle of the high weeds.'; **Laawáskwe nóonj-saak=xoonéexiin.** 'I was sticking out of the weeds up to my neck.'

**laawaskwíhkeew** VII be the middle of the grass. *conj 3rd sg* **laawaskwíh=keek**. *ptcpl* **laawaskwíhkeek**.

**láawate** PC long ago. **Láawate áayleek.** 'What happened years ago.'

**laawatóohaweew** VTA charge s.o. a certain amount. *ind 1st sg* **ndulaawa=tóohawaaw, ndulaawatóohawa**. *ind 3rd sg* **wtulaawatoohawáawal**. *ind inv* **ndulaawatóohaakw**. *ind I-you* **ktulaawatóohool**. *conj 3rd sg* **laa=watóohawaat**. *imp* **laawatóohaw**. *ptcpl* **eelaawatóohawaat**.

**laawatóoheew** VAIO charge a certain price for s.t. *ind 1st sg* **ndulaawa=tóoheen**. *ind 3rd sg* **wtulaawatóo=heen**. *conj 3rd sg* **laawatóoheet**. *imp* **laawatóoheel**. *ptcpl* **eelaawatóoheet**.

**láawatuw** VAI have a certain value, cost a certain amount *(s.t. animate)*. *ind 1st sg* **nduláawati, nduláawatiim**. *conj 3rd sg* **láawatiit**. *ptcpl* **eeláawatiit**.

**láawatuw** VII have a certain value, cost a certain amount. *conj 3rd sg* **láawa=tiik**. *ptcpl* **eeláawatiik**.

**laawcheenáakwsuw** VAI look hopeless, look overwhelming, appear to be hopeless. **Laawcheenáakwsuw máh kiikiisheechpíiwi.** 'He's hopeless, he's never getting dressed.' *ind 1st sg* **laawcheenáakwsi, laawcheenáak=wsiim**. *conj 3rd sg* **laawcheenáakw=siit**. *ptcpl* **laawcheenáakwsiit**.

**laawéelŭmeew** VTA give up on s.o. *ind 1st sg* **laawéelŭmaaw, laawéelŭma**. *ind 3rd sg* **wŭlaaweelŭmáawal**. *ind inv* **laawéelŭmukw**. *ind I-you* **kŭlaa=wéelŭmul**. *conj 3rd sg* **laawéelŭmaat**. *imp* **laawéelum**. *ptcpl* **laawéelŭmaat**.

**laaweelúndam** VOTI1A give up. *ind 1st sg* **laaweelúndam**. *conj 3rd sg* **laa=weelúndang**. *imp* **laaweelúndah**. *ptcpl* **laaweelúndang**.

**laaweelúndam** VTI1A give up over s.t. *ind 1st sg* **laaweelúndamun**. *ind 3rd sg* **wŭlaaweelúndamun**. *conj 1st sg* **laaweelúndamaan**. *conj 3rd sg* **laaweelúndang**. *imp* **laaweelúndah**. *ptcpl* **laaweelúndang**.

**laaweelúnzuw** VAI give up. *ind 1st sg* **laaweelúnzi, laaweelúnziim**. *conj 3rd sg* **laaweelúnziit**. *imp* **laawee=lúnziil**. *ptcpl* **laaweelúnziit**.

**laaweewapóoshiish** NA bobcat, wildcat. *pl* **laaweewapooshíishak**. *dimin* **laa=weewapooshíishush**. *obv* **laawee=wapooshíishal**.

**laaweewii-** PN wild. **Laawéewii-miichŭwáakan.** 'Wild food.'

**laaweewiikíipush** NA pheasant. *pl* **laa=weewiikíipshak**. *dimin* **laaweewii=**

kíipshush. *obv* **laaweewiikíipshal**.
**laawii-** PV middle. *ptcpl* **láawii-**.
**láawii-tpíhkat** VII be midnight. *conj 3rd sg* **láawii-tpíhkahk**. *ptcpl* **láawii-tpíhkahk**.
**laawiilawéeheew** VTA give up on s.o. *ind 1st sg* **laawiilawéehaaw**, **laawii=lawéeha**. *ind 3rd sg* **wŭlaawiilawee=háawal**. *ind inv* **laawiilawéehukw**. *ind I-you* **kŭlaawiilawéehul**. *conj 3rd sg* **laawiilawéehaat**. *imp* **laawíila=weeh**. *ptcpl* **laawiilawéehaat**.
**laawiináakwat** VII look overwhelming, look hopeless, appear to be hopeless. *conj 3rd sg* **laawiináakwahk**. *ptcpl* **laawiináakwahk**.
**laawiináakwsuw** VAI look overwhelming, look hopeless, appear to be hopeless. *ind 1st sg* **laawiináakwsi**, **laa=wiináakwsiim**. *conj 3rd sg* **laawii=náakwsiit**. *ptcpl* **laawiináakwsiit**.
**laawíinam** VTI 1B find that s.t. appears hopeless. *ind 1st sg* **laawíinamun**. *ind 3rd sg* **wŭlaawíinamun**. *conj 1st sg* **laawíinamaan**. *conj 3rd sg* **laawíinang**. *ptcpl* **laawíinang**.
**laawíinaweew** VTA find that s.o. appears hopeless; regret seeing s.o. *ind 1st sg* **laawíinawaaw**, **laawíinawa**. *ind 3rd sg* **wŭlaawiinawáawal**. *ind inv* **laa=wíinaakw**. *ind I-you* **kŭlaawíinool**. *conj 3rd sg* **laawíinawaat**. *imp* **laawíinaw**. *ptcpl* **laawíinawaat**.
**laawihtáakwat** VII sound far away. *conj 3rd sg* **laawihtáakwahk**. *ptcpl* **laawihtáakwahk**.
**laawihtáakwsuw** VAI sound far away. *ind 1st sg* **laawihtáakwsi**, **laawih=táakwsiim**. *conj 3rd sg* **laawihtáak=wsiit**. *ptcpl* **laawihtáakwsiit**.
**laawootéenay** PC middle of the town, middle of the village. **Laawootéenay áhte.** 'It's there in the middle of town.'
**laawsoohaáleew** VTA make s.o. live, revive s.o. *ind 1st sg* **ndulaawsoohaá=laaw**, **ndulaawsoohaála**. *ind 3rd sg* **wtulaawsoohaaláawal**. *ind inv* **ndulaawsoohaálukw**. *ind I-you* **ktulaawsoohaálul**. *conj 3rd sg* **laaw=soohaálaat**. *imp* **laawsóohaal**. *ptcpl* **eelaawsoohaálaat**.
**laawsóoheew** VAIO make s.o. live, revive s.o. *ind 1st sg* **ndulaawsóoheen**. *ind 3rd sg* **wtulaawsoohéenal**. *conj 3rd sg* **laawsóoheet**. *imp* **laawsóoheel**. *ptcpl* **eelaawsóoheet**.
**láawsuw** VAI live in a certain manner. *ind 1st sg* **nduláawsi**, **nduláawsiim**. *conj 3rd sg* **láawsiit**. *imp* **láawsiil**. *ptcpl* **eeláawsiit**.
**laawúndeew** VII be the middle of a room. *conj 3rd sg* **laawúndeek**. *ptcpl* **laawúndeek**.
**lacháaheew** VTA treat s.o. in a certain manner. *ind 1st sg* **ndulacháahaaw**, **ndulacháaha**. *ind 3rd sg* **wtulach=aaháawal**. *ind inv* **ndulacháahukw**. *ind I-you* **ktulacháahul**. *conj 3rd sg* **lacháahaat**. *imp* **láchaah**. *ptcpl* **eelacháahaat**.
**laháhkweew** VAI hit something in a certain manner, hit something in a certain direction. **Wáhli nduláhkwe.** 'I hit it a long way.' *ind 1st sg* **ndul=háhkwe**, **ndulháhkweem**. *conj 3rd sg* **laháhkweet**. *imp* **laháhkweel**. *ptcpl* **eelháhkweet**.
**láham** VOTI 1A paddle in a certain manner, paddle in a certain direction. *ind 1st sg* **ndúlham**. *conj 3rd sg* **láhang**. *imp* **láhah**, **láhih**. *ptcpl* **éelhang**.
**láham** VTI 1A contact s.t. in a certain manner. **Kóolu- ná -aláhŭmun.** 'You got it right ('you hit it right').' *ind 1st sg* **ndulhámun**. *ind 3rd sg* **wtulhám=un**. *conj 1st sg* **láhŭmaan**. *conj 3rd sg* **láhang**. *imp* **láhah**. *ptcpl* **éelhang**.
**lahiingwéexiin** VAI look in a certain direction, look in a certain manner. **Eeheeshandéekanung lahiingwée=xiin.** 'He's looking out the window.'

*ind 1st sg* **ndulhiingwéexiin**, **ndul=hiingwéexi**. *conj 3rd sg* **lahiingwée=xiing**. *imp* **lahiingwéexiil**. *ptcpl* **eelhiingwéexiing**, **eelhiingwéexiit**.

**láhkameew** VII be a certain kind of weather, be a certain kind of day. **Thá láhkameew?** 'What's the weather like?' *conj 3rd sg* **láhkameek**. *ptcpl* **eelákameek**.

**lahkéewuw** VAI be a certain nationality, be a certain breed, be a certain make, have a certain characteristic. **Palíi eelahkeewíhtiit.** 'Other races.' *ind 1st sg* **ndulahkéewi**, **ndulahkée=wiim**. *conj 3rd sg* **lahkéewiit**. *ptcpl* **eelahkéewiit**.

**láhtakat** VII be string in a certain manner, be string in a certain direction. *conj 3rd sg* **láhtakahk**. *ptcpl* **eeláh=takahk**.

**lahtakíhleew** VAI run in a certain manner, run in a certain direction. **Wii=kwáhmshung ndulahtakíhla.** 'I'm going to the bathroom.' *ind 1st sg* **ndulahtakíhla**, **ndulahtakíhlaam**. *conj 3rd sg* **lahtakíhlaat**. *imp* **lahta=kíhlaal**. *ptcpl* **eelahtakíhlaat**.

**lahtkwéehaaw** VTA get credit, be given credit; 'get trusted'. *usually with indefinite subject. ind 1st sg* **ndulaht=kwéehke**. *indef subject* **lahtkwée=haaw**. *conj 3rd sg* **lahtkwéehund**. *ptcpl* **eelahtkwéehund**.

**lahŭmáweew** VTAO throw s.t. to s.o.; knock s.t. to s.o. *(using a tool or instrument). ind 1st sg* **ndulhámawaan**. *ind 3rd sg* **wtulhámawaan**. *ind inv* **ndulhamáakwun**. *ind I-you* **ktul=hamóolun**. *conj 1st sg* **lahŭmáwaan**. *conj 3rd sg* **lahŭmáwaat**. *imp* **láhŭmaw**. *ptcpl* **eelhámawaat**.

**làkehkíimeew** VTA teach s.o. a certain way. *ind 1st sg* **ndulakehkíimaaw**, **ndulakehkíima**. *ind 3rd sg* **wtula=kehkiimáawal**. *ind inv* **ndulakehkíi=mukw**. *ind I-you* **ktulakehkíimul**. *conj 3rd sg* **làkehkíimaat**. *imp* **làkéhkiim**. *ptcpl* **eelakehkíimaat**.

**làkíihuw** VAI be lucky. *ind 1st sg* **làkíi=hi**, **làkíihiim**. *conj 3rd sg* **làkíihiit**. *ptcpl* **làkíihiit**. *From English* lucky.

**lakóosuw** VAI climb in a certain manner, climb in a certain direction, climb up. *ind 1st sg* **ndulakóosi**, **ndulakóosiim**. *conj 3rd sg* **lakóosiit**. *imp* **lakóosiil**. *ptcpl* **eelakóosiit**.

**lákuw** VAI dress in a certain manner. *ind 1st sg* **ndúlakwi**, **ndúlakwiim**. *conj 3rd sg* **lákwiit**. *imp* **lákwiil**. *ptcpl* **éelakwiit**.

**lalóhkeew** VAI work in a certain manner, work in a certain place, be engaged in a certain activity. **Ngwíila- kwéek -làlóhke.** 'I've go nothing to do.'; **Kwéek ktulalóhke?** 'What are you doing?' *ind 1st sg* **ndulalóhke**, **ndul=alóhkeem**. *conj 3rd sg* **lalóhkeet**. *imp* **lalóhkeel**. *ptcpl* **eelalóhkeet**.

**lamalúsuw** VAI feel a certain way, have a certain physical sensation. **Làma=lúsuw wŭlóngwanuw.** 'He thinks he's so good ('has wings')'; **Thá há ktul=amálsi?** 'How do you feel?' *ind 1st sg* **ndulamálsi**, **ndulamálsiim**. *conj 3rd sg* **lamalúsiit**. *ptcpl* **eelamálsiit**.

**làmándam** VTI1A feel s.t. as a sensation in one's body. *ind 1st sg* **ndulamán=damun**. *ind 3rd sg* **wtulamándamun**. *conj 1st sg* **làmándamaan**. *conj 3rd sg* **làmándang**. *ptcpl* **eelamándang**.

**làmóoleew** VTA stick s.t. animate into something in a certain manner, stick s.t. animate into something in a certain direction, stick s.t. animate into something. *ind 1st sg* **ndulamóolaaw**, **ndulamóola**. *ind 3rd sg* **wtulamoo=láawal**. *ind inv* **ndulamóolukw**. *ind I-you* **ktulamóolul**. *conj 3rd sg* **làmóolaat**. *imp* **lámool**. *ptcpl* **eela=móolaat**.

**làmóotoow** VTI2 stick s.t. into something in a certain manner, stick s.t. into something in a certain direction, stick s.t. into something. **Mbáksung ndul=amóotoon xwúsal.** 'I stuck the wood in the box.' *ind 1st sg* **ndulamóotoon**. *ind 3rd sg* **wtulamóotoon**. *conj 1st sg* **làmóotawaan**. *conj 3rd sg* **làmóo=taakw**. *imp* **làmóotool**. *ptcpl* **eela=móotaakw**.

**làmwíhleew** VAI stick into something a certain manner, stick into something in a certain direction. **Píinj làmwíh=leew náxkung.** 'A pin went into my arm.' *conj 3rd sg* **lamwíhlaat**. *ptcpl* **eelamwíhlaat**.

**lamwíhleew** VII stick into something in a certain manner, stick into something a certain direction. **Palalíikaaxkw làmwíhle náxkung.** 'A sliver went in my hand.' *conj 3rd sg* **lamwíhlaak**. *ptcpl* **eelamwíhlaak**. *intensive reduplication* **ihŭlamwíhleew**.

**lápuw** VAI sit in a certain manner, sit in a certain direction. **Wtéeng lápuw.** 'She's sitting in the back.' *ind 1st sg* **ndúlapi**, **ndúlapiim**. *conj 3rd sg* **lápiit**. *imp* **lápiil**. *ptcpl* **éelapiit**.

**làpŭláhksun** NI rubber overshoe. *pl* **làpŭlahksúnal**. *poss* **làpŭlahksún=um**. *loc* **làpŭlahksúnung**. *dimin* **làpŭlahkshúnush**. *From English* rubber.

**láshŭlush** NA Russell. *obv* **làshŭlúshal**. *From English* Russell.

**latawáapuw** VAI see in a certain manner, see in a certain direction. *ind 1st sg* **ndulatawáapi**, **ndulatawáapiim**. *conj 3rd sg* **latawáapiit**. *imp* **lata=wáapiil**. *ptcpl* **eelatawáapiit**.

**latéexun** VII be a road or path going in a certain direction, be a certain kind of road or path. **Kóhpii làtéexun.** 'There's a road going to the bush.' *conj 3rd sg* **latéexung**. *ptcpl* **eela=téexung**.

**laxéexiin** VAI have one's ears lying in a certain manner, have one's ears lying in a certain direction. **Áhkiing làxée=xiin.** 'His ears are hanging down to the ground.' *ind 1st sg* **ndulxéexiin**, **ndulxéexi**. *conj 3rd sg* **laxéexiing**. *imp* **laxéexiil**. *ptcpl* **eelxéexiing**.

**laxkáameew** VTA scold s.o. *ind 1st sg* **laxkáamaaw**, **laxkáama**. *ind 3rd sg* **wŭlaxkaamáawal**. *conj 3rd sg* **lax=káamaat**. *imp* **láxkaam**. *ptcpl* **leex=káamaat**.

**laxkáangeew** VAI scold people. *ind 1st sg* **laxkáange**, **laxkáangeem**. *conj 3rd sg* **laxkáangeet**. *imp* **laxkáan=geel**. *ptcpl* **leexkáangeet**.

**laxkalákayeew** VAI be extremely lazy. *considered impolite*. *ind 1st sg* **laxk=alákaya**, **laxkalákayaam**. *conj 3rd sg* **laxkalákayaat**. *ptcpl* **leexkalá=kayaat**.

**láxkameew** VTA find that s.t. animate has a sour taste. *ind 1st sg* **láxkamaaw**, **láxkama**. *ind 3rd sg* **wŭlaxkamáa=wal**. *conj 3rd sg* **láxkamaat**. *ptcpl* **léexkamaat**.

**laxkamálsuw** VAI feel lazy. *ind 1st sg* **laxkamálsi**, **laxkamálsiim**. *conj 3rd sg* **laxkamálsiit**. *ptcpl* **leexkamálsiit**.

**laxkándam** VTI 1A find that s.t. has a sour taste. *ind 1st sg* **laxkándamun**. *ind 3rd sg* **wŭlaxkándamun**. *conj 1st sg* **laxkándamaan**. *conj 3rd sg* **lax=kándang**. *ptcpl* **leexkándang**.

**laxkeelawúsuw** VAI be tired of playing. *ind 1st sg* **laxkeelawúsi**, **laxkeela=wúsiim**. *conj 3rd sg* **laxkeelawúsiit**. *ptcpl* **leexkeelawúsiit**.

**laxkiipóokwat** VII have a bitter taste, have a sour taste. *conj 3rd sg* **laxkii=póokwahk**. *ptcpl* **leexkiipóokwahk**.

**laxkiipóokwsuw** VAI have a bitter taste, have a sour taste *(s.t. animate)*. *ind 1st sg* **laxkiipóokwsi**, **laxkiipóok=wsiim**. *conj 3rd sg* **laxkiipóokwsiit**. *ptcpl* **leexkiipóokwsiit**.

**laxkiipóokwun** VII have a bitter taste, have a sour taste. *conj 3rd sg* **laxkii=**

**póokwung**. *ptcpl* **leexkiipóokwung**.

**láxksuw** VAI be angry, be frustrated, be discouraged, be annoyed, be put-out; be bitter, be sour *(of foods)*. *ind 1st sg* **láxksi**, **láxksiim**. *conj 3rd sg* **láxksiit**. *ptcpl* **léexksiit**.

**laxktúyeew** VAI be extremely lazy. *ind 1st sg* **laxktúya**, **laxktúyaam**. *conj 3rd sg* **laxktúyaat**. *ptcpl* **leexk=túyaat**.

**láxkun** VII be bitter, taste bitter, taste sour, taste strong. *conj 3rd sg* **láxkung**. *ptcpl* **léexkung**.

**láxun** VII be wind in a certain direction, be a certain kind of wind. *conj 3rd sg* **láxung**. *ptcpl* **éelxung**.

**léew** VII be, happen. **Léew nú kwáy.** 'It's true.' *conj 3rd sg* **léek**. *ptcpl* **éeleek**.

**léekham** VTI 1A write on s.t., write s.t. down. *ind 1st sg* **nduleekhámun**. *ind 3rd sg* **wtuleekhámun**. *conj 1st sg* **leekhámaan**. *conj 3rd sg* **léekhang**. *imp* **léekhah**. *ptcpl* **eeléekhang**.

**leekhámaweew** VTA write to s.o. *ind 1st sg* **nduleekhámawaaw**, **nduleek=hámawa**. *ind 3rd sg* **wtuleekhama=wáawal**. *ind inv* **nduleekhámaakw**. *ind I-you* **ktuleekhámool**. *conj 3rd sg* **leekhámawaat**. *imp* **leekhámaw**. *ptcpl* **eeleekhámawaat**.

**léekheew** VTA write on s. t. animate. *ind 1st sg* **nduléekhaaw**, **nduléekha**. *ind 3rd sg* **wtuleekháawal**. *ind inv* **ndul=éekhookw**. *ind I-you* **ktuléekhool**. *conj 3rd sg* **léekhaat**. *imp* **léekhaw**. *ptcpl* **eeléekhaat**.

**leekhíikeew** VAI write, write a letter. *ind 1st sg* **nduleekhíike**, **nduleekhíi=keem**. *conj 3rd sg* **leekhíikeet**. *imp* **leekhíikeel**. *ptcpl* **eeleekhíikeet**.

**léekuw** NI sand. **Leekóohung lú ka=wíhleew.** 'He fell into the sand.'; **Wshaphóosh'shung ktúnda-katáa=tam leekóohush.** 'You need a little bit of sand in the pail.' *loc* **leekóo=hung**. *dimin* **leekóohush**.

**leekŭwatéexun** VII be a sandy road, be a sandy path. *conj 3rd sg* **leekŭwatée=xung**. *ptcpl* **leekŭwatéexung**.

**léelaa** PC in the middle. **Léelaa lùma=tápi.** 'I'm sitting in the middle.'; **Léelaa pŭmúsuw.** 'He's walking in the middle.' *See* **leeláawii**.

**leeláawii** PC in the middle. **Éenda-leeláawii -payáane.** 'When I had gone half way.' *See* **léelaa**.

**leeláawŭlunj** NI middle finger. *pl* **lee=laawŭlúnjal**. *dimin* **leelaawŭlún=jush**.

**leelawúsuw** VAI play a certain game, play at a certain game. **Músu- kwéek -leelawúsiin.** 'He's playing at different things.'; **Kwéek ktuleelawúsi?** 'What are you playing?' *ind 1st sg* **nduleelawúsi**, **nduleelawúsiim**. *conj 3rd sg* **leelawúsiit**. *imp* **leelawúsiil**. *ptcpl* **eeleelawúsiit**.

**léelham** VOTI 1A make tracks in a certain direction, make tracks in a certain manner. **Yéelak léelham.** 'He's making tracks the other way.' *ind 1st sg* **nduléelham**. *conj 3rd sg* **léelhang**. *imp* **léelhah**. *ptcpl* **eeléelhang**.

**léelŭmeew** VTA let s.o. *(do something)*. *followed by verbal complement in the subordinative*. **Nduléelŭmaaw shookŭlúshal míichiin.** 'I let him eat some candy.' *ind 1st sg* **nduléelŭ=maaw**, **nduléelŭma**. *ind 3rd sg* **wtuleelŭmáawal**. *ind inv* **nduléelŭ=mukw**. *ind I-you* **ktuléelŭmul**. *conj 3rd sg* **léelŭmaat**. *imp* **léelum**. *ptcpl* **eeléelŭmaat**.

**leelúndam** VOTI 1A think, think in a certain manner. **Ngwúteel ktuleelun=damóhna.** 'We (inclusive) think alike.' *ind 1st sg* **nduleelúndam**. *conj 3rd sg* **leelúndang**. *imp* **leelúndah**. *ptcpl* **eeleelúndang**.

**leelúndam** VTI 1A think about s.t., think about s.t. in a certain manner. **Aa=**

yáakwu máh kwéek nduleelunda=móowun nehnayóongus mbóxka=piin. 'After a while I didn't think anything of riding a horse.' *ind 1st sg* **nduleelúndamun**. *ind 3rd sg* **wtul=eelúndamun**. *conj 1st sg* **leelúnda=maan**. *conj 3rd sg* **leelúndang**. *imp* **leelúndah**. *ptcpl* **eeleelúndang**.

**leenhíikeew** VAIO pay a certain amount for s.t. **Níish ndálaas nduleenhíi=keen.** 'I paid two dollars for it.' *ind 1st sg* **nduleenhíikeen**. *ind 3rd sg* **wtuleenhíikeen**. *conj 3rd sg* **leenhíi=keet**. *imp* **leenhíikeel**. *ptcpl* **eeleen=híikeet**. *See* **lalóhkeew**.

**léeshŭlush** NA Lazarus. *obv* **leeshŭ=lúshal**. *From English* Lazarus.

**leetíisuw** VAI be arrogant, have an attitude, think oneself better than others, to put on airs *(of women)*. *ind 1st sg* **leetíisi**, **leetíisiim**. *conj 3rd sg* **leetíi=siit**. *ptcpl* **leetíisiit**. *See* **oxkweewŭ=lúnzuw**.

**léew** VTA say to s.o., tell s.o. *ind 1st sg* **ndúlaaw**, **ndúla**. *ind 3rd sg* **wtuláa=wal**. *ind inv* **ndúkw**. *ind I-you* **ktúlul**. *conj 3rd sg* **láat**. *imp* **úl**. *ptcpl* **éelaat**.

**léexeew** VAI breathe. *ind 1st sg* **léexe**, **léexeem**. *conj 3rd sg* **léexeet**. *imp* **léexeel**. *ptcpl* **léexeet**.

**leexéesuw** VAI be light snow, be powdery snow. *conj 3rd sg* **leexéesiit**. *ptcpl* **leexéesiit**.

**leexéewan** NI breath. *poss* **leexéewan**.

**leexéewsuw** VAI breathe heavily. *ind 1st sg* **leexéewsi**, **leexéewsiim**. *conj 3rd sg* **leexéewsiit**. *imp* **leexéewsiil**. *ptcpl* **leexéewsiit**.

**léhlapiit** VAI as one likes, as one wishes. *usually only in conjunct order*. **Léh=lapiit lúnum.** 'He can do what he wants.'; **Shiikóowuw léhlapiit-uch kwáy éew.** 'She's a widow, she can go where she likes.' *conj 3rd sg* **léhlapiit**.

**lehleewhíikan** NI fan. *pl* **lehleewhíika=nal**. *poss* **lehleewhíikan**. *loc* **leh=leewhíikanung**. *dimin* **lehleewhíi=kanush**.

**lehleewhúnzuw** VAI fan oneself. *ind 1st sg* **lehleewhúnzi**, **lehleewhúnziim**. *conj 3rd sg* **lehleewhúnziit**. *imp* **leh=leewhúnziil**. *ptcpl* **lehleewhúnziit**.

**lehlookíhlaash** NA raspberry. *pl* **lehloo=kihláashak**. *loc* **lehlookihláashung**. *dimin* **lehlookihláashush**. *obv* **leh=lookihláashal**.

**lehlóosiing** NI nettle. *pl* **lehloosíingiil**. *See* **lehlóosŭweeng**.

**lehlóosŭweek** NI poison ivy. *pl* **lehloo=sŭwéekal**.

**lehlóosŭweeng** NI nettle. *pl* **lehloosŭ=wéengiil**. *See* **lehlóosiing**.

**lehlxawalóoyeek** NI fork. *pl* **lehlxawa=looyéekal**. *poss* **lehlxawalooyéekum**. *loc* **lehlxawalooyéekung**. *dimin* **lehlxawalooyéekush**.

**létul** NA letter. *pl* **létŭlak**. *poss* **létŭlum**. *loc* **létulung**. *dimin* **léchŭlush**. *obv* **létŭlal**. *From English* letter.

**líi** PC here, there, thus, so. **Wéemu asiiskŭwatéexun táa líi.** 'The roads are muddy everywhere.' *See* **lí**, **lú**.

**líiheew** VTA make s.o. *(do something)*. *followed by verbal complement in the subordinative*. **Ndulíihaan piilalóh=keen.** 'I made him clean house.'; **Ndulíihkwun nŭmánxeen.** 'He made me cut firewood.' *ind 1st sg* **ndulíi=haan**. *ind 3rd sg* **wtulíihaan**. *ind inv* **ndulíihkwun**. *ind I-you* **ktulíihŭlun**. *conj 3rd sg* **líihaat**. *imp* **líih**. *ptcpl* **eelíihaat**.

**liikáapawuw** VAI stand in a certain manner, stand in a certain direction. **Palíi liikáapawuw.** 'He's standing out of the way.'; **Músu-liikáapawiin.** 'He's fidgeting as he stands.' *ind 1st sg* **nduliikáapawi**, **nduliikáapawiim**. *conj 3rd sg* **liikáapawiit**. *imp* **liikáapawiil**. *ptcpl* **eeliikáapawiit**.

**líikuw** VAI grow in a certain place, grow in a certain manner *(s.t. animate)*. *ind*

*1st sg* **ndulíiki**, **ndulíikiim**. *conj 3rd sg* **líikiit**. *imp* **líikiil**. *ptcpl* **eelíikiit**.

**liikwáaleew** VTA move s.t. animate in a certain direction, move s.t. animate in a certain manner *(using something held in the hand)*. **Wtéeng wtulii=kwaaláawal.** 'He moved him to the back.' *ind 1st sg* **nduliikwáalaaw**, **nduliikwáala**. *ind 3rd sg* **wtulii=kwaaláawal**. *ind inv* **nduliikwáa=lukw**. *ind I-you* **ktuliikwáalul**. *conj 3rd sg* **liikwáalaat**. *imp* **líikwaal**. *ptcpl* **eeliikwáalaat**.

**líikwam** VTI 1A move s.t. in a certain direction, move s.t. in a certain manner *(using something held in the hand)*. **Shayéemung ndulíikwamun.** 'I moved it to the front.'; **Yéelak líi=kwah!** 'Move it over there!' *ind 1st sg* **ndulíikwamun**. *ind 3rd sg* **wtulíi=kwamun**. *conj 1st sg* **líikwamaan**. *conj 3rd sg* **líikwang**. *imp* **líikwah**. *ptcpl* **eelíikwang**.

**liikwsíhleew** VAI slide in a certain manner, slide in a certain direction. *ind 1st sg* **nduliikwsíhla**, **nduliikwsíh=laam**. *conj 3rd sg* **liikwsíhlaat**. *imp* **liikwsíhlaal**. *ptcpl* **eeliikwsíhlaat**.

**líikwsuw** VAI crawl in a certain manner, crawl in a certain direction. *ind 1st sg* **ndulíikwsi**, **ndulíikwsiim**. *conj 3rd sg* **líikwsiit**. *imp* **líikwsiil**. *ptcpl* **eelíikwsiit**.

**líilŭnuw** NA leader, person in position of authority. *pl* **liilŭnúwak**. *obv* **liilŭ=núwal**.

**liináakwat** VII have a certain appearance. *conj 3rd sg* **liináakwahk**. *ptcpl* **eeliináakwahk**.

**liináakwsuw** VAI have a certain appearance. *ind 1st sg* **nduliináakwsi**, **nduliináakwsiim**. *conj 3rd sg* **lii=náakwsiit**. *ptcpl* **eeliináakwsiit**.

**líinam** VOTI 1A be treated in a certain manner. **Nóolu-líinam.** 'I'm well treated.'; **Ndáhwu-líinam.** 'I have a hard time, I have bad luck.' *ind 1st sg* **ndulíinam**. *conj 3rd sg* **líinang**. *ptcpl* **eelíinang**.

**liináxkeew** VAI have one's hands in a certain position. **Nzheewandíika=nung nduliináxke.** 'I had my hands in my pockets.' *ind 1st sg* **nduliináx=ke**, **nduliináxkeem**. *conj 3rd sg* **liináxkeet**. *imp* **liináxkeel**. *ptcpl* **eeliináxkeet**. *moderative reduplication* **aaylíinaxkeew**.

**liindawáakan** NA lantern. *pl* **liinda=wáakanak**. *poss* **liindawáakan**. *loc* **liindawáakanung**. *dimin* **liindawáa=kanush**. *obv* **liindawáakanal**. *See* **niindawáakan**.

**líineew** VAI have a certain disease, have a disease in a certain place. **Kwéek éet há ndulíine.** 'I wonder what disease I have.'; **Ndáyung ndúnda-líine.** 'I have a sore stomach.' *ind 1st sg* **ndulíine**, **ndulíineem**. *conj 3rd sg* **líineet**. *ptcpl* **eelíineet**.

**liingwéexiin** VAI look in a certain direction, look in a certain manner. **Máh nŭweewiiháawu tá eeliingwéexiit.** 'I don't know where he's looking.' *ind 1st sg* **nduliingwéexiin**, **nduliin=gwéexi**. *conj 3rd sg* **liingwéexiing**. *imp* **liingwéexiil**. *ptcpl* **eeliingwée=xiing**, **eeliingwéexiit**.

**liingwéexŭmeew** VTA make s.o. look in a certain direction, make s.o. face in a certain direction. **Yéelak nduliin=gwéexŭmaaw naaníitus.** 'I put the doll facing over there.' *ind 1st sg* **nduliingwéexŭmaaw**, **nduliingwée=xŭma**. *ind 3rd sg* **wtuliingweexŭ=máawal**. *ind inv* **nduliingwéexŭ=mukw**. *ind I-you* **ktuliingwéexŭmul**. *conj 3rd sg* **liingwéexŭmaat**. *imp* **liingwéexum**. *ptcpl* **eeliingwée=xŭmaat**.

**liinjkwéeneew** VTA roll s.o. in a certain direction, roll s.o. in a certain manner. *ind 1st sg* **nduliinjkwéenaaw**,

**nduliinjkwéena**. *ind 3rd sg* **wtul=iinjkweenáawal**. *ind inv* **nduliinj=kwéenukw**. *ind I-you* **ktuliinjkwée=nul**. *conj 3rd sg* **liinjkwéenaat**. *imp* **líinjkween**. *ptcpl* **eeliinjkwéenaat**.

**liinjkwéenum** VTI 1A roll s.t. in a certain manner, roll s.t. in a certain direction. *ind 1st sg* **nduliinjkwéenŭmun**. *ind 3rd sg* **wtuliinjkwéenŭmun**. *conj 1st sg* **liinjkwéenŭmaan**. *conj 3rd sg* **liinjkwéenung**. *imp* **liinjkwéenih**. *ptcpl* **eeliinjkwéenung**.

**liinjkweeyáaheew** VAIO roll s.t. in a certain manner, roll s.t. in a certain direction. *ind 1st sg* **nduliinjkweeyáa=heen**. *ind 3rd sg* **wtuliinjkwee=yáaheen**. *conj 3rd sg* **liinjkweeyáa=heet**. *imp* **liinjkweeyáaheel**. *ptcpl* **eeliinjkweeyáaheet**.

**liinjkwéhleew** VAI roll in a certain manner, roll in a certain direction *(s.t. animate)*. *ind 1st sg* **nduliinjkwéhla**, **nduliinjkwéhlaam**. *conj 3rd sg* **liinjkwéhlaat**. *imp* **liinjkwéhlaal**. *ptcpl* **eeliinjkwéhlaat**.

**liinjkwéhleew** VII roll in a certain manner, roll in a certain direction. *conj 3rd sg* **liinjkwéhlaak**. *ptcpl* **eeliinj=kwéhlaak**.

**liitéeheew** VAI think. **Ngwúteel ktiitee=háhna.** 'We (inclusive) agree, we think the same.'; **Ngwúteel liiteehée=wak.** 'They agree, they think the same.' *ind 1st sg* **ndiitéeha**, **ndiitée=haam**. *conj 3rd sg* **liitéehaat**. *imp* **liitéehaal**. *ptcpl* **eeliitéehaat**.

**liitŭyéepuw** VAI sit on one's backside in a certain manner, sit on one's backside in a certain direction. **Shayée=mung liitŭyéepuw.** 'He slid to the front (of the chair).'; **Msú-liitŭyée=puw.** 'He's sitting this way and that way.' *ind 1st sg* **nduliitŭyéepi**, **ndul=iitŭyéepiim**. *conj 3rd sg* **liitŭyéepiit**. *imp* **liitŭyéepiil**. *ptcpl* **eeliitŭyéepiit**.

**liitŭyéhleew** VAI go in a certain direction, go in a certain manner. **Wáhlu ktuliitŭyéhla.** 'You went far.'; **Msú-liitŭyéhleew.** 'He went here and there.' *ind 1st sg* **nduliitŭyéhla**, **ndul=iitŭyéhlaam**. *conj 3rd sg* **liitŭyéh=laat**. *imp* **liitŭyéhlaal**. *ptcpl* **eeliitŭ=yéhlaat**. *considered impolite.*

**liiwamálsuw** VAI feel better. *ind 1st sg* **liiwamálsi**, **liiwamálsiim**. *conj 3rd sg* **liiwamálsiit**. *ptcpl* **liiwamálsiit**.

**liiwíixun** VII be short *(of a measurement)*. **Pasiikáaxkwal liiwíixŭnool.** 'The boards are not long enough.' *conj 3rd sg* **liiwíixung**. *ptcpl* **liiwíixung**.

**liiwíhlateew** VAIO be short of s.t., lack s.t. **Liiwíhlateew pambíilal.** 'He ran short of paper.'; **Liiwíhlata chángiish.** 'I'm short a little bit.' *ind 1st sg* **liiwíhlataan**. *ind 3rd sg* **wuliiwíhla=taan**. *conj 3rd sg* **liiwíhlataat**. *ptcpl* **liiwíhlataat**.

**liiwíhleew** VAI be short *(of a measurement)*. **Liiwíhleew pámbiil.** 'The paper wasn't long enough.' *conj 3rd sg* **liiwíhlaat**. *ptcpl* **liiwíhlaat**.

**liiwíhleew** VAIO run short of s.t., lack s.t. **Liiwíhleew pasiikáaxkwal.** 'He ran out of boards.' *ind 1st sg* **liiwíhla**. *conj 3rd sg* **liiwíhlaat**.

**liiwíhleew** VII be short *(of a measurement)*. **Liiwíhleew wshapakwíiwan.** 'The cloth wasn't long enough.' *conj 3rd sg* **liiwíhlaak**. *ptcpl* **liiwíhlaak**.

**líixiin** VAI lie in a certain manner, lie in a certain direction. *ind 1st sg* **ndulíi=xiin**, **ndulíixi**. *conj 3rd sg* **líixiing**. *imp* **líixiil**. *ptcpl* **eelíixiing**.

**líixsuw** VAI speak a certain language, speak a certain dialect. **Palíi ayulíix=suw.** 'He speaks another language or dialect.' *ind 1st sg* **ndulíixsi**, **ndul=íixsiim**. *conj 3rd sg* **líixsiit**. *imp* **líixsiil**. *ptcpl* **eelíixsiit**. *intensive reduplication* **ayulíixsuw**.

**líixun** VII lie in a certain manner, lie in a certain direction. **Eehundaxpóonung**

**ehŭlíixung.** 'Table cloth.' *conj 3rd sg* **líixung**. *ptcpl* **eelíixung**.

**lí** PC here, there, thus, so. **Áhkiing lí súkwiiw** 'He spat on the ground.'; **Wiiwŭnóoxwe lí áaneeng.** 'He went around the road.' *See* **líi**, **lú**.

**li-** PV in a certain manner, in a certain direction. **Mbéehaaw wtúli-piinjíi=keen.** 'I waited until he came in.'; **Nál wtúlu- wiikwáhmung -piin=jíikwsiin.** 'Then he crawled inside the house.' *ptcpl* **éeli-**. *See* **eeli-**, **eel-**, **lu-**.

**líhkam** VTI1A do something to s.t. in a certain manner, do something to s.t. in a certain direction *(using the foot or body).* **Pálii ndulíhkamun.** 'I shoved it to the side.' *ind 1st sg* **ndulíhkamun**. *ind 3rd sg* **wtulíhka=mun**. *conj 1st sg* **líhkamaan**. *conj 3rd sg* **líhkang**. *imp* **líhkah**. *ptcpl* **eelíhkang**.

**líhkaweew** VTA do something to s.o. in a certain manner, do something to s.o. in a certain direction *(using the foot or body).* *ind 1st sg* **ndulíhkawaaw**, **ndulíhkawa**. *ind 3rd sg* **wtulihka=wáawal**. *ind inv* **ndulíhkaakw**. *ind I-you* **ktulíhkool**. *conj 3rd sg* **líhka=waat**. *imp* **líhkaw**. *ptcpl* **eelíh=kawaat**.

**líhleew** VAI go in a certain manner, go in a certain direction, fly in a certain manner, fly in a certain direction, proceed in a certain manner, proceed in a certain direction. **Mbíing ktulíhla shùkéhla ksaakaandpée=xiin.** 'You fell in the water but your head is sticking out.' *ind 1st sg* **ndulíhla**, **ndulíhlaam**. *conj 3rd sg* **líhlaat**. *imp* **líhlaal**. *ptcpl* **eelíhlaat**.

**lihlpúneew** VAI be smart, be industrious, like to work. *ind 1st sg* **lihlpúna**, **lihlpúnaam**. *conj 3rd sg* **lihlpúnaat**. *ptcpl* **lihlpúnaat**.

**lihtáakwsuw** VAI have a certain sound, make a certain sound *(s.t. animate).* **Káal lihtáakwsuw alúmu-lookíh=leew.** 'The car sounds like it's going to break down.' *ind 1st sg* **ndulih=táakwsi**, **ndulihtáakwsiim**. *conj 3rd sg* **lihtáakwsiit**. *ptcpl* **eelihtáakwsiit**.

**lihtéexiin** VAI fall in a certain manner, fall in a certain direction *(s.t. animate).* **Palíi-lihtéexiin.** 'He fell out of place.'; **Nŭmúsu-lihtéexiin.** 'I fell this way and that way.' *ind 1st sg* **ndulihtéexiin**, **ndulihtéexi**. *conj 3rd sg* **lihtéexiing**. *imp* **lihtéexiil**. *ptcpl* **eelihtéexiing**, **eelihtéexiit**.

**lihtéexun** VII fall in a certain manner, fall in a certain direction. **Shayée=mung lihtéexun.** 'It fell to the front.' *conj 3rd sg* **lihtéexung**. *ptcpl* **eelih=téexung**.

**líshpet** NA Elizabeth. *obv* **lìshpétal**. *From English* Elizabeth.

**lóoham** VTI1B point at s.t. *ind 1st sg* **ndulóohŭmun**. *ind 3rd sg* **wtulóo=hŭmun**. *conj 1st sg* **lóohŭmaan**. *conj 3rd sg* **lóohang**. *imp* **lóohah**. *ptcpl* **eelóohang**.

**lóoheew** VTA point at s.o. *ind 1st sg* **ndulóohaaw**, **ndulóoha**. *ind 3rd sg* **wtuloohaáwal**. *ind inv* **ndulóohookw**. *ind I-you* **ktulóohul**. *conj 3rd sg* **lóohaat**. *imp* **lóoh**. *ptcpl* **eelóohaat**.

**loohŭmáasuw** VAIO show s.o., show s.t. *ind 1st sg* **nduloohŭmáasiin**. *ind 3rd sg* **wtuloohŭmáasiin**. *conj 3rd sg* **loohŭmáasiit**. *imp* **loohŭmáasiil**. *ptcpl* **eeloohŭmáasiit**.

**loohŭmáweew** VTAO show s.t. to s.o. *ind 1st sg* **nduloohŭmáwaan**. *ind 3rd sg* **wtuloohŭmáwaan**. *ind inv* **nduloo=hŭmáakwun**. *ind I-you* **ktuloohŭ=móolun**. *conj 1st sg* **loohumawaan**. *conj 3rd sg* **loohŭmáwaat**. *imp* **lóohŭmaw**. *ptcpl* **eeloohŭmáwaat**.

**lookaníikeew** VAI have a broken tooth. *ind 1st sg* **lookaníika**, **lookaníikaam**. *conj 3rd sg* **lookaníikaat**. *ptcpl*

**lookaníikaat**.

**lookchéexiin** VAI fall and burst open, lie broken. *ind 1st sg* **lookchéexiin**, **lookchéexi**. *conj 3rd sg* **lookchée=xiing**. *ptcpl* **lookchéexiing**.

**lookchéexun** VII fall and burst open, lie broken. *conj 3rd sg* **lookchéexung**. *ptcpl* **lookchéexung**.

**lóokham** VTI1A break s.t. *(using a tool or instrument)*. *ind 1st sg* **lookhám=un**. *ind 3rd sg* **wŭlookhámun**. *conj 1st sg* **lookhámaan**. *conj 3rd sg* **lóokhang**. *imp* **lóokhah**. *ptcpl* **lóokhang**.

**lóokheew** VTA break s.t. animate *(using a tool or instrument)*. *ind 1st sg* **lóokhaaw**, **lóokha**. *ind 3rd sg* **wŭlookháawal**. *ind inv* **lóokhookw**. *ind I-you* **kŭlóokhool**. *conj 3rd sg* **lóokhaat**. *imp* **lóokhaw**. *ptcpl* **lóokhaat**.

**lookhéewaleew** VTA pull s.t. animate apart, dismantle s.t. animate. *ind 1st sg* **lookhéewalaaw**, **lookhéewala**. *ind 3rd sg* **wŭlookheewaláawal**. *ind inv* **lookhéewalukw**. *ind I-you* **kŭlook=héewalul**. *conj 3rd sg* **lookhéewa=laat**. *imp* **lookhéewal**. *ptcpl* **look=héewalaat**.

**lookhéewatoow** VTI2 pull s.t. apart, dismantle s.t. *ind 1st sg* **lookhéewatoon**. *ind 3rd sg* **wŭlookhéewatoon**. *conj 1st sg* **lookheewatáwaan**. *conj 3rd sg* **lookhéewataakw**. *imp* **lookhéewa=tool**. *ptcpl* **lookhéewataakw**.

**lookíixtoow** VTI2 drop and break s.t. *ind 1st sg* **lookíixtoon**. *ind 3rd sg* **wŭlookíixtoon**. *conj 1st sg* **lookiix=táwaan**. *conj 3rd sg* **lookíixtaakw**. *imp* **lookíixtool**. *ptcpl* **lookíixtaakw**.

**lookíixŭmeew** VTA drop and break s.t. animate. *ind 1st sg* **lookíixŭmaaw**, **lookíixŭma**. *ind 3rd sg* **wŭlookiixŭ=máawal**. *ind inv* **lookíixŭmukw**. *ind I-you* **kŭlookíixŭmul**. *conj 3rd sg* **lookíixŭmaat**. *imp* **lookíixum**. *ptcpl* **lookíixŭmaat**.

**lookíixun** VII be broken, break. *conj 3rd sg* **lookíixung**. *ptcpl* **lookíixung**.

**lookíhkam** VTI1A break s.t. *(using the foot or body)*. *ind 1st sg* **lookíhka=mun**. *ind 3rd sg* **wŭlookíhkamun**. *conj 1st sg* **lookíhkamaan**. *conj 3rd sg* **lookíhkang**. *imp* **lookíhkah**. *ptcpl* **lookíhkang**.

**lookíhkaweew** VTA break s.o. *(using the foot or body)*. *ind 1st sg* **lookíhka=waaw**, **lookíhkawa**. *ind 3rd sg* **wŭlookihkawáawal**. *ind inv* **lookíh=kaakw**. *ind I-you* **kŭlookíhkool**. *conj 3rd sg* **lookíhkawaat**. *imp* **lookíhkaw**. *ptcpl* **lookíhkawaat**.

**lookíhlaleew** VTA break s.t. animate *(quickly)*. *ind 1st sg* **lookíhlalaaw**, **lookíhlala**. *ind 3rd sg* **wŭlookihla=láawal**. *conj 3rd sg* **lookíhlalaat**. *imp* **lookíhlal**. *ptcpl* **lookíhlalaat**.

**lookíhlatoow** VTI2 break s.t. *(quickly)*. *ind 1st sg* **lookíhlatoon**. *ind 3rd sg* **wŭlookíhlatoon**. *conj 1st sg* **lookih=latáwaan**. *conj 3rd sg* **lookíhlataakw**. *imp* **lookíhlatool**. *ptcpl* **lookíhla=taakw**.

**lookíhleew** VAI break down, break *(s.t. animate)*. *ind 1st sg* **lookíhla**, **loo=kíhlaam**. *conj 3rd sg* **lookíhlaat**. *ptcpl* **lookíhlaat**.

**lookíhleew** VII break down, break. *conj 3rd sg* **lookíhlaak**. *ptcpl* **lookíhlaak**.

**lookihtéeham** VTI1A hit and break s.t. *ind 1st sg* **lookihtéehŭmun**. *ind 3rd sg* **wŭlookihtéehŭmun**. *conj 1st sg* **lookihtéehŭmaan**. *conj 3rd sg* **lookihtéehang**. *imp* **lookihtéehih**. *ptcpl* **lookihtéehang**.

**lookihtéeheew** VTA hit and break s.t. animate. *ind 1st sg* **lookihtéehaaw**, **lookihtéeha**. *ind 3rd sg* **wŭlookih=teeháawal**. *ind inv* **lookihtéehookw**. *ind I-you* **kŭlookihtéehool**. *conj 3rd sg* **lookihtéehaat**. *imp* **lookíhteeh**. *ptcpl* **lookihtéehaat**.

**lookihtéextoow** VTI2 drop and break s.t., wreck s.t. *ind 1st sg* **lookih=téextoon**. *ind 3rd sg* **wŭlookihtéex=toon**. *conj 1st sg* **lookihteextáwaan**. *conj 3rd sg* **lookihtéextaakw**. *imp* **lookihtéextool**. *ptcpl* **lookih=téextaakw**.

**lookihtéexŭmeew** VTA drop and break s.t. animate, wreck s.t. animate. *ind 1st sg* **lookihtéexŭmaaw**, **lookihtée=xŭma**. *ind 3rd sg* **wŭlookihteexŭ=máawal**. *ind inv* **lookihtéexŭmukw**. *ind I-you* **kŭlookihtéexŭmul**. *conj 3rd sg* **lookihtéexŭmaat**. *imp* **loo=kihtéexum**. *ptcpl* **lookihtéexŭmaat**.

**lóoksheew** VTA cut s.t. animate. *ind 1st sg* **lóokshaaw**, **lóoksha**. *ind 3rd sg* **wŭlookshaawal**. *ind inv* **lóokshookw**. *ind I-you* **kŭlóokshool**. *conj 3rd sg* **lóokshaat**. *imp* **lóokush**. *ptcpl* **lóokshaat**.

**lookshíikeew** VAI cut things. *ind 1st sg* **lookshíike**, **lookshíikeem**. *conj 3rd sg* **lookshíikeet**. *imp* **lookshíikeel**. *ptcpl* **lookshíikeet**.

**lóokshum** VTI1B cut s.t. *ind 1st sg* **look=shúmun**. *ind 3rd sg* **wŭlookshúmun**. *conj 1st sg* **lookshúmaan**. *conj 3rd sg* **lóokshung**. *imp* **lóokshih**. *ptcpl* **lóokshung**.

**lóokŭneew** VTA break s.t. animate. *ind 1st sg* **lóokŭnaaw**, **lóokŭna**. *ind 3rd sg* **wŭlookŭnáawal**. *ind inv* **lóokŭ=nukw**. *ind I-you* **kŭlóokŭnul**. *conj 3rd sg* **lóokŭnaat**. *imp* **lóokun**. *ptcpl* **lóokŭnaat**.

**lookŭníikeew** VAI break things. *ind 1st sg* **lookŭníike**, **lookŭníikeem**. *conj 3rd sg* **lookŭníikeet**. *imp* **lookŭníi=keel**. *ptcpl* **lookŭníikeet**.

**lóokŭnum** VTI1B break s.t. *ind 1st sg* **lookŭnúmun**. *ind 3rd sg* **wŭlookŭ=númun**. *conj 1st sg* **lookŭnúmaan**. *conj 3rd sg* **lóokŭnung**. *imp* **lóokŭnih**. *ptcpl* **lóokŭnung**.

**lóonzŭweew** VAI sing a hymn. *ind 1st sg* **lóonzŭwe**, **lóonzŭweem**. *conj 3rd sg* **lóonzŭweet**. *imp* **lóonzŭweel**. *ptcpl* **lóonzŭweet**. *moderative reduplication* **laalóonzŭweew**.

**loonzŭweewáakan** NI hymn. *pl* **loon=zŭweewáakanal**. *poss* **loonzŭwee=wáakan**.

**loosáasuw** VAI be burnt *(s.t. animate)*. *conj 3rd sg* **loosáasiit**. *ptcpl* **loo=sáasiit**.

**loosáasuw** VII be burnt. *conj 3rd sg* **loosáasiik**. *ptcpl* **loosáasiik**.

**lóoseew** VTA burn s.o. *ind 1st sg* **lóosaaw**, **lóosa**. *ind 3rd sg* **wŭloosáawal**. *ind inv* **lóosookw**. *ind I-you* **kŭlóosool**. *conj 3rd sg* **lóosaat**. *imp* **lóos**. *ptcpl* **lóosaat**.

**loosóomeew** VTA regret that s.o. leaves. *ind 1st sg* **loosóomaaw**, **loosóoma**. *ind 3rd sg* **wŭloosoomáawal**. *ind inv* **loosóomukw**. *ind I-you* **kŭloosóo=mul**. *conj 3rd sg* **loosóomaat**. *ptcpl* **loosóomaat**.

**lóosum** VTI1B burn s.t. *ind 1st sg* **lóosŭ=mun**. *ind 3rd sg* **wŭlóosŭmun**. *conj 1st sg* **lóosŭmaan**. *conj 3rd sg* **lóosung**. *imp* **lóosih**. *ptcpl* **lóosung**.

**lóosuw** VAI burn *(s.t. animate)*. *ind 1st sg* **lóosi**, **lóosiim**. *conj 3rd sg* **lóosiit**. *imp* **lóosiil**. *ptcpl* **lóosiit**.

**lóoshiin** NA Rosie. *dimin* **looshíinush**. *obv* **looshíinal**. *From English* Rosie.

**lóoteew** VII burn. *conj 3rd sg* **lóoteek**. *ptcpl* **lóoteek**.

**lootéewuw** VAI visit a certain place. *ind 1st sg* **ndulootéewi**, **ndulootéewiim**. *conj 3rd sg* **lootéewiit**. *imp* **lootée=wiil**. *ptcpl* **eelootéewiit**.

**lóowan** VII be winter. **Náh nóom lóowanu.** 'I went there last winter.' *conj 3rd sg* **lóowang**. *ptcpl* **lóowang**.

**loowanámuw** VAI live until winter, survive until winter. *ind 1st sg* **loowa=námwi**, **loowanámwiim**. *conj 3rd sg* **loowanámwiit**. *ptcpl* **loowanámwiit**.

**loowanáxun** VII be a north wind. *conj*

*3rd sg* **loowanáxung**. *ptcpl* **loowa=náxung**.

**loowaneendakwíiwan** NI winter dress. *pl* **loowaneendakwíiwanal**. *poss* **loowaneendakwíiwan**. *loc* **loowa=neendakwíiwanung**. *dimin* **loowa=neenjakwíiwanush**.

**loowanéewung** PC north.

**loowanúwii** PC during the winter.

**loowatawáapuw** VAI look past, look beyond. *ind 1st sg* **loowatawáapi**, **loo=watawáapiim**. *conj 3rd sg* **loowata=wáapiit**. *imp* **loowatawáapiil**. *ptcpl* **loowatawáapiit**.

**loowatawáapuw** VAIO look past s.t., look beyond s.t. *ind 1st sg* **loowatawáa=piin**. *ind 3rd sg* **wŭloowatawáapiin**. *conj 3rd sg* **loowatawáapiit**. *imp* **loo=watawáapiil**. *ptcpl* **loowatawáapiit**.

**loowatóohaweew** VTA charge s.o. a certain amount. *ind 1st sg* **nduloowa=tóohawaaw**, **nduloowatóohawa**. *ind 3rd sg* **wtuloowatoohawáawal**. *ind inv* **nduloowatóohaakw**. *ind I-you* **ktuloowatóohool**. *conj 3rd sg* **loowatóohawaat**. *imp* **loowatóohaw**. *ptcpl* **eeloowatóohawaat**.

**lóowham** VTI1A pass by s.t. *(one's destination)*. *ind 1st sg* **loowhámun**. *ind 3rd sg* **wŭloowhámun**. *conj 1st sg* **loowhámaan**. *conj 3rd sg* **lóowhang**. *imp* **lóowhah**. *ptcpl* **lóowhang**.

**loowhóomeew** VAIO pass by s.o. on horseback, pass by s.t. on horseback. *ind 1st sg* **loowhóomaan**. *ind 3rd sg* **wŭloowhóomaan**. *conj 3rd sg* **loowhóomaat**. *imp* **loowhóomaal**. *ptcpl* **loowhóomaat**.

**lóowiiw** VAI-S pass by. **Náh mbúmu-lóowi.** 'I passed by there.' *ind 1st sg* **lóowi**, **lóowiim**. *conj 3rd sg* **lóowiit**. *imp* **lóowiil**. *ptcpl* **lóowiit**.

**lóowiiw** VAIO pass by s.t. *ind 1st sg* **lóo=wiin**. *ind 3rd sg* **wŭlóowiin**. *conj 3rd sg* **lóowiit**. *imp* **lóowiil**. *ptcpl* **lóowiit**.

**loowíhleew** VAI go by, drive by, fly by, cycle by. *ind 1st sg* **loowíhla**, **loo=wíhlaam**. *conj 3rd sg* **loowíhlaat**. *imp* **loowíhlaal**. *ptcpl* **loowíhlaat**.

**loowíhleew** VAIO go by s.t., drive by s.t., fly by s.t., cycle by s.t. *ind 1st sg* **loowíhlaan**. *ind 3rd sg* **wŭloowíh=laan**. *conj 3rd sg* **loowíhlaat**. *imp* **loowíhlaal**. *ptcpl* **loowíhlaat**.

**lóowŭlaan** VII be rain going by. *conj 3rd sg* **lóowŭlaang**. *ptcpl* **lóowŭlaang**.

**lóoxwaleew** VTA bring s.o., take s.o. along. *ind 1st sg* **ndulóoxwalaaw**, **ndulóoxwala**. *ind 3rd sg* **wtuloo=xwaláawal**. *ind inv* **ndulóoxwalukw**. *ind I-you* **ktulóoxwalul**. *conj 3rd sg* **lóoxwalaat**. *imp* **lóoxwal**. *ptcpl* **eelóoxwalaat**.

**lóoxwatoow** VTI2 bring s.t., take s.t. along. **Kwéekw-uch há ndulóoxwa=to?** 'What shall I bring?' *ind 1st sg* **ndulóoxwatoon**. *ind 3rd sg* **wtulóo=xwatoon**. *conj 1st sg* **looxwatáwaan**. *conj 3rd sg* **lóoxwataakw**. *imp* **lóoxwatool**. *ptcpl* **eelóoxwataakw**.

**lóoxweew** VAI walk in a certain manner, walk in a certain direction. *ind 1st sg* **ndulóoxwe**, **ndulóoxweem**. *conj 3rd sg* **lóoxweet**. *imp* **lóoxweel**. *ptcpl* **eelóoxweet**.

**lohkhámun** NI flour. *poss* **lohkhámu=num**. *loc* **lohkhámŭnung**. *dimin* **lohkhámŭnush**.

**lóhkweew** VAI look in a certain direction, look in a certain manner. *ind 1st sg* **ndulóhkwe**, **ndulóhkweem**. *conj 3rd sg* **lóhkweet**. *imp* **lóhkweel**. *ptcpl* **eelóhkweet**.

**lóhkweew** VAIO look at s.t. in a certain manner, look at s.t. in a certain direction. *ind 1st sg* **ndulóhkween**. *ind 3rd sg* **wtulóhkween**. *conj 3rd sg* **lóhkweet**. *imp* **lóhkweel**. *ptcpl* **eelóhkweet**.

**lohkwéexiin** VAI face in a certain direction, face in a certain manner. *ind 1st sg* **ndulohkwéexiin**, **ndulohkwéexi**.

*conj 3rd sg* **lohkwéexiing**. *imp* **lohkwéexiil**. *ptcpl* **eelohkwéexiing**.

**lohkwéexiin** VAI have one's head hanging in a certain manner, have one's head hanging in a certain direction. *ind 1st sg* **ndulohkwéexiin**, **nduloh=kwéexi**. *conj 3rd sg* **lohkwéexiing**. *imp* **lohkwéexiil**. *ptcpl* **eelohkwée=xiing**.

**lohkwéextoow** VTI2 turn s.t. to face in a certain direction, turn s.t. to face in a certain manner. **Shayéemung ndul=ohkwéextoon.** 'I faced it towards the front.' *ind 1st sg* **ndulohkwéextoon**. *ind 3rd sg* **wtulohkwéextoon**. *conj 1st sg* **lohkweextáwaan**. *conj 3rd sg* **lohkwéextaakw**. *imp* **lohkwéextool**. *ptcpl* **eelohkwéextaakw**.

**lohkwéexŭmeew** VTA turn s.o. to face in a certain direction, turn s.o. to face in a certain manner. *ind 1st sg* **nduloh=kwéexŭmaaw**, **ndulohkwéexŭma**. *ind 3rd sg* **wtulohkweexŭmáawal**. *ind inv* **ndulohkwéexŭmukw**. *ind I-you* **ktulohkwéexŭmul**. *conj 3rd sg* **lohkwéexŭmaat**. *imp* **lohkwéexum**. *ptcpl* **eelohkwéexŭmaat**.

**lohkwéexun** VII face in a certain direction, face in a certain manner. *conj 3rd sg* **lohkwéexung**. *ptcpl* **eeloh=kwéexung**.

**lóngwaam** VAI have a dream. **Ndulón=gwaam wáhkwung ndulakóosi.** 'I dreamt that I climbed up.' *ind 1st sg* **ndulóngwaam**. *conj 3rd sg* **lón=gwaang**. *ptcpl* **eelóngwaang**.

**lóngwaam** VTI3 dream about s.t. *ind 1st sg* **ndulongwáamun**. *ind 3rd sg* **wtulongwáamun**. *conj 1st sg* **long=wáamaan**. *conj 3rd sg* **lóngwaang**. *ptcpl* **eelóngwaang**.

**lóngwan** NID my wing; my armpit. *pl* **lóngwanal**. *poss* **lóngwan**. *loc* **lóngwanung**. *dimin* **lóngwanush**.

**lpákw** VAI cry. *ind 1st sg* **lúpakw**. *emphatic pl* **lpakhátŭwak**. *conj 3rd sg* **lpákuk**. *imp* **lpákih**. *ptcpl* **léepakuk**. *moderative reduplication* **láalpakw**.

**lpwéew** VAI be clever, be smart. *ind 1st sg* **lúpwa**, **lúpwaam**. *conj 3rd sg* **lpwáat**. *ptcpl* **léepwaat**.

**lú** PC here, there, thus, so. *informal.* **Yó lú peechiikwsúwak.** 'They crawled to here.'; **Xwanzhíikanung lú ngatahkéewak.** 'They moved to the United States.' *See* **líi**, **lí**.

**lu-** PV in a certain manner, in a certain direction. *informal.* **Nál há mbápaa-kwíilamun wchápihk, wéemu táa ndúlu-kwíilamun.** 'I looked around for the medicine, I looked for it everywhere.'; **Nál kwáchŭmung ndáan táa ndúlu-aseesahkáaheen.** 'Then I went outside and I threw it as far as I could.' *ptcpl* **éelu-**. *intensive reduplication* **ayulu-**.

**lúchaseew** VTA dye s.t. animate a certain colour. *ind 1st sg* **ndulchásaaw**, **ndul=chása**. *ind 3rd sg* **wtulchasáawal**. *ind inv* **ndulchásookw**. *ind I-you* **ktulchásool**. *conj 3rd sg* **lúchasaat**. *imp* **lúchas**. *ptcpl* **eelchásaat**.

**lúchasum** VTI1B dye s.t., dye s.t. a certain colour. **Niiláxkal ndulchásŭmun.** 'I dyed my hair.' *ind 1st sg* **ndulchásŭ=mun**. *ind 3rd sg* **wtulchásŭmun**. *conj 1st sg* **luchasúmaan**. *conj 3rd sg* **lúchasung**. *imp* **lúchasih**. *ptcpl* **eelchásung**.

**luchéenum** VTI1B roll s.t. in a certain direction, roll s.t. in a certain manner. *ind 1st sg* **ndulchéenŭmun**. *ind 3rd sg* **wtulchéenŭmun**. *conj 1st sg* **luch=éenŭmaan**. *conj 3rd sg* **luchéenung**. *imp* **luchéenih**. *ptcpl* **eelchéenung**.

**luchéesuw** VAI be a certain shape *(s.t. animate)*. *ind 1st sg* **ndulchéesi**, **ndulchéesiim**. *conj 3rd sg* **luchéesiit**. *ptcpl* **eelchéesiit**.

**luchéewuw** VAI lie in a certain manner. **Músu-luchéewiin.** 'He twists and turns.' *ind 1st sg* **ndulchéewi**, **ndul=**

chéewiim. *conj 3rd sg* **luchéewiit.** *ptcpl* **eelchéewiit.**

**luchéeyeew** VII be a certain shape. **Tá luchéeyeew?** 'What shape is it?' *conj 3rd sg* **luchéeyeek.** *ptcpl* **eelchée=yeek.**

**luchéhleew** VAI drive in a certain manner, drive in a certain direction. *ind 1st sg* **ndulchéhla, ndulchéhlaam.** *conj 3rd sg* **luchéhlaat.** *imp* **luchéh=laal.** *ptcpl* **eelchéhlaat.**

**lúkeew** VAI dance in a certain manner, dance in a certain direction. *ind 1st sg* **ndúlka, ndúlkaam.** *conj 3rd sg* **lúkaat.** *imp* **lúkaal.** *ptcpl* **éelkaat.**

**lúkiil** VAI be a certain size. **Nóondaa lúkiil.** 'He is smaller than someone else.' *ind 1st sg* **ndúlkiil.** *conj 3rd sg* **lukíiluk.** *ptcpl* **eelkíiluk.**

**lúkih** PC extent. **Héesh táa lúkih náh ndulootéewi.** 'I go there to visit once in a while.'; **Táa lúkih.** 'Some time ago.'

**lukíhkwi** PC extent, volume, amount. **Táa lukíhkwi.** 'Later on.'; **Tá lukíhkwi póondakat eehundáx=pwiing?** 'How much does the table weigh?'

**lukíhkwun** VII be a certain size. **Nóon=daa lukíhkwun áhpapoon.** 'The chair is smaller (than something else).' *conj 3rd sg* **lukíhkwung.** *ptcpl* **eelkíhkwung.**

**lulóhkeew** VAIO pay a certain amount for s.t. **Níish ndálaas ndulŭlóhkeen.** 'I paid two dollars for it.'; **Kéexu wtulŭlóhkeen?** 'How much did he pay for it?' *ind 1st sg* **ndulŭlóhkeen.** *ind 3rd sg* **wtulŭlóhkeen.** *conj 3rd sg* **lulóhkeet.** *imp* **lulóhkeel.** *ptcpl* **eelŭlóhkeet.** *See* **leenhíikeew.**

**lŭmatáhleew** VTA set s.o. down. *ind 1st sg* **lumatáhlaaw, lumatáhla.** *ind 3rd sg* **wŭlumatahláawal.** *ind inv* **luma=táhlukw.** *ind I-you* **kŭlumatáhlul.** *conj 3rd sg* **lŭmatáhlaat.** *imp* **lŭmátahl.** *ptcpl* **leematáhlaat.**

**lŭmatáhteew** VII sit there. **Wáxkiich lŭmatáhteew.** 'It sits on top.' *conj 3rd sg* **lŭmatáhteek.** *ptcpl* **leema=táhteek.**

**lŭmatáhtoow** VTI2 set s.t. down. *ind 1st sg* **lumatáhtoon.** *ind 3rd sg* **wŭlum=atáhtoon.** *conj 1st sg* **lŭmatáhta=waan.** *conj 3rd sg* **lŭmatáhtaakw.** *imp* **lŭmatáhtool.** *ptcpl* **leema=táhtaakw.**

**lŭmatapihtéexiin** VAI fall while sitting, sit down hard. *ind 1st sg* **lùmatapih=téexiin, lùmatapihtéexi.** *conj 3rd sg* **lŭmatapihtéexiing.** *imp* **lŭmatapih=téexiil.** *ptcpl* **leematapihtéexiing.**

**lŭmátapuw** VAI sit down. *ind 1st sg* **lùmatápi, lùmatápiim.** *conj 3rd sg* **lŭmátapiit.** *imp* **lŭmátapiil.** *ptcpl* **leematápiit.**

**lumbáhkwsuw** VAI have a slender figure, have a slight build, be slim. *ind 1st sg* **lumbáhkwsi, lumbáhkwsiim.** *conj 3rd sg* **lumbáhkwsiit.** *ptcpl* **leembáhkwsiit.**

**lumbíhleew** VAI trot *(especially of horses). ind 1st sg* **lumbíhla, lum=bíhlaam.** *conj 3rd sg* **lumbíhlaat.** *imp* **lumbíhlaal.** *ptcpl* **leembíhlaat.**

**lumtiisíineew** VAI have rheumatism. *ind 1st sg* **lumtiisíine, lumtiisíineem.** *conj 3rd sg* **lumtiisíineet.** *ptcpl* **lumtiisíineet.** *From English* rheumatism.

**lunáapeew** NA Indian, Delaware Indian. *pl* **lunaapéewak.** *obv* **lunaapéewal.**

**lunaapéewuw** VAI be an Indian, be a Delaware Indian. *ind 1st sg* **ndulŭ=naapéewi, ndulŭnaapéewiim.** *conj 3rd sg* **lunaapéewiit.** *ptcpl* **eelŭnaa=péewiit.**

**lunaapéexkweew** NA Indian woman, Delaware woman. *pl* **lunaapeex=kwéewak.** *obv* **lunaapeexkwéewal.**

**lunáhkuy** NI barren land on which nothing grows. *loc* **lunáhkiing.**

**lúnapwaan** NI Indian bread. *pl* **luna=pwáanal**. *poss* **ndulŭnapwáanum**. *loc* **lunapwáanung**. *dimin* **luna=pwáanush**. *bread made with flour, water, baking powder, salt; cooked in oven.*

**lúneew** VTA hand s.o. in a certain direction, hand s.o. in a certain manner. **Wáhkwung ndúlŭnaaw.** 'I lifted him upstairs.' *ind 1st sg* **ndúlŭnaaw**, **ndúlŭna**. *ind 3rd sg* **wtulŭnáawal**. *ind inv* **ndúlŭnukw**. *ind I-you* **ktúlŭ=nul**. *conj 3rd sg* **lúnaat**. *imp* **lún**. *ptcpl* **éelŭnaat**.

**lungíhleew** VAI melt *(s.t. animate)*. *conj 3rd sg* **lungíhlaat**. *ptcpl* **leengíhlaat**.

**lungíhleew** VII melt. *conj 3rd sg* **lun=gíhlaak**. *ptcpl* **leengíhlaak**.

**lungsáasuw** VAI be melted *(s.t. animate, by heat)*. *conj 3rd sg* **lungsáasiit**. *ptcpl* **leengsáasiit**.

**lungsáasuw** VII be melted *(by heat)*. *conj 3rd sg* **lungsáasiik**. *ptcpl* **leengsáasiik**.

**lúngseew** VTA melt s.t. animate. *ind 1st sg* **lúngsaaw**, **lúngsa**. *ind 3rd sg* **wŭ=lungsáawal**. *ind inv* **lúngsookw**. *ind I-you* **kŭlúngsool**. *conj 3rd sg* **lúng=saat**. *imp* **lúngus**. *ptcpl* **léengsaat**.

**lúngsum** VTI 1A melt s.t. *ind 1st sg* **lung=súmun**. *ind 3rd sg* **wŭlungsúmun**. *conj 1st sg* **lungsúmaan**. *conj 3rd sg* **lúngsung**. *imp* **lúngsih**. *ptcpl* **léeng=sung**.

**lúngsuw** VAI melt *(s.t. animate)*. *conj 3rd sg* **lúngsiit**. *ptcpl* **léengsiit**.

**lúngteew** VII melt. *conj 3rd sg* **lúngteek**. *ptcpl* **léengteek**.

**lunii-** PN plain, ordinary. **Lúnii-namées.** 'Any kind of fish.'

**lúnum** VTI 1B do s.t.; hand s.t. in a certain direction, hand s.t. in a certain manner. **Yó lúnih!** 'Hand it here!'; **Kwéek há nú kóonju-lúnŭmun?** 'Why did you do that?' *ind 1st sg* **ndulŭnúmun**. *ind 3rd sg* **wtulŭnúmun**. *conj 1st sg* **lúnŭmaan**. *conj 3rd sg* **lúnung**. *imp* **lúnih**. *ptcpl* **éelŭnung**.

**lunŭmáweew** VTAO hand s.t. to s.o. *ind 1st sg* **ndulŭnúmawaan**. *ind 3rd sg* **wtulŭnúmawaan**. *ind inv* **ndulŭ=numáakwun**. *ind I-you* **ktulŭnum=óolun**. *conj 1st sg* **lunumawaan**. *conj 3rd sg* **lunŭmáwaat**. *imp* **lúnŭmaw**. *ptcpl* **eelŭnúmawaat**.

**lúnuw** NA man. *pl* **lúnŭwak**. *dimin* **lunóosh**. *obv* **lúnŭwal**.

**lunŭweelúnzuw** VAI be a proud man, be arrogant, have an attitude, think that one knows more than anyone else. *ind 1st sg* **ndulŭnuweelúnzi**, **ndulŭ=nuweelúnziim**. *conj 3rd sg* **lunŭ=weelúnziit**. *ptcpl* **eelŭnuweelúnziit**.

**lunŭwéexum** NA male animal. *pl* **lunŭ=weexúmwak**. *dimin* **lunuweexúm=wush**. *obv* **lunŭweexúmwal**.

**lunŭwéhleew** NA rooster, male fowl. *pl* **lunŭwehléewak**. *dimin* **lunŭwéh=leesh**. *obv* **lunŭwehléewal**.

**lunŭwiináakwat** VII look not very nice. *conj 3rd sg* **lunŭwiináakwahk**. *ptcpl* **eelŭnuwiináakwahk**.

**lunŭwiináakwsuw** VAI look not very nice. **Lunŭwiináakwsuw ngáalum.** 'My car doesn't look very nice.' *ind 1st sg* **ndulŭnuwiináakwsi**, **ndulŭ=nuwiináakwsiim**. *conj 3rd sg* **lunŭ=wiináakwsiit**. *ptcpl* **eelŭnuwiináak=wsiit**.

**lunŭwiipóokwat** VII have a not very good taste. *conj 3rd sg* **lunŭwiipóokwahk**. *ptcpl* **eelŭnuwiipóokwahk**.

**lunŭwiipóokwsuw** VAI have a not very good taste *(s.t. animate)*. *conj 3rd sg* **lunŭwiipóokwsiit**. *ptcpl* **eelŭnuwii=póokwsiit**.

**lunŭwíixteew** VAI look homely. *ind 1st sg* **ndulŭnuwíixta**, **ndulŭnuwíix=taam**. *conj 3rd sg* **lunŭwíixtaakw**. *ptcpl* **eelŭnuwíixtaakw**.

**lúpkaash** NA Rebecca. *obv* **lupkáashal**. *From English* Rebecca.

**lupoxkwanéexiin** VAI have one's back in a certain direction, lie with one's back in a certain direction. **Wuláa=kwu ná lupoxkwanéexiin.** 'She had her back turned yesterday.' *ind 1st sg* **ndulpoxkwanéexiin, ndulpoxkwa=néexi**. *conj 3rd sg* **lupoxkwanéexiing**. *imp* **lupoxkwanéexiil**. *ptcpl* **eelpox=kwanéexiing**.
**lúpŭyaan** NA Olivia. *obv* **lùpŭyáanal**. *See* **lúpŭyeen**. *From English* Olivia.
**lúpŭyeen** NA Olivia. *obv* **lùpŭyéenal**. *See* **lúpŭyaan**. *From English* Olivia.
**lústam** VTI1A hear s.t., hear s.t. in a certain manner, hear s.t. in a certain direction. **Ndulsútamun máh koola=malsíiwi.** 'I heard that you weren't well.'; **Kwéek há ktulsútamun?** 'What did you hear?' *ind 1st sg* **ndulsútamun**. *ind 3rd sg* **wtulsút=amun**. *conj 1st sg* **lustámaan**. *conj 3rd sg* **lústang**. *imp* **lústah**. *ptcpl* **eelsútang**.
**lustáweew** VTA hear s.o., hear s.o. in a certain manner, hear s.o. in a certain direction. **Ndulsútawaaw amata=láamuw.** 'I heard him and he sings terribly.' *ind 1st sg* **ndulsútawaaw, ndulsútawa**. *ind 3rd sg* **wtulsuta=wáawal**. *ind inv* **ndulsútaakw**. *ind I-you* **ktulsútool**. *conj 3rd sg* **lustáwaat**. *imp* **lústaw**. *ptcpl* **eelsútawaat**.
**lushiilúndam** VAI marry into a certain family. *ind 1st sg* **ndulshiilúndam**. *conj 3rd sg* **lushiilúndang**. *ptcpl* **eelshiilúndang**. *See* **lushiilúngeew**.
**lushiilúngeew** VAI marry into a certain family. **Kách káa wáak ná wtulshii=lúngeen.** 'It serves him right for marrying into that family.' *ind 1st sg* **ndulshiilúnge, ndulshiilúngeem**. *conj 3rd sg* **lushiilúngeet**. *imp* **lush=iilúngeel**. *ptcpl* **eelshiilúngeet**. *See* **lushiilúndam**.
**lushíimuw** VAI run away in a certain direction, flee in a certain direction. **Wiikwáhmung lushíimuw.** 'He's running towards the house.' *ind 1st sg* **ndulshíimwi, ndulshíimwiim**. *conj 3rd sg* **lùshíimwiit**. *imp* **lushíimwiil**. *ptcpl* **eelshíimwiit**.
**lutaachíindam** VTI1A drag s.t. in a certain direction, drag s.t. in a certain manner. *ind 1st sg* **ndultaachíinda=mun**. *ind 3rd sg* **wtultaachíindamun**. *conj 1st sg* **lutaachíindamaan**. *conj 3rd sg* **lutaachíindang**. *imp* **lutaa=chíindih**. *ptcpl* **eeltaachíindang**.
**lutaachíhleew** VTA drag s.o. in a certain direction, drag s.o. in a certain manner. *ind 1st sg* **ndultaachíhlaaw, ndultaachíhla**. *ind 3rd sg* **wtultaa=chihláawal**. *ind inv* **ndultaachíh=lukw**. *ind I-you* **ktultaachíhlul**. *conj 3rd sg* **lùtaachíhlaat**. *imp* **lutáachihl**. *ptcpl* **eeltaachíhlaat**.
**lutaachíhleew** VAI be dragged in a certain manner, be dragged in a certain direction. *ind 1st sg* **ndultaachíhla, ndultaachíhlaam**. *conj 3rd sg* **lùt=aachíhlaat**. *imp* **lutaachíhlaal**. *ptcpl* **eeltaachíhlaat**.
**lutóonheew** VAI speak in a certain manner. **Wíhwiing- ná -lutóonheew.** 'He likes to stick his noise in.'; **Maama=lóoniish ndultóonhe.** 'I speak slowly.' *ind 1st sg* **ndultóonhe, ndul=tóonheem**. *conj 3rd sg* **lutóonheet**. *imp* **lutóonheel**. *ptcpl* **eeltóonheet**.
**lúweew** VAI make a certain kind of noise. **Wéemi táa ndayŭlúween.** 'I'm making all kinds of noise.' *ind 1st sg* **ndúlŭwe, ndúluweem**. *conj 3rd sg* **lúweet**. *imp* **lúweel**. *ptcpl* **éelŭweet**. *intensive reduplication* **ayúlŭweew**.
**lxakwambíisuw** VAI be tied loosely *(s.t. animate)*. *ind 1st sg* **làxakwámbiisi, làxakwambíisiim**. *conj 3rd sg* **lxak=wambíisiit**. *ptcpl* **leexakwambíisiit**.
**lxakwambíisuw** VII be tied loosely. *conj 3rd sg* **lxakwambíisiik**. *ptcpl* **leexa=**

**kwambíisiik**.

**lxakwíixun** VII be loose, do not adhere tightly *(of lids, of bolts)*. *conj 3rd sg* **lxakwíixung**. *ptcpl* **leexakwíixung**.

**lxakwíhleew** VII get loose. *conj 3rd sg* **lxakwíhlaak**. *ptcpl* **leexakwíhlaak**.

**lxakwihtéexun** VII get bounced loose, get knocked loose. *conj 3rd sg* **lxakwihtéexung**. *ptcpl* **leexakwih=téexung**.

**lxákwŭneew** VTA loosen s.t. animate. *ind 1st sg* **làxakwúnaaw, làxakwúna**. *ind 3rd sg* **wŭlaxakwŭnáawal**. *ind inv* **làxakwúnukw**. *ind I-you* **kŭla=xakwúnul**. *conj 3rd sg* **lxákwŭnaat**. *imp* **lxákwun**. *ptcpl* **leexakwúnaat**.

**lxákwŭnum** VTI1B loosen s.t. *ind 1st sg* **laxakwúnŭmun**. *ind 3rd sg* **wŭlaxa=kwúnŭmun**. *conj 1st sg* **lxakwŭ=númaan**. *conj 3rd sg* **lxákwŭnung**. *imp* **lxákwŭnih**. *ptcpl* **leexakwún=ung**.

**lxawáhkwsuw** VAI be a forked tree. *conj 3rd sg* **lxawáhkwsiit**. *ptcpl* **leexa=wáhkwsiit**.

**lxáweew** VII be forked. *conj 3rd sg* **lxáweek**. *ptcpl* **léexaweek**.

**lxawéelŭmeew** VTA take care of s.o., look after s.o., tend to a responsibility with regard to s.o. **Káta-lxawéelŭ=maa ktahtamoombíilum, chíi amayakaweehéehan.** 'You should take care of your car, don't drive it needlessly.' *ind 1st sg* **làxawéelŭ=maaw, làxawéelŭma**. *ind 3rd sg* **wŭlaxaweelŭmáawal**. *ind inv* **làxa=wéelŭmukw**. *ind I-you* **kŭlaxawée=lŭmul**. *conj 3rd sg* **lxawéelŭmaat**. *imp* **lxawéelum**. *ptcpl* **leexawée=lŭmaat**.

**lxaweelúndam** VTI1B take care of s.t., look after s.t., tend to a responsibility with regard to s.t. **Katá-lxaweelún=dah miichŭwáakan.** 'Take care of the food (said of an empty refrigerator).' *ind 1st sg* **laxaweelúndamun**. *ind 3rd sg* **wŭlaxaweelúndamun**. *conj 1st sg* **lxaweelúndamaan**. *conj 3rd sg* **lxaweelúndang**. *imp* **lxawee=lúndah**. *ptcpl* **leexaweelúndang**.

**lxawíixiin** VAI be about to fall, be placed so as to fall. *ind 1st sg* **làxawíixiin**. *conj 3rd sg* **lxawíixiing**. *ptcpl* **leexa=wíixiing**.

**lxawíixun** VII be about to fall, be placed so as to fall. *conj 3rd sg* **lxawíixung**. *ptcpl* **leexawíixung**.

**lxawóoleew** VTA bother s.o., interrupt s.o. *ind 1st sg* **laxawóolaaw, laxa=wóola**. *ind 3rd sg* **wŭlaxawooláawal**. *ind inv* **laxawóolukw**. *ind I-you* **kŭ=laxawóolul**. *conj 3rd sg* **lxawóolaat**. *imp* **lxáwool**. *ptcpl* **leexawóolaat**.

**lxawóolŭweew** VAI bother people, interrupt people. *ind 1st sg* **làxawóolŭwe, làxawóolŭweem**. *conj 3rd sg* **lxaw=óolŭweet**. *imp* **lxawóolŭweel**. *ptcpl* **leexawóolŭweet**. *intensive reduplication* **làlxawóolŭweew**.

**lxawsiitéesuw** VAI have forked feet *(s.t. animate)*. *ind 1st sg* **làxawusiitéesi, làxawusiitéesiim**. *conj 3rd sg* **lxaw=siitéesiit**. *ptcpl* **leexawusiitéesiit**.

**lxawsiitéeyeew** VII have forked feet. *conj 3rd sg* **lxawsiitéeyeek**. *ptcpl* **leexawusiitéeyeek**.

**lxáwsuw** VAI be forked *(s.t. animate)*. *conj 3rd sg* **lxáwsiit**. *ptcpl* **leexa=wúsiit**.

**lxawŭlunjéesuw** VAI have forked fingers *(s.t. animate)*. *ind 1st sg* **làxawul=unjéesi, làxawulunjéesiim**. *conj 3rd sg* **lxawŭlunjéesiit**. *ptcpl* **leexawul=unjéesiit**.

**lxawŭlunjéeyeew** VII have forked fingers *(as of a fork)*. *conj 3rd sg* **lxaw=ŭlunjéeyeek**. *ptcpl* **leexawulun=jéeyeek**.

**lxeekwáakan** NI rake. *pl* **lxeekwáaka=nal**. *poss* **laxeekwáakan**. *loc* **lxee=kwáakanung**. *dimin* **lxeekwáa=kanush**.

**lxeekwáakeew** VAI rake things, be raking. *ind 1st sg* **làxeekwáake**, **làxee=kwáakeem**. *conj 3rd sg* **lxeekwáa=keet**. *imp* **lxeekwáakeel**. *ptcpl* **leexeekwáakeet**.

**lxéekwam** VTI1A rake s.t. *ind 1st sg* **laxéekwamun**. *ind 3rd sg* **wŭlaxée=kwamun**. *conj 1st sg* **lxéekwamaan**. *conj 3rd sg* **lxéekwang**. *imp* **lxée=kwah**. *ptcpl* **leexéekwang**.

**lxíhleew** VAI get loose *(s.t. animate)*. **Katá-lxíhle.** 'He wants to get loose.' *ind 1st sg* **làxíhla**, **làxíhlaam**. *conj 3rd sg* **lxíhlaat**. *imp* **lxíhlaal**. *ptcpl* **leexíhlaat**.

**lxíhleew** VII get loose. *conj 3rd sg* **lxíhlaak**. *ptcpl* **leexíhlaak**.

**lxúneew** VTA untie s.o., untie s.t. animate. *ind 1st sg* **láxŭnaaw**, **láxŭna**. *ind 3rd sg* **wŭlaxŭnáawal**. *ind inv* **láxŭnukw**. *ind I-you* **kŭláxŭnul**. *conj 3rd sg* **lxúnaat**. *imp* **lxún**. *ptcpl* **léexŭnaat**.

**lxúnum** VTI1B untie s.t. *ind 1st sg* **lax=ŭnúmun**. *ind 3rd sg* **wŭlaxŭnúmun**. *conj 1st sg* **lxúnŭmaan**. *conj 3rd sg* **lxúnung**. *imp* **lxúnih**. *ptcpl* **lée=xŭnung**.

# M

**maachahtakíhleew** VAI run home. *ind 1st sg* **nŭmaachahtakíhla**, **nŭmaa=chahtakíhlaam**. *conj 3rd sg* **maa=chahtakíhlaat**. *imp* **maachahtakíh=laal**. *ptcpl* **maachahtakíhlaat**.

**máachaleew** VTA take s.o. home *(to their place)*. *ind 1st sg* **nŭmáachalaaw**, **nŭmáachala**. *ind 3rd sg* **maachaláa=wal**. *ind inv* **nŭmáachalukw**. *ind I-you* **kŭmáachalul**. *conj 3rd sg* **máa=chalaat**. *imp* **máachal**. *ptcpl* **máa=chalaat**.

**máachatoow** VTI2 take s.t. home *(to where it belongs)*. *ind 1st sg* **nŭmáa=chatoon**. *ind 3rd sg* **máachatoon**. *conj 1st sg* **maachatáwaan**. *conj 3rd sg* **máachataakw**. *imp* **máachatool**. *ptcpl* **máachataakw**.

**máachiiw** VAI-S go home. *ind 1st sg* **nŭ=máachi**, **nŭmáachiim**. *emphatic pl* **maachooltúwak**. *conj 3rd sg* **máa=chiit**. *imp* **máachiil**. *ptcpl* **máachiit**.

**maachiipáhtoow** VTI2 run s.t. home, take s.t. back *(especially of borrowed items)*. *ind 1st sg* **nŭmaachiipáhtoon**. *ind 3rd sg* **maachiipáhtoon**. *conj 1st sg* **maachiipáhtawaan**. *conj 3rd sg* **maachiipáhtaakw**. *imp* **maachii=páhtool**. *ptcpl* **maachiipáhtaakw**.

**maachíipheew** VTA run s.o. home. *ind 1st sg* **nŭmaachíiphaaw**, **nŭmaa=chíipha**. *ind 3rd sg* **maachiipháawal**. *ind inv* **nŭmaachíiphukw**. *ind I-you* **kŭmaachíiphul**. *conj 3rd sg* **maa=chíiphaat**. *imp* **maachíipah**. *ptcpl* **maachíiphaat**.

**máakŭlut** NA Margaret. *obv* **maakŭ=lútal**. *From English* Margaret.

**maaláxkwsiit** NI bean. *pl* **maalaxkw=síital**. *poss* **nŭmaalaxkwsíitum**. *loc* **maalaxkwsíitung**. *dimin* **maalaxk=wshíichush**.

**máaleew** NA glutton, someone who eats a lot, someone who never gets full. *pl* **maaléewak**. *obv* **maaléewal**.

**maaléewuw** VAI be a glutton, be greedy at the table. *ind 1st sg* **nŭmaaléewi**, **nŭmaaléewiim**. *conj 3rd sg* **maalée=wiit**. *ptcpl* **maaléewiit**.

**maaléewuw** VAI play tag. *ind 1st sg* **nŭmaaléewi**, **nŭmaaléewiim**. *conj 3rd sg* **maaléewiit**. *imp* **maaléewiil**. *ptcpl* **maaléewiit**.

**máaliish** NA Molly. *obv* **maalíishal**. *From English* Molly.

**maamaaláxkook** NA garter snake. *pl* **maamaalaxkóokak**. *loc* **maamaa=laxkóokung**. *dimin* **maamaalaxkóo=kush**. *obv* **maamaalaxkóokal**.

**maamáaleew** VII be striped. *conj 3rd sg* **maamáaleek**. *ptcpl* **maamáaleek**.

**maamaalíingwal** NI eyebrows. *usually plural. pl* **maamaalíingwal**. *poss* **nŭmaamaalíingwal**. *See* **maamaa=liingwáawan, maamáawan**.

**maamaaliingwáawan** NI eyebrow. *pl* **maamaaliingwáawanal**. *poss* **nŭmaamaaliingwáawan**. *See* **maamaalíingwal, maamáawan**.

**maamáalsuw** VAI be striped *(s.t. animate). ind 1st sg* **nŭmaamáalsi, nŭmaamáalsiim**. *conj 3rd sg* **maamáalsiit**. *ptcpl* **maamáalsiit**.

**maamaashíixsuw** VAI talk oddly. *ind 1st sg* **nŭmaamaashíixsi, nŭmaamaa=shíixsiim**. *conj 3rd sg* **maamaa=shíixsiit**. *ptcpl* **maamaashíixsiit**.

**maamáawan** NI eyebrow. *pl* **maamáa=wanal**. *poss* **nŭmaamáawan**. *See* **maamaalíingwal, maamaaliin=gwáawan**.

**maamalóoniish** PC kind of slowly, somewhat slowly. **Maamalóoniish pumúsuw.** 'He's walking kind of slowly.'; **Maamalóoniish tóhkiiw.** 'He woke up slowly.' *See* **malóoniish**.

**maamayaníilŭnuw** VAI be lonely. *ind 1st sg* **nŭmaamayaníilŭni, nŭmaa=mayaníilŭniim**. *conj 3rd sg* **maama=yaníilŭniit**. *ptcpl* **maamayaníilŭniit**.

**máamchiish** PC seldom, hardly; very little, a scant amount. **Máamchiish ndalóhke.** 'I seldom work.'; **Máam=chiish aluwíhleew.** 'There's hardly any left over.'

**maanjŭwáawsuw** VAI lead an odd life, lead a strange life. *ind 1st sg* **nŭ=maanjŭwáawsi, nŭmaanjŭwáaw=siim**. *conj 3rd sg* **maanjŭwáawsiit**. *ptcpl* **maanjŭwáawsiit**.

**maanjŭwáween** PR odd person, strange person. *pl* **maanjuwawéeniik**. *obv* **maanjuwawéeniil**.

**maanjŭwúnum** VOTI 1B do odd things. *ind 1st sg* **numaanjuwúnum**. *conj 3rd sg* **maanjŭwúnung**. *ptcpl* **maan=jŭwúnung**. *intensive reduplication* **mahmaanjŭwúnum**.

**máanzakwus** NA fine comb. *pl* **maan=zakwúsak**. *poss* **nŭmaanzakwúsum**. *loc* **maanzakwúsung**. *dimin* **maan=zhakwúshush**. *obv* **maanzakwúsal**. *See* **máasakwus**.

**maanzháapuy** NA bead. *pl* **maanzháa=pŭyak**. *dimin* **maanzháapiish**. *obv* **maanzháapŭyal**.

**máapŭlush** NA marble. *pl* **maapŭlúsh=ak**. *poss* **nŭmaapŭlúshum**. *dimin* **maapŭlúshush**. *obv* **maapulúshal**. *From English* marble.

**maapŭlusheelawúsuw** VAI play marbles. *ind 1st sg* **nŭmaapŭlusheela=wúsi, nŭmaapŭlusheelawúsiim**. *conj 3rd sg* **maapŭlusheelawúsiit**. *imp* **maapŭlusheelawúsiil**. *ptcpl* **maapŭlusheelawúsiit**.

**máasakwus** NA fine comb. *pl* **maasa=kwúsak**. *poss* **nŭmaasakwúsum**. *loc* **maasakwúsung**. *dimin* **maasha=kwúshush**. *obv* **maasakwúsal**. *See* **máanzakwus**.

**máash** PC like, resembling. **Kwŭlúp máash kíineew wihkíiwan.** 'Also it looks sharp, his nose.'; **Máash shŭ=wanakwiináakwsuw.** 'He looks like a White person.'

**maashatawáapuw** VAI see strange things. *ind 1st sg* **nŭmaashatawáapi, nŭmaashatawáapiim**. *conj 3rd sg* **maashatawáapiit**. *ptcpl* **maasha=tawáapiit**. *intensive reduplication* **mahmaashatawáapuw**.

**máashaween** PR strange person. *pl* **maa=shawéeniik**. *obv* **maashawéeniil**.

**maasheelúndam** VOTI 1A have a strange feeling. *ind 1st sg* **numaasheelún=dam**. *conj 3rd sg* **maasheelúndang**. *ptcpl* **maasheelúndang**.

**maashiilatáasuw** VAI make remarks to people, make 'digs' at people, be reluctant to come out and say things to people. *ind 1st sg* **nŭmaashiilatáasi**, **nŭmaashiilatáasiim**. *conj 3rd sg* **maashiilatáasiit**. *ptcpl* **maashiila=táasiit**. *intensive reduplication* **amaashiilatáasuw**.

**maashiilatáweew** VTA make remarks to s.o., make 'digs' at s.o., hint at something to s.o., be reluctant to say something outright to s.o. *ind 1st sg* **nŭmaashiilatáwaaw**, **nŭmaashiila=táwa**. *ind 3rd sg* **maashiilatawáa=wal**. *ind inv* **nŭmaashíilataakw**. *ind I-you* **kŭmaashíilatool**. *conj 3rd sg* **maashiilatáwaat**. *ptcpl* **maashiila=táwaat**. *intensive reduplication* **màmaashiilatawáawal**; *moderative reduplication* **maamaashiilataw=áawal**. *See* **maamaashiilatáweew**.

**maashiilawéeheew** VTA do strange things to s.o.; do things that make s.o. feel strange. *ind 1st sg* **nŭmaashiila=wéehaaw**, **nŭmaashiilawéeha**. *ind 3rd sg* **maashiilaweeháawal**. *ind inv* **nŭmaashiilawéehukw**. *ind I-you* **kŭmaashiilawéehul**. *conj 3rd sg* **maashiilawéehaat**. *imp* **maashíila=weeh**. *ptcpl* **maashiilawéehaat**.

**maashiilawéhtoow** VAI make people feel strange. *ind 1st sg* **nŭmaashii=lawéhto**. *conj 3rd sg* **maashiilawéh=taakw**. *ptcpl* **maashiilawéhtaakw**.

**maashiimáakwat** VII have a strange smell, smell strange. *conj 3rd sg* **maashiimáakwahk**. *ptcpl* **maashii=máakwahk**.

**maashiimáakwsuw** VAI have a strange smell, smell strange *(s.t. animate)*. *ind 1st sg* **nŭmaashiimáakwsi**, **nŭmaashiimáakwsiim**. *conj 3rd sg* **maashiimáakwsiit**. *ptcpl* **maashii=máakwsiit**.

**maashiináakwat** VII look strange, have an odd appearance. *conj 3rd sg* **maa=shiináakwahk**. *ptcpl* **maashiináa=kwahk**.

**maashiináakwsuw** VAI look strange, have an odd appearance. *ind 1st sg* **nŭmaashiináakwsi**, **nŭmaashii=náakwsiim**. *conj 3rd sg* **maashii=náakwsiit**. *ptcpl* **maashiináakwsiit**.

**maashíingweew** VAI have an odd face, have a strange face. *ind 1st sg* **nŭmaa=shíingwa**, **nŭmaashíingwaam**. *conj 3rd sg* **maashíingwaat**. *ptcpl* **maa=shíingwaat**.

**maashiingwéexiin** VAI have a strange look on one's face; have a guilty look on one's face, look guilty of something. *ind 1st sg* **nŭmaashiingwée=xiin**, **nŭmaashiingwéexi**. *conj 3rd sg* **maashiingwéexiing**. *ptcpl* **maa=shiingwéexiing**, **maashiingwéexiit**.

**maashihtáakwat** VII sound odd, sound different, sound strange. *conj 3rd sg* **maashihtáakwahk**. *ptcpl* **maashih=táakwahk**.

**maashihtáakwsuw** VAI sound odd, sound different, sound strange. *ind 1st sg* **nŭmaashihtáakwsi**, **nŭmaa=shihtáakwsiim**. *conj 3rd sg* **maashih=táakwsiit**. *ptcpl* **maashihtáakwsiit**.

**maashóngwaam** VAI have an odd dream. *ind 1st sg* **nŭmaashóngwaam**. *conj 3rd sg* **maashóngwaang**. *ptcpl* **maashóngwaang**. *moderative reduplication* **maamaashóngwaam**.

**maashtoonéexiin** VAI have an odd twist to one's mouth, have an odd twist to one's lips *(indicating a certain attitude)*. *ind 1st sg* **nŭmaashtoonéexiin**, **nŭmaashtoonéexi**. *conj 3rd sg* **maa=shtoonéexiing**. *ptcpl* **maashtoonée=xiing**, **maashtoonéexiit**.

**maashtóonheew** VAI talk oddly. *ind 1st sg* **nŭmaashtóonhe**, **nŭmaash=tóonheem**. *conj 3rd sg* **maashtóon=heet**. *imp* **maashtóonheel**. *ptcpl* **maashtóonheet**. *moderative reduplication* **maamaashtóonheew**.

**máatachuw** VAI have a cold. **Kíhchu-máatachuw.** 'He has a bad cold.' *ind 1st sg* **nŭmáatachi**, **nŭmáatachiim**.

*conj 3rd sg* **máatachiit**. *ptcpl* **máatachiit**.

**maatahtakíhleew** VAI run home. *ind 1st sg* **nŭmaatahtakíhla**, **nŭmaatah=takíhlaam**. *conj 3rd sg* **maatahta=kíhlaat**. *imp* **maatahtakíhlaal**. *ptcpl* **maatahtakíhlaat**.

**maatshíhkaweew** VTA send s.o. home. *ind 1st sg* **nŭmaatshíhkawaaw**, **nŭmaatshíhkawa**. *ind 3rd sg* **maat=shihkawáawal**. *ind inv* **nŭmaatshíh=kaakw**. *ind I-you* **kŭmaatshíhkool**. *conj 3rd sg* **maatshíhkawaat**. *imp* **maatshíhkaw**. *ptcpl* **maatshíh=kawaat**.

**máatŭneew** VTA make s.o.'s condition worse. *ind 1st sg* **nŭmáatŭnaaw**, **nŭmáatŭna**. *ind 3rd sg* **maatŭnáa=wal**. *ind inv* **nŭmáatŭnukw**. *ind I-you* **kŭmáatŭnul**. *conj 3rd sg* **máatŭnaat**. *imp* **máatun**. *ptcpl* **máatŭnaat**.

**máatŭnum** VTI1B make s.t. worse. *ind 1st sg* **nŭmaatŭnúmun**. *ind 3rd sg* **maatŭnúmun**. *conj 1st sg* **maatŭ=númaan**. *conj 3rd sg* **máatŭnung**. *imp* **máatŭnih**. *ptcpl* **máatŭnung**.

**máawapuw** VAI make a contribution, put money in the collection plate. *ind 1st sg* **nŭmáawapi**, **nŭmáawapiim**. *conj 3rd sg* **máawapiit**. *imp* **máawa=piil**. *ptcpl* **máawapiit**. *See* **maawée=wapuw**.

**maawéeheew** VTA gather s.o. up. *ind 1st sg* **nŭmaawéehaaw**, **nŭmaawéeha**. *ind 3rd sg* **maaweeháawal**. *conj 3rd sg* **maawéehaat**. *imp* **máaweeh**. *ptcpl* **maawéehaat**.

**maaweehíinjŭweew** VAI gather the dishes. *ind 1st sg* **nŭmaaweehíinjŭwe**, **nŭmaaweehíinjŭweem**. *conj 3rd sg* **maaweehíinjŭweet**. *imp* **maawee=híinjŭweel**. *ptcpl* **maaweehíinjŭ=weet**.

**maawéehum** VTI1B gather s.t. up. *ind 1st sg* **nŭmaawéehŭmun**. *ind 3rd sg* **maawéehŭmun**. *conj 1st sg* **maa=wéehŭmaan**. *conj 3rd sg* **maawée=hung**. *imp* **maawéehih**. *ptcpl* **maa=wéehung**.

**maaweekwáakeew** VAI gather things, rake things up. *ind 1st sg* **nŭmaa=weekwáake**, **nŭmaaweekwáakeem**. *conj 3rd sg* **maaweekwáakeet**. *imp* **maaweekwáakeel**. *ptcpl* **maawee=kwáakeet**.

**maawéekwam** VTI1A rake s.t. up. *object usually plural*. *ind 1st sg* **nŭmaa=weekwamúnal**. *ind 3rd sg* **maawée=kwamun**. *conj 1st sg* **maawéekwa=maan**. *conj 3rd sg* **maawéekwang**. *imp* **maawéekwah**. *ptcpl* **maawée=kwang**.

**maawéeneew** VTA gather s.o. up *(using the hands)*. *object usually plural*. *ind 1st sg* **nŭmaaweenáawak**. *ind 3rd sg* **maaweenáawal**. *ind inv* **nŭmaa=wéenkook**. *ind I-you* **kŭmaaweenŭ=lóhmwa**. *conj 3rd sg* **maawéenaat**. *imp* **máaween**. *ptcpl* **maawéenaat**.

**maaweeníikan** NI hay rake; collection plate in church. *pl* **maaweeníikanal**. *poss* **nŭmaaweeníikan**. *loc* **maa=weeníikanung**. *dimin* **maaweeníi=kanush**.

**maaweeníikeew** VAI rake things up, rake hay. *ind 1st sg* **nŭmaaweeníike**, **nŭmaaweeníikeem**. *conj 3rd sg* **maaweeníikeet**. *imp* **maaweeníikeel**. *ptcpl* **maaweeníikeet**.

**maaweenjŭweextíikeew** VAI gather up the dishes. *ind 1st sg* **nŭmaaween=jŭweextíike**, **nŭmaaweenjŭweex=tíikeem**. *conj 3rd sg* **maaweenjŭ=weextíikeet**. *imp* **maaweenjŭweex=tíikeel**. *ptcpl* **maaweenjŭ=weextíikeet**.

**maawéenum** VTI1B gather s.t. *(using the hands)*. *ind 1st sg* **nŭmaawéenŭmun**. *ind 3rd sg* **maawéenŭmun**. *conj 1st sg* **maawéenŭmaan**. *conj 3rd sg* **maawéenung**. *imp* **maawéenih**. *ptcpl* **maawéenung**.

**maawéenŭmeew** VAI take up the collection *(in church)*. *ind 1st sg* **nŭmaa=wéenŭma, nŭmaawéenŭmaam**. *conj 3rd sg* **maawéenŭmaat**. *imp* **maa=wéenŭmaal**. *ptcpl* **maawéenŭmaat**.

**maawéewapuw** VAI make a contribution, put money in the collection plate. *ind 1st sg* **nŭmaawéewapi, nŭmaawéewapiim**. *conj 3rd sg* **maawéewapiit**. *imp* **maawéewapiil**. *ptcpl* **maawéewapiit**. *See* **máa=wapuw**.

**maaweewíikaan** NI church. *pl* **maa=weewiikáanal**. *loc* **maaweewiikáa=nung**.

**maawéewuw** VAI attend church, attend a service. *ind 1st sg* **nŭmaawéewi, nŭmaawéewiim**. *conj 3rd sg* **maa=wéewiit**. *imp* **maawéewiil**. *ptcpl* **maawéewiit**.

**maawehléewak** VAI gather together, meet. *usually plural*. *ind 1st pl* **nŭ=maawehláhna**. *conj 3rd sg* **maa=wehláhtiit**. *imp* **maawéhlaakw**. *ptcpl* **maawehláhtiit**.

**maawhúnzuw** VAI gather things up. *ind 1st sg* **nŭmaawhúnzi, nŭmaaw=húnziim**. *conj 3rd sg* **maawhúnziit**. *imp* **maawhúnziil**. *ptcpl* **maaw=húnziit**.

**má** PC preterite particle. **Lúyane áa má, nál áa yú ntápiin.** 'If you had told me, I would have stayed.'; **Maachíite áa má, nŭwiichéewaaw áa.** 'If he had gone home, I would have gone with him.'

**machéekŭneew** VTA fold s.t. animate carelessly. *ind 1st sg* **nŭmachéekŭ=naaw, nŭmachéekŭna**. *ind 3rd sg* **màcheekŭnáawal**. *conj 3rd sg* **machéekŭnaat**. *imp* **machéekun**. *ptcpl* **meechéekŭnaat**. *intensive reduplication* **màmacheekŭnáawal**.

**machéekŭnum** VTI1B fold s.t. carelessly. *ind 1st sg* **nŭmacheekŭnúmun**. *ind 3rd sg* **màcheekŭnúmun**. *conj 1st sg* **macheekŭnúmaan**. *conj 3rd sg* **machéekŭnung**. *imp* **machéekŭnih**. *ptcpl* **meechéekŭnung**.

**machéewayal** NI old things, odds and ends. *usually plural*. *poss* **nŭmach=éewayal**.

**machii-** PN bad. **Machíi-skahúnzuw.** 'Bad boy.'; **Machíi-shŭwánakw.** 'Bad White man.'

**machíi-lpwéew** VAI be too smart for one's own good. *ind 1st sg* **nŭmáchii-lpwá, nŭmáchii-lpwáam**. *conj 3rd sg* **machíi-lpwáat**. *ptcpl* **méechii-lpwáat**.

**machíiheew** VTA spoil s.o. *ind 1st sg* **nŭmachíihaaw, nŭmachíiha**. *ind 3rd sg* **màchiiháawal**. *ind inv* **nŭmachíi=hukw**. *ind I-you* **kŭmachíihul**. *conj 3rd sg* **machíihaat**. *imp* **machíih**. *ptcpl* **meechíihaat**.

**machíikun** VII grow badly. *conj 3rd sg* **machíikung**. *ptcpl* **meechíikung**.

**machíikuw** VAI grow badly. *ind 1st sg* **nŭmachíiki, nŭmachíikiim**. *conj 3rd sg* **machíikiit**. *ptcpl* **meechíikiit**.

**machíilaweew** VAI have an upset stomach *(especially from morning sickness)*. *ind 1st sg* **nŭmachíilawe, nŭmachíilaweem**. *conj 3rd sg* **machíilaweet**. *ptcpl* **meechíilaweet**.

**machíilŭnuw** VAI be separated from one's spouse. *ind 1st sg* **nŭmachíi=lŭni, nŭmachíilŭniim**. *conj 3rd sg* **machíilŭniit**. *ptcpl* **meechíilŭniit**. *See* **chpooxwéewak**.

**machiimáakwat** VII have a bad smell, stink. *conj 3rd sg* **machiimáakwahk**. *ptcpl* **meechiimáakwahk**.

**machiimáakwsuw** VAI have a bad smell, stink *(s.t. animate)*. *ind 1st sg* **nŭ=machiimáakwsi, nŭmachiimáakw=siim**. *conj 3rd sg* **machiimáakwsiit**. *ptcpl* **meechiimáakwsiit**.

**machíimasuw** VAI have a burning smell, smell as if it is burning *(s.t. animate, of something cooking)*. *ind 1st sg*

**nŭmachíimasi**, **nŭmachíimasiim**. *conj 3rd sg* **machíimasiit**. *ptcpl* **meechíimasiit**.

**machiimatásŭmeew** VAI make an unpleasant smell *(of one's cooking)*. *ind 1st sg* **nŭmachiimatásŭma**, **nŭ=machiimatásŭmaam**. *conj 3rd sg* **machiimatásŭmaat**. *ptcpl* **meechii=matásŭmaat**.

**machíimateew** VII have a burning smell, smell as if it is burning *(of something cooking)*. *conj 3rd sg* **machíimateek**. *ptcpl* **meechíimateek**.

**machíinam** VTI1B dislike the looks of s.t. *ind 1st sg* **nŭmachíinamun**. *ind 3rd sg* **màchíinamun**. *conj 1st sg* **machíinamaan**. *conj 3rd sg* **machíi=nang**. *ptcpl* **meechíinang**.

**machíinaweew** VTA dislike the looks of s.o. *ind 1st sg* **nŭmachíinawaaw**, **nŭmachíinawa**. *ind 3rd sg* **màchii=nawáawal**. *ind inv* **nŭmachíinaakw**. *ind I-you* **kŭmachíinool**. *conj 3rd sg* **machíinawaat**. *ptcpl* **meechíi=nawaat**.

**machiipóokwan** VII have an unpleasant taste, taste bad. *conj 3rd sg* **machii=póokwang**. *ptcpl* **meechiipóokwang**.

**machiipóokwat** VII have an upleasant taste, taste bad. *conj 3rd sg* **machii=póokwahk**. *ptcpl* **meechiipóokwahk**.

**machiipóokwsuw** VAI have an unpleasant taste, taste bad *(s.t. animate)*. *ind 1st sg* **nŭmachiipóokwsi**, **nŭmachii=póokwsiim**. *conj 3rd sg* **machii=póokwsiit**. *ptcpl* **meechiipóokwsiit**.

**machiisŭmóoleew** VTA give s.o. something bad to drink. *ind 1st sg* **nŭ=machiisŭmóolaaw**, **nŭmachii=sŭmóola**. *ind 3rd sg* **màchiisŭmoo=láawal**. *ind inv* **nŭmachiisŭmóo=lukw**. *ind I-you* **kŭmachiisŭmóolul**. *conj 3rd sg* **machiisŭmóolaat**. *imp* **machíisŭmool**. *ptcpl* **meechiisŭ=móolaat**.

**machíisŭmuw** VAI be drunk and unpleasant, do bad things while drunk; drink poison *(especially to induce miscarriage)*. *ind 1st sg* **nŭmachíi=sŭmwi**, **nŭmachíisŭmwiim**. *conj 3rd sg* **machíisŭmwiit**. *imp* **machíisŭ=mwiil**. *ptcpl* **meechíisŭmwiit**.

**machiitéeheew** VAI be hard to get along with. *ind 1st sg* **nŭmachiitéeha**, **nŭmachiitéehaam**. *conj 3rd sg* **ma=chiitéehaat**. *ptcpl* **meechiitéehaat**.

**machiixáskwal** NI weeds. *usually plural*. *loc* **machiixáskwung**. *See* **matáskwal**.

**machíiyay** NI grave. *pl* **machíiyayal**.

**machíhleew** VAI run badly *(especially of vehicles)*; decay, go bad, spoil *(s.t. animate)*. *ind 1st sg* **nŭmachíhla**, **nŭmachíhlaam**. *conj 3rd sg* **ma=chíhlaat**. *ptcpl* **meechíhlaat**.

**machíhleew** VII decay, go bad, spoil. *conj 3rd sg* **machíhlaak**. *ptcpl* **mee=chíhlaak**.

**machíhtoow** VTI2 spoil s.t.; use up all of s.t., use up all of s.t. unwisely. **Nŭ=machíhtoon wéemi nzhulpúlum.** 'I spent all of my money.' *ind 1st sg* **nŭmachíhtoon**. *ind 3rd sg* **màchíh=toon**. *conj 1st sg* **machíhtawaan**. *conj 3rd sg* **machíhtaakw**. *imp* **machíhtool**. *ptcpl* **meechíhtaakw**.

**machu-** PN bad. *informal*. **Machú-awéen.** 'A bad person.'

**machu-** PV bad. *informal*. **Machú-léew.** 'Something bad happens.'; **Mbun=oondíhkeen éel-machú-úndaan.** 'I show my feelings because I'm so cross.' *ptcpl* **méechu-**.

**máh** PC here! here it is! take it!

**máh** PC no, not, negative. **Máh téep-kiishtéewi.** 'It's not cooked enough.'; **Máh kihkeesíiwi.** 'He has no parents.' *See* **máhta**.

**máhkahkw** NI pumpkin. *pl* **mahkáh=kwal**. *poss* **nŭmahkáhkwum**. *loc* **mahkáhkwung**. *dimin* **mahkáh=kwush**.

**máhkateew** NI coal, piece of coal. *pl* **mahkatéewal**. *loc* **mahkatéewung**.

**mahkháhkweew** VAI trim trees, cut underbrush. *ind 1st sg* **nŭmahkháh=kwe, nŭmahkháhkweem**. *conj 3rd sg* **mahkháhkweet**. *imp* **mahkháh=kweel**. *ptcpl* **mahkháhkweet**.

**máhkham** VTI1A detach s.t., knock s.t. off. *ind 1st sg* **nŭmahkhámun**. *ind 3rd sg* **mahkhámun**. *conj 1st sg* **mahkhámaan**. *conj 3rd sg* **máhk=hang**. *imp* **máhkhah**. *ptcpl* **máhk=hang**.

**máhkheew** VTA detach s.t. animate, knock s.t. animate off *(using a tool or instrument)*. *ind 1st sg* **nŭmáhk=haaw, nŭmáhkha**. *ind 3rd sg* **mahk=háawal**. *ind inv* **nŭmáhkhookw**. *ind I-you* **kŭmáhkhool**. *conj 3rd sg* **máhkhaat**. *imp* **máhkhaw**. *ptcpl* **máhkhaat**.

**mahkiikwáaleew** VTA scrape s.t. animate off *(using something held in the hand)*. *ind 1st sg* **nŭmahkiikwáa=laaw, nŭmahkiikwáala**. *ind 3rd sg* **mahkiikwaaláawal**. *conj 3rd sg* **mahkiikwáalaat**. *imp* **mahkíikwaal**. *ptcpl* **mahkiikwáalaat**.

**mahkíikwam** VTI1A scrape s.t. off *(using something held in the hand)*. *ind 1st sg* **nŭmahkíikwamun**. *ind 3rd sg* **mahkíikwamun**. *conj 1st sg* **mah=kíikwamaan**. *conj 3rd sg* **mahkíi=kwang**. *imp* **mahkíikwah**. *ptcpl* **mahkíikwang**.

**mahkíixiin** VAI be knocked off, fall off *(s.t. animate)*. *ind 1st sg* **nŭmahkíi=xiin, nŭmahkíixi**. *conj 3rd sg* **mahkíixiing**. *ptcpl* **mahkíixiing**.

**mahkíixtoow** VTI2 knock s.t. off, cause s.t. to be knocked off, detach s.t. *ind 1st sg* **nŭmahkíixtoon**. *ind 3rd sg* **mahkíixtoon**. *conj 1st sg* **mahkiix=táwaan**. *conj 3rd sg* **mahkíixtaakw**. *imp* **mahkíixtool**. *ptcpl* **mahkíix=taakw**.

**mahkíixŭmeew** VTA knock s.t. animate off, cause s.t. animate to be knocked off, detach s.t. animate. *ind 1st sg* **nŭmahkíixŭmaaw, nŭmahkíixŭma**. *ind 3rd sg* **mahkiixŭmáawal**. *ind inv* **nŭmahkíixŭmukw**. *ind I-you* **kŭ=mahkíixŭmul**. *conj 3rd sg* **mahkíi=xŭmaat**. *imp* **mahkíixum**. *ptcpl* **mahkíixŭmaat**.

**mahkíixun** VII be knocked off, fall off. *conj 3rd sg* **mahkíixung**. *ptcpl* **mah=kíixung**.

**mahkíhleew** VAI fall off, come off, become detached *(s.t. animate)*. *ind 1st sg* **nŭmahkíhla, nŭmahkíhlaam**. *conj 3rd sg* **mahkíhlaat**. *ptcpl* **mah=kíhlaat**.

**mahkíhleew** VII fall off, come off, become detached. *conj 3rd sg* **mahkíh=laak**. *ptcpl* **mahkíhlaak**.

**mahkihtéeheew** VTA hit and knock s.t. animate off, hit and detach s.t. animate. *ind 1st sg* **nŭmahkihtéehaaw, nŭmahkihtéeha**. *ind 3rd sg* **mah=kihteeháawal**. *ind inv* **nŭmahkih=téehookw**. *ind I-you* **kŭmahkihtée=hool**. *conj 3rd sg* **mahkihtéehaat**. *imp* **mahkíhteeh**. *ptcpl* **mahkih=téehaat**.

**mahkihtéehum** VTI1B hit and knock s.t. off, hit and detach s.t. *ind 1st sg* **nŭ=mahkihtéehŭmun**. *ind 3rd sg* **mah=kihtéehŭmun**. *conj 1st sg* **mahkih=téehŭmaan**. *conj 3rd sg* **mahkihtée=hung**. *imp* **mahkihtéehih**. *ptcpl* **mahkihtéehung**.

**mahkihtéexiin** VAI be knocked off, be hit and detached. *ind 1st sg* **nŭmah=kihtéexiin, nŭmahkihtéexi**. *conj 3rd sg* **mahkihtéexiing**. *ptcpl* **mahkih=téexiing**.

**mahkihtéextoow** VTI2 hit s.t. and knock it off, hit and detach s.t. *ind 1st sg* **nŭmahkihtéextoon**. *ind 3rd sg* **mah=kihtéextoon**. *conj 1st sg* **mahkih=teextáwaan**. *conj 3rd sg* **mahkih=**

**téextaakw**. *imp* **mahkihtéextool**. *ptcpl* **mahkihtéextaakw**.

**mahkihtéexŭmeew** VTA hit s.t. animate and knock it off, hit and detach s.t. animate. *ind 1st sg* **nŭmahkihtée=xŭmaaw**, **nŭmahkihtéexŭma**. *ind 3rd sg* **mahkihteexŭmáawal**. *ind inv* **nŭmahkihtéexŭmukw**. *ind I-you* **kŭmahkihtéexŭmul**. *conj 3rd sg* **mahkihtéexŭmaat**. *imp* **mahkih=téexum**. *ptcpl* **mahkihtéexŭmaat**.

**mahkihtéexun** VII be knocked off, be hit and detached. *conj 3rd sg* **mah=kihtéexung**. *ptcpl* **mahkihtéexung**.

**máhksun** NI shoe. *pl* **mahksúnal**. *poss* **nŭmáhksun**. *loc* **mahksúnung**. *dimin* **mahkshúnush**.

**mahksunháaleew** VTA put shoes on s.o. *(especially of horses)*. *ind 1st sg* **nŭmahksunháalaaw**, **nŭmahksun=háala**. *ind 3rd sg* **mahksunhaaláa=wal**. *ind inv* **nŭmahksunháalukw**. *ind I-you* **kŭmahksunháalul**. *conj 3rd sg* **mahksunháalaat**. *imp* **mah=ksúnhaal**.

**mahksúnii-mŭkóos** NA shoe tack. *pl* **mahksúnii-mŭkóosak**. *obv* **mah=ksúnii-mŭkóosal**.

**máhksheew** VTA cut a piece off s.t. animate, cut s.t. animate off. *ind 1st sg* **nŭmáhkshaaw**, **nŭmáhksha**. *ind 3rd sg* **mahksháawal**. *ind inv* **nŭmáhk=shookw**. *ind I-you* **kŭmáhkshool**. *conj 3rd sg* **máhkshaat**. *imp* **máh=kush**. *ptcpl* **máhkshaat**.

**máhkshum** VTI 1B cut a piece off s.t., cut s.t. off. *ind 1st sg* **nŭmahkshúmun**. *ind 3rd sg* **mahkshúmun**. *conj 1st sg* **mahkshúmaan**. *conj 3rd sg* **máhk=shung**. *imp* **máhkshih**. *ptcpl* **máhk=shung**.

**máhkŭneew** VTA detach s.t. animate, pull s.t. animate off, take s.t. animate away, remove s.t. animate *(using the hands)*. *ind 1st sg* **nŭmáhkŭnaaw**, **nŭmáh=kŭna**. *ind 3rd sg* **mahkŭnáawal**. *ind inv* **nŭmáhkŭnukw**. *ind I-you* **kŭ=máhkŭnul**. *conj 3rd sg* **máhkŭnaat**. *imp* **máhkun**. *ptcpl* **máhkŭnaat**.

**máhkŭnum** VTI 1B detach s.t., pull s.t. off, take s.t. away, remove s.t. *(using the hands)*. *ind 1st sg* **nŭmahkŭ=númun**. *ind 3rd sg* **mahkŭnúmun**. *conj 1st sg* **mahkŭnúmaan**. *conj 3rd sg* **máhkŭnung**. *imp* **máhkŭnih**. *ptcpl* **máhkŭnung**.

**máhlam** VTI 1A buy s.t. *ind 1st sg* **nŭ=máhlamun**. *ind 3rd sg* **máhlamun**. *conj 1st sg* **máhlamaan**. *conj 3rd sg* **máhlang**. *imp* **máhlah**. *ptcpl* **méh=lang**.

**mahlamáakeew** VAIO sell s.t. *ind 1st sg* **nŭmahlamáakeen**. *ind 3rd sg* **mah=lamáakeen**. *conj 3rd sg* **mahla=máakeet**. *imp* **mahlamáakeel**. *ptcpl* **mehlamáakeet**.

**mahlamwúsuw** VAI shop, go shopping. *ind 1st sg* **nŭmahlamwúsi**, **nŭmah=lamwúsiim**. *conj 3rd sg* **mahla=mwúsiit**. *imp* **mahlamwúsiil**. *ptcpl* **mehlamwúsiit**.

**máhlaweew** VTA buy s.o., buy s.t. animate. *ind 1st sg* **nŭmáhlawaaw**, **nŭmáhlawa**. *ind 3rd sg* **mahlawáa=wal**. *ind inv* **nŭmáhlaakw**. *ind I-you* **kŭmáhlool**. *conj 3rd sg* **máhlawaat**. *imp* **máhlaw**. *ptcpl* **méhlawaat**.

**mahmaashatawáapuw** VAI see black, see things, see spots *(especially after being sick)*. *ind 1st sg* **nŭmahmaa=shatawáapi**, **nŭmahmaashatawáa=piim**. *conj 3rd sg* **mahmaashataw=áapiit**. *ptcpl* **mahmaashatawáapiit**.

**máhta** PC no, not, negative. **Yóh máhta lí sookŭlaanóowi.** 'It's not raining here.'; **Máhta níi njíhnal nihlaawíi=wak awehleeshóoshak.** 'I don't kill birds anymore.' *See* **máh**.

**makóhpuw** VAI pick berries. *ind 1st sg* **nŭmakóhpwi**, **nŭmakóhpwiim**. *conj 3rd sg* **makóhpwiit**. *imp* **makóhpwiil**. *ptcpl* **meekóhpwiit**.

**makóhpuw** VAIO pick s.t. *(of fruits)*. **Nŭmakohpwíinal ooteehíimal.** 'I picked his strawberries.' *ind 1st sg* **nŭmakóhpwiin**. *ind 3rd sg* **màkóh= pwiin**. *conj 3rd sg* **makóhpwiit**. *imp* **makóhpwiil**. *ptcpl* **meekóhpwiit**.

**makúneew** VTA pick s.o. up *(using the hands)*; pick s.t. animate *(off trees)*. *ind 1st sg* **nŭmákŭnaaw**, **nŭmákŭna**. *ind 3rd sg* **màkŭnáawal**. *ind inv* **nŭ= mákŭnukw**. *ind I-you* **kŭmákŭnul**. *conj 3rd sg* **makúnaat**. *imp* **makún**. *ptcpl* **méekŭnaat**.

**makunhaapŭlúsheew** VAI pick apples. *ind 1st sg* **nŭmakŭnahaapŭlúshe**, **nŭmakŭnahaapŭlúsheem**. *conj 3rd sg* **makunhaapŭlúsheet**. *imp* **ma= kunhaapŭlúsheel**. *ptcpl* **meekŭnah= aapŭlúsheet**.

**makúnham** VTI1A pick s.t. up *(using a tool or instrument)*. *ind 1st sg* **nŭ= makŭnáhŭmun**. *ind 3rd sg* **màkŭ= náhŭmun**. *conj 1st sg* **makunhám= aan**. *conj 3rd sg* **makúnhang**. *imp* **makúnhah**. *ptcpl* **meekŭnáhang**.

**makúnheew** VTA pick s.t. animate up *(off the ground)*. **Nŭmakŭnáha aapŭlúshak.** 'I picked up some apples.' *ind 1st sg* **nŭmakŭnáhaaw**, **nŭmakŭnáha**. *ind 3rd sg* **màkŭnah= áawal**. *ind inv* **nŭmakŭnáhukw**. *ind I-you* **kŭmakŭnáhul**. *conj 3rd sg* **makúnhaat**. *imp* **makúnah**. *ptcpl* **meekŭnáhaat**.

**makunhíhpŭneew** VAI pick potatoes. *ind 1st sg* **nŭmakunahíhpŭne**, **nŭmakŭnahíhpŭneem**. *conj 3rd sg* **makunhíhpŭneet**. *imp* **makunhíh= pŭneel**. *ptcpl* **meekŭnahíhpŭneet**.

**makwáandpeew** VAI have a swollen head, have a bump on one's head. *ind 1st sg* **nŭmakwáandpa**, **nŭmakw= áandpaam**. *conj 3rd sg* **makwáand= paat**. *ptcpl* **meekwáandpaat**.

**makwaandpéeheew** VTA give s.o. a swollen head, hit s.o. and give them a lump on the head. *ind 1st sg* **nŭmak= waandpéehaaw**, **nŭmakwaandpée= ha**. *ind 3rd sg* **màkwaandpeeháa= wal**. *ind inv* **nŭmakwaandpéehukw**. *ind I-you* **kŭmakwaandpéehul**. *conj 3rd sg* **makwaandpéehaat**. *imp* **makwáandpeeh**. *ptcpl* **meekwaand= péehaat**.

**makwaandpehtéeheew** VTA hit s.o. and give them a lump on the head. *ind 1st sg* **nŭmakwaandpehtéehaaw**, **nŭ= makwaandpehtéeha**. *ind 3rd sg* **màkwaandpehteeháawal**. *ind inv* **nŭmakwaandpehtéehookw**. *ind I-you* **kŭmakwaandpehtéehool**. *conj 3rd sg* **makwaandpehtéehaat**. *imp* **makwaandpéhteeh**. *ptcpl* **mee= kwaandpehtéehaat**.

**makwíingweew** VAI have a swollen face, have one's face swell up. *ind 1st sg* **nŭmakwíingwe**, **nŭmakwíingweem**. *conj 3rd sg* **makwíingweet**. *ptcpl* **meekwíingweet**.

**makwíisiin** VAIO have s.t. swell up. **Màkwíisiin wtóon.** 'His mouth swelled up.'; **Nŭmakwíisiin ndúkuy.** 'My shoulder swelled up.' *ind 1st sg* **nŭmakwíisiin**. *ind 3rd sg* **màkwíi= siin**. *conj 3rd sg* **makwíisiit**. *ptcpl* **meekwíisiit**. *intensive reduplication* **màmakwíisiin**.

**makwucháaleew** VAI have a swollen nose, have a bump on one's nose. *ind 1st sg* **nŭmakwcháala**, **nŭmakw= cháalaam**. *conj 3rd sg* **makwucháa= laat**. *ptcpl* **meekwcháalaat**.

**makwukaatéeheew** VTA give s.o. a swollen leg, give s.o. a bump on their leg. *ind 1st sg* **nŭmakwkaatéehaaw**, **nŭmakwkaatéeha**. *ind 3rd sg* **màkwkaateeháawal**. *ind inv* **nŭ= makwkaatéehukw**. *ind I-you* **kŭ= makwkaatéehul**. *conj 3rd sg* **ma= kwukaatéehaat**. *imp* **makwukáa= teeh**. *ptcpl* **meekwkaatéehaat**.

**makwukáateew** VAI have a swollen leg,

have a bump on one's leg. *ind 1st sg* **nŭmakwkáata**, **nŭmakwkáataam**. *conj 3rd sg* **makwukáataat**. *ptcpl* **meekwkáataat**.

**makwukaatéhkaweew** VTA kick s.o. and give them a swollen leg, kick s.o. and give them a bump on the leg, sit on s.o. and give them a swollen leg, sit on s.o. and give them a bump on the leg. *ind 1st sg* **nŭmakwkaatéh=kawaaw**, **nŭmakwkaatéhkawa**. *ind 3rd sg* **màkwkaatehkawáawal**. *ind inv* **nŭmakwkaatéhkaakw**. *ind I-you* **kŭmakwkaatéhkool**. *conj 3rd sg* **makwukaatéhkawaat**. *imp* **ma=kwukaatéhkaw**. *ptcpl* **meekwkaa=téhkawaat**.

**makwusíiteew** VAI have one's feet swell up, have swollen feet. *ind 1st sg* **nŭmakwsíita**, **nŭmakwsíitaam**. *conj 3rd sg* **makwusíitaat**. *ptcpl* **meekw=síitaat**. *intensive reduplication* **màmakwusíiteew**.

**makwutóoneew** VAI have a swollen mouth, have a bump on one's mouth. *ind 1st sg* **nŭmakwtóona**, **nŭmakw=tóonaam**. *conj 3rd sg* **makwutóo=naat**. *ptcpl* **meekwtóonaat**.

**malóoniish** PC slowly. **Malóoniish pasúkwiiw Dianne.** 'Dianne got up slowly.' *moderative reduplication* **maamalóoniish**. *See* **maamalóo=niish**.

**màmateenhíikeew** VAI be a bad risk for credit, be a 'poor pay.' *ind 1st sg* **nŭmamateenhíike**, **nŭmamateen=híikeem**. *conj 3rd sg* **màmateenhíi=keet**. *ptcpl* **màmateenhíikeet**.

**màmshamóotoow** VTI2 pile s.t. up. *ind 1st sg* **nŭmamshamóotoon**. *ind 3rd sg* **màmshamóotoon**. *conj 1st sg* **màmshamóotawaan**. *conj 3rd sg* **màmshamóotaakw**. *imp* **màm=shamóotool**. *ptcpl* **màmsham=óotaakw**.

**màmshámuw** VII be heaped up. *conj 3rd sg* **màmshámwiik**. *ptcpl* **màmshámwiik**.

**màmshihléewak** VAI group together. *usually plural*. *ind 1st pl* **nŭmam=shihláhna**. *conj 3rd sg* **màmshih=láhtiit**. *ptcpl* **màmshihláhtiit**.

**mamúkw** VAI be killed in an accident. *ind 1st sg* **nŭmámukw**. *conj 3rd sg* **mamúkwuk**.

**manáaleew** VTA be jealous of s.o. *ind 1st sg* **nŭmanáalaaw**, **nŭmanáala**. *ind 3rd sg* **mànaaláawal**. *ind inv* **nŭmanáalukw**. *ind I-you* **kŭmanáa=lul**. *conj 3rd sg* **manáalaat**. *ptcpl* **meenáalaat**.

**manáasuw** VAI be jealous. *ind 1st sg* **nŭmanáasi**, **nŭmanáasiim**. *conj 3rd sg* **manáasiit**. *ptcpl* **meenáasiit**.

**manáxeew** VAI cut wood. *ind 1st sg* **nŭmánxe**, **nŭmánxeem**. *conj 3rd sg* **manáxeet**. *imp* **manáxeel**. *ptcpl* **méenxeet**.

**mándeew** VII be Monday. **Píish máhta mandéewu.** 'It's not Monday.'; **Éenda-mandéeke náh nóom.** 'I went there last Monday.' *conj 3rd sg* **mándeek**. *From English* Monday.

**mandóomeew** VTA blame s.o., be dissatisfied with s.o.'s actions. *ind 1st sg* **nŭmandóomaaw**, **nŭmandóoma**. *ind 3rd sg* **mandoomáawal**. *ind inv* **nŭmandóomukw**. *ind I-you* **kŭman=dóomul**. *conj 3rd sg* **mandóomaat**. *imp* **mándoom**. *ptcpl* **meendóomaat**.

**mandoomkwúsuw** VAI be blamed. *ind 1st sg* **nŭmandoomkwúsi**, **nŭman=doomkwúsiim**. *conj 3rd sg* **man=doomkwúsiit**. *ptcpl* **meendoom=kwúsiit**.

**mangaaptóoneew** VAI talk loudly. *ind 1st sg* **nŭmangaaptóone**, **nŭman=gaaptóoneem**. *conj 3rd sg* **man=gaaptóoneet**. *ptcpl* **meengaap=tóoneet**.

**mangaléetŭyeew** VAI eat a lot. *ind 1st sg* **nŭmangaléetŭya**, **nŭmangaléetŭ=**

yaam. *conj 3rd sg* **mangaléetŭyaat**. *ptcpl* **meengaléetŭyaat**. *considered impolite.*

**mangateelíingweew** VAI have big eyes. *ind 1st sg* **nŭmangateelíingwe, nŭmangateelíingweem**. *conj 3rd sg* **mangateelíingwaat**. *ptcpl* **meenga=teelíingwaat**. *intensive reduplication* **amangateelíingweew**.

**mangíixsuw** VAI talk loudly. *ind 1st sg* **nŭmangíixsi, nŭmangíixsiim**. *conj 3rd sg* **mangíixsiit**. *imp* **mangíixsiil**. *ptcpl* **meengíixsiit**.

**mangshamóotoow** VTI2 make a big pile of s.t., pile s.t. high. *ind 1st sg* **nŭ=mangshamóotoon**. *ind 3rd sg* **mang=shamóotoon**. *conj 1st sg* **mang=shamóotawaan**. *conj 3rd sg* **mang=shamóotaakw**. *imp* **mangshamóo=tool**. *ptcpl* **meengshamóotaakw**.

**mangshéengweew** VAI have one's eyes bigger than one's belly, take more than one can eat. *ind 1st sg* **nŭmang=shéengwe, nŭmangshéengweem**. *conj 3rd sg* **mangshéengwaat**. *ptcpl* **meengshéengwaat**. *intensive reduplication* **amangshéengweew**.

**mángu-láatam** VOTI1A laugh a lot, laugh out loud. *ind 1st sg* **numángu-láatam**. *conj 3rd sg* **mángu-láatang**. *ptcpl* **méengu-láatang**. *See* **amángu-láatam**.

**mángxeew** VAI have a big ear. *ind 1st sg* **nŭmángxa, nŭmángxaam**. *conj 3rd sg* **mángxaat**. *ptcpl* **méengxaat**.

**mánheel** PC not very, hardly at all. *followed by negative verb.* **Mánheel iiyalohkéewi.** 'He hardly ever works.'; **Mánheel wŭlahkaméewi.** 'It's not a very nice day.'

**maníhleew** VAI die. *ind 1st sg* **nŭman=íhla, nŭmaníhlaam**. *conj 3rd sg* **maníhlaat**. *ptcpl* **meeníhlaat**. *See* **ehkwáawsuw, éhkwi-pŭmáawsuw, éhkwu-pŭmáawsuw**.

**manoongáapameew** VTA look at s.o. angrily. *ind 1st sg* **nŭmanoongáapa=maaw, nŭmanoongáapama**. *ind 3rd sg* **mànoongaapamáawal**. *ind inv* **nŭmanoongáapamukw**. *ind I-you* **kŭmanoongáapamul**. *conj 3rd sg* **manoongáapamaat**. *ptcpl* **manoon=gáapamaat**.

**manoongamálsuw** VAI feel angry about one's illness, feel odd, feel angry. *ind 1st sg* **nŭmanoongamálsi, nŭman=oongamálsiim**. *conj 3rd sg* **manoon=gamálsiit**. *ptcpl* **meenoongamálsiit**.

**manoongchéetŭyeew** VAI be a crabby person. *ind 1st sg* **nŭmanoongchée=tŭya, nŭmanoongchéetŭyaam**. *conj 3rd sg* **manoongchéetŭyaat**. *ptcpl* **meenoongchéetŭyaat**. *considered impolite.*

**manoongeelúndam** VOTI1A feel cross, feel angry. *ind 1st sg* **nŭmanoongee=lúndam**. *conj 3rd sg* **manoongee=lúndang**. *ptcpl* **meenoongeelúndang**. *moderative reduplication* **maama=noongeelúndam**.

**manoongihtáakwsuw** VAI sound angry, be angry-sounding. *ind 1st sg* **nŭ=manoongihtáakwsi, nŭmanoongih=táakwsiim**. *conj 3rd sg* **manoongih=táakwsiit**. *ptcpl* **meenoongihtáakw=siit**.

**manóongsuw** VAI be angry. *ind 1st sg* **nŭmanóongsi, nŭmanóongsiim**. *conj 3rd sg* **manóongsiit**. *ptcpl* **meenóongsiit**.

**manuchooxúmwush** NA weasel. *pl* **manuchooxúmwshak**. *obv* **ma=nuchooxúmwshal**.

**manútoow** NA spirit. *pl* **manutóowak**. *obv* **manutóowal**.

**maskanahkéeyeew** VII be hard ground. *conj 3rd sg* **maskanahkéeyeek**. *ptcpl* **meeskanahkéeyeek**.

**maskanambíileew** VTA tie s.o. firmly. *ind 1st sg* **nŭmaskanambíilaaw, nŭmaskanambíila**. *ind 3rd sg* **mas=kanambiiláawal**. *ind inv* **nŭmaska=**

**nambíilukw**. *ind I-you* **kŭmaska=nambíilul**. *conj 3rd sg* **maskanam=bíilaat**. *imp* **maskanámbiil**. *ptcpl* **meeskanambíilaat**.

**maskanambíisuw** VAI be tied firmly *(s.t. animate)*. *ind 1st sg* **nŭmaskanam=bíisi**, **nŭmaskanambíisiim**. *conj 3rd sg* **maskanambíisiit**. *ptcpl* **meeska=nambíisiit**.

**maskanambíisuw** VII be tied firmly. *conj 3rd sg* **maskanambíisiik**. *ptcpl* **meeskanambíisiik**.

**maskanámbtoow** VTI2 tie s.t. firmly. *ind 1st sg* **nŭmaskanámbtoon**. *ind 3rd sg* **maskanámbtoon**. *conj 1st sg* **maskanambtáwaan**. *conj 3rd sg* **maskanámbtaakw**. *imp* **maska=námbtool**. *ptcpl* **meeskanámbtaakw**.

**máskaneew** VII be strong, be hard. *conj 3rd sg* **máskaneek**. *ptcpl* **méeska=neek**.

**maskaniilúnjeew** VAI close one's hand(s) tightly. *ind 1st sg* **nŭmaska=niilúnje**, **nŭmaskaniilúnjeem**. *conj 3rd sg* **maskaniilúnjeet**. *imp* **maska=niilúnjeel**. *ptcpl* **meeskaniilúnjeet**.

**maskaniilunjéexiin** VAI have one's hand(s) closed tightly. *ind 1st sg* **nŭmaskaniilunjéexiin**, **nŭmaska=niilunjéexi**. *conj 3rd sg* **maskanii=lunjéexiing**. *ptcpl* **meeskaniilun=jéexiing**.

**maskaniináakwat** VII be strong-looking. *conj 3rd sg* **maskaniináakwahk**. *ptcpl* **meeskaniináakwahk**.

**maskaniináakwsuw** VAI be sturdy looking, be strong looking. *ind 1st sg* **nŭ=maskaniináakwsi**, **nŭmaskaniináa=kwsiim**. *conj 3rd sg* **maskaniináa=kwsiit**. *ptcpl* **meeskaniináakwsiit**.

**maskaniitéeheew** VAI be strong willed, be strong in character; be brave. **Éeskwa néeka maskaniiteehéewu.** 'He's not brave yet (usually said of a young person).' *ind 1st sg* **nŭmaska=niitéeha**, **nŭmaskaniitéehaam**. *conj 3rd sg* **maskaniitéehaat**. *imp* **mas=kaniitéehaal**. *ptcpl* **meeskaniitée=haat**.

**maskaníixiin** VAI be a tight fit *(s.t. animate)*. *ind 1st sg* **nŭmaskaníixiin**, **nŭmaskaníixi**. *conj 3rd sg* **maska=níixiing**. *ptcpl* **meeskaníixiing**.

**maskaníixtoow** VTI2 tighten s.t. *ind 1st sg* **nŭmaskaníixtoon**. *ind 3rd sg* **maskaníixtoon**. *conj 1st sg* **maska=niixtáwaan**. *conj 3rd sg* **maskaníix=taakw**. *imp* **maskaníixtool**. *ptcpl* **meeskaníixtaakw**.

**maskaníixŭmeew** VTA tighten s.t. animate, make s.t. animate tight. *ind 1st sg* **nŭmaskaníixŭmaaw**, **nŭmaska=níixŭma**. *ind 3rd sg* **maskaniixŭ=máawal**. *ind inv* **nŭmaskaníixŭ=mukw**. *ind I-you* **kŭmaskaníixŭmul**. *conj 3rd sg* **maskaníixŭmaat**. *imp* **maskaníixum**. *ptcpl* **meeskaníi=xŭmaat**.

**maskaníixun** VII be a tight fit. *conj 3rd sg* **maskaníixung**. *ptcpl* **meeska=níixung**.

**maskanúneew** VTA hold s.o. firmly. *ind 1st sg* **nŭmaskanúnaaw**, **nŭmaska=núna**. *ind 3rd sg* **maskanunáawal**. *ind inv* **nŭmaskanúnukw**. *ind I-you* **kŭmaskanúnul**. *conj 3rd sg* **maska=núnaat**. *imp* **máskanun**. *ptcpl* **meeskanúnaat**.

**maskanúnum** VTI1B hold s.t. firmly. *ind 1st sg* **nŭmaskanúnŭmun**. *ind 3rd sg* **maskanúnŭmun**. *conj 1st sg* **mas=kanúnŭmaan**. *conj 3rd sg* **maska=núnung**. *imp* **maskanúnih**. *ptcpl* **meeskanúnung**.

**maskanúsuw** VAI be strong; be hard *(to eat, s.t. animate)*. *ind 1st sg* **nŭmas=kanúsi**, **nŭmaskanúsiim**. *conj 3rd sg* **maskanúsiit**. *imp* **maskanúsiil**. *ptcpl* **meeskanúsiit**.

**maskanusŭwáakan** NI strength.

**maskchíhleew** VAI defecate while in motion. *ind 1st sg* **nŭmaskchíhla**,

**nŭmaskchíhlaam**. *conj 3rd sg* **maskchíhlaat**. *imp* **maskchíhlaal**. *ptcpl* **meeskchíhlaat**.

**maskchíhtam** VTI 1A defecate in s.t., defecate on s.t. *ind 1st sg* **nŭmask=chíhtamun**. *ind 3rd sg* **maskchíhta=mun**. *conj 1st sg* **maskchíhtamaan**. *conj 3rd sg* **maskchíhtang**. *imp* **maskchíhtah**. *ptcpl* **meeskchíhtang**.

**máskeekw** NI swamp, pond. *pl* **mas=kéekwal**. *poss* **nŭmaskéekwum**. *loc* **maskéekwung**. *dimin* **maskéekwush**.

**masktápuw** VAI defecate while sitting. *ind 1st sg* **nŭmasktápi**, **nŭmasktáp=iim**. *conj 3rd sg* **masktápiit**. *imp* **masktápiil**. *ptcpl* **meesktápiit**.

**masktihtéeheew** VTA beat s.o. until they defecate. *ind 1st sg* **nŭmasktihtée=haaw**, **nŭmasktihtéeha**. *ind 3rd sg* **masktihteeháawal**. *ind inv* **nŭmask=tihtéehookw**. *ind I-you* **kŭmasktih=téehool**. *conj 3rd sg* **masktihtéehaat**. *imp* **masktíhteeh**. *ptcpl* **meesktih=téehaat**.

**masktóoxweew** VAI defecate while walking. *ind 1st sg* **nŭmasktóoxwe**, **nŭmasktóoxweem**. *conj 3rd sg* **masktóoxweet**. *imp* **masktóoxweel**. *ptcpl* **meesktóoxweet**.

**masktóngwaam** VAI defecate while sleeping. *ind 1st sg* **nŭmasktón=gwaam**. *conj 3rd sg* **masktón=gwaang**. *ptcpl* **meesktóngwaang**.

**másktuw** VAI defecate. *ind 1st sg* **nŭmáskti**, **nŭmásktiim**. *conj 3rd sg* **másktiit**. *imp* **másktiil**. *ptcpl* **méesktiit**.

**máskŭneew** VTA hold s.o. tightly. *ind 1st sg* **nŭmáskŭnaaw**, **nŭmáskŭna**. *ind 3rd sg* **maskŭnáawal**. *ind inv* **nŭmáskŭnukw**. *ind I-you* **kŭmás=kŭnul**. *conj 3rd sg* **máskŭnaat**. *imp* **máskun**. *ptcpl* **méeskanaat**.

**mataachŭmóhkaweew** VTA talk badly about s.o. *ind 1st sg* **nŭmataachŭ=móhkawaaw**, **nŭmataachŭmóh=kawa**. *ind 3rd sg* **màtaachŭmohka=wáawal**. *ind inv* **nŭmataachŭmóh=kaakw**. *ind I-you* **kŭmataachŭmóh=kool**. *conj 3rd sg* **mataachŭmóhka=waat**. *imp* **mataachŭmóhkaw**. *ptcpl* **meetaachŭmóhkawaat**.

**mataakanapóoshiish** NA bad cat. *pl* **mataakanapooshíishak**. *poss* **nŭ=mataakanapooshíishum**. *dimin* **mataakanapooshíishush**. *obv* **mataakanapooshíishal**.

**mataakanáween** PR bad person. *pl* **mataakanawéeniik**. *obv* **mataaka=nawéeniil**.

**mataakanáxum** NA bad dog. *pl* **mataa=kanáxŭmwak**. *dimin* **machaaka=náxŭmwush**. *obv* **mataakanáxŭ=mwal**. *See* **matáxum**.

**mataakanii-** PN bad. **Matáakanii-lunaapéewak.** 'Bad Indians.'

**mataangóomeew** VTA be angry with s.o. *ind 1st sg* **nŭmataangóomaaw**, **nŭmataangóoma**. *ind 3rd sg* **màt=aangoomáawal**. *ind inv* **nŭmataan=góomukw**. *ind I-you* **kŭmataangóo=mul**. *conj 3rd sg* **mataangóomaat**. *imp* **matáangoom**. *ptcpl* **meetaan=góomaat**.

**mataapamúkwat** VII be a dull colour. *conj 3rd sg* **mataapamúkwahk**. *ptcpl* **meetaapamúkwahk**.

**mataapamúkwsuw** VAI be a dull colour. *ind 1st sg* **nŭmataapamúkwsi**, **nŭmataapamúkwsiim**. *conj 3rd sg* **mataapamúkwsiit**. *ptcpl* **meetaapa=múkwsiit**.

**matáapan** VII be an unpleasant morning. *conj 3rd sg* **matáapang**. *ptcpl* **meetáapang**.

**mataapasíhkan** NI poison. *pl* **mataa=pasíhkanal**. *poss* **nŭmataapasíh=kanum**. *loc* **mataapasíhkanung**.

**mataapéewuw** VAI be a thief. *ind 1st sg* **nŭmataapéewi**, **nŭmataapéewiim**. *conj 3rd sg* **mataapéewiit**. *ptcpl* **meetaapéewiit**.

**mataaptóoneew** VAI use bad language, tell a lie, perjure oneself. *ind 1st sg* **nŭmataaptóone**, **nŭmataaptóo=neem**. *conj 3rd sg* **mataaptóoneet**. *imp* **mataaptóoneel**. *ptcpl* **meetaap=tóoneet**.

**matáawsuw** VAI lead a bad life, be a sinner. *ind 1st sg* **nŭmatáawsi**, **nŭmat=áawsiim**. *conj 3rd sg* **matáawsiit**. *ptcpl* **meetáawsiit**.

**mataawsuwáakan** NI sin. *pl* **mataaw=suwáakanal**. *poss* **nŭmataawsuw=áakan**.

**matacháaheew** VTA treat s.o. badly. *ind 1st sg* **nŭmatacháahaaw**, **nŭmata=cháaha**. *ind 3rd sg* **màtachaaháa=wal**. *ind inv* **nŭmatacháahukw**. *ind I-you* **kŭmatacháahul**. *conj 3rd sg* **matacháahaat**. *ptcpl* **meetacháa=haat**.

**mataháapeew** NA bad man, good for nothing man, man of poor character. *pl* **matahaapéewak**. *obv* **matahaa=péewal**.

**matahaapéewuw** VAI be a bad person, be a good for nothing person. *ind 1st sg* **nŭmathaapéewi**, **nŭmathaa=péewiim**. *conj 3rd sg* **matahaapée=wiit**. *ptcpl* **meethaapéewiit**.

**matáhkameew** VII be bad weather. *conj 3rd sg* **matáhkameek**. *ptcpl* **mee=táhkameek**.

**matáhkeew** VAI fight. *ind 1st sg* **nŭ=matáhke**, **nŭmatáhkeem**. *emphatic pl* **matahkhátŭwak**. *conj 3rd sg* **matáhkeet**. *imp* **matáhkeel**. *ptcpl* **meetáhkeet**.

**matahkeewíilŭnuw** NA fighting man, soldier. *pl* **matahkeewiilŭnúwak**. *obv* **matahkeewiilŭnúwal**. *rare*.

**matahkháaleew** VTA fight with s.o. *ind 1st sg* **nŭmatahkháalaaw**, **nŭmat=ahkháala**. *ind 3rd sg* **màtahkhaa=láawal**. *ind inv* **nŭmatahkháalukw**. *ind I-you* **kŭmatahkháalul**. *conj 3rd sg* **matahkháalaat**. *imp* **matáhkhaal**. *ptcpl* **meetahkháalaat**.

**matahóxkweew** NA bad woman, good for nothing woman, woman of poor character. *pl* **matahoxkwéewak**. *obv* **matahoxkwéewal**.

**matahoxkwéewuw** VAI be a bad woman, be a good for nothing woman, be a woman of poor character. *ind 1st sg* **nŭmathoxkwéewi**, **nŭmathoxkwée=wiim**. *conj 3rd sg* **matahoxkwéewiit**. *ptcpl* **meethoxkwéewiit**.

**matáht** NA bow. *pl* **matáhtak**. *poss* **nŭmatáhtum**. *dimin* **macháhchush**. *obv* **matáhtal**.

**matahteenamoohaáleew** VTA make s.o. unhappy. *ind 1st sg* **nŭmatahteena=moohaálaaw**, **nŭmatahteenamoo=háala**. *ind 3rd sg* **màtahteenamoo=haaláawal**. *ind inv* **nŭmatahteena=moohaálukw**. *ind I-you* **kŭmatah=teenamoohaálul**. *conj 3rd sg* **ma=tahteenamoohaálaat**. *imp* **matah=teenamóohaal**. *ptcpl* **meetahteena=moohaálaat**.

**matahteenamóoheew** VAIO make s.o. unhappy. *ind 1st sg* **nŭmatahteena=móoheen**. *ind 3rd sg* **màtahteena=moohéenal**. *conj 3rd sg* **matahtee=namóoheet**. *imp* **matahteenamóo=heel**. *ptcpl* **meetahteenamóoheet**.

**matahtéenamuw** VAI be sad. *ind 1st sg* **nŭmatahtéenami**, **nŭmatahtéena=miim**. *conj 3rd sg* **matahtéenamiit**. *ptcpl* **meetahtéenamiit**.

**matákuw** VAI be badly dressed. *ind 1st sg* **nŭmátakwi**, **nŭmátakwiim**. *conj 3rd sg* **matákwiit**. *ptcpl* **méetakwiit**. *intensive reduplication* **amátakuw**.

**matakŭníimeew** VTA talk badly about s.o. *ind 1st sg* **nŭmatakuníimaaw**, **nŭmatakuníima**. *ind 3rd sg* **màta=kuniimáawal**. *ind inv* **nŭmatakuníi=mukw**. *ind I-you* **kŭmatakuníimul**. *conj 3rd sg* **matakŭníimaat**. *imp* **matákŭniim**. *ptcpl* **meetakuníimaat**.

**matáleew** VTA catch up to s.o., overtake

s.o.; catch up to s.o.'s level. *ind 1st sg* **nŭmátalaaw**, **nŭmátala**. *ind 3rd sg* **màtaláawal**. *ind inv* **nŭmátalukw**. *ind I-you* **kŭmátalul**. *conj 3rd sg* **ma=tálaat**. *imp* **matál**. *ptcpl* **méetalaat**.

**matálakay** NA bad person. *pl* **matala=káyak**. *obv* **matalakáyal**. *considered impolite.*

**matalóoham** VTI 1A make s.t. dull *(using a tool or instrument)*. *ind 1st sg* **nŭmatalóohŭmun**. *ind 3rd sg* **màt=alóohŭmun**. *conj 1st sg* **matalóohŭ=maan**. *conj 3rd sg* **matalóohang**. *imp* **matalóohih**. *ptcpl* **meetalóohang**.

**matalóosuw** VAI be dull, have a dull edge, have a dull point *(s.t. animate)*. *ind 1st sg* **nŭmatalóosi**, **nŭmatalóo=siim**. *conj 3rd sg* **matalóosiit**. *ptcpl* **meetalóosiit**.

**matalóoyeew** VII be dull, have a dull edge, have a dull point. *conj 3rd sg* **matalóoyeek**. *ptcpl* **meetalóoyeek**.

**matalóhkeew** VAI do evil. *ind 1st sg* **nŭmatalóhke**, **nŭmatalóhkeem**. *conj 3rd sg* **matalóhkeet**. *imp* **matalóhkeel**. *ptcpl* **meetalóhkeet**.

**matalohkeewáakan** NI evil. *pl* **matal=ohkeewáakanal**.

**matamalúsuw** VAI feel unwell, be sick. *ind 1st sg* **nŭmatamálsi**, **nŭmata=málsiim**. *conj 3rd sg* **matamalúsiit**. *ptcpl* **meetamálsiit**.

**matántoow** NA devil. *pl* **matantóowak**. *obv* **matantóowal**.

**matantoowíineeng** PC hell. **Matantoo=wíineeng-uch kpáam.** 'You'll go to hell.'

**matapóoshiish** NA bad cat. *pl* **matap=ooshíishak**. *loc* **matapooshíishung**. *dimin* **machapooshíishush**. *obv* **matapooshíishal**.

**matápuw** VAI live common-law. *ind 1st sg* **nŭmátapi**, **nŭmátapiim**. *conj 3rd sg* **matápiit**. *imp* **matápiil**. *ptcpl* **méetapiit**.

**matáskwal** NI weeds. *usually plural*. *loc* **matáskwung**. *See* **machiixáskwal**.

**matásun** NA pipe *(for smoking)*. *pl* **matásŭnak**. *poss* **nŭmátasun**. *loc* **matásŭnung**. *dimin* **macháshŭnush**. *obv* **matásŭnal**.

**matatawáapuw** VAI have poor eyesight, have a hard time seeing. **Kŭmata=tawáapi éet.** 'You might have a hard time seeing.' *ind 1st sg* **nŭmatataw=áapi**, **nŭmatatawáapiim**. *conj 3rd sg* **matatawáapiit**. *ptcpl* **meetataw=áapiit**.

**mataxeepóokwat** VII taste awful. *conj 3rd sg* **mataxeepóokwahk**. *ptcpl* **meetxeepóokwahk**.

**mataxktúneew** VAI be a coward. *ind 1st sg* **nŭmataxktúna**, **nŭmataxktún=aam**. *conj 3rd sg* **mataxktúnaat**. *ptcpl* **meetaxktúnaat**.

**matáxum** NA bad dog. *pl* **matáxŭmwak**. *dimin* **macháxŭmwush**. *obv* **matáx=ŭmwal**. *See* **mataakanáxum**.

nŭ**matchóosum** NAD my no-good friend. *pl* **nŭmatchóosŭmak**. *poss* **nŭmat=chóosum**. *3rd poss* **matchóosŭmal**.

**matéelŭmeew** VTA think poorly of s.o., insult s.o.; abuse s.o. *(including physical abuse)*. *ind 1st sg* **nŭmatéelŭ=maaw**, **nŭmatéelŭma**. *ind 3rd sg* **màteelŭmáawal**. *ind inv* **nŭmatée=lŭmukw**. *ind I-you* **kŭmatéelŭmul**. *conj 3rd sg* **matéelŭmaat**. *imp* **ma=téelum**. *ptcpl* **meetéelŭmaat**.

**mateelŭmúkwsuw** VAI be abused. *ind 1st sg* **nŭmateelŭmúkwsi**, **nŭmatee=lŭmúkwsiim**. *conj 3rd sg* **mateelŭ=múkwsiit**. *ptcpl* **meeteelŭmúkwsiit**.

**mateelúndam** VOTI 1A feel sad, be sad, be in a bad mood. *ind 1st sg* **nŭmat=eelúndam**. *conj 3rd sg* **mateelún=dang**. *ptcpl* **meeteelúndang**.

**mateelúnzuw** VAI think badly of oneself. *ind 1st sg* **nŭmateelúnzi**, **nŭ=mateelúnziim**. *conj 3rd sg* **matee=lúnziit**. *ptcpl* **meeteelúnziit**.

**mateeskáleengw** NA bad Black person.

*pl* **mateeskaléengwak**. *dimin* **ma=cheeshkaléengwush**. *obv* **matees=kaléengwal**.

**matéexiin** VAI land, drop, arrive, arrive at a position by falling *(s.t. animate)*. **Níi mbákshung wáxkiich nŭmatée=xiin.** 'I fell on top of the box.'; **Yéelak matéexiin néenaxkw.** 'The ball landed over there.' *ind 1st sg* **nŭmatée=xiin**, **nŭmatéexi**. *conj 3rd sg* **matée=xiing**. *ptcpl* **meetéexiing**.

**matéexun** VII land, drop, arrive, arrive at a position by falling. **Éeli-matée=xung.** 'Where the road goes.' *conj 3rd sg* **matéexung**. *ptcpl* **meetéexung**.

**matóoshkoosh** NA bad pig. *pl* **ma=tooshkóoshak**. *poss* **nŭmatoosh=kóoshum**. *dimin* **machooshkóo=shush**. *obv* **matooshkóoshal**.

**matóngwaam** VAI have a bad dream. *ind 1st sg* **nŭmatóngwaam**. *conj 3rd sg* **matóngwaang**. *ptcpl* **meetón=gwaang**.

**matuchéesuw** VAI be lumpy in shape, be out of shape *(s.t. animate)*. *ind 1st sg* **nŭmatchéesi**, **nŭmatchéesiim**. *conj 3rd sg* **matuchéesiit**. *ptcpl* **meet=chéesiit**. *moderative reduplication* **maamatuchéesuw**.

**matuchéeyeew** VII be lumpy in shape, be out of shape. *conj 3rd sg* **matuch=éeyeek**. *ptcpl* **meetchéeyeek**. *moderative reduplication* **maamatuch=éeyeew**.

**matulŭnáapeew** NA bad Indian. **Nún há oonjíiyayiin ná matulŭnáape.** 'That's where that bad Indian comes from.' *pl* **matulŭnaapéewak**. *obv* **matulŭnaapéewal**.

**matusíisuw** VAI be homely, be ugly. *ind 1st sg* **nŭmatsíisi**, **nŭmatsíisiim**. *conj 3rd sg* **matusíisiit**. *ptcpl* **meetsíisiit**.

**matúsheew** VTA cut s.t. animate incorrectly. *ind 1st sg* **nŭmátshaaw**, **nŭ=mátsha**. *ind 3rd sg* **màtsháawal**. *ind inv* **nŭmátshookw**. *ind I-you* **kŭmát=shool**. *conj 3rd sg* **matúshaat**. *imp* **matúsh**. *ptcpl* **méetshaat**.

**matúshum** VTI1B cut s.t. incorrectly. *ind 1st sg* **nŭmatshúmun**. *ind 3rd sg* **màtshúmun**. *conj 1st sg* **matúshŭ=maan**. *conj 3rd sg* **matúshung**. *imp* **matúshih**. *ptcpl* **méetshung**.

**matutóoneew** VAI have something wrong with the shape of one's mouth, be always saying bad things about people; have a sore mouth. *ind 1st sg* **nŭmattóone**, **nŭmattóoneem**. *conj 3rd sg* **matutóoneet**. *ptcpl* **meet=tóoneet**.

**matutóonheew** VAI use bad language, curse, swear. *ind 1st sg* **nŭmattóonhe**, **nŭmattóonheem**. *conj 3rd sg* **matut=óonheet**. *imp* **matutóonheel**. *ptcpl* **meettóonheet**. *intensive reduplication* **amattóonheew**.

**maw-** PV go *(to do)*; go *(and do)*. **Alúmsuw há wá máw-alóhke.** 'He's gone to work.'; **Náh peeyayáane ngáta-míitsi laawahkwéewŭnii iiyéeskwa máw-kwtawŭniikée=waan.** 'When I got there I wanted to eat at noontime before I went to the funeral.' *ptcpl* **méew-**. *See* **mawii-**, **mawi-**, **mawu-**.

**mawalóhkeew** VAI go to work, go and work. *ind 1st sg* **nŭmawalóhke**, **nŭmawalóhkeem**. *conj 3rd sg* **mawalóhkeet**. *imp* **mawalóhkeel**. *ptcpl* **meewalóhkeet**.

**mawatáhkeew** VAI go and fight. *ind 1st sg* **nŭmawatáhke**, **nŭmawatáhkeem**. *conj 3rd sg* **mawatáhkeet**. *imp* **mawatáhkeel**. *ptcpl* **meewatáhkeet**.

**mawii-** PV go *(to do)*; go *(and do)*. **Mawíi-shkóoluw.** 'He attends school.', **numáwii-shkóoliim**. *ptcpl* **méewii-**. *See* **mawi-**, **maw-**, **mawu-**.

**mawíikeew** VAI stay overnight. *ind 1st sg* **nŭmawíike**, **nŭmawíikeem**. *conj 3rd sg* **mawíikeet**. *imp* **mawíikeel**. *ptcpl* **meewíikeet**.

**mawíisheew** VAI go and urinate. *ind 1st sg* **nŭmawíishe, nŭmawíisheem.** *conj 3rd sg* **mawíisheet.** *imp* **mawíi=sheel.** *ptcpl* **meewíisheet.**

**mawi-** PV go *(to do)*; go *(and do)*. **Máhta sookŭlaanóokwe nŭmáwi-ch -pŭ=námun éenda-neenaxkhwátiing.** 'If it doesn't rain I'll go to the ball game.' *ptcpl* **méewi-.** *See* **mawii-, maw-, mawu-.**

**mawu-** PV go *(to do)*; go *(and do)*. *informal.* **Nŭmáwu-siikwanámwi ootée=neeng.** 'I spent the spring in town.'; **Nŭmáwu-kamukwkáate.** 'I went to put my legs in the water.' *ptcpl* **méewu-.** *See* **maw-, mawii-, mawi-.**

**mawúkeew** VAI go to dance. *ind 1st sg* **nŭmáwka, nŭmáwkaam.** *conj 3rd sg* **mawúkaat.** *imp* **mawúkaal.** *ptcpl* **méewkaat.**

**maxkáaheew** VAI tell a fib, tell lies. *ind 1st sg* **nŭmaxkáahe, nŭmaxkáa=heem.** *conj 3rd sg* **maxkáaheet.** *imp* **maxkáaheel.** *ptcpl* **meexkáaheet.**

**maxkaaláxkwsiit** NI kidney bean. *pl* **maxkaalaxkwsíital.** *poss* **nŭmax=kaaláxkwsiit.** *loc* **maxkaalaxkwsíi=tung.** *dimin* **maxkaalaxkwshíichush.**

**maxkaalóhkweew** VAI have red hair. *ind 1st sg* **nŭmaxkaalóhkwa, nŭmax=kaalóhkwaam.** *conj 3rd sg* **maxkaa=lóhkwaat.** *ptcpl* **meexkaalóhkwaat.**

**maxkáandpeew** VAI be red headed. *ind 1st sg* **nŭmaxkáandpa, nŭmax=káandpaam.** *conj 3rd sg* **maxkáan=dpaat.** *ptcpl* **meexkáandpaat.**

**maxkaapamúkwat** VII be red coloured. *conj 3rd sg* **maxkaapamúkwahk.** *ptcpl* **meexkaapamúkwahk.** *intensive reduplication* **màmaxkaapa=múkwat.**

**maxkaapamúkwsuw** VAI be red coloured *(s.t. animate)*. *ind 1st sg* **nŭmax=kaapamúkwsi, nŭmaxkaapamúkw=siim.** *conj 3rd sg* **maxkaapamúkw=siit.** *ptcpl* **meexkaapamúkwsiit.**

**maxkáapŭweew** VII be red coloured liquid. *conj 3rd sg* **maxkáapŭweek.** *ptcpl* **meexkáapŭweek.**

**máxkachuw** VAI be red with cold. *ind 1st sg* **nŭmáxkachi, nŭmáxkachiim.** *conj 3rd sg* **máxkachiit.** *ptcpl* **méexkachiit.**

**maxkáhtakw** NI red thread. *pl* **max=káhtakwal.** *poss* **nŭmaxkáhtakwum.** *dimin* **maxkáhchakwush.**

**maxkalákayeew** VAI be a liar, tell a lie. *considered impolite. ind 1st sg* **nŭ=maxkalákaya, nŭmaxkalákayaam.** *conj 3rd sg* **maxkalákayaat.** *ptcpl* **meexkalákayaat.**

**máxkalul** VAI rust *(s.t. animate)*. *ind 1st sg* **nŭmáxkalul.** *conj 3rd sg* **maxka=lúluk.** *ptcpl* **meexkalúluk.**

**máxkalut** VII rust. *conj 3rd sg* **máxka=lihk.** *ptcpl* **méexkalihk.**

**máxkasun** NI brick. *pl* **maxkasúnal.** *poss* **nŭmáxkasun.** *loc* **maxkasún=ung.** *dimin* **maxkashúnush.**

**maxkasunháasuw** VII have red bricks on it *(of houses)*. *conj 3rd sg* **maxka=sunháasiik.** *ptcpl* **meexkasunháa=siik.**

**maxkasuníikaan** NI brick house. *pl* **maxkasuniikáanal.** *poss* **nŭmaxka=suníikaan.** *loc* **maxkasuniikáanung.** *dimin* **maxkashuniikáanush.**

**máxkatun** VII be red with cold. *conj 3rd sg* **máxkatung.** *ptcpl* **méexkatung.**

**maxkcháaleew** VAI have a red nose. *ind 1st sg* **nŭmaxkcháala, nŭmaxk=cháalaam.** *conj 3rd sg* **maxkcháa=laat.** *ptcpl* **meexkcháalaat.**

**maxkchàlíingweew** VAI have a red face. *ind 1st sg* **nŭmaxkchàlíingwa, nŭmaxkchàlíingwaam.** *conj 3rd sg* **maxkchàlíingwaat.** *ptcpl* **meexk=chàlíingwaat.**

**maxkchàliingwéhleew** VAI blush. *ind 1st sg* **nŭmaxkchàliingwéhla, nŭmaxkchàliingwéhlaam.** *conj 3rd sg* **maxkchàliingwéhlaat.** *ptcpl*

**meexkchàliingwéhlaat**.
**maxkcháseew** VTA dye s.t. animate red; brown s.t. animate. *ind 1st sg* **nŭmax=kchásaaw**, **nŭmaxkchása**. *ind 3rd sg* **maxkchasáawal**. *ind inv* **nŭmaxk=chásookw**. *ind I-you* **kŭmaxk=chásool**. *conj 3rd sg* **maxkchásaat**. *imp* **máxkchas**. *ptcpl* **meexkchásaat**.
**maxkchásum** VTI 1B dye s.t. red; brown s.t. *(of meat)*. *ind 1st sg* **nŭmaxk=chásŭmun**. *ind 3rd sg* **maxkchás=ŭmun**. *conj 1st sg* **maxkchásŭmaan**. *conj 3rd sg* **maxkchásung**. *imp* **maxkchásih**. *ptcpl* **meexkchásung**.
**maxkchásuw** VAI be dyed red, turn red, burn red *(s.t. animate)*; be red from heat, get a sunburn, be browned *(s.t. animate)*. *ind 1st sg* **nŭmaxkchási**, **nŭmaxkchásiim**. *conj 3rd sg* **maxkchásiit**. *ptcpl* **meexkchásiit**.
**maxkcháteew** VII be dyed red, turn red; be red from heat, be browned *(of meat)*. *conj 3rd sg* **maxkcháteek**. *ptcpl* **meexkcháteek**.
**máxkeew** VII be red. *conj 3rd sg* **máx=keek**. *ptcpl* **méexkeek**.
**maxkeekháasuw** VAI be marked red, have red stripes *(s.t. animate)*. *ind 1st sg* **nŭmaxkeekháasi**, **nŭmaxkeek=háasiim**. *conj 3rd sg* **maxkeekháa=siit**. *ptcpl* **meexkeekháasiit**.
**maxkeekháasuw** VII be marked red, have red stripes. *conj 3rd sg* **maxk=eekháasiik**. *ptcpl* **maxkeekháasiik**. *intensive reduplication* **amaxkeek=háasuw**.
**maxkéetkweek** NA beet. *pl* **maxkeet=kwéekak**. *poss* **nŭmaxkeetkwée=kum**. *obv* **maxkeetkwéekal**.
**maxkeewehlatíikan** NI flag. *pl* **max=keewehlatíikanal**. *rare*.
**maxkii-** PN red. **Máxkii-aníixan.** 'Red shoelace'
**maxkii-** PV red. **Nŭmáxkii-shóohŭmun.** 'I painted it red.' *ptcpl* **méexkii-**.
**maxkíingweew** VAI have a red face. *ind 1st sg* **nŭmaxkíingwa**, **nŭmaxkíin=gwaam**. *conj 3rd sg* **maxkíingwaat**. *ptcpl* **meexkíingwaat**.
**maxkíhleew** VAI have measles, have scarlet fever, turn red. *ind 1st sg* **nŭ=maxkíhla**, **nŭmaxkíhlaam**. *conj 3rd sg* **maxkíhlaat**. *ptcpl* **meexkíhlaat**.
**maxkíhleew** VII turn red. *conj 3rd sg* **maxkíhlaak**. *ptcpl* **meexkíhlaak**.
**máxksuw** VAI be red *(s.t. animate)*. *ind 1st sg* **nŭmáxksi**, **nŭmáxksiim**. *conj 3rd sg* **máxksiit**. *ptcpl* **méexksiit**.
**maxksútam** VTI 1A don't believe s.t., disbelieve s.t. *ind 1st sg* **nŭmaxksút=amun**. *ind 3rd sg* **maxksútamun**. *conj 1st sg* **maxksútamaan**. *conj 3rd sg* **maxksútang**. *ptcpl* **meexksútang**.
**maxksútaweew** VTA don't believe s.o., disbelieve s.o. *ind 1st sg* **nŭmaxks=útawaaw**, **nŭmaxksútawa**. *ind 3rd sg* **maxksutawáawal**. *ind inv* **nŭ=maxksútaakw**. *ind I-you* **kŭmaxk=sútool**. *conj 3rd sg* **maxksútawaat**. *ptcpl* **meexksútawaat**.
**maxkshéengweew** VAI have a red face. *ind 1st sg* **nŭmaxkshéengwe**, **nŭ=maxkshéengweem**. *conj 3rd sg* **maxkshéengweet**. *ptcpl* **meexkshée=ngweet**. *intensive reduplication* **mah=maxkshéengweew**. *See* **maxkshéen=gweew**.
**maxkshéengweew** VAI have red eyes, blush, have a red face. *ind 1st sg* **nŭmaxkshéengwa**, **nŭmaxkshéen=gwaam**. *conj 3rd sg* **maxkshéen=gwaat**. *ptcpl* **maxkshéengwaat**. *See* **maxkshéengweew**.
**maxksheetóoneew** VAI have red lips. *ind 1st sg* **nŭmaxksheetóona**, **nŭmaxk=sheetóonaam**. *conj 3rd sg* **maxk=sheetóonaat**. *ptcpl* **meexkshee=tóonaat**.
**maxktúyeew** VAI tell a lie. *ind 1st sg* **nŭmaxktúya**, **nŭmaxktúyaam**. *conj 3rd sg* **maxktúyaat**. *ptcpl* **meexk=túyaat**. *considered impolite*.

**maxkŭléexiin** VAI be a reddish colour, have a red tinge to it *(s.t. animate)*. *ind 1st sg* **nŭmaxkŭléexiin, nŭmax=kŭléexi**. *conj 3rd sg* **maxkŭléexiing**. *ptcpl* **meexkŭléexiing**.

**maxkŭléexun** VII be a reddish colour, have a red tinge to it. *conj 3rd sg* **max=kŭléexung**. *ptcpl* **meexkŭléexung**.

**máxkw** NA bear. *pl* **máxkwak**. *poss* **nŭmáxkwum**. *dimin* **máxkwush**. *obv* **máxkwal**.

**mayáat** PC one. **Mayáat paxkshiíkan.** 'One knife.'

**mayaawéelŭmeew** VTA be certain about s.o.; have one's mind made up about s.o. *ind 1st sg* **nŭmayaawéelŭmaaw, nŭmayaawéelŭma**. *ind 3rd sg* **mày=aaweelŭmáawal**. *ind inv* **nŭmayaa=wéelŭmukw**. *ind I-you* **kŭmayaa=wéelŭmul**. *conj 3rd sg* **mayaawéelŭ=maat**. *imp* **mayaawéelum**. *ptcpl* **meeyaawéelŭmaat**.

**mayaaweelúndam** VOTI1A be certain, be sure, have one's mind made up. **Kwáy nŭmayaaweelúndam máh há péewu Lyle.** 'Now I'm sure that Lyle's not coming home.'; **Nŭmayaaweelún=dam katá-sóokŭlaan.** 'I'm sure that it's going to rain.' *ind 1st sg* **numay=aaweelúndam**. *conj 3rd sg* **mayaa=weelúndang**. *ptcpl* **meeyaawee=lúndang**.

**mayáawii** PC true, real. **Mayáawii ee=shíinziit.** 'His real name.'; **Mayáawii áanay.** 'The main road.'

**mayaawíixiin** VAI be in order, lie correctly, be lined up straight *(s.t. animate)*; be the main one, be the top person. *ind 1st sg* **nŭmayaawíixiin, nŭmayaawíixi**. *conj 3rd sg* **mayaa=wíixiing**. *ptcpl* **meeyaawíixiing**.

**mayaawíixtoow** VTI2 place s.t. correctly, make s.t. be correctly arranged, straighten s.t. up. *ind 1st sg* **nŭmay=aawíixtoon**. *ind 3rd sg* **màyaawíix=toon**. *conj 1st sg* **mayaawiixtáwaan**. *conj 3rd sg* **mayaawíixtaakw**. *imp* **mayaawíixtool**. *ptcpl* **meeyaawíix=taakw**.

**mayaawíixŭmeew** VTA place s.o. correctly, make s.o. be correctly arranged, straighten s.o. up, arrange s.o. correctly. *ind 1st sg* **nŭmayaawíixŭ=maaw, nŭmayaawíixŭma**. *ind 3rd sg* **màyaawiixŭmáawal**. *ind inv* **nŭ=mayaawíixŭmukw**. *ind I-you* **kŭ=mayaawíixŭmul**. *conj 3rd sg* **ma=yaawíixŭmaat**. *imp* **mayaawíixum**. *ptcpl* **meeyaawíixŭmaat**.

**mayaawíixun** VII be even, be in order, lie correctly. *conj 3rd sg* **mayaawíi=xung**. *ptcpl* **meeyaawíixung**.

**mayaawíhleew** VAI straighten out, go straight; go quickly in the right direction, drive correctly. *ind 1st sg* **nŭ=mayaawíhla, nŭmayaawíhlaam**. *conj 3rd sg* **mayaawíhlaat**. *imp* **ma=yaawíhlaal**. *ptcpl* **meeyaawíhlaat**.

**mayáawsuw** VAI be one, be one of them *(s.t. animate)*. **Mayáawsuw nehna=yóongus.** 'There is one horse.' *ind 1st sg* **nŭmayáawsi, nŭmayáawsiim**. *conj 3rd sg* **mayáawsiit**. *ptcpl* **mee=yáawsiit**.

**mayáawŭneew** VTA straighten s.o. out. *ind 1st sg* **nŭmayáawŭnaaw, nŭ=mayáawŭna**. *ind 3rd sg* **màyaawŭ=náawal**. *ind inv* **nŭmayáawŭnukw**. *ind I-you* **kŭmayáawŭnul**. *conj 3rd sg* **mayáawŭnaat**. *imp* **mayáawun**. *ptcpl* **meeyáawŭnaat**.

**mayaawŭnáxkeew** VAI be right-handed. *ind 1st sg* **nŭmayaawŭnáxka, nŭ=mayaawŭnáxkaam**. *conj 3rd sg* **mayaawŭnáxkaat**. *ptcpl* **meeyaa=wŭnáxkaat**.

**mayáawŭnum** VTI1B straighten s.t. out. *ind 1st sg* **nŭmayaawŭnúmun**. *ind 3rd sg* **màyaawŭnúmun**. *conj 1st sg* **mayaawŭnúmaan**. *conj 3rd sg* **mayáawŭnung**. *imp* **mayáawŭnih**. *ptcpl* **meeyáawŭnung**.

**mayakawéeheew** VAIO waste s.t. **Màm=ayakaweehéenal ahtamoombíilal.** 'He's using the car for no good reason.' *ind 1st sg* **nŭmayakawéeheen**. *ind 3rd sg* **mayakawéeheen**. *conj 3rd sg* **mayakawéeheet**. *ptcpl* **meeya=kawéeheet**. *intensive reduplication* **màmayakawéeheen**.

**mayakíhtoow** VTI2 waste s.t. *ind 1st sg* **nŭmayakíhtoon**. *ind 3rd sg* **màya=kíhtoon**. *conj 1st sg* **mayakíhtawaan**. *conj 3rd sg* **mayakíhtaakw**. *imp* **mayakíhtool**. *ptcpl* **meeyakíhtaakw**.

**mayáksuw** VAI be wasteful. *ind 1st sg* **nŭmayakúsi, nŭmayakúsiim**. *conj 3rd sg* **mayáksiit**. *ptcpl* **meeyakúsiit**. *intensive reduplication* **amayakúsuw**.

**mayaníilŭnuw** VAI be lonely. *ind 1st sg* **nŭmayaníilŭni, nŭmayaníilŭniim**. *conj 3rd sg* **mayaníilŭniit**. *ptcpl* **meeyaníilŭniit**.

**mayaníixkaleew** VTA leave s.o., leave s.o. behind alone, leave s.o. behind and lonely. *ind 1st sg* **nŭmayaníix=kalaaw, nŭmayaníixkala**. *ind 3rd sg* **màyaniixkaláawal**. *ind inv* **nŭmay=aníixkalukw**. *ind I-you* **kŭmaya=níixkalul**. *conj 3rd sg* **mayaníixka=laat**. *imp* **mayaníixkal**. *ptcpl* **meeya=níixkalaat**.

**mbaakíihuw** VAI be balky, refuse to do something. *ind 1st sg* **nùpaakíihi, nùpaakíihiim**. *conj 3rd sg* **mbaakíi=hiit**. *ptcpl* **neepaakíihiit**. *From English* balky.

**mbákii** NA buggy. *pl* **mbakíihak**. *poss* **nùpàkíihum**. *loc* **mbakíihung**. *dimin* **mbakíihush**. *obv* **mbakíihal**. *From English* buggy.

**mbakiihámeew** VAI drive a buggy. *ind 1st sg* **nùpàkiiháma, nùpàkiihám=aam**. *conj 3rd sg* **mbakiihámaat**. *imp* **mbakiihámaal**. *ptcpl* **neepàkii=hámaat**. *From English* buggy.

**mbáks** NI box. *pl* **mbáksal**. *poss* **nùpák=sum**. *loc* **mbáksung**. *dimin* **mbák=shush**. *See* **mbáksh**. *From English* box.

**mbáksh** NI box. *pl* **mbákshal**. *poss* **nùpákshum**. *loc* **mbákshung**. *dimin* **mbákshush**. *See* **mbáks**. *From English* box.

**mbálun** NA barrel. *pl* **mbálŭnak**. *poss* **nùpálun**. *loc* **mbálŭnung**. *dimin* **mbálŭnush**. *obv* **mbálŭnal**. *From English* barrel.

**mbáypul** NA Bible. *pl* **mbáypŭlak**. *poss* **nùpáypul**. *loc* **mbáypŭlung**. *dimin* **mbáypŭlush**. *obv* **mbáypŭlal**. *From English* Bible.

**mbee-** PN also, as well *(before pronouns)*. **Mbée-níi.** 'Me too.'; **Nál mbée-néeka alúmsuw.** 'Then he left too.'

**mbíisus** NI lake. **Níi ndahíixŭmwi mbíissung talí.** 'I went swimming in the lake.' *pl* **mbíissal**. *loc* **mbíissung**.

**mbíl** NA Bill *(man's name)*. *obv* **mbílal**. *From English* Bill.

**mbochŭlanzhíikan** NI butcher's knife. *pl* **mbochŭlanzhíikanal**. *poss* **nùp=òchŭlanzhíikan**. *loc* **mbochŭlan=zhíikanung**. *dimin* **mbochŭlanzhíi=kanush**. *root from English.*

**mbótus** NI boot. *pl* **mbótsal**. *poss* **nùp=ótus, nùpótsum**. *loc* **mbótsung**. *dimin* **mbóch'shush**. *From English* boot.

**mbuwáakan** NI death. *poss* **nùpŭwáa=kan**.

**mbúy** NI water. *loc* **mbíing**.

**mbuyíhleew** VII be water flowing; have water form *(as on sour milk)*. *conj 3rd sg* **mbuyíhlaak**. *ptcpl* **neepŭyíh=laak**. *See* **nanpíhleew**.

**méek** VAIO give s.t. away. **Éewachu-méek shúlpul.** 'She often gives away some money.' *ind 1st sg* **nŭméekun**. *ind 3rd sg* **méekun**. *conj 3rd sg* **méekuk**. *imp* **méekih**. *ptcpl* **méekuk**.

**méelameew** VTA beat s.o. in a race, beat s.o. in a competition. *ind 1st sg* **nŭ=**

**méelamaaw**, **nŭméelama**. *ind 3rd sg* **meelamáawal**. *ind inv* **nŭméela=mukw**. *ind I-you* **kŭméelamul**. *conj 3rd sg* **méelamaat**. *imp* **méelam**. *ptcpl* **méelamaat**.

**meelawíiheew** VTA play with s.o. *ind 1st sg* **nŭmeelawíihaaw**, **nŭmeelawíiha**. *ind 3rd sg* **meelawiiháawal**. *ind inv* **nŭmeelawíihukw**. *ind I-you* **kŭmee=lawíihul**. *conj 3rd sg* **meelawíihaat**. *imp* **méelawiih**. *ptcpl* **meelawíihaat**. *See* **meelawusóomeew**.

**meelawíhtoow** VTI2 play with s.t. *ind 1st sg* **nŭmeelawíhtoon**. *ind 3rd sg* **meelawíhtoon**. *conj 1st sg* **meela=wíhtawaan**. *conj 3rd sg* **meelawíh=taakw**. *imp* **meelawíhtool**. *ptcpl* **meelawíhtaakw**.

**meelawusóomeew** VTA play with s.o. *ind 1st sg* **nŭmeelawusóomaaw**, **nŭmeelawusóoma**. *ind 3rd sg* **mee=lawusoomáawal**. *ind inv* **nŭmeela=wusóomukw**. *ind I-you* **kŭmeela=wusóomul**. *conj 3rd sg* **meelawus=óomaat**. *imp* **meelawúsoom**. *ptcpl* **meelawusóomaat**. *See* **meela=wíiheew**.

**meelawúsuw** VAI play. *ind 1st sg* **nŭ=meelawúsi**, **nŭmeelawúsiim**. *conj 3rd sg* **meelawúsiit**. *imp* **meelawúsiil**. *ptcpl* **meelawúsiit**.

**méeliis** NA Mary. *dimin* **meelíishush**. *obv* **meelíisal**. *From English* Mary.

**meemaxkóhkwees** NA red-headed woodpecker. *pl* **meemaxkohkwéesak**. *obv* **meemaxkohkwéesal**.

**meemeekshéewakw** NI mutton. *pl* **meemeekshéewakwal**.

**meeméekush** NA sheep. *pl* **meeméek=shak**. *dimin* **meeméekshush**. *obv* **meeméekshal**.

**meemeelandawéewak** VAI race, take part in a race. *usually plural*. *ind 1st pl* **nŭmeemeelandawéhna**. *conj 3rd sg* **meemeelandawéhtiit**. *imp* **mee=meelándaweekw**. *ptcpl* **meemee=landawéhtiit**.

**meemeexksíiteew** VAI be barefooted. *ind 1st sg* **nŭmeemeexksíita**, **nŭmee=meexksíitaam**. *conj 3rd sg* **mee=meexksíitaat**. *ptcpl* **meemeexk=síitaat**.

**meemeexksiitéewxeew** VAI walk barefoot. *ind 1st sg* **nŭmeemeexksii=téewxe**, **nŭmeemeexksiitéewxeem**. *conj 3rd sg* **meemeexksiitéewxeet**. *imp* **meemeexksiitéewxeel**. *ptcpl* **meemeexksiitéewxeet**.

**méenaxk** NI fence. *pl* **meenáxkal**. *poss* **nŭmeenáxkum**. *loc* **meenáxkung**. *dimin* **meenáxkush**.

**meenáxkaaxkw** NI fence rail. *pl* **mee=naxkáaxkwal**. *loc* **meenaxkáax=kwung**. *dimin* **meenaxkáaxkwush**.

**meenáxkheew** VAI make a fence. *ind 1st sg* **nŭmeenáxkhe**, **nŭmeenáxkheem**. *conj 3rd sg* **meenáxkheet**. *imp* **meenáxkheel**. *ptcpl* **meenáxkheet**.

**méeneet** NA drunken person, a drunk. *pl* **meenéechiik**. *obv* **meenéechiil**.

**meenéetuw** VAI be drunk, be a drunk. *ind 1st sg* **nŭmeenéeti**, **nŭmeenéetiim**. *conj 3rd sg* **meenéetiit**. *ptcpl* **mee=néetiit**.

**méengweew** NA Oneida Indian. *pl* **meengwéewak**. *obv* **meengwéewal**.

**meengweewíhkeew** VII be a lot of Oneidas; Oneida Town, Ontario. *conj 3rd sg* **meengweewíhkeek**. *ptcpl* **meengweewíhkeek**.

**meengwéexkweew** NA Oneida woman. *pl* **meengweexkwéewak**. *obv* **meen=gweexkwéewal**.

**meexalapóotiis** NA spider. *pl* **meexa=lapootíisak**. *dimin* **meexalapoochíi=shush**. *obv* **meexalapootíisal**.

**méhch** PC now. **Méhch aapalóhkeew.** 'He's returned from working.'; **Méhch há kùsíingwe?** 'Have you washed your face yet?'

**mehchíhkam** VTI1A wear s.t. out. *ind 1st sg* **nŭmehchíhkamun**. *ind 3rd sg*

**mehchíhkamun**. *conj 1st sg* **meh=chíhkamaan**. *conj 3rd sg* **mehchíh=kang**. *imp* **mehchíhkah**. *ptcpl* **meh=chíhkang**.

**mehchíhkaweew** VTA wear s.t. animate out. *ind 1st sg* **nŭmehchíhkawaaw**, **nŭmehchíhkawa**. *ind 3rd sg* **meh=chihkawáawal**. *ind inv* **nŭmehchíh=kaakw**. *ind I-you* **kŭmehchíhkool**. *conj 3rd sg* **mehchíhkawaat**. *imp* **mehchíhkaw**. *ptcpl* **mehchíhkawaat**.

**mehchíhleew** VAI wear out *(s.t. animate)*. *ind 1st sg* **nŭmehchíhla**, **nŭmeh=chíhlaam**. *conj 3rd sg* **mehchíhlaat**. *ptcpl* **mehchíhlaat**.

**mehchíhleew** VII wear out. *conj 3rd sg* **mehchíhlaak**. *ptcpl* **mehchíhlaak**.

**méhchxiish** PC shortly, in a while, in a little while, soon, as soon as. **Méhch=xiish áa mbwahwsúmawa.** 'I'd slap him in the face.'; **Méhchxiish-uch ngiishatúpwi.** 'I'll be done cooking in a little while.' *See* **méhtxii**.

**mehmeelawihtáasiik** NI toy. *pl* **meh=meelawihtaasíikiil**.

**mehmeendawámeew** VTA make up with s.o.; apologize to s.o. *ind 1st sg* **nŭ=mehmeendawámaaw**, **nŭmehmeen=dawáma**. *ind 3rd sg* **mehmeenda=wamáawal**. *ind inv* **nŭmehmeenda=wámukw**. *ind I-you* **kŭmehmeenda=wámul**. *conj 3rd sg* **mehméenda=wamaat**. *imp* **mehméendawam**. *ptcpl* **mehmeendawámaat**.

**mehmeengwéewuw** VAI speak Oneida. *ind 1st sg* **nŭmehmeengwéewi**, **nŭmehmeengwéewiim**. *conj 3rd sg* **mehmeengwéewiit**. *imp* **mehmeen=gwéewiil**. *ptcpl* **mehmeengwéewiit**.

**mehmóonzhŭwees** NA barber. *pl* **meh=moonzhŭwéesak**. *obv* **mehmoon=zhŭwéesal**.

**mehmshúwaleesh** NA peddler. *pl* **meh=mshuwaléeshak**. *obv* **mehmshuwa=léeshal**.

**mehmúndawees** NA person who is never satisfied. *pl* **mehmundawée=sak**. *obv* **mehmundawéesal**.

**méhmuneeng** VII something to drink, a drink. **Méhmŭnéeng míiliil.** 'Give me a drink.' *conj 3rd sg* **méhmŭneeng**

**mehsíhkam** VTI1A wear s.t. out *(of clothing)*. *ind 1st sg* **nŭmehsíhka=mun**. *ind 3rd sg* **mehsíhkamun**. *conj 1st sg* **mehsíhkamaan**. *conj 3rd sg* **mehsíhkang**. *imp* **mehsíhkah**. *ptcpl* **mehsíhkang**.

**mehsíhkaweew** VTA wear s.t. animate out *(of clothing)*. *ind 1st sg* **nŭmeh=síhkawaaw**, **nŭmehsíhkawa**. *ind 3rd sg* **mehsihkawáawal**. *ind inv* **nŭmeh=síhkaakw**. *ind I-you* **kŭmehsíhkool**. *conj 3rd sg* **mehsíhkawaat**. *imp* **mehsíhkaw**. *ptcpl* **mehsíhkawaat**.

**mehtaaptóoneew** VAI be done talking, say all one has to say, run out of things to say. *ind 1st sg* **nŭmehtaap=tóone**, **nŭmehtaaptóoneem**. *conj 3rd sg* **mehtaaptóoneet**. *imp* **mehtaap=tóoneel**. *ptcpl* **mehtaaptóoneet**.

**mehtapáleew** VTA wear s.t. animate out by washing it, wash s.t. animate away, remove s.t. animate by washing; wash s.t. animate completely, wash s.t. animate right out. **Nŭmeh=tapálaaw éenda-leekháasiit.** 'I washed away where the writing was.' *ind 1st sg* **nŭmehtapálaaw**, **nŭmeh=tapála**. *ind 3rd sg* **mehtapaláawal**. *ind inv* **nŭmehtapálukw**. *ind I-you* **kŭmehtapálul**. *conj 3rd sg* **mehta=pálaat**. *imp* **méhtapal**. *ptcpl* **mehtapálaat**.

**mehtapátoow** VTI2 wear s.t. out by washing it; wash s.t. completely, wash s.t. right out, wash s.t. away, remove s.t. by washing. *ind 1st sg* **nŭmehtapát=oon**. *ind 3rd sg* **mehtapátoon**. *conj 1st sg* **mehtapátawaan**. *conj 3rd sg* **mehtapátaakw**. *imp* **mehtapátool**. *ptcpl* **mehtapátaakw**.

**mehtawéeheew** VAIO wear s.t. out. *ind*

*1st sg* **nŭmehtawéeheen**. *ind 3rd sg* **mehtawéeheen**. *conj 3rd sg* **mehta=wéeheet**. *imp* **mehtawéeheel**. *ptcpl* **mehtawéeheet**.

**méhtham** VOTI1A strike out. *ind 1st sg* **numéhtham**. *conj 3rd sg* **méhthang**. *imp* **méhthah**. *ptcpl* **méhthang**. *baseball*.

**méhtseew** VTA burn s.o. up. *ind 1st sg* **nŭméhtsaaw**, **nŭméhtsaaw**. *ind 3rd sg* **mehtsáawal**. *conj 3rd sg* **méhtsaat**. *imp* **méhtus**. *ptcpl* **méhtsaat**.

**méhtsum** VTI1B burn s.t. up. *ind 1st sg* **nŭmehtsúmun**. *ind 3rd sg* **meht=súmun**. *conj 1st sg* **mehtsúmaan**. *conj 3rd sg* **méhtsung**. *imp* **méhtsih**. *ptcpl* **méhtsung**.

**méhtsuw** VAI be burnt up *(s.t. animate)*. *ind 1st sg* **nŭméhtsi**, **nŭméhtsiim**. *conj 3rd sg* **méhtsiit**. *ptcpl* **méhtsiit**.

**méhtsheew** VTA saw up all of s.t. animate, cut up all of s.t. animate. *ind 1st sg* **nŭméhtshaaw**, **nŭméhtsha**. *ind 3rd sg* **mehtsháawal**. *ind inv* **nŭméhtshookw**. *ind I-you* **kŭméht=shool**. *conj 3rd sg* **méhtshaat**. *imp* **méhtush**. *ptcpl* **méhtshaat**.

**mehtshíikeew** VAI cut things up. *ind 1st sg* **nŭmehtshíike**, **nŭmehtshíikeem**. *conj 3rd sg* **mehtshíikeet**. *imp* **mehtshíikeel**. *ptcpl* **mehtshíikeet**.

**méhtshum** VTI1B saw up all of s.t., cut up all of s.t. *ind 1st sg* **nŭmeht=shúmun**. *ind 3rd sg* **mehtshúmun**. *conj 1st sg* **mehtshúmaan**. *conj 3rd sg* **méhtshung**. *imp* **méhtshih**. *ptcpl* **méhtshung**.

**méhtteew** VII be burnt up. *conj 3rd sg* **méhtteek**. *ptcpl* **méhtteek**.

**mehttusíiwu-pehpŭmutóonhees** NA Methodist minister. *pl* **mehttusíiwu-pehpŭmutoonhéesak**. *obv* **mehttus=íiwu-pehpŭmutoonhéesal**. *From English* Methodist.

**méhtxii** PC shortly, in a while, in a little while, soon, as soon as. **Méhtxii ngíish-míitsiin.** 'As soon as I got through eating.'; **Mehtxíiwu-ch páan.** 'He will come in a while.' *See* **méhchxiish**.

**mehtxihkáasuw** VAI come too late. *ind 1st sg* **nŭmehtxihkáasi**, **nŭmehtxih=káasiim**. *conj 3rd sg* **mehtxihkáasiit**. *ptcpl* **mehtxihkáasiit**.

**mehtxíhkaweew** VTA miss s.o., miss meeting s.o. *ind 1st sg* **nŭmehtxíh=kawaaw**, **nŭmehtxíhkawa**. *ind 3rd sg* **mehtxihkawáawal**. *ind inv* **nŭ=mehtxíhkaakw**. *ind I-you* **kŭmeh=txíhkool**. *conj 3rd sg* **mehtxíhka=waat**. *imp* **mehtxíhkaw**. *ptcpl* **mehtxíhkawaat**.

**mehtxíhkeew** VAI come too late, miss an opportunity, miss one's chance. **Kíishi-maawéewiin náh peeyayáa=ne, nŭmehtxíhke.** 'The service was over when I arrived, I came too late.' *ind 1st sg* **nŭmehtxíhke**, **nŭmeh=txíhkeem**. *conj 3rd sg* **mehtxíhkeet**. *ptcpl* **mehtxíhkeet**.

**mhwéew** VTA eat s.t. animate. **Méhch áa ngáta-mhwáaw ná áapŭlush.** 'I ate that apple already.' *ind 1st sg* **nŭmwúhaaw**, **nŭmwúha**. *ind 3rd sg* **mwuháawal**. *ind inv* **nŭmwúhookw**. *ind I-you* **kŭmwúhool**. *conj 3rd sg* **mhwáat**. *imp* **mwúh**. *ptcpl* **mwée=haat**.

**míichuw** VTI3 eat s.t. **Kwíila- kwéek - míichŭwak.** 'They didn't have anything to eat.' *ind 1st sg* **nŭmíichiin**. *ind 3rd sg* **míichiin**. *conj 1st sg* **míichŭyaan**. *conj 3rd sg* **míichiit**. *imp* **míichiil**. *ptcpl* **míichiit**.

**miichŭwáakan** NI food. *poss* **nŭmii=chŭwáakan**.

**míikwan** NA feather. *pl* **míikwanak**. *poss* **nŭmíikwan**. *loc* **míikwanung**. *dimin* **míikwanush**. *obv* **míikwanal**.

**miikwanóowuw** VAI have feathers, have feathers on. **Wéemu táa ndúlu-miikwanóowiin.** 'I'm all covered in feathers.' *ind 1st sg* **nŭmiikwanóowi**, **nŭmiikwanóowiim**. *conj 3rd sg* **miikwanóowiit**. *ptcpl* **miikwanóo=wiit**.

**míikwul** NA crybaby, weakling, coward. *pl* **míikwŭlak**. *dimin* **míikwŭlush**. *obv* **míikwŭlal**.

**míikwŭluw** VAI be a crybaby, be a weakling, be a coward. *ind 1st sg* **nŭmíikwŭli**, **nŭmíikwŭliim**. *conj 3rd sg* **míikwŭliit**. *ptcpl* **míikwŭliit**.

**míileew** VTAO give s.t. to s.o. **Shúlpul nŭmíilaan.** 'I gave him the money.' *ind 1st sg* **nŭmíilaan**. *ind 3rd sg* **míilaan**. *ind inv* **nŭmíilkwun**. *ind I-you* **kŭmíilŭlun**. *conj 3rd sg* **míilaat**. *imp* **míil**. *ptcpl* **míilaat**.

nŭ**miilíhtaakw** NAD my paternal aunt, my father's sister; my cross-aunt. *pl* **numiilihtáakwak**. *3rd poss* **miilih=táakwal**.

**miilkwúsuw** VAI be given *(especially something from heaven)*. *ind 1st sg* **nŭmiilkwúsi**, **nŭmiilkwúsiim**. *conj 3rd sg* **miilkwúsiit**. *ptcpl* **miil=kwúsiit**.

**miiltuwáakan** NI gift. *pl* **miiltuwáa=kanal**. *poss* **nŭmiiltuwáakan**.

**míilŭweew** VAIO give s.o. away to people, give s.t. away to people. *ind 1st sg* **nŭmíilŭween**. *ind 3rd sg* **míilŭ=ween**. *conj 3rd sg* **míiluweet**. *imp* **míilŭweel**. *ptcpl* **míilŭweet**.

**míimiish** NA pigeon. *pl* **miimíishak**. *obv* **miimíishal**.

**míimiiw** NA pigeon, mourning dove. *pl* **miimíiwak**. *obv* **miimíiwal**.

**míingasa** PC better condition, improved condition, better state, improved state. **Míingasa kwáy wŭlú-kpíhle.** 'It's better now, it shuts well (of a door).'; **Míingasa ktáapwi-pá.** 'It's good that you came early.'

**miingasawamálsuw** VAI feel better. *ind 1st sg* **nŭmiingasawamálsi**, **nŭmiin=gasawamálsiim**. *conj 3rd sg* **miin=gasawamálsiit**. *ptcpl* **miingasawa=málsiit**.

**miingasawiináakwsuw** VAI look better *(than before)*. *ind 1st sg* **nŭmiinga=sawiináakwsi**, **nŭmiingasawiináa=kwsiim**. *conj 3rd sg* **miingasawii=náakwsiit**. *ptcpl* **miingasawiináak=wsiit**.

nŭ**míis** NAD my older sister. *pl* **nŭmíisak**. *3rd poss* **míisal**. *dimin* **nŭmíishush**.

**míitsuw** VAI eat. **Ápih nŭmíitsi.** 'I'll eat later.' *ind 1st sg* **nŭmíitsi**, **nŭmíit=siim**. *conj 3rd sg* **míitsiit**. *imp* **míit=siil**. *ptcpl* **míitsiit**.

**miixanáaleew** VTA be ashamed of s.o. *ind 1st sg* **nŭmiixanáalaaw**, **nŭmii=xanáala**. *ind 3rd sg* **miixanaaláawal**. *ind inv* **nŭmiixanáalukw**. *ind I-you* **kŭmiixanáalul**. *conj 3rd sg* **miixa=náalaat**. *imp* **míixanaal**. *ptcpl* **mii=xanáalaat**.

**miixanáatam** VTI 1A be ashamed of s.t. *ind 1st sg* **nŭmiixanáatamun**. *ind 3rd sg* **miixanáatamun**. *conj 1st sg* **miixanáatamaan**. *conj 3rd sg* **mii=xanáatang**. *imp* **miixanáatah**. *ptcpl* **miixanáatang**.

**miixanéelŭmeew** VTA make s.o. feel ashamed. *ind 1st sg* **nŭmiixanéelŭ=maaw**, **nŭmiixanéelŭma**. *ind 3rd sg* **miixaneelŭmáawal**. *ind inv* **nŭmii=xanéelŭmukw**. *ind I-you* **kŭmiixa=néelŭmul**. *conj 3rd sg* **miixanéelŭ=maat**. *imp* **miixanéelum**. *ptcpl* **miixanéelŭmaat**.

**miixaneelúndam** VOTI 1A feel ashamed. *ind 1st sg* **nŭmiixaneelúndam**. *conj 3rd sg* **miixaneelúndang**. *ptcpl* **miixaneelúndang**.

**miixaníiheew** VTA make s.o. ashamed. *ind 1st sg* **nŭmiixaníihaaw**, **nŭmii=xaníiha**. *ind 3rd sg* **miixaniiháawal**. *ind inv* **nŭmiixaníihukw**. *ind I-you* **kŭmiixaníihul**. *conj 3rd sg* **miixa=níihaat**. *imp* **míixaniih**. *ptcpl* **miixa=níihaat**.

**miixaníimeew** VTA make s.o. ashamed by speech, say shameful things to s.o. *ind 1st sg* **nŭmiixaníimaaw**, **nŭmii=xaníima**. *ind 3rd sg* **miixaniimáa=wal**. *ind inv* **nŭmiixaníimukw**. *ind I-you* **kŭmiixaníimul**. *conj 3rd sg* **miixaníimaat**. *imp* **míixaniim**. *ptcpl* **miixaníimaat**.

**miixaniimkwúsuw** VAI be shamed by what someone says. *ind 1st sg* **nŭmiixaniimkwúsi**, **nŭmiixaniim=kwúsiim**. *conj 3rd sg* **miixaniim=kwúsiit**. *ptcpl* **miixaniimkwúsiit**.

**miixaniináakwat** VII look shameful. *conj 3rd sg* **miixaniináakwahk**. *ptcpl* **miixaniináakwahk**.

**miixaniináakwsuw** VAI look shameful. *ind 1st sg* **nŭmiixaniináakwsi**, **nŭmiixaniináakwsiim**. *conj 3rd sg* **miixaniináakwsiit**. *ptcpl* **miixanii=náakwsiit**.

**miixanúsuw** VAI be ashamed. *ind 1st sg* **nŭmiixanúsi**, **nŭmiixanúsiim**. *conj 3rd sg* **miixanúsiit**. *ptcpl* **miixa=núsiit**.

**miixanusŭwáakan** NI shame. *poss* **nŭmiixanusŭwáakan**.

**míixaskwal** NI grass. *usually plural*. *poss* **nŭmiixáskwŭmal**. *loc* **miixás=kwung**. *dimin* **miixáshkwshal**.

**miixaskwíhkeew** VII be a lot of weeds, be a lot of grass. *conj 3rd sg* **miixas=kwíhkeek**. *ptcpl* **miixaskwíhkeek**.

**miixiingwáawan** NA eyelash. *pl* **mii=xiingwáawanal**. *poss* **nŭmiixiin=gwáawan**.

**míhchii** PC in the open. **Míhchii wándak nŭwehlaláawak.** 'I hung the mitts in the open.'

**mihchiitŭyéexiin** VAI have one's back-side exposed, have one's backside sticking out. *ind 1st sg* **nŭmihchiitŭ=yéexiin**, **nŭmihchiitŭyéexi**. *conj 3rd sg* **mihchiitŭyéexiing**. *ptcpl* **mih=chiitŭyéexiing**, **mihchiitŭyéexiit**.

**mihchíixiin** VAI lie down uncovered, lie down exposed, lie down in the open. *ind 1st sg* **nŭmihchíixiin**, **nŭmih=chíixi**. *conj 3rd sg* **mihchíixiing**. *imp* **mihchíixiil**. *ptcpl* **mehchíixiing**.

**mihchiixtáasuw** VAI be uncovered, be exposed to view *(s.t. animate)*. *ind 1st sg* **nŭmihchiixtáasi**, **nŭmih=chiixtáasiim**. *conj 3rd sg* **mihchiix=táasiit**. *ptcpl* **mehchiixtáasiit**.

**mihchiixtáasuw** VII be uncovered, be exposed to view. *conj 3rd sg* **mih=chiixtáasiik**. *ptcpl* **mehchiixtáasiik**.

**mihchiixtáweew** VTAO expose s.t. for s.o.; explain s.t. to s.o. *ind 1st sg* **nŭ=mihchiixtáwaan**. *ind 3rd sg* **mih=chiixtáwaan**. *ind inv* **nŭmihchiix=táakwun**. *ind I-you* **kŭmihchiixtóo=lun**. *conj 3rd sg* **mihchiixtáwaat**. *imp* **mihchíixtaw**. *ptcpl* **mehchiix=táwaat**.

**mihchíixtoow** VTI2 uncover s.t., expose s.t., explain s.t. *ind 1st sg* **nŭmih=chíixtoon**. *ind 3rd sg* **mihchíixtoon**. *conj 1st sg* **mihchiixtáwaan**. *conj 3rd sg* **mihchíixtaakw**. *imp* **mihchíix=tool**. *ptcpl* **mehchíixtaakw**.

**mihchíixŭmeew** VTA uncover s.o., expose s.o., display s.o., cause s.o. to be exposed. *ind 1st sg* **nŭmihchíixŭ=maaw**, **nŭmihchíixŭma**. *ind 3rd sg* **mihchiixŭmáawal**. *ind inv* **nŭmih=chíixŭmukw**. *ind I-you* **kŭmihchíi=xŭmul**. *conj 3rd sg* **mihchíixŭmaat**. *imp* **mihchíixum**. *ptcpl* **mehchíi=xŭmaat**.

**mihchíixun** VII be exposed, be in the open. *conj 3rd sg* **mihchíixung**. *ptcpl* **mehchíixung**.

**mihchíhlaleew** VTA uncover s.o., expose s.o. *ind 1st sg* **nŭmihchíhlalaaw**, **nŭmihchíhlala**. *ind 3rd sg* **mihchih=laláawal**. *ind inv* **nŭmihchíhlalukw**. *ind I-you* **kŭmihchíhlalul**. *conj 3rd sg* **mihchíhlalaat**. *imp* **mihchíhlal**. *ptcpl* **mehchíhlalaat**.

**mihchíhlatoow** VTI2 uncover s.t., expose s.t. *ind 1st sg* **nŭmihchíhlatoon**. *ind 3rd sg* **mihchíhlatoon**. *conj 1st sg* **mihchihlatáwaan**. *conj 3rd sg* **mihchíhlataakw**. *imp* **mihchíh=latool**. *ptcpl* **mehchíhlataakw**.

**mihchíhleew** VAI be found out, be exposed. *ind 1st sg* **nŭmihchíhla, nŭmihchíhlaam**. *conj 3rd sg* **mihchíhlaat**. *ptcpl* **mehchíhlaat**.

**míhchkwshush** NI shrub, bush. *pl* **mihchkwshúshal**. *loc* **mihchkw=shúshung**.

**mihka** PC do reluctantly, be reluctant about doing something; be difficult to do something, be hard to do something. **Míhka nŭmáw-alóhke.** 'I didn't want to go to work (but I did).'; **Míhka mbáskwi.** 'It's hard for me to get up.'

**mihkóomeew** VTA remind s.o., bring something to s.o.'s mind. *ind 1st sg* **nŭmihkóomaaw, nŭmihkóoma**. *ind 3rd sg* **mihkoomáawal**. *ind inv* **nŭ=mihkóomukw**. *ind I-you* **kŭmihkóo=mul**. *conj 3rd sg* **mihkóomaat**. *imp* **míhkoom**. *ptcpl* **mihkóomaat**.

**mihkóhptam** VTI1A recognize the taste of s.t. *ind 1st sg* **nŭmihkohptámun**. *ind 3rd sg* **mihkohptámun**. *conj 1st sg* **mihkohptámaan**. *conj 3rd sg* **mihkóhptang**. *ptcpl* **mihkóhptang**.

**mihkohptámweew** VTA recognize the taste of s.t. animate. *ind 1st sg* **nŭmihkohptámwaaw, nŭmihkohp=támwa**. *ind 3rd sg* **mihkohptàm=wáawal**. *conj 3rd sg* **mihkohp=támwaat**. *ptcpl* **mihkohptámwaat**.

**mihkwchéeneew** VTA feel for s.o., feel s.o. *(using the hands)*. *ind 1st sg* **nŭ=mihkwchéenaaw, nŭmihkwchéena**. *ind 3rd sg* **mihkwcheenáawal**. *ind inv* **nŭmihkwchéenukw**. *ind I-you* **kŭmihkwchéenul**. *conj 3rd sg* **mihkwchéenaat**. *imp* **míhkwcheen**. *ptcpl* **mihkwchéenaat**.

**mihkwchéenum** VTI1B feel for s.t., feel s.t. *(using the hands)*. *ind 1st sg* **nŭ=mihkwchéenŭmun**. *ind 3rd sg* **mihkwchéenŭmun**. *conj 1st sg* **mihkwchéenŭmaan**. *conj 3rd sg* **mihkwchéenung**. *imp* **mihkwchée=nih**. *ptcpl* **mihkwchéenung**.

**mihlóossuw** VAI be an old man. *ind 1st sg* **nŭmihlóossi, nŭmihlóossiim**. *conj 3rd sg* **mihlóossiit**. *ptcpl* **mihlóossiit**.

**mihlóosus** NA old man. *pl* **mihlóossak**. *poss* **nŭmihlóosum**. *3rd poss* **mih=lóosŭmal**. *obv* **mihlóossal**.

**mihmsahtakíhleew** VAI run around, be the 'runaround' type. *ind 1st sg* **nŭ=mihmsahtakíhla, nŭmihmsahta=kíhlaam**. *conj 3rd sg* **mihmsahta=kíhlaat**. *ptcpl* **mihmsahtakíhlaat**.

**mihtáandpeew** VAI be bare headed. *ind 1st sg* **nŭmihtáandpa, nŭmihtáand=paam**. *conj 3rd sg* **mihtáandpaat**. *ptcpl* **mehtáandpaat**.

**mihtaandpéexiin** VAI have one's head exposed, have one's head out in the open. *ind 1st sg* **nŭmihtaandpéexiin, nŭmihtaandpéexi**. *conj 3rd sg* **mih=taandpéexiing**. *ptcpl* **mehtaand=péexiing**.

**mihtaapéhlaleew** VTA hang s.t. animate in the open. *ind 1st sg* **nŭmihtaa=péhlalaaw, nŭmihtaapéhlala**. *ind 3rd sg* **mihtaapehlaláawal**. *ind inv* **nŭmihtaapéhlalukw**. *ind I-you* **kŭmihtaapéhlalul**. *conj 3rd sg* **mihtaapéhlalaat**. *imp* **mihtaapéhlal**. *ptcpl* **mehtaapéhlalaat**.

**mihtaapéhlatoow** VTI2 hang s.t. in the open. *ind 1st sg* **nŭmihtaapéhlatoon**. *ind 3rd sg* **mihtaapéhlatoon**. *conj 1st sg* **mihtaapehlatáwaan**. *conj 3rd sg* **mihtaapéhlataakw**. *imp* **mihtaa=péhlatool**. *ptcpl* **mehtaapéhlataakw**.

**mihtakunóotum** VTI1B explain s.t. *ind 1st sg* **nŭmihtakunóotŭmun**. *ind 3rd sg* **mihtakunóotŭmun**. *conj 1st sg* **mihtakunóotŭmaan**. *conj 3rd sg* **mihtakunóotung**. *imp* **mihtakunóo=**

tih. *ptcpl* **mehtakunóotung**.

**mihtakunootŭmáweew** VTAO explain s.t. to s.o. *ind 1st sg* **nŭmihtakunoo=tŭmáwaan**. *ind 3rd sg* **mihtakunoo=tŭmáwaan**. *ind inv* **nŭmihtakunoo=tŭmáakwun**. *ind I-you* **kŭmihta=kunootŭmóolun**. *conj 3rd sg* **mihta=kunootŭmáwaat**. *imp* **mihtakunóo=tŭmaw**. *ptcpl* **mehtakunootŭ=máwaat**.

**mihtaniikéexiin** VAI have one's teeth exposed. *ind 1st sg* **nŭmihtaniikéexiin**, **nŭmihtaniikéexi**. *conj 3rd sg* **mih=taniikéexiing**. *ptcpl* **mehtanii=kéexiing**.

**míhtapuw** VAI be visible; be born. *ind 1st sg* **nŭmíhtapi**, **nŭmíhtapiim**. *conj 3rd sg* **míhtapiit**. *ptcpl* **méh=tapiit**.

**mihtkaatéexiin** VAI have one's legs showing, have one's legs exposed, have bare legs. *ind 1st sg* **nŭmiht=kaatéexiin**, **nŭmihtkaatéexi**. *conj 3rd sg* **mihtkaatéexiing**. *ptcpl* **mehtkaatéexiing**.

**mihtkwiinóotay** NI basket. *pl* **miht=kwiinóotayal**. *poss* **nŭmihtkwiinóo=tay**. *loc* **mihtkwiinóoteeng**. *dimin* **mihchkwiinóocheesh**.

**mihtkwíhkeew** VII be a lot of trees. *conj 3rd sg* **mihtkwíhkeek**.

**mihtkwunzíhkeew** VII be a lot of bushes. **Éenda-mihtkwunzíhkeek.** 'Where there are a lot of bushes.' *conj 3rd sg* **mihtkwunzíhkeek**.

**míhtkwus** NI stick. *pl* **mihtkwúsal**. *poss* **nŭmihtkwúsum**. *loc* **mihtkwúsung**. *dimin* **mihchkwúshush**.

**mihtpoxkwanéexiin** VAI have one's back exposed, have one's back showing. *ind 1st sg* **nŭmihtpoxkwanéexiin**, **nŭmihtpoxkwanéexi**. *conj 3rd sg* **mihtpoxkwanéexiing**. *ptcpl* **meht=poxkwanéexiing**.

**mihtsiitéexiin** VAI have one's foot exposed, have one's feet showing. *ind 1st sg* **nŭmihtsiitéexiin**, **nŭmihtsii=téexi**. *conj 3rd sg* **mihtsiitéexiing**. *ptcpl* **mehtsiitéexiing**.

**míhtukw** NA tree. *pl* **míhtkwak**. *poss* **nŭmíhtkwum**. *loc* **míhtkwung**. *dimin* **míhchkwush**. *obv* **míhtkwal**.

**mihtŭlúnjeew** VAI have bare hands, have exposed hands. *ind 1st sg* **nŭmihtŭ=lúnja**, **nŭmihtŭlúnjaam**. *conj 3rd sg* **mihtŭlúnjaat**. *ptcpl* **mehtŭlúnjaat**.

**mihtŭlunjéexiin** VAI have bare hands, have no gloves on, have one's hands exposed, have one's hands showing. *ind 1st sg* **nŭmihtŭlunjéexiin**, **nŭ=mihtŭlunjéexi**. *conj 3rd sg* **mihtŭ=lunjéexiing**. *ptcpl* **mehtŭlunjéexiing**.

**mihtŭnáxkeew** VAI have bare hands, have bare arms, have exposed hands, have exposed arms. *ind 1st sg* **nŭmihtŭnáxke**, **nŭmihtŭnáxkeem**. *conj 3rd sg* **mihtŭnáxkeet**. *ptcpl* **mehtŭnáxkeet**.

**mihtŭnaxkéexiin** VAI have one's arms exposed, have bare arms, have one's hands exposed, have bare hands. *ind 1st sg* **nŭmihtŭnaxkéexiin**, **nŭmih=tŭnaxkéexi**. *conj 3rd sg* **mihtŭnax=kéexiing**. *ptcpl* **mehtŭnaxkéexiing**.

**mílalung** PC Melbourne, Ontario. **Héesh mílalung -áhtiit, sóokŭlaan.** 'Every time they go to Melbourne, it's raining.' *From English* Melbourne.

**móokul** NA maul. *pl* **móokŭlak**. *obv* **móokŭlal**. *From Dutch.*

**mookŭlaandpéexiin** VAI get hit on the head with a maul, have a bump on the head. *ind 1st sg* **nŭmookŭlaandpée=xiin**, **nŭmookŭlaandpéexi**. *conj 3rd sg* **mookŭlaandpéexiing**. *ptcpl* **moo=kŭlaandpéexiing**.

**mookŭlihtéeheew** VTA hit s.o. with a maul *(on the head)*. **Ápih nŭmookŭ=lihtéeha.** 'I'm going to hit him with a maul.' *ind 1st sg* **nŭmookŭlihtée=haaw**, **nŭmookŭlihtéeha**. *ind 3rd sg* **mookŭlihteeháawal**. *ind inv* **nŭ=**

**mookŭlihtéehookw**. *ind I-you* **kŭ=mookŭlihtéehool**. *conj 3rd sg* **moo=kŭlihtéehaat**. *imp* **mookŭlíhteeh**. *ptcpl* **mookŭlihtéehaat**.

**moonaalaxkwsíiteew** VAI pull beans, pick beans. *ind 1st sg* **nŭmoonaa=laxkwsíite**, **nŭmoonaalaxkwsíiteem**. *conj 3rd sg* **moonaaláxkwsiit**. *imp* **moonaalaxkwsíiteel**. *ptcpl* **moonaa=laxkwsíiteet**.

**moonaalohkwéhleew** VAI have one's hair fall out. *ind 1st sg* **nŭmoonaa=lohkwéhla**, **nŭmoonaalohkwéh=laam**. *conj 3rd sg* **moonaalohkwéh=laat**. *ptcpl* **moonaalohkwéhlaat**.

**moonáhkeew** NA groundhog. *pl* **moo=nahkéewak**. *obv* **moonahkéewal**.

**moonáhkhookw** VAI get uprooted and fall over *(of trees)*. *ind 1st sg* **nŭ=moonáhkhookw**, *conj 3rd sg* **moo=nahkhóokwuk**. *ptcpl* **moonahk=hóokwuk**.

**moonáskham** VOTI1A be hoeing, hoe things. *ind 1st sg* **numoonáskham**. *conj 3rd sg* **moonáskhang**. *imp* **moonáskhah**. *ptcpl* **moonáskhang**.

**moonáskham** VTI1A hoe s.t. *ind 1st sg* **nŭmoonaskhámun**. *ind 3rd sg* **moo=naskhámun**. *conj 1st sg* **moonask=hámaan**. *conj 3rd sg* **moonáskhang**. *imp* **moonáskhah**. *ptcpl* **moonásk=hang**.

**moonaskhíikeew** VAI be hoeing, hoe things. *ind 1st sg* **nŭmoonaskhíike**, **nŭmoonaskhíikeem**. *conj 3rd sg* **moonaskhíikeet**. *imp* **moonask=híikeel**. *ptcpl* **moonaskhíikeet**.

**móonham** VTI1 dig s.t. up. *ind 1st sg* **nŭmoonhámun**. *ind 3rd sg* **moon=hámun**. *conj 1st sg* **moonhámaan**. *conj 3rd sg* **móonhang**. *imp* **móon=hah**. *ptcpl* **móonhang**.

**móonheew** VTA dig s.o. up. *ind 1st sg* **nŭmóonhaaw**, **nŭmóonha**. *ind 3rd sg* **moonháawal**. *ind inv* **nŭmóon=hookw**. *ind I-you* **kŭmóonhool**. *conj 3rd sg* **móonhaat**. *imp* **móonhaw**. *ptcpl* **móonhaat**.

**moonhíikeew** VAI dig things up. *ind 1st sg* **nŭmoonhíike**, **nŭmoonhíikeem**. *conj 3rd sg* **moonhíikeet**. *imp* **moon=híikeel**. *ptcpl* **moonhíikeet**.

**moonhíhpŭneew** VAI dig up potatoes. *ind 1st sg* **nŭmoonhíhpŭne**, **nŭmoon=híhpŭneem**. *conj 3rd sg* **moonhíh=pŭneet**. *imp* **moonhíhpŭneel**. *ptcpl* **moonhíhpŭneet**.

**móonhookw** VAI be uprooted *(especially of trees)*. *ind 1st sg* **nŭmóonhookw**. *conj 3rd sg* **moonhóokwuk**. *ptcpl* **moonhóokwuk**.

**móonŭneew** VTA pull s.t. animate out *(using the hands)*. *ind 1st sg* **nŭmóo=nŭnaaw**, **nŭmóonŭna**. *ind 3rd sg* **moonŭnáawal**. *ind inv* **nŭmóonŭ=nukw**. *ind I-you* **kŭmóonŭnul**. *conj 3rd sg* **móonŭnaat**. *imp* **móonun**. *ptcpl* **móonŭnaat**.

**móonŭnum** VTI1B pull s.t. out *(using the hands)*. *ind 1st sg* **nŭmoonŭ=númun**. *ind 3rd sg* **moonŭnúmun**. *conj 1st sg* **moonŭnúmaan**. *conj 3rd sg* **móonŭnung**. *imp* **móonŭnih**. *ptcpl* **móonŭnung**.

**móonxookw** VAI be uprooted by the wind. *ind 1st sg* **nŭmóonxookw**. *conj 3rd sg* **moonxóokwuk**. *ptcpl* **moon=xóokwuk**.

**móonzheew** VTA cut s.o.'s hair. *ind 1st sg* **nŭmóonzhaaw**, **nŭmóonzha**. *ind 3rd sg* **moonzháawal**. *ind inv* **nŭ=móonzhookw**. *ind I-you* **kŭmóon=zhool**. *conj 3rd sg* **móonzhaat**. *imp* **móonzh**. *ptcpl* **móonzhaat**.

**moonzháasuw** VAI get one's hair cut. *ind 1st sg* **nŭmoonzháasi**, **nŭmoon=zháasiim**. *conj 3rd sg* **moonzháasiit**. *imp* **moonzháasiil**. *ptcpl* **moonzháa=siit**.

**moonzhihtóonayeew** VAI shave. *ind 1st sg* **nŭmoonzhihtóonaye**, **nŭmoon=zhihtóonayeem**. *conj 3rd sg* **moon=**

zhihtóonayeet. *imp* **moonzhihtóo=nayeel**. *ptcpl* **moonzhihtóonayeet**.

**móonzhuw** VAI shave, be shaving. *ind 1st sg* **nŭmóonzhi, nŭmóonzhiim**. *conj 3rd sg* **móonzhiit**. *imp* **móon=zhiil**. *ptcpl* **móonzhiit**.

**móonzhŭweew** VAI cut people's hair. *ind 1st sg* **nŭmóonzhŭwe, nŭmóon=zhŭweem**. *conj 3rd sg* **móonzhŭ=weet**. *imp* **móonzhŭweel**. *ptcpl* **móonzhŭweet**.

**móos** NA moose. *pl* **móosak**. *poss* **nŭmóosum**. *loc* **móosung**. *dimin* **móoshush**. *obv* **móosal**.

**mooshéandpeew** VAI be bald. *ind 1st sg* **nŭmooshéandpa, nŭmooshéand=paam**. *conj 3rd sg* **mooshéandpaat**. *ptcpl* **mooshéandpaat**. *See* **moosha=káandpeew**.

**mooshakaaméhleew** VAI run naked, run bare. *especially of animals with missing fur*. *ind 1st sg* **nŭmooshakaa=méhla, nŭmooshakaaméhlaam**. *conj 3rd sg* **mooshakaaméhlaat**. *imp* **mooshakaaméhlaal**. *ptcpl* **moosha=kaaméhlaat**.

**mooshakáandpeew** VAI be bald. *ind 1st sg* **nŭmooshakáandpa, nŭmoosha=káandpaam**. *conj 3rd sg* **moosha=káandpaat**. *ptcpl* **mooshakáand=paat**. *See* **mooshéandpeew**.

**móoshakeew** VII be bare, be lacking in fur, be lacking in hair; be lean *(of meat)*. *conj 3rd sg* **móoshakeek**. *ptcpl* **móoshakeek**.

**mooshakíitŭyeew** VAI have no feathers on one's backside. *usually of birds*. *ind 1st sg* **nŭmooshakíitŭya, nŭ=mooshakíitŭyaam**. *conj 3rd sg* **mooshakíitŭyaat**. *ptcpl* **mooshakíi=tŭyaat**.

**mooshakiitŭyéewxeew** VAI walk by with one's backside exposed. *ind 1st sg* **nŭmooshakiitŭyéewxe, nŭmoosha=kiitŭyéewxeem**. *conj 3rd sg* **moo=shakiitŭyéewxeet**. *imp* **mooshakii=tŭyéewxeel**. *ptcpl* **mooshakiitŭ=yéewxeet**.

**mooshakúsuw** VAI be bare, be lacking in fur, be lacking in hair. *ind 1st sg* **nŭmooshakúsi, nŭmooshakúsiim**. *conj 3rd sg* **mooshakúsiit**. *ptcpl* **mooshakúsiit**.

**móoshameew** VTA eat s.t. animate alone, eat s.t. animate with nothing else. *ind 1st sg* **nŭmóoshamaaw, nŭmóoshama**. *ind 3rd sg* **moosha=máawal**. *ind inv* **nŭmóoshamukw**. *ind I-you* **kŭmóoshamul**. *conj 3rd sg* **móoshamaat**. *imp* **móosham**. *ptcpl* **móoshamaat**.

**mooshándam** VTI 1A eat s.t. alone, eat s.t. with nothing else. **Chíi moo=shandamóowi, náxpu-míichiil apwáan.** 'Don't eat it alone, eat it with bread.' *ind 1st sg* **nŭmooshán=damun**. *ind 3rd sg* **mooshándamun**. *conj 1st sg* **mooshándamaan**. *conj 3rd sg* **mooshándang**. *imp* **moo=shándah**. *ptcpl* **mooshándang**. *intensive reduplication* **màmooshán=damun**.

**mooshaníikeew** VAI be toothless, have no teeth. *ind 1st sg* **nŭmooshaníika, nŭmooshaníikaam**. *conj 3rd sg* **mooshaníikaat**. *ptcpl* **moosha=níikaat**.

**mooshéewakw** NI lean meat. *pl* **moo=shéewakwal**. *poss* **nŭmooshéewa=kwum**. *loc* **mooshéewakwung**. *dimin* **mooshéewakwush**.

**móoshkiingw** NA rabbit. *pl* **moosh=kíingwak**. *poss* **nŭmooshkíingwum**. *loc* **mooshkíingwung**. *dimin* **moosh=kíingwush**. *obv* **mooshkíingwal**. *See* **mooshkíingwus**.

**mooshkíingwus** NA rabbit. *pl* **moosh=kíingwsak**. *poss* **nŭmooshkíingw=sum**. *loc* **mooshkíingwsung**. *dimin* **mooshkíingwshush**. *obv* **moosh=kíingwsal**. *See* **móoshkiingw**.

**mooshŭlúnjeew** VAI be empty handed.

*ind 1st sg* **nŭmooshŭlúnja**, **nŭmoo=shŭlúnjaam**. *conj 3rd sg* **mooshŭ=lúnjaat**. *ptcpl* **mooshŭlúnjaat**. *See* **mooshŭlúnjeew**.

**mooshŭlúnjeew** VAI be empty handed. *ind 1st sg* **nŭmooshŭlúnje**, **nŭmoo=shŭlúnjeem**. *conj 3rd sg* **mooshŭ=lúnjeet**. *ptcpl* **mooshŭlúnjeet**. *See* **mooshŭlúnjeew**.

**mooshŭlunjéhleew** VAI go empty handed, go bare handed, don't take anything *(especially to a gathering)*. *ind 1st sg* **nŭmooshŭlunjéhla**, **nŭmoo=shŭlunjéhlaam**. *conj 3rd sg* **moo=shŭlunjéhlaat**. *imp* **mooshŭlun=jéhlaal**. *ptcpl* **mooshŭlunjéhlaat**.

**moowíhleesh** NA dove. *pl* **moowihlée=shak**. *obv* **moowihléeshal**.

**móoxwees** NA white grub. *pl* **mooxwée=sak**. *obv* **mooxwéesal**.

**móoy** NI excrement. *poss* **nŭmóoyum**. *loc* **móoyung**. *See* **mwíichtuy**.

**móoyuw** VAI be covered in excrement. *ind 1st sg* **nŭmóoyi**, **nŭmóoyiim**. *conj 3rd sg* **móoyiit**. *ptcpl* **móoyiit**.

**mohkamíilaan** VII be raining ice. *conj 3rd sg* **mohkamíilaang**. *ptcpl* **mohkamíilaang**.

**móhkamuy** NA ice. *pl* **mohkamúyak**. *loc* **móhkamiing**. *dimin* **móhka=miish**. *obv* **mohkamúyal**.

**mohkamúyuw** VII be icy. *conj 3rd sg* **mohkamúyiik**. *ptcpl* **mohkamúyiik**.

**móhkuw** VAI be bleeding, bleed *(s.t. animate)*. *ind 1st sg* **nŭmóhkwi**. *conj 3rd sg* **móhkwiit**. *ptcpl* **móhkwiit**.

**móhkuw** VII be bleeding, bleed. *conj 3rd sg* **móhkwiik**. *ptcpl* **móhkwiik**.

**móhkw** NI blood. *poss* **nŭmóhkwum**. *loc* **móhkwung**. *dimin* **móhkwush**.

**mohkwáandpeew** VAI have a bloody head. *ind 1st sg* **nŭmohkwáandpa**, **nŭmohkwáandpaam**. *conj 3rd sg* **mohkwáandpaat**. *ptcpl* **mohkw=áandpaat**.

**mohkwahkéeyeew** VII be bloody ground. *conj 3rd sg* **mohkwahkéeyeek**. *ptcpl* **mohkwahkéeyeek**.

**mohkwcháaleew** VAI have a bloody nose. *ind 1st sg* **nŭmohkwcháala**, **nŭ=mohkwcháalaam**. *conj 3rd sg* **mohk=wcháalaat**. *ptcpl* **mohkwcháalaat**.

**mohkwíixiin** VAI be bloody. **Áapchu-mohkwíixiin.** 'He bled to death.' *ind 1st sg* **nŭmohkwíixiin**, **nŭmohkwíi=xi**. *conj 3rd sg* **mohkwíixiing**. *ptcpl* **mohkwíixiing**.

**móngiis** NA monkey. *pl* **mongíisak**. *poss* **nŭmongíisum**. *loc* **mongíisung**. *dimin* **mongíishush**. *obv* **mongíisal**. *From English* monkey.

**mongíisuw** VAI imitate someone's behaviour. *ind 1st sg* **nŭmongíisi**, **nŭ=mongíisiim**. *conj 3rd sg* **mongíisiit**. *imp* **mongíisiil**. *ptcpl* **mongíisiit**. *From English* monkey.

**móxa** PC very. **Móxa wuskiináakwsuw.** 'He looks very young.'; **Móxa wsáamu-xwukíhkwun.** 'It's much too big.'

**móxkam** VTI1A find s.t. *ind 1st sg* **nŭ=móxkamun**. *ind 3rd sg* **móxkamun**. *conj 1st sg* **móxkamaan**. *conj 3rd sg* **móxkang**. *imp* **móxkah**. *ptcpl* **méexkang**.

**móxkaweew** VTA find s.o., find s.t. animate. *ind 1st sg* **nŭmóxkawaaw**, **nŭ=móxkawa**. *ind 3rd sg* **moxkawáa=wal**. *ind inv* **nŭmóxkaakw**. *ind I-you* **kŭmóxkool**. *conj 3rd sg* **móxkawaat**. *imp* **móxkaw**. *ptcpl* **méexkawaat**.

**moxkawúsuw** VAI be stuck *(with a thorn, with a sliver, with a thistle)*. *ind 1st sg* **nŭmoxkawúsi**, **nŭmoxka=wúsiim**. *conj 3rd sg* **moxkawúsiit**. *ptcpl* **meexkawúsiit**.

nŭ**móxoom** NAD my stepfather. *pl* **nŭ=moxóomak**. *3rd poss* **moxóomal**. *dimin* **nŭmoxóomush**.

nŭ**moxóomus** NAD my grandfather. *pl* **nŭmoxóomsak**. *3rd poss* **moxóom=sal**. *dimin* **nŭmoxóomshush**.

nŭ**moxohkwéewsiit** NID my big toe. *pl* **nŭmoxohkweewsíital**. *3rd poss* **moxohkwéewsiit**. *loc* **nŭmoxoh=kweewsíitung**.

nŭ**moxohkwéewŭlunj** NID my thumb. *pl* **nŭmoxohkweewŭlúnjal**. *3rd poss* **moxohkwéewŭlunj**.

**moxŭlunjáawan** NI thumb. *pl* **moxŭ=lunjáawanal**. *poss* **nŭmoxulun=jáawan**. *See* **nŭmoxohkwéewŭlunj**.

nŭ**moxwsiitáawan** NID my big toe. *pl* **nŭmoxwsiitáawanal**. *poss* **mòxw=siitáawan**. *loc* **nŭmoxwsiitáa=wanung**.

**mbuwáatam** VTI 1A die from s.t. *ind 1st sg* **nùpŭwáatamun**. *ind 3rd sg* **wŭnupŭwáatamun**. *conj 1st sg* **mbuwáatamaan**. *conj 3rd sg* **mbuwáatang**. *ptcpl* **neepŭwáatang**.

**msáakchehl** VAI jump about. *ind 1st sg* **nŭmusáakchehl**. *conj 3rd sg* **msaakchéhluk**. *imp* **msaakchéhlih**. *ptcpl* **meesaakchéhluk**.

**msahkéewxeew** VAI travel all over *(mode of transportation unspecified)*. *ind 1st sg* **nŭmusahkéewxe**, **nŭmus=ahkéewxeem**. *conj 3rd sg* **msah=kéewxeet**. *imp* **msahkéewxeel**. *ptcpl* **meesahkéewxeet**.

**msahtakíhleew** VAI run all over. *ind 1st sg* **nŭmusahtakíhla**, **nŭmusahta=kíhlaam**. *conj 3rd sg* **msahtakíhlaat**. *imp* **msahtakíhlaal**. *ptcpl* **meesah=takíhlaat**.

**msakóosuw** VAI climb all over. *ind 1st sg* **nŭmusakóosi**, **nŭmusakóosiim**. *conj 3rd sg* **msakóosiit**. *imp* **msak=óosiil**. *ptcpl* **meesakóosiit**.

**msalóhkeew** VAI work all over. *ind 1st sg* **nŭmusalóhke**, **nŭmusalóhkeem**. *conj 3rd sg* **msalóhkeet**. *imp* **msalóhkeel**. *ptcpl* **meesalóhkeet**.

**mseekhíikeew** VAI write in various places, write all over. *ind 1st sg* **nŭmuseekhíike**, **nŭmuseekhíikeem**. *conj 3rd sg* **mseekhíikeet**. *imp* **mseekhíikeel**. *ptcpl* **meeseekhíikeet**.

**msiikwsíhleew** VAI crawl around, move around. *ind 1st sg* **nŭmusiikwsíhla**, **nŭmusiikwsíhlaam**. *conj 3rd sg* **msiikwsíhlaat**. *imp* **msiikwsíhlaal**. *ptcpl* **meesiikwsíhlaat**.

**msíingw** NA mask, false face mask, scarecrow, someone dressed up with a false face. *pl* **msíingwak**. *loc* **msíingwung**. *dimin* **mshíingwush**. *obv* **msíingwal**.

**msiitŭyéewxeew** VAI go all over, roam with no purpose in mind; throw one's backside about as one goes. *ind 1st sg* **nŭmusiitŭyéewxe**, **nŭmusiitŭyéew=xeem**. *conj 3rd sg* **msiitŭyéewxeet**. *imp* **msiitŭyéewxeel**. *ptcpl* **meesiitŭ=yéewxeet**. *considered impolite*.

**msiitŭyéhleew** VAI roam with no purpose in mind; throw one's behind about as one goes. *ind 1st sg* **nŭmus=iitŭyéhla**, **nŭmusiitŭyéhlaam**. *conj 3rd sg* **msiitŭyéhlaat**. *imp* **msiitŭ=yéhlaal**. *ptcpl* **meesiitŭyéhlaat**. *considered impolite*.

**msíhleew** VAI fly in various directions, drive in various directions, go in various directions, fly, drive. *ind 1st sg* **nŭmusíhla**, **nŭmusíhlaam**. *conj 3rd sg* **msíhlaat**. *imp* **msíhlaal**. *ptcpl* **meesíhlaat**.

**msihtéeheew** VTA knock s.o. around, knock s.o. all over, bounce s.o., hit s.o. various ways. *ind 1st sg* **nŭmus=ihtéehaaw**, **nŭmusihtéeha**. *ind 3rd sg* **musihteeháawal**. *ind inv* **nŭmusihtéehookw**. *ind I-you* **kŭ=musihtéehool**. *conj 3rd sg* **msihtée=haat**. *imp* **msíhteeh**. *ptcpl* **meesih=téehaat**.

**msihtéehum** VTI 1B knock s.t. around, bounce s.t., hit s.t. various ways. *ind 1st sg* **nŭmusihtéehŭmun**. *ind 3rd sg* **musihtéehŭmun**. *conj 1st sg* **msih=téehŭmaan**. *conj 3rd sg* **msihtée=hung**. *imp* **msihtéehih**. *ptcpl*

**meesihtéehung**.

**msihtéexiin** VAI fall all over, bounce around, get hit about. *ind 1st sg* **nŭmusihtéexiin**, **nŭmusihtéexi**. *conj 3rd sg* **msihtéexiing**. *imp* **msihtée=xiil**. *ptcpl* **meesihtéexiing**.

**msóoxweew** VAI travel all over, travel around. *ind 1st sg* **nŭmusóoxwe**, **nŭmusóoxweem**. *conj 3rd sg* **msóo=xweet**. *imp* **msóoxweel**. *ptcpl* **mee=sóoxweet**. *intensive reduplication* **mihmsóoxweew**.

**msu-** PV variously, various places. *informal*. **Msú-líixun.** 'It lies all over.'; **Shúkw ngúmee màmatahkéewak, wáak wá oxkwéesus ngúmee músu-áan, àhalúmsuw.** 'But they were always fighting, and this girl would always go all over, she was always going away.' *ptcpl* **méesu-**. *moderative reduplication* **máamsu-**.

**msú-lápuw** VAI fidget, sit in various ways. *ind 1st sg* **nŭmúsu-lápi**, **nŭmúsu-lápiim**. *conj 3rd sg* **msú-lápiit**. *imp* **msú-lápiil**. *ptcpl* **méesu-lápiit**.

**msúchee** PC hardly, not at all. **Msúchee máh nú léewi.** 'That's not so; no way.'; **Peeyáatu ngúkung wtuláa=wal, "Kwáy máh há njíhnal ngih=kihkŭlooláawu, wáak ngataaláawu msúchee."** 'When he got to my mother's he told her, "Now I'm not going to talk to her anymore and I don't want her at all."'

**msuchee-** PV whole. **Nŭmúschee-ndapwíinak.** 'I cooked them whole.' *ptcpl* **méeschee-**. *See* **msucheewu-**.

**msuchéesuw** VAI be whole, be all in one piece *(s.t. animate)*. **Msuchéesŭwak aapŭlúshak.** 'The apples are whole.' *ind 1st sg* **nŭmuschéesi**, **nŭmus=chéesiim**. *conj 3rd sg* **msuchéesiit**. *ptcpl* **meeschéesiit**.

**msucheewu-** PV whole. **Nŭmuschéewu-sahkaláawak.** 'I boiled them whole.' *ptcpl* **meeschéewu-**. *See* **msuchee-**.

**msuchéeyeew** VII be whole, all in one piece. *conj 3rd sg* **msuchéeyeek**. *ptcpl* **meeschéeyeek**.

**msúneew** VTA rape s.o. **Msúnaaw.** 'She was raped.' *ind 1st sg* **nŭmúsŭnaaw**, **nŭmúsŭna**. *ind 3rd sg* **musŭnáawal**. *ind inv* **nŭmúsŭnukw**. *ind I-you* **kŭmúsŭnul**. *conj 3rd sg* **msúnaat**. *imp* **msún**. *ptcpl* **méesŭnaat**.

**msháaleew** VTA think about s.o., remember s.o. **Awéen éet kŭmusháalukw.** 'Someone must be thinking about you.' *ind 1st sg* **nŭmusháalaaw**, **nŭmusháala**. *ind 3rd sg* **mushaaláa=wal**. *ind inv* **nŭmusháalukw**. *ind I-you* **kŭmusháalul**. *conj 3rd sg* **msháalaat**. *imp* **msháal**. *ptcpl* **meesháalaat**.

**msháatam** VTI 1A think about s.t., remember s.t. *ind 1st sg* **nŭmusháa=tamun**. *ind 3rd sg* **musháatamun**. *conj 1st sg* **msháatamaan**. *conj 3rd sg* **msháatang**. *imp* **msháatah**. *ptcpl* **meesháatang**.

**mshámeew** VTA only eat some of s.t. animate, have a piece of s.t. animate to eat, only eat some of s.t. animate on one's plate. *ind 1st sg* **nŭmúsha=maaw**, **nŭmúshama**. *ind 3rd sg* **mushamáawal**. *ind inv* **nŭmúsha=mukw**. *ind I-you* **kŭmúshamul**. *conj 3rd sg* **mshámaat**. *imp* **mshám**. *ptcpl* **méeshamaat**.

**mshamóoleew** VTA put s.t. animate in a heap, heap s.t. animate up. *object usually plural*. *ind 1st sg* **nŭmusha=mooláawak**. *ind 3rd sg* **mushamoo=láawal**. *ind inv* **nŭmushamóolkook**. *ind I-you* **kŭmushamoolŭlóhmwa**. *conj 3rd sg* **mshamóolaat**. *imp* **mshámool**. *ptcpl* **meeshamóolaat**.

**mshamootíikeew** VAI pile hay up. *ind 1st sg* **nŭmushamootíike**, **nŭmusha=mootíikeem**. *conj 3rd sg* **mshamoo=tíikeet**. *ptcpl* **meeshamootíikeet**.

**mshamóotoow** VTI2 put s.t. in a heap, heap s.t. up. *object usually plural. ind 1st sg* **nŭmushamootóonal**. *ind 3rd sg* **mushamootóonal**. *conj 1st sg* **mshamóotawaan**. *conj 3rd sg* **mshamóotaakw**. *imp* **mshamóotool**. *ptcpl* **meeshamóotaakw**.

**mshámŭwak** VAI be bunched up, be heaped up *(s.t. animate). usually plural. ind 1st pl* **nŭmushamwíhna**. *conj 3rd sg* **mshamwíhtiit**. *ptcpl* **meeshamwíhtiit**.

**mshámŭwal** VII be bunched up, be heaped up. *usually plural. conj 3rd sg* **mshámwiik**. *ptcpl* **meeshamwíikiil**.

**mshándam** VTI1A only eat some of s.t., have a piece of s.t. to eat, only eat part of s.t. on one's plate. *ind 1st sg* **nŭmushándamun**. *ind 3rd sg* **mush=ándamun**. *conj 1st sg* **mshánda=maan**. *conj 3rd sg* **mshándang**. *imp* **mshándah**. *ptcpl* **meeshándang**.

**mshíiheew** VTA transmit an infectious disease to s.o. *ind 1st sg* **nŭmushíi=haaw**, **nŭmushíiha**. *ind 3rd sg* **mush=iiháawal**. *ind inv* **nŭmushíihukw**. *ind I-you* **kŭmushíihul**. *conj 3rd sg* **mshíihaat**. *imp* **mshíih**. *ptcpl* **mee=shíihaat**.

**mshiinaxkéexiin** VAI have one's hands barely touching a surface. **Wéenaa pŭníhleew shùkéhla mshiinaxkée=xiin.** 'He almost fell but he was just hanging on by his fingers.' *ind 1st sg* **nŭmushiinaxkéexiin**, **nŭmushii=naxkéexi**. *conj 3rd sg* **mshiinax=kéexiing**. *imp* **mshiinaxkéexiil**. *ptcpl* **meeshiinaxkéexiing**, **meeshiinax=kéexiit**.

**mshiitŭyéepuw** VAI sit with one's backside barely touching a surface, sit on the edge of something. *ind 1st sg* **nŭmushiitŭyéepi**, **nŭmushiitŭyée=piim**. *conj 3rd sg* **mshiitŭyéepiit**. *imp* **mshiitŭyéepiil**. *ptcpl* **meeshiitŭ=yéepiit**.

**mshíixiin** VAI touch, make contact, be in contact with the ground, be in contact with the floor. *ind 1st sg* **nŭmushíi=xiin**, **nŭmushíixi**. *conj 3rd sg* **mshíi=xiing**. *ptcpl* **meeshíixiing**. *intensive reduplication* **màmshíixiin**.

**mshíixun** VII touch, make contact, be in contact with the ground, be in contact with the floor. **Pŭnaapéhleew wée=naa mshíixun.** 'It's hanging down and it almost touches (the floor).'; **Mshíixŭnool nzíital áhkiing.** 'My feet are touching the floor.' *conj 3rd sg* **mshíixung**. *ptcpl* **meeshíixung**.

**mshúneew** VTA receive s.o., receive s.t. animate. *ind 1st sg* **nŭmúshŭnaaw**, **nŭmúshŭna**. *ind 3rd sg* **mushŭnáa=wal**. *ind inv* **nŭmúshŭnukw**. *ind I-you* **kŭmúshŭnul**. *conj 3rd sg* **mshúnaat**. *imp* **mshún**. *ptcpl* **mée=shŭnaat**.

**mshúnum** VTI1B receive s.t. *ind 1st sg* **nŭmushŭnúmun**. *ind 3rd sg* **mush=ŭnúmun**. *conj 1st sg* **mshúnŭmaan**. *conj 3rd sg* **mshúnung**. *imp* **mshúnih**. *ptcpl* **méeshŭnung**.

**mshusiitéexiin** VAI have one's foot touching down on a surface, have one's foot touching on the floor. *ind 1st sg* **nŭmush'siitéexiin**, **nŭmush'=siitéexi**. *conj 3rd sg* **mshusiitéexiing**. *ptcpl* **meesh'siitéexiing**.

**mtákhweew** VTA cover s.o. up. *ind 1st sg* **nŭmutakwáhaaw**, **nŭmutakwáha**. *ind 3rd sg* **mutakwaháawal**. *ind inv* **nŭmutakwáhookw**. *ind I-you* **kŭ=mutakwáhool**. *conj 3rd sg* **mták=hwaat**. *imp* **mtákwah**. *ptcpl* **meeta=kwáhaat**.

**mtakhwáasuw** VAI be covered up *(s.t. animate). ind 1st sg* **nŭmutakwah=áasi**, **nŭmutakwaháasiim**. *conj 3rd sg* **mtakhwáasiit**. *ptcpl* **meetakwah=áasiit**.

**mtakhwáasuw** VII be covered up. *conj 3rd sg* **mtakhwáasiik**. *ptcpl* **meeta=**

**kwaháasiik**.

**mtákhwam** VTI1A cover s.t. up. *ind 1st sg* **nŭmutakwáhŭmun**. *ind 3rd sg* **mutakwáhŭmun**. *conj 1st sg* **mtak=hwámaan**. *conj 3rd sg* **mtákhwang**. *imp* **mtákhwah**. *ptcpl* **meetakwáh=ang**.

**mŭkíitŭyeew** VAI have a scabby behind. *ind 1st sg* **nŭmukíitŭya**, **nŭmukíitŭ=yaam**. *conj 3rd sg* **mŭkíitŭyaat**. *ptcpl* **meekíitŭyaat**.

**mŭkíhtaneew** VAI have a bloody nose. *ind 1st sg* **nŭmukíhtane**, **nŭmukíh=taneem**. *conj 3rd sg* **mŭkíhtaneet**. *ptcpl* **meekíhtaneet**.

**mŭkóos** NA nail. *pl* **mŭkóosak**. *poss* **nŭmukóosum**. *loc* **mŭkóosung**. *dimin* **mŭkóoshush**. *obv* **mŭkóosal**.

**mŭkúy** NI scab. *pl* **mŭkúyal**. *poss* **nŭmúkuy**.

**mŭkuyáandpeew** VAI have a scabby head, have scabs on one's head. *ind 1st sg* **nŭmukŭyáandpa**, **nŭmukŭ=yáandpaam**. *conj 3rd sg* **mŭkuy=áandpaat**. *ptcpl* **meekŭyáandpaat**.

**mŭkuycháaleew** VAI have a scabby nose, have scabs on one's nose. *ind 1st sg* **nŭmukŭyucháala**, **nŭmukŭ=yucháalaam**. *conj 3rd sg* **mŭkuy=cháaleew**. *ptcpl* **meekŭyucháalaat**.

**mŭkuychàlíingeew** VAI have a scabby face, have scabs on one's face. *ind 1st sg* **nŭmukŭyuchalíingwa**, **nŭmukŭ=yuchalíingwaam**. *conj 3rd sg* **mŭ=kuychàlíingwaat**. *ptcpl* **meekŭ=yuchalíingwaat**.

**mŭkuykáateew** VAI have a scabby leg, have scabs on one's leg. *ind 1st sg* **nŭmukŭyukáata**, **nŭmukŭyukáa=taam**. *conj 3rd sg* **mŭkuykáataat**. *ptcpl* **meekŭyukáataat**.

**mŭkuysíiteew** VAI have a scabby foot, have scabs on one's foot. *ind 1st sg* **nŭmukŭyusíita**, **nŭmukŭyusíitaam**. *conj 3rd sg* **mŭkuysíitaat**. *ptcpl* **meekŭyusíitaat**.

**mŭkúysuw** VAI have a scab, have scabs *(s.t. animate)*. *ind 1st sg* **nŭmukŭyúsi**, **nŭmukŭyúsiim**. *conj 3rd sg* **mŭ=kúysiit**. *ptcpl* **meekŭyúsiit**.

**mŭkuytóoneew** VAI have a scabby mouth, have scabs on one's mouth. *ind 1st sg* **nŭmukŭyutóona**, **nŭ=mukŭyutóonaam**. *conj 3rd sg* **mŭ=kuytóonaat**. *ptcpl* **meekŭyutóonaat**.

**mŭkúyuw** VAI have scabs. *ind 1st sg* **nŭmúkŭyi**, **nŭmúkŭyiim**. *conj 3rd sg* **mŭkúyiit**. *ptcpl* **méekŭyiit**.

**mŭkuyŭnáxkeew** VAI have a scabby hand, have scabs on one's hand, have a scabby arm, have scabs on one's arm. *ind 1st sg* **nŭmukŭyunáxka**, **nŭmukŭyunáxkaam**. *conj 3rd sg* **mŭkuyŭnáxkaat**. *ptcpl* **meekŭyun=áxkaat**.

**mŭláam** VTI3 smell s.t. *(involuntarily)*. *ind 1st sg* **nŭmuláamun**. *ind 3rd sg* **muláamun**. *conj 1st sg* **mŭláamaan**. *conj 3rd sg* **mŭláang**. *ptcpl* **méelaang**.

**mŭláaweew** VTA smell s.o., smell s.t. animate *(involuntarily)*. *ind 1st sg* **nŭmuláawaaw**, **nŭmuláawa**. *ind 3rd sg* **mulaawáawal**. *ind inv* **nŭmuláa=wukw**. *ind I-you* **kŭmuláawul**. *conj 3rd sg* **mŭláawaat**. *ptcpl* **meeláawaat**.

**mŭlakwíhleew** VAI collapse *(s.t. animate)*. *ind 1st sg* **nŭmulakwíhla**, **nŭmulakwíhlaam**. *conj 3rd sg* **mŭlakwíhlaat**. *ptcpl* **meelakwíhlaat**.

**mŭlakwíhleew** VII collapse, cave in. *conj 3rd sg* **mŭlakwíhlaak**. *ptcpl* **meelakwíhlaak**.

**mŭlákwŭnum** VTI1B collapse s.t., tear s.t. down, dismantle s.t. *(using the hands)*. *ind 1st sg* **nŭmulakwúnŭ=mun**. *ind 3rd sg* **mulakwúnŭmun**. *conj 1st sg* **mŭlakwŭnúmaan**. *conj 3rd sg* **mŭlákwŭnung**. *imp* **mŭlák=wŭnih**. *ptcpl* **meelakwúnung**.

**mŭlákwxun** VII be collapsed by the wind. *conj 3rd sg* **mŭlákwxung**. *ptcpl* **meelakwáxung**.

**mŭlándam** VOTI1A throw up, vomit. *ind 1st sg* **nŭmulándam**. *conj 3rd sg* **mŭlándang**. *imp* **mŭlándah**. *ptcpl* **meelándang**. *intensive reduplication* **màmŭlándam**.

**mŭlandamuwiináakwsuw** VAI the way one looks makes someone feel like vomiting, the way one looks makes someone feel like vomiting. *ind 1st sg* **nŭmulandamuwiináakwsi**, **nŭ=mulandamuwiináakwsiim**. *conj 3rd sg* **mŭlandamuwiináakwsiit**. *ptcpl* **meelandamuwiináakwsiit**.

**mŭlánjiiw** VAI-S be left-handed. *ind 1st sg* **nŭmulánji**, **nŭmulánjiim**. *conj 3rd sg* **mŭlánjiit**. *ptcpl* **meelánjiit**. *See* **mŭnánjiiw**.

**mŭleekóonzheew** VAI have a bunch of kids, have a big family. *ind 1st sg* **nŭmuleekóonzhe**, **nŭmuleekóon=zheem**. *conj 3rd sg* **mŭleekóonzheet**. *ptcpl* **meeleekóonzheet**.

**mŭléekuw** VAI multiply; grow as a bunch, grow close together. **Móxa mŭléekuw.** 'It's really multiplied.' *ind 1st pl* **nŭmuleekíhna**. *conj 3rd sg* **mŭléekiit**. *ptcpl* **meeléekiit**.

**mŭleelíingweew** VAI have infected eyes, have pus in one's eyes, have 'sleep' in one's eyes. *ind 1st sg* **nŭmulee=líingwe**, **nŭmuleelíingweem**. *conj 3rd sg* **mŭleelíingweet**. *ptcpl* **meeleelíingweet**.

**mŭléeshiish** NI syrup, molasses. *poss* **nŭmuleeshíishum**. *loc* **mŭleeshíi=shung**. *dimin* **mŭleeshíishush**. *From English* molasses.

**mŭliiháasuw** VAI be infected, have pus in it. *ind 1st sg* **nŭmuliiháasi**, **nŭ=muliiháasiim**. *conj 3rd sg* **mŭliiháa=siit**. *ptcpl* **meeliiháasiit**.

**mŭliiháasuw** VII be infected, have pus in it. *conj 3rd sg* **mŭliiháasiik**. *ptcpl* **meeliiháasiik**.

**mŭliisŭnáaneew** VAI be a crybaby. *ind 1st sg* **nŭmuliisŭnáane**, **nŭmuliisŭ=náaneem**. *conj 3rd sg* **mŭliisŭnáa=neet**. *ptcpl* **meeliisŭnáaneet**.

**mŭlihkáawan** NA pillow, cushion. *pl* **mŭlihkáawanak**. *poss* **nŭmulihkáa=wan**. *loc* **mŭlihkáawanung**. *dimin* **mŭlihkáawanush**. *obv* **mŭlihkáa=wanal**.

**mŭlihkáawan** NI pillow, cushion. *pl* **mŭlihkáawanal**. *poss* **nŭmulihkáa=wan**. *loc* **mŭlihkáawanung**. *dimin* **mŭlihkáawanush**.

**mŭlihkóosuw** VAI use a pillow. *ind 1st sg* **nŭmulihkóosi**, **nŭmulihkóosiim**. *conj 3rd sg* **mŭlihkóosiit**. *imp* **mŭlihkóosiil**. *ptcpl* **meelihkóosiit**.

**mŭlúk** NI milk. *poss* **nŭmúlkum**. *From Dutch.*

**mŭlukáxkook** NA milk snake. *pl* **mŭ=lukaxkóokak**. *obv* **mŭlukaxkóokal**.

**mŭlúy** NI pus. *poss* **nŭmulíihum**.

**mŭluyeelíingweew** VAI have pus in one's eyes, have infected eyes. *ind 1st sg* **nŭmulŭyeelíingwa**, **nŭmulŭyee=líingwaam**. *conj 3rd sg* **mŭluyee=líingwaat**. *ptcpl* **meelŭyeelíingwaat**.

**mŭluyóowuw** VAI be pus-filled, be pussy. *ind 1st sg* **nŭmulŭyóowi**, **nŭ=mulŭyóowiim**. *conj 3rd sg* **mŭluy=óowiit**. *ptcpl* **meelŭyóowiit**.

**mŭluyóowuw** VII be pus-filled, be pussy. *conj 3rd sg* **mŭluyóowiik**. *ptcpl* **meelŭyóowiik**.

**mŭnáheew** VTA give a drink to s.o. *ind 1st sg* **nŭmúnhaaw**, **nŭmúnha**. *ind 3rd sg* **munháawal**. *ind inv* **nŭmún=hookw**. *ind I-you* **kŭmúnhool**. *conj 3rd sg* **mŭnáhaat**. *imp* **mŭnáh**. *ptcpl* **méenhaat**.

**mŭnáhan** NI island. *pl* **mŭnáhŭnal**. *poss* **nŭmúnhan**. *loc* **mŭnáhŭnung**. *dimin* **mŭnáhŭnush**.

**mŭnánjiiw** VAI-S be left-handed. *ind 1st sg* **nŭmunánji**, **nŭmunánjiim**. *conj 3rd sg* **mŭnánjiit**. *ptcpl* **meenánjiit**. *See* **mŭlánjiiw**.

**múndam** VOTI1A grunt, groan. *ind 1st sg*

nŭmúndam. *conj 3rd sg* **múndang**. *imp* **múndah**. *ptcpl* **méendang**. *intensive reduplication* **mihmúndam**.

**mundawámeew** VTA be discontented with s.o. over their actions. *ind 1st sg* **nŭmundawámaaw**, **nŭmunda=wáma**. *ind 3rd sg* **mundawamáawal**. *ind inv* **nŭmundawámukw**. *ind I-you* **kŭmundawámul**. *conj 3rd sg* **mŭn=dawámaat**. *ptcpl* **meendawámaat**.

**múndaweew** VAI moan. *ind 1st sg* **nŭmúndawe**, **nŭmúndaweem**. *conj 3rd sg* **múndaweet**. *imp* **múndaweel**. *ptcpl* **méendaweet**. *intensive reduplication* **mihmúndaweew**.

**mundaweelúndam** VOTI1A be discontented. *ind 1st sg* **nŭmundaweelún=dam**. *conj 3rd sg* **mŭndaweelún=dang**. *ptcpl* **meendaweelúndang**.

**mŭnéew** VAI drink. **Máhta nŭmiimŭ=neewíiwi.** 'I never drink.' *ind 1st sg* **nŭmúne**, **nŭmúneem**. *conj 3rd sg* **mŭnéet**. *imp* **mŭnéel**. *ptcpl* **méeneet**.

**mŭnéew** VAIO drink s.t. *ind 1st sg* **nŭ=múneen**. *ind 3rd sg* **múneen**. *conj 3rd sg* **mŭnéet**. *imp* **mŭnéel**. *ptcpl* **méeneet**.

**mŭneewáakan** NI drinking. **Mŭnee=wáakan-uch kŭníhlkwun.** 'Drinking will kill you.' *poss* **nŭmuneewáa=kan**.

**mŭniikaapawúwak** VAI stand bunched together. *usually plural. ind 1st pl* **nŭmuniikaapawíhna**. *conj 3rd sg* **mŭniikaapawíhtiit**. *imp* **mŭniikáa=pawiikw**. *ptcpl* **meeniikaapawíhtiit**.

**mŭniixíinook** VAI be bunched up together *(s.t. animate). usually plural. ind 1st pl* **nŭmuniixiinóhna**. *conj 3rd sg* **mŭniixiinóhtiit**. *ptcpl* **meeniixii=nóhtiit**.

**mŭníixtoow** VTI2 bunch s.t. up together, put s.t. together in a bunch. *object usually plural. ind 1st sg* **nŭmuniix=tóonal**. *ind 3rd sg* **muniixtóonal**. *conj 1st sg* **mŭniixtáwaan**. *conj 3rd sg* **mŭníixtaakw**. *imp* **mŭníixtool**. *ptcpl* **meeníixtaakw**.

**mŭníixŭmeew** VTA bunch s.o. up together, put s.o. in a bunch. *object usually plural. ind 1st sg* **nŭmuniixŭ=máawak**. *ind 3rd sg* **muniixŭmáa=wal**. *conj 3rd sg* **mŭníixŭmaat**. *imp* **mŭníixum**. *ptcpl* **meeníixŭmaat**.

**mŭníixŭnool** VII be bunched up together. *usually plural. conj 3rd sg* **mŭníixung**. *ptcpl* **meeniixúngiil**.

**múnsiiw** NA Delaware Indian, Munsee Delaware Indian. *pl* **munsíiwak**. *obv* **munsíiwal**. *used at Moraviantown, Ontario for Delawares living at Munceytown, Ontario.*

**múnŭlo** NA Munro *(man's name). obv* **mùnŭlóohal**. *From English* Munro.

**mŭnumohktóonheew** VAI mutter, talk under one's breath. *ind 1st sg* **nŭ=munŭmohktóonhe**, **nŭmunŭmohk=tóonheem**. *conj 3rd sg* **mŭnumohk=tóonheet**. *imp* **mŭnumohktóonheel**. *ptcpl* **meenŭmohktóonheet**.

**múshiin** NI machine, piece of machinery. **Aalŭwíhle nŭmushíinum.** 'My machine won't run.' *pl* **mùshíinal**. *poss* **nŭmushíinum**. *From English* machine.

nŭ**mushúshum** NAD my wife. *pl* **nŭ=mushúshŭmak**. *3rd poss* **mushúsh=ŭmal**. *From English* Mrs.

**mŭtáanheew** VTA bewitch s.o., use medicine to influence s.o. *ind 1st sg* **nŭ=mutáanhaaw**, **nŭmutáanha**. *ind 3rd sg* **mutaanháawal**. *ind inv* **nŭmut=áanhookw**. *ind I-you* **kŭmutáanhool**. *conj 3rd sg* **mŭtáanhaat**. *imp* **mŭtáanhaw**. *ptcpl* **meetáanhaat**.

**mwáakaneew** NA dog. *pl* **mwaakanée=wak**. *poss* **ndálŭmoonz**. *dimin* **mwáakaneesh**. *obv* **mwaakanéewal**.

**mwaakanéewchuy** NI dog excrement. *pl* **mwaakaneewchúyal**.

**mwaakaneewíikaan** NI doghouse. *pl* **mwaakaneewiikáanal**. *loc* **mwaa=**

**kaneewiikáanung**. *dimin* **mwaaka=neewiikáanush**.

**mwíichtuy** NI excrement. *poss* **nŭ=mwíichtuy**. *See* **móoy**.

**mwíitŭyeew** VAI have excrement on one's backside. *ind 1st sg* **nŭmwíitŭ=ya**, **nŭmwíitŭyaam**. *conj 3rd sg* **mwíitŭyaat**. *ptcpl* **mwíitŭyaat**.

**mwiitŭyéewxeew** VAI walk with excrement on one's backside *(indicating a certain attitude)*. *ind 1st sg* **nŭmwii=tŭyéewxe**, **nŭmwiitŭyéewxeem**. *conj 3rd sg* **mwiitŭyéewxeet**. *imp* **mwii=tŭyéewxeel**. *ptcpl* **mwiitŭyéewxeet**.

# N

**naachiichŭwáakaneew** VAI go after food, fetch food. *ind 1st sg* **naachii=chŭwáakane**, **naachiichŭwáaka=neem**. *conj 3rd sg* **naachiichŭwáa=kaneet**. *imp* **naachiichŭwáakaneel**. *ptcpl* **naachiichŭwáakaneet**.

**naachiikwáaleew** VTA fetch s.o. *(using something held in the hand)*. *ind 1st sg* **naachiikwáalaaw**, **naachiikwáa=la**. *ind 3rd sg* **wŭnaachiikwaaláa=wal**. *ind inv* **naachiikwáalukw**. *ind I-you* **kŭnaachiikwáalul**. *conj 3rd sg* **naachiikwáalaat**. *imp* **naachíikwaal**. *ptcpl* **naachiikwáalaat**.

**naachíikwam** VTI1A fetch s.t. *(using something held in the hand)*. *ind 1st sg* **naachíikwamun**. *ind 3rd sg* **wŭ=naachíikwamun**. *conj 1st sg* **naa=chíikwamaan**. *conj 3rd sg* **naa=chíikwang**. *imp* **naachíikwah**. *ptcpl* **naachíikwang**.

**naachíikwsuw** VAIO crawl to fetch s.o., crawl after s.o. *ind 1st sg* **naachíik=wsiin**. *ind 3rd sg* **wŭnaachíikwsiin**. *conj 3rd sg* **naachíikwsiit**. *imp* **naachíikwsiil**. *ptcpl* **naachíikwsiit**.

**naachiináxkeew** VAIO reach out one's hand to get s.t. *ind 1st sg* **naachii=náxkeen**. *ind 3rd sg* **wŭnaachiináx=keen**. *conj 3rd sg* **naachiináxkeet**. *imp* **naachiináxkeel**. *ptcpl* **naachii=náxkeet**.

**naachiinaxkéeneew** VTA reach out one's hand to get s.o. *ind 1st sg* **naachii=naxkéenaaw**, **naachiinaxkéena**. *ind 3rd sg* **wŭnaachiinaxkeenáawal**. *ind inv* **naachiinaxkéenukw**. *ind I-you* **kŭnaachiinaxkéenul**. *conj 3rd sg* **naachiinaxkéenaat**. *imp* **naachii=náxkeen**. *ptcpl* **naachiinaxkéenaat**.

**naachiipáhtoow** VTI2 run to fetch s.t., fetch s.t. *ind 1st sg* **naachiipáhtoon**. *ind 3rd sg* **wŭnaachiipáhtoon**. *conj 1st sg* **naachiipáhtawaan**. *conj 3rd sg* **naachiipáhtaakw**. *imp* **naachii=páhtool**. *ptcpl* **naachiipáhtaakw**.

**naachíipheew** VTA run to fetch s.o., fetch s.o. *ind 1st sg* **naachíiphaaw**, **naachíipha**. *ind 3rd sg* **wŭnaachiip=háawal**. *ind inv* **naachíiphukw**. *ind I-you* **kŭnaachíiphul**. *conj 3rd sg* **naachíiphaat**. *imp* **naachíipah**. *ptcpl* **naachíiphaat**.

**naachŭwáleew** VAI go to fetch a load. *ind 1st sg* **naachŭwále**, **naachŭwál=eem**. *conj 3rd sg* **naachŭwáleet**. *imp* **naachŭwáleel**. *ptcpl* **naachŭwáleet**.

**naachŭwáleew** VAIO go to fetch a load of s.t., fetch and carry a load of something on one's back. *ind 1st sg* **naa=chŭwáleen**. *ind 3rd sg* **wŭnaachŭ=wáleen**. *conj 3rd sg* **naachŭwáleet**. *imp* **naachŭwáleel**. *ptcpl* **naachŭ=wáleet**.

**náahii** PC Moraviantown, Ontario. *'downstream.'*

**naahóosaweew** VTAO sell s.t. to s.o., try to sell s.t. to s.o. **Naahóosaakw wteehíimal.** 'He sold me some strawberries.' *ind 1st sg* **naahóosawaan**. *ind 3rd sg* **wŭnaahóosawaan**. *ind inv* **naahoosáakwun**. *ind I-you* **kŭnaa=hoosóolun**. *conj 3rd sg* **naahóosa=**

**waat**. *imp* **naahóosaw**. *ptcpl* **naa=hóosawaat**.

**naahoosíhtaweew** VTA sell to s.o. *ind 1st sg* **naahoosíhtawaaw**, **naahoo=síhtawa**. *ind 3rd sg* **wŭnaahoosihta=wáawal**. *ind inv* **naahoosíhtaakw**. *ind I-you* **kŭnaahoosíhtool**. *conj 3rd sg* **naahoosíhtawaat**. *imp* **naahoo=síhtaw**. *ptcpl* **naahoosíhtawaat**.

**naahóosuw** VAI peddle, go about selling. *ind 1st sg* **naahóosi**, **naahóosiim**. *conj 3rd sg* **naahóosiit**. *imp* **naa=hóosiil**. *ptcpl* **naahóosiit**.

**naakaayéeke** VII in a while. *usually only in conjunct order*. **Naakaayéeke ápih náh mbá.** 'I'll come in a little while.'; **Naakaayéeke ápih kŭmiit=síhna.** 'We'll eat in a while.' *conj 3rd sg* **naakáayeek**. *dimin* **naakaayée=shiik**.

**náakee** PC for a while, after a while. **Náakee ngáwi.** 'I'm going to sleep for a while.'; **Náake nàkíhlaan ndoo=téewi.** 'I stopped for a while and visited.'

**náakeesh** PC a little while. **Náakeesh-uch shúkw nál-uch paskwiipáh=toon.** 'After a while he'll jump up in a hurry.'; **Náakeesh-uch kpéesi, chíi sháa takwapŭwaaláahan.** 'Wait for a while, don't get married right away.'

**náaleew** VTA go after s.o., fetch s.o. *ind 1st sg* **náalaaw**, **náala**. *ind 3rd sg* **wŭnaaláawal**. *ind inv* **náalukw**. *ind I-you* **kŭnáalul**. *conj 3rd sg* **náalaat**. *imp* **náal**. *ptcpl* **náalaat**.

**naaláasuw** VAI be fetched *(especially the body of a deceased person)*. *ind 1st sg* **naaláasi**, **naaláasiim**. *conj 3rd sg* **naaláasiit**. *ptcpl* **naaláasiit**.

**náalan** PC five.

**naalanaaníhka** PC fifteen.

**naalanaapéeksuw** VAI have five pages *(s.t. animate, of something sheet-like)*. *usually of pieces of paper*. *conj 3rd sg* **naalanaapéeksiit**. *ptcpl* **naalanaapéeksiit**.

**naalanaapóxku** PC five hundred.

**naalanáhtakat** VII be five pieces *(of something string-like)*. *conj 3rd sg* **naalanáhtakahk**. *ptcpl* **naalanáh=takahk**.

**naalanahtéewal** VII be five of them there. *usually plural*. *conj 3rd sg* **naala=náhteek**. *ptcpl* **naalanahtéekiil**.

**naalanalíhkeew** VAI take five steps. *ind 1st sg* **naalanalíhke**, **naalanalíh=keem**. *conj 3rd sg* **naalanalíhkeet**. *imp* **naalanalíhkeel**. *ptcpl* **naalanal=íhkeet**.

**naalanápŭwak** VAI be five of them sitting there, be five of them there. *ind 1st pl* **naalanapíhna**. *conj 3rd sg* **naalanapíhtiit**. *ptcpl* **naalanapíhtiit**.

**naalanatxooxwéewak** VAI walk in fives, be in groups of five. *usually plural*. *ind 1st pl* **naalanatxooxwéhna**. *conj 3rd sg* **naalanatxooxwéhtiit**. *imp* **naalanatxóoxweekw**. *ptcpl* **naala=natxooxwéhtiit**.

**naalaneekíixiin** VAI be in five layers *(s.t. animate, of something sheet-like)*. *ind 1st sg* **naalaneekíixiin**, **naalaneekíixi**. *conj 3rd sg* **naala=neekíixiing**. *ptcpl* **naalaneekíixiing**.

**naalaneekíixun** VII be in five layers *(of something sheet-like)*. *conj 3rd sg* **naalaneekíixung**. *ptcpl* **naalanee=kíixung**.

**naalanéelook** VAI be five pairs, be in five pairs *(s.t. animate)*. *usually plural*. *ind 1st pl* **naalaneelóhna**. *conj 3rd sg* **naalaneelóhtiit**. *ptcpl* **naala=neelóhtiit**.

**naalanéeli** PC five, in fives. **Naalanéeli pihtawíixŭnool.** 'They're stacked in fives.'

**naalanéeltool** VII be five pairs, be in five pairs. *usually plural*. *conj 3rd sg* **naalanéelihk**. *ptcpl* **naalaneelíhkiil**.

**naalaniináxke** PC fifty.

**naalanookwŭnáhkeew** VAI be gone for

five days. *ind 1st sg* **naalanookwŭ=náhke, naalanookwŭnáhkeem**. *conj 3rd sg* **naalanookwŭnáhkeet**. *ptcpl* **naalanookwŭnáhkeet**.

**naalanookwŭnákat** VII be five days. **Naalanookwŭnákate.** 'Five days ago' *conj 3rd sg* **naalanookwŭ=nákahk**. *ptcpl* **naalanookwŭnákahk**.

**naalanóokwŭnii** PC five days.

**naalanúwak** VAI be five, be five of them *(s.t. animate). usually plural. ind 1st pl* **naalaníhna**. *conj 3rd sg* **naala=níhtiit**. *ptcpl* **naalaníhtiit**.

**naalanu-** PN five. **Náalanu-kíishooxkw náh ndúnda-làlóhke.** 'I worked there for five months.' *See* **naalu-**.

**naalanu-** PV five. **Náalanu-pangée=yeew.** 'It's in five slices.' *ptcpl* **náalanu-**. *See* **náalii-**, **náalu-**.

**náalanun** PC five times.

**naalanúnool** VII be five. *usually plural. conj 3rd sg* **náalanung**. *ptcpl* **naala=núngiil**.

**naalii-** PV five. *ptcpl* **náalii-**. *See* **náa=lanu-**, **naalu-**.

**naalu-** PN five. **Náalu-póond txú-poondakúsuw.** 'He weighs five pounds.' *See* **naalanu-**.

**naalu-** PV five. *informal.* **Náalu-pan=géeyeew.** 'It's in five slices.' *ptcpl* **náalu-**. *See* **naalanu-**, **naalii-**.

**naanaxpŭlóhtaweew** VTA imitate the way s.o. talks, imitate s.o.'s speech. *ind 1st sg* **naanaxpŭlóhtawaaw**, **naanaxpŭlóhtawa**. *ind 3rd sg* **wŭ=naanaxpŭlohtawáawal**. *ind inv* **naa=naxpŭlóhtaakw**. *ind I-you* **kŭnaa=naxpŭlóhtool**. *conj 3rd sg* **naanax=pŭlóhtawaat**. *imp* **naanaxpŭlóhtaw**. *ptcpl* **naanaxpŭlóhtawaat**.

**naaneeskàléenguw** VAI be part Black. *ind 1st sg* **naaneeskàléengwi**, **naa=neeskàléengwiim**. *conj 3rd sg* **naa=neeskàléengwiit**. *ptcpl* **naaneeskàl=éengwiit**.

**naaníitus** NA doll. *pl* **naaníitsak**. *poss* **naaníitsum**. *loc* **naaníitsung**. *dimin* **naaníich'shush**. *obv* **naaníitsal**.

**naanxootóonheew** VAI talk by oneself. *ind 1st sg* **naanxootóonhe**, **naan=xootóonheem**. *conj 3rd sg* **naanxoo=tóonheet**. *imp* **naanxootóonheel**. *ptcpl* **naanxootóonheet**.

**naatáasuw** VII be gone after, be brought, be fetched. *conj 3rd sg* **naatáasiik**. *ptcpl* **naatáasiik**.

**naatamáweew** VTAO go after s.t. for s.o., fetch s.t. for s.o. *ind 1st sg* **naata=máwaan**. *ind 3rd sg* **wŭnaatamáw=aan**. *ind inv* **naatamáakwun**. *ind I-you* **kŭnaatamóolun**. *conj 3rd sg* **naatamáwaat**. *imp* **náatamaw**. *ptcpl* **naatamáwaat**.

**naatasánuw** VAIO go after and carry s.t., fetch and carry s.t. *ind 1st sg* **naata=sániin**. *ind 3rd sg* **wŭnaatasániin**. *conj 3rd sg* **naatasániit**. *imp* **naata=sániil**. *ptcpl* **naatasániit**.

**naathéewaleew** VTA go to get a load of s.o. *ind 1st sg* **naathéewalaaw**, **naat=héewala**. *ind 3rd sg* **wŭnaatheewa=láawal**. *ind inv* **naathéewalukw**. *ind I-you* **kŭnaathéewalul**. *conj 3rd sg* **naathéewalaat**. *imp* **naathéewal**. *ptcpl* **naathéewalaat**.

**naathéewasuw** VAI go after something to fetch it, go after something to take it. *ind 1st sg* **naathéewasi**, **naathée=wasiim**. *conj 3rd sg* **naathéewasiit**. *imp* **naathéewasiil**. *ptcpl* **naathée=wasiit**.

**naathéewasuw** VAI go to get a load *(of one's belongings). ind 1st sg* **naat=héewasi**, **naathéewasiim**. *conj 3rd sg* **naathéewasiit**. *imp* **naathéewasiil**. *ptcpl* **naathéewasiit**.

**naathéewatoow** VTI2 go to get a load of s.t. *ind 1st sg* **naathéewatoon**. *ind 3rd sg* **wŭnaathéewatoon**. *conj 1st sg* **naatheewatáwaan**. *conj 3rd sg* **naathéewataakw**. *imp* **naathéewa=tool**. *ptcpl* **naathéewataakw**.

**naathúpeew** VAI fetch water, go after water; go to get liquor. *ind 1st sg* **naathúpe**, **naathúpeem**. *conj 3rd sg* **naathúpeet**. *imp* **naathúpeel**. *ptcpl* **naathúpeet**.

**naattaachíindam** VTI 1A go after and drag s.t., fetch and drag s.t. *ind 1st sg* **naattaachíindamun**. *ind 3rd sg* **wŭnaattaachíindamun**. *conj 1st sg* **naattaachíindamaan**. *conj 3rd sg* **naattaachíindang**. *imp* **naattaa=chíindah**. *ptcpl* **naattaachíindang**.

**naattaachíhleew** VTA go after and drag s.o., go after and drag s.t. animate. *ind 1st sg* **naattaachíhlaaw**, **naat=taachíhla**. *ind 3rd sg* **wŭnaattaa=chihláawal**. *ind inv* **naattaachíh=lukw**. *ind I-you* **kŭnaattaachíhlul**. *conj 3rd sg* **naattaachíhlaat**. *imp* **naattáachihl**. *ptcpl* **naattaachíhlaat**.

**náatum** VTI 1B go after s.t., fetch s.t. *ind 1st sg* **náatŭmun**. *ind 3rd sg* **wŭnáa=tŭmun**. *conj 1st sg* **náatŭmaan**. *conj 3rd sg* **náatung**. *imp* **náatih**. *ptcpl* **náatung**.

**náatŭneew** VTA pick s.o. up. *ind 1st sg* **náatŭnaaw**, **náatŭna**. *ind 3rd sg* **wŭnaatŭnáawal**. *ind inv* **náatŭ=nukw**. *ind I-you* **kŭnáatŭnul**. *conj 3rd sg* **náatŭnaat**. *imp* **náatun**. *ptcpl* **náatŭnaat**.

**naatŭnúkwsuw** VAI be taken away *(especially to heaven)*. *ind 1st sg* **naa=tŭnúkwsi**, **naatŭnúkwsiim**. *conj 3rd sg* **naatŭnúkwsiit**. *ptcpl* **naatŭ=núkwsiit**.

**naatŭnukwsuwáakan** NI being taken away.

**náatŭnum** VTI 1B pick s.t. up. *ind 1st sg* **naatŭnúmun**. *ind 3rd sg* **wŭnaatŭ=númun**. *conj 1st sg* **naatŭnúmaan**. *conj 3rd sg* **náatŭnung**. *imp* **náatŭnih**. *ptcpl* **náatŭnung**.

**naatxákweew** VAI fetch wood, go after wood. *ind 1st sg* **naatxákwe**, **naat=xákweem**. *conj 3rd sg* **naatxákweet**. *imp* **naatxákweel**. *ptcpl* **naatxák=weet**.

**naawáhkeew** VAI follow people. **Wíh=wiing-naawáhkeew.** 'He likes to follow people.' *ind 1st sg* **naawáhke**, **naawáhkeem**. *conj 3rd sg* **naawáh=keet**. *imp* **naawáhkeel**. *ptcpl* **naa=wáhkeet**.

**náawaleew** VTA follow s.o. *ind 1st sg* **náawalaaw**, **náawala**. *ind 3rd sg* **wŭnaawaláawal**. *ind inv* **náawa=lukw**. *ind I-you* **kŭnáawalul**. *conj 3rd sg* **náawalaat**. *imp* **náawal**. *ptcpl* **náawalaat**. *moderative reduplication* **wŭnaanaawaláawal**.

**naawalóotam** VTI 1A follow s.t., follow along with s.t.; follow s.t. *(of religions)*. *ind 1st sg* **naawalóotŭmun**. *ind 3rd sg* **wŭnaawalóotŭmun**. *conj 1st sg* **naawalóotŭmaan**. *conj 3rd sg* **naawalóotang**. *imp* **naawalóotih**. *ptcpl* **naawalóotang**.

**ná** PR that *(animate)*; emphatic. **Ná alíipah wihtawákung** 'Grab him by the ear.'; **Ná há níi.** 'That's me.' *See* **nán**.

**náh** PC there. **Téet náh apúw.** 'Maybe he's there.'; **Oxkwéewak náh apúw=ak wiikwáhmung.** 'There were women in the house.'

**nahkáaleew** VTA rely on s.o., depend on s.o., need s.o.'s help. *ind 1st sg* **nah=káalaaw**, **nahkáala**. *ind 3rd sg* **wŭ=nahkaaláawal**. *ind inv* **nahkáalukw**. *ind I-you* **kŭnahkáalul**. *conj 3rd sg* **nahkáalaat**. *imp* **náhkaal**. *ptcpl* **nehkáalaat**.

**nahkáatum** VTI 1A rely on s.t., depend on s.t. *ind 1st sg* **nahkáatŭmun**. *ind 3rd sg* **wŭnahkáatŭmun**. *conj 1st sg* **nahkáatŭmaan**. *conj 3rd sg* **nah=káatung**. *imp* **nahkáatih**. *ptcpl* **nehkáatung**.

**nahkeeweelúndam** VOTI 1A be hopeful *(especially as one hopes to go to heaven)*. *ind 1st sg* **nahkeeweelún=**

**dam.** *conj 3rd sg* **nahkeeweelún=dang.** *imp* **nahkeeweelúndah.** *ptcpl* **nehkeeweelúndang.**

**nahkéewsuw** VAI be hopeful, be expectant, want help. *ind 1st sg* **nahkéewsi, nahkéewsiim.** *conj 3rd sg* **nahkéew=siit.** *imp* **nahkéewsiil.** *ptcpl* **neh=kéewsiit.**

**nahkeewsuwáakan** NI being hopeful, hopefulness, wanting help.

**nahnakúweew** VAI stutter. *ind 1st sg* **nahnakúwe, nahnakúweem.** *conj 3rd sg* **nahnakúweet.** *ptcpl* **nehnakúweet.** *See* **nànakíixsuw.**

**náhnalii** PC close by. **Awéen há ná náhnalii éenda-lalóhkeet?** 'Who's that close by working?' *See* **náh=naliish, nalíish.**

**náhnaliish** PC close by *(diminutive).* **Náhnaliish ndá.** 'I'm going a little ways.' *See* **náhnalii, nalíish.**

**nahpŭnáleew** VTA reprimand s.o., chew s.o. out. *ind 1st sg* **nahpŭnálaaw, nahpŭnála.** *ind 3rd sg* **wŭnahpŭ=naláawal.** *ind inv* **nahpŭnálukw.** *ind I-you* **kŭnahpŭnálul.** *conj 3rd sg* **nahpŭnálaat.** *imp* **náhpŭnal.** *ptcpl* **nahpŭnálaat.**

**nahtáachuw** VAI be afraid, be nervous. *ind 1st sg* **nahtáachi, nahtáachiim.** *conj 3rd sg* **nahtáachiit.** *ptcpl* **nehtáachiit.**

**nál** PC then, subsequently. **Nál wáak ndalŭmúsiin.** 'Then I left again.'; **Nál wtúlu- wiikwáhmung -piinj=íikwsiin.** 'Then he crawled inside the house.'

**naláhii** PC Munceytown, Ontario. *'up-stream'.* **Náh naláhii ndúlu-pŭmús=iim.** 'I walked to Munceytown.'

**nalawáawsuw** VAI be an unbeliever, don't believe in a Christian way of life; lead a quiet life. *ind 1st sg* **nàl=awáawsi, nàlawáawsiim.** *conj 3rd sg* **nalawáawsiit.** *imp* **nalawáawsiil.** *ptcpl* **neelawáawsiit.**

**nalawáhkeew** VAI be content, be unworried about anything, be unafraid. *ind 1st sg* **nàlawáhke, nàlawáhkeem.** *conj 3rd sg* **nalawáhkeet.** *ptcpl* **neelawáhkeet.** *moderative reduplication* **naanalawáhkeew.**

**nalawamálsuw** VAI feel peaceful. *ind 1st sg* **nàlawamalúsi, nàlawama=lúsiim.** *conj 3rd sg* **nalawamálsiit.** *ptcpl* **neelawamalúsiit.**

**naláwapuw** VAI stay there quietly, be there quietly, live there quietly. *ind 1st sg* **nàlawápi, nàlawápiim.** *conj 3rd sg* **naláwapiit.** *imp* **naláwapiil.** *ptcpl* **neelawápiit.**

**naláwii** PC peacefully, quietly, contentedly. **Naláwii wíikuw.** 'He lives there quietly.' *See* **aayaláwii.**

**nalíish** PC close by. *See* **náhnalíish, náhnalii.**

**nám** VTI1B recognize s.t. *ind 1st sg* **núnamun.** *ind 3rd sg* **wŭnúnamun.** *conj 1st sg* **námaan.** *conj 3rd sg* **náng.** *ptcpl* **néenang.**

**namáaleew** VTA sense s.o.'s presence, sense the presence of s.o. *ind 1st sg* **nàmáalaaw, nàmáala.** *ind 3rd sg* **wŭnamaaláawal.** *ind inv* **namáa=lukw.** *ind I-you* **kŭnamáalul.** *conj 3rd sg* **namáalaat.** *ptcpl* **neemáalaat.**

**namáatam** VTI1A sense s.t.'s presence, sense the presence of s.t. **Nàmáata=mun katá-sóokŭlaan.** 'I feel that it's going to rain.' *ind 1st sg* **nàmáata=mun.** *ind 3rd sg* **wŭnamáatamun.** *conj 1st sg* **namáatamaan.** *conj 3rd sg* **namáatang.** *imp* **neemáatang.** *ptcpl* **neemáatang.**

**namées** NA fish. *pl* **naméesak.** *poss* **nàméesum.** *loc* **naméesung.** *dimin* **naméeshush.** *obv* **naméesal.**

**namées'heew** VAI be fishing, fish. *ind 1st sg* **nàmées'he, nàmées'heem.** *conj 3rd sg* **namées'heet.** *imp* **namées'heel.** *ptcpl* **neemées'heet.**

**namongwáaleew** VTA dream about s.o.,

have a dream about s.o. *ind 1st sg* **nàmongwáalaaw**, **nàmongwáala**. *ind 3rd sg* **wŭnamongwaaláawal**. *ind inv* **nàmongwáalukw**. *ind I-you* **kŭnamongwáalul**. *conj 3rd sg* **na=mongwáalaat**. *imp* **namóngwaal**. *ptcpl* **neemongwáalaat**.

**namongwáatam** VTI 1A dream about s.t., have a dream about s.t. *ind 1st sg* **nàmongwáatŭmun**. *ind 3rd sg* **wŭ=namongwáatŭmun**. *conj 1st sg* **na=mongwáatamaan**. *conj 3rd sg* **na=mongwáatang**. *imp* **namongwáatah**. *ptcpl* **neemongwáatang**.

**nán** PR that *(animate emphatic)*. **Nán há shúkw apaamchéhle.** 'All he does is drive around.' *See* **ná**.

**nànakíixsuw** VAI stutter. *ind 1st sg* **nàn=akíixsi**, **nànakíixsiim**. *conj 3rd sg* **nànakíixsiit**. *imp* **nànakíixsiil**. *ptcpl* **nànakíixsiit**. *See* **nahnakúweew**.

**nángwan** NAD my heel. *pl* **nángwanak**. *3rd poss* **wŭnángwanal**. *loc* **nán=gwanung**. *dimin* **nángwanush**.

**nángwan** NID my heel. *pl* **nángwanal**. *3rd poss* **wŭnángwan**. *loc* **nángwa=nung**. *dimin* **nángwanush**.

**nànkwutíingweew** VAI wink. *ind 1st sg* **nànkwutíingwe**, **nànkwutíingweem**. *conj 3rd sg* **nànkwutíingweet**. *imp* **nànkwutíingweel**. *ptcpl* **nànkwut=íingweet**.

**nanpuyíhleew** VII be water flowing; flow *(of water)*. *conj 3rd sg* **nanpuyíh=laak**. *ptcpl* **nanpuyíhlaak**. *See* **mbuyíhleew**.

**nánuw** NAD my cheek. *pl* **nánŭwak**. *3rd poss* **wŭnánŭwal**. *loc* **nánoong**. *dimin* **nánoosh**.

**nánuw** NID my cheek. *pl* **nánŭwal**. *3rd poss* **wŭnánuw**. *loc* **nánoong**.

**náweew** VTA recognize s.o. *ind 1st sg* **núnawaaw**, **núnawa**. *ind 3rd sg* **wŭnunawáawal**. *ind inv* **núnaakw**. *ind I-you* **kŭnúnool**. *conj 3rd sg* **náwaat**. *ptcpl* **néenawaat**.

**náxk** NID my hand, my arm. *pl* **náxkal**. *3rd poss* **wŭnáxk**. *loc* **náxkung**. *dimin* **náxkush**.

**náxkamay** NID my sleeve. *pl* **náxka=mayal**. *3rd poss* **wŭnáxkamay**.

**naxkóoheew** VTA sing to s.o. *ind 1st sg* **naxkóohaaw**, **naxkóoha**. *ind 3rd sg* **wŭnaxkooháawal**. *ind inv* **naxkóo=hukw**. *ind I-you* **kŭnaxkóohul**. *conj 3rd sg* **naxkóohaat**. *imp* **náxkooh**. *ptcpl* **neexkóohaat**.

**naxkóohŭmeew** VAI sing. *ind 1st sg* **naxkóohŭma**, **naxkóohŭmaam**. *emphatic pl* **naxkoohumáhtŭwak**. *conj 3rd sg* **naxkóohŭmaat**. *imp* **naxkóo=hŭmaal**. *ptcpl* **ŭmaatóohŭmaat**.

**naxkóomeew** VTA answer s.o. *ind 1st sg* **naxkóomaaw**, **naxkóoma**. *ind 3rd sg* **wŭnaxkoomáawal**. *ind inv* **naxkóo=mukw**. *ind I-you* **kŭnaxkóomul**. *conj 3rd sg* **naxkóomaat**. *imp* **náxkoom**. *ptcpl* **neexkóomaat**.

**naxkóotam** VOTI 1A answer. *ind 1st sg* **naxkóotam**. *conj 3rd sg* **naxkóotang**. *imp* **naxkóotah**. *ptcpl* **neexkóotang**.

**naxkóotam** VTI 1A answer s.t. *ind 1st sg* **naxkóotamun**. *ind 3rd sg* **wŭnax=kóotamun**. *conj 1st sg* **naxkóota=maan**. *conj 3rd sg* **naxkóotang**. *imp* **naxkóotih**. *ptcpl* **neexkóotang**.

**náxkush** NID my finger. *pl* **náxkshal**. *3rd poss* **wŭáxkush**. *loc* **náxkshung**.

**naxkwáaleew** VTA give s.o. lice, give s.o. bugs. *ind 1st sg* **naxkwáalaaw**, **naxkwáala**. *ind 3rd sg* **wŭnaxkwaa=láawal**. *ind inv* **naxkwáalukw**. *ind I-you* **kŭnaxkwáalul**. *conj 3rd sg* **naxkwáalaat**. *imp* **náxkwaal**. *ptcpl* **neexkwáalaat**.

**náxkwseew** VTA light s.t. animate, set s.t. animate on fire. *ind 1st sg* **náxk=wsaaw**, **náxkwsa**. *ind 3rd sg* **wŭ=naxkwsáawal**. *ind inv* **náxkwsookw**. *ind I-you* **kŭnáxkwsool**. *conj 3rd sg* **náxkwsaat**. *imp* **náxkwus**. *ptcpl* **néexkwsaat**.

**naxkwsíikeew** VAI set things on fire, set a fire. *ind 1st sg* **naxkwsíike, naxk=wsíikeem**. *conj 3rd sg* **naxkwsíikeet**. *imp* **naxkwsíikeel**. *ptcpl* **neexk=wsíikeet**.

**náxkwsum** VTI1B light s.t., set s.t. on fire. *ind 1st sg* **naxkwsúmun**. *ind 3rd sg* **wŭnaxkwsúmun**. *conj 1st sg* **naxkwsúmaan**. *conj 3rd sg* **náxk=wsung**. *imp* **náxkwsih**. *ptcpl* **néexk=wsung**.

**naxkwsúmaweew** VTAO set s.t. on fire for s.o. *ind 1st sg* **naxkwsúmawaan**. *ind 3rd sg* **wŭnaxkwsúmawaan**. *ind inv* **naxkwsumáakwun**. *ind I-you* **kŭnaxkwsumóolun**. *conj 3rd sg* **naxkwsúmawaat**. *imp* **naxk=wsúmaw**. *ptcpl* **neexkwsúmawaat**.

**náxkwteew** VII burn *(of fires)*. *conj 3rd sg* **náxkwteek**. *ptcpl* **néexkwteek**.

**naxkwtéhleew** VII start up *(of fires, of furnaces)*. *conj 3rd sg* **naxkwtéh=laak**. *ptcpl* **neexkwtéhlaak**.

**náxkwŭnum** VTI1A pick s.t. up. *ind 1st sg* **naxkwŭnúmun**. *ind 3rd sg* **wŭ=naxkwŭnúmun**. *conj 1st sg* **nax=kwŭnúmaan**. *conj 3rd sg* **náxkwŭ=nung**. *imp* **náxkwŭnih**. *ptcpl* **náxkwŭnung**.

**naxpaangóomeew** VTA be related to s.o. as well. *ind 1st sg* **naxpaangóo=maaw, naxpaangóoma**. *ind 3rd sg* **wŭnaxpaangoomáawal**. *ind inv* **naxpaangóomukw**. *ind I-you* **kŭ=naxpaangóomul**. *conj 3rd sg* **nax=paangóomaat**. *imp* **naxpáangoom**. *ptcpl* **neexpaangóomaat**.

**naxpáawsuw** VAIO inherit s.t. *(especially characteristics of personality)*; live with s.t. *ind 1st sg* **naxpáawsiin**. *ind 3rd sg* **wŭnaxpáawsiin**. *conj 3rd sg* **naxpáawsiit**. *imp* **naxpáawsiil**. *ptcpl* **neexpáawsiit**.

**náxpameew** VTA eat s.o. with something. *ind 1st sg* **náxpamaaw, náx=pama**. *ind 3rd sg* **wŭnaxpamáawal**. *conj 3rd sg* **náxpamaat**. *imp* **náxpam**. *ptcpl* **néexpamaat**.

**naxpándam** VTI1A eat s.t. with something. *ind 1st sg* **naxpándamun**. *ind 3rd sg* **wŭnaxpándamun**. *conj 1st sg* **naxpándamaan**. *conj 3rd sg* **nax=pándang**. *imp* **naxpándah**. *ptcpl* **neexpándang**.

**naxpasánuw** VAIO carry s.t. extra, carry s.t. in addition. *ind 1st sg* **naxpasán=iin**. *ind 3rd sg* **wŭnaxpasániin**. *conj 3rd sg* **naxpasániit**. *imp* **naxpasániil**. *ptcpl* **neexpasániit**.

**naxpawéeheew** VAIO use s.t. with something, wear s.t. with something. *ind 1st sg* **naxpawéeheen**. *ind 3rd sg* **wŭnaxpawéeheen**. *conj 3rd sg* **nax=pawéeheet**. *imp* **naxpawéeheel**. *ptcpl* **neexpawéeheet**.

**naxpii-** PV in addition, with something else. **Wŭnáxpii-míichiin.** 'He ate it with something else.' *ptcpl* **néexpii-**.

**naxpíikuw** VAIO grow up with s.o. *ind 1st sg* **naxpíikiin**. *ind 3rd sg* **wŭnax=piikíinal**. *conj 3rd sg* **naxpíikiit**. *imp* **naxpíikiil**. *ptcpl* **neexpíikiit**.

**naxpíhleew** VTA grab s.o. *ind 1st sg* **naxpíhlaaw, naxpíhla**. *ind 3rd sg* **wŭnaxpihláawal**. *ind inv* **naxpíh=lukw**. *ind I-you* **kŭnaxpíhlul**. *conj 3rd sg* **naxpíhlaat**. *imp* **náxpihl**. *ptcpl* **neexpíhlaat**.

**naxpíhleew** VAIO grab s.t., seize and take s.t. along. *ind 1st sg* **naxpíhlaan**. *ind 3rd sg* **wŭnaxpíhlaan**. *conj 3rd sg* **naxpíhlaat**. *imp* **naxpíhlaal**. *ptcpl* **neexpíhlaat**.

**naxpíhtoow** VTI2 grab s.t. *ind 1st sg* **naxpíhtoon**. *ind 3rd sg* **wŭnaxpíh=toon**. *conj 1st sg* **naxpíhtawaan**. *conj 3rd sg* **naxpíhtaakw**. *imp* **naxpíhtool**. *ptcpl* **neexpíhtaakw**.

**naxpóoxwaleew** VTA bring s.o. along as well, take s.o. along as well. *ind 1st sg* **naxpóoxwalaaw, naxpóoxwala**. *ind 3rd sg* **wŭnaxpooxwaláawal**. *ind* *inv* **naxpóoxwalukw**. *ind I-you* **kŭ=naxpóoxwalul**. *conj 3rd sg* **naxpóo=xwalaat**. *imp* **naxpóoxwal**. *ptcpl* **neexpóoxwalaat**.

**naxpóoxwatoow** VTI2 bring s.t. along as well, take s.t. along as well. *ind 1st sg* **naxpóoxwatoon**. *ind 3rd sg* **wŭnax=póoxwatoon**. *conj 1st sg* **naxpoo=xwatáwaan**. *conj 3rd sg* **naxpóo=xwataakw**. *imp* **naxpóoxwatool**. *ptcpl* **neexpóoxwataakw**.

**naxpóoxweew** VAIO take s.t. along as well, take s.t. along in addition. *ind 1st sg* **naxpóoxween**. *ind 3rd sg* **wŭnaxpóoxween**. *conj 3rd sg* **nax=póoxweet**. *imp* **naxpóoxweel**. *ptcpl* **neexpóoxweet**.

**náxpŭnum** VTI1B grab s.t. *ind 1st sg* **naxpŭnúmun**. *ind 3rd sg* **wŭnaxpŭ=númun**. *conj 1st sg* **naxpŭnúmaan**. *conj 3rd sg* **náxpŭnung**. *imp* **náxpŭ=nih**. *ptcpl* **néexpŭnung**.

**nayapáawunii** PC in the morning. **Na=yapáawŭnii-uch kŭnéewul.** 'I'll see you in the morning.' *See* **ayapáa=wŭnii**.

**nayóomeew** VTA carry s.o. on one's back. *ind 1st sg* **nàyóomaaw**, **nàyóoma**. *ind 3rd sg* **wŭnayoomáawal**. *ind inv* **nàyóomukw**. *ind I-you* **kŭnayóomul**. *conj 3rd sg* **nayóomaat**. *imp* **nayóom**. *ptcpl* **neeyóomaat**.

**nayóondam** VTI1A carry s.o. on one's back. *ind 1st sg* **nàyóondamun**. *ind 3rd sg* **wŭnayóondamun**. *conj 1st sg* **nayóondamaan**. *conj 3rd sg* **nayóondang**. *imp* **nayóondah**. *ptcpl* **neeyóondang**.

**ndáaktul** NA doctor. *pl* **ndaaktúlak**. *poss* **nùtaaktúlum**. *dimin* **ndaak=chúlush**. *obv* **ndaaktúlal**. *From English* doctor.

**ndaaktulhámeew** VAI be treated by a doctor. *ind 1st sg* **nùtaaktulháma**, **nùtaaktulhámaam**. *conj 3rd sg* **ndaaktulhámaak**. *imp* **ndaaktul=hámaal**. *ptcpl* **neetaaktulhámaat**. *From English* doctor.

**ndálaas** NI dollar. *singular only, usually with number prenoun*. **Ngwút-ndálaas láawatuw.** 'It costs one dollar.'; **Ngwútaash txú-ndálaas láa=watuw.** 'It costs six dollars.' *From English* dollar.

**ndawáapameew** VTA look around searching for s.o., look out to see s.o., look out for s.o. *ind 1st sg* **nàtawáa=pamaaw**, **nàtawáapama**. *ind 3rd sg* **wŭnatawaapamáawal**. *ind inv* **nàta=wáapamukw**. *ind I-you* **kŭnatawáa=pamul**. *conj 3rd sg* **ndawáapamaat**. *imp* **ndawáapam**. *ptcpl* **neetawáa=pamaat**.

**ndawaapándam** VTI1A look around searching for s.t., look out to see s.t., look out for s.t. *ind 1st sg* **nàtawaa=pándamun**. *ind 3rd sg* **wŭnatawaa=pándamun**. *conj 1st sg* **ndawaapán=damaan**. *conj 3rd sg* **ndawaapán=dang**. *imp* **ndawaapándah**. *ptcpl* **neetawaapándang**.

**ndawáapuw** VAI look around searching; look around *(in expectation of someone or something)*. *ind 1st sg* **nàta=wáapi**, **nàtawáapiim**. *conj 3rd sg* **ndawáapiit**. *imp* **ndawáapiil**. *ptcpl* **neetawáapiit**.

**ndawakóoyeew** VAI look for a cow, look for cows. *ind 1st sg* **nàtawakóoye**, **nàtawakóoyeem**. *conj 3rd sg* **ndaw=akóoyeet**. *imp* **ndawakóoyeel**. *ptcpl* **neetawakóoyeet**.

**ndawapooshíisheew** VAI look for a cat. *ind 1st sg* **nàtawapooshíishe**, **nàtaw=apooshíisheem**. *conj 3rd sg* **ndawa=pooshíisheet**. *imp* **ndawapooshíi=sheel**. *ptcpl* **neetawapooshíisheet**.

**ndáwat** VII be scarce. *conj 3rd sg* **ndáwahk**. *ptcpl* **néetawahk**.

**ndawehnayóongseew** VAI look for horses. *ind 1st sg* **nàtawehnayóong=se**, **nàtawehnayóongseem**. *conj 3rd* *sg* **ndawehnayóongseet**. *imp* **ndaw=ehnayóongseel**. *ptcpl* **neetawehna=yóongseet**.

**ndáwsuw** VAI be scarce *(s.t. animate)*. *conj 3rd sg* **ndáwsiit**. *ptcpl* **neeta=wúsiit**.

**ndawxúmweew** VAI look for a dog. *ind 1st sg* **nàtawáxŭmwe**, **nàtawáxŭ=mweem**. *conj 3rd sg* **ndawxúmweet**. *imp* **ndawxúmweel**. *ptcpl* **neetawáx=ŭmweet**.

**ndóonaleew** VTA challenge s.o. to a fight. *ind 1st sg* **nàtóonalaaw**, **nàt=óonala**. *ind 3rd sg* **wŭnatoonaláa=wal**. *ind inv* **nàtóonalukw**. *ind I-you* **kŭnatóonali**. *conj 3rd sg* **ndóona=laat**. *imp* **ndóonal**. *ptcpl* **neetóo=nalaat**.

**ndootamáweew** VTAO ask s.o. for s.t. *ind 1st sg* **nàtootamáwaan**. *ind 3rd sg* **wŭnatootamáwaan**. *ind inv* **nàt=ootamáakwun**. *ind I-you* **kŭnatoo=tamóolun**. *conj 3rd sg* **ndootamáw=aat**. *imp* **ndóotamaw**. *ptcpl* **neetoo=tamáwaat**.

**ndooxtáweew** VTAO ask s.o. about s.t. *ind 1st sg* **nàtooxtáwaan**. *ind 3rd sg* **wŭnatooxtáwaan**. *ind inv* **nàtoox=táakwun**. *ind I-you* **kŭnatooxtóolun**. *conj 3rd sg* **ndooxtáwaat**. *imp* **ndóoxtaw**. *ptcpl* **neetooxtáwaat**.

**ndóoxtoow** VTI2 ask about s.t. *ind 1st sg* **nàtóoxtoon**. *ind 3rd sg* **wŭnatóox=toon**. *conj 1st sg* **ndooxtáwaan**. *conj 3rd sg* **ndóoxtaakw**. *imp* **ndóoxtool**. *ptcpl* **neetóoxtaakw**.

**ndóoxwŭmeew** VTA ask about s.o. *ind 1st sg* **nàtóoxwŭmaaw**, **nàtóoxwŭ=ma**. *ind 3rd sg* **wŭnatooxwŭmáawal**. *ind inv* **nàtóoxwŭmukw**. *ind I-you* **kŭnatóoxwŭmul**. *conj 3rd sg* **ndóo=xwŭmaat**. *imp* **ndóoxwum**. *ptcpl* **neetóoxwŭmaat**.

**ndumíiheew** VTAO lend s.t to s.o. *ind 1st sg* **nàtŭmíihaan**. *ind 3rd sg* **wŭnatŭ=míihaan**. *ind inv* **nàtŭmíihkwun**. *ind I-you* **kŭnatumíihŭlun**. *conj 3rd sg* **ndumíihaat**. *imp* **ndúmiih**. *ptcpl* **neetŭmíihaat**.

**ndumíihŭweew** VAI lend things, lend things to people. *ind 1st sg* **nàtumíi=hŭwe**, **nàtumíihŭweem**. *conj 3rd sg* **ndumíihŭweet**. *imp* **ndumíihŭweel**. *ptcpl* **neetŭmíihŭweet**.

**ndumíihŭweew** VAIO lend s.t., lend s.t. animate. *ind 1st sg* **natŭmíihŭween**. *ind 3rd sg* **wŭnatumíihŭween**. *conj 3rd sg* **ndumíihŭweet**. *imp* **ndumíi=hŭweel**. *ptcpl* **neetŭmíihŭweet**.

**ndúnaluw** VAI have dinner. *ind 1st sg* **nùtúnali**, **nùtúnaliim**. *conj 3rd sg* **ndúnaliit**. *imp* **ndúnaliil**. *ptcpl* **neetúnaliit**. *From English* dinner.

**ndúpuw** VAI cook. *ind 1st sg* **nátpwi**, **nátpwiim**. *conj 3rd sg* **ndúpwiit**. *imp* **ndúpwiil**. *ptcpl* **néetpwiit**.

**ndúpuw** VAIO cook s.t., cook s.t. animate. **Nŭmuschéewu-ndupwíinak.** 'I cooked them whole.' *ind 1st sg* **nát=pwiin**. *ind 3rd sg* **wŭnátpwiin**. *conj 3rd sg* **ndúpwiit**. *imp* **ndúpwiil**. *ptcpl* **néetpwiit**.

**néek** PR those *(animate)*. *See* **níik**.

**néeka** PR he, him, she, her. **Néeka áashtee.** 'It's his/her turn.'

**neekáawa** PR they, them. *See* **neekŭmáawa**.

**neekumáawa** PR they, them. *See* **neekáawa**.

**neeli-** PV while. *followed by verb in conjunct order.* **Néeli-pŭmáawsiit.** 'While she's alive.'

**néem** VTI 3 see s.t. *ind 1st sg* **néemun**. *ind 3rd sg* **wŭnéemun**. *conj 1st sg* **néemaan**. *conj 3rd sg* **néeng**. *ptcpl* **néeng**.

**neemwáakan** NI sight, seeing the light.

**neenáxkuw** VAI play ball. *ind 1st sg* **neenáxkwi**, **neenáxkwiim**. *conj 3rd sg* **neenáxkwiit**. *imp* **neenáxkwiil**. *ptcpl* **neenáxkwiit**.

**néenaxkw** NA ball. *pl* **neenáxkwak**.

*poss* **neenáxkwum**. *loc* **neenáx=kwung**. *dimin* **neenáxkwush**. *obv* **neenáxkwal**.

**neeneemáhpapoon** NI rocking chair. *pl* **neeneemahpapóonal**. *poss* **neenee=máhpapoon**. *loc* **neeneemahpapóo=nung**. *dimin* **neeneemahpapóonush**.

**neeneemíhleew** VAI rock oneself, be rocking. *ind 1st sg* **neeneemíhla**, **neeneemíhlaam**. *conj 3rd sg* **nee=neemíhlaat**. *imp* **neeneemíhlaal**. *ptcpl* **neeneemíhlaat**.

**neeskàléenguw** VAI be a Black man. *ind 1st sg* **neeskaléengwi**, **neeskaléen=gwiim**. *conj 3rd sg* **neeskaléengwiit**. *ptcpl* **neeskaléengwiit**.

**neeskáleengw** NA Black person. *pl* **neeskàléengwak**. *dimin* **neeskàléen=gwush**. *obv* **neeskàléengwal**.

**neew-** PN four. **Néew-kíishooxkw náh ndúnda-làlóhke.** 'I worked there for four months.'

**neew-** PV four. **Néew-kŭlákuw.** 'It's four o'clock.' *ptcpl* **néew-**.

**neewaaníhka** PC fourteen.

**neewaapéeksuw** VAI have four pages *(s.t. animate, of something sheet-like). usually of pieces of paper. conj 3rd sg* **neewaapéeksiit**. *ptcpl* **neewaapéek=siit**.

**neewaapóxku** PC four hundred.

**néewa** PC four. **Néewa poondakúsuw.** 'He weighs four pounds.'

**neewáhtakat** VII be four pieces *(of something string-like). conj 3rd sg* **neewáhtakahk**. *ptcpl* **neewáhta=kahk**.

**neewalíhkeew** VAI take four steps. *ind 1st sg* **neewalíhke**, **neewalíhkeem**. *conj 3rd sg* **neewalíhkeet**. *imp* **neewalíhkeel**. *ptcpl* **neewalíhkeet**.

**neewataxooxwéewak** VAI walk in groups of four. *usually plural. ind 1st pl* **neewataxooxwéhna**. *conj 3rd sg* **neewataxooxwéhtiit**. *imp* **neewa=taxóoxweekw**. *ptcpl* **neewataxoo=xwéhtiit**.

**neeweekíixiin** VAI be in four layers *(s.t. animate, of something sheet-like). conj 3rd sg* **neeweekíixiing**. *ptcpl* **neeweekíixiing**, **neeweekíixiit**.

**neeweekíixun** VII be in four layers *(of something sheet-like). conj 3rd sg* **neeweekíixung**. *ptcpl* **neeweekí=ixung**.

**neewéeli** PC four, in fours. **Neewéeli pihtawíixŭnool.** 'They're stacked in fours.'

**neewéelook** VAI be four pairs, be four sets *(s.t. animate). usually plural. ind 1st pl* **neeweelóhna**. *conj 3rd sg* **neeweelóhtiit**. *ptcpl* **neeweelóhtiit**.

**neewéeltool** VII be four pairs, be four sets. *usually plural. conj 3rd sg* **neewéelihk**. *ptcpl* **neeweelíhkiil**.

**néeweew** VTA see s.o. *ind 1st sg* **née=waaw**, **néewa**. *ind 3rd sg* **wŭnee=wáawal**. *ind inv* **néewukw**. *ind I-you* **kŭnéewul**. *conj 3rd sg* **néewaat**. *ptcpl* **néewaat**.

**neewiináxke** PC forty.

**neewookwŭnáhkeew** VAI be gone for four days. *ind 1st sg* **neewookwŭ=náhke**, **neewookwŭnáhkeem**. *conj 3rd sg* **neewookwŭnáhkeet**. *ptcpl* **neewookwŭnáhkeet**.

**neewóokwŭnii** PC four days.

**néewŭwak** VAI be four of them, be four *(s.t. animate). usually plural. ind 1st pl* **neewíhna**. *conj 3rd sg* **neewíhtiit**. *ptcpl* **neewíhtiit**.

**néewŭnool** VII be four of them, be four. *usually plural. conj 3rd sg* **néewung**. *ptcpl* **neewúngiil**.

**nehnaahóosiit** VAI peddler. *conj 3rd sg* **nehnaahóosiit**. *pl* **nehnaahoosíhtiit**.

**nehnatúpwiis** NA cook. *pl* **nehnatup=wíisak**. *dimin* **nehnachupwíishush**. *obv* **nehnatupwíisal**.

**nehnayoondíikan** NI pack. *pl* **nehna=yoondíikanal**. *poss* **nehnayoondíi=kan**. *loc* **nehnayoondíikanung**.

*dimin* **nehnayoonjíikanush**.

**nehnayóongsii-mehmahksunhíikeet** VAI blacksmith. *conj 3rd sg* **nehna=yóongsii-mehmahksunhíikeet**. *pl* **nehnayóongsii-mehmahksunhii=kéhtiit**. *See* **shŭmít**.

**nehnayoongsúchuy** NI horse droppings, horse excrement. *pl* **nehnayoong=súchŭyal**.

**nehnayóongus** NA horse. *pl* **nehna=yóongsak**. *poss* **nehnayóongsum**. *loc* **nehnayóongsung**. *dimin* **nehna=yóongshush**. *obv* **nehnayóongsal**.

**nehneenáxkwiis** NA ball player. *pl* **nehneenaxkwíisak**. *dimin* **nehnee=naxkwíishush**. *obv* **nehneenax=kwíisal**.

**nehnihliikíipsheet** NA chicken hawk. *pl* **nehnihliikiipshéhtiit**.

**nehnihliikíipsheet** NA chicken hawk. *pl* **nehnihliikiipshéetak**. *dimin* **neh=nihliikiipshéechush**. *obv* **nehnihlii=kiipshéetal**.

**néwiyaal** PC New Year's Day. **Néwiyaal!** 'Happy New Year!'

**newiyáaliin** VAI celebrate New Year's day. *indefinite subject only*. *indef subject* **newiyáaliin**. *conj 3rd sg* **newi=yáaliing**.

**ngáleew** VTA leave s.o. behind. *ind 1st sg* **núkalaaw**, **núkala**. *ind 3rd sg* **wŭnukaláawal**. *ind inv* **núkalukw**. *ind I-you* **kŭnúkalul**. *conj 3rd sg* **ngálaat**. *imp* **ngál**. *ptcpl* **néekalaat**.

**ngatáhkeew** VAI move, move one's residence. *ind 1st sg* **nùkatáhke**, **nùkatáhkeem**. *conj 3rd sg* **ngatáh=keet**. *imp* **ngatáhkeel**. *ptcpl* **neeka=táhkeet**.

**ngátum** VTI 1B leave s.t. behind. *ind 1st sg* **nùkatúmun**. *ind 3rd sg* **wŭnuka=túmun**. *conj 1st sg* **ngátŭmaan**. *conj 3rd sg* **ngátung**. *imp* **ngátih**. *ptcpl* **néekatung**.

**ngélsak** NA braces, suspenders. *usually plural*. *poss* **nùkèlsúmak**. *dimin* **ngèlshúshak**. *obv* **ngélsal**. *From English* galluses.

**ngiikwáaleew** VTA stop s.o. *(with an elongated object)*; bunt a ball *(in baseball)*. **Nàkiikwáalaaw áng néenaxkw.** 'I bunted the ball.' *ind 1st sg* **nàkiikwáalaaw**, **nàkiikwáala**. *ind 3rd sg* **wŭnakiikwaaláawal**. *ind inv* **nàkiikwáalukw**. *ind I-you* **kŭnakii=kwáalul**. *conj 3rd sg* **ngiikwáalaat**. *imp* **ngíikwaal**. *ptcpl* **neekii=kwáalaat**.

**ngíiskam** VTI 1A meet s.t. *ind 1st sg* **nàkíiskamun**. *ind 3rd sg* **wŭnakíis=kamun**. *conj 1st sg* **ngíiskamaan**. *conj 3rd sg* **ngíiskang**. *imp* **ngíiskah**. *ptcpl* **neekíiskang**.

**ngíiskaweew** VTA meet s.o. *ind 1st sg* **nàkíiskawaaw**, **nàkíiskawa**. *ind 3rd sg* **wŭnakiiskawáawal**. *ind inv* **nàk=íiskaakw**. *ind I-you* **kŭnakíiskool**. *conj 3rd sg* **ngíiskawaat**. *imp* **ngíiskaw**. *ptcpl* **neekíiskawaat**.

**ngíixiin** VAI be stopped, stop. *ind 1st sg* **nàkíixiin**, **nàkíixi**. *conj 3rd sg* **ngíi=xiing**. *imp* **ngíixiil**. *ptcpl* **neekíixiing**.

**ngíhleew** VAI stop. *ind 1st sg* **nàkíhla**, **nàkíhlaam**. *conj 3rd sg* **ngíhlaat**. *imp* **ngíhlaal**. *ptcpl* **neekíhlaat**.

**ngúmee** PC always. **Ngúmee nzhiiwa=sáni.** 'I'm always tired.'; **Ngúmee kaachapíishuw.** 'The little one is always hiding.'

**ngumeewíhleew** VAI be constantly in motion, be constantly in operation. **Ndahámŭlum ngumeewíhleew.** 'My hammer's going all the time.' *ind 1st sg* **nùkŭmeewíhla**, **nùkŭmeewíh=laam**. *conj 3rd sg* **ngumeewíhlaat**. *ptcpl* **neekŭmeewíhlaat**.

**ngumeewíhleew** VII be constantly in motion, be constantly in operation. *conj 3rd sg* **ngumeewíhlaat**. *ptcpl* **neekŭmeewíhlaak**.

**ngumeewihtéeheew** VTA always hit s.o. *ind 1st sg* **nùkŭmeewihtéehaaw**,

**nùkŭmeewihtéeha**. *ind 3rd sg* **wŭnukŭmeewihteeháawaal**. *ind inv* **nùkŭmeewihtéehookw**. *ind I-you* **kŭnukŭmeewihtéehool**. *conj 3rd sg* **ngumeewihtéehaat**. *imp* **ngumee=wíhteeh**. *ptcpl* **neekŭmeewihtée=haat**.

**ngumeewtóonheew** VAI be always talking. *ind 1st sg* **nùkŭmeewtóonhe**, **nùkŭmeewtóonheem**. *conj 3rd sg* **ngumeewtóonheet**. *imp* **ngumeew=tóonheel**. *ptcpl* **neekŭmeewtóon=heet**.

**ngúneew** VTA stop s.o. *ind 1st sg* **nákŭ=naaw**, **nákŭna**. *ind 3rd sg* **wŭnakŭ=náawal**. *ind inv* **nákŭnukw**. *ind I-you* **kŭnákŭnul**. *conj 3rd sg* **ngúnaat**. *imp* **ngún**. *ptcpl* **néekŭnaat**.

**ngúnum** VTI 1B stop s.t. *ind 1st sg* **nàk=ŭnúmun**. *ind 3rd sg* **wŭnakŭnúmun**. *conj 1st sg* **ngúnŭmaan**. *conj 3rd sg* **ngúnung**. *imp* **ngúnih**. *ptcpl* **néekŭnung**.

**ngwut-** PN one. **Ngwút-kíishooxkw náh ndúnda-làlóhke.** 'I worked there for one month.'

**ngwut-** PV one. **Ngwút-pangéeyeew.** 'It's in one piece.'; **Néekwtu-pan=géesiit.** 'One slice.' *ptcpl* **néekwtu-**.

**ngwutaaníhka** PC eleven.

**ngwutaapéeksuw** VAI have one page *(s.t. animate, of something sheet-like). usually of pieces of paper. conj 3rd sg* **ngwutaapéeksiit**. *ptcpl* **neekwtaapéeksiit**.

**ngwutaapóxku** PC one hundred.

**ngwútaash** PC six. **Nóolii txiináxku wáak ngwútaash.** 'Ninety-six.'

**ngwutáhkameew** VII be one day. **Ngwutahkaméeke náh mbá.** 'I'll come in a day.' *conj 3rd sg* **ngwut=áhkameek**. *ptcpl* **neekwtáhkameek**.

**ngwutáhtakat** VII be one piece *(of something string-like). conj 3rd sg* **ngwutáhtakahk**. *ptcpl* **neekwtáh=takahk**.

**ngwutalíhkeew** VAI take one step. *ind 1st sg* **nùkwtàlíhke**, **nùkwtàlíh=keem**. *conj 3rd sg* **ngwutalíhkeet**. *imp* **ngwutalíhkeel**. *ptcpl* **neekw=talíhkeet**.

**ngwutéekat** VII be one page, be one sheet. *conj 3rd sg* **ngwutéekahk**. *ptcpl* **neekwtéekahk**.

**ngwuteekíixiin** VAI be in one layer *(s.t. animate, of something sheet-like).* **Kŭmáhlawaa-uch niisheekíixiit wiikwáhmshii-pámbiil, chíi mahla=wáahan ngwuteekíixiit.** 'Buy two-ply toilet paper, don't buy one-ply.' *conj 3rd sg* **ngwuteekíixiing**. *ptcpl* **neekwteekíixiing**.

**ngwuteekíixun** VII be in one layer *(of something sheet-like). conj 3rd sg* **ngwuteekíixung**. *ptcpl* **neekwtee=kíixung**.

**ngwúteel** PC the same. **Ngwúteel talí.** 'In one place.'; **Ngwúteel apúwak.** 'They stay in the same place; they live together.'

**ngwútii-tpohkweewáhkeew** VAI stay out overnight. *ind 1st sg* **núkwtii-tpohkweewáhke**, **núkwtii-tpoh=kweewáhkeem**. *conj 3rd sg* **ngwútii-tpohkweewáhkeet**. *ptcpl* **néekwtii-tpohkweewáhkeet**.

**ngwutíingweew** VAI have one eye. *ind 1st sg* **nùkwtíingwa**, **nùkwtíin=gwaam**. *conj 3rd sg* **ngwutíingwaat**. *ptcpl* **neekwtíingwaat**.

**ngwutiingwéhleew** VAI be winking. *ind 1st sg* **nùkwtiingwéhla**, **nùkwtiin=gwéhlaam**. *conj 3rd sg* **ngwutiin=gwéhlaat**. *imp* **ngwutiingwéhlaal**. *ptcpl* **neekwtiingwéhlaat**. *intensive reduplication* **nànkwutiingwéhleew**.

**ngwutiingwéhtaweew** VTA wink at s.o. *ind 1st sg* **nùkwtiingwéhtawaaw**, **nùkwtiingwéhtawa**. *ind 3rd sg* **wŭ=nukwtiingwehtawáawal**. *ind inv* **nùkwtiingwéhtaakw**. *ind I-you* **kŭ=nukwtiingwéhtool**. *conj 3rd sg* ngwutiingwéhtawaat. *imp* **ngwut=iingwéhtaw**. *ptcpl* **neekwtiingwéh=tawaat**. *intensive reduplication* **wŭnankwutiingwehtawáawal**.

**ngwúti** PC one.

**ngwutíhleew** VAI faint. *ind 1st sg* **nùkw=tíhla**, **nùkwtíhlaam**. *conj 3rd sg* **ngwutíhlaat**. *ptcpl* **neekwtíhlaat**.

**ngwutihtéexiin** VAI fall and get knocked out. *ind 1st sg* **nùkwtihtéexiin**, **nùk=wtihtéexi**. *conj 3rd sg* **ngwutihtée=xiing**. *ptcpl* **neekwtihtéexiing**.

**ngwutkáateew** VAI have one leg. *ind 1st sg* **nùkwtukáata**, **nùkwtukáataam**. *conj 3rd sg* **ngwutkáataat**. *ptcpl* **neekwtukáataat**.

**ngwutkaatéexiin** VAI use one leg. *ind 1st sg* **nùkwtukaatéexiin**, **nùkwtuk=aatéexi**. *conj 3rd sg* **ngwutkaatée=xiing**. *imp* **ngwutkaatéexiil**. *ptcpl* **neekwtukaatéexiing**.

**ngwutookwŭnáhkeew** VAI be gone overnight. *ind 1st sg* **nùkwtookwŭ=náhke**, **nùkwtookwŭnáhkeem**. *conj 3rd sg* **ngwutookwŭnáhkeet**. *ptcpl* **neekwtookwŭnáhkeet**.

**ngwutóokwŭnii** PC one day.

**ngwutoonáxkeew** VAI use one hand. *ind 1st sg* **nùkwtoonáxke**, **nùkwtoonáx=keem**. *conj 3rd sg* **ngwutoonáxkeet**. *imp* **ngwutoonáxkeel**. *ptcpl* **neek=wtoonáxkeet**.

**ngwutoonáxkwiiw** VAI-S use one hand. *ind 1st sg* **nùkwtoonáxkwi**, **nùkw=toonáxkwiim**. *conj 3rd sg* **ngwutoo=náxkwiit**. *imp* **ngwutoonáxkwiil**. *ptcpl* **neekwtoonáxkwiit**. *See* **ngwutŭnaxkéexiin**.

**ngwutŭláamuw** VAI let out a cry, let out one cry. *ind 1st sg* **nùkwtuláamwi**, **nùkwtuláamwiim**. *conj 3rd sg* **ngwutaláamwiit**. *ptcpl* **neekwtul=áamwiit**.

**ngwútun** PC once, one time. **Ngwútun shúkw ndahtíike.** 'I only bet once.'

**ngwutun-** PV once, one time. **Wŭnúk=wtun- náh -áan.** 'She went there one time.'; **Wíixkwii wŭnúkwtun-páan, wtuláawal ngúkal, "Ngáta-takwap=íhna."** 'All of a sudden one time he came, and he told my mother, "We want to get married."' *ptcpl* **néekwtun-**.

**ngwutŭnáxkeew** VAI have one hand. *ind 1st sg* **nùkwtunáxka**, **nùkwtunáx=kaam**. *conj 3rd sg* **ngwutŭnáxkaat**. *ptcpl* **neekwtunáxkaat**.

**ngwutŭnaxkéexiin** VAI use one hand. *ind 1st sg* **nùkwtunaxkéexiin**, **nùkw=tunaxkéexi**. *conj 3rd sg* **ngwutŭ=naxkéexiing**. *imp* **ngwutŭnaxkéexiil**. *ptcpl* **neekwtunaxkéexiing**. *See* **ngwutoonáxkwiiw**.

**nhíinaakw** VAI be lucky. *ind 1st sg* **nàhíinaakw**. *conj 3rd sg* **nhiináa=kwuk**. *ptcpl* **neehiináakwuk**.

**nhíinaakw** VAIO have something lucky happen *(to oneself)*. *ind 1st sg* **nahii=náakwun**. *ind 3rd sg* **wŭnahiináa=kwun**. *conj 3rd sg* **nhiináakwuk**. *ptcpl* **neehiináakwuk**.

**níi** PR I, me. **Nún há níi nzíin.** 'That's what I said.'; **Níi áashtee.** 'It's my turn.'

**níichaan** NAD my child. *pl* **niicháanak**. *3rd poss* **wŭniicháanal**. *loc* **niicháa=nung**. *dimin* **niicháanush**. *See* **niicháanus**.

**niicháanus** NAD my child. *pl* **niicháan=sak**. *3rd poss* **wŭniicháansal**. *loc* **niicháansung**. *dimin* **niicháanshush**. *See* **níichaan**.

**níik** PR those *(animate)*. *See* **néek**.

**níil** PR that, those *(animate obviative)*.

**níil** PR those *(inanimate)*.

**niilóona** PR we *(exclusive)*.

**níimaaw** VAI-S take one's lunch along. *ind 1st sg* **níima**, **níimaam**. *conj 3rd sg* **níimaat**. *imp* **níimaal**. *ptcpl* **níimaat**.

**niimáawan** NID my lunch. *pl* **niimáa=wanal**. *3rd poss* **wŭniimáawan**. *loc*

**niimáawanung**. *dimin* **niimáawa=nush**.

**niimaawanáheew** VAI make lunch. *ind 1st sg* **niimaawanáhe**, **niimaawa=náheem**. *conj 3rd sg* **niimaawa=náheet**. *imp* **niimaawanáheel**. *ptcpl* **niimaawanáheet**.

**niimaawanáhŭmeew** VAI take a nap. *ind 1st sg* **niimaawanáhŭma**, **nii=maawanáhŭmaam**. *conj 3rd sg* **niimaawanáhŭmaat**. *imp* **niimaa=wanáhŭmaal**. *ptcpl* **niimaawanáh=ŭmaat**.

**niimcheehŭmáakan** NI lacrosse stick. *pl* **niimcheehŭmáakanal**. *poss* **niimcheehumáakan**. *loc* **niimchee=hŭmáakanung**. *dimin* **niimcheehŭ=máakanush**.

**niimchéehŭmeew** VAI play lacrosse. *ind 1st sg* **niimchéehŭma**, **niimchéehŭ=maam**. *emphatic pl* **niimcheehŭ=máhtŭwak**. *conj 3rd sg* **niimchée=hŭmaat**. *imp* **niimchéehŭmaal**. *ptcpl* **niimchéehŭmaat**.

**niindawáakan** NA lantern. *pl* **niinda=wáakanak**. *poss* **niindawáakan**. *loc* **niindawáakanung**. *dimin* **niinja=wáakanush**. *obv* **niindawáakanal**. *See* **liindawáakan**.

**níindaweew** VAI carry a lantern. *ind 1st sg* **níindawe**, **níindaweem**. *conj 3rd sg* **níindaweet**. *imp* **níindaweel**. *ptcpl* **níindaweet**.

**níingiiw** VAI-S growl. *ind 1st sg* **níingi**, **níingiim**. *conj 3rd sg* **níingiit**. *imp* **níingiil**. *ptcpl* **níingiit**.

**niingíhtaweew** VTA growl at s.o. *ind 1st sg* **niingíhtawaaw**, **niingíhtawa**. *ind 3rd sg* **wŭniingihtawáawal**. *ind inv* **niingíhtaakw**. *ind I-you* **kŭniingíh=tool**. *conj 3rd sg* **niingíhtawaat**. *imp* **niingíhtaw**. *ptcpl* **niingíhtawaat**.

**niipáahum** NA moon. *obv* **niipáahŭ=mal**.

**níipaleew** VTA stand s.o. up, stand s.t. animate up. *ind 1st sg* **níipalaaw**, **níipala**. *ind 3rd sg* **wŭniipaláawal**. *ind inv* **níipalukw**. *ind I-you* **kŭníi=palul**. *conj 3rd sg* **níipalaat**. *imp* **níipal**. *ptcpl* **níipalaat**.

**niipatáasuw** VAI be stood up. *conj 3rd sg* **niipatáasiit**. *ptcpl* **niipatáasiik**.

**níipateew** VII stand. *conj 3rd sg* **níipa=teek**. *ptcpl* **níipateek**.

**niipatíikeew** VAI stand things up. *ind 1st sg* **niipatíike**, **niipatíikeem**. *conj 3rd sg* **niipatíikeet**. *imp* **niipatíikeel**. *ptcpl* **niipatíikeet**.

**níipatoow** VTI2 stand s.t. up. *ind 1st sg* **níipatoon**. *ind 3rd sg* **wŭníipatoon**. *conj 1st sg* **niipatáwaan**. *conj 3rd sg* **níipataakw**. *imp* **níipatool**. *ptcpl* **níipataakw**.

**niipawáakchehl** VAI jump to one's feet. *ind 1st sg* **niipawáakchehl**. *conj 3rd sg* **niipawaakchéhluk**. *imp* **niipa=waakchéhlih**. *ptcpl* **niipawaak=chéhluk**.

**niipawaxéexiin** VAI have one's ears standing up. *ind 1st sg* **niipawaxée=xiin**, **niipawaxéexi**. *conj 3rd sg* **niipawaxéexiing**. *ptcpl* **niipawax=éexiing**.

**niipawéelŭmeew** VTA be proud of s.o. *ind 1st sg* **niipawéelŭmaaw**, **niipa=wéelŭma**. *ind 3rd sg* **wŭniipaweelŭ=máawal**. *ind inv* **niipawéelŭmukw**. *ind I-you* **kŭniipawéelŭmul**. *conj 3rd sg* **niipawéelŭmaat**. *imp* **niipawée=lum**. *ptcpl* **niipawéelŭmaat**.

**niipaweelúndam** VTI1A be proud of s.t. *ind 1st sg* **niipaweelúndamun**. *ind 3rd sg* **wŭniipaweelúndamun**. *conj 1st sg* **niipaweelúndamaan**. *conj 3rd sg* **niipaweelúndang**. *imp* **niipawee=lúndah**. *ptcpl* **niipaweelúndang**.

**níipawuw** VAI stand. *ind 1st sg* **níipawi**, **níipawiim**. *conj 3rd sg* **níipawiit**. *imp* **níipawiil**. *ptcpl* **níipawiit**. *mod-erative reduplication* **naaníipawuw**.

**níipun** VII be summer. **Níipŭne.** 'Last summer.'; **Niipúnge.** 'Next summer.'

*conj 3rd sg* **níipung**. *ptcpl* **níipung**.

**niipŭnámuw** VAI live until summer, survive until summer. *ind 1st sg* **niipŭ=námwi**, **niipŭnámwiim**. *conj 3rd sg* **niipŭnámwiit**. *ptcpl* **niipŭnámwiit**.

**niiskaachíimuw** VAI talk dirty. *ind 1st sg* **niiskaachíimwi**, **niiskaachíi=mwiim**. *conj 3rd sg* **niiskaachíi=mwiit**. *imp* **niiskaachíimwiil**. *ptcpl* **niiskaachíimwiit**.

**niiskaalóhkweew** VAI have dirty hair. *ind 1st sg* **niiskaalóhkwa**, **niiskaa=lóhkwaam**. *conj 3rd sg* **niiskaalóh=kwaat**. *ptcpl* **niiskaalóhkwaat**.

**niiskáandpeew** VAI have a dirty head. *ind 1st sg* **niiskáandpa**, **niiskáand=paam**. *conj 3rd sg* **niiskáandpaat**. *ptcpl* **niiskáandpaat**.

**niiskáasŭleew** VII be wasted light. **Ngwútii-tpóhkwe niiskáasŭle.** 'The light was left on overnight.' *conj 3rd sg* **niiskáasŭleew**. *ptcpl* **niiskáa=sŭleek**.

**niiskaláamuw** VAI sing when not wanted, sing and get on someone's nerves, cry, wail. *ind 1st sg* **niiskaláamwi**, **niiskaláamwiim**. *conj 3rd sg* **niiska=láamwiit**. *imp* **niiskaláamwiil**. *ptcpl* **niiskaláamwiit**.

**niiskalóhkeew** VAI make a mess, do a messy job, do dirty work, do unsatisfactory work. *ind 1st sg* **niiskalóhke**, **niiskalóhkeem**. *conj 3rd sg* **niiska=lóhkeet**. *ptcpl* **niiskalóhkeet**. *intensive reduplication* **aniiskalóhkeew**.

**niiskapíikweew** VAI play loud music. *ind 1st sg* **niiskapíikwe**, **niiskapíi=kweem**. *conj 3rd sg* **niiskapíikweet**. *imp* **niiskapíikweel**. *ptcpl* **niiskapíi=kweet**.

**niiskapóoshiish** NA dirty cat. *pl* **niiska=pooshíishak**. *poss* **niiskapooshíi=shum**. *loc* **niiskapooshíishung**. *dimin* **niiskapooshíishush**. *obv* **niiskapooshíishal**.

**niiskcháaleew** VAI have a dirty nose. *ind 1st sg* **niiskcháala**, **niiskcháalaam**. *conj 3rd sg* **niiskcháalaat**. *ptcpl* **niiskcháalaat**.

**niiskchàlíingweew** VAI have a dirty face. *ind 1st sg* **niiskchàlíingwa**, **niisk=chàlíingwaam**. *conj 3rd sg* **niisk=chàlíingwaat**. *ptcpl* **niiskchàlíin=gwaat**.

**niiskcheengwéexiin** VAI have a look of distaste on one's face, turn one's nose up at something. *ind 1st sg* **niisk=cheengwéexiin**, **niiskcheengwéexi**. *conj 3rd sg* **niiskcheengwéexiing**. *ptcpl* **niiskcheengwéexiing**, **niisk=cheengwéexiit**.

**níiskeew** VII be dirty. *conj 3rd sg* **níiskeek**. *ptcpl* **níiskeek**.

**niiskeekhíikeew** VAI write messily. **Wéemi táa ndúlu-niiskeekhíike.** 'I'm writing all over.' *ind 1st sg* **niis=keekhíike**, **niiskeekhíikeem**. *conj 3rd sg* **niiskeekhíikeet**. *imp* **niis=keekhíikeel**. *ptcpl* **niiskeekhíikeet**.

**niiskéelŭmeew** VTA think that s.o. is dirty. *ind 1st sg* **niiskéelŭmaaw**, **niiskéelŭma**. *ind 3rd sg* **wŭniiskee=lŭmáawal**. *ind inv* **niiskéelŭmukw**. *ind I-you* **kŭniiskéelŭmul**. *conj 3rd sg* **niiskéelŭmaat**. *ptcpl* **niiskée=lŭmaat**.

**niiskeelúndam** VTI 1A think that s.t. is dirty. *ind 1st sg* **niiskeelúndamun**. *ind 3rd sg* **wŭniiskeelúndamun**. *conj 1st sg* **niiskeelúndamaan**. *conj 3rd sg* **niiskeelúndang**. *ptcpl* **niiskee=lúndang**.

**niiskíiheew** VTA dirty s.o., make s.o. dirty. *ind 1st sg* **niiskíihaaw**, **niiskíi=ha**. *ind 3rd sg* **wŭniiskiiháawal**. *ind inv* **niiskíihukw**. *ind I-you* **kŭniiskíi=hul**. *conj 3rd sg* **niiskíihaat**. *imp* **níiskiih**. *ptcpl* **niiskíihaat**.

**niiskíikeew** VAI have a dirty house. *ind 1st sg* **niiskíike**, **niiskíikeem**. *conj 3rd sg* **niiskíikeet**. *ptcpl* **niiskíikeet**.

**niiskiiktúkweew** VAI have a dirty knee.

*ind 1st sg* **niiskiiktúkwe**, **niiskiik=túkweem**. *conj 3rd sg* **niiskiiktúk=weet**. *ptcpl* **niiskiiktúkweet**.

**niiskiinááakwat** VII be dirty looking, look dirty. *conj 3rd sg* **niiskiináa=kwahk**. *ptcpl* **niiskiináakwahk**.

**niiskiináakwsuw** VAI be dirty looking, look dirty *(s.t. animate)*. *ind 1st sg* **niiskiináakwsi**, **niiskiináakwsiim**. *conj 3rd sg* **niiskiináakwsiit**. *ptcpl* **niiskiináakwsiit**.

**niiskíhkam** VTI1A make s.t. dirty *(using the foot or body)*; step on s.t. and make it dirty. *ind 1st sg* **niiskíhka=mun**. *ind 3rd sg* **wŭniiskíhkamun**. *conj 1st sg* **niiskíhkamaan**. *conj 3rd sg* **niiskíhkang**. *imp* **niiskíhkah**. *ptcpl* **niiskíhkang**.

**niiskíhkaweew** VTA make s.o. dirty *(using the foot or body)*; step on s.o. and make them dirty. *ind 1st sg* **niiskíh=kawaaw**, **niiskíhkawa**. *ind 3rd sg* **wŭniiskihkawáawal**. *ind inv* **niis=kíhkaakw**. *ind I-you* **kŭniiskíhkool**. *conj 3rd sg* **niiskíhkawaat**. *imp* **niiskíhkaw**. *ptcpl* **niiskíhkawaat**.

**niiskihtáakwat** VII be noisy. *conj 3rd sg* **niiskihtáakwahk**. *ptcpl* **niiskihtáa=kwahk**.

**niiskihtáakwsuw** VAI be noisy. *ind 1st sg* **niiskihtáakwsi**, **niiskihtáakw=siim**. *conj 3rd sg* **niiskihtáakwsiit**. *ptcpl* **niiskihtáakwsiit**.

**niiskihtawákeew** VAI have a dirty ear, have dirty ears. *ind 1st sg* **niiskihta=wáka**, **niiskihtawákaam**. *conj 3rd sg* **niiskihtawákaat**. *ptcpl* **niiskihta=wákaat**.

**niiskíhtoow** VTI2 dirty s.t., make s.t. dirty. *ind 1st sg* **niiskíhtoon**. *ind 3rd sg* **wŭniiskíhtoon**. *conj 1st sg* **niis=kíhtawaan**. *conj 3rd sg* **niiskíhtaakw**. *imp* **niiskíhtool**. *ptcpl* **niiskíhtaakw**.

**niiskkáateew** VAI have a dirty leg; have a dark leg. *ind 1st sg* **niiskkáata**, **niiskkáataam**. *conj 3rd sg* **niiskkáa=taat**. *ptcpl* **niiskkáataat**. *intensive reduplication* **aniiskkáateew**.

**niiskóhkweew** VAI have dirty hair, have a dirty head. *ind 1st sg* **niiskóhkwa**, **niiskóhkwaam**. *conj 3rd sg* **niiskóh=kwaat**. *ptcpl* **niiskóhkwaat**.

**niiskpáleew** VTA get s.o. wet, make s.o. wet. *ind 1st sg* **niiskpálaaw**, **niisk=pála**. *ind 3rd sg* **wŭniiskpaláawal**. *ind inv* **niiskpálukw**. *ind I-you* **kŭ=niiskpálul**. *conj 3rd sg* **niiskpálaat**. *imp* **níiskpal**. *ptcpl* **niiskpálaat**.

**niiskpáteew** VII get wet. *conj 3rd sg* **niiskpáteek**. *ptcpl* **níiskpateek**.

**niiskpátoow** VTI2 get s.t. wet, make s.t. wet. *ind 1st sg* **niiskpátoon**. *ind 3rd sg* **wŭniiskpátoon**. *conj 1st sg* **niisk=pátawaan**. *conj 3rd sg* **niiskpátaakw**. *imp* **niiskpátool**. *ptcpl* **niiskpátaakw**.

**níiskpeew** VAI get wet. *ind 1st sg* **níiskpe**, **níiskpeem**. *conj 3rd sg* **níiskpeet**. *ptcpl* **níiskpeet**.

**níiskpeew** VII get wet. *conj 3rd sg* **níiskpeek**. *ptcpl* **níiskpeek**.

**niiskpéekat** VII be dirty water. *conj 3rd sg* **niiskpéekahk**. *ptcpl* **niiskpée=kahk**.

**niiskpéhleew** VII leak badly. **Ehŭliin=gwáhteek wúnj-niiskpéhleew.** 'There's a bad leak from the stovepipe.' *conj 3rd sg* **niiskpéhlaak**. *ptcpl* **niiskpéhlaak**.

**níiskpuy** NI dirty water. *loc* **níiskpiing**.

**niisksíiteew** VAI have a dirty foot. *ind 1st sg* **niisksíita**, **niisksíitaam**. *conj 3rd sg* **niisksíitaat**. *ptcpl* **niisksíitaat**. *intensive reduplication* **aniisksíiteew**.

**níisksuw** VAI be dirty. *ind 1st sg* **níisksi**, **níisksiim**. *conj 3rd sg* **níisksiit**. *ptcpl* **níisksiit**.

**niisktóoneew** VAI have a dirty mouth. *ind 1st sg* **niisktóona**, **niisktóonaam**. *conj 3rd sg* **niisktóonaat**. *ptcpl* **niisktóonaat**.

**niisktóonheew** VAI talk a lot, gossip; talk dirty. *ind 1st sg* **niisktóonhe**,

**niisktóonheem**. *conj 3rd sg* **niisk=tóonheet**. *imp* **niisktóonheel**. *ptcpl* **niisktóonheet**.

**niisktuyéemuw** VAI talk a lot. *ind 1st sg* **niisktuyéemwi**, **niisktuyéemwiim**. *conj 3rd sg* **niisktuyéemwiit**. *ptcpl* **niisktuyéemwiit**. *considered impolite.*

**níiskŭlaan** VII be unpleasant weather. *conj 3rd sg* **níiskŭlaang**. *ptcpl* **níiskŭlaang**.

**niiskŭlaníikameew** VAI have a runny nose. *ind 1st sg* **niiskŭlaníikama**, **niiskŭlaníikamaam**. *conj 3rd sg* **niiskŭlaníikamaat**. *ptcpl* **niiskŭlan=íikamaat**.

**níiskŭneew** VTA touch and dirty s.o., make s.o. dirty *(using the hands)*. *ind 1st sg* **níiskŭnaaw**, **níiskŭna**. *ind 3rd sg* **wŭniiskŭnáawal**. *ind inv* **níiskŭ=nukw**. *ind I-you* **kŭníiskŭnul**. *conj 3rd sg* **níiskŭnaat**. *imp* **níiskun**. *ptcpl* **níiskŭnaat**.

**niiskŭnáxkeew** VAI have a dirty hand. *ind 1st sg* **niiskŭnáxka**, **niiskŭnáx=kaam**. *conj 3rd sg* **niiskŭnáxkaat**. *ptcpl* **niiskŭnáxkaat**. *intensive reduplication* **aniiskŭnáxkeew**.

**níiskŭnum** VTI 1A touch and dirty s.t., make s.t. dirty *(using the hands)*. *ind 1st sg* **niiskŭnúmun**. *ind 3rd sg* **wŭniiskŭnúmun**. *conj 1st sg* **niiskŭ=númaan**. *conj 3rd sg* **níiskŭnung**. *imp* **níiskŭnih**. *ptcpl* **níiskŭnung**.

**níiskŭweew** VAI make an irritating noise, make an annoying noise. *ind 1st sg* **níiskŭwe**, **níiskŭweem**. *conj 3rd sg* **níiskŭweet**. *ptcpl* **níiskŭweet**.

**níiskŭweew** VII make an irritating noise, make an annoying noise. *conj 3rd sg* **níiskŭweek**. *ptcpl* **níiskŭweek**.

**níiskwan** NAD my elbow. *pl* **níiskwa=nak**. *3rd poss* **wŭníiskwanal**. *loc* **níiskwanung**. *dimin* **níiskwanush**.

**níiskwan** NID my elbow. *pl* **níiskwanal**. *3rd poss* **wŭníiskwan**. *loc* **níiskwa=nung**. *dimin* **níiskwanush**.

**níiskxum** NA dirty dog. *pl* **niiskxúmwak**. *loc* **niiskxúmwung**. *dimin* **niishk=xúmwush**. *obv* **niiskxúmwal**.

**niish-** PN two. **Níish-kíishooxkw náh ndúnda-làlóhke.** 'I worked there for two months.'; **Níish-póond txú-poondakúsuw.** 'He weighs two pounds.'

**niish-** PV two. **Kŭníish-alaawhúnzi.** 'You are using two canes.' *ptcpl* **níish-**. *See* **niishu-**.

**niishaaníhka** PC twelve.

**niishaapéeksuw** VAI have two pages *(s.t. animate, of something sheet-like)*. *usually of pieces of paper. conj 3rd sg* **niishaapéeksiit**. *ptcpl* **niishaapée=ksiit**.

**níishaash** PC seven.

**níisha** PC two.

**niisháhkameew** VII be two days. *conj 3rd sg* **niisháhkameek**. *ptcpl* **nii=sháhkameek**.

**niisháhtakat** VII be two pieces *(of something string-like)*. *conj 3rd sg* **nii=sháhtakahk**. *ptcpl* **niisháhtakahk**.

**niishaláamuw** VAI sing together. *ind 1st sg* **niishaláamwi**, **niishaláamwiim**. *conj 3rd sg* **niishaláamwiit**. *imp* **nii=shaláamwiil**. *ptcpl* **niishaláamwiit**.

**niishalíhkeew** VAI take two steps. *ind 1st sg* **niishalíhke**, **niishalíhkeem**. *conj 3rd sg* **niishalíhkeet**. *imp* **niishalíhkeel**. *ptcpl* **niishalíhkeet**.

**niishalohkéemeew** VTA work with s.o. *ind 1st sg* **niishalohkéemaaw**, **nii=shalohkéema**. *ind 3rd sg* **wŭniisha=lohkeemáawal**. *ind inv* **niishaloh=kéemukw**. *ind I-you* **kŭniishaloh=kéemul**. *conj 3rd sg* **niishalohkée=maat**. *imp* **niishalóhkeem**. *ptcpl* **niishalohkéemaat**.

**niishapóomeew** VTA sit with s.o. *ind 1st sg* **niishapóomaaw**, **niishapóoma**. *ind 3rd sg* **wŭniishapoomáawal**. *ind inv* **niishapóomukw**. *ind I-you* **kŭ=**

**niishapóomul**. *conj 3rd sg* **niisha=póomaat**. *imp* **níishapoom**. *ptcpl* **niishapóomaat**.

**niishataxooxwéewak** VAI walk in groups of two. *usually plural. ind 1st pl* **nii=shataxooxwéhna**. *conj 3rd sg* **nii=shataxooxwéhtiit**. *imp* **niishatax=óoxweekw**. *ptcpl* **niishataxooxwéh=tiit**.

**niishéekat** VII be double, be in two layers *(of something sheet-like). conj 3rd sg* **niishéekahk**. *ptcpl* **niishéekahk**.

**niisheekíixiin** VAI be in two layers *(s.t. animate, of something sheet-like). conj 3rd sg* **niisheekíixiing**. *ptcpl* **niisheekíixiing, niisheekíixiit**.

**niisheekíixun** VII be in two layers *(of something sheet-like). conj 3rd sg* **niisheekíixung**. *ptcpl* **niishee=kíixung**.

**niishéeksuw** VAI be double, be in two layers *(s.t. animate, of something sheet-like). conj 3rd sg* **niishéeksiit**. *ptcpl* **niishéeksiit**.

**niisheelawúsŭwak** VAI play together. *usually plural. ind 1st pl* **niishee=lawusíhna**. *conj 3rd sg* **niisheela=wusíhtiit**. *imp* **niisheelawúsiikw**. *ptcpl* **niisheelawusíhtiit**.

**niishéeli** PC two, in twos. **Niishéeli pihtawíixŭnool.** 'They're stacked in twos.'; **Níi néem niishéeli éenda-náxkwteek.** 'I saw two fires.'

**niishéelook** VAI be two pairs, be two sets *(s.t. animate). usually plural. ind 1st pl* **niisheelóhna**. *indef subject* **niishéelun**. *conj 3rd sg* **niisheelóh=tiit**. *ptcpl* **niisheelóhtiit**.

**niishéeltool** VII be two pairs, be two sets. *usually plural. conj 3rd sg* **niishée=lihk**. *ptcpl* **niisheelíhkiil**.

**níishii** PC two **Níishii ndoxkwamúnal.** 'I sewed them in twos.'

**níishii-takwápuw** VAI sit on one's knees. *ind 1st sg* **níishii-takwápi, níishii-takwápiim**. *conj 3rd sg* **níishii-takwápiit**. *imp* **níishii-takwápiil**. *ptcpl* **níishii-takwápiit**.

**níishii-takwíixiin** VAI kneel, fall on one's knees. *ind 1st sg* **níishii-takwíixiin, níishii-takwíixi**. *conj 3rd sg* **níishii-takwíixiing**. *imp* **níishii-takwíixiil**. *ptcpl* **níishii-takwíixiing**.

**niishíitakuw** VAI kneel down. *ind 1st sg* **niishíitakwi, niishíitakwiim**. *conj 3rd sg* **niishíitakwiit**. *imp* **niishíita=kwiil**. *ptcpl* **niishíitakwiit**.

**niishiitakwíhtaweew** VTA kneel to s.o. *ind 1st sg* **niishiitakwíhtawaaw, nii=shiitakwíhtawa**. *ind 3rd sg* **wŭnii=shiitakwihtawáawal**. *ind inv* **niishii=takwíhtaakw**. *ind I-you* **kŭniishiita=kwíhtool**. *conj 3rd sg* **niishiitakwíh=tawaat**. *imp* **niishiitakwíhtaw**. *ptcpl* **niishiitakwíhtawaat**.

**niishkéemeew** VTA dance with s.o. *ind 1st sg* **niishkéemaaw, niishkéema**. *ind 3rd sg* **wŭniishkeemáawal**. *ind inv* **niishkéemukw**. *ind I-you* **kŭ=niishkéemul**. *conj 3rd sg* **niishkée=maat**. *imp* **níishkeem**. *ptcpl* **niish=kéemaat**. *See* **wiitkéemeew**.

**niishookwŭnáhkeew** VAI be gone for two days. *ind 1st sg* **niishookwŭ=náhke, niishookwŭnáhkeem**. *conj 3rd sg* **niishookwŭnáhkeet**. *ptcpl* **niishookwŭnáhkeet**.

**niishookwŭnákat** VII be two days. **Nii=shookwŭnákate náh éew.** 'He went there two days ago.'; **Niishookwŭ=nakáhke náh éew.** 'He's going there in two days.' *conj 3rd sg* **niishoo=kwŭnákahk**. *ptcpl* **niishookwŭ=nákahk**.

**niishóokwŭnii** PC two days.

**niishooxwéewak** VAI walk in twos, walk as a pair. *usually plural. ind 1st pl* **niishooxwéhna**. *conj 3rd sg* **niishoo=xwéhtiit**. *imp* **niishóoxweekw**. *ptcpl* **niishooxwéhtiit**.

**niishohkwéepŭwak** VAI sit in twos. *usually plural. ind 1st pl* **niishohkwee=**

**píhna**. *conj 3rd sg* **niishohkweepíh=tiit**. *imp* **niishohkwéepiikw**. *ptcpl* **niishohkweepíhtiit**.

**níishŭwak** VAI be two of them. *ind 1st pl* **niishíhna**. *conj 3rd sg* **níishíhtiit**. *ptcpl* **niishíhtiit**.

**niishu-** PV two. **Níishu-pangéeyeew.** 'It's in two pieces.' *ptcpl* **níishu-**. *See* **niish-**.

**níishun** PC two times.

**níishŭnool** VII be two of them. *usually plural*. *conj 3rd sg* **níishung**. *ptcpl* **niishúngiil**.

**niixahtakíhleew** VAI run downhill. *ind 1st sg* **niixahtakíhla**, **niixahtakíh=laam**. *conj 3rd sg* **niixahtakíhlaat**. *imp* **niixahtakíhlaal**. *ptcpl* **niixahta=kíhlaat**.

**niixakóosuw** VAI come down, climb down. *ind 1st sg* **niixakóosi**, **niixa=kóosiim**. *conj 3rd sg* **niixakóosiit**. *imp* **niixakóosiil**. *ptcpl* **niixakóosiit**.

**níixiiw** VAI-S come down, descend, get out of a vehicle. *ind 1st sg* **níixi**, **níi=xiim**. *conj 3rd sg* **níixiit**. *imp* **níixiil**. *ptcpl* **níixiit**.

**niixíikwsuw** VAI crawl downwards. *ind 1st sg* **niixíikwsi**, **niixíikwsiim**. *conj 3rd sg* **niixíikwsiit**. *imp* **niixíikwsiil**. *ptcpl* **niixíikwsiit**. *See* **chiixíikwsuw**.

**niixsheetóonayeew** VAI have one's lips sticking out, pout. *ind 1st sg* **niix=sheetóonaya**, **niixsheetóonayaam**. *conj 3rd sg* **niixsheetóonayaat**. *ptcpl* **niixsheetóonayaat**.

**níixŭneew** VTA lower s.o., take s.o. down. *ind 1st sg* **níixŭnaaw**, **níixŭna**. *ind 3rd sg* **wŭniixŭnáawal**. *ind inv* **níi=xŭnukw**. *ind I-you* **kŭníixŭnul**. *conj 3rd sg* **níixŭnaat**. *imp* **níixun**. *ptcpl* **níixŭnaat**.

**níixŭnum** VTI 1B lower s.t., take s.t. down. *ind 1st sg* **niixŭnúmun**. *ind 3rd sg* **wŭniixŭnúmun**. *conj 1st sg* **niixŭ=númaan**. *conj 3rd sg* **níixŭnung**. *imp* **níixŭnih**. *ptcpl* **níixŭnung**.

**níhleew** VTA kill s.o.; beat s.o. up. *ind 1st sg* **níhlaaw**, **níhla**. *ind 3rd sg* **wŭnihláawal**. *ind inv* **níhlukw**. *ind I-you* **kŭníhlul**. *conj 3rd sg* **níhlaat**. *imp* **níhl**. *ptcpl* **néhlaat**.

**nihlaakanáxŭmweew** VAI kill a dog; beat a dog. *ind 1st sg* **nihlaakanáxŭ=mwe**, **nihlaakanáxŭmweem**. *conj 3rd sg* **nihlaakanáxŭmweet**. *imp* **nihlaakanáxŭmweel**. *ptcpl* **nehlaa=kanáxŭmweet**.

**nihláaleew** VTA own s.o. *ind 1st sg* **nih=láalaaw**, **nihláala**. *ind 3rd sg* **wŭ=nihlaaláawal**. *ind inv* **nihláalukw**. *ind I-you* **kŭnihláalul**. *conj 3rd sg* **nihláalaat**. *imp* **níhlaal**. *ptcpl* **nehláalaat**.

**nihlaapeewháaleew** VTA set s.o. free. *ind 1st sg* **nihlaapeewháalaaw**, **nih=laapeewháala**. *ind 3rd sg* **wŭnihlaa=peewhaaláawal**. *ind inv* **nihlaapeew=háalukw**. *ind I-you* **kŭnihlaapeew=háalul**. *conj 3rd sg* **nihlaapeewháa=laat**. *imp* **nihlaapéewhaal**. *ptcpl* **nehlaapeewháalaat**.

**nihlaapéewheew** VAIO free s.o. *ind 1st sg* **nihlaapeewhéenal**. *ind 3rd sg* **wŭ=nihlaapéewheen**. *conj 3rd sg* **nih=laapéewheet**. *imp* **nihlaapéewheel**. *ptcpl* **nehlaapéewhaat**.

**nihlaapéewuw** VAI be free, be unmarried, have no attachments. *ind 1st sg* **nih=laapéewi**, **nihlaapéewiim**. *conj 3rd sg* **nihlaapéewiit**. *ptcpl* **nehlaa=péewiit**.

**nihláatam** VTI 1A own s.t. *ind 1st sg* **nihláatŭmun**. *ind 3rd sg* **wŭnihláa=tamun**. *conj 1st sg* **nihláatamaan**. *conj 3rd sg* **nihláatang**. *imp* **nihláa=tih**. *ptcpl* **nehláatang**.

**nihlaawsoohάaleew** VTA set s.o. free, make s.o. free. *ind 1st sg* **nihlaaw=soohάalaaw**, **nihlaawsoohάala**. *ind 3rd sg* **wŭnihlaawsoohaaláawal**. *ind inv* **nihlaawsoohάalukw**. *ind I-you* **kŭnihlaawsoohάalul**. *conj 3rd sg*

**nihlaawsooháalaat**. *imp* **nihlaaw=sóohaal**. *ptcpl* **nehlaawsooháalaat**. *See* **nihlaawsóoheew**.

**nihlaawsóoheew** VAIO set s.o. free, make s.o. free. *ind 1st sg* **nihlaawsóoheen**. *ind 3rd sg* **wŭnihlaawsoohéenal**. *conj 3rd sg* **nihlaawsóoheet**. *imp* **nihlaawsóoheel**. *ptcpl* **nehlaawsóo=heet**. *See* **nihlaawsooháaleew**.

**nihlatóhweew** VAI kill a deer. *ind 1st sg* **nihlatóhwe**, **nihlatóhweem**. *conj 3rd sg* **nihlatóhweet**. *imp* **nihlatóhweel**. *ptcpl* **nehlatóhweet**.

**nihlawehleeshóosheew** VAI kill a bird. *ind 1st sg* **nihlawehleeshóoshe**, **nihlawehleeshóosheem**. *conj 3rd sg* **nihlawehleeshóosheet**. *imp* **nihla=wehleeshóosheel**. *ptcpl* **nehlaweh=leeshóosheet**.

**nihlawiilpíisheew** VAI kill a louse. *ind 1st sg* **nihlawiilpíishe**, **nihlawiilpíi=sheem**. *conj 3rd sg* **nihlawiilpíisheet**. *imp* **nihlawiilpíisheel**. *ptcpl* **nehla=wiilpíisheet**.

**nihlaxkóokeew** VAI kill a snake. *ind 1st sg* **nihlaxkóoke**, **nihlaxkóokeem**. *conj 3rd sg* **nihlaxkóokeet**. *imp* **nihlaxkóokeel**. *ptcpl* **nehlaxkóokeet**.

**nihláxkweew** VAI kill a bear. *ind 1st sg* **nihláxkwe**, **nihláxkweem**. *conj 3rd sg* **nihláxkweet**. *imp* **nihláxkweel**. *ptcpl* **nehláxkweet**. *See* **nihliimáx=kweew**.

**níhlii** PC by oneself. **Níhlii kpákamaaw khákay.** 'You hit yourself.'; **Níhlii nŭwéechpii.** 'I got dressed by my-self.'

**nihliikíipsheew** VAI kill a chicken. *ind 1st sg* **nihliikíipshe**, **nihliikíipsheem**. *conj 3rd sg* **nihliikíipsheet**. *imp* **nih=liikíipsheel**. *ptcpl* **nehliikíipsheet**.

**nihliimáxkweew** VAI kill a bear. *ind 1st sg* **nihliimáxkwe**, **nihliimáxkweem**. *conj 3rd sg* **nihliimáxkweet**. *imp* **nihliimáxkweel**. *ptcpl* **nehliimáx=kweet**. *See* **nihláxkweew**.

**nihlkwúsuw** VAI be killed. *ind 1st sg* **nihlkwúsi**, **nihlkwúsiim**. *conj 3rd sg* **nihlkwúsiit**. *ptcpl* **nehlkwúsiit**.

**nihloochéeweew** VAI kill a fly. *ind 1st sg* **nihloochéewe**, **nihloochéeweem**. *conj 3rd sg* **nihloochéeweet**. *imp* **nihloochéeweel**. *ptcpl* **nehloochée=weet**.

**níhlŭweew** VAI murder, kill people. *ind 1st sg* **níhlŭwe**, **níhlŭweem**. *conj 3rd sg* **níhlŭweet**. *imp* **níhlŭweel**. *ptcpl* **néhlŭweet**.

**nihlxúmweew** VAI kill an animal; beat an animal. *ind 1st sg* **nihlxúmwe**, **nihlxúmweem**. *conj 3rd sg* **nihl=xúmweet**. *imp* **nihlxúmweel**. *ptcpl* **nehlxúmweet**.

**nihtaa-** PV skillfully, know how to *(do something)*. **Wŭníhtaa- wéemi kwéek -saakíhtoon.** 'He watches everything.'; **Níhtaa-pŭmutóon=heew.** 'He's a good preacher.' *ptcpl* **néhtaa-**.

**níhtaa-píchuw** VAI be a good pitcher. *ind 1st sg* **níhtaa-píchi**, **níhtaa-píchiim**. *conj 3rd sg* **níhtaa-píchiit**. *ptcpl* **néhtaa-píchiit**.

**nihtaawáaheew** VAI throw well. *ind 1st sg* **nihtaawáahe**, **nihtaawáaheem**. *conj 3rd sg* **nihtaawáaheet**. *imp* **nih=taawáaheel**. *ptcpl* **nehtaawáaheet**.

**nihtaawaaptóoneew** VAI be a good speaker *(also of a child learning how to speak)*; be good at speaking, be good at public speaking. *ind 1st sg* **nihtaawaaptóone**, **nihtaawaaptóo=neem**. *conj 3rd sg* **nihtaawaaptóo=neet**. *ptcpl* **nehtaawaaptóoneet**.

**nihtaawakíinzuw** VAI read skillfully, be able to read properly. *ind 1st sg* **nih=taawakíinzi**, **nihtaawakíinziim**. *conj 3rd sg* **nihtaawakíinziit**. *ptcpl* **neh=taawakíinziit**.

**nihtaawaláamuw** VAI be a good singer. *ind 1st sg* **nihtaawaláamwi**, **nihtaa=waláamwiim**. *conj 3rd sg* **nihtaawa=**

láamwiit. *ptcpl* **nehtaawaláamwiit**.

**nihtaawalóhkeew** VAI work well, do one's work correctly. *ind 1st sg* **nih=taawalóhke**, **nihtaawalóhkeem**. *conj 3rd sg* **nihtaawalóhkeet**. *imp* **nih=taawalóhkeel**. *ptcpl* **nehtaawa=lóhkeet**.

**nihtaawatúpuw** VAI be a good cook. *ind 1st sg* **nihtaawatúpwi**, **nihtaawa=túpwiim**. *conj 3rd sg* **nihtaawa=túpwiit**. *ptcpl* **nehtaawatúpwiit**.

**nihtaawayáxkham** VOTI1A shoot skillfully, be a good shot. *ind 1st sg* **nih=taawayáxkham**. *conj 3rd sg* **nihtaa=wayáxkhang**. *ptcpl* **nehtaawa=yáxkhang**.

**nihtáhtoow** VTI2 know how to do s.t. *ind 1st sg* **nihtáhtoon**. *ind 3rd sg* **wŭnihtáhtoon**. *conj 1st sg* **nihtáhta=waan**. *conj 3rd sg* **nihtáhtaakw**. *ptcpl* **nehtáhtaakw**.

**nihtamáweew** VTAO kill s.o. for s.o. *ind 1st sg* **nihtamáwaan**. *ind 3rd sg* **wŭ=nihtamáwaan**. *ind inv* **nihtamáa=kwun**. *ind I-you* **kŭnihtamóolun**. *conj 3rd sg* **nihtamáwaat**. *imp* **níhtamaw**. *ptcpl* **nehtamáwaat**.

**níhtoow** VTI2 kill s.t. **Kwéek kŭníhto?** 'What did you kill?' *ind 1st sg* **níh=toon**. *ind 3rd sg* **wŭníhtoon**. *conj 1st sg* **níhtawaan**. *conj 3rd sg* **níhtaakw**. *imp* **níhtool**. *ptcpl* **néhtaakw**.

**nján** NA John. *dimin* **njánush**. *obv* **njánal**. *From English* John.

**njékpiin** NA Jacobina. *obv* **njèkpíinal**. *From English* Jacobina.

**njíhnal** PC more. **Njíhnal kwéek káta-weewíhto?** 'Do you want to know some more?'; **Kwáy máh há njíhnal nŭwiicheewáawu.** 'I don't go with her anymore.'

**njík** NA nickname for person named Julia. *obv* **njíkal**.

**njóoliish** NA Julia. *dimin* **njoolíishush**. *obv* **njoolíishal**. *From English* Julia.

**nooch-** PV start to. *informal*. **Nóoch-tohtoongtóone.** 'He's starting to yawn.'; **Náakeesh shúkw manóong=suw, nál wáak méhtxii amíimunz wtulkíilun nál wáak wŭnóoch-wiichéewaan.** 'He was angry for a while, and then as soon as the baby was born he started to go with her (the woman) again.' *ptcpl* **nóoch-**. *See* **noochi-**.

**noochaawsáweew** VTA take care of s.o.'s child for them. *ind 1st sg* **noochaaw=sáwaaw**, **noochaawsáwa**. *ind 3rd sg* **wŭnoochaawsawáawal**. *ind inv* **noocháawsaakw**. *ind I-you* **kŭnoo=cháawsool**. *conj 3rd sg* **noochaaw=sáwaat**. *imp* **noocháawsaw**. *ptcpl* **noochaawsáwaat**.

**noocháawsuw** VAI take care of a child, babysit. *ind 1st sg* **noocháawsi**, **noo=cháawsiim**. *conj 3rd sg* **noocháawsiit**. *imp* **noocháawsiil**. *ptcpl* **noocháaw=siit**.

**noochíikuw** VAI start to grow. **Áawiis noochíikuw, méhch alumíikuw.** 'He was slow to start growing, he's growing now.' *ind 1st sg* **noochíiki**, **noo=chíikiim**. *conj 3rd sg* **noochíikiit**. *ptcpl* **noochíikiit**.

**noochíikwsuw** VAI start to crawl. *ind 1st sg* **noochíikwsi**, **noochíikwsiim**. *conj 3rd sg* **noochíikwsiit**. *imp* **noochíik=wsiil**. *ptcpl* **noochíikwsiit**.

**noochíikwsuw** VAI start to crawl. *ind 1st sg* **noochíikwsi**, **noochíikwsiim**. *conj 3rd sg* **noochíikwsiit**. *imp* **noochíik=wsiil**. *ptcpl* **noochíikwsiit**.

**noochiilŭnúweew** VAI look for a man. *ind 1st sg* **noochiilŭnúwe**, **noochii=lŭnúweem**. *conj 3rd sg* **noochiilŭ=núweet**. *imp* **noochiilŭnúweel**. *ptcpl* **noochiilŭnúweet**.

**noochi-** PV start to. **Nóochi-apáamsuw.** 'He's starting to walk.'; **Nóochi-apáamsi.** 'I'm starting to walk.' *ptcpl* **nóochi-**. *See* **nooch-**.

**noochu-** PV start to. *informal*. **Kwáy íin**

**nóochu-neenáxkuw.** 'Now he's starting to play ball.' *ptcpl* **nóochu-**. *See* **nooch-**, **noochi-**.
**nóolii** PC nine. **Nóoli txaaníhka.** 'Nineteen.'
**noonáakan** NID my breast, my nipple. *pl* **noonáakanal**. *3rd poss* **wŭnoonáa=kan**. *loc* **noonáakanung**.
**noonáaleew** VTA suck s.o., feed at s.o.'s breast, nurse from s.o. *ind 1st sg* **noonáalaaw**, **noonáala**. *ind 3rd sg* **wŭnoonaaláawal**. *ind inv* **noonáa=lukw**. *ind I-you* **kŭnoonáalul**. *conj 3rd sg* **noonáalaat**. *imp* **nóonaal**. *ptcpl* **noonáalaat**.
**nóondaa** PC less *(than someone or something else)*. **Nóondaa ndúndxu-poondakúsi.** 'I weigh less.'; **Nóon=daa lúkiil.** 'He's smaller.'
**noondaawíixun** VII be not enough of something. *conj 3rd sg* **noondaa=wíixung**. *ptcpl* **noondaawíixung**.
**noondayeelúnzuw** VAI think oneself inferior. *ind 1st sg* **noondayeelúnzi**, **noondayeelúnziim**. *conj 3rd sg* **noondayeelúnziit**. *ptcpl* **noondayee=lúnziit**.
**noondéexiin** VAI be deficient, be lacking, be short of something, be not quite enough of something *(s.t. animate)*; fall short. *ind 1st sg* **noondéexiin**, **noondéexi**. *conj 3rd sg* **noondée=xiing**. *ptcpl* **noondéexiing**.
**noondéextoow** VTI2 lack s.t., lack sufficiently of s.t. *(to cover something, to reach something)*. *ind 1st sg* **noon=déextoon**. *ind 3rd sg* **wŭnoondéex=toon**. *conj 1st sg* **noondeextáwaan**. *conj 3rd sg* **noondéextaakw**. *ptcpl* **noondéextaakw**.
**noondéexŭmeew** VTA lack s.t. animate *(of commodities)*. **Noondéexŭma pambíilak.** 'I have not quite enough paper.' *ind 1st sg* **noondéexŭmaaw**, **noondéexŭma**. *ind 3rd sg* **wŭnoon=deexŭmáawal**. *ind inv* **noondéexŭ=mukw**. *ind I-you* **kŭnoondéexŭmul**. *conj 3rd sg* **noondéexŭmaat**. *ptcpl* **noondéexŭmaat**.
**noondéexun** VII be deficient, be lacking, be short of something, be not quite enough of something. *conj 3rd sg* **noondéexung**. *ptcpl* **noondéexung**.
**noondéeyeew** VII be short, be lacking. *conj 3rd sg* **noondéeyeek**. *ptcpl* **noondéeyeek**.
**noondéhleew** VAIO run short of s.t., be lacking s.t. *(a commodity)*. **Noondéh=laan pámbiil.** 'I ran short of the paper.' *ind 1st sg* **wŭnoondéhlaan**. *ind 3rd sg* **noondéhlaan**. *conj 3rd sg* **noondéhlaat**. *ptcpl* **noondéhlaat**.
**noonóosuw** VAI nurse *(of a child)*. *ind 1st sg* **noonóosi**, **noonóosiim**. *conj 3rd sg* **noonóosiit**. *imp* **noonóosiil**. *ptcpl* **noonóosiit**.
**noonzhéesuw** VAI carry a baby. *ind 1st sg* **noonzhéesi**, **noonzhéesiim**. *conj 3rd sg* **noonzhéesiit**. *imp* **noonzhée=siil**. *ptcpl* **noonzhéesiit**. *See* **noon=zhéewasuw**.
**noonzhéewasuw** VAI carry a baby. *ind 1st sg* **noonzhéewasi**, **noonzhéewa=siim**. *conj 3rd sg* **noonzhéewasiit**. *imp* **noonzhéewasiil**. *ptcpl* **noon=zhéewasiit**. *See* **noonzhéesuw**.
**noospépul** NA newspaper. *pl* **noospép=ŭlal**. *poss* **noospépŭlum**. *loc* **noos=pépŭlung**. *dimin* **noospépŭlush**. *obv* **noospépŭlal**. *From English* newspaper.
**nootalóhkeew** VAI start working. *ind 1st sg* **nootalóhke**, **nootalóhkeem**. *conj 3rd sg* **nootalóhkeet**. *imp* **nootalóh=keel**. *ptcpl* **nootalóhkeet**.
**nóotapuw** VAI begin to stay there, begin to stay here. *ind 1st sg* **nóotapi**, **nóo=tapiim**. *conj 3rd sg* **nóotapiit**. *imp* **nóotapiil**. *ptcpl* **nóotapiit**.
**nootíikeew** VAI stay at home alone. *ind 1st sg* **nootíike**, **nootíikeem**. *conj 3rd sg* **nootíikeet**. *imp* **nootíikeel**. *ptcpl*

**nootíikeet**.

**nootíikees** NI stick placed across the door to indicate that no one is at home. *pl* **nootiikéesal**.

**nootoxkwéeweew** VAI look for a woman. *ind 1st sg* **nootoxkwéewe, noo=toxkwéeweem**. *conj 3rd sg* **nootox=kwéeweet**. *imp* **nootoxkwéeweel**. *ptcpl* **nootoxkwéeweet**.

**noottóonheew** VAI start to talk. *ind 1st sg* **noottóonhe, noottóonheem**. *conj 3rd sg* **noottóonheet**. *imp* **noottóon=heel**. *ptcpl* **noottóonheet**.

**nóotŭweew** VAI start to make noise. *ind 1st sg* **nóotŭwe, nóotŭweem**. *conj 3rd sg* **nóotŭweet**. *imp* **nóotŭweel**. *ptcpl* **nóotŭweet**.

**nóhleew** VTA nurse s.o. *ind 1st sg* **nóh=laaw, nóhla**. *ind 3rd sg* **wŭnohláawal**. *ind inv* **nóhlukw**. *ind I-you* **kŭnóhlul**. *conj 3rd sg* **nóhlaat**. *imp* **nóhl**. *ptcpl* **nóhlaat**.

**nohláawasuw** VAI nurse a baby. *ind 1st sg* **nohláawasi, nohláawasiim**. *conj 3rd sg* **nohláawasiit**. *imp* **nohláawa=siil**. *ptcpl* **nohláawasiit**.

**nohtáakwat** VII be understood. *conj 3rd sg* **nohtáakwahk**. *ptcpl* **neenohtáa=kwahk**.

**nohtáakwsuw** VAI be understood. *ind 1st sg* **nunohtáakwsi, nùnohtáak=wsiim**. *conj 3rd sg* **nohtáakwsiit**. *ptcpl* **neenohtáakwsiit**.

**nohtáasuw** VAI understand. *ind 1st sg* **nùnohtáasi, nùnohtáasiim**. *conj 3rd sg* **nohtáasiit**. *ptcpl* **neenohtáasiit**.

**nóhtam** VTI 1A understand s.t. *ind 1st sg* **nùnóhtamun**. *ind 3rd sg* **wŭnunóh=tamun**. *conj 1st sg* **nóhtamaan**. *conj 3rd sg* **nóhtang**. *ptcpl* **neenóhtang**.

**nóhtameew** VAI understand. *ind 1st sg* **nùnóhtama, nùnóhtamaam**. *conj 3rd sg* **nóhtamaakw**. *ptcpl* **neenóh=tamaakw**.

**nóhtaweew** VTA understand s.o. *ind 1st sg* **nùnóhtawaaw, nùnóhtawa**. *ind 3rd sg* **wŭnunohtawáawal**. *ind inv* **nùnóhtaakw**. *ind I-you* **kŭnunóh=tool**. *conj 3rd sg* **nóhtawaat**. *ptcpl* **neenóhtawaat**.

**nú** PR that *(inanimate)*. **Nú óonj-tóhpu-chpapiinéewa amiimúnzak.** 'That's the reason why the children were (born) far apart.'; **Kŭnéemun há nú?** 'Did you see it?' *See* **nún**.

**nún** PR that *(inanimate emphatic)*. **Nún éet há.** 'That must be it.'; **Nún áa ndulŭnúmun.** 'That's what I should do.' *See* **nú**.

**núngachuw** VAI shiver from the cold. *ind 1st sg* **núngachi, núngachiim**. *conj 3rd sg* **núngachiit**. *ptcpl* **néengachiit**.

**nungatayéhleew** VAI have one's stomach shaking. *ind 1st sg* **nungatayéh=la, nungatayéhlaam**. *conj 3rd sg* **nungatayéhlaat**. *ptcpl* **neengata=yéhlaat**.

**nungíhleew** VAI shake *(s.t. animate)*. *ind 1st sg* **nungíhla, nungíhlaam**. *conj 3rd sg* **nungíhlaat**. *ptcpl* **neengíhlaat**.

**nungíhleew** VII shake. *conj 3rd sg* **nungíhlaak**. *ptcpl* **neengíhlaak**.

**nungkaatéhleew** VAI have one's legs shaking; be afraid. *ind 1st sg* **nung=kaatéhla, nungkaatéhlaam**. *conj 3rd sg* **nungkaatéhlaat**. *ptcpl* **neengkaa=téhlaat**.

**nungohkwéhleew** VAI have one's head shaking *(involuntarily)*. *ind 1st sg* **nungohkwéhla, nungohkwéhlaam**. *conj 3rd sg* **nungohkwéhlaat**. *ptcpl* **neengohkwéhlaat**.

**nvootíhtaweew** VTA vote for s.o. *ind 1st sg* **nùfootíhtawaaw, nùfootíhtawa**. *ind 3rd sg* **wŭnufootihtawáawal**. *ind inv* **nùfootíhtaakw**. *ind I-you* **kŭnuf=ootíhtool**. *conj 3rd sg* **nvootíhtawaat**. *imp* **nvootíhtaw**. *ptcpl* **neefootíhta=waat**. *From English* vote.

**nvóotuw** VAI vote, cast a vote. **Máw-nvóotuw.** 'He's going to vote.' *ind*

*1st sg* **nùfóoti**, **nùfóotiim**. *conj 3rd sg* **nvóotiit**. *imp* **nvóotiil**. *ptcpl* **nee=fóotiit**. *From English* vote.

**nxáaleew** VTA watch for s.o., watch out for s.o., be wary of s.o. *ind 1st sg* **naxáalaaw**, **naxáala**. *ind 3rd sg* **wŭnaxaaláawal**. *ind inv* **naxáalukw**. *ind I-you* **kŭnaxáalul**. *conj 3rd sg* **nxáalaat**. *imp* **nxáal**. *ptcpl* **nee=xáalaat**.

**nxaangwéewak** VAI lie in threes. *usually plural. ind 1st pl* **naxaangwéhna**. *conj 3rd sg* **nxaangwéhtiit**. *imp* **nxáangweekw**. *ptcpl* **neexaan=gwéhtiit**.

**nxaaníhka** PC thirteen.

**nxaapéeksuw** VAI have three pages *(s.t. animate, of something sheet-like). usually of pieces of paper. ind 1st sg* **naxaapéeksi**, **naxaapéeksiim**. *conj 3rd sg* **nxaapéeksiit**. *ptcpl* **neexaa=péeksiit**.

**nxaapóxku** PC three hundred.

**nxáasuw** VAI watch out, be wary. **Nxáa=siil! Ktumshóokwun-uch.** 'Look out! It'll cut you!' *ind 1st sg* **naxáasi**, **naxáasiim**. *conj 3rd sg* **nxáasiit**. *imp* **nxáasiil**. *ptcpl* **neexáasiit**.

**nxáatam** VTI1A be wary of s.t. *ind 1st sg* **naxáatŭmun**. *ind 3rd sg* **wŭnaxáa=tŭmun**. *conj 1st sg* **nxáatŭmaan**. *conj 3rd sg* **nxáatang**. *imp* **nxáatih**. *ptcpl* **neexáatang**.

**nxáawapuw** VAI be in danger. *ind 1st sg* **naxáawapi**, **naxáawapiim**. *conj 3rd sg* **nxáawapiit**. *ptcpl* **neexáawapiit**.

**nxaawéelŭmeew** VTA watch out for s.o., be wary of what may happen to s.o. *ind 1st sg* **nàxaawéelŭmaaw**, **nàxaa=wéelŭma**. *ind 3rd sg* **wŭnaxaawee=lŭmáawal**. *ind inv* **nàxaawéelŭ=mukw**. *ind I-you* **kŭnaxaawéelŭmul**. *conj 3rd sg* **nxaawéelŭmaat**. *ptcpl* **neexaawéelŭmaat**.

**nxáh** PC three. **Níi nŭmoxóomus wáak nóohum kxánŭwak nxáh amii=múnzal.** 'My grandfather and my grandmother had three children.'

**nxáhtakat** VII be three *(of something string-like). conj 3rd sg* **nxáhtakahk**. *ptcpl* **neexáhtakahk**.

**nxahtéewal** VII be three of them there. *usually plural. conj 3rd sg* **nxáhteek**. *ptcpl* **neexahtéekiil**.

**nxambíileew** VTA tie s.o. in threes. *object usually plural. ind 1st sg* **nax=ambiiláawak**. *ind 3rd sg* **wŭnaxam=biiláawal**. *ind inv* **naxambíilkook**. *ind I-you* **kŭnaxambiilŭlóhmwa**. *conj 3rd sg* **nxambíilaat**. *imp* **nxám=biil**. *ptcpl* **neexambíilaat**.

**nxambíisŭwak** VAI be tied in threes *(s.t. animate). usually plural. ind 1st pl* **naxambiisíhna**. *conj 3rd sg* **nxam=biisíhtiit**. *ptcpl* **neexambiisíhtiit**.

**nxambíisŭwal** VII be tied in threes. *conj 3rd sg* **nxambíisiik**. *ptcpl* **neexam=biisíikiil**.

**nxámbtoow** VTI2 tie s.t. in threes. *object usually plural. ind 1st sg* **naxamb=tóonal**. *ind 3rd sg* **wŭnaxambtóonal**. *conj 1st sg* **nxambtáwaan**. *conj 3rd sg* **nxámbtaakw**. *imp* **nxámbtool**. *ptcpl* **neexámbtaakw**.

**nxápŭwak** VAI be three of them sitting there. *usually plural. ind 1st pl* **naxa=píhna**. *conj 3rd sg* **nxapíhtiit**. *ptcpl* **neexapíhtiit**.

**nxatxooxwéewak** VAI walk in threes. *usually plural. ind 1st pl* **naxatax=ooxwéhna**. *conj 3rd sg* **nxatxoo=xwéhtiit**. *imp* **nxatxóoxweekw**. *ptcpl* **neexataxooxwéhtiit**.

**nxeekíixiin** VAI be in three layers *(s.t. animate, of something sheet-like). conj 3rd sg* **nxeekíixiing**. *ptcpl* **neexeekíixiing**.

**nxeekíixun** VII be in three layers *(of something sheet-like). conj 3rd sg* **nxeekíixung**. *ptcpl* **neexeekíixung**.

**nxéelook** VAI be three pairs, be three sets, be three of them, be three in number *(s.t. animate). usually plural. ind 1st pl* **naxeelóhna**. *indef subject* **nxéelun**. *conj 3rd sg* **nxeelóhtiit**. *ptcpl* **neexeelóhtiit**.

**nxéeli** PC three, in threes. **Nxéeli pihta=wíixŭnool mbáksal.** 'The boxes are stacked in threes.'

**nxéeltool** VII be three of them, be three in number, be in three pairs. *usually plural. conj 3rd sg* **nxéelihk**. *ptcpl* **neexeelíhkiil**.

**nxíiwak** VAI-S be three of them. *ind 1st pl* **naxíhna**. *conj 3rd sg* **nxíhtiit**. *ptcpl* **neexíhtiit**.

**nxiikaapawúwak** VAI stand in threes, be three standing there. *usually plural. ind 1st pl* **naxiikaapawíhna**. *conj 3rd sg* **nxiikaapawíhtiit**. *imp* **nxiikáapa=wiikw**. *ptcpl* **neexiikaapawíhtiit**.

**nxiilŭnúwak** VAI live together in threes, stay together in threes. *usually plural. ind 1st pl* **naxiilŭníhna**. *conj 3rd sg* **nxiilŭníhtiit**. *imp* **nxíilŭniikw**. *ptcpl* **neexiilŭníhtiit**.

**nxiináxke** PC thirty.

**nxóo** PC alone. **Nxóo nŭwíiki.** 'I live alone.'

**nxoo-** PV alone, on its own; the most, the best *(of something)*. **Wŭnáxoo-kwŭnáhkwsiin.** 'He's the tallest.'; **Náxoo-nihtaawatúpwiin.** 'I'm the best cook.' *ptcpl* **néexoo-**.

**nxooháalŭnuw** VAI live alone, be on one's own. *ind 1st sg* **naxooháalŭni**, **naxoohéalŭniim**. *conj 3rd sg* **nxoo=háalŭniit**. *imp* **nxoohéalŭniil**. *ptcpl* **neexoohéalŭniit**.

**nxoohóowuw** VAI be by oneself, be on one's own, be the only one in a family. *ind 1st sg* **naxoohóowi**, **naxoo=hóowiim**. *conj 3rd sg* **nxoohóowiit**. *ptcpl* **neexoohóowiit**.

**nxookwŭnáhkeew** VAI be gone for three days. *ind 1st sg* **naxookwŭnáhke**, **naxookwŭnáhkeem**. *conj 3rd sg* **nxookwŭnáhkeet**. *ptcpl* **neexoo=kwŭnáhkeet**.

**nxookwŭnákat** VII be three days. **Nxoo=kwŭnákate.** 'Three days ago.' *conj 3rd sg* **nxookwŭnákahk**. *ptcpl* **nee=xookwŭnákahk**.

**nxóokwŭnii** PC three days, for three days.

**nxootóonheew** VAI talk to oneself. *ind 1st sg* **naxootóonhe**, **naxootóon=heem**. *conj 3rd sg* **nxootóonheet**. *imp* **nxootóonheel**. *ptcpl* **neexoo=tóonheet**. *intensive reduplication* **naanxootóonheew**.

**nxóoxweew** VAI go by oneself. *ind 1st sg* **naxóoxwe**, **naxóoxweem**. *conj 3rd sg* **nxóoxweet**. *imp* **nxóoxweel**. *ptcpl* **neexóoxweet**.

**nxohkwéepuw** VAI sit alone. *ind 1st sg* **naxohkwéepi**, **naxohkwéepiim**. *conj 3rd sg* **nxohkwéepiit**. *imp* **nxoh=kwéepiil**. *ptcpl* **neexohkwéepiit**.

**nxohkwéepŭwak** VAI sit in threes. *usually plural. ind 1st pl* **naxohkwee=píhna**. *conj 3rd sg* **nxohkweepíhtiit**. *imp* **nxohkwéepiikw**. *ptcpl* **neexoh=kweepíhtiit**.

**nxú** PC three. **Nxú mbihtawákwi.** 'I am covered in three layers, I am dressed in three layers.'; **Nxú pangéesuw.** 'It is in three pieces.'

**nxu-** PN three. **Nxú-ndálaas láawatuw.** 'It cost three dollars.'

**nxu-** PV three. **Nxú-kŭlákuw.** 'It's three o'clock.'; **Néexu-pangéeyeek.** 'Three pieces.' *ptcpl* **néexu-**.

**nxún** PC three times.

**nxúnool** VII be three of them, be three in number. *usually plural. conj 3rd sg* **nxúng**. *ptcpl* **neexúngiil**.

**nzáapaan** NI cornmeal mush, oatmeal. *poss* **nùsaapáanum**, **nzaapáanum**. *loc* **nzaapáanung**.

**nzukaalakíingweew** VAI have dark eyes. *ind 1st sg* **nuskaalakíingwe**, **nus=kaalakíingweem**. *conj 3rd sg* **nzuk=aalakíingweet**. *ptcpl* **neeskaala=**

**kíingweet**.

**nzukaalóhkweew** VAI have black hair. *ind 1st sg* **nuskaalóhkwa**, **nuskaa=lóhkwaam**. *conj 3rd sg* **nzukaalóh=kwaat**. *ptcpl* **neeskaalóhkwaat**.

**nzukaapamúkwat** VII look dark, be dark-looking. *conj 3rd sg* **nzukaa=pamúkwahk**. *ptcpl* **neeskaapa=múkwahk**.

**nzukaapamúkwsuw** VAI look dark, be dark-looking. *ind 1st sg* **nuskaapa=múkwsi**, **nuskaapamúkwsiim**. *conj 3rd sg* **nzukaapamúkwsiit**. *ptcpl* **neeskaapamúkwsiit**.

**nzukáhtakw** NI black thread, black string. *pl* **nzukáhtakwal**. *poss* **nus=káhtakwum**. *loc* **nzukáhtakwung**. *dimin* **nzukáhchakwush**.

**nzukakumáhkwat** VII be a black cloud. *conj 3rd sg* **nzukakumáhkwahk**. *ptcpl* **neeskakumáhkwahk**.

**nzukamóxool** NA black boat. *pl* **nzuka=moxóolak**. *poss* **nuskámxool**, **nus=kamxóolum**. *loc* **nzukamoxóolung**. *dimin* **nzhukamoxóolush**. *obv* **nzukamoxóolal**.

**nzukamóxool** NI black boat. *pl* **nzuka=moxóolal**. *poss* **nuskámxool**, **nus=kamxóolum**. *loc* **nzukamoxóolung**. *dimin* **nzhukamoxóolush**.

**nzukasunáanay** NI railroad, railroad track. *pl* **nzukasunáanayal**. *loc* **nzukasunáaneeng**.

**nzukcháseew** VTA scorch s.t. animate, blacken s.t. animate *(by heat)*; dye s.t. animate. *ind 1st sg* **nuskúchasaaw**, **nuskúchasa**. *ind 3rd sg* **wŭnus=kuchasáawal**. *conj 3rd sg* **nzuk=chásaat**. *imp* **nzúkchas**. *ptcpl* **nees=kúchasaat**.

**nzukchásum** VTI1B blacken s.t. *(by heat)*; dye s.t. black. *ind 1st sg* **nus=kuchasúmun**. *ind 3rd sg* **wŭnus=kuchasúmun**. *conj 1st sg* **nzukchás=ŭmaan**. *conj 3rd sg* **nzukchásung**. *imp* **nzukchásih**. *ptcpl* **neeskúch=asung**.

**nzukchásuw** VAI be burnt black *(s.t. animate)*; be dyed black. *ind 1st sg* **nuskúchasi**, **nuskúchasiim**. *conj 3rd sg* **nzukchásiit**. *ptcpl* **neeskúchasiit**.

**nzukcháteew** VII be burnt black; be dyed black. *conj 3rd sg* **nzukcháteek**. *ptcpl* **neeskúchateek**.

**nzúkchuy** NI black excrement.

**nzúkeew** VII be black. *conj 3rd sg* **nzúk=eek**. *ptcpl* **néeskeek**.

**nzukeekháasuw** VAI be marked black, have a black mark, have a black stripe *(s.t. animate)*. *ind 1st sg* **nuskeek=háasi**, **nuskeekháasiim**. *conj 3rd sg* **nzukeekháasiit**. *ptcpl* **neeskeek=háasiit**.

**nzukeekháasuw** VII be marked black, have a black mark, have a black stripe. *conj 3rd sg* **nzukeekháasiik**. *ptcpl* **neeskeekháasiik**.

**nzukii-** PN black. **Nzúkii-lehlookih=láashak.** 'Black raspberries.'; **Nzúkii-aníixan.** 'Black shoelace.'

**nzukii-** PV black. **Nzúkii-kwáalxeek.** 'Black smoke.' *ptcpl* **néeskii-**.

**nzúkii-koothámeew** VAI wear a black coat. *ind 1st sg* **núskii-kootháma**, **núskii-koothámaam**. *conj 3rd sg* **nzúkii-koothámaat**. *imp* **nzúkii-koothámaal**. *ptcpl* **néeskii-koothámaat**.

**nzukíhleew** VAI turn black *(s.t. animate)*. *ind 1st sg* **nuskíhla**, **nuskíhlaam**. *conj 3rd sg* **nzukíhlaat**. *ptcpl* **neeskíhlaat**.

**nzukíhleew** VII turn black. *conj 3rd sg* **nzukíhlaak**. *ptcpl* **neeskíhlaak**.

**nzukihtóonay** NI black beard, black whiskers. *pl* **nzukihtóonayal**. *poss* **nuskihtóonayal**.

**nzukihtóonayeew** VAI have a black beard, have a black mustache. *ind 1st sg* **nuskihtóonaya**, **nuskihtóona=**

**yaam**. *conj 3rd sg* **nzukihtóonayaat**. *ptcpl* **neeskihtóonayaat**.

**nzúksuw** VAI be black *(s.t. animate)*. *ind 1st sg* **nuskúsi**, **nuskúsiim**. *conj 3rd sg* **nzúksiit**. *ptcpl* **neeskúsiit**. *intensive reduplication* **aneeskusúwak**; *moderative reduplication* **naan=súksuw**.

**nzukshapakwíiwan** NI black cloth. *pl* **nzukshapakwíiwanal**. *poss* **nus=kushapakwíiwan**. *loc* **nzukshapa=kwíiwanung**. *dimin* **nzukshapak=wíiwanush**.

**nzukshéengweew** VAI have a black eye. *ind 1st sg* **nuskshéengwa**, **nusk=shéengwaam**. *conj 3rd sg* **nzuk=shéengwaat**. *ptcpl* **neeskshéen=gwaat**.

**nzuktóoneew** VAI have a black mouth. *ind 1st sg* **nuskùtóona**, **nuskùtóo=naam**. *conj 3rd sg* **nzuktóonaat**. *ptcpl* **neesktóonaat**.

**nzukŭléexiin** VAI be dark-coloured, be a blackish colour, have a black tinge to it *(s.t. animate)*. *ind 1st sg* **nuskùl=éexiin**, **nuskùléexi**. *conj 3rd sg* **nzukŭléexiing**. *ptcpl* **neeskùléexiing**.

**nzukŭléexun** VII be dark-coloured, be a blackish colour, have a black tinge to it. *conj 3rd sg* **nzukŭléexung**. *ptcpl* **neeskùléexung**.

**nzukxásuw** VAI be tanned. *ind 1st sg* **nuskáxasi**, **nuskáxasiim**. *conj 3rd sg* **nzukxásiit**. *ptcpl* **neeskáxasiit**.

# OO

**óocheew** NA fly. *pl* **oochéewak**. *dimin* **óocheesh**. *obv* **oochéewal**. *See* **oochéewees**.

**oochéewees** NA fly. *pl* **oocheewéesak**. *dimin* **oocheewéeshush**. *obv* **oo=cheewéesal**. *See* **óocheew**.

**nóohum** NAD my grandmother. *pl* **nóo=hŭmak**. *3rd poss* **óohŭmal**. *dimin* **nóohŭmush**.

**nóohŭmus** NAD my stepmother. *pl* **noo=hŭmúsak**. *3rd poss* **oohŭmúsal**. *dimin* **noohŭmúshush**.

**oolihkaapamúkwat** VII be blue in colour, be blue-coloured. *conj 3rd sg* **oolihkaapamúkwahk**. *ptcpl* **oolih=kaapamúkwahk**.

**oolihkaapamúkwsuw** VAI be blue in colour, be blue-coloured *(s.t. animate)*. *ind 1st sg* **ndoolihkaapa=múkwsi**, **ndoolihkaapamúkwsiim**. *conj 3rd sg* **oolihkaapamúkwsiit**. *ptcpl* **oolihkaapamúkwsiit**.

**oolihkáhtakw** NI blue thread, blue string. *pl* **oolihkáhtakwal**. *poss* **ndoolihkáhtakwum**. *dimin* **oolih=káhchakwush**.

**oolihkakumáhkwat** VII be a blue cloud, be blue *(of clouds)*. *conj 3rd sg* **oolihkakumáhkwahk**. *ptcpl* **oolih=kakumáhkwahk**.

**oolíhkeew** VII be blue. *conj 3rd sg* **oolíhkeek**. *ptcpl* **oolíhkeek**.

**oolihkii-** PN blue. **Oolíhkii-tiihíinjuw.** 'A blue teacup.'

**oolihkii-** PV blue. **Ndoolíhkii-shóohŭ=mun.** 'I painted it blue.' *ptcpl* **oolíhkii-**.

**oolihkíhleew** VAI turn blue *(s.t. animate)*. *ind 1st sg* **ndoolihkíhla**, **ndoolihkíh=laam**. *conj 3rd sg* **oolihkíhlaat**. *ptcpl* **oolihkíhlaat**.

**oolihkíhleew** VII turn blue. *conj 3rd sg* **oolihkíhlaak**. *ptcpl* **oolihkíhlaak**.

**oolihkpáleew** VTA put blueing on s.t. animate. *ind 1st sg* **ndoolihkpálaaw**, **ndoolihkpála**. *ind 3rd sg* **wtoolihk=paláawal**. *ind inv* **ndoolihkpálukw**. *ind I-you* **ktoolihkpálul**. *conj 3rd sg* **oolihkpálaat**. *imp* **oolíhkpal**. *ptcpl* **oolihkpálaat**.

**oolihkpatíikan** NI blueing. *poss* **ndoo=**

**lihkpatíikan**. *material used for whitening clothes.*

**oolihkpatíikeew** VAI use blueing. *ind 1st sg* **ndoolihkpatíike, ndoolihkpatíi=keem**. *conj 3rd sg* **oolihkpatíikeet**. *imp* **oolihkpatíikeel**. *ptcpl* **oolihk=patíikeet**.

**oolihkpátoow** VTI2 put blueing on s.t. *ind 1st sg* **ndoolihkpátoon**. *ind 3rd sg* **wtoolihkpátoon**. *conj 1st sg* **oo=lihkpátawaan**. *conj 3rd sg* **oolihk=pátaakw**. *imp* **oolihkpátool**. *ptcpl* **oolihkpátaakw**.

**oolíhksuw** VAI be blue *(s.t. animate)*. *ind 1st sg* **ndoolíhksi, ndoolíhksiim**. *conj 3rd sg* **oolíhksiit**. *ptcpl* **oolíhk=siit**.

**oolihkŭléexiin** VAI be a blueish colour, have a blue tinge to it *(s.t. animate)*. *ind 1st sg* **ndoolihkŭléexiin, ndoo=lihkŭléexi**. *conj 3rd sg* **oolihkŭlée=xiing**. *ptcpl* **oolihkŭléexiing**.

**oolihkŭléexun** VII be a blueish colour, have a blue tinge to it. *conj 3rd sg* **oolihkŭléexung**. *ptcpl* **oolihkŭ=léexung**.

**ooshawáawsuw** VAI lead a sad life. *ind 1st sg* **ndooshawáawsi, ndoosha=wáawsiim**. *conj 3rd sg* **ooshawáaw=siit**. *ptcpl* **ooshawáawsiit**.

**ooshawahtéenamuw** VAI grieve. *ind 1st sg* **ndooshawahtéenami, ndoosha=wahtéenamiim**. *conj 3rd sg* **oosha=wahtéenamiit**. *ptcpl* **ooshawahtée=namiit**.

**ooshawamalúsuw** VAI grieve, feel grief. *ind 1st sg* **ndooshawamalúsi, ndoo=shawamalúsiim**. *conj 3rd sg* **oosha=wamalúsiit**. *ptcpl* **ooshawamalúsiit**.

**ooshaweelúndam** VOTI1A grieve, feel grief, be sad. *ind 1st sg* **ndoosha=weelúndam**. *conj 3rd sg* **ooshawee=lúndang**. *ptcpl* **ooshaweelúndang**.

**ooshawiináakwsuw** VAI look sad, look to be grieving. *ind 1st sg* **ndoosha=wiináakwsi, ndooshawiináakwsiim**. *conj 3rd sg* **ooshawiináakwsiit**. *ptcpl* **ooshawiináakwsiit**.

**ooshawihtáakwsuw** VAI make sounds of grief, sound full of grief *(especially of singing)*. *ind 1st sg* **ndooshawih=táakwsi, ndooshawihtáakwsiim**. *conj 3rd sg* **ooshawihtáakwsiit**. *ptcpl* **ooshawihtáakwsiit**.

**ooshawutoonéexiin** VAI be about to cry *(especially of a baby that looks sad)*. *ind 1st sg* **ndooshawutoonéexiin, ndooshawutoonéexi**. *conj 3rd sg* **ooshawutoonéexiing**. *ptcpl* **oosha=wutoonéexiing**.

**ooshawutoonéhleew** VAI have an expression on one's face indicating that one is about to cry. *ind 1st sg* **ndoo=shawutoonéhla, ndooshawutoonéh=laam**. *conj 3rd sg* **ooshawutoonéh=laat**. *ptcpl* **ooshawutoonéhlaat**. *intensive reduplication* **ohooshawut=oonéhleew**.

**ootéenay** NI town; land. *pl* **ootéenayal**. *poss* **ndootéenay**. *loc* **ootéeneeng**. *dimin* **oochéeneesh**.

**ooteenayápuw** VAI live in town. *ind 1st sg* **ndooteenayápi, ndooteenayáp=iim**. *conj 3rd sg* **ooteenayápiit**. *imp* **ooteenayápiil**. *ptcpl* **ooteenayápiit**.

**ooteewáaleew** VTA visit s.o. *ind 1st sg* **ndooteewáalaaw, ndooteewáala**. *ind 3rd sg* **wtooteewaaláawal**. *ind inv* **ndooteewáalukw**. *ind I-you* **ktootee=wáalul**. *conj 3rd sg* **ooteewáalaat**. *imp* **ootéewaal**. *ptcpl* **ooteewáalaat**.

**ootéewuw** VAI visit. *ind 1st sg* **ndootéewi, ndootéewiim**. *conj 3rd sg* **ootéewiit**. *imp* **ootéewiil**. *ptcpl* **ootéewiit**.

**nóox** NAD my father. *pl* **nóoxwak**. *3rd poss* **óoxwal**.

**nóoxwiis** NAD my grandchild. *pl* **noo=xwíisak**. *3rd poss* **ooxwíisal**. *dimin* **nooxwíishush**.

**nóoxwush** NAD my uncle, my father's brother; parallel uncle. *pl* **nóoxw=shak**. *3rd poss* **óoxwshal**.

# O

**ohkóowuw** VII be maggots. **Éeli-ohkóowiik.** 'Because there are maggots.' *conj 3rd sg* **ohkóowiik**. *ptcpl* **ohkóowiik**.

**óhkw** NA maggot. *pl* **óhkwak**. *dimin* **óhkwush**. *obv* **óhkwal**.

**óhkwaan** NA pothook. *pl* **ohkwáanak**. *obv* **ohkwáanal**.

n**ohkwtóomus** NAD my stepchild. *pl* **nohkwtóomsak**. *3rd poss* **ohk=wtóomsal**. *dimin* **nohkwchóom=shush**.

**óhleew** VTA get s.o. from a certain place. **Táa néek éet wéhlak.** 'I don't know where I got him.' *ind 1st sg* **nóhlaaw**, **nóhla**. *ind 3rd sg* **ohláawal**. *ind inv* **nóhlukw**. *ind I-you* **kóhlul**. *conj 3rd sg* **óhlaat**. *imp* **óhl**. *ptcpl* **wéhlaat**.

**óhpun** NA potato. *pl* **óhpŭnak**. *poss* **ndóhpŭnum**. *loc* **óhpŭnung**. *dimin* **óhpŭnush**. *obv* **óhpŭnal**.

**ohpwáasuw** VII be smoked. *conj 3rd sg* **ohpwáasiik**. *ptcpl* **ohpwáasiik**.

**óhpweew** VAI smoke a pipe, smoke tobacco. *ind 1st sg* **ndóhpwa**, **ndóh=pwaam**. *conj 3rd sg* **óhpwaat**. *imp* **óhpwaal**. *ptcpl* **óhpwaat**.

**óhpweew** VAI smoke s.t. *(of tobacco)*. **Ndóhpwa shíkaash.** 'I smoked a cigar.' *ind 1st sg* **ndohpwaan**. *ind 3rd sg* **wtohpwaanal**. *conj 3rd sg* **óh=pwaat**. *imp* **óhpwaal**. *ptcpl* **óhpwaat**.

**oxkwáakeew** VAI sew. *ind 1st sg* **ndox=kwáake**, **ndoxkwáakeem**. *conj 3rd sg* **oxkwáakeet**. *imp* **oxkwáakeel**. *ptcpl* **eexkwáakeet**, **oxkwáakeet**.

**oxkwáaleew** VTA sew s.t. animate. *ind 1st sg* **ndoxkwáalaaw**, **ndoxkwáala**. *ind 3rd sg* **wtoxkwaaláawal**. *ind inv* **ndoxkwáalukw**. *ind I-you* **kutox=kwáalul**. *conj 3rd sg* **oxkwáalaat**. *imp* **óxkwaal**. *ptcpl* **eexkwáalaat**, **oxkwáalaat**.

**oxkwáasuw** VII be sewn. *conj 3rd sg* **oxkwáasiik**. *ptcpl* **oxkwáasiik**.

**óxkwam** VTI1 sew s.t. *ind 1st sg* **ndóx=kwamun**. *ind 3rd sg* **wtóxkwamun**. *conj 1st sg* **óxkwamaan**. *conj 3rd sg* **óxkwang**. *imp* **óxkwah**. *ptcpl* **óx=kwang**, **éexkwang**.

nd**oxkwéehum** NAD my sister *(man speaking)*. *pl* **ndoxkwéehŭmak**. *3rd poss* **wtoxkwéehŭmal**.

**oxkweekángan** NI neck. **Ktahtíike koxkweekánganum!** 'That's right! ('You bet your neck!').' *pl* **oxkwee=kánganal**. *poss* **noxkweekángan**, **ndoxkweekángan**. *loc* **oxkweekán=ganung**. *dimin* **oxkweekánganush**.

**oxkwéesus** NA girl. *pl* **oxkwéessak**. *poss* **ndoxkwéessum**. *dimin* **oxkwée=shush**. *obv* **oxkwéessal**.

**oxkwéew** NA woman. *pl* **oxkwéewak**. *poss* **ndoxkwéehum**. *obv* **oxkwée=wal**.

**oxkweeweelúnzuw** VAI be arrogant, have an attitude, think oneself better than others, to put on airs *(of women)*. *ind 1st sg* **ndoxkweeweelúnzi**, **ndox=kweeweelúnziim**. *conj 3rd sg* **ox=kweeweelúnziit**. *ptcpl* **eexkweewee=lúnziit**, **oxkweeweelúnziit**. *See* **leetíisuw**.

**oxkweewiináakwsuw** VAI look like an adult woman. *ind 1st sg* **ndoxkwee=wiináakwsi**, **ndoxkweewiináakw=siim**. *conj 3rd sg* **oxkweewiináakw=siit**. *ptcpl* **eexkweewiináakwsiit**, **oxkweewiináakwsiit**.

**oxkwéexum** NA female dog; female of animal species. *pl* **oxkwéexŭmwak**. *dimin* **oxkwéexŭmwush**. *obv* **ox=**

**kwéexŭmwal**.

**oxkwéhleew** NA hen, female bird. *pl* **oxkwehléewak**. *dimin* **oxkwéhleesh**. *obv* **oxkwehléewal**.

# P

**paakaandpéeheew** VTA hit s.o. on the head. *ind 1st sg* **mbaakaandpée=haaw**, **mbaakaandpéeha**. *ind 3rd sg* **paakaandpeeháawal**. *ind inv* **mbaa=kaandpéehukw**. *ind I-you* **kpaa=kaandpéehul**. *conj 3rd sg* **paa=kaandpéehaat**. *imp* **paakáandpeeh**. *ptcpl* **paakaandpéehaat**.

**paakaandpéexiin** VAI bump one's head. *ind 1st sg* **mbaakaandpéexiin**, **mbaakaandpéexi**. *conj 3rd sg* **paa=kaandpéexiing**. *ptcpl* **paakaand=péexiing**.

**paakaandpéexŭmeew** VTA bang s.o.'s head against something. *ind 1st sg* **mbaakaandpéexŭmaaw**, **mbaa=kaandpéexŭma**. *ind 3rd sg* **paa=kaandpeexŭmáawal**. *ind inv* **mbaa=kaandpéexŭmukw**. *ind I-you* **kpaa=kaandpéexŭmul**. *conj 3rd sg* **paa=kaandpéexŭmaat**. *imp* **paakaand=péexum**. *ptcpl* **paakaandpéexŭ=maat**.

**paakaasiitŭyéeheew** VTA spank s.o., give s.o. a spanking. *ind 1st sg* **mbaa=kaasiitŭyéehaaw**, **mbaakaasiitŭ=yéeha**. *ind 3rd sg* **paakaasiitŭyee=háawal**. *ind inv* **mbaakaasiitŭyée=hukw**. *ind I-you* **kpaakaasiitŭyée=hul**. *conj 3rd sg* **paakaasiitŭyéehaat**. *imp* **paakaasíitŭyeeh**. *ptcpl* **paa=kaasiitŭyéehaat**. *moderative reduplication* **paapaakaasiitŭyeeháawal**.

**paakchaaléexiin** VAI bump one's nose against something. *ind 1st sg* **mbaak=chaaléexiin**, **mbaakchaaléexi**. *conj 3rd sg* **paakchaaléexiing**. *ptcpl* **paakchaaléexiing**, **paakchaaléexiit**.

**páakham** VTI1A bump against s.t. *(with something)*. *ind 1st sg* **mbaakhámun**. *ind 3rd sg* **paakhámun**. *conj 1st sg* **paakhámaan**. *conj 3rd sg* **páakhang**. *imp* **páakhah**. *ptcpl* **páakhang**.

**páakiim** NI cranberry. *pl* **paakíimal**. *poss* **mbaakíimum**. *loc* **paakíimung**. *dimin* **paakíimush**.

**paakiimíinzhuy** NA cranberry bush. *pl* **paakiimíinzhŭyak**. *obv* **paakiimíin=zhŭyal**.

**paakiingwéexiin** VAI bump one's face against something. *ind 1st sg* **mbaa=kiingwéexiin**, **mbaakiingwéexi**. *conj 3rd sg* **paakiingwéexiing**. *ptcpl* **paakiingwéexiing**, **paakiingwéexiit**.

**paakihtéeheew** VTA bump s.t. animate against something. **Mbaakihtéehaaw ngútko.** 'I bumped my knee against something.' *ind 1st sg* **mbaakihtée=haaw**, **mbaakihtéeha**. *ind 3rd sg* **paakihteeháawal**. *ind inv* **mbaakih=téehookw**. *ind I-you* **kpaakihtéehool**. *conj 3rd sg* **paakihtéehaat**. *imp* **paakíhteeh**. *ptcpl* **paakihtéehaat**.

**paakihtéehum** VTI1B bump into something with s.t. *ind 1st sg* **mbaakih=téehŭmun**. *ind 3rd sg* **paakihtéehŭ=mun**. *conj 1st sg* **paakihtéehŭmaan**. *conj 3rd sg* **paakihtéehung**. *imp* **paakihtéehih**. *ptcpl* **paakihtéehung**.

**paakihtéexiin** VAI fall and bump *(against something)*; bump into an object. **Meenáxkung mbaakihtéexiin.** 'I bumped into the fence.' *ind 1st sg* **mbaakihtéexiin**, **mbaakihtéexi**. *conj 3rd sg* **paakihtéexiing**. *ptcpl* **paa=kihtéexiing**.

**paakihtéextoow** VTI2 fall and bump against s.t. *(with something)*. **Wíhkaat paakihtéextoon.** 'He bumped his leg against something.' *ind 1st sg* **mbaa=kihtéextoon**. *ind 3rd sg* **paakihtéex=toon**. *conj 1st sg* **paakihteextáwaan**. *conj 3rd sg* **paakihtéextaakw**. *imp* paakihtéextool. *ptcpl* **paakihtéex=taakw**.

**paakihtéexŭmeew** VTA fall and bump into s.o., fall and bump s.o. *(with something)*. *ind 1st sg* **mbaakihtée=xŭmaaw**, **mbaakihtéexŭma**. *ind 3rd sg* **paakihteexŭmáawal**. *ind inv* **mbaakihtéexŭmukw**. *ind I-you* **kpaakihtéexŭmul**. *conj 3rd sg* **paa=kihtéexŭmaat**. *imp* **paakihtéexum**. *ptcpl* **paakihtéexŭmaat**.

**paakihtéexun** VII fall and bump *(against something)*; bump into an object. **Paakihtéexun níhkaat.** 'It bumped into my leg.'; **Paakihtéexun kpáh=oon.** 'The door banged against something.' *conj 3rd sg* **paakihtéexung**. *ptcpl* **paakihtéexung**.

**paakíhtoow** VTI2 bump s.t. **Mbaakíh=toon níhkaat.** 'I bumped my leg.' *ind 1st sg* **mbaakíhtoon**. *ind 3rd sg* **paa=kíhtoon**. *conj 1st sg* **paakíhtawaan**. *conj 3rd sg* **paakíhtaakw**. *imp* **paa=kíhtool**. *ptcpl* **paakíhtaakw**.

**paakkaatéexiin** VAI bump one's leg against something. *ind 1st sg* **mbaak=kaatéexiin**, **mbaakkaatéexi**. *conj 3rd sg* **paakkaatéexiing**. *ptcpl* **paak=kaatéexiing**, **paakkaatéexiit**.

**paaksiitéexiin** VAI stub one's toe. *ind 1st sg* **mbaaksiitéexiin**, **mbaaksiitéexi**. *conj 3rd sg* **paaksiitéexiing**. *ptcpl* **paaksiitéexiing**.

**paaktoonéexiin** VAI bump one's mouth. *ind 1st sg* **mbaaktoonéexiin**, **mbaak=toonéexi**. *conj 3rd sg* **paaktoonée=xiing**. *ptcpl* **paaktoonéexiing**.

**paakŭnaxkéexiin** VAI bump one's hand against something. *ind 1st sg* **mbaa=kŭnaxkéexiin**, **mbaakŭnaxkéexi**. *conj 3rd sg* **paakŭnaxkéexiing**. *ptcpl* **paakŭnaxkéexiing**.

**paakwáakan** NI noise. **Móxa paa=kwáakan.** 'They're awfully noisy.'

**paakweenztoonháaleew** VTA talk lots to s.o., talk too much to s.o. *ind 1st sg* **mbaakweenztoonháalaaw**, **mbaa=kweenztoonháala**. *ind 3rd sg* **paa=kweenztoonhaaláawal**. *ind inv* **mbaakweenztoonháalukw**. *ind I-you* **kpaakweenztoonháalul**. *conj 3rd sg* **paakweenztoonháalaat**. *imp* **paa=kweenztóonhaal**. *ptcpl* **paakweenz=toonháalaat**.

**paakwéenzuw** VAI talk lots, make noise. *ind 1st sg* **mbaakwéenzi**, **mbaa=kwéenziim**. *conj 3rd sg* **paakwéen=ziit**. *imp* **paakwéenziil**. *ptcpl* **paa=kwéenziit**.

**paakxehtéeheew** VTA slap s.o. across the face *(close to the ears)*; slap s.o. across the ears. *ind 1st sg* **mbaak=xehtéehaaw**, **mbaakxehtéeha**. *ind 3rd sg* **paakxehteeháawal**. *ind inv* **mbaakxehtéehookw**. *ind I-you* **kpaakxehtéehool**. *conj 3rd sg* **paak=xehtéehaat**. *imp* **paakxéhteeh**. *ptcpl* **paakxehtéehaat**. *moderative reduplication* **paapaakxehteeháawal**.

**paaláaheew** VAIO throw s.t. over; throw s.t. farther than intended. **Mbaaláa=heen wiikwáhmung.** 'I threw it over the house.' *ind 1st sg* **mbaaláaheen**. *ind 3rd sg* **paaláaheen**. *conj 3rd sg* **paaláaheet**. *imp* **paaláaheel**. *ptcpl* **paaláaheet**.

**paaláakchehl** VAIO jump over s.t., jump over s.o. *(farther than intended)*. *ind 1st sg* **mbaalaakchéhlun**. *ind 3rd sg* **paalaakchéhlun**. *conj 3rd sg* **paa=laakchéhluk**. *imp* **paalaakchéhlih**. *ptcpl* **paalaakchéhluk**.

**paalaakchéhleew** VAIO jump over s.o., jump over s.t. *(farther than intended)*. *ind 1st sg* **mbaalaakchéhlaan**. *ind 3rd sg* **paalaakchéhlaan**. *conj 3rd sg* **paalaakchéhlaat**. *imp* **paalaak=chéhlaal**. *ptcpl* **paalaakchéhlaat**.

**paalaapéhlaleew** VTA hang s.t. animate over something. *ind 1st sg* **mbaalaa=péhlalaaw**, **mbaalaapéhlala**. *ind 3rd sg* **paalaapehlaláawal**. *ind inv* **mbaa=**

**laapéhlalukw**. *ind I-you* **kpaalaa=péhlalul**. *conj 3rd sg* **paalaapéhla=laat**. *imp* **paalaapéhlal**. *ptcpl* **paa=laapéhlalaat**.

**paalaapéhlatoow** VTI2 hang s.t. over something. *ind 1st sg* **mbaalaapéh=latoon**. *ind 3rd sg* **paalaapéhlatoon**. *conj 1st sg* **paalaapehlatáwaan**. *conj 3rd sg* **paalaapéhlataakw**. *imp* **paa=laapéhlatool**. *ptcpl* **paalaapéhla=taakw**.

**paalaapéhleew** VAI have a hangover. *ind 1st sg* **mbaalaapéhla**, **mbaalaapéh=laam**. *conj 3rd sg* **paalaapéhlaat**. *ptcpl* **paalaapéhlaat**.

**paalahkwéextoow** VTI2 pile s.t. over something *(of something wood- or stick-like)*. *ind 1st sg* **mbaalahkwéex=toon**. *ind 3rd sg* **paalahkwéextoon**. *conj 1st sg* **paalahkweextáwaan**. *conj 3rd sg* **paalahkwéextaakw**. *imp* **paa=lahkwéextool**. *ptcpl* **paalahkwéex=taakw**.

**paaláhleew** VTA overfill s.t. animate. *ind 1st sg* **mbaaláhlaaw**, **mbaaláhla**. *ind 3rd sg* **paalahláawal**. *conj 3rd sg* **paaláhlaat**. *imp* **páalahl**. *ptcpl* **paa=láhlaat**.

**paaláhteew** VII overflow, be filled over the top. *conj 3rd sg* **paaláhteek**. *ptcpl* **paaláhteek**.

**paaláhtoow** VTI2 overfill s.t. *ind 1st sg* **mbaaláhtoon**. *ind 3rd sg* **paaláhtoon**. *conj 1st sg* **paaláhtawaan**. *conj 3rd sg* **paaláhtaakw**. *imp* **paaláhtool**. *ptcpl* **paaláhtaakw**.

**paalakóosuw** VAI climb over. *ind 1st sg* **mbaalakóosi**, **mbaalakóosiim**. *conj 3rd sg* **paalakóosiit**. *imp* **paalakóo=siil**. *ptcpl* **paalakóosiit**.

**paalalíhkeew** VAIO step over s.t., step over s.o. *ind 1st sg* **mbaalalíhkeen**. *ind 3rd sg* **paalalíhkeen**. *conj 3rd sg* **paalalíhkeet**. *imp* **paalalíhkeel**. *ptcpl* **paalalíhkeet**.

**páalapuw** VAI overflow, be full over the top *(s.t. animate)*. *conj 3rd sg* **páala=piit**. *ptcpl* **páalapiit**.

**paalatawáapuw** VAIO look over s.t., look over s.o., look past s.t., look past s.o. *ind 1st sg* **mbaalatawáapiin**. *ind 3rd sg* **paalatawáapiin**. *conj 3rd sg* **paalatawáapiit**. *imp* **paalatawáapiil**. *ptcpl* **paalatawáapiit**.

**paalchásŭmeew** VAI boil over *(of one's cooking)*; have one's cooking boil over. *ind 1st sg* **mbaalchásŭma**, **mbaalchásŭmaam**. *conj 3rd sg* **paal=chásŭmaat**. *ptcpl* **paalchásŭmaat**.

**paalchásuw** VAI boil over, overflow *(s.t. animate, from being heated)*. *ind 1st sg* **mbaalchási**, **mbaalchásiim**. *conj 3rd sg* **paalchásiit**. *ptcpl* **paalchásiit**.

**paalcháteew** VII boil over, overflow *(from being heated)*. *conj 3rd sg* **paalcháteek**. *ptcpl* **paalcháteek**.

**paalháhkweew** VAIO hit s.t. over something *(farther than intended)*. *ind 1st sg* **mbaalháhkween**. *ind 3rd sg* **paal=háhkween**. *conj 3rd sg* **paalháh=kweet**. *imp* **paalháhkweel**. *ptcpl* **paalháhkweet**.

**páalham** VTI1A hit s.t. way over something, knock s.t. way over something *(using a tool or instrument)*; knock s.t. over something. *ind 1st sg* **mbaal=hámun**. *ind 3rd sg* **paalhámun**. *conj 1st sg* **paalhámaan**. *conj 3rd sg* **páalhang**. *imp* **páalhah**. *ptcpl* **páal=hang**.

**páalheew** VTA hit s.t. animate a long way over, knock s.t. animate way over something *(using a tool or instrument)*. *ind 1st sg* **mbáalhaaw**, **mbáal=ha**. *ind 3rd sg* **paalháawal**. *ind inv* **mbáalhookw**. *ind I-you* **kpáalhool**. *conj 3rd sg* **páalhaat**. *imp* **páalhaw**. *ptcpl* **páalhaat**.

**paalhiingwéexiin** VAI peek over, look over something. *ind 1st sg* **mbaal=hiingwéexiin**, **mbaalhiingwéexi**. *conj 3rd sg* **paalhiingwéexiing**. *imp*

**paalhiingwéexiil**. *ptcpl* **paalhiin=gwéexiing**, **paalhiingwéexiit**.

**paalíikwam** VTI1A spill s.t. *(while using a tool)*. *ind 1st sg* **mbaalíikwamun**. *ind 3rd sg* **paalíikwamun**. *conj 1st sg* **paalíikwamaan**. *conj 3rd sg* **paalíi=kwang**. *imp* **paalíikwah**. *ptcpl* **paa=líikwang**.

**paalíixiin** VAI hang over something, lie over something *(s.t. animate)*. *ind 1st sg* **mbaalíixiin**, **mbaalíixi**. *conj 3rd sg* **paalíixiing**. *imp* **paalíixiil**. *ptcpl* **paalíixiing**, **paalíixiit**.

**paalíixtoow** VTI2 put s.t. over something; make s.t. overlap. *ind 1st sg* **mbaalíixtoon**. *ind 3rd sg* **paalíix=toon**. *conj 1st sg* **paaliixtáwaan**. *conj 3rd sg* **paalíixtaakw**. *imp* **paalíixtool**. *ptcpl* **paalíixtaakw**.

**paalíixŭmeew** VTA put s.t. animate over something. *ind 1st sg* **mbaalíixŭ=maaw**, **mbaalíixŭma**. *ind 3rd sg* **paaliixŭmáawal**. *ind inv* **mbaalíixŭ=mukw**. *ind I-you* **kpaalíixŭmul**. *conj 3rd sg* **paalíixŭmaat**. *imp* **paalíixum**. *ptcpl* **paalíixŭmaat**.

**paalíixun** VII hang over something, lie over something. *conj 3rd sg* **paalíi=xung**. *ptcpl* **paalíixung**.

**paalíhkam** VTI1A step over s.t. *ind 1st sg* **mbaalíhkamun**. *ind 3rd sg* **paa=líhkamun**. *conj 1st sg* **paalíhka=maan**. *conj 3rd sg* **paalíhkang**. *imp* **paalíhkah**. *ptcpl* **paalíhkang**.

**paalíhkaweew** VTA step over s.o., step over s.t. animate. *ind 1st sg* **mbaalíh=kawaaw**, **mbaalíhkawa**. *ind 3rd sg* **paalihkawáawal**. *ind inv* **mbaalíh=kaakw**. *ind I-you* **kpaalíhkool**. *conj 3rd sg* **paalíhkawaat**. *imp* **paalíhkaw**. *ptcpl* **paalíhkawaat**.

**paalíhleew** VAI go over, flow over. *conj 3rd sg* **paalíhlaat**. *ptcpl* **paalíhlaak**.

**paalíhleew** VII go over, flow over. *conj 3rd sg* **paalíhlaak**. *ptcpl* **paalíhlaak**.

**paalihtéeheew** VTA hit s.t. animate over *(farther than intended)*. *ind 1st sg* **mbaalihtéehaaw**, **mbaalihtéeha**. *ind 3rd sg* **paalihteeháawal**. *ind inv* **mbaalihtéehookw**. *ind I-you* **kpaa=lihtéehookw**. *conj 3rd sg* **paalihtée=haat**. *imp* **paalíhteeh**. *ptcpl* **paalih=téehaat**.

**paalíhtoow** VTI2 make s.t. over something. *ind 1st sg* **mbaalíhtoon**. *ind 3rd sg* **paalíhtoon**. *conj 1st sg* **paa=líhtawaan**. *conj 3rd sg* **paalíhtaakw**. *imp* **paalíhtool**. *ptcpl* **paalíhtaakw**.

**paalpáteew** VII overflow *(of heated liquid, of radiator, of container that boils over)*. *conj 3rd sg* **paalpáteek**. *ptcpl* **paalpáteek**.

**páalpeew** VAI overflow *(s.t. animate, of containers)*. *conj 3rd sg* **páalpeet**. *ptcpl* **páalpeet**.

**páalpeew** VAIO overfill s.t.; make s.t. overflow. *ind 1st sg* **mbáalpeen**. *ind 3rd sg* **páalpeen**. *conj 3rd sg* **páal=peet**. *imp* **páalpeel**. *ptcpl* **páalpeet**.

**páalpeew** VII overflow *(of containers)*. *conj 3rd sg* **páalpeek**. *ptcpl* **páalpeek**.

**páalŭneew** VTA put s.o. over the top of something *(using the hands)*. *ind 1st sg* **mbáalŭnaaw**, **mbáalŭna**. *ind 3rd sg* **paalŭnáawal**. *ind inv* **mbáalŭ=nukw**. *ind I-you* **kpáalŭnul**. *conj 3rd sg* **páalŭnaat**. *imp* **páalun**. *ptcpl* **páalŭnaat**.

**páalŭnum** VTI1A put s.t. over the top of something *(using the hands)*. *ind 1st sg* **mbaalŭnúmun**. *ind 3rd sg* **paalŭ=númun**. *conj 1st sg* **paalunúmaan**. *conj 3rd sg* **páalŭnung**. *imp* **páalŭnih**. *ptcpl* **páalŭnung**.

**paanáhksun** NI wide shoe. *pl* **paanah=ksúnal**. *poss* **mbaanáhksun**. *loc* **paanahksúnung**. *dimin* **paanahk=shúnush**.

**paanalóowŭyeew** VII have a wide blade. *conj 3rd sg* **paanalóowŭyeek**. *ptcpl* **paanalóowŭyeek**.

**paanatéexun** VII be a wide road. *conj*

*3rd sg* **paanatéexung**. *ptcpl* **paana=téexung**.

**páaneew** VII be wide. *conj 3rd sg* **páa=neek**. *ptcpl* **páaneek**.

**páanham** VTI 1A dig s.t. up. **Mbaan=hámun éepiit.** 'I dug it up where he is.' *ind 1st sg* **mbaanhámun**. *ind 3rd sg* **paanhámun**. *conj 1st sg* **paan=hámaan**. *conj 3rd sg* **páanhang**. *imp* **páanhah**. *ptcpl* **páanhang**.

**páanheew** VTA dig s.o. up, dig s.t. animate up. *ind 1st sg* **mbáanhaaw**, **mbáanha**. *ind 3rd sg* **paanháawal**. *ind inv* **mbáanhookw**. *ind I-you* **kpáanhookw**. *conj 3rd sg* **páanhaat**. *imp* **páanhaw**. *ptcpl* **páanhaat**.

**paansíiteew** VAI have wide feet. *ind 1st sg* **mbaansíita**, **mbaansíitaam**. *conj 3rd sg* **paansíitaat**. *ptcpl* **paansíitaat**.

**paantoonháasuw** VAI have a wide mouth. *ind 1st sg* **mbaantoonháasi**, **mbaantoonháasiim**. *conj 3rd sg* **paantoonháasiit**. *ptcpl* **paantoon=háasiit**.

**paapaakalóohuw** VAI whoop. *ind 1st sg* **mbaapaakalóohi**, **mbaapaakalóo=hiim**. *conj 3rd sg* **paapaakalóohiit**. *imp* **paapaakalóohiil**. *ptcpl* **paapaa=kalóohiit**.

**paasáandpeew** VAI have a swollen head, have one's head swell up. *ind 1st sg* **mbasáandpa**, **mbasáandpaam**. *conj 3rd sg* **paasáandpaat**. *ptcpl* **paa=sáandpaat**.

**páasapwaan** NI baker's bread, bread made with yeast. *pl* **paasapwáanal**. *poss* **mbaasapwáanum**. *loc* **paasa=pwáanung**. *dimin* **paashapwáanush**.

**paasatáyeew** VAI have a swollen stomach, be bloated, have gas. *ind 1st sg* **mbaasatáya**, **mbaasatáyaam**. *conj 3rd sg* **paasatáyaat**. *ptcpl* **paasa=táyaat**.

**paasawiixíikan** NI yeast. *poss* **mbaasa=wiixíikan**. *loc* **paasawiixíikanung**. *dimin* **paasawiixíikanush**.

**paasawíixun** VII rise *(of yeast)*. *conj 3rd sg* **paasawíixung**. *ptcpl* **paasawíi=xung**.

**paascháaleew** VAI have a swollen nose, have one's nose swell up. *ind 1st sg* **mbaascháala**, **mbaascháalaam**. *conj 3rd sg* **paascháalaat**. *ptcpl* **paas=cháalaat**.

**paaschàlíingweew** VAI have a swollen face. *ind 1st sg* **mbaaschàlíingwa**, **mbaaschàlíingwaam**. *conj 3rd sg* **paaschàlíingwaat**. *ptcpl* **paaschàl=íingwaat**. *See* **paasíingweew**.

**páasiiw** VAI-S swell up *(s.t. animate)*. **Páasiiw ngútko.** 'My knee swelled up.' *ind 1st sg* **mbáasi**, **mbáasiim**. *conj 3rd sg* **páasiit**. *ptcpl* **páasiit**.

**páasiiw** VII-S swell up. *conj 3rd sg* **páa=siik**. *ptcpl* **páasiik**.

**paasiiktúkweew** VAI have a swollen knee. *ind 1st sg* **mbaasiiktúkwa**, **mbaasiiktúkwaam**. *conj 3rd sg* **paasiiktúkwaat**. *ptcpl* **paasiik=túkwaat**.

**paasíilaneew** VAI have a swollen udder, have a swollen breast. *ind 1st sg* **mbaasíilana**, **mbaasíilanaam**. *conj 3rd sg* **paasíilanaat**.

**paasíingweew** VAI have a swollen face, have one's face swell up. *ind 1st sg* **mbaasíingwa**, **mbaasíingwaam**. *conj 3rd sg* **paasíinkwaat**. *ptcpl* **paasíingwaat**. *See* **paaschàlíin=gweew**.

**paaskáateew** VAI have a swollen leg, have one's leg swell up. *ind 1st sg* **mbaaskáata**, **mbaaskáataam**. *conj 3rd sg* **paaskáataat**. *ptcpl* **paas=káataat**.

**páaspeew** VII swell from moisture, swell in moisture. **Xwús páaspeew.** 'The wood is swollen from dampness.' *conj 3rd sg* **páaspeek**. *ptcpl* **páaspeek**.

**paassíiteew** VAI have swollen feet. *ind 1st sg* **mbaassíita**, **mbaassíitaam**.

*conj 3rd sg* **paassíitaat**. *ptcpl* **paas=síitaat**.

**paasŭnáxkeew** VAI have a swollen hand. *ind 1st sg* **mbaasŭnáxka**, **mbaasŭ=náxkaam**. *conj 3rd sg* **paasŭnáx=kaat**. *ptcpl* **paasŭnáxkaat**.

**paasxóoneew** VAI have a swollen neck, have one's neck swell up. *ind 1st sg* **mbaasxóona**, **mbaasxóonaam**. *conj 3rd sg* **paasxóonaat**. *ptcpl* **paas=xóonaat**.

**páasteew** VII rise. *conj 3rd sg* **páasteek**. *ptcpl* **páasteek**.

**páaw** NA peacock, peahen. *pl* **páawak**. *From Dutch.*

**paawsúwahkw** NA poplar tree. *pl* **paaw=suwáhkwak**. *loc* **paawsuwáhkwung**. *obv* **paawsuwáhkwal**.

**paaxkeehúnzuw** VAI take the covers off oneself. *ind 1st sg* **mbaaxkeehúnzi**, **mbaaxkeehúnziim**. *conj 3rd sg* **paaxkeehúnziit**. *imp* **paaxkee=húnziil**. *ptcpl* **paaxkeehúnziit**.

**paaxkéeneew** VTA uncover s.o. *(using the hands)*. *ind 1st sg* **mbaaxkée=naaw**, **mbaaxkéena**. *ind 3rd sg* **paaxkeenáawal**. *ind inv* **mbaaxkée=nukw**. *ind I-you* **kpaaxkéenukw**. *conj 3rd sg* **paaxkéenaat**. *imp* **páaxkeen**. *ptcpl* **paaxkéenaat**.

**paaxkéenum** VTI1B uncover s.t. *(using the hands)*. *ind 1st sg* **mbaaxkée=nŭmun**. *ind 3rd sg* **paaxkéenŭmun**. *conj 1st sg* **paaxkéenŭmaan**. *conj 3rd sg* **paaxkéenung**. *imp* **paaxkée=nih**. *ptcpl* **paaxkéenung**.

**paaxkéexiin** VAI lie uncovered. *ind 1st sg* **mbaaxkéexiin**, **mbaaxkéexi**. *conj 3rd sg* **paaxkéexiing**. *imp* **paaxkée=xiil**. *ptcpl* **paaxkéexiing**.

**paaxkéexun** VII lie uncovered. *conj 3rd sg* **paaxkéexung**. *ptcpl* **paaxkéexung**.

**paaxkeeyáaheew** VAIO throw the cover off s.o., throw the cover off s.t. *ind 1st sg* **mbaaxkeeyáaheen**. *ind 3rd sg* **paaxkeeyáaheen**. *conj 3rd sg* **paax=keeyáaheet**. *imp* **paaxkeeyáaheel**. *ptcpl* **paaxkeeyáaheet**.

**pahchíilateew** VAI choke *(from food going down the wrong way)*. *ind 1st sg* **mbahchíilata**, **mbahchíilataam**. *conj 3rd sg* **pahchíilataat**. *ptcpl* **pahchíi=lataat**. *intensive reduplication* **pah=pahchíilateew**.

**pahchíinam** VTI1A mistake s.t. for something else. *ind 1st sg* **mbahchíina=mun**. *ind 3rd sg* **pahchíinamun**. *conj 1st sg* **pahchíinamaan**. *conj 3rd sg* **pahchíinang**. *ptcpl* **pahchíinang**.

**pahchíinaweew** VTA mistake s.o. for someone else. *ind 1st sg* **mbahchíi=nawaaw**, **mbahchíinawa**. *ind 3rd sg* **pahchiinawáawal**. *ind inv* **mbah=chíinaakw**. *ind I-you* **kpahchíinool**. *conj 3rd sg* **pahchíinawaat**. *ptcpl* **pahchíinawaat**.

**pahchi-** PV by accident, in error. **Mbáhchi-tŭmúshaaw.** 'I cut him by accident.' *ptcpl* **páhchi-**. *See* **pahchu-**.

**pahchíhkaweew** VTA kick s.o. by accident. *ind 1st sg* **mbahchíhkawaaw**, **mbahchíhkawa**. *ind 3rd sg* **pah=chihkawáawal**. *ind inv* **mbahchíh=kaakw**. *ind I-you* **kpahchíhkool**. *conj 3rd sg* **pahchíhkawaat**. *ptcpl* **pahchíhkawaat**.

**pahchóoleew** VTA cheat s.o. **Ngáta-péechi-pahpahchóolukw.** 'He's coming here to cheat me.' *ind 1st sg* **mbahchóolaaw**, **mbahchóola**. *ind 3rd sg* **pahchooláawal**. *ind inv* **mbahchóolukw**. *ind I-you* **kpah=chóolul**. *conj 3rd sg* **pahchóolaat**. *imp* **páhchool**. *ptcpl* **pahchóolaat**. *intensive reduplication* **pahpah=chooláawal**.

**pahchoolŭweewiinάakwsuw** VAI look deceptive, look misleading. *ind 1st sg* **mbahchoolŭweewiinάakwsi**, **mbah=choolŭweewiinάakwsiim**. *conj 3rd sg* **pahchoolŭweewiinάakwsiit**. *ptcpl*

**pahchoolŭweewiináakwsiit**.

**pahchóhkeew** VAI cheat, cheat people. *ind 1st sg* **mbahchóhke, mbahchóh=keem**. *conj 3rd sg* **pahchóhkeet**. *imp* **pahchóhkeel**. *ptcpl* **pahchóhkeet**. *intensive reduplication* **pahpahchóh=keew**.

**pahchu-** PV by accident, in error. *informal*. **Páhchu- kwéek -úw.** 'He said it by accident.'; **Mbáhchu-ahpalíh=keen.** 'I stepped on it by accident.' *ptcpl* **páhchu-**. *See* **pahchi-**.

**páhkŭnum** VII be dark. **Éelkih-páhkŭ=nung.** 'Because it was so dark.' *conj 3rd sg* **páhkŭnung**. *ptcpl* **páhkŭnung**.

**pahkŭnumwíhleew** VII get dark *(rapidly)*. **Wchiimáhteew pahkŭnum=wíhleew.** 'The light went out and it got dark quickly.' *conj 3rd sg* **pah=kŭnumwíhlaak**. *ptcpl* **pahkŭnum=wíhlaak**.

**pahkwtéeyeew** VII be a clearing. *conj 3rd sg* **pahkwtéeyeek**. *ptcpl* **pahk=wtéeyeek**.

**pahpaakaláamuw** VAI whoop. *ind 1st sg* **mbahpaakaláamwi, mbahpaa=kaláamwiim**. *conj 3rd sg* **pahpaa=kaláamwiit**. *imp* **pahpaakaláamwiil**. *ptcpl* **pahpaakaláamwiit**.

**pahpáhkuw** NA ruffed grouse, partridge. *pl* **pahpáhkŭwak**. *obv* **pahpáh=kŭwal**.

**pahtaaptóoneew** VAI mistakenly reveal some information; 'let the cat out of the bag.' *ind 1st sg* **mbahtaaptóone, mbahtaaptóoneem**. *conj 3rd sg* **pahtaaptóoneet**. *ptcpl* **pahtaap=tóoneet**.

**páhtameew** VTA eat s.t. animate by accident. *ind 1st sg* **mbáhtamaaw, mbáhtama**. *ind 3rd sg* **pahtamáa=wal**. *ind inv* **mbáhtamukw**. *ind I-you* **kpáhtamul**. *conj 3rd sg* **páhtamaat**. *ptcpl* **páhtamaat**.

**pahtamáweew** VTA pray to s.o. *ind 1st sg* **mbahtamáwaaw, mbahtamáwa**. *ind 3rd sg* **pahtamawáawal**. *ind inv* **mbáhtamaakw**. *ind I-you* **kpáhta=mool**. *conj 3rd sg* **pahtamáwaat**. *imp* **páhtamaw**. *ptcpl* **pahtamáwaat**.

**pahtamáwaas** NA God. *obv* **pahta=mawáasal**.

**pahtamawáasuw** VAI be God. *ind 1st sg* **mbahtamawáasi, mbahtamawáa=siim**. *conj 3rd sg* **pahtamawáasiit**. *ptcpl* **pahtamawáasiit**.

**pahtamáweew** VAI pray. *ind 1st sg* **mbahtamáwe, mbahtamáweem**. *conj 3rd sg* **pahtamáweet**. *imp* **pahtamáweel**. *ptcpl* **pahtamáweet**.

**pahtamaweelúnzuw** VAI think that one is God. *ind 1st sg* **mbahtamawee=lúnzi, mbahtamaweelúnziim**. *conj 3rd sg* **pahtamaweelúnziit**. *ptcpl* **pahtamaweelúnziit**.

**pahtamaweelxáweew** VTA pray to s.o., pray for s.o. *ind 1st sg* **mbahtamaw=eelxáwaaw, mbahtamaweelxáwa**. *ind 3rd sg* **pahtamaweelxawáawal**. *ind inv* **mbahtamawéelxookw**. *ind I-you* **kpahtamawéelxool**. *conj 3rd sg* **pahtamaweelxáwaat**. *imp* **pahta=mawéelxaw**. *ptcpl* **pahtamaweel=xáwaat**.

**pahtamawíikaan** NI church. *pl* **pahta=mawíikaanal**. *loc* **pahtamawiikáa=nung**. *dimin* **pahchamawiikáanush**.

**pahtándam** VTI 1A eat s.t. by accident. *ind 1st sg* **mbahtándamun**. *ind 3rd sg* **pahtándamun**. *conj 1st sg* **pah=tándamaan**. *conj 3rd sg* **pahtándang**. *ptcpl* **páhtandang**.

**páhtham** VTI 1A hit s.t. by accident. *ind 1st sg* **mbahthámun**. *ind 3rd sg* **pahthámun**. *conj 1st sg* **pahthám=aan**. *conj 3rd sg* **páhthang**. *ptcpl* **páhthang**.

**páhtheew** VTA hit s.o. by accident. *ind 1st sg* **mbáhthaaw, mbáhtha**. *ind 3rd sg* **pahtháawal**. *ind inv* **mbáht=hookw**. *ind I-you* **kpáhthool**. *conj 3rd sg* **páhthaat**. *ptcpl* **páhthaat**.

**páhthookw** VAI get hit by accident. *ind 1st sg* **mbáhthookw, mbáhthookw**. *conj 3rd sg* **pahthóokwuk**.

**pahtihtéeham** VTI1A hit s.t. by accident. *ind 1st sg* **mbahtihtéehŭmun**. *ind 3rd sg* **pahtihtéehŭmun**. *conj 1st sg* **pahtihtéehŭmaan**. *conj 3rd sg* **pah=tihtéehang**. *ptcpl* **pahtihtéehang**.

**pahtihtéeheew** VTA hit s.o. by accident. *ind 1st sg* **mbahtihtéehaaw, mbah=tihtéeha**. *ind 3rd sg* **pahtihteeháa=wal**. *ind inv* **mbahtihtéehookw**. *ind I-you* **kpahtihtéehool**. *conj 3rd sg* **pahtihtéehaat**. *ptcpl* **pahtihtéehaat**.

**páhtsheew** VTA cut s.o. by accident, cut s.t. animate by accident. *ind 1st sg* **mbáhtshaaw, mbáhtsha**. *ind 3rd sg* **pahtsháawal**. *ind inv* **mbáhtshookw**. *ind I-you* **kpáhtshool**. *conj 3rd sg* **páhtshaat**. *ptcpl* **páhtshaat**.

**páhtshum** VTI1B cut s.t. by accident. *ind 1st sg* **mbahtshúmun**. *ind 3rd sg* **pahtshúmun**. *conj 1st sg* **paht=shúmaan**. *conj 3rd sg* **páhtshung**. *ptcpl* **páhtshung**.

**páhtŭneew** VTA pick s.o. up by mistake, touch s.o. by mistake. *ind 1st sg* **mbáhtŭnaaw, mbáhtŭna**. *ind 3rd sg* **pahtŭnáawal**. *ind inv* **mbáhtŭnukw**. *ind I-you* **kpáhtŭnul**. *conj 3rd sg* **páhtŭnaat**. *ptcpl* **páhtŭnaat**.

**páhtŭnum** VTI1B pick s.t. up by mistake, touch s.t. by mistake. *ind 1st sg* **mbahtŭnúmun**. *ind 3rd sg* **pahtŭ=númun**. *conj 1st sg* **pahtŭnúmaan**. *conj 3rd sg* **páhtŭnung**. *ptcpl* **páhtŭnung**.

**pàhŭníikan** NI sifter. *pl* **pàhŭníikanal**. *poss* **mbahŭníikan**. *loc* **pàhŭníi=kanung**. *dimin* **pàhŭníikanush**. *See* **pawŭníikan**.

**pàhŭníikeew** VAI sift things, be sifting. *ind 1st sg* **mbahŭníike, mbahŭníi=keem**. *conj 3rd sg* **pàhŭníikeet**. *imp* **pàhŭníikeel**. *ptcpl* **pàhŭníikeet**.

**pàkáandpeew** VAI have a flat head. *ind 1st sg* **mbakáandpa, mbakáand=paam**. *conj 3rd sg* **pàkáandpaat**. *ptcpl* **pàkáandpaat**.

**pàkaandpéhleew** VAI have a flat head *(of blow adders)*; have one's head go flat *(when blowing)*. *ind 1st sg* **mbakaandpéhla, mbakaandpéh=laam**. *conj 3rd sg* **pàkaandpéhlaat**. *ptcpl* **pàkaandpéhlaat**.

**pakahíikan** NI barn, threshing barn. *pl* **pakahíikanal**. *loc* **pakahíikanung**.

**pakáhŭmeew** VAI thresh grain. *ind 1st sg* **mbakháma, mbakhámaam**. *conj 3rd sg* **pakáhŭmaat**. *imp* **pakáhŭ=maal**. *ptcpl* **peekhámaat**.

**pakámeew** VTA hit s.o. *ind 1st sg* **mbák=amaaw, mbákama**. *ind 3rd sg* **pàk=amáawal**. *ind inv* **mbákamukw**. *ind I-you* **kpákamul**. *conj 3rd sg* **pakám=aat**. *imp* **pakám**. *ptcpl* **péekamaat**. *intensive reduplication* **pàpakamáa=wal**.

**pakándam** VTI1A hit s.t. *ind 1st sg* **mbakándamun**. *ind 3rd sg* **pàkán=damun**. *conj 1st sg* **pakándamaan**. *conj 3rd sg* **pakándang**. *imp* **pakán=dah**. *ptcpl* **peekándang**.

**pakandíikan** NI club, baseball bat. *pl* **pakandíikanal**. *poss* **mbakandíikan**. *loc* **pakandíikanung**. *dimin* **pakan=jíikanush**.

**pakásŭmeew** VAI crack nuts. *ind 1st sg* **mbakasúma, mbakasúmaam**. *conj 3rd sg* **pakásŭmaat**. *imp* **pakásŭ=maal**. *ptcpl* **peekasúmaat**.

**pàkatéexiin** VAI lie on one's stomach. *ind 1st sg* **mbakatéexiin, mbakatée=xi**. *conj 3rd sg* **pàkatéexiing**. *imp* **pàkatéexiil**. *ptcpl* **pàkatéexiing, pàkatéexiit**.

**pàkatéexun** VII be a flat road, be a flat driveway. *conj 3rd sg* **pàkatéexung**. *ptcpl* **pàkatéexung**.

**pàkatéhleew** VAI roll over onto one's stomach. *ind 1st sg* **mbakatéhla, mbakatéhlaam**. *conj 3rd sg* **pàka=**

**téhlaat**. *imp* **pàkatéhlaal**. *ptcpl* **pàkatéhlaat**.

**pàkcháaleew** VAI have a flat nose. *ind 1st sg* **mbakcháala**, **mbakcháalaam**. *conj 3rd sg* **pàkcháalaat**. *ptcpl* **pàkcháalaat**.

**pàkchaalehtéexiin** VAI hit and flatten one's nose against something. *ind 1st sg* **mbakchaalehtéexiin**, **mbak=chaalehtéexi**. *conj 3rd sg* **pàkchaa=lehtéexiing**. *ptcpl* **pàkchaalehtée=xiing**, **pàkchaalehtéexiit**.

**pàkchéeheew** VTA flatten s.o. *ind 1st sg* **mbakchéehaaw**, **mbakchéeha**. *ind 3rd sg* **pàkcheeháawal**. *ind inv* **mbakchéehukw**. *ind I-you* **kpak=chéehul**. *conj 3rd sg* **pàkchéehaat**. *imp* **pákcheeh**. *ptcpl* **pàkchéehaat**.

**pàkchéehum** VTI1B flatten s.t. *ind 1st sg* **mbakchéehŭmun**. *ind 3rd sg* **pàk=chéehŭmun**. *conj 1st sg* **pàkchéehŭ=maan**. *conj 3rd sg* **pàkchéehung**. *imp* **pàkchéehih**. *ptcpl* **pàkchéehung**.

**pàkchéeneew** VTA flatten s.o. *(using the hands)*. *ind 1st sg* **mbakchéenaaw**, **mbakchéena**. *ind 3rd sg* **pàkchee=náawal**. *ind inv* **mbakchéenukw**. *ind I-you* **kpakchéenul**. *conj 3rd sg* **pàkchéenaat**. *imp* **pákcheen**. *ptcpl* **pàkchéenaat**.

**pàkchéenum** VTI1B flatten s.t., straighten s.t. *(using the hands)*. *ind 1st sg* **mbakchéenŭmun**. *ind 3rd sg* **pàk=chéenŭmun**. *conj 1st sg* **pàkchéenŭ=maan**. *conj 3rd sg* **pàkchéenung**. *imp* **pàkchéenih**. *ptcpl* **pàkchéenung**.

**pàkchéesuw** VAI be flat *(s.t. animate)*. *ind 1st sg* **mbakchéesi**, **mbakchée=siim**. *conj 3rd sg* **pàkchéesiit**. *ptcpl* **pàkchéesiit**.

**pàkchéeyeew** VII be flat. *conj 3rd sg* **pàkchéeyeek**. *ptcpl* **pàkchéeyeek**.

**pàkchéhkam** VTI1A flatten s.t. *(using the foot or body)*. *ind 1st sg* **mbak=chéhkamun**. *ind 3rd sg* **pàkchéhka=mun**. *conj 1st sg* **pàkchéhkamaan**. *conj 3rd sg* **pàkchéhkang**. *imp* **pàkchéhkah**. *ptcpl* **pàkchéhkang**.

**pàkchéhkaweew** VTA flatten s.o. *(using the foot or body)*. *ind 1st sg* **mbak=chéhkawaaw**, **mbakchéhkawa**. *ind 3rd sg* **pàkchehkawáawal**. *ind inv* **mbakchéhkaakw**. *ind I-you* **kpak=chéhkool**. *conj 3rd sg* **pàkchéhka=waat**. *imp* **pàkchéhkaw**. *ptcpl* **pàk=chéhkawaat**.

**pàkchehtéexiin** VAI fall on one's stomach, land on one's stomach; fall flat, fall face down. *ind 1st sg* **mbak=chehtéexiin**, **mbakchehtéexi**. *conj 3rd sg* **pàkchehtéexiing**. *ptcpl* **pàk=chehtéexiing**.

**pákeew** VII be flat. *conj 3rd sg* **pákeek**. *ptcpl* **pákeek**.

**pákham** VTI1A flatten s.t. *(using a tool or instrument)*. *ind 1st sg* **mbak=hámun**. *ind 3rd sg* **pàkhámun**. *conj 1st sg* **pàkhámaan**. *conj 3rd sg* **pák=hang**. *imp* **pákhah**. *ptcpl* **pákhang**.

**pákheew** VTA flatten s.o., flatten s.t. animate *(using a tool or instrument)*. *ind 1st sg* **mbákhaaw**, **mbákha**. *ind 3rd sg* **pàkháawal**. *ind inv* **mbákhookw**. *ind I-you* **kpákhool**. *conj 3rd sg* **pàk=haat**. *imp* **pákhaw**. *ptcpl* **pákhaat**.

**pàkii-** PN flat. **Pákii-amóxool.** 'Flat-bottomed boat.'

**pakíileew** VTA throw s.o. away, throw s.t. animate away. *ind 1st sg* **mbakíilaaw**, **mbakíila**. *ind 3rd sg* **pàkiiláawal**. *ind inv* **mbakíilukw**. *ind I-you* **kpakíilul**. *conj 3rd sg* **pakíilaat**. *imp* **pakíil**. *ptcpl* **peekíilaat**.

**pàkiingwehtéexiin** VAI hit and flatten one's face against something. *ind 1st sg* **mbakiingwehtéexiin**, **mbakiin=gwehtéexi**. *conj 3rd sg* **pàkiingweh=téexiing**. *ptcpl* **pàkiingwehtéexiing**, **pàkiingwehtéexiit**.

**pàkíinjuw** NI plate. *pl* **pàkíinjŭwal**. *poss* **mbakiinjóohum**. *loc* **pàkiin=jóohung**. *dimin* **pàkíinjoosh**.

**pakíitoow** VTI2 throw s.t. away. *ind 1st sg* **mbakíitoon**. *ind 3rd sg* **pàkíitoon**. *conj 1st sg* **pakíitawaan**. *conj 3rd sg* **pakíitaakw**. *imp* **pakíitool**. *ptcpl* **peekíitaakw**.

**pàkíitŭyeew** VAI have a flat backside. *ind 1st sg* **mbakíitŭya, mbakíitŭyaam**. *conj 3rd sg* **pàkíitŭyaat**. *ptcpl* **pàkíi=tŭyaat**.

**pàkíhkam** VTI1A flatten s.t. *(using the foot or body)*. *ind 1st sg* **mbakíhka=mun**. *ind 3rd sg* **pàkíhkamun**. *conj 1st sg* **pàkíhkamaan**. *conj 3rd sg* **pàkíhkang**. *imp* **pàkíhkah**. *ptcpl* **pàkíhkang**.

**pàkíhkaweew** VTA flatten s.o. *(using the foot or body)*. *ind 1st sg* **mbakíhka=waaw, mbakíhkawa**. *ind 3rd sg* **pàkihkawáawal**. *ind inv* **mbakíh=kaakw**. *ind I-you* **kpakíhkool**. *conj 3rd sg* **pàkíhkawaat**. *imp* **pàkíhkaw**. *ptcpl* **pàkíhkawaat**.

**pàkíhleew** VII go flat. *conj 3rd sg* **pàk=íhlaak**. *ptcpl* **pàkíhlaak**.

**pàkihtéeheew** VTA hit and flatten s.o., hit and flatten s.t. animate. *ind 1st sg* **mbakihtéehaaw, mbakihtéeha**. *ind 3rd sg* **pàkihteeháawal**. *ind inv* **mbakihtéehookw**. *ind I-you* **kpak=ihtéehool**. *conj 3rd sg* **pàkihtéehaat**. *imp* **pàkíhteeh**. *ptcpl* **pàkihtéehaat**.

**pàkihtéehum** VTI1B hit and flatten s.t. *ind 1st sg* **mbakihtéehŭmun**. *ind 3rd sg* **pàkihtéehŭmun**. *conj 1st sg* **pàk=ihtéehŭmaan**. *conj 3rd sg* **pàkihtée=hung**. *imp* **pàkihtéehih**. *ptcpl* **pàk=ihtéehung**.

**páksuw** VAI be flat *(s.t. animate)*. *ind 1st sg* **mbáksi, mbáksiim**. *conj 3rd sg* **páksiit**. *ptcpl* **páksiit**.

**pákŭneew** VTA flatten s.o., flatten s. t. animate *(using the hands)*. *ind 1st sg* **mbákŭnaaw, mbákŭna**. *ind 3rd sg* **pàkŭnáawal**. *ind inv* **mbákŭnukw**. *ind I-you* **kpákŭnul**. *conj 3rd sg* **pák=ŭnaat**. *imp* **pákun**. *ptcpl* **pákŭnaat**.

**pákŭnum** VTI1B flatten s.t. *ind 1st sg* **mbakŭnúmun**. *ind 3rd sg* **pàkŭ=númun**. *conj 1st sg* **pàkŭnúmaan**. *conj 3rd sg* **pákŭnung**. *imp* **pákŭnih**. *ptcpl* **pákŭnung**.

**paláham** VTI1A miss hitting s.t. *(using a tool or instrument)*. *ind 1st sg* **mbal=hámun**. *ind 3rd sg* **pàlhámun**. *conj 1st sg* **paláhŭmaan**. *conj 3rd sg* **pa=láhang**. *imp* **paláhah**. *ptcpl* **péelhang**.

**paláheew** VTA miss hitting s.o., miss hitting s.t. animate *(using a tool or instrument)*. *ind 1st sg* **mbálhaaw, mbálha**. *ind 3rd sg* **pàlháawal**. *ind inv* **mbálhookw**. *ind I-you* **kpálhool**. *conj 3rd sg* **paláhaat**. *ptcpl* **péelhaat**.

**palalíikaaxkw** NI sliver. *pl* **palaliikáax=kwal**. *loc* **palaliikáaxkwung**. *dimin* **palaliikáaxkwush**.

**palámeew** VTA drop s.t. animate from one's mouth, have s.t. animate fall out of one's mouth, miss one's mouth with s.t. animate *(of food)*. *ind 1st sg* **mbálamaaw, mbálama**. *ind 3rd sg* **pàlamáawal**. *ind inv* **mbálamukw**. *ind I-you* **kpálamul**. *conj 3rd sg* **palámaat**. *ptcpl* **péelamaat**.

**palándam** VOTI1A drop food from one's mouth, have food fall out of one's mouth, miss one's mouth while eating. *ind 1st sg* **mbalándam**. *conj 3rd sg* **palándang**. *ptcpl* **peelándang**. *intensive reduplication* **pàpalándam**.

**palándam** VTI1A drop s.t. from one's mouth, have s.t. fall out of one's mouth, miss one's mouth with s.t. *ind 1st sg* **mbalándamun**. *ind 3rd sg* **pàlándamun**. *conj 1st sg* **palánda=maan**. *conj 3rd sg* **palándang**. *ptcpl* **peelándang**.

**palapíhleew** VAI miss one's seat while sitting down, fall while sitting. *ind 1st sg* **mbalapíhla, mbalapíhlaam**. *conj 3rd sg* **palapíhlaat**. *ptcpl* **peelapíh=laat**.

**palápuw** VAI miss one's seat while sitting down, fall while sitting. *ind 1st sg* **mbálapi**, **mbálapiim**. *conj 3rd sg* **palápiit**. *ptcpl* **péelapiit**.

**palíi** PC elsewhere, somewhere else. **Palíi luchéhlaal!** 'Drive somewhere else!'; **Palíi áal!** 'Go away!' *See* **palí**, **palíiwi**.

**palii-** PV elsewhere, somewhere else. **Mbálii-áhtoon.** 'I put it elsewhere.'; **Palíi-lóoxwe.** 'He went the other way.' *ptcpl* **péelii-**. *See* **palu-**.

**paliikáapawuw** VAI stand over, stand somewhere else, stand elsewhere. *ind 1st sg* **mbaliikáapawi**, **mbaliikáa=pawiim**. *conj 3rd sg* **paliikáapawiit**. *imp* **paliikáapawiil**. *ptcpl* **peelii=káapawiit**.

**palíiwi** PC elsewhere, somewhere else. **Palíiwi íin wŭniipalaawáawal.** 'They stood him somewhere else.' *See* **palí**, **palíi**.

**palí** PC elsewhere, somewhere else. *informal.* **Palí lúnih nú asún wúnju-eehundaxpóonung.** 'Take the stone off the table.' *See* **palíi**, **palíiwi**.

**palíhkam** VTI1A miss stepping on s.t. *ind 1st sg* **mbalíhkamun**. *ind 3rd sg* **pàlíhkamun**. *conj 1st sg* **palíhka=maan**. *conj 3rd sg* **palíhkang**. *imp* **palíhkah**. *ptcpl* **peelíhkang**.

**palíhkaweew** VTA miss stepping on s.o., miss stepping on s.t. animate. *ind 1st sg* **mbalíhkawaaw**, **mbalíhkawa**. *ind 3rd sg* **pàlihkawáawal**. *ind inv* **mbalíhkaakw**. *ind I-you* **kpalíhkool**. *conj 3rd sg* **palíhkawaat**. *imp* **palíhkaw**. *ptcpl* **peelíhkawaat**.

**palíhleew** VAI miss an event, miss a regular event. *ind 1st sg* **mbalíhla**, **mbalíhlaam**. *conj 3rd sg* **palíhlaat**. *ptcpl* **peelíhlaat**.

**palihtéeham** VTI1A miss at hitting s.t. *ind 1st sg* **mbalihtéehŭmun**. *ind 3rd sg* **pàlihtéehŭmun**. *conj 1st sg* **palih=téehŭmaan**. *conj 3rd sg* **palihtée=hang**. *imp* **palihtéehih**. *ptcpl* **peelih=téehang**.

**palihtéeheew** VTA miss at hitting s.o., miss at hitting s.t. animate. *ind 1st sg* **mbalihtéehaaw**, **mbalihtéeha**. *ind 3rd sg* **pàlihteeháawal**. *ind inv* **mbalihtéehookw**. *ind I-you* **kpalih=téehool**. *conj 3rd sg* **palihtéehaat**. *imp* **palíhteeh**. *ptcpl* **peelihtéehaat**.

**palíhtoow** VTI2 make a mistake in doing s.t. **Mbalíhtoon shookŭlápwaan.** 'I made a mistake in making the cake.' *ind 1st sg* **mbalíhtoon**. *ind 3rd sg* **pàlíhtoon**. *conj 1st sg* **palíhtawaan**. *conj 3rd sg* **palíhtaakw**. *ptcpl* **pee=líhtaakw**.

**palu-** PV elsewhere, somewhere else. *informal.* **Mbálu-íin.** 'I said it in a hurry.' *ptcpl* **péelu-**. *See* **palii-**.

**palúneew** VTA drop s.o. *ind 1st sg* **mbál=ŭnaaw**, **mbálŭna**. *ind 3rd sg* **pàlŭ=náawal**. *ind inv* **mbálŭnukw**. *ind I-you* **kpálŭnul**. *conj 3rd sg* **palúnaat**. *imp* **palún**. *ptcpl* **péelŭnaat**.

**palúnum** VTI1B drop s.t. **Pàlŭnúmun lí kóonung.** 'He dropped it in the snow.' *ind 1st sg* **mbalŭnúmun**. *ind 3rd sg* **pàlŭnúmun**. *conj 1st sg* **palúnŭmaan**. *conj 3rd sg* **palúnung**. *imp* **palúnih**. *ptcpl* **péelŭnung**.

**palustáweew** VTA disbelieve s.o. *ind 1st sg* **mbalsútawaaw**, **mbalsútawa**. *ind 3rd sg* **pàlsutawáawal**. *ind inv* **mbalsútaakw**. *ind I-you* **kpalsútool**. *conj 3rd sg* **palústawaat**. *imp* **pa=lústaw**. *ptcpl* **peelsútawaat**.

**palústam** VTI1A disbelieve s.t. **Kwéek mbúndam, mbalsútam.** 'I didn't believe what I heard.' *ind 1st sg* **mbal=sútamun**. *ind 3rd sg* **pàlsútamun**. *conj 1st sg* **palustámaan**. *conj 3rd sg* **palústang**. *imp* **palústah**. *ptcpl* **peelsútang**.

**pámbiil** NA book, paper, letter. **Xúwii-pambíilak.** 'Old books.' *pl* **pambíi=lak**. *poss* **mbambíilum**. *loc* **pambíi=lung**. *dimin* **pambíilush**. *obv* **pam=**

**bíilal**. *From Dutch.*
**pambiilhíikeew** VAI put up wallpaper. *ind 1st sg* **mbambiilhíike, mbam=biilhíikeem**. *conj 3rd sg* **pambiilhíi=keet**. *imp* **pambiilhíikeel**. *ptcpl* **peembiilhíikeet**.
**pambiiliinóotay** NI paper bag. *pl* **pam=biiliinóotayal**. *poss* **mbambiilii=nóotay**.
**pambíilush** NA little bit of paper, Kleenex. *pl* **pambíilshak**. *poss* **mbambíil=shum**. *loc* **pambíilshung**. *obv* **pam=bíilshal**.
**pán** NA frying pan. *pl* **pának**. *poss* **mbánum**. *loc* **pánung**. *dimin* **pánush**. *obv* **pánal**. *From Dutch.*
**pánapwaan** NI pan bread. *pl* **pàna=pwáanal**. *poss* **mbanapwáanum**. *loc* **pànapwáanung**. *dimin* **pànapwáa=nush**. *cooked on top of the stove at low heat with no grease.*
**pangéesuw** VAI be in pieces, be in slices *(s.t. animate). usually with number particle.* **Nxú pangéesuw.** 'It's in three slices.'; **Kéexu pangéesuw.** 'It's in several pieces.' *conj 3rd sg* **pangéesiit**. *ptcpl* **peengéesiit**.
**pangéesheew** VTA cut s.t. animate in pieces, cut s.t. animate in slices. **Níisha mbangéeshaaw.** 'I cut him in two pieces.' *ind 1st sg* **mbangée=shaaw, mbangéesha**. *ind 3rd sg* **pangeesháawal**. *conj 3rd sg* **pan=géeshaat**. *imp* **pángeesh**. *ptcpl* **peen=géeshaat**.
**pangéeshum** VTI 1A cut s.t. in pieces, cut s.t. in slices. **Níisha mbangéeshŭ=mun.** 'I cut it in two pieces.' *ind 1st sg* **mbangéeshŭmun**. *ind 3rd sg* **pangéeshŭmun**. *conj 1st sg* **pangée=shŭmaan**. *conj 3rd sg* **pangéeshung**. *imp* **pangéeshih**. *ptcpl* **peengée=shung**.
**pangéeyeew** VII be in pieces, be in slices. *usually with number particle.* **Néew-pangéeyeew.** 'It's in four slices.'; **Amángu-pangéeyeew.** 'It's in big pieces' *conj 3rd sg* **pangéeyeek**.
**pángpeew** VAI drip, be dripping *(s.t. animate). ind 1st sg* **mbángpe, mbáng=peem**. *conj 3rd sg* **pángpeet**. *ptcpl* **péengpeet**.
**pángpeew** VII drip, be dripping. **Kíhchu-pángpe.** 'It's really dripping.' *conj 3rd sg* **pángpeek**. *ptcpl* **péengpeek**. *intensive reduplication* **pahpáng=peew**.
**pánkook** NA pancake. *pl* **pankóokak**. *poss* **mbankóokum**. *loc* **pankóo=kung**. *dimin* **pankóokush**. *obv* **pankóokal**. *From Dutch.*
**papaa-** PV about, around, here and there. **Nxóo há mbápaa-kàkawíhlaan.** 'I keep falling about by myself.'; **Náa=keesh wiitaawsoomáawal wiita=weemáachiil, nál wáak pàkíilaan, nál wáak nzhíisal pápaa-kwíila=waan.** 'She lived with her husband for a while, then she left him, and then she went looking for my uncle.' *ptcpl* **péepaa-**. *See* **apaamu-**.
**pàpalaachíimuw** VAI say something in a hurry, leave something out of a story, don't tell the whole story. *ind 1st sg* **mbapalaachíimwi, mbapalaachíi=mwiim**. *conj 3rd sg* **pàpalaachíi=mwiit**. *imp* **pàpalaachíimwiil**. *ptcpl* **pàpalaachíimwiit**.
**pàpsákeew** VII be spotted. *conj 3rd sg* **pàpsákeek**. *ptcpl* **pàpsákeek**.
**pàpsáksuw** VAI be spotted *(s.t. animate). ind 1st sg* **mbapsáksi, mbapsáksiim**. *conj 3rd sg* **pàpsáksiit**. *ptcpl* **pàp=sáksiit**.
**pàpsákuw** VAI be sticky. *ind 1st sg* **mbapsákwi, mbapsákwiim**. *conj 3rd sg* **pàpsákwiit**. *ptcpl* **pàpsákwiit**.
**pàpsákŭlaan** VII be sprinkling rain. *conj 3rd sg* **pàpsákŭlaang**. *ptcpl* **pàp=sákŭlaang**.
**pàptukaashŭwíhleew** VAI swim zigzag. *ind 1st sg* **mbaptukaashŭwíhla**,

**mbaptukaashŭwíhlaam**. *conj 3rd sg* **pàptukaashŭwíhlaat**. *imp* **pàptuk= aashŭwíhlaal**. *ptcpl* **pàptukaashŭ= wíhlaat**.

**pàptukáhtakat** VII be crooked *(of something string-like)*. *conj 3rd sg* **pàp= tukáhtakahk**. *ptcpl* **pàptukáh= takahk**.

**pàptukahtakíhleew** VAI run zigzag. *ind 1st sg* **mbaptukahtakíhla, mbap= tukahtakíhlaam**. *conj 3rd sg* **pàp= tukahtakíhlaat**. *imp* **pàptukahta= kíhlaal**. *ptcpl* **pàptukahtakíhlaat**.

**pàptukatéexun** VII be a crooked road. *conj 3rd sg* **pàptukatéexung**. *ptcpl* **pàptukatéexung**.

**pàptukchéhleew** VAI drive crookedly. *ind 1st sg* **mbaptukchéhla, mbap= tukchéhlaam**. *conj 3rd sg* **pàptuk= chéhlaat**. *imp* **pàptukchéhlaal**. *ptcpl* **pàptukchéhlaat**.

**pàptúkeew** VII be crooked, be winding. **Pàptúkeew nú síipuw.** 'The river is winding.' *conj 3rd sg* **pàptúkeek**. *ptcpl* **pàptúkeek**.

**pàptukeekháasuw** VII be written crookedly. *conj 3rd sg* **pàptukeekháasiik**. *ptcpl* **pàptukeekháasiik**.

**pàptukéelham** VOTI1A leave crooked tracks. *ind 1st sg* **mbàptukéelham**. *conj 3rd sg* **pàptukéelhang**. *imp* **pàptukéelhah**. *ptcpl* **pàptukéelhang**.

**pàptukhóomeew** VAI go crookedly while riding on horseback. *ind 1st sg* **mbaptukhóoma, mbaptukhóo= maam**. *conj 3rd sg* **pàptukhóomaat**. *imp* **pàptukhóomaal**. *ptcpl* **pàptuk= hóomaat**.

**pàptukiikwáakeew** VAI sew things crookedly. *ind 1st sg* **mbaptukii= kwáake, mbaptukiikwáakeem**. *conj 3rd sg* **pàptukiikwáakeet**. *imp* **pàp= tukiikwáakeel**. *ptcpl* **pàptukii= kwáakeet**.

**pàptukiikwáaleew** VTA sew s.t. animate crookedly. *ind 1st sg* **mbaptukii= kwáalaaw, mbaptukiikwáala**. *ind 3rd sg* **pàptukiikwaaláawal**. *ind inv* **mbaptukiikwáalukw**. *ind I-you* **kpaptukiikwáalul**. *conj 3rd sg* **pàp= tukiikwáalaat**. *imp* **pàptukíikwaal**. *ptcpl* **pàptukiikwáalaat**.

**pàptukíikwam** VTI1A sew s.t. crookedly. *ind 1st sg* **mbaptukíikwamun**. *ind 3rd sg* **pàptukíikwamun**. *conj 1st sg* **pàptukíikwamaan**. *conj 3rd sg* **pàptukíikwang**. *imp* **pàptukíikwah**. *ptcpl* **pàptukíikwang**.

**pàptukiikwsíhleew** VAI wriggle, go crookedly. *ind 1st sg* **mbaptukiikw= síhla, mbaptukiikwsíhlaam**. *conj 3rd sg* **pàptukiikwsíhlaat**. *imp* **pàp= tukiikwsíhlaal**. *ptcpl* **pàptukiikw= síhlaat**.

**pàptukíixiin** VAI lie crookedly *(s.t. animate)*. *ind 1st sg* **mbaptukíixiin, mbaptukíixi**. *conj 3rd sg* **pàptukíi= xiing**. *ptcpl* **pàptukíixiing**.

**pàptukíixun** VII lie crookedly. *conj 3rd sg* **pàptukíixung**. *ptcpl* **pàptuk= íixung**.

**pàptukíhleew** VAI go crookedly, fly crookedly, fly on an erratic course. *ind 1st sg* **mbaptukíhla, mbaptuk= íhlaam**. *conj 3rd sg* **pàptukíhlaat**. *imp* **pàptukíhlaal**. *ptcpl* **pàptuk= íhlaat**.

**pàptukóoxweew** VAI walk crookedly, walk on a crooked road. *ind 1st sg* **mbaptukóoxwe, mbaptukóoxweem**. *conj 3rd sg* **pàptukóoxweet**. *imp* **pàptukóoxweel**. *ptcpl* **pàptukóo= xweet**.

**pàptukshíimuw** VAI run away crookedly. *ind 1st sg* **mbaptukshíimwi, mbap= tukshíimwiim**. *conj 3rd sg* **pàptuk= shíimwiit**. *imp* **pàptukshíimwiil**. *ptcpl* **pàptukshíimwiit**.

**pàptukshíhkaweew** VTA chase s.o. crookedly. *ind 1st sg* **mbaptukshíh= kawaaw, mbaptukshíhkawa**. *ind 3rd sg* **pàptukshihkawáawal**. *ind inv*

**mbaptukshíhkaakw**. *ind I-you* **kpaptukshíhkool**. *conj 3rd sg* **pàp=tukshíhkawaat**. *imp* **pàptukshíh=kaw**. *ptcpl* **pàptukshíhkawaat**.

**pàptúkwŭneew** VTA bunch s.t. animate up, crumple s.t. animate up. *ind 1st sg* **mbaptúkwŭnaaw**, **mbaptúkwŭna**. *ind 3rd sg* **pàptukwŭnáawal**. *ind inv* **mbaptúkwŭnukw**. *ind I-you* **kpap=túkwŭnul**. *conj 3rd sg* **pàptúkwŭ=naat**. *imp* **pàptúkwun**. *ptcpl* **pàp=túkwŭnaat**.

**pàptúkwŭnum** VTI1B bunch s.t. up, crumple s.t. up. *ind 1st sg* **mbaptuk=wŭnúmun**. *ind 3rd sg* **pàptukwŭ=númun**. *conj 1st sg* **pàptukwŭnúm=aan**. *conj 3rd sg* **pàptúkwŭnung**. *imp* **pàptúkwŭnih**. *ptcpl* **pàptúkwŭnung**.

**pàptukíikwsuw** VAI crawl zigzag. *ind 1st sg* **mbaptukíikwsi**, **mbaptukíi=kwsiim**. *conj 3rd sg* **pàptukíikwsiit**. *imp* **pàptukíikwsiil**. *ptcpl* **pàptuk=íikwsiit**.

**pàpŭlakaachíimuw** VAI leave out part of the story while talking. *ind 1st sg* **mbapŭlakaachíimwi**, **mbapŭla=kaachíimwiim**. *conj 3rd sg* **pàpŭla=kaachíimwiit**. *imp* **pàpŭlakaachíi=mwiil**. *ptcpl* **pàpŭlakaachíimwiit**.

**pàpŭlakaapamúkwat** VII have disorganized colours, have mixed up colours. *conj 3rd sg* **pàpŭlakaapamúk=wahk**. *ptcpl* **pàpŭlakaapamúkwahk**.

**pàpŭlakaapamúkwsuw** VAI have disorganized colours, have mixed up colours *(s.t. animate)*. *ind 1st sg* **mbapŭ=lakaapamúkwsi**, **mbapŭlakaapa=múkwsiim**. *conj 3rd sg* **pàpŭlakaa=pamúkwsiit**. *ptcpl* **pàpŭlakaapa=múkwsiit**.

**pàpŭlakéechpuw** VAI dress haphazardly, dress hurriedly, throw on one's clothes. *ind 1st sg* **mbapŭlakéechpi**, **mbapŭlakéechpiim**. *conj 3rd sg* **pàpŭlakéechpiit**. *imp* **pàpŭlakéech=piil**. *ptcpl* **pàpŭlakéechpiit**.

**pàpxangakwíiwan** NI quilt. *pl* **pàpxan=gakwíiwanal**. *poss* **mbapxangakwíi=wanum**. *loc* **pàpxangakwíiwanung**. *dimin* **pàpxangakwiíwanush**.

**pàpxoowaashŭwíhleew** VAI swim fast. *ind 1st sg* **mbàpxoowaashŭwíhla**, **mbàpxoowaashŭwíhlaam**. *conj 3rd sg* **pàpxoowaashŭwíhlaat**. *imp* **pàp=xoowaashŭwíhlaal**. *ptcpl* **pàpxoo=waashŭwíhlaat**.

**pàpxoowíhleew** VAI go fast *(in or on a vehicle or bicycle)*. *ind 1st sg* **mbap=xoowíhla**, **mbapxoowíhlaam**. *conj 3rd sg* **pàpxoowíhlaat**. *imp* **pàpxoo=wíhlaal**. *ptcpl* **pàpxoowíhlaat**.

**pasáandpeew** VAI have a cracked head, have a cut on one's head. *ind 1st sg* **mbasáandpa**, **mbasáandpaam**. *conj 3rd sg* **pasáandpaat**. *ptcpl* **pee=sáandpaat**.

**pasaandpéexiin** VAI have a cracked head, have a cut on one's head; fall and crack one's head, fall and cut one's head. *ind 1st sg* **mbasaandpéexiin**, **mbasaandpéexi**. *conj 3rd sg* **pa=saandpéexiing**. *ptcpl* **peesaand=péexiing**.

**pasaaxchánaweew** VTA part s.o.'s hair. *ind 1st sg* **mbasaaxchánawaaw**, **mbasaaxchánawa**. *ind 3rd sg* **pàs=aaxchanawáawal**. *ind inv* **mbasaax=chánaakw**. *ind I-you* **kpasaaxchán=ool**. *conj 3rd sg* **pasaaxchánawaat**. *imp* **pasaaxchánaw**. *ptcpl* **pasaax=chánawaat**.

**pasaaxcháneew** VAI part one's hair, have one's hair parted. *ind 1st sg* **mbasaax=chána**, **mbasaaxchánaam**. *conj 3rd sg* **pasaaxchánaat**. *imp* **pasaax=chánaal**. *ptcpl* **peesaaxchánaat**.

**pasaháhkweew** VAI split wood. *ind 1st sg* **mbas'háhkwe**, **mbas'háhkweem**. *conj 3rd sg* **pasaháhkweet**. *imp* **pa=saháhkweel**. *ptcpl* **pees'háhkweet**. *intensive reduplication* **apas'háh=kweew**.

**pasáham** VTI1A split s.t. *(using a tool or instrument)*. *ind 1st sg* **mbas'hámun**. *ind 3rd sg* **pàs'hámun**. *conj 1st sg* **pasáhŭmaan**. *conj 3rd sg* **pasáhang**. *imp* **pasáhah**. *ptcpl* **pées'hang**. *intensive reduplication* **pàpasáhŭmun**.

**pasáheew** VTA split s.t. animate *(using a tool or instrument)*. *ind 1st sg* **mbás'=haaw, mbás'ha**. *ind 3rd sg* **pàs'háa=wal**. *ind inv* **mbás'hookw**. *ind I-you* **kpás'hool**. *conj 3rd sg* **pasáhaat**. *imp* **pasáh**. *ptcpl* **pées'haat**.

**pasáhkameew** PC half a day.

**pasát** VII be cracked, be split in two, be in half. **Sháxk éet pasát.** 'It must be cracked.' *conj 3rd sg* **pasáhk**. *ptcpl* **péesahk**.

**paseeskáleengw** NA part Black person. *pl* **paseeskàléengwak**. *dimin* **pasees=kàléengwush**. *obv* **paseeskàléen=gwal**.

**paseewáatam** VOTI1A be silly. *ind 1st sg* **mbaseewáatam**. *conj 3rd sg* **pasee=wáatang**. *ptcpl* **peeseewáatang**.

**pasíi** PC half. **Néew-kŭlák wáak pasíi.** 'It's four-thirty.'

**pasiikaaxkhwáasuw** VII have boards on it, be covered in boards. **Wíikŭyaan pasiikaaxkhwáasuw.** 'My house has boards on it.' *conj 3rd sg* **pasii=kaaxkhwáasiik**. *ptcpl* **peesiikaaxk=hwáasiik**.

**pasiikáaxkw** NI board. *pl* **pasiikáax=kwal**. *poss* **mbasiikáaxkwum**. *loc* **pasiikáaxkwung**. *dimin* **pasiikáax=kwush**.

**pasiikaaxkwíikaan** NI frame house, board house. *pl* **pasiikaaxkwíikaa=nal**. *poss* **mbasiikaaxkwíikaan**. *loc* **pasiikaaxkwiikáanung**. *dimin* **pashiikaaxkwiikáanush**.

**pasíitŭyeew** VAI have a crack in one's buttocks. *ind 1st sg* **mbasíitŭya, mbasíitŭyaam**. *conj 3rd sg* **pasíitŭ=yaat**. *ptcpl* **peesíitŭyaat**.

**pasiitŭyeewáakan** NI crack in the buttocks. *poss* **mbasiitŭyeewáakan**. *loc* **pasiitŭyeewáakanung**.

**pasíixtoow** VTI2 crack s.t., drop and crack s.t.; break s.t. in half. *ind 1st sg* **mbasíixtoon**. *ind 3rd sg* **pàsíixtoon**. *conj 1st sg* **pasiixtáwaan**. *conj 3rd sg* **pasíixtaakw**. *imp* **pasíixtool**. *ptcpl* **peesíixtaakw**.

**pasíixŭmeew** VTA crack s.t. animate, drop and crack s.t. animate; break s.t. animate in half. *ind 1st sg* **mbasíixŭ=maaw, mbasíixŭma**. *ind 3rd sg* **pàs=iixŭmáawal**. *ind inv* **mbasíixŭmukw**. *ind I-you* **kpasíixŭmul**. *conj 3rd sg* **pasíixŭmaat**. *imp* **pasíixum**. *ptcpl* **peesíixŭmaat**.

**pasíhkam** VTI1A split s.t. *(using the foot or body)*. *ind 1st sg* **mbasíhkamun**. *ind 3rd sg* **pàsíhkamun**. *conj 1st sg* **pasíhkamaan**. *conj 3rd sg* **pasíh=kang**. *imp* **pasíhkah**. *ptcpl* **peesíh=kang**.

**pasíhkaweew** VTA split s.t. animate *(using the foot or body)*. *ind 1st sg* **mbasíhkawaaw, mbasíhkawa**. *ind 3rd sg* **pàsihkawáawal**. *ind inv* **mbasíhkaakw**. *ind I-you* **kpasíhkool**. *conj 3rd sg* **pasíhkawaat**. *imp* **pasíhkaw**. *ptcpl* **peesíhkawaat**.

**pasíhleew** VAI split in two. *ind 1st sg* **mbasíhla, mbasíhlaam**. *conj 3rd sg* **pasíhlaat**. *ptcpl* **peesíhlaat**.

**pasíhleew** VII split in two. *conj 3rd sg* **pasíhlaak**. *ptcpl* **peesíhlaak**.

**pasihtéeham** VTI1A hit and split s.t. *ind 1st sg* **mbasihtéehŭmun**. *ind 3rd sg* **pàsihtéehŭmun**. *conj 1st sg* **pasih=téehŭmaan**. *conj 3rd sg* **pasihtée=hang**. *imp* **pasihtéehih**. *ptcpl* **pee=sihtéehang**.

**pasihtéextoow** VTI2 drop s.t. and split it in two. *ind 1st sg* **mbasihtéextoon**. *ind 3rd sg* **pàsihtéextoon**. *conj 1st sg* **pasihteextáwaan**. *conj 3rd sg* **pasih=téextaakw**. *imp* **pasihtéextool**. *ptcpl* **peesihtéextaakw**.

**pasihtéexŭmeew** VTA drop s.t. animate and split it in two. *ind 1st sg* **mbas=ihtéexŭmaaw**, **mbasihtéexŭma**. *ind 3rd sg* **pàsihteexŭmáawal**. *ind inv* **mbasihtéexŭmukw**. *ind I-you* **kpas=ihtéexŭmul**. *conj 3rd sg* **pasihtéexŭ=maat**. *imp* **pasihtéexum**. *ptcpl* **pee=sihtéexŭmaat**.

**pasihtéexun** VII fall and split in two. *conj 3rd sg* **pasihtéexung**. *ptcpl* **peesihtéexung**.

**pasuchéhkam** VTI 1A kick s.t. *ind 1st sg* **mbaschéhkamun**. *ind 3rd sg* **pàs=chéhkamun**. *conj 1st sg* **pasuchéh=kamaan**. *conj 3rd sg* **pasuchéhkang**. *imp* **pasuchéhkah**. *ptcpl* **peeschéh=kang**.

**pasuchéhkaweew** VTA kick s.o. **Kwíh=chu-paapasuchehkawáawal.** 'He really kicked him about.' *ind 1st sg* **mbaschéhkawaaw**, **mbaschéhkawa**. *ind 3rd sg* **pàschehkawáawal**. *ind inv* **mbaschéhkaakw**. *ind I-you* **kpas=chéhkool**. *conj 3rd sg* **pasuchéhka=waat**. *imp* **pasuchéhkaw**. *ptcpl* **peeschéhkawaat**. *intensive reduplication* **pàpasuchehkawáawal**.

**pasúkwiiw** VAI-S get up from sitting. *ind 1st sg* **mbáskwi**, **mbáskwiim**. *conj 3rd sg* **pasúkwiit**. *imp* **pasúkwiil**. *ptcpl* **péeskwiit**.

**pasukwiipáhtoow** VAI get up in a hurry. *ind 1st sg* **mbaskwiipáhto**. *conj 3rd sg* **pasukwiipáhtaakw**. *imp* **pasuk=wiipáhtool**. *ptcpl* **peeskwiipáh=taakw**.

**pasukwtóonheew** VAI 'testify' at a religious meeting, 'testify' in church. *ind 1st sg* **mbaskwutóonhe**, **mbaskwut=óonheem**. *conj 3rd sg* **pasukwtóon=heet**. *imp* **pasukwtóonheel**. *ptcpl* **peeskwutóonheet**. *intensive reduplication* **pàpasukwtóonheew**, **apas=kwutóonheew**.

**pasúlam** VTI 1A split s.t. by forceful contact, split s.t. by shot, split s.t. by hitting it with a projectile. *ind 1st sg* **mbasŭlámun**. *ind 3rd sg* **pàsŭlám=un**. *conj 1st sg* **pasúlamaan**. *conj 3rd sg* **pasúlang**. *imp* **pasúlah**. *ptcpl* **péesŭlang**.

**pasúlaweew** VTA split s.t. animate by forceful contact, split s.t. animate by shot, split s.t. animate with a projectile. *ind 1st sg* **mbasŭláwaaw**, **mbas=ŭláwa**. *ind 3rd sg* **pàsŭlawáawal**. *ind inv* **mbásŭlaakw**. *ind I-you* **kpásŭ=lool**. *conj 3rd sg* **pasúlawaat**. *imp* **pasúlaw**. *ptcpl* **peesŭláwaat**.

**pasúneew** VTA tear s.t. animate, split s.t. animate in two. *ind 1st sg* **mbásŭ=naaw**, **mbásŭna**. *ind 3rd sg* **pàsŭ=náawal**. *ind inv* **mbásŭnukw**. *ind I-you* **kpásŭnul**. *conj 3rd sg* **pasúnaat**. *imp* **pasún**. *ptcpl* **péesŭnaat**.

**pasúnum** VTI 1B tear s.t., split s.t. in two. *ind 1st sg* **mbasŭnúmun**. *ind 3rd sg* **pàsŭnúmun**. *conj 1st sg* **pasúnŭ=maan**. *conj 3rd sg* **pasúnung**. *imp* **pasúnih**. *ptcpl* **péesŭnung**.

**pasusiitéexiin** VAI trip, stub one's toe. *ind 1st sg* **mbassiitéexiin**, **mbassii=téexi**. *conj 3rd sg* **pasusiitéexiing**. *ptcpl* **peessiitéexiing**, **peessiitéexiit**.

**pasusiitéhkaweew** VTA trip s.o. *ind 1st sg* **mbassiitéhkawaaw**, **mbassiitéh=kawa**. *ind 3rd sg* **pàssiitehkawáa=wal**. *ind inv* **mbassiitéhkaakw**. *ind I-you* **kpassiitéhkool**. *conj 3rd sg* **pa=susiitéhkawaat**. *imp* **pasusiitéhkaw**. *ptcpl* **peessiitéhkawaat**.

**pasúsuw** VAI be cracked, be split in two, be in half *(s.t. animate)*. *ind 1st sg* **mbássi**, **mbássiim**. *conj 3rd sg* **pa=súsiit**. *ptcpl* **péessiit**.

**pasúsheew** VTA cut s.t. animate in two, cut s.t. animate in half, split s.t. animate in two by cutting it. *ind 1st sg* **mbás'shaaw**, **mbás'sha**. *ind 3rd sg* **pàs'sháawal**. *ind inv* **mbás'shookw**. *ind I-you* **kpás'shool**. *conj 3rd sg* **pasúshaat**. *imp* **pasúsh**. *ptcpl* **pées'=**

**shaat**.

**pasúshum** VTI 1B cut s.t. in two, cut s.t. in half, split s.t. in two by cutting it. *ind 1st sg* **mbas'shúmun**. *ind 3rd sg* **pàs'shúmun**. *conj 1st sg* **pasúshŭ=maan**. *conj 3rd sg* **pasúshung**. *imp* **pasúshih**. *ptcpl* **pées'shung**.

**pasúweew** VAIO deny s.t. *ind 1st sg* **mbásŭween**. *ind 3rd sg* **pásŭween**. *conj 3rd sg* **pasúweet**. *imp* **pasúweel**. *ptcpl* **péesŭweet**.

**pawáaheew** VAIO shake s.t., shake s.t. out. *ind 1st sg* **mbawáaheen**. *ind 3rd sg* **pawáaheen**. *conj 3rd sg* **pawáa=heet**. *imp* **pawáaheel**. *ptcpl* **pee=wáaheet**. *intensive reduplication* **pàpawáaheen**.

**pawalsóoheew** VAIO make s.o. rich. *ind 1st sg* **mbawalusóoheen**. *ind 3rd sg* **pàwalusoohéenal**. *conj 3rd sg* **pawalsóoheet**. *imp* **pawalsóoheel**. *ptcpl* **peewalusóoheet**.

**pawálsuw** VAI be rich. *ind 1st sg* **mbaw=alúsi**, **mbawalúsiim**. *conj 3rd sg* **pawálsiit**. *ptcpl* **peewalúsiit**.

**pawiingweehíikeew** VAI shell corn. *ind 1st sg* **mbawiingweehíike**, **mbaw=iingweehíikeem**. *conj 3rd sg* **pa=wiingweehíikeet**. *imp* **pawiingwee=híikeel**. *ptcpl* **peewiingweehíikeet**.

**pawíhleew** VAI fall off *(s.t. animate, as fruits from a tree or bush)*. *ind 1st sg* **mbawíhla**, **mbawíhlaam**. *conj 3rd sg* **pawíhlaat**. *ptcpl* **peewíhlaat**. *intensive reduplication* **apawíhleew**. *See* **apawíhleew**.

**pawíhleew** VII fall off *(as a leaf)*; shed *(as hair)*. *conj 3rd sg* **pawíhlaak**. *ptcpl* **peewíhlaak**. *intensive reduplication* **apawíhleew**. *See* **apawíhleew**.

**pawunáasuw** VII be sifted. *conj 3rd sg* **pawunáasiik**. *ptcpl* **peewŭnáasiik**.

**pawuníikan** NI sifter. *pl* **pawuníikanal**. *poss* **mbawŭníikan**. *loc* **pawuníika=nung**. *dimin* **pawuníikanush**.

**pawuníikeew** VAI sift things. *ind 1st sg* **mbawŭníike**, **mbawŭníikeem**. *conj 3rd sg* **pawuníikeet**. *imp* **pawuníi=keel**. *ptcpl* **peewŭníikeet**.

**pawúnum** VTI 1B sift s.t. *ind 1st sg* **mbawŭnúmun**. *ind 3rd sg* **pàwŭ=númun**. *conj 1st sg* **pawúnŭmaan**. *conj 3rd sg* **pawúnung**. *imp* **pawúnih**. *ptcpl* **péewŭnung**.

**paxkawápuw** VAI sit doubled over, sit doubled up. *ind 1st sg* **mbaxkawápi**, **mbaxkawápiim**. *conj 3rd sg* **paxka=wápiit**. *imp* **paxkawápiil**. *ptcpl* **peex=kawápiit**. *See* **paxkawohkwéepuw**.

**paxkawiikwáakeew** VAI sew around the edges, put a hem on. *ind 1st sg* **mbax=kawiikwáake**, **mbaxkawiikwáa=keem**. *conj 3rd sg* **paxkawiikwáa=keet**. *imp* **paxkawiikwáakeel**. *ptcpl* **peexkawiikwáakeet**.

**paxkawiikwáaleew** VTA sew s.t. animate up, sew around the edge of s.t. animate. *ind 1st sg* **mbaxkawiikwáa=laaw**, **mbaxkawiikwáala**. *ind 3rd sg* **paxkawiikwaaláawal**. *ind inv* **mbax=kawiikwáalukw**. *ind I-you* **kpaxka=wiikwáalul**. *conj 3rd sg* **paxkawii=kwáalaat**. *imp* **paxkawíikwaal**. *ptcpl* **peexkawiikwáalaat**.

**paxkawiikwáasuw** VII be sewn along the edges, be sewn up. *conj 3rd sg* **paxkawiikwáasiik**. *ptcpl* **peexka=wiikwáasiik**.

**paxkawíikwam** VTI 1A sew around the edge of s.t., turn up and sew s.t. *ind 1st sg* **mbaxkawíikwamun**. *ind 3rd sg* **paxkawíikwamun**. *conj 1st sg* **paxkawíikwamaan**. *conj 3rd sg* **paxkawíikwang**. *imp* **paxkawíi=kwah**. *ptcpl* **peexkawíikwang**.

**paxkawiinaxkéesuw** VAI fold one's arms, have one's arms folded. *ind 1st sg* **mbaxkawiinaxkéesi**, **mbaxka=wiinaxkéesiim**. *conj 3rd sg* **paxka=wiinaxkéesiit**. *imp* **paxkawiinax=kéesiil**. *ptcpl* **peexkawiinaxkéesiit**. *See* **paxkawiinaxkéexiin**.

**paxkawiinaxkéexiin** VAI fold one's arms, have one's arms folded. *ind 1st sg* **mbaxkawiinaxkéexiin**, **mbaxka=wiinaxkéexi**. *conj 3rd sg* **paxkawii=naxkéexiing**. *imp* **paxkawiinaxkée=xiil**. *ptcpl* **peexkawiinaxkéexiing**, **peexkawiinaxkéexiit**. *See* **peexka=wiinaxkéesuw**.

**paxkawohkwéepuw** VAI sit doubled over, sit doubled up. *ind 1st sg* **mbax=kawohkwéepi**, **mbaxkawohkwée=piim**. *conj 3rd sg* **paxkawohkwée=piit**. *imp* **paxkawohkwéepiil**. *ptcpl* **peexkawohkwéepiit**.

**paxkawúneew** VTA fold s.o., fold s.t. animate *(using the hands)*. *ind 1st sg* **mbaxkawúnaaw**, **mbaxkawúna**. *ind 3rd sg* **paxkawunáawal**. *ind inv* **mbaxkawúnukw**. *ind I-you* **kpax=kawúnul**. *conj 3rd sg* **paxkawúnaat**. *imp* **páxkawun**. *ptcpl* **peexkawún=aat**.

**paxkawúnum** VTI1B fold s.t. *(using the hands)*. *ind 1st sg* **mbaxkawúnŭmun**. *ind 3rd sg* **paxkawúnŭmun**. *conj 1st sg* **paxkawúnŭmaan**. *conj 3rd sg* **paxkawúnung**. *imp* **paxkawúnih**. *ptcpl* **peexkawúnung**.

**páxkeew** VAI turn *(off the road)*. **Yóon-uch ktúnda-páxkeen.** 'This is where you turn (off).' *ind 1st sg* **mbáxke**, **mbáxkeem**. *conj 3rd sg* **páxkeet**. *imp* **páxkeel**. *ptcpl* **péexkeet**.

**paxkéexiin** VAI be at the side of the road, park at the side of the road *(s.t. animate)*. *ind 1st sg* **mbaxkéexiin**, **mbaxkéexi**. *conj 3rd sg* **paxkéexiing**. *imp* **paxkéexiil**. *ptcpl* **peexkéexiing**, **peexkéexiit**.

**paxkéhleew** VAI turn *(off the road)*. *ind 1st sg* **mbaxkéhla**, **mbaxkéhlaam**. *conj 3rd sg* **paxkéhlaat**. *imp* **pax=kéhlaal**. *ptcpl* **peexkéhlaat**.

**paxkíixtoow** VTI2 break s.t. *(of something string-like)*. *ind 1st sg* **mbax=kíixtoon**. *ind 3rd sg* **paxkíixtoon**. *conj 1st sg* **paxkiixtáwaan**. *conj 3rd sg* **paxkíixtaakw**. *imp* **paxkíixtool**. *ptcpl* **peexkíixtaakw**.

**paxkíhleew** VII break *(of something string-like)*. *conj 3rd sg* **paxkíhlaak**. *ptcpl* **peexkíhlaak**.

**páxksheew** VTA cut through s.t. animate, cut and break s.t. animate, cut s.t. animate *(of something string-like)*. *ind 1st sg* **mbáxkshaaw**, **mbáxksha**. *ind 3rd sg* **paxksháawal**. *ind inv* **mbáxk=shookw**. *ind I-you* **kpáxkshool**. *conj 3rd sg* **páxkshaat**. *imp* **páxkush**. *ptcpl* **péexkshaat**.

**paxkshíikan** NI knife. *pl* **paxkshíikanal**. *poss* **mbaxkshíikan**. *loc* **paxkshíi=kanung**. *dimin* **paxkshíikanush**.

**paxkshíikeew** VAI cut things *(of something string-like)*. *ind 1st sg* **mbaxk=shíike**, **mbaxkshíikeem**. *conj 3rd sg* **paxkshíikeet**. *imp* **paxkshíikeel**. *ptcpl* **peexkshíikeet**.

**páxkshum** VTI1B cut through s.t., cut and break s.t., cut s.t. *(of something string-like)*. *ind 1st sg* **mbaxkshúm=un**. *ind 3rd sg* **paxkshúmun**. *conj 1st sg* **paxkshúmaan**. *conj 3rd sg* **páxk=shung**. *imp* **páxkshih**. *ptcpl* **péexk=shung**.

**paxkshúweew** VAI cut things up *(of animate objects)*. *ind 1st sg* **mbaxk=shúwe**, **mbaxkshúweem**. *conj 3rd sg* **paxkshúweet**. *imp* **paxkshúweel**. *ptcpl* **peexkshúweet**.

**páxkŭneew** VTA break s.t. animate, break s.t. animate off; pick s.t. animate. **Aapŭlúshak mbáxkŭna.** 'I picked some apples.' *ind 1st sg* **mbáxkŭ=naaw**, **mbáxkŭna**. *ind 3rd sg* **pax=kŭnáawal**. *ind inv* **mbáxkŭnukw**. *ind I-you* **kpáxkŭnul**. *conj 3rd sg* **páxkŭnaat**. *imp* **páxkun**. *ptcpl* **péexkŭnaat**.

**paxkŭnaapŭlúsheew** VAI pick apples *(off the tree)*. *ind 1st sg* **mbaxkŭ=naapŭlúshe**, **mbaxkŭnaapŭlúsh=**

eem. *conj 3rd sg* **paxkŭnaapŭlúsh=eet**. *imp* **paxkŭnaapŭlúsheel**. *ptcpl* **peexkŭnaapŭlúsheet**.

**paxkŭniichèlíiseew** VAI pick cherries *(off the stems)*. *ind 1st sg* **mbaxkŭ=niichèlíise**, **mbaxkŭniichèlíiseem**. *conj 3rd sg* **paxkŭniichèlíiseet**. *imp* **paxkŭniichèlíiseel**. *ptcpl* **peexkŭnii=chèlíiseet**.

**paxkŭníikeew** VAI pick things. *ind 1st sg* **mbaxkŭníike**, **mbaxkŭníikeem**. *conj 3rd sg* **paxkŭníikeet**. *imp* **paxkŭníikeel**. *ptcpl* **peexkŭníikeet**.

**páxkŭnum** VTI 1B break s.t., break s.t. off *(of strings, using the hands)*; pick s.t. *ind 1st sg* **mbaxkŭnúmun**. *ind 3rd sg* **paxkŭnúmun**. *conj 1st sg* **paxkŭnúmaan**. *conj 3rd sg* **páxkŭ=nung**. *imp* **páxkŭnih**. *ptcpl* **péex=kŭnung**.

**páxkwŭleew** VAI bloom, be blooming *(of flowers)*. *conj 3rd sg* **páxkwŭleet**. *ptcpl* **péexkwŭleet**.

**páy** NA pie. *pl* **páyak**. *poss* **mbáyum**. *loc* **páyung**. *dimin* **páyush**. *obv* **páyal**. *From English* pie.

**payáhkwameew** VTA be glad to eat s.t. animate *(not having had it for some time)*. *ind 1st sg* **mbayáhkwamaaw**, **payáhkwama**. *ind 3rd sg* **pàyahkwa=máawal**. *conj 3rd sg* **payáhkwa=maat**. *ptcpl* **peeyáhkwamaat**.

**payahkwándam** VTI 1A be glad to eat s.t. *(not having had it for some time)*. *ind 1st sg* **mbayahkwándamun**. *ind 3rd sg* **pàyahkwándamun**. *conj 1st sg* **payahkwándamaan**. *conj 3rd sg* **payahkwándang**. *ptcpl* **peeyah=kwándang**.

**payahkwiináakwsuw** VAI be glad to see someone. *ind 1st sg* **mbayahkwii=náakwsi**, **mbayahkwiináakwsiim**. *conj 3rd sg* **payahkwiináakwsiit**. *ptcpl* **peeyahkwiináakwsiit**.

**payahkwíinam** VTI 1A be glad to see s.t. *ind 1st sg* **mbayahkwíinamun**. *ind 3rd sg* **pàyahkwíinamun**. *conj 1st sg* **payahkwíinamaan**. *conj 3rd sg* **pa=yahkwíinang**. *ptcpl* **peeyahkwíi=nang**.

**payahkwíinaweew** VTA be glad to see s.o. *ind 1st sg* **mbayahkwíinawaaw**, **mbayahkwíinawa**. *ind 3rd sg* **pày=ahkwiinawáawal**. *ind inv* **mbayah=kwíinaakw**. *ind I-you* **kpayahkwíi=nool**. *conj 3rd sg* **payahkwíinawaat**. *ptcpl* **peeyahkwíinawaat**.

**payahkwsútam** VTI 1A be glad to hear s.t., be glad to listen to s.t. *ind 1st sg* **mbayahkwsútamun**. *ind 3rd sg* **pày=ahkwsútamun**. *conj 1st sg* **payah=kwsútamaan**. *conj 3rd sg* **payahkw=sútang**. *ptcpl* **peeyahkwsútang**.

**payahkwsútaweew** VTA be glad to hear s.o., be glad to listen to s.o. *ind 1st sg* **mbayahkwsútawaaw**, **mbayahkw=sútawa**. *ind 3rd sg* **pàyahkwsuta=wáawal**. *ind inv* **mbayahkwsútaakw**. *ind I-you* **kpayahkwsútool**. *conj 3rd sg* **payahkwsútawaat**. *ptcpl* **peeyah=kwsútawaat**.

**payahkwu-** PV be glad about something. **Mbayáhkwu-alúmsi.** 'I'm glad I left.'; **Mbayáhko-péech-máachi.** 'I'm glad I went home.' *ptcpl* **pee=yáhkwu-**.

**payáxkhaaw** VTA be struck by lightning. *indefinite subject only*. **Mbayaxk=hóoke.** 'I was struck by lightning.' *indef subject* **payáxkhaaw**. *conj 3rd sg* **payáxkhoond**. *ptcpl* **peeyáxk=hoond**.

**payáxkham** VOTI 1A shoot. *ind 1st sg* **mbayáxkham**. *conj 3rd sg* **payáxk=hang**. *imp* **payáxkhah**. *ptcpl* **peeyáx=khang**. *intensive reduplication* **apay=áxkham**.

**payáxkham** VTI 1A shoot s.t., shoot at s.t. *ind 1st sg* **mbayaxkhámun**. *ind 3rd sg* **pàyaxkhámun**. *conj 1st sg* **payaxkhámaan**. *conj 3rd sg* **payáx=khang**. *imp* **payáxkhah**. *ptcpl* **pee=**

**yáxkhang.**

**payáxkheew** VTA shoot s.o. *ind 1st sg* **mbayáxkhaaw, mbayáxkha.** *ind 3rd sg* **pàyaxkháawal.** *ind inv* **mbayáx=khookw.** *ind I-you* **kpayáxkhool.** *conj 3rd sg* **payáxkhaat.** *imp* **payáx=khaw.** *ptcpl* **peeyáxkhaat.**

**payaxkhíikan** NI gun, rifle. *pl* **payaxk=híikanal.** *poss* **mbayaxkhíikan.** *loc* **payaxkhíikanung.** *dimin* **payaxk=híikanush.**

**payaxkhíikeew** VAI shoot. *ind 1st sg* **mbayaxkhíike, mbayaxkhíikeem.** *conj 3rd sg* **payaxkhíikeet.** *imp* **pa=yaxkhíikeel.** *ptcpl* **peeyaxkhíikeet.**

**payaxkhóotam** VOTI1A shoot off a gun. *ind 1st sg* **mbayaxkhóotam.** *conj 3rd sg* **payaxkhóotang.** *imp* **payaxkhóo=tah.** *ptcpl* **peeyaxkhóotang.**

**payaxkhóotam** VTI1A shoot at s.t. *ind 1st sg* **mbayaxkhóotamun.** *ind 3rd sg* **pàyaxkhóotamun.** *conj 1st sg* **payaxkhóotamaan.** *conj 3rd sg* **pa=yaxkhóotang.** *imp* **payaxkhóotah.** *ptcpl* **peeyaxkhóotang.**

**páyund** NA dipper, cup with handle. *pl* **pàyúndak.** *poss* **mbayúndum.** *loc* **pàyúndung.** *dimin* **pàyúnjush.** *obv* **pàyúndal.**

**pchihtáhleew** VTAO ask s.o. to bring s.t. *ind 1st sg* **mbuchihtáhlaan.** *ind 3rd sg* **pùchihtáhlaan.** *ind inv* **mbuchih=táhlkwun.** *ind I-you* **kpuchihtáhlŭ=lun.** *conj 3rd sg* **pchihtáhlaat.** *imp* **pchíhtahl.** *ptcpl* **peechihtáhlaat.**

**pchúkwu-meelíishush** NA little round Mary. *obv* **pchúkwu-meelíish'shal.** *a nickname.*

**peech-** PV here, to here, towards the speaker. **Méhchxiish láapii mbéech-lúkw, "Máhta nŭmoxkamóowŭnal. Máhta yóh ahteewíiwal."** 'Soon he called me back, "I didn't find them. They're not here."'; **Àhalúmsuw kehkeexookwŭnáhke, wáak áng nzhíis péeyaat péech-wiicheewáatu, wŭlú áng kéhla áalu- kwéek -lúnum.** 'She would leave for several days, and when my uncle came (to visit) if she came with him he couldn't do anything.' *ptcpl* **péech-.** *See* **peechi-, peechu-.**

**peech'chéhleew** VAI drive in this direction, drive here, come here driving, drive toward the speaker. *ind 1st sg* **mbeech'chéhla, mbeech'chéhlaam.** *conj 3rd sg* **peech'chéhlaat.** *imp* **peech'chéhlaal.** *ptcpl* **peech'chéh=laat.** *See* **peetchéhleew.**

**peechíikwsuw** VAI crawl here, crawl towards the speaker. *ind 1st sg* **mbee=chíikwsi, mbeechíikwsiim.** *conj 3rd sg* **peechíikwsiit.** *imp* **peechíikwsiil.** *ptcpl* **peechíikwsiit.**

**peechíimeew** VTA call s.o. over, call s.o. here. *ind 1st sg* **mbeechíimaaw, mbeechíima.** *ind 3rd sg* **peechii=máawal.** *ind inv* **mbeechíimukw.** *ind I-you* **kpeechíimul.** *conj 3rd sg* **peechíimaat.** *imp* **péechiim.** *ptcpl* **peechíimaat.**

**peechiinjkweeyáaheew** VAIO roll s.t. to here, roll s.t. towards the speaker. *ind 1st sg* **mbeechiinjkweeyáaheen.** *ind 3rd sg* **peechiinjkweeyáaheen.** *conj 3rd sg* **peechiinjkweeyáaheet.** *imp* **peechiinjkweeyáaheel.** *ptcpl* **pee=chiinjkweeyáaheet.**

**peechiinjkwéhleew** VAI roll here, roll towards the speaker. **Méhch wáak peechiinjkwéhleew.** 'He's rolling this way (of a fat person).' *ind 1st sg* **mbeechiinjkwéhla, mbeechiinj=kwéhlaam.** *conj 3rd sg* **peechiinj=kwéhlaat.** *imp* **peechiinjkwéhlaal.** *ptcpl* **peechiinjkwéhlaat.**

**peechiipáhtoow** VTI2 bring s.t. here in a hurry. *ind 1st sg* **mbeechiipáhtoon.** *ind 3rd sg* **peechiipáhtoon.** *conj 1st sg* **peechiipáhtawaan.** *conj 3rd sg* **peechiipáhtaakw.** *imp* **peechiipáh=tool.** *ptcpl* **peechiipáhtaakw.**

**peechíipheew** VTA bring s.o. here in a hurry. *ind 1st sg* **mbeechíiphaaw, mbeechíipha**. *ind 3rd sg* **peechiip=háawal**. *ind inv* **mbeechíiphukw**. *ind I-you* **kpeechíiphul**. *conj 3rd sg* **peechíiphaat**. *imp* **peechíipah**. *ptcpl* **peechíiphaat**.

**peechíisheew** VAI urinate in this direction, urinate to here. *ind 1st sg* **mbee=chíishe, mbeechíisheem**. *conj 3rd sg* **peechíisheet**. *imp* **peechíisheel**. *ptcpl* **peechíisheet**.

**peechi-** PV here, to here, towards the speaker. **Ngáta-péechi-pahpah=chóolukw.** 'He's coming here to cheat me.'; **Mbéech-piinjíike.** 'I came inside.' *ptcpl* **péechi-**. *See* **peechu-, peech-**.

**peechíhleew** VAI come here flying, fly towards the speaker. *ind 1st sg* **mbeechíhla, mbeechíhlaam**. *conj 3rd sg* **peechíhlaat**. *imp* **peechíhlaal**. *ptcpl* **peechíhlaat**.

**peechu-** PV here, to here, towards the speaker. *informal*. **Mbéechu-nax=kóomukw.** 'He answered me.'; **Mbéechu-pŭmúsi.** 'I came walking.' *ptcpl* **péechu-**. *See* **peechi-, peech-**.

**péeheew** VTA wait for s.o. *ind 1st sg* **mbéehaaw, mbéeha**. *ind 3rd sg* **pee=háawal**. *ind inv* **mbéehukw**. *ind I-you* **kpéehul**. *conj 3rd sg* **péehaat**. *imp* **péeh**. *ptcpl* **péehaat**.

**peekáawsuw** VAI be tired of living. *ind 1st sg* **mbeekáawsi, mbeekáawsiim**. *conj 3rd sg* **peekáawsiit**. *ptcpl* **peekáawsiit**.

**peekahtéenamuw** VAI be tired of feeling a certain way, be tired of living. *ind 1st sg* **mbeekahtéenami, mbeekah=téenamiim**. *conj 3rd sg* **peekahtée=namiit**. *ptcpl* **peekahtéenamiit**.

**peekalóhkeew** VAI be tired of working. *ind 1st sg* **mbeekalóhke, mbeeka=lóhkeem**. *conj 3rd sg* **peekalóhkeet**. *ptcpl* **peekalóhkeet**.

**péekameew** VTA be tired of eating s.t. animate. *ind 1st sg* **mbéekamaaw, mbéekama**. *ind 3rd sg* **peekamáa=wal**. *ind inv* **mbéekamukw**. *ind I-you* **kpéekamul**. *conj 3rd sg* **péekamaat**. *ptcpl* **péekamaat**.

**peekándam** VTI 1A be tired of eating s.t. *ind 1st sg* **mbeekándamun**. *ind 3rd sg* **peekándamun**. *conj 1st sg* **pee=kándamaan**. *conj 3rd sg* **peekán=dang**. *ptcpl* **peekándang**.

**peekatáhkeew** VAI be tired of fighting. *ind 1st sg* **mbeekatáhke, mbeeka=táhkeem**. *conj 3rd sg* **peekatáhkeet**. *ptcpl* **peekatáhkeet**.

**peekeekhíikeew** VAI be tired of writing. *ind 1st sg* **mbeekeekhíike, mbee=keekhíikeem**. *conj 3rd sg* **peekeek=híikeet**. *ptcpl* **peekeekhíikeet**.

**peekiikanáaxiin** VAI be tired of lying in bed. *ind 1st sg* **mbeekiikanáaxiin, mbeekiikanáaxi**. *conj 3rd sg* **peekii=kanáaxiing**. *ptcpl* **peekiikanáaxiing**.

**peekiikwáakeew** VAI be tired of sewing. *ind 1st sg* **mbeekiikwáake, mbee=kiikwáakeem**. *conj 3rd sg* **peekii=kwáakeet**. *ptcpl* **peekiikwáakeet**.

**peekiilawéeheew** VTA be tired of s.o., find s.o. tiresome. *ind 1st sg* **mbee=kiilawéehaaw, mbeekiilawéeha**. *ind 3rd sg* **peekiilaweeháawal**. *ind inv* **mbeekiilawéehukw**. *ind I-you* **kpee=kiilawéehul**. *conj 3rd sg* **peekiila=wéehaat**. *ptcpl* **peekiilawéehaat**.

**peekíinam** VTI 1A be tired of looking at s.t., find s.t. tiresome to look at. *ind 1st sg* **mbeekíinamun**. *ind 3rd sg* **peekíinamun**. *conj 1st sg* **peekíina=maan**. *conj 3rd sg* **peekíinang**. *ptcpl* **peekíinang**.

**peekíinaweew** VTA be tired of looking at s.o., find s.o. tiresome to look at. *ind 1st sg* **mbeekíinawaaw, mbeekíi=nawa**. *ind 3rd sg* **peekiinawáawal**. *ind inv* **mbeekíinaakw**. *ind I-you* **kpeekíinool**. *conj 3rd sg* **peekíina=**

**waat**. *ptcpl* **peekíinawaat**.

**peeksútam** VTI 1A be tired of listening to s.t. *ind 1st sg* **mbeeksútamun**. *ind 3rd sg* **peeksútamun**. *conj 1st sg* **peeksútamaan**. *conj 3rd sg* **peek=sútang**. *ptcpl* **peeksútang**.

**peeksútaweew** VTA be tired of listening to s.o. *ind 1st sg* **mbeeksútawaaw**, **mbeeksútawa**. *ind 3rd sg* **peeksut=awáawal**. *ind inv* **mbeeksútaakw**. *ind I-you* **kpeeksútool**. *conj 3rd sg* **peeksútawaat**. *ptcpl* **peeksútaakw**.

**peeku-** PV (be) tired of. *informal*. **Péeku-shungíixiin.** 'He is tired of lying down.' *ptcpl* **péeku-**.

**peengwahkéeyeew** VII be dry ground. *conj 3rd sg* **peengwahkéeyeek**. *ptcpl* **peengwahkéeyeek**.

**peengwáhkhwam** VTI 1A dry s.t. *ind 1st sg* **mbeengwahkhwámun**. *ind 3rd sg* **peengwahkhwámun**. *conj 1st sg* **peengwahkhwámaan**. *conj 3rd sg* **peengwáhkhwang**. *imp* **peengwáh=khwah**. *ptcpl* **peengwáhkhwang**.

**peengwahkhwíikan** NI tea towel. *pl* **peengwahkhwíikanal**. *poss* **mbeen=gwahkhwíikan**. *loc* **peengwahk=hwíikanung**. *dimin* **peengwahk=hwíikanush**. *See* **peengwiikwáakan**.

**peengwahkhwíikeew** VAI dry the dishes. *ind 1st sg* **mbeengwahkhwíike**, **mbeengwahkhwíikeem**. *conj 3rd sg* **peengwahkhwíikeet**. *imp* **peen=gwahkhwíikeel**. *ptcpl* **peengwahk=hwíikeet**. *See* **peengwiikwáakeew**.

**péengwat** VII be dry *(after being wet)*. **Péengwatool keeshiixtàwáaniil.** 'My washing is dry.' *conj 3rd sg* **péengwahk**. *ptcpl* **péengwahk**.

**peengwii-** PN dried. **Péengwii-asún.** 'Dried stone.'

**peengwiikwáakan** NI tea towel. *pl* **peengwiikwáakanal**. *poss* **mbeen=gwiikwáakan**. *loc* **peengwiikwáa=kanung**. *dimin* **peengwiikwáaka=nush**. *See* **peengwahkhwíikan**.

**peengwiikwáakeew** VAI dry the dishes. *ind 1st sg* **mbeengwiikwáake**, **mbeengwiikwáakeem**. *conj 3rd sg* **peengwiikwáakeet**. *imp* **peengwii=kwáakeel**. *ptcpl* **peengwiikwáakeet**. *See* **peengwahkhwíikeew**.

**peengwiikwáaleew** VTA dry s.o. *(with a towel)*; wipe s.o. off *(with a towel)*. *ind 1st sg* **mbeengwiikwáalaaw**, **mbeengwiikwáala**. *ind 3rd sg* **peen=gwiikwaaláawal**. *ind inv* **mbeen=gwiikwáalukw**. *ind I-you* **kpeen=gwiikwáalul**. *conj 3rd sg* **peengwii=kwáalaat**. *imp* **peengwíikwaal**. *ptcpl* **peengwiikwáalaat**.

**peengwíikwam** VTI 1A dry s.t. *(with a towel)*; wipe s.t. off *(with a towel)*. *ind 1st sg* **mbeengwíikwamun**. *ind 3rd sg* **peengwíikwamun**. *conj 1st sg* **peengwíikwamaan**. *conj 3rd sg* **peengwíikwang**. *imp* **peengwíikwah**. *ptcpl* **peengwíikwang**.

**peengwíixŭmeew** VTA change s.o.'s diaper; make s.o. be dry. *ind 1st sg* **mbeengwíixŭmaaw**, **mbeengwíixŭ=ma**. *ind 3rd sg* **peengwiixŭmáawal**. *ind inv* **mbeengwíixŭmukw**. *ind I-you* **kpeengwíixŭmul**. *conj 3rd sg* **peengwíixŭmaat**. *imp* **peengwíixum**. *ptcpl* **peengwíixŭmaat**.

**peengwíhleew** VII be dried, dry out. *conj 3rd sg* **peengwíhlaak**. *ptcpl* **peen=gwíhlaak**.

**péengwseew** VTA dry s.o., dry s.t. animate *(by heat)*. *ind 1st sg* **mbéeng=wsaaw**, **mbéengwsa**. *ind 3rd sg* **peengwsáawal**. *ind inv* **mbéeng=wsookw**. *ind I-you* **kpéengwsool**. *conj 3rd sg* **péengwsaat**. *imp* **péeng=wus**. *ptcpl* **péengwsaat**.

**peengwsíikan** NI clothes dryer. *pl* **peengwsíikanal**. *poss* **mbeengwsíi=kan**. *loc* **peengwsíikanung**. *dimin* **peengwshíikanush**.

**péengwsum** VTI 1B dry s.t. *(by heat)*. *ind 1st sg* **mbeengwsúmun**. *ind 3rd sg*

**peengwsúmun**. *conj 1st sg* **peeng=wsúmaan**. *conj 3rd sg* **péengwsung**. *imp* **péengwsih**. *ptcpl* **péengwsung**.

**péengwsuw** VAI be dried by heat *(s.t. animate, after being wet). ind 1st sg* **mbéengwsi**, **mbéengwsiim**. *conj 3rd sg* **péengwsiit**. *ptcpl* **péengwsiit**.

**péengwteew** VII be dried by heat *(after being wet). conj 3rd sg* **péengwteek**. *ptcpl* **péengwteek**.

**péengwun** VII be dry *(after being wet). conj 3rd sg* **péengwung**. *ptcpl* **péengwung**.

**péengwŭneew** VTA dry s.o., wring s.o. out. *ind 1st sg* **mbéengwŭnaaw**, **mbéengwŭna**. *ind 3rd sg* **peengwŭ=náawal**. *ind inv* **mbéengwŭnukw**. *ind I-you* **kpéengwŭnul**. *conj 3rd sg* **péengwŭnaat**. *imp* **péengwun**. *ptcpl* **péengwŭnaat**.

**péengwŭnum** VTI1B dry s.t., wring s.t. out *(using the hands). ind 1st sg* **mbeengwŭnúmun**. *ind 3rd sg* **peen=gwŭnúmun**. *conj 1st sg* **peengwŭ=númaan**. *conj 3rd sg* **péengwŭnung**. *imp* **péengwŭnih**. *ptcpl* **péengwŭ=nung**.

**péengxookw** VAI be dried by the wind, be dried out by the wind *(s.t. animate). ind 1st sg* **mbéengxookw**, **mbéengxookw**. *conj 3rd sg* **peeng=xóokwuk**. *ptcpl* **peengxóokwuk**.

**péengxwakw** NI piece of dried wood. *pl* **peengxwákwal**. *poss* **mbeeng=xwákwum**. *loc* **peengxwákwung**. *dimin* **peengxwákwush**.

**péengxwun** VII be dried by the wind, be dried out by the wind. *conj 3rd sg* **péengxwung**. *ptcpl* **péengxwung**.

**péepakang** NI sweet flag. **Nzhash=kwándamun péepakang.** 'I chewed the sweet flag.' *pl* **peepakángal**.

**peepáxkwŭleesh** NA flower. *pl* **peepax=kwŭléeshak**. *poss* **mbeepaxkwŭlée=shum**. *loc* **peepaxkwŭléeshung**. *dimin* **peepaxkwŭléeshush**. *obv* **pee=paxkwŭléeshal**. *See* **pehpáxkwŭ=leesh**.

**peepaxkwŭleesh'háasuw** VAI have flowers on it *(s.t. animate). ind 1st sg* **mbeepaxkwŭleesh'háasi**, **mbee=paxkwŭleesh'háasiim**. *conj 3rd sg* **peepaxkwŭleesh'háasiit**. *ptcpl* **pee=paxkwŭleesh'háasiit**.

**peepaxkwŭleesh'háasuw** VII have flowers on it. *conj 3rd sg* **peepaxkwŭ=leesh'háasiik**. *ptcpl* **peepaxkwŭ=leesh'háasiik**.

**peepiishlóngwanaash** NA bat. *pl* **pee=piishlongwanáashak**. *obv* **peepiish=longwanáashal**.

**péesuw** VAI wait, be waiting. **Méhch ngwúnii-péesi.** 'I've been waiting for a long time.' *ind 1st sg* **mbéesi**, **mbée=siim**. *conj 3rd sg* **péesiit**. *imp* **péesiil**. *ptcpl* **péesiit**.

**péeshŭweew** VTA bring s.o., bring s.t. animate. *ind 1st sg* **mbéeshŭwaaw**, **mbéeshŭwa**. *ind 3rd sg* **peeshŭwáa=wal**. *ind inv* **mbéeshookw**. *ind I-you* **kpéeshool**. *conj 3rd sg* **péeshŭwaat**. *imp* **péeshuw**. *ptcpl* **péeshŭwaat**.

**peetaachíimuw** VAI bring news, spread the word. *ind 1st sg* **mbeetaachíi=mwi**, **mbeetaachíimwiim**. *conj 3rd sg* **peetaachíimwiit**. *imp* **peetaachíi=mwiil**. *ptcpl* **peetaachíimwiit**.

**peetaachŭmóhkaweew** VTA bring news to here from s.o., bring news to s.o. *ind 1st sg* **mbeetaachŭmóhkawaaw**, **mbeetaachŭmóhkawa**. *ind 3rd sg* **peetaachŭmohkawáawal**. *ind inv* **mbeetaachŭmóhkaakw**. *ind I-you* **kpeetaachŭmóhkool**. *conj 3rd sg* **peetaachŭmóhkawaat**. *imp* **peetaa=chŭmóhkaw**. *ptcpl* **peetaachŭmóh=kawaat**.

**peetaahóosuw** VAI come here to sell things, come here selling things. *ind 1st sg* **mbeetaahóosi**, **mbeetaahóo=siim**. *conj 3rd sg* **peetaahóosiit**. *imp* **peetaahóosiil**. *ptcpl* **peetaahóosiit**.

**peetaapamúkwat** VII be visible from here. *conj 3rd sg* **peetaapamúkwahk**. *ptcpl* **peetaapamúkwahk**. **peetaa=pamúkwsuw** VAI be visible from here *(s.t. animate)*. *ind 1st sg* **mbeetaapa=múkwsi**, **mbeetaapamúkwsiim**. *conj 3rd sg* **peetaapamúkwsiit**. *ptcpl* **peetaapamúkwsiit**.

**peetáapan** VII be daylight coming, be daylight. *conj 3rd sg* **peetáapang**. *ptcpl* **peetáapang**.

**peetáasŭleew** VAI shine in this direction, shine here *(s.t. animate, of lights)*. *conj 3rd sg* **peetáasŭleet**. *ptcpl* **peetáasŭleet**.

**peetáasŭleew** VII shine in this direction, shine here *(of lights)*. *conj 3rd sg* **peetáasŭleek**. *ptcpl* **peetáasŭleek**.

**peetáashŭweew** VAI swim in this direction, swim here, swim this way. *ind 1st sg* **mbeetáashŭwe**, **mbeetáashŭ=weem**. *conj 3rd sg* **peetáashŭweet**. *imp* **peetáashŭweel**. *ptcpl* **peetáa=shŭweet**.

**peetaashŭwíhleew** VAI swim in this direction, swim here, swim this way. **Eéskwa káamung peetaashŭwíh=laakw.** 'Before he got across to the other side.' *ind 1st sg* **mbeetaashŭ=wíhla**, **mbeetaashŭwíhlaam**. *conj 3rd sg* **peetaashŭwíhlaat**. *imp* **pee=taashŭwíhlaal**. *ptcpl* **peetaashŭ=wíhlaat**.

**peetáathookw** VAI float here, float in this direction. *ind 1st sg* **mbeetáat=hookw**. *conj 3rd sg* **peetaathóo=kwuk**. *ptcpl* **peetaathóokwuk**.

**peetáathun** VII float here, float in this direction. *conj 3rd sg* **peetáathung**. *ptcpl* **peetáathung**.

**peetáawsuw** VAI live to a certain age, live until now. **Náh mbeetáawsi éenda-áalu- tá -ayáan.** 'I've lived to the age where I can't go anywhere.' *ind 1st sg* **mbeetáawsi**, **mbeetáaw=siim**. *conj 3rd sg* **peetáawsiit**. *imp* **peetáawsiil**. *ptcpl* **peetáawsiit**.

**peetahtakíhleew** VAI run here, run in this direction, come here running. *ind 1st sg* **mbeetahtakíhla**, **mbeetahtakíh=laam**. *conj 3rd sg* **peetahtakíhlaat**. *imp* **peetahtakíhlaal**. *ptcpl* **peetah=takíhlaat**. *See* **peetaaméhleew**.

**peetaaméhleew** VAI run here, run in this direction, come here running. *ind 1st sg* **mbeetaaméhla**, **mbeetaaméh=laam**. *conj 3rd sg* **peetaaméhlaat**. *imp* **peetaaméhlaal**. *ptcpl* **peetaa=méhlaat**. *See* **peetahtakíhleew**.

**peetakóosuw** VAI climb here, climb towards speaker. *ind 1st sg* **mbeeta=kóosi**, **mbeetakóosiim**. *conj 3rd sg* **peetakóosiit**. *imp* **peetakóosiil**. *ptcpl* **peetakóosiit**.

**peetakumáhkwat** VII be clouds coming in this direction. *conj 3rd sg* **peeta=kumáhkwahk**. *ptcpl* **peetakumáh=kwahk**.

**peetaláamuw** VAI come here singing, come in this direction singing. *ind 1st sg* **mbeetaláamwi**, **mbeetaláa=mwiim**. *conj 3rd sg* **peetaláamwiit**. *imp* **peetaláamwiil**. *ptcpl* **peeta=láamwiit**.

**peetanóongsuw** VAI come here angry, come in this direction while angry. *ind 1st sg* **mbeetanóongsi**, **mbeeta=nóongsiim**. *conj 3rd sg* **peetanóong=siit**. *ptcpl* **peetanóongsiit**.

**peetasánuw** VAIO bring s.t. in this direction *(towards the speaker)*; bring s.t. this way. **Mbeetasániin nŭmóxwsal.** 'I brought my wood this way.' *ind 1st sg* **mbeetasániin**. *ind 3rd sg* **peeta=sániin**. *conj 3rd sg* **peetasániit**. *imp* **peetasániil**. *ptcpl* **peetasániit**.

**péetaweew** VTAO bring s.t. for s.o. *ind 1st sg* **mbéetawaan**. *ind 3rd sg* **pée=tawaan**. *ind inv* **mbeetáakwun**. *ind I-you* **kpeetóolun**. *conj 3rd sg* **péeta=waat**. *imp* **péetaw**. *ptcpl* **péetawaat**.

**peetawéeheew** VAIO use s.t. to come here,

use s.t. to come in this direction. *ind 1st sg* **mbeetawéeheen**. *ind 3rd sg* **peetawéeheen**. *conj 3rd sg* **peeta=wéeheet**. *imp* **peetawéeheel**. *ptcpl* **peetawéeheet**.

**peetchéhleew** VAI drive in this direction, drive here, come here driving, drive toward the speaker. *ind 1st sg* **mbeet=chéhla**, **mbeetchéhlaam**. *conj 3rd sg* **peetchéhlaat**. *imp* **peetchéhlaal**. *ptcpl* **peetchéhlaat**. *See* **peech'chéh=leew**.

**peeteekhámaweew** VTA write to s.o. *ind 1st sg* **mbeeteekhámawaaw**, **mbee=teekhámawa**. *ind 3rd sg* **peeteek=hamawáawal**. *ind inv* **mbeeteek=hámaakw**. *ind I-you* **kpeeteekhám=ool**. *conj 3rd sg* **peeteekhámawaat**. *imp* **peeteekhámaw**. *ptcpl* **peeteek=hámawaat**.

**peeteekhíikeew** VAI write a letter, write a letter to here. *ind 1st sg* **mbeeteek=híike**, **mbeeteekhíikeem**. *conj 3rd sg* **peeteekhíikeet**. *imp* **peeteekhíikeel**. *ptcpl* **peeteekhíikeet**.

**peetéelham** VAI make tracks coming this way, make tracks coming towards the speaker. *ind 1st sg* **mbeetéelham**. *conj 3rd sg* **peetéelhang**. *imp* **pee=téelhah**. *ptcpl* **peetéelhang**.

**peeteelúndam** VOTI1A come to this conclusion. *ind 1st sg* **mbeeteelúndam**. *conj 3rd sg* **peeteelúndang**. *ptcpl* **peeteelúndang**.

**peetéewtam** VOTI1A come here crying, come towards the speaker crying. *ind 1st sg* **mbeetéewtam**. *conj 3rd sg* **peetéewtang**. *imp* **peetéewtah**. *ptcpl* **peetéewtang**.

**péetham** VOTI1A row this way, come here paddling, paddle towards the speaker. *ind 1st sg* **mbéetham**. *conj 3rd sg* **péethang**. *imp* **péethah**. *ptcpl* **péethang**.

**peethámeew** VAI paddle this way in the water. *ind 1st sg* **mbeethάma**, **mbeet=hámaam**. *conj 3rd sg* **peethámaat**. *imp* **peethámaal**. *ptcpl* **peethámaat**.

**peethiingwéexiin** VAI look in this direction, look over here. *ind 1st sg* **mbeet=hiingwéexiin**, **mbeethiingwéexi**. *conj 3rd sg* **peethiingwéexiing**. *imp* **peethiingwéexiil**. *ptcpl* **peethiin=gwéexiing**, **peethiingwéexiit**.

**peethóomeew** VAI come here riding on horseback, ride towards the speaker. *ind 1st sg* **mbeethóoma**, **mbeethóo=maam**. *conj 3rd sg* **peethóomaat**. *imp* **peethóomaal**. *ptcpl* **peethóomaat**.

**peethúpeew** VAI bring water in this direction, bring water towards the speaker. *ind 1st sg* **mbeethúpe**, **mbeet=húpeem**. *conj 3rd sg* **peethúpeet**. *imp* **peethúpeel**. *ptcpl* **peethúpeet**.

**péetoow** VTI2 bring s.t. **Nún há nóonj-péetoon.** 'That's why I brought it.' *ind 1st sg* **mbéetoon**. *ind 3rd sg* **péetoon**. *conj 1st sg* **péetawaan**. *conj 3rd sg* **péetaakw**. *imp* **péetool**. *ptcpl* **péetaakw**.

**peetootéewuw** VAI come here to visit, come here visiting. *ind 1st sg* **mbee=tootéewi**, **mbeetootéewiim**. *conj 3rd sg* **peetootéewiit**. *imp* **peetootéewiil**. *ptcpl* **peetootéewiit**.

**peetóoxweew** VAI walk here, walk in this direction, come here walking. *ind 1st sg* **mbeetóoxwe**, **mbeetóoxweem**. *conj 3rd sg* **peetóoxweet**. *imp* **pee=tóoxweel**. *ptcpl* **peetóoxweet**.

**peetsiitéexiin** VAI have one's feet here, have one's feet sticking this way. **Áalu- náh -peetsiitéexiin.** 'He can't get his feet there.' *ind 1st sg* **mbeet=siitéexiin**, **mbeetsiitéexi**. *conj 3rd sg* **peetsiitéexiing**. *imp* **peetsiitéexiil**. *ptcpl* **peetsiitéexiing**, **peetsiitéexiit**.

**peetshíimuw** VAI run away to here, escape to here. *ind 1st sg* **mbeetshíi=mwi**, **mbeetshíimwiim**. *conj 3rd sg* **peetshíimwiit**. *imp* **peetshíimwiil**. *ptcpl* **peetshíimwiit**.

**peetshíhkaweew** VTA chase s.o. to here, chase s.o. in this direction, drive s.o. to here. *ind 1st sg* **mbeetshíhka=waaw**, **mbeetshíhkawa**. *ind 3rd sg* **peetshihkawáawal**. *ind inv* **mbeet=shíhkaakw**. *ind I-you* **kpeetshíhkool**. *conj 3rd sg* **peetshíhkawaat**. *imp* **peetshíhkaw**. *ptcpl* **peetshíhkawaat**.

**peettáachiind** VTI3 drag s.t. to here, drag s.t. towards the speaker. *ind 1st sg* **mbeettaachíindun**. *ind 3rd sg* **peettaachíindun**. *conj 1st sg* **peet=taachíindawaan**. *conj 3rd sg* **peet=taachíinduk**. *imp* **peettaachíindih**. *ptcpl* **peettaachíinduk**. *See* **peettaa=chíindam**.

**peettaachíindam** VTI1A drag s.t. to here, drag s.t. towards the speaker. *ind 1st sg* **mbettaachíindamun**. *ind 3rd sg* **peettaachíindamun**. *conj 1st sg* **peettaachíindamaan**. *conj 3rd sg* **peettaachíindang**. *imp* **peettaa=chíindah**. *ptcpl* **peettaachíindang**. *See* **peettáachiind**.

**peettaachíhleew** VTA drag s.o. to here, drag s.t. animate to here, drag s.o. towards the speaker, drag s.t. animate towards the speaker. *ind 1st sg* **mbeet=taachíhlaaw**, **mbeettaachíhla**. *ind 3rd sg* **peettaachihláawal**. *ind inv* **mbeettaachíhlukw**. *ind I-you* **kpeet=taachíhlul**. *conj 3rd sg* **peettaachíh=laat**. *imp* **peettáachihl**. *ptcpl* **peet=taachíhlaat**.

**péetŭlaan** VII be rain coming in this direction. *conj 3rd sg* **péetŭlaang**. *ptcpl* **péetŭlaang**.

**peetŭnúmaweew** VTAO hand s.t. to s.o. *ind 1st sg* **mbeetŭnúmawaan**. *ind 3rd sg* **peetŭnúmawaan**. *ind inv* **mbeetŭnumáakwun**. *ind I-you* **kpeetŭnumóolun**. *conj 3rd sg* **peetŭ=númawaat**. *imp* **peetŭnúmaw**. *ptcpl* **peetŭnúmawaat**.

**péetxookw** VAI be blown in this direction by the wind, be blown here by the wind. *ind 1st sg* **mbéetxookw**. *conj 3rd sg* **peetxóokwuk**. *ptcpl* **peetxóokwuk**.

**péetxun** VII blow in this direction *(of the wind)*; be the wind coming here, be blown here by the wind. **Wíixkwii péetxun.** 'The wind came up all of a sudden.' *conj 3rd sg* **péetxung**. *ptcpl* **péetxung**.

**péew** VAI come, come here. **Péexoot náh kpá.** 'You're almost there.' *ind 1st sg* **mbá**, **mbáam**. *conj 3rd sg* **páat**. *imp* **páal**. *ptcpl* **péeyaat**.

**péexoot** PC soon, nearly. **Péexoot ngáwiim.** 'I'm almost sleeping.'; **Péexoot éet sóokŭlaan.** 'It must be going to rain pretty soon.'

**peexŭwaaméhleew** VAI run close by. *ind 1st sg* **mbeexŭwaaméhla**, **mbeexŭ=waaméhlaam**. *conj 3rd sg* **peexŭ=waaméhlaat**. *imp* **peexŭwaaméhlaal**. *ptcpl* **peexŭwaaméhlaat**.

**péexŭwat** VII be near; be soon. **Péexŭwat sóokŭlaan.** 'It will rain soon.' *conj 3rd sg* **péexŭwahk**. *ptcpl* **péexŭwahk**.

**peexŭwéelŭmeew** VTA think s.o. to be close. *ind 1st sg* **mbeexuwéelŭmaaw**, **mbeexŭwéelŭma**. *ind 3rd sg* **peexŭ=weelŭmáawal**. *ind inv* **mbeexŭwée=lŭmukw**. *ind I-you* **kpeexŭwéelŭmul**. *conj 3rd sg* **peexŭwéelŭmaat**. *ptcpl* **peexuwéelŭmaat**.

**peexŭweelúndam** VTI1A think s.t. to be close. *ind 1st sg* **mbeexŭweelúnda=mun**. *ind 3rd sg* **peexŭweelúndamun**. *conj 1st sg* **peexŭweelúndamaan**. *conj 3rd sg* **peexŭweelúndang**. *ptcpl* **peexŭweelúndang**.

**péexŭwii** PC close, up close. **Péexŭwii ndúlu-pŭnáwaaw.** 'I looked at him up close.'; **Péexŭwii wsháyii péew.** 'He came close to the edge.'

**peexŭwiikáaleew** VTA live near s.o., live close to s.o. *ind 1st sg* **mbeexŭwii=káalaaw**, **mbeexŭwiikáala**. *ind 3rd sg* **peexŭwiikaaláawal**. *ind inv* mbeexŭwiikáalukw. *ind I-you* kpee=xŭwiikáalul. *conj 3rd sg* peexŭwii=káalaat. *imp* peexŭwíikaal. *ptcpl* peexŭwiikáalaat.

**peexŭwíikwsuw** VAI crawl close by. *ind 1st sg* **mbeexŭwíikwsi, mbeexŭ=wíikwsiim**. *conj 3rd sg* **peexŭwíik=wsiit**. *imp* **peexŭwíikwsiil**. *ptcpl* **peexŭwíikwsiit**.

**peexŭwiináakwat** VII appear to be close by, look to be close by. *conj 3rd sg* **peexŭwiináakwahk**. *ptcpl* **peexŭ=wiináakwahk**.

**peexŭwiináakwsuw** VAI appear to be close by, look to be close by *(s.t. animate)*. *ind 1st sg* **mbeexŭwiináakwsi, mbeexŭwiináakwsiim**. *conj 3rd sg* **peexŭwiináakwsiit**. *ptcpl* **peexŭwii=náakwsiit**.

**peexŭwíhkam** VTI 1A get close to s.t. *ind 1st sg* **mbeexŭwíhkamun**. *ind 3rd sg* **peexŭwíhkamun**. *conj 1st sg* **peexŭ=wíhkamaan**. *conj 3rd sg* **peexŭwíh=kang**. *imp* **peexŭwíhkah**. *ptcpl* **peexŭwíhkang**.

**peexŭwíhkaweew** VTA get close to s.o. *ind 1st sg* **mbeexŭwíhkawaaw, mbeexŭwíhkawa**. *ind 3rd sg* **peexŭ=wihkawáawal**. *conj 3rd sg* **peexŭ=wíhkawaat**. *imp* **peexŭwíhkaw**. *ptcpl* **peexŭwíhkawaat**.

**peexŭwíhleew** VAI get close, approach, fly close by, go close by. *ind 1st sg* **mbeexŭwíhla, mbeexŭwíhlaam**. *conj 3rd sg* **peexŭwíhlaat**. *imp* **peexŭwíhlaal**. *ptcpl* **peexŭwíhlaat**.

**peexŭwíhleew** VII get close, approach, fly close by, go close by. *conj 3rd sg* **peexŭwíhlaak**. *ptcpl* **peexŭwíhlaak**.

**peexŭwihtáakwat** VII sound close by. *conj 3rd sg* **peexŭwihtáakwahk**. *ptcpl* **peexŭwihtáakwahk**.

**peexŭwihtáakwsuw** VAI sound close by *(s.t. animate)*. *ind 1st sg* **mbeexŭ=wihtáakwsi, mbeexŭwihtáakwsiim**. *conj 3rd sg* **peexŭwihtáakwsiit**. *ptcpl* **peexŭwihtáakwsiit**.

**peexŭwóoxweew** VAI walk close by. *ind 1st sg* **mbeexŭwóoxwe, mbeexŭ=wóoxweem**. *conj 3rd sg* **peexŭwóo=xweet**. *imp* **peexŭwóoxweel**. *ptcpl* **peexŭwóoxweet**.

**peexŭwuchéhleew** VAI drive close by. *ind 1st sg* **mbeexŭwuchéhla, mbee=xŭwuchéhlaam**. *conj 3rd sg* **peexŭ=wuchéhlaat**. *imp* **peexŭwuchéhlaal**. *ptcpl* **peexŭwuchéhlaat**.

**péexwiish** PC near to, close by, nearly. **Péexwiish wihkwáameew.** 'He has a little ways to the end (of the road).'; **Péexwiish náh ndá.** 'I'm not going far.'

**peeyéewuw** VII come, come here. **Pee=yéewuw wúlu-léek.** 'Something good is coming' *conj 3rd sg* **peeyéewiik**. *ptcpl* **peeyéewiik**. *See* **peeyéeyuw**.

**peeyéeyuw** VII come, come here. **Pee=yéeyuw téeheek.** 'The cold weather is here.'; **Peeyéeyuw wiinamalsuw=áakan.** 'The sickness is coming.' *conj 3rd sg* **peeyéeyiik**. *ptcpl* **peeyéeyiik**. *See* **peeyéewuw**.

**péhkiik** PC reluctantly, (do) reluctantly; finally. **Péhkiik náh ndá.** 'I went there reluctantly.'; **Mbeeteekháma=waa, péhkiik naxkóomukw.** 'I wrote to him and he finally answered me.'

**pehpáasteek** NI rice. *pl* **pehpaastéekiil**.

**pehpáasteek** NI rice. *pl* **pehpaastéekal**.

**pehpáxkwŭleesh** NA flower. *pl* **pehpax=kwŭléeshak**. *poss* **mbehpaxkwŭlée=shum**. *loc* **pehpaxkwŭléeshung**. *dimin* **pehpaxkwŭléeshush**. *obv* **pehpaxkwŭléeshal**. *See* **peepáx=kwŭleesh**.

**pehpeechkwéekush** NA carrot. *pl* **peh=peechkwéekshak**. *obv* **pehpeech=kwéekshal**.

**pehpéetkweek** NA turnip. *pl* **pehpeet=kwéekak**. *obv* **pehpeetkwéekal**.

**pehpehtáhkuw** VII thunder, be thundering. *conj 3rd sg* **pehpehtáhkwiik**.

*ptcpl* **pehpehtáhkwiik**. *See* **peh=táhkuw**.

**pehpéhtŭlaan** VII rain on and off, rain intermittently. *conj 3rd sg* **pehpéhtŭ=laang**. *ptcpl* **pehpéhtŭlaang**.

**pehpíchiis** NA pitcher *(baseball)*. *pl* **pehpìchíisak**. *obv* **pehpìchíisal**. *From English* pitcher.

**pehpóolŭwees** NA runaway. *pl* **pehpoo=lŭwéesak**. *dimin* **pehpoolŭwéeshush**. *obv* **pehpoolŭwéesal**.

**pehpootáalŭwees** NA blow adder. *pl* **pehpootaalŭwéesak**. *poss* **mbeh=pootaalŭwéesum**. *loc* **pehpootaa=lŭwéesung**. *dimin* **pehpoochaalŭ=wéeshush**. *obv* **pehpootaalŭwéesal**.

**pehpóxkapiis** NA horse rider. *pl* **peh=poxkapíisak**. *dimin* **pehpoxkapíi=shush**. *obv* **pehpoxkapíisal**.

**pehpoxkwahtíikan** NI cupboard. *pl* **pehpoxkwahtíikanal**. *poss* **mbeh=poxkwahtíikan**. *loc* **pehpoxkwah=tíikanung**. *dimin* **pehpoxkwahchíi=kanush**.

**pehpŭlakíixtaang** VII short apron. *conj 3rd sg* **pehpŭlakíixtaang** *pl* **pehpŭ=lakiixtaangiil**.

**pehpŭmutóonhees** NA preacher. *pl* **pehpŭmutoonhéesak**. *poss* **mbeh=pŭmutoonhéesum**. *obv* **pehpŭmut=oonhéesal**.

**pehpunáwsuw** VAI look in a mirror. *ind 1st sg* **mbehpŭnáwsi**, **mbehpŭnáw=siim**. *conj 3rd sg* **pehpŭnáwsiit**. *imp* **pehpŭnáwsiil**. *ptcpl* **pehpŭnáwsiit**.

**pehpŭnáwus** NA mirror. *pl* **pehpŭnáw=sak**. *poss* **mbehpŭnáwsum**. *loc* **pehpŭnáwsung**. *dimin* **pehpunáw=shush**. *obv* **pehpŭnáwsal**.

**pehtáhkuw** VII thunder, be thundering. *conj 3rd sg* **pehtáhkwiik**. *ptcpl* **pehtáhkwiik**. *moderative reduplication* **paapehtáhkuw**. *See* **pehpeh=táhkuw**.

**pehtchásuw** VAI get hot *(all of a sudden)*. **Pehpehtchásuw.** 'She has hot flashes.' *ind 1st sg* **mbehtchási**, **mbehtchásiim**. *conj 3rd sg* **peht=chásiit**. *ptcpl* **pehtchásiit**. *intensive reduplication* **pehpehtchásuw**.

**péhtoow** VTI2 wait for s.t. *ind 1st sg* **mbéhtoon**. *ind 3rd sg* **péhtoon**. *conj 1st sg* **péhtawaan**. *conj 3rd sg* **péh=taakw**. *imp* **péhtool**. *ptcpl* **péhtaakw**.

**pékiis** NA Becky. *obv* **pèkíisal**. *From English* Becky.

**pénsul** NI pencil. *pl* **pensúlal**. *poss* **mbensúlum**. *loc* **pensúlung**. *dimin* **penshúlush**. *From English* pencil.

**pépul** NI pepper. *poss* **mbépŭlum**. *loc* **pépŭlung**. *dimin* **pépŭlush**. *From English* pepper.

**pèpŭlíinjuw** NI pepper shaker. *pl* **pèpŭ=líinjŭwal**. *poss* **mbepŭliinjóohum**. *loc* **pèpŭliinjóohung**. *dimin* **pèpŭ=líinjoosh**.

**píikat** VII be shredded, be torn up. *conj 3rd sg* **píikahk**. *ptcpl* **píikahk**.

**piikchásuw** VAI fall to pieces, fall apart *(s.t. animate, in cooking)*. *ind 1st sg* **mbiikchási**, **mbiikchásiim**. *conj 3rd sg* **piikchásiit**. *ptcpl* **piikchásiit**.

**piikcháteew** VII fall to pieces, fall apart *(in cooking)*. *conj 3rd sg* **piikcháteek**. *ptcpl* **piikcháteek**.

**piikchéesuw** VAI fall to pieces, fall apart *(in cooking)*. *ind 1st sg* **mbiik=chéesi**, **mbiikchéesiim**. *conj 3rd sg* **piikchéesiit**. *ptcpl* **piikchéesiit**.

**piikháhkweew** VAI chop up wood. *ind 1st sg* **mbiikháhkwe**, **mbiikháh=kweem**. *conj 3rd sg* **piikháhkweet**. *imp* **piikháhkweel**. *ptcpl* **piikháh=kweet**.

**píikham** VTI1A dice s.t., cut s.t. up into small pieces, chop s.t. up, crack s.t. *ind 1st sg* **mbiikhámun**. *ind 3rd sg* **piikhámun**. *conj 1st sg* **piikhámaan**. *conj 3rd sg* **píikhang**. *imp* **píikhah**. *ptcpl* **píikhang**.

**píikheew** VTA dice s.t. animate, cut s.t. animate up into small pieces, chop s.t. animate, crack s.t. animate. *ind 1st sg* **mbíikhaaw**, **mbíikha**. *ind 3rd sg* **piikháawal**. *ind inv* **mbíikhookw**. *ind I-you* **kpíikhool**. *conj 3rd sg* **píik=haat**. *imp* **píikhaw**. *ptcpl* **píikhaat**.

**piikhéewaleew** VTA take s.t. animate apart to pieces. *ind 1st sg* **mbiikhée=walaaw**, **mbiikhéewala**. *ind 3rd sg* **piikheewaláawal**. *ind inv* **mbiikhée=walukw**. *ind I-you* **kpiikhéewalul**. *conj 3rd sg* **piikhéewalaat**. *imp* **piikhéewal**. *ptcpl* **piikhéewalaat**.

**piikhéewatoow** VTI2 take s.t. apart to pieces. *ind 1st sg* **mbiikhéewatoon**. *ind 3rd sg* **piikhéewatoon**. *conj 1st sg* **piikheewatáwaan**. *conj 3rd sg* **piikhéewataakw**. *imp* **piikhéewatool**. *ptcpl* **piikhéewataakw**.

**piikíhleew** VAI go to pieces, fall to pieces. *conj 3rd sg* **piikíhlaat**. *ptcpl* **piikíhlaat**.

**piikíhleew** VII go to pieces, fall to pieces. *conj 3rd sg* **piikíhlaak**. *ptcpl* **piikíh=laak**.

**piikihtéexun** VII be broken into pieces. *conj 3rd sg* **piikihtéexung**. *ptcpl* **piikihtéexung**.

**píiksuw** VAI be shredded, be torn up *(s.t. animate)*. *ind 1st sg* **mbíiksi**, **mbíik=siim**. *conj 3rd sg* **píiksiit**. *ptcpl* **píiksiit**.

**píiksheew** VTA cut s.t. animate up, cut s.t. animate into pieces. *ind 1st sg* **mbíikshaaw**, **mbíiksha**. *ind 3rd sg* **piiksháawal**. *ind inv* **mbíikshookw**. *ind I-you* **kpíikshool**. *conj 3rd sg* **píikshaat**. *imp* **píikush**. *ptcpl* **píikshaat**.

**piikshíikeew** VAI be discing, use a disc *(of farming equipment)*. *ind 1st sg* **mbiikshíike**, **mbiikshíikeem**. *conj 3rd sg* **piikshíikeet**. *imp* **piikshíikeel**. *ptcpl* **piikshíikeet**.

**píikshum** VTI1B cut s.t. up, cut s.t. into pieces. *ind 1st sg* **mbiikshúmun**. *ind 3rd sg* **piikshúmun**. *conj 1st sg* **piik=shúmaan**. *conj 3rd sg* **píikshung**. *imp* **píikshih**. *ptcpl* **píikshung**.

**piikshúmaweew** VTAO cut s.t. up for s.o. *ind 1st sg* **mbiikshúmawaan**. *ind 3rd sg* **piikshúmawaan**. *ind inv* **mbiik=shumáakwun**. *ind I-you* **kpiikshum=óolun**. *conj 1st sg* **piikshumawaan**. *conj 3rd sg* **piikshúmawaat**. *imp* **piikshúmaw**. *ptcpl* **piikshúmawaat**.

**píikŭneew** VTA crumble s.t. animate, break s.t. animate up into pieces, shred s.t. animate *(using the hands)*. *ind 1st sg* **mbíikŭnaaw**, **mbíikŭna**. *ind 3rd sg* **piikŭnáawal**. *ind inv* **mbíikŭnukw**. *ind I-you* **kpíikŭnul**. *conj 3rd sg* **píikŭnaat**. *imp* **píikun**. *ptcpl* **píikŭnaat**.

**piikŭníikeew** VAI shred things, break things into pieces. *ind 1st sg* **mbii=kŭníike**, **mbiikŭníikeem**. *conj 3rd sg* **piikŭníikeet**. *imp* **piikŭníikeel**. *ptcpl* **piikŭníikeet**.

**píikŭnum** VTI1B crumble s.t., break s.t. up into pieces, shred s.t. *(using the hands)*. *ind 1st sg* **mbiikŭnúmun**. *ind 3rd sg* **piikŭnúmun**. *conj 1st sg* **pii=kŭnúmaan**. *conj 3rd sg* **píikŭnung**. *imp* **píikŭnih**. *ptcpl* **píikŭnung**.

**piikŭnúmeew** VAI break up bread in milk, break bread into liquid, break crackers into liquid. *ind 1st sg* **mbii=kŭnúma**, **mbiikŭnúmaam**. *conj 3rd sg* **piikŭnúmaat**. *imp* **piikŭnúmaal**. *ptcpl* **piikŭnúmaat**.

**piikwshaalóhkweew** VAI have tangled hair, have matted hair, have messy hair. *ind 1st sg* **mbiikwshaalóhkwa**, **mbiikwshaalóhkwaam**. *conj 3rd sg* **piikwshaalóhkwaat**. *ptcpl* **piikw=shaalóhkwaat**.

**piikwsháandpeew** VAI have messy hair. *ind 1st sg* **mbiikwsháandpa**, **mbiik=wsháandpaam**. *conj 3rd sg* **piikw=sháandpaat**. *ptcpl* **piikwsháand=paat**.

**piikwshákuw** VAI dress raggedly, wear

ragged clothing. *ind 1st sg* **mbiikw=shákwi**, **mbiikwshákwiim**. *conj 3rd sg* **piikwshákwiit**. *imp* **piikwshák=wiil**. *ptcpl* **piikwshákwiit**.

**píikwsheew** VII be ragged, bushy. *conj 3rd sg* **píikwsheek**. *ptcpl* **píikw=sheek**.

**piikwshihtóonayeew** VAI have a ragged beard, have a messy beard. *ind 1st sg* **mbiikwshihtóonaya**, **mbiikwshih=tóonayaam**. *conj 3rd sg* **piikwshih=tóonayaat**. *ptcpl* **piikwshihtóona=yaat**.

**piikwshúsuw** VAI be ragged, be bushy *(s.t. animate)*. *ind 1st sg* **mbiikwshúsi**, **mbiikwshúsiim**. *conj 3rd sg* **piikw=shúsiit**. *ptcpl* **piikwshúsiit**.

**piilahksúneew** VAI have clean shoes. *ind 1st sg* **mbiilahksúna**, **mbiilahksún=aam**. *conj 3rd sg* **piilahksúnaat**. *ptcpl* **piilahksúnaat**.

**píilakush** NA peach. *pl* **píilakush**. *poss* **mbiilakúshum**. *loc* **piilakúshung**. *dimin* **piilakúshush**. *obv* **piilakúshal**. *See* **píilkush**. *From Dutch.*

**piilalóhkeew** VAI clean up. *ind 1st sg* **mbiilalóhke**, **mbiilalóhkeem**. *conj 3rd sg* **piilalóhkeet**. *imp* **piilalóhkeel**. *ptcpl* **piilalóhkeet**.

**piilapóoshiish** NA clean cat. *pl* **piila=pooshíishak**. *poss* **mbiilapooshíi=shum**. *loc* **piilapooshíishung**. *dimin* **piilapooshíishush**. *obv* **piilapoo=shíishal**.

**piilchàlíingweew** VAI have a clean face. *ind 1st sg* **mbiilchàlíingwa**, **mbiil=chàlíingwaam**. *conj 3rd sg* **piilchàl=íingwaat**. *ptcpl* **piilchàlíingwaat**.

**piilháhkweew** VAI clear away under-brush, be underbrushing. *ind 1st sg* **mbiilháhkwe**, **mbiilháhkweem**. *conj 3rd sg* **piilháhkweet**. *imp* **piilháh=kweel**. *ptcpl* **piilháhkweet**.

**piilhúnzuw** VAI clean oneself up. *ind 1st sg* **mbiilhúnzi**, **mbiilhúnziim**. *conj 3rd sg* **piilhúnziit**. *imp* **piilhúnziil**. *ptcpl* **piilhúnziit**.

**piilii-** PN clean. **Píilii-waapasáanay.** 'A clean sheet.'; **Píilii-pàkíinjuw.** 'A clean plate.'

**piilíiheew** VTA clean s.o., clean s.o. up. *ind 1st sg* **mbiilíihaaw**, **mbiilíiha**. *ind 3rd sg* **piiliiháawal**. *ind inv* **mbiilíi=hukw**. *ind I-you* **kpiilíihul**. *conj 3rd sg* **piilíihaat**. *imp* **píiliih**. *ptcpl* **pii=líihaat**.

**piilíikeew** VAI have a clean house. *ind 1st sg* **mbiilíike**, **mbiilíikeem**. *conj 3rd sg* **piilíikeet**. *imp* **piilíikeel**. *ptcpl* **piilíikeet**.

**piiliiktúkweew** VAI have clean knees. *ind 1st sg* **mbiiliiktúkwa**, **mbiiliiktúk=waam**. *conj 3rd sg* **piiliiktúkwaat**. *ptcpl* **piiliiktúkwaat**. *See* **piiliiktúk=weew**.

**piiliiktúkweew** VAI have clean knees. *ind 1st sg* **mbiiliiktúkwe**, **mbiiliiktúk=weem**. *conj 3rd sg* **piiliiktúkweet**. *ptcpl* **piiliiktúkweet**. *See* **piiliiktúk=weew**.

**piiliikwáaleew** VTA wipe s.o. clean *(with something held in the hand)*. *ind 1st sg* **mbiiliikwáalaaw**, **mbiiliikwáala**. *ind 3rd sg* **piiliikwaaláawal**. *ind inv* **mbiiliikwáalukw**. *ind I-you* **kpiilii=kwáalul**. *conj 3rd sg* **piiliikwáalaat**. *imp* **piilíikwaal**. *ptcpl* **piiliikwáalaat**.

**piilíikwam** VTI1A wipe s.t. clean *(with something held in the hand)*. *ind 1st sg* **mbiilíikwamun**. *ind 3rd sg* **piilíi=kwamun**. *conj 1st sg* **piilíikwamaan**. *conj 3rd sg* **piilíikwang**. *imp* **piilíi=kwah**. *ptcpl* **piilíikwang**.

**piiliináakwat** VII be clean looking, have a clean appearance. *conj 3rd sg* **pii=liináakwahk**. *ptcpl* **piiliináakwahk**.

**piiliináakwsuw** VAI be clean looking, have a clean appearance *(s.t. animate)*. *ind 1st sg* **mbiiliináakwsi**, **mbiilii=náakwsiim**. *conj 3rd sg* **piiliináakw=siit**. *ptcpl* **piiliináakwsiit**.

**piilihtawákeew** VAI have a clean ear. *ind*

*1st sg* **mbiilihtawáke, mbiilihta=wákeem**. *conj 3rd sg* **piilihtawákeet**. *ptcpl* **piilihtawákeet**. *See* **píilxeew**.

**piilíhtoow** VTI2 clean s.t., clean s.t. up. *ind 1st sg* **mbiilíhtoon**. *ind 3rd sg* **piilíhtoon**. *conj 1st sg* **piilíhtawaan**. *conj 3rd sg* **piilíhtaakw**. *imp* **piilíh=tool**. *ptcpl* **piilíhtaakw**.

**píilkush** NA peach. *pl* **piilkúshak**. *poss* **mbiilkúshum**. *loc* **piilkúshung**. *dimin* **piilkúshush**. *obv* **piilkúshal**. *See* **píilakush**. *From Dutch.*

**piilsíiteew** VAI have clean feet. *ind 1st sg* **mbiilsíita, mbiilsíitaam**. *conj 3rd sg* **piilsíitaat**. *ptcpl* **piilsíitaat**.

**píilsuw** VAI be clean *(s.t. animate)*. *ind 1st sg* **mbíilsi, mbíilsiim**. *conj 3rd sg* **píilsiit**. *ptcpl* **píilsiit**.

**piilŭnáxkeew** VAI have clean hands. *ind 1st sg* **mbiilŭnáxka, mbiilŭnáxkaam**. *conj 3rd sg* **piilŭnáxkaat**. *ptcpl* **piilŭnáxkaat**.

**píilut** VII be clean. *conj 3rd sg* **píilihk**. *ptcpl* **píilihk**.

**píilxeew** VAI have a clean ear. *ind 1st sg* **mbíilxa, mbíilxaam**. *conj 3rd sg* **píilxaat**. *ptcpl* **píilxaat**. *See* **piilih=tawákeew**.

**piimáangweew** VAI lie crookedly *(s.t. animate)*. *ind 1st sg* **mbiimáangwe, mbiimáangweem**. *conj 3rd sg* **piimáangweet**. *ptcpl* **piimáangweet**.

**piimaapéhleew** VAI hang crookedly *(s.t. animate)*. *ind 1st sg* **mbiimaapéhla, mbiimaapéhlaam**. *conj 3rd sg* **pii=maapéhlaat**. *ptcpl* **piimaapéhlaat**.

**piimaapéhleew** VII hang crookedly. *conj 3rd sg* **piimaapéhlaak**. *ptcpl* **pii=maapéhlaak**.

**piimahkéeyeew** VII be uneven ground, be crooked ground. *conj 3rd sg* **pii=mahkéeyeek**. *ptcpl* **piimahkéeyeek**. *intensive reduplication* **pihpiimah=kéeyeew**.

**piimaníikeew** VAI have a crooked tooth. *ind 1st sg* **mbiimaníika, mbiimaníi=kaam**. *conj 3rd sg* **piimaníikaat**. *ptcpl* **piimaníikaat**. *intensive reduplication* **apiimaníikeew**.

**píimapuw** VAI sit crookedly. *ind 1st sg* **mbíimapi, mbíimapiim**. *conj 3rd sg* **píimapiit**. *imp* **píimapiil**. *ptcpl* **píimapiit**.

**piimateelíingweew** VAI be cross-eyed. *ind 1st sg* **mbiimateelíingwa, mbii=mateelíingwaam**. *conj 3rd sg* **pii=mateelíingwaat**. *ptcpl* **piimateelíin=gwaat**.

**piimatéexun** VII be a crooked road. *conj 3rd sg* **piimatéexung**. *ptcpl* **piima=téexung**. *intensive reduplication* **pihpiimatéexun**.

**piimchéesuw** VAI be lopsided, be uneven, lean to one side. *ind 1st sg* **mbiim=chéesi, mbiimchéesiim**. *conj 3rd sg* **piimchéesiit**. *imp* **piimchéesiil**. *ptcpl* **piimchéesiit**.

**piimchéexiin** VAI lean over, sit crookedly, lie crookedly. *ind 1st sg* **mbiimchée=xiin, mbiimchéexi**. *conj 3rd sg* **piimchéexiing**. *imp* **piimchéexiil**. *ptcpl* **piimchéexiing**.

**piimchéeyeew** VII be lopsided, be uneven. *conj 3rd sg* **piimchéeyeek**. *ptcpl* **piimchéeyeek**.

**piimchéhleew** VAI fall sideways, drive crookedly. *ind 1st sg* **mbiimchéhla, mbiimchéhlaam**. *conj 3rd sg* **piim=chéhlaat**. *imp* **piimchéhlaal**. *ptcpl* **piimchéhlaat**.

**píimeew** VII be crooked, be lopsided, be uneven. **Ktaláawan píimeew.** 'Your cane is crooked.' *conj 3rd sg* **píimeek**. *ptcpl* **píimeek**.

**piimíikaan** NI house that leans. *pl* **pii=miikáanal**. *poss* **mbiimiikáanum**. *loc* **piimiikáanung**. *dimin* **piimii=káanush**.

**piimíikeew** VAI have a house that's leaning. *ind 1st sg* **mbiimíike, mbiimíi=keem**. *conj 3rd sg* **piimíikeet**. *ptcpl* **piimíikeet**.

**piimíikun** VII grow unevenly, grow crookedly, come up crooked. *conj 3rd sg* **piimíikung**. *ptcpl* **piimíikung**.

**piimíikuw** VAI grow unevenly, grow crookedly, come up crooked *(s.t. animate)*. *ind 1st sg* **mbiimíiki**, **mbii=míikiim**. *conj 3rd sg* **piimíikiit**. *ptcpl* **piimíikiit**.

**piimíikwsuw** VAI crawl sideways, crawl on the diagonal. *ind 1st sg* **mbii=míikwsi**, **mbiimíikwsiim**. *conj 3rd sg* **piimíikwsiit**. *ptcpl* **piimíikwsiit**.

**piimiitŭyéewxeew** VAI walk with a limp, walk with one hip higher than the other. *ind 1st sg* **mbiimiitŭyéewxe**, **mbiimiitŭyéewxeem**. *conj 3rd sg* **piimiitŭyéewxeet**. *imp* **piimiitŭ=yéewxeel**. *ptcpl* **piimiitŭyéewxeet**.

**piimiitŭyéexiin** VAI stand lopsided, stand with one leg higher than the other. *ind 1st sg* **mbiimiitŭyéexiin**, **mbiimiitŭyéexi**. *conj 3rd sg* **piimii=tŭyéexiing**. *imp* **piimiitŭyéexiil**. *ptcpl* **piimiitŭyéexiing**.

**piimíixiin** VAI lean over, lean to one side *(s.t. animate)*; be crooked, lean. **Koosáamu-kshú-wiiwŭníhlaan éenda-aashŭwatéexung, kwŭlúp kpiimíixiin.** 'You drove around the Four Corners too fast and you were leaning.' *ind 1st sg* **mbiimíixiin**, **mbiimíixi**. *conj 3rd sg* **piimíixiing**. *imp* **piimíixiil**. *ptcpl* **piimíixiing**.

**piimíixtoow** VTI2 lean s.t. to one side, put s.t. on crooked. *ind 1st sg* **mbii=míixtoon**. *ind 3rd sg* **piimíixtoon**. *conj 1st sg* **piimiixtáwaan**. *conj 3rd sg* **piimíixtaakw**. *imp* **piimíixtool**. *ptcpl* **piimíixtaakw**.

**piimíixŭmeew** VTA lean s.o. to one side, lean s.t. animate to one side. *ind 1st sg* **mbiimíixŭmaaw**, **mbiimíixŭma**. *ind 3rd sg* **piimiixŭmáawal**. *ind inv* **mbiimíixŭmukw**. *ind I-you* **kpiimíi=xŭmul**. *conj 3rd sg* **piimíixŭmaat**. *imp* **piimíixum**. *ptcpl* **piimíixŭmaat**.

**piimíixun** VII lean over, lean to one side; be on crooked. *conj 3rd sg* **piimíi=xung**. *ptcpl* **piimíixung**.

**piimíhleew** VAI lean to one side. *ind 1st sg* **mbiimíhla**, **mbiimíhlaam**. *conj 3rd sg* **piimíhlaat**. *imp* **piimíhlaal**. *ptcpl* **piimíhlaat**.

**piimíhleew** VII lean to one side. *conj 3rd sg* **piimíhlaak**. *ptcpl* **piimíhlaak**.

**piimihtéeheew** VTA hit s.o. and knock them sideways. *ind 1st sg* **mbiimih=téehaaw**, **mbiimihtéeha**. *ind 3rd sg* **piimihteeháawal**. *ind inv* **mbiimih=téehookw**. *ind I-you* **kpiimihtéehool**. *conj 3rd sg* **piimihtéehaat**. *imp* **piimíhteeh**. *ptcpl* **piimihtéehaat**.

**piimihtéehum** VTI1B hit s.t. and knock it sideways. *ind 1st sg* **mbiimihtée=hŭmun**. *ind 3rd sg* **piimihtéehŭmun**. *conj 1st sg* **piimihtéehŭmaan**. *conj 3rd sg* **piimihtéehung**. *imp* **piimih=téehih**. *ptcpl* **piimihtéehung**.

**piimihtéexiin** VAI fall sideways *(s.t. animate)*. *ind 1st sg* **mbiimihtéexiin**, **mbiimihtéexi**. *conj 3rd sg* **piimih=téexiing**. *ptcpl* **piimihtéexiing**.

**piimihtéexun** VII fall sideways. *conj 3rd sg* **piimihtéexung**. *ptcpl* **piimihtée=xung**.

**piimkaatéeyeew** VII have crooked legs. *conj 3rd sg* **piimkaatéeyeek**. *ptcpl* **piimkaatéeyeek**.

**piimóhkweew** VAI cock one's head, turn one's head, look to the side. *ind 1st sg* **mbiimóhkwe**, **mbiimóhkweem**. *conj 3rd sg* **piimóhkweet**. *imp* **piimóhkweel**. *ptcpl* **piimóhkweet**.

**piimohkwéepuw** VAI sit crookedly. *ind 1st sg* **mbiimohkwéepi**, **mbiimoh=kwéepiim**. *conj 3rd sg* **piimohkwée=piit**. *imp* **piimohkwéepiil**. *ptcpl* **piimohkwéepiit**.

**piimoxkwaníikeew** VAI have crooked teeth. *ind 1st sg* **mbiimoxkwaníika**, **mbiimoxkwaníikaam**. *conj 3rd sg* **piimoxkwaníikaat**. *ptcpl* **piimox=**

**kwaníikaat**.

**piimóxkweew** VII be twisted *(especially of iron). conj 3rd sg* **piimóxkweek**. *ptcpl* **piimóxkweek**.

**piimoxkwíixiin** VAI lie crosswise, be twisted, be at an angle, lie at an angle, be lopsided. *ind 1st sg* **mbii=moxkwíixiin**, **mbiimoxkwíixi**. *conj 3rd sg* **piimoxkwíixiing**. *ptcpl* **piimoxkwíixiing**.

**piimoxkwíixun** VII be twisted, be at an angle, lie at an angle, be lopsided, lie on its side, be misaligned *(of a misbuttoned shirt). conj 3rd sg* **piimox=kwíixung**. *ptcpl* **piimoxkwíixung**.

**piimpóxkwaneew** VAI have a crooked back. *ind 1st sg* **mbiimpóxkwana**, **mbiimpóxkwanaam**. *conj 3rd sg* **piimpóxkwanaat**. *ptcpl* **piimpóx=kwanaat**.

**píimsuw** VAI lean to one side *(s.t. animate). ind 1st sg* **mbíimsi**, **mbíim=siim**. *conj 3rd sg* **píimsiit**. *ptcpl* **píimsiit**.

**píimsheew** VTA cut s.t. animate lopsided, cut s.t. animate unevenly. *ind 1st sg* **mbíimshaaw**, **mbíimsha**. *ind 3rd sg* **piimsháawal**. *ind inv* **mbíimshookw**. *ind I-you* **kpíimshool**. *conj 3rd sg* **píimshaat**. *imp* **píimush**. *ptcpl* **píimshaat**.

**píimshum** VTI 1B cut s.t. lopsided, cut s.t. unevenly. *ind 1st sg* **mbiim=shúmun**. *ind 3rd sg* **piimshúmun**. *conj 1st sg* **piimshúmaan**. *conj 3rd sg* **píimshung**. *imp* **píimshih**. *ptcpl* **píimshung**.

**piimtoonéexiin** VAI have a crooked mouth, have a lopsided mouth. *ind 1st sg* **mbiimtoonéexiin**, **mbiimtoo=néexi**. *conj 3rd sg* **piimtoonéexiing**. *ptcpl* **piimtoonéexiing**.

**píimŭlam** VTI 1A knock s.t. sideways, knock s.t. crooked *(by shot, by physical contact, with a projectile). ind 1st sg* **mbiimŭlámun**. *ind 3rd sg* **piimŭ=lámun**. *conj 1st sg* **piimŭlámaan**. *conj 3rd sg* **píimŭlang**. *imp* **píimŭlah**. *ptcpl* **píimŭlang**.

**piimŭláweew** VTA knock s.o. sideways, knock s.t. crooked *(by shot, by physical contact, with a projectile). ind 1st sg* **mbiimŭláwaaw**, **mbiimŭláwa**. *ind 3rd sg* **piimŭlawáawal**. *ind inv* **mbíimŭlaakw**. *ind I-you* **kpíimŭlool**. *conj 3rd sg* **piimŭláwaat**. *imp* **píimŭlaw**. *ptcpl* **piimŭláwaat**.

**píimŭneew** VTA tilt s.o., tip s.o., cause s.o. to be on the diagonal, bend s.o. *(using the hands). ind 1st sg* **mbíi=mŭnaaw**, **mbíimŭna**. *ind 3rd sg* **piimŭnáawal**. *ind inv* **mbíimŭnukw**. *ind I-you* **kpíimŭnul**. *conj 3rd sg* **píimŭnaat**. *imp* **píimun**. *ptcpl* **píi=mŭnaat**.

**piimŭnáhtaan** NI thread. *pl* **piimŭnah=táanal**. *poss* **mbiimŭnahtáanum**. *dimin* **piimŭnahcháanush**. *See* **piimŭnáhtakw**.

**piimŭnáhtakw** NI thread. *pl* **piimŭnáh=takwal**. *poss* **mbiimŭnáhtakwum**. *loc* **piimŭnáhtakwung**. *dimin* **pii=mŭnáhchakwush**. *See* **piimŭnáh=taan**.

**píimŭnum** VTI 1B tilt s.t., tip s.t., cause s.t. to be on the diagonal, bend s.t. *(using the hands). ind 1st sg* **mbii=mŭnúmun**. *ind 3rd sg* **piimŭnúmun**. *conj 1st sg* **piimŭnúmaan**. *conj 3rd sg* **píimŭnung**. *imp* **píimŭnih**. *ptcpl* **píimŭnung**.

**piimŭnúmaweew** VTA cheat s.o., shortchange s.o. *ind 1st sg* **mbiimŭnúma=waaw**, **mbiimŭnúmawa**. *ind 3rd sg* **piimŭnumawáawal**. *ind inv* **mbii=mŭnúmaakw**. *ind I-you* **kpiimŭ=númool**. *conj 3rd sg* **piimŭnúma=waat**. *imp* **piimŭnúmaw**. *ptcpl* **piimŭnúmawaat**.

**piindáakchehl** VAI jump inside. *ind 1st sg* **mbiindáakchehl**. *conj 3rd sg* **piindaakchéhluk**. *imp* **piindaak=**

**chéhlih**. *ptcpl* **piindaakchéhluk**.

**piindáameew** VAI lie inside, lie inside something. *ind 1st sg* **mbiindáame, mbiindáameem**. *conj 3rd sg* **piin=dáameet**. *imp* **piindáameel**. *ptcpl* **piindáameet**.

**piindáameew** VII lie inside, lie inside something. **Wihtawákal péech-piindaaméewal.** 'He was listening from the other room. ('His ears were lying inside here.')' *conj 3rd sg* **piindáameek**. *ptcpl* **piindáameek**.

**piindahtakíhleew** VAI run inside. *ind 1st sg* **mbiindahtakíhla, mbiindahta=kíhlaam**. *conj 3rd sg* **piindahtakíh=laat**. *imp* **piindahtakíhlaal**. *ptcpl* **piindahtakíhlaat**.

**piindashíikaneew** VAI put on one's socks. *ind 1st sg* **mbiindashíikana, mbiindashíikanaam**. *conj 3rd sg* **piindashíikanaat**. *imp* **piindashíi=kanaal**. *ptcpl* **piindashíikanaat**.

**píindaweew** VTAO put s.t. on for s.o. *(of clothing)*. *ind 1st sg* **mbíindawaan**. *ind 3rd sg* **píindawaan**. *ind inv* **mbiindáakwun**. *ind I-you* **kpiindóo=lun**. *conj 3rd sg* **píindawaat**. *imp* **píindaw**. *ptcpl* **píindawaat**.

**píindham** VTI1A insert s.t., put s.t. inside. *ind 1st sg* **mbiindhámun**. *ind 3rd sg* **piindhámun**. *conj 1st sg* **piindhámaan**. *conj 3rd sg* **píindhang**. *imp* **píindhah**. *ptcpl* **píindhang**.

**piindhéembteew** VAI put on one's shirt. *ind 1st sg* **mbiindhéembta, mbiind=héembtaam**. *conj 3rd sg* **piind=héembtaat**. *imp* **piindhéembtaal**. *ptcpl* **piindhéembtaat**.

**piindhéewaleew** VTA take s.o. inside, take s.t. animate inside, take a load of s.t. animate inside. *ind 1st sg* **mbiind=héewalaaw, mbiindhéewala**. *ind 3rd sg* **piindheewaláawal**. *ind inv* **mbiindhéewalukw**. *ind I-you* **kpiindhéewalul**. *conj 3rd sg* **piind=héewalaat**. *imp* **piindhéewal**. *ptcpl* **piindhéewalaat**.

**piindhéewatoow** VTI2 take s.t. inside, take a load of s.t. inside. *ind 1st sg* **mbiindhéewatoon**. *ind 3rd sg* **piind=héewatoon**. *conj 1st sg* **piindheewa=táwaan**. *conj 3rd sg* **piindhéewa=taakw**. *imp* **piindhéewatool**. *ptcpl* **piindhéewataakw**.

**piindhíikan** NA baloney, sausage. *pl* **piindhíikanak**. *poss* **mbiindhíikan**. *loc* **piindhíikanung**. *dimin* **piinjhíi=kanush**. *obv* **piindhíikanal**.

**piindhíikanush** NA sausage. *pl* **piind=hiikanúshak**. *poss* **mbiindhíikanush**. *loc* **piindhiikanúshung**. *obv* **piind=hiikanúshal**.

**piindóoxwaleew** VTA take s.o. inside, take s.t. animate inside, bring s.o. inside. *ind 1st sg* **mbiindóoxwalaaw, mbiindóoxwala**. *ind 3rd sg* **piindoo=xwaláawal**. *ind inv* **mbiindóoxwa=lukw**. *ind I-you* **kpiindóoxwalul**. *conj 3rd sg* **piindóoxwalaat**. *imp* **piindóoxwal**. *ptcpl* **piindóoxwalaat**.

**piindóoxwatoow** VTI2 take s.t. inside, bring s.t. inside. *ind 1st sg* **mbiin=dóoxwatoon**. *ind 3rd sg* **piindóo=xwatoon**. *conj 1st sg* **piindooxwa=táwaan**. *conj 3rd sg* **piindóoxwa=taakw**. *imp* **piindóoxwatool**. *ptcpl* **piindóoxwataakw**.

**piindshíiheew** VTA take s.o. inside, chase s.o. inside, send s.o. inside; drive s.o. inside *(of animals)*. *ind 1st sg* **mbiindshíihaaw, mbiindshíiha**. *ind 3rd sg* **piindshiiháawal**. *ind inv* **mbiindshíihukw**. *ind I-you* **kpiind=shíihul**. *conj 3rd sg* **piindshíihaat**. *imp* **píindshiih**. *ptcpl* **piindshíihaat**.

**piindshíimuw** VAI run away inside the house, flee inside the house. *ind 1st sg* **mbiindshíimwi, mbiindshíimwiim**. *conj 3rd sg* **piindshíimwiit**. *imp* **piindshíimwiil**. *ptcpl* **piindshíi=mwiit**.

**piindshíhkaweew** VTA chase s.o. inside,

send s.o. inside; drive s.o. inside *(of animals)*. *ind 1st sg* **mbiindshíhka=waaw**, **mbiindshíhkawa**. *ind 3rd sg* **piindshihkawáawal**. *ind inv* **mbiind=shíhkaakw**. *ind I-you* **kpiindshíh=kool**. *conj 3rd sg* **piindshíhkawaat**. *imp* **piindshíhkaw**. *ptcpl* **piindshíh=kawaat**.

**píindŭneew** VTA put s.o. inside. *ind 1st sg* **mbíindŭnaaw**, **mbíindŭna**. *ind 3rd sg* **piindŭnáawal**. *ind inv* **mbíin=dŭnukw**. *ind I-you* **kpíindŭnul**. *conj 3rd sg* **píindŭnaat**. *imp* **píindun**. *ptcpl* **píindŭnaat**.

**piindŭnáasuw** VII be put on, be put inside. **Pasíikaaxkw piindŭnáasuw wíikwahm.** 'The boards were put inside the house.' *conj 3rd sg* **piindŭ=náasiik**. *ptcpl* **piindŭnáasiik**.

**piindŭnahksúneew** VAI put on one's shoes. *ind 1st sg* **mbiindŭnahksúne**, **mbiindŭnahksúneem**. *conj 3rd sg* **piindŭnahksúneet**. *imp* **piindŭnah=ksúneel**. *ptcpl* **piindŭnahksúneet**.

**piindŭnahksunéeneew** VTA put shoes on s.o. *ind 1st sg* **mbiindŭnahksun=éenaaw**, **mbiindŭnahksunéena**. *ind 3rd sg* **piindŭnahksuneenáawal**. *ind inv* **mbiindŭnahksunéenukw**. *ind I-you* **kpiindŭnahksunéenul**. *conj 3rd sg* **piindŭnahksunéenaat**. *imp* **piin=dŭnahksúneen**. *ptcpl* **piindŭnahk=sunéenaat**.

**piindŭniiwándeew** VAI put on one's mitts. *ind 1st sg* **mbiindŭniiwánde**, **mbiindŭniiwándeem**. *conj 3rd sg* **piindŭniiwándeet**. *imp* **piindŭnii=wándeel**. *ptcpl* **piindŭniiwándeet**.

**píindŭnum** VTI1B put s.t. inside. *ind 1st sg* **mbiindŭnúmun**. *ind 3rd sg* **piin=dŭnúmun**. *conj 1st sg* **piindŭnúm=aan**. *conj 3rd sg* **píindŭnung**. *imp* **píindŭnih**. *ptcpl* **píindŭnung**.

**piindxákweew** VAI bring wood inside. *ind 1st sg* **mbiindxákwe**, **mbiind=xákweem**. *conj 3rd sg* **piindxákweet**. *imp* **piindxákweel**. *ptcpl* **piindxák=weet**.

**píinj** NA pin. *pl* **píinjak**. *poss* **mbíinjum**. *loc* **píinjung**. *dimin* **píinjush**. *obv* **píinjal**. *From Dutch.*

**piinjíikeew** VAI come inside. **Péech-piinjíikeew.** 'He came in.' *ind 1st sg* **mbiinjíike**, **mbiinjíikeem**. *conj 3rd sg* **piinjíikeet**. *imp* **piinjíikeel**. *ptcpl* **piinjíikeet**.

**piinjiikéhleew** VAI go inside quickly, run inside, enter a dwelling running. *ind 1st sg* **mbiinjiikéhla**, **mbiinjii=kéhlaam**. *conj 3rd sg* **piinjiikéhlaat**. *imp* **piinjiikéhlaal**. *ptcpl* **piinjiikéh=laat**.

**piinjíikwsuw** VAI crawl inside. **Nál wtúlu- wiikwáhmung -piinjíikw=siin.** 'Then he crawled into the house.' *ind 1st sg* **mbiinjíikwsi**, **mbiinjíikw=siim**. *conj 3rd sg* **piinjíikwsiit**. *imp* **piinjíikwsiil**. *ptcpl* **piinjíikwsiit**.

**piinjiipáhtoow** VAI hurry inside. *ind 1st sg* **mbiinjiipáhto**, **mbiinjiipáhtoom**. *conj 1st sg* **piinjiipahtawaane**. *conj 3rd sg* **piinjiipáhtaakw**. *imp* **piinjii=páhtool**. *ptcpl* **piinjiipáhtaakw**.

**piinjiipáhtoow** VAIO hurry inside with s.t. *ind 1st sg* **mbiinjiipáhtoon**. *ind 3rd sg* **piinjiipáhtoon**. *conj 1st sg* **piinjiipáhtawaan**. *conj 3rd sg* **piin=jiipáhtaakw**. *imp* **piinjiipáhtool**. *ptcpl* **piinjiipáhtaakw**.

**piinjíipheew** VTA hurry inside with s.o. *ind 1st sg* **mbiinjíiphaaw**, **mbiin=jíipha**. *ind 3rd sg* **piinjiiphaawal**. *ind inv* **mbiinjíiphukw**. *ind I-you* **kpiinjíiphul**. *conj 3rd sg* **piinjíiphaat**. *imp* **piinjíipah**. *ptcpl* **piinjíiphaat**.

**piinjíhlatoow** VTI2 put s.t. in, put s.t. inside. *ind 1st sg* **mbiinjíhlatoon**. *ind 3rd sg* **piinjíhlatoon**. *conj 1st sg* **piinjihlatáwaan**. *conj 3rd sg* **piinjíh=lataakw**. *imp* **piinjíhlatool**. *ptcpl* **piinjíhlataakw**.

**piinjíhleew** VAI go inside, fly inside,

drive inside, fall inside. *ind 1st sg* **mbiinjíhla, mbiinjíhlaam**. *conj 3rd sg* **piinjíhlaat**. *imp* **piinjíhlaal**. *ptcpl* **piinjíhlaat**.

**piipíinam** VTI I choose s.t. *ind 1st sg* **mbiipíinamun**. *ind 3rd sg* **piipíina=mun**. *conj 1st sg* **piipíinamaan**. *conj 3rd sg* **piipíinang**. *imp* **piipíinah**. *ptcpl* **piipíinang**.

**piipíinaweew** VTA choose s.o. *ind 1st sg* **mbiipíinawaaw, mbiipíinawa**. *ind 3rd sg* **piipiinawáawal**. *ind inv* **mbii=píinaakw**. *ind I-you* **kpiipíinool**. *conj 3rd sg* **piipíinawaat**. *imp* **piipíinaw**. *ptcpl* **piipíinawaat**.

**píipush** NA man's nickname. *obv* **píipshal**.

**píiskeew** VII be night. **Piiskéeke náh ndá.** 'I went there last night.'; **Piis=kéeke-uch náh ndá.** 'I'll go there tonight.' *conj 3rd sg* **píiskeek**. *ptcpl* **píiskeek**.

**piiskéewŭnii** PC night, at night. **Piiskée=wŭnii áng shúkw.** 'Just at night.'

**piiskéhleew** VII get to be night. *conj 3rd sg* **piiskéhlaak**. *ptcpl* **piiskéhlaak**.

**piisŭlaapéhleew** VII hang loosely, hang limply, hang wrinkled. *conj 3rd sg* **piisŭlaapéhlaak**. *ptcpl* **piisŭlaa=péhlaak**.

**piisŭláapŭlush** NA shrivelled apple. *pl* **piisŭlaapŭlúshak**. *loc* **piisŭlaapŭ=lúshung**. *dimin* **piishŭlaapŭlúshush**. *obv* **piisŭlaapŭlúshal**.

**piisŭlamalúsuw** VAI feel weak. *ind 1st sg* **mbiisŭlamalúsi, mbiisŭlama=lúsiim**. *conj 3rd sg* **piisŭlamalúsiit**. *ptcpl* **piisŭlamalúsiit**.

**píisŭleew** VII be limp; be wrinkled. **Píisŭleew nŭweendakwíiwan.** 'My dress is wrinkled.' *conj 3rd sg* **píisŭleek**. *ptcpl* **píisŭleek**.

**piisŭlíixun** VII be loose, be a loose fit *(of clothes)*. *conj 3rd sg* **piisŭlíixung**. *ptcpl* **piisŭlíixung**.

**piisŭlíhleew** VAI get weak, get shrivelled. *ind 1st sg* **mbiisŭlíhla, mbiisŭlíh=laam**. *conj 3rd sg* **piisŭlíhlaat**. *ptcpl* **piisŭlíhlaat**.

**piisŭlihtáakwat** VII sound weak. *conj 3rd sg* **piisŭlihtáakwahk**. *ptcpl* **piisŭlihtáakwahk**.

**piisŭlihtáakwsuw** VAI sound weak. *ind 1st sg* **mbiisŭlihtáakwsi, mbiisŭlih=táakwsiim**. *conj 3rd sg* **piisŭlih=táakwsiit**. *ptcpl* **piisŭlihtáakwsiit**.

**piisŭlihtéexiin** VAI fall due to be being weak, fall due to being limp. *ind 1st sg* **mbiisŭlihtéexiin, mbiisŭlihtéexi**. *conj 3rd sg* **piisŭlihtéexiing**. *ptcpl* **piisŭlihtéexiing**.

**piisŭlóoxweew** VAI walk limply. *ind 1st sg* **mbiisŭlóoxwe, mbiisŭlóoxweem**. *conj 3rd sg* **piisŭlóoxweet**. *imp* **piisŭ=lóoxweel**. *ptcpl* **piisŭlóoxweet**. *intensive reduplication* **apiisŭlóoxweew**.

**piisŭlúpeew** VAI be soaking wet, be drenched, be limp from water. *ind 1st sg* **mbiisŭlúpe, mbiisŭlúpeem**. *conj 3rd sg* **piisŭlúpeet**. *ptcpl* **piisŭlúpeet**.

**piisŭlúpeew** VII be soaking wet, be drenched, be limp from water. *conj 3rd sg* **piisŭlúpeek**. *ptcpl* **piisŭlúpeek**.

**piisŭlúsuw** VAI be limp, be weak, be a weakling. *ind 1st sg* **mbiisŭlúsi, mbiisŭlúsiim**. *conj 3rd sg* **piisŭlúsiit**. *ptcpl* **piisŭlúsiit**.

**píish** PC indeed, yes; **Píish ndúlaan shukéhla wánsiin.** 'I told him but he still forgot.'; **Píish áa ná káta-alóolaaw.** 'You should hire him.'

**píishkw** NA nighthawk. *pl* **píishkwak**. *obv* **píishkwal**.

**píiwameew** VTA leave scraps of s.t. animate behind, don't eat all of s.t. animate *(of food)*. *ind 1st sg* **mbíiwa=maaw, mbíiwama**. *ind 3rd sg* **piiwa=máawal**. *ind inv* **mbíiwamukw**. *ind I-you* **kpíiwamul**. *conj 3rd sg* **píiwa=maat**. *imp* **píiwam**. *ptcpl* **píiwamaat**.

**piiwándam** VTI I A leave scraps of s.t. behind *(of food)*; don't eat all of s.t.

**Chángiish mbiiwándamun.** 'I left a little bit.' *ind 1st sg* **mbiiwándamun**. *ind 3rd sg* **piiwándamun**. *conj 1st sg* **piiwándamaan**. *conj 3rd sg* **piiwán=dang**. *imp* **piiwándah**. *ptcpl* **piiwán=dang**.

**piiwíiheew** VTA have s.o. remaining, have s.o. left over. *ind 1st sg* **mbii=wíihaaw**, **mbiiwíiha**. *ind 3rd sg* **piiwiiháawal**. *ind inv* **mbiiwíihukw**. *ind I-you* **kpiiwíihul**. *conj 3rd sg* **piiwíihaat**. *ptcpl* **piiwíihaat**.

**piiwíixiin** VAI be left over, be one of the survivors. *ind 1st sg* **mbiiwíixiin**, **mbiiwíixi**. *conj 3rd sg* **piiwíixiing**. *ptcpl* **piiwíixiing**.

**piiwíhleew** VII be left over. *conj 3rd sg* **piiwíhlaak**. *ptcpl* **piiwíhlaak**.

**piiwíhtoow** VTI2 have s.t. remaining, have s.t. left over. *ind 1st sg* **mbiiwíh=toon**. *ind 3rd sg* **piiwíhtoon**. *conj 1st sg* **piiwíhtawaan**. *conj 3rd sg* **pii=wíhtaakw**. *ptcpl* **piiwíhtaakw**.

**píiwŭneew** VTA have s.o. left over, have s.o. unused. *ind 1st sg* **mbíiwŭnaaw**, **mbíiwŭna**. *ind 3rd sg* **piiwŭnáawal**. *ind inv* **mbíiwŭnukw**. *ind I-you* **kpíi=wŭnul**. *conj 3rd sg* **píiwŭnaat**. *imp* **píiwun**. *ptcpl* **píiwŭnaat**.

**píiwŭnum** VTI1B have s.t. left over, have s.t. unused. *ind 1st sg* **mbiiwŭnúm=un**. *ind 3rd sg* **piiwŭnúmun**. *conj 1st sg* **piiwŭnúmaan**. *conj 3rd sg* **píi=wŭnung**. *imp* **píiwŭnih**. *ptcpl* **píiwŭ=nung**.

**píhkeew** VII be numb. **Náxk píhkeew.** 'My hand is numb.' *conj 3rd sg* **píhkeek**. *ptcpl* **píhkeek**.

**píhksuw** VAI be numb *(s.t. animate)*. **Pasíi mbíhksi.** 'I'm half numb (of someone who had a stroke).' *ind 1st sg* **mbíhksi**, **mbíhksiim**. *conj 3rd sg* **píhksiit**. *ptcpl* **píhksiit**.

**píhkŭweew** VII be numb. *conj 3rd sg* **píhkŭweek**. *ptcpl* **píhkŭweek**.

**pihkŭwíhleew** VAI get numb. *ind 1st sg* **mbihkŭwíhla**, **mbihkŭwíhlaam**. *conj 3rd sg* **pihkŭwíhlaat**. *ptcpl* **pihkŭwíhlaat**.

**pihkŭwíhleew** VII get numb. *conj 3rd sg* **pihkŭwíhlaak**. *ptcpl* **pihkŭwíhlaak**.

**pihkŭwúsuw** VAI be numb *(s.t. animate)*. **Pihkŭwúsuw ngútko.** 'My knee is numb.' *ind 1st sg* **mbihkŭ=wúsi**, **mbihkŭwúsiim**. *conj 3rd sg* **pihkŭwúsiit**. *ptcpl* **pihkŭwúsiit**.

**pihkwamálsuw** VAI feel numb, have a sensation of numbness. *ind 1st sg* **mbihkwamálsi**, **mbihkwamálsiim**. *conj 3rd sg* **pihkwamálsiit**. *ptcpl* **pihkwamálsiit**.

**pihkwíhleew** VAI get numb *(s.t. animate)*. *ind 1st sg* **mbihkwíhla**, **mbihkwíh=laam**. *conj 3rd sg* **pihkwíhlaat**. *ptcpl* **pihkwíhlaat**.

**pihpiischàlíingweew** VAI have a wrinkled face. *ind 1st sg* **mbihpiischàl=íingwa**, **mbihpiischàlíingwaam**. *conj 3rd sg* **pihpiischàlíingwaat**. *ptcpl* **pihpiischàlíingwaat**. *See* **pihpiisŭlíingweew**.

**pihpiisŭlíingweew** VAI have a wrinkled face. *ind 1st sg* **mbihpiisŭlíingwa**, **mbihpiisŭlíingwaam**. *conj 3rd sg* **pihpiisŭlíingwaat**. *ptcpl* **pihpiisŭ=líingwaat**. *See* **pihpiischàlíingweew**.

**pihpiisŭlunáxkee** VAI have wrinkled hands. *ind 1st sg* **mbihpiisŭlunáxke**, **mbihpiisŭlunáxkeem**. *conj 3rd sg* **pihpiisŭlunáxkeet**. *ptcpl* **pihpiisŭ=lunáxkeet**.

**pihpíhtawi-takwápuw** VAI have two wives. *ind 1st sg* **mbihpíhtawi-takwápi**, **mbihpíhtawi-takwápiim**. *conj 3rd sg* **pihpíhtawi-takwápiit**. *ptcpl* **pihpíhtawi-takwápiit**.

**píht** PC maybe, perhaps. **Píht éet katá-wíineew.** 'Maybe it will snow.'; **Píht áa kíish- áa -kawíim.** 'You might be able to sleep.'

**píhtameew** VTA eat s.t. animate by accident. *ind 1st sg* **mbíhtamaaw**, **mbíh=**

**tama**. *ind 3rd sg* **pihtamáawal**. *ind inv* **mbíhtamukw**. *ind I-you* **kpíh=tamul**. *conj 3rd sg* **píhtamaat**. *ptcpl* **píhtamaat**. *See* **pahtamáawal**.

**pihtándam** VTI 1A eat s.t. by accident. *ind 1st sg* **mbihtándamun**. *ind 3rd sg* **pihtándamun**. *conj 1st sg* **pihtán=damaan**. *conj 3rd sg* **pihtándang**. *ptcpl* **pihtándang**. *See* **pahtánda=mun**.

**pihtawahéembteew** VAI wear an extra shirt. *ind 1st sg* **mbihtawahéembta**, **mbihtawahéembtaam**. *conj 3rd sg* **pihtawahéembtaat**. *imp* **pihtawah=éembtaal**. *ptcpl* **pihtawahéembtaat**.

**pihtawáhksun** NI rubber overshoe. *pl* **pihtawahksúnal**. *poss* **mbihtawáh=ksun**. *loc* **pihtawahksúnung**. *dimin* **pihchawahkshúnush**.

**pihtawahksúneew** VAI wear more than one pair of shoes, wear more than one layer of footwear; wear overshoes. *ind 1st sg* **mbihtawahksúne**, **mbih=tawahksúneem**. *conj 3rd sg* **pihta=wahksúneet**. *imp* **pihtawahksúneel**. *ptcpl* **pihtawahksúneet**.

**pihtawákuw** VAI have (extra) clothes in layers, have on more clothes than someone else. **Nxú mbihtawákwi.** 'I am covered in three layers, I am dressed in three layers.' *ind 1st sg* **mbihtawákwi**, **mbihtawákwiim**. *conj 3rd sg* **pihtawákwiit**. *imp* **pihtawákwiil**. *ptcpl* **pihtawákwiit**.

**pihtawashíikaneew** VAI wear more than one pair of socks. *ind 1st sg* **mbihta=washíikane**, **mbihtawashíikaneem**. *conj 3rd sg* **pihtawashíikaneet**. *imp* **pihtawashíikaneel**. *ptcpl* **pihta=washíikaneet**.

**píhtaweew** VII be in layers, be double. **Níishu-píhtawe.** 'It is in two layers.'; **Nxéeli píhtaweew.** 'It's in three layers.' *conj 3rd sg* **píhtaweek**. *ptcpl* **píhtaweek**.

**pihtawii-** PV double, doubled, one over the other. **Mbíhtawii-pambiilhíike.** 'I papered over the other wallpaper.' *ptcpl* **píhtawii-**.

**pihtawíikaan** NI lean-to *(addition to house)*. *pl* **pihtawiikáanal**. *poss* **mbihtawiikáanum**. *loc* **pihtawii=káanung**. *dimin* **pihtawiikáanush**.

**pihtawiikaapawúwak** VAI stand in rows, stand several deep. *usually plural*. *ind 1st pl* **mbihtawiikaapawíh=na**. *conj 3rd sg* **pihtawiikaapawíh=tiit**. *imp* **pihtawiikáapawiikw**. *ptcpl* **pihtawiikaapawíhtiit**.

**pihtawiikóoteew** VAI wear more than one coat. *ind 1st sg* **mbihtawiikóote**, **mbihtawiikóoteem**. *conj 3rd sg* **pih=tawiikóoteet**. *imp* **pihtawiikóoteel**. *ptcpl* **pihtawiikóoteet**.

**pihtawíikun** VII grow double. *conj 3rd sg* **pihtawíikung**. *ptcpl* **pihtawíi=kung**.

**pihtawíikuw** VAI grow double. *ind 1st sg* **mbihtawíiki**, **mbihtawíikiim**. *conj 3rd sg* **pihtawíikiit**. *ptcpl* **pihtawíi=kiit**.

**pihtawiikwáakan** NI lining *(of coats, of quilts)*. *pl* **pihtawiikwáakanal**. *poss* **mbihtawiikwáakan**. *loc* **pihtawii=kwáakanung**. *dimin* **pihchawii=kwáakanush**.

**pihtawiikwáaleew** VTA make a lining in s.t. animate. *ind 1st sg* **mbihtawii=kwáalaaw**, **mbihtawiikwáala**. *ind 3rd sg* **pihtawiikwaaláawal**. *ind inv* **mbihtawiikwáalukw**. *ind I-you* **kpihtawiikwáalul**. *conj 3rd sg* **pih=tawiikwáalaat**. *imp* **pihtawíikwaal**. *ptcpl* **pihtawiikwáalaat**.

**pihtawíikwam** VTI 1A make a lining for s.t. *ind 1st sg* **mbihtawíikwamun**. *ind 3rd sg* **pihtawíikwamun**. *conj 1st sg* **pihtawíikwamaan**. *conj 3rd sg* **pihtawíikwang**. *imp* **pihtawíikwah**. *ptcpl* **pihtawíikwang**.

**pihtawiipŭlóokeew** VAI wear more than one pair of pants. *ind 1st sg* **mbihta=**

wiipŭlóoka, mbihtawiipŭlóokaam. *conj 3rd sg* **pihtawiipŭlóokaat**. *imp* **pihtawiipŭlóokaal**. *ptcpl* **pihtawii=pŭlóokaat**.

**pihtawíixiin** VAI be double, lie double, be in layers *(s.t. animate)*. *ind 1st sg* **mbihtawíixiin, mbihtawíixi**. *conj 3rd sg* **pihtawíixiing**. *ptcpl* **pihtawíi=xiing, pihtawíixiit**.

**pihtawíixtoow** VTI2 make s.t. be double, cause s.t. to be double, lay s.t. in a layer on top of something else. *ind 1st sg* **mbihtawíixtoon**. *ind 3rd sg* **pihtawíixtoon**. *conj 1st sg* **pihta=wiixtáwaan**. *conj 3rd sg* **pihtawíix=taakw**. *imp* **pihtawíixtool**. *ptcpl* **pihtawíixtaakw**. *intensive reduplication* **pihpihtawíixtoon**.

**pihtawíixŭmeew** VTA make s.t. animate be double, cause s.t. animate to be double, lay s.t. animate in a layer on top of something else. *ind 1st sg* **mbihtawíixŭmaaw, mbihtawíixŭ=ma**. *ind 3rd sg* **pihtawiixŭmáawal**. *ind inv* **mbihtawíixŭmukw**. *ind I-you* **kpihtawíixŭmul**. *conj 3rd sg* **pihta=wíixŭmaat**. *imp* **pihtawíixum**. *ptcpl* **pihtawíixŭmaat**.

**pihtawíixun** VII be double, lie double, be in layers. **Niishéeli pihtawíixŭ=nool wiikwáhmal.** 'Two-story houses.' *conj 3rd sg* **pihtawíixung**. *ptcpl* **pihtawíixung**. *intensive reduplication* **pihpihtawíixun**.

**pihtawúsuw** VAI be in layers, be double *(s.t. animate)*. *ind 1st sg* **mbihtawúsi, mbihtawúsiim**. *conj 3rd sg* **pihta=wúsiit**. *ptcpl* **pihtawúsiit**.

**píhteew** NI foam.

**pihteewáapŭweew** VII be a foamy liquid. *conj 3rd sg* **pihteewáapŭweek**. *ptcpl* **pihteewáapŭweek**.

**píhtsheew** VTA cut s.o. by accident, cut s.t. animate by accident. *ind 1st sg* **mbíhtshaaw, mbíhtsha**. *ind 3rd sg* **pihtsháawal**. *ind inv* **mbíht=shookw**. *ind I-you* **kpíhtshool**. *conj 3rd sg* **píhtshaat**. *See* **páhtsheew**.

**píhtshum** VTI1B cut s.t. by accident. *ind 1st sg* **mbihtshúmun**. *ind 3rd sg* **pihtshúmun**. *conj 1st sg* **pihtshúm=aan**. *conj 3rd sg* **píhtshung**. *ptcpl* **píhtshung**. *See* **páhtshum**.

**píind** VTI3 put s.t. on *(of clothing)*. **Mbíindun mbulóokum.** 'I put my pants on.' *ind 1st sg* **mbíindun**. *ind 3rd sg* **píindun**. *conj 1st sg* **píinda=waan**. *conj 3rd sg* **píinduk**. *imp* **píindih**. *ptcpl* **píinduk**.

**píkchul** NA picture. *pl* **pìkchúlak**. *poss* **mbikchúlum**. *loc* **pìkchúlung**. *dimin* **pìkchúlush**. *obv* **pìkchúlal**. *From English* picture.

**pimpŭlíingweew** VAI have pimples on one's face. *ind 1st sg* **mbimpŭlíin=gwa, mbimpŭlíingwaam**. *conj 3rd sg* **pimpŭlíingwaat**. *ptcpl* **pimpŭ=líingwaat**. *From English* pimple.

**pkóhkweew** VAI look through a hole, look through an opening, look through something. *ind 1st sg* **mbukóhkwe, mbukóhkweem**. *conj 3rd sg* **pkóh=kweet**. *imp* **pkóhkweel**. *ptcpl* **pee=kóhkweet**.

**pkúw** NA gum, pitch. *poss* **mbukóohum**. *dimin* **pkúwush**. *obv* **pkúwal**.

**pkwáaheew** VAIO throw something through a hole; drop s.t. in a hole. *ind 1st sg* **mbukwáaheen**. *ind 3rd sg* **pukwáaheen**. *conj 3rd sg* **pkwáaheet**. *imp* **pkwáaheel**. *ptcpl* **peekwáaheet**.

**pkwáakchehl** VAI jump through a hole. *ind 1st sg* **mbukwáakchehl**. *conj 3rd sg* **pkwaakchéhluk**. *imp* **pkwaak=chéhlih**. *ptcpl* **peekwaakchéhluk**.

**pkwáham** VTI1A make a hole in s.t. *(using a tool or instrument)*. *ind 1st sg* **mbukhwámun**. *ind 3rd sg* **pùk=hwámun**. *conj 1st sg* **pkwáhŭmaan**. *conj 3rd sg* **pkwáhang**. *imp* **pkwáhih**. *ptcpl* **péekhwang**.

**pkwáheew** VTA make a hole in s.t. animate *(using a tool or instrument)*. *ind 1st sg* **mbúkhwaaw**, **mbúkhwa**. *ind 3rd sg* **pùkhwáawal**. *ind inv* **mbúk=hookw**. *ind I-you* **kpúkhool**. *conj 3rd sg* **pkwáhaat**. *imp* **pkwáh**. *ptcpl* **péekhwaat**.

**pkwahiingwéexiin** VAI look out from an opening. *ind 1st sg* **mbukhwiin=gwéexiin**, **mbukhwiingwéexi**. *conj 3rd sg* **pkwahiingwéexiing**. *imp* **pkwahiingwéexiil**. *ptcpl* **peekhwiin=gwéexiing**.

**pkwaskwíhleew** VAI fall through the ice. *ind 1st sg* **mbukwaskwíhla**, **mbuk=waskwíhlaam**. *conj 3rd sg* **pkwas=kwíhlaat**. *imp* **pkwaskwíhlaal**. *ptcpl* **peekwaskwíhlaat**.

**pkwát** VII have a hole, be a hole. *conj 3rd sg* **pkwáhk**. *ptcpl* **péekwahk**. *intensive reduplication* **pápkwat**.

**pkwiikanáaxiin** VAI have bedsores. *ind 1st sg* **mbukwiikanáaxiin**, **mbuk=wiikanáaxi**. *conj 3rd sg* **pkwiika=náaxiing**. *ptcpl* **peekwiikanáaxiing**.

**pkwíikwsuw** VAI crawl through an opening. *ind 1st sg* **mbukwíikwsi**, **mbuk=wíikwsiim**. *conj 3rd sg* **pkwíikwsiit**. *imp* **pkwíikwsiil**. *ptcpl* **peekwíikw=siit**.

**pkwíhkam** VTI 1A make a hole in s.t. *(using the foot or body)*. *ind 1st sg* **mbukwíhkamun**. *ind 3rd sg* **pùk=wíhkamun**. *conj 1st sg* **pkwíhka=maan**. *conj 3rd sg* **pkwíhkang**. *imp* **pkwíhkah**. *ptcpl* **peekwíhkang**.

**pkwíhkaweew** VTA step on s.o. and make a hole in them. *ind 1st sg* **mbukwíh=kawaaw**, **mbukwíhkawa**. *ind 3rd sg* **pukwihkawáawal**. *ind inv* **mbuk=wíhkaakw**. *ind I-you* **kpukwíhkool**. *conj 3rd sg* **pkwíhkawaat**. *imp* **pkwíhkaw**. *ptcpl* **peekwíhkawaat**.

**pkwíhleew** VAI fall through an opening. *ind 1st sg* **mbukwíhla**, **mbukwíh=laam**. *conj 3rd sg* **pkwíhlaat**. *ptcpl* **peekwíhlaat**.

**pkwíhleew** VII fall through an opening. *conj 3rd sg* **pkwíhlaak**. *ptcpl* **pee=kwíhlaak**.

**pkwihtéeham** VTI 1A hit s.t. and make a hole in it. *ind 1st sg* **mbukwihtéehŭ=mun**. *ind 3rd sg* **pukwihtéehŭmun**. *conj 1st sg* **pkwihtéehŭmaan**. *conj 3rd sg* **pkwihtéehang**. *imp* **pkwih=téehih**. *ptcpl* **peekwihtéehang**.

**pkwihtéeheew** VTA hit s.o. and make a hole in them. *ind 1st sg* **mbukwih=téehaaw**, **mbukwihtéeha**. *ind 3rd sg* **pukwihteeháawal**. *ind inv* **mbuk=wihtéehookw**. *ind I-you* **kpukwih=téehool**. *conj 3rd sg* **pkwihtéehaat**. *imp* **pkwíhteeh**. *ptcpl* **peekwihtée=haat**.

**pkwihteehíikan** NI awl, chisel. *pl* **pkwihteehíikanal**. *poss* **mbukwih=teehíikan**. *loc* **pkwihteehíikanung**. *dimin* **pkwihcheehíikanush**.

**pkwuchéeneew** VTA open s.t. animate up, operate on s.o. *(as a doctor)*; make a hole in s.o., take the insides out of s.o. **Pkwuchéenaaw.** 'He had an operation.' *ind 1st sg* **mbukwchée=naaw**, **mbukwchéena**. *ind 3rd sg* **pukwcheenáawal**. *ind inv* **mbukw=chéenukw**. *ind I-you* **kpukwchéenul**. *conj 3rd sg* **pkwuchéenaat**. *imp* **pkwúcheen**. *ptcpl* **peekwchéenaat**.

**pkwucheenáasuw** VII have a hole made in it. *conj 3rd sg* **pkwucheenáasiik**. *ptcpl* **peekwcheenáasiik**.

**pkwucheeníikeew** VAI operate *(of doctors)*; take out the insides of things. *ind 1st sg* **mbukwcheeníike**, **mbukwcheeníikeem**. *conj 3rd sg* **pkwucheeníikeet**. *imp* **pkwuchee=níikeel**. *ptcpl* **peekwcheeníikeet**.

**pkwuchéenum** VTI 1B make a hole in s.t., open s.t. up. *ind 1st sg* **mbukwchée=nŭmun**. *ind 3rd sg* **pukwchéenŭmun**. *conj 1st sg* **pkwuchéenŭmaan**. *conj 3rd sg* **pkwuchéenung**. *imp* **pkwuch=éenih**. *ptcpl* **peekwchéenung**.

**pkwukáateew** VAI have a hole in one's leg. *ind 1st sg* **mbukwkáata, mbuk=wkáataam**. *conj 3rd sg* **pkwukáa=taat**. *ptcpl* **peekwkáataat**.

**pkwúlam** VTI1A make a hole in s.t. by forceful contact, make a hole in s.t. with an instrument, make a hole in s.t. with a projectile. *ind 1st sg* **mbukwŭlámun**. *ind 3rd sg* **pukwŭ=lámun**. *conj 1st sg* **pkwúlamaan**. *conj 3rd sg* **pkwúlang**. *imp* **pkwúlah**. *ptcpl* **péekwŭlang**.

**pkwúlaweew** VTA make a hole in s.t. animate by forceful contact, make a hole in s.t. animate with an instrument, make a hole in s.t. animate with a projectile. *ind 1st sg* **mbuk=wŭláwaaw, mbukwŭláwa**. *ind 3rd sg* **pukwŭlawáawal**. *ind inv* **mbúk=wŭlaakw**. *ind I-you* **kpúkwŭlool**. *conj 3rd sg* **pkwúlawaat**. *imp* **pkwúlaw**. *ptcpl* **peekwŭláwaat**.

**pkwúneew** VTA make a hole in s.o., make a hole in s.t. animate. *ind 1st sg* **mbúkwŭnaaw, mbúkwŭna**. *ind 3rd sg* **pukwŭnáawal**. *ind inv* **mbúkwŭ=nukw**. *ind I-you* **kpúkwŭnul**. *conj 3rd sg* **pkwúnaat**. *imp* **pkwún**. *ptcpl* **péekwŭnaat**.

**pkwúnum** VTI1B insert s.t. in a hole, make a hole in s.t. *(using the hands)*. *ind 1st sg* **mbukwŭnúmun**. *ind 3rd sg* **pùkwŭnúmun**. *conj 1st sg* **pkwúnŭmaan**. *conj 3rd sg* **pkwún=ung**. *imp* **pkwúnih**. *ptcpl* **péekwŭ=nung**.

**pkwusiitéeyeew** VII have a hole in the sole of something *(of shoes or boots)*. *conj 3rd sg* **pkwusiitéeyeek**. *ptcpl* **peekwsiitéeyeek**.

**pkwúsuw** VAI have a hole, have holes *(s.t. animate)*. **Pámbiil pkwúsuw.** 'The paper has holes in it.' *ind 1st sg* **mbúkwsi, mbúkwsiim**. *conj 3rd sg* **pkwúsiit**. *ptcpl* **péekwsiit**.

**pkwúsheew** VTA cut a hole in s.o. *ind 1st sg* **mbúkwshaaw, mbúkwsha**. *ind 3rd sg* **pùkwsháawal**. *ind inv* **mbúkwshookw**. *ind I-you* **kpúkw=shool**. *conj 3rd sg* **pkwúshaat**. *imp* **pkwúsh**. *ptcpl* **péekwshaat**.

**pkwushéesuw** VAI have a hole in it *(s.t animate)*. *ind 1st sg* **mbukwshéesi, mbukwshéesiim**. *conj 3rd sg* **pkwushéesiit**. *ptcpl* **peekwshéesiit**.

**pkwushéeyeew** VII have a hole, be a hole in something. *conj 3rd sg* **pkwushéeyeek**. *ptcpl* **peekwshée=yeek**.

**pkwushíikan** NI awl. *pl* **pkwushíika=nal**. *poss* **mbukwshíikan**. *loc* **pkwushíikanung**. *dimin* **pkwushíi=kanush**.

**pkwushíikeew** VAI cut holes in things. *ind 1st sg* **mbukwshíike, mbukw=shíikeem**. *conj 3rd sg* **pkwushíikeet**. *imp* **pkwushíikeel**. *ptcpl* **peekw=shíikeet**.

**pkwúshum** VTI1B cut a hole in s.t. *ind 1st sg* **mbukwshúmun**. *ind 3rd sg* **pùkwshúmun**. *conj 1st sg* **pkwúsh=ŭmaan**. *conj 3rd sg* **pkwúshung**. *imp* **pkwúshih**. *ptcpl* **péekwshung**.

**póocheew** VII be the inside angle of a corner. **Eénda-póocheek máw-níipatool chiikhíikan.** 'Go stand the broom in the corner.' *conj 3rd sg* **póocheek**. *ptcpl* **póocheek**.

**pooktiimáakwsuw** VAI smell like a fart. *ind 1st sg* **mbooktiimáakwsi, mbooktiimáakwsiim**. *conj 3rd sg* **pooktiimáakwsiit**. *ptcpl* **pooktii=máakwsiit**.

**pooktohkwéepuw** VAI fart while sitting down. *ind 1st sg* **mbooktohkwéepi, mbooktohkwéepiim**. *conj 3rd sg* **pooktohkwéepiit**. *ptcpl* **pooktoh=kwéepiit**.

**pooktóngwaam** VAI fart while sleeping. *ind 1st sg* **mbooktóngwaam, mbooktóngwaam**. *conj 3rd sg* **pooktóngwaang**. *ptcpl* **pooktón=**

**gwaang**.

**póoktuw** VAI fart. **Katá-póoktuw.** 'He wants to fart.' *ind 1st sg* **mbóokti**, **mbóoktiim**. *conj 3rd sg* **póoktiit**. *ptcpl* **póoktiit**.

**póoleew** VTA escape from s.o. *ind 1st sg* **mbóolaaw**, **mbóola**. *ind 3rd sg* **pooláawal**. *ind inv* **mbóolukw**. *ind I-you* **kpóolul**. *conj 3rd sg* **póolaat**. *imp* **póol**. *ptcpl* **póolaat**.

**póolŭweew** VAI escape. *ind 1st sg* **mbóolŭwe**, **mbóolŭweem**. *conj 3rd sg* **póolŭweet**. *imp* **póolŭweel**. *ptcpl* **póolŭweet**.

**poonáaheew** VAIO let go of s.o., let go of s.t. *ind 1st sg* **mboonáaheen**. *ind 3rd sg* **poonáaheen**. *conj 3rd sg* **poo=náaheet**. *imp* **poonáaheel**. *ptcpl* **poonáaheet**.

**póond** NI pound. *singular only, usually with number prenoun*. **Níish-poond txu-poondakúsuw.** 'He weighs two pounds.'; **Ngwútaash txú-poonda=kúsuw.** 'He weighs six pounds.' *From Dutch*.

**póondakat** VII weigh a certain amount, have a certain weight. *usually with number particle*. **Kéexu póondakat?** 'How much does it weigh?'; **Níishu póondakat.** 'It weighs two pounds.' *conj 3rd sg* **póondakahk**. *ptcpl* **póondakahk**. *From Dutch*.

**poondakúsuw** VAI weigh a certain amount, have a certain weight *(s.t. animate)*. *usually with number particle*. **Néewa poondakúsŭwak.** 'They weigh four pounds.' *ind 1st sg* **mboondakúsi**, **mboondakúsiim**. *conj 3rd sg* **poondakúsiit**. *ptcpl* **poondakúsiit**. *From Dutch*.

**poondháasuw** VAI be weighed *(s.t. animate)*. *ind 1st sg* **mboondháasi**, **mboondháasiim**. *conj 3rd sg* **poond=háasiit**. *ptcpl* **poondháasiit**. *From Dutch*.

**poondháasuw** VII be weighed. *conj 3rd sg* **poondháasiit**. *ptcpl* **poondháa=siik**. *From Dutch*.

**póondham** VTI1A weigh s.t. *ind 1st sg* **mboondhámun**. *ind 3rd sg* **poond=hámun**. *conj 1st sg* **poondhámaan**. *conj 3rd sg* **póondhang**. *imp* **póond=hah**. *ptcpl* **póondhang**. *From Dutch*.

**póondheew** VAIO weigh s.o., weigh s.t. *ind 1st sg* **mbóondheen**. *ind 3rd sg* **póondheen**. *conj 3rd sg* **póondheet**. *imp* **póondheel**. *ptcpl* **póondheet**. *From Dutch*.

**póondheew** VTA weigh s.o. *ind 1st sg* **mbóondhaaw**, **mbóondha**. *ind 3rd sg* **poondháawal**. *ind inv* **mbóond=hookw**. *ind I-you* **kpóondhool**. *conj 3rd sg* **póondhaat**. *imp* **póondhaw**. *ptcpl* **póondhaat**. *From Dutch*.

**poondhíikan** NI measuring scales. *pl* **poondhíikanal**. *poss* **mboondhíikan**. *loc* **poondhíikanung**. *dimin* **poonj=híikanush**. *From Dutch*.

**poondhíikeew** VAI weigh things. *ind 1st sg* **mboondhíike**, **mboondhíikeem**. *conj 3rd sg* **poondhíikeet**. *imp* **poondhíikeel**. *ptcpl* **poondhíikeet**. *From Dutch*.

**poonéelŭmeew** VTA give up on s.o.; let go of s.o. *(especially of someone who has died)*. *ind 1st sg* **mboonéelŭ=maaw**, **mboonéelŭma**. *ind 3rd sg* **pooneelŭmáawal**. *ind inv* **mboonée=lŭmukw**. *ind I-you* **kpoonéelŭmul**. *conj 3rd sg* **poonéelŭmaat**. *imp* **poonéelum**. *ptcpl* **poonéelŭmaat**.

**pooneelundáasuw** VAI forgive people. *ind 1st sg* **mbooneelundáasi**, **mboo=neelundáasiim**. *conj 3rd sg* **poonee=lundáasiit**. *ptcpl* **pooneelundáasiit**.

**pooneelundáasuw** VII be forgiven. *conj 3rd sg* **pooneelundáasiik**. *ptcpl* **pooneelundáasiik**.

**pooneelúndam** VTI1A give s.t. up, let go of s.t.; let s.t. go *(of debts)*. *ind 1st sg* **mbooneelúndamun**. *ind 3rd sg* **poo=neelúndamun**. *conj 1st sg* **poonee=**

**lúndamaan**. *conj 3rd sg* **pooneelún=dang**. *imp* **pooneelúndah**. *ptcpl* **pooneelúndang**.

**pooneelundamáweew** VTA forgive s.o. *ind 1st sg* **mbooneelundamáwaaw**, **mbooneelundamáwa**. *ind 3rd sg* **pooneelundamawáawal**. *ind inv* **mbooneelúndamaakw**. *ind I-you* **kpooneelúndamool**. *conj 3rd sg* **pooneelundamáwaat**. *imp* **poonee=lúndamaw**. *ptcpl* **pooneelunda=máwaat**.

**pooneelundamuwáakan** NI forgiveness.

**pooníiheew** VTA leave s.o. alone, have nothing to with s.o., let s.o. go, give up on s.o., break up with s.o., give up making s.t. animate. *ind 1st sg* **mboo=níihaaw**, **mbooníiha**. *ind 3rd sg* **poo=niiháawal**. *ind inv* **mbooníihukw**. *ind I-you* **kpooníihul**. *conj 3rd sg* **poo=níihaat**. *imp* **póoniih**. *ptcpl* **pooníi=haat**.

**pooníhtoow** VTI2 let s.t. go, give s.t. up, give up doing s.t., give up making s.t. *ind 1st sg* **mbooníhtoon**. *ind 3rd sg* **pooníhtoon**. *conj 1st sg* **pooníhta=waan**. *conj 3rd sg* **pooníhtaakw**. *imp* **pooníhtool**. *ptcpl* **pooníhtaakw**.

**póonŭneew** VTA let go of s.o., give s.o. up, let s.o. go, free s.o. *ind 1st sg* **mbóonŭnaaw**, **mbóonŭna**. *ind 3rd sg* **poonŭnáawal**. *ind inv* **mbóonŭ=nukw**. *ind I-you* **kpóonŭnul**. *conj 3rd sg* **póonŭnaat**. *imp* **póonun**. *ptcpl* **póonŭnaat**.

**póonŭnum** VTI1B let go of s.t., give s.t. up. *ind 1st sg* **mboonŭnúmun**. *ind 3rd sg* **poonŭnúmun**. *conj 1st sg* **poonŭ=númaan**. *conj 3rd sg* **póonŭnung**. *imp* **póonŭnih**. *ptcpl* **póonŭnung**.

**póonxeew** VAI put wood on the fire. **Noosáamu- askxákwal -póonxe.** 'I put in too much green wood.' *ind 1st sg* **mbóonxe**, **mbóonxeem**. *conj 3rd sg* **póonxeet**. *imp* **póonxeel**. *ptcpl* **póonxeet**.

**poosáakchehl** VAI jump on board. *ind 1st sg* **mboosáakchehl**. *conj 3rd sg* **poosaakchéhluk**. *imp* **poosaak=chéhlih**. *ptcpl* **poosaakchéhluk**.

**póosiiw** VAI-S get on board a vehicle. *ind 1st sg* **mbóosi**, **mbóosiim**. *conj 3rd sg* **póosiit**. *imp* **póosiil**. *ptcpl* **póosiit**.

**poosóoleew** VTA give s.o. a ride. *ind 1st sg* **mboosóolaaw**, **mboosóola**. *ind 3rd sg* **poosooláawal**. *ind inv* **mboo=sóolukw**. *ind I-you* **kpoosóolul**. *conj 3rd sg* **poosóolaat**. *imp* **póosool**. *ptcpl* **poosóolaat**.

**póoshiish** NA cat. *pl* **pooshíishak**. *poss* **mbooshíishum**. *dimin* **pooshíishush**. *obv* **pooshíishal**. *From Dutch.*

**pooshíish'chuy** NI cat excrement, cat droppings. *loc* **pooshíish'chiing**.

**póosht** NI post, fencepost. *pl* **póoshtal**. *poss* **mbóoshtum**. *loc* **póoshtung**. *dimin* **póoshchush**. *From English* post.

**pootáaleew** VTA blow at s.o., blow on s.o. *ind 1st sg* **mbootáalaaw**, **mbootáala**. *ind 3rd sg* **pootaaláawal**. *ind inv* **mbootáalukw**. *ind I-you* **kpootáalul**. *conj 3rd sg* **pootáalaat**. *imp* **póotaal**. *ptcpl* **pootáalaat**. *intensive reduplication* **pohpootaaláawal**.

**pootáatam** VTI1A blow at s.t., blow on s.t. *ind 1st sg* **mbootáatŭmun**. *ind 3rd sg* **pootáatŭmun**. *conj 1st sg* **pootáatŭmaan**. *conj 3rd sg* **pootáa=tang**. *imp* **pootáatih**. *ptcpl* **pootáa=tang**. *intensive reduplication* **poh=pootáatamun**.

**pootaatíikan** NA horn. *pl* **pootaatíika=nak**. *poss* **mbootaatíikan**. *loc* **poo=taatíikanung**. *dimin* **poochaachíi=kanush**. *obv* **pootaatíikanal**.

**pootaatíikanush** NA whistle. *pl* **poo=taatiikanúshak**. *poss* **mbootaatíi=kanush**. *loc* **pootaatiikanúshung**. *obv* **pootaatiikanúshal**.

**pootaatíikeew** VAI blow at things, blow

on things. *ind 1st sg* **mbootaatíike**, **mbootaatíikeem**. *conj 3rd sg* **poo=taatíikeet**. *imp* **pootaatíikeel**. *ptcpl* **pootaatíikeet**.

**pooteewáatamiiw** NA Potawatomi. *pl* **pooteewaatamíiwak**. *obv* **pootee=waatamíiwal**.

**pooteewaatamíixsuw** VAI speak Potawatomi. *ind 1st sg* **mbooteewaata=míixsi**, **mbooteewaatamíixsiim**. *conj 3rd sg* **pooteewaatamíixsiit**. *imp* **pooteewaatamíixsiil**. *ptcpl* **pootee=waatamíixsiit**.

**póotul** NI butter. *poss* **mbóotŭlum**. *loc* **póotŭlung**. *dimin* **póochŭlush**. *From Dutch.*

**pootŭláham** VTI1A put butter on s.t. *ind 1st sg* **mbootŭláhŭmun**. *ind 3rd sg* **pootŭláhŭmun**. *conj 1st sg* **pootŭ=láhŭmaan**. *conj 3rd sg* **pootŭláhang**. *imp* **pootŭláhih**. *ptcpl* **pootŭláhang**.

**pootŭláheew** VAI make butter. *ind 1st sg* **mbootŭláhe**, **mbootŭláheem**. *conj 3rd sg* **pootŭláheet**. *imp* **pootŭláheel**. *ptcpl* **pootŭláheet**. *See* **pootŭlah=íikeew**.

**pootŭláheew** VTA put butter on s.t. animate *(using a tool or instrument)*. *ind 1st sg* **mbootŭláhaaw**, **mbootŭláha**. *ind 3rd sg* **pootŭlaháawal**. *ind inv* **mbootŭláhookw**. *ind I-you* **kpootŭ=láhool**. *conj 3rd sg* **pootŭláhaat**. *imp* **póotŭlah**. *ptcpl* **pootŭláhaat**.

**pootŭlahíikeew** VAI make butter. *ind 1st sg* **mbootŭlahíike**, **mbootŭlahíi=keem**. *conj 3rd sg* **pootŭlahíikeet**. *imp* **pootŭlahíikeel**. *ptcpl* **pootŭlah=íikeet**. *See* **pootŭláheew**.

**pootŭlupéexun** VII cream. **Pootŭlup=éexung máhlam.** 'He bought some butter.' *conj 3rd sg* **pootŭlupéexung**. *ptcpl* **pootŭlupéexung**.

**póoxpeew** VII be fragile, be delicate. *conj 3rd sg* **póoxpeek**. *ptcpl* **póoxpeek**.

**póoxpsuw** VAI be fragile, be delicate *(s.t. animate)*; be delicate in health. *ind 1st sg* **mbóoxpsi**, **mbóoxpsiim**. *conj 3rd sg* **póoxpsiit**. *ptcpl* **póoxp=siit**.

**pòháhkweew** VAI cut splints, cut splints of wood for baskets. *ind 1st sg* **mbohάhkwe**, **mbohάhkweem**. *conj 3rd sg* **pòháhkweet**. *imp* **pòháh=kweel**. *ptcpl* **pòháhkweet**.

**póham** VTI1A knock on s.t. *(especially of drums)*; tap on s.t. *ind 1st sg* **mbohámun**. *ind 3rd sg* **pòhámun**. *conj 1st sg* **pòhámaan**. *conj 3rd sg* **póhang**. *imp* **póhah**. *ptcpl* **póhang**. *intensive reduplication* **pàpòhámun**.

**pòhámeew** VAI beat a drum, play a drum. *ind 1st sg* **mbohάma**, **mbohámaam**. *conj 3rd sg* **pòhámaat**. *imp* **pòhám=aal**. *ptcpl* **pòhámaat**.

**pòhíikeew** VAI knock, rap *(on a door)*. *ind 1st sg* **mbohíike**, **mbohíikeem**. *conj 3rd sg* **pòhíikeet**. *imp* **pòhíikeel**. *ptcpl* **pòhíikeet**. *intensive reduplication* **pàpòhíikeew**.

**pohkwalóhkeew** VAI stop working, break off working, quit before one is done *(without necessarily having completed a task)*. *ind 1st sg* **mboh=kwalóhke**, **mbohkwalóhkeem**. *conj 3rd sg* **pohkwalóhkeet**. *imp* **poh=kwalóhkeel**. *ptcpl* **pohkwalóhkeet**.

**póhkweew** VII be broken off. *conj 3rd sg* **póhkweek**. *ptcpl* **póhkweek**.

**pohkwii-** PV stop before one finishes *(doing something)*. **Mbóhkwii-apwáanhe.** 'I quit making bread.'; **Mbóhkwii-punámun.** 'I quit looking at it.' *ptcpl* **póhkwii-**. *See* **pohkwu-**.

**pohkwíhlatoow** VTI2 use s.t. up. *ind 1st sg* **mbohkwíhlatoon**. *ind 3rd sg* **pohkwíhlatoon**. *conj 1st sg* **poh=kwihlatáwaan**. *conj 3rd sg* **poh=kwíhlataakw**. *imp* **pohkwíhlatool**. *ptcpl* **pohkwíhlataakw**.

**pohkwíhleew** VAI be broke, have spent all one's money. *ind 1st sg* **mboh=kwíhla**, **mbohkwíhlaam**. *conj 3rd sg*

**pohkwíhlaat**. *ptcpl* **pohkwíhlaat**.

**pohkwíhleew** VAIO run out of something. **Pohkwíhlaan wŭyóos.** 'He ran out of meat.' *ind 1st sg* **mbohkwíh=laan**. *ind 3rd sg* **pohkwíhlaan**. *conj 3rd sg* **pohkwíhlaat**. *ptcpl* **pohkwíh=laat**.

**póhkwsheew** VTA cut the last of s.t. animate, cut s.t. animate off at the end. *ind 1st sg* **mbóhkwshaaw**, **mbóhk=wsha**. *ind 3rd sg* **pohkwsháawal**. *ind inv* **mbóhkwshookw**. *ind I-you* **kpóhkwshool**. *conj 3rd sg* **póhk=wshaat**. *imp* **póhkwush**. *ptcpl* **póhkwshaat**.

**póhkwshum** VTI1B cut the last of s.t., cut s.t. off at the end. *ind 1st sg* **mbohkwshúmun**. *ind 3rd sg* **pohk=wshúmun**. *conj 1st sg* **pohkwshúm=aan**. *conj 3rd sg* **póhkwshung**. *imp* **póhkwshih**. *ptcpl* **póhkwshung**.

**pohkwu-** PV stop before one finishes *(doing something)*. *informal*. **Póh=kwu-míitsuw.** 'He stopped while eating.' *ptcpl* **póhkwu-**. *See* **pohkwii-**.

**póhkwun** VII be broken off, be blunt. *conj 3rd sg* **póhkwung**. *ptcpl* **póh=kwung**.

**póhkwŭneew** VTA take all of s.t. animate, take the last piece of s.t. animate. *ind 1st sg* **mbóhkwŭnaaw**, **mbóhkwŭna**. *ind 3rd sg* **pohkwŭnáawal**. *ind inv* **mbóhkwŭnukw**. *ind I-you* **kpóh=kwŭnul**. *conj 3rd sg* **póhkwŭnaat**. *imp* **póhkwun**. *ptcpl* **póhkwŭnaat**.

**póhkwŭnum** VTI1B take all of s.t., take the last piece of s.t.; quit while doing s.t. *ind 1st sg* **mbohkwŭnúmun**. *ind 3rd sg* **pohkwŭnúmun**. *conj 1st sg* **pohkwŭnúmaan**. *conj 3rd sg* **póh=kwŭnung**. *imp* **póhkwŭnih**. *ptcpl* **póhkwŭnung**.

**pohpóokwush** NA quail. *pl* **pohpóokw=shak**. *obv* **pohpóokwshal**.

**pohpohkwíixsuw** VAI leave out words when one speaks. *ind 1st sg* **mboh=pohkwíixsi**, **mbohpohkwíixsiim**. *conj 3rd sg* **pohpohkwíixsiit**. *ptcpl* **pohpohkwíixsiit**.

**pòhwíixiin** VAI fall with a thud. *ind 1st sg* **mbohwíixiin**, **mbohwíixi**. *conj 3rd sg* **pòhwíixiing**. *ptcpl* **pòhwíixiing**.

**pòhwíixtoow** VTI2 throw s.t. down with a thud, drop s.t. so that it makes a thud. *ind 1st sg* **mbohwíixtoon**. *ind 3rd sg* **pòhwíixtoon**. *conj 1st sg* **pòhwiix=táwaan**. *conj 3rd sg* **pòhwíixtaakw**. *imp* **pòhwíixtool**. *ptcpl* **pòhwíix=taakw**.

**pòhwíixŭmeew** VTA throw s.o. down with a thud, drop s.o. so that they make a thud. *ind 1st sg* **mbohwíixŭmaaw**, **mbohwíixŭma**. *ind 3rd sg* **pòhwii=xŭmáawal**. *ind inv* **mbohwíixŭ=mukw**. *ind I-you* **kpohwíixŭmul**. *conj 3rd sg* **pòhwíixŭmaat**. *imp* **pòhwíixum**. *ptcpl* **pòhwíixŭmaat**.

**pòhwíixun** VII fall and make a noise, fall and make a dull noise, fall with a thud. *conj 3rd sg* **pòhwíixung**. *ptcpl* **pòhwíixung**.

**pòhwsiitéexiin** VAI stamp with one's feet, keep time with one's feet. *ind 1st sg* **mbohwsiitéexiin**, **mbohwsii=téexi**. *conj 3rd sg* **pòhwsiitéexiing**. *imp* **pòhwsiitéexiil**. *ptcpl* **pòhwsii=téexiing**.

**pòhwtoonéexiin** VAI pout. *ind 1st sg* **mbohwtoonéexiin**, **mbohwtoonéexi**. *conj 3rd sg* **pòhwtoonéexiing**. *ptcpl* **pòhwtoonéexiing**.

**pòhwŭníikan** NI drum. *pl* **pòhwŭníika=nal**. *poss* **mbohwŭníikan**. *loc* **pòh=wŭníikanung**. *dimin* **pòhwŭníika=nush**.

**pòhwŭníikeew** VAI beat a drum, play a drum. *ind 1st sg* **mbohwŭníike**, **mbohwŭníikeem**. *conj 3rd sg* **pòh=wŭníikeet**. *imp* **pòhwŭníikeel**. *ptcpl* **pòhwŭníikeet**.

**pòhwŭnúmeew** VAI beat a drum, play a drum; beat *(on a black ash log, so* *that strips of wood will come off). ind 1st sg* **mbohwŭnúma, mbohwŭ=númaam**. *conj 3rd sg* **pòhwŭnúm=aat**. *imp* **pòhwŭnúmaal**. *ptcpl* **pòhwŭnúmaat**.

**pókhwiit** NA guinea fowl. *pl* **pòkhwíi=tak**. *poss* **mbokhwíitum**. *dimin* **pòkhwíichush**. *obv* **pòkhwíital**.

**pókwus** NA bedbug. *pl* **pókwsak**. *poss* **mbókwsum**. *dimin* **pókwshush**. *obv* **pókwsal**.

**ponghwáaleew** VTA throw powder on s.o., throw dust on s.o., throw sand on s.o., throw dirt on s.o. *ind 1st sg* **mbonghwáalaaw, mbonghwáala**. *ind 3rd sg* **ponghwaaláawal**. *ind inv* **mbonghwáalukw**. *ind I-you* **kpóng=hwáalul**. *conj 3rd sg* **ponghwáalaat**. *imp* **pónghwaal**. *ptcpl* **ponghwáa=laat**.

**ponghwúnzuw** VAI powder oneself, give oneself a dustbath. *ind 1st sg* **mbong=hwúnzi, mbonghwúnziim**. *conj 3rd sg* **ponghwúnziit**. *imp* **ponghwún=ziil**. *ptcpl* **ponghwúnziit**.

**pongóohuw** VAI be dusty. *ind 1st sg* **mbongóohi, mbongóohiim**. *conj 3rd sg* **pongóohiit**. *ptcpl* **pongóohiit**.

**pongóowuw** VII be dusty. *conj 3rd sg* **pongóowiik**. *ptcpl* **pongóowiik**.

**póngw** NI dust. *poss* **mbóngwum**. *loc* **póngwung**. *dimin* **póngwush**.

**póngwsuw** VAI be dusty. *ind 1st sg* **mbóngwsi, mbóngwsiim**. *conj 3rd sg* **póngwsiit**. *ptcpl* **póngwsiit**.

**póngwush** NA moth. *pl* **póngwshak**. *obv* **póngwshal**.

**pòwahkéeyeew** VII be a hill, be a mound. *conj 3rd sg* **pòwahkéeyeek**. *ptcpl* **pòwahkéeyeek**. *intensive reduplication* **pohpòwahkéeyeew**.

**pòwcháteew** VII have lumps protruding from a surface *(of food cooking)*. *conj 3rd sg* **pòwcháteek**. *ptcpl* **pòwchát=eek**.

**pòwíixiin** VAI stick up in a lump *(s.t. animate)*. *ind 1st sg* **mbowíixiin, mbowíixi**. *conj 3rd sg* **pòwíixiing**. *ptcpl* **pòwíixiing**.

**pòwíixun** VII stick up in a lump. *conj 3rd sg* **pòwíixung**. *ptcpl* **pòwíixung**.

**poxkakóosuw** VAI climb up onto something. **Poxkakóosuw nehnayóong=sung.** 'She climbed up onto the horse.' *ind 1st sg* **mboxkakóosi, mboxkakóosiim**. *conj 3rd sg* **poxka=kóosiit**. *imp* **poxkakóosiil**. *ptcpl* **peexkakóosiit**.

**poxkapíishush** NA chipmunk. *pl* **pox=kapíish'shak**. *obv* **poxkapíish'shal**.

**póxkapuw** VAI sit astride something; sit straddling something. *ind 1st sg* **mbóxkapi, mbóxkapiim**. *conj 3rd sg* **póxkapiit**. *imp* **póxkapiil**. *ptcpl* **péexkapiit**. *See* **póxkwapuw**.

**poxkohkwéepuw** VAI sit upon something, sit astride. *ind 1st sg* **mbox=kohkwéepi, mboxkohkwéepiim**. *conj 3rd sg* **poxkohkwéepiit**. *imp* **poxkohkwéepiil**. *ptcpl* **peexkoh=kwéepiit**.

**poxkwáhleew** VTA place s.o. on top *(of something)*. *ind 1st sg* **mboxkwáh=laaw, mboxkwáhla**. *ind 3rd sg* **pox=kwahláawal**. *ind inv* **mboxkwáh=lukw**. *ind I-you* **kpoxkwáhlul**. *conj 3rd sg* **poxkwáhlaat**. *imp* **póxkwahl**. *ptcpl* **peexkwáhlaat**.

**poxkwáhteew** VII sit upon something. *conj 3rd sg* **poxkwáhteek**. *ptcpl* **peexkwáhteek**.

**poxkwáhtoow** VTI2 place s.t. on top *(of something)*. *ind 1st sg* **mboxkwáh=toon**. *ind 3rd sg* **poxkwáhtoon**. *conj 1st sg* **poxkwáhtawaan**. *conj 3rd sg* **poxkwáhtaakw**. *imp* **poxkwáhtool**. *ptcpl* **peexkwáhtaakw**.

**póxkwapuw** VAI sit astride something; sit straddling something. *ind 1st sg* **mbóxkwapi, mbóxkwapiim**. *conj 3rd sg* **póxkwapiit**. *imp* **póxkwapiil**. *ptcpl* **péexkwapiit**. *See* **póxkapuw**.

**poxkwchéepuw** VAI perch upon something. *ind 1st sg* **mboxkwchéepi**, **mboxkwchéepiim**. *conj 3rd sg* **poxkwchéepiit**. *imp* **poxkwchéepiil**. *ptcpl* **peexkwchéepiit**.

**poxkwiikáapawuw** VAI stand upon something. *ind 1st sg* **mboxkwii=káapawi**, **mboxkwiikáapawiim**. *conj 3rd sg* **poxkwiikáapawiit**. *imp* **poxkwiikáapawiil**. *ptcpl* **peexkwii=káapawiit**.

**poxkwsíiteew** VAI put one's feet upon something. *ind 1st sg* **mboxkwsíite**, **mboxkwsíiteem**. *conj 3rd sg* **poxkw=síiteet**. *imp* **poxkwsíiteel**. *ptcpl* **peexkwsíiteet**.

**poxkwsiitéepuw** VAI put one's feet up, sit with one's feet upon something. *ind 1st sg* **mboxkwsiitéepi**, **mbox=kwsiitéepiim**. *conj 3rd sg* **poxkwsii=téepiit**. *imp* **poxkwsiitéepiil**. *ptcpl* **peexkwsiitéepiit**.

**poxkwsiitéexiin** VAI have one's feet up on something. *ind 1st sg* **mboxkwsii=téexiin**, **mboxkwsiitéexi**. *conj 3rd sg* **poxkwsiitéexiing**. *imp* **poxkwsiitée=xiil**. *ptcpl* **peexkwsiitéexiing**.

**psakohkwéepŭwak** VAI sit close together. *usually plural. ind 1st pl* **mbusakohkweepíhna**. *conj 3rd sg* **psakohkweepíhtiit**. *imp* **psakoh=kwéepiikw**. *ptcpl* **peesakohkwee=píhtiit**. *See* **psakwapúwak**.

**psákwamuw** VAI be stuck on, be stuck together *(s.t. animate). ind 1st sg* **mbusakwámwi**, **mbusakwámwiim**. *conj 3rd sg* **psákwamwiit**. *ptcpl* **peesakwámwiit**.

**psákwamuw** VII be stuck on, be stuck together. *conj 3rd sg* **psákwamwiik**. *ptcpl* **peesakwámwiik**.

**psakwapúwak** VAI sit close together. *usually plural. ind 1st pl* **mbusa=kwapíhna**. *conj 3rd sg* **psakwapíhtiit**. *imp* **psákwapiikw**. *ptcpl* **peesa=kwapíhtiit**. *See* **psakohkwéepŭwak**.

**psákweew** VII be sticky. *conj 3rd sg* **psákweek**. *ptcpl* **péesakweek**. *intensive reduplication* **pàpsákweew**.

**psakwii-** PN sticky. **Psákwii-pámbiil** 'Sticky paper.' *ptcpl* **peesakwii-**.

**psakwiixíinook** VAI lie close together, be close together, lie close to something. *usually plural. ind 1st pl* **mbusakwiixiinóhna**. *conj 3rd sg* **psakwiixiinóhtiit**. *imp* **psakwíi=xiikw**. *ptcpl* **peesakwiixiinóhtiit**.

**psakwíixtoow** VTI2 put s.t. close together; stick s.t. up against something. *ind 1st sg* **mbusakwíixtoon**. *ind 3rd sg* **pusakwíixtoon**. *conj 1st sg* **psak=wiixtáwaan**. *conj 3rd sg* **psakwíix=taakw**. *imp* **psakwíixtool**. *ptcpl* **peesakwíixtaakw**.

**psakwíixŭmeew** VTA put s.o. close together, put s.t. animate close together, stick s.o. up against something. *object usually plural. ind 1st sg* **mbusa=kwiixŭmáawak**. *ind 3rd sg* **pusa=kwiixŭmáawal**. *ind inv* **mbusakwíi=xŭmukw**. *ind I-you* **kpusakwiixŭ=mulóhmwa**. *conj 3rd sg* **psakwíixŭ=maat**. *imp* **psakwíixum**. *ptcpl* **pee=sakwíixŭmaat**.

**psakwíixun** VII lie close together, be close together, lie close to something. **Psakwíixun áhpapoon kpahóo=nung.** 'The chair is up against the door.' *conj 3rd sg* **psakwíixung**. *ptcpl* **peesakwíixung**.

**psakwihtéeheew** VTA crucify s.o.; nail s.o. up, nail s.o. down. **Psakwihtée=haa.** 'He was crucified.' *ind 1st sg* **mbusakwihtéehaaw**, **mbusakwih=téeha**. *ind 3rd sg* **pusakwihtee=háawal**. *ind inv* **mbusakwihtée=hookw**. *ind I-you* **kpusakwihtéehool**. *conj 3rd sg* **psakwihtéehaat**. *imp* **psakwíhteeh**. *ptcpl* **peesakwihtée=haat**.

**psakwihteeháasuw** VAI be crucified. *ind 1st sg* **mbusakwihteeháasi**, **mbusa=**

**kwihteeháasiim**. *conj 3rd sg* **psak= wihteeháasiit**. *ptcpl* **peesakwihtee= háasiit**.

**psakwpáleew** VTA paste s.o. together, glue s.o. together. *object usually plural*. *ind 1st sg* **mbusakwupaláawak**. *ind 3rd sg* **pusakwupaláawal**. *ind inv* **mbusakwupalúkook**. *ind I-you* **kpusakwupalulóhmwa**. *conj 3rd sg* **psakwpálaat**. *imp* **psákwpal**. *ptcpl* **peesakwúpalaat**.

**psakwpátoow** VTI2 paste s.t. together, glue s.t. together. *object usually plural*. **Mbusakwupatóonal xwúsal.** 'I glued the pieces of wood together.' *ind 1st sg* **mbusakwupatóonal**. *ind 3rd sg* **pusakwupatóonal**. *conj 1st sg* **psakwpátawaan**. *conj 3rd sg* **psakw= pátaakw**. *imp* **psakwpátool**. *ptcpl* **peesakwúpataakw**.

**psakwpéhlaleew** VTA glue s.t. animate together, paste s.t. animate. *ind 1st sg* **mbusakwupéhlalaaw**, **mbusakwup= éhlala**. *ind 3rd sg* **pusakwupehla= láawal**. *ind inv* **mbusakwupéhla= lukw**. *ind I-you* **kpusakwupéhlalul**. *conj 3rd sg* **psakwpéhlalaat**. *imp* **psakwpéhlal**. *ptcpl* **peesakwupéhla= laat**.

**psakwpéhlatoow** VTI2 glue s.t. together, paste s.t. *ind 1st sg* **mbusakwupéh= latoon**. *ind 3rd sg* **pusakwupéhla= toon**. *conj 1st sg* **psakwpehlatáw= aan**. *conj 3rd sg* **psakwpéhlataakw**. *imp* **psakwpéhlatool**. *ptcpl* **peesa= kwupéhlataakw**.

**psákwsuw** VAI be sticky *(s.t. animate)*. *ind 1st sg* **mbusakwúsi**, **mbusa= kwúsiim**. *conj 3rd sg* **psákwsiit**. *ptcpl* **peesakwúsiit**.

**psakwŭlúnjeew** NA black squirrel. *pl* **psakwŭlunjéewak**. *obv* **psakwŭ= lunjéewal**.

**psákwŭnum** VTI1B glue s.t., stick s.t. together. *ind 1st sg* **mbusakwúnŭmun**. *ind 3rd sg* **pusakwúnŭmun**. *conj 1st sg* **psakwŭnúmaan**. *conj 3rd sg* **psákwŭnung**. *imp* **psákwŭnih**. *ptcpl* **peesakwúnung**.

**psúm** VOTI1B have something in one's eye. *ind 1st sg* **mbúsum**. *conj 3rd sg* **psúng**. *ptcpl* **péesung**.

**psundháasuw** VAI be buried. **Yóon pusundháasiin.** 'He is buried here.' *ind 1st sg* **mbusundháasi**, **mbus= undháasiim**. *conj 3rd sg* **psundháa= siit**. *ptcpl* **peesundháasiit**.

**psúndham** VTI1A bury s.t., cover s.t. over. *ind 1st sg* **mbusundhámun**. *ind 3rd sg* **pusundhámun**. *conj 1st sg* **psundhámaan**. *conj 3rd sg* **psúnd= hang**. *imp* **psúndhah**. *ptcpl* **peesúnd= hang**.

**psúndheew** VTA bury s.o., cover s.o. over. **Psúndhaaw.** 'He was covered up, buried.' *ind 1st sg* **mbusúndhaaw**, **mbusúndha**. *ind 3rd sg* **pusundháa= wal**. *ind inv* **mbusúndhookw**. *ind I-you* **kpusúndhool**. *conj 3rd sg* **psúndhaat**. *imp* **psúndhaw**. *ptcpl* **peesúndhaat**.

**psúndpeew** VAI be covered with water. *ind 1st sg* **mbusúndpe**, **mbusúnd= peem**. *conj 3rd sg* **psúndpeet**. *ptcpl* **peesúndpeet**.

**psúndpeew** VAIO cover s.t. with water. *ind 1st sg* **mbusúndpeen**. *ind 3rd sg* **pusúndpeen**. *conj 3rd sg* **psúndpeet**. *imp* **psúndpeel**. *ptcpl* **peesúndpeet**.

**psúndpeew** VII be covered with water. *conj 3rd sg* **psúndpeek**. *ptcpl* **pee= súndpeek**.

**pshihki-** PN nice, good. **Pshíhki-lúnuw.** 'A good man.' *See* **pshihku-**.

**pshihku-** PN nice, good. *informal*. **Pshíhku-nehnayóongus.** 'A nice horse.'; **Pshíhku-mwáakaneew.** 'A nice dog.' *See* **pshihki-**.

**pshihku-** PV nice, good. *informal*. **Pshíhku-únd.** 'He has a nice disposition.' *ptcpl* **peeshíhku-**.

**pshíhku-awéenuw** VAI be a nice person.

*ind 1st sg* **mbushíhku-awéeni**, **mbushíhku-awéeniim**. *conj 3rd sg* **pshíhku-awéeniit**. *ptcpl* **peeshíhku-awéeniit**.

**pshúm** NA nickname. *obv* **pshúmal**.

**ptáheew** VTA catch s.t. animate with a hook. **Níishŭwak waasíingwak mbutháawak.** 'I caught two pickerel.' *ind 1st sg* **mbúthaaw**, **mbútha**. *ind 3rd sg* **putháawal**. *ind inv* **mbút=hookw**. *ind I-you* **kpúthool**. *conj 3rd sg* **ptáhaat**. *imp* **ptáh**. *ptcpl* **péethaat**.

**ptukohkwéepuw** VAI sit with one's legs folded; sit hunched over. *ind 1st sg* **mbutkohkwéepi**, **mbutkohkwée=piim**. *conj 3rd sg* **ptukohkwéepiit**. *imp* **ptukohkwéepiil**. *ptcpl* **peet=kohkwéepiit**. *See* **ptúkwapuw**.

**ptukwaaláxkwsiit** NI pea. *pl* **ptukwaa=laxkwsíital**. *poss* **mbutkwaaláxk=wsiit**.

**ptukwáhtakw** NI rope. *pl* **ptukwáhta=kwal**. *poss* **mbutkwáhtakwum**. *loc* **ptukwáhtakwung**. *dimin* **pchuk=wáhchakwush**.

**ptúkwapuw** VAI sit with one's legs folded; sit hunched over. *ind 1st sg* **mbut=kwápi**, **mbutkwápiim**. *conj 3rd sg* **ptúkwapiit**. *imp* **ptúkwapiil**. *ptcpl* **peetkwápiit**. *See* **ptukohkwéepuw**.

**ptukwchéenum** VTI1B make a hole in s.t. *ind 1st sg* **mbutkwuchéenŭmun**. *ind 3rd sg* **putkwuchéenŭmun**. *conj 1st sg* **ptukwchéenŭmaan**. *conj 3rd sg* **ptukwchéenung**. *imp* **ptukw=chéenih**. *ptcpl* **peetkwuchéenung**.

**ptukwchéesuw** VAI be round in shape *(s.t. animate)*. *ind 1st sg* **mbut=kwuchéesi**, **mbutkwuchéesiim**. *conj 3rd sg* **ptukwchéesiit**. *ptcpl* **peet=kwuchéesiit**.

**ptukwchéeyeew** VII be round in shape. *conj 3rd sg* **ptukwchéeyeek**. *ptcpl* **peetkwuchéeyeek**.

**ptúkweew** VII be round. *conj 3rd sg* **ptúkweek**. *ptcpl* **péetkweek**.

**ptukweehundáxpoon** NI round table. *pl* **ptukweehundaxpóonal**. *poss* **mbut=kweehundáxpoon**.

**ptukwíim** NI walnut. *pl* **ptukwíimal**. *poss* **mbutkwíimum**. *loc* **ptukwíi=mung**. *dimin* **pchukwíimush**.

**ptukwiimíinzhuy** NA walnut tree. *pl* **ptukwiimíinzhŭyak**. *obv* **ptukwii=míinzhŭyal**.

**ptukwíixiin** VAI be curled up, lie curled up *(s.t. animate)*. *ind 1st sg* **mbut=kwíixiin**, **mbutkwíixi**. *conj 3rd sg* **ptukwíixiing**. *imp* **ptukwíixiil**. *ptcpl* **peetkwíixiing**.

**ptukwíixtoow** VTI2 curl s.t. up. *ind 1st sg* **mbutkwíixtoon**. *ind 3rd sg* **put=kwíixtoon**. *conj 1st sg* **ptukwiixtáw=aan**. *conj 3rd sg* **ptukwíixtaakw**. *imp* **ptukwíixtool**. *ptcpl* **peetkwíixtaakw**.

**ptukwíixŭmeew** VTA curl s.o. up. *ind 1st sg* **mbutkwíixŭmaaw**, **mbut=kwíixŭma**. *ind 3rd sg* **putkwiixŭ=máawal**. *ind inv* **mbutkwíixŭmukw**. *ind I-you* **kputkwíixŭmul**. *conj 3rd sg* **ptukwíixŭmaat**. *imp* **ptukwíixum**. *ptcpl* **peetkwíixŭmaat**.

**ptukwíixun** VII be curled up, lie curled up. *conj 3rd sg* **ptukwíixung**. *ptcpl* **peetkwíixung**.

**ptukwpoxkwanéexiin** VAI have round shoulders. *ind 1st sg* **mbutkwupox=kwanéexiin**, **mbutkwupoxkwanée=xi**. *conj 3rd sg* **ptukwpoxkwanée=xiing**. *ptcpl* **peetkwupoxkwanée=xiing**.

**ptúkwsuw** VAI be round *(s.t. animate)*; be full *(of the moon)*. *ind 1st sg* **mbutkwúsi**, **mbutkwúsiim**. *conj 3rd sg* **ptúkwsiit**. *ptcpl* **peetkwúsiit**.

**ptúkwsheew** VTA cut s.t. animate in a round shape. *ind 1st sg* **mbutkwúsh=aaw**, **mbutkwúsha**. *ind 3rd sg* **put=kwusháawal**. *ind inv* **mbutkwúsh=ookw**. *ind I-you* **kputkwúshool**. *conj 3rd sg* **ptúkwshaat**. *imp* **ptúkwush**. *ptcpl* **peetkwúshaat**.

**ptúkwshum** VTI 1B cut s.t. in a round shape. *ind 1st sg* **mbutkwúshŭmun**. *ind 3rd sg* **putkwúshŭmun**. *conj 1st sg* **ptukwshúmaan**. *conj 3rd sg* **ptúkwshung**. *imp* **ptúkwshih**. *ptcpl* **peetkwúshung**.

**ptúkwŭlunj** NI fist. *pl* **ptukwŭlúnjal**. *See* **ptukwŭlunjeewáakan**.

**ptukwŭlúnjeew** VAI have one's hand clenched in a fist. *ind 1st sg* **mbut=kwulúnje**, **mbutkwulúnjeem**. *conj 3rd sg* **ptukwŭlúnjeet**. *ptcpl* **peet=kwulúnjeet**. *See* **ptukwŭlunjéexiin**.

**ptukwŭlunjeewáakan** NI fist. *pl* **ptuk=wŭlunjeewáakanal**. *See* **ptúkwŭlunj**.

**ptukwŭlunjéexiin** VAI have one's hand clenched in a fist. *ind 1st sg* **mbut=kwulunjéexiin**, **mbutkwulunjéexi**. *conj 3rd sg* **ptukwŭlunjéexiing**. *ptcpl* **peetkwulunjéexiing**, **peet=kwulunjéexiit**. *See* **ptukwŭlúnjeew**.

**ptukwŭlunjhámeew** VAI make a fist. *ind 1st sg* **mbutkwulunjháma**, **mbutkwulunjhámaam**. *conj 3rd sg* **ptukwŭlunjhámaat**. *imp* **ptukwŭ=lunjhámaal**. *ptcpl* **peetkwulunj=hámaat**.

**ptúkwŭneew** VTA roll s.t. animate up *(using the hands)*. *ind 1st sg* **mbut=kwúnaaw**, **mbutkwúna**. *ind 3rd sg* **putkwunáawal**. *ind inv* **mbutkwún=ukw**. *ind I-you* **kputkwúnul**. *conj 3rd sg* **ptúkwŭnaat**. *imp* **ptúkwun**. *ptcpl* **peetkwúnaat**.

**ptúkwŭnum** VTI 1B roll s.t. up *(using the hands)*. *ind 1st sg* **mbutkwúnŭmun**. *ind 3rd sg* **putkwúnŭmun**. *conj 1st sg* **ptukwŭnúmaan**. *conj 3rd sg* **ptúkwŭnung**. *imp* **ptúkwŭnih**. *ptcpl* **peetkwúnung**.

**pŭlakiingwáalaaw** VTA have one's cataracts removed. *indefinite subject only*. *conj 3rd sg* **pŭlakiingwáalund**. *ptcpl* **peelakiingwáalund**.

**pŭlakiingwéeneew** VTA remove s.o.'s cataracts. *ind 1st sg* **mbulakiingwée=naaw**, **mbulakiingwéena**. *ind 3rd sg* **pulakiingweenáawal**. *ind inv* **mbul=akiingwéenukw**. *ind I-you* **kpula=kiingwéenul**. *conj 3rd sg* **pŭlakiin=gwéenaat**. *imp* **pŭlakíingwéen**. *ptcpl* **peelakiingwéenaat**.

**pŭlakihtéeheew** VTA hit s.o. and knock the covering off them, hit s.o. and knock the skin off them. *ind 1st sg* **mbulakihtéehaaw**, **mbulakihtéeha**. *ind 3rd sg* **pulakihteehéawal**. *ind inv* **mbulakihtéehookw**. *ind I-you* **kpul=akihtéehool**. *conj 3rd sg* **pŭlakih=téehaat**. *imp* **pŭlakíhteeh**. *ptcpl* **peelakihtéehaat**.

**pŭlakihteeháasuw** VAI have the covering of something be hit and knocked off, have the skin of something be hit and knocked off. *ind 1st sg* **mbula=kihteeháasi**, **mbulakihteeháasiim**. *conj 3rd sg* **pŭlakihteeháasiit**. *ptcpl* **peelakihteeháasiit**. *intensive reduplication* **pàpŭlakihteeháasuw**.

**pŭláksheew** VTA cut s.t. animate off, cut a piece off s.t. animate. *ind 1st sg* **mbulakúshaaw**, **mbulakúsha**. *ind 3rd sg* **pulakusháawal**. *ind inv* **mbul=akúshookw**. *ind I-you* **kpulakúshool**. *conj 3rd sg* **pŭlákshaat**. *imp* **pŭlák=ush**. *ptcpl* **peelakúshaat**.

**pŭlákshum** VTI 1B cut s.t. off, cut a piece off s.t. *ind 1st sg* **mbulakúshŭmun**. *ind 3rd sg* **pulakúshŭmun**. *conj 1st sg* **pŭlakshúmaan**. *conj 3rd sg* **pŭ=lákshung**. *imp* **pŭlákshih**. *ptcpl* **peelakúshung**.

**pŭlákŭneew** VTA take the covering off s.t. animate, take the outer layer off s.t. animate, remove the shell from s.t. animate. *ind 1st sg* **mbulakún=aaw**, **mbulakúna**. *ind 3rd sg* **pula=kŭnáawal**. *ind inv* **mbulakúnukw**. *ind I-you* **kpulakúnul**. *conj 3rd sg* **pŭlákŭnaat**. *imp* **pŭlákun**. *ptcpl* **peelakúnaat**.

**pŭlákŭnum** VTI 1A take the covering off

s.t., take the outer layer off s.t., remove the shell from s.t. *ind 1st sg* **mbulakúnŭmun**. *ind 3rd sg* **pula=kúnŭmun**. *conj 1st sg* **pŭlakŭnúm=aan**. *conj 3rd sg* **pŭlákŭnung**. *imp* **pŭlákŭnih**. *ptcpl* **peelakúnung**.

**pŭlánzhŭmaan** NA Frenchman. *pl* **pŭlanzhŭmáanak**. *dimin* **pŭlanzhŭ=máanush**. *obv* **pŭlanzhŭmáanal**. *From Dutch.*

**pŭléew** NA turkey. *pl* **pŭléewak**. *obv* **pŭléewal**.

**pŭléewii-míikwan** NA turkey feather. *pl* **pŭléewii-míikwanak**. *poss* **mbulée=wii-míikwanum**. *dimin* **pŭléewii-míikwanush**. *obv* **pŭléewii-míikwa=nal**.

**pŭliisóohŭweew** VAI drool. *ind 1st sg* **mbuliisóohŭwe, mbuliisóohŭweem**. *conj 3rd sg* **pŭliisóohŭweet**. *ptcpl* **peeliisóohŭweet**.

**pŭlóok** NI pants. *pl* **pŭlóokal**. *poss* **mbulóokum**. *loc* **pŭlóokung**. *dimin* **pŭlóokush**. *From Dutch.*

**pŭlúpiin** NA Phillipine. *obv* **pŭlupíinal**. *woman's name. From English* Phillipine.

**pŭlupihtéeheew** VTA beat s.o. to death. *ind 1st sg* **mbulpihtéehaaw, mbul=pihtéeha**. *ind 3rd sg* **pulpihteeháa=wal**. *ind inv* **mbulpihtéehookw**. *ind I-you* **kpulpihtéehul**. *conj 3rd sg* **pŭlupihtéehaat**. *imp* **pŭlupíhteeh**. *ptcpl* **peelpihtéehaat**. *intensive reduplication* **pàpeelpihteeháawal**.

**pŭlupihtéexiin** VAI fall and die, be beaten to death, get hit and die. *ind 1st sg* **mbulpihtéexiin, mbulpihtéexi**. *conj 3rd sg* **pŭlupihtéexiing**. *ptcpl* **peel=pihtéexiing**.

**pŭmáameew** VAI be in a line, be lined up, be in a line there, lie there in a line. **Pumáameen séhkeek wíi=kwahm.** 'He was lying across the length of the house.'; **Áxkook pŭ=máameew áaneeng.** 'The snake was lying on the road.' *ind 1st sg* **mbum=áame, mbumáameem**. *conj 3rd sg* **pŭmáameet**. *ptcpl* **peemáameet**.

**pŭmáameew** VII be in a line, be lined up, lie. **Peemáameek ptukwáhtakw.** 'The rope is lying straight.'; **Áanaay yéelak pŭmáameew.** 'There's a road over there.' *conj 3rd sg* **pŭmáameek**. *ptcpl* **peemáameek**.

**pŭmaapéeneew** VTA lead s.o. along with a string, lead s.o. by with a string; lead s.o. along by the reins, lead s.o. by by the reins *(of horses)*. *ind 1st sg* **mbumaapéenaaw, mbumaapéena**. *ind 3rd sg* **pumaapeenáawal**. *ind inv* **mbumaapéenukw**. *ind I-you* **kpum=aapéenul**. *conj 3rd sg* **pŭmaapée=naat**. *imp* **pŭmáapeen**. *ptcpl* **pee=maapéenaat**.

**pŭmáaphookw** VAI float by, float along, float away. *ind 1st sg* **mbumáap=hookw**. *conj 3rd sg* **pŭmaaphóo=kwuk**. *imp* **pŭmaaphóokwih**. *ptcpl* **peemaaphóokwuk**.

**pŭmaapŭwéhleew** VII flow by, flow along *(of water)*. *conj 3rd sg* **pŭmaa=pŭwéhlaak**. *ptcpl* **peemaapŭwéh=laak**.

**pŭmaashóokeew** VAI wade in the water. *ind 1st sg* **mbumaashóoke, mbum=aashóokeem**. *conj 3rd sg* **pŭmaa=shóokeet**. *imp* **pŭmaashóokeel**. *ptcpl* **peemaashóokeet**.

**pŭmáashŭwiiw** VAI-S swim. *ind 1st sg* **mbumáashŭwi, mbumáashŭwiim**. *conj 3rd sg* **pŭmáashŭwiit**. *imp* **pŭ=máashŭwiil**. *ptcpl* **peemáashŭwiit**.

**pŭmáashŭwihl** VAI swim, go swimming. *ind 1st sg* **mbumáashŭwihl**. *conj 3rd sg* **pŭmaashŭwíhluk**. *imp* **pŭmaa=shŭwíhlih**. *ptcpl* **peemaashŭwíhluk**.

**pŭmaashŭwíhleew** VAI swim. *ind 1st sg* **mbumaashŭwíhla, mbumaashŭ=wíhlaam**. *conj 3rd sg* **pŭmaashŭ=wíhlaat**. *imp* **pŭmaashŭwíhlaal**. *ptcpl* **peemaashŭwíhlaat**.

**pŭmáatham** VAI go by in a boat, go along in a boat, float by in a boat, float along in a boat. *ind 1st sg* **mbumáatham**. *conj 3rd sg* **pŭmáat=hang**. *imp* **pŭmáathah**. *ptcpl* **pee=máathang**.

**pŭmáathookw** VAI float by, float along. **Yú pùmaathóokwun.** 'He floated right by here.' *ind 1st sg* **mbumáat=hookw**. *conj 3rd sg* **pŭmaathóo=kwuk**. *ptcpl* **peemaathóokwuk**.

**pŭmáathun** VII float, float by, float along. *conj 3rd sg* **pŭmáathung**. *ptcpl* **peemáathung**.

**pŭmaawsoohááleew** VTA make s.o. live, save s.o., give s.o. a reason to live. *ind 1st sg* **mbumaawsoohááalaaw**, **mbumaawsoohááala**. *ind 3rd sg* **pum=aawsoohaaláawal**. *ind inv* **mbum=aawsoohháalukw**. *ind 1-you* **kpum=aawsoohháalul**. *conj 3rd sg* **pŭmaaw=soohháalaat**. *imp* **pŭmaawsóohaal**. *ptcpl* **peemaawsoohháalaat**.

**pŭmáawsuw** VAI live, be alive, be living. *ind 1st sg* **mbumáawsi**, **mbumáaw=siim**. *conj 3rd sg* **pŭmáawsiit**. *ptcpl* **peemáawsiit**.

**pŭmaawsuwáakan** NI life. *poss* **mbum=aawsuwáakan**.

**pŭmáham** VOTI1A float, paddle by, paddle along, paddle a watercraft. **Wshíhwe pŭmáham.** 'The duck is paddling by.' *ind 1st sg* **mbúmham**. *conj 3rd sg* **pŭmáhang**. *imp* **pŭmáh=ah**. *ptcpl* **péemhang**.

**pŭmáhan** VII float, float by, float along. *conj 3rd sg* **pŭmáhang**. *ptcpl* **péem=hang**.

**pŭmáhookw** VAI float by, float along. *ind 1st sg* **mbúmhookw**. *conj 3rd sg* **pŭmahóokwuk**. *ptcpl* **peemhóo=kwuk**.

**pŭmahóomeew** VAI ride by on horseback, ride along on horseback. *ind 1st sg* **mbumhóoma**, **mbumhóo=maam**. *conj 3rd sg* **pŭmahóomaat**. *imp* **pŭmahóomaal**. *ptcpl* **peem=hóomaat**.

**pŭmahtakíhleew** VAI run by, run along. *ind 1st sg* **mbumahtakíhla**, **mbumahtakíhlaam**. *conj 3rd sg* **pŭmahtakíhlaat**. *imp* **pŭmahta=kíhlaal**. *ptcpl* **peemahtakíhlaat**.

**pŭmáxookw** VAI be blown along by the wind, be blown by by the wind *(s.t. animate)*. *ind 1st sg* **mbúmxookw**. *conj 3rd sg* **pŭmaxóokwuk**. *ptcpl* **peemxóokwuk**.

**pŭmáxun** VII be blown along by the wind, be blown by by the wind. *conj 3rd sg* **pŭmáxung**. *ptcpl* **péemxung**.

**pumbahkéeyeew** VII slope down *(of the ground)*; be a hill. **Éenda-pum=bahkéeyeek ndúlu-pŭmúsi.** 'I walked to the hill.' *conj 3rd sg* **pum=bahkéeyeek**. *ptcpl* **peembahkée=yeek**.

**púmbiiw** VAI-S go downhill. *ind 1st sg* **mbúmbi**, **mbúmbiim**. *conj 3rd sg* **púmbiit**. *imp* **púmbiil**. *ptcpl* **péem=biit**.

**pumbíhleew** VAI go downhill, fall downhill, slide downhill. *ind 1st sg* **mbumbíhla**, **mbumbíhlaam**. *conj 3rd sg* **pŭmbíhlaat**. *imp* **pŭmbíh=laal**. *ptcpl* **peembíhlaat**.

**pŭmiich'chéewxeew** VAI walk sideways. *ind 1st sg* **mbumiich'chéew=xe**, **mbumiich'chéewxeem**. *conj 3rd sg* **pŭmiich'chéewxeet**. *imp* **pŭ=miich'chéewxeel**. *ptcpl* **peemiich'=chéewxeet**. *See* **pumiitchéewxeew**.

**pŭmíichii** PC beside, alongside. **Pŭ=míichii púmsiin.** 'He's walking beside me.'

**pŭmiichiikáapawuw** VAI stand sideways, stand beside someone. *ind 1st sg* **mbumiichiikáapawi**, **mbumii=chiikáapawiim**. *conj 3rd sg* **pŭmii=chiikáapawiit**. *imp* **pŭmiichiikáa=pawiil**. *ptcpl* **peemiichiikáapawiit**.

**pŭmiichíikun** VII grow crookedly,

grow sideways. **Pŭmiichíikun níipiit.** 'My tooth came up crooked.' *conj 3rd sg* **pŭmiichíikung**. *ptcpl* **peemiichíikung**.

**pŭmiichíikuw** VAI grow crookedly, grow sideways. *ind 1st sg* **mbumii=chíiki, mbumiichíikiim**. *conj 3rd sg* **pŭmiichíikiit**. *ptcpl* **peemiichíikiit**.

**pŭmiichíixiin** VAI lie crookedly, lie sideways, lie on one's side. *ind 1st sg* **mbumiichíixiin, mbumiichíixi**. *conj 3rd sg* **pŭmiichíixiing**. *imp* **pŭmiichíixiil**. *ptcpl* **peemiichíixiing**.

**pŭmiichíixun** VII lie crookedly, lie sideways, lie on it's side. *conj 3rd sg* **pŭmiichíixung**. *ptcpl* **peemiichíi=xung**.

**pŭmíikwsuw** VAI crawl by, crawl along. *ind 1st sg* **mbumíikwsi, mbumíikw=siim**. *conj 3rd sg* **pŭmíikwsiit**. *imp* **pŭmíikwsiil**. *ptcpl* **peemíikwsiit**.

**pŭmiinéeheew** VTA argue with s.o., quarrel with s.o. *ind 1st sg* **mbumii=néehaaw, mbumiinéeha**. *ind 3rd sg* **pumiineeháawal**. *ind inv* **mbumii=néehukw**. *ind I-you* **kpumiinéehul**. *conj 3rd sg* **pŭmiinéehaat**. *imp* **pŭmíineeh**. *ptcpl* **peemiinéehaat**.

**pŭmiineehíikeew** VAI argue, quarrel. *ind 1st sg* **mbumiineehíike, mbumii=neehíikeem**. *conj 3rd sg* **pŭmiinee=híikeet**. *imp* **pŭmiineehíikeel**. *ptcpl* **peemiineehíikeet**.

**pŭmiinjkweeyáaheew** VAIO roll s.t. by, roll s.t. along. *ind 1st sg* **mbumiinj=kweeyáaheen**. *ind 3rd sg* **pumiinj=kweeyáaheen**. *conj 3rd sg* **pŭmiinj=kweeyáaheet**. *imp* **pŭmiinjkwee=yáaheel**. *ptcpl* **peemiinjkweeyáa=heet**.

**pŭmiinjkwéhleew** VAI roll by, roll along. *ind 1st sg* **mbumiinjkwéhla, mbumiinjkwéhlaam**. *conj 3rd sg* **pŭmiinjkwéhlaat**. *imp* **pŭmiinj=kwéhlaal**. *ptcpl* **peemiinjkwéhlaat**.

**pŭmiinjkwéhleew** VII roll by, roll along. *conj 3rd sg* **pŭmiinjkwéhlaak**. *ptcpl* **peemiinjkwéhlaak**.

**pŭmiipáhtoow** VTI2 hurry by with s.t., hurry along with s.t. *ind 1st sg* **mbumiipáhtoon**. *ind 3rd sg* **pumii=páhtoon**. *conj 1st sg* **pŭmiipáhta=waan**. *conj 3rd sg* **pŭmiipáhtaakw**. *imp* **pŭmiipáhtool**. *ptcpl* **peemii=páhtaakw**.

**pŭmíipheew** VTA take s.o. by in a hurry, take s.o. along in a hurry. *ind 1st sg* **mbumíiphaaw, mbumíipha**. *ind 3rd sg* **pumiipháawal**. *ind inv* **mbumíip=hukw**. *ind I-you* **kpumíiphul**. *conj 3rd sg* **pŭmíiphaat**. *imp* **pŭmíipah**. *ptcpl* **peemíiphaat**.

**pŭmíitapuw** VAI sit sideways. *ind 1st sg* **mbumíitapi, mbumíitapiim**. *conj 3rd sg* **pŭmíitapiit**. *imp* **pŭmíitapiil**. *ptcpl* **peemíitapiit**. *See* **pŭmiitoh=kwéepuw**.

**pŭmiitchéewxeew** VAI walk sideways. *ind 1st sg* **mbumiitchéewxe, mbum=iitchéewxeem**. *conj 3rd sg* **pŭmiit=chéewxeet**. *imp* **pŭmiitchéewxeel**. *ptcpl* **peemiitchéewxeet**. *See* **pŭ=miich'chéewxeew**.

**pŭmiitóhkweew** VAI look sideways, turn one's head. *ind 1st sg* **mbumiitóhkwe, mbumiitóhkweem**. *conj 3rd sg* **pŭ=miitóhkweet**. *imp* **pŭmiitóhkweel**. *ptcpl* **peemiitóhkweet**.

**pŭmiitohkwéepuw** VAI sit sideways. *ind 1st sg* **mbumiitohkwéepi, mbumii=tohkwéepiim**. *conj 3rd sg* **pŭmiitoh=kwéepiit**. *imp* **pŭmiitohkwéepiil**. *ptcpl* **peemiitohkwéepiit**. *See* **pŭmíitapuw**.

**pŭmíixiin** VAI be crooked, be on crooked. *ind 1st sg* **mbumíixiin, mbumíixi**. *conj 3rd sg* **pŭmíixiing**. *ptcpl* **pee=míixiing**.

**pŭmíixun** VII be crooked. *conj 3rd sg* **pŭmíixung**. *ptcpl* **peemíixung**.

**pŭmíhleew** VAI fly by, fly along, go by, go along, drive by, drive along, pedal by, pedal along. *ind 1st sg* **mbumíhla, mbumíhlaam**. *conj 3rd sg* **pŭmíh=laat**. *imp* **pŭmíhlaal**. *ptcpl* **peemíh=laat**.

**pŭmohkáasuw** VAI win. *ind 1st sg* **mbumohkáasi, mbumohkáasiim**. *conj 3rd sg* **pŭmohkáasiit**. *ptcpl* **peemohkáasiit**.

**pŭmu-** PV by, along. **Náh mbúmu-laashíhla.** 'I ran by in a flash.' *ptcpl* **péemu-**.

**pŭmuchéhleew** VAI drive by, drive along. *ind 1st sg* **mbumchéhla, mbum=chéhlaam**. *conj 3rd sg* **pŭmuchéh=laat**. *imp* **pŭmuchéhlaal**. *ptcpl* **peemchéhlaat**.

**pŭmúneew** VTA beat s.o. in a competition, best s.o., do better than s.o. *ind 1st sg* **mbúmŭnaaw, mbúmŭna**. *ind 3rd sg* **pumŭnáawal**. *ind inv* **mbúm=ŭnukw**. *ind I-you* **kpúmŭnul**. *conj 3rd sg* **pŭmúnaat**. *imp* **pŭmún**. *ptcpl* **péemŭnaat**.

**pŭmunóotam** VTI1A overcome s.t., get the better of s.t. *ind 1st sg* **mbŭmŭ=nóotamun**. *ind 3rd sg* **pumŭnóota=mun**. *conj 1st sg* **pŭmunóotamaan**. *conj 3rd sg* **pŭmunóotang**. *imp* **pŭmunóotih**. *ptcpl* **peemŭnóotang**. *See* **pŭmúnum**.

**pŭmúnum** VTI1A overcome s.t., get the better of s.t. *ind 1st sg* **mbumŭnúm=un**. *ind 3rd sg* **pumŭnúmun**. *conj 1st sg* **pŭmúnŭmaan**. *conj 3rd sg* **pŭmúnung**. *imp* **pŭmúnih**. *ptcpl* **péemŭnung**. *See* **pŭmunóotam**.

**pŭmúsuw** VAI walk by, walk along; run *(of equipment)*. *ind 1st sg* **mbúmsi, mbúmsiim**. *conj 3rd sg* **pŭmúsiit**. *imp* **pŭmúsiil**. *ptcpl* **péemsiit**. *moderative reduplication* **paapŭmúsuw**.

**pŭmushíhkaweew** VTA drive s.t. animate, pilot s.t. animate. **Pŭmushih=kawáawak nehnayóongsak.** 'The horses are being driven.' *ind 1st sg* **mbumshíhkawaaw, mbumshíhka=wa**. *ind 3rd sg* **pumshihkawáawal**. *ind inv* **mbumshíhkaakw**. *ind I-you* **kpumshíhkool**. *conj 3rd sg* **pŭ=mushíhkawaat**. *imp* **pŭmushíhkaw**. *ptcpl* **peemshíhkawaat**.

**pŭmutáachiind** VTI3 drag s.t. by, drag s.t. along. *ind 1st sg* **mbumtaachíin=dun**. *ind 3rd sg* **pumtaachíindun**. *conj 1st sg* **pŭmutaachíindawaan**. *conj 3rd sg* **pŭmutaachíinduk**. *imp* **pŭmutaachíindih**. *ptcpl* **peemtaa=chíinduk**.

**pŭmutaachíhleew** VTA drag s.o. by, drag s.o. along. *ind 1st sg* **mbumtaachíh=laaw, mbumtaachíhla**. *ind 3rd sg* **pumtaachihláawal**. *ind inv* **mbum=taachíhlukw**. *ind I-you* **kpumtaa=chíhlul**. *conj 3rd sg* **pŭmutaachíh=laat**. *imp* **pŭmutáachihl**. *ptcpl* **peemtaachíhlaat**.

**pŭmutoonháaleew** VTA preach to s.o. *ind 1st sg* **mbumtoonháalaaw, mbumtoonháala**. *ind 3rd sg* **pum=toonhaaláawal**. *ind inv* **mbumtoon=háalukw**. *ind I-you* **kpumtoonháa=lul**. *conj 3rd sg* **pŭmutoonháalaat**. *imp* **pŭmutóonhaal**. *ptcpl* **peem=toonháalaat**.

**pŭmutóonheew** VAI preach. *ind 1st sg* **mbumtóonhe, mbumtóonheem**. *conj 3rd sg* **pŭmutóonheet**. *imp* **pŭmutóonheel**. *ptcpl* **peemtóonheet**.

**pŭmúwaleew** VTA carry s.o. on one's back. *ind 1st sg* **mbumŭwálaaw, mbumŭwála**. *ind 3rd sg* **pumŭwal=áawal**. *ind inv* **mbumŭwálukw**. *ind I-you* **kpumŭwálul**. *conj 3rd sg* **pŭmúwalaat**. *imp* **pŭmúwal**. *ptcpl* **peemŭwálaat**.

**pŭmúwaleew** VAI carry a load on one's back. *ind 1st sg* **mbumŭwále, mbumŭwáleem**. *conj 3rd sg* **pŭ=múwaleet**. *imp* **pŭmúwaleel**. *ptcpl* **peemŭwáleet**.

**pŭmúwees** NA boil. **Aláamii-pŭmúwees apúw.** 'There was a boil inside.' *pl*

**pŭmuwéesak**. *loc* **pŭmuwéesung**. *dimin* **pŭmuwéeshush**. *obv* **pŭmuw=éesal**. *See* **pŭmúweew**.

**pŭmúweew** NA boil. *pl* **pŭmuwéewak**. *obv* **pŭmuwéewal**. *See* **pŭmúwees**.

**pŭmúy** NI grease. *loc* **pŭmíing**.

**pŭnaaháaleew** VTA throw s.o. down, throw s.o. in. *ind 1st sg* **mbunaaháa=laaw, mbunaaháala**. *ind 3rd sg* **punaahaaláawal**. *ind inv* **mbunaa=háalukw**. *ind I-you* **kpunaaháalul**. *conj 3rd sg* **pŭnaaháalaat**. *imp* **pŭnáahaal**. *ptcpl* **peenaaháalaat**.

**pŭnáaheew** VAIO throw s.t. down, throw s.t. in. *ind 1st sg* **mbunáaheen**. *ind 3rd sg* **punáaheen**. *conj 3rd sg* **pŭnáaheet**. *imp* **pŭnáaheel**. *ptcpl* **peenáaheet**.

**pŭnáakchehl** VAI jump down. *ind 1st sg* **mbunáakchehl**. *conj 3rd sg* **pŭnaak=chéhluk**. *imp* **pŭnaakchéhlih**. *ptcpl* **peenaakchéhluk**.

**pŭnaapéhlaleew** VTA hang s.o. down. *ind 1st sg* **mbunaapéhlalaaw, mbun=aapéhlala**. *ind 3rd sg* **punaapehla=láawal**. *ind inv* **mbunaapéhlalukw**. *ind I-you* **kpunaapéhlalul**. *conj 3rd sg* **pŭnaapéhlalaat**. *imp* **pŭnaapéh=lal**. *ptcpl* **peenaapéhlalaat**.

**pŭnaapéhlatoow** VTI2 hang s.t. down. *ind 1st sg* **mbunaapéhlatoon**. *ind 3rd sg* **punaapéhlatoon**. *conj 1st sg* **pŭ=naapehlatáwaan**. *conj 3rd sg* **pŭnaa=péhlataakw**. *imp* **pŭnaapéhlatool**. *ptcpl* **peenaapéhlataakw**.

**pŭnaapéhleew** VAI hang down *(s.t. animate)*. *ind 1st sg* **mbunaapéhla, mbunaapéhlaam**. *conj 3rd sg* **pŭ=naapéhlaat**. *ptcpl* **peenaapéhlaat**.

**pŭnaapéhleew** VII hang down. *conj 3rd sg* **pŭnaapéhlaak**. *ptcpl* **peenaapéh=laak**.

**pŭnaapŭwéhleew** VII flow down *(of liquids)*. *conj 3rd sg* **pŭnaapŭwéhlaak**. *ptcpl* **peenaapŭwéhlaak**.

**pŭnáasuw** VAI look on. **Xwéelook lún=ŭwak pŭnáasŭwak éenda-neenaxk=hwátiing.** 'Lots of people watched the baseball game.' *ind 1st sg* **mbunáasi, mbunáasiim**. *conj 3rd sg* **pŭnáasiit**. *imp* **pŭnáasiil**. *ptcpl* **peenáasiit**.

**pŭnáham** VOTI1A earn money, earn a wage. *ind 1st sg* **mbúnham**. *conj 3rd sg* **pŭnáhang**. *ptcpl* **péenhang**.

**pŭnáham** VTI1A earn s.t. *ind 1st sg* **mbunhámun**. *ind 3rd sg* **punhámun**. *conj 1st sg* **pŭnáhŭmaan**. *conj 3rd sg* **pŭnáhang**. *imp* **pŭnáhih**. *ptcpl* **péenhang**.

**pŭnahkwíixun** VII go down *(of water)*. *conj 3rd sg* **pŭnahkwíixung**. *ptcpl* **peenahkwíixung**.

**pŭnám** VTI1A look at s.t. *ind 1st sg* **mbúnamun**. *ind 3rd sg* **púnamun**. *conj 1st sg* **pŭnámaan**. *conj 3rd sg* **pŭnáng**. *imp* **pŭnáh**. *ptcpl* **péenang**.

**pŭnáweew** VTA look at s.o., look at s.t. animate. *ind 1st sg* **mbúnawaaw, mbúnawa**. *ind 3rd sg* **punawáawal**. *ind inv* **mbúnaakw**. *ind I-you* **kpún=ool**. *conj 3rd sg* **pŭnáwaat**. *imp* **pŭnáw**. *ptcpl* **péenawaat**. *moderative reduplication* **paapŭnawáawal**.

**pŭnawéelŭmeew** VTA think about s.o. *ind 1st sg* **mbunawéelŭmaaw, mbunawéelŭma**. *ind 3rd sg* **puna=weelŭmáawal**. *ind inv* **mbunawée=lŭmukw**. *ind I-you* **kpunawéelŭmul**. *conj 3rd sg* **pŭnawéelŭmaat**. *imp* **pŭnawéelum**. *ptcpl* **peenawéelŭ=maat**.

**pŭnaweelúndam** VOTI1A think. *ind 1st sg* **mbunaweelúndam**. *conj 3rd sg* **pŭnaweelúndang**. *imp* **pŭnawee=lúndah**. *ptcpl* **peenaweelúndang**.

**pŭnaweelúndam** VTI1A think about s.t. *ind 1st sg* **mbunaweelúndamun**. *ind 3rd sg* **punaweelúndamun**. *conj 1st sg* **pŭnaweelúndamaan**. *conj 3rd sg* **pŭnaweelúndang**. *imp* **pŭnawee=lúndah**. *ptcpl* **peenaweelúndang**.

**pundáakwat** VII be heard. *conj 3rd sg*

**pundáakwahk**. *ptcpl* **peendáa=kwahk**.

**pundáakwsuw** VAI be heard *(s.t. animate). ind 1st sg* **mbundáakwsi**, **mbundáakwsiim**. *conj 3rd sg* **pundáakwsiit**. *ptcpl* **peendáakwsiit**.

**púndam** VTI 1A hear s.t. **Máh kóolu-pundamóowun.** 'You didn't hear it correctly.' *ind 1st sg* **mbúndamun**. *ind 3rd sg* **púndamun**. *conj 1st sg* **púndamaan**. *conj 3rd sg* **púndang**. *ptcpl* **péendang**.

**pundamóoheew** VAIO make s.o. hear. *ind 1st sg* **mbundamóoheen**. *ind 3rd sg* **pundamoohéenal**. *conj 3rd sg* **pundamóoheet**. *imp* **pundamóoheel**. *ptcpl* **peendamóoheet**.

**púndaweew** VTA hear s.o. *ind 1st sg* **mbúndawaaw**, **mbúndawa**. *ind 3rd sg* **pundawáawal**. *ind inv* **mbún=daakw**. *ind I-you* **kpúndool**. *conj 3rd sg* **púndawaat**. *ptcpl* **péendawaat**.

**pŭniitŭyéepuw** VAI fall on one's backside while sitting. *ind 1st sg* **mbunii=tŭyéepi**, **mbuniitŭyéepiim**. *conj 3rd sg* **pŭniitŭyéepiit**. *ptcpl* **peeniitŭ=yéepiit**.

**pŭníhkam** VTI 1A knock s.t. down, knock s.t. over *(using the foot or body). ind 1st sg* **mbuníhkamun**. *ind 3rd sg* **puníhkamun**. *conj 1st sg* **pŭníhka=maan**. *conj 3rd sg* **pŭníhkang**. *imp* **pŭníhkah**. *ptcpl* **peeníhkang**.

**pŭníhkaweew** VTA knock s.o. down, knock s.o. over, knock s.o. off something *(using the foot or body).* **Mbun=íhkawaaw wúnj-apíineeng.** 'I knocked him off the bed.' *ind 1st sg* **mbun=íhkawaaw**, **mbuníhkawa**. *ind 3rd sg* **punihkawáawal**. *ind inv* **mbuníh=kaakw**. *ind I-you* **kpuníhkool**. *conj 3rd sg* **pŭníhkawaat**. *imp* **pŭníhkaw**. *ptcpl* **peeníhkawaat**.

**pŭníhleew** VAI fall down off of something. *ind 1st sg* **mbuníhla**, **mbuníh=laam**. *conj 3rd sg* **pŭníhlaat**. *ptcpl* **peeníhlaat**.

**pŭníhleew** VII fall down off of something. *conj 3rd sg* **pŭníhlaak**. *ptcpl* **peeníhlaak**.

**pŭnihtéeham** VTI 1A knock s.t. down from something, knock s.t. off. *ind 1st sg* **mbunihtéehŭmun**. *ind 3rd sg* **punihtéehŭmun**. *conj 1st sg* **pŭnih=téehŭmaan**. *conj 3rd sg* **pŭnihtée=hang**. *imp* **pŭnihtéehih**. *ptcpl* **pee=nihtéehang**.

**pŭnihtéeheew** VTA hit s.o. and knock them down, hit s.o. and knock them off, hit s.o. and knock them over. *ind 1st sg* **mbunihtéehaaw**, **mbunihtée=ha**. *ind 3rd sg* **punihteeháawal**. *ind inv* **mbunihtéehookw**. *ind I-you* **kpunihtéehul**. *conj 3rd sg* **pŭnihtée=haat**. *imp* **pŭníhteeh**. *ptcpl* **peenih=téehaat**.

**pŭnihtéexiin** VAI fall down. **Apíineeng wúnj-pŭnihtéexiin.** 'He fell out of bed.' *ind 1st sg* **mbunihtéexiin**, **mbunihtéexi**. *conj 3rd sg* **pŭnihtée=xiing**. *ptcpl* **peenihtéexiing**.

**pŭnoondíhkeew** VAIO display s.t. of importance, show s.t. of importance, display s.t. *(of one's feelings)*; show s.t. *(of one's feelings).* **Kpunoondíh=keen máh ktahwaaláawi.** 'You showed that you didn't love her.' *ind 1st sg* **mbunoondíhkeen**. *ind 3rd sg* **punoondíhkeen**. *conj 3rd sg* **pŭ=noondíhkeet**. *imp* **pŭnoondíhkeel**. *ptcpl* **peenoondíhkeet**.

**pŭnoondŭláweew** VTA show one's feelings to s.o. *ind 1st sg* **mbunoondŭ=láwaaw**, **mbunoondŭláwa**. *ind 3rd sg* **punoondŭlawáawal**. *ind inv* **mbunóondŭlaakw**. *ind I-you* **kpun=óondŭlool**. *conj 3rd sg* **pŭnoondŭ=láwaat**. *imp* **pŭnóondŭlaw**. *ptcpl* **peenoondŭláwaat**.

**pŭnóngwaam** VAI fall out of bed while sleeping. *ind 1st sg* **mbunóngwaam**. *conj 3rd sg* **pŭnóngwaang**. *ptcpl*

**peenóngwaang**.

**pŭnóngxwiin** VAI fall out of bed while sleeping. *ind 1st sg* **mbunóngxwiin**. *conj 3rd sg* **pŭnóngxwiing**. *ptcpl* **peenóngxwiing**, **peenóngxwiit**.

**pŭyóol** NI violin. *pl* **pŭyóolal**. *poss* **mbuyóolum**. *loc* **pŭyóolung**. *dimin* **pŭyóolush**. *From Dutch.*

**pŭyoolhámeew** VAI play the violin. *ind 1st sg* **mbuyoolháma**, **mbuyoolhámaam**. *conj 3rd sg* **pŭyoolhámaat**. *imp* **pŭyoolhámaal**. *ptcpl* **pŭyoolhámaat**.

**pwáawameew** VTA be unable to bite s.o. *ind 1st sg* **mbwáawamaaw**, **mbwáawama**. *ind 3rd sg* **pwaawamáawal**. *ind inv* **mbwáawamukw**. *ind I-you* **kpwáawamul**. *conj 3rd sg* **pwáawamaat**. *ptcpl* **pwáawamaat**.

**pwaawándam** VTI 1A be unable to bite s.t. *ind 1st sg* **mbwaawándamun**. *ind 3rd sg* **pwaawándamun**. *conj 1st sg* **pwaawándamaan**. *conj 3rd sg* **pwaawándang**. *ptcpl* **pwaawándang**.

**pwaawásktuw** VAI be constipated, be unable to defecate. *ind 1st sg* **mbwaawáskti**, **mbwaawásktiim**. *conj 3rd sg* **pwaawásktiit**. *ptcpl* **pwaawásktiit**. *See* **aalŭwásktuw**.

**pwáawham** VTI 1A be unable to hit s.t. *(using a tool or instrument). ind 1st sg* **mbwaawhámun**. *ind 3rd sg* **pwaawhámun**. *conj 1st sg* **pwaawhámaan**. *conj 3rd sg* **pwáawhang**. *ptcpl* **pwáawhang**.

**pwáawheew** VTA be unable to hit s.o. *(using a tool or instrument). ind 1st sg* **mbwáawhaaw**, **mbwáawha**. *ind 3rd sg* **pwaawháawal**. *ind inv* **mbwáawhookw**. *ind I-you* **kpwáawhool**. *conj 3rd sg* **pwáawhaat**. *ptcpl* **pwáawhaat**.

**pwaawii-** PV unable to. **Pwáawii-kunjchúnŭmun.** 'He can't push it.'; **Mbwáawii-wtúnŭmun.** 'I can't pull it.' *ptcpl* **pwáawii-**.

**pwáawsheew** VTA be unable to cut s.o. *ind 1st sg* **mbwáawshaaw**, **mbwáawsha**. *ind 3rd sg* **pwaawsháawal**. *ind inv* **mbwáawshookw**. *ind I-you* **kpwáawshool**. *conj 3rd sg* **pwáawshaat**. *ptcpl* **pwáawshaat**.

**pwáawshum** VTI 1A be unable to cut s.t. *ind 1st sg* **mbwaawshúmun**. *ind 3rd sg* **pwaawshúmun**. *conj 1st sg* **pwaawshúmaan**. *conj 3rd sg* **pwáawshung**. *ptcpl* **pwáawshung**.

**pwáawŭneew** VTA be unable to lift s.o. *ind 1st sg* **mbwáawŭnaaw**, **mbwáawŭna**. *ind 3rd sg* **pwaawŭnáawal**. *ind inv* **mbwáawŭnukw**. *ind I-you* **kpwáawŭnul**. *conj 3rd sg* **pwáawŭnaat**. *ptcpl* **pwáawŭnaat**.

**pwáawŭnum** VTI 1A be unable to lift s.t. *ind 1st sg* **mbwaawŭnúmun**. *ind 3rd sg* **pwaawŭnúmun**. *conj 1st sg* **pwaawŭnúmaan**. *conj 3rd sg* **pwáawŭnung**. *ptcpl* **pwáawŭnung**.

**pwahkaandpéexiin** VAI crack one's head. *ind 1st sg* **mbwahkaandpéexiin**, **mbwahkaandpéexi**. *conj 3rd sg* **pwahkaandpéexiing**. *ptcpl* **pwahkaandpéexiing**.

**pwáhkamaash** NA plum. *pl* **pwahkamáashak**. *poss* **mbwahkamáasum**. *dimin* **pwahkamáashush**. *obv* **pwahkamáashal**.

**pwáhkamaash** NI plum. *pl* **pwahkamáashal**. *poss* **mbwahkamáashum**. *loc* **pwahkamáashung**. *dimin* **pwahkamáashush**.

**pwáhkham** VTI 1A crack s.t. *ind 1st sg* **mbwahkhámun**. *ind 3rd sg* **pwahkhámun**. *conj 1st sg* **pwahkhámaan**. *conj 3rd sg* **pwáhkhang**. *imp* **pwáhkhah**. *ptcpl* **pwáhkhang**.

**pwahkháweew** VAI hatch *(of chicks). ind 1st sg* **mbwahkháwe**, **mbwahkháweem**. *conj 3rd sg* **pwahkháweet**. *imp* **pwahkháweel**. *ptcpl* **pwahkháweet**.

**pwáhkheew** VTA crack s.t. animate. *ind 1st sg* **mbwáhkhaaw, mbwáhkha**. *ind 3rd sg* **pwahkháawal**. *ind inv* **mbwáhkhookw**. *ind I-you* **kpwáhk=hool**. *conj 3rd sg* **pwáhkhaat**. *imp* **pwáhkhaw**. *ptcpl* **pwáhkhaat**.

**pwahkihtéeham** VTI 1A hit and crack s.t. *ind 1st sg* **mbwahkihtéehŭmun**. *ind 3rd sg* **pwahkihtéehŭmun**. *conj 1st sg* **pwahkihtéehŭmaan**. *conj 3rd sg* **pwahkihtéehang**. *imp* **pwahkih=téehih**. *ptcpl* **pwahkihtéehang**.

**pwahkihtéeheew** VTA hit and crack s.o., hit and crack s.t. animate. *ind 1st sg* **mbwahkihtéehaaw, mbwahkih=téeha**. *ind 3rd sg* **pwahkihteeháa=wal**. *ind inv* **mbwahkihtéehookw**. *ind I-you* **kpwahkihtéehul**. *conj 3rd sg* **pwahkihtéehaat**. *imp* **pwahkíh=teeh**. *ptcpl* **pwahkihtéehaat**.

**pwahkpéhleew** VAI have smallpox. *ind 1st sg* **mbwahkpéhla, mbwahkpéh=laam**. *conj 3rd sg* **pwahkpéhlaat**. *ptcpl* **pwahkpéhlaat**.

**pwáhkseew** VTA make s.t. animate explode, make s.t. animate blow up *(from heat)*. *ind 1st sg* **mbwáhksaaw, mbwáhksa**. *ind 3rd sg* **pwahksáa=wal**. *ind inv* **mbwáhksookw**. *ind I-you* **kpwáhksool**. *conj 3rd sg* **pwáhk=saat**. *imp* **pwáhkus**. *ptcpl* **pwáhksaat**.

**pwáhksum** VTI 1B make s.t. explode, make s.t. blow up *(from heat)*. *ind 1st sg* **mbwahksúmun**. *ind 3rd sg* **pwahksúmun**. *conj 1st sg* **pwahk=súmaan**. *conj 3rd sg* **pwáhksung**. *imp* **pwáhksih**. *ptcpl* **pwáhksung**.

**pwáhksuw** VAI explode, blow up, burst *(from heat, s.t. animate)*. *ind 1st sg* **mbwáhksi, mbwáhksiim**. *conj 3rd sg* **pwáhksiit**. *ptcpl* **pwáhksiit**.

**pwáhkteew** VII explode, blow up, burst *(from heat)*. *conj 3rd sg* **pwáhkteek**. *ptcpl* **pwáhkteek**.

**pwahpwaawíikwham** VOTI 1A hiccup. *ind 1st sg* **mbwahpwaawíikwham**. *conj 3rd sg* **pwahpwaawíikwhang**. *ptcpl* **pwahpwaawíikwhang**.

**pwàhwiingwéeheew** VTA slap s.o. in the face *(loud enough to be heard)*. *ind 1st sg* **mbwahwiingwéehaaw, mbwah=wiingwéeha**. *ind 3rd sg* **pwàhwiin=gweeháawal**. *ind inv* **mbwahwiin=gwéehookw**. *ind I-you* **kpwahwiin=gwéehool**. *conj 3rd sg* **pwàhwiin=gwéehaat**. *imp* **pwàhwíingweeh**. *ptcpl* **pwàhwiingwéehaat**.

**pwàhwíixiin** VAI fall and make a noise, fall and make a dull noise, fall with a thud, fall down hard, fall flat on one's face. *ind 1st sg* **mbwahwíixiin, mbwahwíixi**. *conj 3rd sg* **pwàhwíi=xiing**. *ptcpl* **pwàhwíixiing, pwàh=wíixiit**.

**pwàhwíixun** VII fall and make a noise, fall and make a dull noise, fall with a thud. *conj 3rd sg* **pwàhwíixung**. *ptcpl* **pwàhwíixung**.

**pwàhwihtéeheew** VTA slap s.o. *(loud e-nough to be heard)*. *ind 1st sg* **mbwah=wihtéehaaw, mbwahwihtéeha**. *ind 3rd sg* **pwàhwihteeháawal**. *ind inv* **mbwahwihtéehookw**. *ind I-you* **kpwahwihtéehool**. *conj 3rd sg* **pwàhwihtéehaat**. *imp* **pwàhwíhteeh**. *ptcpl* **pwàhwihtéehaat**.

**pwàhwihtéexiin** VAI fall down and make a noise. *ind 1st sg* **mbwahwihtéexiin, mbwahwihtéexi**. *conj 3rd sg* **pwàh=wihtéexiing**. *ptcpl* **pwàhwihtéexiing**.

**pwàhwsiitéexiin** VAI make noise with one's feet. *ind 1st sg* **mbwahwsii=téexiin, mbwahwsiitéexi**. *conj 3rd sg* **pwàhwsiitéexiing**. *imp* **pwàhwsii=téexiil**. *ptcpl* **pwàhwsiitéexiing**.

**pwàhwsúmaweew** VTA slap s.o. in the face *(loud enough to be heard)*. *ind 1st sg* **mbwahwsúmawaaw, mbwah=wsúmawa**. *ind 3rd sg* **pwàhwsuma=wáawal**. *ind inv* **mbwahwsúmaakw**. *ind I-you* **kpwahwsúmool**. *conj 3rd sg* **pwàhwsúmawaat**. *imp* **pwàhw=**

**súmaw**. *ptcpl* **pwàhwsúmawaat**.

**pwàhwsheengwéeheew** VTA slap s.o. in the face *(loud enough to be heard). ind 1st sg* **mbwahwsheengwéehaaw**, **mbwahwsheengwéeha**. *ind 3rd sg* **pwàhwsheengweeháawal**. *ind inv* **mbwahwsheengwéehukw**. *ind I-you* **kpwahwsheengwéehul**. *conj 3rd sg* **pwàhwsheengwéehaat**. *imp* **pwàh=wshéengweeh**. *ptcpl* **pwàhwsheen=gwéehaat**.

**pwàhwsheengwéexiin** VAI hit one's face hard against something. *ind 1st sg* **mbwahwsheengwéexiin**, **mbwah=wsheengwéexi**. *conj 3rd sg* **pwàhw=sheengwéexiing**. *ptcpl* **pwàhw=sheengwéexiing**, **pwàhwsheen=gwéexiit**.

**pxáakw** VAI choke. *ind 1st sg* **mbáx=aakw**. *conj 3rd sg* **pxáakwuk**. *ptcpl* **peexáakwuk**. *intensive reduplication* **pápxaakw**.

**pxánghweew** VTA patch s.t. animate. *ind 1st sg* **mbaxánghwaaw**, **mbaxáng=hwa**. *ind 3rd sg* **paxanghwáawal**. *ind inv* **mbaxánghookw**. *ind I-you* **kpaxánghool**. *conj 3rd sg* **pxáng=hwaat**. *imp* **pxánghwaw**. *ptcpl* **peexánghwaat**.

**pxanghwáasuw** VAI be patched, have patches *(s.t. animate). ind 1st sg* **mbaxanghwáasi**, **mbaxanghwáa=siim**. *conj 3rd sg* **pxanghwáasiit**. *ptcpl* **peexanghwáasiit**.

**pxanghwáasuw** VII be patched, have patches. *conj 3rd sg* **pxanghwáasiik**. *ptcpl* **peexanghwáasiik**.

**pxánghwam** VTI1A patch s.t. *ind 1st sg* **mbaxanghwámun**. *ind 3rd sg* **pax=anghwámun**. *conj 1st sg* **pxang=hwámaan**. *conj 3rd sg* **pxánghwang**. *imp* **pxánghwah**. *ptcpl* **peexáng=hwang**.

**pxanghwíikeew** VAI patch things. *ind 1st sg* **mbaxanghwíike**, **mbaxanghwíi=keem**. *conj 3rd sg* **pxanghwíikeet**. *imp* **pxanghwíikeel**. *ptcpl* **peexang=hwíikeet**.

**pxwaapŭlúsheew** VAI peel apples. *ind 1st sg* **mboxwaapŭlúshe**, **mboxwaa=pŭlúsheem**. *conj 3rd sg* **pxwaapŭ=lúsheet**. *imp* **pxwaapŭlúsheel**. *ptcpl* **peexaapŭlúsheet**. *See* **pxwashaa=pŭlúsheew**.

**pxwásŭmeew** VAI lye corn. *ind 1st sg* **mboxwasúma**, **mboxwasúmaam**. *conj 3rd sg* **pxwásŭmaat**. *imp* **pxwás=ŭmaal**. *ptcpl* **peexasúmaat**.

**pxwásheew** VTA peel s.t. animate. *ind 1st sg* **mbóxwashaaw**, **mbóxwasha**. *ind 3rd sg* **poxwasháawal**. *ind inv* **mbóxwashookw**. *ind I-you* **kpóxwa=shool**. *conj 3rd sg* **pxwáshaat**. *imp* **pxwásh**. *ptcpl* **péexashaat**.

**pxwashaapŭlúsheew** VAI peel apples. *ind 1st sg* **mboxwashaapŭlúshe**, **mboxwashaapŭlúsheem**. *conj 3rd sg* **pxwashaapŭlúsheet**. *imp* **pxwash=aapŭlúsheel**. *ptcpl* **peexashaapŭ=lúsheet**. *See* **pxwaapŭlúsheew**.

**pxwashíhpŭneew** VAI peel potatoes. *ind 1st sg* **mboxwashíhpŭne**, **mboxwa=shíhpŭneem**. *conj 3rd sg* **pxwashíh=pŭneet**. *imp* **pxwashíhpŭneel**. *ptcpl* **peexashíhpŭneet**.

**pxwíineew** VTA skin s.t. animate, remove the covering from s.t. animate. *ind 1st sg* **mboxwíinaaw**, **mboxwíina**. *ind 3rd sg* **poxwiináawal**. *ind inv* **mbox=wíinukw**. *ind I-you* **kpoxwíinul**. *conj 3rd sg* **pxwíinaat**. *imp* **pxwíin**. *ptcpl* **peexíinaat**.

**pxwíinam** VTI1A skin s.t., remove the covering from s.t.; shell s.t. *(of corn). ind 1st sg* **mboxwíinamun**. *ind 3rd sg* **poxwíinamun**. *conj 1st sg* **pxwíinamaan**. *conj 3rd sg* **pxwíi=nang**. *imp* **pxwíinih**. *ptcpl* **peexíi=nang**.

**pxwiináskweew** VAI husk corn. *ind 1st sg* **mboxwiináskwe**, **mboxwiinás=kweem**. *conj 3rd sg* **pxwiináskweet**.

*imp* **pxwiináskweel**. *ptcpl* **peexii=náskweet**.

**pxwíiskeew** VII be skinned, be peeled off *(of bedsores, of blisters)*. *conj 3rd sg* **pxwíiskeek**. *ptcpl* **peexwíiskeek**.

**pxwíiskham** VTI 1A skin s.t. *(especially of body parts)*. *ind 1st sg* **mbox=wiiskhámun**. *ind 3rd sg* **poxwiisk=hámun**. *conj 1st sg* **pxwiiskhámaan**. *conj 3rd sg* **pxwíiskhang**. *ptcpl* **peexíiskhang**.

**pxwíisksuw** VAI have an open sore, be skinned, be peeled off *(of bedsores, of blisters)*. *ind 1st sg* **mboxwíisksi**, **mboxwíisksiim**. *conj 3rd sg* **pxwíisk=siit**. *ptcpl* **peexwíisksiit**.

**pxwíixiin** VAI peel, be peeled *(s.t. animate)*. *ind 1st sg* **mboxwíixiin**, **mboxwíixi**. *conj 3rd sg* **pxwíixiing**. *ptcpl* **peexíixiing**.

**pxwíixun** VII peel, be peeled. **Ndáxay pxwíixun.** 'My skin is peeling.' *conj 3rd sg* **pxwíixung**. *ptcpl* **peexwíi=xung**.

# S

**saakáandpeew** VAI have one's head sticking out. **Máh neewáawi shúkw péech-saakáandpeew.** 'I didn't see him but his head was sticking out.' *ind 1st sg* **nzaakáandpa**, **nzaa=káandpaam**. *conj 3rd sg* **saakáand=paat**. *ptcpl* **saakáandpaat**.

**saakaandpéexiin** VAI have one's head sticking out, lie with one's head sticking out, stick one's head out. *ind 1st sg* **nzaakaandpéexiin**, **nzaakaand=péexi**. *conj 3rd sg* **saakaandpéexiing**. *imp* **saakaandpéexiil**. *ptcpl* **saa=kaandpéexiing**, **saakaandpéexiit**.

**saakaapéhleew** VAI hang down. *ind 1st sg* **nzaakaapéhla**, **nzaakaapéhlaam**. *conj 3rd sg* **saakaapéhlaat**. *imp* **saakaapéhlaal**. *ptcpl* **saakaapéhlaat**.

**saakaapéhleew** VII hang down. *conj 3rd sg* **saakaapéhlaak**. *ptcpl* **saakaa=péhlaak**.

**saakangwanéexiin** VAI have one's heel sticking out, stick one's heel out. *ind 1st sg* **nzaakangwanéexiin**, **nzaa=kangwanéexi**. *conj 3rd sg* **saakan=gwanéexiing**. *imp* **saakangwanée=xiil**. *ptcpl* **saakangwanéexiing**, **saakangwanéexiit**.

**saakatayéewxeew** VAI walk with one's belly sticking out, have one's belly sticking out as one walks. *ind 1st sg* **nzaakatayéewxe**, **nzaakatayéew=xeem**. *conj 3rd sg* **saakatayéewxeet**. *imp* **saakatayéewxeel**. *ptcpl* **saaka=tayéewxeet**.

**saakatayéexiin** VAI stick one's belly out, have one's belly sticking out. *ind 1st sg* **nzaakatayéexiin**, **nzaakatayéexi**. *conj 3rd sg* **saakatayéexiing**. *imp* **saakatayéexiil**. *ptcpl* **saakatayée=xiing**, **saakatayéexiit**.

**saakhóosuw** VAI have one's slip sticking out. *ind 1st sg* **nzaakhóosi**, **nzaak=hóosiim**. *conj 3rd sg* **saakhóosiit**. *ptcpl* **saakhóosiit**.

**saakíiheew** VTA watch s.o., watch for s.o., watch out for s.o. *ind 1st sg* **nzaakíihaaw**, **nzaakíiha**. *ind 3rd sg* **wsaakiiháawal**. *ind inv* **nzaakíihukw**. *ind I-you* **ksaakíihul**. *conj 3rd sg* **saakíihaat**. *imp* **sáakiih**. *ptcpl* **saa=kíihaat**.

**saakíikun** VII sprout, come up *(of plants)*. *conj 3rd sg* **saakíikung**. *ptcpl* **saakíikung**.

**saakíikuw** VAI sprout, come up *(s.t. animate, of plants)*. *ind 1st sg* **nzaakíiki**, **nzaakíikiim**. *conj 3rd sg* **saakíikiit**. *ptcpl* **saakíikiit**.

**saakiitŭyéexiin** VAI stick one's backside out, have one's backside sticking out. *ind 1st sg* **nzaakiitŭyéexiin**, **nzaa=kiitŭyéexi**. *conj 3rd sg* **saakiitŭyée=**

xiing. *imp* **saakiitŭyéexiil**. *ptcpl* **saakiitŭyéexiing**, **saakiitŭyéexiit**.

**saakíixiin** VAI stick out *(s.t. animate)*. *ind 1st sg* **nzaakíixiin**, **nzaakíixi**. *conj 3rd sg* **saakíixiing**. *ptcpl* **saa=kíixiing**.

**saakíixtoow** VTI2 stick s.t. out. *ind 1st sg* **nzaakíixtoon**. *ind 3rd sg* **wsaa=kíixtoon**. *conj 1st sg* **saakiixtáwaan**. *conj 3rd sg* **saakíixtaakw**. *imp* **saakíixtool**. *ptcpl* **saakíixtaakw**.

**saakíixun** VII stick out. **Wshúkwŭnay saakíixun.** 'His tail is sticking out.' *conj 3rd sg* **saakíixung**. *ptcpl* **saa=kíixung**.

**saakíhleew** VII stick out. **Saakíhleew ksuwétŭlum.** 'Your sweater was sticking out.' *conj 3rd sg* **saakíhlaak**. *ptcpl* **saakíhlaak**.

**saakíhtoow** VTI2 watch s.t., watch for s.t., watch out for s.t. **Wŭníhtaa-wéemi kwéek -saakíhtoon.** 'He watches everything.' *ind 1st sg* **nzaa=kíhtoon**. *ind 3rd sg* **wsaakíhtoon**. *conj 1st sg* **saakíhtawaan**. *conj 3rd sg* **saakíhtaakw**. *imp* **saakíhtool**. *ptcpl* **saakíhtaakw**.

**saakohkwéexiin** VAI lie with one's head sticking out, have one's head sticking out. **Mbíing nóonj-saakohkwéexiin.** 'My head was sticking out of the water'; **Nŭmutakwaháasi shùkéhla nzaakohkwéexiin.** 'I was covered up but my head was sticking out.' *ind 1st sg* **nzaakohkwéexiin**, **nzaakoh=kwéexi**. *conj 3rd sg* **saakohkwée=xiing**. *imp* **saakohkwéexiil**. *ptcpl* **saakohkwéexiing**, **saakohkwéexiit**.

**saakpéhleew** VAI get measles, get chicken pox, come out in blotches, come out in spots. *ind 1st sg* **nzaak=péhla**, **nzaakpéhlaam**. *conj 3rd sg* **saakpéhlaat**. *ptcpl* **saakpéhlaat**.

**saakpéhleew** VII come out *(of liquid)*. *conj 3rd sg* **saakpéhlaak**. *ptcpl* **saakpéhlaak**.

**saaksíiteew** VAI have one's foot sticking out. *ind 1st sg* **nzaaksíita**, **nzaaksíi=taam**. *conj 3rd sg* **saaksíitaat**. *ptcpl* **saaksíitaat**.

**saaksiitéexiin** VAI stick one's feet out, have one's feet sticking out. *ind 1st sg* **nzaaksiitéexiin**, **nzaaksiitéexi**. *conj 3rd sg* **saaksiitéexiing**. *imp* **saaksiitéexiil**. *ptcpl* **saaksiitéexiing**, **saaksiitéexiit**.

**sáakun** VII sprout, come up *(out of the ground)*. *conj 3rd sg* **sáakung**. *ptcpl* **sáakung**. *moderative reduplication* **saasáakun**.

**saakŭnaxkéexiin** VAI stick one's hand out, have one's hand sticking out. *ind 1st sg* **nzaakŭnaxkéexiin**, **nzaakŭ=naxkéexi**. *conj 3rd sg* **saakŭnaxkée=xiing**. *imp* **saakŭnaxkéexiil**. *ptcpl* **saakŭnaxkéexiing**, **saakŭnaxkée=xiit**.

**sáakŭnum** VTI1B stick s.t. out. *ind 1st sg* **nzaakŭnúmun**. *ind 3rd sg* **wsaa=kŭnúmun**. *conj 1st sg* **saakŭnúmaan**. *conj 3rd sg* **sáakŭnung**. *imp* **sáakŭ=nih**. *ptcpl* **sáakŭnung**.

**sáakuw** VAI sprout, come up *(out of the ground)*. *ind 1st sg* **nzáaki**, **nzáakiim**. *conj 3rd sg* **sáakiit**. *imp* **sáakiil**. *ptcpl* **sáakiit**.

**saakxoonéexiin** VAI stick one's neck out, have one's neck sticking out. *ind 1st sg* **nzaakxoonéexiin**, **nzaakxoonée=xi**. *conj 3rd sg* **saakxoonéexiing**. *imp* **saakxoonéexiil**. *ptcpl* **saakxoonée=xiing**, **saakxoonéexiit**.

**sáalaak** NI log. *pl* **saaláakal**. *poss* **nzaa=láakum**. *loc* **saaláakung**. *dimin* **shaaláakush**. *From English* saw log.

**saaláakheew** VAI cut logs. *ind 1st sg* **nzaaláakhe**, **nzaaláakheem**. *conj 3rd sg* **saaláakheet**. *imp* **saaláakheel**. *ptcpl* **saaláakheet**.

**sáangweew** VAI bawl, holler; make noise *(of vocal sounds)*. **Chkwálak saan=gwéewak.** 'The frogs are bawling.' *ind*

*1st sg* **nzáangwe**, **nzáangweem**. *conj 3rd sg* **sáangweet**. *imp* **sáangweel**. *ptcpl* **sáangweet**.

**sáapameew** VTA lick s.o., lick s.t. animate. *ind 1st sg* **nzáapamaaw**, **nzáa=pama**. *ind 3rd sg* **wsaapamáawal**. *ind inv* **nzáapamukw**. *ind I-you* **ksáapamul**. *conj 3rd sg* **sáapamaat**. *imp* **sáapam**. *ptcpl* **sáapamaat**.

**saapándam** VTI1A lick s.t. *ind 1st sg* **nzaapándamun**. *ind 3rd sg* **wsaa=pándamun**. *conj 1st sg* **saapánda=maan**. *conj 3rd sg* **saapándang**. *imp* **saapándah**. *ptcpl* **saapándang**.

**sáapheew** VTA sting s.o. *ind 1st sg* **nzáaphaaw**, **nzáapha**. *ind 3rd sg* **wsaapháawal**. *ind inv* **nzáaphookw**. *ind I-you* **ksáaphool**. *conj 3rd sg* **sáaphaat**. *imp* **sáaphaw**. *ptcpl* **sáaphaat**.

**saapiilanúweew** VAI stick out one's tongue. *ind 1st sg* **nzaapiilanúwe**, **nzaapiilanúweem**. *conj 3rd sg* **saapiilanúweet**. *imp* **saapiilanúweel**. *ptcpl* **saapiilanúweet**. *intensive reduplication* **sahsaapiilanúweew**.

**saapiilanuwéexiin** VAI have one's tongue sticking out. *ind 1st sg* **nzaa=piilanuwéexiin**, **nzaapiilanuwéexi**. *conj 3rd sg* **saapiilanuwéexiing**. *imp* **saapiilanuwéexiil**. *ptcpl* **saapiila=nuwéexiing**, **saapiilanuwéexiit**.

**saapiilanuwéhtaweew** VTA stick one's tongue out at s.o. *ind 1st sg* **nzaa=piilanuwéhtawaaw**, **nzaapiilanuw=éhtawa**. *ind 3rd sg* **wsaapiilanuw=ehtawáawal**. *ind inv* **nzaapiilanuw=éhtaakw**. *ind I-you* **ksaapiilanuw=éhtool**. *conj 3rd sg* **saapiilanuw=éhtawaat**. *imp* **saapiilanuwéhtaw**. *ptcpl* **saapiilanuwéhtawaat**.

**saapŭléexiin** VAI shine brightly, be brilliant *(especially light)*; wear bright colours. *ind 1st sg* **nzaapŭléexiin**, **nzaapŭléexi**. *conj 3rd sg* **saapŭlée=xiing**. *ptcpl* **saapŭléexiing**.

**saapŭléexun** VII shine brightly, be brilliant, be brightly coloured *(especially light)*. *conj 3rd sg* **saapŭléexung**. *ptcpl* **saapŭléexung**.

**saapŭléhleew** VII be lightning. *conj 3rd sg* **saapŭléhlaak**. *ptcpl* **saapŭléhlaak**. *intensive reduplication* **saasaapŭ=léhleew**.

**saasiingtuyéewuw** VAI take one's time. **Kŭníhtaa-saasiingtuyéewi.** 'You know how to take your time.' *ind 1st sg* **nzaasiingtuyéewi**, **nzaasiing=tuyéewiim**. *conj 3rd sg* **saasiing=tuyéewiit**. *ptcpl* **saasiingtuyéewiit**. *considered impolite*.

**saasiitéepookw** VAI have cold feet. *ind 1st sg* **nzaasiitéepookw**, **nzaasiitée=pookw**. *conj 3rd sg* **saasiiteepóo=kwuk**. *ptcpl* **saasiiteepóokwuk**. *See* **thusíiteew**.

**saasŭlunjéepookw** VAI have cold hands. *ind 1st sg* **nzaasŭlunjéepookw**. *conj 3rd sg* **saasŭlunjeepóokwuk**. *ptcpl* **saasŭlunjeepóokwuk**. *See* **thunáx=keew**.

**sahkáaheew** VAIO throw s.t. a certain distance. **Wáhlu nzahkáaheen.** 'I threw it far.' *ind 1st sg* **nzahkáaheen**. *ind 3rd sg* **wsahkáaheen**. *conj 3rd sg* **sahkáaheet**. *imp* **sahkáaheel**. *ptcpl* **sehkáaheet**.

**sahkáalakat** VII be a certain depth, be a certain length *(of holes)*. **Ngwúteel sahkáalakat.** 'It is the same depth (of a hole).' *conj 3rd sg* **sahkáalakahk**. *ptcpl* **sehkáalakahk**.

**sahkaandpéexiin** VAI have one's head lying the length of something. **Kíixkii kpahóonung sahkaandpéexiin.** 'His head was by the door.' *ind 1st sg* **nzahkaandpéexiin**, **nzahkaandpée=xi**. *conj 3rd sg* **sahkaandpéexiing**. *imp* **sahkaandpéexiil**. *ptcpl* **seh=kaandpéexiing**, **sehkaandpéexiit**.

**sahkáawsuw** VAI live a certain length of time. **Siikwángu sahkaawsuyáane.**

'If I live until springtime.' *ind 1st sg* **nzahkáawsi**. *conj 3rd sg* **sahkáaw=siit**. *ptcpl* **sehkáawsiit**.

**sahkáhkeew** VAI be gone a certain length of time. **Níish-kíishooxkw sahkáh=keew.** 'He was gone for two months.'; **Thá sahkáhke?** 'How long has he been gone?' *ind 1st sg* **nzahkáhke**, **nzahkáhkeem**. *conj 3rd sg* **sahkáh=keet**. *ptcpl* **sehkáhkeet**.

**sahkáhkwat** VII be a certain height. **Tá sahkáhkwat wíikwahm?** 'How tall is the house?' *conj 3rd sg* **sahkáh=kwahk**. *ptcpl* **sehkáhkwahk**.

**sahkáhkwsuw** VAI be a certain height *(s.t. animate)*. **Táa éet thá wsah=káhkwsiin.** 'I wonder how tall he is.'; **Thá wsahkáhkwsiin?** 'How tall is he?' *ind 1st sg* **nzahkáhkwsi**, **nzah=káhkwsiim**. *conj 3rd sg* **sahkáhk=wsiit**. *ptcpl* **sehkáhkwsiit**.

**sáhkaleew** VTA boil s.t. animate. *ind 1st sg* **nzáhkalaaw**, **nzáhkala**. *ind 3rd sg* **wsahkaláawal**. *ind inv* **nzáhkalukw**. *ind I-you* **ksáhkalul**. *conj 3rd sg* **sáhkalaat**. *imp* **sáhkal**.

**sahkatáhkeew** VAI fight for a certain length of time, fight until now. *ind 1st sg* **nzahkatáhke**, **nzahkatáhkeem**. *conj 3rd sg* **sahkatáhkeet**. *imp* **sahkatáhkeel**. *ptcpl* **sehkatáhkeet**.

**sahkatíikeew** VAI boil things. *ind 1st sg* **nzahkatíike**, **nzahkatíikeem**. *conj 3rd sg* **sahkatíikeet**. *imp* **sahkatíi=keel**. *ptcpl* **sahkatíikeet**.

**sáhkatoow** VTI2 boil s.t. *ind 1st sg* **nzáh=katoon**. *ind 3rd sg* **wsáhkatoon**. *conj 1st sg* **sahkatáwaan**. *conj 3rd sg* **sáhkataakw**. *imp* **sáhkatool**.

**sáhkeew** VII be a certain length. **Thá sáhkeew pasíikaaxkw?** 'How long is the board?'; **Séhkeek wíikwahm.** 'The length of the house.' *conj 3rd sg* **sáhkeek**. *ptcpl* **séhkeek**.

**sáhkii** PC a certain length *(of time, measurement)*. **Sáhkii nóoli kíishooxkw.** 'For nine months.'

**sahkii-** PV a certain length *(of time, measurement)*. *ptcpl* **séhkii-**. *See* **sahku-**.

**sahkóoxweew** VAI walk so far, go so far, go a certain distance. **Móxa wáhlu sahkóoxweew.** 'He went very far.' *ind 1st sg* **nzahkóoxwe**, **nzahkóo=xweem**. *conj 3rd sg* **sahkóoxweet**. *imp* **sahkóoxweel**. *ptcpl* **sehkóo=xweet**. *See* **asahkóoxweew**.

**sahksiitéexiin** VAI have one's feet lying the length of something. **Wsháyee apíineeng sahksiitéexiin.** 'His feet are at the edge of the bed.' *ind 1st sg* **nzahksiitéexiin**, **nzahksiitéexi**. *conj 3rd sg* **sahksiitéexiing**. *imp* **sahksii=téexiil**. *ptcpl* **sehksiitéexiing**.

**sáhksuw** VAI be a certain length. **Thá wsáhksiin ná áxkook?** 'How long is the snake?' *ind 1st sg* **nzáhksi**, **nzáh=ksiim**. *conj 3rd sg* **sáhksiit**. *ptcpl* **séhksiit**.

**sáhksuw** VAI boil *(s.t. animate)*. *conj 3rd sg* **sáhksiit**. *ptcpl* **séhksiit**.

**sáhkteew** VII boil. *conj 3rd sg* **sáhkteek**. *ptcpl* **séhkteek**.

**sahku** PC a certain length *(of time, measurement)*. *informal*. **Kwúnii-wii=taawsoomáawal, tá sáhku shíi=kaanzh lúkih wtalŭwihkawáawal nzhíisal.** 'He lived with her for a long time, and she really dominated my uncle for a long time.'

**sahku-** PV a certain length *(of time, measurement)*. *informal*. **Séhku-wáapang ndalóhke.** 'I've been working since this morning.'; **Mbéehaaw sáhku-níish-kŭlakíike.** 'I waited for him until two o'clock.' *ptcpl* **séhku-**. *See* **sahkii-**.

**sahkúndeew** VII be a certain length *(of rooms)*. **Asahkóoxweew sehkún=deek.** 'He was pacing back and forth in the room.' *conj 3rd sg* **sahkúndeek**. *ptcpl* **sehkúndeek**.

**sahsáapŭlaan** VII be sprinkling rain.

*conj 3rd sg* **sahsáapŭlaang**. *ptcpl* **sahsáapŭlaang**.

**sahsakándŭwak** VAI bite each other. *ind 1st pl* **nzahsakandíhna**. *indef subject* **sahsakándiin**. *conj 3rd sg* **sahsa=kandíhtiit**. *imp* **sahsakándiikw**. *ptcpl* **sahsakandíhtiit**.

**sahsanákwtiis** NA wart. *pl* **sahsanak=wtíisak**. *obv* **sahsanakwtíisal**.

**sakáhkwŭneew** VTA hold s.o.'s hand. *ind 1st sg* **nzakáhkwŭnaaw**, **nzak=áhkwŭna**. *ind 3rd sg* **wsakahkwŭ=náawal**. *ind inv* **nzakáhkwŭnukw**. *ind I-you* **ksakáhkwŭnul**. *conj 3rd sg* **sakáhkwŭnaat**. *imp* **sakáhkwun**. *ptcpl* **seekáhkwŭnaat**.

**sakahtakuníikanal** NI reins. *usually plural*. *poss* **nzakahtakuníikanal**. *loc* **sakahtakuníikanung**. *dimin* **shakahchakuniikanúshal**.

**sakámeew** VTA bite s.o. *ind 1st sg* **nzákamaaw**, **nzákama**. *ind 3rd sg* **wsakamáawal**. *ind inv* **nzákamukw**. *ind I-you* **ksákamul**. *conj 3rd sg* **sakámaat**. *imp* **sakám**. *ptcpl* **sée=kamaat**.

**sakándam** VTI 1A bite s.t. *ind 1st sg* **nzakándamun**. *ind 3rd sg* **wsakán=damun**. *conj 1st sg* **sakándamaan**. *conj 3rd sg* **sakándang**. *imp* **sakán=dah**. *ptcpl* **seekándang**.

**sakandawéewak** VAI bite each other. *ind 1st pl* **nzakandawéhna**. *conj 3rd sg* **sakandawéhtiit**. *imp* **sakánda=weekw**. *ptcpl* **seekandawéhtiit**.

**sakaxéehoon** NI earring. *pl* **sakaxee=hóonal**. *poss* **nzakxéehoon**. *loc* **sa=kaxeehóonung**. *dimin* **shakaxee=hóonush**. *See* **skaxeehóonay**, **sakax=eehóonay**.

**sakaxeehóonay** NI earring. *pl* **sakaxee=hóonayal**. *poss* **nzakxeehóonay**. *See* **skaxeehóonay**, **sakaxéehoon**.

**sakaxeehoonháméew** VAI wear earrings. *ind 1st sg* **nzakxeehoonháma**, **nzak=xeehoonhámaam**. *conj 3rd sg* **sakax=eehoonhámaat**. *imp* **sakaxeehoon=hámaal**. *ptcpl* **seekxeehoonhámaat**. *See* **skaxéehuw**.

**sakeehíikan** NA ladder. *pl* **sakeehíika=nak**. *poss* **nzakeehíikan**. *loc* **sakee=híikanung**. *dimin* **shakeehíikanush**. *obv* **sakeehíikanal**.

**sakíimeew** NA mosquito. *pl* **sakiimée=wak**. *obv* **sakiiméewal**.

**sakiinaxkéeneew** VTA shake hands with s.o., hold hands with s.o. *ind 1st sg* **nzakiinaxkéenaaw**, **nzakiinaxkée=na**. *ind 3rd sg* **wsakiinaxkeenáawal**. *ind inv* **nzakiinaxkéenukw**. *ind I-you* **ksakiinaxkéenul**. *conj 3rd sg* **sakii=naxkéenaat**. *imp* **sakiináxkeen**. *ptcpl* **seekiinaxkéenaat**.

**sakiindpéeneew** VTA pull s.o.'s hair, pull on s.o.'s hair. *ind 1st sg* **nzakiind=péenaaw**, **nzakiindpéena**. *ind 3rd sg* **wsakiindpeenáawal**. *ind inv* **nzak=iindpéenukw**. *ind I-you* **ksakiind=péenul**. *conj 3rd sg* **sakiindpéenaat**. *imp* **sakíindpeen**. *ptcpl* **seekiindpée=naat**.

**sáksak** NA burr. *pl* **sàksákak**. *dimin* **shàkshákush**. *obv* **sàksákal**.

**sakukaatéeheew** VTA grab s.o.'s leg. *ind 1st sg* **nzakkaatéehaaw**, **nzakkaa=téeha**. *ind 3rd sg* **wsakkaateeháa=wal**. *ind inv* **nsakkaatéehookw**. *ind I-you* **ksakkaatéehool**. *conj 3rd sg* **sakukaatéehaat**. *imp* **sakukáateeh**. *ptcpl* **seekkaatéehaat**.

**sakukaatéeneew** VTA grab s.o. by the leg, pull on s.o.'s leg. *ind 1st sg* **nzakkaatéenaaw**, **nzakkaatéena**. *ind 3rd sg* **wsakkaateenáawal**. *ind inv* **nzakkaatéenukw**. *ind I-you* **ksakkaatéenul**. *conj 3rd sg* **sakuk=aatéenaat**. *imp* **sakukáateen**. *ptcpl* **seekkaatéenaat**.

**sakúneew** VTA grab s.o. by the hand, tug at s.o, pull on s.o. *ind 1st sg* **nzákŭ=naaw**, **nzákŭna**. *ind 3rd sg* **wsakŭ=náawal**. *ind inv* **nzákŭnukw**. *ind I-*

*you* **ksákŭnul**. *conj 3rd sg* **sakúnaat**. *imp* **sakún**. *ptcpl* **séekŭnaat**.

**sakunaxkéexiin** VAI have one's hand(s) sticking out. *ind 1st sg* **nzakŭnax=kéexiin, nzakŭnaxkéexi**. *conj 3rd sg* **sakunaxkéexiing**. *ptcpl* **seekŭnax=kéexiing**.

**sakúnum** VTI 1B grab s.t. by the hand, tug and pull on s.t. *ind 1st sg* **nzakŭ=númun**. *ind 3rd sg* **wsakŭnúmun**. *conj 1st sg* **sakúnŭmaan**. *conj 3rd sg* **sakúnung**. *imp* **sakúnih**. *ptcpl* **sée=kŭnung**.

**sàkwáawsuw** VAI lead an unsettled life, lead a restless life. *ind 1st sg* **nzak=wáawsi, nzakwáawsiim**. *conj 3rd sg* **sàkwáawsiit**. *ptcpl* **sàkwáawsiit**.

**sàkwahtéenamuw** VAI be worried. *ind 1st sg* **nzakwahtéenami, nzakwah=téenamiim**. *conj 3rd sg* **sàkwahtée=namiit**. *ptcpl* **sàkwahtéenamiit**.

**sàkwamálsuw** VAI be restless, be bothered, feel restless. *ind 1st sg* **nzak=wamálsi, nzakwamálsiim**. *conj 3rd sg* **sàkwamálsiit**. *ptcpl* **sàkwamál=siit**.

**sàkwáxktiis** NA bothersome person, worry-wart. *pl* **sàkwaxktíisak**. *dimin* **sàkwaxktíishush**. *obv* **sàkwaxktíi=sal**. *See* **sàkwáxktuy**.

**sàkwáxktuy** NA bothersome person, worry-wart. *pl* **sakwaxktúyak**. *obv* **sàkwaxktúyal**. *See* **sàkwáxktiis**.

**sàkwaxktúyeew** VAI be a nuisance. *ind 1st sg* **nzàkwaxktúya, nzàkwaxk=túyaam**. *conj 3rd sg* **sàkwaxktúyaat**. *ptcpl* **sàkwaxktúyaat**.

**sàkwéelŭmeew** VTA worry about s.o. *ind 1st sg* **nzakwéelŭmaaw, nzakwéelŭ=ma**. *ind 3rd sg* **wsakweelŭmáawal**. *ind inv* **nzakwéelŭmukw**. *ind I-you* **ksakwéelŭmul**. *conj 3rd sg* **sàkwéelŭmaat**. *imp* **sàkwéelum**. *ptcpl* **sàkwéelŭmaat**.

**sàkweelúndam** VOTI 1A be worried. *ind 1st sg* **nzakweelúndam**. *conj 3rd sg* **sàkweelúndang**. *ptcpl* **sàkweelún=dang**.

**sàkweelúndam** VTI 1A worry about s.t. *ind 1st sg* **nzakweelúndamun**. *ind 3rd sg* **wsakweelúndamun**. *conj 1st sg* **sàkweelúndamaan**. *conj 3rd sg* **sàkweelúndang**. *imp* **sàkweelúndah**. *ptcpl* **sàkweelúndang**.

**sàkwíiheew** VTA worry about s.o. *ind 1st sg* **nzakwíihaaw, nzakwíiha**. *ind 3rd sg* **wsakwiiháawal**. *ind inv* **nzakwíi=hukw**. *ind I-you* **ksakwíihul**. *conj 3rd sg* **sàkwíihaat**. *imp* **sákwiih**. *ptcpl* **sàkwíihaat**.

**sàkwiilawéeheew** VTA worry s.o., make s.o. worry. *ind 1st sg* **nzakwiilawée=haaw, nzakwiilawéeha**. *ind 3rd sg* **wsakwiilaweeháawal**. *ind inv* **nzak=wiilawéehukw**. *ind I-you* **ksakwii=lawéehul**. *conj 3rd sg* **sàkwiilawée=haat**. *ptcpl* **sàkwiilawéehaat**.

**sàkwiináakwat** VII look troubled. *conj 3rd sg* **sàkwiináakwahk**. *imp* **sàkwii=náakwahk**.

**sàkwiináakwsuw** VAI look troubled. *ind 1st sg* **nzakwiináakwsi, nzakwii=náakwsiim**. *conj 3rd sg* **sàkwii=náakwsiit**. *ptcpl* **sàkwiináakwsiit**.

**sákwsuw** VAI be worried, be upset, be irritable, be restless. *ind 1st sg* **nzákwsi, nzákwsiim**. *conj 3rd sg* **sákwsiit**. *ptcpl* **sákwsiit**.

**salápwaan** NI fry bread. *pl* **salapwáa=nal**. *poss* **nzalapwáanum**. *loc* **salap=wáanung**. *dimin* **shalapwáanush**. *made with flour, water, baking powder, salt; cooked in grease on stove.*

**saláseew** VTA fry s.t. animate. *ind 1st sg* **nzálasaaw, nzálasa**. *ind 3rd sg* **wsalasáawal**. *ind inv* **nzálasookw**. *ind I-you* **ksálasool**. *conj 3rd sg* **salásaat**. *imp* **salás**. *ptcpl* **séelasaat**.

**salásŭm** VTI 1B fry s.t. *ind 1st sg* **nzala=súmun**. *ind 3rd sg* **wsalasúmun**. *conj 1st sg* **salásŭmaan**. *conj 3rd sg* **sa=lásung**. *imp* **salásih**. *ptcpl* **séelasung**.

**salásŭmeew** VAI cook by frying *(of cooks)*. *ind 1st sg* **nzalasúma**, **nzala=súmaam**. *conj 3rd sg* **salásŭmaat**. *imp* **salásŭmaal**. *ptcpl* **seelasúmaat**.

**salaxkíhleew** VAI be surprised, be shocked, be startled. *ind 1st sg* **nzalaxkíh=la**, **nzalaxkíhlaam**. *conj 3rd sg* **salaxkíhlaat**. *ptcpl* **seelaxkíhlaat**. *intensive reduplication* **sàsalaxkíhleew**.

**salaxkihtéeheew** VTA hit s.o. and startle them. *ind 1st sg* **nzalaxkihtéehaaw**, **nzalaxkihtéeha**. *ind 3rd sg* **wsalax=kihteeháawal**. *ind inv* **nzalaxkihtée=hookw**. *ind I-you* **ksalaxkihtéehool**. *conj 3rd sg* **salaxkihtéehaat**. *imp* **sa=laxkíhteeh**. *ptcpl* **seelaxkihtéehaat**.

**samwámbtoow** VTI2 tie s.t. shut. *ind 1st sg* **nzamwámbtoon**. *ind 3rd sg* **wsamwámbtoon**. *conj 1st sg* **sa=mwambtáwaan**. *conj 3rd sg* **sa=mwámbtaakw**. *imp* **samwámbtool**. *ptcpl* **seemwámbtaakw**.

**samwiikwáaleew** VTA sew s.t. animate shut *(of an opening)*. *ind 1st sg* **nzamwiikwáalaaw**, **nzamwiikwáa=la**. *ind 3rd sg* **wsamwiikwaaláawal**. *ind inv* **nzamwiikwáalukw**. *ind I-you* **ksamwiikwáalul**. *conj 3rd sg* **samwiikwáalaat**. *imp* **samwíikwaal**. *ptcpl* **seemwiikwáalaat**.

**samwiikwáasuw** VAI be sewn shut. *conj 3rd sg* **samwiikwáasiit**. *ptcpl* **see=mwiikwáasiit**.

**samwiikwáasuw** VII be sewn shut. *conj 3rd sg* **samwiikwáasiik**. *ptcpl* **see=mwiikwáasiik**.

**samwíikwam** VTI1A sew s.t. shut *(of an opening)*. *ind 1st sg* **nzamwíikwa=mun**. *ind 3rd sg* **wsamwíikwamun**. *conj 1st sg* **samwíikwamaan**. *conj 3rd sg* **samwíikwang**. *imp* **samwíi=kwah**. *ptcpl* **seemwíikwang**.

**samwúnum** VTI1B hold s.t. shut. *ind 1st sg* **nzamwŭnúmun**. *ind 3rd sg* **wsam=wŭnúmun**. *conj 1st sg* **samwúnŭ=maan**. *conj 3rd sg* **samwúnung**. *imp* **samwúnih**. *ptcpl* **séemwŭnung**.

**samwushéengweew** VAI have one's eyes swollen shut. *ind 1st sg* **nzamw=shéengwa**, **nzamwshéengwaam**. *conj 3rd sg* **samwushéengwaat**. *ptcpl* **seemwshéengwaat**. *intensive reduplication* **asamwshéengweew**.

**samwusheengwéexiin** VAI have one's eyes swollen shut. *ind 1st sg* **nzam=wsheengwéexiin**, **nzamwsheen=gwéexi**. *conj 3rd sg* **samwusheen=gwéexiing**. *ptcpl* **seemwsheengwée=xiing**.

**samwutoonéexiin** VAI close one's lips tightly, have one's lips tightly closed. *ind 1st sg* **nzamwtoonéexiin**, **nzam=wtoonéexi**. *conj 3rd sg* **samwutoo=néexiing**. *imp* **samwutoonéexiil**. *ptcpl* **seemwtoonéexiing**.

**saníikuw** VAI blow one's nose. *ind 1st sg* **nzaníikwi**, **nzaníikwiim**. *conj 3rd sg* **saníikwiit**. *imp* **saníikwiil**. *ptcpl* **seeníikwiit**. *intensive reduplication* **sahsaníikuw**.

**sápaluw** VAI eat supper. *ind 1st sg* **nzápali**, **nzápaliim**. *conj 3rd sg* **sáp=aliit**. *imp* **sápaliil**. *ptcpl* **sápaliit**. *From English* supper.

**sàsaláamuw** VAI cry a great deal, cry hard. *ind 1st sg* **nzasaláamwi**, **nzas=aláamwiim**. *conj 3rd sg* **sàsaláa=mwiit**. *ptcpl* **sàsaláamwiit**.

**sàsaláxkŭweew** VAI shriek, be shrill. *ind 1st sg* **nzasaláxkŭwe**, **nzasaláxkŭ=weem**. *conj 3rd sg* **sàsaláxkŭweek**. *imp* **sàsaláxkŭweel**. *ptcpl* **sàsaláx=kŭweet**.

**sàsamwuchiingwéhleew** VAI blink. *ind 1st sg* **nzasamwuchiingwéhla**, **nzasamwuchiingwéhlaam**. *conj 3rd sg* **sàsamwuchiingwéhlaat**. *imp* **sàs=amwuchiingwéhlaal**. *ptcpl* **sàsa=mwuchiingwéhlaat**.

**sàsápeew** VII be spotted. *conj 3rd sg* **sàsápeek**. *ptcpl* **sàsápeek**.

**sàsàpeekháasuw** VAI have spots on it,

have a line of spots on it, be marked with spots *(s.t. animate)*. *ind 1st sg* **nzasàpeekháasi**, **nzasàpeekháasiim**. *conj 3rd sg* **sàsàpeekháasiit**. *ptcpl* **sàsàpeekháasiit**.

**sàsàpeekháasuw** VII have spots on it, have a line of spots on it, be marked with spots. *conj 3rd sg* **sàsàpeek=háasiik**. *ptcpl* **sàsàpeekháasiik**.

**sàsàpéekham** VTI 1A put spots on s.t., make a line of spots on s.t., mark s.t. with spots. *ind 1st sg* **nzasàpeek=hámun**. *ind 3rd sg* **wsasàpeekhám=un**. *conj 1st sg* **sàsàpeekhámaan**. *conj 3rd sg* **sàsàpéekhang**. *imp* **sàsàpéekhah**. *ptcpl* **sàsàpéekhang**.

**sàsàpéekheew** VTA put spots on s.o., make a line of spots on s.o., mark spots on s.o. *ind 1st sg* **nzasàpéek=haaw**, **nzasàpéekha**. *ind 3rd sg* **wsasàpeekháawal**. *ind inv* **nzasàp=éekhookw**. *ind I-you* **ksasàpéekhool**. *conj 3rd sg* **sàsàpéekhaat**. *imp* **sàsàpéekhaw**. *ptcpl* **sàsàpéekhaat**.

**sàsápsuw** VAI be spotted *(s.t. animate)*. *ind 1st sg* **nzasápsi**, **nzasápsiim**. *conj 3rd sg* **sàsápsiit**. *ptcpl* **sàsápsiit**.

**sàséeham** VTI 1A sow s.t. *(of seeds)*; scatter s.t. *ind 1st sg* **nzaséehŭmun**. *ind 3rd sg* **wsaséehŭmun**. *conj 1st sg* **sàséehŭmaan**. *conj 3rd sg* **sàséehang**. *imp* **sàséehih**. *ptcpl* **sàséehang**.

**sàsehshíhkaweew** VTA scatter s.o. *object usually plural. ind 1st sg* **nzas=ehshihkawáawak**. *ind 3rd sg* **wsas=ehshihkawáawal**. *ind inv* **nzaseh=shihkaakóona**. *conj 3rd sg* **sàseh=shíhkawaat**. *imp* **sàsehshíhkaw**. *ptcpl* **sàsehshíhkawaat**.

**sàskápeew** VII be somewhat wet. *conj 3rd sg* **sàskápeek**.

**sátateew** VII be Saturday. *conj 3rd sg* **sátateek**. *See* **sátteew**. *From English* Saturday.

**sátteew** VII be Saturday. **Ootéeneeng ndá éenda-sàttéeke.** 'I went to town last Saturday.' *conj 3rd sg* **sátteek**. *See* **sátateew**. *From English* Saturday.

**sayaandpéexiin** VAI have messy hair. *ind 1st sg* **nzayaandpéexiin**, **nzay=aandpéexi**. *conj 3rd sg* **sayaandpée=xiing**. *ptcpl* **seeyaandpéexiing**.

**sayaandpéhleew** VAI have one's hair blowing about. *ind 1st sg* **nzayaand=péhla**, **nzayaandpéhlaam**. *conj 3rd sg* **sayaandpéhlaat**. *ptcpl* **seeyaand=péhlaat**. *intensive reduplication* **sàsayaandpéhleew**.

**sayaaxksiitéexiin** VAI spread one's toes apart, have one's toes spread apart. *ind 1st sg* **nzayaaxksiitéexiin**, **nzay=aaxksiitéexi**. *conj 3rd sg* **sayaaxksii=téexiing**. *imp* **sayaaxksiitéexiil**. *ptcpl* **seeyaaxksiitéexiing**.

**sayaaxkŭlunjéexiin** VAI spread one's fingers apart, have one's fingers spread apart. *ind 1st sg* **nzayaaxkŭ=lunjéexiin**, **nzayaaxkŭlunjéexi**. *conj 3rd sg* **sayaaxkŭlunjéexiing**. *imp* **sayaaxkŭlunjéexiil**. *ptcpl* **seeyaax=kŭlunjéexiing**, **seeyaaxkŭlunjéexiit**.

**sayeexíinook** VAI lie scattered, be scattered. *usually plural.* **Sayeexíinook pambíilak.** 'The papers are scattered.' *conj 3rd sg* **sayeexiinóhtiit**. *ptcpl* **seeyeexiinóhtiit**.

**sayéexŭnool** VII be scattered, lie scattered. *usually plural.* **Sayéexŭnool koolaakanúsal.** 'Your dishes are scattered.' *conj 3rd sg* **sayéexung**. *ptcpl* **seeyeexúngiil**.

**séekaween** PR restless person, active person. *pl* **seekawéeniik**. *obv* **seeka=wéeniil**.

**seekawéenuw** VAI be a restless person, be an active person. *ind 1st sg* **nzee=kawéeni**, **nzeekawéeniim**. *conj 3rd sg* **seekawéeniit**. *ptcpl* **seekawéeniit**.

**séeksuw** VAI be a restless person, be an active person; be hard to handle. *ind 1st sg* **nzéeksi**, **nzéeksiim**. *conj 3rd sg* **séeksiit**. *ptcpl* **séeksiit**.

**seesahkáaheew** VAIO throw s.t. as far as one can. **Nál kwáchŭmung ndáan táa ndúlu-aseesahkáaheen.** 'Then I went outside and I threw it as far as I could.' *ind 1st sg* **nzeesahkáaheen**. *ind 3rd sg* **wseesahkáaheen**. *conj 3rd sg* **seesahkáaheet**. *ptcpl* **seesahkáa=heet**.

**seexeekawíiheew** VTA whip s.o. *ind 1st sg* **nzeexeekawíihaaw**, **nzeexeeka=wíiha**. *ind 3rd sg* **wseexeekawiiháa=wal**. *ind inv* **nzeexeekawíihukw**. *ind I-you* **kseexeekawíihul**. *conj 3rd sg* **seexeekawíihaat**. *imp* **seexéekawiih**. *ptcpl* **seexeekawíihaat**.

**seexeekawíihŭweew** VAI whip people. *ind 1st sg* **nzeexeekawíihŭwe**, **nzee=xeekawíihŭweem**. *conj 3rd sg* **see=xeekawíihŭweet**. *imp* **seexeekawíi=hŭweel**. *ptcpl* **seexeekawíihŭweet**.

**seexeekawihtéeheew** VTA whip s.o. *ind 1st sg* **nzeexeekawihtéehaaw**, **nzee=xeekawihtéeha**. *ind 3rd sg* **wseexee=kawihteeháawal**. *ind inv* **nzeexee=kawihtéehookw**. *ind I-you* **kseexee=kawihtéehool**. *conj 3rd sg* **seexeeka=wihtéehaat**. *imp* **seexeekawíhteeh**. *ptcpl* **seexeekawihtéehaat**.

**seeyéeheew** VAIO scatter s.t., throw s.t. about. *ind 1st sg* **nzeeyáaheen**. *ind 3rd sg* **wseeyéeheen**. *conj 3rd sg* **seeyáaheet**. *imp* **seeyáaheel**. *ptcpl* **seeyáaheet**. *intensive reduplication* **wsàseeyáaheen**.

**séhleew** VII splatter, shatter, splash, scatter. *conj 3rd sg* **séhlaak**. *ptcpl* **séhlaak**. *intensive reduplication* **sàséhleew**.

**sehsookhúpees** NA bartender. *pl* **seh=sookhupéesak**. *obv* **sehsookhupée=sal**.

**sehtéeheew** VTA hit s.o. and shatter them. *ind 1st sg* **nzehtéehaaw**, **nzehtéeha**. *ind 3rd sg* **wsehteeháawal**. *conj 3rd sg* **sehtéehaat**. *imp* **séhteeh**. *ptcpl* **sehtéehaat**.

**sehtéexiin** VAI fall and shatter *(s.t. animate)*. *conj 3rd sg* **sehtéexiing**. *ptcpl* **sehtéexiing**. *intensive reduplication* **sàsehtéexiin**.

**sehtéextoow** VTI2 drop s.t. and make it shatter, hit s.t. and make it shatter. *ind 1st sg* **nzehtéextoon**. *ind 3rd sg* **wseh=téextoon**. *conj 1st sg* **sehteextáwaan**. *conj 3rd sg* **sehtéextaakw**. *imp* **seh=téextool**. *ptcpl* **sehtéextaakw**. *intensive reduplication* **wsasehtéextoon**.

**sehtéexŭmeew** VTA drop s.o. and make them shatter, hit s.o. and make them shatter. *ind 1st sg* **nzehtéexŭmaaw**, **nzehtéexŭma**. *ind 3rd sg* **wsehtee=xŭmáawal**. *ind inv* **nzehtéexŭmukw**. *ind I-you* **ksehtéexŭmul**. *conj 3rd sg* **sehtéexŭmaat**. *imp* **sehtéexum**. *ptcpl* **sehtéexŭmaat**. *intensive reduplication* **wsasehteexŭmáawal**.

**sehtéexun** VII fall and shatter. *conj 3rd sg* **sehtéexung**. *ptcpl* **sehtéexung**. *intensive reduplication* **sàsehtéexun**.

**sèkháaleew** VTA dismiss s.o., fire s.o. *ind 1st sg* **nzekháalaaw**, **nzekháala**. *ind 3rd sg* **wsekhaaláawal**. *ind inv* **nzekháalukw**. *ind I-you* **ksekháalul**. *conj 3rd sg* **sèkháalaat**. *imp* **sékhaal**. *ptcpl* **sèkháalaat**.

**siihŭnáasuw** VII be drained *(especially of wells)*. *conj 3rd sg* **siihŭnáasiik**. *ptcpl* **siihŭnáasiik**.

**síikhweew** VTA rub s.t. animate *(using a tool or instrument)*. *ind 1st sg* **nzíik=hwaaw**, **nzíikhwa**. *ind 3rd sg* **wsiik=hwáawal**. *ind inv* **nzíikhookw**. *ind I-you* **ksíikhool**. *conj 3rd sg* **síikhwaat**. *imp* **síikhwaw**. *ptcpl* **síikhwaat**.

**síikhwam** VTI1A rub s.t. *(of clothes on a washboard)*. *ind 1st sg* **nziikhwám=un**. *ind 3rd sg* **wsiikhwámun**. *conj 1st sg* **siikhwámaan**. *conj 3rd sg* **síikhwang**. *imp* **síikhwah**. *ptcpl* **síikhwang**.

**siikhwíikan** NI washboard. *pl* **siikhwíi=kanal**. *poss* **nziikhwíikan**. *loc* **siik=hwíikanung**. *dimin* **shiikhwíikanush**.

**siikhwíikeew** VAI use a washboard. *ind 1st sg* **nziikhwíike**, **nziikhwíikeem**. *conj 3rd sg* **siikhwíikeet**. *imp* **siik=hwíikeel**. *ptcpl* **siikhwíikeet**.
**siikwaandpéeneew** VTA rub s.o. on the head, pet s.o. on the head. *ind 1st sg* **nziikwaandpéenaaw**, **nziikwaand=péena**. *ind 3rd sg* **wsiikwaandpee=náawal**. *ind inv* **nziikwaandpée=nukw**. *ind I-you* **ksiikwaandpéenul**. *conj 3rd sg* **siikwaandpéenaat**. *imp* **siikwáandpeen**. *ptcpl* **siikwaand=péenaat**.
**síikwameew** VTA lick s.o., rub s.o. with the mouth. *ind 1st sg* **nzíikwamaaw**, **nzíikwama**. *ind 3rd sg* **wsiikwamáa=wal**. *ind inv* **nzíikwamukw**. *ind I-you* **ksíikwamul**. *conj 3rd sg* **síikwamaat**. *imp* **síikwam**. *ptcpl* **síikwamaat**.
**síikwan** VII be spring. **Siikwánge ngáta-náh -á.** 'I want to go there next spring.'; **Síikwane náh nóom.** 'I went there last spring.' *conj 3rd sg* **síi=kwang**. *ptcpl* **síikwang**.
**siikwanámuw** VAI live until springtime, survive until springtime. *ind 1st sg* **nziikwanámwi**, **nziikwanámwiim**. *conj 3rd sg* **siikwanámwiit**. *ptcpl* **siikwanámwiit**.
**siikwándam** VTI 1A lick s.t., rub on s.t. with the mouth. *ind 1st sg* **nzii=kwándamun**. *ind 3rd sg* **wsiikwán=damun**. *conj 1st sg* **siikwándamaan**. *conj 3rd sg* **siikwándang**. *imp* **sii=kwándah**. *ptcpl* **siikwándang**.
**siikwanéewung** PC south, in the south.
**siikwanúwii** PC during springtime, happen during springtime.
**siikwíixiin** VAI rub against something, rub up against something. *ind 1st sg* **nziikwíixiin**, **nziikwíixi**. *conj 3rd sg* **siikwíixiing**. *imp* **siikwíixiil**. *ptcpl* **siikwíixiing**.
**siikwíixun** VII rub against something, rub up against something. *conj 3rd sg* **siikwíixung**. *ptcpl* **siikwíixung**.
**síikwŭneew** VTA rub s.o., pet s.o. *(using the hands)*. *ind 1st sg* **nzíikwŭnaaw**, **nzíikwŭna**. *ind 3rd sg* **wsiikwŭnáa=wal**. *ind inv* **nzíikwŭnukw**. *ind I-you* **ksíikwŭnul**. *conj 3rd sg* **síikwŭnaat**. *imp* **síikwun**. *ptcpl* **síikwŭnaat**. *moderative reduplication* **wsaasiikwŭ=náawal**.
**síikwŭnum** VTI 1B rub s.t. *(using the hands)*. *ind 1st sg* **nziikwŭnúmun**. *ind 3rd sg* **wsiikwŭnúmun**. *conj 1st sg* **siikwŭnúmaan**. *conj 3rd sg* **síikwŭnung**. *imp* **síikwŭnih**. *ptcpl* **síikwŭnung**. *moderative reduplication* **wsaasiikwŭnúmun**.
**síineew** VTA milk s.o. *ind 1st sg* **nzíi=naaw**, **nzíina**. *ind 3rd sg* **wsiináawal**. *ind inv* **nzíinukw**. *ind I-you* **ksíinul**. *conj 3rd sg* **síinaat**. *imp* **síin**. *ptcpl* **síinaat**.
**síingeew** VII be the outside angle of a corner. **Éenda-síingeek wíikwahm.** 'The corner of the house.' *conj 3rd sg* **síingeek**. *ptcpl* **síingeek**.
**siingiikamíikat** VII be the corner *(of the house)*. *conj 3rd sg* **siingiikamíikahk**. *ptcpl* **siingiikamíikahk**.
**siingiitŭyéexiin** VAI stick one's backside out, have one's backside sticking up. *ind 1st sg* **nziingiitŭyéexiin**, **nziin=giitŭyéexi**. *conj 3rd sg* **siingiitŭyée=xiing**. *imp* **siingiitŭyéexiil**. *ptcpl* **siingiitŭyéexiing**.
**síingsuw** VAI be the outside angle of a corner *(s.t. animate)*. *ind 1st sg* **nzíingsi**. *conj 3rd sg* **síingsiit**. *ptcpl* **síingsiit**.
**siiníikeew** VAI be milking, milk an animal. *ind 1st sg* **nziiníike**, **nziiníikeem**. *conj 3rd sg* **siiníikeet**. *imp* **siiníikeel**. *ptcpl* **siiníikeet**.
**síipuw** NI river. *pl* **síipŭwal**. *loc* **síipoong**. *dimin* **shíipoosh**.
**síisameew** VTA rub one's mouth on s.o., lap s.o., lick s.o. *ind 1st sg* **nzíisa=maaw**, **nzíisama**. *ind 3rd sg* **wsiisa=máawal**. *ind inv* **nzíisamukw**. *ind I-*

*you* **ksíisamul**. *conj 3rd sg* **síisamaat**. *imp* **síisam**. *ptcpl* **síisamaat**.

**siisándam** VTI1A rub one's mouth on s.t, lick s.t. *ind 1st sg* **nziisándamun**. *ind 3rd sg* **wsiisándamun**. *conj 1st sg* **siisándamaan**. *conj 3rd sg* **siisán=dang**. *imp* **siisándah**. *ptcpl* **siisán=dang**.

**siisiingwáaleew** VTA scratch s.o. on the face. *ind 1st sg* **nziisiingwáalaaw**, **nziisiingwáala**. *ind 3rd sg* **wsiisiin=gwaaláawal**. *ind inv* **nziisiingwáa=lukw**. *ind I-you* **ksiisiingwáalul**. *conj 3rd sg* **siisiingwáalaat**. *imp* **siisíin=gwaal**. *ptcpl* **siisiingwáalaat**.

**síisŭneew** VTA scratch s.o., claw s.o. *(using the hands)*. *ind 1st sg* **nzíisŭnaaw**, **nzíisŭna**. *ind 3rd sg* **wsiisŭnáawal**. *ind inv* **nzíisŭnukw**. *ind I-you* **ksíisŭ=nul**. *conj 3rd sg* **síisŭnaat**. *imp* **síisun**. *ptcpl* **síisŭnaat**.

**siisŭníikeew** VAI scratch things. *ind 1st sg* **nziisŭníike**, **nziisŭníikeem**. *conj 3rd sg* **siisŭníikeet**. *imp* **siisŭníikeel**. *ptcpl* **siisŭníikeet**.

**síisŭnum** VTI1B scratch s.t., claw s.t. *(using the hands)*. *ind 1st sg* **nziisŭ=númun**. *ind 3rd sg* **wsiisŭnúmun**. *conj 1st sg* **siisŭnúmaan**. *conj 3rd sg* **síisŭnung**. *imp* **síisŭnih**. *ptcpl* **síi=sŭnung**.

**síixiin** VAI be scraped, have a scrape mark on it *(s.t. animate)*. *ind 1st sg* **nzíixiin**, **nzíixi**. *conj 3rd sg* **síixiing**. *ptcpl* **síixiing**, **síixiit**. *intensive reduplication* **sihsíixiin**.

**siixiipahkwáawan** NI cornstalk. *pl* **sii=xiipahkwáawanal**. *loc* **siixiipah=kwáawanung**. *dimin* **shiixiipah=kwáawanush**.

**síixtoow** VTI2 scrape s.t., make a scrape mark on s.t. *ind 1st sg* **nzíixtoon**. *ind 3rd sg* **wsíixtoon**. *conj 1st sg* **siix=táwaan**. *conj 3rd sg* **síixtaakw**. *imp* **síixtool**. *ptcpl* **síixtaakw**. *intensive reduplication* **wsihsíixtoon**.

**síixŭmeew** VTA scrape s.o., make a scrape mark on s.o. *ind 1st sg* **nzíixŭmaaw**, **nzíixŭma**. *ind 3rd sg* **wsiixŭmáawal**. *ind inv* **nzíixŭmukw**. *ind I-you* **ksíi=xŭmul**. *conj 3rd sg* **síixŭmaat**. *imp* **síixum**. *ptcpl* **síixŭmaat**. *intensive reduplication* **wsihsiixŭmáawal**.

**síixun** VII be scraped, have a scrape mark on it. *conj 3rd sg* **síixung**. *ptcpl* **síi=xung**. *intensive reduplication* **sih=síixun**.

**sihkpatíikeew** VAI boil dry. *ind 1st sg* **nzihkpatíike**, **nzihkpatíikeem**. *conj 3rd sg* **sihkpatíikeet**. *ptcpl* **sihkpat=íikeet**.

**sihkpéeneew** VTA strain s.t. animate. *ind 1st sg* **nzihkpéenaaw**, **nzihkpéena**. *ind 3rd sg* **wsihkpeenáawal**. *ind inv* **nzihkpéenukw**. *ind I-you* **ksihkpée=nul**. *conj 3rd sg* **sihkpéenaat**. *imp* **síhkpeen**. *ptcpl* **sihkpéenaat**.

**sihkpeeníikan** NI sieve. *pl* **sihkpeeníi=kanal**. *poss* **nzihkpeeníikan**. *loc* **sihkpeeníikanung**. *dimin* **shihkpee=níikanush**.

**sihkpeeníikeew** VAI strain things. *ind 1st sg* **nzihkpeeníike**, **nzihkpeeníikeem**. *conj 3rd sg* **sihkpeeníikeet**. *imp* **sihk=peeníikeel**. *ptcpl* **sihkpeeníikeet**.

**sihkpéenum** VTI1B strain s.t. *ind 1st sg* **nzihkpéenŭmun**. *ind 3rd sg* **wsihk=péenŭmun**. *conj 1st sg* **sihkpéenŭ=maan**. *conj 3rd sg* **sihkpéenung**. *imp* **sihkpéenih**. *ptcpl* **sihkpéenung**.

**sihkpéesuw** VAI be boiled dry *(s.t. animate)*. *ind 1st sg* **nzihkpéesi**, **nzihk=péesiim**. *conj 3rd sg* **sihkpéesiit**. *ptcpl* **sihkpéesiit**.

**sihkpeewchásuw** VAI boil dry. *ind 1st sg* **nzihkpeewchási**, **nzihkpeewchás=iim**. *conj 3rd sg* **sihkpeewchásiit**. *ptcpl* **sihkpeewchásiit**.

**sihkpeewcháteew** VII boil dry. *conj 3rd sg* **sihkpeewcháteek**. *ptcpl* **sihk=peewcháteek**.

**sihkpéhleew** VII run dry *(of an amount*

*of water). conj 3rd sg* **sihkpéhlaak**. *ptcpl* **sihkpéhlaak**.

**síhlaleew** VTA drain s.t. animate. *ind 1st sg* **nzíhlalaaw**, **nzíhlala**. *ind 3rd sg* **wsihlaláawal**. *conj 3rd sg* **síhlalaat**. *imp* **síhlal**. *ptcpl* **síhlalaat**.

**síhlatoow** VTI2 drain s.t. *ind 1st sg* **nzíhlatoon**. *ind 3rd sg* **wsíhlatoon**. *conj 1st sg* **sihlatáwaan**. *conj 3rd sg* **síhlataakw**. *imp* **síhlatool**. *ptcpl* **síhlataakw**.

**síhleew** VII go down *(of the water level). conj 3rd sg* **síhlaak**. *ptcpl* **síhlaak**. *intensive reduplication* **sihsíhleew**.

**sihtaníineew** VAI have a runny nose. *ind 1st sg* **nzihtaníine**, **nzihtaníineem**. *conj 3rd sg* **sihtaníineet**. *ptcpl* **sihta=níineet**.

**silkaháasuw** VII have ribbons on it. *conj 3rd sg* **silkaháasiik**. *ptcpl* **silkaháa=siik**.

**sìlkáhŭmeew** VAI wear a ribbon. *ind 1st sg* **nzìlkáhŭma**, **nzìlkáhŭmaam**. *conj 3rd sg* **sìlkáhŭmaat**. *imp* **sìl=káhŭmaal**. *ptcpl* **sìlkáhŭmaat**.

**silkeendakwíiwan** NI silk dress. *pl* **silkeendakwíiwanal**. *poss* **nzilkeen=dakwíiwan**, **nzilkeendakwíiwanum**. *loc* **silkeendakwíiwanung**. *dimin* **silkeendakwíiwanush**.

**síluk** NI ribbon. *pl* **sílkal**. *poss* **nzílkum**. *dimin* **shíkush**.

**skáchmaan** NA Scottish person. *pl* **skachmáanak**. *obv* **skachmáanal**.

**skahúnzuw** NA boy. *pl* **skahúnzŭwak**. *dimin* **shkahúnzhoosh**. *obv* **skahún=zŭwal**.

**skapáandpeew** VAI have wet hair. *ind 1st sg* **nzukapáandpa**, **nzuka=páandpaam**. *conj 3rd sg* **skapáand=paat**. *ptcpl* **seekapáandpaat**.

**skapachásuw** VAI sweat, be damp from heat, be wet from heat. *ind 1st sg* **nzukapáchasi**, **nzukapáchasiim**. *conj 3rd sg* **skapachásiit**. *ptcpl* **seekapáchasiit**.

**skapacháteew** VII be damp from heat, be wet from heat. *conj 3rd sg* **skapa=cháteek**. *ptcpl* **seekapáchateek**.

**skapahkéeyeew** VII be wet ground. *conj 3rd sg* **skapahkéeyeek**. *ptcpl* **seeka=pahkéeyeek**.

**skapáhksun** NI wet shoe. *pl* **skapahk=súnal**. *poss* **nzukapáhksun**. *loc* **skapahksúnung**. *dimin* **shkapahk=shúnush**.

**skapahksúneew** VAI have wet shoes. *ind 1st sg* **nzukapahksúna**, **nzukapah=ksúnaam**. *conj 3rd sg* **skapahksún=aat**. *ptcpl* **seekapahksúnaat**.

**skapáskat** VII be wet grass. *conj 3rd sg* **skapáskahk**. *ptcpl* **seekapáskahk**. *See* **skapáskwat**.

**skapáskwat** VII be wet grass. *conj 3rd sg* **skapáskwahk**. *ptcpl* **seekapás=kwahk**. *See* **skapáskat**.

**skápeew** VII be wet. *conj 3rd sg* **skáp=eek**. *ptcpl* **séekapeek**.

**skapeewáhkameew** VII be a wet day. *conj 3rd sg* **skapeewáhkameek**. *ptcpl* **seekapeewáhkameek**.

**skaphháaleew** VTA dampen s.o., dampen s.t. animate. *ind 1st sg* **nzukpaháa=laaw**, **nzukpaháala**. *ind 3rd sg* **wsukpahaaláawal**. *ind inv* **nzukpah=áalukw**. *ind I-you* **ksukpaháalul**. *conj 3rd sg* **skaphháalaat**. *imp* **skáp=haal**. *ptcpl* **seekpaháalaat**.

**skaphháatoow** VTI2 dampen s.t. *ind 1st sg* **nzukapaháatoon**. *ind 3rd sg* **wsukapaháatoon**. *conj 1st sg* **skap=háatawaan**. *conj 3rd sg* **skaphháa=taakw**. *imp* **skaphháatool**. *ptcpl* **seekapaháataakw**.

**skapíixiin** VAI be damp, be wet *(s.t. animate). ind 1st sg* **nzukapíixiin**, **nzuk=apíixi**. *conj 3rd sg* **skapíixiing**. *ptcpl* **seekapíixiing**.

**skapíixun** VII be damp, be wet. *conj 3rd sg* **skapíixung**. *ptcpl* **seekapíixung**.

**skapsíiteew** VAI have wet feet. *ind 1st sg* **nzukapusíita**, **nzukapusíitaam**. *conj*

*3rd sg* **skapsíitaat**. *ptcpl* **seekapusíi=taat**.

**skápsuw** VAI be wet. *ind 1st sg* **nzuka=púsi**, **nzukapúsiim**. *conj 3rd sg* **skápsiit**. *ptcpl* **seekapúsiit**.

**skaxeehóonay** NI earring. *pl* **skaxee=hóonayal**. *See* **sakaxéehoon**, **skax=éehoon**.

**skaxéehuw** VAI wear earrings. *ind 1st sg* **nzakxéehi**, **nzakxéehiim**. *conj 3rd sg* **skaxéehiit**. *imp* **skaxéehiil**. *ptcpl* **seekxéehiit**. *See* **sakaxeehoonhám=eew**.

nu**skíinjukw** NID my eye; my face. *pl* **nuskíinjkwal**. *3rd poss* **wuskíinjukw**. *loc* **nuskíinjkwung**. *dimin* **nush=kíinjkwush**.

**sóochul** NA soldier. *pl* **sóochŭlak**. *dimin* **shóochŭlush**. *obv* **sóochŭlal**. *From English* soldier.

**sóochŭluw** VAI be in the army, join the army. *ind 1st sg* **nzóochŭli**, **nzóo=chŭliim**. *conj 3rd sg* **sóochŭliit**. *imp* **sóochŭliil**. *ptcpl* **sóochŭliit**.

**sookáaheew** VAIO spill s.t, pour s.t. away. *ind 1st sg* **nzookáaheen**. *ind 3rd sg* **wsookáaheen**. *conj 3rd sg* **sookáa=heet**. *imp* **sookáaheel**. *ptcpl* **sookáa=heet**.

**sookáhlaleew** VTA spill s.t. animate, pour s.t. animate out. *ind 1st sg* **nzookáhlalaaw**, **nzookáhlala**. *ind 3rd sg* **wsookahlaláawal**. *ind inv* **nzookáhlalukw**. *ind I-you* **ksookáh=lalul**. *conj 3rd sg* **sookáhlalaat**. *imp* **sookáhlal**. *ptcpl* **sookáhlalaat**.

**sookáhlatoow** VTI2 spill s.t., pour s.t. out. *ind 1st sg* **nzookáhlatoon**. *ind 3rd sg* **wsookáhlatoon**. *conj 1st sg* **sookahlatáwaan**. *conj 3rd sg* **soo=káhlataakw**. *imp* **sookáhlatool**. *ptcpl* **sookáhlataakw**.

**sookáhleew** VAI spill out, spill, be spilt *(s.t. animate)*. *conj 3rd sg* **sookáhlaat**. *ptcpl* **sookáhlaat**.

**sookáhleew** VII spill out, spill, be spilt. *conj 3rd sg* **sookáhlaak**. *ptcpl* **soo=káhlaak**. *intensive reduplication* **sohsookáhleew**.

**sookalúndam** VTI1A sprinkle s.t. with water, spray s.t. with water. *ind 1st sg* **nzookalúndamun**. *ind 3rd sg* **wsoo=kalúndamun**. *conj 1st sg* **sookalún=damaan**. *conj 3rd sg* **sookalúndang**. *imp* **sookalúndah**. *ptcpl* **sookalúndang**.

**sookalúndaweew** VTA sprinkle s.o. with water, spray s.o. with water. *ind 1st sg* **nzookalúndawaaw**, **nzookalún=dawa**. *ind 3rd sg* **wsookalundawáa=wal**. *ind inv* **nzookalúndaakw**. *ind I-you* **ksookalúndool**. *conj 3rd sg* **sookalúndawaat**. *imp* **sookalúndaw**. *ptcpl* **sookalúndawaat**.

**sookalundíikeew** VAI sprinkle things with water. *ind 1st sg* **nzookalundíi=ke**, **nzookalundíikeem**. *conj 3rd sg* **sookalundíikeet**. *imp* **sookalundíi=keel**. *ptcpl* **sookalundíikeet**.

**sóokham** VTI1A spill s.t., pour s.t. away. *ind 1st sg* **nzookhámun**. *ind 3rd sg* **wsookhámun**. *conj 1st sg* **sookhám=aan**. *conj 3rd sg* **sóokhang**. *imp* **sóokhah**. *ptcpl* **sóokhang**.

**sóokheew** VTA spill s.t. animate out, pour s.t. animate away. **Nzookháa=wak óhpŭnak.** 'I got the potatoes out (of a container).' *ind 1st sg* **nzóok=haaw**, **nzóokha**. *ind 3rd sg* **wsook=háawal**. *ind inv* **nzóokhookw**. *ind I-you* **ksóokhool**. *conj 3rd sg* **sóokhaat**. *imp* **sóokhaw**. *ptcpl* **sóokhaat**.

**sookhíingweew** VAI bathe one's eyes; put drops in one's eyes. *ind 1st sg* **nzookhíingwa**, **nzookhíingwaam**. *conj 3rd sg* **sookhíingwaat**. *imp* **soo=khíingwaal**. *ptcpl* **sookhíingwaat**.

**sookhúpatoow** VTI2 soak s.t. in liquid. *ind 1st sg* **nzookhúpatoon**. *ind 3rd sg* **wsookhúpatoon**. *conj 1st sg* **sookhupatáwaan**. *conj 3rd sg* **sook=húpataakw**. *imp* **sookhúpatool**. *ptcpl*

**sookhúpataakw**.

**sookhupeesíikaan** NI hotel; drinking establishment, bootlegger's place. *pl* **sookhupeesiikáanal**. *loc* **sookhup=eesiikáanung**.

**sookhúpeew** NA bootlegger. *pl* **sook=hupéewak**. *obv* **sookhupéewal**.

**sookpáleew** VTA soak s.o. *ind 1st sg* **nzookpálaaw**, **nzookpála**. *ind 3rd sg* **wsookpaláawal**. *ind inv* **nzookpál=ukw**. *ind I-you* **ksookpálul**. *conj 3rd sg* **sookpálaat**. *imp* **sóokpal**. *ptcpl* **sookpálaat**.

**sookpatíikeew** VAI soak things. *ind 1st sg* **nzookpatíike**, **nzookpatíikeem**. *conj 3rd sg* **sookpatíikeet**. *imp* **sookpatíikeel**. *ptcpl* **sookpatíikeet**.

**sookpátoow** VTI2 soak s.t. *ind 1st sg* **nzookpátoon**. *ind 3rd sg* **wsookpát=oon**. *conj 1st sg* **sookpátawaan**. *conj 3rd sg* **sookpátaakw**. *imp* **sookpát=ool**. *ptcpl* **sookpátaakw**.

**sookpéenŭmeew** VAI pour out a liquid. *ind 1st sg* **nzookpéenŭma**, **nzook=péenŭmaam**. *conj 3rd sg* **sookpée=nŭmaat**. *imp* **sookpéenŭmaal**. *ptcpl* **sookpéenŭmaat**.

**sookpéhleew** VII spill, fall down, come down *(of water)*. *conj 3rd sg* **sook=péhlaak**. *ptcpl* **sookpéhlaak**.

**sóokŭlaan** VII rain, be raining. **Katá-ch sookŭláange wíikŭyaan-uch ndápi.** 'If it rains I'll stay at home.' *conj 3rd sg* **sóokŭlaang**. *ptcpl* **sóokŭlaang**. *intensive reduplication* **sohsóokŭlaan**; *moderative reduplication* **saasóokŭ=laan**.

**sookŭnupáaleew** VTA baptize s.o. *ind 1st sg* **nzookŭnupáalaaw**, **nzookŭnup=áala**. *ind 3rd sg* **wsookŭnupaaláa=wal**. *ind inv* **nzookŭnupáalukw**. *ind I-you* **ksookŭnupáalul**. *conj 3rd sg* **sookŭnupáalaat**. *imp* **sookŭnúpaal**. *ptcpl* **sookŭnupáalaat**.

**sookŭnupáasuw** VAI be baptized. *ind 1st sg* **nzookŭnupáasi**, **nzookŭnup=áasiim**. *conj 3rd sg* **sookŭnupáasiit**. *ptcpl* **sookŭnupáasiit**.

**sookŭnupaasŭwáakan** NI Baptism. *pl* **sookŭnupaasŭwáakanal**. *poss* **nzookŭnupaasŭwáakan**.

**sohpwíingweew** VAI have one's eyes closed, close one's eyes. *ind 1st sg* **nzohpwíingwe**, **nzohpwíingweem**. *conj 3rd sg* **sohpwíingweet**. *imp* **soh=pwíingweel**. *ptcpl* **sohpwíingweet**.

**sohpwiingwéexiin** VAI have one's eyes closed. *ind 1st sg* **nzohpwiingwée=xiin**, **nzohpwiingwéexi**. *conj 3rd sg* **sohpwiingwéexiing**. *imp* **sohpwiin=gwéexiil**. *ptcpl* **sohpwiingwéexiing**, **sohpwiingwéexiit**.

**sótii** NI baking soda. *poss* **nzòtíihum**. *dimin* **sòtíihush**. *From English* soda.

**spwíikŭwak** VAI grow close together *(s.t. animate)*. *usually plural*. *conj 3rd sg* **spwiikíhtiit**. *ptcpl* **seepwiikíhtiit**.

**spwíikŭnool** VII grow close together. *usually plural*. *conj 3rd sg* **spwíikung**. *ptcpl* **seepwiikúngiil**.

**spwiikwáakeew** VAI sew things closed. *ind 1st sg* **nzupwiikwáake**, **nzup=wiikwáakeem**. *conj 3rd sg* **spwii=kwáakeet**. *imp* **spwiikwáakeel**. *ptcpl* **seepwiikwáakeet**.

**spwiikwáaleew** VTA sew s.o. closed. *ind 1st sg* **nzupwiikwáalaaw**, **nzupwii=kwáala**. *ind 3rd sg* **wsupwiikwaa=láawal**. *ind inv* **nzupwiikwáalukw**. *ind I-you* **ksupwiikwáalul**. *conj 3rd sg* **spwiikwáalaat**. *imp* **spwíikwaal**. *ptcpl* **seepwiikwáalaat**.

**spwíikwam** VTI1A sew s.t. closed. *ind 1st sg* **nzupwíikwamun**. *ind 3rd sg* **wsupwíikwamun**. *conj 1st sg* **spwíi=kwamaan**. *conj 3rd sg* **spwíikwang**. *imp* **spwíikwah**. *ptcpl* **seepwíi=kwang**.

**spwíingweew** VAI have small eyes *(as if closed)*. *ind 1st sg* **nzupwíingwe**, **nzupwíingweem**. *conj 3rd sg* **spwíin=gweet**. *ptcpl* **seepwíingweet**.

**spwiingwéewii-páhkŭnum** VII be extra dark out, be awfully dark. *conj 3rd sg* **spwiingwéewii-páhkŭnung**. *ptcpl* **seepwiingwéewii-páhkŭnung**.

**spwiingwéexiin** VAI have one's eye's half closed. *ind 1st sg* **nzupwiin= gwéexiin**, **nzupwiingwéexi**. *conj 3rd sg* **spwiingwéexiing**. *ptcpl* **seepwiin= gwéexiing**.

**spwihtkwíhkeew** VII be a lot of thick trees, be a lot of dense trees, be a dense forest. *conj 3rd sg* **spwiht= kwíhkeek**. *ptcpl* **seepwihtkwíhkeek**.

**spwuch'híingweew** VAI blink. *ind 1st sg* **nzupwchahíingwa**, **nzupwchah= íingwaam**. *conj 3rd sg* **spwuch'híin= gwaat**. *imp* **spwuch'híingwaal**. *ptcpl* **seepwchahíingwaat**.

**spwutóoneew** VAI pout, close one's mouth. *ind 1st sg* **nzupwtóona**, **nzupwtóonaam**. *conj 3rd sg* **spwut= óonaat**. *ptcpl* **seepwtóonaat**.

**spwutoonéexiin** VAI close one's mouth tightly, have one's mouth closed, have one's lips pursed; pout. *ind 1st sg* **nzupwtoonéexiin**, **nzupwtoonée= xi**. *conj 3rd sg* **spwutoonéexiing**. *ptcpl* **seepwtoonéexiing**, **seepwtoo= néexiit**.

**sùkhwáaleew** VTA spit at s.o. *ind 1st sg* **nzukhwáalaaw**, **nzukhwáala**. *ind 3rd sg* **wsukhwaaláawal**. *ind inv* **nzukhwáalukw**. *ind I-you* **ksuk= hwáalul**. *conj 3rd sg* **sùkhwáalaat**. *imp* **súkhwaal**. *ptcpl* **sùkhwáalaat**.

**súkwiiw** VAI spit. *ind 1st sg* **nzúkwi**, **nzúkwiim**. *conj 3rd sg* **súkwiit**. *imp* **súkwiil**. *ptcpl* **súkwiit**. *intensive re- duplication* **sahsúkwiiw**.

**sùkwiináakan** NI spit, saliva. *pl* **sùk= wiináakanal**. *poss* **nzùkwiináakan**.

**sŭláamuw** VAI let out a cry. *ind 1st sg* **nzuláamwi**, **nzuláamwiim**. *conj 3rd sg* **sŭláamwiit**. *ptcpl* **seeláamwiit**. *See* **sàsaláamuw**.

**sŭluskihtéeham** VTI1A press the insides out of s.t., squeeze the insides out of s.t. *ind 1st sg* **nzuluskihtéehŭmun**. *ind 3rd sg* **wsuluskihtéehŭmun**. *conj 1st sg* **sŭluskihtéehŭmaan**. *conj 3rd sg* **sŭluskihtéehang**. *imp* **sŭluskih= téehih**. *ptcpl* **seeluskihtéehang**.

**sŭluskihtéeheew** VTA press the insides out of s.o., squeeze the insides out of s.o. *ind 1st sg* **nzuluskihtéehaaw**, **nzuluskihtéeha**. *ind 3rd sg* **wsulus= kihteeháawal**. *ind inv* **nzuluskihtée= hookw**. *ind I-you* **ksuluskihtéehool**. *conj 3rd sg* **sŭluskihtéehaat**. *imp* **sŭ= luskíhteeh**. *ptcpl* **seeluskihtéehaat**.

**sŭluskóonzheew** VAI have a lot of chil- dren. *ind 1st sg* **nzuluskóonzhe**, **nzuluskóonzheem**. *conj 3rd sg* **sŭ= luskóonzheet**. *ptcpl* **seeluskóon= zheet**.

**sŭlúskŭneew** VTA press s.o., squeeze s.o. *(using the hands)*. *ind 1st sg* **nzulús= kŭnaaw**, **nzulúskŭna**. *ind 3rd sg* **wsuluskŭnáawal**. *ind inv* **nzulúskŭ= nukw**. *ind I-you* **ksulúskŭnul**. *conj 3rd sg* **sŭlúskŭnaat**. *imp* **sŭlúskun**. *ptcpl* **seelúskŭnaat**.

**sŭlúskŭnum** VTI1B press s.t., squeeze s.t. *(using the hands)*. *ind 1st sg* **nzuluskŭnúmun**. *ind 3rd sg* **wsul= uskŭnúmun**. *conj 1st sg* **sŭluskŭ= númaan**. *conj 3rd sg* **sŭlúskŭnung**. *imp* **sŭlúskŭnih**. *ptcpl* **seelúskŭnung**.

**sŭwétul** NI sweater. *pl* **sŭwétŭlal**. *poss* **nzuwétŭlum**. *loc* **sŭwétŭlung**. *dimin* **shŭwéchŭlush**. *From English* sweater.

# SH

**sháa** PC right away, immediately. **Yó, kwáy sháa ngwiilamúnal.** 'Okay, I'll look for them right away.'; **Sháa ngúk wtúlaan nóohŭmal wáak nŭmoxóomsal.** 'My mother told my grandmother and my grandfather right away.' *See* **sháawu**.

**sháakpuy** NI well. *pl* **shaakpúyal**. *loc* **sháakpiing**. *dimin* **sháakpiish**.

**shaapwaalhóosuw** VAI wear a diaper. *ind 1st sg* **nzhaapwaalhóosi**, **nzhaapwaalhóosiim**. *conj 3rd sg* **shaapwaalhóosiit**. *imp* **shaap=waalhóosiil**. *ptcpl* **shaapwaalhóosiit**.

**shaapwíhleew** VAI have diarrhea. *ind 1st sg* **nzhaapwíhla**, **nzhaapwíhlaam**. *conj 3rd sg* **shaapwíhlaat**. *ptcpl* **shaapwíhlaat**.

**shaapwshéeshum** VTI1B cut through s.t. *ind 1st sg* **nzhaapwshéeshŭmun**. *ind 3rd sg* **wshaapwshéeshŭmun**. *conj 1st sg* **shaapwshéeshŭmaan**. *conj 3rd sg* **shaapwshéeshung**. *imp* **shaap=wshéeshih**. *ptcpl* **shaapwshéeshung**.

**shaapwshéeyeew** VII be a hole through something. *conj 3rd sg* **shaapwshée=yeek**. *ptcpl* **shaapwshéeyeek**.

**shaashŭwánakuw** VAI be part White. **Sháxk éet shaashŭwánakuw.** 'He must be part White.' *ind 1st sg* **nzhaashŭwánakwi**, **nzhaashŭwa=nákwiim**. *conj 3rd sg* **shaashŭwán=akwiit**. *ptcpl* **shaashŭwánakwiit**.

**shaawanéewung** PC south. **Shaawa=néewung wúndxun.** 'The wind is from the south.'

**sháawu** PC right away, immediately. **Máh sháawu kŭnunoolóowu.** 'I didn't recognize you right away.'; **Ayásku-ch sháawu ktahkíiheem.** 'You'll have to plant right away.' *See* **sháa**.

**shaaxkaachíimuw** VAI tell the truth. *ind 1st sg* **nzhaaxkaachíimwi**, **nzhaax=kaachíimwiim**. *conj 3rd sg* **shaax=kaachíimwiit**. *imp* **shaaxkaachíi=mwiil**. *ptcpl* **shaaxkaachíimwiit**.

**shaaxkaalóhkweew** VAI have straight hair. *ind 1st sg* **nzhaaxkaalóhkwe**, **nzhaaxkaalóhkweem**. *conj 3rd sg* **shaaxkaalóhkweet**. *ptcpl* **shaaxkaa=lóhkweet**.

**shaaxkáameew** VII be in a straight row, be in a straight line. **Shaaxkáameew ehkíihayaan.** 'What I planted is in a straight row.' *conj 3rd sg* **shaaxkáa=meek**. *ptcpl* **shaaxkáameek**.

**shaaxkáanay** NI straight road. *pl* **shaax=káanayal**. *loc* **shaaxkáaneeng**.

**shaaxkaapéewuw** VAI be honest. *ind 1st sg* **nzhaaxkaapéewi**, **nzhaaxkaa=péewiim**. *conj 3rd sg* **shaaxkaapée=wiit**. *imp* **shaaxkaapéewiil**. *ptcpl* **shaaxkaapéewiit**.

**shaaxkaaptóoneew** VAI speak the exact truth. *ind 1st sg* **nzhaaxkaaptóone**, **nzhaaxkaaptóoneem**. *conj 3rd sg* **shaaxkaaptóoneet**. *imp* **shaaxkaap=tóoneel**. *ptcpl* **shaaxkaaptóoneet**. *intensive reduplication* **ashaaxkaap=tóoneew**.

**shaaxkahkéexun** VII be level earth. *conj 3rd sg* **shaaxkahkéexung**. *ptcpl* **shaaxkahkéexung**.

**shaaxkahkéeyeew** VII be level ground. *conj 3rd sg* **shaaxkahkéeyeek**. *ptcpl* **shaaxkahkéeyeek**.

**shaaxkáhtakat** VII be straight *(of something string-like). conj 3rd sg* **shaax=káhtakahk**. *ptcpl* **shaaxkáhtakahk**.

**shaaxkahtakúsuw** VAI be straight *(s.t. animate, of something string-like). ind 1st sg* **nzhaaxkahtakúsi**, **nzhaax=kahtakúsiim**. *conj 3rd sg* **shaaxkah=takúsiit**. *ptcpl* **shaaxkahtakúsiit**.

**sháaxkat** VII be straight. *conj 3rd sg* **sháaxkahk**. *ptcpl* **sháaxkahk**.

**shaaxkàtéexun** VII be a straight road. *conj 3rd sg* **shaaxkàtéexung**. *ptcpl* **shaaxkàtéexung**.

**sháaxkeew** VII be straight. *conj 3rd sg* **sháaxkeek**. *ptcpl* **sháaxkeek**.

**shaaxkeekháasuw** VAI be marked in a straight line, be written in a straight line. *ind 1st sg* **nzhaaxkeekháasi**, **nzhaaxkeekháasiim**. *conj 3rd sg* **shaaxkeekháasiit**. *ptcpl* **shaaxkeek=**

**háasiit**.

**shaaxkeekháasuw** VII be marked in a straight line. *conj 3rd sg* **shaaxkeek=háasiik**. *ptcpl* **shaaxkeekháasiik**.

**shaaxkéekham** VTI1A make a mark on s.t. in a straight line, mark s.t. in a straight line. *ind 1st sg* **nzhaaxkeek=hámun**. *ind 3rd sg* **wshaaxkeek=hámun**. *conj 1st sg* **shaaxkeekhám=aan**. *conj 3rd sg* **shaaxkéekhang**. *imp* **shaaxkéekhah**. *ptcpl* **shaaxkéek=hang**.

**shaaxkéekheew** VTA make a mark on s.o. in a straight line, mark s.o. in a straight line. *ind 1st sg* **nzhaaxkéek=haaw**, **nzhaaxkéekha**. *ind 3rd sg* **wshaaxkeekháawal**. *ind inv* **nzhaax=kéekhookw**. *ind I-you* **kshaaxkéek=hool**. *conj 3rd sg* **shaaxkéekhaat**. *imp* **shaaxkéekhaw**. *ptcpl* **shaaxkéek=haat**.

**shaaxkeekhíikeew** VAI make a straight line of things, write in a straight line. *ind 1st sg* **nzhaaxkeekhíike**, **nzhaax=keekhíikeem**. *conj 3rd sg* **shaax=keekhíikeet**. *imp* **shaaxkeekhíikeel**. *ptcpl* **shaaxkeekhíikeet**. *intensive re-duplication* **ashaaxkeekhíikeew**.

**shaaxkéelŭmeew** VTA be certain about s.o. *ind 1st sg* **nzhaaxkéelŭmaaw**, **nzhaaxkéelŭma**. *ind 3rd sg* **wshaax=keelŭmáawal**. *ind inv* **nzhaaxkéelŭ=mukw**. *ind I-you* **kshaaxkéelŭmul**. *conj 3rd sg* **shaaxkéelŭmaat**. *imp* **shaaxkéelum**. *ptcpl* **shaaxkéelŭ=maat**.

**shaaxkeelúndam** VOTI1A be certain. *ind 1st sg* **nzhaaxkeelúndam**. *conj 3rd sg* **shaaxkeelúndang**. *ptcpl* **shaax=keelúndang**. *intensive reduplication* **ashaaxkeelúndam**.

**shaaxkeelúndam** VTI1A be certain about s.t. *ind 1st sg* **nzhaaxkeelúndamun**. *ind 3rd sg* **wshaaxkeelúndamun**. *conj 1st sg* **shaaxkeelúndamaan**. *conj 3rd sg* **shaaxkeelúndang**. *ptcpl* **shaaxkeelúndang**.

**shaaxkiikáapawuw** VAI stand straight. **Kŭníhtaa-shaaxkiikáapawi.** 'You know how to stand straight.' *ind 1st sg* **nzhaaxkiikáapawi**, **nzhaaxkii=káapawiim**. *conj 3rd sg* **shaaxkii=káapawiit**. *imp* **shaaxkiikáapawiil**. *ptcpl* **shaaxkiikáapawiit**.

**shaaxkiikwáakeew** VAI sew things straight; straighten things *(with a tool)*. *ind 1st sg* **nzhaaxkiikwáake**, **nzhaaxkiikwáakeem**. *conj 3rd sg* **shaaxkiikwáakeet**. *imp* **shaaxkii=kwáakeel**. *ptcpl* **shaaxkiikwáakeet**. *intensive reduplication* **ashaaxkii=kwáakeew**.

**shaaxkiikwáaleew** VTA sew s.t. animate straight; poke s.o. straight, straighten s.o. out *(with a tool)*. *ind 1st sg* **nzhaaxkiikwáalaaw**, **nzhaaxkii=kwáala**. *ind 3rd sg* **wshaaxkiikwaa=láawal**. *ind inv* **nzhaaxkiikwáalukw**. *ind I-you* **kshaaxkiikwáalul**. *conj 3rd sg* **shaaxkiikwáalaat**. *imp* **shaaxkíikwaal**. *ptcpl* **shaaxkii=kwáalaat**.

**shaaxkíikwam** VTI1A sew s.t. straight; poke s.t. straight, straighten s.t. *(with a tool)*. *ind 1st sg* **nzhaaxkíikwa=mun**. *ind 3rd sg* **wshaaxkíikwamun**. *conj 1st sg* **shaaxkíikwamaan**. *conj 3rd sg* **shaaxkíikwang**. *imp* **shaax=kíikwah**. *ptcpl* **shaaxkíikwang**.

**shaaxkíixiin** VAI lie straight. *ind 1st sg* **nzhaaxkíixiin**, **nzhaaxkíixi**. *conj 3rd sg* **shaaxkíixiing**. *imp* **shaaxkíixiil**. *ptcpl* **shaaxkíixiing**, **shaaxkíixiit**.

**shaaxkíixtoow** VTI2 straighten s.t., lay s.t. straight. *ind 1st sg* **nzhaaxkíix=toon**. *ind 3rd sg* **wshaaxkíixtoon**. *conj 1st sg* **shaaxkiixtáwaan**. *conj 3rd sg* **shaaxkíixtaakw**. *imp* **shaax=kíixtool**. *ptcpl* **shaaxkíixtaakw**.

**shaaxkíixŭmeew** VTA straighten s.o., lay s.o. straight. *ind 1st sg* **nzhaaxkíixŭ=maaw**, **nzhaaxkíixŭma**. *ind 3rd sg*

**wshaaxkiixŭmáawal**. *ind inv* **nzhaa=xkíixŭmukw**. *ind I-you* **kshaaxkíi=xŭmul**. *conj 3rd sg* **shaaxkíixŭmaat**. *imp* **shaaxkíixum**. *ptcpl* **shaaxkíixŭ=maat**.

**shaaxkíixun** VII lie straight. *conj 3rd sg* **shaaxkíixung**. *ptcpl* **shaaxkíixung**.

**shaaxkíhkam** VTI1A straighten s.t., straighten s.t. out *(using the foot or body)*. *ind 1st sg* **nzhaaxkíhkamun**. *ind 3rd sg* **wshaaxkíhkamun**. *conj 1st sg* **shaaxkíhkamaan**. *conj 3rd sg* **shaaxkíhkang**. *imp* **shaaxkíhkah**. *ptcpl* **shaaxkíhkang**.

**shaaxkíhkaweew** VTA straighten s.o., straighten s.o. out *(using the foot or body)*. *ind 1st sg* **nzhaaxkíhkawaaw**, **nzhaaxkíhkawa**. *ind 3rd sg* **wshaax=kihkawáawal**. *ind inv* **nzhaaxkíh=kaakw**. *ind I-you* **kshaaxkíhkool**. *conj 3rd sg* **shaaxkíhkawaat**. *imp* **shaaxkíhkaw**. *ptcpl* **shaaxkíhka=waat**.

**shaaxkíhleew** VAI go straight, fly straight. *ind 1st sg* **nzhaaxkíhla**, **nzhaaxkíhlaam**. *conj 3rd sg* **shaax=kíhlaat**. *imp* **shaaxkíhlaal**. *ptcpl* **shaaxkíhlaat**.

**shaaxkíhleew** VII go straight. *conj 3rd sg* **shaaxkíhlaak**. *ptcpl* **shaaxkíh=laak**.

**shaaxkihtéeham** VTI1A hit and straighten s.t. *ind 1st sg* **nzhaaxkihtéehŭ=mun**. *ind 3rd sg* **wshaaxkihtée=hŭmun**. *conj 1st sg* **shaaxkihtéehŭ=maan**. *conj 3rd sg* **shaaxkihtéehang**. *imp* **shaaxkihtéehih**. *ptcpl* **shaax=kihtéehang**.

**shaaxkihtéeheew** VTA hit and straighten s.o., hit and straighten s.t. animate. *ind 1st sg* **nzhaaxkihtéehaaw**, **nźhaax=kihtéeha**. *ind 3rd sg* **wshaaxkihtee=háawal**. *ind inv* **nzhaaxkihtéehookw**. *ind I-you* **kshaaxkihtéehool**. *conj 3rd sg* **shaaxkihtéehaat**. *imp* **shaaxkíh=teeh**. *ptcpl* **shaaxkihtéehaat**.

**shaaxkíhtoow** VTI2 straighten s.t. *ind 1st sg* **nzhaaxkíhtoon**. *ind 3rd sg* **wshaaxkíhtoon**. *conj 1st sg* **shaax=kíhtawaan**. *conj 3rd sg* **shaaxkíh=taakw**. *imp* **shaaxkíhtool**. *ptcpl* **shaaxkihtaakw**.

**shaaxkóoxweew** VAI walk directly to one's destination, go directly to one's destination; follow a good path in life. *ind 1st sg* **nzhaaxkóoxwe**, **nzhaax=kóoxweem**. *conj 3rd sg* **shaaxkóo=xweet**. *imp* **shaaxkóoxweel**. *ptcpl* **shaaxkóoxweet**.

**shaaxkóhkweew** VAI look straight ahead. *ind 1st sg* **nzhaaxkóhkwe**, **nzhaax=kóhkweem**. *conj 3rd sg* **shaaxkóh=kweet**. *imp* **shaaxkóhkweel**. *ptcpl* **shaaxkóhkweet**. *See* **shaaxkhiin=gwéexiin**.

**shaaxkohkwéepuw** VAI sit straight. *ind 1st sg* **nzhaaxkohkwéepi**, **nzhaax=kohkwéepiim**. *conj 3rd sg* **shaax=kohkwéepiit**. *imp* **shaaxkohkwée=piil**. *ptcpl* **shaaxkohkwéepiit**.

**shaaxkúneew** VTA straighten s.o. *(using the hands)*. *ind 1st sg* **nzhaaxkúnaaw**, **nzhaaxkúna**. *ind 3rd sg* **wshaax=kùnáawal**. *ind inv* **nzhaaxkúnukw**. *ind I-you* **kshaaxkúnul**. *conj 3rd sg* **shaaxkúnaat**. *imp* **sháaxkun**. *ptcpl* **shaaxkúnaat**.

**shaaxkùnaxkéexiin** VAI stick one's hand out straight, have one's hand(s) out straight. *ind 1st sg* **nzhaaxkùnax=kéexiin**, **nzhaaxkùnaxkéexi**. *conj 3rd sg* **shaaxkùnaxkéexiing**. *imp* **shaaxkùnaxkéexiil**. *ptcpl* **shaax=kùnaxkéexiing**.

**shaaxkúnum** VTI1B straighten s.t. *(using the hands)*. *ind 1st sg* **nzhaax=kúnŭmun**. *ind 3rd sg* **wshaaxkún=ŭmun**. *conj 1st sg* **shaaxkúnŭmaan**. *conj 3rd sg* **shaaxkúnung**. *imp* **shaaxkúnih**. *ptcpl* **shaaxkúnung**.

**shaaxkúsuw** VAI be straight *(s.t. animate)*. *ind 1st sg* **nzhaaxkúsi**, **nzhaa=**

xkúsiim. *conj 3rd sg* **shaaxkúsiit**. *ptcpl* **shaaxkúsiit**.

**shaaxkútseew** VTA iron s.t. animate *(of clothing). ind 1st sg* **nzhaaxkútsaaw, nzhaaxkútsa**. *ind 3rd sg* **wshaax=kùtsáawal**. *ind inv* **nzhaaxkútsookw**. *ind I-you* **kshaaxkútsool**. *conj 3rd sg* **shaaxkútsaat**. *imp* **shaaxkútus**. *ptcpl* **shaaxkútsaat**.

**shaaxkùtsíikan** NI clothes iron. *pl* **shaa=xkùtsíikanal**. *poss* **nzhaaxkùtsíikan**. *loc* **shaaxkùtsíikanung**. *dimin* **shaa=xkùch'shíikanush**. *See* **chiingaal=síikan**.

**shaaxkútsum** VTI1B iron s.t. *(of clothing). ind 1st sg* **nzhaaxkùtsúmun**. *ind 3rd sg* **wshaaxkùtsúmun**. *conj 1st sg* **shaaxkùtsúmaan**. *conj 3rd sg* **shaaxkútsung**. *imp* **shaaxkútsih**. *ptcpl* **shaaxkútsung**.

**shaaxkiingwéexiin** VAI have a straight face, have a sober face, have a poker face. *ind 1st sg* **nzhaaxkiingwéexiin, nzhaaxkiingwéexi**. *conj 3rd sg* **shaaxkiingwéexiing**. *ptcpl* **shaax=kiingwéexiing, shaaxkiingwéexiit**.

**shahkamóoleew** VTA feed s.o. by hand. *ind 1st sg* **nzhahkamóolaaw, nzhah=kamóola**. *ind 3rd sg* **wshahkamoo=láawal**. *ind inv* **nzhahkamóolukw**. *ind I-you* **kshahkamóolul**. *conj 3rd sg* **shahkamóolaat**. *imp* **sháhkmool**. *ptcpl* **shahkamóolaat**. *intensive reduplication* **wshahshahkamooláawal**.

**shàhwáaleew** VTA be in a hurry *(for s.o. to do something)*; be in a hurry for s.o. to die. **Nzhahwáalaaw ootéeneeng wtáan.** 'I'm in a hurry for him to go to town.' *ind 1st sg* **nzhahwáalaaw, nzhahwáala**. *ind 3rd sg* **wshahwaa=láawal**. *ind inv* **nzhahwáalukw**. *ind I-you* **kshahwáalul**. *conj 3rd sg* **shàhwáalaat**. *ptcpl* **shèhwáalaat**. *See* **shawáaleew**.

**shàhwáapeew** VAIO hesitate about s.t. *ind 1st sg* **nzhahwáapeen**. *ind 3rd sg* **wshahwáapeen**. *conj 3rd sg* **shàh=wáapeet**. *imp* **shàhwáapeel**. *ptcpl* **shèhwáapeet**.

**shàhwalóhkeew** VAI work slowly. *ind 1st sg* **nzhahwalóhke, nzhahwalóh=keem**. *conj 3rd sg* **shàhwalóhkeet**. *imp* **shàhwalóhkeel**. *ptcpl* **shèhwa=lóhkeet**.

**shahwi-** PV slow. **Níi áa ngíish-sháhwi-kúndka.** 'I can dance slow.' *ptcpl* **shehwi-**.

**sháhwkeew** VAI dance slowly. *ind 1st sg* **nzháhwka, nzháhwkaam**. *conj 3rd sg* **sháhwkaat**. *imp* **sháhwkaal**. *ptcpl* **shéhwkaat**.

**shàkiinóotay** NI bag. *pl* **shàkiinóotayal**. *poss* **nzhàkiinóotay**. *loc* **shàkiinóo=teeng**. *dimin* **shàkiinóocheesh**.

**shalapwáanush** NI doughnut. *pl* **sha=lapwáanshal**. *poss* **nzhalapwáan=shum**. *loc* **shalapwáanshung**.

**shamaatpùníikan** NA greasy wagon. *pl* **shamaatpùníikanak**. *poss* **nzham=aatpùníikan**. *loc* **shamaatpùníika=nung**. *dimin* **shamaachpùníikanush**. *obv* **shamaatpùníikanal**.

**shamaatpùníikaneew** VAI grease a buggy. *ind 1st sg* **nzhamaatpùníi=kane, nzhamaatpùníikaneem**. *conj 3rd sg* **shamaatpùníikanaat**. *imp* **shamaatpùníikanaal**. *ptcpl* **shee=maatpùníikanaat**.

**shaméew** VII be greasy. *conj 3rd sg* **shaméek**. *ptcpl* **shéemeek**.

**shamóoshkoosh** NA greasy pig. *pl* **sha=mooshkóoshak**. *poss* **nzhamoosh=kóoshum**. *loc* **shamooshkóoshung**. *dimin* **shamooshkóoshush**. *obv* **shamooshkóoshal**.

**shamóhkweew** VAI have greasy hair. *ind 1st sg* **nzhamóhkwa, nzhamóh=kwaam**. *conj 3rd sg* **shamóhkwaat**. *ptcpl* **sheemóhkwaat**.

**shamuchéepuw** VAI eat greasy food. **Noosáami-shamuchéepwi.** 'I ate too much greasy food.' *ind 1st sg* **nzham=**

chéepwi, nzhamchéepwiim. *conj 3rd sg* **shamuchéepwiit**. *imp* **sha=muchéepwiil**. *ptcpl* **sheemchéepwiit**.

**shamúneew** VTA put grease on s.o., put grease on s.t. animate. *ind 1st sg* **nzhámŭnaaw**, **nzhámŭna**. *ind 3rd sg* **wshamŭnáawal**. *ind inv* **nzhámŭ=nukw**. *ind I-you* **kshámŭnul**. *conj 3rd sg* **shamúnaat**. *imp* **shamún**. *ptcpl* **shéemŭnaat**.

**shamunáxkeew** VAI have greasy hands. *ind 1st sg* **nzhamŭnáxka**, **nzhamŭ=náxkaam**. *conj 3rd sg* **shamunáx=kaat**. *ptcpl* **sheemŭnáxkaat**.

**shamuníikan** NI oil for greasing. *poss* **nzhamŭníikan**. *loc* **shamuníika=nung**. *dimin* **shamuníikanush**.

**shamuníiwu-káanoos** NA oil for greasing. *obv* **shamuníiwu-kaanóosal**.

**shamúnum** VTI 1B put grease on s.t. *ind 1st sg* **nzhamŭnúmun**. *ind 3rd sg* **wshamŭnúmun**. *conj 1st sg* **sha=múnŭmaan**. *conj 3rd sg* **shamún=ung**. *imp* **shamúnih**. *ptcpl* **shée=mŭnung**.

**shamúsuw** VAI be greasy *(s.t. animate)*. *ind 1st sg* **nzhámsi**, **nzhámsiim**. *conj 3rd sg* **shamúsiit**. *ptcpl* **shéemsiit**.

**shamutóoneew** VAI have a greasy mouth. *ind 1st sg* **nzhamtóona**, **nzhamtóo=naam**. *conj 3rd sg* **shamutóonaat**. *ptcpl* **sheemtóonaat**.

**shándham** VOTI 1A kick out one's legs, stretch out one's legs; maneuver *(of trains)*. *ind 1st sg* **nzhándham**. *conj 3rd sg* **shándhang**. *imp* **shándhah**. *ptcpl* **shéendhang**. *intensive reduplication* **shàshándham**.

**shàshkíisŭmuw** VAI drink until one urinates. *ind 1st sg* **nzhashkíisŭmwi**, **nzhashkíisŭmwiim**. *conj 3rd sg* **shashkíisŭmwiit**. *imp* **shàshkíisŭ=mwiil**. *ptcpl* **shashkíisŭmwiit**.

**shàshkwáheew** VTA pound s.t. animate, mash s.t. animate. *ind 1st sg* **nzhash=kwáhaaw**, **nzhashkwáha**. *ind 3rd sg* **wshashkwaháawal**. *ind inv* **nzhash=kwáhookw**. *ind I-you* **kshashkwáh=ool**. *conj 3rd sg* **shashkwáhaat**. *imp* **sháshkwah**. *ptcpl* **shashkwáhaat**.

**shashkwakíindam** VTI 1A memorize s.t. *ind 1st sg* **nzhashkwakíindamun**. *ind 3rd sg* **wshashkwakíindamun**. *conj 1st sg* **shashkwakíindamaan**. *conj 3rd sg* **shashkwakíindang**. *imp* **shàshkwakíindah**. *ptcpl* **shash=kwakíindang**.

**shàshkwakíinzuw** VAI say things from memory, recite from memory. *ind 1st sg* **nzhashkwakíinzi**, **nzhashkwak=íinziim**. *conj 3rd sg* **shashkwakíin=ziit**. *imp* **shàshkwakíinziil**. *ptcpl* **shashkwakíinziit**.

**shàshkwámeew** VTA chew s.t. animate. **Pkóohal shashkwámeew.** 'He's chewing some gum.' *ind 1st sg* **nzhashkwámaaw**, **nzhashkwáma**. *ind 3rd sg* **wshashkwamáawal**. *ind inv* **nzhashkwámukw**. *ind I-you* **kshashkwámul**. *conj 3rd sg* **shash=kwámaat**. *imp* **sháshkwam**. *ptcpl* **shashkwámaat**.

**shàshkwámuw** VAI chew, be chewing. *ind 1st sg* **nzhashkwámwi**, **nzhash=kwámwiim**. *conj 3rd sg* **shash=kwámwiit**. *imp* **shàshkwámwiil**. *ptcpl* **shashkwámwiit**.

**shàshkwándam** VTI 1A chew s.t. *ind 1st sg* **nzhashkwándamun**. *ind 3rd sg* **wshashkwándamun**. *conj 1st sg* **shashkwándamaan**. *conj 3rd sg* **shashkwándang**. *imp* **shàshkwán=dah**. *ptcpl* **shashkwándang**.

**shawáałeew** VTA be in a hurry *(for s.o. to do something)*; be in a hurry for s.o. to die. *ind 1st sg* **nzhawáalaaw**, **nzhawáala**. *ind 3rd sg* **wshawaaláa=wal**. *ind inv* **nzhawáalukw**. *ind I-you* **kshawáalul**. *conj 3rd sg* **shawáalaat**. *ptcpl* **shewáalaat**. *See* **shàhwáaleew**.

**shawaláamuw** VAI starve; starve to death. *ind 1st sg* **nzhawaláamwi**, nzhawaláamwiim. *conj 3rd sg* **shawaláamwiit**. *ptcpl* **sheewa=láamwiit**.

**shawamalúsuw** VAI feel weak. *ind 1st sg* **nzhawamálsi**, **nzhawamálsiim**. *conj 3rd sg* **shawamalúsiit**. *ptcpl* **sheewamálsiit**.

**shawéew** VII be weak. **Shawéew náxk.** 'My hand is weak.' *conj 3rd sg* **shawéek**. *ptcpl* **shéeweek**.

**shaweelúndam** VOTI1A be in a hurry. *ind 1st sg* **nzhaweelúndam**. *conj 3rd sg* **shaweelúndang**. *ptcpl* **sheewee=lúndang**.

**shàwéexiin** VAI lie on one's side. *ind 1st sg* **nzhawéexiin**, **nzhawéexi**. *conj 3rd sg* **shàwéexiing**. *imp* **shàwéexiil**.

**shawiináakwat** VII look weak. *conj 3rd sg* **shawiináakwahk**. *ptcpl* **sheewii=náakwahk**.

**shawiináakwsuw** VAI look weak. *ind 1st sg* **nzhawiináakwsi**, **nzhawiináak=wsiim**. *conj 3rd sg* **shawiináakwsiit**. *ptcpl* **sheewiináakwsiit**.

**shawíipasuw** VAI be wilted *(s.t. animate)*. *ind 1st sg* **nzhawíipasi**, **nzhawíipa=siim**. *conj 3rd sg* **shawíipasiit**. *ptcpl* **sheewíipasiit**.

**shawíipateew** VII be wilted. *conj 3rd sg* **shawíipateek**. *ptcpl* **sheewíipateek**.

**shawíhleew** VAI be tired out, be exhausted. *ind 1st sg* **nzhawíhla**, **nzhawíh=laam**. *conj 3rd sg* **shawíhlaat**. *ptcpl* **sheewíhlaat**. *intensive reduplication* **ashawíhleew**.

**shawúpeew** VAI be weak from being in the water. *ind 1st sg* **nzháwpe**, **nzháwpeem**. *conj 3rd sg* **shawúpeet**. *ptcpl* **shéewpeet**.

**shawúsuw** VAI be weak. *ind 1st sg* **nzháwsi**, **nzháwsiim**. *conj 3rd sg* **shawúsiit**. *ptcpl* **shéewsiit**.

**sháxk** PC must be. *informal*. **Sháxk éet pasát.** 'It must be cracked.'; **Sháxk éet shaashŭwánakuw.** 'He must be part white.' *See* **sháxkii**.

**sháxkii** PC must be. **Sháxkii ayásku náh ndá.** 'I guess I'll have to go.' *See* **sháxk**.

**shayee-** PV first. **Nzháyee-míitsi.** 'I eat before, I eat ahead of the others.'; **Néeka shayée-ktuniikóote.** 'He took his coat off first.' *ptcpl* **shéeyee-**.

**shayéemung** PC in the lead, in front. **Shayéemung níipiit éhteek.** 'My front tooth.'; **Shayéemung lú áan=dapuw.** 'She changed her seat to the front.' *See* **shéemung**.

**shayeewaaméhleew** VAI run ahead, be leading in a race. *ind 1st sg* **nzhayee=waaméhla**, **nzhayeewaaméhlaam**. *conj 3rd sg* **shayeewaaméhlaat**. *imp* **shayeewaaméhlaal**. *ptcpl* **sheeyee=waaméhlaat**.

**shayeewahtakíhleew** VAI run ahead, be leading in a race. *ind 1st sg* **nzhayee=wahtakíhla**, **nzhayeewahtakíhlaam**. *conj 3rd sg* **shayeewahtakíhlaat**. *imp* **shayeewahtakíhlaal**. *ptcpl* **sheeyee=wahtakíhlaat**.

**shayeewchéhleew** VAI drive ahead, drive in the lead, drive first. *ind 1st sg* **nzhayeewchéhla**, **nzhayeewchéh=laam**. *conj 3rd sg* **shayeewchéhlaat**. *imp* **shayeewchéhlaal**. *ptcpl* **shee=yeewchéhlaat**.

**shayéewi** PC first. *See* **shayée**.

**shayeewiikwsíhleew** VAI crawl ahead. *ind 1st sg* **nzhayeewiikwsíhla**, **nzhayeewiikwsíhlaam**. *conj 3rd sg* **shayeewiikwsíhlaat**. *imp* **shayee=wiikwsíhlaal**. *ptcpl* **sheeyeewiikw=síhlaat**.

**shayeewíikwsuw** VAI crawl ahead, crawl in the lead. *ind 1st sg* **nzhayeewíik=wsi**, **nzhayeewíikwsiim**. *conj 3rd sg* **shayeewíikwsiit**. *imp* **shayeewíikw=siil**. *ptcpl* **sheeyeewíikwsiit**.

**shayéewxeew** VAI walk in the lead, walk in front, go ahead, walk ahead. **Wíh=wiing-shayéewxeew.** 'He likes to be ahead.'; **Wíhwiing-shàshayéew=**

**xeew.** 'He always likes to go ahead.' *ind 1st sg* **nzhayéewxe**, **nzhayéew=xeem**. *conj 3rd sg* **shayéewxeet**. *imp* **shayéewxeel**. *ptcpl* **sheeyéewxeet**. *intensive reduplication* **shàshayéew=xeew**.

**shayéexiin** VAI be first, be first in line, be first in a competition. *ind 1st sg* **nzhayéexiin**, **nzhayéexi**. *conj 3rd sg* **shayéexiing**. *imp* **shayéexiil**. *ptcpl* **sheeyéexiing**.

**shayéextoow** VTI2 put s.t. in the front, put s.t. in the lead. *ind 1st sg* **nzhay=éextoon**. *ind 3rd sg* **wshayéextoon**. *conj 1st sg* **shayeextáwaan**. *conj 3rd sg* **shayéextaakw**. *ptcpl* **sheeyéex=taakw**.

**shayéexŭmeew** VTA put s.o. in the front, put s.o. in the lead. *ind 1st sg* **nzhay=éexŭmaaw**, **nzhayéexŭma**. *ind 3rd sg* **wshayeexŭmáawal**. *ind inv* **nzhayéexŭmukw**. *ind I-you* **kshay=éexŭmul**. *conj 3rd sg* **shayéexŭmaat**. *imp* **shayéexum**. *ptcpl* **sheeyéexŭ=maat**.

**shayéexun** VII be at the front, be in the lead. *conj 3rd sg* **shayéexung**. *ptcpl* **sheeyéexung**.

**shayéhleew** VAI be in the lead, go first, fly first, run first, drive first, proceed first, go ahead, run ahead. **Cheeng=shíishiit éel-péechi-shayéhlaat.** 'The little one came in first.' *ind 1st sg* **nzhayéhla**, **nzhayéhlaam**. *conj 3rd sg* **shayéhlaat**. *imp* **shayéhlaal**. *ptcpl* **sheeyéhlaat**.

**shée** PC for shame! **Shée! Kpalŭnúm=un.** 'For shame! You dropped it!'

**shéeliish** NA Sarah. *obv* **sheelíishal**. *From English* Sarah.

**shéemung** PC in the lead, in front. **Shéemung líhle.** 'It fell forward, it went to the front.' *See* **shayéemung**.

**shéetoon** NI lip. *pl* **sheetóonal**. *poss* **nzhéetoon**.

**sheetoonéexiin** VAI have one's lips sticking out, stick one's lips out. *ind 1st sg* **nzheetoonéexiin**, **nzheetoonéexi**. *conj 3rd sg* **sheetoonéexiing**. *imp* **sheetoonéexiil**. *ptcpl* **sheetoonée=xiing**, **sheetoonéexiit**. *indicates that one is pouting or angry.*

**sheetoonohkwéepuw** VAI sit with one's lips sticking out. *ind 1st sg* **nzhee=toonohkwéepi**, **nzheetoonohkwée=piim**. *conj 3rd sg* **sheetoonohkwée=piit**. *imp* **sheetoonohkwéepiil**. *ptcpl* **sheetoonohkwéepiit**.

**sheewandíikan** NA pocket. *pl* **sheewan=díikanak**. *poss* **nzheewandíikan**. *loc* **sheewandíikanung**. *dimin* **sheewan=jíikanush**. *obv* **sheewandíikanal**.

**sheexkalaaméhleew** VAI run naked. *ind 1st sg* **nzheexkalaaméhla**, **nzheex=kalaaméhlaam**. *conj 3rd sg* **sheex=kalaaméhlaat**. *imp* **sheexkalaaméh=laal**. *ptcpl* **sheexkalaaméhlaat**.

**sheexkaláangweew** VAI lie naked. *ind 1st sg* **nzheexkaláangwe**, **nzheexka=láangweem**. *conj 3rd sg* **sheexka=láangweet**. *imp* **sheexkaláangweel**. *ptcpl* **sheexkaláangweet**.

**shéexkalii-kawíiw** VAI sleep naked. *ind 1st sg* **nzhéexkalii-kawí**, **nzhéexkalii-kawíim**. *conj 3rd sg* **shéexkalii-kawíit**. *imp* **shéexkalii-kawíil**. *ptcpl* **shéexkalii-kawíit**. *See* **sheexkalón=gwaam**.

**sheexkaliikáapawuw** VAI stand naked. *ind 1st sg* **nzheexkaliikáapawi**, **nzheexkaliikáapawiim**. *conj 3rd sg* **sheexkaliikáapawiit**. *imp* **sheexka=liikáapawiil**. *ptcpl* **sheexkaliikáa=pawiit**.

**sheexkalíhleew** VAI get naked. *ind 1st sg* **nzheexkalíhla**, **nzheexkalíhlaam**. *conj 3rd sg* **sheexkalíhlaat**. *imp* **sheexkalíhlaal**. *ptcpl* **sheexkalíhlaat**.

**sheexkalohkwéepuw** VAI sit naked. *ind 1st sg* **nzheexkalohkwéepi**, **nzheex=kalohkwéepiim**. *conj 3rd sg* **sheex=kalohkwéepiit**. *imp* **sheexkaloh=**

**kwéepiil**. *ptcpl* **sheexkalohkwéepiit**.

**sheexkalóngwaam** VAI sleep naked. *ind 1st sg* **nzheexkalóngwaam**. *conj 3rd sg* **sheexkalóngwaang**. *imp* **sheex=kalóngwaah**. *ptcpl* **sheexkalón=gwaang**. *See* **shéexkalii-kawíiw**.

**sheexkalúneew** VTA undress s.o., take off all of s.o.'s clothes. **Kách wáak ápih shúkw nzheexkalúnukw.** 'She's just going to undress me again.' *ind 1st sg* **nzheexkalúnaaw**, **nzheexka=lúna**. *ind 3rd sg* **wsheexkalŭnáawal**. *ind inv* **nzheexkalúnukw**. *ind I-you* **ksheexkalúnul**. *conj 3rd sg* **sheex=kalúnaat**. *imp* **shéexkalun**. *ptcpl* **sheexkalúnaat**.

**sheexkalúsuw** VAI be naked. *ind 1st sg* **nzheexkalúsi**, **nzheexkalúsiim**. *conj 3rd sg* **sheexkalúsiit**. *ptcpl* **sheex=kalúsiit**.

**shehshíikaleek** NI lace curtain, transparent curtain. *pl* **shehshiikaléekal**.

**shehshiipihláak apíikwan** NI accordion. *pl* **shehshiipihláakiil apíikwa=nal**. *'musical instrument that stretches in and out.'*

**shehshkoolháalŭwees** NA schoolteacher. *pl* **shehshkoolhaalŭwéesak**. *obv* **shehshkoolhaalŭwéesal**.

**shehshkoolhaalŭweesóxkweew** NA woman schoolteacher. *pl* **shehshkool=haalŭweesoxkwéewak**. *obv* **shehsh=koolhaalŭweesoxkwéewal**.

**shehshoohíikeeng** NI paint brush. *pl* **shehshoohiikéengiil**.

**shéntii** NI shanty. *pl* **shentíihal**. *poss* **nzhentíihum**. *loc* **shentíihung**. *dimin* **shentíihush**. *From English* shanty.

**shentiihámeew** VAI live in a shanty. *ind 1st sg* **nzhentiiháma**, **nzhentiihám=aam**. *conj 3rd sg* **shentiihámaat**. *imp* **shentiihámaal**. *ptcpl* **shentiihámaat**. *From English* shanty.

**shíifush** NA Cephas *(man's name)*. *dimin* **shíifshush**. *obv* **shíifshal**. *From English* Cephas.

**shíikaanzh** PC very, extremely, intensely. **Shíikaanzh lúkih nŭwiiníihukw.** 'She really made me mad.'; **Shíi=kaanzh lúkih wŭlíhleew.** 'It really runs well.' *See* **shihshíikaanzh**.

**shiikalaalóhkweew** VAI have thin hair, have fine hair. *ind 1st sg* **nzhiikalaa=lóhkwe**, **nzhiikalaalóhkweem**. *conj 3rd sg* **shiikalaalóhkweet**. *ptcpl* **shiikalaalóhkweet**.

**shiikalahóosuw** VAI wear a sheer dress, wear a transparent dress. *ind 1st sg* **nzhiikalahóosi**, **nzhiikalahóosiim**. *conj 3rd sg* **shiikalahóosiit**. *imp* **shiikalahóosiil**. *ptcpl* **shiikalah=óosiit**.

**shíikaleew** VII be transparent, be thin *(of material)*. *conj 3rd sg* **shíikaleek**. *ptcpl* **shíikaleek**.

**shiikaleeheeshandéekan** NA screen window. *pl* **shiikaleeheeshandée=kanak**. *poss* **nzhiikaleeheeshandée=kan**. *loc* **shiikaleeheeshandéeka=nung**. *dimin* **shiikaleeheeshanjée=kanush**. *obv* **shiikaleeheeshandée=kanal**.

**shiikalúsuw** VAI be transparent, be thin *(s.t. animate, of material)*. *ind 1st sg* **nzhiikalúsi**, **nzhiikalúsiim**. *conj 3rd sg* **shiikalúsiit**. *ptcpl* **shiikalúsiit**.

**shiikóowuw** VAI be widowed, be a widower. *ind 1st sg* **nzhiikóowi**, **nzhii=kóowiim**. *conj 3rd sg* **shiikóowiit**. *ptcpl* **shiikóowiit**.

**shiikóxkweew** NA widow. *pl* **shiikox=kwéewak**. *obv* **shiikoxkwéewal**.

**shiikwíineew** VAI be an orphan. *ind 1st sg* **nzhiikwíine**, **nzhiikwíineem**. *conj 3rd sg* **shiikwíineet**. *ptcpl* **shiikwíi=neet**.

**shíikwsheew** VTA cut s.t. animate closely. *ind 1st sg* **nzhíikwshaaw**, **nzhíi=kwsha**. *ind 3rd sg* **wshiikwsháawal**. *ind inv* **nzhíikwshookw**. *ind I-you* **kshíikwshool**. *conj 3rd sg* **shíikw=shaat**. *imp* **shíikwush**. *ptcpl* **shíikw=**

**shaat**.

**shíikwshum** VTI 1A cut s.t. closely. *ind 1st sg* **nzhiikwshúmun**. *ind 3rd sg* **wshiikwshúmun**. *conj 1st sg* **shii=kwshúmaan**. *conj 3rd sg* **shíikw=shung**. *imp* **shíikwshih**. *ptcpl* **shíikwshung**.

**shíikwŭneew** VTA take all of s.t. animate out. *ind 1st sg* **nzhíikwŭnaaw**, **nzhíi=kwŭna**. *ind 3rd sg* **wshiikwŭnáawal**. *ind inv* **nzhíikwŭnukw**. *ind I-you* **kshíikwŭnul**. *conj 3rd sg* **shíikwŭ=naat**. *ptcpl* **shíikwŭnaat**.

**shíikwŭnum** VTI 1A take all of s.t. out *(of something)*. *ind 1st sg* **nzhiikwŭ=númun**. *ind 3rd sg* **wshiikwŭnúmun**. *conj 1st sg* **shiikwŭnúmaan**. *conj 3rd sg* **shíikwŭnung**. *imp* **shíikwŭnih**. *ptcpl* **shíikwŭnung**.

**shiindáasuw** VII have a certain name, be named. *conj 3rd sg* **shiindáasiik**. *ptcpl* **eeshiindáasiik**.

**shiing-** PV unwillingly, refuse to do. *informal*. **Shíing-siiníikeew.** 'He wouldn't milk the cow.'; **Shíing-alumsúwak.** 'They didn't want to leave.' *ptcpl* **shíing-**. *See* **shiingi-**, **shiingu-**.

**shiingáalŭweew** VAI hate people. *ind 1st sg* **nzhiingáalŭwe**, **nzhiingáalŭ=weem**. *conj 3rd sg* **shiingáalŭweet**. *ptcpl* **shiingáalŭweet**.

**shiingáatam** VTI 1A dislike s.t. *ind 1st sg* **nzhiingáatamun**. *ind 3rd sg* **wshiin=gáatamun**. *conj 1st sg* **shiingáata=maan**. *conj 3rd sg* **shiingáatang**. *ptcpl* **shiingáatang**.

**shiingahkíiheew** VAI be reluctant to plant. *ind 1st sg* **nzhiingahkíihe**, **nzhiingahkíiheem**. *conj 3rd sg* **shiingahkíiheet**. *ptcpl* **shiingahkíi=heet**.

**shiingalóhkeew** VAI be unwilling to work. *ind 1st sg* **nzhiingalóhke**, **nzhiingalóhkeem**. *conj 3rd sg* **shiin=galóhkeet**. *ptcpl* **shiingalóhkeet**.

**shíingapuw** VAI dislike where one is. *ind 1st sg* **nzhíingapi**, **nzhíingapiim**. *conj 3rd sg* **shíingapiit**. *ptcpl* **shíin=gapiit**.

**shíingapuw** VAIO dislike it where one is, dislike it where one stays. *ind 1st sg* **nzhíingapiin**. *ind 3rd sg* **wshíinga=piin**. *conj 3rd sg* **shíingapiit**. *ptcpl* **shíingapiit**.

**shiingeelúndam** VOTI 1A be reluctant. *ind 1st sg* **nzhiingeelúndam**. *conj 3rd sg* **shiingeelúndang**. *ptcpl* **shiingeelún=dang**.

**shiingiináasuw** VAI be hateful; dislike people. *ind 1st sg* **nzhiingiináasi**, **nzhiingiináasiim**. *conj 3rd sg* **shiin=giináasiit**. *ptcpl* **shiingiináasiit**.

**shiingíinam** VTI 1A hate s.t.; dislike s.t. *ind 1st sg* **nzhiingíinamun**. *ind 3rd sg* **wshiingíinamun**. *conj 1st sg* **shiingíinamaan**. *conj 3rd sg* **shiin=gíinang**. *ptcpl* **shiingíinang**.

**shiingíinaweew** VTA hate s.o., dislike s.o. *ind 1st sg* **nzhiingíinawaaw**, **nzhiingíinawa**. *ind 3rd sg* **wshiingii=nawáawal**. *ind inv* **nzhiingíinaakw**. *ind I-you* **kshiingíinool**. *conj 3rd sg* **shiingíinawaat**. *ptcpl* **shiingíina=waat**.

**shiingi-** PV unwillingly, refuse to do. **Wshíingi-leelŭmáawal.** 'He wouldn't let them (do something).'; **Nzhíingi-wiichéewukw.** 'He wouldn't go with me.' *ptcpl* **shíingi-**. *See* **shiing-**, **shiingu-**.

**shiingóoxweew** VAI be unwilling to go, be reluctant to go. *ind 1st sg* **nzhiin=góoxwe**, **nzhiingóoxweem**. *conj 3rd sg* **shiingóoxweet**. *ptcpl* **shiingóo=xweet**.

**shiingsútam** VTI 1A dislike listening to s.t., dislike the sound of s.t. *ind 1st sg* **nzhiingsútamun**. *ind 3rd sg* **wshiing=sútamun**. *conj 1st sg* **shiingsúta=maan**. *conj 3rd sg* **shiingsútang**. *ptcpl* **shiingsútang**.

**shiingsútaweew** VTA dislike listening to s.o., dislike the sound of s.o., dislike hearing about s.o. *ind 1st sg* **nzhiing=sútawaaw**, **nzhiingsútawa**. *ind 3rd sg* **wshiingsutawáawal**. *ind inv* **nzhiingsútaakw**. *ind I-you* **kshiing=sútool**. *conj 3rd sg* **shiingsútawaat**. *ptcpl* **shiingsútawaat**.

**shiingu-** PV unwillingly, refuse to do. *informal*. **Shíingu-póosiiw.** 'He wouldn't get in.'; **Shíingu-míitsuw.** 'He wouldn't eat' *ptcpl* **shíingu-**. *See* **shiing-**, **shiingi-**.

**shíinzuw** VAI have a certain name, be named. *ind 1st sg* **ndushíinzi**, **ndush=íinziim**. *conj 3rd sg* **shíinziit**. *ptcpl* **eeshíinziit**.

**shiinzŭwáakan** NI name. *pl* **shiinzŭ=wáakanal**. *poss* **ndushiinzŭwáakan**.

**shiinzŭwáaleew** VTA call s.o. by a certain name. *ind 1st sg* **ndushiinzŭ=wáalaaw**, **ndushiinzŭwáala**. *ind 3rd sg* **wtushiinzuwaaláawal**. *ind inv* **ndushiinzuwáalukw**. *ind I-you* **ktushiinzŭwáalul**. *conj 3rd sg* **shiinzŭwáalaat**. *imp* **shíinzŭwaal**. *ptcpl* **eeshiinzŭwáalaat**.

**shiipáameew** VAI be stretched out *(s.t. animate)*. *ind 1st sg* **nzhiipáame**, **nzhiipáameem**. *conj 3rd sg* **shii=páameet**. *ptcpl* **shiipáameet**.

**shiipáameew** VII be stretched out. *conj 3rd sg* **shiipáameek**. *ptcpl* **shiipáa=meek**.

**shiipáhkhwam** VTI1A spread s.t. out, roll s.t. out *(using a tool or instrument)*. *ind 1st sg* **nzhiipahkhwámun**. *ind 3rd sg* **wshiipahkhwámun**. *conj 1st sg* **shiipahkhwámaan**. *conj 3rd sg* **shiipáhkhwang**. *imp* **shiipáhkhwah**. *ptcpl* **shiipáhkhwang**.

**shiipahkhwíikeew** VAI use a roller. *ind 1st sg* **nzhiipahkhwíike**, **nzhiipahk=hwíikeem**. *conj 3rd sg* **shiipahk=hwíikeet**. *imp* **shiipahkhwíikeel**. *ptcpl* **shiipahkhwíikeet**.

**shiipchéesuw** VAI be stretched out. *ind 1st sg* **nzhiipchéesi**, **nzhiipchéesiim**. *conj 3rd sg* **shiipchéesiit**. *ptcpl* **shiipchéesiit**.

**shiipchéewuw** VAI stretch, be stretching. *ind 1st sg* **nzhiipchéewi**, **nzhiip=chéewiim**. *conj 3rd sg* **shiipchéewiit**. *imp* **shiipchéewiil**. *ptcpl* **shiipchée=wiit**. *intensive reduplication* **shih=shiipchéewuw**.

**shiipchéexiin** VAI lie spread out. *ind 1st sg* **nzhiipchéexiin**, **nzhiipchéexi**. *conj 3rd sg* **shiipchéexiing**. *imp* **shiipchéexiil**. *ptcpl* **shiipchéexiing**.

**shiipchéextoow** VTI2 lay s.t. down spread open. *ind 1st sg* **nzhiipchéex=toon**. *ind 3rd sg* **wshiipchéextoon**. *conj 1st sg* **shiipcheextáwaan**. *conj 3rd sg* **shiipchéextaakw**. *imp* **shiip=chéextool**. *ptcpl* **shiipchéextaakw**.

**shiipchéexŭmeew** VTA lay s.o. down and spread them out. *ind 1st sg* **nzhiipchéexŭmaaw**, **nzhiipchéexŭ=ma**. *ind 3rd sg* **wshiipcheexŭmáa=wal**. *ind inv* **nzhiipchéexŭmukw**. *ind I-you* **kshiipchéexŭmul**. *conj 3rd sg* **shiipchéexŭmaat**. *imp* **shiipchée=xum**. *ptcpl* **shiipchéexŭmaat**.

**shiipchéexun** VII lie spread out. *conj 3rd sg* **shiipchéexung**. *ptcpl* **shiipchée=xung**.

**shiipháasuw** VAI be spread out *(s.t. animate)*. *ind 1st sg* **nzhiipháasi**, **nzhiipháasiim**. *conj 3rd sg* **shiip=háasiit**. *ptcpl* **shiipháasiit**.

**shiipháasuw** VII be spread out. *conj 3rd sg* **shiipháasiik**. *ptcpl* **shiipháasiik**.

**shíipham** VTI1A spread s.t. out. *ind 1st sg* **nzhiiphámun**. *ind 3rd sg* **wshiip=hámun**. *conj 1st sg* **shiiphámaan**. *conj 3rd sg* **shíiphang**. *imp* **shíiphah**. *ptcpl* **shíiphang**.

**shíipheew** VTA spread s.o. out. *ind 1st sg* **nzhíiphaaw**, **nzhíipha**. *ind 3rd sg* **wshiipháawal**. *ind inv* **nzhíiphookw**. *ind I-you* **kshíiphool**. *conj 3rd sg*

**shíiphaat**. *imp* **shíiphaw**. *ptcpl* **shíiphaat**.

**shiipii-** PV stretch, stretched. **Nzhíipii-kŭlahkhwámun.** 'I stretched it out and tacked it down.' *ptcpl* **shíipii-**.

**shiipiináxkeew** VAI stretch out one's arm. *ind 1st sg* **nzhiipiináxke**, **nzhii=piináxkeem**. *conj 3rd sg* **shiipiináx=keet**. *imp* **shiipiináxkeel**. *ptcpl* **shii=piináxkeet**.

**shiipíixiin** VAI lie stretched out, be stretched out *(s.t. animate)*. *ind 1st sg* **nzhiipíixiin**, **nzhiipíixi**. *conj 3rd sg* **shiipíixiing**. *imp* **shiipíixiil**. *ptcpl* **shiipíixiing**, **shiipíixiit**.

**shiipíixtoow** VTI2 stretch s.t. out, lay s.t. out. *ind 1st sg* **nzhiipíixtoon**. *ind 3rd sg* **wshiipíixtoon**. *conj 1st sg* **shii=piixtáwaan**. *conj 3rd sg* **shiipíix=taakw**. *imp* **shiipíixtool**. *ptcpl* **shii=píixtaakw**.

**shiipíixŭmeew** VTA stretch s.o. out, lay s.o. out. *ind 1st sg* **nzhiipíixŭmaaw**, **nzhiipíixŭma**. *ind 3rd sg* **wshiipii=xŭmáawal**. *ind inv* **nzhiipíixŭmukw**. *ind I-you* **kshiipíixŭmul**. *conj 3rd sg* **shiipíixŭmaat**. *imp* **shiipíixum**. *ptcpl* **shiipíixŭmaat**.

**shiipíixun** VII lie stretched out, be stretched out. *conj 3rd sg* **shiipíi=xung**. *ptcpl* **shiipíixung**.

**shiipíhleew** VII stretch, spread, spread out. *conj 3rd sg* **shiipíhlaak**. *ptcpl* **shiipíhlaak**. *intensive reduplication* **shihshiipíhleew**.

**shiipóoshush** NI creek. *pl* **shiipóosh'=shal**. *loc* **shiipóosh'shung**.

**shíipŭneew** VTA stretch s.t. animate *(us-ing the hands)*. *ind 1st sg* **nzhíipŭ=naaw**, **nzhíipŭna**. *ind 3rd sg* **wshii=pŭnáawal**. *ind inv* **nzhíipŭnukw**. *ind I-you* **kshíipŭnul**. *conj 3rd sg* **shíi=pŭnaat**. *imp* **shíipun**. *ptcpl* **shíipŭ=naat**.

**shiipŭnáasuw** VAI be stretched out *(s.t. animate)*. *ind 1st sg* **nzhiipŭnáasi**, **nzhiipŭnáasiim**. *conj 3rd sg* **shiipŭ=náasiit**. *ptcpl* **shiipŭnáasiit**.

**shiipŭnáasuw** VII be stretched out. *conj 3rd sg* **shiipŭnáasiik**. *ptcpl* **shiipŭ=náasiik**.

**shiipŭnáxkeew** VAI stretch one's hands out. *ind 1st sg* **nzhiipŭnáxka**, **nzhii=pŭnáxkaam**. *conj 3rd sg* **shiipŭnáx=kaat**. *ptcpl* **shiipŭnáxkaat**.

**shiipŭnaxkéexiin** VAI stretch one's hand out, have one's hand stretched out. *ind 1st sg* **nzhiipŭnaxkéexiin**, **nzhii=pŭnaxkéexi**. *conj 3rd sg* **shiipŭnax=kéexiing**. *imp* **shiipŭnaxkéexiil**. *ptcpl* **shiipŭnaxkéexiing**.

**shíipŭnum** VTI1B stretch s.t. *(using the hands)*. *ind 1st sg* **nzhiipŭnúmun**. *ind 3rd sg* **wshiipŭnúmun**. *conj 1st sg* **shiipŭnúmaan**. *conj 3rd sg* **shíi=pŭnung**. *imp* **shíipŭnih**. *ptcpl* **shíi=pŭnung**.

**shiipŭwámeew** VTA whistle at s.o. *ind 1st sg* **nzhiipŭwámaaw**, **nzhiipŭ=wáma**. *ind 3rd sg* **wshiipuwamáa=wal**. *ind inv* **nzhiipŭwámukw**. *ind I-you* **kshiipŭwámul**. *conj 3rd sg* **shii=pŭwámaat**. *imp* **shíipŭwam**. *ptcpl* **shiipŭwámaat**. *intensive reduplica-tion* **wshihshiipŭwamáawal**.

**shíipŭweew** VAI whistle. *ind 1st sg* **nzhíipŭwe**, **nzhíipŭweem**. *conj 3rd sg* **shíipŭweet**. *imp* **shíipŭweel**. *ptcpl* **shíipŭweet**.

**shiiwaaméhleew** VAI be tired from run-ning, be tired of running. *ind 1st sg* **nzhiiwaaméhla**, **nzhiiwaaméhlaam**. *conj 3rd sg* **shiiwaaméhlaat**. *ptcpl* **shiiwaaméhlaat**.

**shiiwaapéekŭlush** NA bluebird. *pl* **shii=waapeekŭlúshak**. *obv* **shiiwaapee=kŭlúshal**. *rare*.

**shiiwaasíitŭyeew** VAI have a tired back-side, have a sore backside. *ind 1st sg* **nzhiiwaasíitŭya**, **nzhiiwaasíitŭ=yaam**. *conj 3rd sg* **shiiwaasíitŭyaat**. *ptcpl* **shiiwaasíitŭyaat**.

**shiiwaláamuw** VAI be tired of singing. *ind 1st sg* **nzhiiwaláamwi**, **nzhiiwa=láamwiim**. *conj 3rd sg* **shiiwaláa=mwiit**. *ptcpl* **shiiwaláamwiit**.

**shiiwamálsuw** VAI feel tired, feel restless *(especially when sick)*. *ind 1st sg* **nzhiiwamálsi**, **nzhiiwamálsiim**. *conj 3rd sg* **shiiwamálsiit**. *ptcpl* **shiiwa=málsiit**.

**shíiwang** NI salt.

**shiiwangáapoow** NI salt water. *loc* **shii=wangáapoong**.

**shiiwangíinjuw** NI salt shaker. *pl* **shii=wangíinjŭwal**. *dimin* **shiiwangíin=joosh**.

**shíiwapuw** VAI be tired of sitting. *ind 1st sg* **nzhíiwapi**, **nzhíiwapiim**. *conj 3rd sg* **shíiwapiit**. *ptcpl* **shíiwapiit**. *See* **shiiwohkwéepuw**.

**shiiwasánuw** VAI be tired. *ind 1st sg* **nzhiiwasáni**, **nzhiiwasániim**. *conj 3rd sg* **shiiwasániit**. *ptcpl* **shiiwa=sániit**.

**shiiweelúndam** VOTI 1A be sad, be grieving. *ind 1st sg* **nzhiiweelúndam**. *conj 3rd sg* **shiiweelúndang**. *ptcpl* **shii=weelúndang**.

**shiiweelúndam** VTI 1A be sad about s.t., be sorry about s.t. *ind 1st sg* **nzhii=weelúndamun**. *ind 3rd sg* **wshiiwee=lúndamun**. *conj 1st sg* **shiiweelún=damaan**. *conj 3rd sg* **shiiweelún=dang**. *ptcpl* **shiiweelúndang**.

**shiiwiikáapawuw** VAI be tired of standing. *ind 1st sg* **nzhiiwiikáapawi**, **nzhiiwiikáapawiim**. *conj 3rd sg* **shiiwiikáapawiit**. *ptcpl* **shiiwiikáa=pawiit**.

**shiiwíikwsuw** VAI be tired of crawling. *ind 1st sg* **nzhiiwíikwsi**, **nzhiiwíikw=siim**. *conj 3rd sg* **shiiwíikwsiit**. *ptcpl* **shiiwíikwsiit**.

**shiiwiilawéeheew** VTA make s.o. tired, tire s.o. out; disappoint s.o. *ind 1st sg* **nzhiiwiilawéehaaw**, **nzhiiwiilawée=ha**. *ind 3rd sg* **wshiiwiilaweeháawal**. *ind inv* **nzhiiwiilawéehukw**. *ind I-you* **kshiiwiilawéehul**. *conj 3rd sg* **shii=wiilawéehaat**. *imp* **shiiwíilaweeh**. *ptcpl* **shiiwiilawéehaat**.

**shiiwiitŭyéepuw** VAI be tired of sitting on one's backside, have a sore backside from sitting down. *ind 1st sg* **nzhiiwiitŭyéepi**, **nzhiiwiitŭyéepiim**. *conj 3rd sg* **shiiwiitŭyéepiit**. *ptcpl* **shiiwiitŭyéepiit**.

**shiiwóoxweew** VAI be tired from walking. *ind 1st sg* **nzhiiwóoxwe**, **nzhii=wóoxweem**. *conj 3rd sg* **shiiwóo=xweet**. *ptcpl* **shiiwóoxweet**.

**shiiwohkwéepuw** VAI be tired of sitting. *ind 1st sg* **nzhiiwohkwéepi**, **nzhii=wohkwéepiim**. *conj 3rd sg* **shiiwoh=kwéepiit**. *ptcpl* **shiiwohkwéepiit**. *See* **shíiwapuw**.

**shiiwsiitéexiin** VAI have tired feet. *ind 1st sg* **nzhiiwsiitéexiin**, **nzhiiwsii=téexi**. *conj 3rd sg* **shiiwsiitéexiing**. *ptcpl* **shiiwsiitéexiing**, **shiiwsiitée=xiit**.

**shiiwu-** PV tired of, be tired of. *informal*. **Nzhíiwu-péesi.** 'I'm tired of waiting.'; **Nzhíiwu-péehaaw.** 'I'm tired of waiting for him.' *ptcpl* **shíiwu-**.

**shiiwŭnaxkéexiin** VAI have a tired hand. *ind 1st sg* **nzhiiwŭnaxkéexiin**, **nzhiiwŭnaxkéexi**. *conj 3rd sg* **shii=wŭnaxkéexiing**. *ptcpl* **shiiwŭnax=kéexiing**, **shiiwŭnaxkéexiit**.

**shíhkwameew** VTA leave s.t. animate behind on one's plate *(of food)*. *ind 1st sg* **nzhíhkwamaaw**, **nzhíhkwa=ma**. *ind 3rd sg* **wshihkwamáawal**. *ind inv* **nzhíhkwamukw**. *ind I-you* **kshíhkwamul**. *conj 3rd sg* **shíhkwa=maat**. *imp* **shíhkwam**. *ptcpl* **shíh=kwamaat**.

**shihkwándam** VTI 1A leave s.t. behind on one's plate *(of food)*. *ind 1st sg* **nzhihkwándamun**. *ind 3rd sg* **wshihkwándamun**. *conj 1st sg* **shihkwándamaan**. *conj 3rd sg*

**shihkwándang**. *imp* **shihkwándah**. *ptcpl* **shihkwándang**.

**shihkwihtáasuw** VAI rob people, take things from people by force. *ind 1st sg* **nzhihkwihtáasi**, **nzhihkwihtáa=siim**. *conj 3rd sg* **shihkwihtáasiit**. *ptcpl* **shihkwihtáasiit**.

**shihkwíhtaweew** VTAO take s.t. from s.o. by force, force s.o. to do s.t. *ind 1st sg* **nzhihkwíhtawaan**. *ind 3rd sg* **wshihkwíhtawaan**. *ind inv* **nzhih=kwihtáakwun**. *ind I-you* **kshih=kwihtóolun**. *conj 3rd sg* **shihkwíh=tawaat**. *imp* **shihkwíhtaw**. *ptcpl* **shihkwíhtawaat**.

**shíhleew** VAI run in a certain manner, run in a certain direction, go in a certain manner, go in a certain direction. **Náhnalii shíhleew.** 'He was running close by.' *ind 1st sg* **ndushíhla**, **ndushíhlaam**. *conj 3rd sg* **shíhlaat**. *imp* **shíhlaal**. *ptcpl* **eeshíhlaat**.

**shihshíikaanzh** PC very, extremely, intensely. **Shihshíikaanzh lúkih xwáchu-áxkook.** 'A great big snake.'; **Shihshíikaanzh lúkih níiskpe.** 'I got really wet.' *See* **shíikaanzh**.

**shihshŭwánakuw** VAI speak English. *ind 1st sg* **nzhihshŭwánakwi**, **nzhih=shŭwánakwiim**. *conj 3rd sg* **shih=shŭwánakwiit**. *imp* **shihshŭwána=kwiil**. *ptcpl* **shihshŭwánakwiit**.

**shíkaash** NA cigar. **Ndóhpwaan wshikáashŭmal.** 'I smoked his cigar.' *pl* **shìkáashak**. *poss* **nzhikáashum**. *loc* **shìkáashung**. *dimin* **shìkáashush**. *obv* **shìkáashal**. *See* **shúkaal**. *From English* cigar.

**shílpaa** NA Sylvia. *obv* **shìlpáahal**. *From English* Sylvia.

**shkáakwus** NA skunk. *pl* **shkáakwsak**. *dimin* **shkáakwshush**. *obv* **shkáak=wsal**.

**shkápuw** VAI urinate while sitting. *ind 1st sg* **nzhúkapi**, **nzhúkapiim**. *conj 3rd sg* **shkápiit**. *ptcpl* **shéekapiit**. *See* **shkohkwéepuw**.

**shkíiw** VAI-S urinate. *ind 1st sg* **nzhúki**, **nzhúkiim**. *conj 3rd sg* **shkíit**. *imp* **shkíil**. *ptcpl* **shéekiit**.

**shkíingwaam** VAI urinate while sleeping. *ind 1st sg* **nzhukíingwaam**. *conj 3rd sg* **shkíingwaang**. *ptcpl* **sheekíin=gwaang**.

**shkíiwan** NI urine. *poss* **nzhukíiwan**. *loc* **shkíiwanung**.

**shkíhleew** VAI urinate while in motion, urinate while walking. *ind 1st sg* **nzhukíhla**, **nzhukíhlaam**. *conj 3rd sg* **shkíhlaat**. *ptcpl* **sheekíhlaat**.

**shkoolháalŭweew** VAI teach school. *ind 1st sg* **nzhukoolháalŭwe**, **nzhukool=háalŭweem**. *conj 3rd sg* **shkoolháa=lŭweet**. *imp* **shkoolháalŭweel**. *ptcpl* **sheekoolháalŭweet**.

**shkóoluw** VAI attend school. *ind 1st sg* **nzhukóoli**, **nzhukóoliim**. *conj 3rd sg* **shkóoliit**. *imp* **shkóoliil**. *ptcpl* **shee=kóoliit**. *from Dutch.*

**shkohkwéepuw** VAI urinate while sitting. *ind 1st sg* **nzhukohkwéepi**, **nzhuk=ohkwéepiim**. *conj 3rd sg* **shkoh=kwéepiit**. *ptcpl* **sheekohkwéepiit**. *See* **shkápuw**.

**shkúp** NA playing card; shovel. *pl* **shkúpak**. *poss* **nzhúkpum**. *loc* **shkúpung**. *dimin* **shkúpush**. *obv* **shkúpal**. *From Dutch.*

**shkuphámeew** VAI play cards. *ind 1st sg* **nzhukpáhŭma**, **nzhukpáhŭmaam**. *conj 3rd sg* **shkuphámaat**. *imp* **shkuphámaal**. *ptcpl* **sheekpáhŭ=maat**.

**shkwáham** VTI1A pound s.t., crush s.t., grind s.t. *(using a tool or instrument)*. *ind 1st sg* **nzhukhwámun**. *ind 3rd sg* **wshukhwámun**. *conj 1st sg* **shkwáh=ŭmaan**. *conj 3rd sg* **shkwáhang**. *imp* **shkwáhih**. *ptcpl* **shéekhwang**.

**shkwáheew** VTA pound s.o., crush s.o., grind s.o. *(using a tool or instrument)*. *ind 1st sg* **nzhúkhwaaw**, **nzhúkhwa**.

*ind 3rd sg* **wshukhwáawal**. *ind inv* **nzhúkhookw**. *ind I-you* **kshúkhool**. *conj 3rd sg* **shkwáhaat**. *imp* **shkwáh**. *ptcpl* **shéekhwaat**.

**shkwahíikan** NI mill, grinder. *pl* **shkwahíikanal**. *poss* **nzhukhwíikan**. *loc* **shkwahíikanung**. *dimin* **shkwahíikanush**.

**shkwahíikeew** VAI pound things, grind things. *ind 1st sg* **nzhukhwíike**, **nzhukhwíikeem**. *conj 3rd sg* **shkwahíikeet**. *imp* **shkwahíikeel**. *ptcpl* **sheekhwíikeet**.

**shkwáteew** VAI have a miscarriage. *ind 1st sg* **nzhúkwata**, **nzhúkwataam**. *conj 3rd sg* **shkwátaat**. *ptcpl* **shée=kwataat**.

**shkwíixtoow** VTI2 crush s.t. **Nzhuk=wíixtoon náxkush.** 'I crushed my finger.' *ind 1st sg* **nzhukwíixtoon**. *ind 3rd sg* **wshukwíixtoon**. *conj 1st sg* **shkwiixtáwaan**. *conj 3rd sg* **shkwíix=taakw**. *imp* **shkwíixtool**. *ptcpl* **sheekwíixtaakw**.

**shkwíixŭmeew** VTA crush s.o. **Nzhuk=wíixŭmaaw áxkook.** 'I crushed the snake.' *ind 1st sg* **nzhukwíixŭmaaw**, **nzhukwíixŭma**. *ind 3rd sg* **wshuk=wiixŭmáawal**. *ind inv* **nzhukwíixŭ=mukw**. *ind I-you* **kshukwíixŭmul**. *conj 3rd sg* **shkwíixŭmaat**. *imp* **shkwíixum**. *ptcpl* **sheekwíixŭmaat**.

**shkwíhkam** VTI1A crush s.t., squash s.t. *(using the foot or body). ind 1st sg* **nzhukwíhkamun**. *ind 3rd sg* **wshuk=wíhkamun**. *conj 1st sg* **shkwíhka=maan**. *conj 3rd sg* **shkwíhkang**. *imp* **shkwíhkah**. *ptcpl* **sheekwíhkang**.

**shkwíhkaweew** VTA crush s.o., squash s.o. *(using the foot or body). ind 1st sg* **nzhukwíhkawaaw**, **nzhukwíhka=wa**. *ind 3rd sg* **wshukwihkawáawal**. *ind inv* **nzhukwíhkaakw**. *ind I-you* **kshukwíhkool**. *conj 3rd sg* **shkwíh=kawaat**. *imp* **shkwíhkaw**. *ptcpl* **sheekwíhkawaat**.

**shkwíhleew** VAI be crushed down, get reduced in cooking. *ind 1st sg* **nzhuk=wíhla**, **nzhukwíhlaam**. *conj 3rd sg* **shkwíhlaat**. *ptcpl* **sheekwíhlaat**.

**shkwihtéeham** VTI1A smash s.t., squash s.t., flatten s.t. *ind 1st sg* **nzhukwih=téehŭmun**. *ind 3rd sg* **wshukwihtée=hŭmun**. *conj 1st sg* **shkwihtéehŭ=maan**. *conj 3rd sg* **shkwihtéehang**. *imp* **shkwihtéehah**. *ptcpl* **sheekwih=téehang**.

**shkwihtéeheew** VTA smash s.t. animate, squash s.t. animate, flatten s.t. animate. *ind 1st sg* **nzhukwihtéehaaw**, **nzhukwihtéeha**. *ind 3rd sg* **wshuk=wihteeháawal**. *ind inv* **nzhukwih=téehookw**. *ind I-you* **kshukwihtée=hool**. *conj 3rd sg* **shkwihtéehaat**. *imp* **shkwíhteeh**. *ptcpl* **sheekwihtée=haat**.

**shkwihtéexiin** VAI fall and get crushed. *ind 1st sg* **nzhukwihtéexiin**, **nzhuk=wihtéexi**. *conj 3rd sg* **shkwihtée=xiing**. *ptcpl* **sheekwihtéexiing**.

**shkwihtéexŭmeew** VTA hit and crush s.o. *ind 1st sg* **nzhukwihtéexŭmaaw**, **nzhukwihtéexŭma**. *ind 3rd sg* **wshukwihteexŭmáawal**. *ind inv* **nzhukwihtéexŭmukw**. *ind I-you* **kshukwihtéexŭmul**. *conj 3rd sg* **shkwihtéexŭmaat**. *imp* **shkwih=téexum**. *ptcpl* **sheekwihtéexŭmaat**.

**shkwúchasuw** VAI fall apart in cooking, boil down, be cooked down *(s.t. animate). ind 1st sg* **nzhukwchási**, **nzhukwchásiim**. *conj 3rd sg* **shkwúchasiit**. *ptcpl* **sheekwchásiit**.

**shkwúchateew** VII fall apart in cooking, boil down, be cooked down. *conj 3rd sg* **shkwúchateek**. *ptcpl* **sheekw=cháteek**.

**shkwúneew** VTA squeeze s.t. animate. *ind 1st sg* **nzhúkwŭnaaw**, **nzhúk=wŭna**. *ind 3rd sg* **wshukwŭnáawal**. *ind inv* **nzhúkwŭnukw**. *ind I-you* **kshúkwŭnul**. *conj 3rd sg* **shkwúnaat**.

*imp* **shkwún**. *ptcpl* **shéekwŭnaat**.

**shkwundíikan** NI pliers. *pl* **shkwun=díikanal**. *poss* **nzhukwundíikan**. *loc* **shkwundíikanung**. *dimin* **shkwun=jíikanush**.

**shkwunéesuw** VAI like to follow people. *ind 1st sg* **nzhukwŭnéesi**, **nzhukwŭ=néesiim**. *conj 3rd sg* **shkwunéesiit**. *ptcpl* **sheekwŭnéesiit**.

**shkwúnum** VTI 1B squeeze s.t. *ind 1st sg* **nzhukwŭnúmun**. *ind 3rd sg* **wshuk=wŭnúmun**. *conj 1st sg* **shkwúnŭ=maan**. *conj 3rd sg* **shkwúnung**. *imp* **shkwúnih**. *ptcpl* **shéekwŭnung**.

**shkwúteew** VII be burnt up, fall to pieces, be in pieces after being cooked. *conj 3rd sg* **shkwúteek**. *ptcpl* **shéekwteek**.

**shkwútsuw** VAI be burnt up, fall to pieces, be in pieces after being cooked *(s.t. animate)*. *ind 1st sg* **nzhukw=túsi**, **nzhukwtúsiim**. *conj 3rd sg* **shkwútsiit**. *ptcpl* **sheekwtúsiit**.

**shmák** NI smock. *pl* **shmákal**. *poss* **nzhumákum**. *loc* **shmákung**. *dimin* **shmákush**. *From English* smock.

**shmakhámeew** VAI wear a smock. *ind 1st sg* **nzhumàkháma**, **nzhumàk=hámaam**. *conj 3rd sg* **shmakhám=aat**. *imp* **shmakhámaal**. *ptcpl* **shmakhámaat**.

**shooháasuw** VAI be painted *(s.t. animate)*. *ind 1st sg* **nzhooháasi**, **nzhoo=háasiim**. *conj 3rd sg* **shooháasiit**. *ptcpl* **shooháasiit**.

**shooháasuw** VII be painted. *conj 3rd sg* **shooháasiik**. *ptcpl* **shooháasiik**.

**shóoham** VTI 1A paint s.t.; rub s.t. on, rub s.t. *ind 1st sg* **nzhóohŭmun**. *ind 3rd sg* **wshóohŭmun**. *conj 1st sg* **shóohŭmaan**. *conj 3rd sg* **shóohang**. *imp* **shóohah**. *ptcpl* **shóohang**.

**shóoheew** VTA paint s.o.; rub s.o., rub on s.o. *ind 1st sg* **nzhóohaaw**, **nzhóoha**. *ind 3rd sg* **wshooháawal**. *ind inv* **nzhóohookw**. *ind I-you* **kshóohool**. *conj 3rd sg* **shóohaat**. *imp* **shóoh**. *ptcpl* **shóohaat**.

**shoohíikan** NI paint; paint brush. *pl* **shoohíikanal**. *poss* **nzhoohíikan**. *loc* **shoohíikanung**. *dimin* **shoohíika=nush**.

**shoohíikeew** VAI paint things, be painting. *ind 1st sg* **nzhoohíike**, **nzhoo=híikeem**. *conj 3rd sg* **shoohíikeet**. *imp* **shoohíikeel**. *ptcpl* **shoohíikeet**.

**shoohúnzuw** VAI put on makeup. *ind 1st sg* **nzhoohúnzi**, **nzhoohúnziim**. *conj 3rd sg* **shoohúnziit**. *imp* **shoohúnziil**. *ptcpl* **shoohúnziit**.

**shóokul** NI sugar. *poss* **nzhóokŭlum**. *loc* **shóokŭlung**. *dimin* **shóokŭlush**. *From Dutch.*

**shookŭlaaháaleew** VTA put sugar on s.o., put sugar on s.t. animate. *ind 1st sg* **nzhookŭlaaháalaaw**, **nzhookŭ=laaháala**. *ind 3rd sg* **wshookŭlaa=haaláawal**. *ind inv* **nzhookŭlaaháa=lukw**. *ind I-you* **kshookŭlaaháalul**. *conj 3rd sg* **shookŭlaaháalaat**. *imp* **shookŭláahaal**. *ptcpl* **shookŭlaa=háalaat**.

**shookŭláapoow** NI sap; Kool-Aid, soft drink, sweet drink. *poss* **nzhookŭ=laapóohum**. *loc* **shookŭláapoong**. *dimin* **shookŭlaapóohush**.

**shookŭlaháasuw** VAI have sugar on it, have sugar in it *(s.t. animate)*. *ind 1st sg* **nzhookŭlaháasi**, **nzhookŭlaháa=siim**. *conj 3rd sg* **shookŭlaháasiik**. *ptcpl* **shookŭlaháasiit**.

**shookŭlaháasuw** VII have sugar on it, have sugar in it. *conj 3rd sg* **shookŭ=laháasiik**. *ptcpl* **shookŭlaháasiik**.

**shookŭláham** VTI 1A put sugar on s.t. *ind 1st sg* **nzhookŭláhŭmun**. *ind 3rd sg* **wshookŭláhŭmun**. *conj 1st sg* **shookŭláhŭmaan**. *conj 3rd sg* **shoo=kŭláhang**. *imp* **shookŭláhih**. *ptcpl* **shookŭláhang**.

**shookŭlápwaan** NI cake. *pl* **shookŭ=lapwáanal**. *poss* **nzhookŭlapwáa=num**. *loc* **shookŭlapwáanung**. *dimin*

**shookŭlapwáanush**.

**shookŭlapwáanheew** VAI make a cake. *ind 1st sg* **nzhookŭlapwáanhe**, **nzhookŭlapwáanheem**. *conj 3rd sg* **shookŭlapwáanheet**. *imp* **shookŭ=lapwáanheel**. *ptcpl* **shookŭlap=wáanheet**.

**shookŭlapwáanush** NI cookie. *pl* **shoo=kŭlapwáanshal**. *poss* **nzhookŭlap=wáanshum**. *loc* **shookŭlapwáan=shung**.

**shookŭlíinjuw** NI sugar bowl. *pl* **shoo=kŭlíinjŭwal**. *loc* **shookŭlíinjoong**. *dimin* **shookŭlíinjoosh**.

**shookŭliipóokwan** VII have a sweet taste, be sweet in taste. *conj 3rd sg* **shookŭliipóokwang**. *ptcpl* **shookŭ=liipóokwang**. *See* **shookŭliipóokwat**.

**shookŭliipóokwat** VII have a sweet taste, be sweet in taste. *conj 3rd sg* **shookŭliipóokwahk**. *ptcpl* **shookŭ=liipóokwahk**. *See* **shookŭliipóo=kwan**.

**shookŭliipóokwsuw** VAI have a sweet taste, be sweet in taste. *ind 1st sg* **nzhookŭliipóokwsi**, **nzhookŭlii=póokwsiim**. *conj 3rd sg* **shookŭlii=póokwsiit**. *ptcpl* **shookŭliipóokwsiit**.

**shookŭlíhleew** VAI get diabetes, develop diabetes, have diabetes. *ind 1st sg* **nzhookŭlíhla**, **nzhookŭlíhlaam**. *conj 3rd sg* **shookŭlíhlaat**. *ptcpl* **shookŭ=líhlaat**.

**shóokŭlush** NI candy. *pl* **shookŭlúshal**. *poss* **nzhookŭlúshum**. *loc* **shookŭ=lúshung**.

**shoopéekal** NI moccasin. *usually plural*. *poss* **nzhoopéekŭmal**. *loc* **shoopée=kung**. *dimin* **shoopéekshal**.

**shóhweew** VAI make noise. *usually of non-humans*. **Shohwéewak aweh=leeshóoshak.** 'The birds are making noise.' *ind 1st sg* **nzhóhwe**, **nzhóh=weem**. *conj 3rd sg* **shóhweet**. *imp* **shóhweel**. *ptcpl* **shóhweet**.

**shóhwkeew** VAI make a shuffling noise while dancing. *ind 1st sg* **nzhóhwka**, **nzhóhwkaam**. *conj 3rd sg* **shóhw=kaat**. *imp* **shóhwkaal**. *ptcpl* **shóhw=kaat**.

**shòhwsiitéexiin** VAI make a noise while shuffling one's feet. *ind 1st sg* **nzhohwsiitéexiin**, **nzhohwsiitéexi**. *conj 3rd sg* **shòhwsiitéexiing**. *imp* **shòhwsiitéexiil**. *ptcpl* **shòhwsiitée=xiing**, **shòhwsiitéexiit**.

**shòhwŭnáakwsuw** VAI make a lot of noise. **Aapíikwus táa wtúnda-shòh=wŭnáakwsiin.** 'The mouse was making a lot of noise somewhere.' *ind 1st sg* **nzhohwŭnáakwsi**, **nzhohwŭ=náakwsiim**. *conj 3rd sg* **shòhwŭ=náakwsiit**. *ptcpl* **shòhwŭnáakwsiit**.

**shòhwŭníikan** NI rattle. *pl* **shòhwŭníi=kanal**. *poss* **nzhohwŭníikan**. *loc* **shòhwŭníikanung**. *dimin* **shòhwŭ=níikanush**.

**shòhwŭníikeew** VAI use a rattle, make a rattling sound. *ind 1st sg* **nzhohwŭ=níike**, **nzhohwŭníikeem**. *conj 3rd sg* **shòhwŭníikeet**. *imp* **shòhwŭníikeel**. *ptcpl* **shòhwŭníikeet**. *See* **shóhwŭ=númeew**.

**shòhwŭnúmeew** VAI use a rattle, make a rattling sound. *ind 1st sg* **nzhohwŭ=núma**, **nzhohwŭnúmaam**. *conj 3rd sg* **shòhwŭnúmaat**. *imp* **shòhwŭ=númaal**. *ptcpl* **shòhwŭnúmaat**. *See* **shòhwŭníikeew**.

**shpánzhpeekw** NI muskmelon. *pl* **shpanzhpéekwal**. *loc* **shpanzh=péekwung**. *dimin* **shpanzhpée=kwush**.

**shték** NI haystack. *pl* **shtékal**. *poss* **nzhutékum**. *loc* **shtékung**. *dimin* **shtékush**. *From English* stack.

**shtépul** NI stable, log stable. *pl* **shtépŭ=lal**. *poss* **nzhutépŭlum**. *loc* **shtépŭ=lung**. *dimin* **shtépŭlush**. *From English* stable.

**shúkaal** NA cigar. *pl* **shukáalak**. *obv* **shukáalal**. *See* **shíkaash**. *From Eng-*

*lish* cigar.

**shùkéhla** PC only. **Písh ndúlaan shùkéhla wánsiin.** 'I told him but he still forgot.'; **Shùkéhla mŭnéew tíi.** 'He only drinks tea.'

**shúkw** PC but, only. **Akulkúsŭwak, wéemu kwéek ndukwŭnéewa, wáak ngihkiixkŭnúkook, shúkw msúchee máh nùnohtawaawíiwak.** 'They were laughing, saying all sorts of things to me, and touching me, but I didn't understand them.'; **Shúkw kàkpíixiin.** 'But he's in my way.'

**shŭláash** NI lettuce. *pl* **shŭláashal**. *poss* **nzhuláashum**. *loc* **shŭláashung**. *dimin* **shŭláashush**. *From Dutch.*

**shŭléechush** NA sleigh. *pl* **shŭléech'=shak**. *obv* **shŭléech'shal**.

**shŭléet** NA sled. *pl* **shŭléetak**. *obv* **shŭléetal**.

**shúlpul** NI money. *poss* **nzhulpúlum**. *dimin* **shulpúlush**. *From Dutch.*

**shulpùliinóotay** NI purse. *pl* **shulpulii=nóotayal**. *poss* **nzhulpùliinóotay**. *loc* **shulpùliinóoteeng**. *dimin* **shulpùlii=nóocheesh**.

**shŭmít** NA blacksmith. *pl* **shŭmítak**. *obv* **shŭmítal**. *See* **nehnayóongsii-mehmahksunhíikeet**. *From Dutch.*

**shúndahkw** NA cedar tree. *pl* **shundáh=kwak**. *loc* **shundáhkwung**. *obv* **shundáhkwal**.

**shŭnék** NA Snake *(family name)*. *obv* **shŭnékal**. *From English* Snake.

**shungawíinjuw** NI saucer. *pl* **shunga=wíinjŭwal**. *loc* **shungawiinjóohung**. *dimin* **shungawíinjoosh**.

**shungíixiin** VAI lie down. *ind 1st sg* **nzhungíixiin**, **nzhungíixi**. *conj 3rd sg* **shungíixiing**. *imp* **shungíixiil**. *ptcpl* **sheengíixiing**, **sheengíixiit**. *moderative reduplication* **shaashun=gíixiin**.

**shungíixtoow** VTI2 lay s.t. down. *ind 1st sg* **nzhungíixtoon**. *ind 3rd sg* **wshun=gíixtoon**. *conj 1st sg* **shungiixtáwaan**. *conj 3rd sg* **shungíixtaakw**. *imp* **shungíixtool**. *ptcpl* **sheengíixtaakw**.

**shungíixŭmeew** VTA lay s.o. down. *ind 1st sg* **nzhungíixŭmaaw**, **nzhun=gíixŭma**. *ind 3rd sg* **wshungiixŭ=máawal**. *ind inv* **nzhungíixŭmukw**. *ind I-you* **kshungíixŭmul**. *conj 3rd sg* **shungíixŭmaat**. *imp* **shungíixum**. *ptcpl* **sheengíixŭmaat**.

**shungíixun** VII lie, recline. *conj 3rd sg* **shungíixung**. *ptcpl* **sheengíixung**.

**shŭwáapoow** NI vinegar. *poss* **nzhuw=aapóohum**. *loc* **shŭwaapóohung**.

**shŭwahháasuw** VAI be salted *(s.t. animate)*. *ind 1st sg* **nzhuwháasi**, **nzhuwháasiim**. *conj 3rd sg* **shŭwah=áasiit**. *ptcpl* **sheewháasiit**.

**shŭwahháasuw** VII be salted. **Máh téep-shŭwahháasiiwu.** 'It doesn't have enough salt.' *conj 3rd sg* **shŭwahháa=siik**. *ptcpl* **sheewháasiik**.

**shŭwáham** VTI1A salt s.t., put salt on s.t., preserve s.t. in salt. *ind 1st sg* **nzhuwhámun**. *ind 3rd sg* **wshuw=hámun**. *conj 1st sg* **shŭwáhŭmaan**. *conj 3rd sg* **shŭwáhang**. *imp* **shŭ=wáhah**. *ptcpl* **shéewhang**.

**shŭwáheew** VTA salt s.t. animate, put salt on s.t. animate, preserve s.t. animate in salt. *ind 1st sg* **nzhúwhaaw**, **nzhúwha**. *ind 3rd sg* **wshuwháawal**. *ind inv* **nzhúwhookw**. *ind I-you* **kshúwhool**. *conj 3rd sg* **shŭwáhaat**. *imp* **shŭwáh**. *ptcpl* **shéewhaat**.

**shŭwálul** VAI be sour, turn sour, spoil *(s.t. animate)*. **Wsáami-shŭwálŭlook.** 'They are too sour.' *ind 1st sg* **nzhúw=alul**. *conj 3rd sg* **shŭwálŭluk**. *ptcpl* **sheewalúluk**.

**shŭwálut** VII be sour, turn sour, spoil. *conj 3rd sg* **shŭwálihk**. *ptcpl* **shée=walihk**.

**shŭwán** VII be salty, be sour. *conj 3rd sg* **shŭwáng**. *ptcpl* **shéewang**.

**shŭwanakóxkweew** NA White woman. *pl* **shŭwanakoxkwéewak**. *poss* nzhuwanakoxkwéehum. *dimin* shŭwanakóxkweesh. *obv* shŭwana=koxkwéewal.

**shŭwánakuw** VAI be a White person. *ind 1st sg* **nzhuwanákwi**, **nzhuwa=nákwiim**. *conj 3rd sg* **shŭwánakwiit**. *ptcpl* **sheewanákwiit**.

**shŭwánakw** NA White man. *pl* **shŭ=wánakwak**. *poss* **nzhuwanákwum**. *dimin* **shŭwánakwush**. *obv* **shŭ=wánakwal**.

**shŭwanakwamalúsuw** VAI feel like a White person. *ind 1st sg* **nzhuwa=nakwamálsi**, **nzhuwanakwamál=siim**. *conj 3rd sg* **shŭwanakwama=lúsiit**. *ptcpl* **sheewanakwamálsiit**.

**shŭwanakweelúnzuw** VAI think of oneself as a White person. *ind 1st sg* **nzhuwanakweelúnzi**, **nzhuwa=nakweelúnziim**. *conj 3rd sg* **shŭ=wanakweelúnziit**. *ptcpl* **sheewanak=weelúnziit**.

**shŭwánakwii-apwáan** NI white bread, baker's bread. *pl* **shŭwánakwii-apwáanal**. *poss* **nzhuwanákwii-apwáanum**. *loc* **shŭwánakwii-apwáanung**. *dimin* **shŭwánakwii-apwáanush**. *See* **wáapapwaan**.

**shŭwanakwiináakwsuw** VAI look like a White person. *ind 1st sg* **nzhuwa=nakwiináakwsi**, **nzhuwanakwii=náakwsiim**. *conj 3rd sg* **shŭwana=kwiináakwsiit**. *ptcpl* **sheewanak=wiináakwsiit**.

**shŭwanakwíhleew** VAI become White, act like a White person. *ind 1st sg* **nzhuwanakwíhla**, **nzhuwanakwíh=laam**. *conj 3rd sg* **shŭwanakwíhlaat**. *ptcpl* **sheewanakwíhlaat**.

**shŭwánpuy** NI ocean, sea, salt water.

**shŭwáskw** NI rhubarb. *pl* **shŭwáskwal**. *poss* **nzhuwáskwum**. *loc* **shŭwás=kwung**. *dimin* **shŭwáshkwush**.

**shŭwéeka** PC Six Nations, Ontario.

**shŭwéewakw** NI salt pork. *pl* **shŭwée=wakwal**. *poss* **nzhuwéewakwum**. *loc* **shŭwéewakwung**. *dimin* **shŭwéewa=kwush**.

**shŭwii-** PN sour. **Shŭwíi-kòkómush.** 'Brine pickle.'

**shŭwíi-képuch** NI sauerkraut. *pl* **shŭwíi-kepúchal**. *poss* **nzhúwii-kèpúchum**.

**shŭwíi-kòkòmsháheew** VAI make brine pickles. *ind 1st sg* **nzhúwii-kòkòm=sháhe**, **nzhúwii-kòkòmsháheem**. *conj 3rd sg* **shŭwíi-kòkòmsháheet**. *imp* **shŭwíi-kòkòmsháheel**. *ptcpl* **shéewii-kòkòmsháheet**.

**shŭwíi-mŭlúk** NI buttermilk, sour milk. *poss* **nzhúwii-mŭlúkum**. *loc* **shŭwíi-mŭlúkung**. *dimin* **shŭwíi-mŭlúkush**.

**shŭwíip** NI whip. *pl* **shŭwíipal**. *poss* **nzhuwíipum**. *loc* **shŭwíipung**. *dimin* **shŭwíipush**. *From Dutch.*

**shŭwiipóokwan** VII taste sour, have a sour taste. *conj 3rd sg* **shŭwiipóo=kwang**. *ptcpl* **sheewiipóokwang**. *See* **shŭwiipóokwat**.

**shŭwiipóokwat** VII taste sour, have a sour taste. *conj 3rd sg* **shŭwiipóo=kwahk**. *ptcpl* **sheewiipóokwahk**. *See* **shŭwiipóokwan**.

**shŭwiipóokwsuw** VAI taste sour, have a sour taste *(s.t. animate)*. *ind 1st sg* **nzhuwiipóokwsi**, **nzhuwiipóokw=siim**. *conj 3rd sg* **shŭwiipóokwsiit**. *ptcpl* **sheewiipóokwsiit**.

**shŭwúl** VAI be salty, be sour *(s.t. animate)*. *ind 1st sg* **nzhúwul**. *conj 3rd sg* **shŭwúluk**. *ptcpl* **shéewŭluk**.

**sh'xéeham** VTI 1A search s.t. *ind 1st sg* **nzhaxéehŭmun**. *ind 3rd sg* **wshaxée=hŭmun**. *conj 1st sg* **sh'xéehŭmaan**. *conj 3rd sg* **sh'xéehang**. *imp* **sh'xéehih**. *ptcpl* **sheexéehang**.

**sh'xéeheew** VTA search s.o. *ind 1st sg* **nzhaxéehaaw**, **nzhaxéeha**. *ind 3rd sg* **wshaxeeháawal**. *ind inv* **nzhaxéeh=ookw**. *ind I-you* **kshaxéehool**. *conj 3rd sg* **sh'xéehaat**. *imp* **sh'xéeh**. *ptcpl* **sheexéehaat**.

**sh'xeehíikeew** VAI search, snoop, be

snooping. *ind 1st sg* **nzhaxeehíike**, **nzhaxeehíikeem**. *conj 3rd sg* **sh'xee=híikeet**. *imp* **sh'xeehíikeel**. *ptcpl* **sheexeehíikeet**. *intensive reduplication* **shàsh'xeehíikeew**.

**sh'xiikwáaleew** VTA hollow s.t. animate out. *ind 1st sg* **nzhaxiikwáalaaw**, **nzhaxiikwáala**. *ind 3rd sg* **wshaxii=kwaaláawal**. *ind inv* **nzhaxiikwáa=lukw**. *ind I-you* **kshaxiikwáalul**. *conj 3rd sg* **sh'xiikwáalaat**. *imp* **sh'xíi=kwaal**. *ptcpl* **sheexiikwáalaat**.

**sh'xíikweew** VII be hollow. *conj 3rd sg* **sh'xíikweek**. *ptcpl* **sheexíikweet**.

**sh'xíikwsuw** VAI be hollow *(s.t. animate)*. *ind 1st sg* **nzhaxíikwsi**, **nzhax=íikwsiim**. *conj 3rd sg* **sh'xíikwsiit**. *ptcpl* **sheexíikwsiit**.

**sh'xiikwshéesuw** VAI be hollow *(s.t. animate)*. *conj 3rd sg* **sh'xiikwshée=siit**. *ptcpl* **sheexiikwshéesiit**.

**sh'xiikwshéeyeew** VII be hollow. *conj 3rd sg* **sh'xiikwshéeyeek**. *ptcpl* **sheexiikwshéeyeek**.

**sh'xíikwun** VII be hollow. *conj 3rd sg* **sh'xíikwung**. *ptcpl* **sheexíikwung**.

# T

**táa** PC emphatic. **Táa níik éet kwéekw wéenj-péetaakw.** 'I don't know why he brought it.'; **Wéemu táa ndúlu-kwíilamun.** 'I looked everywhere for it.'

**táas** PC might *(undeclared intention)*. **Táas-uch ootéeneeng ndá.** 'I might go to town.'; **Táas-uch nŭmáw-maawéewi.** 'I might go to church.'

**táas** PC one time, emphatic. **Noohŭmáya táas ndúkw.** 'My late grandmother told me.'

**táasa** PC might *(undeclared intention)*. **Táasa áa nŭmáhlamun.** 'I might buy it.'; **Táasa áa ootéeneeng ndá.** 'I might go to town.'

**táataskw** NA sleigh. *pl* **taatáskwak**. *poss* **ndaatáskwum**. *loc* **taatás=kwung**. *dimin* **taatáshkwush**. *obv* **taatáskwal**.

**taatpùníikan** NA wagon. *pl* **taatpùníi=kanak**. *poss* **ndaatpùníikan**. *loc* **taatpùníikanung**. *dimin* **chaach=pùníikanush**. *obv* **taatpùníikanal**.

**taatpùniikanáhŭmeew** VAI use a wagon. *ind 1st sg* **ndaatpùniikanáhŭma**, **ndaatpùniikanáhŭmaam**. *conj 3rd sg* **taatpùniikanáhŭmaat**. *imp* **taat=pùniikanáhŭmaal**. *ptcpl* **taatptùnii=kanáhŭmaat**.

**taatxooxwíisuw** VAI have great-grandchildren. *ind 1st sg* **ndaatxooxwíisi**, **ndaatxooxwíisiim**. *conj 3rd sg* **taat=xooxwíisiit**. *ptcpl* **taatxooxwíisiit**.

**táatxun** PC not very often, a few times. **Táatxun noochapíhkum nŭmúneen.** 'I drank my medicine a few times.'; **Ootéeneeng táatxun ndá.** 'I didn't go to town very often.'

**taatxupéekat** VII be shallow water. *conj 3rd sg* **taatxupéekahk**. *ptcpl* **taat=xupéekahk**. *See* **chaachxupeeka=chúshuw**.

**taaxkshéengweew** VAI pull one's eyes down, have one's eyes pulled down. *ind 1st sg* **ndaaxkshéengwe**, **ndaax=kshéengweem**. *conj 3rd sg* **taaxk=shéengweet**. *imp* **taaxkshéengweel**. *ptcpl* **taaxkshéengweet**. *intensive reduplication* **ataaxkshéengweew**.

**taaxksheengwéeneew** VTA pull s.o.'s eye down, hold s.o.'s eye open. *ind 1st sg* **ndaaxksheengwéenaaw**, **ndaaxksheengwéena**. *ind 3rd sg* **wtaaxksheengweenáawal**. *ind inv* **ndaaxksheengwéenukw**. *ind I-you* **ktaaxksheengwéenul**. *conj 3rd sg* **taaxksheengwéenaat**. *imp* **taaxk=shéengween**. *ptcpl* **taaxksheen=gwéenaat**.

**taaxksheengwéexiin** VAI have pulled-down eyes. *ind 1st sg* **ndaaxksheen=gwéexiin**, **ndaaxksheengwéexi**. *conj 3rd sg* **taaxksheengwéexiing**. *ptcpl* **taaxksheengwéexiing**, **taaxksheen=gwéexiit**.

**taaxkshéenum** VTI1B pull s.t. down. *ind 1st sg* **ndaaxkshéenŭmun**. *ind 3rd sg* **wtaaxkshéenŭmun**. *conj 1st sg* **taaxkshéenŭmaan**. *conj 3rd sg* **taaxkshéenung**. *imp* **taaxkshéenih**. *ptcpl* **taaxkshéenung**.

**taaxpéhleew** VAI regain consciousness, come to one's senses, sober up. **Wíixkwii méhch ndaaxpéhla.** 'I came to all of a sudden.'; **Lúkih ndaaxpéhlaan.** 'I just came to.' *ind 1st sg* **ndaaxpéhla**, **ndaaxpéhlaam**. *conj 3rd sg* **taaxpéhlaat**. *ptcpl* **taax=péhlaat**.

**tá** PC how. **Tá éew?** 'Where is he going?'; **Tá wúndakw wíikiin?** 'Where does he live?' *See* **thá**.

**táhtaas** PC sometimes. **Táhtaas áng nŭwiingándamun.** 'Sometimes I like the taste of it.'

**tahtáhwŭneew** VAI play tag. *ind 1st sg* **ndahtáhwŭna**, **ndahtáhwŭnaam**. *conj 3rd sg* **tahtáhwŭnaat**. *imp* **tahtáhwŭnaal**. *ptcpl* **tahtáhwŭnaat**.

**tahtakáapŭweew** VII be thick *(of liquids)*. *conj 3rd sg* **tahtakáapŭweek**. *ptcpl* **tehtakáapŭweek**.

**táhtakan** VII be thick in consistency. *conj 3rd sg* **táhtakang**. *ptcpl* **téhtakang**.

**tahtakii-** PN thick in consistency. **Táhtakii-mŭlúk.** 'Thick milk.'

**tàhwiipáhtoow** VTI2 grab s.t. in a hurry. *ind 1st sg* **ndahwiipáhtoon**. *ind 3rd sg* **wtahwiipáhtoon**. *conj 1st sg* **tàh=wiipáhtawaan**. *conj 3rd sg* **tàhwii=páhtaakw**. *imp* **tàhwiipáhtool**. *ptcpl* **tèhwiipáhtaakw**.

**tàhwíipheew** VTA grab s.o. in a hurry. *ind 1st sg* **ndahwíiphaaw**, **ndahwíip=ha**. *ind 3rd sg* **wtahwiipháawal**. *ind inv* **ndahwíiphukw**. *ind I-you* **ktah=wíiphul**. *conj 3rd sg* **tàhwíiphaat**. *imp* **tàhwíipah**. *ptcpl* **tèhwíiphaat**.

**táhwŭneew** VTA catch s.o.; arrest s.o. *ind 1st sg* **ndáhwŭnaaw**, **ndáhwŭna**. *ind 3rd sg* **wtahwŭnáawal**. *ind inv* **ndáhwŭnukw**. *ind I-you* **ktáhwŭnul**. *conj 3rd sg* **táhwŭnaat**. *imp* **táhwun**. *ptcpl* **téhwŭnaat**.

**táhwŭnum** VTI1B catch s.t. *ind 1st sg* **ndahwŭnúmun**. *ind 3rd sg* **wtahwŭ=númun**. *conj 1st sg* **tàhwŭnúmaan**. *conj 3rd sg* **táhwŭnung**. *imp* **táh=wŭnih**. *ptcpl* **téhwŭnung**.

**takwáakuw** VII be fall, be autumn. **Takwaakíike náh ndá.** 'I'm going there next fall.'; **Takwáakuw náh ndá.** 'I went there last fall.' *conj 3rd sg* **takwáakiik**.

**takwaakwŭnúwii** PC during the fall, during the autumn.

**takwaangwéewak** VAI lie together. *usually plural*. *ind 1st pl* **ndakwaan=gwéhna**. *conj 3rd sg* **takwaangwéh=tiit**. *imp* **takwáangweekw**. *ptcpl* **teekwaangwéhtiit**.

**takwaapŭwehléewal** VII be mixed together in a liquid. *conj 3rd sg* **ta=kwaapŭwéhlaak**. *ptcpl* **teekwaapŭ=wehláakiil**.

**takwáchuw** VAI be cold. *ind 1st sg* **ndákwachi**, **ndákwachiim**. *conj 3rd sg* **takwáchiit**. *ptcpl* **téekwachiit**.

**takwachŭwiináakwsuw** VAI look cold. *ind 1st sg* **ndakwachuwiináakwsi**, **ndakwachuwiináakwsiim**. *conj 3rd sg* **takwachŭwiináakwsiit**. *ptcpl* **teekwachuwiináakwsiit**.

**takwaháakan** NI mortar. *pl* **takwaháa=kanal**. *poss* **ndakhwáakan**. *loc* **takwaháakanung**. *dimin* **chakwah=áakanush**.

**takwahtéewal** VII be there together. *usually plural*. *conj 3rd sg* **takwáh=teek**. *ptcpl* **teekwahtéekiil**.

**takwalooníikan** NI scissors. *pl* **takwal=**

**ooníikanal**. *poss* **ndakwalooníikan**. *loc* **takwalooníikanung**. *dimin* **chakwalooníikanush**.

**takwambíileew** VTA tie s.o. together. *object usually plural. ind 1st sg* **ndakwambiiláawak**. *ind 3rd sg* **wtakwambiiláawal**. *ind inv* **ndak=wambíilkook**. *ind I-you* **ktakwam=biilŭlóhmwa**. *conj 3rd sg* **takwam=bíilaat**. *imp* **takwámbiil**. *ptcpl* **teekwambíilaat**.

**takwambíisŭwak** VAI be tied together *(s.t. animate). usually plural. ind 1st pl* **ndakwambiisíhna**. *conj 3rd sg* **takwambiisíhtiit**. *ptcpl* **teekwam=biisíhtiit**.

**takwambíisŭwal** VII be tied together. *usually plural. conj 3rd sg* **takwam=bíisiik**. *ptcpl* **teekwambiisíikiil**.

**takwámbtoow** VTI2 tie s.t. together. *object usually plural. ind 1st sg* **ndak=wambtóonal**. *ind 3rd sg* **wtakwamb=tóonal**. *conj 1st sg* **takwambtáwaan**. *conj 3rd sg* **takwámbtaakw**. *imp* **takwámbtool**. *ptcpl* **teekwámb=taakw**.

**takwámŭwak** VAI be stuck together *(s.t. animate). usually plural. ind 1st pl* **ndakwamwíhna**. *conj 3rd sg* **ta=kwamwíhtiit**. *ptcpl* **teekwamwíhtiit**.

**takwámŭwal** VII be stuck together. *usually plural. conj 3rd sg* **takwámwiik**. *ptcpl* **teekwamwíikiil**. *intensive reduplication* **tahtakwámŭwal**.

**takwápuw** VAI get married. **Ngáta-takwápi.** 'I want to get married.' *ind 1st sg* **ndákwapi**, **ndákwapiim**. *conj 3rd sg* **takwápiit**. *imp* **takwápiil**. *ptcpl* **téekwapiit**. *See* **wiitawéengeew**.

**takwapŭwáaleew** VTA marry s.o. *ind 1st sg* **ndakwapuwáalaaw**, **ndakwa=puwáala**. *ind 3rd sg* **wtakwapuwaa=láawal**. *ind inv* **ndakwapuwáalukw**. *ind I-you* **ktakwapuwáalul**. *conj 3rd sg* **takwapŭwáalaat**. *imp* **takwápŭ=waal**. *ptcpl* **teekwapuwáalaat**.

**takwátun** VII be frozen together. *conj 3rd sg* **takwátung**. *ptcpl* **téekwatung**.

**takwáx** NA turtle. *pl* **takwáxak**. *dimin* **chakwáxush**. *obv* **takwáxal**.

**takwíikŭwak** VAI grow together. *usually plural. ind 1st pl* **ndakwiikíhna**. *conj 3rd sg* **takwiikíhtiit**. *ptcpl* **teekwii=kíhtiit**.

**takwíikŭnool** VII grow together. *usually plural. conj 3rd sg* **takwíikung**. *ptcpl* **teekwiikúngiil**.

**takwiikwáakeew** VAI sew things together. *ind 1st sg* **ndakwiikwáake**, **ndakwiikwáakeem**. *conj 3rd sg* **takwiikwáakeet**. *imp* **takwiikwáa=keel**. *ptcpl* **teekwiikwáakeet**. *intensive reduplication* **tàtakwiikwáa=keew**.

**takwiikwáaleew** VTA sew s.t. animate together. *ind 1st sg* **ndakwiikwáa=laaw**, **ndakwiikwáala**. *ind 3rd sg* **wtakwiikwaaláawal**. *ind inv* **ndak=wiikwáalukw**. *ind I-you* **ktakwii=kwáalul**. *conj 3rd sg* **takwiikwáa=laat**. *imp* **takwíikwaal**. *ptcpl* **tee=kwiikwáalaat**.

**takwíikwam** VTI1 sew s.t. together. *ind 1st sg* **ndakwíikwamun**. *ind 3rd sg* **wtakwíikwamun**. *conj 1st sg* **takwíi=kwamaan**. *conj 3rd sg* **takwíikwang**. *imp* **takwíikwah**. *ptcpl* **teekwíi=kwang**.

**takwiináxke** PC twenty.

**takwiipóoleew** VTA hold a feast for s.o. *ind 1st sg* **ndakwiipóolaaw**, **ndak=wiipóola**. *ind 3rd sg* **wtakwiipooláa=wal**. *ind inv* **ndakwiipóolukw**. *ind I-you* **ktakwiipóolul**. *conj 3rd sg* **takwiipóolaat**. *imp* **takwíipool**. *ptcpl* **tekwiipóolaat**.

**takwíipuw** VAI hold a feast. *ind 1st sg* **ndakwíipwi**, **ndakwíipwiim**. *conj 3rd sg* **takwíipwiit**. *imp* **takwíipwiil**. *ptcpl* **teekwíipwiit**.

**takwiipŭláawan** NI hoe. *pl* **takwiipŭ=láawanal**. *poss* **ndakwiipŭláawan**.

*loc* **takwiipŭláawanung**. *dimin* **chakwiipŭláawanush**. *See* **akwiipŭ=láawan**.

**takwiipwáakan** NI feast. *pl* **takwii=pwáakanal**. *poss* **ndakwiipwáakan**.

**takwiixíinook** VAI be close together, lie close together. *usually plural. ind 1st pl* **ndakwiixiinóhna**. *conj 3rd sg* **takwiixiinóhtiit**. *imp* **takwíixiikw**. *ptcpl* **teekwiixiinóhtiit**.

**takwíixtoow** VTI2 lay s.t. together, join s.t. together. *object usually plural. ind 1st sg* **ndakwiixtóonal**. *ind 3rd sg* **wtakwiixtóonal**. *conj 1st sg* **takwiix=táwaan**. *conj 3rd sg* **takwíixtaakw**. *imp* **takwíixtool**. *ptcpl* **teekwíix=taakw**.

**takwíixŭmeew** VTA lay s.o. together, join s.o. together. *object usually plural. ind 1st sg* **ndakwiixŭmáawak**. *ind 3rd sg* **wtakwiixŭmáawal**. *ind inv* **ndakwiixŭmúkook**. *ind I-you* **ktakwiixŭmulóhmwa**. *conj 3rd sg* **takwíixŭmaat**. *imp* **takwíixum**. *ptcpl* **teekwíixŭmaat**.

**takwíixŭnool** VII be close together, lie close together. *usually plural. conj 3rd sg* **takwíixung**. *ptcpl* **teekwii=xúngiil**.

**takwíhleew** VII come together, join together. *conj 3rd sg* **takwíhlaak**. *ptcpl* **teekwíhlaak**.

**takwihléewak** VAI come together, join together, band together. *usually plural. ind 1st pl* **ndakwihláhna**. *conj 3rd sg* **takwihláhtiit**. *imp* **takwíh=laakw**. *ptcpl* **teekwihláhtiit**.

**takwihtéehum** VTI1B nail s.t. together, hit s.t. and join it together. *ind 1st sg* **ndakwihtéehŭmun**. *ind 3rd sg* **wtakwihtéehŭmun**. *conj 1st sg* **ta=kwihtéehŭmaan**. *conj 3rd sg* **ta=kwihtéehung**. *imp* **takwihtéehih**. *ptcpl* **teekwihtéehung**.

**takwihteexíinook** VAI hit together. *usually plural. ind 1st pl* **ndakwihtee=xiinóhna**. *conj 3rd sg* **takwihteexii=nóhtiit**. *ptcpl* **teekwihteexiinóhtiit**.

**takwihtéexŭnool** VII hit together. *usually plural. conj 3rd sg* **takwihtée=xung**. *ptcpl* **teekwihteexúngiil**.

**takwukaatéexiin** VAI have one's legs together. *ind 1st sg* **ndakwkaatéexiin**, **ndakwkaatéexi**. *conj 3rd sg* **takwuk=aatéexiing**. *ptcpl* **teekwkaatéexiing**.

**takwúneew** VTA put s.t. animate together *(using the hands)*. *ind 1st sg* **ndákwŭ=naaw**, **ndákwŭna**. *ind 3rd sg* **wtak=wŭnáawal**. *ind inv* **ndákwŭnukw**. *ind I-you* **ktákwŭnul**. *conj 3rd sg* **takwúnaat**. *imp* **takwún**. *ptcpl* **tée=kwŭnaat**.

**takwundaméewak** VAI work together, help each other. *ind 1st pl* **ndakwun=damáhna**. *conj 3rd sg* **takwunda=máhtiit**. *imp* **takwúndamaakw**. *ptcpl* **teekwundamáhtiit**.

**takwúndaweew** VAI have one's arms around people. *ind 1st sg* **ndakwún=dawe**, **ndakwúndaweem**. *conj 3rd sg* **takwúndaweet**. *imp* **takwúndaweel**. *ptcpl* **teekwúndaweet**.

**takwundíikan** NI pincers. *pl* **takwun=díikanal**. *poss* **ndakwundíikan**. *loc* **takwundíikanung**. *dimin* **takwun=díikanush**.

**takwúnum** VTI1B put s.t. together *(using the hands)*. *ind 1st sg* **ndakwŭnúm=un**. *ind 3rd sg* **wtakwŭnúmun**. *conj 1st sg* **takwúnŭmaan**. *conj 3rd sg* **takwúnung**. *imp* **takwúnih**. *ptcpl* **téekwŭnung**. *intensive reduplication* **wtatakwúnŭmun**.

**taláawsuw** VAI live there. *ind 1st sg* **ndundaláawsi**, **ndundaláawsiim**. *conj 3rd sg* **taláawsiit**. *ptcpl* **eenda=láawsiit**.

**talahkíiheew** VAI plant things in a certain place, plant things there. *ind 1st sg* **ndundalahkíihe**, **ndundalahkíi=heem**. *conj 3rd sg* **talahkíiheet**. *imp* **talahkíiheel**. *ptcpl* **eendalahkíiheet**.

**talalóhkeew** VAI work in a certain place, work there. *ind 1st sg* **ndundalalóh=ke, ndundalalóhkeem**. *conj 3rd sg* **talalóhkeet**. *imp* **talalóhkeel**. *ptcpl* **eendalalóhkeet**.

**talámŭwak** VAI hang there. *usually plural*. **Wéemi táa talámŭwak.** 'They're hanging all over.'; **Talámŭwak aapŭlúshak ngwúteel talí.** 'The apples are hanging there bunched together.' *ind 1st pl* **ndundalamwíhna**. *conj 3rd sg* **talamwíhtiit**. *ptcpl* **eendalamwíhtiit**.

**talatawáapameew** VTA see s.o. in a certain place. **Wiikwáhmung ndunda=latawáapamaaw.** 'I saw him in the house.' *ind 1st sg* **ndundalatawáa=pamaaw, ndundalatawáapama**. *ind 3rd sg* **wtundalatawaapamáawal**. *ind inv* **ndundalatawáapamukw**. *ind I-you* **ktundalatawáapamul**. *conj 3rd sg* **talatawáapamaat**. *ptcpl* **een=dalatawáapamaat**.

**talatawaapándam** VTI I A see s.t. in a certain place. **Wiikwáhmung ndun=dalatawaapándamun.** 'I saw it in the house.' *ind 1st sg* **ndundalata=waapándamun**. *ind 3rd sg* **wtunda=latawaapándamun**. *conj 1st sg* **talatawaapándamaan**. *conj 3rd sg* **talatawaapándang**. *ptcpl* **eendalat=awaapándang**.

**talatawáapuw** VAI see something in a certain place. **Kóhpii talatawáapuw.** 'He saw it in the forest.' *ind 1st sg* **ndundalatawáapi, ndundalatawáa=piim**. *conj 3rd sg* **talatawáapiit**. *ptcpl* **eendalatawáapiit**.

**taleelawúsuw** VAI play in a certain place, play there. **Kwáchŭmung taleela=wúsuw.** 'He's playing outside.' *ind 1st sg* **ndundaleelawúsi, ndunda=leelawúsiim**. *conj 3rd sg* **taleela=wúsiit**. *imp* **taleelawúsiil**. *ptcpl* **een=daleelawúsiit**.

**talíineew** VAI have an illness in a certain part of one's body. **Wihkáatung talíineew.** 'His leg is sore.' *ind 1st sg* **ndundalíine, ndundalíineem**. *conj 3rd sg* **talíineet**. *ptcpl* **eendalíineet**.

**taliinghwáhkweew** VAI make a noise on metal, hit something metallic that makes noise. *ind 1st sg* **ndaliing=hwáhkwe, ndaliinghwáhkweem**. *conj 3rd sg* **taliinghwáhkweet**. *imp* **taliinghwáhkweel**. *ptcpl* **teeliing=hwáhkweet**.

**taliinghwíikeew** VAI ring a bell; make a ringing noise *(on metal)*. *ind 1st sg* **ndaliinghwíike, ndaliinghwíikeem**. *conj 3rd sg* **taliinghwíikeet**. *imp* **taliinghwíikeel**. *ptcpl* **teeliinghwíi=keet**.

**talíingweew** VII ring, be ringing. *conj 3rd sg* **talíingweek**. *ptcpl* **teelíingweek**.

**taliingwíixiin** VAI ring, be ringing. *conj 3rd sg* **taliingwíixiing**. *ptcpl* **teeliin=gwíixiing, teeliingwíixiit**.

**taliingwíixun** VII ring, be ringing. *conj 3rd sg* **taliingwíixung**. *ptcpl* **teeliin=gwíixung**.

**taliingwihtéexun** VII ring, make a ringing noise, make a tinny noise. *conj 3rd sg* **taliingwihtéexung**. *ptcpl* **tee=liingwihtéexung**.

**taliingwŭníikan** NA bell. *pl* **taliingwŭ=níikanak**. *poss* **ndaliingwŭníikan**. *loc* **taliingwŭníikanung**. *dimin* **cha=liingwŭníikanush**. *obv* **taliingwŭ=níikanal**.

**taliingwŭníikan** NI bell. *pl* **taliingwŭ=níikanal**. *poss* **ndaliingwŭníikan**. *loc* **taliingwŭníikanung**. *dimin* **cha=liingwŭníikanush**.

**taliingwŭnúmeew** VAI ring a bell. *ind 1st sg* **ndaliingwŭnúma, ndaliin=gwŭnúmaam**. *conj 3rd sg* **taliin=gwŭnúmaat**. *imp* **taliingwŭnúmaal**. *ptcpl* **teeliingwŭnúmaat**.

**talí** PC here, there, in a certain place. **Mohkamúyuw talí mbíing.** 'It's icy in the water.'; **Chíipayal néeweew**

**kúshtung talí.** 'He saw ghosts in a coffin.' *See* **talú**.

**talú** PC here, there, in a certain place. **Akushíilaan yóon talú.** 'It rains heavily here.'; **Kóonung talú kŭláhkweew.** 'He got stuck in the snow.' *See* **talí**.

**talúweew** VAI make noise in a certain place. **Péexwiish talúweew.** 'He's making noise close by.' *ind 1st sg* **ndundalúwe**, **ndundalúweem**. *conj 3rd sg* **talúweet**. *imp* **talúweel**. *ptcpl* **eendalúweet**.

**tamákeew** VII bend at a joint. *conj 3rd sg* **tamákeek**. *ptcpl* **téemakeek**.

**tamakíhkam** VTI 1A step on and bend s.t. *(of a pedal)*. *ind 1st sg* **ndama=kíhkamun**. *ind 3rd sg* **wtamakíhka=mun**. *conj 1st sg* **tamakíhkamaan**. *conj 3rd sg* **tamakíhkang**. *imp* **tamakíhkah**. *ptcpl* **teemakíhkang**.

**tamakíhleew** VAI bend at a joint. *ind 1st sg* **ndamakíhla**, **ndamakíhlaam**. *conj 3rd sg* **tamakíhlaat**. *ptcpl* **teemakíhlaat**. *intensive reduplication* **tàtamakíhleew**.

**tamakíhleew** VII bend at a joint. *conj 3rd sg* **tamakíhlaak**. *ptcpl* **teema=kíhlaak**. *intensive reduplication* **tàtamakíhleew**.

**tamakohkwéhleew** VAI nod one's head. *ind 1st sg* **ndamakohkwéhla**, **ndamakohkwéhlaam**. *conj 3rd sg* **tamakohkwéhlaat**. *imp* **tamakoh=kwéhlaal**. *ptcpl* **teemakohkwéhlaat**. *intensive reduplication* **tàtamakoh=kwéhleew**, **atamakohkwéhleew**. *See* **tàtamohkwaandpéhleew**.

**tamáksuw** VAI be bent over, be doubled up. *ind 1st sg* **ndamakúsi**, **ndama=kúsiim**. *conj 3rd sg* **tamáksiit**. *ptcpl* **teemakúsiit**.

**tamákŭneew** VTA press down on s.o., push down on s.o., bend s.o. at a joint *(using the hands)*. *ind 1st sg* **ndama=kúnaaw**, **ndamakúna**. *ind 3rd sg* **wtamakunáawal**. *ind inv* **ndama=kúnukw**. *ind I-you* **ktamakúnul**. *conj 3rd sg* **tamákŭnaat**. *imp* **tamákun**. *ptcpl* **teemakúnaat**.

**tamákŭnum** VTI 1B press down on s.t., push down on s.t., bend s.t. at a joint *(using the hands)*. *ind 1st sg* **ndama=kúnŭmun**. *ind 3rd sg* **wtamakúnŭ=mun**. *conj 1st sg* **tamakŭnúmaan**. *conj 3rd sg* **tamákŭnung**. *imp* **ta=mákŭnih**. *ptcpl* **teemakúnung**. *intensive reduplication* **wtatamakŭ=númun**.

**tamongwíhleew** VAI roar, go by roaring; run well. *ind 1st sg* **ndamongwíhla**, **ndamongwíhlaam**. *conj 3rd sg* **ta=mongwíhlaat**. *ptcpl* **teemongwíh=laat**.

**tamongwíhleew** VII roar, go by roaring. *conj 3rd sg* **tamongwíhlaak**. *ptcpl* **teemongwíhlaak**.

**tangaawatóoheew** VAIO lower the price of s.t. *ind 1st sg* **ndangaawatóoheen**. *ind 3rd sg* **wtangaawatóoheen**. *conj 3rd sg* **tangaawatóoheet**. *imp* **tan=gaawatóoheel**. *ptcpl* **teengaawatóo=heet**.

**tangáawatuw** VII have a low price. *conj 3rd sg* **tangáawatiik**. *ptcpl* **teengáa=watiik**.

**tángaloonz** NI bullet. *pl* **tangalóonzal**. *rare*.

**tángameew** VTA stab s.o. *ind 1st sg* **ndángamaaw**, **ndángama**. *ind 3rd sg* **wtangamáawal**. *ind inv* **ndánga=mukw**. *ind I-you* **ktángamul**. *conj 3rd sg* **tángamaat**. *imp* **tángam**. *ptcpl* **téengamaat**.

**tangamíikan** NA sword, spear. *pl* **tan=gamíikanak**. *poss* **ndangamíikan**. *loc* **tangamíikanung**. *dimin* **changa=míikanush**. *obv* **tangamíikanal**.

**tangamíikan** NI sword, spear. *pl* **tan=gamíikanal**. *poss* **ndangamíikan**. *loc* **tangamíikanung**. *dimin* **changamíi=kanush**. *See* **tangandíikan**.

**tangandíikan** NI sword, spear. *pl* **tan=gandíikanal**. *poss* **ndangandíikan**. *loc* **tangandíikanung**. *dimin* **chan=ganjíikanush**. *See* **tangamíikan**.

**tangeelúndam** VOTI 1A feel lowly, think little *(of oneself)*. *ind 1st sg* **ndan=geelúndam**. *conj 3rd sg* **tangee=lúndang**. *ptcpl* **teengeelúndang**.

**tángii** PC some, a little bit, a small amount. **Tángii nú yéelak áhte apwáan.** 'There's a bit of bread there.'; **Tángii káta-míitsi?** 'Do you want to eat a little bit?' *See* **chángiish**, **changíiwiish**.

**tangii-** PV some, a little bit, a small amount. **Méhch há kíish-tángii-hulŭníixsi?** 'Can you speak a little Delaware now?' *ptcpl* **téengii-**.

**tashakíhleew** VAI be ripped, be torn *(s.t. animate)*. *ind 1st sg* **ndashakíhla**, **ndashakíhlaam**. *conj 3rd sg* **tashak=íhlaat**. *ptcpl* **teeshakíhlaat**.

**tashakíhleew** VII be ripped, be torn. *conj 3rd sg* **tashakíhlaak**. *ptcpl* **teeshakíhlaak**.

**tashakihtéeheew** VTA hit and cut s.o. *ind 1st sg* **ndashakihtéehaaw**, **ndashakihtéeha**. *ind 3rd sg* **wtasha=kihteeháawal**. *ind inv* **ndashakih=téehookw**. *ind I-you* **ktashakihtée=hool**. *conj 3rd sg* **tashakihtéehaat**. *imp* **tashakíhteeh**. *ptcpl* **teeshakih=téehaat**. *intensive reduplication* **wtatashakihteeháawal**.

**tashákŭneew** VTA tear s.t. animate *(using the hands)*. *ind 1st sg* **ndasha=kúnaaw**, **ndashakúna**. *ind 3rd sg* **wtashakunáawal**. *ind inv* **ndasha=kúnukw**. *ind I-you* **ktashakúnul**. *conj 3rd sg* **tashákŭnaat**. *imp* **ta=shákun**. *ptcpl* **teeshakúnaat**.

**tashákŭnum** VTI 1B tear s.t. *(using the hands)*. *ind 1st sg* **ndashakúnŭmun**. *ind 3rd sg* **wtashakúnŭmun**. *conj 1st sg* **tashakŭnúmaan**. *conj 3rd sg* **tashákŭnung**. *imp* **tashákŭnih**. *ptcpl* **teeshakúnung**.

**tàtamakohkwaandpéhleew** VAI nod one's head. *ind 1st sg* **ndatamakoh=kwaandpéhla**, **ndatamakohkwaan=dpéhlaam**. *conj 3rd sg* **tàtamakoh=kwaandpéhlaat**. *imp* **tàtamakoh=kwaandpéhlaal**. *ptcpl* **tàtamakoh=kwaandpéhlaat**.

**tàtamakohkwéhlaash** NA bug species with nodding head. *pl* **tàtamakoh=kwehláashak**. *obv* **tàtamakohkweh=láashal**. *See* **tàtamakohkwehláa=shiit**.

**tàtamakohkwehláashiit** NA bug species with nodding head. *pl* **tàtamakoh=kwehlaashíhtiit**. *See* **tàtamakoh=kwehláash**.

**tàtapásuw** VAI shield oneself, dodge from something. *ind 1st sg* **ndata=pási**, **ndatapásiim**. *conj 3rd sg* **tàt=apásiit**. *imp* **tàtapásiil**.

**tàtùpáalakat** VII be a tunnel. *conj 3rd sg* **tàtùpáalakahk**. *ptcpl* **tàtùpáa=lakahk**.

**tàtúpxun** VII blow around *(of the wind)*; be blown around by the wind. *conj 3rd sg* **tàtúpxung**. *ptcpl* **tàtúpxung**.

**tawaapéhleew** VII hang open, be open. *conj 3rd sg* **tawaapéhlaak**. *ptcpl* **teewaapéhlaak**.

**tawáxookw** VAI be blown open by the wind *(s.t. animate)*. *conj 3rd sg* **tawaxóokwuk**. *ptcpl* **teewxóokwuk**.

**tawáxun** VII be blown open by the wind. **Tawáxun kpáhoon.** 'The door was blown open by the wind.' *conj 3rd sg* **tawáxung**. *ptcpl* **téewxung**.

**taweenáxkŭneew** VTA open the gate for s.o. *ind 1st sg* **ndaweenáxkŭnaaw**, **ndaweenáxkŭna**. *ind 3rd sg* **wtaw=eenaxkŭnáawal**. *ind inv* **ndawee=náxkŭnukw**. *ind I-you* **ktaweenáx=kŭnul**. *conj 3rd sg* **taweenáxkŭnaat**. *imp* **taweenáxkun**. *ptcpl* **teeweenáx=kŭnaat**.

**taweenaxkŭníikan** NI gate. *pl* **tawee=**

naxkŭníikanal. *poss* **ndaweenaxkŭ=níikan**. *loc* **taweenaxkŭníikanung**. *dimin* **chaweenaxkŭníikanush**. *See* **tehtaweenaxkŭníikan**.

**tawiikwáakan** NA key. *pl* **tawiikwáa=kanak**. *poss* **ndawiikwáakan**. *loc* **tawiikwáakanung**. *dimin* **chawii=kwáakanush**. *obv* **tawiikwáakanal**.

**tawiikwáaleew** VTA unlock s.t. animate. *ind 1st sg* **ndawiikwáalaaw**, **ndaw=iikwáala**. *ind 3rd sg* **wtawiikwaa=láawal**. *ind inv* **ndawiikwáalukw**. *ind I-you* **ktawiikwáalul**. *conj 3rd sg* **tawiikwáalaat**. *imp* **tawíikwaal**. *ptcpl* **teewiikwáalaat**.

**tawiikwáasuw** VAI be unlocked *(s.t. animate)*. *ind 1st sg* **ndawiikwáasi**, **ndawiikwáasiim**. *conj 3rd sg* **tawii=kwáasiit**. *ptcpl* **teewiikwáasiit**.

**tawiikwáasuw** VII be unlocked. *conj 3rd sg* **tawiikwáasiik**. *ptcpl* **teewiikwáa=siik**.

**tawíikwam** VTI1A unlock s.t. *ind 1st sg* **ndawíikwamun**. *ind 3rd sg* **wtawíi=kwamun**. *conj 1st sg* **tawíikwamaan**. *conj 3rd sg* **tawíikwang**. *imp* **tawíi=kwah**. *ptcpl* **teewíikwang**.

**tawíikwŭnum** VTI1B unlock s.t. *ind 1st sg* **ndawiikwŭnúmun**. *ind 3rd sg* **wtawiikwŭnúmun**. *conj 1st sg* **tawii=kwunúmaan**. *conj 3rd sg* **tawíikwŭ=nung**. *imp* **tawíikwŭnih**. *ptcpl* **tee=wíikwŭnung**.

**tawíixiin** VAI be open *(s.t. animate)*. *ind 1st sg* **ndawíixiin**, **ndawíixi**. *conj 3rd sg* **tawíixiing**. *ptcpl* **teewíixiing**.

**tawíixtoow** VTI2 leave s.t. open. *ind 1st sg* **ndawíixtoon**. *ind 3rd sg* **wtawíix=toon**. *conj 1st sg* **tawiixtáwaan**. *conj 3rd sg* **tawíixtaakw**. *imp* **tawíixtool**. *ptcpl* **teewíixtaakw**.

**tawíixŭmeew** VTA leave s.t. animate open. *ind 1st sg* **ndawíixŭmaaw**, **ndawíixŭma**. *ind 3rd sg* **wtawiixŭ=máawal**. *ind inv* **ndawíixŭmukw**. *ind I-you* **ktawíixŭmul**. *conj 3rd sg* **tawíixŭmaat**. *imp* **tawíixum**. *ptcpl* **teewíixŭmaat**.

**tawíixun** VII be open. **Taatawíixun kwúphoon.** 'His door is open.' *conj 3rd sg* **tawíixung**. *ptcpl* **teewíixung**. *moderative reduplication* **taatawíi=xun**.

**táwsun** NI thousand. *singular only, with number particle or prenoun*. **Kawíiw ngwúti táwsun txú-katúne.** 'He's sleeping for a thousand years.'; **Níish-táwsun.** 'Two thousand.' *From English* thousand.

**tawúneew** VTA open s.t. animate. *ind 1st sg* **ndáwŭnaaw**, **ndáwŭna**. *ind 3rd sg* **wtawŭnáawal**. *ind inv* **ndáwŭ=nukw**. *ind I-you* **ktáwŭnul**. *conj 3rd sg* **tawúnaat**. *imp* **tawún**. *ptcpl* **téewŭnaat**.

**tawúnum** VTI1B open s.t. *(using the hands)*. *ind 1st sg* **ndawŭnúmun**. *ind 3rd sg* **wtawŭnúmun**. *conj 1st sg* **tawúnŭmaan**. *conj 3rd sg* **tawúnung**. *imp* **tawúnih**. *ptcpl* **téewŭnung**.

**tawushéextoow** VTI2 leave s.t. wide open. *ind 1st sg* **ndawshéextoon**. *ind 3rd sg* **wtawshéextoon**. *conj 1st sg* **tawusheextáwaan**. *conj 3rd sg* **ta=wushéextaakw**. *imp* **tawushéextool**. *ptcpl* **teewshéextaakw**.

**tawushéexŭmeew** VTA leave s.t. animate wide open. *ind 1st sg* **ndawshéexŭ=maaw**, **ndawshéexŭma**. *ind 3rd sg* **wtawsheexŭmáawal**. *conj 3rd sg* **tawushéexŭmaat**. *imp* **tawushée=xum**. *ptcpl* **teewshéexŭmaat**.

**tayáaxkwaan** NI bridge. *pl* **tayaax=kwáanal**. *poss* **ndayáaxkwaan**. *loc* **tayaaxkwáanung**. *dimin* **chayaax=kwáanush**.

**teep-** PV enough, sufficiently. *informal*. **Máh téep-kiishtéewi.** 'It's not cooked enough.'; **Ktéep-kxáni?** 'Do you have enough?' *ptcpl* **téep-**. *See* **teepu-**.

**teepáalakat** VII be deep enough *(of*

*holes). conj 3rd sg* **teepáalakahk**. *ptcpl* **teepáalakahk**.

**teepaawatóoheew** VAIO charge a fair price for s.t. *ind 1st sg* **ndeepaawa=tóoheen**. *ind 3rd sg* **wteepaawatóo=heen**. *conj 3rd sg* **teepaawatóoheet**. *imp* **teepaawatóoheel**. *ptcpl* **teepaa=watóoheet**.

**teepáawatuw** VAI be a fair price *(s.t. animate). ind 1st sg* **ndeepáawati**, **ndeepáawatiim**. *conj 3rd sg* **teepáa=watiit**. *ptcpl* **teepáawatiit**.

**teepáawatuw** VII be a fair price. *conj 3rd sg* **teepáawatiik**. *ptcpl* **teepáa=watiik**.

**téepamuw** VII fit *(into something)*; 'it fits.' **Nzíit téepamuw mahksúnung.** 'My foot fits into the shoe.' *conj 3rd sg* **téepamwiik**. *ptcpl* **téepamwiik**.

**teepéelook** VAI be enough *(s.t. animate). usually plural. ind 1st pl* **ndeepee=lóhna**. *conj 3rd sg* **teepeelóhtiit**. *ptcpl* **teepeelóhtiit**.

**teepéeltool** VII be enough of them. *usu-ally plural. conj 3rd sg* **teepéelihk**. *ptcpl* **teepeelíhkiil**.

**teepéelŭmeew** VTA be satisfied with s.o. *ind 1st sg* **ndeepéelŭmaaw**, **ndee=péelŭma**. *ind 3rd sg* **wteepeelŭmáa=wal**. *ind inv* **ndeepéelŭmukw**. *ind I-you* **kteepéelŭmul**. *conj 3rd sg* **tee=péelŭmaat**. *imp* **teepéelum**. *ptcpl* **teepéelŭmaat**.

**teepeelúndam** VOTI1A be satisfied. *ind 1st sg* **ndeepeelúndam**. *conj 3rd sg* **teepeelúndang**. *ptcpl* **teepeelúndang**.

**teepeelúndam** VTI1A be satisfied with s.t. **Ndeepeelúndamun weendaawsúy=aan.** 'I'm satisfied with the way I live.' *ind 1st sg* **ndeepeelúndamun**. *ind 3rd sg* **wteepeelúndamun**. *conj 1st sg* **teepeelúndamaan**. *conj 3rd sg* **teepeelúndang**. *imp* **teepeelúndah**. *ptcpl* **teepeelúndang**.

**teepíikun** VII be ready, be ripe, be fully grown. *conj 3rd sg* **teepíikung**. *ptcpl* **teepíikung**.

**teepíikuw** VAI be ready, be ripe, be fully grown *(s.t. animate). ind 1st sg* **ndee=píiki**, **ndeepíikiim**. *conj 3rd sg* **tee=píikiit**. *ptcpl* **teepíikiit**.

**teepiilawéeheew** VTA make s.o. content, satisfy s.o. **Ndeepiilawéehaaw.** 'S/he satisfies me.' *ind 1st sg* **ndeepiila=wéehaaw**, **ndeepiilawéeha**. *ind 3rd sg* **wteepiilaweeháawal**. *ind inv* **ndeepiilawéehukw**. *ind I-you* **ktee=piilawéehul**. *conj 3rd sg* **teepiila=wéehaat**. *imp* **teepíilaweeh**. *ptcpl* **teepiilawéehaat**.

**teepiilaweehkwúsuw** VAI be satisfied. *ind 1st sg* **ndeepiilaweehkwúsi**, **ndeepiilaweehkwúsiim**. *conj 3rd sg* **teepiilaweehkwúsiit**. *ptcpl* **teepiila=weehkwúsiit**.

**teepíisŭmuw** VAI have enough to drink. **Méhch kteepíisŭmwi?** 'Did you have enough to drink?' *ind 1st sg* **ndeepíisŭmwi**, **ndeepíisŭmwiim**. *conj 3rd sg* **teepíisŭmwiit**. *ptcpl* **teepíisŭmwiit**.

**teepiitéeheew** VAI be satisfied. *ind 1st sg* **ndeepiitéeha**, **ndeepiitéehaam**. *conj 3rd sg* **teepiitéehaat**. *ptcpl* **teepiitée=haat**.

**teepíhkam** VTI1A fit s.t. *(of clothing)*; 'it fits'. **Ndeepíhkamun.** 'It fits me.'; **Ndeepíhkamun máhksun.** 'The shoe fits me.' *ind 1st sg* **ndeepíhka=mun**. *ind 3rd sg* **wteepíhkamun**. *conj 1st sg* **teepíhkamaan**. *conj 3rd sg* **teepíhkang**. *ptcpl* **teepíhkang**.

**teepíhkaweew** VTA fit s.t. animate *(of clothing)*; 'it fits'. **Ndeepihkawáa=wak.** 'They fit me.'; **Wteepihka=wáawal wándal.** 'The mitt fits him.' *ind 1st sg* **ndeepíhkawaaw**, **ndee=píhkawa**. *ind 3rd sg* **wteepihkawáa=wal**. *ind inv* **ndeepíhkaakw**. *ind I-you* **kteepíhkool**. *conj 3rd sg* **teepíh=kawaat**. *ptcpl* **teepíhkawaat**.

**teepíhlaleew** VTA have enough of s.t.

animate. *ind 1st sg* **ndeepíhlalaaw**, **ndeepíhlala**. *ind 3rd sg* **wteepihla=láawal**. *ind inv* **ndeepíhlalukw**. *ind I-you* **kteepíhlalul**. *conj 3rd sg* **teepíh=lalaat**. *ptcpl* **teepíhlalaat**.

**teepíhlatoow** VTI2 have enough of s.t. *ind 1st sg* **ndeepíhlatoon**. *ind 3rd sg* **wteepíhlatoon**. *conj 1st sg* **teepihla=táwaan**. *conj 3rd sg* **teepíhlataakw**. *imp* **teepíhlatool**. *ptcpl* **teepíhla=taakw**.

**teepu-** PV enough, sufficiently. *informal*. **Téepu-lukíhkwun.** 'It is big enough.'; **Méhch áa ktéepu-moonzháasi.** 'It's time you got a haircut.' *ptcpl* **téepu-**. *See* **teep-**.

**téet** PC maybe. **Ngushiipáandpa, téet ndawiilpíishi.** 'I have an itchy head, maybe I'm lousy.'; **Nzháwsi, téet ngatóopwi.** 'I'm weak, maybe I'm hungry.'

**téetawii** PC between. **Mwáakane téeta=wii níipawuw mihtkwíhke.** 'The dog is standing between the trees.'; **Tée=tawii apwáanung ndáhtoon wŭyóos.** 'I put the meat between the slices of bread.'

**teetawiikáapawuw** VAI stand between something. *ind 1st sg* **ndeetawiikáa=pawi**, **ndeetawiikáapawiim**. *conj 3rd sg* **teetawiikáapawiit**. *imp* **teetawii=káapawiil**. *ptcpl* **teetawiikáapawiit**.

**téexii** PC anyway, regardless, go ahead and do something. **Téexii nátpwiin máh awéen péewi.** 'I just went ahead and cooked, but no one came.'; **Téexii ngwúteel apúwak.** 'They went ahead and lived together.'

**tehtàhwŭníikees** NA policeman. *pl* **teh=tàhwŭniikéesak**. *obv* **tehtàhwŭnii=kéesal**.

**tehtaweenaxkŭníikan** NI gate. *pl* **teh=taweenaxkŭníikanal**. *poss* **ndehta=weenaxkŭníikan**. *loc* **tehtaweenax=kŭníikanung**. *dimin* **chehchawee=naxkŭníikanush**. *See* **taweenaxkŭ=níikan**.

**téksak** NA tacks. *usually plural*. *poss* **ndeksúmak**. *dimin* **tékshush**. *obv* **téksal**. *From English* tacks.

**témbul** NI Thamesville, Ontario. **Tém=bul wíikuw.** 'He lives in Thames-ville.' *From English* Thamesville.

**tháapŭweew** VII be cold water. *conj 3rd sg* **tháapŭweek**. *ptcpl* **teeháapŭweek**.

**thá** PC how *(question word)*. **Thá wá ná lúnuw?** 'Where is the man?' *See* **tá**.

**tháhkameew** VII be a cold day. *conj 3rd sg* **tháhkameek**. *ptcpl* **teeháhka=meek**.

**thahkéeyeew** VII be cold ground. *conj 3rd sg* **thahkéeyeek**. *ptcpl* **teehah=kéeyeek**.

**tháxun** VII be a cold wind. *conj 3rd sg* **tháxung**. *ptcpl* **téehxung**. *moderative reduplication* **taatháxun**.

**théew** VII be cold. *conj 3rd sg* **théek**. *ptcpl* **téeheek**.

**théewakw** NI cold meat. *pl* **théewa=kwal**. *poss* **ndahéewakwum**. *loc* **théewakwung**. *dimin* **théewakwush**.

**thii-** PN cold. **Thíi-tíi** 'Cold tea.'

**thíi-láakuw** VII be a cool evening. *conj 3rd sg* **thíi-láakwiik**. *ptcpl* **téehii-láakwiik**.

**thíi-tpíhkat** VII be a cold night. *conj 3rd sg* **thíi-tpíhkahk**. *ptcpl* **téehii-tpíhkahk**.

**thiikamíikat** VII be cold, be cool *(of houses, of rooms)*. *conj 3rd sg* **thii=kamíikahk**. *ptcpl* **teehiikamíikahk**.

**thiináakwat** VII be cold looking, look cold. *conj 3rd sg* **thiináakwahk**. *ptcpl* **teehiináakwahk**.

**thiináakwsuw** VAI be cold looking, look cold *(s.t. animate)*. *ind 1st sg* **ndahii=náakwsi**, **ndahiináakwsiim**. *conj 3rd sg* **thiináakwsiit**. *ptcpl* **teehiináakw=siit**.

**thíingweew** VAI have a cold face. *ind 1st sg* **ndahíingwa**, **ndahíingwaam**. *conj*

*3rd sg* **thíingwaat**. *ptcpl* **teehíin=gwaat**.

**thíisŭmuw** VAI have a drink of something cold. *ind 1st sg* **ndahíisŭmwi**, **ndahíisŭmwiim**. *conj 3rd sg* **thíi=sŭmwiit**. *imp* **thíisŭmwiil**. *ptcpl* **teehíisŭmwiit**.

**thíixŭmuw** VAI swim, be in swimming, be in the water; take a bath. *ind 1st sg* **ndahíixŭmwi**, **ndahíixŭmwiim**. *conj 3rd sg* **thíixŭmwiit**. *imp* **thíixŭmwiil**. *ptcpl* **teehíixŭmwiit**.

**thíhlaleew** VTA cool s.o. down. *ind 1st sg* **ndahíhlalaaw**, **ndahíhlala**. *ind 3rd sg* **wtahihlaláawal**. *ind inv* **ndahíhlalukw**. *ind I-you* **ktahíhlalul**. *conj 3rd sg* **thíhlalaat**. *imp* **thíhlal**. *ptcpl* **teehíhlalaat**.

**thíhlatoow** VTI2 cool s.t. down. *ind 1st sg* **ndahíhlatoon**. *ind 3rd sg* **wtahíh=latoon**. *conj 1st sg* **thihlatáwaan**. *conj 3rd sg* **thíhlataakw**. *imp* **thíh=latool**. *ptcpl* **teehíhlataakw**.

**thíhleew** VII become cold, get cold. *conj 3rd sg* **thíhlaak**. *ptcpl* **teehíhlaak**.

**thunáxkeew** VAI have a cold hand. *ind 1st sg* **ndahŭnáxka**, **ndahŭnáxkaam**. *conj 3rd sg* **thunáxkaat**. *ptcpl* **tee=hŭnáxkaat**. *intensive reduplication* **atahŭnáxkeew**. *See* **saasŭlunjée=pookw**.

**thupéekat** VII be cold water. *conj 3rd sg* **thupéekahk**. *ptcpl* **teehpéekahk**.

**thupéekw** NI spring well; cold water. *pl* **thupéekwal**. *poss* **ndahpéekwum**. *loc* **thupéekwung**.

**thúpuy** NI cold water. *loc* **thúpiing**.

**thusíiteew** VAI have cold feet. *ind 1st sg* **ndahsíita**, **ndahsíitaam**. *conj 3rd sg* **thusíitaat**. *ptcpl* **teehsíitaat**. *intensive reduplication* **atahsíiteeẃ**. *See* **saasiitéepookw**.

**thúsuw** VAI be cold *(s.t. animate)*. *ind 1st sg* **ndáhsi**, **ndáhsiim**. *conj 3rd sg* **thúsiit**. *ptcpl* **téehsiit**.

**tíi** NI tea. *poss* **ndíihum**. *loc* **tíihung**. *From English* tea.

**tiiheemhwáanus** NA teaspoon. *pl* **tii=heemhwáansak**. *obv* **tiiheemhwáan=sal**.

**tiihíinjuw** NI teacup. *pl* **tiihíinjŭwal**. *poss* **ndiihiinjóohum**. *dimin* **chii=hiinjóohush**.

**tíihoos** NA tea kettle. *pl* **tiihóosak**. *poss* **ndiihóosum**. *loc* **tiihóosung**. *dimin* **chiihóoshush**. *obv* **tiihóosal**.

**tíipat** NA tea pot. *pl* **tiipátak**. *poss* **ndii=pátum**. *loc* **tiipátung**. *dimin* **chii=páchush**. *obv* **tiipátal**. *From English* teapot.

**tíitiis** NA blue jay. *pl* **tiitíisak**. *obv* **tii=tíisal**.

**tiiwchéhleew** VAI drive and make a loud noise, make a rattling noise while driving *(of wagon wheels)*. *ind 1st sg* **ndiiwchéhla**, **ndiiwchéhlaam**. *conj 3rd sg* **tiiwchéhlaat**. *imp* **tiiwchéh=laal**. *ptcpl* **tiiwchéhlaat**.

**tiiwháhkweew** VAI pound and make a noise, hit and make a noise *(on wood, on solid objects)*. *ind 1st sg* **ndiiw=háhkwe**, **ndiiwháhkweem**. *conj 3rd sg* **tiiwháhkweet**. *imp* **tiiwháhkweel**. *ptcpl* **tiiwháhkweet**.

**tiiwíixiin** VAI fall and make a loud noise *(s.t. animate)*. *ind 1st sg* **ndiiwíixiin**, **ndiiwíixi**. *conj 3rd sg* **tiiwíixiing**. *ptcpl* **tiiwíixiing**.

**tiiwíixtoow** VTI2 throw s.t down hard so as to make a loud noise, set s.t down hard so as to make a loud noise. *ind 1st sg* **ndiiwíixtoon**. *ind 3rd sg* **wtii=wíixtoon**. *conj 1st sg* **tiiwiixtáwaan**. *conj 3rd sg* **tiiwíixtaakw**. *imp* **tii=wíixtool**. *ptcpl* **tiiwíixtaakw**.

**tiiwíixŭmeew** VTA throw s.o. down hard so as to make a loud noise, set s.o. down hard so as to make a loud noise. *ind 1st sg* **ndiiwíixŭmaaw**, **ndiiwíi=xŭma**. *ind 3rd sg* **wtiiwiixŭmáawal**. *ind inv* **ndiiwíixŭmukw**. *ind I-you* **ktiiwíixŭmul**. *conj 3rd sg* **tiiwíixŭ=**

maat. *imp* **tiiwíixum**. *ptcpl* **tiiwíixŭ=maat**.

**tiiwíixun** VII fall and make a loud noise. *conj 3rd sg* **tiiwíixung**. *ptcpl* **tiiwíi=xung**.

**tiiwóoxweew** VAI walk and make a loud noise. *ind 1st sg* **ndiiwóoxwe**, **ndii=wóoxweem**. *conj 3rd sg* **tiiwóoxweet**. *imp* **tiiwóoxweel**. *ptcpl* **tiiwóoxweet**.

**tihkambíisoon** NA belt. *pl* **tihkambii=sóonak**. *poss* **ndihkambíisoon**. *loc* **tihkambiisóonung**. *dimin* **tihkam=biishóonush**. *obv* **tihkambiisóonal**.

**tíhlam** VTI1A chop s.t. down with an ax, cut s.t. down with an ax. **Ndíhlam xwús.** 'I chopped some wood.' *ind 1st sg* **ndíhlamun**. *ind 3rd sg* **wtíh=lamun**. *conj 1st sg* **tíhlamaan**. *conj 3rd sg* **tíhlang**. *imp* **tíhlah**. *ptcpl* **tíhlang**.

**tíhlaweew** VTA chop s.o. down with an ax, cut s.o. down with an ax. *ind 1st sg* **ndíhlawaaw**, **ndíhlawa**. *ind 3rd sg* **wtihlawáawal**. *conj 3rd sg* **tíhla=waat**. *imp* **tíhlaw**.

**tíhtpan** VII be bitter in taste. *conj 3rd sg* **tíhtpang**. *ptcpl* **tíhtpang**.

**tihtpihtáasuw** VAI wave at people, wave for people. *ind 1st sg* **ndihtpihtáasi**, **ndihtpihtáasiim**. *conj 3rd sg* **tiht=pihtáasiit**. *imp* **tihtpihtáasiil**. *ptcpl* **tihtpihtáasiit**.

**tihtpíhtaweew** VTA wave to s.o., wave at s.o. *ind 1st sg* **ndihtpíhtawaaw**, **ndihtpíhtawa**. *ind 3rd sg* **wtihtpih=tawáawal**. *ind inv* **ndihtpíhtaakw**. *ind I-you* **ktihtpíhtool**. *conj 3rd sg* **tihtpíhtawaat**. *imp* **tihtpíhtaw**. *ptcpl* **tihtpíhtawaat**.

**tíhtpuw** VAI be waving, wave. *ind 1st sg* **ndíhtpi**, **ndíhtpiim**. *conj 3rd sg* **tíht=piit**. *imp* **tíhtpiil**. *ptcpl* **tíhtpiit**.

**tíhtŭyaak** NA ring. *pl* **tihtŭyáakak**. *poss* **ndihtŭyáakum**. *loc* **tihtŭyáakung**. *dimin* **tihtŭyáakush**. *obv* **tihtŭyáa=kal**.

**tíhtŭyaak** NI ring. *pl* **tihtŭyáakal**. *poss* **ndihtŭyáakum**. *loc* **tihtŭyáakung**. *dimin* **tihtŭyáakush**.

**tihtŭyaakhámeew** VAI wear a ring. *ind 1st sg* **ndihtŭyaakháma**, **ndihtŭ=yaakhámaam**. *conj 3rd sg* **tihtŭ=yaakhámaat**. *imp* **tihtŭyaakhámaal**. *ptcpl* **tihtŭyaakhámaat**.

**tóongapuw** VAI sit with one's legs open, sit with one's legs spread apart. *ind 1st sg* **ndóongapi**, **ndóongapiim**. *conj 3rd sg* **tóongapiit**. *imp* **tóonga=piil**. *ptcpl* **tóongapiit**. *See* **toongoh=kwéepuw**.

**toongchéexiin** VAI lie sprawled, lie spread out, lie flat. *ind 1st sg* **ndoong=chéexiin**, **ndoongchéexi**. *conj 3rd sg* **toongchéexiing**. *ptcpl* **toongchée=xiing**.

**toongchéextoow** VTI2 leave s.t. open *(as a door)*. *ind 1st sg* **ndoongchéex=toon**. *ind 3rd sg* **wtoongchéextoon**. *conj 1st sg* **toongcheextáwaan**. *conj 3rd sg* **toongchéextaakw**. *imp* **toong=chéextool**. *ptcpl* **toongchéextaakw**.

**toongchéexŭmeew** VTA leave s.t. animate open. *ind 1st sg* **ndoongchée=xŭmaaw**, **ndoongchéexŭma**. *ind 3rd sg* **wtoongcheexŭmáawal**. *ind inv* **ndoongchéexŭmukw**. *ind I-you* **ktoongchéexŭmul**. *conj 3rd sg* **toongchéexŭmaat**. *imp* **toongchée=xum**. *ptcpl* **toongchéexŭmaat**.

**toongchéexun** VII lie sprawled, lie spread out, lie flat. *conj 3rd sg* **toong=chéexung**. *ptcpl* **toongchéexung**.

**toongiikáapawuw** VAI stand with one's legs open, stand with one's legs spread apart. *ind 1st sg* **ndoongii=káapawi**, **ndoongiikáapawiim**. *conj 3rd sg* **toongiikáapawiit**. *imp* **toon=giikáapawiil**. *ptcpl* **toongiikáapa=wiit**.

**toongiingwéexiin** VAI have one's eyes open *(especially of a dead person)*. *ind 1st sg* **ndoongiingwéexiin**,

**ndoongiingwéexi**. *conj 3rd sg* **toon=giingwéexiing**. *ptcpl* **toongiingwée=xiing**.

**toongíixiin** VAI be spread out, have one's legs open. *ind 1st sg* **ndoongíixiin**, **ndoongíixi**. *conj 3rd sg* **toongíixiing**. *ptcpl* **toongíixiing**.

**toongíixun** VII be spread out, be open *(as sole of shoe flapping)*; be open, be apart *(as a shirt)*. *conj 3rd sg* **toongíixung**. *ptcpl* **toongíixung**.

**toongíhleew** VII open up, come open. *conj 3rd sg* **toongíhlaak**. *ptcpl* **toongíhlaak**.

**toongkaatéexiin** VAI have one's legs spread apart. *ind 1st sg* **ndoongkaa=téexiin**, **ndoongkaatéexi**. *conj 3rd sg* **toongkaatéexiing**. *imp* **toongkaa=téexiil**. *ptcpl* **toongkaatéexiing**.

**toongohkwéepuw** VAI sit with one's legs open, sit with one's legs spread apart. *ind 1st sg* **ndoongohkwéepi**, **ndoon=gohkwéepiim**. *conj 3rd sg* **toongoh=kwéepiit**. *imp* **toongohkwéepiil**. *ptcpl* **toongohkwéepiit**. *See* **tóonga=puw**.

**toongtoonéexiin** VAI have one's mouth open. *ind 1st sg* **ndoongtoonéexiin**, **ndoongtoonéexi**. *conj 3rd sg* **toong=toonéexiing**. *imp* **toongtoonéexiil**. *ptcpl* **toongtoonéexiing**.

**tóhkiiw** VAI-S wake up. *ind 1st sg* **ndóhki**, **ndóhkiim**. *conj 3rd sg* **tóhkiit**. *imp* **tóhkiil**. *ptcpl* **tóhkiit**.

**tohkíiheew** VTA wake s.o. up. *ind 1st sg* **ndohkíihaaw**, **ndohkíiha**. *ind 3rd sg* **wtohkiiháawal**. *ind inv* **ndohkíi=hukw**. *ind I-you* **ktohkíihul**. *conj 3rd sg* **tohkíihaat**. *imp* **tóhkiih**. *ptcpl* **tohkíihaat**.

**tohkíimeew** VTA wake s.o. up by calling to them. **Akwáawu kwéek áa ktoh=kíimkwun.** 'Anything can wake you up.' *ind 1st sg* **ndohkíimaaw**, **ndoh=kíima**. *ind 3rd sg* **wtohkiimáawal**. *ind inv* **ndohkíimukw**. *ind I-you* **ktohkíimul**. *conj 3rd sg* **tohkíimaat**. *imp* **tóhkiim**. *ptcpl* **tohkíimaat**.

**tohkíhleew** VAI wake up. *ind 1st sg* **ndohkíhla**, **ndohkíhlaam**. *conj 3rd sg* **tohkíhlaat**. *imp* **tohkíhlaal**. *ptcpl* **tohkíhlaat**.

**tóhkŭneew** VTA wake s.o. up *(using the hands)*. *ind 1st sg* **ndóhkŭnaaw**, **ndóhkŭna**. *ind 3rd sg* **wtohkŭnáa=wal**. *ind inv* **ndóhkŭnukw**. *ind I-you* **któhkŭnul**. *conj 3rd sg* **tóhkŭnaat**. *imp* **tóhkun**. *ptcpl* **tóhkŭnaat**.

**tohpalóhkeew** VAI do a lot of work, work a lot. *ind 1st sg* **ndohpalóhke**, **ndohpalóhkeem**. *conj 3rd sg* **tohpa=lóhkeet**. *imp* **tohpalóhkeel**. *ptcpl* **tohpalóhkeet**.

**tohphéewasuw** VAI carry a big load. *ind 1st sg* **ndohphéewasi**, **ndohphéewa=siim**. *conj 3rd sg* **tohphéewasiit**. *imp* **tohphéewasiil**. *ptcpl* **tohphéewasiit**.

**tohpi-** PV a lot, lots. **Tóhpi-léexeel!** 'Take a deep breath.' *ptcpl* **tóhpi-**. *See* **tohpu-**.

**tohpshamóoleew** VTA pile up a lot of s.t. animate, pile s.t. animate up high. *ind 1st sg* **ndohpshamóolaaw**, **ndohp=shamóola**. *ind 3rd sg* **wtohpsham=ooláawal**. *ind inv* **ndohpshamóo=lukw**. *ind I-you* **ktohpshamóolul**. *conj 3rd sg* **tohpshamóolaat**. *imp* **tohpshámool**. *ptcpl* **tohpshamóo=laat**.

**tohpshamóotoow** VTI2 pile up a lot of s.t., pile s.t. up high. *ind 1st sg* **ndohp=shamóotoon**. *ind 3rd sg* **wtohp=shamóotoon**. *conj 1st sg* **tohpsham=óotawaan**. *conj 3rd sg* **tohpshamóo=taakw**. *imp* **tohpshamóotool**. *ptcpl* **tohpshamóotaakw**.

**tohpshámuw** VAI be piled high *(s.t. animate)*. *conj 3rd sg* **tohpshámwiit**. *ptcpl* **tohpshámwiit**.

**tohpshámuw** VII be piled high. *conj 3rd sg* **tohpshámwiik**. *ptcpl* **tohpshám=wiik**.

**tohpu-** PV a lot, lots. *informal.* **Tóhpu-mŭnéew.** 'He had too much to drink.'; **Ndóhpu-kwúndam.** 'I swallowed too much.' *ptcpl* **tóhpu-**. *See* **tohpi-**.

**tóhpun** VII be frost. *conj 3rd sg* **tóhpung**. *ptcpl* **tóhpung**.

**tohtoongtóoneew** VAI yawn. *ind 1st sg* **ndohtoongtóone, ndohtoongtóo=neem**. *conj 3rd sg* **tohtoongtóoneet**. *ptcpl* **tohtoongtóoneet**.

**tpuskhíikan** NI something used for measuring, ruler, measuring tape, measuring stick. *pl* **tpuskhíikanal**. *poss* **ndupuskhíikan**. *loc* **tpuskhíi=kanung**. *dimin* **chpushkhíikanush**.

**tpuskhíikeew** VAI measure things. *ind 1st sg* **ndupuskhíike, ndupuskhíi=keem**. *conj 3rd sg* **tpuskhíikeet**. *imp* **tpuskhíikeel**. *ptcpl* **teepuskhíikeet**.

**tpúskhweew** VTA measure the size of s.o, measure the height of s.o., measure s.t. animate out, fill s.t. animate to the brim *(as a pail)*. *ind 1st sg* **ndup=úskhwaaw, ndupúskhwa**. *ind 3rd sg* **wtupuskhwáawal**. *ind inv* **ndupúsk=hookw**. *ind I-you* **ktupúskhool**. *conj 3rd sg* **tpúskhwaat**. *imp* **tpúskhwaw**. *ptcpl* **teepúskhwaat**.

**tpúskhwam** VTI1A measure the size of s.t., measure the height of s.t., measure s.t. out. *ind 1st sg* **ndupusk=hwámun**. *ind 3rd sg* **wtupuskhwám=un**. *conj 1st sg* **tpuskhwámaan**. *conj 3rd sg* **tpúskhwang**. *imp* **tpúskhwah**. *ptcpl* **teepúskhwang**.

**tpuskhwúpeew** VAIO fill s.t. to the brim with water. *ind 1st sg* **ndupusk=hwúpeen**. *ind 3rd sg* **wtupuskhwúp=een**. *conj 3rd sg* **tpuskhwúpeet**. *imp* **tpuskhwúpeel**. *ptcpl* **teepuskhwúp=eet**.

**tpuskŭwáapŭweew** VAIO make s.t. level with the top of a container *(of liquids)*. *ind 1st sg* **ndupuskŭwáapŭ=ween**. *ind 3rd sg* **wtupuskŭwáapŭ=ween**. *conj 3rd sg* **tpuskŭwáapŭ=weet**. *imp* **tpuskŭwáapŭweel**. *ptcpl* **teepuskŭwáapŭweet**.

**tpuskŭwáapŭweew** VII contain liquid level with the top *(of containers)*; be level with the top of a container *(of liquids)*. *conj 3rd sg* **tpuskŭwáapŭ=week**. *ptcpl* **teepuskŭwáapŭweek**.

**tpuskŭwáhleew** VTA place s.t. animate level with the top of container. *ind 1st sg* **ndupuskŭwáhlaaw, ndupuskŭ=wáhla**. *ind 3rd sg* **wtupuskŭwahláa=wal**. *ind inv* **ndupuskŭwáhlukw**. *ind I-you* **ktupuskŭwáhlul**. *conj 3rd sg* **tpuskŭwáhlaat**. *imp* **tpúskŭwahl**. *ptcpl* **teepuskŭwáhlaat**.

**tpuskŭwáhteew** VII be full to the brim, be level with the top *(of non-liquids)*. *conj 3rd sg* **tpuskŭwáhteek**. *ptcpl* **teepuskŭwáhteek**.

**tpuskŭwáhtoow** VTI2 place s.t. level with the top of container. *ind 1st sg* **ndupuskŭwáhtoon**. *ind 3rd sg* **wtup=uskŭwáhtoon**. *conj 1st sg* **tpuskŭ=wáhtawaan**. *conj 3rd sg* **tpuskŭ=wáhtaakw**. *imp* **tpuskŭwáhtool**. *ptcpl* **teepuskŭwáhtaakw**.

**tpuskŭwápuw** VAI be level with the top *(s.t. animate, of non-liquids)*. *ind 1st sg* **ndupuskŭwápi, ndupuskŭwáp=iim**. *conj 3rd sg* **tpuskŭwápiit**. *ptcpl* **teepuskŭwápiit**.

**tpuskŭwíixtoow** VTI2 fit s.t. level, fit s.t. evenly. **Ndupuskŭwíixtoon ndaa=kongwéepuy.** 'My hat is on evenly.' *ind 1st sg* **ndupuskuwíixtoon**. *ind 3rd sg* **wtupuskŭwíixtoon**. *conj 1st sg* **tpuskŭwiixtáwaan**. *conj 3rd sg* **tpuskŭwíixtaakw**. *imp* **tpuskŭwíix=tool**. *ptcpl* **teepuskŭwíixtaakw**.

**tpuskŭwíixun** VII be level, be on level, be even, be on even; be even with something. *conj 3rd sg* **tpuskŭwíi=xung**. *ptcpl* **teepuskŭwíixung**.

**tpuskŭwúpeew** VAI contain liquid level with the top *(s.t. animate)*; be liquid level to the top of container. *ind 1st sg* **ndpuskŭwúpe**, **ndpuskŭwúpeem**. *conj 3rd sg* **tpuskŭwúpeet**. *ptcpl* **teepuskŭwúpeet**.

**tpuskŭwúpeew** VAIO fill s.t. level to the top *(of liquids)*. *ind 1st sg* **ndupus=kŭwúpeen**. *ind 3rd sg* **wtupuskŭ=wúpeen**. *conj 3rd sg* **tpuskŭwúpeet**. *imp* **tpuskŭwúpeel**. *ptcpl* **teepuskŭ=wúpeet**.

**tpuskŭwúpeew** VII contain liquid level with the top, be liquid level to the top of container. *conj 3rd sg* **tpuskŭ=wúpeek**. *ptcpl* **teepuskŭwúpeek**.

**tputaawáhkuy** NI collectively held land, land that belongs to the band. *loc* **tputaawáhkiing**.

**tputáawii** PC in common, collective, owned by the band. **Tpútaawii ndáaktul.** 'Doctor for everyone; doctor hired by Indian Affairs.'; **Tputáa=wii éenda-maawéhlaang.** 'The community hall.'

**tputoohaaléewak** VTA gang up on s.o. *subject usually plural. ind 1st sg* **nduptoohaaláawŭna**. *ind 3rd sg* **wtuptoohaalaawáawal**. *ind inv* **nduptoohálkook**. *conj 3rd sg* **tput=oohaaláhtiit**. *imp* **tputoohálooh**. *ptcpl* **teeptoohaaláhtiit**.

**tŭlúmb** NI Jew's harp. *pl* **tŭlúmbal**. *poss* **ndulúmbum**. *dimin* **tŭlúmbush**. *From Dutch.*

**tŭlumbhámeew** VAI play Jew's harp. *ind 1st sg* **ndulumbháma**, **ndulumb=hámaam**. *conj 3rd sg* **tŭlumbhám=aat**. *imp* **tŭlumbhámaal**. *ptcpl* **tŭlumbhámaat**.

**tŭmaháhkweew** VAI chop with an ax, cut down trees, trim trees. *ind 1st sg* **ndumháhkwe**, **ndumháhkweem**. *conj 3rd sg* **tŭmaháhkweet**. *imp* **tŭmaháhkweel**. *ptcpl* **teemháh=kweet**. *intensive reduplication* **tàtŭmaháhkweew**.

**tŭmáham** VTI 1A cut s.t. down, chop s.t. off, cut s.t. down, cut s.t. off. *ind 1st sg* **ndumhámun**. *ind 3rd sg* **wtum=hámun**. *conj 1st sg* **tŭmáhŭmaan**. *conj 3rd sg* **tŭmáhang**. *imp* **tŭmáhih**. *ptcpl* **téemhang**.

**tŭmáheew** VTA chop s.t. animate down, chop s.t. animate off, cut s.t. animate down, cut s.t. animate off. *ind 1st sg* **ndúmhaaw**, **ndúmha**. *ind 3rd sg* **wtumháawal**. *ind inv* **ndúmhookw**. *ind I-you* **ktúmhool**. *conj 3rd sg* **tŭmáhaat**. *imp* **tŭmáh**. *ptcpl* **téem=haat**. *intensive reduplication* **wtatŭ=maháawal**.

**tŭmahíikan** NI ax. *pl* **tŭmahíikanal**. *poss* **ndumhíikan**. *loc* **tumahíika=nung**. *dimin* **chŭmahíikanush**.

**tŭmáhkwat** VII be cut off, be severed. *conj 3rd sg* **tŭmáhkwahk**. *ptcpl* **tee=máhkwahk**.

**tŭmáhkweew** VAI cut down trees. *ind 1st sg* **ndumáhkwe**, **ndumáhkweem**. *conj 3rd sg* **tŭmáhkweet**. *ptcpl* **tee=máhkweet**.

**tŭmáhkwsuw** VAI be cut off *(of trees)*. *ind 1st sg* **ndumáhkwsi**, **ndumáhk=wsiim**. *conj 3rd sg* **tŭmáhkwsiit**. *ptcpl* **teemáhkwsiit**.

**tŭmáhkwsheew** VTA cut s.t. animate off, cut a limb off s.t. animate *(of trees)*. *ind 1st sg* **ndumáhkwshaaw**, **ndum=áhkwsha**. *ind 3rd sg* **wtumahkw=sháawal**. *ind inv* **ndumáhkwshookw**. *ind I-you* **ktumáhkwshool**. *conj 3rd sg* **tŭmáhkwshaat**. *imp* **tŭmáh=kwush**. *ptcpl* **teemáhkwshaat**.

**tŭmahkwsháasuw** VII be cut off, be severed. *conj 3rd sg* **tŭmahk=wsháasiik**. *ptcpl* **teemahkwsháasiik**.

**tŭmáhkwshum** VTI 1B cut s.t. off *(of something wooden)*. *ind 1st sg* **ndum=ahkwshúmun**. *ind 3rd sg* **wtumahk=wshúmun**. *conj 1st sg* **tŭmahk=wshúmaan**. *conj 3rd sg* **tŭmáhk=wshung**. *imp* **tŭmáhkwshih**. *ptcpl* **teemáhkwshung**.

**tŭmáhookw** VAI be cut down, be knocked over, be broken off *(s.t. animate)*. **Tŭmáhookw míhtukw.** 'The tree was knocked over, broken off.' *ind 1st sg* **ndúmhookw**. *conj 3rd sg* **tŭmahóokwuk**. *ptcpl* **teemhóokwuk**.

**tŭmaskhíikan** NI scythe. *pl* **tŭmaskhíi=kanal**. *poss* **ndumaskhíikan**. *loc* **tumaskhíikanung**. *dimin* **chŭmash=khíikanush**.

**tŭmaskhíikeew** VAI cut weeds *(with a scythe)*; cut with a scythe. *ind 1st sg* **ndumaskhíike, ndumaskhíikeem**. *conj 3rd sg* **tŭmaskhíikeet**. *imp* **tŭ=maskhíikeel**. *ptcpl* **teemaskhíikeet**.

**tŭmáxookw** VAI be blown over by the wind, be broken off by the wind, be severed by the wind *(s.t. animate)*. *ind 1st sg* **ndúmxookw**. *conj 3rd sg* **tŭmaxóokwuk**. *ptcpl* **teemxóokwuk**.

**tŭmáxun** VII be blown over by the wind, be broken off by the wind, be severed by the wind. *conj 3rd sg* **tŭmáxung**. *ptcpl* **téemxung**.

**tùmétoos** NA tomato. *pl* **tùmètóosak**. *poss* **ndùmètóosum**. *loc* **tùmètóo=sung**. *dimin* **chùmèchóoshush**. *obv* **tùmètóosal**. *From English* tomatoes.

**tŭmiikwéeheew** VTA break s.o.'s neck, sever s.o. at the neck, break s.o. at the neck, cut s.o. off at the neck. *ind 1st sg* **ndumiikwéehaaw, ndumiikwée=ha**. *ind 3rd sg* **wtumiikweeháawal**. *ind inv* **ndumiikwéehukw**. *ind I-you* **ktumiikwéehul**. *conj 3rd sg* **tŭmii=kwéehaat**. *imp* **tŭmíikweeh**. *ptcpl* **teemiikwéehaat**.

**tŭmiikwéeneew** VTA break s.o.'s neck *(using the hands)*. *ind 1st sg* **ndumii=kwéenaaw, ndumiikwéena**. *ind 3rd sg* **wtumiikweenáawal**. *ind inv* **ndumiikwéenukw**. *ind I-you* **ktumii=kwéenul**. *conj 3rd sg* **tŭmiikwéenaat**. *imp* **tŭmíikween**. *ptcpl* **teemiikwée=naat**.

**tŭmiikwéexiin** VAI have a broken neck. *ind 1st sg* **ndumiikwéexiin, ndumii=kwéexi**. *conj 3rd sg* **tŭmiikwéexiing**. *ptcpl* **teemiikwéexiing**.

**tŭmiikwéexŭmeew** VTA drop s.o. and sever their neck. *ind 1st sg* **ndumii=kwéexŭmaaw, ndumiikwéexŭma**. *ind 3rd sg* **wtumiikweexŭmáawal**. *ind inv* **ndumiikwéexŭmukw**. *ind I-you* **ktumiikwéexŭmul**. *conj 3rd sg* **tŭmiikwéexŭmaat**. *imp* **tŭmiikwée=xum**. *ptcpl* **teemiikwéexŭmaat**.

**tŭmiikwehtéeheew** VTA hit and break s.o.'s neck. *ind 1st sg* **ndumiikweh=téehaaw, ndumiikwehtéeha**. *ind 3rd sg* **wtumiikwehteeháawal**. *ind inv* **ndumiikwehtéehookw**. *ind I-you* **ktumiikwehtéehool**. *conj 3rd sg* **tŭmiikwehtéehaat**. *imp* **tŭmiikwéh=teeh**. *ptcpl* **teemiikwehtéehaat**.

**tŭmíixtoow** VTI2 have s.t. drop and break off, have s.t. drop and be severed. *ind 1st sg* **ndumíixtoon**. *ind 3rd sg* **wtumíixtoon**. *conj 1st sg* **tŭmiix=táwaan**. *conj 3rd sg* **tŭmíixtaakw**. *imp* **tŭmíixtool**. *ptcpl* **teemíixtaakw**.

**tŭmíixun** VII fall and break off, be severed. *conj 3rd sg* **tŭmíixung**. *ptcpl* **teemíixung**.

**tŭmíhleew** VAI break off *(s.t. animate)*. *ind 1st sg* **ndumíhla, ndumíhlaam**. *conj 3rd sg* **tŭmíhlaat**. *ptcpl* **teemíh=laat**.

**tŭmíhleew** VII break off. **Wtaláawan tŭmíhleew.** 'His cane broke off.' *conj 3rd sg* **tŭmíhlaak**. *ptcpl* **teemíhlaak**.

**tŭmihtéeham** VTI1A hit and sever s.t., cut s.t. off. *ind 1st sg* **ndumihtéehŭ=mun**. *ind 3rd sg* **wtumihtéehŭmun**. *conj 1st sg* **tŭmihtéehŭmaan**. *conj 3rd sg* **tŭmihtéehang**. *imp* **tŭmih=téehah**. *ptcpl* **teemihtéehang**.

**tŭmihtéeheew** VTA hit and sever s.t. animate, cut s.t. animate off. *ind 1st sg* **ndumihtéehaaw, ndumihtéeha**. *ind 3rd sg* **wtumihteeháawal**. *conj 3rd sg* **tŭmihtéehaat**. *imp* **tŭmíhteeh**.

*ptcpl* **teemihtéehaat**.

**tŭmukáateew** VAI have a cut-off leg, have one's leg severed. *ind 1st sg* **ndumkáata**, **ndumkáataam**. *conj 3rd sg* **tŭmukáataat**. *ptcpl* **teemkáa=taat**.

**tŭmúneew** VTA break s.o., sever s.o. *(using the hands)*. *ind 1st sg* **ndúmŭ=naaw**, **ndúmŭna**. *ind 3rd sg* **wtumŭ=náawal**. *ind inv* **ndúmŭnukw**. *ind I-you* **ktúmŭnul**. *conj 3rd sg* **tŭmún=aat**. *imp* **tŭmún**. *ptcpl* **téemŭnaat**.

**tŭmúnum** VTI 1B break s.t., sever s.t. *(using the hands)*. *ind 1st sg* **ndumŭ=númun**. *ind 3rd sg* **wtumŭnúmun**. *conj 1st sg* **tŭmúnŭmaan**. *conj 3rd sg* **tŭmúnung**. *imp* **tŭmúnih**. *ptcpl* **téemŭnung**.

**tŭmúsheew** VTA cut s.t. animate, cut and sever s.t. animate. *ind 1st sg* **ndúm=shaaw**, **ndúmsha**. *ind 3rd sg* **wtum=sháawal**. *ind inv* **ndúmshookw**. *ind I-you* **ktúmshool**. *conj 3rd sg* **tŭ=múshaat**. *imp* **tŭmúsh**. *ptcpl* **téem=shaat**.

**tŭmushahkwáakan** NI saw, hand saw. *pl* **tŭmushahkwáakanal**. *poss* **ndumshahkwáakan**. *loc* **tŭmush=ahkwáakanung**. *dimin* **chŭmushah=kwáakanush**.

**tŭmusháhkweew** VAI saw timber, cut logs. *ind 1st sg* **ndumsháhkwe**, **ndumsháhkweem**. *conj 3rd sg* **tŭ=musháhkweet**. *imp* **tŭmusháhkweel**. *ptcpl* **teemsháhkweet**. *intensive reduplication* **tàtŭmusháhkweew**.

**tŭmushíikeew** VAI cut things, cut grass. *ind 1st sg* **ndumshíike**, **ndumshíi=keem**. *conj 3rd sg* **tŭmushíikeet**. *imp* **tŭmushíikeel**. *ptcpl* **teemshíikeet**.

**tŭmúshum** VTI 1B saw s.t., cut and sever s.t. *ind 1st sg* **ndumshúmun**. *ind 3rd sg* **wtumshúmun**. *conj 1st sg* **tŭ=múshŭmaan**. *conj 3rd sg* **tŭmúsh=ung**. *imp* **tŭmúshih**. *ptcpl* **téem=shung**.

**túndeew** NI fire. *pl* **tundéewal**. *poss* **ndundéehum**. *loc* **tundéewung**.

**tundeewaatpùníikan** NI train. *pl* **tun=deewaatpùníikanal**. *loc* **tundee=waatpùníikanung**.

**tundeewháweew** VTA light a fire for s.o., make a fire for s.o. *ind 1st sg* **ndun=deewháwaaw**, **ndundeewháwa**. *ind 3rd sg* **wtundeewhawáawal**. *ind inv* **ndundéewhaakw**. *ind I-you* **ktun=déewhool**. *conj 3rd sg* **tundeewháw=aat**. *imp* **tundéewhaw**. *ptcpl* **teen=deewháwaat**.

**tundéewheew** VAI make a fire. *ind 1st sg* **ndundéewhe**, **ndundéewheem**. *conj 3rd sg* **tundéewheet**. *imp* **tundéew=heel**. *ptcpl* **teendéewheet**.

**tùpáaheew** VAIO spin and throw s.t., throw and spin s.t., twirl s.t. around. **Néhtaa-píchiit wtupaahéenal áng neenáxkwal.** 'A good pitcher throws the ball with a spin to it.' *ind 1st sg* **ndupáaheen**. *ind 3rd sg* **wtupáaheen**. *conj 3rd sg* **tùpáaheet**. *imp* **tùpáa=heel**. *ptcpl* **tùpáaheet**.

**tùpáhkhweew** VTA wind s.t. animate *(as a clock)*; crank s.t. animate *(as a car)*. *ind 1st sg* **ndupáhkhwaaw**, **ndup=áhkhwa**. *ind 3rd sg* **wtupahkhwáa=wal**. *ind inv* **ndupáhkhookw**. *ind I-you* **ktupáhkhool**. *conj 3rd sg* **tùp=áhkhwaat**. *imp* **tùpáhkhwaw**. *ptcpl* **tùpáhkhwaat**.

**tùpáhkhwam** VTI 1A turn s.t., screw s.t., wind s.t., drive s.t. in *(of screws)*. *ind 1st sg* **ndupahkhwámun**. *ind 3rd sg* **wtupahkhwámun**. *conj 1st sg* **tùp=ahkhwámaan**. *conj 3rd sg* **tùpáhk=hwang**. *imp* **tùpáhkhwah**. *ptcpl* **tùpáhkhwang**.

**tùpambíileew** VTA tie s.o. up. *ind 1st sg* **ndupambíilaaw**, **ndupambíila**. *ind 3rd sg* **wtupambiiláawal**. *ind inv* **ndupambíilukw**. *ind I-you* **ktupam=bíilul**. *conj 3rd sg* **tùpambíilaat**. *imp* **tùpámbiil**. *ptcpl* **tùpambíilaat**.

**tùpambíisuw** VAI be tied up *(s.t. animate). ind 1st sg* **ndupambíisi**, **ndupambíisiim**. *conj 3rd sg* **tùpam=bíisiit**. *ptcpl* **tùpambíisiit**.

**tùpambíisuw** VII be tied up. *conj 3rd sg* **tùpambíisiik**. *ptcpl* **tùpambíisiik**.

**tùpámbtoow** VTI2 wrap s.t. around, tie s.t. up. *ind 1st sg* **ndupámbtoon**. *ind 3rd sg* **wtupámbtoon**. *conj 1st sg* **tùpambtáwaan**. *conj 3rd sg* **tùp=ámbtaakw**. *imp* **tùpámbtool**. *ptcpl* **tùpámbtaakw**.

**tùpchéhleew** VAI roll, roll around. *ind 1st sg* **ndupchéhla**, **ndupchéhlaam**. *conj 3rd sg* **tùpchéhlaat**. *imp* **tùp=chéhlaal**. *ptcpl* **tùpchéhlaat**. *intensive reduplication* **tàtupchéhleew**.

**tùpchéhleew** VII roll, roll around. *conj 3rd sg* **tùpchéhlaak**. *ptcpl* **tùpchéh=laak**.

**tùpháaleew** VTA wrap s.o. up. *ind 1st sg* **ndupháalaaw**, **ndupháala**. *ind 3rd sg* **wtuphaaláawal**. *ind inv* **ndup=háalukw**. *ind I-you* **ktupháalul**. *conj 3rd sg* **tùpháalaat**. *imp* **túphaal**. *ptcpl* **tùpháalaat**.

**tùpháasuw** VAI be rolled up, be tied up *(s.t. animate). ind 1st sg* **ndupháasi**, **ndupháasiim**. *conj 3rd sg* **tùpháasiit**. *ptcpl* **tùpháasiit**.

**tùpháasuw** VII be rolled up, be tied up. *conj 3rd sg* **tùpháasiik**. *ptcpl* **tùp=háasiik**.

**túpham** VTI1A wrap s.t. around something, roll s.t. up. *ind 1st sg* **ndup=hámun**. *ind 3rd sg* **wtuphámun**. *conj 1st sg* **tùphámaan**. *conj 3rd sg* **túp=hang**. *imp* **túphah**. *ptcpl* **túphang**.

**túpheew** VTA wrap s.t. animate around something, roll s.o. up, tie s.o. up. *ind 1st sg* **ndúphaaw**, **ndúpha**. *ind 3rd sg* **wtupháawal**. *ind inv* **ndúphookw**. *ind I-you* **ktúphool**. *conj 3rd sg* **túphaat**. *imp* **túphaw**. *ptcpl* **túphaat**.

**tùpiinjkweeyáaheew** VAIO roll s.t around. *ind 1st sg* **ndupiinjkwee=yáaheen**. *ind 3rd sg* **wtupiinjkwee=yáaheen**. *conj 3rd sg* **tùpiinjkwee=yáaheet**. *imp* **tùpiinjkweeyáaheel**. *ptcpl* **tùpiinjkweeyáaheet**.

**tùpiinjkwéhleew** VAI roll over, roll around, roll along *(s.t. animate). ind 1st sg* **ndupiinjkwéhla**, **ndupiinj=kwéhlaam**. *conj 3rd sg* **tùpiinj=kwéhlaat**. *imp* **tùpiinjkwéhlaal**. *ptcpl* **tùpiinjkwéhlaat**.

**tùpiinjkwéhleew** VII roll over, roll around, roll along. *conj 3rd sg* **tùp=iinjkwéhlaak**. *ptcpl* **tùpiinjkwéh=laak**.

**tùpíixiin** VAI turn over. *ind 1st sg* **ndup=íixiin**, **ndupíixi**. *conj 3rd sg* **tùpíi=xiing**. *ptcpl* **tùpíixiing**.

**tùpíixtoow** VTI2 turn s.t. around, turn s.t. over. *ind 1st sg* **ndupíixtoon**. *ind 3rd sg* **wtupíixtoon**. *conj 1st sg* **tùp=iixtáwaan**. *conj 3rd sg* **tùpíixtaakw**. *imp* **tùpíixtool**. *ptcpl* **tùpíixtaakw**.

**tùpíixŭmeew** VTA turn s.o. around, turn s.o. over. *ind 1st sg* **ndupíixŭmaaw**, **ndupíixŭma**. *ind 3rd sg* **wtupiixŭ=máawal**. *ind inv* **ndupíixŭmukw**. *ind I-you* **ktupíixŭmul**. *conj 3rd sg* **tùpíixŭmaat**. *imp* **tùpíixum**. *ptcpl* **tùpíixŭmaat**.

**tùpíhleew** VAI go around, rotate, spin *(s.t. animate). ind 1st sg* **ndupíhla**, **ndupíhlaam**. *conj 3rd sg* **tùpíhlaat**. *ptcpl* **tùpíhlaat**.

**tùpíhleew** VII go around, rotate, spin. *conj 3rd sg* **tùpíhlaak**. *ptcpl* **tùpíh=laak**.

**tùpihtéeham** VTI1A hit s.t. and make it go around, hit s.t. and make it spin around. *ind 1st sg* **ndupihtéehŭmun**. *ind 3rd sg* **wtupihtéehŭmun**. *conj 1st sg* **tùpihtéehŭmaan**. *conj 3rd sg* **tùpihtéehang**. *imp* **tùpihtéehih**. *ptcpl* **tùpihtéehang**.

**tùpihtéeheew** VTA hit s.o. and make them go around, hit s.o. and make them spin around. *ind 1st sg* **ndupih=**

**téehaaw**, **ndupihtéeha**. *ind 3rd sg* **wtupihteehaawal**. *ind inv* **ndupih=téehookw**. *ind I-you* **ktupihtéehool**. *conj 3rd sg* **tùpihtéehaat**. *imp* **tùpíhteeh**. *ptcpl* **tùpihtéehaat**.

**túpŭneew** VTA turn s.o. around, crank s.t. animate *(using the hands)*. *ind 1st sg* **ndúpŭnaaw**, **ndúpŭna**. *ind 3rd sg* **wtupŭnáawal**. *ind inv* **ndúpŭnukw**. *ind I-you* **ktúpŭnul**. *conj 3rd sg* **túpŭnaat**. *imp* **túpun**. *ptcpl* **túp=ŭnaat**.

**tùpŭníikan** NI crank, handle for turning, hand grinder. *pl* **tùpŭníikanal**. *poss* **ndupŭníikan**. *loc* **tùpŭníikanung**. *dimin* **tùpŭníikanush**.

**tùpŭníikeew** VAI turn a crank, crank things, turn things around. *ind 1st sg* **ndupŭníike**, **ndupŭníikeem**. *conj 3rd sg* **tùpŭníikeet**. *imp* **tùpŭníikeel**. *ptcpl* **tùpŭníikeet**.

**túpŭnum** VTI1B turn s.t. around, crank s.t. *(using the hands)*. *ind 1st sg* **ndupŭnúmun**. *ind 3rd sg* **wtupŭ=númun**. *conj 1st sg* **tùpŭnúmaan**. *conj 3rd sg* **túpŭnung**. *imp* **túpŭnih**. *ptcpl* **túpŭnung**.

**túpxookw** VAI be blown around by the wind, be spun around by the wind. *ind 1st sg* **ndúpxookw**. *conj 3rd sg* **tùpxóokwuk**. *ptcpl* **tùpxóokwuk**. *intensive reduplication* **tàtúpxookw**.

**túpxun** VII be blown around by the wind, be spun around by the wind. *conj 3rd sg* **túpxung**. *ptcpl* **túpxung**.

**txaaníhka** PC so many times. *with number particles to form numbers 16-19.* **Níishaash txaaníhka.** 'Seventeen.'; **Ngwútaash txaaníhka.** 'Sixteen.'

**txaapóxke** PC so many hundred. *with number particles to form numbers 600-900.* **Ngwútaash txaapóxke.** 'Six hundred.'

**txáhtakat** VII be so many pieces *(of something string-like).* **Ngwútaash txáhtakat.** 'Six pieces of string.' *conj 3rd sg* **txáhtakahk**. *ptcpl* **eendxáh=takahk**.

**txahtéewal** VII be so many there, be so many of them there. *usually plural; usually with number particle.* **Níi=shaash txahtéewal.** 'There are seven of them there.' *conj 3rd sg* **txáhteek**. *ptcpl* **eendxahtéekiil**.

**txalíhkeew** VAI take so many steps. **Ngwútaash txalíhkeew.** 'He took six steps.' *ind 1st sg* **ndundxalíhke**, **ndundxalíhkeem**. *conj 3rd sg* **txal=íhkeet**. *imp* **txalíhkeel**. *ptcpl* **eend=xalíhkeet**.

**txápŭwak** VAI be so many of them there. *usually plural; usually with number particle.* **Ngwútaash txápŭwak.** 'There's six of them there.' *ind 1st pl* **ndundxapíhna**. *conj 3rd sg* **txapíh=tiit**. *ptcpl* **eendxapíhtiit**.

**txatxooxwéewak** VAI be so many of them walking. *usually plural; usually with number particle.* **Ngwútaash ktund=xatxooxwéhna** 'We were walking in sixes.' *ind 1st pl* **ndundxatxooxwéh=na**. *conj 3rd sg* **txatxooxwéhtiit**. *ptcpl* **eendxatxooxwéhtiit**.

**txeekíixiin** VAI be in so many layers *(s.t. animate, of something sheet-like). usually with number particle.* **Ngwút=aash txeekíixiin.** 'It is in six layers.' *ind 1st sg* **ndundxeekíixiin**, **ndund=xeekíixi**. *conj 3rd sg* **txeekíixiing**. *ptcpl* **eendxeekíixiing**.

**txeekíixun** VII be so many layers *(of something sheet-like). usually with number particle.* **Xáash txeekíixun.** 'It is in eight layers.' *conj 3rd sg* **txeekíixung**. *ptcpl* **eendxeekíixung**.

**txéelook** VAI be so many of them, be so many of them in pairs *(s.t. animate). usually plural; usually with number particle.* **Xáash txéelook.** 'They are in eight pairs.' *ind 1st pl* **ndundxee=lóhna**. *conj 3rd sg* **txeelóhtiit**. *ptcpl* **eendxeelóhtiit**.

**txéeli** PC in groups of so many. **Ngwút=aash txéeli pihtawíixŭnool.** 'They're stacked in sixes.'; **Xáash txéelook.** 'They are in eight pairs.'

**txéeltool** VII be so many; be so many pairs. *usually plural; usually with number particle.* **Ngwútaash txéel=tool.** 'They are in six pairs.' *conj 3rd sg* **txéelihk**. *ptcpl* **eendxeelíhkiil**.

**txii-** PV so many, so many times. **Éenda-neewaaníhka -txíi-katúnge.** 'When he was fourteen years old.'; **Naala=naaníhka txíi-katúm.** 'He is fifteen years old.' *ptcpl* **éendxii-**. *See* **txu-**.

**txiináxke** PC multiple of twenty *(in counting). with number particle for numbers 60-90.* **Xáash txiináxke.** 'Eighty.'

**txíhlateew** VAI lack a commodity, run out of something. *ind 1st sg* **ndund=xíhlata, ndundxíhlataam**. *conj 3rd sg* **txíhlataat**. *ptcpl* **eendxíhlataat**.

**txíhleew** VAI be all gone *(s.t. animate).* **Txihléewak naméesak.** 'The fish are all gone.' *ind 1st sg* **ndundxíhla, ndundxíhlaam**. *conj 3rd sg* **txíhlaat**. *ptcpl* **eendxíhlaat**.

**txíhleew** VII be all gone. *conj 3rd sg* **txíhlaak**. *ptcpl* **eendxíhlaak**.

**txookwŭnáhkeew** VAI be gone for so many days. *usually with number particle.* **Ngwútaash ndundxookwŭ=náhke.** 'I was gone for six days.' *ind 1st sg* **ndundxookwŭnáhke, ndund=xookwŭnáhkeem**. *conj 3rd sg* **txoo=kwŭnáhkeet**. *ptcpl* **eendxookwŭ=náhkeet**.

**txóokwŭnii** PC so many days. *usually with number particle.* **Ngwútaash txóokwŭnii.** 'Six days.'

**txu-** PN so many, so many times. *informal.* **Nóolii txú-kíishooxkw.** 'Nine months.'

**txu-** PV so many, so many times. *informal.* **Neewaaníhka txú-katúngu.** 'Fourteen years old.'; **Ngwútaash ndúndxu-kundŭweewŭnáhke.** 'I was gone for six weeks.' *ptcpl* **éendxu-**. *See* **txii-**.

**txú-katúm** VAI be so many years of age *(with number preverb).* **Wíimbat ndúndxii-katúm.** 'I'm ten years old.' *ind 1st sg* **ndúndxii-katúm**. *conj 3rd sg* **txú-katúng**. *ptcpl* **éendxu-katúng**.

**txún** PC so many times. **Xáash txún.** 'Eight times.'

**txúnool** VII be so many of them. *usually plural; usually with number particle.* **Ngwútaash txúnool paxkshíikanal.** 'There are six knives.' *conj 3rd sg* **txúng**. *ptcpl* **eendxúngiil**.

**txúwak** VAI be so many *(s.t. animate). usually plural; usually with number particle.* **Ngwútaash txúwak lúnŭ=wak.** 'There are six men.'; **Wéenaa ngwutaapóxke txúwak.** 'There were almost one hundred of them.' *ind 1st pl* **ndundxíhna**. *conj 3rd sg* **txíhtiit**. *ptcpl* **eendxíhtiit**.

# U

nd**uloohíikan** NID my pointing finger. *pl* **nduloohíikanal**. *3rd poss* **wtuloohíi=kan**. *See* nd**aloohíikan**.

nd**ulŭnóohum** NAD my brother *(woman speaking). pl* **ndulŭnóohŭmak**. *3rd poss* **wtulŭnóohŭmal**.

**únd** VAI be so. **Áhwi-únd.** 'He's hard to get along with.' *ind 1st sg* **ndúnd**. *conj 3rd sg* **únduk**. *ptcpl* **éenduk**.

**uskwáandu** PC doorstep, threshold of house.

**uspáakchehl** VAI jump up, jump upwards. *ind 1st sg* **nduspáakchehl**. *conj 3rd sg* **uspaakchéhluk**. *imp* **uspaakchéhlih**. *ptcpl* **eespaakchéh=luk**.

**uspaalŭwéexiin** VAI have one's tail up. *ind 1st sg* **nduspaalŭwéexiin**, **ndus=paalŭwéexi**. *conj 3rd sg* **uspaalŭ=wéexiing**. *imp* **uspaalŭwéexiil**. *ptcpl* **eespaalŭwéexiing**.

**uspaawatóoheew** VAIO raise the price of s.t. *ind 1st sg* **nduspaawatóoheen**. *ind 3rd sg* **wtuspaawatóoheen**. *conj 3rd sg* **uspaawatóoheet**. *imp* **uspaa=watóoheel**. *ptcpl* **eespaawatóoheet**.

**uspaawúngeew** VAI go uphill *(on a road)*. *ind 1st sg* **nduspaawúnge**, **nduspaawúngeem**. *conj 3rd sg* **uspaawúngeet**. *imp* **uspaawúngeel**. *ptcpl* **eespaawúngeet**.

**uspáhkhweew** VTA raise s.t. animate up, lift s.t. animate up *(using a tool or instrument)*. *ind 1st sg* **nduspáhk=hwaaw**, **nduspáhkhwa**. *ind 3rd sg* **wtuspahkhwáawal**. *ind inv* **ndus=páhkhookw**. *ind I-you* **ktuspáhk=hool**. *conj 3rd sg* **uspáhkhwaat**. *imp* **uspáhkhwaw**. *ptcpl* **eespáhkhwaat**.

**uspáhkhwam** VTI1A raise s.t. up, lift s.t. up *(using a tool or instrument)*. *ind 1st sg* **nduspahkhwámun**. *ind 3rd sg* **wtuspahkhwámun**. *conj 1st sg* **us=pahkhwámaan**. *conj 3rd sg* **us=páhkhwang**. *imp* **uspáhkhwah**. *ptcpl* **eespáhkhwang**.

**uspakóosuw** VAI go up, climb up. *ind 1st sg* **nduspakóosi**, **nduspakóosiim**. *conj 3rd sg* **uspakóosiit**. *imp* **uspa=kóosiil**. *ptcpl* **eespakóosiit**.

**uspchéhleew** VAI drive up. *ind 1st sg* **nduspchéhla**, **nduspchéhlaam**. *conj 3rd sg* **uspchéhlaat**. *imp* **uspchéh=laal**. *ptcpl* **eespchéhlaat**.

**uspíikwsuw** VAI crawl up. *ind 1st sg* **nduspíikwsi**, **nduspíikwsiim**. *conj 3rd sg* **uspíikwsiit**. *imp* **uspíikwsiil**. *ptcpl* **eespíikwsiit**.

**uspiináxkeew** VAI raise one's hand. *ind 1st sg* **nduspiináxke**, **nduspiináx=keem**. *conj 3rd sg* **uspiináxkeet**. *imp* **uspiináxkeel**. *ptcpl* **eespiináxkeet**.

**uspíixiin** VAI be up, be in a raised position. *ind 1st sg* **nduspíixiin**, **nduspíi=xi**. *conj 3rd sg* **uspíixiing**. *ptcpl* **eespíixiing**.

**uspíixtoow** VTI2 lift s.t. up. *ind 1st sg* **nduspíixtoon**. *ind 3rd sg* **wtuspíix=toon**. *conj 1st sg* **uspiixtáwaan**. *conj 3rd sg* **uspíixtaakw**. *imp* **uspíixtool**. *ptcpl* **eespíixtaakw**.

**uspíixŭmeew** VTA lift s.o. up, lift s.t. animate up. *ind 1st sg* **nduspíixŭ=maaw**, **nduspíixŭma**. *ind 3rd sg* **wtuspiixŭmáawal**. *ind inv* **nduspíi=xŭmukw**. *ind I-you* **ktuspíixŭmul**. *conj 3rd sg* **uspíixŭmaat**. *imp* **uspíi=xum**. *ptcpl* **eespíixŭmaat**.

**uspíixun** VII be up, be in a raised position. *conj 3rd sg* **uspíixung**. *ptcpl* **eespíixung**.

**uspíhleew** VAI go up, come up, start to come up. *ind 1st sg* **nduspíhla**, **nduspíhlaam**. *conj 3rd sg* **uspíhlaat**. *imp* **uspíhlaal**. *ptcpl* **eespíhlaat**.

**uspíhleew** VII go up, come up, start to come up. *conj 3rd sg* **uspíhlaak**. *ptcpl* **eespíhlaak**.

**uspihtéexiin** VAI be thrown upwards, hit something and bounce, bounce. *ind 1st sg* **nduspihtéexiin**, **nduspihtéexi**. *conj 3rd sg* **uspihtéexiing**. *imp* **us=pihtéexiil**. *ptcpl* **eespihtéexiing**.

**uspihtéexŭmeew** VTA make s.o. bounce. *ind 1st sg* **nduspihtéexŭmaaw**, **ndus=pihtéexŭma**. *ind 3rd sg* **wtuspihtee=xŭmáawal**. *ind inv* **nduspihtéexŭ=mukw**. *ind I-you* **ktuspihtéexŭmul**. *conj 3rd sg* **uspihtéexŭmaat**. *imp* **us=pihtéexum**. *ptcpl* **eespihtéexŭmaat**.

**uspkáateew** VAI put one's leg up, raise one's legs. *ind 1st sg* **nduspkáate**,

**nduspkáateem**. *conj 3rd sg* **uspkáa=teet**. *imp* **uspkáateel**. *ptcpl* **eespkáa=teet**.

**uspkaatéepuw** VAI sit with one's legs up, raise one's legs while sitting. *ind 1st sg* **nduspkaatéepi**, **nduspkaa=téepiim**. *conj 3rd sg* **uspkaatéepiit**. *imp* **uspkaatéepiil**. *ptcpl* **eespkaa=téepiit**. *moderative reduplication* **aayuspkaatéepuw**. *See* **uspkaatée=wapuw**.

**uspkaatéewapuw** VAI sit with one's legs up, raise one's legs while sitting. *ind 1st sg* **nduspkaatéewapi**, **ndusp=kaatéewapiim**. *conj 3rd sg* **uspkaa=téewapiit**. *imp* **uspkaatéewapiil**. *ptcpl* **eespkaatéewapiit**. *See* **usp=kaatéepuw**.

**uspkaatéexiin** VAI raise one's legs up, have one's legs raised up. *ind 1st sg* **nduspkaatéexiin**, **nduspkaatéexi**. *conj 3rd sg* **uspkaatéexiing**. *imp* **uspkaatéexiil**. *ptcpl* **eespkaatée=xiing**.

**uspootŭyéexiin** VAI stick one's backside out, have one's backside sticking out. *ind 1st sg* **nduspootŭyéexiin**, **ndus=pootŭyéexi**. *conj 3rd sg* **uspootŭyée=xiing**. *imp* **uspootŭyéexiil**. *ptcpl* **eespootŭyéexiing**.

**uspóhkweew** VAI raise one's head, look up. *ind 1st sg* **nduspóhkwe**, **ndus=póhkweem**. *conj 3rd sg* **uspóhkweet**. *imp* **uspóhkweel**. *ptcpl* **eespóhkweet**.

**uspohkwéhleew** VAI lift up one's head. *ind 1st sg* **nduspohkwéhla**, **ndus=pohkwéhlaam**. *conj 3rd sg* **uspoh=kwéhlaat**. *imp* **uspohkwéhlaal**. *ptcpl* **eespohkwéhlaat**.

**uspsheetóonayeew** VAI stick one's lips up, have one's lips sticking out. *ind 1st sg* **nduspsheetóonaya**, **ndusp=sheetóonayaam**. *conj 3rd sg* **usp=sheetóonayaat**. *imp* **uspsheetóona=yaal**. *ptcpl* **eespsheetóonayaat**.

**usptáachihleew** VTA drag s.o. up. *ind 1st sg* **ndusptaachíhlaaw**, **ndusp=taachíhla**. *ind 3rd sg* **wtusptaachih=láawal**. *ind inv* **ndusptaachíhlukw**. *ind I-you* **ktusptaachíhlul**. *conj 3rd sg* **usptaachíhlaat**. *imp* **usptáachihl**. *ptcpl* **eesptaachíhlaat**.

**uspŭléeneew** VTA turn s.t. animate up *(of lanterns, of flames)*. *ind 1st sg* **nduspŭléenaaw**, **nduspŭléena**. *ind 3rd sg* **wtuspŭleenáawal**. *ind inv* **nduspŭléenukw**. *ind I-you* **ktuspŭ=léenul**. *conj 3rd sg* **uspŭléenaat**. *imp* **úspŭleen**. *ptcpl* **eespŭléenaat**.

**uspŭléenum** VTI1B turn s.t. up *(as a stove)*. *ind 1st sg* **nduspŭléenŭmun**. *ind 3rd sg* **wtuspŭléenŭmun**. *conj 1st sg* **uspŭléenŭmaan**. *conj 3rd sg* **uspŭléenung**. *imp* **uspŭléenih**. *ptcpl* **eespŭléenung**.

**úspŭneew** VTA lift s.o. up, make s.o. go up *(using the hands)*. *ind 1st sg* **ndúspŭnaaw**, **ndúspŭna**. *ind 3rd sg* **wtuspŭnáawal**. *ind inv* **ndúspŭnukw**. *ind I-you* **ktúspŭnul**. *conj 3rd sg* **úspŭnaat**. *imp* **úspun**. *ptcpl* **éespŭ=naat**.

**uspŭníikan** NI lifter, hook, something to lift with. *pl* **uspŭníikanal**. *poss* **nduspŭníikan**. *loc* **uspŭníikanung**. *dimin* **ushpŭníikanush**.

**úspŭnum** VTI1B lift s.t. up, make s.t. go up *(using the hands)*. *ind 1st sg* **nduspŭnúmun**. *ind 3rd sg* **wtuspŭ=númun**. *conj 1st sg* **uspŭnúmaan**. *conj 3rd sg* **úspŭnung**. *imp* **úspŭnih**. *ptcpl* **éespŭnung**.

**uspxéexiin** VAI raise one's ears, have one's ears raised. *ind 1st sg* **ndusp=xéexiin**, **nduspxéexi**. *conj 3rd sg* **uspxéexiing**. *imp* **uspxéexiil**. *ptcpl* **eespxéexiing**.

**úw** VAI say, say so. **Nún ná há níi nzíin.** 'That's what I'd say.' *ind 1st sg* **nzí**, **nzíim**. *conj 3rd sg* **íit**. *imp* **íil**. *ptcpl*

**éeyiit**.

**úw** VAIO say s.t. **Máh ngíish-íiwun.** 'I can't say it.' *ind 1st sg* **nzíin**. *ind 3rd sg* **wsíin**. *conj 3rd sg* **íit**. *imp* **íil**. *ptcpl* **éeyiit**.

# W

**wáak** PC and. **Nál wáak ndalŭmúsiin.** 'And then I left.'

**waakatéexun** VII be a winding road. *conj 3rd sg* **waakatéexung**. *ptcpl* **waakatéexung**.

**waakchéesuw** VAI have a bent shape, be bent, be curved *(s.t. animate)*. *ind 1st sg* **nŭwaakchéesi**, **nŭwaakchéesiim**. *conj 3rd sg* **waakchéesiit**. *ptcpl* **waakchéesiit**.

**waakchéeyeew** VII have a bent shape, be bent, be curved. **Waakchéeyeew ktaláawan.** 'Your cane is bent.' *conj 3rd sg* **waakchéeyeek**. *ptcpl* **waak=chéeyeek**.

**waakchéhlashiish** NA grasshopper. *pl* **waakchehlashíishak**. *obv* **waak=chehlashíishal**.

**wáakeew** VII be bent, be curved. *conj 3rd sg* **wáakeek**. *ptcpl* **wáakeek**.

**wáakham** VTI 1A bend s.t. *(using a tool or instrument)*. *ind 1st sg* **nŭwaak=hámun**. *ind 3rd sg* **waakhámun**. *conj 1st sg* **waakhámaan**. *conj 3rd sg* **wáakhang**. *imp* **wáakhah**. *ptcpl* **wáakhang**.

**wáakheew** VTA bend s.t. animate *(using a tool or instrument)*. *ind 1st sg* **nŭwáakhaaw**, **nŭwáakha**. *ind 3rd sg* **waakháawal**. *ind inv* **nŭwáakhookw**. *ind I-you* **kŭwáakhool**. *conj 3rd sg* **wáakhaat**. *imp* **wáakhaw**. *ptcpl* **wáakhaat**.

**waakhóotŭyeew** VAI have a deformed hip, have one hip higher than the other, have a lopsided hip. *ind 1st sg* **nŭwaakhóotŭya**, **nŭwaakhóotŭ=yaam**. *conj 3rd sg* **waakhóotŭyaat**. *ptcpl* **waakhóotŭyaat**.

**waakhootŭyéewxeew** VAI walk bent over with one's behind sticking out. *ind 1st sg* **nŭwaakhootŭyéewxe**, **nŭwaakhootŭyéewxeem**. *conj 3rd sg* **waakhootŭyéewxeet**. *imp* **waak=hootŭyéewxeel**. *ptcpl* **waakhootŭ=yéewxeet**.

**waakíikun** VII grow crookedly. *conj 3rd sg* **waakíikung**. *ptcpl* **waakíikung**.

**waakíikuw** VAI grow crookedly *(s.t. animate)*. *ind 1st sg* **nŭwaakíiki**, **nŭwaa=kíikiim**. *conj 3rd sg* **waakíikiit**. *ptcpl* **waakíikiit**.

**waakiikwáakeew** VAI sew things crookedly. *ind 1st sg* **nŭwaakiikwáake**, **nŭwaakiikwáakeem**. *conj 3rd sg* **waakiikwáakeet**. *imp* **waakiikwáa=keel**. *ptcpl* **waakiikwáakeet**.

**waakiikwáaleew** VTA sew s.t. animate crookedly. *ind 1st sg* **nŭwaakii=kwáalaaw**, **nuwaakiikwáala**. *ind 3rd sg* **waakiikwaaláawal**. *ind inv* **nŭ=waakiikwáalukw**. *ind I-you* **kŭwaa=kiikwáalul**. *conj 3rd sg* **waakii=kwáalaat**. *imp* **waakíikwaal**. *ptcpl* **waakiikwáalaat**.

**waakíikwam** VTI 1A sew s.t. crookedly. *ind 1st sg* **nŭwaakíikwamun**. *ind 3rd sg* **waakíikwamun**. *conj 1st sg* **waa=kíikwamaan**. *conj 3rd sg* **waakíi=kwang**. *imp* **waakíikwah**. *ptcpl* **waakíikwang**.

**waakihtéeham** VTI 1A hit and bend s.t. *ind 1st sg* **nŭwaakihtéehŭmun**. *ind 3rd sg* **waakihtéehŭmun**. *conj 1st sg* **waakihtéehŭmaan**. *conj 3rd sg* **waakihtéehang**. *imp* **waakihtéehih**. *ptcpl* **waakihtéehang**.

**waakihtéeheew** VTA hit and bend s.t. animate. *ind 1st sg* **nŭwaakihtée=haaw**, **nŭwaakihtéeha**. *ind 3rd sg* **waakihteeháawal**. *ind inv* **nŭwaa=kihtéehookw**. *ind I-you* **kŭwaakih=**

téehool. *conj 3rd sg* **waakihtéehaat**. *imp* **waakíhteeh**. *ptcpl* **waakihtée=haat**.

**waakihtéexiin** VAI be hit and get bent *(s.t. animate)*. *ind 1st sg* **nŭwaakih=téexiin**, **nŭwaakihtéexi**. *conj 3rd sg* **waakihtéexiing**. *ptcpl* **waakihtée=xiing**.

**waakihtéextoow** VTI2 hit and bend s.t., hit s.t. and cause it to become bent. *ind 1st sg* **nŭwaakihtéextoon**. *ind 3rd sg* **waakihtéextoon**. *conj 1st sg* **waakihteextáwaan**. *conj 3rd sg* **waakihtéextaakw**. *imp* **waakihtéex=tool**. *ptcpl* **waakihtéextaakw**.

**waakihtéexŭmeew** VTA hit and bend s.t. animate, hit s.t. animate and cause it to become bent. *ind 1st sg* **nŭwaa=kihtéexŭmaaw**, **nŭwaakihtéexŭma**. *ind 3rd sg* **waakihteexŭmáawal**. *ind inv* **nŭwaakihtéexŭmukw**. *ind I-you* **kŭwaakihtéexŭmul**. *conj 3rd sg* **waakihtéexŭmaat**. *imp* **waakihtée=xum**. *ptcpl* **waakihtéexŭmaat**.

**waakihtéexun** VII hit and get bent. *conj 3rd sg* **waakihtéexung**. *ptcpl* **waa=kihtéexung**.

**waakóoxweew** VAI walk bent over, walk stooped over. *ind 1st sg* **nŭwaakóo=xwe**, **nŭwaakóoxweem**. *conj 3rd sg* **waakóoxweet**. *imp* **waakóoxweel**. *ptcpl* **waakóoxweet**.

**waakohkwéepuw** VAI sit bent over. *ind 1st sg* **nŭwaakohkwéepi**, **nŭwaa=kohkwéepiim**. *conj 3rd sg* **waakoh=kwéepiit**. *imp* **waakohkwéepiil**. *ptcpl* **waakohkwéepiit**.

**waakpóxkwaneew** VAI be humpbacked. *ind 1st sg* **nŭwaakpóxkwana**, **nŭwaakpóxkwanaam**. *conj 3rd sg* **waakpóxkwanaat**. *ptcpl* **waakpóx=kwanaat**.

**waakpoxkwanéepuw** VAI sit hunched over. *ind 1st sg* **nŭwaakpoxkwanée=pi**, **nŭwaakpoxkwanéepiim**. *conj 3rd sg* **waakpoxkwanéepiit**. *imp* **waakpoxkwanéepiil**. *ptcpl* **waak=poxkwanéepiit**.

**waakpoxkwanéexiin** VAI be hunched over. *ind 1st sg* **nŭwaakpoxkwanée=xiin**, **nŭwaakpoxkwanéexi**. *conj 3rd sg* **waakpoxkwanéexiing**. *ptcpl* **waakpoxkwanéexiing**.

**wáaksuw** VAI be bent, be bent over, be curved *(s.t. animate)*. *ind 1st sg* **nŭwáaksi**, **nŭwáaksiim**. *conj 3rd sg* **wáaksiit**. *ptcpl* **wáaksiit**.

**wáakul** NA Walker *(man's name)*. *obv* **wáakŭlal**. *From English* Walker.

**wáakŭneew** VTA bend s.t. animate *(using the hands)*. *ind 1st sg* **nŭwáakŭ=naaw**, **nŭwáakŭna**. *ind 3rd sg* **waa=kŭnáawal**. *ind inv* **nŭwáakŭnukw**. *ind I-you* **kŭwáakŭnul**. *conj 3rd sg* **wáakŭnaat**. *imp* **wáakun**. *ptcpl* **wáakŭnaat**.

**wáakŭnum** VTI1B bend s.t. *(using the hands)*. *ind 1st sg* **nŭwaakŭnúmun**. *ind 3rd sg* **waakŭnúmun**. *conj 1st sg* **waakŭnúmaan**. *conj 3rd sg* **wáakŭ=nung**. *imp* **wáakŭnih**. *ptcpl* **wáakŭ=nung**.

**waalahkéeyeew** VII be a hole in the ground. *conj 3rd sg* **waalahkéeyeek**. *ptcpl* **waalahkéeyeek**.

**waalakéeyeew** VII have a hole in it. *conj 3rd sg* **waalakéeyeek**. *ptcpl* **waala=kéeyeek**. *intensive reduplication* **wahwaalakéeyeew**.

**wáalakw** NI pit, hole in ground *(especially for storing vegetables in winter)*. *pl* **wáalakwal**. *loc* **wáalakwung**. *dimin* **wáalakwush**.

**waalatéexiin** VAI lie on one's stomach. *ind 1st sg* **nŭwaalatéexiin**, **nŭwaa=latéexi**. *conj 3rd sg* **waalatéexiing**. *imp* **waalatéexiil**. *ptcpl* **waalatée=xiing**.

**wáaleew** VII have a hole, have a hollow, be concave. *conj 3rd sg* **wáaleek**. *ptcpl* **wáaleek**.

**waalháaleew** VTA bury s.o. *ind 1st sg*

**nŭwaalháalaaw**, **nŭwaalháala**. *ind 3rd sg* **waalhaaláawal**. *ind inv* **nŭ=waalháalukw**. *ind I-you* **kŭwaal=háalul**. *conj 3rd sg* **waalháalaat**. *imp* **wáalhaal**. *ptcpl* **waalháalaat**.

**waalháasuw** VAI be buried *(s.t. animate)*. *ind 1st sg* **nŭwaalháasi**, **nŭwaalháa=siim**. *conj 3rd sg* **waalháasiit**. *ptcpl* **waalháasiit**.

**waalhaatáasuw** VII be buried. *conj 3rd sg* **waalhaatáasiik**. *ptcpl* **waalhaa=táasiik**.

**waalháatoow** VTI2 bury s.t. *ind 1st sg* **nŭwaalháatoon**. *ind 3rd sg* **waal=háatoon**. *conj 1st sg* **waalháata=waan**. *conj 3rd sg* **waalháataakw**. *imp* **waalháatool**. *ptcpl* **waalháa=taakw**.

**wáalheew** VAI dig a hole. *ind 1st sg* **nŭwáalhe**, **nŭwáalheem**. *conj 3rd sg* **wáalheet**. *imp* **wáalheel**. *ptcpl* **wáalheet**.

**wáalpool** NI Walpole Island, Ontario. **Waalpóolung ndá.** 'I'm going to Walpole Island.' *loc* **waalpóolung**. *From English* Walpole.

**wáalsuw** VAI have a hole, have a hollow, be concave *(s.t. animate)*. *ind 1st sg* **nŭwáalsi**, **nŭwáalsiim**. *conj 3rd sg* **wáalsiit**. *ptcpl* **wáalsiit**.

**waalshéeyeew** VII have a hole, be a hole. *conj 3rd sg* **waalshéeyeek**. *ptcpl* **waalshéeyeek**.

**wáamwiis** NA bullfrog. *pl* **waamwíisak**. *dimin* **waamwíishush**. *obv* **waa=mwíisal**.

**waangóomeew** VTA kiss s.o. *ind 1st sg* **nŭwaangóomaaw**, **nŭwaangóoma**. *ind 3rd sg* **waangoomáawal**. *ind inv* **nŭwaangóomukw**. *ind I-you* **kŭ=waangóomul**. *conj 3rd sg* **waangóo=maat**. *imp* **wáangoom**. *ptcpl* **waan=góomaat**.

**waapaaláxkwsiit** NI white bean. *pl* **waapaalaxkwsíital**. *loc* **waapaa=laxkwsíitung**. *dimin* **waapaalaxk=wshíichush**.

**waapáandpeew** VAI have grey hair. *ind 1st sg* **nŭwaapáandpa**, **nŭwaapáan=dpaam**. *conj 3rd sg* **waapáandpaat**. *ptcpl* **waapáandpaat**.

**waapaapamúkwat** VII be white. *conj 3rd sg* **waapaapamúkwahk**. *ptcpl* **waapaapamúkwahk**.

**waapáhtakw** NI white thread. *pl* **waa=páhtakwal**. *poss* **nŭwaapáhtakwum**. *loc* **waapáhtakwung**. *dimin* **waa=páhchakwush**.

**waapamálsuw** VAI feel that one is White, think that one is White. *ind 1st sg* **nŭwaapamálsi**, **nŭwaapamálsiim**. *conj 3rd sg* **waapamálsiit**. *ptcpl* **waapamálsiit**.

**wáapan** VII be dawn. **Méhch wáapan.** 'It's daylight now.'; **Waapánge.** 'Tomorrow.' *conj 3rd sg* **wáapang**. *ptcpl* **wáapang**.

**waapanáaxiin** VAI live until morning *(of a sick person)*. *ind 1st sg* **nŭwaapa=náaxiin**, **nŭwaapanáaxi**. *conj 3rd sg* **waapanáaxiing**. *ptcpl* **waapanáa=xiing**.

**waapanáheew** VAI see daylight, live to daylight. *ind 1st sg* **nŭwaapanáhe**, **nŭwaapanáheem**. *conj 3rd sg* **waa=panáheet**. *ptcpl* **waapanáheet**.

**waapanámuw** VAI live until morning. *ind 1st sg* **nŭwaapanámwi**, **nŭwaa=panámwiim**. *conj 3rd sg* **waapa=námwiit**. *ptcpl* **waapanámwiit**.

**wáapapwaan** NI white bread, baker's bread. *pl* **waapapwáanal**. *poss* **nŭ=waapapwáanum**. *loc* **waapapwáa=nung**; *dimin* **waapapwáanush**. *See* **shuwánakwii-apwáan**.

**waapasáanay** NI blanket. *pl* **waapasáa=nayal**. *poss* **nŭwaapasáanay**.

**waapasíiskuw** NI clay. *loc* **waapasíis=koong**.

**waapcháseew** VTA dye s.t. animate white; heat s.t. animate up and whiten it *(when washing clothes)*. *ind 1st sg*

**nŭwaapchásaaw**, **nŭwaapchása**. *ind 3rd sg* **waapchasáawal**. *ind inv* **nŭ=waapchásookw**. *ind I-you* **kŭwaap=chásool**. *conj 3rd sg* **waapchásaat**. *imp* **wáapchas**. *ptcpl* **waapchásaat**.

**waapchásum** VTI1B dye s.t. white; heat s.t. up and whiten it *(when washing clothes)*. *ind 1st sg* **nŭwaapchásŭ=mun**. *ind 3rd sg* **waapchásŭmun**. *conj 1st sg* **waapchásŭmaan**. *conj 3rd sg* **waapchásung**. *imp* **waap=chásih**. *ptcpl* **waapchásung**.

**wáapeew** VII be white. *conj 3rd sg* **wáapeek**. *ptcpl* **wáapeek**.

**waapeeliingwéexiin** VAI see the whites of someone's eyes. *ind 1st sg* **nŭ=waapeeliingwéexiin**, **nŭwaapeeliin=gwéexi**. *conj 3rd sg* **waapeeliingwée=xiing**. *ptcpl* **waapeeliingwéexiing**.

**waaphátiin** VAI be a wake going on. *usually indefinite subject only*. **Katá-waaphátiin.** 'There's going to be a wake.' *indef subject* **waaphátiin**. *conj 3rd sg* **waaphátiing**.

**waaphéembteew** VAI wear a white shirt, have a white shirt on. *ind 1st sg* **nŭwaaphéembta**, **nŭwaaphéemb=taam**. *conj 3rd sg* **waaphéembtaat**. *imp* **waaphéembtaal**. *ptcpl* **waap=héembtaat**.

**waapii-** PN white. **Wáapii-kóon.** 'White snow.'; **Wáapii-aníixan.** 'White shoelace.'

**waapii-** PV white. **Nŭwáapii-shóohŭ=mun.** 'I painted it white.' *ptcpl* **wáapii-**. *See* **waapu-**.

**waapíikaan** NI white house. *pl* **waapii=káanal**. *poss* **nŭwaapíikaan**. *loc* **waapiikáanung**. *dimin* **waapiikáa=nush**.

**waapíikwan** NA white feather. *pl* **waa=píikwanak**. *poss* **nŭwaapíikwan**. *loc* **waapíikwanung**. *dimin* **waapíikwa=nush**. *obv* **waapíikwanal**.

**wáapiim** NI chestnut. *pl* **waapíimal**. *loc* **waapíimung**. *dimin* **waapíimush**.

**waapíhleew** VII turn white. *conj 3rd sg* **waapíhlaak**. *ptcpl* **waapíhlaak**.

**waapihtóonay** NI white beard. *pl* **waa=pihtóonayal**.

**waapihtóonayeew** VAI have a grey beard, have a white beard. *ind 1st sg* **nŭwaapihtóonaya**, **nŭwaapihtóo=nayaam**. *conj 3rd sg* **waapihtóona=yaat**. *ptcpl* **waapihtóonayaat**.

**waapóhkweew** VAI have white hair. *ind 1st sg* **nŭwaapóhkwa**, **nŭwaapóh=kwaam**. *conj 3rd sg* **waapóhkwaat**. *ptcpl* **waapóhkwaat**.

**wáapsuw** VAI be white *(s.t. animate)*. *ind 1st sg* **nŭwáapsi**, **nŭwáapsiim**. *conj 3rd sg* **wáapsiit**. *ptcpl* **wáapsiit**. *moderative reduplication* **waawáap=suw**.

**waapsuwíhleew** NA goose. *pl* **waap=suwihléewak**. *obv* **waapsuwihlée=wal**.

**waaptihkíhleew** VAI turn pale. *ind 1st sg* **nŭwaaptihkíhla**, **nŭwaaptihkíh=laam**. *conj 3rd sg* **waaptihkíhlaat**. *ptcpl* **waaptihkíhlaat**.

**waaptíhksuw** VAI be pale, turn pale. *ind 1st sg* **nŭwaaptíhksi**, **nŭwaaptíhk=siim**. *conj 3rd sg* **waaptíhksiit**. *ptcpl* **waaptíhksiit**.

**waapu-** PV white. *informal*. **Wáapu-làmalúsuw.** 'He feels that he is White.'; **Awáapu-sàsápe** 'It has white dots.' *ptcpl* **wáapu-**. *intensive reduplication* **awaapu-**. *See* **waapii-**.

**waapŭléexiin** VAI be light in colour *(s.t. animate)*; be a whitish colour, have a white tinge to it *(s.t. animate)*. *ind 1st sg* **nŭwaapŭléexiin**, **nŭwaapŭléexi**. *conj 3rd sg* **waapŭléexiing**. *ptcpl* **waapŭléexiing**, **waapŭléexiit**.

**waapŭléexun** VII be light in colour; be a whitish colour, have a whitish tinge to it. *conj 3rd sg* **waapŭléexung**. *ptcpl* **waapŭléexung**.

**waasaláangweew** NA shining star. *pl* **waasalaangwéewak**. *obv* **waasa=**

**laangwéewal**.

**waasatéexiin** VAI lie on one's back. *ind 1st sg* **nŭwaasatéexiin**, **nŭwaasatée=xi**. *conj 3rd sg* **waasatéexiing**. *imp* **waasatéexiil**. *ptcpl* **waasatéexiing**.

**waaseeliingohkwéepuw** VAI sit with shining eyes *(especially in the dark)*. *ind 1st sg* **nŭwaaseeliingohkwéepi**, **nŭwaaseeliingohkwéepiim**. *conj 3rd sg* **waaseeliingohkwéepiit**. *imp* **waa=seeliingohkwéepiil**. *ptcpl* **waasee=liingohkwéepiit**.

**waaseeliingwéexiin** VAI have shiny eyes *(especially in the dark)*. *ind 1st sg* **nŭwaaseeliingwéexiin**, **nŭwaasee=liingwéexi**. *conj 3rd sg* **waaseeliin=gwéexiing**. *ptcpl* **waaseeliingwée=xiing**.

**wáasiingw** NA pickerel. *pl* **waasíingwak**. *poss* **nŭwaasíingwum**. *loc* **waasíin=gwung**. *dimin* **waashíingwush**. *obv* **waasíingwal**.

**waasŭláandeew** VII shine, be shining out *(of the weather)*; be a sunny day. *conj 3rd sg* **waasŭláandeek**. *ptcpl* **waasŭláandeek**.

**waasŭlahksúneew** VAI have shiny shoes. *ind 1st sg* **nŭwaasŭlahksúna**, **nŭ=waasŭlahksúnaam**. *conj 3rd sg* **waasŭlahksúnaat**. *ptcpl* **waasŭlah=ksúnaat**.

**waasŭleeníikan** NA light, lamp. *pl* **waa=sŭleeníikanak**. *poss* **nŭwaasŭleeníi=kan**. *loc* **waasŭleeníikanung**. *dimin* **waashŭleeníikanush**. *obv* **waasŭ=leeníikanal**.

**waasŭléenŭmeew** VAI turn on the light. *ind 1st sg* **nŭwaasŭléenŭma**, **nŭ=waasŭléenŭmaam**. *conj 3rd sg* **waasŭléenŭmaat**. *imp* **waasŭ=léenŭmaal**. *ptcpl* **waasŭléenŭmaat**.

**wáasŭleew** VII shine, be light; be a light on. **Kíi wíikŭyan wáasŭleew?** 'Are you home? ('Is your house shining?').' *conj 3rd sg* **wáasŭleek**. *ptcpl* **wáasŭleek**.

**waasŭléexiin** VAI shine *(of the sun)*; be shiny *(s.t. animate)*. *ind 1st sg* **nŭ=waasŭléexiin**, **nŭwaasŭléexi**. *conj 3rd sg* **waasŭléexiing**. *ptcpl* **waasŭ=léexiing**.

**waasŭleextíikeew** VAI shine things, polish things. *ind 1st sg* **nŭwaasŭ=leextíike**, **nŭwaasŭleextíikeem**. *conj 3rd sg* **waasŭleextíikeet**. *imp* **waasŭ=leextíikeel**. *ptcpl* **waasŭleextíikeet**.

**waasŭléextoow** VTI2 shine s.t., make s.t. shine. *ind 1st sg* **nŭwaasŭléextoon**. *ind 3rd sg* **waasŭléextoon**. *conj 1st sg* **waasŭleextáwaan**. *conj 3rd sg* **waasŭléextaakw**. *imp* **waasŭléex=tool**. *ptcpl* **waasŭléextaakw**.

**waasŭléexŭmeew** VTA shine s.t. animate, make s.t. animate shine. *ind 1st sg* **nŭwaasuléexŭmaaw**, **nŭwaasulée=xŭma**. *ind 3rd sg* **waasuleexŭmáa=wal**. *ind inv* **nŭwaasuléexŭmukw**. *ind I-you* **kŭwaasuléexŭmul**. *conj 3rd sg* **waasŭléexŭmaat**. *imp* **waasŭlée=xum**. *ptcpl* **waasŭléexŭmaat**.

**waasŭléexun** VII shine, be shiny. *conj 3rd sg* **waasŭléexung**. *ptcpl* **waasŭ=léexung**.

**waatŭlamóokan** NI watermelon. *pl* **waatŭlamóokanal**. *poss* **nŭwaatŭ=lamóokanum**. *loc* **waatŭlamóoka=nung**. *dimin* **waatŭlamóokanush**. *From Dutch.*

nŭ**waawíikan** NID my back. *3rd poss* **waawíikan**. *loc* **nŭwaawíikanung**. *See* n**aawíikan**.

**waawiikaníineew** VAI have a backache, have a sore back. *ind 1st sg* **nŭwaa=wiikaníine**, **nŭwaawiikaníineem**. *conj 3rd sg* **waawiikaníineet**. *ptcpl* **waawiikaníineet**.

**waaxamóhkweew** VAI be shiny bald, be completely bald. *ind 1st sg* **nŭwaa=xamóhkwa**, **nŭwaaxamóhkwaam**. *conj 3rd sg* **waaxamóhkwaat**. *ptcpl* **waaxamóhkwaat**. *moderative reduplication* **waawaaxamóhkweew**.

**wáaxaweew** NA sunflower. *pl* **waaxa=wéewak**. *obv* **waaxawéewal**.

**waaxeelíingweew** VAI have light-coloured eyes; have grey eyes. *ind 1st sg* **nŭwaaxeelíingwa**, **nŭwaaxeelíin=gwaam**. *conj 3rd sg* **waaxeelíin=gwaat**. *ptcpl* **waaxeelíingwaat**. *intensive reduplication* **wàwaaxeelíin=gweew**.

**waaxéeyeew** VII be bright out *(at night)*; be daylight. **Alúmu-waaxéeyeew.** 'It gets bright out'; **Wúsku-waaxée=yeew.** 'There's a new moon.' *conj 3rd sg* **waaxéeyeek**. *ptcpl* **waaxéeyeek**.

**waaxéhleew** VII be bright out. **Méhch waaxéhleew.** 'It's bright out now.' *conj 3rd sg* **waaxéhlaak**. *ptcpl* **waa=xéhlaak**.

**wá** PR this *(animate)*. *used in animate 'where' questions*. **Shúkw ngúmee màmatahkéewak, wáak wá ox=kwéesus ngúmee músu-áan, àha=lúmsuw.** 'But they always fought, and this girl was always going all over, she would frequently go away.'; **Tá wá ná lúnuw?** 'Where is the man?' *See* **wán**.

**wách** NA watch. *pl* **wáchak**. *poss* **nŭwáchum**. *dimin* **wáchush**. *obv* **wáchal**. *From English* watch.

**wách** PC I wonder. **Wách xéet néeka alúmsuw.** 'I wonder if he left.'; **Wách xéet wŭlamalúsuw.** 'I wonder if he's well.' *See* **wéech**.

**wahkwéelŭneew** VTA put a collar on s.o., put a scarf on s.o. *ind 1st sg* **nŭwah=kwéelŭnaaw**, **nŭwahkwéelŭna**. *ind 3rd sg* **wahkweelŭnáawal**. *ind inv* **nŭwahkwéelŭnukw**. *ind I-you* **kŭ=wahkwéelŭnul**. *conj 3rd sg* **wah=kwéelŭnaat**. *imp* **wahkwéelun**.

**wahkwéelŭnuw** VAI have something around one's neck. *ind 1st sg* **nŭwah=kwéelŭni**, **nŭwahkwéelŭniim**. *conj 3rd sg* **wahkwéelŭniit**. *imp* **wah=kwéelŭniil**. *ptcpl* **wahkwéelŭniit**.

**wahkwéelŭnuw** VAIO wear s.t. around one's neck. **Wahkwéelŭnuw maan=zháapŭyal.** 'She's got beads around her neck.' *ind 1st sg* **nŭwahkwée=lŭniin**. *ind 3rd sg* **wahkwéelŭniin**. *conj 3rd sg* **wahkwéelŭniit**. *imp* **wahkwéelŭniil**. *ptcpl* **wahkwéelŭ=niit**.

**wáhkwung** PC up, upwards, upstairs. **Ndulóngwaam wáhkwung ndula=kóosi.** 'I dreamt I climbed up.'

**wáhleesh** PC in a hurry. **Wáhleesh manáxeel!** 'Chop wood in a hurry!'

**wáhli** PC far. **Wáhli laháhkweew mée=naxk, paalíhleew meenáxkung lí.** 'He hit it a long way to the fence, and it went over the fence.' *See* **wáhlu**.

**wáhlu** PC far. *informal*. **Wáhlu áhteew.** 'It is far away.'; **Wáhlu wíikuw.** 'He lives far away.' *See* **wáhli**.

**wahlŭmahtéewal** VII be far apart. *usually plural*. *conj 3rd sg* **wahlŭmáh=teek**. *ptcpl* **wahlŭmahtéekiil**.

**wahlŭmápŭwak** VAI sit far apart, be far apart, be far away. *ind 1st pl* **nŭwah=lŭmapíhna**. *conj 3rd sg* **wahlŭmap=íhtiit**. *imp* **wahlŭmápiikw**. *ptcpl* **wahlŭmapíhtiit**.

**wáhlŭmat** VII be far away. *conj 3rd sg* **wáhlŭmahk**. *ptcpl* **wáhlŭmahk**.

**wahlŭmiikaapawúwak** VAI stand far apart. *usually plural*. *ind 1st pl* **nŭ=wahlŭmiikaapawíhna**. *conj 3rd sg* **wahlŭmiikaapawíhtiit**. *imp* **wahlŭ=miikáapawiikw**. *ptcpl* **wahlŭmii=kaapawíhtiit**.

**wahlŭmiikéewak** VAI live far apart. *usually plural*. *ind 1st pl* **nŭwahlŭmii=kéhna**. *conj 3rd sg* **wahlŭmiikéhtiit**. *imp* **wahlŭmíikeekw**. *ptcpl* **wahlŭ=miikéhtiit**.

**wahlŭmihtáakwat** VII sound far away. *conj 3rd sg* **wahlŭmihtáakwahk**. *ptcpl* **wahlŭmihtáakwahk**.

**wahlŭmihtáakwsuw** VAI sound far away *(s.t. animate)*. *ind 1st sg* **nŭwahlŭ=**

**mihtáakwsi**, **nŭwahlŭmihtáakw=siim**. *conj 3rd sg* **wahlŭmihtáakw=siit**. *ptcpl* **wahlŭmihtáakwsiit**.

**wahlŭmukéewak** VAI dance far apart. *usually plural. ind 1st pl* **nŭwahlŭ=mukáhna**. *conj 3rd sg* **wahlŭmuk=áhtiit**. *imp* **wahlŭmúkaal**. *ptcpl* **wahlŭmukáhtiit**.

**wáhpan** NA lung. *pl* **wáhpanak**. *poss* **nŭwáhpanum**. *obv* **wáhpanal**.

**wahwaasŭléhleew** VII be lightning. *conj 3rd sg* **wahwaasŭléhlaak**. *ptcpl* **wahwaasŭléhlaak**.

**wáhwal** NI egg. *pl* **wáhwalal**. *poss* **nŭwáhwalum**. *loc* **wáhwalung**. *dimin* **wáhwalush**.

**wáhwheew** VAI lay an egg. *ind 1st sg* **nŭwáhwhe**, **nŭwáhwheem**. *conj 3rd sg* **wáhwheet**. *imp* **wáhwheel**. *ptcpl* **wáhwheet**.

**wán** PR this *(animate, emphatic)*. **Wán há níi.** 'It's me.' *See* **wá**.

**wanáatam** VAI be out of one's mind. *ind 1st sg* **nŭwanáatam**. *conj 3rd sg* **wanáatang**. *ptcpl* **weenáatang**.

**wanahkwateelúndam** VOTI1A be out of one's mind with grief. *ind 1st sg* **nuwanahkwateelúndam**. *conj 3rd sg* **wanahkwateelúndang**. *ptcpl* **wee=nahkwateelúndang**.

**wanahkwatéhleew** VAI be out of one's mind, be unconscious. *ind 1st sg* **nŭwanahkwatéhla**, **nŭwanahkwa=téhlaam**. *conj 3rd sg* **wanahkwatéh=laat**. *ptcpl* **weenahkwatéhlaat**.

**wanahtakíhleew** VAI run out of sight. *ind 1st sg* **nŭwanahtakíhla**, **nŭwan=ahtakíhlaam**. *conj 3rd sg* **wanahta=kíhlaat**. *imp* **wanahtakíhlaal**. *ptcpl* **weenahtakíhlaat**.

**wánd** NA mitt. *pl* **wándak**. *poss* **nŭwán=dum**. *loc* **wándung**. *dimin* **wánjush**. *obv* **wándal**. *From Dutch.*

**wándheew** VAI make mitts. *ind 1st sg* **nŭwándhe**, **nŭwándheem**. *conj 3rd sg* **wándheet**. *imp* **wándheel**. *ptcpl* **wándheet**.

**waníipakuw** VAI have leaves on it *(s.t. animate)*. *conj 3rd sg* **waníipakwiit**. *ptcpl* **weeníipakwiit**.

**waníipakw** NI leaf. *pl* **waníipakwal**. *loc* **waníipakwung**. *dimin* **waníipa=kwush**.

**waníisŭmuw** VAI be very drunk. *ind 1st sg* **nŭwaníisŭmwi**, **nŭwaníisŭ=mwiim**. *conj 3rd sg* **waníisŭmwiit**. *ptcpl* **weeníisŭmwiit**.

**waníhleew** VAI go out of sight. *ind 1st sg* **nŭwaníhla**, **nŭwaníhlaam**. *conj 3rd sg* **waníhlaat**. *ptcpl* **weeníhlaat**.

**wanohtáasuw** VAI hide, hide out of sight. *ind 1st sg* **nŭwanohtáasi**, **nŭ=wanohtáasiim**. *conj 3rd sg* **wanoh=táasiit**. *imp* **wanohtáasiil**. *ptcpl* **wee=nohtáasiit**.

**wanóhtaweew** VTA hide from s.o. *(especially to keep the doors locked while at home)*. *ind 1st sg* **nŭwanóhta=waaw**, **nŭwanóhtawa**. *ind 3rd sg* **wànohtawáawal**. *ind inv* **nŭwanóh=taakw**. *ind 1-you* **kŭwanóhtool**. *conj 3rd sg* **wanóhtawaat**. *imp* **wanóhtaw**. *ptcpl* **weenóhtawaat**.

**wanúpaleew** VTA cover s.o. over with water, cover s.t. animate over with water. *ind 1st sg* **nŭwanpálaaw**, **nŭ=wanpála**. *ind 3rd sg* **wànpaláawal**. *ind inv* **nŭwanpálukw**. *ind 1-you* **kŭ=wanpálul**. *conj 3rd sg* **wanúpalaat**. *imp* **wanúpal**. *ptcpl* **weenpálaat**.

**wanúpatoow** VTI2 cover s.t. over with water. *ind 1st sg* **nŭwanpátoon**. *ind 3rd sg* **wànpátoon**. *conj 1st sg* **wa=nupatáwaan**. *conj 3rd sg* **wanúpa=taakw**. *imp* **wanúpatool**. *ptcpl* **ween=pátaakw**.

**wanúpeew** VAI be covered over with water *(s.t. animate)*. *ind 1st sg* **nŭ=wánpe**, **nŭwánpeem**. *conj 3rd sg* **wanúpeet**. *ptcpl* **wéenpeet**.

**wanúpeew** VII be covered over with water. *conj 3rd sg* **wanúpeek**. *ptcpl*

**wéenpeek**.

**wanúsuw** VAI forget. **Ngúmee wahwa=núsiin.** 'He always forgets.' *ind 1st sg* **nŭwánsi**, **nŭwánsiim**. *conj 3rd sg* **wanúsiit**. *ptcpl* **wéensiit**. *intensive reduplication* **wahwanúsuw**.

**wanúsuw** VAIO forget s.o., forget s.t. **Chíi wanusíiwu kŭniimáawan.** 'Don't forget your lunch.' *ind 1st sg* **nŭwánsiin**. *ind 3rd sg* **wánsiin**. *conj 3rd sg* **wanúsiit**. *ptcpl* **wéensiit**.

**watéeneew** VAI have diarrhea, have stomach flu. *ind 1st sg* **nŭwatéene**, **nŭ=watéeneem**. *conj 3rd sg* **watéeneet**. *ptcpl* **weetéeneet**.

**wàwchihkwíhleew** VII have cramps. *conj 3rd sg* **wàwchihkwíhlaak**. *ptcpl* **wàwchihkwíhlaak**.

**wàwtamiitŭyéhleew** VAI go slowly. *ind 1st sg* **nŭwàwtamiitŭyéhla**, **nŭwàw=tamiitŭyéhlaam**. *conj 3rd sg* **wàw=tamiitŭyéhlaat**. *imp* **wàwtamiitŭ=yéhlaal**. *ptcpl* **wàwtamiitŭyéhlaat**. *considered impolite*.

**wàwtamóoxweew** VAI walk slowly, walk in a relaxed fashion. *ind 1st sg* **nŭwawtamóoxwe**, **nŭwawtamóo=xweem**. *conj 3rd sg* **wàwtamóo=xweet**. *imp* **wàwtamóoxweel**. *ptcpl* **wàwtamóoxweet**.

**wàwtámsuw** VAI work slowly, work to to suit oneself. *ind 1st sg* **nŭwaw=támsi**, **nŭwawtámsiim**. *conj 3rd sg* **wàwtámsiit**. *imp* **wàwtámsiil**. *ptcpl* **wàwtámsiit**.

**wàwŭyamoxkchéhleew** VAI move around, stir. *ind 1st sg* **nŭwàwŭyam=oxkchéhla**, **nŭwàwŭyamoxkchéh=laam**. *conj 3rd sg* **wàwŭyamoxk=chéhlaat**. *imp* **wàwŭyamoxkchéh=laal**. *ptcpl* **wàwŭyamoxkchéhlaat**.

**wáwxwukw** VAI cough *(more than once). ind 1st sg* **nŭwáwxwukw**. *conj 3rd sg* **wàwxwúkwuk**. *imp* **wàw=xwúkwih**. *ptcpl* **wàwxwúkwuk**. *See* **xwúkw**.

**waxkáandpe** PC top of head.

**wáxkan** NI bone. *pl* **wáxkanal**. *poss* **nŭwáxkan**. *loc* **wáxkanung**. *dimin* **wáxkanush**.

**wáxkaniim** NI seed. *pl* **waxkaníimal**. *dimin* **waxkaníimush**.

**waxkanúsak** NA lamb's quarters. *usually plural. obv* **waxkanúsal**.

**waxkanúsŭw** VAI be thin, be skinny. *ind 1st sg* **nŭwaxkanúsi**, **nŭwaxkanús=iim**. *conj 3rd sg* **waxkanúsiit**. *ptcpl* **weexkanúsiit**.

**wáxkiich** PC above, on top of. *informal.* **Níi mbákshung wáxkiich nŭmatée=xiin.** 'I fell on top of the box.'; **Wáx=kiich eehundáxpwiing kwéek ndáh=toon.** 'I put something on top of the table.' *See* **waxkíichi**.

**waxkíichi** PC above, on top of. **Waxkíi=chi apánzhŭyung.** 'On top of the timbers.' *See* **waxkíich**.

**waxkíitaakw** PC the top of the roof, the top of the house. **Waxkíitaakw wun=jíikuw.** 'The top of the roof leaks.'

**waxkiitáangweew** VAI lie on top of something. *ind 1st sg* **nŭwaxkiitáan=gwe**, **nŭwaxkiitáangweem**. *conj 3rd sg* **waxkiitáangweet**. *imp* **waxkii=táangweel**. *ptcpl* **weexkiitáangweet**.

**waxkiitáawung** PC top of the hill.

**waxkiitapíinaye** PC on top of the bed. **Nzhungíixiin waxkiitapíinaye.** 'I was lying on top of the bed.'

**waxkiiteehundaxpóone** PC on top of the table.

**waxkiitihtéexiin** VAI fall on top of something, lie on top of something. *ind 1st sg* **nŭwaxkiitihtéexiin**, **nŭwaxkii=tihtéexi**. *conj 3rd sg* **waxkiitihtée=xiing**. *ptcpl* **weexkiitihtéexiing**.

**waxkiitihtéexun** VII fall on top of something, lie on top of something. *conj 3rd sg* **waxkiitihtéexung**. *ptcpl* **weexkiitihtéexung**.

**wáyun** NI wine. **Wáyun mŭnáhtiin.** 'People are drinking wine.' *poss*

**nŭwáyunum**. *loc* **wáyŭnung**. *dimin* **wáyŭnush**. *From English* wine.

**wchápihk** NI medicine. *pl* **wchapíhkal**. *poss* **noochapíhkum**. *loc* **wchapíh=kung**. *dimin* **wchapíhkush**.

**wchapíhkxakw** NI root. *pl* **wchapihk=xákwal**. *poss* **noochapihkxákwum**. *loc* **wchapihkxákwung**. *dimin* **wchapihkxákwush**.

**wchéht** NA muscle. *pl* **wchéhtak**. *poss* **noochéhtum**. *obv* **wchéhtal**.

**wchíikwsuw** VAI disappear, crawl out of sight. *ind 1st sg* **noochíikwsi**, **noo=chíikwsiim**. *conj 3rd sg* **wchíikwsiit**. *imp* **wchíikwsiil**. *ptcpl* **weechíikw=siit**.

**wchiimahtawásuw** VAI have one's fire go out. *ind 1st sg* **noochiimahtawási**, **noochiimahtawásiim**. *conj 3rd sg* **wchiimahtawásiit**. *ptcpl* **weechii=mahtawásiit**.

**wchiimáhteew** VII go out *(of fires)*; be burnt up *(in a fire)*. *conj 3rd sg* **wchii=máhteek**. *ptcpl* **weechiimáhteek**.

**wchiimahtéeham** VTI1A put s.t. out, extinguish s.t. *(of fires)*. **Piiskéeku awéen oochiimahtéehŭmun wíikŭ=yaan.** 'Last night someone turned off the lights at my place.' *ind 1st sg* **noochiimahtéehŭmun**. *ind 3rd sg* **oochiimahtéehŭmun**. *conj 1st sg* **wchiimahtéehŭmaan**. *conj 3rd sg* **wchiimahtéehang**. *imp* **wchiimah=téehih**. *ptcpl* **weechiimahtéehang**.

**wchiimahtéeheew** VTA put s.t. animate out, extinguish s.t. animate *(of fires)*. *ind 1st sg* **noochiimahtéehaaw**, **noo=chiimahtéeha**. *ind 3rd sg* **oochii=mahteeháawal**. *conj 3rd sg* **wchii=mahtéehaat**. *imp* **wchiimáhteeh**. *ptcpl* **weechiimahtéehaat**.

**wchiimahtéhleew** VII be gone out, go out quickly *(of fires)*. *conj 3rd sg* **wchiimahtéhlaak**. *ptcpl* **weechii=mahtéhlaak**.

**wchiimambíileew** VTA tie s.o. in a knot. *ind 1st sg* **noochiimambíilaaw**, **noo=chiimambíila**. *ind 3rd sg* **oochii=mambiiláawal**. *ind inv* **noochiimam=bíilukw**. *ind I-you* **koochiimambíi=lul**. *conj 3rd sg* **wchiimambíilaat**. *imp* **wchiimámbiil**. *ptcpl* **weechii=mambíilaat**.

**wchiimambíisuw** VAI be tied up in a knot, be tied in a knot. *ind 1st sg* **noochiimambíisi**, **noochiimambíi=siim**. *conj 3rd sg* **wchiimambíisiit**. *ptcpl* **weechiimambíisiit**.

**wchiimambíisuw** VII be tied up in a knot, be tied in a knot. *conj 3rd sg* **wchiimambíisiik**. *ptcpl* **weechii=mambíisiik**.

**wchiimámbtoow** VTI2 tie s.t. in a knot. *ind 1st sg* **noochiimámbtoon**. *ind 3rd sg* **oochiimámbtoon**. *conj 1st sg* **wchiimambtáwaan**. *conj 3rd sg* **wchiimámbtaakw**. *imp* **wchiimám=btool**. *ptcpl* **weechiimámbtaakw**.

**wchíimapuw** VAI stay away for good. *ind 1st sg* **noochíimapi**, **noochíima=piim**. *conj 3rd sg* **wchíimapiit**. *imp* **wchíimapiil**. *ptcpl* **weechíimapiit**.

**wchíimham** VTI1A lock s.t. *ind 1st sg* **noochiimhámun**. *ind 3rd sg* **oo=chiimhámun**. *conj 1st sg* **wchiim=hámaan**. *conj 3rd sg* **wchíimhang**. *imp* **wchíimhah**. *ptcpl* **weechíim=hang**.

**wchíimheew** VTA lock s.t. animate. *ind 1st sg* **noochíimhaaw**, **noochíimha**. *ind 3rd sg* **oochiimháawal**. *ind inv* **noochíimhookw**. *ind I-you* **koo=chíimhool**. *conj 3rd sg* **wchíimhaat**. *imp* **wchíimhaw**. *ptcpl* **weechíim=haat**.

**wchiimhíikan** NA lock. *pl* **wchiimhíi=kanak**. *poss* **noochiimhíikan**. *loc* **wchiimhíikanung**. *dimin* **wchiim=híikanush**. *obv* **wchiimhíikanal**.

**wchiimwáhkeew** VAI go away for good, stay away for good. *ind 1st sg* **noo=chiimwáhke**, **noochiimwáhkeem**.

*conj 3rd sg* **wchiimwáhkeet**. *imp* **wchiimwáhkeel**. *ptcpl* **weechii=mwáhkeet**.

**wchiimwii-** PV for good, permanently. **Koochíimwii-kpáhŭmun.** 'You shut it for good.'; **Noochíimwii-aníhtoon.** 'I lost it for good.' *ptcpl* **weechíi=mwii-**.

**wchiipiisóowuw** VII be a tingling sensation, have pins and needles *(of body parts)*. **Ndaaktúlung ndáam éelunáxk -wchiipiisóowiik.** 'I went to the doctor because my arm was numb.' *conj 3rd sg* **wchiipiisóowiik**. *ptcpl* **weechiipiisóowiik**.

**wchiipíisuw** VAI have a fit, have a seizure, have an epileptic seizure. *ind 1st sg* **noochiipíisi, noochiipíisiim**. *conj 3rd sg* **wchiipíisiit**. *ptcpl* **wee=chiipíisiit**.

**wchihkwáandpeew** VAI have a lump on one's head, have a bump on one's head. *ind 1st sg* **noochihkwáandpa, noochihkwáandpaam**. *conj 3rd sg* **wchihkwáandpaat**. *ptcpl* **weechih=kwáandpaat**.

**wchíhkweew** VII have a lump, have a bump. *conj 3rd sg* **wchíhkweek**. *ptcpl* **weechíhkweek**. *intensive reduplication* **wàwchíikweew**.

**wchihkwíhleew** VAI get a lump, get a bump. *ind 1st sg* **noochihkwíhla, noochihkwíhlaam**. *conj 3rd sg* **wchihkwíhlaat**. *ptcpl* **weechihkwíh=laat**.

**wchihkwíhleew** VAI have a cramp. *ind 1st sg* **noochihkwíhla, noochih=kwíhlaam**. *conj 3rd sg* **wchihkwíh=laat**. *ptcpl* **weechihkwíhlaat**. *intensive reduplication* **wàwchihkwíh=leew**.

**wchihkwíhleew** VII get a lump, get a bump. *conj 3rd sg* **wchihkwíhlaak**. *ptcpl* **weechihkwíhlaak**.

**wchíhkwsuw** VAI have a knot *(s.t. animate)*; have a lump, have a bump. *ind 1st sg* **noochíhkwsi, noochíhkwsiim**. *conj 3rd sg* **wchíhkwsiit**. *ptcpl* **wee=chíhkwsiit**. *intensive reduplication* **wàwchíhkwsuw**.

**wchíhleew** VAI disappear, go out of sight *(s.t. animate)*; shrink *(s.t. animate)*. **Eeheeshandéekan lí któhkweew, nál táa wtúlu-wchíhlaan, káata=puw.** 'He was looking out the window, then he disappeared, he's hiding.' *ind 1st sg* **noochíhla, noochíhlaam**. *conj 3rd sg* **wchíhlaat**. *ptcpl* **weechíhlaat**.

**wchíhleew** VII disappear, go out of sight; shrink. **Wíil wchíhleew.** 'His head disappeared out of sight.' *conj 3rd sg* **wchíhlaak**. *ptcpl* **weechíhlaak**.

**wchóosŭmeew** VTA be s.o.'s friend, be friends with s.o. *ind 1st sg* **noochóo=sŭmaaw, noochóosŭma**. *ind 3rd sg* **oochoosŭmáawal**. *ind inv* **noochóo=sŭmúkw**. *ind I-you* **koochóosŭmul**. *conj 3rd sg* **wchóosŭmaat**. *imp* **wchóosum**. *ptcpl* **weechóosŭmaat**.

**wchoosúndŭwak** VAI be friends *(with each other)*. *usually plural*. *ind 1st pl* **noochoosundíhna**. *conj 3rd sg* **wchoosundíhtiit**. *ptcpl* **weechoo=sundíhtiit**.

**wchúleew** VII be wrinkled. **Wchuléewal ehakwíingiil.** 'The clothes are wrinkled.' *conj 3rd sg* **wchúleek**. *ptcpl* **wéechŭleek**.

**wchuleendakwíiwan** NI wrinkled dress. *pl* **wchuleendakwíiwanal**. *poss* **noo=chŭleendakwíiwan**. *loc* **wchuleen=dakwíiwanung**. *dimin* **wchuleenda=kwíiwanush**.

**wchulhéembteew** VAI have a wrinkled shirt. *ind 1st sg* **noochŭlahéembta, noochŭlahéembtaam**. *conj 3rd sg* **wchulhéembtaat**. *ptcpl* **weechulah=éembtaat**.

**wchulíingweew** VAI have a wrinkled face, have a contorted face. *ind 1st sg* **noochŭlíingwa, noochŭlíingwaam**. *conj 3rd sg* **wchulíingwaat**. *ptcpl*

**weechŭlíingwaat**.

**wchuliingwéexiin** VAI have a wrinkled face, have a contorted face, pout, be in a temper, be discontented *(as if about to cry)*. *ind 1st sg* **noochŭliin=gwéexiin**, **noochŭliingwéexi**. *conj 3rd sg* **wchuliingwéexiing**. *ptcpl* **weechŭliingwéexiing**.

**wchúlsuw** VAI be wrinkled *(s.t. animate)*. **Wándak wchulsúwak.** 'The mitts are wrinkled.' *ind 1st sg* **noochŭlúsi**, **noochŭlúsiim**. *conj 3rd sg* **wchúlsiit**. *ptcpl* **weechŭlúsiit**.

**wchupahkiiháakan** NI garden. *pl* **wchupahkiiháakanal**. *poss* **nooch=pahkiiháakan**. *loc* **wchupahkiiháa=kanung**. *dimin* **wchupahkiiháaka=nush**.

**wchupáhleew** VTA fill s.t. animate up. *ind 1st sg* **noochpáhlaaw**, **noochpáhla**. *ind 3rd sg* **oochpahláawal**. *ind inv* **noochpáhlukw**. *ind I-you* **kooch=páhlul**. *conj 3rd sg* **wchupáhlaat**. *imp* **wchúpahl**. *ptcpl* **weechpáhlaat**.

**wchupŭlaalóhkweew** VAI have curly hair. *ind 1st sg* **noochpulaalóhkwa**, **noochpulaalóhkwaam**. *conj 3rd sg* **wchupŭlaalóhkwaat**. *ptcpl* **weech=pulaalóhkwaat**. *See* **wchupŭláand=peew**.

**wchupŭláandpeew** VAI have curly hair. *ind 1st sg* **noochpuláandpa**, **nooch=puláandpaam**. *conj 3rd sg* **wchupŭ=láandpaat**. *ptcpl* **weechpuláandpaat**. *See* **wchupŭlaalóhkweew**.

**wchúpŭleew** VII be curly. *conj 3rd sg* **wchúpŭleek**. *ptcpl* **weechpúleek**.

**wchupŭlúneew** VTA bunch s.t. animate up. *ind 1st sg* **noochpúlŭnaaw**, **noochpúlŭna**. *ind 3rd sg* **oochpulŭ=náawal**. *ind inv* **noochpúlŭnukw**. *ind I-you* **koochpúlŭnul**. *conj 3rd sg* **wchupŭlúnaat**. *imp* **wchúpŭlun**. *ptcpl* **weechpúlŭnaat**.

**wchupŭlúnum** VTI1B bunch s.t. up. *ind 1st sg* **noochpulŭnúmun**. *ind 3rd sg* **oochpulŭnúmun**. *conj 1st sg* **wchup=ŭlúnŭmaan**. *conj 3rd sg* **wchupŭ=lúnung**. *imp* **wchupŭlúnih**. *ptcpl* **weechpúlŭnung**.

**wchupŭlúsuw** VAI be wrinkled, be bunched up *(s.t. animate)*. *ind 1st sg* **noochpúlsi**, **noochpúlsiim**. *conj 3rd sg* **wchupŭlúsiit**. *ptcpl* **weechpúlsiit**.

**wchuwáapŭweew** VAIO fill s.t with liquid. *ind 1st sg* **noochŭwáapŭween**. *ind 3rd sg* **oochŭwáapŭween**. *conj 3rd sg* **wchuwáapŭweet**. *imp* **wchuwáapŭweel**. *ptcpl* **weechŭwáa=pŭweet**.

**wchuwáhleew** VTA fill s.t. animate up *(with non-liquid)*. *ind 1st sg* **noochŭ=wáhlaaw**, **noochŭwáhla**. *ind 3rd sg* **oochŭwahláawal**. *ind inv* **noochŭ=wáhlukw**. *ind I-you* **koochŭwáhlul**. *conj 3rd sg* **wchuwáhlaat**. *imp* **wchúwahl**. *ptcpl* **weechŭwáhlaat**.

**wchuwáhteew** VII be full *(with non-liquid)*. *conj 3rd sg* **wchuwáhteek**. *ptcpl* **weechŭwáhteek**.

**wchuwáhtoow** VTI2 fill s.t. up *(with non-liquid)*. *ind 1st sg* **noochŭwáhtoon**. *ind 3rd sg* **oochŭwáhtoon**. *conj 1st sg* **wchuwáhtawaan**. *conj 3rd sg* **wchuwáhtaakw**. *imp* **wchuwáhtool**. *ptcpl* **weechŭwáhtaakw**.

**wchúwapuw** VAI be full *(s.t. animate, with non-liquid)*. *ind 1st sg* **noochŭ=wápi**, **noochŭwápiim**. *conj 3rd sg* **wchúwapiit**. *ptcpl* **weechŭwápiit**.

**wchuwíixiin** VAI be full *(s.t. animate)*. *conj 3rd sg* **wchuwíixiing**. *ptcpl* **weechŭwíixiing**.

**wchuwíixtoow** VTI2 fill s.t. *ind 1st sg* **noochŭwíixtoon**. *ind 3rd sg* **oochŭ=wíixtoon**. *conj 1st sg* **wchuwiixtáw=aan**. *conj 3rd sg* **wchuwíixtaakw**. *imp* **wchuwíixtool**. *ptcpl* **weechŭ=wíixtaakw**.

**wchuwíixŭmeew** VTA fill s.t. animate. *ind 1st sg* **noochŭwíixŭmaaw**, **noo=chŭwíixŭma**. *ind 3rd sg* **oochŭwii=**

xŭmáawal. *conj 3rd sg* **wchuwíixŭ=maat**. *imp* **wchuwíixum**. *ptcpl* **wee=chŭwíixŭmaat**.

**wchuwíixun** VII be full. *conj 3rd sg* **wchuwíixung**. *ptcpl* **weechŭwíi=xung**.

**wchúwpeew** VAI be full of water, be full of liquids *(s.t. animate)*. *ind 1st sg* **noochŭwúpe, noochŭwúpeem**. *conj 3rd sg* **wchúwpeet**. *ptcpl* **weechŭ=wúpeet**.

**wchúwpeew** VAIO fill s.t. up with water, fill s.t. up with liquid. *ind 1st sg* **noochŭwúpeen**. *ind 3rd sg* **oochŭ=wúpeen**. *conj 3rd sg* **wchúwpeet**. *imp* **wchúwpeel**. *ptcpl* **weechŭwúp=eet**.

**wchúwpeew** VII be full of water, be full of liquids. **Shiipóosh'shal weew=chuwpéewal.** 'The creeks are full of water.' *conj 3rd sg* **wchúwpeek**. *ptcpl* **weechŭwúpeek**. *distributive reduplication* **weewchuwpéewal**.

**wchuwpéhleew** VAI fill up with liquid *(s.t. animate)*. *ind 1st sg* **noochŭ=wupéhla, noochŭwupéhlaam**. *conj 3rd sg* **wchuwpéhlaat**. *ptcpl* **wee=chŭwupéhlaat**.

**wchuwpéhleew** VII fill up with liquid. *conj 3rd sg* **wchuwpéhlaak**. *ptcpl* **weechŭwupéhlaak**.

**wéech** PC I wonder. **Wéech xéet lí ootéeneeng katá-éew.** 'I wonder if he's going to town.'; **Wéech xéet nú?** 'Would that be it?' *See* **wách**.

**wéechiis** NA fishworm. *pl* **weechíisak**. *dimin* **weechíishush**. *obv* **weechíisal**.

**weechpóoleew** VTA dress s.o. *ind 1st sg* **nŭweechpóolaaw, nŭweechpóola**. *ind 3rd sg* **weechpooláawal**. *ind inv* **nŭweechpóolukw**. *ind I-you* **kŭ=weechpóolul**. *conj 3rd sg* **weech=póolaat**. *imp* **wéechpool**. *ptcpl* **weechpóolaat**.

**wéechpuw** VAI get dressed, get ready. *ind 1st sg* **nŭwéechpi, nŭwéechpiim**. *conj 3rd sg* **wéechpiit**. *imp* **wéechpiil**. *ptcpl* **wéechpiit**.

**weechpúneew** VTA dress s.o., get s.o. ready. *ind 1st sg* **nŭweechpúnaaw, nŭweechpúna**. *ind 3rd sg* **weech=punáawal**. *ind inv* **nŭweechpúnukw**. *ind I-you* **kŭweechpúnul**. *conj 3rd sg* **weechpúnaat**. *imp* **wéechpun**. *ptcpl* **weechpúnaat**.

**weemachéekaniish** NA little person. *pl* **weemacheekaníishak**. *obv* **weema=cheekaníishal**. *live in woods and rarely show themselves to people*.

**weemalóhkeew** VAIO get rid of s.t., completely dispose of s.t., sell all of s.t. **Nŭweemalóhkeen nehláatamaan.** 'I gave away all of my belongings.' *ind 1st sg* **nŭweemalóhkeen**. *ind 3rd sg* **weemalóhkeen**. *conj 3rd sg* **weema=lóhkeet**. *imp* **weemalóhkeel**. *ptcpl* **weemalóhkeet**.

**weemawéeheew** VAIO use s.t. up, use up all of s.t. *ind 1st sg* **nŭweemawée=heen**. *ind 3rd sg* **weemawéeheen**. *conj 3rd sg* **weemawéeheet**. *imp* **weemawéeheel**. *ptcpl* **weemawée=heet**.

**weemíiheew** VTA destroy all of s.o., kill all of s.o., get rid of all of s.o. *object usually plural*. *ind 1st sg* **nŭweemii=háawak**. *ind 3rd sg* **weemiiháawal**. *ind inv* **nŭweemíihkook**. *ind I-you* **kŭweemiihŭlóhmwa**. *conj 3rd sg* **weemíihaat**. *imp* **wéemiih**. *ptcpl* **weemíihaat**.

**weemíixkaleew** VTA leave s.o. alone, leave s.o. behind *(at home, in a competition)*; leave everyone behind. **Nŭweemiixkalukéhna.** 'We were left behind (by the deceased).' *ind 1st sg* **nŭweemíixkalaaw, nŭweemíixkala**. *ind 3rd sg* **weemiixkaláawal**. *ind inv* **nŭweemíixkalukw**. *ind I-you* **kŭweemíixkalul**. *conj 3rd sg* **wee=míixkalaat**. *imp* **weemíixkal**. *ptcpl* **weemíixkalaat**.

**wéemi** PC all. **Wéemi kwéek.** 'Everything.' *See* **wéemu**.

**weemíhlaleew** VTA use up all of s.t. animate. *ind 1st sg* **nŭweemíhlalaaw**, **nŭweemíhlala**. *ind 3rd sg* **weemih=laláawal**. *ind inv* **nŭweemíhlalukw**. *ind I-you* **kŭweemíhlalul**. *conj 3rd sg* **weemíhlalaat**. *imp* **weemíhlal**. *ptcpl* **weemíhlalaat**.

**weemíhlatoow** VTI2 use s.t. up, use up all of s.t.; spend all of it *(of money)*. *ind 1st sg* **nŭweemíhlatoon**. *ind 3rd sg* **weemíhlatoon**. *conj 1st sg* **wee=mihlatáwaan**. *conj 3rd sg* **weemíh=lataakw**. *imp* **weemíhlatool**. *ptcpl* **weemíhlataakw**.

**weemíhleew** VII be all gone, be used up. *conj 3rd sg* **weemíhlaak**. *ptcpl* **wee=míhlaak**.

**weemihtéeheew** VTA hit all of s.o. *object usually plural*. *ind 1st sg* **nŭwee=mihteeháawak**. *ind 3rd sg* **weemih=teeháawal**. *ind inv* **nŭweemihtéeh=kook**. *ind I-you* **kŭweemihteehŭlóh=mwa**. *conj 3rd sg* **weemihtéehaat**. *imp* **weemíhteeh**. *ptcpl* **weemihtée=haat**.

**weemihtéeham** VTI1A hit all of s.t. *object usually plural*. **Nŭweemihtee=hŭmúnal mihtkwúsal.** 'I chopped down all of the bushes.' *ind 1st sg* **nŭweemihteehŭmúnal**. *ind 3rd sg* **weemihteehŭmúnal**. *conj 1st sg* **weemihtéehŭmaan**. *conj 3rd sg* **weemihtéehang**. *imp* **weemihtée=hah**. *ptcpl* **weemihtéehang**.

**weemooltúwak** VAI be all gone, everybody is gone. *ind 1st pl* **nŭweemool=tíhna**. *indef subject* **weemóoltiin**. *conj 3rd sg* **weemooltíhtiit**. *ptcpl* **weemooltíhtiit**.

**wéemu** PC all. *informal*. **Wéemu talí wŭlatéexun kóhpii.** 'There are a lot of good roads in the bush.'; **Wéemu kwéek ndúkook.** 'They said all sorts of things to me.' *See* **wéemi**.

**wéenaa** PC almost, nearly. **Wéenaa kŭláchuw.** 'He almost froze to death.'; **Wéenaa aaptahpáasuw.** 'He nearly got scared to death.'

**weendáameew** VAI fish with a line. *ind 1st sg* **nŭweendáame**, **nŭweendáa=meem**. *conj 3rd sg* **weendáameet**. *imp* **weendáameel**. *ptcpl* **weendáa=meet**.

**weendakwíiwan** NI dress; coat. *pl* **weendakwíiwanal**. *poss* **nŭweenda=kwíiwan**. *loc* **weendakwíiwanung**. *dimin* **weenjakwíiwanush**.

**wéenzteew** VII be Wednesday. *conj 3rd sg* **wéenzteek**. *ptcpl* **wéenzteek**. *From English* Wednesday.

**wéenzhteew** VII be Wednesday. **Wéen=zhteek náh éew.** 'She's going there on Wednesday.'; **Éenda-weenzhtée=ke náh nóom.** 'I went there last Wednesday.' *conj 3rd sg* **wéenzhteek**. *From English* Wednesday.

**wéest** NI blouse. *pl* **wéestal**. *poss* **nŭ=wéestum**. *See* **wéyst**. *From English* waist.

**weesthámeew** VAI wear a blouse. *ind 1st sg* **nŭweesthàma**, **nŭweesthámaam**. *conj 3rd sg* **weesthámaat**. *imp* **weesthámaal**. *ptcpl* **weesthámaat**. *See* **weysthámeew**.

**wéetu** PC in a while. **Ápih wéetu ndalŭ=músi.** 'I'm leaving soon.'

**weetŭmu-** PV while. *followed by verb in the conjunct order*. **Wéetŭmu-poonxáyaan.** 'While I was stoking the fire.'; **Náh mbá wéetŭmu-alóhkeet.** 'I came while he was working.' *ptcpl* **wéetŭmu-**.

**weewáatam** VAI come to, be aware. **Máh weewaatamóowi.** 'He doesn't know what's going on around him.' *ind 1st sg* **nŭweewáatam**. *conj 3rd sg* **weewáatang**. *ptcpl* **weewáatang**.

**weeweetŭyéepuw** VAI be squatting, squat. *ind 1st sg* **nŭweeweetŭyéepi**, **nŭweeweetŭyéepiim**. *conj 3rd sg* weeweetŭyéepiit. *imp* weeweetŭ=yéepiil. *ptcpl* weeweetŭyéepiit.

**weewehkáasoon** NI swing. *pl* **weeweh=kaasóonal**. *poss* **nŭweewehkáasoon**. *loc* **weewehkaasóonung**. *dimin* **weewehkaashóonush**.

**weewehkáasuw** VAI swing, be swinging. *ind 1st sg* **nŭweewehkáasi**, **nŭwee=wehkáasiim**. *conj 3rd sg* **weeweh=káasiit**. *imp* **weewehkáasiil**. *ptcpl* **weewehkáasiit**.

**weewíiheew** VTA know s.o. *ind 1st sg* **nŭweewíihaaw**, **nŭweewíiha**. *ind 3rd sg* **weewiiháawal**. *ind inv* **nŭweewíi=hukw**. *ind I-you* **kŭweewíihul**. *conj 3rd sg* **weewíihaat**. *ptcpl* **weewíi=haat**.

**weewíhtoow** VTI2 know s.t. *ind 1st sg* **nŭweewíhtoon**. *ind 3rd sg* **weewíh=toon**. *conj 1st sg* **weewíhtawaan**. *conj 3rd sg* **weewíhtaakw**. *ptcpl* **weewíhtaakw**.

**wéewsuw** VAI know the news, hear the news, know what's going on. *ind 1st sg* **nŭwéewsi**, **nŭwéewsiim**. *conj 3rd sg* **wéewsiit**. *ptcpl* **wéewsiit**. *See* **wihwéewsuw**.

**weewŭlaalakíingweew** VAI have nice eyes. *ind 1st sg* **nŭweewŭlaalakíin=gwa**, **nŭweewŭlaalakíingwaam**. *conj 3rd sg* **weewulaalakíingwaat**. *ptcpl* **weewŭlaalakíingwaat**.

**weewŭliináakwsuw** VAI be cute looking. *ind 1st sg* **nŭweewŭliináakwsi**, **nŭweewŭliináakwsiim**. *conj 3rd sg* **weewŭliináakwsiit**. *ptcpl* **weewŭlii=náakwsiit**.

**weewúndakwii** PC on both sides of something. **Weewúndakwii áaneeng wíikŭwak.** 'They live on both sides of the road.'; **Weewúndakwii pŭ=músŭwak.** 'They're walking on both sides (of you).'

**wehkáathoos** NA iron kettle with legs. *pl* **wehkaathóosak**. *loc* **wehkaat=hóosung**. *obv* **wehkaathóosal**. *See* **wihkáathoos**, **wihkaathóosus**.

**wehkwáhleew** VAI be the last of one's family, be last of one's lineage. *ind 1st sg* **nŭwehkwáhla**, **nŭwehkwáh=laam**. *conj 3rd sg* **wehkwáhlaat**. *ptcpl* **wehkwáhlaat**.

**wéhlaleew** VTA hang s.o. up, hang s.t. animate up. *ind 1st sg* **nŭwéhlalaaw**, **nŭwéhlala**. *ind 3rd sg* **wehlaláawal**. *ind inv* **nŭwéhlalukw**. *ind I-you* **kŭwéhlalul**. *conj 3rd sg* **wéhlalaat**. *imp* **wéhlal**. *ptcpl* **wéhlalaat**.

**wéhlatoow** VTI2 hang s.t. up. *ind 1st sg* **nŭwéhlatoon**. *ind 3rd sg* **wéhlatoon**. *conj 1st sg* **wehlatáwaan**. *conj 3rd sg* **wéhlataakw**. *imp* **wéhlatool**. *ptcpl* **wéhlataakw**.

**wéhleew** VAI hang, be hanging *(s.t. animate)*. **Wéhleew píkchul.** 'The picture is hanging up.' *ind 1st sg* **nŭ=wéhla**, **nŭwéhlaam**. *conj 3rd sg* **wéhlaat**. *ptcpl* **wéhlaat**.

**wéhleew** VII hang, be hanging. **Wéhleew ngóotum.** 'My coat is hanging up.' *conj 3rd sg* **wéhlaak**. *ptcpl* **wéhlaak**.

**wehwahkwéelŭniing** NI scarf, collar, necktie, horse's collar. *pl* **wehwah=kweelŭníingal**. *poss* **nŭwehwah=kweelŭníingum**.

**wehwahkweelŭniingháasuw** VII have a collar on it. *conj 3rd sg* **wehwah=kweelŭniingháasiik**. *ptcpl* **wehwah=kweelŭniingháasiik**.

**wehwéemwaaleew** VTA make fun of s.o. *ind 1st sg* **nŭwehweemwáalaaw**, **nŭwehweemwáala**. *ind 3rd sg* **weh=weemwaaláawal**. *ind inv* **nŭwehwee=mwáalukw**. *ind I-you* **kŭwehwee=mwáalul**. *conj 3rd sg* **wehweemwáa=laat**. *imp* **wehwéemwaal**. *ptcpl* **wehweemwáalaat**.

**wehweemwáalŭweew** VAI make fun of people. *ind 1st sg* **nŭwehweemwáa=lŭwe**, **nŭwehweemwáalŭweem**. *conj 3rd sg* **wehweemwáalŭweet**. *imp* **wehweemwáalŭweel**. *ptcpl* **weh=**

**weemwáalŭweet**.

**wehwíinŭwees** NA beggar. *pl* **wehwii=nŭwéesak**. *dimin* **wehwiinŭwée=shush**. *obv* **wehwiinŭwéesal**.

**wehwtúnŭwees** NA mermaid. *pl* **weh=wtunŭwéesak**. *obv* **wehwtunŭwée=sal**. *lives in Thames River near Moraviantown.*

**wéhwunj-shoohíikeeng** NI paint brush. *pl* **wéhwunj-shoohiikéengiil**.

**wekóoliis** NA whipporwhill. *pl* **wekoo=líisak**. *dimin* **wekoolíishush**. *obv* **wekoolíisal**.

**wéyst** NI blouse. *pl* **wéystal**. *poss* **nŭ=wéystum**. *dimin* **wéysh'chush**. *See* **wéest**. *From English* waist.

**weysthámeew** VAI wear a blouse. *ind 1st sg* **nŭweystháma**, **nŭweysthámaam**. *conj 3rd sg* **weysthámaat**. *imp* **weysthámaal**. *ptcpl* **weysthámaat**. *See* **weesthámeew**.

**wiichéeweew** VTA accompany s.o., go with s.o. **Wíhwiing- wéemu awéeniil lúnŭwal -wiicheewáawal.** 'She liked to go around with any man at all.' *ind 1st sg* **nŭwiichéewaaw**, **nŭwiichée=wa**. *ind 3rd sg* **wiicheewáawal**. *ind inv* **nŭwiichéewukw**. *ind I-you* **kŭ=wiichéewul**. *conj 3rd sg* **wiichéewaat**. *imp* **wíicheew**. *ptcpl* **wiichéewaat**.

**wiichii-** PV with, accompanying. **Nŭ=wíichii-maawéewi.** 'I went to the service with someone.' *ptcpl* **wíichii-**.

**wiichkúneew** VAI help people, help out. *ind 1st sg* **nŭwiichkúne**, **nŭwiich=kúneem**. *conj 3rd sg* **wiichkúneet**. *imp* **wiichkúneel**. *ptcpl* **wiichkúneet**. *moderative reduplication* **waawiich=kúneew**.

**wiichóohŭweew** VAI participate, take part, take part in a game, take part in a fight. *ind 1st sg* **nŭwiichóohŭwe**, **nŭwiichóohŭweem**. *conj 3rd sg* **wiichóohŭweet**. *imp* **wiichóohŭweel**. *ptcpl* **wiichóohŭweet**.

**wíichŭmeew** VTA help s.o. **Káta-wíi=chŭmul.** 'I want to help you.' *ind 1st sg* **nŭwíichŭmaaw**, **nŭwíichŭma**. *ind 3rd sg* **wiichŭmáawal**. *ind inv* **nŭwíi=chŭmukw**. *ind I-you* **kŭwíichŭmul**. *conj 3rd sg* **wíichŭmaat**. *imp* **wíi=chum**. *ptcpl* **wíichŭmaat**.

**wiichúndam** VTI1A help with s.t. *(of a project)*; second s.t. *(of a motion at a meeting)*. *ind 1st sg* **nŭwiichúnda=mun**. *ind 3rd sg* **wiichúndamun**. *conj 1st sg* **wiichúndamaan**. *conj 3rd sg* **wiichúndang**. *imp* **wiichúndah**. *ptcpl* **wiichúndang**.

**wíikheew** VAI build a house. *ind 1st sg* **nŭwíikhe**, **nŭwíikheem**. *conj 3rd sg* **wíikheet**. *imp* **wíikheel**. *ptcpl* **wíik=heet**.

**wíikuw** VAI dwell there, live there. **Wíi=kŭyaan.** 'My house.'; **Wíikŭyan.** 'Your house.' *ind 1st sg* **nŭwíiki**, **nŭwíikiim**. *conj 3rd sg* **wíikiit**. *ptcpl* **wíikiit**.

**wíikwahm** NI house. **Wíikŭuyaan.** 'My house, where I live.'; **Wíikiit.** 'His house, where he lives.' *pl* **wiikwáh=mal**. *loc* **wiikwáhmung**. *dimin* **wii=kwáhmush**. *See* **wíikuw**.

**wiikwáhmush** NI outhouse, toilet. *pl* **wiikwáhmshal**. *loc* **wiikwáhm=shung**.

**wiiláawan** NI antler, horn. *pl* **wiiláawa=nal**. *poss* **nŭwiiláawan**. *dimin* **wii=láawanush**.

**wiilawaakongwéepuy** NI fancy hat. *pl* **wiilawaakongwéepŭyal**. *poss* **nŭ=wiilawaakongwéepuy**.

**wiilawahkwéelŭnuw** VAI wear something around the neck, wear a scarf, wear jewellery. *ind 1st sg* **nŭwiila=wahkwéelŭni**, **nŭwiilawahkwéelŭ=niim**. *conj 3rd sg* **wiilawahkwéelŭ=niit**. *imp* **wiilawahkwéelŭniil**. *ptcpl* **wiilawahkwéelŭniit**.

**wiilawáhpapoon** NI fancy chair. *pl* **wii=lawahpapóonal**. *poss* **nŭwiilawáh=papoon**. *loc* **wiilawahpapóonung**.

*dimin* **wiilawahpapóonush**.

**wiilawii-** PN fancy. **Wíilawii-káal.** 'A fancy car.'

**wiilawiináakwat** VII be fancy looking. *conj 3rd sg* **wiilawiináakwahk**. *ptcpl* **wiilawiináakwahk**.

**wiilawiináakwsuw** VAI be fancy looking *(s.t. animate)*; be dressed up fancily. **Móxa wiilawiináakwsuw.** 'He's dressed up fancy.' *ind 1st sg* **nŭwii=lawiináakwsi**, **nŭwiilawiináakw=siim**. *conj 3rd sg* **wiilawiináakwsiit**. *ptcpl* **wiilawiináakwsiit**.

**wiilawíiyayuw** VAI act fancily. *ind 1st sg* **nŭwiilawíiyayi**, **nŭwiilawíiyayiim**. *conj 3rd sg* **wiilawíiyayiit**. *ptcpl* **wii=lawíiyayiit**.

**wiilawihtáakwat** VII sound fancy. *conj 3rd sg* **wiilawihtáakwahk**. *ptcpl* **wiilawihtáakwahk**.

**wiilawihtáakwsuw** VAI sound fancy *(s.t. animate)*. *ind 1st sg* **nŭwiilawih=táakwsi**, **nŭwiilawihtáakwsiim**. *conj 3rd sg* **wiilawihtáakwsiit**. *ptcpl* **wii=lawihtáakwsiit**.

**wiilawóoxweew** VAI have a fancy walk, walk fancily. *ind 1st sg* **nŭwiilawóo=xwe**, **nŭwiilawóoxweem**. *conj 3rd sg* **wiilawóoxweet**. *imp* **wiilawóoxweel**. *ptcpl* **wiilawóoxweet**.

**wíilaxkii-píinj** NA hair pin. *pl* **wiiláxkii-píinjak**. *poss* **nŭwiiláxkii-píinjum**. *dimin* **wiiláxkii-píinjush**. *obv* **wiiláxkii-píinjal**.

**wíilaxkii-píinj** NI hair pin. *pl* **wiiláxkii-píinjal**. *poss* **nŭwiiláxkii-píinjum**. *dimin* **wiiláxkii-píinjush**.

**wiilíineew** VAI have a headache. *ind 1st sg* **nŭwiilíine**, **nŭwiilíineem**. *emphatic pl* **wiiliinhátŭwak**. *conj 3rd sg* **wiilíineet**. *ptcpl* **wiilíineet**.

**wíimb** NI heartwood of tree, spine.

**wiimbámbtoow** VTI2 turn s.t. up and tie it *(of a horse's tail, of a person's hair)*; do s.t. up in a bun *(of someone's hair)*. *ind 1st sg* **nŭwiimbámbtoon**. *ind 3rd sg* **wiimbámbtoon**. *conj 1st sg* **wiim=bambtáwaan**. *conj 3rd sg* **wiim=bámbtaakw**. *imp* **wiimbámbtool**. *ptcpl* **wiimbámbtaakw**.

**wíimbat** PC ten. **Wíimbat txú-kŭlakíi=ke.** 'Ten o'clock.'

**wiimbíhleew** VAI wriggle, squirm. *ind 1st sg* **nŭwiimbíhla**, **nŭwiimbíh=laam**. *conj 3rd sg* **wiimbíhlaat**. *imp* **wiimbíhlaal**. *ptcpl* **wiimbíhlaat**. *intensive reduplication* **wihwiimbíh=leew**.

**wíimbŭnum** VTI1B twist and turn s.t., turn s.t. up *(of hair)*. *ind 1st sg* **nŭ=wiimbŭnúmun**. *ind 3rd sg* **wiimbŭ=númun**. *conj 1st sg* **wiimbŭnúmaan**. *conj 3rd sg* **wíimbŭnung**. *imp* **wíim=bŭnih**. *ptcpl* **wíimbŭnung**.

**wiinamálsuw** VAI be sick. *ind 1st sg* **nŭwiinamálsi**, **nŭwiinamálsiim**. *conj 3rd sg* **wiinamálsiit**. *ptcpl* **wiinamálsiit**.

**wiinamámeew** VTA be sore in s.t. animate *(of body parts)*; hurt s.t. animate. **Nguchkóohush nŭwiinamámaaw.** 'I hurt my little knee.' *ind 1st sg* **nŭwii=namámaaw**, **nŭwiinamáma**. *ind 3rd sg* **wiinamamáawal**. *conj 3rd sg* **wiinamámaat**. *ptcpl* **wiinamámaat**.

**wiinamándam** VTI1A be sore in s.t. *(of body parts)*; hurt s.t. **Wiinamánda=mun wsíit.** 'His foot is sore.' *ind 1st sg* **nŭwiinamándamun**. *ind 3rd sg* **wiinamándamun**. *conj 1st sg* **wiina=mándamaan**. *conj 3rd sg* **wiina=mándang**. *ptcpl* **wiinamándang**.

**wiinawámeew** VTAO beg s.o. for s.t. *ind 1st sg* **nŭwiinawámaan**. *ind 3rd sg* **wiinawámaan**. *ind inv* **nŭwiina=wámkwun**. *ind I-you* **kŭwiinawám=ŭlun**. *conj 3rd sg* **wiinawámaat**. *imp* **wíinawam**. *ptcpl* **wiinawámaat**.

**wiindáasuw** VII be named, be mentioned. *conj 3rd sg* **wiindáasiik**. *ptcpl* **wiindáasiik**.

**wíindam** VTI1A name s.t., mention s.t.

by name, call s.t. by name. *ind 1st sg* **nŭwíindamun**. *ind 3rd sg* **wíinda=mun**. *conj 1st sg* **wíindamaan**. *conj 3rd sg* **wíindang**. *imp* **wíindah**. *ptcpl* **wíindang**.

**wíineew** VII be snowing. **Éenda-wii=néeke.** 'When it was snowing.' *conj 3rd sg* **wíineek**. *ptcpl* **wíineek**.

**wiingáaleew** VTA like to do something with s.o. *requires complement in subordinative mode*. **Nŭwiingáalaaw nŭmeelawíihaan.** 'I like to play with him.' *ind 1st sg* **nŭwiingáalaaw**, **nŭ=wiingáala**. *ind 3rd sg* **wiingaaláa=wal**. *ind inv* **nŭwiingáalukw**. *ind I-you* **kŭwiingáalul**. *conj 3rd sg* **wiin=gáalaat**. *ptcpl* **wiingáalaat**.

**wiingáapŭweew** VAI like water. *ind 1st sg* **nŭwiingáapŭwe**, **nŭwiingáapŭ=weem**. *conj 3rd sg* **wiingáapŭweet**. *ptcpl* **wiingáapŭweet**.

**wiingáatam** VTI1A like s.t. **Nŭwiingáa=tamun nŭmíitsiin.** 'I like to eat.' *ind 1st sg* **nŭwiingáatamun**. *ind 3rd sg* **wiingáatamun**. *conj 1st sg* **wiingáa=tamaan**. *conj 3rd sg* **wiingáatang**. *ptcpl* **wiingáatang**.

**wiingáawsuw** VAI have a good time, have fun. *ind 1st sg* **nŭwiingáawsi**, **nŭwiingáawsiim**. *conj 3rd sg* **wiin=gáawsiit**. *ptcpl* **wiingáawsiit**.

**wiingalóhkeew** VAI like to work. *ind 1st sg* **nŭwiingalóhke**, **nŭwiingalóh=keem**. *conj 3rd sg* **wiingalóhkeet**. *ptcpl* **wiingalóhkeet**.

**wíingameew** VTA like the taste of s.t. animate. *ind 1st sg* **nŭwíingamaaw**, **nŭwíingama**. *ind 3rd sg* **wiinga=máawal**. *ind inv* **nŭwíingamukw**. *ind I-you* **kŭwíingamul**. *conj 3rd sg* **wíingamaat**. *ptcpl* **wíingamaat**.

**wíingan** VII taste good. **Míingasa wíin=gan.** 'It tastes better.' *conj 3rd sg* **wíingang**. *ptcpl* **wíingang**.

**wiingándam** VTI1A like the taste of s.t. **Máh wiingandamóowun.** 'He didn't like the taste of it.' *ind 1st sg* **nŭ=wiingándamun**. *ind 3rd sg* **wiingán=damun**. *conj 1st sg* **wiingándamaan**. *conj 3rd sg* **wiingándang**. *ptcpl* **wiingándang**.

**wíingapuw** VAI like it where one is. *ind 1st sg* **nŭwíingapi**, **nŭwíingapiim**. *conj 3rd sg* **wíingapiit**. *ptcpl* **wíinga=piit**.

**wiingatáhkeew** VAI like to fight. *ind 1st sg* **nŭwiingatáhke**, **nŭwiingatáh=keem**. *conj 3rd sg* **wiingatáhkeet**. *ptcpl* **wiingatáhkeet**.

**wiingatawáapuw** VAI like looking at things, enjoy the view. *ind 1st sg* **nŭwiingatawáapi**, **nŭwiingatawáa=piim**. *conj 3rd sg* **wiingatawáapiit**. *ptcpl* **wiingatawáapiit**.

**wiingchéepuw** VAI enjoy one's food. *ind 1st sg* **nŭwiingchéepwi**, **nŭwiing=chéepwiim**. *conj 3rd sg* **wiingchée=pwiit**. *ptcpl* **wiingchéepwiit**.

**wiingeelawúsuw** VAI enjoy playing, have fun while playing. *ind 1st sg* **nŭwiin=geelawúsi**, **nŭwiingeelawúsiim**. *conj 3rd sg* **wiingeelawúsiit**. *imp* **wiin=geelawúsiil**. *ptcpl* **wiingeelawúsiit**.

**wiingeelúndam** VAI be glad, be happy. *ind 1st sg* **nŭwiingeelúndam**. *conj 3rd sg* **wiingeelúndang**. *ptcpl* **wiin=geelúndang**.

**wiingeelúndam** VTI1A be happy about s.t., be glad about s.t. *ind 1st sg* **nŭ=wiingeelúndamun**. *ind 3rd sg* **wiin=geelúndamun**. *conj 1st sg* **wiingee=lúndamaan**. *conj 3rd sg* **wiingee=lúndang**. *ptcpl* **wiingeelúndang**.

**wiingiilawéemeew** VTA tell something to s.o. and make them happy. *ind 1st sg* **nŭwiingiilawéemaaw**, **nŭwiingii=lawéema**. *ind 3rd sg* **wiingiilawee=máawal**. *ind inv* **nŭwiingiilawée=mukw**. *ind I-you* **kŭwiingiilawée=mul**. *conj 3rd sg* **wiingiilawéemaat**. *imp* **wiingíilaweem**. *ptcpl* **wiingiila=wéemaat**.

**wiingiilŭnúweew** VAI be fond of men, like all the men, be 'boy-crazy.' *ind 1st sg* **nŭwiingiilŭnúwe**, **nŭwiingii=lŭnúweem**. *conj 3rd sg* **wiingíilŭ=nuweet**. *ptcpl* **wiingiilŭnúweet**.

**wiingiimáakwat** VII smell good, be good smelling, have a good smell. *conj 3rd sg* **wiingiimáakwahk**. *ptcpl* **wiingiimáakwahk**.

**wiingiimáakwsuw** VAI smell good, be good smelling, have a good smell *(s.t. animate)*. *ind 1st sg* **nŭwiingiimáak=wsi**, **nŭwiingiimáakwsiim**. *conj 3rd sg* **wiingiimáakwsiit**. *ptcpl* **wiingii=máakwsiit**.

**wiingiimáaleew** VTA like the smell of s.o. *ind 1st sg* **nŭwiingiimáalaaw**, **nŭwiingiimáala**. *ind 3rd sg* **wiingii=maláawal**. *ind inv* **nŭwiingiimáa=lukw**. *ind I-you* **kŭwiingiimáalul**. *conj 3rd sg* **wiingiimáalaat**. *ptcpl* **wiingiimáalaat**.

**wiingiimáatam** VTI 1A like the smell of s.t. *ind 1st sg* **nŭwiingiimáatamun**. *ind 3rd sg* **wiingiimáatamun**. *conj 1st sg* **wiingiimáatamaan**. *conj 3rd sg* **wiingiimáatang**. *ptcpl* **wiingii=máatang**.

**wiingíimaskw** NI sweetgrass. *pl* **wiin=giimáskwal**. *poss* **nŭwiingiimás=kwum**. *loc* **wiingiimáskwung**. *dimin* **wiingiimáshkwush**.

**wiingiimasúmeew** VAI have a nice smell *(of something cooking)*. *ind 1st sg* **nŭwiingiimasúma**, **nŭwiingiima=súmaam**. *conj 3rd sg* **wiingiima=súmaat**. *ptcpl* **wiingiimasúmaat**.

**wiingíimateew** VII have a nice smell *(of something cooking)*. *conj 3rd sg* **wiingíimateek**. *ptcpl* **wiingíimateek**.

**wiingíinam** VTI 1A like the look of s.t. *ind 1st sg* **nŭwiingíinamun**. *ind 3rd sg* **wiingíinamun**. *conj 1st sg* **wiin=gíinamaan**. *conj 3rd sg* **wiingíinang**. *ptcpl* **wiingíinang**.

**wiingíinaweew** VTA like the look of s.o. *ind 1st sg* **nŭwiingíinawaaw**, **nŭ=wiingíinawa**. *ind 3rd sg* **wiingiina=wáawal**. *ind inv* **nŭwiingíinaakw**. *ind I-you* **kŭwiingíinool**. *conj 3rd sg* **wiingíinawaat**. *ptcpl* **wiingíinawaat**.

**wiingíisŭmuw** VAI like to drink. *ind 1st sg* **nŭwiingíisŭmwi**, **nŭwiingíisŭ=mwiim**. *conj 3rd sg* **wiingíisŭmwiit**. *ptcpl* **wiingíisŭmwiit**.

**wiingóoxweew** VAI be glad to go. **Móxa nŭwiingooxwéhna.** 'We were so glad to go.' *ind 1st sg* **nŭwiingóoxwe**, **nŭwiingóoxweem**. *conj 3rd sg* **wiin=góoxweet**. *ptcpl* **wiingóoxweet**.

**wiingoxkwéeweew** VAI like women, be 'girl-crazy.' *ind 1st sg* **nŭwiingox=kwéewe**, **nŭwiingoxkwéeweem**. *conj 3rd sg* **wiingoxkwéeweet**. *ptcpl* **wiingoxkwéeweet**.

**wiingsútam** VTI 1A like the sound of s.t., like to listen to s.t. **Nŭwiingsuta=múnal.** 'They (inanimate) sound good to me.' *ind 1st sg* **nŭwiingsútamun**. *ind 3rd sg* **wiingsútamun**. *conj 1st sg* **wiingsútamaan**. *conj 3rd sg* **wiing=sútang**. *ptcpl* **wiingsútang**.

**wiingsútaweew** VTA like the sound of s.o., like the sound of s.t. animate, like to listen to s.o. *ind 1st sg* **nŭ=wiingsútawaaw**, **nŭwiingsútawa**. *ind 3rd sg* **wiingsutawáawal**. *ind inv* **nŭwiingsútaakw**. *ind I-you* **kŭ=wiingsútool**. *conj 3rd sg* **wiingsúta=waat**. *imp* **wiingsútaw**. *ptcpl* **wiing=sútawaat**.

**wiingu-** PV like to. *informal*. **Níi áa kŭwíingu-wiicheewŭlóhmwa.** 'I'd like to go with you (plural).'; **Kŭ=wíingu-néewul.** 'I'm glad to see you.' *ptcpl* **wíingu-**. *See* **wihwiing-**.

**wíingul** VAI taste good *(s.t. animate)*. *conj 3rd sg* **wíingŭluk**. *ptcpl* **wíin=gŭluk**.

**wíingŭleew** VII burn well. *conj 3rd sg* **wíingŭleek**. *ptcpl* **wíingŭleek**.

**wiingxéexiin** VAI like to listen, enjoy listening, enjoy hearing something. **Wiingxéexiin há wá.** 'This one likes to listen.' *ind 1st sg* **nŭwiingxéexiin, nŭwiingxéexi**. *conj 3rd sg* **wiing=xéexiing**. *ptcpl* **wiingxéexiing, wiingxéexiit**.

**wiiníiheew** VTA make s.o. angry. *ind 1st sg* **nŭwiiníihaaw, nŭwiiníiha**. *ind 3rd sg* **wiiniiháawal**. *ind inv* **nŭwii=níihukw**. *ind I-you* **kŭwiiníihul**. *conj 3rd sg* **wiiníihaat**. *imp* **wíiniih**. *ptcpl* **wiiníihaat**.

**wiiníingwus** NA mink. *pl* **wiiníingwsak**. *dimin* **wiiníingwshush**. *obv* **wii=níingwsal**.

**wiinóonzhuy** NA onion. *pl* **wiinóon=zhŭyak**. *obv* **wiinóonzhŭyal**.

**wíinŭweew** VAI beg. *ind 1st sg* **nŭwíi=nŭwe, nŭwíinŭweem**. *conj 3rd sg* **wíinŭweet**. *imp* **wíinŭweel**. *ptcpl* **wíinŭweet**.

**wíinŭweew** VAIO beg for s.t., ask for s.t. *ind 1st sg* **nŭwíinŭween**. *ind 3rd sg* **wíinuween**. *conj 3rd sg* **wíinŭweet**. *imp* **wíinŭweel**. *ptcpl* **wíinŭweet**.

**wiipawáhksun** NI narrow shoe. *pl* **wii=pawahksúnal**. *poss* **nŭwiipawáh=ksun**. *loc* **wiipawahksúnung**. *dimin* **wiipawahkshúnush**.

**wíipaweew** VII be narrow. **Wiipawée=shuw nú síipuw.** 'The river is narrow.' *conj 3rd sg* **wíipaweek**. *ptcpl* **wíipaweek**.

**wiipawúsuw** VAI be wide *(s.t. animate)*. *ind 1st sg* **nŭwiipawúsi, nŭwiipa=wúsiim**. *conj 3rd sg* **wiipawúsiit**. *ptcpl* **wiipawúsiit**.

**wiipiithámeew** VAI wear dentures, wear false teeth. *ind 1st sg* **nŭwiipiitháma, nŭwiipiithámaam**. *conj 3rd sg* **wii=piithámaat**. *imp* **wiipiithámaal**. *ptcpl* **wiipiithámaat**.

**wiipíituw** VAI have teeth. *ind 1st sg* **noowiipíiti, noowiipíitiim**. *conj 3rd sg* **wiipíitiit**. *ptcpl* **weewíipiit**.

**wiipongwaalakíingweew** VAI have grey eyes. *ind 1st sg* **nŭwiipongwaala=kíingwa, nŭwiipongwaalakíin=gwaam**. *conj 3rd sg* **wiipongwaala=kíingwaat**. *ptcpl* **wiipongwaalakíin=gwaat**.

**wiipongwaalakíingweew** VAI have grey eyes, have brown eyes. *ind 1st sg* **nŭ=wiipongwaalakíingwe, nŭwiipon=gwaalakíingweem**. *conj 3rd sg* **wii=pongwaalakíingweet**. *ptcpl* **wiipon=gwaalakíingweet**.

**wiipongwaalóhkweew** VAI have brown hair. *ind 1st sg* **nŭwiipongwaalóh=kwa, nŭwiipongwaalóhkwaam**. *conj 3rd sg* **wiipongwaalóhkwaat**. *ptcpl* **wiipongwaalóhkwaat**.

**wiipongwaapamúkwat** VII be brown coloured, be grey coloured. *conj 3rd sg* **wiipongwaapamúkwahk**. *ptcpl* **wiipongwaapamúkwahk**.

**wiipongwaapamúkwsuw** VAI be brown coloured, be grey coloured *(s.t. animate)*. *ind 1st sg* **nŭwiipongwaapa=múkwsi, nŭwiipongwaapamúkw=siim**. *conj 3rd sg* **wiipongwaapa=múkwsiit**. *ptcpl* **wiipongwaapa=múkwsiit**.

**wiipongwahkéeyeew** VII be brown earth, be grey earth. *conj 3rd sg* **wiipon=gwahkéeyeek**. *ptcpl* **wiipongwah=kéeyeek**.

**wiipongwáhtakw** NI brown thread, grey thread. *pl* **wiipongwáhtakwal**. *poss* **nŭwiipongwáhtakwum**. *loc* **wii=pongwáhtakwung**. *dimin* **wiipon=gwáhchakwush**.

**wiipongwcháseew** VTA dye s.t. animate brown, dye s.t. animate grey. *ind 1st sg* **nŭwiipongwchásaaw, nŭwii=pongwchása**. *ind 3rd sg* **wiipong=wchasáawal**. *ind inv* **nŭwiipong=wchásookw**. *ind I-you* **kŭwiipong=wchásool**. *conj 3rd sg* **wiipong=wchásaat**. *imp* **wiipóngwchas**. *ptcpl* **wiipongwchásaat**.

**wiipongwchásum** VTI1B dye s.t. brown,

dye s.t. grey. *ind 1st sg* **nŭwiipong=wchásŭmun**. *ind 3rd sg* **wiipongw=chásŭmun**. *conj 1st sg* **wiipong=wchásŭmaan**. *conj 3rd sg* **wiipong=wchásung**. *imp* **wiipongwchásih**. *ptcpl* **wiipongwchásung**.

**wiipóngweew** VII be brown, be grey. *conj 3rd sg* **wiipóngweek**. *ptcpl* **wiipóngweek**.

**wiipongwii-** PV brown, grey. **Nŭwii=póngwii-shóohŭmun.** 'I painted it brown, grey.' *ptcpl* **wiipóngwii-**.

**wiipongwíhleew** VAI turn brown, turn grey *(s.t. animate)*. *ind 1st sg* **nŭwii=pongwíhla**, **nŭwiipongwíhlaam**. *conj 3rd sg* **wiipongwíhlaat**. *ptcpl* **wiipongwíhlaat**.

**wiipongwíhleew** VII turn brown, turn grey. *conj 3rd sg* **wiipongwíhlaak**. *ptcpl* **wiipongwíhlaak**.

**wiipóngwsuw** VAI be brown, be grey *(s.t. animate)*. *ind 1st sg* **nŭwiipóngwsi**, **nŭwiipóngwsiim**. *conj 3rd sg* **wii=póngwsiit**. *ptcpl* **wiipóngwsiit**.

**wiipongwŭléexiin** VAI be a brownish colour, have a brown tinge to it, be a greyish colour, have a grey tinge to it *(s.t. animate)*. *ind 1st sg* **nŭwiipon=gwŭléexiin**, **nŭwiipongwŭléexi**. *conj 3rd sg* **wiipongwŭléexiing**. *ptcpl* **wiipongwŭléexiing**.

**wiipongwŭléexun** VII be a brownish colour, have a brown tinge to it, be a greyish colour, have a grey tinge to it. *conj 3rd sg* **wiipongwŭléexung**. *ptcpl* **wiipongwŭléexung**.

**wiisáamapwaan** NI corn meal bread, Johnny cake. *pl* **wiisaamapwáanal**. *poss* **nŭwiisáamapwaan**. *loc* **wiisaa=mapwáanung**. *dimin* **wiishaama=pwáanush**.

**wiisaawaapamúkwat** VII be yellow coloured. *conj 3rd sg* **wiisaawaapa=múkwahk**. *ptcpl* **wiisaawaapa=múkwahk**.

**wiisaawaapamúkwsuw** VAI be yellow coloured *(s.t. animate)*. *ind 1st sg* **nŭwiisaawaapamúkwsi**, **nŭwiisaa=waapamúkwsiim**. *conj 3rd sg* **wii=saawaapamúkwsiit**. *ptcpl* **wiisaa=waapamúkwsiit**.

**wiisaawáhtakw** NI yellow thread. *pl* **wiisaawáhtakwal**. *poss* **nŭwiisaa=wáhtakwum**. *loc* **wiisaawáhta=kwung**. *dimin* **wiishaawáhcha=kwush**.

**wiisaawaníikwus** NA red squirrel. *pl* **wiisaawaníikwsak**. *dimin* **wiishaa=waníikwshush**. *obv* **wiisaawaníikw=sal**.

**wiisaawcháseew** VTA dye s.t. animate yellow, dye s.t. animate brown. *ind 1st sg* **nŭwiisaawchásaaw**, **nŭwii=saawchása**. *ind 3rd sg* **wiisaawchas=áawal**. *ind inv* **nŭwiisaawchásookw**. *ind 1-you* **kŭwiisaawchásool**. *conj 3rd sg* **wiisaawchásaat**. *imp* **wii=sáawchas**. *ptcpl* **wiisaawchásaat**.

**wiisaawchásum** VTI1B dye s.t. yellow, dye s.t. brown. *ind 1st sg* **nŭwiisaaw=chásŭmun**. *ind 3rd sg* **wiisaawchás=ŭmun**. *conj 1st sg* **wiisaawchásŭ=maan**. *conj 3rd sg* **wiisaawchásung**. *imp* **wiisaawchásih**. *ptcpl* **wiisaaw=chásung**.

**wiisáaweew** VII be yellow. *conj 3rd sg* **wiisáaweek**. *ptcpl* **wiisáaweek**.

**wiisaawii-** PN yellow. **Wiisáawii-maa=laxkwsíital.** 'Yellow beans.'; **Wii=sáawii-kàshayéemal.** 'Yellow green beans.'

**wiisaawii-** PV yellow. **Nŭwiisáawii-shoohŭmúnal.** 'I painted them yellow.' *ptcpl* **wiisáawii-**.

**wiisáawii-maaláxkwsiit** NI yellow bean. *pl* **wiisáawii-maalaxkwsíital**. *poss* **nŭwiisáawii-maalaxkwsíitum**. *loc* **wiisáawii-maalaxkwsíitung**. *dimin* **wiisháawii-maalaxkwshíichush**.

**wiisaawíhleew** VAI turn yellow, turn brown *(s.t. animate)*. *ind 1st sg* **nŭwiisaawíhla**, **nŭwiisaawíhlaam**.

*conj 3rd sg* **wiisaawíhlaat**. *ptcpl* **wiisaawíhlaat**.

**wiisaawíhleew** VII turn yellow, turn brown. *conj 3rd sg* **wiisaawíhlaak**. *ptcpl* **wiisaawíhlaak**.

**wiisáawsuw** VAI be yellow *(s.t. animate)*. *ind 1st sg* **nŭwiisáawsi**, **nŭ=wiisáawsiim**. *conj 3rd sg* **wiisáawsiit**. *ptcpl* **wiisáawsiit**.

**wiisaawŭléexiin** VAI be a yellowish colour, have a yellow tinge to it. *ind 1st sg* **nŭwiisaawŭléexiin**, **nŭwiisaa=wŭléexi**. *conj 3rd sg* **wiisaawŭlée=xiing**. *ptcpl* **wiisaawŭléexiing**.

**wiisaawŭléexun** VII be a yellowish colour, have a yellowish tinge to it. *conj 3rd sg* **wiisaawŭléexung**. *ptcpl* **wii=saawŭléexung**.

**wiisaawxásuw** VAI turn reddish-brown, turn yellow, turn orange *(s.t. animate, by heat)*. *ind 1st sg* **nŭwiisaawxási**, **nŭwiisaawxásiim**. *conj 3rd sg* **wii=saawxásiit**. *ptcpl* **wiisaawxásiit**.

**wiisaawxáteew** VII turn reddish-brown, turn yellow *(by heat)*; be a ripened colour *(of grain ready to harvest)*. *conj 3rd sg* **wiisaawxáteek**. *ptcpl* **wiisaawxáteek**.

**wíisakeew** VII be sore, be tender; sting *(of sores)*. *conj 3rd sg* **wíisakeek**. *ptcpl* **wíisakeek**.

**wíisakiim** NI grape, raisin. *pl* **wiisakíi=mal**. *loc* **wiisakíimung**. *dimin* **wii=shakíimush**.

**wiisakíhleew** VAI get sore, hurt, have a pain, have a sharp pain, have a brief pain. **Ngútko wiisakíhleew.** 'My knee had a sharp pain.' *ind 1st sg* **nŭ=wiisakíhla**, **nŭwiisakíhlaam**. *conj 3rd sg* **wiisakíhlaat**. *ptcpl* **wiisakíhlaat**.

**wiisakíhleew** VII get sore, hurt, have a pain, have a sharp pain, have a brief pain. *conj 3rd sg* **wiisakíhlaak**. *ptcpl* **wiisakíhlaak**.

**wiisakúsuw** VAI be sore, be tender; sting *(of sores)*. *ind 1st sg* **nŭwiisakúsi**, **nŭwiisakúsiim**. *conj 3rd sg* **wiisa=kúsiit**. *ptcpl* **wiisakúsiit**.

**wiisóoheew** VAIO fatten s.o., fatten s.t. *ind 1st sg* **nŭwiisóoheen**. *ind 3rd sg* **wiisoohéenal**. *conj 3rd sg* **wiisóoheet**. *imp* **wiisóoheel**. *ptcpl* **wiisóoheet**.

**wiisóowuw** VII be fatty *(of meat)*. *conj 3rd sg* **wiisóowiik**. *ptcpl* **wiisóowiik**.

**wíisuw** VAI be fat. *ind 1st sg* **nŭwíisi**, **nŭwíisiim**. *conj 3rd sg* **wíisiit**. *ptcpl* **wíisiit**. *moderative reduplication* **waawíisuw**.

**wiisŭwatéelŭnuw** NA fat man. *pl* **wiisŭ=wateelŭnúwak**. *obv* **wiisŭwateelŭ=núwal**.

**wiisŭwóxkweew** NA fat woman. *pl* **wii=sŭwoxkwéewak**. *obv* **wiisŭwox=kwéewal**.

**wiisháasuw** VAI be afraid, be scared. *ind 1st sg* **nŭwiisháasi**, **nŭwiisháasiim**. *conj 3rd sg* **wiisháasiit**. *ptcpl* **wii=sháasiit**.

**wiis'háhkweew** VAI tap trees. *ind 1st sg* **nŭwiis'háhkwe**, **nŭwiis'háhkweem**. *conj 3rd sg* **wiis'háhkweet**. *imp* **wiis'háhkweel**. *ptcpl* **wiis'háhkweet**.

**wíishaleew** VTA frighten s.o., scare s.o. *ind 1st sg* **nŭwíishalaaw**, **nŭwíisha=la**. *ind 3rd sg* **wiishaláawal**. *ind inv* **nŭwíishalukw**. *ind I-you* **kŭwíisha=lul**. *conj 3rd sg* **wíishalaat**. *imp* **wíishal**. *ptcpl* **wíishalaat**.

**wiishalúweew** VAI frighten people, scare people. *ind 1st sg* **nŭwiishalúwe**, **nŭwiishalúweem**. *conj 3rd sg* **wii=shalúweet**. *imp* **wiishalúweel**. *ptcpl* **wiishalúweet**.

**wiishalúwees** NA rattlesnake. *pl* **wiisha=luwéesak**. *dimin* **wiishaluwéeshush**. *obv* **wiishaluwéesal**. *See* **wiisha=lúweew**.

**wiishalúweew** NA rattlesnake. *pl* **wii=shaluwéewak**. *obv* **wiishaluwéewal**. *See* **wiishalúwees**.

**wiitaachíimuw** VAI take part in a discussion. *ind 1st sg* **nŭwiitaachíimwi**,

**nŭwiitaachíimwiim**. *conj 3rd sg* **wiitaachíimwiit**. *imp* **wiitaachíi=mwiil**. *ptcpl* **wiitaachíimwiit**.

**wiitaaméhleew** VAI run as well, run with. *ind 1st sg* **nŭwiitaaméhla**, **nŭwiitaaméhlaam**. *conj 3rd sg* **wiitaaméhlaat**. *imp* **wiitaaméhlaal**. *ptcpl* **wiitaaméhlaat**.

**wiitaawsóomeew** VTA live with s.o. *ind 1st sg* **nŭwiitaawsóomaaw**, **nŭwii=taawsóoma**. *ind 3rd sg* **wiitaawsoo=máawal**. *ind inv* **nŭwiitaawsóo=mukw**. *ind I-you* **kŭwiitaawsóomul**. *conj 3rd sg* **wiitaawsóomaat**. *imp* **wiitáawsoom**. *ptcpl* **wiitaawsóo=maat**.

**wiitaláamuw** VAI sing along. *ind 1st sg* **nŭwiitaláamwi**, **nŭwiitaláamwiim**. *conj 3rd sg* **wiitaláamwiit**. *imp* **wii=taláamwiil**. *ptcpl* **wiitaláamwiit**.

**wiitalóhkeew** VAI work along with others, work with others. *ind 1st sg* **nŭ=wiitalóhke**, **nŭwiitalóhkeem**. *conj 3rd sg* **wiitalóhkeet**. *imp* **wiitalóh=keel**. *ptcpl* **wiitalóhkeet**.

**wiitapóomeew** VTA eat with s.o., stay with s.o. *ind 1st sg* **nŭwiitapóomaaw**, **nŭwiitapóoma**. *ind 3rd sg* **wiitapoo=máawal**. *ind inv* **nŭwiitapóomukw**. *ind I-you* **kŭwiitapóomul**. *conj 3rd sg* **wiitapóomaat**. *imp* **wíitapoom**. *ptcpl* **wiitapóomaat**.

**wíitapuw** VAI be here too, be present. *ind 1st sg* **nŭwíitapi**, **nŭwíitapiim**. *conj 3rd sg* **wíitapiit**. *imp* **wíitapiil**. *ptcpl* **wíitapiit**.

**wiitatáhkeew** VAI join in the fighting. *ind 1st sg* **nŭwiitatáhke**, **nŭwiita=táhkeem**. *conj 3rd sg* **wiitatáhkeet**. *imp* **wiitatáhkeel**. *ptcpl* **wiitatáhkeet**.

**wiitawéemak** VTA my wife, my husband, my spouse. **Wiitaweemáachiil.** 'His wife, her husband, his or her spouse.'; **Wiitawéemat.** 'Your wife, your husband, your spouse.' *conj 3rd sg* **wii=tawéemak**. *ptcpl* **wiitaweemáachiil**.

**wiitawéemeew** VTA marry s.o. *ind 1st sg* **nŭwiitawéemaaw**, **nŭwiitawéema**. *ind 3rd sg* **wiitaweemáawal**. *ind inv* **nŭwiitawéemukw**. *ind I-you* **kŭwii=tawéemul**. *conj 3rd sg* **wiitawée=maat**. *imp* **wíitaweem**. *ptcpl* **wiita=wéemaat**.

**wiitawéengeew** VAI get married. *ind 1st sg* **nŭwiitawéenge**, **nŭwiitawéen=geem**. *conj 3rd sg* **wiitawéengeet**. *imp* **wiitawéengeel**. *ptcpl* **wiita=wéengeet**. *See* **takwápuw**.

**wíiteew** VAI go along, accompany. *ind 1st sg* **nŭwíite**, **nŭwíiteem**. *conj 3rd sg* **wíiteet**. *imp* **wíiteel**. *ptcpl* **wíiteet**.

**wiithóomeew** VTA ride on horseback with s.o. *ind 1st sg* **nŭwiithóomaaw**, **nŭwiithóoma**. *ind 3rd sg* **wiithoo=máawal**. *ind inv* **nŭwiithóomukw**. *ind I-you* **kŭwiithóomul**. *conj 3rd sg* **wiithóomaat**. *imp* **wíithoom**. *ptcpl* **wiithóomaat**.

**wíitkeew** VAI take part in a dance. *ind 1st sg* **nŭwíitka**, **nŭwíitkaam**. *conj 3rd sg* **wíitkaat**. *imp* **wíitkaal**. *ptcpl* **wíitkaat**.

**wiitkéemeew** VTA dance with s.o. *ind 1st sg* **nŭwiitkéemaaw**, **nŭwiitkée=ma**. *ind 3rd sg* **wiitkeemáawal**. *ind inv* **nŭwiitkéemukw**. *ind I-you* **kŭ=wiitkéemul**. *conj 3rd sg* **wiitkéemaat**. *imp* **wíitkeem**. *ptcpl* **wíitkéemaat**. *See* **wiitkéemeew**.

nŭ**wíitkoxkw** NAD my sister. *pl* **nŭwiit=kóxkwak**. *3rd poss* **wiitkóxkwal**. *dimin* **nŭwiitkóxkwush**.

**wiitóoxweew** VAI go along *(with others)*. *ind 1st sg* **nŭwiitóoxwe**, **nŭwiitóo=xweem**. *conj 3rd sg* **wiitóoxweet**. *imp* **wiitóoxweel**. *ptcpl* **wiitóoxweet**.

**wiitóngwaam** VAI sleep with someone, sleep as well. *ind 1st sg* **nŭwiitón=gwaam**. *conj 3rd sg* **wiitóngwaang**. *imp* **wiitóngwaah**. *ptcpl* **wiitón=gwaang**.

**wiittóonheew** VAI take part in a conversation, butt into a conversation. *ind 1st sg* **nŭwiittóonhe, nŭwiittóon=heem**. *conj 3rd sg* **wiittóonheet**. *imp* **wiittóonheel**. *ptcpl* **wiittóonheet**.

**wiiwŭlaháakanal** NI harness. *usually plural. poss* **nŭwiiwŭlaháakanal**. *dimin* **wiiwŭlahaakanúshal**.

**wiiwŭnaashŭwíhleew** VAI swim in a circle, swim around something. *ind 1st sg* **nŭwiiwŭnaashŭwíhla, nŭwiiwŭ=naashŭwíhlaam**. *conj 3rd sg* **wiiwŭ=naashŭwíhlaat**. *imp* **wiiwŭnaashŭ=wíhlaal**. *ptcpl* **wiiwŭnaashŭwíhlaat**.

**wiiwŭnahtakíhleew** VAI run in a circle, run around something. *ind 1st sg* **nŭ=wiiwŭnahtakíhla, nŭwiiwunahta=kíhlaam**. *conj 3rd sg* **wiiwŭnahta=kíhlaat**. *imp* **wiiwŭnahtakíhlaal**. *ptcpl* **wiiwŭnahtakíhlaat**.

**wiiwŭnambíileew** VTA tie something around s.o. *ind 1st sg* **nŭwiiwŭnam=bíilaaw, nŭwiiwŭnambíila**. *ind 3rd sg* **wiiwŭnambiiláawal**. *ind inv* **nŭ=wiiwŭnambíilukw**. *ind I-you* **kŭwii=wŭnambíilul**. *conj 3rd sg* **wiiwŭ=nambíilaat**. *imp* **wiiwŭnámbiil**. *ptcpl* **wiiwŭnambíilaat**.

**wiiwŭnámbtoow** VTI2 tie something around s.t.; 'put s.t. up' *(of someone's hair). ind 1st sg* **nŭwiiwŭnámbtoon**. *ind 3rd sg* **wiiwŭnámbtoon**. *conj 1st sg* **wiiwŭnambtáwaan**. *conj 3rd sg* **wiiwŭnámbtaakw**. *imp* **wiiwŭ=námbtool**. *ptcpl* **wiiwŭnámbtaakw**.

**wiiwŭnéekham** VTI1A draw a circle around s.t., draw a circle on s.t., circle s.t. *ind 1st sg* **nŭwiiwŭneekhám=un**. *ind 3rd sg* **wiiwŭneekhámun**. *conj 1st sg* **wiiwŭneekhámaan**. *conj 3rd sg* **wiiwŭnéekhang**. *imp* **wiiwŭ=néekhah**. *ptcpl* **wiiwŭnéekhang**.

**wiiwŭnéekheew** VTA draw a circle around a picture of s.o., draw a circle on a picture of s.o., circle a picture of s.o. *ind 1st sg* **nŭwiiwŭnéekhaaw, nŭwiiwŭnéekha**. *ind 3rd sg* **wiiwŭ=neekháawal**. *ind inv* **nŭwiiwŭnéek=hookw**. *ind I-you* **kŭwiiwŭnéekhool**. *conj 3rd sg* **wiiwŭnéekhaat**. *imp* **wiiwŭnéekhaw**. *ptcpl* **wiiwŭnéek=haat**.

**wiiwŭneekhíikeew** VAI draw a circle around things, circle things. *ind 1st sg* **nŭwiiwŭneekhíike, nŭwiiwŭ=neekhíikeem**. *conj 3rd sg* **wiiwŭ=neekhíikeet**. *imp* **wiiwŭneekhíikeel**. *ptcpl* **wiiwŭneekhíikeet**.

**wiiwŭniikaapawúwak** VAI stand in a circle. *usually plural. ind 1st pl* **nŭ=wiiwŭniikaapawíhna**. *conj 3rd sg* **wiiwŭniikaapawíhtiit**. *imp* **wiiwŭ=niikáapawiikw**. *ptcpl* **wiiwŭniikaa=pawíhtiit**.

**wiiwŭniikwáakeew** VAI sew around the edges. *ind 1st sg* **nŭwiiwŭniikwáake, nŭwiiwŭniikwáakeem**. *conj 3rd sg* **wiiwŭniikwáakeet**. *imp* **wiiwŭnii=kwáakeel**. *ptcpl* **wiiwŭniikwáakeet**.

**wiiwŭniikwáaleew** VTA sew around the edges of s.t. animate. *ind 1st sg* **nŭ=wiiwŭniikwáalaaw, nŭwiiwŭnii=kwáala**. *ind 3rd sg* **wiiwŭniikwaa=láawal**. *ind inv* **nŭwiiwŭniikwáa=lukw**. *ind I-you* **kŭwiiwŭniikwáalul**. *conj 3rd sg* **wiiwŭniikwáalaat**. *imp* **wiiwŭníikwaal**. *ptcpl* **wiiwŭnii=kwáalaat**.

**wiiwŭníikwam** VTI1A sew around the edges of s.t. *ind 1st sg* **nŭwiiwŭníi=kwamun**. *ind 3rd sg* **wiiwŭníikwa=mun**. *conj 1st sg* **wiiwŭníikwamaan**. *conj 3rd sg* **wiiwŭníikwang**. *imp* **wiiwŭníikwah**. *ptcpl* **wiiwŭníi=kwang**.

**wiiwŭníikwsuw** VAI crawl in a circle, crawl around something. *ind 1st sg* **nŭwiiwŭníikwsi, nŭwiiwŭníikw=siim**. *conj 3rd sg* **wiiwŭníikwsiit**. *imp* **wiiwŭníikwsiil**. *ptcpl* **wiiwŭ=níikwsiit**.

**wiiwŭniinjkwéhlaleew** VTA roll s.o. around in a circle. *ind 1st sg* **nŭwii=**

wŭniinjkwéhlalaaw, **nŭwiiwŭ=niinjkwéhlala**. *ind 3rd sg* **wiiwŭ=niinjkwehlaláawal**. *ind inv* **nŭwii=wŭniinjkwéhlalukw**. *ind I-you* **kŭ=wiiwŭniinjkwéhlalul**. *conj 3rd sg* **wiiwŭniinjkwéhlalaat**. *imp* **wiiwŭ=niinjkwéhlal**. *ptcpl* **wiiwŭniinj=kwéhlalaat**.

**wiiwŭniinjkwéhlatoow** VTI2 roll s.t. around in a circle. *ind 1st sg* **nŭwii=wŭniinjkwéhlatoon**. *ind 3rd sg* **wiiwŭniinjkwéhlatoon**. *conj 1st sg* **wiiwŭniinjkwehlatáwaan**. *conj 3rd sg* **wiiwŭniinjkwéhlataakw**. *imp* **wiiwŭniinjkwéhlatool**. *ptcpl* **wiiwŭ=niinjkwéhlataakw**.

**wiiwŭniinjkwéhleew** VAI roll around, roll in a circle *(s.t. animate)*. *ind 1st sg* **nŭwiiwŭniinjkwéhla, nŭwiiwŭ=niinjkwéhlaam**. *conj 3rd sg* **wiiwŭ=niinjkwéhlaat**. *imp* **wiiwŭniinj=kwéhlaal**. *ptcpl* **wiiwŭniinjkwéh=laat**.

**wiiwŭniixíinook** VAI be placed around something, be placed all around something. *ind 1st pl* **nŭwiiwŭniixii=nóhna**. *conj 3rd sg* **wiiwŭniixiinóh=tiit**. *ptcpl* **wiiwŭniixiinóhtiit**.

**wiiwŭníixtoow** VTI2 put s.t. around something, put s.t. all around something. *object usually plural. ind 1st sg* **nŭwiiwŭniixtóonal**. *ind 3rd sg* **wii=wŭniixtóonal**. *conj 1st sg* **wiiwŭ=niixtáwaan**. *conj 3rd sg* **wiiwŭníix=taakw**. *imp* **wiiwŭníixtool**. *ptcpl* **wiiwŭníixtaakw**.

**wiiwŭníixŭmeew** VTA put s.t. animate around something, put s.t. animate all around something. *object usually plural. ind 1st sg* **nŭwiiwŭniixŭmáa=wak**. *ind 3rd sg* **wiiwŭniixŭmáawal**. *ind inv* **nŭwiiwŭniixŭmúkook**. *ind I-you* **kŭwiiwŭniixŭmulóhmwa**. *conj 3rd sg* **wiiwŭníixŭmaat**. *imp* **wiiwŭ=níixum**. *ptcpl* **wiiwŭníixŭmaat**.

**wiiwŭníixŭnool** VII be placed around something, be placed all around something. *usually plural. conj 3rd sg* **wii=wŭníixung**. *ptcpl* **wiiwŭniixúngiil**.

**wiiwŭníhkamook** VTI1A surround s.t. *subject usually plural. ind 1st sg* **nŭ=wiiwŭnihkamúneen**. *ind 3rd sg* **wii=wŭnihkamunéewa**. *conj 1st sg* **wii=wŭníhkameengw**. *conj 3rd sg* **wii=wŭnihkamóhtiit**. *imp* **wiiwŭníhka=mookw**. *ptcpl* **wiiwŭnihkamóhtiit**.

**wiiwŭnihkawéewak** VTA surround s.o. *subject usually plural. ind 1st sg* **nŭwiiwŭnihkawáawuna**. *ind 3rd sg* **wiiwŭnihkawaawáawal**. *ind inv* **nŭ=wiiwŭnihkáakook**. *ind I-you* **kŭwii=wŭnihkoolóhmwa**. *conj 3rd sg* **wii=wŭnihkawáhtiit**. *imp* **wiiwŭníhka=wooh**. *ptcpl* **wiiwŭnihkawáhtiit**.

**wiiwŭníhleew** VAI go in a circle, go around, roll in a circle *(s.t. animate)*. *ind 1st sg* **nŭwiiwŭníhla, nŭwiiwŭ=níhlaam**. *conj 3rd sg* **wiiwŭníhlaat**. *imp* **wiiwŭníhlaal**. *ptcpl* **wiiwŭníh=laat**. *intensive reduplication* **wihwii=wŭníhleew**.

**wiiwŭníhleew** VII go in a circle, go around, roll in a circle. *conj 3rd sg* **wiiwŭníhlaak**. *ptcpl* **wiiwŭníhlaak**. *intensive reduplication* **wihwiiwŭ=níhleew**.

**wiiwŭnóoxweew** VAI walk around something. *ind 1st sg* **nŭwiiwŭnóoxwe, nŭwiiwŭnóoxweem**. *conj 3rd sg* **wiiwŭnóoxweet**. *imp* **wiiwŭnóo=xweel**. *ptcpl* **wiiwŭnóoxweet**.

**wiiwŭnohkwéepŭwak** VAI sit in a circle. *usually plural. ind 1st pl* **nuwiiwŭ=nohkweepíhna**. *conj 3rd sg* **wiiwŭ=nohkweepíhtiit**. *imp* **wiiwŭnoh=kwéepiikw**. *ptcpl* **wiiwŭnohkwee=píhtiit**.

**wiiwŭnuchéhleew** VAI drive in a circle, drive around something. *ind 1st sg* **nŭwiiwŭnuchéhla, nŭwiiwŭnuch=éhlaam**. *conj 3rd sg* **wiiwŭnuchéh=laat**. *imp* **wiiwŭnuchéhlaal**. *ptcpl*

**wiiwŭnuchéhlaat**.

**wiiwŭnúsheew** VTA cut s.t. animate around the edge. *ind 1st sg* **nŭwii=wŭnúshaaw**, **nŭwiiwŭnúsha**. *ind 3rd sg* **wiiwŭnusháawal**. *ind inv* **nŭwii=wŭnúshookw**. *ind I-you* **kŭwiiwŭ=núshool**. *conj 3rd sg* **wiiwŭnúshaat**. *imp* **wíiwŭnush**. *ptcpl* **wiiwŭnúshaat**.

**wiiwŭnúshum** VTI1B cut s.t. around the edge. *ind 1st sg* **nŭwiiwŭnúshŭmun**. *ind 3rd sg* **wiiwŭnúshŭmun**. *conj 1st sg* **wiiwŭnúshŭmaan**. *conj 3rd sg* **wiiwŭnúshung**. *imp* **wiiwŭnúshih**. *ptcpl* **wiiwŭnúshung**. *intensive reduplication* **wihwiiwŭnúshŭmun**.

**wíixcheew** NA wolf. *pl* **wiixchéewak**. *obv* **wiixchéewal**.

**wiixéekan** NI body hair. *pl* **wiixéekanal**. *poss* **nŭwiixéekan**. *loc* **wiixéeka=nung**. *dimin* **wiixéekanush**.

**wiixeekanóowuw** VAI be hairy. *ind 1st sg* **nŭwiixeekanóowi**, **nŭwiixeeka=nóowiim**. *conj 3rd sg* **wiixeekanóo=wiit**. *ptcpl* **wiixeekanóowiit**.

**wiixeekanóowuw** VII be hairy *(as a chair)*. *conj 3rd sg* **wiixeekanóowiik**. *ptcpl* **wiixeekanóowiik**.

**wíixka** PC never. **Máhta wíixka péewi.** 'He never came.'; **Máh wíixka náh noomóowi.** 'I never went there.'

**wiixkweepíileew** VTA wrap s.o. up. *ind 1st sg* **nŭwiixkweepíilaaw**, **nŭwiix=kweepíila**. *ind 3rd sg* **wiixkweepii=láawal**. *ind inv* **nŭwiixkweepíilukw**. *ind I-you* **kŭwiixkweepíilul**. *conj 3rd sg* **wiixkweepíilaat**. *imp* **wiixkwée=piil**. *ptcpl* **wiixkweepíilaat**.

**wiixkweepíisuw** VAI be wrapped up *(s.t. animate)*. *ind 1st sg* **nŭwiixkweepíi=si**, **nŭwiixkweepíisiim**. *conj 3rd sg* **wiixkweepíisiit**. *ptcpl* **wiixkweepíi=siit**.

**wiixkweepíisuw** VII be wrapped up. *conj 3rd sg* **wiixkweepíisiik**. *ptcpl* **wiixkweepíisiik**.

**wiixkweeptíikan** NI bandage, wrapping paper, material used for wrapping. *pl* **wiixkweeptíikanal**. *poss* **nŭwiix=kweeptíikan**. *loc* **wiixkweeptíika=nung**. *dimin* **wiixkweepchíikanush**.

**wiixkwéeptoow** VTI2 wrap s.t. up. *ind 1st sg* **nŭwiixkwéeptoon**. *ind 3rd sg* **wiixkwéeptoon**. *conj 1st sg* **wiix=kweeptáwaan**. *conj 3rd sg* **wiix=kwéeptaakw**. *imp* **wiixkwéeptool**. *ptcpl* **wiixkwéeptaakw**.

**wíixkwii** PC all of a sudden. **Wíixkwii wtakŭniimaawáawal.** 'All of a sudden they started talking about him.'; **Kwáalŭmal wíixkwii ngíhleew.** 'His car stopped all of a sudden.'

**wiixŭwaxkóokus** NA caterpillar. *pl* **wii=xŭwaxkóoksak**. *dimin* **wiixŭwax=kóokshush**. *obv* **wiixŭwaxkóoksal**.

**wíixŭweew** VII be hairy. *conj 3rd sg* **wíixŭweek**. *ptcpl* **wíixŭweek**.

**wiixŭwíingweew** VAI have a hairy face. *ind 1st sg* **nŭwiixŭwíingwe**, **nŭwii=xŭwíingweem**. *conj 3rd sg* **wiixŭ=wíingweet**. *ptcpl* **wiixŭwíingweet**.

**wiixŭwihtóonayeew** VAI have a bushy beard. *ind 1st sg* **nŭwiixŭwihtóo=naya**, **nŭwiixŭwihtóonayaam**. *conj 3rd sg* **wiixŭwihtóonayaat**. *ptcpl* **wiixŭwihtóonayaat**.

**wiixŭwúsuw** VAI be hairy. **Mwáaka=neew wiixŭwúsuw.** 'The dog is furry.' *ind 1st sg* **nŭwiixŭwúsi**, **nŭ=wiixŭwúsiim**. *conj 3rd sg* **wiixŭwús=iit**. *ptcpl* **wiixŭwúsiit**.

**wihkáathoos** NA iron kettle with legs. *pl* **wihkaathóosak**. *loc* **wihkaathóo=sung**. *obv* **wihkaathóosal**. *See* **wihkaathóosus**, **wehkáathoos**.

**wihkaathóosus** NA iron kettle with legs. *pl* **wihkaathóossak**. *loc* **wehkaat=hóossung**. *obv* **wihkaathóossal**. *See* **wihkáathoos**, **wehkáathoos**.

**wihkaatíineew** VAI have a sore leg, have a lame leg. *ind 1st sg* **nŭwihkaatíine**, **nŭwihkaatíineem**. *conj 3rd sg* **wih=kaatíineet**. *ptcpl* **wihkaatíineet**.

**wihkaatŭnáasuw** VII be braided. *conj 3rd sg* **wihkaatŭnáasiik**. *ptcpl* **wehkaatŭnáasiik**.

**wihkáatŭnum** VTI1B braid s.t. *(of hair, of mats)*. *ind 1st sg* **nŭwihkaatŭ=númun**. *ind 3rd sg* **wihkaatŭnúmun**. *conj 1st sg* **wihkaatŭnúmaan**. *conj 3rd sg* **wihkáatŭnung**. *imp* **wihkáa=tŭnih**. *ptcpl* **wehkáatŭnung**.

**wihkwáameew** VII be at the end of a row, be at the end of a line, be at the end of something. **Péexwiish wih=kwáameew.** 'It is a little ways to the end of it.'; **Méhch kwáy éenda-wihkwaámeek kpáhna.** 'We've come to the end now.' *conj 3rd sg* **wih=kwáameek**. *ptcpl* **wihkwáameek**.

**wihkwáanay** NI the end of the road. *loc* **wihkwáaneeng**.

**wihkwáhleew** VAI be the last of one's family. *ind 1st sg* **nŭwihkwáhla**, **nŭwihkwáhlaam**. *conj 3rd sg* **wih=kwáhlaat**. *ptcpl* **wihkwáhlaat**.

**wíhkwanahkw** NI tree stump. *pl* **wih=kwanáhkwal**. *loc* **wihkwanáh=kwung**. *dimin* **wihkwanáhkwush**.

**wihkwatéexun** VII be the end of the road. *conj 3rd sg* **wihkwatéexung**. *ptcpl* **wihkwatéexung**.

**wíhkweew** VII come to an end, be the end of something. *conj 3rd sg* **wíh=kweek**. *ptcpl* **wíhkweek**.

**wihkwiitŭyéhleew** VAIO run out of s.t. *ind 1st sg* **nŭwihkwiitŭyéhlaan**. *ind 3rd sg* **wihkwiitŭyéhlaan**. *conj 3rd sg* **wihkwiitŭyéhlaat**. *ptcpl* **wih=kwiitŭyéhlaat**. *considered impolite*.

**wihkwíhleew** VAIO run out of s.t. *ind 1st sg* **nŭwihkwíhlaa**. *ind 3rd sg* **wih=kwíhlaan**. *conj 3rd sg* **wihkwíhlaat**. *ptcpl* **wihkwíhlaat**.

**wíhleew** VTA name s.o., mention s.o. by name, call s.o. by name. **Ndáaylu-wíhlaaw.** 'I call him by that name.' *ind 1st sg* **nŭwíhlaaw**, **nŭwíhla**. *ind 3rd sg* **wihláawal**. *ind inv* **nŭwíhlukw**. *ind I-you* **kŭwíhlul**. *conj 3rd sg* **wíhlaat**. *imp* **wíhl**. *ptcpl* **wíhlaat**.

**wihlkwúsuw** VAI be named, be mentioned by name. *ind 1st sg* **nŭwihl=kwúsi**, **nŭwihlkwúsiim**. *conj 3rd sg* **wihlkwúsiit**. *ptcpl* **wihlkwúsiit**.

**wihpéemeew** VTA sleep with s.o. *ind 1st sg* **nŭwihpéemaaw**, **nŭwihpéema**. *ind 3rd sg* **wihpeemáawal**. *ind inv* **nŭwihpéemukw**. *ind I-you* **kŭwih=péemul**. *conj 3rd sg* **wihpéemaat**. *imp* **wíhpeem**. *ptcpl* **wihpéemaat**.

**wihpéendŭwak** VAI sleep with each other, sleep together. *usually plural*. *ind 1st pl* **nŭwihpeendíhna**. *conj 3rd sg* **wihpeendíhtiit**. *imp* **wihpéen=diikw**. *ptcpl* **wihpeendíhtiit**.

**wihpóomeew** VTA eat with s.o. *ind 1st sg* **nŭwihpóomaaw**, **nŭwihpóoma**. *ind 3rd sg* **wihpoomáawal**. *ind inv* **nŭwihpóomukw**. *ind I-you* **kŭwih=póomul**. *conj 3rd sg* **wihpóomaat**. *imp* **wíhpoom**. *ptcpl* **wihpóomaat**.

**wihtawakíineew** VAI have an earache. *ind 1st sg* **nŭwihtawakíine**, **nŭwih=tawakíineem**. *conj 3rd sg* **wihta=wakíineet**. *ptcpl* **wihtawakíineet**.

nŭ**wihtóonay** NAD beard, whiskers. *pl* **nuwihtóonayak**. *3rd poss* **wihtóo=nayal**.

**wihtóonayuw** VAI have a beard, have a mustache, have whiskers. *ind 1st sg* **noowihtóonayi**, **noowihtóonayiim**. *conj 3rd sg* **wihtóonayiit**. *ptcpl* **wee=wihtóonayiit**.

**wihtóonayuw** VII have tassels *(of corn)*. *conj 3rd sg* **wihtóonayiik**. *ptcpl* **wihtóonayiik**.

**wihwchiipíisuw** VAI be afflicted with epilepsy, have epilepsy. *ind 1st sg* **nŭwihwchiipíisi**, **nŭwihwchiipíi=siim**. *conj 3rd sg* **wihwchiipíisiit**. *ptcpl* **wihwchiipíisiit**.

**wihwéewsuw** VAI know all the news, hear everything, hear all the gossip. *ind 1st sg* **nŭwihwéewsi**, **nŭwih=**

**wéewsiim**. *conj 3rd sg* **wihwéewsiit**. *ptcpl* **wihwéewsiit**. *See* **wéewsuw**.

**wihwiimbchéhleew** VAI wriggle. *ind 1st sg* **nŭwihwiimbchéhla, nŭwih=wiimbchéhlaam**. *conj 3rd sg* **wih=wiimbchéhlaat**. *imp* **wihwiimb=chéhlaal**. *ptcpl* **wihwiimbchéhlaat**.

**wihwiimbíixun** VII be curled, lie curled up. *conj 3rd sg* **wihwiimbíixung**. *ptcpl* **wihwiimbíixung**.

**wihwiing-** PV like to. **Wíhwiing-naa=wáhkeew.** 'He likes to follow people.'; **Wíhwiing- kwéek -úw** 'He likes to talk.' *ptcpl* **wíhwiing-**. *See* **wiingu-**.

**wihwiingaashóokeew** VAI like to wade in the water. *ind 1st sg* **nŭwihwiin=gaashóoke, nŭwihwiingaashóo=keem**. *conj 3rd sg* **wihwiingaashóo=keet**. *ptcpl* **wihwiingaashóokeet**.

**wihwshiipŭwéewuw** VAI speak Ojibwe. *ind 1st sg* **nŭwihwshiipŭwéewi, nŭwihwshiipŭwéewiim**. *conj 3rd sg* **wihwshiipŭwéewiit**. *imp* **wihwshii=pŭwéewiil**. *ptcpl* **wihwshiipŭwée=wiit**.

**wihwŭnaamíiwuw** VAI speak Unami. *ind 1st sg* **nŭwihwŭnaamíiwi, nŭwihwŭnaamíiwiim**. *conj 3rd sg* **wihwŭnaamíiwiit**. *imp* **wihwŭnaa=míiwiil**. *ptcpl* **wihwŭnaamiiwiit**.

**wsaa-** PV too much, excessively. **Wsáa-kwŭnéew.** 'It's too long.'; **Wsáa-laanzhíhkan pakandíikan.** 'The bat's too heavy.' *ptcpl* **wéesaa-**. *See* **wsaami-, wsaamu-**.

**wsaamcháseew** VTA overcook s.o., overheat s.o. *ind 1st sg* **noosaamchásaaw, noosaamchása**. *ind 3rd sg* **oosaam=chasáawal**. *ind inv* **noosaamchás=ookw**. *ind I-you* **koosaamchásool**. *conj 3rd sg* **wsaamchásaat**. *imp* **wsáamchas**. *ptcpl* **weesaamchásaat**.

**wsaamchásuw** VAI be overcooked, be overheated. *ind 1st sg* **noosaamchási, noosaamchásiim**. *conj 3rd sg* **wsaamchásiit**. *ptcpl* **weesaamchásiit**.

**wsaamchásum** VTI 1B overcook s.t., overheat s.t. *ind 1st sg* **noosaamchásŭ=mun**. *ind 3rd sg* **oosaamchásŭmun**. *conj 1st sg* **wsaamchásŭmaan**. *conj 3rd sg* **wsaamchásung**. *imp* **wsaam=chásih**. *ptcpl* **weesaamchásung**.

**wsaamíikun** VII grow too much, be overgrown. *conj 3rd sg* **wsaamíikung**. *ptcpl* **weesaamíikung**.

**wsaamíikuw** VAI grow too much, be overgrown. *ind 1st sg* **noosaamíiki, noosaamíikiim**. *conj 3rd sg* **wsaa=míikiit**. *ptcpl* **weesaamíikiit**.

**wsaamíisŭmuw** VAI drink too much. *ind 1st sg* **noosaamíisŭmwi, noosaamíi=sŭmwiim**. *conj 3rd sg* **wsaamíisŭ=mwiit**. *ptcpl* **weesaamíisŭmwiit**.

**wsaamíixun** VII be too much of something. *conj 3rd sg* **wsaamíixung**. *ptcpl* **weesaamíixung**.

**wsaami-** PV too much, excessively. **Wsáami-kihtamúneew.** 'He is too lazy.'; **Wsáami-xwushéeyeew.** 'It's too big, the hole is too deep.' *ptcpl* **weesáami-**. *See* **wsaa-, wsaamu-**.

**wsaamihtéeheew** VTA hit s.o. too much, hit s.o. too hard. *ind 1st sg* **noosaa=mihtéehaaw, noosaamihtéeha**. *ind 3rd sg* **oosaamihteeháawal**. *ind inv* **noosaamihtéehookw**. *ind I-you* **koosaamihtéehool**. *conj 3rd sg* **wsaamihtéehaat**. *imp* **wsaamíhteeh**. *ptcpl* **weesaamihtéehaat**.

**wsaamóoxweew** VAI walk too much. *ind 1st sg* **noosaamóoxwe, noosaamóo=xweem**. *conj 3rd sg* **wsaamóoxweet**. *ptcpl* **weesaamóoxweet**.

**wsaamóngwaam** VAI oversleep, sleep late, sleep in. *ind 1st sg* **noosaamón=gwaam**. *conj 3rd sg* **wsaamón=gwaang**. *ptcpl* **weesaamóngwaang**.

**wsaamu-** PV too much, excessively. *informal*. **Sháa wtulaawáawal kwiis=sùwáawal, "Chíi takwapŭwaaláa=han, wsáamu-mihmsahtakíhle."**

'Right away they told their son, "Don't marry her, she runs around too much."'; **Wsáamu-chahkwée=shuw ktaláawan.** 'Your cane is too short.' *ptcpl* **weesáamu-**. *intensive reduplication* **wàwsaamu-**. *See* **wsaa=mi-**, **wsaa-**.

**wsaamŭlóosuw** VAI overeat. *ind 1st sg* **noosaamŭlóosi**, **noosaamŭlóosiim**. *conj 3rd sg* **wsaamŭlóosiit**. *ptcpl* **weesaamŭlóosiit**.

**wsíitahkw** NI ax-handle. *pl* **wsiitáhkwal**. *poss* **noosiitáhkwum**. *loc* **wsiitáh=kwung**. *dimin* **wshiicháhkwush**.

**wsíhkaaw** VII-S be sunset. *conj 3rd sg* **wsíhkaak**. *ptcpl* **weesíhkaak**. *See* **wsíhkaan**.

**wsíhkaan** VII be sunset. **Alúmu-wsíh=kaan.** 'It was starting to be sunset.' *conj 3rd sg* **wsíhkaang**. *ptcpl* **wee=síhkaang**. *See* **wsíhkaaw**.

**wshaaxahkéeyeew** VII be slippery ground. *conj 3rd sg* **wshaaxahkée=yeek**. *ptcpl* **weeshaaxahkéeyeek**.

**wsháaxan** VII be slippery. *conj 3rd sg* **wsháaxang**. *ptcpl* **weesháaxang**.

**wshaaxíhleew** VAI slip. *ind 1st sg* **nooshaaxíhla**, **nooshaaxíhlaam**. *conj 3rd sg* **wshaaxíhlaat**. *ptcpl* **weeshaaxíhlaat**.

**wshaaxsáapaan** NI porridge made from water and flour rubbed together. *poss* **nooshaaxsáapaan**.

**wsháaxsuw** VAI be slippery *(s.t. animate)*. *ind 1st sg* **noosháaxsi**, **noo=sháaxsiim**. *conj 3rd sg* **wsháaxsiit**. *ptcpl* **weesháaxsiit**.

**wsháaxŭlaan** VII be sleeting. *conj 3rd sg* **wsháaxŭlaang**. *ptcpl* **weesháaxŭ=laang**.

**wshákay** NI shell. *pl* **wshákayal**. *loc* **wshákeeng**. *dimin* **wshákeesh**.

**wshanzhíhleew** VAI slip, slip sideways. *ind 1st sg* **nooshanzhíhla**, **nooshan=zhíhlaam**. *conj 3rd sg* **wshanzhíh=laat**. *ptcpl* **weeshanzhíhlaat**.

**wshapakwíiwan** NI cloth, cotton, rag. *pl* **wshapakwíiwanal**. *poss* **noosha=pakwíiwan**. *loc* **wshapakwíiwa=nung**. *dimin* **wshapakwíiwanush**.

**wshapakwiiwaníikaan** NI tent. *pl* **wshapakwiiwaniikáanal**. *poss* **noo=shapakwiiwaníikaan**. *loc* **wshapa=kwiiwaniikáanung**. *dimin* **wshapa=kwiiwaniikáanush**.

**wshápan** VII be thin *(as cake that didn't rise, slice of bread, meat, board)*. *conj 3rd sg* **wshápang**. *ptcpl* **wée=shapang**.

**wsháphoos** NA pail. *pl* **wshaphóosak**. *poss* **nooshapáhoos**. *loc* **wshaphóo=sung**. *dimin* **wshaphóoshush**. *obv* **wshaphóosal**.

**wshaphóosameekw** NA shiner *(fish species)*. *pl* **wshaphoosaméekwak**. *loc* **wshaphoosaméekwung**. *dimin* **wshaphoosaméekwush**. *obv* **wshap=hoosaméekwal**.

**wshaphoosíinjuw** NI tin pan. *pl* **wshap=hoosíinjŭwal**. *dimin* **wshaphoosíin=joosh**.

**wshapiiwu-** PN thin. *informal*. **Wshap=íiwu-kehkaasiingwéehiin.** 'Thin towel.'

**wshápsuw** VAI be thin *(s.t. animate)*. *ind 1st sg* **nooshapúsi**, **nooshapúsiim**. *conj 3rd sg* **wshápsiit**. *ptcpl* **wee=shapúsiit**.

**wshápsheew** VTA slice s.t. animate thinly. *ind 1st sg* **nooshapúshaaw**, **noosha=púsha**. *ind 3rd sg* **ooshapusháawal**. *ind inv* **nooshapúshookw**. *ind I-you* **kooshapúshool**. *conj 3rd sg* **wsháp=shaat**. *imp* **wshápush**. *ptcpl* **wee=shapúshaat**.

**wshapsháasuw** VAI be sliced thin *(s.t. animate)*. *ind 1st sg* **nooshapusháasi**, **nooshapusháasiim**. *conj 3rd sg* **wshapsháasiit**. *ptcpl* **weeshapush=áasiit**.

**wshapsháasuw** VII be sliced thin. *conj 3rd sg* **wshapsháasiik**. *ptcpl* **wee=**

**shapusháasiik**.

**wshápshum** VTI 1B slice s.t. thinly. *ind 1st sg* **nooshapúshŭmun**. *ind 3rd sg* **ooshapúshŭmun**. *conj 1st sg* **wshap=shúmaan**. *conj 3rd sg* **wshápshung**. *imp* **wshápshih**. *ptcpl* **weeshapúsh=ung**.

**wshapu-** PV thin. *informal.* **Wshápu-pangéeyeew.** 'It's in thin pieces.' *ptcpl* **wéeshapu-**.

**wshayaawúnge** PC edge of the hill.

**wshayapíineeng** PC at the edge of the bed.

**wsháyee** PC at the edge of something. **Wsháyee mbíing pŭmúsuw.** 'He's walking at the edge of the water.' *See* **wsháyii**, **wsháyiish**.

**wsháyii** PC at the edge of something. **Pámbiil wsháyii eehundaxpóonung ndáhlaaw.** 'I put the book at the edge of the table.' *See* **wsháye**, **wsháyiish**.

**wsháyiish** PC at the edge of something *(diminutive)*. **Wsháyiish ngáwi.** 'I sleep at the edge.' *See* **wsháyee**, **wsháyii**.

**wsháype** PC lake, edge of water. **Wsháype nóom.** 'I went out to the lake.'

**wsheewandiikanaháasuw** VII have pockets, have pockets on it. *conj 3rd sg* **wsheewandiikanaháasiik**. *ptcpl* **weesheewandiikanaháasiik**.

**wshéexakw** NI wood chip. *pl* **wshéexa=kwal**. *poss* **nooshéexakwum**. *loc* **wshéexakwung**. *dimin* **wshéexa=kwush**.

**wsheexakwáheew** VAI gather wood chips. *ind 1st sg* **noosheexakwáhe**, **noosheexakwáheem**. *conj 3rd sg* **wsheexakwáheet**. *imp* **wsheexa=kwáheel**. *ptcpl* **weesheexakwáheet**.

**wshíimeew** VTA run away from s.o., flee from s.o. *ind 1st sg* **nooshíimaaw**, **nooshíima**. *ind 3rd sg* **ooshiimáa=wal**. *ind inv* **nooshíimukw**. *ind I-you* **kooshíimul**. *conj 3rd sg* **wshíimaat**. *imp* **wshíim**. *ptcpl* **weeshíimaat**.

**wshíimuw** VAI run away, flee. *ind 1st sg* **nooshíimwi**, **nooshíimwiim**. *conj 3rd sg* **wshíimwiit**. *imp* **wshíimwiil**. *ptcpl* **weeshíimwiit**.

**wshíipŭweew** NA Ojibwe Indian. *pl* **wshiipŭwéewak**. *obv* **wshiipŭwée=wal**.

**wshiipŭwéexkweew** NA Ojibwe woman. *pl* **wshiipŭweexkwéewak**. *dimin* **wshiipŭwéexkweesh**. *obv* **wshiipŭ=weexkwéewal**.

**wshíixay** NI nest. *pl* **wshíixayal**.

**wshiixayáheew** VAI make a nest. *ind 1st sg* **nooshiixayáhe**, **nooshiixayáheem**. *conj 3rd sg* **wshiixayáheet**. *imp* **wshiixayáheel**. *ptcpl* **weeshiixayáh=eet**.

**wshíhweew** NA duck. *pl* **wshihwéewak**. *obv* **wshihwéewal**.

**wshulpúlŭmuw** VAI have money. *ind 1st sg* **nooshulpúlŭmi**, **nooshulpúlŭ=miim**. *conj 3rd sg* **wshulpúlŭmiit**. *ptcpl* **weeshulpúlŭmiit**.

**wtáansuw** VAI have a daughter. *ind 1st sg* **nootáansi**, **nootáansiim**. *conj 3rd sg* **wtáansiit**. *ptcpl* **weetáansiit**.

**wtáansuw** VAIO be s.o.'s daughter, have s.o. as a daughter. *ind 1st sg* **noo=táansiin**. *ind 3rd sg* **ootaansíinal**. *conj 3rd sg* **wtáansiit**. *ptcpl* **wee=táansiit**.

**wtakahkéeyeew** VII be soft ground. *conj 3rd sg* **wtakahkéeyeek**. *ptcpl* **weeta=kahkéeyeek**.

**wtákaneew** VII be warm out, be mild out. *conj 3rd sg* **wtákaneek**. *ptcpl* **weetakáneek**.

**wtakanii-** PV mild. **Éelii-wtákanii-láakwiik.** 'Because it is a mild evening.'; **Wtákanii-tpíhkat.** 'It's a warm night.' *ptcpl* **weetakánii-**.

**wtákanii-tpíhkat** VII be a warm night, be a mild night. *conj 3rd sg* **wtáka=nii-tpíhkahk**. *ptcpl* **weetakánii-tpíhkahk**.

**wtákeew** VII be damp, be wet, be soft. **Wtákeew íiyaach keeshiixtàwáaniil.** 'My washing's still damp.' *conj 3rd sg* **wtákeek**. *ptcpl* **wéetakeek**.

**wtakíixiin** VAI get damp, become soft from dampness *(s.t. animate)*. *ind 1st sg* **nootakíixiin**, **nootakíixi**. *conj 3rd sg* **wtakíixiing**. *ptcpl* **weetakíixiing**, **weetakíixiit**.

**wtakíixtoow** VTI2 soften s.t. *(with liquid)*. *ind 1st sg* **nootakíixtoon**. *ind 3rd sg* **ootakíixtoon**. *conj 1st sg* **wtakiixtáwaan**. *conj 3rd sg* **wtak=íixtaakw**. *imp* **wtakíixtool**. *ptcpl* **weetakíixtaakw**.

**wtakíixun** VII get damp, become soft from dampness. *conj 3rd sg* **wtakíi=xung**. *ptcpl* **weetakíixung**.

**wtakpáleew** VTA soften s.o. in water. *ind 1st sg* **nootakúpalaaw**, **nootakúpala**. *ind 3rd sg* **ootakupaláawal**. *ind inv* **nootakúpalukw**. *ind I-you* **koota=kúpalul**. *conj 3rd sg* **wtakpálaat**. *imp* **wtákpal**. *ptcpl* **weetakúpalaat**.

**wtakpátoow** VTI2 soften s.t. in water. *ind 1st sg* **nootakúpatoon**. *ind 3rd sg* **ootakúpatoon**. *conj 1st sg* **wtakpát=awaan**. *conj 3rd sg* **wtakpátaakw**. *imp* **wtakpátool**. *ptcpl* **weetakúpa=taakw**.

**wtákpeew** VAI be soft from dampness *(s.t. animate)*. **Pambíilak wtakpée=wak.** 'The papers are softened from being in water.' *ind 1st sg* **noota=kúpe**, **nootakúpeem**. *conj 3rd sg* **wtákpeet**. *ptcpl* **weetakúpeet**.

**wtákpeew** VII be soft from dampness. *conj 3rd sg* **wtákpeek**. *ptcpl* **weeta=kúpeek**.

**wtáksuw** VAI be damp, be wet, be soft *(s.t. animate)*. *ind 1st sg* **nootakúsi**, **nootakúsiim**. *conj 3rd sg* **wtáksiit**. *ptcpl* **weetakúsiit**.

**wtákŭneew** VTA soften s.t. animate. *ind 1st sg* **nootakúnaaw**, **nootakúna**. *ind 3rd sg* **ootakunáawal**. *ind inv* **noota=kúnukw**. *ind I-you* **kootakúnul**. *conj 3rd sg* **wtákŭnaat**. *imp* **wtákun**. *ptcpl* **weetakúnaat**.

**wtakŭnáxkeew** VAI have soft hands. *ind 1st sg* **nootakunáxka**, **nootakunáx=kaam**. *conj 3rd sg* **wtakŭnáxkaat**. *ptcpl* **weetakunáxkaat**.

**wtalŭmóonzuw** VAIO have s.o. for a pet, keep s.o. as a pet. *ind 1st sg* **noota=lumóonziin**. *ind 3rd sg* **ootalumoon=zíinal**. *conj 3rd sg* **wtalŭmóonziit**. *ptcpl* **weetalumóonziit**. *See* **alum=óonzuw**.

**wtamalóhkeew** VAI be busy. *ind 1st sg* **nootamalóhke**, **nootamalóhkeem**. *conj 3rd sg* **wtamalóhkeet**. *ptcpl* **weetamalóhkeet**.

**wtáxeew** VTA visit s.o. *ind 1st sg* **nóot=xaaw**, **nóotxa**. *ind 3rd sg* **óotxáawal**. *ind inv* **nóotxookw**. *ind I-you* **kóot=xool**. *conj 3rd sg* **wtáxaat**. *imp* **wtáx**. *ptcpl* **wéetxaat**.

**wtéehiim** NI strawberry. *pl* **wteehíimal**. *poss* **nooteehíimum**. *dimin* **wtee=híimush**.

**wteehíineew** VAI have heart trouble. *ind 1st sg* **nooteehíine**, **nooteehíineem**. *conj 3rd sg* **wteehíineet**. *ptcpl* **wee=teehíineet**.

**wtéeng** PC behind, at the back, in back of. **Wtéeng nóom.** 'I came from behind.'; **Niipíital wtéeng ehtéekiil.** 'My back teeth.'

**wteengíixiin** VAI be behind, be behind someone or something. *ind 1st sg* **nooteengíixiin**, **nooteengíixi**. *conj 3rd sg* **wteengíixiing**. *ptcpl* **weeteen=gíixiing**, **weeteengíixiit**.

**wtéeskw** NI corn husk, corn husk mat. *pl* **wtéeskwal**. *poss* **nootéeskwum**. *loc* **wtéeskwung**. *dimin* **wchéesh=kwush**.

**wtéeskwii-ehahpalíhkeeng** NI corn husk mat. *pl* **wtéeskwii-ehahpalih=kéengiil**.

**wtéhkaweew** VTA follow and come behind s.o., come behind s.o., come from behind s.o. *ind 1st sg* **nootéh=kawaaw, nootéhkawa**. *ind 3rd sg* **ootehkawáawal**. *ind inv* **nootéh=kaakw**. *ind I-you* **kootéhkool**. *conj 3rd sg* **wtéhkawaat**. *imp* **wtéhkaw**. *ptcpl* **weetéhkawaat**.

**wtóoxuw** VAI have a father. *ind 1st sg* **nootóoxwi, nootóoxwiim**. *conj 3rd sg* **wtóoxwiit**. *ptcpl* **weetóoxwiit**.

**wtóoxuw** VAIO have s.o. as a father, think of s.o. as one's father. **Wán há nzhíis shúkw nootóoxwiin.** 'He is my uncle but I think of him as my father.' *ind 1st sg* **nootóoxwiin**. *ind 3rd sg* **ootooxwíinal**. *conj 3rd sg* **wtóo=xwiit**. *ptcpl* **weetóoxwiit**.

**wtooxwíisuw** VAI have a grandchild. *ind 1st sg* **nootooxwíisi, nootooxwíisiim**. *conj 3rd sg* **wtooxwíisiit**. *ptcpl* **wee=tooxwíisiit**.

**wtooxwíisuw** VAIO have s.o. as a grandchild, be s.o.'s grandchild. *ind 1st sg* **nootooxwíisiin**. *ind 3rd sg* **ootoo=xwiisíinal**. *conj 3rd sg* **wtooxwíisiit**. *ptcpl* **weetooxwíisiit**.

**wtohwaníingweew** VAI have a sty in one's eye. *ind 1st sg* **nootòhwaníin=gwe, nootòhwaníingweem**. *conj 3rd sg* **wtohwaníingweet**. *ptcpl* **weetòh=waníingweet**.

**wtohwaníingwus** NA moth. *pl* **wtohwa=níingwsak**. *obv* **wtohwaníingwsal**.

**wtóhwanuw** VAI have branches, have antlers. *ind 1st sg* **nootóhwani, noo=tóhwaniim**. *conj 3rd sg* **wtóhwaniit**. *ptcpl* **weetóhwaniit**.

**wtuléeneew** VTA turn s.t. animate down *(of lights or sources of heat)*. *ind 1st sg* **nootŭléenaaw, nootŭléena**. *ind 3rd sg* **ootŭleenáawal**. *ind inv* **noo=tŭléenukw**. *ind I-you* **kootŭléenul**. *conj 3rd sg* **wtuléenaat**. *imp* **wtúleen**. *ptcpl* **weetŭléenaat**.

**wtuléenum** VTI1B turn s.t. down *(of lights or sources of heat)*. *ind 1st sg* **nootŭléenŭmun**. *ind 3rd sg* **ootŭlée=nŭmun**. *conj 1st sg* **wtuléenŭmaan**. *conj 3rd sg* **wtuléenung**. *imp* **wtul=éenih**. *ptcpl* **weetŭléenung**.

**wtúneew** VTA pull s.o., pull at s.o. **Nŭ=wawtúnukw.** 'He kept pulling at me.' *ind 1st sg* **nóotŭnaaw, nóotŭna**. *ind 3rd sg* **ootŭnáawal**. *ind inv* **nóotŭ=nukw**. *ind I-you* **kóotŭnul**. *conj 3rd sg* **wtúnaat**. *imp* **wtún**. *ptcpl* **wéetŭ=naat**. *intensive reduplication* **wàw=tunáawal**.

**wtuníikan** NI harness tug, harness gear. *pl* **wtuníikanal**. *poss* **nootŭníikan**. *loc* **wtuníikanung**. *dimin* **wtuníika=nush**.

**wtuníikeew** VAI pull things. *ind 1st sg* **nootŭníike, nootŭníikeem**. *conj 3rd sg* **wtuníikeet**. *imp* **wtuníikeel**. *ptcpl* **weetŭníikeet**.

**wtúnum** VTI1B pull s.t., pull at s.t. **Ngáta-wtúnŭmun.** 'I want to pull it.' *ind 1st sg* **nootŭnúmun**. *ind 3rd sg* **ootŭnúmun**. *conj 1st sg* **wtúnŭmaan**. *conj 3rd sg* **wtúnung**. *imp* **wtúnih**. *ptcpl* **wéetŭnung**.

**wtúpaleew** VTA shrink s.t. animate, shrink s.o. *(in water)*. *ind 1st sg* **nootpálaaw, nootpála**. *ind 3rd sg* **ootpaláawal**. *conj 3rd sg* **wtúpalaat**. *imp* **wtúpal**. *ptcpl* **weetpálaat**.

**wtúpatoow** VTI2 shrink s.t. *(in water)*. *ind 1st sg* **nootpátoon**. *ind 3rd sg* **ootpátoon**. *conj 1st sg* **wtupatáwaan**. *conj 3rd sg* **wtúpataakw**. *imp* **wtúp=atool**. *ptcpl* **weetpátaakw**.

**wtúpeew** VAI shrink *(s.t. animate, in water)*. *ind 1st sg* **nóotpe, nóotpeem**. *conj 3rd sg* **wtúpeet**. *ptcpl* **wéetpeet**.

**wtúpeew** VII shrink *(in water)*. *conj 3rd sg* **wtúpeek**. *ptcpl* **wéetpeek**.

**wtutaachíindam** VTI1A pull and drag s.t. *ind 1st sg* **noottaachíindamun**. *ind 3rd sg* **oottaachíindamun**. *conj 1st sg* **wtutaachíindamaan**. *conj 3rd sg* **wtutaachíindang**. *imp* **wtutaa=**

**chíindah**. *ptcpl* **weettaachíindang**.

**wtutaachíhleew** VTA pull and drag s.o., pull and drag s.t. animate. *ind 1st sg* **noottaachíhlaaw**, **noottaachíhla**. *ind 3rd sg* **oottaachihláawal**. *ind inv* **noottaachíhlukw**. *ind I-you* **koot=taachíhlul**. *conj 3rd sg* **wtutaachíh=laat**. *imp* **wtutáachihl**. *ptcpl* **weet=taachíhlaat**.

**wŭlaachíimuw** VAI give a good account of onself, tell a favourable story. *ind 1st sg* **noolaachíimwi**, **noolaachíi=mwiim**. *conj 3rd sg* **wŭlaachíimwiit**. *imp* **wŭlaachíimwiil**. *ptcpl* **weelaa=chíimwiit**.

**wŭláaheew** VAI take good aim *(with a gun)*; throw well. *ind 1st sg* **nooláa=he**, **nooláaheem**. *conj 3rd sg* **wŭláa=heet**. *imp* **wŭláaheel**. *ptcpl* **weeláa=heet**. *intensive reduplication* **awul=áaheew**.

**wŭlaakanaamíinzhuy** NA American elm. *pl* **wŭlaakanaamíinzhŭyak**. *obv* **wŭlaakanaamíinzhŭyal**.

**wŭlaakanahóonzhuy** NA American elm. *pl* **wŭlaakanahóonzhŭyak**. *obv* **wŭlaakanahóonzhŭyal**.

**wŭláakanus** NI dish. *pl* **wŭlaakanúsal**. *poss* **nooláakanus**. *loc* **wŭlaakanús=ung**. *dimin* **wŭlaakanúshush**.

**wŭláakuw** VII be evening. **Wulaakwíi=ke-uch náh mbá.** 'I'll go this evening.'; **Peetootéewuw weelaakwíike** 'He came to visit last evening.' *conj 3rd sg* **wŭláakwiik**. *ptcpl* **weeláa=kwiik**.

**wŭláakwe** PC yesterday. **Wuláakwe nŭmáhlam kshíiteew.** 'I bought some soup yesterday.'

**wŭlaakwŭnúwii** PC during the evening. **Wŭlaakwŭnúwii áng nŭmáw-paapŭmúsi.** 'I walk around in the evenings.'

**wŭlaalóhkweew** VAI have fine hair, have nice hair, have good hair. *ind 1st sg* **noolaalóhkwa**, **noolaalóhkwaam**. *conj 3rd sg* **wŭlaalóhkwaat**. *ptcpl* **weelaalóhkwaat**.

**wŭláamat** VII be fine in grain, be fine grained *(of flour, of sand)*. *conj 3rd sg* **wŭláamahk**. *ptcpl* **weeláamahk**.

**wŭlaaméewak** VAI be in a straight line, be in a row *(s.t. animate)*. *usually plural*. *ind 1st pl* **noolaaméhna**. *conj 3rd sg* **wŭlaaméhtiit**. *imp* **wŭláa=meekw**. *ptcpl* **weelaaméhtiit**.

**wŭlaaméewal** VII be in a straight line, be in a row. *usually plural*. *conj 3rd sg* **wŭláameek**. *ptcpl* **weelaaméekiil**.

**wŭlaameexíinook** VAI be lined up, be in a straight line, line up. *usually plural*. *ind 1st pl* **noolaameexiinóhna**. *conj 3rd sg* **wŭlaameexiinóhtiit**. *imp* **wŭlaaméexiikw**. *ptcpl* **weelaamee=xiinóhtiit**.

**wŭlaaméextoow** VTI2 line s.t. up. *object usually plural*. *ind 1st sg* **noolaa=meextóonal**. *ind 3rd sg* **oolaameex=tóonal**. *conj 1st sg* **wŭlaameextáw=aan**. *conj 3rd sg* **wŭlaaméextaakw**. *imp* **wŭlaaméextool**. *ptcpl* **weelaa=méextaakw**.

**wŭlaaméexŭmeew** VTA line s.o. up, line s.t. animate up. *object usually plural*. *ind 1st sg* **noolaameexŭmáawak**. *ind 3rd sg* **oolaameexŭmáawal**. *ind inv* **noolaameexŭmúkook**. *ind I-you* **koolaameexŭmulóhmwa**. *conj 3rd sg* **wŭlaaméexŭmaat**. *imp* **wŭlaa=méexum**. *ptcpl* **weelaaméexŭmaat**.

**wŭlaaméexŭnool** VII be lined up, be in a straight line, line up. *usually plural*. *conj 3rd sg* **wŭlaaméexung**. *ptcpl* **weelaameexúngiil**.

**wŭlaamii-** PN fine grained. **Wŭláamii-léekuw.** 'Fine sand.'

**wŭláamsheew** VTA cut s.t. animate finely. *ind 1st sg* **nooláamshaaw**, **noo=láamsha**. *ind 3rd sg* **oolaamsháawal**. *ind inv* **nooláamshookw**. *ind I-you* **kooláamshool**. *conj 3rd sg* **wŭláam=shaat**. *imp* **wŭláamush**. *ptcpl* **wee=**

**láamshaat**.

**wŭláamshum** VTI I B cut s.t. finely. *ind 1st sg* **noolaamshúmun**. *ind 3rd sg* **oolaamshúmun**. *conj 1st sg* **wŭ=laamshúmaan**. *conj 3rd sg* **wŭláam=shung**. *imp* **wŭláamshih**. *ptcpl* **wee=láamshung**.

**wŭláamweew** VAI tell the truth, make a deal. *ind 1st sg* **nooláamwe, nooláa=mweem**. *conj 3rd sg* **wŭláamweet**. *imp* **wŭláamweel**. *ptcpl* **weeláa=mweet**.

**wŭlaamweewáakan** NI truth.

**wŭláandeew** VII shine *(of the sun)*. *conj 3rd sg* **wŭláandeek**. *ptcpl* **weeláan=deek**.

**wŭlaandéhleew** VII become sunny. *conj 3rd sg* **wŭlaandéhlaak**. *ptcpl* **wee=laandéhlaak**.

**wŭláandpeew** VAI have a good head on one's shoulders. *ind 1st sg* **nooláan=dpa, nooláandpaam**. *conj 3rd sg* **wŭláandpaat**. *ptcpl* **weeláandpaat**.

**wŭlaangóomeew** VTA be friends with s.o. *ind 1st sg* **noolaangóomaaw, noolaangóoma**. *ind 3rd sg* **oolaan=goomáawal**. *ind inv* **noolaangóo=mukw**. *ind I-you* **koolaangóomul**. *conj 3rd sg* **wŭlaangóomaat**. *imp* **wŭláangoom**. *ptcpl* **weelaangóo=maat**.

**wŭlaangoondŭwáakan** NI friendship. *pl* **wŭlaangoondŭwáakanal**. *poss* **noo=laangoondŭwáakan**.

**wŭlaapamúkwat** VII be brightly coloured. *conj 3rd sg* **wŭlaapa=múkwahk**. *ptcpl* **weelaapamúk=wahk**.

**wŭlaapamúkwsuw** VAI be brightly coloured *(s.t. animate)*. *ind 1st sg* **noo=laapamúkwsi, noolaapamúkwsiim**. *conj 3rd sg* **wŭlaapamúkwsiit**. *ptcpl* **weelaapamúkwsiit**.

**wŭlaapasíhkan** NI good medicine. *pl* **wŭlaapasíhkan**. *poss* **noolapasíh=kan**.

**wŭlaapéemeew** VTA think that s.o. is handy, find s.o. handy, be helpful towards s.o., be good for s.o. *ind 1st sg* **noolaapéemaaw, noolaapéema**. *ind 3rd sg* **oolaapeemáawal**. *ind inv* **noolaapéemukw**. *ind I-you* **koolaa=péemul**. *conj 3rd sg* **wŭlaapéemaat**. *ptcpl* **weelaapéemaat**.

**wŭlaapéendam** VTI I A think that s.t. is handy, find s.t. handy, think that s.t. is useful, find s.t. useful. **Noolaapéen=damun noochapíhkum.** 'My medicine is good for me.' *ind 1st sg* **noo=laapéendamun**. *ind 3rd sg* **oolaa=péendamun**. *conj 1st sg* **wŭlaapéen=damaan**. *conj 3rd sg* **wŭlaapéen=dang**. *ptcpl* **weelaapéendang**.

**wŭlaapéenzuw** VAI be helpful, be handy, be useful. *ind 1st sg* **noolaapéenzi, noolaapéenziim**. *conj 3rd sg* **wŭlaa=péenziit**. *ptcpl* **weelaapéenziit**.

**wŭlaapéewuw** VAI be helpful, be handy. *ind 1st sg* **noolaapéewi, noolaapée=wiim**. *conj 3rd sg* **wŭlaapéewiit**. *ptcpl* **weelaapéewiit**.

**wŭlaaptoonáaleew** VTA say something good about s.o. *ind 1st sg* **noolaap=toonáalaaw, noolaaptoonáala**. *ind 3rd sg* **oolaaptoonaaláawal**. *ind inv* **noolaaptoonáalukw**. *ind I-you* **koo=laaptoonáalul**. *conj 3rd sg* **wŭlaap=toonáalaat**. *imp* **wŭlaaptóonaal**. *ptcpl* **weelaaptoonáalaat**.

**wŭlaaptóoneew** VAI say good things, preach. *ind 1st sg* **noolaaptóone, noolaaptóoneem**. *conj 3rd sg* **wŭlaaptóoneet**. *imp* **wŭlaaptóoneel**. *ptcpl* **weelaaptóoneet**.

**wŭláapŭweew** VII be clear liquid. *conj 3rd sg* **wŭláapŭweek**. *ptcpl* **weeláa=pŭweek**.

**wŭláasŭleew** VII be bright light. *conj 3rd sg* **wŭláasŭleek**. *ptcpl* **weeláasŭ=leek**.

**wŭláawsuw** VAI live well. *ind 1st sg* **nooláawsi, nooláawsiim**. *conj 3rd sg* wŭláawsiit. *ptcpl* **weeláawsiit**.

**wŭlacháaheew** VTA treat s.o. well. *ind 1st sg* **noolacháahaaw**, **noolacháa=ha**. *ind 3rd sg* **oolachaaháawal**. *ind inv* **noolacháahukw**. *ind I-you* **koo=lacháahul**. *conj 3rd sg* **wŭlacháa=haat**. *imp* **wŭláchaah**. *ptcpl* **weela=cháahaat**.

**wŭlahkachíhteew** VII be good shade, give good shade. *conj 3rd sg* **wŭlah=kachíhteek**. *ptcpl* **weelahkachíh=teek**.

**wŭláhkameew** VII be a nice day. *conj 3rd sg* **wŭláhkameek**. *ptcpl* **weeláh=kameek**.

**wŭlahkéeyeew** VII be even ground, be smooth ground. *conj 3rd sg* **wŭlah=kéeyeek**. *ptcpl* **weelahkéeyeek**.

**wŭlahkweexíinook** VAI be piled up neatly, be piled up nicely, be piled up properly *(s.t. animate, of something wood- or stick-like). usually plural. conj 3rd sg* **wŭlahkweexiinóhtiit**. *ptcpl* **weelahkweexiinóhtiit**.

**wŭlahkweextíikeew** VAI pile up wood, pile things up *(of something wood- or stick-like). ind 1st sg* **noolahkweex=tíike**, **noolahkweextíikeem**. *conj 3rd sg* **wŭlahkweextíikeet**. *imp* **wŭlah=kwéextiikeel**. *ptcpl* **weelahkweex=tíikeet**.

**wŭlahkwéextoow** VTI2 store s.t., pile s.t. up *(of something wood- or stick-like). object usually plural. ind 1st sg* **noolahkweextóonal**. *ind 3rd sg* **oolahkweextóonal**. *conj 1st sg* **wŭlahkweextáwaan**. *conj 3rd sg* **wŭlahkwéextaakw**. *imp* **wŭlah=kwéextool**. *ptcpl* **weelahkwéex=taakw**.

**wŭlahkwéexŭmeew** VTA store s.t. animate, pile s.t. animate up *(of something wood- or stick-like). object usually plural. ind 1st sg* **noolahkwee=xŭmáawak**. *ind 3rd sg* **oolahkwee=xŭmáawal**. *ind inv* **noolahkweexŭ=múkook**. *ind I-you* **koolahkweexŭ=mulóhmwa**. *conj 3rd sg* **wŭlah=kwéexŭmaat**. *imp* **wŭlahkwéexum**. *ptcpl* **weelahkwéexŭmaat**.

**wŭlahkwéexŭnool** VII be piled up neatly, be piled up nicely, be piled up properly *(of something wood- or stick-like). usually plural. conj 3rd sg* **wŭ=lahkwéexung**. *ptcpl* **weelahkwee=xúngiil**.

**wŭláhkwsuw** VAI have a trim shape, have a good shape, have a good figure. *ind 1st sg* **nooláhkwsi**, **noo=láhkwsiim**. *conj 3rd sg* **wŭláhkwsiit**. *ptcpl* **weeláhkwsiit**.

**wŭláhleew** VTA put s.t. animate away, keep s.t. animate. *ind 1st sg* **nooláh=laaw**, **nooláhla**. *ind 3rd sg* **oolahláa=wal**. *ind inv* **nooláhlukw**. *ind I-you* **kooláhlul**. *conj 3rd sg* **wŭláhlaat**. *imp* **wŭláhl**. *ptcpl* **weeláhlaat**.

**wŭlahtáasuw** VAI put things away, store things; be buried. *ind 1st sg* **noolah=táasi**, **noolahtáasiim**. *conj 3rd sg* **wŭlahtáasiit**. *ptcpl* **weelahtáasiit**.

**wŭlahtáasuw** VII be stored, be put away. *conj 3rd sg* **wŭlahtáasiik**. *ptcpl* **wee=lahtáasiik**.

**wŭláhtakat** VII be good, be straight, be a good strand of thread, be fine *(of something stringlike). conj 3rd sg* **wŭláhtakahk**. *ptcpl* **weeláhtakahk**.

**wŭlahtéenamuw** VAI be happy, be in good spirits. *ind 1st sg* **noolahtée=nami**, **noolahtéenamiim**. *conj 3rd sg* **wŭlahtéenamiit**. *ptcpl* **weelahtée=namiit**. *intensive reduplication* **wàw=ŭlahteenamúwak**.

**wŭláhtoow** VTI2 put s.t. away, store s.t. **Ngáta-wŭláhtoon.** 'I want to put it away.' *ind 1st sg* **nooláhtoon**. *ind 3rd sg* **ooláhtoon**. *conj 1st sg* **wŭláhta=waan**. *conj 3rd sg* **wŭláhtaakw**. *imp* **wŭláhtool**. *ptcpl* **weeláhtaakw**.

**wŭlakíimeew** VTA read s.t. animate correctly. *ind 1st sg* **noolakíimaaw**,

**noolakíima**. *ind 3rd sg* **oolakiimáa=wal**. *ind inv* **noolakíimukw**. *ind I-you* **koolakíimul**. *conj 3rd sg* **wŭlakíi=maat**. *imp* **wŭlákim**. *ptcpl* **weelakíi=maat**.

**wŭlakíindam** VTI1A read s.t. correctly. *ind 1st sg* **noolakíindamun**. *ind 3rd sg* **oolakíindamun**. *conj 1st sg* **wŭ=lakíindamaan**. *conj 3rd sg* **wŭlak=íindang**. *imp* **wŭlakíindah**. *ptcpl* **weelakíindang**.

**wŭlákshuy** NI guts, intestines, innards. *pl* **wŭlakshúyal**.

**wŭlakŭníimeew** VTA say good things about s.o., praise s.o. *ind 1st sg* **noo=lakuníimaaw**, **noolakuníima**. *ind 3rd sg* **oolakuniimáawal**. *ind inv* **noolakuníimukw**. *ind I-you* **koola=kuníimul**. *conj 3rd sg* **wŭlakuníi=maat**. *imp* **wŭlákŭniim**. *ptcpl* **wee=lakuníimaat**. *intensive reduplication* **wàwŭlakŭniimáawal**.

**wŭlakŭniimkwúsuw** VAI be praised, have a good name. *ind 1st sg* **noola=kuniimkwúsi**, **noolakuniimkwús=iim**. *conj 3rd sg* **wŭlakuniimkwúsiit**. *ptcpl* **weelakuniimkwúsiit**.

**wŭlakwunáheew** VTA dress s.o. nicely; put bedcovers on s.o. *ind 1st sg* **noo=lakwúnhaaw**, **noolakwúnha**. *ind 3rd sg* **oolakwunháawal**. *ind inv* **noola=kwúnhookw**. *ind I-you* **koolakwún=hool**. *conj 3rd sg* **wŭlakwŭnáhaat**. *imp* **wŭlákwunah**. *ptcpl* **weelakwún=haat**.

**wŭlalóhkeew** VAI do good work. *ind 1st sg* **noolalóhke**, **noolalóhkeem**. *conj 3rd sg* **wŭlalóhkeet**. *imp* **wŭlaloh=keel**. *ptcpl* **weelalóhkeet**.

**wŭlamalúsuw** VAI feel well. *ind 1st sg* **noolamálsi**, **noolamálsiim**. *conj 3rd sg* **wŭlamalúsiit**. *ptcpl* **weelamálsiit**.

**wŭlámameew** VTA find that s.o. feels better, find that s.o. feels good; feel comfortable with s.o. *ind 1st sg* **noo=lamámaaw**, **noolamáma**. *ind 3rd sg* **oolamamáawal**. *ind inv* **noolamám=ukw**. *ind I-you* **koolamámul**. *conj 3rd sg* **wŭlámamaat**. *ptcpl* **weela=mámaat**.

**wŭlamándam** VTI1A find that s.t. feels better, find that s.t. feels good. **Noo=lamándamun náxk.** 'My hand feels better.'; **Mahksúnal noolamanda=múnal.** 'My shoes feel good.' *ind 1st sg* **noolamándamun**. *ind 3rd sg* **oo=lamándamun**. *conj 1st sg* **wŭlam=ándamaan**. *conj 3rd sg* **wŭlamán=dang**. *ptcpl* **weelamándang**.

**wŭlambíileew** VTA put a harness on s.o., tie s.o up properly, tie s.o. up well. *ind 1st sg* **noolambíilaaw**, **noolam=bíila**. *ind 3rd sg* **oolambiiláawal**. *ind inv* **noolambíilukw**. *ind I-you* **koo=lambíilul**. *conj 3rd sg* **wŭlambíilaat**. *imp* **wŭlámbiil**. *ptcpl* **weelambíilaat**.

**wŭlambtíikeew** VAI put a harness on. *ind 1st sg* **noolambtíike**, **noolamb=tíikeem**. *conj 3rd sg* **wŭlambtíikeet**. *imp* **wŭlambtíikeel**. *ptcpl* **weelam=btíikeet**.

**wŭlámbtoow** VTI2 tie s.t. up properly, tie s.t. up well. **Koolámbtoon éenda-kshihteexíinge.** 'You bandaged it up where he got hurt.' *ind 1st sg* **noo=lámbtoon**. *ind 3rd sg* **oolámbtoon**. *conj 1st sg* **wŭlambtáwaan**. *conj 3rd sg* **wŭlámbtaakw**. *imp* **wŭlámbtool**. *ptcpl* **weelámbtaakw**.

**wŭlamkwaaháaleew** VTA pile s.t. animate up, make s.t. animate into mounds. *ind 1st sg* **noolàmkwaa=háalaaw**, **noolàmkwaaháala**. *ind 3rd sg* **oolàmkwaahaaláawal**. *conj 3rd sg* **wŭlamkwaaháalaat**. *imp* **wŭlam=kwáahaal**. *ptcpl* **weelàmkwaaháa=laat**.

**wŭlamkwaaháatoow** VTI2 pile s.t. up, make s.t. into mounds. *ind 1st sg* **noolàmkwaaháatoon**. *ind 3rd sg* **oolàmkwaaháatoon**. *conj 1st sg* **wŭlamkwaaháatawaan**. *conj 3rd sg*

**wŭlamkwaaháataakw**. *imp* **wŭlam=kwaaháatool**. *ptcpl* **weelàmkwaa=háataakw**.

**wŭlamkwáaheew** VAIO make s.t. into a pile, make s.t. into a mound. *ind 1st sg* **noolàmkwáaheen**. *ind 3rd sg* **oo=làmkwáaheen**. *conj 3rd sg* **wŭlam=kwáaheet**. *imp* **wŭlamkwáaheel**. *ptcpl* **weelàmkwáaheet**.

**wŭlamkwáham** VTI1A pile s.t. up, make s.t. into mounds. *ind 1st sg* **noolàm=kwáhŭmun**. *ind 3rd sg* **oolàmkwáh=ŭmun**. *conj 1st sg* **wŭlamkwáhŭ=maan**. *conj 3rd sg* **wŭlamkwáhang**. *imp* **wŭlamkwáhih**. *ptcpl* **weelàm=kwáhang**.

**wŭlamkwahíikeew** VAI pile things up, make mounds, make things into mounds *(as when hilling potatoes)*. *ind 1st sg* **noolàmkwahíike**, **noo=làmkwahíikeem**. *conj 3rd sg* **wŭ=lamkwahíikeet**. *imp* **wŭlamkwahíi=keel**. *ptcpl* **weelàmkwahíikeet**.

**wŭlámkweew** VII be in a mound, be in a hill. *conj 3rd sg* **wŭlámkweek**. *ptcpl* **weelámkweek**.

**wŭlamkwiixíinook** VAI be piled up *(s.t. animate)*. *object usually plural*. **Wŭ=lamkwiixíinook aapŭlúshak.** 'The apples are piled up.' *conj 3rd sg* **wŭ=lamkwiixiinóhtiit**. *ptcpl* **weelàm=kwiixiinóhtiit**.

**wŭlamkwiixtóowal** VTI2 pile s.t. up. *object usually plural*. *ind 1st sg* **oolàm=kwiixtóonal**. *ind 3rd sg* **oolàm=kwiixtóonal**. *conj 1st sg* **wŭlam=kwiixtáwaan**. *conj 3rd sg* **wŭlam=kwíixtaakw**. *imp* **wŭlamkwíixtool**. *ptcpl* **weelàmkwíixtaakw**.

**wŭlamkwíixŭméew** VTA pile s.t. animate up; build a hill around s.t. animate *(of potatoes)*. *object usually plural*. *ind 1st sg* **noolamkwiixŭ=máawak**. *ind 3rd sg* **oolamkwiixŭ=máawal**. *conj 3rd sg* **wŭlamkwíixŭ=maat**. *imp* **wŭlamkwíixum**. *ptcpl* **weelàmkwíixŭmaat**.

**wŭlamkwíixŭnool** VII be piled up. *usually plural*. **Wŭlamkwíixŭnool mii=xáskwal.** 'The grass is piled up.' *conj 3rd sg* **wŭlamkwíixung**. *ptcpl* **wee=làmkwiixúngiil**.

**wŭlamkwihtáasuw** VAI make a mound of things. *ind 1st sg* **noolàmkwih=táasi**, **noolàmkwihtáasiim**. *conj 3rd sg* **wŭlamkwihtáasiit**. *imp* **wŭlam=kwihtáasiil**. *ptcpl* **weelàmkwihtáa=siit**.

**wŭlamookanáapŭlush** NA pear. *pl* **wŭ=lamookanaapŭlúshak**. *dimin* **wŭ=lamookanaapŭlúshush**. *obv* **wŭlam=ookanaapŭlúshal**.

**wŭlanáhkeew** VAI make the bed, fix the bed. *ind 1st sg* **noolanáhke**, **noola=náhkeem**. *conj 3rd sg* **wŭlanáhkeet**. *imp* **wŭlanáhkeel**. *ptcpl* **weelanáh=keet**.

**wŭlápuw** VAI be in a nice place, be well seated; have a good home *(of an adopted child or a person in heaven)*. *ind 1st sg* **nóolapi**, **nóolapiim**. *conj 3rd sg* **wŭlápiit**. *ptcpl* **wéelapiit**.

**wŭlásanuw** VAIO take s.t. along, carry s.t. **Noolasániin kŭlooshliihiiwáa=kanal.** 'I carried the groceries.' *ind 1st sg* **noolasániin**. *ind 3rd sg* **oola=sániin**. *conj 3rd sg* **wŭlásaniit**. *ptcpl* **weelasániit**.

**wŭláskat** VII be good grass. *conj 3rd sg* **wŭláskahk**. *ptcpl* **weeláskahk**.

**wŭlaskŭneextíikeew** VAI pack up one's things, be packing up. *ind 1st sg* **noolaskŭneextíike**, **noolaskŭneex=tíikeem**. *conj 3rd sg* **wŭlaskŭneex=tíikeet**. *imp* **wŭlaskŭneextíikeel**. *ptcpl* **weelaskŭneextíikeet**.

**wŭlatawáapuw** VAI see a long way, have good eyesight. *ind 1st sg* **noo=latawáapi**, **noolatawáapiim**. *conj 3rd sg* **wŭlatawáapiit**. *ptcpl* **weela=tawáapiit**.

**wŭlatéexteew** VAI make a good road,

make a good path, have a good road, have a good path. *ind 1st sg* **noola=téexta, noolatéextaam**. *conj 3rd sg* **wŭlatéextaat**. *imp* **wŭlatéextaal**. *ptcpl* **weelatéextaat**.

**wŭlatéexun** VII be a good road, be a good path. *conj 3rd sg* **wŭlatéexung**. *ptcpl* **weelatéexung**.

**wŭlawéexteew** VAI have neat hair, have plastered-down hair. *ind 1st sg* **noo=lawéexta, noolawéextaam**. *conj 3rd sg* **wŭlawéextaat**. *ptcpl* **weelawéex=taat**.

**wŭláxakw** NI kindling, piece of kindling. *pl* **wŭláxakwal**. *poss* **noolxákwum**. *loc* **wŭláxakwung**. *dimin* **wŭláxa=kwush**.

**wŭlaxakwáheew** VAI make kindling, gather kindling. *ind 1st sg* **noolxák=hwe, noolxákhweem**. *conj 3rd sg* **wŭlaxakwáheet**. *imp* **wŭlaxakwáh=eel**. *ptcpl* **weelxákhweet**.

**wŭlaxakwáheew** VAIO make kindling of s.t. **Ngáta-wŭlaxakwahéenal.** 'I want to make kindling of them.' *ind 1st sg* **noolxákhween**. *ind 3rd sg* **oolxákhween**. *conj 3rd sg* **wŭlaxa=kwáheet**. *imp* **wŭlaxakwáheel**. *ptcpl* **weelxákhweet**.

**wŭláxun** VII be a nice wind. *conj 3rd sg* **wŭláxung**. *ptcpl* **wéelxung**. *intensive reduplication* **awúlxun**.

**wŭléekham** VTI1A write s.t. down. *ind 1st sg* **nooleekhámun**. *ind 3rd sg* **ooleekhámun**. *conj 1st sg* **wŭleek=hámaan**. *conj 3rd sg* **wŭléekhang**. *imp* **wŭléekhah**. *ptcpl* **weeléekhang**.

**wŭléekheew** VTA make a mark on s.o., make a mark on s.t. animate, write on s.t. animate. **Nooléekha pámbiil.** 'I'm writing a letter.' *ind 1st sg* **noo=léekhaaw, nooléekha**. *ind 3rd sg* **oo=leekháawal**. *ind inv* **nooléekhookw**. *ind I-you* **kooléekhool**. *conj 3rd sg* **wŭléekhaat**. *imp* **wŭléekhaw**. *ptcpl* **weeléekhaat**.

**wŭléekŭneew** VTA fold s.t. animate *(of something sheet-like)*. *ind 1st sg* **nooléekŭnaaw, nooléekŭna**. *ind 3rd sg* **ooleekŭnáawal**. *conj 3rd sg* **wŭ=léekŭnaat**. *imp* **wŭléekun**. *ptcpl* **weeléekŭnaat**.

**wŭléekŭnum** VTI1B fold s.t. *(of something sheet-like)*. *ind 1st sg* **noolee=kŭnúmun**. *ind 3rd sg* **ooleekŭnúm=un**. *conj 1st sg* **wŭleekŭnúmaan**. *conj 3rd sg* **wŭléekŭnung**. *ptcpl* **weeléekŭnung**. *intensive reduplication* **wàwŭleekŭnúmun**.

**wŭleeláhkameew** VII be moonlight. *conj 3rd sg* **wŭleeláhkameek**. *ptcpl* **wee=leeláhkameek**.

**wŭléelham** VOTI1A make good tracks. *ind 1st sg* **nooléelham**. *conj 3rd sg* **wŭléelhang**. *imp* **wŭléelhah**. *ptcpl* **weeléelhang**.

**wŭleelúndam** VOTI1A be glad, be happy. *ind 1st sg* **nooleelúndam**. *conj 3rd sg* **wŭleelúndang**. *ptcpl* **weeleelúndang**.

**wŭleelúndam** VTI1A be glad about s.t., be happy about s.t. *ind 1st sg* **noolee=lúndamun**. *ind 3rd sg* **ooleelúnda=mun**. *conj 1st sg* **wŭleelúndamaan**. *conj 3rd sg* **wŭleelúndang**. *imp* **wŭleelúndah**. *ptcpl* **weeleelúndang**.

**wŭleelúnzuw** VAI think well of oneself, think highly of oneself. *ind 1st sg* **nooleelúnzi, nooleelúnziim**. *conj 3rd sg* **wŭleelúnziit**. *ptcpl* **weeleelúnziit**.

**wŭleewáatam** VOTI1A be sane. *ind 1st sg* **nooleewáatam**. *conj 3rd sg* **wŭ=leewáatang**. *ptcpl* **weeleewáatang**.

**wŭlé** PC really, indeed, that's right, well. **Kàkawóngxwiin? Wŭlé!** 'Are you sleepy?' 'That's right!'

**wŭli-** PV nice, good. **Wŭlí-shkwúna=yeew.** 'He has a nice tail.' *ptcpl* **wéeli-**. *See* **wŭlu-**.

**wŭlíi-pŭnáweew** VTA think well of s.o., respect s.o. *ind 1st sg* **nóolii-pŭnáw=aaw, nóolii-pŭnáwa**. *ind 3rd sg* **óolii-pŭnawáawal**. *ind inv* **nóolii-pŭ=**

**náakw**. *ind I-you* **kóolii-pŭnóol**. *conj 3rd sg* **wŭlíi-punáwaat**. *imp* **wŭlíi-pŭnáw**. *ptcpl* **wéelii-pŭnáwaat**.

**wŭlíiheew** VTA make s.t. animate. *ind 1st sg* **noolíihaaw**, **noolíiha**. *ind 3rd sg* **ooliiháawal**. *conj 3rd sg* **wŭlíihaat**. *imp* **wŭlíih**. *ptcpl* **weelíihaat**.

**wŭlíihukw** VTA do good for s.o., give s.o. luck. *inanimate subject only*. **Noolíihkwun wchápihk.** 'The medicine did me good.'; **Noolíihkwun wiikwáhmung wúnj-kchúyaan.** 'It did me good to get out of the house.' *conj 3rd sg* **wŭlíihkwaan**. *ptcpl* **weelíihkwaan**.

**wŭlíikun** VII grow well. *conj 3rd sg* **wŭlíikung**. *ptcpl* **weelíikung**.

**wŭlíikuw** VAI grow big, grow well *(s.t. animate)*. *ind 1st sg* **noolíiki**, **noolíi=kiim**. *conj 3rd sg* **wŭlíikiit**. *ptcpl* **weelíikiit**.

**wŭliikwamáweew** VTA comb s.o.'s hair. *ind 1st sg* **nooliikwamáwaaw**, **noo=liikwamáwa**. *ind 3rd sg* **ooliikwa=mawáawal**. *ind inv* **noolíikwa=maakw**. *ind I-you* **koolíikwamool**. *conj 3rd sg* **wŭliikwamáwaat**. *imp* **wŭlíikwamaw**. *ptcpl* **weeliikwa=máwaat**.

**wŭlíikwameew** VAI comb one's (own) hair. *ind 1st sg* **noolíikwama**, **noo=líikwamaam**. *conj 3rd sg* **wŭlíikwa=maat**. *imp* **wŭlíikwamaal**. *ptcpl* **weelíikwamaat**.

**wŭliilawéeheew** VTA make s.o. feel good. *ind 1st sg* **nooliilawéehaaw**, **nooliilawéeha**. *ind 3rd sg* **ooliila=weeháawal**. *ind inv* **nooliilawée=hukw**. *ind I-you* **kooliilawéehul**. *conj 3rd sg* **wŭliilawéehaat**. *imp* **wŭlíi=laweeh**. *ptcpl* **weeliilawéehaat**.

**wŭliilawéemeew** VTA talk to s.o. and make them feel good. *ind 1st sg* **noo=liilawéemaaw**, **nooliilawéema**. *ind 3rd sg* **ooliilaweemáawal**. *ind inv* **nooliilawéemukw**. *ind I-you* **koolii=lawéemul**. *conj 3rd sg* **wŭliilawée=maat**. *imp* **wŭlíilaweem**. *ptcpl* **wee=liilawéemaat**.

**wŭliináakwat** VII look good, be nice looking, have a nice appearance. *conj 3rd sg* **wŭliináakwahk**. *ptcpl* **weelii=náakwahk**.

**wŭliináakwsuw** VAI look good, be nice looking, have a nice appearance, be pretty *(s.t. animate)*. *ind 1st sg* **noo=liináakwsi**, **nooliináakwsiim**. *conj 3rd sg* **wŭliináakwsiit**. *ptcpl* **weelii=náakwsiit**.

**wŭlíinam** VTI1A like the looks of s.t., admire s.t. *ind 1st sg* **noolíinamun**. *ind 3rd sg* **oolíinamun**. *conj 1st sg* **wŭlíinamaan**. *conj 3rd sg* **wŭlíinang**. *ptcpl* **weelíinang**.

**wŭlíinaweew** VTA like the looks of s.o., admire s.o. *ind 1st sg* **noolíinawaaw**, **noolíinawa**. *ind 3rd sg* **ooliinawáa=wal**. *ind inv* **noolíinaakw**. *ind I-you* **koolíinool**. *conj 3rd sg* **wŭlíinawaat**. *ptcpl* **weelíinawaat**.

**wŭliinjkwéhleew** VAI roll straight *(s.t. animate)*. *ind 1st sg* **nooliinjkwéhla**, **nooliinjkwéhlaam**. *conj 3rd sg* **wŭ=liinjkwéhlaat**. *ptcpl* **weeliinjkwéh=laat**.

**wŭliinjkwéhleew** VII roll straight. *conj 3rd sg* **wŭliinjkwéhlaak**. *ptcpl* **wee=liinjkwéhlaak**.

**wŭliinjŭweextíikeew** VAI set the table. *ind 1st sg* **nooliinjŭweextíike**, **noo=liinjŭweextíikeem**. *conj 3rd sg* **wŭ=liinjŭweextíikeet**. *imp* **wŭliin=jŭweextíikeel**. *ptcpl* **weeliinjŭweex=tíikeet**.

**wŭliipóokwat** VII taste good. *conj 3rd sg* **wŭliipóokwahk**. *ptcpl* **weelii=póokwahk**.

**wŭliipóokwsuw** VAI taste good *(s.t. animate)*. *ind 1st sg* **nooliipóokwsi**, **nooliipóokwsiim**. *conj 3rd sg* **wŭ=liipóokwsiit**. *ptcpl* **weeliipóokwsiit**.

**wŭliitéeheew** VAI be nice, be good, be

pleasant, be good-natured. *ind 1st sg* **nooliitéeha, nooliitéehaam**. *conj 3rd sg* **wŭliitéehaat**. *ptcpl* **weeliitéehaat**.

**wŭlíixiin** VAI lie down, be in bed, lie in bed. **Kwáy nŭmáwi-wuliíxiin, nŭmáw-kawí.** 'I'm going to lie down, I'm going to sleep.' *ind 1st sg* **noolíi=xiin, noolíixi**. *conj 3rd sg* **wŭlíixiing**. *imp* **wŭlíixiil**. *ptcpl* **weelíixiing**.

**wŭlíixsuw** VAI speak well. *ind 1st sg* **noolíixsi, noolíixsiim**. *conj 3rd sg* **wŭlíixsiit**. *imp* **wŭlíixsiil**. *ptcpl* **weelíixsiit**. *intensive reduplication* **awulíixsuw**.

**wŭliixtáakeew** VAIO get s.t. fixed. *ind 1st sg* **nooliixtáakeen**. *ind 3rd sg* **ooliixtáakeen**. *conj 3rd sg* **wŭliix=táakeet**. *imp* **wŭliixtáakeel**. *ptcpl* **weeliixtáakeet**.

**wŭliixtáasuw** VAI fix things. *ind 1st sg* **nooliixtáasi, nooliixtáasiim**. *conj 3rd sg* **wŭliixtáasiit**. *imp* **wŭliixtáa=siil**. *ptcpl* **weeliixtáasiit**.

**wŭliixtáasuw** VII be fixed, be repaired. *conj 3rd sg* **wŭliixtáasiik**. *ptcpl* **weeliixtáasiik**.

**wŭliixtáweew** VTAO fix s.t. for s.o. *ind 1st sg* **nooliixtáwaan**. *ind 3rd sg* **ooliixtáwaan**. *ind inv* **nooliixtáa=kwun**. *ind I-you* **kooliixtóolun**. *conj 1st sg* **wuliixtawaan**. *conj 3rd sg* **wŭliixtáwaat**. *imp* **wŭlíixtaw**. *ptcpl* **weeliixtáwaat**.

**wŭlíixtoow** VTI2 fix s.t., repair s.t. *ind 1st sg* **noolíixtoon**. *ind 3rd sg* **oolíix=toon**. *conj 1st sg* **wŭliixtáwaan**. *conj 3rd sg* **wŭlíixtaakw**. *imp* **wŭlíixtool**. *ptcpl* **weelíixtaakw**.

**wŭlíixŭmeew** VTA fix s.t. animate, repair s.t. animate; put s.o. to bed. *ind 1st sg* **noolíixŭmaaw, noolíixŭma**. *ind 3rd sg* **ooliixŭmáawal**. *ind inv* **noolíixŭmukw**. *ind I-you* **koolíixŭ=mul**. *conj 3rd sg* **wŭlíixŭmaat**. *imp* **wŭlíixum**. *ptcpl* **weelíixŭmaat**.

**wŭlíixun** VII be correct, be good. **Ktaa=kongwéepuy wŭlíixun.** 'Your hat looks good on you.' *conj 3rd sg* **wŭ=líixung**. *ptcpl* **weelíixung**.

**wŭlíhkam** VTI1A find s.t. too small, find that s.t. doesn't fit, be too small for s.t. *(of clothing)*. **Noolíhkamun.** 'It's too small for me, it doesn't fit me.'; **Noolíhkamun ndahéembut.** 'My shirt doesn't fit.' *ind 1st sg* **noolíh=kamun**. *ind 3rd sg* **oolíhkamun**. *conj 1st sg* **wŭlíhkamaan**. *conj 3rd sg* **wŭlíhkang**. *ptcpl* **weelíhkang**.

**wŭlíhkaweew** VTA find s.t. animate too small, find that s.t. animate doesn't fit, be too small for s.t. animate *(of clothing)*. **Noolihkawáawak.** 'They are too small, they don't fit me.'; **Noolíhkawaaw nŭwánd.** 'My mitt doesn't fit.' *ind 1st sg* **noolíhkawaaw, noolíhkawa**. *ind 3rd sg* **oolihkawáa=wal**. *ind inv* **noolíhkaakw**. *ind I-you* **koolíhkool**. *conj 3rd sg* **wŭlíhkawaat**. *ptcpl* **weelíhkawaat**.

**wŭlíhlaleew** VTA find s.o. useful. *ind 1st sg* **noolíhlalaaw, noolíhlala**. *ind 3rd sg* **oolihlaláawal**. *ind inv* **noolíhla=lukw**. *ind I-you* **koolíhlalul**. *conj 3rd sg* **wŭlíhlalaat**. *ptcpl* **weelíhlalaat**.

**wŭlíhlatoow** VTI2 find s.t. useful. *ind 1st sg* **noolíhlatoon**. *ind 3rd sg* **oo=líhlatoon**. *conj 1st sg* **wŭlihlatáw=aan**. *conj 3rd sg* **wŭlíhlataakw**. *imp* **wŭlíhlatool**. *ptcpl* **weelíhlataakw**.

**wŭlíhleew** VAI run well *(s.t. animate)*. *ind 1st sg* **noolíhla, noolíhlaam**. *conj 3rd sg* **wŭlíhlaat**. *ptcpl* **weelíhlaat**.

**wŭlíhleew** VII run well. *conj 3rd sg* **wŭlíhlaak**. *ptcpl* **weelíhlaak**.

**wŭlihtáakwat** VII sound good, sound nice. *conj 3rd sg* **wŭlihtáakwahk**. *ptcpl* **weelihtáakwahk**.

**wŭlihtáakwsuw** VAI sound good, sound nice *(s.t. animate)*. *ind 1st sg* **noolih=táakwsi, noolihtáakwsi**. *conj 3rd sg* **wŭlihtáakwsiit**. *ptcpl* **weelihtáakw=siit**.

**wŭlíhtaweew** VTAO make s.t. for s.o. *ind 1st sg* **noolíhtawaan**. *ind 3rd sg* **oo=líhtawaan**. *ind inv* **noolihtáakwun**. *ind I-you* **koolihtóolun**. *conj 1st sg* **wulihtawaan**. *conj 3rd sg* **wŭlíhta=waat**. *imp* **wŭlíhtaw**. *ptcpl* **weelíhta=waat**.

**wŭlíhtoow** VTI2 make s.t. **Kíhchi-meenaxkáaxkwal -wulihtóowak.** 'They made lots of fence rails.' *ind 1st sg* **noolíhtoon**. *ind 3rd sg* **oolíh=toon**. *conj 1st sg* **wŭlíhtawaan**. *conj 3rd sg* **wŭlíhtaakw**. *imp* **wŭlíhtool**. *ptcpl* **weelíhtaakw**.

**wŭlihtóonayeew** VAI have a nice beard, have a nice mustache. *ind 1st sg* **noolihtóonaya, noolihtóonayaam**. *conj 3rd sg* **wŭlihtóonayaat**. *ptcpl* **weelihtóonayaat**.

**wŭlóngwaam** VAI have a good dream. **Ngúmee nŭwaawŭlóngwaam.** 'I always have good dreams.' *ind 1st sg* **noolóngwaam**. *conj 3rd sg* **wŭlón=gwaang**. *ptcpl* **weelóngwaang**. *moderative reduplication* **waawŭlón=gwaam**.

**wŭlú** PC really, indeed, that's right, well. **Wŭlú máh neewáawi.** 'I didn't see him.'; **Wulú ndáalu-nóhtawaaw.** 'I can't understand him.' *See* **wŭlé**.

**wŭlu-** PV nice, good. *informal*. **Níishŭ=wak nehnayóongsak ngaxaníhna, mayáawsuw móxa wúlu-únd.** 'We had two horses, and one was very nice.'; **Óolu-tapaaláawal yóol ox=kwéessal wáak oolaliiháawal, shúkw wá oxkwéesus ngúmee alúmsuw.** 'He supported that girl well and treated her well, but this girl would always leave.' *ptcpl* **wéelu-**. *See* **wŭlii-**.

**wŭlú-líiheew** VTA treat s.o. well, be good to s.o. *ind 1st sg* **nóolu-líihaaw, nóo=lu-líiha**. *ind 3rd sg* **óolu-liiháawal**. *ind inv* **nóolu-líihukw**. *ind I-you* **kóolu-líihul**. *conj 3rd sg* **wŭlú-líi=haat**. *imp* **wŭlú-líih**. *ptcpl* **wéelu-líihaat**.

**wŭlú-líinam** VOTI1A be treated well. *ind 1st sg* **nóolu-líinam**. *conj 3rd sg* **wŭlú-líinang**. *ptcpl* **wéelu-líinang**.

**wŭlúchasuw** VAI be nicely browned *(s.t. animate)*. *ind 1st sg* **noolachási, noolachásiim**. *conj 3rd sg* **wŭlúcha=siit**. *ptcpl* **weelachásiit**.

**wŭlúchateew** VII be nicely browned. *conj 3rd sg* **wŭlúchateek**. *ptcpl* **weelacháteek**.

**wŭluchéesuw** VAI be pretty, be evenly shaped, be nicely shaped *(s.t. animate)*. *ind 1st sg* **noolchéesi, nool=chéesiim**. *conj 3rd sg* **wŭluchéesiit**. *ptcpl* **weelchéesiit**.

**wŭluchéeyeew** VII be pretty, be evenly shaped, be nicely shaped, be smoothly shaped. *conj 3rd sg* **wŭluchée=yeek**. *ptcpl* **weelchéeyeek**.

**wŭlulawásuw** VAI have a good fire. *ind 1st sg* **noolŭláwasi, noolŭláwasiim**. *conj 3rd sg* **wŭlulawásiit**. *ptcpl* **wee=lŭláwasiit**.

**wŭlúleew** VAI burn well *(s.t. animate)*. *ind 1st sg* **nóolŭle, nóolŭleem**. *conj 3rd sg* **wŭlúleet**. *ptcpl* **wéelŭleet**.

**wŭlúleew** VII burn well. *conj 3rd sg* **wŭlúleek**. *ptcpl* **wéelŭleek**.

**wŭluléewuw** VAI be in full bloom *(of flowers)*. *conj 3rd sg* **wŭluléewiit**. *ptcpl* **weelŭléewiit**.

**wŭluléexiin** VAI be brightly coloured, be dressed up. *ind 1st sg* **noolŭléexiin, noolŭléexi**. *conj 3rd sg* **wŭluléexiing**. *ptcpl* **weelŭléexiing, weelŭléexiit**. *See* **ktakŭléexiin**.

**wŭluléexun** VII be brightly coloured. *conj 3rd sg* **wŭluléexung**. *ptcpl* **weelŭléexung**. *See* **ktakŭléexun**.

**wŭlúneew** VTA fix s.o. up; grab s.o., grasp s.o. **Nóolŭnaaw mwáakaneew wtéeng oxkweekánganung.** 'I grabbed the dog by the back of the neck.' *ind 1st sg* **nóolŭnaaw, nóolŭna**. *ind*

*3rd sg* **oolŭnáawal**. *ind inv* **nóolŭ=nukw**. *ind I-you* **kóolŭnul**. *conj 3rd sg* **wŭlúnaat**. *imp* **wŭlún**. *ptcpl* **wéelŭnaat**.

**wŭlúnum** VTI1B grab s.t. **Ngíish- áa -wŭlúnŭmun xwús.** 'I could go and grab the wood.' *ind 1st sg* **noolŭ=númun**. *ind 3rd sg* **oolŭnúmun**. *conj 1st sg* **wŭlúnŭmaan**. *conj 3rd sg* **wŭlúnung**. *imp* **wŭlúnih**. *ptcpl* **wée=lŭnung**.

**wŭlupéekat** VII be clear water, be good water. *conj 3rd sg* **wŭlupéekahk**. *ptcpl* **weelpéekahk**.

**wŭlupéenum** VTI1B add water to s.t. *(to make a drink or medicine).* **Ngáta-wŭlupéenŭmun.** 'I want to make a drink.' *ind 1st sg* **noolpéenŭmun**. *ind 3rd sg* **oolpéenŭmun**. *conj 1st sg* **wŭlupéenŭmaan**. *conj 3rd sg* **wŭ=lupéenung**. *imp* **wŭlupéenih**. *ptcpl* **weelpéenung**.

**wŭlústam** VOTI1A believe; become a Christian, become a believer. *ind 1st sg* **noolsútam**. *conj 3rd sg* **wŭlústang**. *imp* **wŭlústah**. *ptcpl* **weelsútang**.

**wŭlústam** VTI1A believe s.t. *ind 1st sg* **noolsútamun**. *ind 3rd sg* **oolsúta=mun**. *conj 1st sg* **wŭlustámaan**. *conj 3rd sg* **wŭlústang**. *imp* **wŭlústah**. *ptcpl* **weelsútang**.

**wŭlúsuw** VAI be pretty, be good, be nice *(s.t. animate). ind 1st sg* **nóolsi**, **nóol=siim**. *conj 3rd sg* **wŭlúsiit**. *ptcpl* **wéel=siit**. *intensive reduplication* **awul=súwak**; *moderative reduplication* **waawŭlúsuw**.

**wŭlúsheew** VTA cut s.t. animate nicely, cut s.t. animate in a pattern. *ind 1st sg* **nóolshaaw**, **nóolsha**. *ind 3rd sg* **ool=sháawal**. *ind inv* **nóolshookw**. *ind I-you* **kóolshool**. *conj 3rd sg* **wŭlúshaat**. *imp* **wŭlúsh**. *ptcpl* **wéelshaat**.

**wŭlustáweew** VTA believe s.o. *ind 1st sg* **noolsútawaaw**, **noolsútawa**. *ind 3rd sg* **oolsutawáawal**. *ind inv* **noolsút=aakw**. *ind I-you* **koolsútool**. *conj 3rd sg* **wŭlustáwaat**. *imp* **wŭlústaw**. *ptcpl* **weelsútawaat**.

**wŭlushíikeew** VAI cut a pattern, cut things nicely. *ind 1st sg* **noolshíike**, **noolshíikeem**. *conj 3rd sg* **wŭlushíi=keet**. *imp* **wŭlushíikeel**. *ptcpl* **weel=shíikeet**.

**wŭlúshum** VTI1B cut s.t. nicely, cut s.t. in a pattern. *ind 1st sg* **noolshúmun**. *ind 3rd sg* **oolshúmun**. *conj 1st sg* **wŭlúshŭmaan**. *conj 3rd sg* **wŭlúsh=ung**. *imp* **wŭlúshih**. *ptcpl* **wéelshung**. *intensive reduplication* **wàwŭlúshŭ=mun**.

**wŭlút** VII be pretty, be good, be nice. *conj 3rd sg* **wŭlíhk**. *ptcpl* **wéelihk**.

**wúm** VAI come from a certain place, come from there. **Chétum wúm.** 'He came from Chatham.' *ind 1st sg* **nóom**. *conj 3rd sg* **wúng**. *ptcpl* **wéeng**.

**wŭnamongáapŭlush** NA pear. *pl* **wŭ=namongaapŭlúshak**. *dimin* **wŭnam=ongaapŭlúshush**. *obv* **wŭnamon=gaapŭlúshal**.

**wŭnaxkwíhtahkw** NI branch. *pl* **wŭ=naxkwihtáhkwal**. *loc* **wŭnaxkwih=táhkwung**. *dimin* **wŭnaxkwihtáh=kwush**.

**wúnd** VTI3 get s.t. from a certain place, get s.t. from somewhere. **Chétum nóondun.** 'I got it in Chatham.' *ind 1st sg* **nóondun**. *ind 3rd sg* **óondun**. *conj 1st sg* **wúndawaan**. *conj 3rd sg* **wúnduk**. *imp* **wúndih**. *ptcpl* **wéen=duk**.

**wundáakchehl** VAI jump from a certain place, jump for a certain reason. **Wáhlu noondáakchehl.** 'I jumped from far away.' *ind 1st sg* **noon=dáakchehl**. *conj 3rd sg* **wundaak=chéhluk**. *imp* **wundaakchéhlih**. *ptcpl* **weendaakchéhluk**.

**wundaaméhleew** VAI take a big start in a competition, take a jump in a competition, take a leap in a competition, get a running start. *ind 1st sg* **noon=daaméhla, noondaaméhlaam**. *conj 3rd sg* **wundaaméhlaat**. *imp* **wun=daaméhlaal**. *ptcpl* **weendaaméhlaat**.

**wundaapéhlatoow** VTI2 hang s.t. from a certain place, hang s.t. for a certain reason. **Yéelak noondaapéhlatoon.** 'I hung it over there.' *ind 1st sg* **noondaapéhlatoon**. *ind 3rd sg* **oon=daapéhlatoon**. *conj 1st sg* **wundaa=pehlatáwaan**. *conj 3rd sg* **wundaa=péhlataakw**. *imp* **wundaapéhlatool**. *ptcpl* **weendaapéhlataakw**.

**wundaapéhleew** VAI hang from a certain place, hang for a certain reason. *ind 1st sg* **noondaapéhla, noondaa=péhlaam**. *conj 3rd sg* **wundaapéh=laat**. *ptcpl* **weendaapéhlaat**.

**wundaapéhleew** VII hang from a certain place, have for a certain reason. *conj 3rd sg* **wundaapéhlaak**. *ptcpl* **ween=daapéhlaak**.

**wundaaptóoneew** VAI talk from a certain place, talk for a certain reason, holler from a certain place, holler for a certain reason; call from a certain place, call for a certain reason *(especially on the telephone)*. **Wáhlu noondaaptóone.** 'I talked from far away.' *ind 1st sg* **noondaaptóone, noondaaptóoneem**. *conj 3rd sg* **wundaaptóoneet**. *imp* **wundaaptóo=neel**. *ptcpl* **weendaaptóoneet**.

**wundáasŭleew** VAI shine from a certain place, shine for a certain reason *(s.t. animate, of lamps)*. *ind 1st sg* **noon=dáasŭle, noondáasŭleem**. *conj 3rd sg* **wundáasŭleet**. *ptcpl* **weendáasŭ=leet**.

**wundáasŭleew** VII shine from a certain place, shine for a certain reason. *conj 3rd sg* **wundáasŭleek**. *ptcpl* **ween=dáasŭleek**.

**wundáawsuw** VAIO live from s.o., live from s.t. **Oondáawsiin mùshúshŭ=mal wshulpúlum.** 'He lives from his wife's money.'; **Noondáawsiin peen=hámaan.** 'I live from what I earn.' *ind 1st sg* **noondáawsiin**. *ind 3rd sg* **oondáawsiin**. *conj 3rd sg* **wun=dáawsiit**. *imp* **wundáawsiil**. *ptcpl* **weendáawsiit**.

**wúndakw** PC direction. **Tá wúndakw wíikiin?** 'Where does he live?'; **Kíi palíi wúndakw ktulíikwsi.** 'You crawled the other way.'

**wundambíisuw** VAI be tied from a certain place; be tied for a certain reason. **Mwáakanew wundambíisuw póostung.** 'The dog is tied to the post' *ind 1st sg* **noondambíisi, noon=dambíisiim**. *conj 3rd sg* **wundam=bíisiit**. *imp* **wundambíisiil**. *ptcpl* **weendambíisiit**.

**wundambíisuw** VII be tied from a certain place; be tied for a certain reason. *conj 3rd sg* **wundambíisiik**. *ptcpl* **weendambíisiik**.

**wundatawáapuw** VAI look from a certain place, look from there. **Wiikwáh=mung noondatawáapi.** 'I looked from the house.' *ind 1st sg* **noonda=tawáapi, noondatawáapiim**. *conj 3rd sg* **wundatawáapiit**. *imp* **wun=datawáapiil**. *ptcpl* **weendatawáa=piit**.

**wundatéexun** VII be a road that comes from a certain place. **Kóhpii wunda=téexun.** 'The road leads from the forest.' *conj 3rd sg* **wundatéexung**. *ptcpl* **weendatéexung**.

**wundchéhleew** VAI drive from a certain place, drive for a certain reason. **Chétum wundchehléewak.** 'They were driving from Chatham.' *ind 1st sg* **noondchéhla, noondchéhlaam**. *conj 3rd sg* **wundchéhlaat**. *imp* **wundchéhlaal**. *ptcpl* **weendchéh=laat**. *See* **wunjchéhleew**.

**wúndeew** VII boil, come to a boil. *conj 3rd sg* **wúndeek**. *ptcpl* **wéendeek**.

**wundeelawúsuw** VAI play for a cause,

play for a certain reason *(especially to gamble).* **Noondeelawúsi shúlpul.** 'I played for money.'; **Noondeela=wúsi máapŭlush.** 'I played for marbles.' *ind 1st sg* **noondeelawúsi**, **noondeelawúsiim**. *conj 3rd sg* **wun=deelawúsiit**. *imp* **wundeelawúsiil**. *ptcpl* **weendeelawúsiit**.

**wundéewtam** VAI cry for a certain reason. **Kwéek wundéewtam?** 'What's he crying for?'; **Noondéewtam shookŭlúshal.** 'I was crying about the candies.' *ind 1st sg* **noondéewtam**. *conj 3rd sg* **wundéewtang**. *ptcpl* **weendéewtang**.

**wundhiingwéexiin** VAI look from a certain place, look for a certain reason. *ind 1st sg* **noondhiingwéexiin**, **noondhiingwéexi**. *conj 3rd sg* **wund=hiingwéexiing**. *imp* **wundhiingwée=xiil**. *ptcpl* **weendhiingwéexiing**.

**wundihtéexiin** VAI bump into something. **Kpáhoon noondihtéexiin.** 'I bumped into the door.' *ind 1st sg* **noondihtée=xiin**, **noondihtéexi**. *conj 3rd sg* **wun=dihtéexiing**. *ptcpl* **weendihtéexiing**.

**wundóoxweew** VAIO borrow s.t. *ind 1st sg* **noondóoxween**. *ind 3rd sg* **oon=dóoxween**. *conj 3rd sg* **wundóoxweet**. *imp* **wundóoxweel**. *ptcpl* **weendóo=xweet**.

**wúndpeew** VAI leak *(s.t. animate).* **Wúndpeew wsháphoos.** 'The pail is leaking.' *ind 1st sg* **nóondpe**, **nóond=peem**. *conj 3rd sg* **wúndpeet**. *ptcpl* **wéendpeet**.

**wúndpeew** VII leak. *conj 3rd sg* **wúnd=peek**. *ptcpl* **wéendpeek**.

**wundsútam** VTI 1A hear s.t. from a certain place, hear s.t. for a certain reason. **Kóhpii noondsútamun.** 'I heard it from the forest.' *ind 1st sg* **noond=sútamun**. *ind 3rd sg* **oondsútamun**. *conj 1st sg* **wundsútamaan**. *conj 3rd sg* **wundsútang**. *imp* **wundsútah**. *ptcpl* **weendsútang**.

**wundsútaweew** VTA hear s.o. from a certain direction, hear s.o. for a certain reason. *ind 1st sg* **noondsúta=waaw**, **noondsútawa**. *ind 3rd sg* **oondsutawáawal**. *ind inv* **noondsút=aakw**. *ind 1-you* **koondsútool**. *conj 3rd sg* **wundsútawaat**. *imp* **wund=sútaw**. *ptcpl* **weendsútawaat**.

**wundshíimuw** VAI run away from a certain place, flee from a certain place. **Wiikwáhmung wundshíimuw.** 'He's running away from the house.' *ind 1st sg* **noondshíimwi**, **noondshíimwiim**. *conj 3rd sg* **wundshíimwiit**. *imp* **wundshíimwiil**. *ptcpl* **weendshíi=mwiit**.

**wúndxun** VII blow from a certain direction *(of the wind).* **Yéelak wúndxun.** 'The wind is blowing from over there.' *conj 3rd sg* **wúndxung**. *ptcpl* **wéendxung**.

**wungáaleew** VTA bark at s.o. *ind 1st sg* **noongáalaaw**, **noongáala**. *ind 3rd sg* **oongaaláawal**. *ind inv* **noongáalukw**. *ind 1-you* **koongáalul**. *conj 3rd sg* **wungáalaat**. *imp* **wúngaal**. *ptcpl* **weengáalaat**. *intensive reduplication* **wihwungaaláawal**.

**wungáatam** VTI 1A bark at s.t.; want s.t. that someone else has. *ind 1st sg* **noongáatamun**. *ind 3rd sg* **oongáa=tamun**. *conj 1st sg* **wungáatamaan**. *conj 3rd sg* **wungáatang**. *imp* **wun=gáatah**. *ptcpl* **weengáatang**.

**wúngeew** VAI bark, be barking. *ind 1st sg* **nóonge**, **nóongeem**. *conj 3rd sg* **wúngeet**. *imp* **wúngeel**. *ptcpl* **wéen=geet**. *intensive reduplication* **wih=wúngeew**.

**wŭniicháanuw** VAI have a child, have children. *ind 1st sg* **nooniicháani**, **nooniicháaniim**. *conj 3rd sg* **wŭnii=cháaniit**. *ptcpl* **weeniicháaniit**.

**wunj-** PN place; reason. *informal.* **Máh mahkshaawíiwal wúnj-xwacháh=kwung.** 'They didn't cut them off the big trees.'; **Njiixíikwsi wúnj-míht=kwung.** 'I crawled down from the tree.' *See* **wunju-**.

**wunj-** PV from a certain place; for a certain reason. *informal.* **Waxkiitáa=wung nóonj-niixahtakíhla.** 'I ran down from the top of the hill'; **Mbíing nóonj-saakohkwéexiin.** 'My head was sticking out of the water.' *ptcpl* **wéenj-**. *See* **wunji-**, **wunju-**.

**wunjchéhleew** VAI drive from a certain place, drive from there. **Naláhii wunjchehléewak.** 'They were driving from Munceytown.' *ind 1st sg* **noonjchéhla**, **noonjchéhlaam**. *conj 3rd sg* **wunjchéhlaat**. *imp* **wunj=chéhlaal**. *ptcpl* **weenjchéhlaat**. *See* **wundchéhleew**.

**wunjíiheew** VTA make s.t. animate from something, make s.t. animate for a certain reason. *ind 1st sg* **noonjíi=haaw**, **noonjíiha**. *ind 3rd sg* **oonjii=háawal**. *conj 3rd sg* **oonjíihaat**. *imp* **wúnjiih**. *ptcpl* **weenjíihaat**.

**wunjíikun** VII grow from a certain source, grow for a certain reason. *conj 3rd sg* **wunjíikung**. *ptcpl* **weenjíi=kung**.

**wunjíikun** VII leak. *conj 3rd sg* **wunjíi=kung**. *ptcpl* **weenjíikung**.

**wunjíikuw** VAI grow from a certain source, grow for a certain reason. *conj 3rd sg* **wunjíikiit**. *ptcpl* **weenjíikiit**.

**wunjíikuw** VAI leak *(s.t. animate)*. **Tíi=hoos wunjíikuw.** 'The teakettle is leaking.' *ind 1st sg* **noonjíiki**, **noon=jíikiim**. *conj 3rd sg* **wunjíikiit**. *ptcpl* **weenjíikiit**.

**wunjíikuw** VII leak, be leaking. *conj 3rd sg* **wunjíikiik**. *ptcpl* **weenjíikiik**.

**wunjíikwsuw** VAI crawl from a certain place, crawl for a certain reason. **Yéelak noonjíikwsi.** 'I crawled from over there.' *ind 1st sg* **noonjíikwsi**, **noonjíikwsiim**. *conj 3rd sg* **wun=jíikwsiit**. *imp* **wunjíikwsiil**. *ptcpl* **weenjíikwsiit**.

**wunjíimeew** VTA call s.o., summon s.o. *ind 1st sg* **noonjíimaaw**, **noonjíima**. *ind 3rd sg* **oonjiimáawal**. *ind inv* **noonjíimukw**. *ind I-you* **koonjíimul**. *conj 3rd sg* **wunjíimaat**. *imp* **wún=jiim**. *ptcpl* **weenjíimaat**. *intensive reduplication* **wihwunjiimáawal**.

**wunjíixiin** VAI come from a certain place. *ind 1st sg* **noonjíixiin**, **noon=jíixi**. *conj 3rd sg* **wunjíixiing**. *ptcpl* **weenjíixiing**.

**wunjíixun** VII come from a certain place. **Áaneeng wunjíixŭnool.** 'They came from the road.' *conj 3rd sg* **wunjíi=xung**. *ptcpl* **weenjíixung**.

**wunjíiyayuw** VAI be from there, be from a certain place. **Wunjiiyayúwak shŭwéeka.** 'They are from Six Nations.'; **Xwanzhíikanung wunjíiya=yuw.** 'He's from the United States.' *ind 1st sg* **noonjíiyayi**, **noonjíiya=yiim**. *conj 3rd sg* **wunjíiyayiit**. *ptcpl* **weenjíiyayiit**.

**wunji-** PV from a certain place; for a certain reason. **Wiikwáhmung nóonji-kchíim.** 'I came out of the house.' *ptcpl* **wéenjii-**. *See* **wunj-**, **wunju-**.

**wunjíhleew** VAI come from a certain place *(quickly)*. *ind 1st sg* **noonjíhla**, **noonjíhlaam**. *conj 3rd sg* **wunjíh=laat**. *imp* **wunjíhlaal**. *ptcpl* **ween=jíhlaat**.

**wunjíhtoow** VTI2 make s.t. from something, make s.t. for a certain reason. *ind 1st sg* **noonjíhtoon**. *ind 3rd sg* **oonjíhtoon**. *conj 1st sg* **wunjíhta=waan**. *conj 3rd sg* **wunjíhtaakw**. *imp* **wunjíhtool**. *ptcpl* **weenjíhtaakw**.

**wunju-** PN place; reason. *informal.* **Wúnju-eehundaxpóonung.** 'Off the table.'; **Máh njíhnal shkuphamee=wíiwak wúnju-shúlpul.** 'They didn't play cards for money any more.' *See* **wunj-**.

**wunju-** PV from a certain place; for a

certain reason. *informal.* **Kwéek há nú kóonju-lúnŭmun?** 'Why did you do that?'; **Nehnayóongsung wúnju-níixiiw.** 'He got off the horse.' *ptcpl* **wéenju-**. *See* **wunj-**, **wunji-**.

**wunzáasuw** VAI be boiled *(s.t. animate). ind 1st sg* **noonzáasi**, **noonzáasiim**. *conj 3rd sg* **wunzáasiit**. *ptcpl* **ween=záasiit**.

**wunzáasuw** VII be boiled. *conj 3rd sg* **wunzáasiik**. *ptcpl* **weenzáasiik**.

**wúnzeew** VTA boil s.o., bring s.o. to a boil. *ind 1st sg* **nóonzaaw**, **nóonza**. *ind 3rd sg* **oonzáawal**. *ind inv* **nóon=zookw**. *ind I-you* **kóonzool**. *conj 3rd sg* **wúnzaat**. *imp* **wúnz**. *ptcpl* **wéen=zaat**.

**wúnzuw** VAI boil, come to a boil *(s.t. animate). ind 1st sg* **nóonzi**, **nóon=ziim**. *conj 3rd sg* **wúnziit**. *ptcpl* **wéenziit**.

**wúnzum** VTI1B boil s.t., bring s.t. to a boil. *ind 1st sg* **nóonzŭmun**. *ind 3rd sg* **óonzŭmun**. *conj 1st sg* **wúnzŭ=maan**. *conj 3rd sg* **wúnzung**. *imp* **wúnzih**. *ptcpl* **wéenzung**.

**wuskáhksun** NI new shoe. *pl* **wuskah=ksúnal**. *poss* **nooskáhksun**. *loc* **wus=kahksúnung**. *dimin* **wushkahk=shúnush**.

**wuskahksúneew** VAI have new shoes. *ind 1st sg* **nooskahksúna**, **nooskah=ksúnaam**. *conj 3rd sg* **wuskahksún=aat**. *ptcpl* **weeskahksúnaat**.

**wuskáhpapoon** NI new chair. *pl* **wus=kahpapóonal**. *poss* **nooskáhpapoon**. *loc* **wuskahpapóonung**. *dimin* **wushkahpapóonush**.

**wúskakuw** VAI wear new clothes. *ind 1st sg* **nóoskakwi**, **nóoskakwiim**. *conj 3rd sg* **wúskakwiit**. *imp* **wúska=kwiil**. *ptcpl* **wéeskakwiit**. *intensive reduplication* **awúskakuw**.

**wúskapuw** VAI be new *(especially of ba-bies)*; be a new moon. *ind 1st sg* **nóoskapi**, **nóoskapiim**. *conj 3rd sg* **wúskapiit**. *ptcpl* **wéeskapiit**.

**wuskehnayóongus** NA young horse. *pl* **wuskehnayóongsak**. *poss* **nooskeh=nayóongsum**. *dimin* **wuskehna=yóongshush**. *obv* **wuskehnayóong=sal**.

**wuskii-** PN new; young. **Wúskii-pám=biil.** 'A new book.'

**wuskíikaan** NI new house. *pl* **wuskii=káanal**. *poss* **nooskíikaan**. *loc* **wus=kiikáanung**. *dimin* **wushkiikáanush**.

**wuskíilŭnuw** NA young man. *pl* **wus=kiilŭnúwak**. *dimin* **wushkíilŭnoosh**. *obv* **wuskiilŭnúwal**.

**wuskiináakwat** VII look new, look young. *conj 3rd sg* **wuskiináakwahk**. *ptcpl* **weeskiináakwahk**.

**wuskiináakwsuw** VAI look new, look young. *ind 1st sg* **nooskiináakwsi**, **nooskiináakwsiim**. *conj 3rd sg* **wus=kiináakwsiit**. *ptcpl* **weeskiináakw=siit**.

**wuskiinjkwahíikanal** NI eyeglasses, glasses. *usually plural. poss* **noos=kiinjkwahíikanal**. *loc* **wuskiinj=kwahíikanung**. *dimin* **wushkiinj=kwahiikanúshal**.

**wuskiinjkwáhŭmeew** VAI wear eye-glasses, wear glasses. *ind 1st sg* **nooskiinjkwáhŭma**, **nooskiinj=kwáhŭmaam**. *conj 3rd sg* **wuskiinj=kwáhŭmaat**. *imp* **wuskiinjkwáhŭ=maal**. *ptcpl* **weeskiinjkwáhŭmaat**.

**wuskiinjkwíineew** VAI have sore eyes. *ind 1st sg* **nooskiinjkwíine**, **noos=kiinjkwíineem**. *conj 3rd sg* **wus=kiinjkwíineet**. *ptcpl* **weeskiinjkwíi=neet**.

**wuskiixáskwal** NI fresh grass, green grass. *usually plural. loc* **wuskiixás=kwung**.

**wuskíhpun** NA new potato. *pl* **wuskíh=pŭnak**. *poss* **nooskíhpun**. *loc* **wus=kíhpŭnung**. *dimin* **wushkíhpŭnush**. *obv* **wuskíhpŭnal**.

**wuskíhtukw** NA young tree. *pl* **wus=**

**kíhtkwak**. *poss* **nooskíhtkwum**. *loc* **wuskíhtkwung**. *dimin* **wushkíhch=kwush**. *obv* **wuskíhtkwal**.

**wuskóoshkoosh** NA young pig, new pig. *pl* **wuskooshkóoshak**. *poss* **noos=kooshkóoshum**. *loc* **wuskooshkóo=shung**. *dimin* **wushkooshkóoshush**. *obv* **wuskooshkóoshal**.

**wuskóxkweew** NA young woman. *pl* **wuskoxkwéewak**. *obv* **wuskox=kwéewal**.

**wúsksuw** VAI be new, be young *(s.t. animate)*. *ind 1st sg* **nóosksi**, **nóosksiim**. *conj 3rd sg* **wúsksiit**. *ptcpl* **wéesksiit**.

**wuskshapakwíiwan** NI new cloth. *pl* **wuskshapakwíiwanal**. *poss* **noosk=shapakwíiwan**. *loc* **wuskshapa=kwíiwanung**. *dimin* **wuskshapa=kwíiwanush**.

**wúskun** VII be new, be young. *conj 3rd sg* **wúskung**. *ptcpl* **wéeskung**.

**wuskxáskwiim** NI new corn, green corn. *pl* **wuskxaskwíimal**. *poss* **nooskxas=kwíimum**. *loc* **wuskxaskwíimung**. *dimin* **wushkxashkwíimush**.

**wúskxum** NA young dog. *pl* **wuskxúm=wak**. *poss* **nóoskxum**. *dimin* **wushk=xúmwush**. *obv* **wuskxúmwal**.

**wúshkii** NI whiskey. *poss* **nooshkíihum**. *loc* **wushkíihung**. *dimin* **wushkíi=hush**. *From English* whiskey.

**wŭyakaapŭlúsheew** VAI have plenty of apples. *ind 1st sg* **nooyakaapŭlúsha**, **nooyakaapŭlúshaam**. *conj 3rd sg* **wŭyakaapŭlúshaat**. *ptcpl* **weeya=kaapŭlúshaat**.

**wŭyakaashŭwíhleew** VAI swim often, swim a lot. *ind 1st sg* **nooyakaashŭ=wíhla**, **nooyakaashŭwíhlaam**. *conj 3rd sg* **wŭyakaashŭwíhlaat**. *imp* **wŭyakaashŭwíhlaal**. *ptcpl* **weeya=kaashŭwíhlaat**.

**wŭyakáawsuw** VAI be hard to handle, don't obey the rules, be 'out of hand.' *ind 1st sg* **nooyakáawsi**, **nooya=káawsiim**. *conj 3rd sg* **wŭyakáaw=siit**. *ptcpl* **weeyakáawsiit**.

**wŭyakahtakíhleew** VAI run around, run wild, run all over. *ind 1st sg* **nooya=kahtakíhla**, **nooyakahtakíhlaam**. *conj 3rd sg* **wŭyakahtakíhlaat**. *imp* **wŭyakahtakíhlaal**. *ptcpl* **weeya=kahtakíhlaat**.

**wŭyákakuw** VAI have plenty of clothes. *ind 1st sg* **nooyakákwi**, **nooyakák=wiim**. *conj 3rd sg* **wŭyákakwiit**. *ptcpl* **weeyakákwiit**.

**wŭyakaskeelŭmuwiináakwsuw** VAI the way one looks makes someone feel like throwing up, the way one looks makes someone feel like vomiting. *ind 1st sg* **nooyakaskeelŭmuwii=náakwsi**, **nooyakaskeelŭmuwii=náakwsiim**. *conj 3rd sg* **wŭyakas=keelŭmuwiináakwsiit**. *ptcpl* **weeya=kaskeelŭmuwiináakwsiit**.

**wŭyakaskíileew** VTA make s.o. nauseous, make s.o. throw up, make s.o. vomit. *ind 1st sg* **nooyakaskíilaaw**, **nooya=kaskíila**. *ind 3rd sg* **ooyakaskiiláa=wal**. *ind inv* **nooyakaskíilukw**. *ind I-you* **kooyakaskíilul**. *conj 3rd sg* **wŭyakaskíilaat**. *imp* **wŭyakáskiil**. *ptcpl* **weeyakaskíilaat**.

**wŭyakaskíilaweew** VAI feel nauseous, feel sick to one's stomach. *ind 1st sg* **nooyakaskíilawe**, **nooyakaskíila=weem**. *conj 3rd sg* **wŭyakaskíila=weet**. *ptcpl* **weeyakaskíilaweet**.

**wŭyakaskíhleew** VAI feel sick, feel like throwing up, feel like vomiting. *ind 1st sg* **nooyakaskíhla**, **nooyakaskíh=laam**. *conj 3rd sg* **wŭyakaskíhlaat**. *ptcpl* **weeyakaskíhlaat**.

**wŭyákat** VII be in abundance, be plenty. *conj 3rd sg* **wŭyákahk**. *ptcpl* **wée=yakahk**.

**wŭyakiichŭwáakaneew** VAI have lots of food, have an abundance of food. *ind 1st sg* **nooyakiichŭwáakane**, **nooya=kiichŭwáakaneem**. *conj 3rd sg* **wŭ=yakiichŭwáakaneet**. *ptcpl* **weeyak=**

**iichŭwáakaneet**.

**wŭyakíipuw** VAI have plenty to eat, have an abundance of food. *ind 1st sg* **nooyakíipwi**, **nooyakíipwiim**. *conj 3rd sg* **wŭyakíipwiit**. *ptcpl* **weeya=kíipwiit**.

**wŭyakíisŭmuw** VAI have plenty to drink. *ind 1st sg* **nooyakíisŭmwi**, **nooya=kíisŭmwiim**. *conj 3rd sg* **wŭyakíisŭ=mwiit**. *ptcpl* **weeyakíisŭmwiit**.

**wŭyakíhleew** VAI go back and forth, ride back and forth, fly back and forth. **Káalak wŭyakihléewak.** 'The cars are going back and forth.' *ind 1st sg* **nooyakíhla**, **nooyakíhlaam**. *conj 3rd sg* **wŭyakíhlaat**. *imp* **wŭyakíh=laal**. *ptcpl* **weeyakíhlaat**.

**wŭyaksúwak** VAI be in abundance, be plenty *(s.t. animate). usually plural. ind 1st pl* **nooyakusíhna**. *conj 3rd sg* **wŭyaksíhtiit**. *ptcpl* **weeyakusíhtiit**.

**wŭyaku-** PV often. *informal.* **Máh nóo=yaku-neewáawu.** 'I don't see him often.'; **Wŭyáku-pŭmihléewak.** 'They fly by often.' *ptcpl* **wéeyaku-**. *See* **eewachu-**, **yáanee**.

**wŭyamoxkáaheew** VAIO shake s.t. up. *ind 1st sg* **nooyamoxkáaheen**. *ind 3rd sg* **ooyamoxkáaheen**. *conj 3rd sg* **wŭyamoxkáaheet**. *imp* **wŭyamox=káaheel**. *ptcpl* **weeyamoxkáaheet**.

**wŭyamoxkháasuw** VAI be stirred, be stirred up *(s.t. animate). ind 1st sg* **nooyamoxkháasi**, **nooyamoxkháa=siim**. *conj 3rd sg* **wŭyamoxkháasiit**. *ptcpl* **weeyamoxkháasiit**.

**wŭyamoxkháasuw** VII be stirred, be stirred up. **Méhch wŭyamoxkháa=suw.** 'It's stirred up now.' *conj 3rd sg* **wŭyamoxkháasiik**. *ptcpl* **weeya=moxkháasiik**.

**wŭyamóxkham** VOTI1A stir things. *ind 1st sg* **nooyamóxkham**. *conj 3rd sg* **wŭyamóxkhang**. *imp* **wŭyamóxk=hah**. *ptcpl* **weeyamóxkhang**.

**wŭyamóxkham** VTI1A stir s.t. *ind 1st sg* **nooyamoxkhámun**. *ind 3rd sg* **oo=yamoxkhámun**. *conj 1st sg* **wuyam=oxkhámaan**. *conj 3rd sg* **wŭyamóx=khang**. *imp* **wŭyamóxkhah**. *ptcpl* **weeyamóxkhang**.

**wŭyamóxkheew** VTA stir s.t. animate. *ind 1st sg* **nooyamóxkhaaw**, **nooya=móxkha**. *ind 3rd sg* **ooyamoxkháa=wal**. *ind inv* **nooyamóxkhookw**. *ind I-you* **kooyamóxkhool**. *conj 3rd sg* **wŭyamóxkhaat**. *imp* **wŭyamóxk=haw**. *ptcpl* **weeyamóxkhaat**.

**wŭyamoxkhíikan** NI stirring stick, object used for stirring. *pl* **wŭyamoxk=híikanal**. *poss* **nooyamoxkhíikan**. *loc* **wŭyamoxkhíikanung**. *dimin* **wŭyamoxkhíikanush**.

**wŭyamoxkhíikeew** VAI stir things. *ind 1st sg* **nooyamoxkhíike**, **nooyamox=khíikeem**. *conj 3rd sg* **wŭyamoxk=híikeet**. *imp* **wŭyamoxkhíikeel**. *ptcpl* **weeyamoxkhíikeet**.

**wŭyamoxkíhleew** VII get shaken up. *conj 3rd sg* **wŭyamoxkíhlaak**. *ptcpl* **weeyamoxkíhlaak**.

**wŭyamoxkihtéexiin** VAI fall and get shaken up, be hit and get shaken up. *ind 1st sg* **nooyamoxkihtéexiin**, **nooyamoxkihtéexi**. *conj 3rd sg* **wŭ=yamoxkihtéexiing**. *ptcpl* **weeya=moxkihtéexiing**, **weeyamoxkih=téexiit**.

**wŭyamoxkíhtoow** VTI2 shake and stir s.t., agitate s.t. *ind 1st sg* **nooyamox=kíhtoon**. *ind 3rd sg* **ooyamoxkíh=toon**. *conj 1st sg* **wuyamoxkíhta=waan**. *conj 3rd sg* **wŭyamoxkíh=taakw**. *imp* **wŭyamoxkíhtool**. *ptcpl* **weeyamoxkíhtaakw**.

**wŭyamóxkŭnum** VTI1B stir s.t. *(using the hands). ind 1st sg* **nooyamox=kŭnúmun**. *ind 3rd sg* **ooyamoxkŭ=númun**. *conj 1st sg* **wuyamoxkŭ=númaan**. *conj 3rd sg* **wŭyamóxkŭ=nung**. *imp* **wŭyamóxkŭnih**. *ptcpl* **weeyamóxkŭnung**.

**wŭyóos** NI meat. *pl* **wŭyóosal**. *poss* **nooyóosum**. *loc* **wŭyóosung**. *dimin* **wŭyóoshush**.
**wŭyoosŭniikáawan** NI gums. *poss* **nooyoosŭniikáawan**, **nooyoosŭnii=káawanum**.

# X

**xáa** PC emphatic, should. **Káta- xáa - keeshéetsiin kshulpúlum.** 'You should try to save your money.'; **Táas xáa máachiiw.** 'I wish he'd go home'
**xáash** PC eight. **Xáash txaaníhka.** 'Eighteen.'
**xámeew** VTA feed s.o. *ind 1st sg* **ndáxa=maaw**, **ndáxama**. *ind 3rd sg* **wtaxa=máawal**. *ind inv* **ndáxamukw**. *ind I-you* **ktáxamul**. *conj 3rd sg* **xámaat**. *imp* **xám**. *ptcpl* **éexamaat**.
**xámeew** VTAO feed s.t. to s.o. **Ndáxa=maan óhpŭnal.** 'I fed her the potatoes.'; **Wŭyóos ndáxamaan.** 'I fed him the meat.' *ind 1st sg* **ndáxamaan**. *ind 1st sg* **ndaxamúkwun**. *ind 3rd sg* **wtáxamaan**. *ind I-you* **ktaxamúlun**. *conj 3rd sg* **xámaat**. *imp* **xám**. *ptcpl* **éexamaat**.
**xángeew** VAI feed people. *ind 1st sg* **ndaxánge**, **ndaxángeem**. *conj 3rd sg* **xángeet**. *imp* **xángeel**. *ptcpl* **eexán=geet**.
nxánz NAD my older brother. *pl* **nxán=zak**. *3rd poss* **xwánzal**. *dimin* **nxán=zhush**.
**xáy** NA hide, skin. *pl* **xáyak**. *poss* **ndáx=ayum**. *dimin* **xáyush**. *obv* **xáyal**.
**xayáhksun** NI leather shoe. *pl* **xayah=ksúnal**. *poss* **ndaxayáhksun**. *loc* **xayahksúnung**. *dimin* **xayahkshún=ush**.
**xáyii-aníixan** NI leather shoelace. *pl* **xáyii-aníixanal**. *poss* **ndáxayii-aníixan**. *loc* **xáyii-aníixanung**. *dimin* **xáyii-aníixanush**.
**xáyii-kóot** NI leather coat. *pl* **xáyii-kóotal**. *poss* **ndáxayii-kóotum**. *loc* **xáyii-kóotung**. *dimin* **xáyii-kóo=chush**.
**xáyii-wánd** NA leather glove. *pl* **xáyii-wándak**. *poss* **ndáxayii-wándum**. *dimin* **xáyii-wánjush**. *obv* **xáyii-wándal**.
**xayiinóotay** NI leather bag. *pl* **xayii=nóotayal**. *poss* **ndaxayiinóotay**.
**xéet** PC maybe, emphatic. **Máh xéet ná.** 'That's not the one.'; **Wách xéet náh péew.** 'I wonder if he's there yet.'
**xéetiis** PC mildly derogatory expression.
nxíisŭmus NAD my younger brother, my younger sister, my younger sibling. *pl* **nxiisŭmúsak**. *3rd poss* **xwiisŭmúsal**.
nxúm NAD my daughter-in-law. *pl* **nxúmak**. *3rd poss* **xwúmal**. *dimin* **nxúmush**.
**xuwáhksun** NI old shoe. *pl* **xuwahk=súnal**. *poss* **nŭmoxwŭwáhksun**. *loc* **xuwahksúnung**. *dimin* **xuwahk=shúnush**.
**xúwahkw** NA old tree. *pl* **xuwáhkwak**. *poss* **nŭmoxwŭwáhkwum**. *loc* **xuw=áhkwung**. *dimin* **xuwáhkwush**. *obv* **xuwáhkwal**.
**xuwáhpapoon** NI old chair. *pl* **xuwah=papóonal**. *poss* **nŭmoxwŭwáhpa=poon**. *loc* **xuwahpapóonung**. *dimin* **xuwahpapóonush**.
**xuwáskwal** NI old grass, weeds. *usually plural*. *loc* **xuwáskwung**. *See* **xuwii=xáskwal**.
**xuweendakwíiwan** NI old dress. *pl* **xuweendakwíiwanal**. *poss* **nŭmox=wŭweendakwíiwan**. *loc* **xuweenda=kwíiwanung**. *dimin* **xuweenjakwíi=wanush**.
**xúwii** PC old. **Xúwii éhakwiing.** 'Old clothing.' *See* **xúwu**.
**xuwii-** PN old. **Xúwii-pambíilak.** 'Old books.'; **Xúwii-kiikíipush.** 'Old chicken.'

**xuwíikaan** NI old house. *pl* **xuwiikáa=nal**. *poss* **nŭmoxwŭwíikaan**. *loc* **xuwiikáanung**. *dimin* **xuwiikáanush**.

**xuwiixáskwal** NI old grass, weeds. *usually plural*. *loc* **xuwiixáskwung**. *See* **xuwáskwal**.

**xuwíiyayuw** VAI be old, be worn out *(s.t. animate)*. *ind 1st sg* **nŭmoxwŭ=wíiyayi**, **nŭmoxwŭwíiyayiim**. *conj 3rd sg* **xuwíiyayiit**. *ptcpl* **meexŭwíi=yayiit**.

**xuwíiyayuw** VII be old, be worn out. *conj 3rd sg* **xuwíiyayiik**. *ptcpl* **mee=xŭwíiyayiit**.

**xuwihlóosus** NA old man. *pl* **xuwih=lóossak**. *poss* **nŭmoxwŭwihlóossum**. *obv* **xuwihlóossal**.

**xuwíhtukw** NA old tree. *pl* **xuwíhtkwak**. *loc* **xuwíhtkwung**. *dimin* **xuwíhch=kwush**. *obv* **xuwíhtkwal**.

**xuwóoshkoosh** NA old pig. *pl* **xuw=ooshkóoshak**. *poss* **nŭmoxwŭ=wooshkóoshum**. *loc* **xuwooshkóo=shung**. *dimin* **xuwooshkóoshush**. *obv* **xuwooshkóoshal**.

**xúwu** PC old. *informal*. **Xúwu kwéekwiil awéehe.** 'He wears old things.' *See* **xúwii**.

**xúwxum** NA old dog. *pl* **xuwxúmwak**. *loc* **xuwxúmwung**. *dimin* **xuwxúm=wush**. *obv* **xuwxúmwal**.

**xwaalakaxóoneew** VAI have a deep voice. *ind 1st sg* **nŭmoxwaalakax=óona**, **nŭmoxwaalakaxóonaam**. *conj 3rd sg* **xwaalakaxóonaat**. *ptcpl* **meexaalakaxóonaat**.

**xwaalakiingwéexiin** VAI have one's eyes open, have big eyes. *ind 1st sg* **nŭ=moxwaalakiingwéexiin**, **nŭmox=waalakiingwéexi**. *conj 3rd sg* **xwaa=lakiingwéexiing**. *ptcpl* **meexaala=kiingwéexiing**, **meexaalakiingwée=xiit**.

**xwáalŭwees** NA fox. *pl* **xwaalŭwéesak**. *poss* **nŭmoxwaalŭwéesum**. *dimin* **xwaalŭwéeshush**. *obv* **xwaalŭwée=sal**.

**xwáandpeew** VAI have a big head. *ind 1st sg* **nŭmoxwáandpa**, **nŭmox=wáandpaam**. *conj 3rd sg* **xwáand=paat**. *ptcpl* **meexáandpaat**.

**xwaapakiingwéexiin** VAI have one's eyes wide open, have big eyes. *ind 1st sg* **nŭmoxwaapakiingwéexiin**, **nŭmoxwaapakiingwéexi**. *conj 3rd sg* **xwaapakiingwéexiing**. *ptcpl* **meexaapakiingwéexiing**.

**xwáapŭweew** VII be a lot of water, be a large amount of water. *conj 3rd sg* **xwáapŭweek**. *ptcpl* **meexáapŭweek**.

**xwaawatóoheew** VAIO charge a lot for s.t. *ind 1st sg* **nŭmoxwaawatóoheen**. *ind 3rd sg* **moxwaawatóoheen**. *conj 3rd sg* **xwaawatóoheet**. *imp* **xwaa=watóoheel**. *ptcpl* **meexaawatóoheet**.

**xwáawatuw** VAI be expensive *(s.t. animate)*. *ind 1st sg* **nŭmoxwáawati**, **nŭmoxwáawatiim**. *conj 3rd sg* **xwáawatiit**. *ptcpl* **meexáawatiit**.

**xwáawatuw** VII be expensive. *conj 3rd sg* **xwáawatiik**. *ptcpl* **meexáawatiik**.

**xwáchahkw** NA big tree. *pl* **xwacháh=kwak**. *poss* **nŭmoxwacháhkwum**. *loc* **xwacháhkwung**. *obv* **xwacháh=kwal**.

**xwachii-** PN big. **Xwáchii-áxkook.** 'A big snake.'; **Xwáchii-kiikíipush.** 'Big chicken.' *See* **xwachu-**.

**xwachíikeew** VAI have a big house. *ind 1st sg* **nŭmoxwachíike**, **nŭmoxwa=chíikeem**. *conj 3rd sg* **xwachíikeet**. *ptcpl* **meexachíikeet**. *See* **xwíikeew**.

**xwachiináakwat** VII look big. *conj 3rd sg* **xwachiináakwahk**. *ptcpl* **meexa=chiináakwahk**.

**xwachiináakwsuw** VAI look big *(s.t. animate)*. *ind 1st sg* **nŭmoxwachii=náakwsi**, **nŭmoxwachiináakwsiim**. *conj 3rd sg* **xwachiináakwsiit**. *ptcpl* **meexachiináakwsiit**.

**xwachíinjuw** NI big dish. *pl* **xwachíin=jŭwal**. *poss* **nŭmoxwachiinjóohum**.

*loc* **xwachíinjoong**.
**xwachi-** PN big. **Xwáchi-táataskw.** 'A sled.' *See* **xwachii-**, **xwachu-**.
**xwachíhpun** NA big potato. *pl* **xwach=íhpŭnak**. *poss* **nŭmoxwachíhpŭ=num**. *loc* **xwachíhpŭnung**. *obv* **xwachíhpŭnal**.
**xwachu-** PN big. *informal*. **Xwáchu-eehundáxpoon.** 'A big table.' *See* **xwachii-**.
**xwáhkŭyeew** VAI have a lot of land. *ind 1st sg* **nŭmoxwáhkŭye**, **nŭmoxwáh=kŭyeem**. *conj 3rd sg* **xwáhkŭyeet**. *ptcpl* **meexáhkŭyeet**.
**xwáhkwat** VII be big, be big around the middle, be big in girth. *conj 3rd sg* **xwáhkwahk**. *ptcpl* **meexáhkwahk**.
**xwahkwíixun** VII be high water, be deep water, be a flood, be flooding. *conj 3rd sg* **xwahkwíixung**. *ptcpl* **mee=xahkwíixung**.
**xwáhkwsuw** VAI be big, be big around the middle, be big in girth. *ind 1st sg* **nŭmoxwáhkwsi**, **nŭmoxwáhkwsiim**. *conj 3rd sg* **xwáhkwsiit**. *ptcpl* **mee=xáhkwsiit**.
**xwáhtakat** VII be big, be coarse *(of something stringlike)*. *conj 3rd sg* **xwáhtakahk**. *ptcpl* **meexáhtakahk**.
**xwáhteew** VII be deep snow. *conj 3rd sg* **xwáhteek**. *ptcpl* **meexáhteek**.
**xwalóhkeew** VAIO pay a lot for s.t., pay too much for s.t. *ind 1st sg* **nŭmox=walóhkeen**. *ind 3rd sg* **moxwalóh=keen**. *conj 3rd sg* **xwalóhkeet**. *imp* **xwalóhkeel**. *ptcpl* **meexalóhkeet**.
**xwanzhíikan** NA American. *pl* **xwan=zhíikanak**. *obv* **xwanzhíikanal**.
**xwanzhíikan** NI big knife; the United States. *pl* **xwanzhíikanal**. *poss* **nŭ=moxwanzhíikan**. *loc* **xwanzhíika=nung**. *See* **xwatanzhíikan**.
**xwaskóonzhuy** NI corn cob. *pl* **xwas=kóonzhŭyal**. *See* **xwashkóonzhuy**.
**xwásktuw** VAI defecate a large amount, go to the bathroom a lot. *ind 1st sg* **nŭmoxwáskti**, **nŭmoxwásktiim**. *conj 3rd sg* **xwásktiit**. *imp* **xwásktiil**. *ptcpl* **meexásktiit**. *See* **amangásktuw**.
**xwáskwcheew** VAI have a big belly. *ind 1st sg* **nŭmoxwáskwcha**, **nŭmox=wáskwchaam**. *conj 3rd sg* **xwásk=wchaat**. *ptcpl* **meexáskwchaat**. *See* **xwaskwchiimóotayeew**.
**xwaskwchiimóotayeew** VAI have a big belly. *ind 1st sg* **nŭmoxwaskwchii=móotaya**, **nŭmoxwaskwchiimóota=yaam**. *conj 3rd sg* **xwaskwchiimóo=tayaat**. *ptcpl* **meexaskwchiimóota=yaat**. *See* **xwáskwcheew**.
**xwáskwiim** NI corn. *pl* **xwaskwíimal**. *poss* **nŭmoxwaskwíimum**. *loc* **xwas=kwíimung**. *dimin* **xwashkwíimush**.
**xwaskwíimapwaan** NI corn bread. *pl* **xwaskwiimapwáanal**. *poss* **nŭmox=waskwíimapwaan**. *loc* **xwaskwii=mapwáanung**. *dimin* **xwashkwii=mapwáanush**. *See* **xwaskwiimŭ=nápwaan**.
**xwaskwiimŭnápwaan** NI corn bread. *pl* **xwaskwiimŭnapwáanal**. *poss* **nŭ=moxwaskwiimŭnápwaan**. *loc* **xwas=kwiimŭnapwáanung**. *dimin* **xwash=kwiimŭnapwáanush**. *See* **xwas=kwíimapwaan**.
**xwáskwus** NA muskrat; big muskrat. *pl* **xwáskwsak**. *dimin* **xwáshkwshush**. *obv* **xwáskwsal**. *See* **xwáshkwshush**.
**xwashkóonzhuy** NI corn cob. *pl* **xwash=kóonzhŭyal**. *See* **xwaskóonzhuy**.
**xwáshkwshush** NA muskrat; Little Muskrat *(nickname)*. *pl* **xwashk=wshúshak**. *obv* **xwashkwshúshal**. *See* **xwáskwus**.
**xwataaníitus** NA big doll. *pl* **xwataa=níitsak**. *poss* **nŭmoxwataaníitsum**. *loc* **xwataaníitsung**. *obv* **xwataa=níitsal**.
**xwataapíikwus** NA rat. *pl* **xwataapíik=wsak**. *poss* **nŭmoxwataapíikwsum**. *obv* **xwataapíikwsal**.
**xwataatpùníikan** NA wagon. *pl* **xwat=**

**aatpùníikanak**. *poss* **nŭmoxwataat=pùniíkan**. *loc* **xwataatpùníikanung**. *obv* **xwataatpùníikanal**.

**xwataatpùníikan** NI wagon. *pl* **xwat=aatpùníikanal**. *poss* **nŭmoxwataat=pùníikan**. *loc* **xwataatpùníikanung**.

**xwataatpùniikanáhŭmeew** VAI use a wagon. *ind 1st sg* **nŭmoxwataat=pùniikanáhŭma**, **nŭmoxwataat=pùniikanáhŭmaam**. *conj 3rd sg* **xwataatpùniikanáhŭmaat**. *imp* **xwataatpùniikanáhŭmaal**. *ptcpl* **meexataatpùniikanáhŭmaat**.

**xwátameekw** NA big fish. *pl* **xwata=méekwak**. *poss* **nŭmoxwatamée=kwum**. *loc* **xwataméekwung**. *obv* **xwataméekwal**.

**xwatanzhíikan** NI big knife; the United States. *pl* **xwatanzhíikanal**. *poss* **nŭ=moxwatanzhíikan**. *See* **xwanzhíi=kan**.

**xwatáxkook** NA big snake. *pl* **xwatax=kóokak**. *obv* **xwataxkóokal**.

**xwateemhwáanus** NA tablespoon. *pl* **xwateemhwáansak**. *poss* **nŭmox=wateemhwáansum**. *obv* **xwateem=hwáansal**.

**xwatóoshkoosh** NA big pig. *pl* **xwat=ooshkóoshak**. *poss* **nŭmoxwatoosh=kóoshum**. *obv* **xwatooshkóoshal**.

**xwatootéenay** NI big town, city. *pl* **xwatootéenayal**. *loc* **xwatootée=neeng**.

**xwatootéenayuw** VAI have a lot of land. *ind 1st sg* **nŭmoxwatootéenayi**, **nŭ=moxwatootéenayiim**. *conj 3rd sg* **xwatootéenayiit**. *ptcpl* **meexatoo=téenayiit**. *See* **kihtootéenayuw**.

**xwátxum** NA big dog. *pl* **xwatxúmwak**. *obv* **xwatxúmwal**.

**xwéelook** VAI be many of them *(s.t. animate)*. *usually plural*. **Xwéelook kchooltúwak.** 'Many of them came out.' *ind 1st pl* **numoxweelóhna**. *indef subject* **xwéelun**. *conj 3rd sg* **xweelóhtiit**. *ptcpl* **meexeelóhtiit**.

**xweelaangwéewak** VAI be many of them lying together. *usually plural*. *ind 1st pl* **nŭmoxweelaangwéhna**. *conj 3rd sg* **xweelaangwéhtiit**. *ptcpl* **meexee=laangwéhtiit**.

**xweelaapéeksuw** VAI have many pages *(of books)*. *conj 3rd sg* **xweelaapéek=siit**. *ptcpl* **meexeelaapéeksiit**.

**xweelatéexun** VII be many roads. *conj 3rd sg* **xweelatéexung**. *ptcpl* **mee=xéelatung**.

**xwéelham** VOTI I A make a lot of tracks, make many tracks. *ind 1st sg* **nŭmox=wéelham**. *conj 3rd sg* **xwéelhang**. *imp* **xwéelhah**. *ptcpl* **meexéelhang**. *See* **kaanzhéelham**.

**xwéeli** PC very, many, a lot. **Xwéeli kwéek kŭmóxkam.** 'You'll find lots of things.'; **Xwéeli íin ngúmee kwéek móxkam.** 'He always found plenty, it is said.' *See* **xwéelu**.

**xweeliikaapawúwak** VAI be many of them standing *(in a group)*. *usually plural*. *ind 1st pl* **nŭmoxweeliikaa=pawíhna**. *conj 3rd sg* **xweeliikaapa=wíhtiit**. *ptcpl* **meexeeliikaapawíhtiit**.

**xweelkóoyeew** VAI have many cows. *ind 1st sg* **nŭmoxweelkóoye**, **nŭmox=weelkóoyeem**. *conj 3rd sg* **xweel=kóoyeet**. *ptcpl* **meexeelkóoyeet**.

**xweelookwŭnáhkeew** VAI be gone for many nights, be gone for many days. *ind 1st sg* **nŭmoxweelookwŭnáhke**, **nŭmoxweelookwŭnáhkeem**. *conj 3rd sg* **xweelookwŭnáhkeet**. *ptcpl* **meexeelookwŭnáhkeet**.

**xweelookwŭnákat** VII be many nights, be many days. *conj 3rd sg* **xweeloo=kwŭnákahk**. *ptcpl* **meexeelookwŭ=nákahk**.

**xweelóonzheew** VAI have many children. *ind 1st sg* **nŭmoxweelóonzhe**, **nŭ=moxweelóonzheem**. *conj 3rd sg* **xweelóonzheet**. *ptcpl* **meexeelóon=zheet**.

**xwéelpeew** VII be a lot of water. *conj 3rd*

*sg* **xwéelpeek**. *ptcpl* **meexéelpeek**.

**xweelshamóoleew** VTA pile up a lot of s.t. animate. *object usually plural. ind 1st sg* **nŭmoxweelshamooláawak**. *ind 3rd sg* **xweelshamooláawal**. *conj 3rd sg* **xweelshamóolaat**. *imp* **xweel=shámool**. *ptcpl* **meexeelshamóolaat**.

**xweelshamóotoow** VTI2 pile up a lot of s.t. *object usually plural. ind 1st sg* **nŭmoxweelshamootóonal**. *ind 3rd sg* **moxweelshamootóonal**. *conj 1st sg* **xweelshamóotawaan**. *conj 3rd sg* **xweelshamóotaakw**. *imp* **xweel=shamóotool**. *ptcpl* **meexeelshamóo=taakw**.

**xwéeltool** VII be many. *usually plural. conj 3rd sg* **xwéelihk**. *ptcpl* **meexee=líhkiil**.

**xwéelu** PC very, many, a lot. *informal.* **Wtuláawal, "Pŭnáh nú tiihíinjuw! Nùkatúmaakw xwéelu shúlpul."** 'She told her, "Look in the cup! He left me a lot of money."'; **Kwáy éel-náatŭnat ngúmee-uch xwéelu kwéek kŭmóxkam.** 'Now because you picked him up you'll always find lots of things.' *See* **xwéeli**.

**xwéelŭmeew** VTA think a lot of s.o., think highly of s.o., have a high regard for s.o. *ind 1st sg* **nŭmoxwéelŭmaaw, nŭmoxwéelŭma**. *ind 3rd sg* **moxwee=lŭmáawal**. *ind inv* **nŭmoxwéelŭ=mukw**. *ind I-you* **kŭmoxwéelŭmul**. *conj 3rd sg* **xwéelŭmaat**. *imp* **xwée=lum**. *ptcpl* **meexéelŭmaat**.

**xweelŭmúkwsuw** VAI be well thought of. *ind 1st sg* **nŭmoxweelŭmúkwsi, nŭmoxweelŭmúkwsiim**. *conj 3rd sg* **xweelŭmúkwsiit**. *ptcpl* **meexeelŭ=múkwsiit**.

**xwéelun** PC many times. **Xwéelun ootéeneeng nóom.** 'I went to town several times.'

**xweelúndam** VTI1A think a lot of s.t., think highly of s.t., have a high regard for s.t. *ind 1st sg* **nŭmoxwee=lúndamun**. *ind 3rd sg* **moxweelún=damun**. *conj 1st sg* **xweelúndamaan**. *conj 3rd sg* **xweelúndang**. *imp* **xwee=lúndah**. *ptcpl* **meexeelúndang, mee=xweelúndang**.

**xweelúnzuw** VAI be proud. *ind 1st sg* **nŭmoxweelúnzi, nŭmoxweelúnziim**. *conj 3rd sg* **xweelúnziit**. *ptcpl* **mee=xeelúnziit**.

**xweenhíikeew** VAI pay a lot. *ind 1st sg* **nŭmoxweenhíike, nŭmoxweenhíi=keem**. *conj 3rd sg* **xweenhíikeet**. *imp* **xweenhíikeel**. *ptcpl* **meexeenhíikeet**.

**xwii-** PV big. **Nŭmóxwii-kaalháma.** 'I'm driving a big car.'; **Xwíi-kaal=hámeew.** 'He/she is driving a big car.' *ptcpl* **méexii-**.

**xwíikeew** VAI have a big house. *ind 1st sg* **nŭmoxwíikee, nŭmoxwíikeem**. *conj 3rd sg* **xwíikeet**. *ptcpl* **meexíi=keet**. *See* **xwachíikeew**.

**xwíilaneew** VAI have big breasts; have big udders *(of a cow). ind 1st sg* **nŭmoxwíilana, nŭmoxwíilanaam**. *conj 3rd sg* **xwíilanaat**. *ptcpl* **mee=xíilanaat**.

**xwíingweew** VAI have a big face. *ind 1st sg* **nŭmoxwíingwa, nŭmoxwíin=gwaam**. *conj 3rd sg* **xwíingwaat**. *ptcpl* **meexíingwaat**.

**xwíisŭmuw** VAI take a big drink, take a lot of liquid, drink a lot *(including non-alcoholic beverages). ind 1st sg* **nŭ=moxwíisŭmwi, nŭmoxwíisŭmwiim**. *conj 3rd sg* **xwíisŭmwiit**. *imp* **xwíisŭmwiil**. *ptcpl* **meexíisŭmwiit**.

**xwíisheew** VAI urinate a lot. *ind 1st sg* **nŭmoxwíishe, nŭmoxwíisheem**. *conj 3rd sg* **xwíisheet**. *imp* **xwíisheel**. *ptcpl* **meexíisheet**.

**xwíixsuw** VAI speak loudly. *ind 1st sg* **nŭmoxwíixsi, nŭmoxwíixsiim**. *conj 3rd sg* **xwíixsiit**. *imp* **xwíixsiil**. *ptcpl* **meexíixsiit**.

**xwíhk** NA liver. *pl* **xwíhkak**. *obv* **xwíh=kal**.

**xwucháaleew** VAI have a big nose. *ind 1st sg* **nŭmoxwcháala, nŭmoxw=cháalaam**. *conj 3rd sg* **xwucháalaat**. *ptcpl* **meexcháalaat**.

**xwuchéesuw** VAI be big, have a big shape. **Xwuchéesuw míhtukw.** 'The tree is big.' *ind 1st sg* **nŭmoxwchée=si, nŭmoxwchéesiim**. *conj 3rd sg* **xwuchéesiit**. *ptcpl* **meexchéesiit**.

**xwuchéeyeew** VII be big *(of a body)*. **Xwuchéeyeew nzíit.** 'My foot's swollen.' *conj 3rd sg* **xwuchéeyeek**. *ptcpl* **meexchéeyeek**.

**xwukáateew** VAI have a big leg, have big legs. *ind 1st sg* **nŭmoxwkáata, nŭmoxwkáataam**. *conj 3rd sg* **xwukáataat**. *ptcpl* **meexkáataat**. *See* **amangkáateew**.

**xwúkiil** VAI be big. *ind 1st sg* **nŭmóxw=kiil**. *conj 3rd sg* **xwukíiluk**. *ptcpl* **meexkíiluk**.

**xwukíhkwun** VII be big. **Meexkíhkwung kwáy ndawéeheen.** 'I'm using the big one now.' *conj 3rd sg* **xwukíh=kwung**. *ptcpl* **meexkíhkwung**.

**xwúkw** VAI cough *(once)*. *ind 1st sg* **nóoxukw**. *conj 3rd sg* **xwúkwuk**. *imp* **xwúkwih**. *intensive reduplication* **wáwxwukw**. *See* **wáwxwukw**.

**xwukwíineew** VAI have a cough, have a coughing disease. *ind 1st sg* **noox=kwíine, nooxkwíineem**. *conj 3rd sg* **xwukwíineet**.

**xwulóhkeew** VAIO pay a lot for s.t., pay too much for s.t. *ind 1st sg* **nŭmox=wŭlóhkeen**. *ind 3rd sg* **moxwŭlóh=keen**. *conj 3rd sg* **xwulóhkeet**. *ptcpl* **meexŭlóhkeet**.

**xwúndeew** VII be a large room. *conj 3rd sg* **xwúndeek**. *ptcpl* **meexúndeek**.

**xwúpeew** VII be a lot of water *(as in a puddle or ditch)*. *conj 3rd sg* **xwúpeek**. *ptcpl* **méexpeek**.

**xwupéekat** VII be deep water, be a lot of water. *conj 3rd sg* **xwupéekahk**. *ptcpl* **meexpéekahk**.

**xwús** NI wood, piece of wood. *pl* **xwús=al**. *poss* **nŭmóxwsum**. *loc* **xwúsung**. *dimin* **xwúshush**.

**xwusapíikwan** NI clarinet, wooden musical instrument. *pl* **xwusapíikwanal**. *poss* **nŭmoxwsapíikwan**. *loc* **xwus=apíikwanung**. *dimin* **xwushapíikwa=nush**.

**xwusíinjuw** NI wooden cup, wooden dish. *pl* **xwusíinjŭwal**. *poss* **nŭmox=wsiinjóohum**.

**xwusíiteew** VAI have big feet. *ind 1st sg* **nŭmoxwsíita, nŭmoxwsíitaam**. *conj 3rd sg* **xwusíitaat**. *ptcpl* **meexsíitaat**. *See* **amangsíiteew**.

**xwushamóotoow** VTI2 pile s.t. high, pile up many of s.t. *ind 1st sg* **nŭmoxw=shamóotoon**. *ind 3rd sg* **moxwsham=óotoon**. *conj 1st sg* **xwushamóota=waan**. *conj 3rd sg* **xwushamóotaakw**. *imp* **xwushamóotool**. *ptcpl* **meex=shamóotaakw**.

**xwushéeyeew** VII be big, be deep *(of holes)*. *conj 3rd sg* **xwushéeyeek**. *ptcpl* **meexshéeyeek**.

**xwutóoneew** VAI have a big mouth. *ind 1st sg* **nŭmoxwtóona, nŭmoxwtóo=naam**. *conj 3rd sg* **xwutóonaat**. *ptcpl* **meextóonaat**.

# Y

**yáanee** PC always, often. **Yáanee ngakawíhla.** 'I fall down a lot.'; **Yáanee peetootéewuw.** 'He visits here often.' *See* **wŭyaku-**, **eewachu-**.

**yáapee** PC along the bank, down by the river, close to the river. **Yáapee mbúmsi.** 'I walked along the shore.'

**yáawii** PC on one side. **Yáawii kchah=kwŭnaxkáashi.** 'You have a short arm on one side.'; **Yáawii shúkw**

**ndundalahkíihe.** 'I just planted on one side.'

**yángiis** NA Yankee, American. *pl* **yan=gíisak**. *obv* **yangíisal**. *See* **yéengiis**. *From English* Yankee.

**yangwtéehoon** NI apron. *pl* **yangwtee=hóonal**. *loc* **yangwteehóonung**. *dimin* **yangwcheehóonush**.

**yéelak** PR over there. **Yéelak awási ndáhtoon.** 'I put it over there on the other side.'

**yéengiis** NA Yankee, American. *pl* **yeen=gíisak**. *obv* **yeengíisal**. *See* **yángiis**. *From English* Yankee.

**yehyaapéhlaash** NA yellow legs, shorebird. *pl* **yehyaapehláashak**. *obv* **yehyaapehláashal**.

**yó** PC o.k, all right.

**yóok** PR these *(animate)*.

**yóol** PR these *(inanimate)*.

**yóol** PR this, these *(animate obviative)*.

**yóolak** PR way over there, over there a considerable distance.

**yóon** PR this *(inanimate emphatic)*. **Yóon lí áatookw.** 'Let's go this way.'; **Yóon wáak wsáamu-kshúteew.** 'This one's too hot also.'

**yóh** PC here. **Yóh lúnih!** 'Pass it here.'; **Yóh áal!** 'Come here!'

**yóhkwa** PC let's, I'd better, we'd better. **Yóhkwa alumsíitookw.** 'Let's leave.'; **Yóhkwa nŭmáwu-kawíin.** 'I'd better go to sleep.'

**yú** PR this *(inanimate)*; here. *used in inanimate 'where' questions.* **Yú tiihíinjuw.** 'This teacup.'; **Thá yú?** 'Where is it?'

# Z

**nzíit** NID my foot. *pl* **nzíital**. *3rd poss* **wsíit**. *loc* **nzíitung**. *dimin* **nzhíi=chush**.

**nzóokan** NID my hip. *pl* **nzóokanal**. *3rd poss* **wsóokan**. *loc* **nzóokanung**.

**nzúkwiis** NAD my mother-in-law. *pl* **nzukwíisak**. *3rd poss* **wsukwíisal**.

**nzupóotuy** NID my anus. *3rd poss* **wsupóotuy**.

# ZH

**nzheemóotay** NID my stomach. *poss* **noosheemóotay**.

**nzhíichush** NID my toe. *pl* **nzhíich'shal**. *3rd poss* **wshíichush**. *loc* **nzhíich'=shung**.

**nzhiilíhloos** NAD my father-in-law. *pl* **nzhiilihlóosak**. *3rd poss* **wshiilih=lóosal**.

**nzhíis** NAD my uncle, my mother's brother; my cross-uncle. *pl* **nzhíisak**. *3rd poss* **wshíisal**.

**nzhúkwŭnay** NID my tail. *3rd poss* **wshúkwŭnay**. *loc* **nzhúkwŭneeng**.

DELAWARE-ENGLISH DICTIONARY

# A

**able** ADJ **be able to tell the difference between people, 'make strange'** *(of babies)* chihchpiináasuw VAI, chpii=náasuw VAI; **able to, be able to** kiish- PV **Now you won't be able to abuse me anymore.** 'Kwáy máh há njíhnal kíish-mateelŭmíiwu.', **You can write.** 'Kíish- áa -leekhíike.'; **can do something** *(that was previously impossible)* kang- PV *informal* **That's the reason why I was able to sit on top of the horse.** 'Nál nú nóonj-káng-náh wáxkiich lŭmátapiin nehna=yóongsung.'; **read skillfully, be able to read properly** nihtaawakíinzuw VAI.

**about** ADV **about, approximately** apáa=mu PC **And as I left from there suddenly I thought, "I'll look for them outside around here."** 'Nál náh nóonj-alúmsiin wíixkwii ndíit, "Ngwiilamúnal kwáchŭmung apáamu yú talí."', **He worked there about two years.** 'Apáamu níish-katúne náh talalóhkeew.'; **about, around, here and there** apaamu- PV **I fell about by myself.** 'Nxóo mbapáamu-kawíhla.'; **about, around, here and there** papaa- PV **I keep falling about by myself.** 'Nxóo há mbápaa-kàkawíh=laan.', **She lived with her husband for a while, then she left him, and then she went looking for my uncle.** 'Náakeesh wiitaawsoomáawal wiita=weemáachiil, nál wáak pàkíilaan, nál wáak nzhíisal pápaa-kwíilawaan.'; **be about to cry** *(especially of a baby that looks sad)* ooshawutoonéexiin VAI; **be about to fall, be placed so as to fall** lxawíixiin VAI, lxawíixun VII; **have an expression on one's face indicating that one is about to cry** ooshawutoonéhleew VAI.

**above** ADV **above, on top of** waxkíichi PC **On top of the timbers.** 'Waxkíi=chi apánzhŭyung.'; **above, on top of** wáxkiich PC *informal* **I fell on top of the box.** 'Níi mbákshung wáxkiich nŭmatéexiin.', **I put something on top of the table.** 'Wáxkiich eehun=dáxpwiing kwéek ndáhtoon.'

**abundance** N **be in abundance, be plenty** wŭyaksúwak VAI *usually plural,* wŭyákat VII; **have lots of food, have an abundance of food** wŭyakii=chŭwáakaneew VAI; **have plenty to eat, have an abundance of food** wŭyakíipuw VAI.

**abuse** VT **think poorly of s.o., insult s.o., abuse s.o.** *(including physical abuse)* matéelŭmeew VTA; **be abused** mateelŭmúkwsuw VAI.

**abuse verbally** VT **criticize s.o., abuse s.o. verbally, 'run s.o. down'** akush=akuníimeew VTA, akushíimeew VTA.

**accident** N **by accident, in error** pahchi- PV **I cut him by accident.** 'Mbáhchi-tŭmúshaaw.'; **by accident, in error** pahchu- PV *informal* **He said it by accident.** 'Páhchu- kwéek -úw.', **I stepped on it by accident.** 'Mbáhchu-ahpalíhkeen.'; **cut s.o. by accident** páhtsheew VTA, píhtsheew VTA; **cut s.t. by accident** páhtshum VTI1B, píhtshum VTI1B; **eat s.t. animate by accident** páhtameew VTA, píhtameew VTA; **eat s.t. by accident** pahtándam VTI1A, pihtándam VTI1A; **get hit by accident** páhthookw VAI; **hit s.o. by accident** pahtihtéeheew VTA, páhtheew VTA; **hit s.t. by accident** pahtihtéeham VTI1A, páhtham VTI1A; **kick s.o. by accident** pah=chíhkaweew VTA; **be killed in an accident** mamúkw VAI.

**accompany** VT **accompany s.o., go with s.o.** wiichéeweew VTA **She liked to go around with any man at all.** 'Wíhwiing- wéemu awéeniil lúnŭwal

-wiicheewáawal.'; **go along, accompany** wíiteew VAI; **with, accompanying** wiichii- PV **I went to the service with someone.** 'Nŭwíichii-maawée=wi.'

**accordion** N shehshiipihláak apíikwan NI.

**ache** N **feel s.t. as an ache, feel s.t. as a pain, feel s.t. as a soreness in one's body** amándam VTI1A.

**ache** VI **be sore, be tender, ache** *(of body parts)* kiihíicheew VII; **be sore, be tender, ache** kiihíitsuw VAI.

**achievement** N **be jealous of s.o.'s achievements, be jealous of s.o.'s possessions, be envious of s.o.** kxée=lŭmeew VTA.

**across** ADV **crawl across** aashŭwíikw=suw VAI; **drive across** aashŭwuchéh=leew VAI; **drive back, drive across** *(the river)* kwaxkchéhleew VAI; **go across, drive across, pedal across, fly across** aashŭwíhleew VAI; **go across, take a shortcut** kaxkéeweew VAI; **reach across** aashŭwiináxkeew VAI; **run across** aashtéhleew VAI; **run across** *(the road)* aashŭwahtakíhleew VAI; **swim across** kwaxkaashŭwíh=leew VAI; **take s.o. across in a hurry** aashŭwíipheew VTA; **take s.t. across in a hurry** aashŭwiipáhtoow VTI2; ADV **tie s.t. across** aashŭwámbtoow VTI2; **wade here and there in the water, wade around in the water, wade across** apaamaashóokeew VAI; **walk across** aashŭwóoxweew VAI.

**across** PREP **go across the water** kwáx=kakeew VAI; **over across the river** kaamŭnúwiing PC; **row across the water, paddle across the water** kwaxkhámeew VAI; **slap s.o. across the face** *(close to the ears)*, **slap s.o. across the ears** paakxehtéeheew VTA; **walk across the water** aashŭwaak=chóoxwee VAI.

**act** VI **act fancily** wiilawíiyayuw VAI; **act like a baby, feel babyish, don't want to act one's age** *(especially of children)* changeelunzhíishuw VAI; **act oddly, act strangely, make faces** amáashŭnum VOTI1; **act shy** apwaa=líiyayuw VAI; **act strangely** amaa=shíiyayuw VAI; **become White, act like a White person** shŭwanakwíh=leew VAI.

**act up** VI **make faces, act up, act out of the ordinary** achíipŭnum VOTI1.

**action** N **advise people against a course of action** kwihtíhkeew VAI; **discontented with s.o. over their actions** múndawameew VTA; **completed action** kiish- PV **I went to town after he paid me.** 'Ootéeneeng ndá kíish-eenhawíite.'

**active** ADJ **be a restless person, be an active person** seekawéenuw VAI; **be a restless person, be an active person, be hard to handle** séeksuw VAI; **restless person, active person** séeka=ween PR.

**activity** N **be finished an activity** eh=koohaawatúwak VAI *usually plural*; **work in a certain manner, work in a certain place, be engaged in a certain activity** lalóhkeew VAI **I've go nothing to do.** 'Ngwíila- kwéek -làlóhke.', **What are you doing?** 'Kwéek ktulalóhke?'

**add to** VT **add on to a story, interpret** aanihkwaachíimuw VAI; **add on to s.t., lengthen s.t., make s.t. longer** aanihkwíhtoow VTI2; **add on to s.t. animate, lengthen s.t. animate, make s.t. animate longer** aanihkwíi=heew VTA; **add on to s.t. animate, extend s.t. animate** aaníhkhweew VTA; **add on to s.t., extend s.t.** aaníhkhwam VTI1A; **add water to s.t.** *(to make a drink or medicine)* wŭlupéenum VTI1B **I want to make a drink.** 'Ngáta-wŭlupéenŭmun.'

**adder** N **blow adder** pehpootáalŭwees

NA.

**addition** N **in addition, with something else** naxpii- PV **He ate it with something else.** 'Wŭnáxpii-míichiin.'

**admire** VT **like the looks of s.o., admire s.o.** wŭlíinaweew VTA; **like the looks of s.t., admire s.t.** wŭlíinam VTI1A.

**adult** N **adult male, adult man** kihkŭ=wíilŭnuw NA, kíhkwu-lúnuw NA; **adult woman** kíhkwu-óxkweew NA; **be grown-up, be an adult** kihkŭ=waweénuw VAI; **look like an adult woman** oxkweewiinráakwsuw VAI; **unmarried adult woman** kihkaa=péexkweew NA.

**advise** VT **advise people against a course of action** kwihtíhkeew VAI; **advise s.o. against a course of action, advise s.o. against an intention** kwíhtŭleew VTA.

**afraid** ADJ **be afraid** kwihtu- PV *informal* **I'm afraid to eat.** 'Ngwíhtu-míitsi.', **He's afraid to go along.** 'Kwíhtu-wíiteew.'; **be afraid of people** kxúw=eew VAI; **be afraid of s.o., be wary of s.o.** kxwéew VTA; **be afraid of s.t.** kxwáatam VTI1A; **be afraid, be nervous** nahtáachuw VAI; **be afraid, be scared** wiisháasuw VAI; **have one's legs shaking, be afraid** nungkaa=téhleew VAI.

**again** ADV láapii PC **Now go and hunt again.** 'Kwáy láapii máw-aláwiil.', **He fixed it again.** 'Láapii oolíix=toon.'; **hit s.t. again** aandihtéeham VTI1A.

**against** PREP **advise s.o. against a course of action, advise s.o. against an intention** kwíhtŭleew VTA; **bang s.o.'s head against something** paa=kaandpéexŭmeew VTA; **be struck in the eye, brush against something which goes into the eye** laapsheen=gwéexiin VAI; **brush up against s.o.** *(using the foot or body)* chaskíhka=weew VTA; **brush up against s.o.** *(using a tool or instrument)* cháskheew VTA; **brush up against s.t.** *(using the foot or body)* chaskíhkam VTI1A; **brush up against s.t.** *(using a tool or instrument)* cháskham VTI1A; **brush up against something** chaskíixiin VAI, chaskíixun VII, laalíixiin VAI, laalíixun VII; **bump against s.t.** *(with something)* páakham VTI1A; **bump one's face against something** paa=kiingwéexiin VAI; **bump one's hand against something** paakŭnaxkéexiin VAI; **bump one's leg against something** paakkaatéexiin VAI; **bump one's nose against something** paa=kchaaléexiin VAI; **bump s.t. animate against something** paakihtéeheew VTA **I bumped my knee against something.** 'Mbaakihtéehaaw ngút=ko.'; **contact and brush up against s.o.** laalihtéexŭmeew VTA; **contact and brush up against s.t.** laalihtéex=toow VTI2; **fall and bump** *(against something)*, **bump into an object** paakihtéexun VII **It bumped into my leg.** 'Paakihtéexun níhkaat.', **The door banged against something.** 'Paakihtéexun kpáhoon.'; **fall and bump against s.t.** *(with something)* paakihtéextoow VTI2 **He bumped his leg against something.** 'Wíhkaat paakihtéextoon.'; **rub against something, rub up against something** siikwíixiin VAI, siikwíixun VII; **rub against something and fall, brush up against something and fall** laa=lihtéexiin VAI.

**age** N **act like a baby, feel babyish, don't want to act one's age** *(especially of children)* changeelunzhíi=shuw VAI; **be a man who died of old age** aaptihlóosuw VAI **I'm just about dying of old age.** 'Péexoot ndaaptih=lóosi.'; **be a woman who died of old age** áapchii-kihtoxkwéesuw VAI; **be so many years of age** *(with number* *preverb)* katúm VAI **He is fifteen years old.** 'Naalanaaníhka txíi-katúm.'; **be so many years of age** *(with number preverb)* txú-katúm VAI **I'm ten years old.** 'Wíimbat ndúndxii-katúm.'; **look old, be old-looking, look older than one's age** kihkŭwiináakwsuw VAI.

**agent** N **Indian agent** échun NA **I'm going to the agent's.** 'Échŭnung ndá.'

**agitate** VT **shake and stir s.t., agitate s.t.** wŭyamoxkíhtoow VTI2.

**ago** ADV **long ago** láawate PC **What happened years ago.** 'Láawate áayleek.'; **some time ago** chíingu PC **I went to town some time ago.** 'Chíingu ootée= neeng nóom.', **I talked to the clever one recently.** 'Chíingu léepwaat ngihkŭlóolaaw.'

**ahead** ADV **be in the lead, go first, fly first, run first, drive first, proceed first, go ahead, run ahead** shayéh= leew VAI **The little one came in first.** 'Cheengshíishiit éel-péechi-shayéh= laat.'; **crawl ahead** shayeewiikwsíh= leew VAI; **crawl ahead, crawl in the lead** shayeewíikwsuw VAI; **drive ahead, drive in the lead, drive first** shayeewchéhleew VAI; **look straight ahead** shaaxkóhkweew VAI; **run ahead, be leading in a race** shayee= waaméhleew VAI; **run ahead, be leading in a race** shayeewahtakíh= leew VAI; **walk in the lead, walk in front, go ahead, walk ahead** sha= yéewxeew VAI **He likes to be ahead.** 'Wíhwiing-shayéewxeew.', **He always likes to go ahead.** 'Wíhwiing-shàshayéewxeew.'

**aim** N **take good aim** *(with a gun)*, **throw well** wŭláaheew VAI.

**airs** N **be arrogant, have an attitude, think oneself better than others, to put on airs** *(of women)* leetíisuw VAI, oxkweeweelúnzuw VAI.

**Albert** N élput NA *man's name.*

**alight** VI **land, land on the ground, alight** awáhleew VAI **I landed over there.** 'Yéelak ndúlu-awáhla.'

**alike** ADV **look the same, look alike** eeyŭliinaakwsúwak VAI *usually plural.*

**alive** ADV **be independent, be smart, be alive, be strong** *(especially a sick person who gets up because he or she is feeling better)* àhwaapéewuw VAI; **live, be alive, be living** pŭmáawsuw VAI.

**all** ADJ wéemi PC **Everything.** 'Wéemi kwéek.'; **all** wéemu PC *informal* **There are a lot of good roads in the bush.** 'Wéemu talí wŭlatéexun kóhpii.', **They said all sorts of things to me.** 'Wéemu kwéek ndúkook.'; **be all gone** txíhleew VAI **The fish are all gone.** 'Txihléewak naméesak.'; **be all gone** txíhleew VII; **be all gone, be used up** weemíhleew VII; **be all gone, everybody is gone** weemooltúwak VAI; **destroy all of s.o., kill all of s.o., get rid of all of s.o.** weemíiheew VTA *object usually plural*; **get rid of s.t., completely dispose of s.t., sell all of s.t.** weemalóhkeew VAIO **I gave away all of my belongings.** 'Nŭweema= lóhkeen nehláatamaan.'; **hit all of s.o.** weemihtéeheew VTA *object usually plural;* **hit all of s.t.** weemihtée= ham VTI1A *object usually plural* **I chopped down all of the bushes.** 'Nŭweemihteehŭmúnal mihtkwúsal.'; **saw up all of s.t. animate, cut up all of s.t. animate** méhtsheew VTA; **saw up all of s.t., cut up all of s.t.** méht= shum VTI1B; **spoil s.t., use up all of s.t., use up all of s.t. unwisely** ma= chíhtoow VTI2 **I spent all of my money.** 'Nŭmachíhtoon wéemi nzhulpúlum.'; **take all of s.t. animate out** shíikwŭneew VTA; **take all of s.t. animate, take the last piece of s.t. animate** póhkwŭneew VTA; **take all of s.t. out** *(of something)* shíikwŭnum VTI1A; **take all of s.t., take the last piece of s.t., quit while doing s.t.** póhkwŭnum VTI1B; **undress s.o., take off all of s.o.'s clothes** sheexkalúneew VTA **She's just going to undress me again.** 'Kách wáak ápih shúkw nzheexkalúnukw.'; **use s.t. up, use up all of s.t.** weemawée=heew VAIO; **use s.t. up, use up all of s.t., spend all of it** *(of money)* wee=míhlatoow VTI2; **use up all of s.t. animate** weemíhlaleew VTA.

**all over** ADV **climb all over** msakóosuw VAI; ADV **fall all over, bounce around, get hit about** msihtéexiin VAI; **go all over, roam with no purpose in mind, throw one's backside about as one goes** msiitŭyéewxeew VAI; **run all over** msahtakíhleew VAI; **run around, run wild, run all over** wŭ=yakahtakíhleew VAI; **travel all over** *(mode of transportation unspecified)* msahkéewxeew VAI; **travel all over, travel around** msóoxweew VAI; **work all over** msalóhkeew VAI; **write in various places, write all over** mseek=híikeew VAI.

**all right** ADJ **o.k, all right** yó PC.

**almost** ADV **almost hit s.o., 'nick' s.o.** chaskihtéeheew VTA; **almost, nearly** wéenaa PC **He almost froze to death.** 'Wéenaa kŭláchuw.', **He nearly got scared to death.** 'Wéenaa aaptah=páasuw.'

**alone** ADJ nxóo PC **I live alone.** 'Nxóo nŭwíiki.'; **alone, on its own, the most, the best** *(of something)* nxoo- PV **He's the tallest.** 'Wŭnáxoo-kwŭnáhkwsiin.', **I'm the best cook.** 'Náxoo-nihtaawatúpwiin.'; **eat s.t. alone, eat s.t. with nothing else** mooshándam VTI1A **Don't eat it alone, eat it with bread.** 'Chíi mooshandamóowi, náxpu-míichiil apwáan.'; **eat s.t. animate alone, eat s.t. animate with nothing else** móo=shameew VTA; **leave s.o. alone, leave s.o. behind** *(at home, in a competition)*, **leave everyone behind** wee=míixkaleew VTA **We were left behind (by the deceased).** 'Nŭweemiixka=lukéhna.'; **leave s.o., leave s.o. behind alone, leave s.o. behind and lonely** mayaníixkaleew VTA; **live alone, be on one's own** nxooháalŭ=nuw VAI; **sit alone** nxohkwéepuw VAI; **stay at home alone** nootíikeew VAI.

**along** ADV **by, along** pŭmu- PV **I ran by in a flash.** 'Náh mbúmu-laashíhla.'; **along the bank, down by the river, close to the river** yáapee PC **I walked along the shore.** 'Yáapee mbúmsi.'; **go along** *(with others)* wiitóoxweew VAI.

**alongside** ADV **beside, alongside** pŭmíi=chii PC **He's walking beside me.** 'Pŭmíichii púmsiin.'

**also** ADV ámbee PC **Me too.** 'Ámbee níi.', **I'm going to go too.** 'Ámbee-uch nŭwíite.'; **also, as well** *(before pronouns)* mbee- PN **Me too.** 'Mbée-níi.', **Then he left too.** 'Nál mbée-néeka alúmsuw.'; **also, emphatic** kwŭlúp PC **I went that way, and also he went the other way.** 'Níi nú wún=dakw ndá, kwŭlúp néeka yéelak wún=dakw éew.', **He thinks he's a real angel ('He thinks he has wings').** 'Kwŭlúp liitéeheew wŭlóngwanuw.'

**alter** VT **change s.t., alter s.t., make s.t. over** aanjíhtoow VTI2.

**always** ADV ngúmee PC **I'm always tired.** 'Ngúmee nzhiiwasáni.', **The little one is always hiding.** 'Ngúmee kaachapíishuw.'; **always hit s.o.** ngumeewihtéeheew VTA; **always, often** yáanee PC **I fall down a lot.** 'Yáanee ngakawíhla.', **He visits here often.** 'Yáanee peetootéewuw.'; **be always talking** ngumeewtóonheew VAI.

**amazing** ADJ **great, wonderful, amaz-**

**ing** kaanzhu- PV **Something wonderful happened.** 'Káanzhu-léew.'

**American** N xwanzhíikan NA; **American elm** wŭlaakanahóonzhuy NA; **Yankee, American** yángiis NA, yéengiis NA.

**amount** N kéexu PC *informal* **How much does it weigh?** 'Kéexu póondakat?', **How old are you?** 'Kéexu ktúndxii-katúm?'; **extent, volume, amount** lukíhkwi PC **Later on.** 'Táa lukíh=kwi.', **How much does the table weigh?** 'Tá lukíhkwi póondakat eehundáxpwiing?'; **certain amount, certain extent** eelkih- PV *followed by verb in conjunct order* **It's getting close to when I want to leave.** 'Pee=xŭwíhle éelkih-katá-alumsúyaan.', **It's time to eat.** 'Éelkih-miitsáh=tiing.'; **seldom, hardly, very little, a scant amount** máamchiish PC **I seldom work.** 'Máamchiish ndalóhke.', **There's hardly any left over.** 'Máamchiish aluwíhleew.'; **some, a little bit, a small amount** tangii- PV **Can you speak a little Delaware now?** 'Méhch há kíish-tángii-hulŭ=níixsi?'; **some, a little bit, a small amount** tángii PC **There's a bit of bread there.** 'Tángii nú yéelak áhte apwáan.', **Do you want to eat a little bit?** 'Tángii káta-míitsi?'; **be a lot of water, be a large amount of water** xwáapŭweew VII; **charge s.o. a certain amount** laawatóohaweew VTA; **charge s.o. a certain amount** loo=watóohaweew VTA; **defecate a large amount, go to the bathroom a lot** amangásktuw VA, xwásktuw VAI; **have a certain value, cost a certain amount** láawatuw VAI, láawatuw VII; **have an overwhelming amount of work to do** laawalóhkeew VAI; **pay a certain amount for s.t.** lulóhkeew VAIO **I paid two dollars for it.** 'Níish ndálaas ndulŭlóhkeen.', **How much did he pay for it?** 'Kéexu wtulŭlóh=keen?'; **weigh a certain amount, have a certain weight** poondakúsuw VAI *usually with number particle* **They weigh four pounds.** 'Néewa poon=dakúsŭwak.'; **weigh a certain amount, have a certain weight** póondakat VII *usually with number particle* **How much does it weigh?** 'Kéexu póondakat?', **It weighs two pounds.** 'Níishu póondakat.'

**and** CJ wáak PC **And then I left.** 'Nál wáak ndalŭmúsiin.'

**anew** ADV **hit s.o. anew, hit s.o. another time** aandihtéeheew VTA.

**angle** N **be the inside angle of a corner** póocheew VII **Go stand the broom in the corner.** 'Eénda-póocheek máw-níipatool chiikhíikan.'; **be the outside angle of a corner** síingeew VII **The corner of the house.** 'Éenda-síingeek wíikwahm.'; **be the outside angle of a corner** síingsuw VAI; **be twisted, be at an angle, lie at an angle, be lopsided, lie on its side, be misaligned** *(of a misbuttoned shirt)* piimoxkwíixun VII; **lie crosswise, be twisted, be at an angle, lie at an angle, be lopsided** piimoxkwíixiin VAI.

**Anglican** N **Anglican minister** eeng=lushmaaníiwu-pehpŭmutóonhees NA.

**angry** ADJ **make s.o. angry** wiiníiheew VTA; **be angry** manóongsuw VAI; kwŭnutoonéexiin **be angry, be frustrated, be discouraged, be annoyed, be put-out, be bitter, be sour** *(of foods)* láxksuw VAI; **be through being angry** ehkwanóongsuw VAI; **be very angry, go into a rage** kihta=nóongsuw VAI; **come here angry, come in this direction while angry** peetanóongsuw VAI; **feel angry about one's illness, feel odd, feel angry** manoongamálsuw VAI; **feel cross, feel angry** manoongeelúndam VOTI1; **get angry very easily** ayaapŭwanóong=

suuw VAI; **look at s.o. angrily** ma=noongáapameew VTA; **sound angry, be angry-sounding** manoongih=táakwsuw VAI.

**angry with** VT **be angry with s.o.** ma=taangóomeew VTA.

**animal** N awéeyayus NA; **be milking, milk an animal** siiníikeew VAI; **female dog, female of animal species** oxkwéexum NA; **kill an animal, beat an animal** nihlxúmweew VAI; **make a noise like an animal, make a crowing noise** akeenjíimuw VAI; **male animal** lunŭwéexum NA.

**annoy** VT **annoy s.o.** chaniilawéeheew VTA; **be angry, be frustrated, be discouraged, be annoyed, be put-out, be bitter, be sour** *(of foods)* láxksuw VAI; **be annoyed about s.t.** chanee=lúndam VTI1A; **be annoyed, be discouraged** chaneelúndam VOTI1.

**annoying** ADJ **make an irritating noise, make an annoying noise** níiskŭweew VII, níiskŭweew VAI.

**another** ADJ **hit s.o. anew, hit s.o. another time** aandihtéeheew VTA; **hit s.o. anew, hit s.o. another time** aandihtéeheew VTA.

**answer** VI naxkóotam VOTI1.

**answer** VT **answer s.o.** naxkóomeew VTA; **answer s.t.** naxkóotam VTI1A.

**ant** N eelíikwus NA.

**antler** N **antler, horn** wiiláawan NI; **have branches, have antlers** wtóhwanuw VAI.

**anus** N **my anus** nzupóotuy NID.

**any** ADJ **either, any** akwáawu PC **I want anything.** 'Akwáawu kwéekw ngat=áatam.', **I can go anywhere.** 'Akwáa=wu táa ndá.'

**anything** N **go empty handed, go bare handed, don't take anything** *(especially to a gathering)* mooshŭlun=jéhleew VAI.

**anyway** ADV alóot PC **I'll eat anyway.** 'Wáak-uch alóot nŭmíitsi.', **He was glad to see me anyway.** 'Alóot nŭwíingu-néewukw.'; **anyway** *(contrary to expectation)* hachíingi PC **I went there anyways.** 'Hachíingi náh ndá.', **He went ahead and did it.** 'Hachíingi wtulŭnúmun.'; **anyway, regardless, go ahead and do something** téexii PC **I just went ahead and cooked, but no one came.** 'Téexii nátpwiin máh awéen péewi.', **They went ahead and lived together.** 'Téexii ngwúteel apúwak.'

**apart** ADV **be apart** chpahtéewal VII *usually plural*; **be apart, be isolated, be separated from other people** chpúsuw VAI; **be apart, be separated** chpiixíinook VAI *usually plural*, chpíixŭnool VII *usually plural*; **be apart, be separated by birth or location** chpápŭwak VAI *usually plural*; **be far apart** *(of trees)* awahlŭmahk=wsúwak VAI *usually plural*; **be far apart** awahlŭmahtéewal VII *usually plural*, wahlŭmahtéewal VII *usually plural*; **be separated from one's spouse, live apart** chpooxwéewak VAI *usually plural*; **be spread out, be open** *(as sole of shoe flapping)*, **be open, be apart** *(as a shirt)* toongíi=xun VII; **come apart** chpíhleew VII; **dance far apart** wahlŭmukéewak VAI *usually plural*; **grow apart** chàchpíi=kŭwak VAI *usually plural*, chàchpíi=kŭnool VII *usually plural*; **have one's legs spread apart** toongkaatéexiin VAI; **live far apart** wahlŭmiikéewak VAI *usually plural*; **place s.o. apart, place s.t. animate apart** chpáhleew VTA *object usually plural*; **place s.t. apart, set s.t. aside** chpáhtoow VTI2 *object usually plural*; **pull s.t. animate apart, dismantle s.t. animate** lookhéewaleew VTA; **pull s.t. apart, dismantle s.t.** lookhéewatoow VTI2; **sit far apart** awahlŭmohkwéepŭwak VAI *usually plural*; **sit far apart, be**

**far apart, be far away** wahlŭmápŭ=wak VAI; **stand far apart** wahlŭmii=kaapawúwak VAI *usually plural*; **take s.t. animate apart, take s.o. apart** *(using a tool or instrument)* chpáhk=hweew VTA; **take s.t. apart** *(using a tool or instrument)* chpáhkhwam VTI1A.

**apologize to** VT **make up with s.o., apologize to s.o.** mehmeendawámeew VTA.

**appear** VI **appear to be close by, look to be close by** peexŭwiináakwat VII, peexŭwiináakwsuw VAI; **find that s.o. appears hopeless, regret seeing s.o.** laawíinaweew VTA; **find that s.t. appears hopeless** laawíinam VTI1B; **look overwhelming, look hopeless, appear to be hopeless** laawchee=náakwsuw VAI **He's hopeless, he's never getting dressed.** 'Laawchee=náakwsuw máh kiikiisheechpíiwi.'; **look overwhelming, look hopeless, appear to be hopeless** laawiináakwat VII, laawiináakwsuw VAI.

**appearance** N **be clean looking, have a clean appearance** piiliináakwat VII, piiliináakwsuw VAI; **be plain looking, have a plain appearance** kahkanii=náakwat VII, kahkaniináakwsuw VAI; **have a certain appearance** liináa=kwat VII, liináakwsuw VAI; **look good, be nice looking, have a nice appearance** wŭliináakwat VII, wŭliináakw=suw VAI; **look strange, have an odd appearance** maashiináakwat VII, maashiináakwsuw VAI; **look terrible, be terrible looking, have a frightful appearance** chiipiináakwat VII, chii=piináakwsuw VAI.

**apple** N áapŭlush NA; **apple, Apple** *(man's name)* áapul NA **The late Apple.** 'Aapŭláya.'; **apple tree** aapŭ=lúshahkw NA; **dried apple** kaaháa=pŭlush NA; **have plenty of apples** wŭyakaapŭlúsheew VAI; **peel apples** pxwaapŭlúsheew VAI, pxwashaapŭ=lúsheew VAI; **pick apples** makunhaa=pŭlúsheew VAI; **pick apples** *(off the tree)* paxkŭnaapŭlúsheew VAI; **shrivelled apple** piisŭláapŭlush NA; **work in an apple orchard** aapŭlúsh'heew VAI.

**approach** VI **get close, approach, fly close by, go close by** peexŭwíhleew VAI, peexŭwíhleew VII.

**approximately** ADV **about, approximately** apáamu PC **And as I left from there suddenly I thought, "I'll look for them outside around here."** 'Nál náh nóonj-alúmsiin wíixkwii ndíit, "Ngwiilamúnal kwáchŭmung apáamu yú talí."', **He worked there about two years.** 'Apáamu níish-katúne náh talalóhkeew.'

**apron** N yangwtéehoon NI; **short apron** pehpŭlakíixtaang VII.

**argue** VI **argue, quarrel** pŭmiineehíi=keew VAI; VT **argue with s.o., quarrel with s.o.** pŭmiinéeheew VTA.

**argument** N **take s.o.'s side in an argument, speak on s.o.'s behalf in an argument, defend s.o.** ihkáameew VTA.

**arm** N **my hand, my arm** náxk NID; **break s.o.'s arm, break s.o.'s hand** kaxkŭnaxkéeheew VTA; **break s.o.'s arm, break s.o.'s hand** kaxkŭnax=kéexŭmeew VTA; **fold one's arms, have one's arms folded** paxkawii=naxkéesuw VAI, paxkawiinaxkéexiin VAI; **have a broken arm, have a broken hand** kaxkŭnaxkéexiin VAI, kaxkŭnáxkeew VAI; **have a long arm, reach a long way** kwŭniináxkeew VAI, kwŭniináxkeew VAI; **have a scabby hand, have scabs on one's hand, have a scabby arm, have scabs on one's arm** mŭkuyŭnáxkeew VAI; **have a scratch on one's arm, have a scratch on one's hand** kchaxkŭnáxkeew VAI; **have a short**

**arm** *(diminutive)* chahkwŭnaxkée=shuw VAI; **have a sore arm, have a sore hand** kiihiitŭnáxkeew VAI; **have bare hands, have bare arms, have exposed hands, have exposed arms** mihtŭnáxkeew VAI; **have long arms** akwaanŭnáxkeew VAI; **have one's arms around people** takwúndaweew VAI; **have one's arms exposed, have bare arms, have one's hands exposed, have bare hands** mihtŭnax=kéexiin VAI; **have one's arms linked** laapiinaxkeeniikéewak VAI *usually plural*; **have one's arms out** ktunax=kéexiin VAI, ktunŭnaxkéexiin VAI; **have one's arms together, have one's arms intertwined** laapiinaxkéexiin VAI; **have short arms** *(diminutive)* achahkwŭnaxkéeshuw VAI; **hold s.o. tightly around the waist, have one's arms around s.t. animate** kaskatée=neew VTA; **hold s.t. tightly, have one's arms around s.t.** kaskatéenum VTI1B; **lead s.o. by the arm, take s.o. by the arm, be arm in arm with s.o.** laa=piinaxkéeneew VTA, laapiináxkeew VAIO; **stretch out one's arm** shiipii=náxkeew VAI.

**armpit** N **my wing, my armpit** lóng=wan NID; **perspire from one's armpits** ashiilóngwaneew VAI.

**army** N **be in the army, join the army** sóochŭluw VAI.

**around** ADV **about, around, here and there** papaa- PV **I keep falling about by myself.** 'Nxóo há mbápaa-kàka=wíhlaan.', **She lived with her husband for a while, then she left him, and then she went looking for my uncle.** 'Náakeesh wiitaawsoomáawal wiitaweemáachiil, nál wáak pàkíi=laan, nál wáak nzhíisal pápaa-kwíila=waan.'; **about, around, here and there** apaamu- PV **I fell about by myself.** 'Nxóo mbapáamu-kawíhla.'; **be blown around by the wind, be spun around by the wind** túpxookw VAI, túpxun VII; **blow around** *(of the wind)*, **be blown around by the wind** tàtúpxun VII; **chase s.o. around** apaamshíhkaweew VTA; **crawl around, move around** msiikwsíh=leew VAI; **float here and there, float about, float around** apaamáathookw VAI, apaamáathun VII; **go around, rotate, spin** tùpíhleew VAI, tùpíhleew VII; **go in a circle, go around, roll in a circle** wiiwŭníhleew VAI, wiiwŭníh=leew VII; **knock s.o. around, knock s.o. all over, bounce s.o., hit s.o. various ways** msihtéeheew VTA; **move around, stir** wàwŭyamoxkchéhleew VAI; **roll around, roll in a circle** wiiwŭniinjkwéhleew VAI; **roll over, roll around, roll along** tùpiinjkwéh=leew VAI, tùpiinjkwéhleew VII; **roll s.o. around in a circle** wiiwŭniinj=kwéhlaleew VTA; **roll s.t around** tùpiinjkweeyáaheew VAIO; **roll, roll around** tùpchéhleew VAI; **travel all over, travel around** msóoxweew VAI; **turn a crank, crank things, turn things around** tùpŭníikeew VAI; **turn s.o. around, crank s.t. animate** *(using the hands)* túpŭneew VTA; **turn s.t. around, crank s.t.** *(using the hands)* túpŭnum VTI1B; **wrap s.t. around, tie s.t. up** tùpámbtoow VTI2.

**around** PREP **be big, be big around the middle, be big in girth** xwáhkwat VII, xwáhkwsuw VAI; **be placed around something, be placed all around something** wiiwŭniixíinook VAI, wiiwŭníixŭnool VII *usually plural*; **crawl in a circle, crawl around something** wiiwŭníikwsuw VAI; **cut s.t. animate around the edge** wii=wŭnúsheew VTA; **cut s.t. around the edge** wiiwŭnúshum VTI1B; **drive in a circle, drive around something** wiiwŭnuchéhleew VAI; **have one's arms around people** takwúndaweew

VAI; **have something around one's neck** wahkwéelŭnuw VAI; **hold s.o. tightly around the waist, have one's arms around s.t. animate** kaskatée=neew VTA; **hold s.t. tightly, have one's arms around s.t.** kaskatéenum VTI1B; **put s.o. over something, put s.o. on something, put s.o. around something** laapíixŭmeew VTA; **put s.t. animate around something, put s.t. animate all around something** wii=wŭníixŭmeew VTA *object usually plural*; **put s.t. around something, put s.t. all around something** wiiwŭ=níixtoow VTI2 *object usually plural*; **put s.t. over something, put s.t. on something, put s.t. around something** laapíixtoow VTI2; **run in a circle, run around something** wiiwŭ=nahtakíhleew VAI; **sew around the edge of s.t., turn up and sew s.t.** paxkawíikwam VTI1A; **sew around the edges** wiiwŭniikwáakeew VAI; **sew around the edges of s.t.** wiiwŭ=níikwam VTI1A; **sew around the edges of s.t. animate** wiiwŭniikwáa=leew VTA; **sew s.t. animate up, sew around the edge of s.t. animate** paxkawiikwáaleew VTA; **swim in a circle, swim around something** wiiwŭnaashŭwíhleew VAI; **tie something around s.o.** wiiwŭnambíileew VTA; **tie something around s.t., 'put s.t. up'** *(of someone's hair)* wiiwŭ=námbtoow VTI2; **walk around something** wiiwŭnóoxweew VAI; **wrap s.t. animate around something, roll s.o. up, tie s.o. up** túpheew VTA; **wrap s.t. around something, roll s.t. up** túp=ham VTI1A.

**arrange** VT **place s.o. correctly, make s.o. be correctly arranged, straighten s.o. up, arrange s.o. correctly** mayaawíixŭmeew VTA; **place s.t. correctly, make s.t. be correctly arranged, straighten s.t. up** mayaa=wíixtoow VTI2.

**arrest** VT **catch s.o., arrest s.o.** táhwŭneew VTA.

**arrogant** ADJ **be a proud man, be arrogant, have an attitude, think that one knows more than anyone else** lunŭweelúnzuw VAI; **be arrogant, have an attitude, think oneself better than others, to put on airs** *(of women)* leetíisuw VAI, oxkweewee=lúnzuw VAI.

**arrow** N **my arrow** níip NID.

**as** ADV **as one likes, as one wishes** léh=lapiit VAI *usually only in conjunct order* **He can do what he wants.** 'Léh=lapiit lúnum.', **She's a widow, she can go where she likes.** 'Shiikóo=wuw léhlapiit-uch kwáy éew.'

**as well** ADV **also, as well** *(before pronouns)* mbee- PN **Me too.** 'Mbée-níi.', **Then he left too.** 'Nál mbée-néeka alúmsuw.'; ADV **be related to s.o. as well** naxpaangóomeew VTA; **bring s.o. along as well, take s.o. along as well** naxpóoxwaleew VTA; **bring s.t. along as well, take s.t. along as well** naxpóoxwatoow VTI2; **run as well, run with** wiitaaméhleew VAI; **take s.t. along as well, take s.t. along in addition** naxpóoxweew VAIO.

**ashamed** ADJ amiixanii- PV **He/she laughs nervously.** 'Amíixanii-kŭlúksuw.'; **ashamed** amiixu- PV *informal* **He/she snickers.** 'Amíixu-láatam.'; **be ashamed** miixanúsuw VAI; **be ashamed of s.o.** miixanáa=leew VTA; **be ashamed of s.t.** miixa=náatam VTI1A; **feel ashamed** miixa=neelúndam VOTI1; **make s.o. ashamed** miixaníiheew VTA; **make s.o. ashamed by speech, say shameful things to s.o.** miixaníimeew VTA; **make s.o. feel ashamed** miixanéelŭmeew VTA.

**aside** ADV **place s.t. apart, set s.t. aside** chpáhtoow VTI2 *object usually plural.*

**ask** VI **ask, ask people** kwchiimóhkeew

VAI.

**ask** VT **ask s.o.** kwchiimóoleew VTA; **ask s.o. to bring s.t.** pchihtáhleew VTAO; **ask, ask people** kwchiimóhkeew VAI.

**ask about** VT **ask about s.o.** ndóoxwŭ=meew VTA; **ask about s.t.** ndóoxtoow VTI2; VT **ask s.o. about s.t.** ndoox=táweew VTAO.

**ask for** VT **ask s.o. for s.t.** ndootamáw=eew VTAO; **beg for s.t., ask for s.t.** wíinŭweew VAIO.

**ass** N **my behind, my backside, my ass** naasíituy NID.

**astride** ADV **sit astride something, sit straddling something** póxkapuw VAI, póxkwapuw VAI; **sit upon something, sit astride** poxkohkwéepuw VAI.

**attachment** N **be free, be unmarried, have no attachments** nihlaapéewuw VAI.

**attack** VT **attack s.o., come up to s.o.** kwihlóotaweew VTA.

**attend** VT **attend church, attend a service** maawéewuw VAI; **attend school** shkóoluw VAI.

**attitude** N **be arrogant, have an attitude, think oneself better than others, put on airs** *(of women)* leetíisuw VAI, oxkweeweelúnzuw VAI.

**Augustine** N àkwúshtiin NA.

**aunt** N **my maternal aunt, my mother's sister, my parallel aunt** ngúkush NAD; **my paternal aunt, my father's sister, my cross-aunt** nŭmiilíhtaakw NAD.

**authority** N **leader, person in position of authority** líilŭnuw NA.

**automobile** N **car, automobile** ahta=móombiil NA; **drive a car, use an automobile** ahtamoombiilhámeew VAI.

**autumn** N **be fall, be autumn** takwáa=kuw VII **I'm going there next fall.** 'Takwaakíike náh ndá.', **I went there last fall.** 'Takwáakuw náh ndá.'; **during the fall, during the autumn** takwaakwŭnúwii PC.

**aware** ADV **come to, be aware** weewáa=tam VAI **He doesn't know what's going on around him.** 'Máh weewaa=tamóowi.'

**away** ADV **be away a long time** kwŭnáh=keew VAI; **being taken away** naatŭ=nukwsuwáakan NI; **blow away in the wind, be blown away by the wind** alúmxookw VAI, alúmxun VII; **carry s.t. away** alumasánuw VAIO; **carry s.t. away in a pack or bundle** alumŭ=wáleew VAIO; **carry s.t. away, carry s.t. away in a pack** alumŭwaléhleew VAIO; **carry something away quickly** alumasaníhleew VAIO; **cart away a load** *(of one's belongings)* alumhée=wasuw VAI; **climb away, climb up** alumakóosuw VAI; **crawl away** alum=íikwsuw VAI; **drive away** alumchéh=leew VAI; **drive away with s.o.** alum=chéhlaleew VTA; **float away** alumáat=hookw VAI, alumáathun VII; **fly away, go away, pedal away** alumíhleew VAI; **give s.o. away to people, give s.t. away to people** míilŭweew VAIO; **go away crying** aluméewtam VOTI1; **go away with things** alumŭwaléh=leew VAI; **jump away** alumáakchehl VAI; **leave running, run away, start to run** alumahtakíhleew VAI; **ride away on horseback** alumhóomeew VAI; **roll away** alumiinjkwéhleew VAI; **roll s.t. away** alumiinjkweeyáaheew VAIO; **run away from s.o., flee from s.o.** wshíimeew VTA; **run away in a hurry** kihtshíimuw VAI; **run away, flee** alumshíimuw VAI, wshíimuw VAI; **shine going away** *(of lights)* alumáa=sŭleew VII; **shine going away** *(of lights)* alumáasŭleew VAI; **sound far away** laawihtáakwat VII, laawih=táakwsuw VAI; **swim away** alumáa=shŭweew VAI; **swim away, float away** alumaashŭwíhleew VAI; **swim away, float away** alumáashŭwihl VAI; **take s.o. away in a hurry** alumíipheew

VTA; **take s.t. away in a hurry** alum=iipáhtoow VTI2; **wear s.t. animate out by washing it, wash s.t. animate away, remove s.t. animate by washing, wash s.t. animate completely, wash s.t. animate right out** mehta=páleew VTA **I washed away where the writing was.** 'Nŭmehtapálaaw éenda-leekháasiit.'

**awful** ADJ **find that s.o. sounds awful** chiipsútaweew VTA; **find that s.t. sounds awful** chiipsútam VTI1A; **taste awful** mataxeepóokwat VII.

**awl** N pkwushíikan NI; **awl, chisel** pkwihteehíikan NI.

**ax** N tŭmahíikan NI; **chop s.o. down with an ax, cut s.o. down with an ax** tíhlaweew VTA; **chop s.t. down with an ax, cut s.t. down with an ax** tíhlam VTI1A **I chopped some wood.** 'Ndíhlam xwús.'; **chop with an ax, cut down trees, trim trees** tŭmaháh=kweew VAI.

**ax-handle** N wsíitahkw NI.

# B

**baby** N amiimúnzhush NA; **act like a baby, feel babyish, don't want to act one's age** *(especially of children)* changeelunzhíishuw VAI; **carry a baby** noonzhéesuw VAI, noonzhée=wasuw VAI; **nurse a baby** nohláawa=suw VAI.

**babyish** ADJ **act like a baby, feel babyish, don't want to act one's age** *(especially of children)* changeelunzhíi=shuw VAI.

**babysit** VI **take care of a child, babysit** noocháawsuw VAI.

**bachelor** N kihkáapeew NA.

**back** ADJ **my back of neck** nihtángan NID.

**back** ADV **back, return** kwaxku- PV *informal* **I gave it back.** 'Ngwáxku-méekun.'; **behind, at the back, in back of** wtéeng PC **I came from behind.** 'Wtéeng nóom.', **My back teeth.** 'Niipíital wtéeng ehtéekiil.'; **come back from planting** aapahkíi=heew VAI; **drive back, drive across** *(the river)* kwaxkchéhleew VAI; **go to fetch a load of s.t., fetch and carry a load of something on one's back** naachŭwáleew VAIO; **lean back while sitting** aamchéepuw VAI; **sit back** áamapuw VAI.

**back** N **my back** naawíikan NID, nŭwaa=wíikan NID; **carry a heavy load on one's back** laanzhihkŭwáleew VAI; **carry a load on one's back** pŭmúw=aleew VAI; **carry s.o. on one's back** nayóomeew VTA; **carry s.o. on one's back** nayóondam VTI1A; **carry s.o. on one's back** pŭmúwaleew VTA; **finish packing a load on one's back, be finished packing a load on one's back, be already packed** kiishŭwál=heew VAI; **have a backache, have a sore back** waawiikaníineew VAI; **have a crooked back** piimpóxkwaneew VAI; **have one's back exposed, have one's back showing** mihtpoxkwa=néexiin VAI; **have one's back in a certain direction, lie with one's back in a certain direction** lupox=kwanéexiin VAI **She had her back turned yesterday.** 'Wuláakwu ná lupoxkwanéexiin.'; **lie on one's back** waasatéexiin VAI; **scratch one's back, have an itchy back** kshiippóxkwa=neew VAI; **scratch s.o.'s back** kshiip=poxkwanéeneew VTA.

**back and forth** ADJ **be blown back and forth by the wind** kwàkwchúkxookw VAI, kwàkwchúkxwun VII; **be blown back and forth by the wind, be shaken by the wind** apáwxookw VAI, apáwxun VII; **be moved back and forth, be shaken back and forth**

kwàkwchúkhookw VAI; **shake back and forth, sway back and forth** apawíhleew VII; **shake one's head, move one's head back and forth** kwàkwchukohkwéhleew VAI; **shake s.o. back and forth, move s.o. back and forth, wave s.o. back and forth, rock s.o. back and forth** kwàkw=chukwaaháaleew VTA; **shake s.t. back and forth, move s.t. back and forth, wave s.t. back and forth, rock s.t. back and forth** kwàkwchukwáaheew VAIO; **go back and forth, ride back and forth, fly back and forth** wŭ=yakíhleew VAI **The cars are going back and forth.** 'Káalak wŭyakih=léewak.'; **pace back and forth** asahkóoxweew VAI; **shake back and forth, sway back and forth** apawíh=leew VAI.

**backache** N **have a backache, have a sore back** waawiikaníineew VAI.

**backside** N **my behind, my backside, my ass** naasíituy NID; **be tired of sitting on one's backside, have a sore backside from sitting down** shiiwii=tŭyéepuw VAI; **fall on one's backside while sitting** pŭniitŭyéepuw VAI; **go all over, roam with no purpose in mind, throw one's backside about as one goes** msiitŭyéewxeew VAI; **have a flat backside** pàkíitŭyeew VAI; **have a tight backside, have a tight ass** kpaasíitŭyeew VAI; **have a tired backside, have a sore backside** shii=waasíitŭyeew VAI; **have excrement on one's backside** mwíitŭyeew VAI; **have no feathers on one's backside** mooshakíitŭyeew VAI *usually of birds;* **have one's backside exposed, have one's backside sticking out** mihchii=tŭyéexiin VAI; **roam with no purpose in mind, throw one's behind about as one goes** msiitŭyéhleew VAI; **sit on one's backside in a certain manner, sit on one's backside in a certain direction** liitŭyéepuw VAI **He slid to the front (of the chair).** 'Shayée=mung liitŭyéepuw.', **He's sitting this way and that way.** 'Msú-liitŭyée=puw.'; **sit with one's backside barely touching a surface, sit on the edge of something** mshiitŭyéepuw VAI; **stick one's backside out, have one's backside sticking out** saakii=tŭyéexiin VAI, uspootŭyéexiin VAI; **stick one's backside out, have one's backside sticking up** siingiitŭyéexiin VAI; **walk by with one's backside exposed** mooshakiitŭyéewxeew VAI; **walk with excrement on one's backside** *(indicating a certain attitude)* mwiitŭyéewxeew VAI.

**backwards** ADJ **be shy, be 'backwards'** achíipsuw VAI; **crawl backwards** ashahkcheewíikwsuw VAI; **drive backwards** ashahkchéhleew VAI; **fall backwards** aamihtéexun VII, aapa=míhleew VAI; **fall backwards, be knocked over, be knocked down** aamihtéexiin VAI; **run backwards** ashahkcheewahtakíhleew VAI; ADJ **shy person, 'backwards' person** cheh=chíipsiit NA; **swim backwards** ashahkcheewaashŭwíhleew VAI; **hit s.o. and knock them over, hit s.o. and make them fall backwards** aamihtéeheew VTA; **hit s.t. and knock it over, hit s.t. and make it fall backwards** aamihtéeham VTI1A; **make s.o. fall backwards** aamihtée=xŭmeew VTA; **make s.t. fall backwards** aamihtéextoow VTI2; **tip something over, tip something backwards, knock something over, knock something over backwards** aamáaheew VAIO; **walk backwards** ashahkchéewxeew VAI.

**bad** ADJ machii- PN **Bad boy.** 'Machíi-skahúnzuw.', **Bad White man.** 'Machíi-shŭwánakw.'; machu- PN *informal* **A bad person.** 'Machú-awéen.'; **bad** mataakanii- PN **Bad Indians.** 'Matáakanii-lunaapéewak.'; machu- PV *informal* **Something bad happens.** 'Machú-léew.', **I show my feelings because I'm so cross.** 'Mbunoondíhkeen éel-machú-ún=daan.'; **bad Black person** matees=káleengw NA; **bad Indian** matulŭ=náapeew NA **That's where that bad Indian comes from.** 'Nún há oonjíi=yayiin ná matulŭnáape.'; **bad cat** mataakanapóoshiish NA, matapóo=shiish NA; **bad dog** mataakanáxum NA, matáxum NA; **bad man, good for nothing man, man of poor character** matahaápeew NA; **bad person** mataakanáween PR, matálakay NA *considered impolite;* **bad pig** ma=tóoshkoosh NA; **bad woman, good for nothing woman, woman of poor character** matahóxkweew NA; **be a bad person, be a good for nothing person** matahaapéewuw VAI; **be a bad risk for credit, be a 'poor pay'** màmateenhíikeew VAI; **be a bad thunderstorm** akaanzháhkweew VII; **be a bad woman, be a good for nothing woman, be a woman of poor character** matahoxkwéewuw VAI; **be a bad worker, do bad deeds** amatalóhkeew VAI; **be bad weather** matáhkameew VII; **be drunk and unpleasant, do bad things while drunk, drink poison** *(especially to induce miscarriage)* machíisŭmuw VAI; **be in terrible shape, have a terrible figure, have a terrible shape, be in a bad shape** chiipáhkwsuw VAI; **decay, go bad, spoil** machíhleew VII; **feel sad, be sad, be in a bad mood** ma=teelúndam VOTI1; **give s.o. something bad to drink** machiisŭmóoleew VTA; **have a bad dream** chiipóngwaam VAI, matóngwaam VAI; **have a bad smell, stink** machiimáakwat VII, machii=máakwsuw VAI; **have a bad thought, think bad thoughts, have bad feelings** chiipahtéenamuw VAI; **have an unpleasant taste, taste bad** machii=póokwsuw VAI, machiipóokwan VII, machiipóokwat VII; **have bad shoes** achiipahksúneew VAI; **have bad teeth** amataníikeew VAI; **have evil thoughts, have bad thoughts** *(as if without regret)* chiipiitéeheew VAI; **lead a bad life, be a sinner** matáawsuw VAI; **odd person, bad person, person who does bad things** chíipaween PR; **shoot badly, be a bad shot** amatayáxkham VOTI1; **use bad language, curse, swear** matutóonheew VAI; **use bad language, tell a lie, perjure oneself** mataaptóoneew VAI; **wake after a bad dream, wake up screaming, have a nightmare** akiiwóngxwiin VAI.

**badly** ADV **be badly dressed** matákuw VAI; **grow badly** machíikun VII, ma=chíikuw VII; **leak badly** niiskpéhleew VII **There's a bad leak from the stovepipe.** 'Ehŭliingwáhteek wúnj-niiskpéhleew.'; **read badly, be a poor reader** amatakíinzuw VAI; **run badly** *(especially of vehicles)*, **decay, go bad, spoil** machíhleew VAI; **sew badly** amachiikwáakeew VAI; **shoot badly, be a bad shot** amatayáxkham VOTI1; **sing badly** amataláamuw VAI; **talk badly about s.o.** mataachŭmóh=kaweew VTA, matakŭníimeew VTA; **talk terribly, talk badly, use foul language** chiiptóonheew VAI; **think badly of oneself** mateelúnzuw VAI; **treat s.o. badly** matacháaheew VTA; **walk badly, have a hard time walking** amatóoxweew VAI.

**bag** N shàkiinóotay NI; **leather bag** xayiinóotay NI; **paper bag** pambiilii=nóotay NI.

**bail out** VT **pry s.o. out** *(using a tool or instrument)*, **bail s.o. out of jail** ktáhkhweew VTA.

**baker's bread** N **white bread, baker's**

**bread** shŭwánakwii-apwáan NI, wáa=papwaan NI; **baker's bread, bread made with yeast** páasapwaan NI.

**baking soda** N sótii NI.

**bald** ADJ **be bald** mooshakáandpeew VAI, mooshááandpeew VAI; **be shiny bald, be completely bald** waaxamóhkweew VAI.

**balky** ADJ **be balky, be stubborn** achee=xáakwsuw VAI; **be balky, refuse to do something** mbaakíihuw VAI.

**ball** N néenaxkw NA; **ball player** nehnee=náxkwiis NA; **play ball** neenáxkuw VAI; **stop s.o.** *(with an elongated object)*, **bunt a ball** *(in baseball)* ngii=kwáaleew VTA **I bunted the ball.** 'Nàkiikwáalaaw áng néenaxkw.'

**baloney** N **baloney, sausage** piindhíikan NA.

**band** N **collectively held land, land that belongs to the band** tputaawáh=kuy NI; **in common, collective, owned by the band** tputáawii PC **Doctor for everyone; doctor hired by Indian Affairs.** 'Tpútaawii ndáaktul.', **The community hall.** 'Tputáawii éenda-maawéhlaang.'

**band** VI **come together, join together, band together** takwihléewak VAI *usually plural.*

**bandage** N **bandage, wrapping paper, material used for wrapping** wiix=kweeptíikan NI.

**bang** VT **bang s.o.'s head against something** paakaandpéexŭmeew VTA.

**bank** N **along the bank, down by the river, close to the river** yáapee PC **I walked along the shore.** 'Yáapee mbúmsi.'

**Baptism** N sookŭnupaasŭwáakan NI.

**baptize** VT **baptize s.o.** sookŭnupáaleew VTA; **be baptized** sookŭnupáasuw VAI.

**barber** N mehmóonzhŭwees NA.

**bare** ADJ **be bare headed** mihtáandpeew VAI; **be bare, be lacking in fur, be lacking in hair** mooshakúsuw VAI; **be bare, be lacking in fur, be lacking in hair**, **be lean** *(of meat)* móosha=keew VII; **be bare, be stripped bare** chíikweew VII **The forest is bare.** 'Chíikweew kóhpii.'; **be bare, be stripped bare** chíikwsuw VAI **The tree is bare.** 'Chíikwsuw míhtukw.'; **eat s.t. animate bare, strip s.t. animate to the bone** chíikwameew VTA; **eat s.t. bare, strip s.t. to the bone** chiikwándam VTI1A **The horse ate the grass to the ground.** 'Nehna=yóongus wchiikwándamun miixás=kwal.'; **have bare hands, have bare arms, have exposed hands, have exposed arms** mihtŭnáxkeew VAI; **have bare hands, have exposed hands** mihtŭlúnjeew VAI; **have bare hands, have no gloves on, have one's hands exposed, have one's hands showing** mihtŭlunjéexiin VAI; **have bare shins** *(of a woman not wearing stockings)* amehchkáxkwaneew VAI; **have one's arms exposed, have bare arms, have one's hands exposed, have bare hands** mihtŭnaxkéexiin VAI; **have one's legs showing, have one's legs exposed, have bare legs** miht=kaatéexiin VAI; **run naked, run bare** mooshakaaméhleew VAI *especially of animals with missing fur.*

**bare handed** ADJ **go empty handed, go bare handed, don't take anything** *(especially to a gathering)* mooshŭ=lunjéhleew VAI.

**barefoot** ADJ **be barefooted** meemeex=ksíiteew VAI; **walk barefoot** mee=meexksiitéewxeew VAI.

**bark** N hwákees NA.

**bark** VI **bark, be barking** wúngeew VAI.

**bark at** VT **bark at s.o.** wungáaleew VTA; **bark at s.t., want s.t. that someone else has** wungáatam VTI1A.

**barn** N **barn, threshing barn** pakahíi=kan NI; **cow shed, cow barn** kooyíi=kaan NI.

**barrel** N mbálun NA.
**barren** ADJ **barren land on which nothing grows** lunáhkuy NI.
**bartender** N sehsookhúpees NA.
**baseball bat** N **club, baseball bat** pakandíikan NI.
**basket** N mihtkwiinóotay NI; **cut splints, cut splints of wood for baskets** pòháhkweew VAI.
**bat** *(animal)* N peepiishlóngwanaash NA.
**bath** N **swim, be in swimming, be in the water, take a bath** thíixŭmuw VAI.
**bathe** VT **bathe one's eyes, put drops in one's eyes** sookhíingweew VAI.
**bathroom** N **come out, go out, go to the bathroom** kchíiw VAI-S **I came out of the house.** 'Wiikwáhmung nóonj-kchíim.'
**batting** N **cotton batting** kátoon NI.
**bawl** VI **bawl, holler, make noise** *(of vocal sounds)* sáangweew VAI **The frogs are bawling.** 'Chkwálak saan=gwéewak.'
**be** VI **be from there, be from a certain place** wunjíiyayuw VAI **They are from Six Nations.** 'Wunjiiyayúwak shŭ=wéeka.', **He's from the United States.** 'Xwanzhíikanung wunjíiya=yuw.'; **be here too, be present** wíi=tapuw VAI; **be so** únd VAI **He's hard to get along with.** 'Áhwi-únd.'
**bead** N maanzháapuy NA.
**bean** N maaláxkwsiit NI; **green bean** káshayeem NI; **kidney bean** maxkaa=láxkwsiit NI; **pull beans, pick beans** moonaalaxkwsíiteew VAI; **white bean** waapaaláxkwsiit NI; **yellow bean** wiisáawii-maaláxkwsiit NI.
**bear** N máxkw NA; **kill a bear** nihliimáx=kweew VAI, nihláxkweew VAI.
**beard** N **my beard, my whiskers** nŭ=wihtóonay NAD, nihtóonay NAD; **black beard, black whiskers** nzukihtóonay NI; **have a heavy beard** kaanzhihtóo=nayeew VAI; **have a beard, have a mustache, have whiskers** wihtóona=yuw VAI; **have a black beard, have a black mustache** nzukihtóonayeew VAI; **have a bushy beard** wiixŭwih=tóonayeew VAI; **have a grey beard, have a white beard** waapihtóona=yeew VAI; **have a long beard, have long whiskers** kwŭnihtóonayeew VAI; **have a nice beard, have a nice mustache** wŭlihtóonayeew VAI; **have a ragged beard, have a messy beard** piikwshihtóonayeew VAI; **have a small beard, have a small mustache** chan=gihchoonayéeshuw VAI; **white beard** waapihtóonay NI.
**beat** VT **beat s.o. in a competition, best s.o., do better than s.o.** pŭmúneew VTA; **beat s.o. in a race, beat s.o. in a competition** méelameew VTA.
**beat** VT **beat a drum, play a drum** pòhwŭníikeew VAI; **beat a drum, play a drum, beat** *(on a black ash log, so that strips of wood will come off)* pòhwŭnúmeew VAI; **beat s.o. to death** pŭlupihtéeheew VTA; **beat s.o. until they defecate** masktihtéeheew VTA; **fall and die, be beaten to death, get hit and die** pŭlupihtéexiin VAI; **kill a dog, beat a dog** nihlaakanáxŭ=mweew VAI; **kill an animal, beat an animal** nihlxúmweew VAI.
**beat up** VT **kill s.o., beat s.o. up** níhleew VTA.
**beaver** N amóxkw NA.
**because** CJ **because, in a certain manner, in a certain direction** eel- PV *followed by verb in conjunct order* **Now it must be because he had overcome the medicine.** 'Nál xéet ná kwáy éel- wchápihk -aluwíhkang.', **Because you picked him up you'll always find lots of things (to hunt).** 'Kwáy éel-náatŭnat ngúmee-uch xwéelu kwéek kŭmóxkam.'; **because, in a certain manner, in a certain direction** eeli- PV *followed by verb in*

*conjunct order* **She wanted to kill him because he had cracked the eggs.** 'Kwáta-nihláawal éeli- wáhwal -pwáhkhang.'

**Becky** N pékiis NA.

**become** VI **become White, act like a White person** shŭwanakwíhleew VAI; **become silly, become crazy** kpuch=éhleew VAI; **believe, become a Christian, become a believer** wŭlústam VOTI1.

**bed** N apíinay NI; **at the edge of the bed** wshayapíineeng PC; **be tired of lying in bed** peekiikanáaxiin VAI; **fall out of bed while of sleeping** pŭnón=gwaam VAI, pŭnóngxwiin VAI; **fix s.t. animate, repair s.t. animate, put s.o. to bed** wŭlíixŭmeew VTA; **get s.o. into sitting position, raise s.o., raise s.o. in bed** *(from lying down)* aa=mwíhkŭneew VTA; **lie down, be in bed, lie in bed** wŭlíixiin VAI **I'm going to lie down, I'm going to sleep.** 'Kwáy nŭmáwi-wulixiin, nŭmáw-kawí.'; **make the bed, fix the bed** wŭlanáhkeew VAI; **on top of the bed** waxkiitapíinaye PC **I was lying on top of the bed.** 'Nzhungíixiin wax=kiitapíinaye.'; **send s.o. to bed** ka=wushíhkaweew VTA; **turn over from one side to the other, turn over in bed** kwŭlupatéexiin VAI.

**bedbug** N pókwus NA.

**bedcover** N **put bedcovers on s.o.** akwúnheew VTA.

**bedding material** N anaanzŭwahíikan NI.

**bedsore** N **have bedsores** pkwiikanáa=xiin VAI.

**bee** N áamweew NA.

**beef** N kooyéewakw NI.

**beet** N maxkéetkweek NA.

**before** PREP iiyéeskwa PC *followed by conjunct verb* **I fixed the car before he left.** 'Noolíixŭmaaw káal iiyées=kwa alúmsiikw.', **I tried it on before I bought it.** 'Nzháyee-kwchíhlatoon iiyéeskwa máhlamaan.'; **stop before one finishes** *(doing something)* pohkwii- PV **I quit making bread.** 'Mbóhkwii-apwáanhe.', **I quit looking at it.** 'Mbóhkwii-punámun.'; **stop before one finishes** *(doing something)* pohkwu- PV *informal* **He stopped while eating.** 'Póhkwu-míitsuw.'

**beg** VI wíinŭweew VAI.

**beg for** VT **beg for s.t., ask for s.t.** wíi=nŭweew VAIO; **beg s.o. for s.t.** wiina=wámeew VTAO.

**beggar** N wehwíinŭwees NA.

**begin** VI **begin to** alu- PV **I'm starting to feed him.** 'Ndálu-xámaaw.', **I'm starting to feel better.** 'Ndálu-wŭlamalúsi.'; **begin to** alumu- PV **They're starting to grow badly.** 'Alúmu-machíikŭnool.', **It (water level) is starting to go down.** 'Alúmu-síhleew.'; **begin raining** alúmŭlaan VII; **begin to stay there, begin to stay here** nóotapuw VAI.

**behaviour** N **imitate someone's behaviour** mongíisuw VAI.

**behind** ADV **be behind, be behind someone or something** wteengíixiin VAI; **behind, at the back, in back of** wtéeng PC **I came from behind.** 'Wtéeng nóom.', **My back teeth.** 'Niipíital wtéeng ehtéekiil.'; **leave s.o. alone, leave s.o. behind** *(at home, in a competition)*, **leave everyone behind** weemíixkaleew VTA **We were left behind (by the deceased).** 'Nŭ=weemiixkalukéhna.'; **leave s.o., leave s.o. behind alone, leave s.o. behind and lonely** mayaníixkaleew VTA; **leave s.t. animate behind on one's plate** *(of food)* shíhkwameew VTA; **leave s.t. behind** ngátum VTI1B; **leave s.t. behind on one's plate** *(of food)* shihkwándam VTI1A.

**behind** N **my behind, my backside, my ass** naasíituy NID; **fall on one's behind**

*(especially when squatting down)* aamootŭyéhleew VAI; **have a scabby behind** mŭkíitŭyeew VAI; **walk bent over with one's behind sticking out** waakhootŭyéewxeew VAI.

**behind** PREP **follow and come behind s.o., come behind s.o., come from behind s.o.** wtéhkaweew VTA.

**believe** VI **believe, become a Christian, become a believer** wŭlústam VOTI1.

**believe** VT **believe s.o.** wŭlustáweew VTA; **believe s.t.** wŭlústam VTI1A; **don't believe s.o., disbelieve s.o.** maxksútaweew VTA; **don't believe s.t., disbelieve s.t.** maxksútam VTI1A.

**believer** N **believe, become a Christian, become a believer** wŭlústam VOTI1.

**bell** N taliingwŭníikan NI; taliingwŭníi=kan NA; **ring a bell, make a ringing noise** *(on metal)* taliinghwíikeew VAI; **ring a bell** taliingwŭnúmeew VAI.

**belly** N **have a big belly** xwaskwchii=móotayeew VAI, xwáskwcheew VAI; **stick one's belly out, have one's belly sticking out** saakatayéexiin VAI; **walk with one's belly sticking out, have one's belly sticking out as one walks** saakatayéewxeew VAI.

**belongings** N **go to get a load** *(of one's belongings)* naathéewasuw VAI.

**belt** N tihkambíisoon NA.

**bend** N **have a bend in it** kwŭlúkwat VII **The road has a bend in it.** 'Kwŭ=lúkwat áanay.'

**bend** VI **bend at a joint** tamakíhleew VAI, tamakíhleew VII, tamákeew VII.

**bend** VT **bend s.t.** *(using a tool or instrument)* wáakham VTI1A; **bend s.t.** *(using the hands)* wáakŭnum VTI1B; **bend s.t. animate** *(using a tool or instrument)* wáakheew VTA; **bend s.t. animate** *(using the hands)* wáakŭ=neew VTA; **be bent, be bent over, be curved** wáakeew VII, wáaksuw VAI; **be hit and get bent** waakihtéexiin VAI; **have a bent shape, be bent, be curved** waakchéesuw VAI, waakchée=yeew VII **Your cane is bent.** 'Waak=chéeyeew ktaláawan.'; **hit and bend s.t.** waakihtéeham VTI1A; **hit and bend s.t. animate** waakihtéeheew VTA; **hit and bend s.t. animate, hit s.t. animate and cause it to become bent** waakihtéexŭmeew VTA; **hit and bend s.t., hit s.t. and cause it to become bent** waakihtéextoow VTI2; **hit and get bent** waakihtéexun VII; **press down on s.o., push down on s.o., bend s.o. at a joint** *(using the hands)* tamákŭneew VTA; **press down on s.t., push down on s.t., bend s.t. at a joint** *(using the hands)* tamákŭnum VTI1B; **step on and bend s.t.** *(of a pedal)* tamakíhkam VTI1A; **tilt s.o., tip s.o., cause s.o. to be on the diagonal, bend s.o.** *(using the hands)* píi=mŭneew VTA; **tilt s.t., tip s.t., cause s.t. to be on the diagonal, bend s.t.** *(using the hands)* píimŭnum VTI1B.

**bend over** VI **be bending over** ahtée=wuw VAI; **bend over** ahtéhleew VAI; **bend over, be hunched over, be bent over** ahtéexiin VAI.

**bend over** VT **knock s.o. over, push s.o. over, bend s.o. over, tilt s.o. over** *(using the hands)* áamŭneew VTA; **knock s.t. over, push s.t. over, bend s.t. over, tilt s.t. over** *(using the hands)* áamŭnum VTI1B; **be bent over, be doubled up** tamáksuw VAI; **be bent, be bent over, be curved** wáakeew VII, wáaksuw VAI.

**bent over** VI **bend over, be hunched over, be bent over** ahtéexiin VAI; **sit bent over** waakohkwéepuw VAI; **sit bent over, sit hunched over** ahtee=wohkwéepuw VAI; **walk bent over with one's behind sticking out** waakhootŭyéewxeew VAI; **walk bent over, walk stooped over** waakóo=xweew VAI.

**berry** N **pick berries** makóhpuw VAI.

**beside** PREP **beside, alongside** pŭmíichii PC **He's walking beside me.** 'Pŭmíi=chii púmsiin.'; **stand sideways, stand beside someone** pŭmiichii=káapawuw VAI.

**best** VT **beat s.o. in a competition, best s.o., do better than s.o.** pŭmúneew VTA.

**bet** VI **bet, play for money** ahtíikeew VAI.

**betray** VT **betray s.o., tell on s.o., betray s.o.'s confidence** kchíhlaleew VTA.

**better** ADJ **better condition, improved condition, better state, improved state** míingasa PC **It's better now, it shuts well (of a door).** 'Míingasa kwáy wŭlú-kpíhle.', **It's good that you came early.** 'Míingasa ktáapwipá.'; **feel better** liiwamálsuw VAI; **beat s.o. in a competition, best s.o., do better than s.o.** pŭmúneew VTA; **feel better** miingasawamálsuw VAI; **find that s.o. feels better, find that s.o. feels good, feel comfortable with s.o.** wŭlámameew VTA; **find that s.t. feels better, find that s.t. feels good** wŭlamándam VTI1A **My hand feels better.** 'Noolamándamun náxk.', **My shoes feel good.** 'Mahksúnal noolamandamúnal.'; **look better** *(than before)* miingasawiináakwsuw VAI; **think oneself better than s.o.** aluweelunzíhtaweew VTA; **think oneself better than s.o. else** aluweelún=zuw VAIO.

**between** PREP **between** téetawii PC **The dog is standing between the trees.** 'Mwáakane téetawii níipawuw miht=kwíhke.', **I put the meat between the slices of bread.** 'Téetawii apwáa=nung ndáhtoon wŭyóos.'; **stand between something** teetawiikáapawuw VAI.

**bewitch** VT **bewitch s.o., use medicine to influence s.o.** mŭtáanheew VTA.

**beyond** ADV **look past, look beyond** loowatawáapuw VAI.

**beyond** PREP **look past s.t., look beyond s.t.** loowatawáapuw VAIO.

**Bible** N mbáypul NA.

**big** ADJ **be big** xwukíhkwun VII **I'm using the big one now.** 'Meexkíh=kwung kwáy ndawéeheen.'; **be big** xwúkiil VAI, amangkíilook VAI *usually plural,* amangéewal VII *usually plural;* **be big, have a big shape** xwuch=éesuw VAI **The tree is big.** 'Xwuchée=suw míhtukw.'; **be big** *(of a body)* xwuchéeyeew VII **My foot's swollen.** 'Xwuchéeyeew nzíit.'; **big** amanga=chii- PN *usually plural only* **Big chickens.** 'Amángachii-kiikíipshak.'; **big** amangu- PV **It's in big pieces.** 'Aman=gu-pangéeyeew.', **I gathered a lot of flowers.** 'Nŭmángu-ayúwa pehpax=kwŭléeshak.'; **big** xwachi- PN **A sled.** 'Xwáchi-táataskw.'; **big** xwachii- PN **A big snake.** 'Xwáchii-áxkook.', **Big chicken.** 'Xwáchii-kiikíipush.'; **big** xwachu- PN *informal* **A big table.** 'Xwáchu-eehundáxpoon.'; **big** xwii- PV **I'm driving a big car.** 'Nŭmóxwii-kaalháma.', **He/she is driving a big car.** 'Xwíi-kaalhámeew.'; **big, very** kihchi- PV **There is a heavy frost.** 'Kíhchi-tóhpun.', **They're praying hard.** 'Kíhchi-pahtamawéewak.'; **big, very** kihchu- PV *informal* **They're painting them.** 'Kwíhchu-shoohŭ=múnal.', **Everybody is cutting cordwood** 'Kíhchu-kaatxakhwátiin.'; **be a big pile** *(as of hay)* amangshámuw VII; **be a big puddle** amangpeekíixun VII; **be big eyed** *(after seeing something unusual)*, **lie with one's eyes open** *(especially if one cannot sleep)* amangaalakiingwéexiin VAI; **be big, be big around the middle, be big in girth** xwáhkwat VII, xwáhkwsuw VAI; **be big, be coarse** *(of something stringlike)* xwáhtakat VII; **be big, be deep** *(of holes)* xwushéeyeew VII; **big**

dish xwachíinjuw NI; **big dog** xwát=xum NA; **big doll** xwataaníitus NA; **big fish** xwátameekw NA; **big houses** amangachiikáanal NI *usually plural;* **big knife, the United States** xwan=zhíikan NI; **big knife, the United States** xwatanzhíikan NI; **big pig** xwatóoshkoosh NA; **big potato** xwachíhpun NA; **big river** kihtsíipuw NI; **big snake** xwatáxkook NA; **big town, city** kihtootéenay NI, xwatoo=téenay NI; **big tree** xwáchahkw NA; **carry a big load** tohphéewasuw VAI; **fight vigourously, have a big fight** kihtatáhkeew VAI; **grow big, grow well** wŭlíikuw VAI; **have a big belly** xwaskwchiimóotayeew VAI, xwásk=wcheew VAI; **have a big ear** máng=xeew VAI; **have a big face** xwíingweew VAI; **have a big head** xwáandpeew VAI; **have a big house** xwachíikeew VAI, xwíikeew VAI; **have a big leg, have big legs** xwukáateew VAI; **have a big mouth** xwutóoneew VAI; **have a big nose** xwucháaleew VAI; **have a bunch of kids, have a big family** mŭleekóonzheew VAI; **have big breasts** amangíilaneew VAI; **have big breasts, have big udders** *(of a cow)* xwíilaneew VAI; **have big cheeks** amangŭnánŭweew VAI; **have big ears** amángxeew VAI; **have big eyes** a=mangaalakíingweew VAI, mangatee=líingweew VAI; **have big feet** amang=síiteew VAI, xwusíiteew VAI; **have big legs** amangkáateew VAI; **have big shoes** amangahksúneew VAI; **have one's eyes bigger than one's belly, take more than one can eat** mang=shéengweew VAI; **have one's eyes open, have big eyes** xwaalakiin=gwéexiin VAI; **have one's eyes wide open, have big eyes** xwaapakiin=gwéexiin VAI; **look big** xwachiináa=kwat VII, xwachiináakwsuw VAI; **make a big hole, make a deep hole** kwŭnáalheew VAI; **make a big pile of s.t., pile s.t. high** mangshamóotoow VTI2; **make a lot of noise, make a big noise** amángŭweew VAI; **musk-rat, big muskrat** xwáskwus NA; **take a big drink, take a lot of liquid, drink a lot** *(including non-alcoholic beverages)* xwíisŭmuw VAI; **toe** N **my big toe** nŭmoxwsiitáawan NID, nŭ=moxohkwéewsiit NID.

**Bill** N mbíl NA *man's name.*

**bird** N awehléeshoosh NA; **bluebird** shiiwaapéekŭlush NA; **hawk, large bird** awéhleew NA; **hen, female bird** oxkwéhleew NA; **kill a bird** nihla=wehleeshóosheew VAI.

**birthday** N **have a birthday** áanjii-katúm VAI.

**bit** N **bit for horse's bridle** kehkŭlún=dang NI.

**bit** N **some, a small amount, a little bit** changíiwiish PC **I don't drink but I drink a little bit.** 'Máhta níi nŭmun=éewi changíiwiish shúkw nŭmúne.'; **some, a small amount, a little bit** chángiish PC **There's just a little frost.** 'Chángiish shúkw tóhpun.', **I left a little bit of the food.** 'Chán=giish mbiiwándamun.'

**bite** N **take a bite out of s.o.** kwashám=eew VTA; **take a bite out of s.t.** kwa=shándam VTI1A.

**bite** VT **bite s.o.** sakámeew VTA; **bite s.o., bite s.o. hard** akúshameew VTA; **bite s.t.** sakándam VTI1A; **bite s.t. and injure it** kshándam VTI1A; **bite s.t., bite s.t. hard** akushándam VTI1A; **be unable to bite s.o.** pwáawameew VTA; **be unable to bite s.t.** pwaawán=dam VTI1A; **bite and injure s.o.** kshámeew VTA; **bite each other** sah=sakándŭwak VAI, sakandawéewak VAI.

**bitter** ADJ **be angry, be frustrated, be discouraged, be annoyed, be put out, be bitter, be sour** *(of foods)* láxksuw VAI; **be bitter in taste** tíhtpan

VII; **be bitter, taste bitter, taste sour, taste strong** láxkun VII; **have a bitter taste, have a sour taste** laxkiipóo=kwat VII, laxkiipóokwsuw VAI, laxkii=póokwun VII.

**black** ADJ **be black** nzúkeew VII, nzúk=suw VAI; **black** nzukii- PN **Black raspberries.** 'Nzúkii-lehlookihláashak.', **Black shoelace.** 'Nzúkii-aníixan.'; **black** nzukii- PV **Black smoke.** 'Nzúkii-kwáalxeek.'; **be burnt black, be dyed black** nzukchásuw VAI, nzukcháteew VII; **be dark-coloured, be a blackish colour, have a black tinge to it** nzukŭléexiin VAI, nzukŭ=léexun VII; **be marked black, have a black mark, have a black stripe** nzukeekháasuw VAI, nzukeekháasuw VII; **black beard, black whiskers** nzukihtóonay NI; **black boat** nzuka=móxool NA, nzukamóxool NI; **black cloth** nzukshapakwíiwan NI; **black excrement** nzúkchuy NI; **black squirrel** psakwŭlúnjeew NA; **black thread, black string** nzukáhtakw NI; **scorch s.t. animate, blacken s.t. animate** *(by heat)*, **dye s.t. animate** nzuk=cháseew VTA; **blacken s.t.** *(by heat)*, **dye s.t. black** nzukchásum VTI1B; ADJ **be a black cloud** nzukakumáhkwat VII; **have a black beard, have a black mustache** nzukihtóonayeew VAI; **have a black eye** nzukshéengweew VAI; **have a black mouth** nzuktóoneew VAI; **have black hair** nzukaalóhkweew VAI; **see black, see things, see spots** *(especially after being sick)* mah=maashatawáapuw VAI; **turn black** nzukíhleew VAI, nzukíhleew VII; **wear a black coat** nzúkii-koothámeew VAI.

**Black** N **Black person** neeskáleengw NA; **bad Black person** mateeskál=eengw NA; **be a Black man** neeskàl=éenguw VAI; **be part Black** naanees=kàléenguw VAI; **part Black person** paseeskáleengw NA.

**black cap** N ehkwáhkwalus NA.

**blacksmith** N nehnayóongsii-mehmah=ksunhíikeet VA, shŭmít NA.

**blade** N **have a wide blade** paanalóo=wŭyeew VII.

**blame** VT **blame s.o. for s.t.** akwíimeew VTAO; **blame s.o., be dissatisfied with s.o.'s actions** mandóomeew VTA; **be blamed** mandoomkwúsuw VAI.

**blanket** N waapasáanay NI.

**bleed** VI **be bleeding, bleed** móhkuw VAI, móhkuw VII; **bleed to death** aaptupéhleew VAI.

**blind** ADJ **be blind** akeepíingweew VAI.

**blinder** N **put blinders on s.o.** *(especially of horses)* kpiingwéexŭmeew VTA.

**blindfold** VT **blindfold s.o.** kpiingwée=neew VTA.

**blink** VI spwuch'híingweew VAI, sàsa=mwuchiingwéhleew VAI.

**bloated** ADJ **have a swollen stomach, be bloated, have gas** paasatáyeew VAI.

**block** VT **can s.t. animate, put s.t. animate in cans, block s.o., plug s.t. animate, fill in the cracks of s.t. animate, winterize s.t. animate** *(especially of windows)* kpáskheew VTA.

**blood** N móhkw NI.

**bloody** ADJ **be bloody** mohkwíixiin VAI **He bled to death.** 'Áapchu-moh=kwíixiin.'; **be bloody ground** moh=kwahkéeyeew VII; **have a bloody head** mohkwáandpeew VAI; **have a bloody nose** mohkwcháaleew VAI, mŭkíhtaneew VAI.

**bloom** VI **bloom, be blooming** *(of flowers)* páxkwŭleew VAI; **be in full bloom** *(of flowers)* wŭluléewuw VAI.

**blotch** N **get measles, get chicken pox, come out in blotches, come out in spots** saakpéhleew VAI.

**blouse** N wéest NI, wéyst NI; **wear a blouse** weesthámeew VAI, weysthám=eew VAI.

**blow** VI **be windy, be blowing** *(of the wind)* ksháxun VII; **blow from a certain direction** *(of the wind)* wúndxun VII **The wind is blowing from over there.** 'Yéelak wúndxun.'; **have one's hair blowing about** sayaandpéhleew VAI.

**blow** VT **be blown along by the wind, be blown by by the wind** pŭmáx=ookw VAI, pŭmáxun VII; **be blown around by the wind, be spun around by the wind** túpxookw VAI, túpxun VII; **blow around** *(of the wind)*, **be blown around by the wind** tàtúpxun VII; **be blown back and forth by the wind** kwàkwchúkxookw VAI, kwàk=wchúkxwun VII; **be blown back and forth by the wind, be shaken by the wind** apáwxookw VAI, apáwxun VII; **be blown in this direction by the wind, be blown here by the wind** péetxookw VAI, péetxun VII **The wind came up all of a sudden.** 'Wíixkwii péetxun.'; **be blown open by the wind** tawáxookw VAI, tawáxun VII **The door was blown open by the wind.** 'Tawáxun kpáhoon.'; **be shut in by the wind, be blown shut by the wind** kpáxookw VAI, kpáxun VII; **be turned by the wind, be blown by the wind** *(of something sheet-like)* aapéekxookw VAI *usually of pieces of paper;* **blow in this direction** *(of the wind)*, **be the wind coming here, be blown here by the wind** péetxun VII **The wind came up all of a sudden.** 'Wíixkwii péetxun.'; **blow away in the wind, be blown away by the wind** alúmxookw VAI, alúmxun VII; **blow one's nose** saníikuw VAI.

**blow adder** N pehpootáalŭwees NA.

**blow at** VT **blow at s.o., blow on s.o.** pootáaleew VTA; VT **blow at s.t., blow on s.t.** pootáatam VTI1A; **blow at things, blow on things** pootaatíikeew VAI.

**blow on** VT **blow at s.o., blow on s.o.** pootáaleew VTA; **blow at s.t., blow on s.t.** pootáatam VTI1A; **blow at things, blow on things** pootaatíikeew VAI.

**blow over** VT **be blown over by the wind** áamxookw VAI, áamxun VII; **be blown over by the wind, be broken off by the wind, be severed by the wind** tŭmáxookw VAI, tŭmáxun VII; **be knocked over by the wind, be blown over by the wind** kawáxookw VAI, kawáxun VII.

**blow up** VI **explode, blow up, burst** *(from heat)* pwáhksuw VAI pwáhkteew VII; **make s.t. animate explode, make s.t. animate blow up** *(from heat)* pwáhkseew VTA; **make s.t. explode, make s.t. blow up** *(from heat)* pwáhksum VTI1B.

**blue** ADJ **be blue** oolíhkeew VII, oolíh=ksuw VAI; **blue** oolihkii- PN **A blue teacup.** 'Oolíhkii-tiihíinjuw.'; **blue** oolihkii- PV **I painted it blue.** 'Ndoo=líhkii-shóohŭmun.'; **be a blue cloud, be blue** *(of clouds)* oolihkakumáh=kwat VII; **be a blueish colour, have a blue tinge to it** oolihkŭléexiin VAI, oolihkŭléexun VII; **be blue in colour, be blue-coloured** oolihkaapamúkwat VII, oolihkaapamúkwsuw VAI; **turn blue** oolihkíhleew VAI, oolihkíhleew VII; **blue thread, blue string** oolih=káhtakw NI.

**blue jay** N tíitiis NA.

**bluebird** N shiiwaapéekŭlush NA.

**blueing** N oolihkpatíikan NI; **put blueing on s.t.** oolihkpátoow VTI2; **put blueing on s.t. animate** oolihkpáleew VTA; **use blueing** oolihkpatíikeew VAI.

**blunt** ADJ **be broken off, be blunt** póh=kwun VII.

**blush** VI maxkchàliingwéhleew VAI; **have red eyes, blush, have a red face** maxkshéengweew VAI.

**board** N pasíikaaxkw NI; **frame house, board house** pasiikaaxkwíikaan NI;

**have boards on it, be covered in boards** pasiikaaxkhwáasuw VII **My house has boards on it.** 'Wíikŭyaan pasiikaaxkhwáasuw.'

**boast** VI akíinŭweew VAI.

**boat** N amóxool NA, amóxool NI; **black boat** nzukamóxool NA, nzukamóxool NI; **cross in a boat** kwaxkakáham VOTI1; **go by in a boat, go along in a boat, float by in a boat, float along in a boat** pŭmáatham VAI; **sail a boat, use a boat** amoxoolhámeew VAI, amoxóolham VOTI1; **upset, turn over in a boat, turn over in a car** koox=káaweew VAI.

**bobbed** ADJ **have a bobbed tail, have a cut-off tail** *(diminutive)* chŭmoochŭ=yéeshuw VAI.

**bobcat** N **bobcat, wildcat** laaweewa=póoshiish NA.

**body** N **my body** nhákay NID; **feel s.t. as a sensation in one's body** làmándam VTI1A; **feel s.t. as an ache, feel s.t. as a pain, feel s.t. as a soreness in one's body** amándam VTI1A; **have a long shape, have a long body** kwŭnoo=chéeyeew VII **And it was short, it was wrapped around in a bundle, and it was a rectangular little thing.** 'Kéhla wáak chahkwéeshuw, tàtùp=háasuw, kwŭnoocheeyéeshuw.'; **have a long shape, have a long body** kwŭnuchéeyeew VII; **inside my body** ndalaamhákeeng NID.

**body hair** N wiixéekan NI.

**body part** N **feeling, sensation, feeling in a sore body part** amandamuw=áakan NI.

**boil** N pŭmúwees NA **There was a boil inside.** 'Aláamii-pŭmúwees apúw.'; **boil** pŭmúweew NA.

**boil** N **boil s.o., bring s.o. to a boil** wúnzeew VTA; **boil s.t., bring s.t. to a boil** wúnzum VTI1B.

**boil** VI **boil, come to a boil** wúndeew VII, wúnzuw VAI; **boil** sáhksuw VAI; sáhkteew VII; **boil dry** sihkpatíikeew VAI, sihkpeewchásuw VAI, sihkpeew=cháteew VII; **boil dry, boil down** ihkpéesuw VAI, ihkpéeteew VII; **boil over** *(of one's cooking)*, **have one's cooking boil over** paalchásŭmeew VAI; **fall apart in cooking, boil down, be cooked down** shkwúcha=suw VAI, shkwúchateew VII; **boil over, overflow** *(from being heated)*, paal=chásuw VAI; paalcháteew VII; **put s.o. on to boil** chóoskŭneew VTA.

**boil** VT **boil s.o., bring s.o. to a boil** wúnzeew VTA; **boil s.t., bring s.t. to a boil** wúnzum VTI1B; **boil s.o.** sáhka=leew VTA; **boil s.t.** sáhkatoow VTI2; **boil s.t. down** ihkpéesum VTI1B; **be boiled** wunzáasuw VAI, wunzáasuw VII; **be boiled dry** sihkpéesuw VAI; **boil things** sahkatíikeew VAI; **boiled cornbread** chooskŭnápwaan NI; **put s.t. on to boil** chóoskŭnum VTI1B.

**bone** N wáxkan NI; **eat s.t. animate bare, strip s.t. animate to the bone** chíi=kwameew VTA; **eat s.t. bare, strip s.t. to the bone** chiikwándam VTI1A **The horse ate the grass to the ground.** 'Nehnayóongus wchiikwándamun miixáskwal.'

**book** N **book, paper, letter** pámbiil NA **Old books.** 'Xúwii-pambíilak.'

**boot** N mbótus NI.

**bootlegger** N sookhúpeew NA; **hotel, drinking establishment, bootlegger's place** sookhupeesíikaan NI.

**born** VI **be born** kiishíikuw VAI; **be visible, be born** míhtapuw VAI.

**borrow** VT **borrow s.t.** wundóoxweew VAIO.

**both** ADJ éeylii PC **Both my feet are sore.** 'Éeylii nŭwiinamándamun nzíital.', **I bought both horses.** 'Éeylii nehna=yóongsak nŭmahlawáawak.'; **on both sides of something** weewúndakwii PC **They live on both sides of the road.** 'Weewúndakwii áaneeng wíikŭwak.',

**They're walking on both sides (of you).** 'Weewúndakwii pŭmúsŭwak.'

**bother** VT **bother s.o., interrupt s.o.** lxawóoleew VTA; **bother people, interrupt people** lxawóolŭweew VAI; **be restless, be bothered, feel restless** sàkwamálsuw VAI.

**bothersome** ADJ **bothersome person, worry-wart** sàkwáxktiis NA, sàkwáx=ktuy NA.

**bottle** N **bottle, jar** eeheeshaapamúk=wahk NA, eeheesháapamukw NA.

**bottle** VT **bottle s.t., put s.t. in cans, block s.t.** kpáskham VTI1A.

**bottom** N **bottom of a hill** alaamaa=wúnge PC.

**bounce** VI kwaxkwíixun VII; **rebound off something, bounce back and fall, fall back** *(s.t. animate)*, **be a foul ball** *(baseball)* kwaxkwíixiin VAI; **fall all over, bounce around, get hit about** msihtéexiin VAI; **make s.o. bounce** uspihtéexŭmeew VTA; **be thrown upwards, hit something and bounce, bounce** uspihtéexiin VAI.

**bounce** VT **bounce s.t. animate** *(off something)* kwaxkwíixŭmeew VTA; **get bounced loose, get knocked loose** lxakwihtéexun VII; **knock s.o. around, knock s.o. all over, bounce s.o., hit s.o. various ways** msihtée=heew VTA; **knock s.t. around, bounce s.t., hit s.t. various ways** msihtée=hum VTI1B.

**bow** N matáht NA.

**bowl** N **sugar bowl** shookŭlíinjuw NI.

**bowlegged** ADJ **be bowlegged** awaak=káateew VAI.

**box** N mbáks NI, mbáksh NI.

**boy** N skahúnzuw NA.

**boy-crazy** ADJ **be fond of men, like all the men, be 'boy-crazy'** wiingiilŭ=núweew VAI.

**braces** N **braces, suspenders** ngélsak NA *usually plural.*

**brag** VI **brag, say great things** *(especially when making a speech)* akaan=zhaaptóoneew VAI; **talk a lot, brag** kaanzhíixsuw VAI; **tell a tall tale, tell an exciting story, brag** kaanzhaa=chíimuw VAI.

**braid** VT **braid s.t.** *(of hair, of mats)* wihkáatŭnum VTI1B; **be braided** wihkaatŭnáasuw VII.

**brain** N **my brain** ndúmb NID.

**branch** N wŭnaxkwíhtahkw NI; **my branch, my limb** ndóhwan NID; **have branches, have antlers** wtóhwanuw VAI.

**brave** ADJ **be strong willed, be strong in character, be brave** maskaniitée=heew VAI **He's not brave yet (usually said of a young person).** 'Éeskwa néeka maskaniiteehéewu.'

**bread** N apwáan NI; **Indian bread** lúna=pwaan NI; **baker's bread, bread made with yeast** páasapwaan NI; **pan bread** pánapwaan NI; **white bread, baker's bread** shŭwánakwii-apwáan NI, wáapapwaan NI; **corn bread** xwaskwiimŭnápwaan NI, xwaskwíi=mapwaan NI; **corn meal bread, Johnny cake** wiisáamapwaan NI; **dried-out bread** káahapwaan NI; **fry bread** salápwaan NI; **make bread** apwáanheew VAI.

**break** VI **be broken, break** lookíixun VII; **break** *(of something string-like)* paxkíhleew VII; **break down, break** lookíhleew VAI, lookíhleew VII.

**break** VT **break s.o., sever s.o.** *(using the hands)* tŭmúneew VTA; **break s.t.** *(using the foot or body)*, **step on and break s.t.** kaxkíhkam VTI **I stepped on his leg and broke it.** 'Ngaxkíh=kamun wíhkaat.'; **break s.o.** kaxkíi=xŭmeew VTA; **break s.t.** kaxkíixtoow VTI2; **break s.t.** *(using the hands)* káxkŭnum VTI1B; **break s.t.** *(using the foot or body)* lookíhkam VTI1A; **break s.t.** *(quickly)* lookíhlatoow

VTI2; **break s.t.** *(using a tool or instrument)* lóokham VTI1A; **break s.t.** lóokŭnum VTI1B; **break s.t.** *(of something string-like)* paxkíixtoow VTI2; **break s.t. animate** *(using the foot or body)*, **step on and break s.t. animate** kaxkíhkaweew VTA; **break s.t. animate** *(using the hands)* káxkŭ=neew VTA; **break s.t. animate** *(quickly)* lookíhlaleew VTA; **break s.t. animate** *(using a tool or instrument)* lóokheew VTA; **break s.t. animate** lóokŭneew VTA; **break s.t. animate, break s.t. animate off, pick s.t. animate** páxkŭneew VTA **I picked some apples.** 'Aapŭlúshak mbáxkŭna.'; **break s.t., break s.t. off** *(of strings, using the hands)*, **pick s.t.** páxkŭnum VTI1B; **break s.t., run s.t. over** káxk=ham VTI1A; **break s.t., sever s.t.** *(using the hands)* tŭmúnum VTI1B; **break s.o.** *(using the foot or body)* lookíh=kaweew VTA; **be broken** kaxkíhleew VII, kaxkíhleew VAI; **be broken** kax=kíixiin VAI, kaxkíixun VII; **be broken into pieces** piikihtéexun VII; **break s.o.'s arm, break s.o.'s hand** kaxkŭ=naxkéeheew VTA; **break s.o.'s arm, break s.o.'s hand** kaxkŭnaxkéexŭ=meew VTA; **break s.o.'s leg** kaxkkaa=téeheew VTA; **break s.o.'s leg** *(using the foot or body)*, **step on and break s.o.'s leg** kaxkkaatéhkaweew VTA; **break s.o.'s neck** kaxkxoonéeheew VTA; **break s.o.'s neck** *(using the hands)* kaxkxoonéeneew VTA, tŭmii=kwéeneew VTA; **break s.o.'s neck, sever s.o. at the neck, break s.o. at the neck, cut s.o. off at the neck** tŭmiikwéeheew VTA; **break s.o.'s nose** kaxkchaaléeheew VTA; **break things** lookŭníikeew VAI; **break up bread in milk, break bread into liquid, break crackers into liquid** piikŭnúmeew VAI; **crack s.t. animate, drop and crack s.t. animate, break s.t. animate in half** pasíixŭmeew VTA; **crack s.t., drop and crack s.t., break s.t. in half** pasíixtoow VTI2; **crumble s.t. animate, break s.t. animate up into pieces, shred s.t. animate** *(using the hands)* píikŭneew VTA; **cut through s.t. animate, cut and break s.t. animate, cut s.t. animate** *(of something string-like)* páxksheew VTA; **cut through s.t., cut and break s.t., cut s.t.** *(of something string-like)* páxkshum VTI1B; **drop and break s.t.** lookíixtoow VTI2; **drop and break s.t. animate** lookíixŭmeew VTA; **drop and break s.t. animate, wreck s.t. animate** lookihtéexŭmeew VTA; **drop and break s.t., wreck s.t.** lookih=téextoow VTI2; **fall and burst open, lie broken** lookchéexiin VAI, look=chéexun VII; **have a broken arm, have a broken hand** kaxkŭnaxkée=xiin VAI, kaxkŭnáxkeew VAI; **have a broken leg** kaxkkáateew VAI; **have a broken neck** tŭmiikwéexiin VAI; **have a broken nose** kaxkcháaleew VAI; **have a broken tooth** kaxkaniikéexiin VAI, lookaníikeew VAI; **have one's nose broken, have a broken nose** kaxkchaaléexiin VAI; **hit and break s.o.** kaxkihtéeheew VTA; **hit and break s.o.'s neck** tŭmiikwehtéeheew VTA; **hit and break s.t.** kaxkihtéeham VTI1A; **hit and break s.t.** lookihtée=ham VTI1A; **hit and break s.t. animate** lookihtéeheew VTA; **shred things, break things into pieces** piikŭníikeew VAI.

**break down** VI **break down, break** lookíhleew VAI, lookíhleew VII.

**break of day** N **be the break of day, be clearing** *(of the sky)* alúmu-waaxéh=leew VII.

**break off** VI **break off** tŭmíhleew VAI, tŭmíhleew VII **His cane broke off.** 'Wtaláawan tŭmíhleew.'; **break off in chunks** kwashíhleew VII; **fall out**

**in chunks, be a chunk falling out, have a chip fall out, have a chunk fall out, break off** kwàkwashíhleew VII; **have s.t. drop and break off, have s.t. drop and be severed** tŭ=míixtoow VTI2.

**break off** VT **break a piece off s.t. animate, break a chunk off s.t. animate** *(using the hands)* kwashúneew VTA; **break a piece off s.t., break a chunk off s.t.** *(using the hands)* kwashúnum VTI1B; **break s.t. animate, break s.t. animate off, pick s.t. animate** páx=kŭneew VTA **I picked some apples.** 'Aapŭlúshak mbáxkŭna.'; **break s.t., break s.t. off** *(of strings, using the hands)*, **pick s.t.** páxkŭnum VTI1B; **be blown over by the wind, be broken off by the wind, be severed by the wind** tŭmáxookw VAI, tŭmáxun VII; **be broken off** póhkweew VII; **be broken off, be blunt** póhkwun VII; **be cut down, be knocked over, be broken off** tŭmáhookw VAI **The tree was knocked over, broken off.** 'Tŭmáh=ookw míhtukw.'; **fall and break off, be severed** tŭmíixun VII; **get run over, be broken off** káxkhookw VAI.

**break up** VT **break up bread in milk, break bread into liquid, break crackers into liquid** piikŭnúmeew VAI; **crumble s.t., break s.t. up into pieces, shred s.t.** *(using the hands)* píikŭnum VTI1B; **leave s.o. alone, have nothing to with s.o., let s.o. go, give up on s.o., break up with s.o., give up making s.t. animate** pooníi=heew VTA.

**breast** N **my breast, my nipple** noo=náakan NID; **have a swollen udder, have a swollen breast** paasíilaneew VAI; **have big breasts** amangíilaneew VAI; **have big breasts, have big udders** *(of a cow)* xwíilaneew VAI; **have long breasts, have long udders** *(of a cow)* akwaaníilaneew VAI.

**breath** N leexéewan NI; **mutter, talk under one's breath** mŭnumohktóon=heew VAI.

**breathe** VI léexeew VAI; **breathe heavily** leexéewsuw VAI.

**breed** N **be a certain nationality, be a certain breed, be a certain make, have a certain characteristic** lah=kéewuw VAI **Other races.** 'Palíi eelahkeewíhtiit.'

**brick** N máxkasun NI; **brick house** max=kasuníikaan NI; **have red bricks on it** *(of houses)* maxkasunháasuw VII.

**bridge** N tayáaxkwaan NI.

**bridle** N **bit for horse's bridle** kehkŭ=lúndang NI; **horse's bridle** laaptoo=néepuy NI; **take the bridle off s.o.** ktohkwéeneew VTA.

**brief** ADJ **get sore, hurt, have a pain, have a sharp pain, have a brief pain** wiisakíhleew VII, wiisakíhleew VAI **My knee had a sharp pain.** 'Ngútko wiisakíhleew.'

**briefly** ADV **see s.o. briefly, see s.o. for a moment** laashíinaweew VTA; **see s.t. briefly, see s.t. for a moment** laashíinam VTI1A; **touch s.t. briefly, touch s.t. for a moment** láashu-lúnum VTI1A.

**bright** ADJ **be bright light** wŭláasŭleew VII; **be bright out** *(at night)*, **be daylight** waaxéeyeew VII **It gets bright out** 'Alúmu-waaxéeyeew.', **There's a new moon.** 'Wúsku-waaxéeyeew.'; **be bright out** waaxéhleew VII **It's bright out now.** 'Méhch waaxéh=leew.'; **be brightly coloured, wear bright colours** ktakŭléexiin VAI; **be brightly coloured** ktakŭléexun VII, wŭluléexun VII, wŭlaapamúkwsuw VAI; **shine brightly, be brilliant** *(especially light)*, **wear bright colours** saapŭléexiin VAI; **be brightly coloured, be dressed up** wŭluléexiin VAI; **shine brightly, be brilliant, be brightly coloured** *(especially light)* saapŭléexun VII.

**brilliant** ADJ **shine brightly, be brilliant, be brightly coloured** *(especially light)* saapŭléexun VII.

**brim** N **be full to the brim, be level with the top** *(of non-liquids)* tpus=kŭwáhteew VII; **fill s.t. to the brim with water** tpuskhwúpeew VAIO.

**bring** VT **bring s.o., bring s.t. animate** péeshŭweew VTA; **bring s.t.** péetoow VTI2 **That's why I brought it.** 'Nún há nóonj-péetoon.'; **ask s.o. to bring s.t.** pchihtáhleew VTAO; **bring a load of s.t., go by with a load of s.t., haul a load of s.t.** éewatoow VTI2 **I hauled a load of hay.** 'Ndéewato miixás=kwal.'; **bring news to here from s.o., bring news to s.o.** peetaachŭmóhka=weew VTA; **bring news, spread the word** peetaachíimuw VAI; **bring s.o. here in a hurry** peechíipheew VTA; **bring s.t. here in a hurry** peechii=páhtoow VTI2; **bring s.t. in this direction** *(towards the speaker)*, **bring s.t. this way** peetasánuw VAIO **I brought my wood this way.** 'Mbeetasániin nŭmóxwsal.'; **bring water in this direction, bring water towards the speaker** peethúpeew VAI; **bring wood inside** piindxákweew VAI; **remind s.o., bring something to s.o.'s mind** mihkóomeew VTA; **be gone after, be brought, be fetched** naatáasuw VII.

**bring along** VT **bring s.o. along as well, take s.o. along as well** naxpóoxwa=leew VTA; **bring s.o., take s.o. along** lóoxwaleew VTA; **bring s.t. along as well, take s.t. along as well** naxpóo=xwatoow VTI2; **bring s.t., take s.t. along** lóoxwatoow VTI2 **What shall I bring?** 'Kwéekw-uch há ndulóo=xwato?'

**bring back** VT **return s.o., bring s.o. back** kwaxkóoxwaleew VTA; **return s.t., bring s.t. back** kwaxkóoxwa=toow VTI2.

**bring for** VT **bring s.t. for s.o.** péeta=weew VTAO.

**bring inside** VT **take s.o. inside, take s.t. animate inside, bring s.o. inside** piindóoxwaleew VTA; **take s.t. inside, bring s.t. inside** piindóoxwatoow VTI2.

**broke** ADJ **be broke, have spent all one's money** pohkwíhleew VAI.

**broom** N chiikhíikan NI.

**brother** N **my brother** *(woman speaking)* ndulŭnóohum NAD; **my brother** *(man speaking)* nímat NAD; **my brother** *(man speaking)* níimatus NAD; **my older brother** nxánz NAD; **my paternal uncle, my mother's brother, my cross-uncle** nzhíis NAD; **my uncle, my father's brother, parallel uncle** nóoxwush NAD; **my younger brother, my younger sister, my younger sibling** nxíisŭmus NAD.

**brother-in-law** N **my sister-in-law** *(man speaking)*, **my brother-in-law** *(woman speaking)* níilum NAD.

**brown** ADJ **be brown, be grey** wiipón=gweew VII, wiipóngwsuw VAI; **brown, grey** wiipongwii- PV **I painted it brown, grey.** 'Nŭwiipóngwii-shóo=hŭmun.'; **be a brownish colour, have a brown tinge to it, be a greyish colour, have a grey tinge to it** wiipongwŭléexiin VAI, wiipongwŭ=léexun VII; **be brown coloured, be grey coloured** wiipongwaapamúkwat VII, wiipongwaapamúkwsuw VAI; **be brown earth, be grey earth** wiipon=gwahkéeyeew VII; **brown thread, grey thread** wiipongwáhtakw NI; **dye s.t. animate brown, dye s.t. animate grey** wiipongwcháseew VTA; **dye s.t. animate yellow, dye s.t. animate brown** wiisaawcháseew VTA; **dye s.t. brown, dye s.t. grey** wiipongwchás=um VTI1B; **dye s.t. yellow, dye s.t. brown** wiisaawchásum VTI1B; **have brown hair** wiipongwaalóhkweew

VAI; **have grey eyes, have brown eyes** wiipongwaalakíingweew VAI; **turn brown, turn grey** wiipongwíh=leew VAI, wiipongwíhleew VII; **turn reddish-brown, turn yellow** *(by heat)*, **be a ripened colour** *(of grain ready to harvest)* wiisaawxáteew VII; **turn reddish-brown, turn yellow, turn orange** *(by heat)* wiisaawxásuw VAI; **turn yellow, turn brown** wiisaa=wíhleew VAI; wiisaawíhleew VII.

**brown** VT **dye s.t. animate red, brown s.t. animate** maxkcháseew VTA; **dye s.t. red, brown s.t.** *(of meat)* maxk=chásum VTI1B; **be dyed red, turn red, be red from heat, be browned** *(of meat)* maxkcháteew VII; **be dyed red, turn red, burn red** *(s.t. animate)*, **be red from heat, get a sunburn, be browned** maxkchásuw VAI; **be nicely browned** wŭlúchasuw VAI, wŭlúcha=teew VII.

**brush** N **paint, paint brush** shoohíikan NI, shehshoohíikeeng NI; **paint brush** wéhwunj-shoohíikeeng NI.

**brush** VT **brush one's teeth** kshiixaníi=keew VAI; **brush s.t., rub s.t.** *(using a tool or instrument)* láalham VTI1A.

**brush against** VT **brush up against s.o.** *(using the foot or body)* chaskíhka=weew VTA, laalíhkaweew VTA; **brush up against s.o.** *(using a tool or instrument)* cháskheew VTA; **brush up against s.t.** *(using the foot or body)* chaskíhkam VTI1A, laalíhkam VTI1A; **brush up against s.t.** *(using a tool or instrument)* cháskham VTI1A; **brush up against something** chaskíixiin VAI, chaskíixun VII, laalíixiin VAI, laa=líixun VII; **contact and brush up against s.o.** laalihtéexŭmeew VTA; **contact and brush up against s.t.** laalihtéextoow VTI2; **have one's feet brushing against a surface, have one's feet contacting a surface** chasksiitéexiin VAI; **rub against something and fall, brush up against something and fall** laalihtéexiin VAI; **rub s.o., brush up against s.t. animate, pet s.o., caress s.o.** *(using the hands)* láalŭneew VTA; **be struck in the eye, brush against something which goes into the eye** laapsheen=gwéexiin VAI.

**bug** N **insect, bug** axkóokus NA; **give s.o. lice, give s.o. bugs** naxkwáaleew VTA.

**bug species** N **bug species with nodding head** tàtamakohkwehláashiit NA, tàtamakohkwéhlaash NA.

**buggy** N mbákii NA; **drive a buggy** mbakiihámeew VAI; **grease a buggy** shamaatpùníikaneew VAI.

**build** N **have a slender figure, have a slight build, be slim** lumbáhkwsuw VAI; **have a slight build, be slim** laangáhkwsuw VAI.

**build** VT **build a house** wíikheew VAI; **finish building a house** kiishíikheew VAI; **pile s.t. animate up, build a hill around s.t. animate** *(of potatoes)* wŭlamkwíixŭméew VTA *object usually plural.*

**bullet** N tángaloonz NI.

**bullfrog** N wáamwiis NA.

**bump** N **get a lump, get a bump** wchih=kwíhleew VAI, wchihkwíhleew VII; **get hit on the head with a maul, have a bump on the head** mookŭlaandpée=xiin VAI; **give s.o. a swollen leg, give s.o. a bump on their leg** makwukaa=téeheew VTA; **have a lump, have a bump** wchíhkweew VII; **have a knot, have a lump, have a bump** wchíhk=wsuw VAI; **have a lump on one's head, have a bump on one's head** wchihkwáandpeew VAI; **have a swollen head, have a bump on one's head** makwáandpeew VAI; **have a swollen leg, have a bump on one's leg** makwukáateew VAI; **have a swollen mouth, have a bump on one's**

**mouth** makwutóoneew VAI; **have a swollen nose, have a bump on one's nose** makwucháaleew VAI; **kick s.o. and give them a swollen leg, kick s.o. and give them a bump on the leg, sit on s.o. and give them a swollen leg, sit on s.o. and give them a bump on the leg** makwukaatéhka=weew VTA.

**bump** VT **bump one's head** paakaand=péexiin VAI; **bump one's mouth** paak=toonéexiin VAI; **bump s.t.** paakíhtoow VTI2 **I bumped my leg.** 'Mbaakíh=toon níhkaat.'; **fall and bump into s.o., fall and bump s.o.** *(with something)* paakihtéexŭmeew VTA.

**bump against** VT **bump against s.t.** *(with something)* páakham VTI1A; **bump one's face against something** paakiingwéexiin VAI; **bump one's hand against something** paakŭnax=kéexiin VAI; **bump one's leg against something** paakkaatéexiin VAI; **bump one's nose against something** paak=chaaléexiin VAI; **bump s.t. animate against something** paakihtéeheew VTA **I bumped my knee against something.** 'Mbaakihtéehaaw ngútko.'; **fall and bump** *(against something)*, **bump into an object** paakihtéexiin VAI **I bumped into the fence.** 'Mee=náxkung mbaakihtéexiin.'; **fall and bump** *(against something)*, **bump into an object** paakihtéexun VII **It bumped into my leg.** 'Paakihtéexun níhkaat.', **The door banged against something.** 'Paakihtéexun kpáhoon.'; **fall and bump against s.t.** *(with something)* paakihtéextoow VTI2 **He bumped his leg against something.** 'Wíhkaat paakihtéextoon.'

**bump into** VT **bump into something** wundihtéexiin VAI **I bumped into the door.** 'Kpáhoon noondihtéexiin.'; **bump into something with s.t.** paa=kihtéehum VTI1B; **fall and bump** *(against something)*, **bump into an object** paakihtéexiin VAI **I bumped into the fence.** 'Meenáxkung mbaa=kihtéexiin.'; **fall and bump** *(against something)*, **bump into an object** paakihtéexun VII **It bumped into my leg.** 'Paakihtéexun níhkaat.', **The door banged against something.** 'Paakihtéexun kpáhoon.'; **fall and bump into s.o., fall and bump s.o.** *(with something)* paakihtéexŭmeew VTA.

**bunch** N **bunch s.o. up together, put s.o. in a bunch** mŭníixŭmeew VTA *object usually plural;* **bunch s.t. up together, put s.t. together in a bunch** mŭníixtoow VTI2 *object usually plural;* **have a bunch of kids, have a big family** mŭleekóonzheew VAI; **multiply, grow as a bunch, grow close together** mŭléekuw VAI **It's really multiplied.** 'Móxa mŭléekuw.'; **stand in a bunch, be bunched up standing together** kohpakiikaapa=wúwak VAI *usually plural.*

**bunch** VT **be wrinkled, be bunched up** wchupŭlúsuw VAI; **stand bunched together** mŭniikaapawúwak VAI *usually plural.*

**bunch up** VT **bunch s.o. up together, put s.o. in a bunch** mŭníixŭmeew VTA *object usually plural;* **bunch s.t. animate up** wchupŭlúneew VTA; **bunch s.t. animate up, crumple s.t. animate up** pàptúkwŭneew VTA; **bunch s.t. up** wchupŭlúnum VTI1B; **bunch s.t. up together, put s.t. together in a bunch** mŭníixtoow VTI2 *object usually plural;* **bunch s.t. up, crumple s.t. up** pàptúkwŭnum VTI1B; **be bunched up together** mŭniixíi=nook VAI *usually plural,* mŭníixunool VII *usually plural;* **be bunched up, be heaped up** mshámŭwak VAI *usually plural,* mshámŭwal VII *usually plural.*

**bundle** N **carry s.t. away in a pack or**

**bundle** alumŭwáleew VAIO.

**bunt** VT **stop s.o.** *(with an elongated object)*, **bunt a ball** *(in baseball)* ngii=kwáaleew VTA **I bunted the ball.** 'Nàkiikwáalaaw áng néenaxkw.'

**burn** VI **burn** lóosuw VAI, lóoteew VII; **be dyed red, turn red, burn red** *(s.t. animate)*, **be red from heat, get a sunburn, be browned** maxkchásuw VAI; **burn** *(of fires)* náxkwteew VII; **burn well** wíingŭleew VII, wŭlúleew VII; **burn well** wŭlúleew VAI, machíi=masuw VAI; **have a burning smell, smell as if it is burning** *(of something cooking)* machíimateew VII; **stop burning** ehkwchásuw VAI, eh=kwcháteew VII; **stop burning, cease burning** éhkwsuw VAI, éhkwteew VII.

**burn** VT **burn s.o.** lóoseew VTA; **burn s.t.** lóosum VTI1B; **be burnt** loosáa=suw VII, loosáasuw VAI; **be burnt black, be dyed black** nzukchásuw VAI nzukcháteew VII.

**burn up** VT **burn s.o. up** méhtseew VTA; **burn s.t. up** méhtsum VTI1B; **be burnt up** méhtsuw VAI, méhtteew VII; **be burnt up, fall to pieces, be in pieces after being cooked** shkwút=suw VAI, shkwúteew VII; **go out** *(of fires)*, **be burnt up** *(in a fire)* wchii=máhteew VII; **be burnt up** méhtteew VII.

**burr** N sáksak NA.

**burst** VI **explode, blow up, burst** *(from heat)* pwáhksuw VAI, pwáhkteew VII; **fall and burst open, lie broken** lookchéexiin VAI, lookchéexun VII.

**bury** VT **bury s.o.** waalháaleew VTA; **bury s.o., cover s.o. over** psúndheew VTA **He was covered up, buried.** 'Psúndhaaw.'; **bury s.t.** waalháatoow VTI2; **bury s.t., cover s.t. over** psúnd=ham VTI1A; **be buried** kwtawŭnáasuw VAI, psundháasuw VAI **He is buried here.** 'Yóon pusundháasiin.'; **be buried** waalháasuw VAI, waalhaatáasuw VII; **put things away, store things, be buried** wŭlahtáasuw VAI.

**bush** N **shrub, bush** míhchkwshush NI; **thistle bush** kaawúnzhahkw NA; **be a lot of bushes** mihtkwunzíhkeew VII **Where there are a lot of bushes.** 'Éenda-mihtkwunzíhkeek.'; **cranberry bush** paakiimíinzhuy NA; **forest, in the bush** kóhpii PC **There are lots of good roads in the bush.** 'Wéemi talí wŭlatéexun kóhpii.', **They went in the bush.** 'Kóhpii éewak.'

**bushy** ADJ **be ragged, be bushy** píikw=sheew VII, piikwshúsuw VAI; **have a bushy beard** wiixŭwihtóonayeew VAI.

**business** N **be put through** *(of a motion at a meeting, of business)* eeshoo=xwatáasuw VII; **take s.t. through something** *(of a matter of business)* eeshóoxwatoow VTI2.

**busy** ADJ **be busy** wtamalóhkeew VAI.

**but** CJ **but, only** shúkw PC **They were laughing, saying all sorts of things to me, and touching me, but I didn't understand them.** 'Akulkúsŭwak, wéemu kwéek ndukwŭnéewa, wáak ngihkiixkŭnúkook, shúkw msúchee máh nùnohtawaawíiwak.', **But he's in my way.** 'Shúkw kàkpíixiin.'

**butcher's knife** N mbochŭlanzhíikan NI.

**butt in** VI **butt in, disrupt the conversation** ìhŭlutóonheew VAI; **take part in a conversation, butt into a conversation** wiittóonheew VAI.

**butter** N póotul NI; **make butter** pootŭ=lahíikeew VAI, pootŭláheew VAI; **put butter on s.t.** pootŭláham VTI1A; **put butter on s.t. animate** *(using a tool or instrument)* pootŭláheew VTA.

**butterfly** N kaakáapush NA.

**buttermilk** N **buttermilk, sour milk** shŭwíi-mŭlúk NI.

**buttocks** N **crack in the buttocks** pasiitŭyeewáakan NI; **have a crack in**

one's buttocks pasíitŭyeew VAI.

**button** N kŭnóop NA; **button hole** kŭ=noopáalakw NI; **button shoe** kŭnoo=páhksun NI; **have buttons** kŭnoop=háasuw VII; **have buttons** kŭnoop=háasuw VAI; **have round ('button') eyes** kŭnoopaalakíingweew VAI.

**button** VT **button s.t. up, do s.t. up tightly, make a down payment on s.t.** kŭláhkhwam VTI1A; **be buttoned, be hooked up** kŭlahkhwáasuw VII; **fasten things, button things, hook things up** kŭlahkhwíikeew VAI.

**buy** VT **buy s.o., buy s.t. animate** máh=laweew VTA; **buy s.t.** máhlam VTI1A; **get s.o., buy s.o., keep s.o., have s.o.** ayúweew VTA; **buy s.o. clothes to wear, get s.o. clothes to wear, dress s.o.** akwúneew VTA; **get s.t. animate cheaply, buy s.t. animate cheaply** aapŭwíiheew VTA; **get s.t. cheaply, buy s.t. cheaply** aapŭwíhtoow VTI2 **Get it as cheaply as you can.** 'Kángu-uch lúkih -aapŭwíhtawan.'; **get s.t., buy s.t., keep s.t., have s.t.** ayúm VTI1B.

**by** PREP **by, along** pŭmu- PV **I ran by in a flash.** 'Náh mbúmu-laashíhla.'; **hurry by with s.t., hurry along with s.t.** pŭmiipáhtoow VTI2; **take s.o. by in a hurry, take s.o. along in a hurry** pŭmíipheew VTA.

# C

**cabbage** N képuch NI.

**cake** N shookŭlápwaan NI; **make a cake** shookŭlapwáanheew VAI.

**calendar** N aalŭmuníikan NI.

**call** VT **call s.o. by a certain name** shiinzŭwáaleew VTA; **call s.o. over, call s.o. here** peechíimeew VTA; **call s.o., summon s.o.** wunjíimeew VTA; **name s.o., mention s.o. by name, call s.o. by name** wíhleew VTA **I call him by that name.** 'Ndáaylu-wíh=laaw.'; **name s.t., mention s.t. by name, call s.t. by name** wíindam VTI1A; **talk from a certain place, talk for a certain reason, holler from a certain place, holler for a certain reason, call from a certain place, call for a certain reason** *(especially on the telephone)* wundaap=tóoneew VAI **I talked from far away.** 'Wáhlu noondaaptóone.'

**call over** VT **call s.o. over, call s.o. here** peechíimeew VTA.

**call to** VT **wake s.o. up by calling to them** tohkíimeew VTA **Anything can wake you up.** 'Akwáawu kwéek áa ktohkíimkwun.'

**calm** ADJ **have a calm mind** kŭlamee=lúndam VOTI1; **have a peaceful mind, have a calm mind** kŭlamahtéena=muw VAI.

**camera** N kteekhíikan NI.

**can** N **bottle s.t., put s.t. in cans, block s.t.** kpáskham VTI1A; **can s.t. animate, put s.t. animate in cans** kéenheew VTA; **can s.t., put s.t. in cans** kéen=ham VTI1A; **can things, put things in cans** keenhíikeew VAI; **oil can** kaa=noosiilamóokan NA.

**can** VI **can do something** *(that was previously impossible)* kangu- PV *informal* **Can you do it?** 'Kángu- áa há nú -kíish-lúnŭmun?', **Can he do it?** 'Kwángu- áa há nú -kíish-lúnŭmun?'; **should, would, can, could** áa PC **We (inclusive) should hide.** 'Kiilóona áa kaatapíhna.', **I'd really like to go with you (plural).** 'Píish áa móxa kŭwíingu-wiicheewŭlóhmwa.'; **throw s.t. as far as one can** seesahkáaheew VAIO **Then I went outside and I threw it as far as I could.** 'Nál kwáchŭmung ndáan táa ndúlu-asee=sahkáaheen.'

**can** VT **can s.t. animate, put s.t. animate**

**in cans, block s.o., plug s.t. animate, fill in the cracks of s.t. animate, winterize s.t. animate** *(especially of windows)* kpáskheew VTA; **can s.t. animate, put s.t. animate in cans** kéenheew VTA; **can s.t., put s.t. in cans** kéenham VTI1A; **can things, put things in cans** keenhíikeew VAI.

**candy** N shóokŭlush NI.

**cane** N aláawan NI; **use a cane** alaaw=húnzuw VAI; **go quickly using a cane** kshalaawhúnzuw VAI.

**cap** N kép NI.

**car** N **car, automobile** ahtamóombiil NA; **car, train car** káal NA; **be hit, be trapped, be hit by a car** kŭláhookw VAI; **drive a car, use a car** kaalhám=eew VAI; **drive a car, use an automobile** ahtamoombiilhámeew VAI; **have a car** kwáalŭmuw VAI; **upset, turn over in a boat, turn over in a car** kooxkáaweew VAI.

**card** N **playing card, shovel** shkúp NA.

**cards** N **play cards** shkuphámeew VAI.

**care** N **take care of a child, babysit** noocháawsuw VAI; **take care of s.o.'s child for them** noochaawsáweew VTA; **take care of s.t., look after s.t., tend to a responsibility with regard to s.t.** lxaweelúndam VTI1B **Take care of the food (said of an empty refrigerator).** 'Katá-lxaweelúndah miichŭ=wáakan.'; lxawéelŭmeew VTA **You should take care of your car, don't drive it needlessly.** 'Káta-lxawéelŭ=maa ktahtamoombíilum, chíi amaya=kaweehéehan.'

**carelessly** ADV **carelessly, bad** amachu-PV **I fold it carelessly.** 'Nŭmámachu-wŭleekŭnúmun.'; **fold s.t. animate carelessly** machéekŭneew VTA; **fold s.t. carelessly** machéekŭnum VTI1B.

**caress** VT **rub s.o., brush up against s.t. animate, pet s.o., caress s.o.** *(using the hands)* láalŭneew VTA.

**carpet** N **carpet, rug** ehahpalíhkeeng VII.

**carrot** N pehpeechkwéekush NA.

**carry** VT **hold s.o., hold on to s.o., hold on tightly to s.o., carry s.o.** *(using the hands)* kŭlúneew VTA; **hold s.t., hold onto s.t., hold on tightly to s.t., carry s.t.** *(using the hands)* kŭlúnum VTI1B; **carry s.o. on one's back** nayóomeew VTA; **carry s.t. on one's back** nayóondam VTI1A; **carry a baby** noonzhéesuw VAI, noonzhée=wasuw VAI; **carry a big load** tohp=héewasuw VAI; **carry a heavy load on one's back** laanzhihkŭwáleew VAI; **carry a lantern** níindaweew VAI; **carry a load on one's back** pŭmúw=aleew VAI; **carry s.o. on one's back** pŭmúwaleew VTA; **carry s.t. extra, carry s.t. in addition** naxpasánuw VAIO; **carry something around** apaamasánuw VAI; **go after and carry s.t., fetch and carry s.t.** naatasánuw VAIO; **go to fetch a load of s.t., fetch and carry a load of something on one's back** naachŭwáleew VAIO; **hide s.t. while carrying it** kaatasánuw VAIO; **take s.t. along, carry s.t.** wŭ=lásanuw VAIO **I carried the groceries.** 'Noolasániin kŭlooshliihiiwáakanal.'

**carry away** VT **carry s.t. away in a pack or bundle** alumŭwáleew VAIO; **carry s.t. away, carry s.t. away in a pack** alumŭwaléhleew VAIO; **carry something away quickly** alumasan=íhleew VAIO; **carry s.t. away** aluma=sánuw VAIO.

**cart away** VT **cart away a load** *(of one's belongings)* alumhéewasuw VAI.

**casket** N **chest, trunk, small box, casket, coffin** kúsht NI.

**cat** N póoshiish NA; **bad cat** mataa=kanapóoshiish NA, matapóoshiish NA; **cat excrement, cat droppings** poo=shíish'chuy NI; **clean cat** piilapóo=shiish NA; **dirty cat** niiskapóoshiish NA; **look for a cat** ndawapooshíi=

sheew VAI.

**cataract** N **have one's cataracts removed** pŭlakiingwáalaaw VTA *indefinite subject only.* **remove s.o.'s cataracts** pŭlakiingwéeneew VTA.

**catch** VT **catch s.o., arrest s.o.** táhwŭ=neew VTA; **catch s.t.** táhwŭnum VTI 1B; **catch s.t. animate with a hook** ptáheew VTA **I caught two pickerel.** 'Níishŭwak waasíingwak mbutháa=wak.'

**catch up to** VT **catch up to s.o., overtake s.o., catch up to s.o.'s level** matáleew VTA.

**catcher** N kehkéchiis NA *baseball.*

**caterpillar** N wiixŭwaxkóokus NA.

**Catholic** N keeslukíiwi-pehpŭmutóon=hees NA.

**caulk** VT **plug things up, caulk things, fill in chinks** kpaskhíikeew VAI.

**cave in** VI **collapse, cave in** mŭlakwíh=leew VII.

**cease** VI **stop, cease** ehkwi- PV **I couldn't see him.** 'Ndéhkwi-néewa.'; **stop, cease** ehkwu- PV *informal* **He quit breathing.** 'Éhkwu-léexeew.', **The service is over.** 'Éhkwu-maawée=wiin.'; **stop burning, cease burning** éhkwsuw VAI, éhkwteew VII; **stop cutting s.t. animate, cease cutting s.t. animate** éhkwsheew VTA; **stop cutting s.t., cease cutting s.t.** éhkwshum VTI 1B; **stop cutting things, cease cutting things** ehkwshíikeew VAI; **stop talking, cease talking** ehkwtóon=heew VAI; **stop urinating, cease urinating, quit urinating** ehkwíisheew VAI.

**cedar** N **cedar tree** shúndahkw NA.

**celebrate** VT **celebrate Christmas** kŭlushmíshiin VAI *usually with indefinite subject only;* **celebrate Easter, be Easter** *(indefinite subject)* íisŭliin VAI; **celebrate New Year's day** newi=yáaliin VAI *indefinite subject only.*

**cellar** N **root cellar** ahkuyáalakw NI.

**Cephas** N *(man's name)* shíifush NA.

**certain** ADJ **be certain** shaaxkeelúndam VOTI 1; **be certain about s.o.** shaax=kéelŭmeew VTA; **be certain about s.t.** shaaxkeelúndam VTI 1A; **be certain, be sure, have one's mind made up** mayaaweelúndam VOTI 1 **Now I'm sure that Lyle's not coming home.** 'Kwáy nŭmayaaweelúndam máh há péewu Lyle.', **I'm sure that it's going to rain.** 'Nŭmayaaweelúndam katá-sóokŭlaan.'; **be certain about s.o., have one's mind made up about s.o.** mayaawéelŭmeew VTA; **be certain about s.o.** shaaxkéelŭmeew VTA; **be certain about s.t.** shaaxkee=lúndam VTI 1A.

**certain** ADJ **because, in a certain manner, in a certain direction** eel- PV *followed by verb in conjunct order* **Now it must be because he had overcome the medicine.** 'Nál xéet ná kwáy éel- wchápihk -aluwíhkang.', **Because you picked him up you'll always find lots of things (to hunt).** 'Kwáy éel-náatŭnat ngúmee-uch xwéelu kwéek kŭmóxkam.'; **because, in a certain manner, in a certain direction** eeli- PV *followed by verb in conjunct order* **She wanted to kill him because he had cracked the eggs.** 'Kwáta-nihláawal éeli- wáhwal -pwáhkhang.'; **in a certain manner, in a certain direction** li- PV **I waited until he came in.** 'Mbéehaaw wtúli-piinjíikeen.', **Then he crawled inside the house.** 'Nál wtúlu- wiikwáhmung -piinjíikwsiin.'; **in a certain manner, in a certain direction** lu- PV *informal* **I looked around for the medicine, I looked for it everywhere.** 'Nál há mbápaa-kwíilamun wchápihk, wéemu táa ndúlu-kwíilamun.', **Then I went outside and I threw it as far as I could.** 'Nál kwáchŭmung ndáan táa ndúlu-aseesahkáaheen.'; **do some-**

**thing to s.o. in a certain manner, do something to s.o. in a certain direction** *(using the foot or body)* líhka=weew VTA; **do something to s.t. in a certain manner, do something to s.t. in a certain direction** *(using the foot or body)* líhkam VTI1A **I shoved it to the side.** 'Pálii ndulíhkamun.'; **look in a certain direction, look in a certain manner** liingwéexiin VAI **I don't know where he's looking.** 'Máh nŭweewiiháawu tá eeliingwée=xiit.'; **shine a light in a certain direction, shine a light in a certain manner** laasŭléenŭmeew VAI; **shine in a certain direction** *(of the sun)* láandeew VII; **shine s.t. in a certain direction, shine s.t. in a certain manner** *(of lights)* laasŭléenum VTI1A, laasŭléenŭmeew VAIO **I shone the lantern over there.** 'Yeelak ndulaa=sŭléenŭmaan waasŭleeníikan.'; **speak in a certain manner** lutóonheew VAI **He likes to stick his noise in.** 'Wíh=wiing- ná -lutóonheew.', **I speak slowly.** 'Maamalóoniish ndultóonhe.'

**chair** N áhpapoon NI; **fancy chair** wii=lawáhpapoon NI; **new chair** wuskáh=papoon NI; **old chair** xuwáhpapoon NI; **rocking chair** neeneemáhpapoon NI; **trade chairs, change chairs** aashŭwahpapoonéewak VAI *usually plural;* **trade chairs, change chairs** aashŭwahpapóonheew VAI.

**challenge** VT **challenge s.o. to a fight** ndóonaleew VTA.

**change** VI **change**, **take a turn for the worse, have one's medical condition worsen** aanjíhleew VAI.

**change** VT **change s.t., alter s.t., make s.t. over** aanjíhtoow VTI2; **change one's clothes** aashŭwákuw VAI, áan=dakuw VAI; **change one's pants** aa=shŭwiipŭlóokeew VAI; **change one's place while sitting** áandapuw VAI; **change one's shirt** aandhéembteew VAI, aashŭwahéembteew VAI; **change one's socks** aashŭwashíikaneew VAI; **change s.o.'s diaper**, **make s.o. be dry** peengwíixŭmeew VTA; **change seats, sit somewhere else** aandapíh=leew VAI; **trade chairs, change chairs** aashŭwahpapoonéewak VAI *usually plural,* aashŭwahpapóonheew VAI; **trade shoes, change one's shoes** aashŭwahksúneew VAI.

**chapped** ADJ **have rough hands, have chapped hands** kaaxkŭnáxkeew VAI.

**character** N **be strong willed, be strong in character**, **be brave** maskaniitée=heew VAI **He's not brave yet (usually said of a young person).** 'Éeskwa néeka maskaniiteehéewu.'

**characteristic** N **be a certain nationality, be a certain breed, be a certain make, have a certain characteristic** lahkéewuw VAI **Other races.** 'Palíi eelahkeewíhtiit.'; **have a certain characteristic** *(of people)*, **be a certain type of person** laapéewuw VAI **He's good for nothing.** 'Máh kwéek laapeewíiwu.'

**charge** VT **charge a certain price for s.t.** laawatóoheew VAIO; **charge a fair price for s.t.** teepaawatóoheew VAIO; **charge a lot** amangaawatóoheew VAI **You charge too much.** 'Kóosaa-amangaawatóohe.'; **charge a lot for s.t.** xwaawatóoheew VAIO; **charge s.o. a certain amount** laawatóohaweew VTA; **charge s.o. a certain amount** loowatóohaweew VTA.

**chase** VT **chase s.o. around** apaam=shíhkaweew VTA; **chase s.o. crookedly** pàptukshíhkaweew VTA; **chase s.o. inside, send s.o. inside**, **drive s.o. inside** *(of animals)* piindshíhka=weew VTA; **take s.o. inside, chase s.o. inside, send s.o. inside**, **drive s.o. inside** *(of animals)* piindshíiheew VTA; **chase s.o. into the water** chooxpw=shíiheew VTA; **chase s.o. into the wa-**

ter, drive s.o. into the water kamuk=wshíiheew VTA; chase s.o. out of the water chooxpwshíhkaweew VTA; chase s.o. to here, chase s.o. in this direction, drive s.o. to here peet=shíhkaweew VTA.

**Chatham** N **Chatham, Ontario** chétum NI **He's going to Chatham.** 'Chétum éew.'

**cheap** ADJ **be cheap, be inexpensive** aapŭwáawatuw VAI, aapŭwáawatuw VII; **get s.t. cheap, pay a little for s.t.** aapŭwalóhkeew VAIO.

**cheaply** ADV **get s.t. animate cheaply, buy s.t. animate cheaply** aapŭwíi=heew VTA; **get s.t. cheaply, buy s.t. cheaply** aapŭwíhtoow VTI2 **Get it as cheaply as you can.** 'Kángu-uch lúkih -aapŭwíhtawan.'

**cheat** VT **cheat s.o.** pahchóoleew VTA **He's coming here to cheat me.** 'Ngáta-péechi-pahpahchóolukw.'; **cheat s.o., shortchange s.o.** piimŭ=númaweew VTA; **cheat, cheat people** pahchóhkeew VAI.

**checkers** N koonjcháashak NA *usually plural*; **play checkers** koonjcháashuw VAI.

**cheek** N **my cheek** nánuw NAD, nánuw NID; **have big cheeks** amangŭnánŭ=weew VAI; .

**cherry** N chéeliis NA, chéliis NA; **pick cherries** *(off the stems)* paxkŭnii=chèlíiseew VAI; **pick cherries, work in a cherry orchard** cheelíis'heew VAI, chèlíis'heew VAI.

**chest** N **chest, trunk, small box, casket, coffin** kúsht NI.

**chest** N **my chest** ndóolheew NID.

**chestnut** N wáapiim NI.

**chew** VI **chew, be chewing** shàsh=kwámuw VAI.

**chew** VT **chew s.t.** shàshkwándam VTI1A; **chew s.t. animate** shàshkwámeew VTA **He's chewing some gum.** 'Pkóo=hal shashkwámeew.'; **chew tobacco** cháahuw VAI.

**chew out** VT **reprimand s.o., chew s.o. out** nahpŭnáleew VTA.

**chicken** N kiikíipush NA; **chicken droppings, chicken excrement** kiikiip=shúchuy NI; **chicken house** kiikiip=shíikaan NI; **cluck, make a noise like a chicken** kwŭlukhwámeew VAI; **kill a chicken** nihliikíipsheew VAI.

**chicken hawk** N nehnihliikíipsheet NA.

**chicken pox** N **get measles, get chicken pox, come out in blotches, come out in spots** saakpéhleew VAI; **have chicken pox** kiikiipshupéhleew VAI.

**chief** N kíhkay NA; **be chief, be the leader** kíhkayuw VAI; **make s.o. chief, make s.o. be the leader** kihkayúm=heew VAIO.

**child** N amíimunz NA; **my child** niicháa=nus NAD, níichaan NAD; **be a child** amiimúnzuw VAI; **have a child, have children** wŭniicháanuw VAI; **have a lot of children** sŭluskóonzheew VAI; **have many children** xweelóonzheew VAI; **take care of a child, babysit** noocháawsuw VAI; **take care of s.o.'s child for them** noochaawsáweew VTA.

**chimney pipe** N ehŭliingwáhteek NI.

**chink** N **plug things up, caulk things, fill in chinks** kpaskhíikeew VAI.

**chip** N **wood chip** wshéexakw NI; **be chipped, have a chip missing** kwa=shát VII, kwashúsuw VAI; **fall out in chunks, be a chunk falling out, have a chip fall out, have a chunk fall out, break off** kwàkwashíhleew VII, kwàkwashíhleew VAI; **gather wood chips** wsheexakwáheew VAI; **have a chipped tooth, have a chip off one's tooth** kwashaníikeew VAI.

**chip** VT **drop and chip s.t.** kwashih=téextoow VTI2; **drop and chip s.t. animate** kwashihtéexŭmeew VTA; **be chipped, have a chip missing, have a chunk missing** kwashát VII, kwa=shúsuw VAI; **crack, fall and crack,**

**fall and get chipped** kwashihtéexiin VII, kwashihtéexun VAI; **have a chipped spout** kwashutóoneew VAI; **have a chipped tooth, have a chip off one's tooth** kwashaníikeew VAI.

**chipmunk** N poxkapíishush NA.

**chisel** N **awl, chisel** pkwihteehíikan NI.

**choke** VI pxáakw VAI, aapchíilateew VAI, **choke** *(from food going down the wrong way)* pahchíilateew VAI.

**choke** VT **choke s.o., strangle s.o.** kchiixkwéeneew VTA.

**choose** VT **choose s.o.** piipíinaweew VTA; **choose s.t.** piipíinam VTI1.

**chop** VT **chop s.t. animate down, chop s.t. animate off, cut s.t. animate down, cut s.t. animate off** tŭmáheew VTA; **chop s.t. down, chop s.t. off, cut s.t. down, cut s.t. off** tŭmáham VTI1A; **chop s.t. animate down with an ax, cut s.t. animate down with an ax** tíhlaweew VTA; **chop s.t. down with an ax, cut s.t. down with an ax** tíhlam VTI1A **I chopped some wood.** 'Ndíhlam xwús.'; **chop with an ax, cut down trees, trim trees** tŭmaháh=kweew VAI; **chop down a tree** aam=háhkweew VAI.

**chop up** VT **chop up wood** piikháh=kweew VAI; **dice s.t. animate, cut s.t. animate up into small pieces, chop s.t. animate, crack s.t. animate** píik=heew VTA; **dice s.t., cut s.t. up into small pieces, chop s.t. up, crack s.t.** píikham VTI1A.

**chore** N **finish one's chores, be finished one's chores, get through one's chores** kiishanáakwsuw VAI.

**Christian** N **Christian Indian, Moravian convert** kéendŭwees NA; **be an unbeliever, don't believe in a Christian way of life, lead a quiet life** nalawáawsuw VAI; **believe, become a Christian, become a believer** wŭlústam VOTI1.

**Christmas** N kŭlúshmish NI; **celebrate Christmas** kŭlushmíshiin VAI *usually with indefinite subject only.*

**chunk** N **be chipped, have a chip missing, have a chunk missing** kwa=shúsuw VAI; **break a piece off s.t. animate, break a chunk off s.t. animate** *(using the hands)* kwashúneew VTA; **break a piece off s.t., break a chunk off s.t.** *(using the hands)* kwashúnum VTI1B; **break off in chunks** kwashíhleew VII; **fall out in chunks, be a chunk falling out, have a chip fall out, have a chunk fall out, break off** kwàkwashíhleew VAI, kwàkwashíhleew VII.

**church** N kundŭweewíikaan NI, maa=weewíikaan NI, pahtamawíikaan NI, éenda-maawéewiing VII; **'testify' at a religious meeting, 'testify' in church** pasukwtóonheew VAI; **attend church, attend a service** maawéewuw VAI.

**cigar** N shíkaash NA **I smoked his cigar.** 'Ndóhpwaan wshikáashŭmal.'; **cigar** shúkaal NA.

**circle** N **crawl in a circle, crawl around something** wiiwŭníikwsuw VAI; **draw a circle around a picture of s.o., draw a circle on a picture of s.o., circle a picture of s.o.** wiiwŭnéek=heew VTA; **draw a circle around s.t., draw a circle on s.t., circle s.t.** wii=wŭnéekham VTI1A; **draw a circle around things, circle things** wiiwŭ=neekhíikeew VAI; **drive in a circle, drive around something** wiiwŭ=nuchéhleew VAI; **go in a circle, go around, roll in a circle** wiiwŭníhleew VAI, wiiwŭníhleew VII; **roll around, roll in a circle** wiiwŭniinjkwéhleew VAI; **roll s.o. around in a circle** wii=wŭniinjkwéhlaleew VTA; **roll s.t. around in a circle** wiiwŭniinjkwéh=latoow VTI2; **run in a circle, run around something** wiiwŭnahtakíh=leew VAI; **sit in a circle** wiiwŭnoh=kwéepŭwak VAI *usually plural;* **stand**

in a circle wiiwŭniikaapawúwak VAI *usually plural;* **swim in a circle, swim around something** wiiwŭnaa=shŭwíhleew VAI.

**city** N **big town, city** kihtootéenay NI, xwatootéenay NI.

**Clara** N **Clara, Clarisse** kŭléshii NA.

**clarinet** N **clarinet, wooden musical instrument** xwusapíikwan NI.

**Clarisse** N **Clara, Clarisse** kŭléshii NA.

**claw** VT **scratch s.o., claw s.o.** *(using the hands)* síisŭneew VTA; **scratch s.t., claw s.t.** *(using the hands)* síi=sŭnum VTI1B.

**clay** N waapasíiskuw NI; **clay pot** asiiskŭwahóosus NA, asiiskŭwáhoos NA.

**clean** ADJ **be clean** píilsuw VAI, píilut VII; **be clean looking, have a clean appearance** piiliináakwat VII, piilii=náakwsuw VAI; **clean** piilii- PN **A clean sheet.** 'Píilii-waapasáanay.', **A clean plate.** 'Píilii-pàkíinjuw.'; **clean cat** piilapóoshiish NA; **have a clean ear** piilihtawákeew VAI, píilxeew VAI; **have a clean face** piilchàlíingweew VAI; **have a clean house** piilíikeew VAI; **have clean feet** piilsíiteew VAI; **have clean fingernails** apiilíhkasheew VAI; **have clean hands** piilŭnáxkeew VAI; **have clean knees** piiliiktúkweew VAI; **have clean shoes** piilahksúneew VAI; **have clean teeth** apiilaníikeew VAI; **wear clean clothes** apíilakuw VAI; **wipe s.o. clean** *(with something held in the hand)* piiliikwáaleew VTA; **wipe s.t. clean** *(with something held in the hand)* piilíikwam VTI1A.

**clean** VT **clean s.o., clean s.o. up** piilíi=heew VTA; **clean s.t., clean s.t. up** piilíhtoow VTI2.

**clean up** VI piilalóhkeew VAI; **clean oneself up** piilhúnzuw VAI; **clean s.o., clean s.o. up** piilíiheew VTA; **clean s.t., clean s.t. up** piilíhtoow VTI2.

**clear** ADJ **be clear liquid** wŭláapŭweew VII; **be clear water, be good water** wŭlupéekat VII.

**clear** VI **be the break of day, be clearing** *(of the sky)* alúmu-waaxéhleew VII.

**clear away** VT **clear away underbrush, be underbrushing** piilháhkweew VAI.

**clearing** N **be a clearing** pahkwtéeyeew VII.

**clench** VT **have one's hand clenched in a fist** ptukwŭlunjéexiin VAI, ptukwŭ=lúnjeew VAI.

**clever** ADJ **be clever, be smart** lpwéew VAI.

**climb** VI **climb in a certain manner, climb in a certain direction, climb up** lakóosuw VAI; **climb all over** msakóosuw VAI; **climb away, climb up** alumakóosuw VAI; **climb here, climb towards speaker** peetakóosuw VAI; **climb out of sight** kaatakóosuw VAI; **climb over** paalakóosuw VAI; **climb straight up** kundakóosuw VAI; **go up, climb up** uspakóosuw VAI.

**climb** VT **climb up a long flight of stairs** kwŭnakóosuw VAI; **climb up onto something** poxkakóosuw VAI **She climbed up onto the horse.** 'Poxkakóosuw nehnayóongsung.'

**climb down** VI **come down, climb down** niixakóosuw VAI.

**climb up** VI **climb in a certain manner, climb in a certain direction, climb up** lakóosuw VAI.

**clock** N **clock, hour of the day** kŭlák NA **You will come at four o'clock.** 'Néew-kŭlák-uch kúnj kpá.'

**close** ADJ **be close together** kchukáh=teew VII; **be close together, lie close together** takwiixíinook VAI *usually plural,* takwíixŭnool VII *usually plural;* **be in a group of people crowded close together, make one's way through the crowd** kàkchúkamuw VAI; **close, up close** péexŭwii PC **I looked at him up close.** 'Péexŭwii ndúlu-pŭnáwaaw.', **He came close to the edge.** 'Péexŭwii wsháyii péew.'; **get close to s.o.** peexŭwíhkaweew VTA; **get close to s.t.** peexŭwíhkam VTI1A; **get close, approach, fly close by, go close by** peexŭwíhleew VAI, peexŭwíhleew VII; **grow close together** kchukíikŭwak VAI *usually plural,* spwíikŭwak VAI *usually plural,* spwíi=kŭnool VII *usually plural;* **lie close together** kchukaangwéewak VAI *usually plural;* **lie close together, be close together, lie close to something** psakwiixíinook VAI *usually plural,* psakwíixun VII **The chair is up against the door.** 'Psakwíixun áhpa=poon kpahóonung.'; **live near s.o., live close to s.o.** peexŭwiikáaleew VTA; **put s.o. close together, put s.t. animate close together, stick s.o. up against something** psakwíixŭmeew VTA *object usually plural;* **put s.t. close together**, **stick s.t. up against something** psakwíixtoow VTI2; **sit close together** kchukapúwak VAI *usually plural,* kchukohkwéepŭwak VAI *usually plural,* psakohkwéepŭwak VAI *usually plural,* psakwapúwak VAI *usually plural;* **stand close together** kchukiikaapawúwak VAI *usually plural;* **think s.o. to be close** peexŭwée=lŭmeew VTA; **think s.t. to be close** peexŭweelúndam VTI1A.

**close** VI kpíhleew VII.

**close** VT **shut s.o. out, shut s.o. in, close s.t. animate** kpáheew VTA; **shut s.t. out, shut s.t. in, close s.t.** kpáham VTI1A; **close things up, shut things in, shut things out** kpahíikeew VAI; **be closed, be shut in, be shut out** kpaháasuw VII; **close one's hand(s) tightly** maskaniilúnjeew VAI; **close one's lips tightly, have one's lips tightly closed** samwutoonéexiin VAI; **close one's mouth tightly, have one's mouth closed, have one's lips pursed**, **pout** spwutoonéexiin VAI; **hang closed, be closed** kpaapéhleew VII; **have one's eye's half closed** spwiingwéexiin VAI, sohpwiingwée=xiin VAI; **have one's eyes closed, close one's eyes** sohpwíingweew VAI, sohpwíingweew VAI; **have one's hand(s) closed tightly** maskaniilun=jéexiin VAI; **pout, close one's mouth** spwutóoneew VAI; **sew s.o. closed** spwiikwáaleew VTA; **sew s.t. closed** spwíikwam VTI1A; **sew things closed** spwiikwáakeew VAI.

**close by** ADV **appear to be close by, look to be close by** peexŭwiinéakwat VII, peexŭwiinéakwsuw VAI; **close by** nalíish PC; **close by** náhnalii PC **Who's that close by working?** 'Awéen há ná náhnalii éenda-lalóhkeet?'; **close by** *(diminutive)* náhnaliish PC **I'm going a little ways.** 'Náhnaliish ndá.'; **crawl close by** peexŭwíikwsuw VAI; **drive close by** peexŭwuchéhleew VAI; **near to, close by, nearly** péexwiish PC **He has a little ways to the end (of the road).** 'Péexwiish wihkwáa=meew.', **I'm not going far.** 'Pée=xwiish náh ndá.'; **run close by** pee=xŭwaaméhleew VAI; **sound close by** peexŭwihtáakwat VII, peexŭwihtáak=wsuw VAI; **walk close by** peexŭwóo=xweew VAI.

**closely** ADV **be closely related to s.o.**, **want to be related to s.o.** àhwaan=góomeew VTA; **cut s.t. animate closely** *(as whiskers)* chíikwsheew VTA; **cut s.t. animate closely** shíikwsheew VTA; **cut s.t. closely** chíikwshum VTI1B; **cut s.t. closely** shíikwshum VTI1A.

**cloth** N **cloth, cotton, rag** wshapakwíi=wan NI; **black cloth** nzukshapakwíi=wan NI; **cloth for wiping** kaas'híikan NI; **new cloth** wuskshapakwíiwan NI.

**clothes** N **buy s.o. clothes to wear, get s.o. clothes to wear, dress s.o.** akwúneew VTA; **change one's clothes**

aashŭwákuw VAI; **change one's clothes** áandakuw VAI; **dress haphazardly, dress hurriedly, throw on one's clothes** pàpŭlakéechpuw VAI; **get undressed, take off one's clothes** ktunéechpuw VAI; **have (extra) clothes in layers, have on more clothes than someone else** pihtawákuw VAI **I am covered in three layers, I am dressed in three layers.** 'Nxú mbihta= wákwi.'; **have plenty of clothes** wŭyákakuw VAI; **muddy clothes** asíiskŭwii-éhakwiing NI; **take s.o.'s clothes off for s.o., take s.t. out for s.o.** ktunŭmáweew VTAO; **undress s.o., take off all of s.o.'s clothes** sheexkalúneew VTA **She's just going to undress me again.** 'Kách wáak ápih shúkw nzheexkalúnukw.'; **wear clean clothes** apíilakuw VAI; **wear dirty clothes** aníiskakuw VAI; **wear new clothes** wúskakuw VAI.

**clothes dryer** N peengwsíikan NI.

**clothes iron** N chiingaalsíikan NI, shaax= kùtsíikan NI.

**clothes pin** N kŭlahkhwíikan NI.

**clothing** N éhakwiing VII; **dress raggedly, wear ragged clothing** piikwshák= uw VAI; **have an item of clothing undone** *(especially fly of pants)* kchax= kíixteew VAI; **put s.t. on** *(of clothing)* píind VTI3 **I put my pants on.** 'Mbíin= dun mbulóokum.'; **put s.t. on for s.o.** *(of clothing)* píindaweew VTAO.

**cloud** N akúmahkw NA; **be a black cloud** nzukakumáhkwat VII; **be a blue cloud, be blue** *(of clouds)* oolihka= kumáhkwat VII; **be clouds coming in this direction** peetakumáhkwat VII.

**cloudy** ADJ **be cloudy** akumáhkwat VII.

**club** N **club, baseball bat** pakandíikan NI.

**cluck** VI **cluck, make a noise like a chicken** kwŭlukhwámeew VAI.

**coal** N **coal, piece of coal** máhkateew NI; **coal oil** káanoos NA.

**coarse** ADJ **be big, be coarse** *(of something stringlike)* xwáhtakat VII; **be rough, be coarse** kaaxkashúsuw VAI, káaxkasheew VII; **rough, coarse** kaaxkashii- PN **Coarse flour.** 'Káax= kashii-lohkhámun.', **Coarse cloth.** 'Káaxkashii-wshapakwíiwan.'

**coat** N kóot NI; **dress, coat** weenda= kwíiwan NI; **leather coat** xáyii-kóot NI; **wear a black coat** nzúkii-koot= hámeew VAI; **wear a coat** koothám= eew VAI; **wear a coat with a long tail** kwŭníi-shkwúnayii-koothámeew VAI; **wear a long coat, have a long coat on** kwŭníi-koothámeew VAI; **wear more than one coat** pihtawiikóoteew VAI.

**cob** N **corn cob** xwaskóonzhuy, xwash= kóonzhuy NI.

**coffin** N **chest, trunk, small box, casket, coffin** kúsht NI.

**cold** ADJ **be cold** takwáchuw VAI, théew VII, thúsuw VAI; **cold** thii- PN **Cold tea.** 'Thíi-tíi'; **be a cold day** tháhkameew VII; **be a cold night** thíi-tpíhkat VII; **be a cold wind** tháxun VII; **be cold ground** thahkéeyeew VII; **be cold looking, look cold** thiináakwat VII, thiináakwsuw VAI; **be cold water** thupéekat VII, tháapŭweew VII; **be cold, be cool** *(of houses, of rooms)* thiikamíikat VII; **become cold, get cold** thíhleew VII; **cold meat** thée= wakw NI; **cold water** thúpuy NI; **get cold easily** ayáhwachuw VAI; **have a cold face** thíingweew VAI; **have a cold hand** thunáxkeew VAI; **have a drink of something cold** thíisŭmuw VAI; **have cold feet** saasiitéepookw VAI, thusíiteew VAI; **have cold hands** saasŭlunjéepookw VAI; **look cold** takwachŭwiináakwsuw VAI; **spring well, cold water** thupéekw NI.

**cold** N **have a cold** máatachuw VAI **He has a bad cold.** 'Kíhchu-máata= chuw.'; **be red with cold** máxkachuw

VAI, máxkatun VII; **shiver from the cold** núngachuw VAI.

**collapse** VI mŭlakwíhleew VAI, mŭlak=wíhleew VII.

**collapse** VT **collapse s.t., tear s.t. down, dismantle s.t.** *(using the hands)* mŭlákwŭnum VTI1B; **be collapsed by the wind** mŭlákwxun VII.

**collar** N kálul NI; **have a collar on it** wehwahkweelŭniingháasuw VII; **put a collar on s.o., put a scarf on s.o.** wahkwéelŭneew VTA; **scarf, collar, necktie, horse's collar** wehwah=kwéelŭniing NI.

**collection** N **take up the collection** *(in church)* maawéenŭmeew VAI; **plate** N **hay rake, collection plate in church** maaweeníikan NI.

**collection plate** N **make a contribution, put money in the collection plate** maawéewapuw VAI, máawapuw VAI.

**collective** ADJ **collectively held land, land that belongs to the band** tput=aawáhkuy NI; **in common, collective, owned by the band** tputáawii PC **Doctor for everyone; doctor hired by Indian Affairs.** 'Tpútaawii ndáaktul.', **The community hall.** 'Tputáawii éenda-maawéhlaang.'

**colour** N **be a blueish colour, have a blue tinge to it** oolihkŭléexiin VAI, oolihkŭléexun VII; **be a brownish colour, have a brown tinge to it, be a greyish colour, have a grey tinge to it** wiipongwŭléexiin VAI, wiipon=gwŭléexun VII; **be blue in colour, be blue-coloured** oolihkaapamúkwat VII, oolihkaapamúkwsuw VAI; **be a dull colour** mataapamúkwat VII, mataapa=múkwsuw VAI; **be a greenish colour, have a green tinge to it** askaskwŭ=léexiin VAI, askaskwŭléexun VII; **be a plain colour, be plain coloured** kahkanaapamúkwat VII, kahkanaa=pamúkwsuw VAI; **be a reddish colour, have a red tinge to it** maxkŭ=léexiin VAI, maxkŭléexun VII; **be a yellowish colour, have a yellow tinge to it** wiisaawŭléexiin VAI, wii=saawŭléexun VII; **be brightly coloured, wear bright colours** ktakŭ=léexiin VAI; **be brown coloured, be grey coloured** wiipongwaapamúkwat VII, wiipongwaapamúkwsuw VAI; **be dark-coloured, be a blackish colour, have a black tinge to it** nzukŭ=léexiin VAI, nzukŭléexun VII; **be green in colour, be green-coloured** askas=kwaapamúkwat VII, askaskwaapa=múkwsuw VAI; **be light in colour** *(s.t. animate)*, **be a whitish colour, have a white tinge to it** waapŭléexiin VAI, waapŭléexun VII; **be red coloured liquid** maxkáapŭweew VII; **dye s.t. animate a certain colour** lúchaseew VTA; **dye s.t., dye s.t. a certain colour** lúchasum VTI1B **I dyed my hair.** 'Niiláxkal ndulchásŭmun.'; **have disorganized colours, have mixed up colours** pàpŭlakaapamúkwat VII, pàpŭlakaapamúkwsuw VAI; **shine brightly, be brilliant** *(especially light)*, **wear bright colours** saapŭ=léexiin VAI.

**colour** VT **be brightly coloured** ktakŭ=léexun VII, wŭlaapamúkwat VII, wŭ=luléexun VII, wŭlaapamúkwsuw VAI; **be brightly coloured, be dressed up** wŭluléexiin VAI; **be brightly coloured, wear bright colours** ktakŭléexiin VAI; **be coloured in a certain manner, be seen in a certain manner** laapamúkwat VII **It can be seen through.** 'Éeshu-laapamúkwat.'; **be coloured in a certain manner** *(s.t. animate)*, **be seen in a certain manner** laapamúkwsuw VAI; **be red coloured** maxkaapamúkwat VII, max=kaapamúkwsuw VAI; **be yellow coloured** wiisaawaapamúkwat VII, wiisaawaapamúkwsuw VAI; **have light-coloured eyes, have grey eyes**

waaxeelíingweew VAI; **shine brightly, be brilliant, be brightly coloured** *(especially light)* saapŭléexun VII.

**comb** N chiixíikan NA; **fine comb** máan=zakwus NA, máasakwus NA.

**comb** VT **comb one's (own) hair** wŭlíi=kwameew VAI; **comb s.t.** *(of hair)* chíixham VTI1A; **comb s.o.'s hair** wŭliikwamáweew VTA; **comb s.o.'s hair for them** chiixhámaweew VTAO.

**come** VI **come, come here** péew VAI **You're almost there.** 'Péexoot náh kpá.'; **come from a certain place** *(quickly)* wunjíhleew VAI; **come from a certain place** wunjíixiin VAI, wun=jíixun VII **They came from the road.** 'Áaneeng wunjíixŭnool.'; **come from a certain place, come from there** wúm VAI **He came from Chatham.** 'Chétum wúm.'; **come here angry, come in this direction while angry** peetanóongsuw VAI; **come here crying, come towards the speaker crying** peetéewtam VOTI1; **come here flying, fly towards the speaker** pee=chíhleew VAI; **come here riding on horseback, ride towards the speaker** peethóomeew VAI; **come here singing, come in this direction singing** peetaláamuw VAI; **come here to sell things, come here selling things** peetaahóosuw VAI; **come here to visit, come here visiting** peetootée=wuw VAI; **come out** *(of water)* ktup=éhleew VII; **come to this conclusion** peeteelúndam VOTI1; **come together, join together** takwíhleew VII, ta=kwihléewak VAI *usually plural;* **come too late** mehtxihkáasuw VAI; **come too late, miss an opportunity, miss one's chance** mehtxíhkeew VAI **The service was over when I arrived, I came too late.** 'Kíishi-maawéewiin náh peeyayáane, nemehtxíhke.'; **come, come here** peeyéewuw VII **Something good is coming** 'Peeyée=wuw wúlu-léek.'; **come, come here** peeyéeyuw VII **The cold weather is here.** 'Peeyéeyuw téeheek.', **The sickness is coming.** 'Peeyéeyuw wiinamalsuwáakan.'; **go up, come up, start to come up** uspíhleew VAI, uspíhleew VII; **row this way, come here paddling, paddle towards the speaker** péetham VOTI1; **run here, run in this direction, come here running** peetahtakíhleew VAI; **walk here, walk in this direction, come here walking** peetóoxweew VAI; **use s.t. to come here, use s.t. to come in this direction** peetawéeheew VAIO; **come across swimming, swim across towards the speaker** peetaashŭwíh=leew VAI **Before he got across to the other side.** 'Eéskwa káamung pee=taashŭwíhlaakw.'; **come apart** chpíhleew VII.

**come back** VI **return, come back** kwáxkiiw VAI-S **I'm back.** 'Méhch wáak mbéech-kwáxki.'; **come back from cutting wood** aapanáxeew VAI; **come back from dancing, return from dancing** áapkeew VAI; **come back from hunting** aapaláwiiw VAI-S; **come back from planting** aapahkíi=heew VAI; **come back from working** aapalóhkeew VAI.

**come behind** VT **follow and come behind s.o., come behind s.o., come from behind s.o.** wtéhkaweew VTA.

**come down** VI **come down, climb down** niixakóosuw VAI; **come down, descend, get out of a vehicle** níixiiw VAI-S.

**come inside** VI **come inside** piinjíikeew VAI **He came in.** 'Péech-piinjíikeew.'

**come off** VI **fall off, come off, become detached** mahkíhleew VAI, mahkíh=leew VII.

**come out** VI **come out, go out, go to the bathroom** kchíiw VAI-S **I came out of the house.** 'Wiikwáhmung nóonj-kchíim.'; **fall out, run out, come out** kchíhleew VAI, kchíhleew VII; **come out** *(of liquid)* saakpéhleew VII.

**come through** VI **be the sun coming through** eeshŭláandeew VII.

**come to** VI **come to, be aware** weewáa=tam VAI **He doesn't know what's going on around him.** 'Máh weewaa=tamóowi.'; **regain consciousness, come to one's senses, sober up** taaxpéhleew VAI **I came to all of a sudden.** 'Wíixkwii méhch ndaax=péhla.', **I just came to.** 'Lúkih ndaaxpéhlaan.'

**come up** VI **be the sun coming up** ktanaxkíhleew VII **East, where the sun comes up.** 'Éhunda-ktanaxkíh=laak.'; **grow unevenly, grow crookedly, come up crooked** piimíikuw VAI, piimíikun VII; **sprout, come up** saakíikuw VAI, saakíikun VII; **sprout, come up** *(out of the ground)* sáakuw VAI, sáakun VII.

**come up to** VT **attack s.o., come up to s.o.** kwihlóotaweew VTA.

**comfortable** ADJ **find that s.o. feels better, find that s.o. feels good, feel comfortable with s.o.** wŭlámameew VTA.

**commodity** N **lack a commodity, run out of something** txíhlateew VAI.

**common** ADJ **in common, collective, owned by the band** tputáawii PC **Doctor for everyone; doctor hired by Indian Affairs.** 'Tpútaawii ndáaktul.', **The community hall.** 'Tputáawii éenda-maawéhlaang.'

**common-law** N **live common-law** ma=tápuw VAI.

**compete** VI **want to fight, want to compete** katoonáasuw VAI; VT **want to fight s.o., want to kill s.o., want to compete with s.o.** katóonaleew VTA.

**competent** ADJ **think s.o. to be smart, have a high opinion of s.o., think s.o. competent** kshéelŭmeew VTA.

**competition** N **be first, be first in line, be first in a competition** shayéexiin VAI; **beat s.o. in a race, beat s.o. in a competition** méelameew VTA; **take a big start in a competition, take a jump in a competition, take a leap in a competition, get a running start** wundaaméhleew VAI.

**complete** VT **completed action** kiish- PV **I went to town after he paid me.** 'Ootéeneeng ndá kíish-eenhawíite.'

**completely** ADV **be shiny bald, be completely bald** waaxamóhkweew VAI; **get rid of s.t., completely dispose of s.t., sell all of s.t.** weemalóhkeew VAIO **I gave away all of my belongings.** 'Nŭweemalóhkeen nehláata=maan.'; **wear s.t. out by washing it, wash s.t. completely, wash s.t. right out, wash s.t. away, remove s.t. by washing** mehtapátoow VTI2.

**completion** N **cook s.t. animate done, cook s.t. animate to completion** kíish'seew VTA; **cook s.t. done, cook s.t. to completion** kíish'sum VTI1B.

**conclusion** N **come to this conclusion** peeteelúndam VOTI1.

**condemn** VT **condemn s.o., want s.o. to die, think s.o. incapable of doing something** kundéelŭmeew VTA; **be condemned to die for evil deeds, die deservedly, be thought incapable** kundeelŭmúkwsuw VAI.

**condemnation** N **condemnation, being thought incapable** kundeelŭmukw=suwáakan NI.

**condition** N **be in a frightening condition, be in a dangerous condition** kxwaawíixiin VAI, kxwaawíixun VII; **better condition, improved condition, better state, improved state** míingasa PC **It's better now, it shuts well (of a door).** 'Míingasa kwáy wŭlú-kpíhle.', **It's good that you came early.** 'Míingasa ktáapwi-pá.';

**change, take a turn for the worse, have one's medical condition worsen** aanjíhleew VAI; **make s.o.'s condition worse** máatŭneew VTA.

**confused** ADJ **be mixed up, be confused** chàchanaandpéhleew VAI.

**conscious** ADJ **regain consciousness, come to one's senses, sober up** taaxpéhleew VAI **I came to all of a sudden.** 'Wíixkwii méhch ndaax=péhla.', **I just came to.** 'Lúkih ndaaxpéhlaan.'

**considerable** ADJ **way over there, over there a considerable distance** yóo=lak PR.

**consistency** N **be thick in consistency** táhtakan VII; **thick in consistency** tahtakii- PN **Thick milk.** 'Táhtakii-mŭlúk.'

**constantly** ADV **be constantly in motion, be constantly in operation** ngumeewíhleew VAI **My hammer's going all the time.** 'Ndahámŭlum ngumeewíhleew.'; **be constantly in motion, be constantly in operation** ngumeewíhleew VII.

**constipated** ADJ **be constipated** kpas=kíhleew VAI, kpíitŭyeew VAI, aalŭwás=ktuw VAI, pwaawásktuw VAI.

**contact** N **make a hole in s.t. animate by forceful contact, make a hole in s.t. animate with an instrument, make a hole in s.t. animate with a projectile** pkwúlaweew VTA; **make a hole in s.t. by forceful contact, make a hole in s.t. with an instrument, make a hole in s.t. with a projectile** pkwúlam VTI1A; **run into s.o., make physical contact with s.o.** alíhkaweew VTA; **run into s.t., make physical contact with s.t.** alíhkam VTI1A; **touch, make contact, be in contact with the ground, be in contact with the floor** mshíixiin VAI, mshíixun VII **It's hanging down and it almost touches (the floor).** 'Pŭ=naapéhleew wéenaa mshíixun.', **My feet are touching the floor.** 'Mshíi=xŭnool nzíital áhkiing.'

**contact** VT **contact and brush up against s.o.** laalihtéexŭmeew VTA; **contact and brush up against s.t.** laalihtéextoow VTI2; **contact s.t. in a certain manner** láham VTI1A **You got it right ('you hit it right').** 'Kóolu-ná -aláhŭmun.'; **have one's feet brushing against a surface, have one's feet contacting a surface** chasksiitéexiin VAI; **touch s.o., make contact with s.o., run into s.o., hit s.o.** aláheew VTA; **touch s.t., run into s.t., drive into s.t., make contact with s.t. forcefully, hit s.t.** aláham VTI1A **I ran into it.** 'Ná ndalhámun.'

**contain** VT **contain liquid level with the top** *(s.t. animate)*, **be liquid level to the top of container** tpuskŭwúp=eew VAI.

**container** N ahtíikan NI; **container, trunk** ehahtíikeeng VII; **make s.t. level with the top of a container** *(of liquids)* tpuskŭwáapŭweew VAIO; **place s.t. animate level with the top of container** tpuskŭwáhleew VTA; **place s.t. level with the top of container** tpuskŭwáhtoow VTI2.

**content** ADJ **be content, be unworried about anything, be unafraid** nalaw=áhkeew VAI; **make s.o. content, satisfy s.o.** teepiilawéeheew VTA **He/she satisfies me.** 'Ndeepiilawéehaaw.'

**contentedly** ADV **peacefully, quietly, contentedly** naláwii PC **He lives there quietly.** 'Naláwii wíikuw.'; **peacefully, quietly, contentedly** aayaláwii PC **He's sitting quietly.** 'Aayaláwii laalŭmátapuw.', **They're playing quietly.** 'Aayaláwii meela=wúsŭwak.'

**contorted** ADJ **have a wrinkled face, have a contorted face** wchulíin=gweew VAI; **have one's face wrin-**

**kled, have one's face contorted, pout, be in a temper, be discontented** *(as if about to cry)* wchuliin=gwéexiin VAI.

**contribution** N **make a contribution, put money in the collection plate** maawéewapuw VAI, máawapuw VAI.

**conversation** N **butt in, disrupt the conversation** ìhŭlutóonheew VAI; **take part in a conversation, butt into a conversation** wiittóonheew VAI.

**convert** N **Christian Indian, Moravian convert** kéendŭwees NA.

**cook** N nehnatúpwiis NA, **be a good cook** nihtaawatúpuw VAI.

**cook** VI **be done cooking, be finished cooking** *(of cooks)* kiishatúpuw VAI; **be crushed down, get reduced in cooking** shkwíhleew VAI; **be done cooking, be finished cooking** kíish'=suw VAI, kíishteew VII; **cook** ndúpuw VAI; **cook by frying** *(of cooks)* sa=lásŭmeew VAI; **fall apart in cooking, boil down, be cooked down** shkwúchasuw VAI, shkwúchateew VII.

**cook** VT **cook s.t., cook s.t. animate** ndúpuw VAIO **I cooked them whole.** 'Nŭmuschéewu-ndupwíinak.'; **cook s.t. animate done, cook s.t. animate to completion** kíish'seew VTA; **cook s.t. done, cook s.t. to completion** kíish'sum VTI1B; **undercook s.t. animate, cook s.t. animate raw** ask=cháseew VTA; **undercook s.t., cook s.t. raw** askchásum VTI1B; **undercook s.t., cook s.t. raw, cook s.t. rare** askatúpuw VAIO; **be burnt up, fall to pieces, be in pieces after being cooked** shkwúteew VII, shkwútsuw VAI; **be done cooking, be finished cooking** *(of cooks)* kiishatúpuw VAI; **fall apart in cooking, boil down, be cooked down** shkwúchasuw VAI.

**cookie** N shookŭlapwáanush NI.

**cooking** N **boil over** *(of one's cooking)*, **have one's cooking boil over** paal=chásŭmeew VAI.

**cool** ADJ **be a cool evening** thíi-láakuw VII; **be cold, be cool** *(of houses, of rooms)* thiikamíikat VII.

**cool down** VT **cool s.o. down** thíhlaleew VTA; **cool s.t. down** thíhlatoow VTI2.

**cordwood** N káatxakw NI; **cut cordwood** kaatxákhweew VAI.

**cork** N **plug, cork** kpaskhíikan NI, kpas=kŭníikan NI.

**corn** N xwáskwiim NI; **corn soup** kaa=háhkwteew NI; **green corn** askxás=kwiim NI; **husk corn** pxwiináskweew VAI; **lye corn** pxwásŭmeew VAI; **new corn, green corn** wuskxáskwiim NI; **shell corn** pawiingweehíikeew VAI.

**corn bread** N xwaskwiimápwaan NI, xwaskwiimŭnápwaan NI.

**corn cob** N xwaskóonzhuy NI; xwash=kóonzhuy NI.

**corn husk** N **corn husk mat** wtéeskwii-ehahpalíhkeeng NI; **corn husk, corn husk mat** wtéeskw NI.

**corn meal** N **corn meal bread, Johnny cake** wiisáamapwaan NI.

**cornbread** N **boiled cornbread** choos=kŭnápwaan NI.

**corner** N **be the corner** *(of the house)* siingiikamíikat VII; **be the inside angle of a corner** póocheew VII **Go stand the broom in the corner.** 'Eénda-póocheek máw-níipatool chiikhíikan.'; **be the outside angle of a corner** síingeew VII **The corner of the house.** 'Éenda-síingeek wíi=kwahm.'; **be the outside angle of a corner** síingsuw VAI.

**cornmeal** N **cornmeal mush, oatmeal** nzáapaan NI.

**cornstalk** N siixiipahkwáawan NI.

**correct** ADJ **be correct, be good** wŭlíi=xun VII **Your hat looks good on you.** 'Ktaakongwéepuy wŭlíixun.'

**correctly** ADV **be even, be in order, lie correctly** mayaawíixun VII; **place s.o.**

**correctly, make s.o. be correctly arranged, straighten s.o. up, arrange s.o. correctly** mayaawíixŭmeew VTA; **place s.t. correctly, make s.t. be correctly arranged, straighten s.t. up** mayaawíixtoow VTI2; **read s.t. animate correctly** wŭlakíimeew VTA; **read s.t. correctly** wŭlakíindam VTI1A; **straighten out, go straight, go quickly in the right direction, drive correctly** mayaawíhleew VAI; **work well, do one's work correctly** nihtaawalóhkeew VAI.

**corset** N **jacket, corset, vest** chékut NI.

**cost** VI **have a certain value, cost a certain amount** láawatuw VAI, láawatuw VII; **be expensive, cost a lot** aman=gaawatúwal VII *usually plural.*

**cotton** ADJ **cotton batting** kátoon NI; **cloth, cotton, rag** wshapakwíiwan NI.

**cough** N **have a cough, have a coughing disease** xwukwíineew VAI; **have whooping cough** aapchíhleew VAI, àhaapchíhleew VAI.

**cough** VI xwúkw VAI *once*, wáwxwukw VAI *more than once*.

**could** VI **should, would, can, could** áa PC **We (inclusive) should hide.** 'Kii=lóona áa kaatapíhna.', **I'd really like to go with you (plural).** 'Píish áa móxa kŭwíingu-wiicheewŭlóhmwa.'

**council** N **hold a council** aachŭmoh=kéewak VAI *usually plural.*

**count** VI **read, count** akíinzuw VAI.

**count** VT **count s.t. animate, read s.t. animate** akíimeew VTA; **read s.t., count s.t.** akíindam VTI1A.

**cousin** N **my female cousin** ndaang=wsóxkweew NAD; **my male cousin** ndáangwus NAD.

**cover** N **dress s.o. nicely, put bedcovers on s.o.** wŭlakwunáheew VTA; **take the covers off oneself** paaxkeehúnzuw VAI; **throw the cover off s.o., throw the cover off s.t.** paaxkeeyáaheew VAIO.

**cover** VT **cover s.o. up** mtákhweew VTA; **cover s.t. up** mtákhwam VTI1A; **bury s.o., cover s.o. over** psúndheew VTA **He was covered up, buried.** 'Psúnd=haaw.'; **bury s.t., cover s.t. over** psúndham VTI1A; **be covered in excrement** móoyuw VAI; **be covered in shingles** *(of a house)* apahahkáasuw VII; **be covered in snow, have snow on oneself** koonóowuw VAI **I'm all covered in snow.** 'Wéemu táa ndúlukoonóowiin.'; **be covered with water** psúndpeew VII, psúndpeew VAI; **be covered, have a lid, be frozen over** kpátun VII; **cover one's ears, have one's ears covered** kpaxéexiin VAI, kpoxwéexiin VAI; **cover s.o.'s ears** *(using the hands)* kpaxéeneew VTA, kpoxwéeneew VTA; **cover s.o.'s ears** kpaxéexŭmeew VTA; **cover s.t. with water** psúndpeew VAIO; **have boards on it, be covered in boards** pasii=kaaxkhwáasuw VII **My house has boards on it.** 'Wíikŭyaan pasii=kaaxkhwáasuw.'

**cover over** VT **be covered over with water** wanúpeew VAI, wanúpeew VII; **cover s.o. over with water, cover s.t. animate over with water** wanúpa=leew VTA; **cover s.t. over with water** wanúpatoow VTI2; **be covered up** mtakhwáasuw VAI, mtakhwáasuw VII.

**covering** N **have the covering of something be hit and knocked off, have the skin of something be hit and knocked off** pŭlakihteeháasuw VAI; **hit s.o. and knock the covering off them, hit s.o. and knock the skin off them** pŭlakihtéeheew VTA; **skin s.t. animate, remove the covering from s.t. animate** pxwíineew VTA; **skin s.t., remove the covering from s.t., shell s.t.** *(of corn)* pxwíinam VTI1A; **take the covering off s.t. animate, take the outer layer off s.t. animate, remove the shell from s.t.**

**animate** pŭlákŭneew VTA; **take the covering off s.t., take the outer layer off s.t., remove the shell from s.t.** pŭlákŭnum VTI1A.

**cow** N kóowuy NA; **cow droppings, cow excrement** kóoychuy NI; **cow shed, cow barn** kooyíikaan NI; **have many cows** xweelkóoyeew VAI; **look for a cow, look for cows** ndawakóoyeew VAI.

**coward** N **crybaby, weakling, coward** míikwul NA; **be a coward** mataxk=túneew VAI; **be a crybaby, be a weakling, be a coward** míikwŭluw VAI.

**crabby** ADJ **be a crabby person** ma=noongchéetŭyeew VAI.

**crack** N **crack in the buttocks** pasiitŭ=yeewáakan NI; **have a crack in one's buttocks** pasíitŭyeew VAI.

**crack** VI **crack, fall and crack, fall and get chipped** kwashihtéexun VII.

**crack** VT **crack s.t.** pwáhkham VTI1A; **crack s.t. animate** pwáhkheew VTA; **crack s.t. animate, drop and crack s.t. animate, break s.t. animate in half** pasíixŭmeew VTA; **crack s.t., drop and crack s.t., break s.t. in half** pasíixtoow VTI2; **hit and crack s.o., hit and crack s.t. animate** pwahkihtéeheew VTA; **hit and crack s.t.** pwahkihtéeham VTI1A; **dice s.t. animate, cut s.t. animate up into small pieces, chop s.t. animate, crack s.t. animate** píikheew VTA; **dice s.t., cut s.t. up into small pieces, chop s.t. up, crack s.t.** píikham VTI1A; **have a cracked head, have a cut on one's head, fall and crack one's head, fall and cut one's head** pa=saandpéexiin VAI; **have a cracked head, have a cut on one's head** pa=sáandpeew VAI; **be cracked, be split in two, be in half** pasát VII **It must be cracked.** 'Sháxk éet pasát.'; **be cracked, be split in two, be in half** pasúsuw VAI; **crack nuts** pakásŭmeew VAI; **crack one's head** pwahkaand=péexiin VAI.

**cradleboard** N ambíisoon NI.

**cramp** N **have a cramp** wchihkwíhleew VAI; **have cramps** wàwchihkwíhleew VII.

**cranberry** N páakiim NI; **cranberry bush** paakiimíinzhuy NA.

**crank** N **crank, handle for turning, hand grinder** tùpŭníikan NI.

**crank** VT **turn s.o. around, crank s.t. animate** *(using the hands)* túpŭneew VTA; **turn s.t. around, crank s.t.** *(using the hands)* túpŭnum VTI1B; **wind s.t. animate** *(as a clock)*, **crank s.t. animate** *(as a car)* tùpáhkhweew VTA; **turn a crank, crank things, turn things around** tùpŭníikeew VAI.

**crawl** VI **crawl in a certain manner, crawl in a certain direction** líikwsuw VAI; **crawl across** aashŭwíikwsuw VAI; **crawl ahead** shayeewiikwsíh=leew VAI; **crawl ahead, crawl in the lead** shayeewíikwsuw VAI; **crawl around, move around** msiikwsíh=leew VAI; **crawl away** alumíikwsuw VAI; **crawl backwards** ashahkchee=wíikwsuw VAI; **crawl by, crawl along** pŭmíikwsuw VAI; **crawl close by** peexŭwíikwsuw VAI; **crawl down** chiixíikwsuw VAI; **crawl downwards** niixíikwsuw VAI; **crawl from a certain place, crawl for a certain reason** wunjíikwsuw VAI **I crawled from over there.** 'Yéelak noonjíikwsi.'; **crawl here and there, crawl about** apaamíikwsuw VAI; **crawl here, crawl towards the speaker** peechíikwsuw VAI; **crawl in a circle, crawl around something** wiiwŭníikwsuw VAI; **crawl inside** piinjíikwsuw VAI **Then he crawled into the house.** 'Nál wtúlu- wiikwáhmung -piinjíikwsiin.'; **crawl out** kchíikwsuw VAI; **crawl quickly** kshiikwsíhleew VAI, kshíik=

wsuw VAI; **crawl sideways, crawl on the diagonal** piimíikwsuw VAI; **crawl slowly** ashahwíikwsuw VAI, chkaw=iikwshíishuw VAI; **crawl through** *(a space)* eeshíikwsuw VAI; **crawl through an opening** pkwíikwsuw VAI; **crawl to fetch s.o., crawl after s.o.** naachíikwsuw VAIO; **crawl up** uspíikwsuw VAI; **crawl zigzag** pàp=tukíikwsuw VAI; **disappear, crawl out of sight** wchíikwsuw VAI; **sneak around crawling, crawl secretly** kiimíikwsuw VAI; **start to crawl** noochíikwsuw VAI **turn around while crawling** kwŭlupíikwsuw VAI; **be tired of crawling** shiiwíikwsuw VAI.

**crazy** ADJ **be crazy from drinking, be silly from drinking** kpucheewíisŭ=muw VAI; **become silly, become crazy** kpuchéhleew VAI.

**creak** VI kàktóohŭweew VII; **creak, squeak, make a creaking sound, make a squeaking sound** *(s.t animate)* kíiskŭweew VAI, kíiskŭweew VII; **creak, squeak** kwíiskwsuw VAI, kwíiskweew VII.

**cream** N pootŭlupéexun VII **He bought some butter.** 'Pootŭlupéexung máh=lam.'

**Creator** N **the Creator, He who created us** kiisheelŭmúkweengw VTA *conjunct order form only.*

**credit** N **be a bad risk for credit, be a 'poor pay'** màmateenhíikeew VAI; **get credit, be given credit, 'get trusted'** lahtkwéehaaw VTA *usually with indefinite subject.*

**creek** N shiipóoshush NI.

**cricket** N chŭlóochŭloosh NA.

**criticize** VT **criticize s.o., abuse s.o. verbally, 'run s.o. down'** akusha=kuníimeew VTA, akushíimeew VTA.

**crooked** ADJ **be crooked** pŭmíixiin VAI pŭmíixun VII, ; **be crooked, be lopsided, be uneven** píimeew VII **Your cane is crooked.** 'Ktaláawan píi=meew.'; **be crooked, be winding** pàptúkeew VII **The river is winding.** 'Pàptúkeew nú síipuw.'; **be a crooked road** piimatéexun VII, pàptuka=téexun VII; **be crooked** *(of something string-like)* pàptukáhtakat VII; **be uneven ground, be crooked ground** piimahkéeyeew VII; **grow crooked, grow sideways** pŭmiichíikun VII **My tooth came up crooked.** 'Pŭmiichíi=kun níipiit.'; **have a crooked back** piimpóxkwaneew VAI; **have a crooked mouth, have a lopsided mouth** piimtoonéexiin VAI; **have a crooked tooth** piimaníikeew VAI; **have crooked legs** piimkaatéeyeew VII; **have crooked teeth** apiimaníikeew VAI; **have crooked teeth** piimoxkwaníikeew VAI; **knock s.o. sideways, knock s.t. crooked** *(by shot, by physical contact, with a projectile)* piimŭláweew VTA; **knock s.t. sideways, knock s.t. crooked** *(by shot, by physical contact, with a projectile)* píimŭlam VTI1A; **lean over, lean to one side** *(s.t. animate)*, **be crooked, lean** piimíixiin VAI **You drove around the Four Corners too fast and you were leaning.** 'Koosáamu-kshú-wiiwŭníhlaan éen=da-aashŭwatéexung, kwŭlúp kpiimíi=xiin.'; **lean over, lean to one side, be on crooked** piimíixun VII; **lean s.t. to one side, put s.t. on crooked** pii=míixtoow VTI2; **leave crooked tracks** pàptukéelham VOTI1; **walk crookedly, walk on a crooked road** pàptukóo=xweew VAI.

**crookedly** ADV **be written crookedly** pàptukeekháasuw VII; **chase s.o. crookedly** pàptukshíhkaweew VTA; **drive crookedly** pàptukchéhleew VAI; **fall sideways, drive crookedly** piim=chéhleew VAI; **go crookedly while riding on horseback** pàptukhóo=meew VAI; **go crookedly, fly crookedly, fly on an erratic course** pàp=

tukíhleew VAI; **grow crookedly** waa=kíikuw VAI; waakíikun VII; **grow crookedly, grow sideways** pŭmii=chíikuw VAI; **grow unevenly, grow crookedly, come up crooked** piimíi=kuw VAI, piimíikun VII; **hang crookedly** piimaapéhleew VII, piimaapéh=leew VAI; **lean over, sit crookedly, lie crookedly** piimchéexiin VAI; **lie crookedly** piimáangweew VAI; **lie crookedly** pàptukíixiin VAI, pàptukíi=xun VII; **lie crookedly, lie sideways, lie on it's side** pŭmiichíixun VII, pŭmiichíixiin VAI; **run away crookedly** pàptukshíimuw VAI; **sew s.t. animate crookedly** pàptukiikwáaleew VTA, waakiikwáaleew VTA; **sew s.t. crookedly** pàptukíikwam VTI1A, waa=kíikwam VTI1A; **sew things crookedly** pàptukiikwáakeew VAI, waakii=kwáakeew VAI; **sit crookedly** piimoh=kwéepuw VAI, píimapuw VAI; **walk crookedly, walk on a crooked road** pàptukóoxweew VAI; **wriggle, go crookedly** pàptukiikwsíhleew VAI.

**cross** N aashtehteehíikan NI; **crucify s.o., put s.o. on the cross** aashtehtéeheew VTA.

**cross** VI **cross in a boat** kwaxkakáham VOTI1.

**cross** VT **cross one's legs** aashŭwiix=kéexiin VAI; **cross s.t.** aashŭwíixtoow VTI2; **have one's legs crossed** aashŭ=wukaatéexiin VAI.

**cross-eyed** ADJ **be cross-eyed** piimatee=líingweew VAI.

**crossroad** N **be a crossroads, the Four Corners** *(main intersection near band office at Moraviantown, Ontario)* aashŭwatéexun VII **I'm going to the Four Corners.** 'Aashŭwatéexun numáw-níipawi.'

**crosswise** ADV **lie crosswise, be twisted, be at an angle, lie at an angle, be lopsided** piimoxkwíixiin VAI.

**crow** N áahaas NA, aaháasuw NA.

**crow** VI **make a noise like an animal, make a crowing noise** akeenjíimuw VAI; **start off singing** *(especially in church)*, **burst out crowing** *(of roosters)* kundaláamuw VAI.

**crowd out** VT **crowd s.o. out** achíika=weew VTA.

**crowded** ADJ **be in a group of people crowded close together, make one's way through the crowd** kàkchúka=muw VAI.

**crucify** VT **crucify s.o., nail s.o. up, nail s.o. down** psakwihtéeheew VTA **He was crucified.** 'Psakwihtéehaa.'; **crucify s.o., put s.o. on the cross** aashtehtéeheew VTA; **be crucified** psakwihteeháasuw VAI.

**crumble** VT **crumble s.t. animate, break s.t. animate up into pieces, shred s.t. animate** *(using the hands)* píikŭneew VTA; **crumble s.t., break s.t. up into pieces, shred s.t.** *(using the hands)* píikŭnum VTI1B.

**crumple** VT **bunch s.t. animate up, crumple s.t. animate up** pàptúkwŭ=neew VTA; **bunch s.t. up, crumple s.t. up** pàptúkwŭnum VTI1B.

**crush** VT **crush s.o.** shkwíixŭmeew VTA **I crushed the snake.** 'Nzhukwíixŭ=maaw áxkook.'; **crush s.o., squash s.o.** *(using the foot or body)* shkwíh=kaweew VTA; **crush s.t.** shkwíixtoow VTI2 **I crushed my finger.** 'Nzhuk=wíixtoon náxkush.'; **crush s.t., squash s.t.** *(using the foot or body)* shkwíhkam VTI1A; **pound s.o., crush s.o., grind s.o.** *(using a tool or instrument)* shkwáheew VTA; **pound s.t., crush s.t., grind s.t.** *(using a tool or instrument)* shkwáham VTI1A; **hit and crush s.o.** shkwihtéexŭmeew VTA; **be crushed down, get reduced in cooking** shkwíhleew VAI; **fall and get crushed** shkwihtéexiin VAI.

**cry** N **let out a cry** sŭláamuw VAI; **let out a cry, let out one cry** ngwutŭ=

láamuw VAI.

**cry** VI lpákw VAI, chaangíhleew VAI; **be about to cry** *(especially of a baby that looks sad)* ooshawutoonéexiin VAI; **come here crying, come towards the speaker crying** peetéewtam VOTI1; **cry** *(while doing something)* chaangii- PV **I was crying as I left him behind.** 'Njáangii-ngálaaw.', **She was crying as she washed the dishes.** 'Cháangii-kshiixíinjŭweew.'; **cry** *(while doing something)* chaangu- PV *informal* **I was crying while I pushed him down.** 'Njáangu-kundaaháalaaw.', **He was crying as he left.** 'Cháangu-alúmsuw.'; **cry a great deal, cry hard** sàsaláamuw VAI; **cry for a certain reason** wundéewtam VAI **What's he crying for?** 'Kwéek wundéew=tam?', **I was crying about the candies.** 'Noondéewtam shookŭlúshal.'; **go away crying** aluméewtam VOTI1; **go here and there crying, go about crying** apaaméewtam VOTI1; **have an expression on one's face indicating that one is about to cry** ooshawut=oonéhleew VAI; **hit s.o. and make them cry** chaangihtéeheew VTA; **knock s.o. down and make them cry** chaangihtéexŭmeew VTA; **make s.o. cry** *(using the foot or body)*, **kick s.o. and make them cry** chaangíh=kaweew VTA; **sing when not wanted, sing and get on someone's nerves, cry, wail** niiskaláamuw VAI; **talk to s.o. and make them cry** chaang=toonháaleew VTA; **talk to s.o. and make them cry** chaangíimeew VTA; **throw s.o. and make them cry** chaangaaháaleew VTA; **throw s.o. and make them cry** chaangáaheew VAIO.

**crybaby** N **crybaby, weakling, coward** míikwul NA; **be a crybaby** mŭliisŭ=náaneew VAI; **be a crybaby, be a weakling, be a coward** míikwŭluw VAI.

**cucumber** N kòkómush NI, kòmkómush NI.

**cup** N **dipper, cup with handle** páyund NA; **teacup** tiihíinjuw NI; **wooden cup, wooden dish** xwusíinjuw NI.

**cupboard** N pehpoxkwahtíikan NI.

**cure** VT **cure s.o., heal s.o.** kiikéeheew VTA; **cure people** kiikéehŭweew VAI; **be cured, be healed** kíikeew VAI.

**curl** VT **curl s.t. up** ptukwíixtoow VTI2; **be curled up, lie curled up** ptukwíi=xiin VAI, ptukwíixun VII; **be curled, lie curled up** wihwiimbíixun VII; **curl s.o. up** ptukwíixŭmeew VTA.

**curly** ADJ **be curly** wchúpŭleew VII; **have curly hair** wchupŭlaalóhkweew VAI, wchupŭláandpeew VAI.

**curse** VI **use bad language, curse, swear** matutóonheew VAI.

**curtain** N kpaapehlatíikan NI; **lace curtain, transparent curtain** shehshíi=kaleek NI.

**curved** ADJ **be bent, be bent over, be curved** wáaksuw VAI, wáakeew VII; **have a bent shape, be bent, be curved** waakchéesuw VAI, waakchée=yeew VII **Your cane is bent.** 'Waak=chéeyeew ktaláawan.'

**cushion** N **cushion, saddle** eháhpapiing NI; **pillow, cushion** mŭlihkáawan NI, mŭlihkáawan NA.

**cut** N **have a cracked head, have a cut on one's head, fall and crack one's head, fall and cut one's head** pa=saandpéexiin VAI; **have a cracked head, have a cut on one's head** pasáandpeew VAI.

**cut** VT **be unable to cut s.o.** pwáaw=sheew VTA; **be unable to cut s.t.** pwáawshum VTI1A; **cut through s.t. animate, cut and break s.t. animate, cut s.t. animate** *(of something string-like)* páxksheew VTA; **cut through s.t., cut and break s.t., cut s.t.** *(of something string-like)* páxk=shum VTI1B; **cut a hole in s.o.** pkwúsh=

eew VTA; **cut a hole in s.t.** pkwúshum VTI1B; **cut a pattern, cut things nicely** wŭlushíikeew VAI; **cut and knock over s.t. animate** áamsheew VTA; **cut and knock s.t. over** áam=shum VTI1B; **cut cordwood** kaat=xákhweew VAI; **cut holes in things** pkwushíikeew VAI; **cut logs** saaláak=heew VAI; **cut people's hair** móon=zhŭweew VAI; **come back from cutting wood** aapanáxeew VAI; **cut s.o. by accident** páhtsheew VTA, píht=sheew VTA; **cut s.t.** lóokshum VTI1B; **cut s.t. and make a point on it, cut a point on s.t.** chpwúshum VTI1B; **cut s.t. and make it square, cut s.t. square** ashawéeshum VTI1B; **cut s.t. and sharpen it, sharpen s.t. by cutting** kíinshum VTI1B; **cut s.t. animate** lóoksheew VTA; **cut s.t. animate and make a point on it, cut a point on s.t. animate** chpwúsheew VTA; **cut s.t. animate and make it square, cut s.t. animate square** ashawéesheew VTA; **cut s.t. animate finely** wŭláam=sheew VTA; **cut s.t. animate in a round shape** ptúkwsheew VTA; **cut s.t. animate in pieces, cut s.t. animate in slices** pangéesheew VTA **I cut him in two pieces.** 'Níisha mban=géeshaaw.'; **cut s.t. animate in two, cut s.t. animate in half, split s.t. animate in two by cutting it** pasúsh=eew VTA; **cut s.t. animate incorrectly** matúsheew VTA; **cut s.t. animate lopsided, cut s.t. animate unevenly** píimsheew VTA; **cut s.t. animate nicely, cut s.t. animate in a pattern** wŭ=lúsheew VTA; **cut s.t. animate short** cháhkwsheew VTA **I cut the window (glass) short.** 'Njáhkwshaaw ee=heeshandéekan.'; **cut s.t. animate smoothly, scrape s.t. animate smooth, cut s.t. animate lightly, trim s.t. animate** láalsheew VTA; **cut s.t. animate thickly** kohpakúsheew VTA; **cut s.t. animate, cut and sever s.t. animate** tŭmúsheew VTA; **cut s.t. by accident** píhtshum VTI1B; **cut s.t. finely** wŭláamshum VTI1B; **cut s.t. in a round shape** ptúkwshum VTI1B; **cut s.t. in pieces, cut s.t. in slices** pan=géeshum VTI1A **I cut it in two pieces.** 'Níisha mbangéeshŭmun.'; **cut s.t. in two, cut s.t. in half, split s.t. in two by cutting it** pasúshum VTI1B; **cut s.t. incorrectly** matúshum VTI1B; **cut s.t. lopsided, cut s.t. unevenly** píimshum VTI1B; **cut s.t. nicely, cut s.t. in a pattern** wŭlúshum VTI!B; **cut s.t. short** cháhkwshum VTI1B; **cut s.t. smoothly, scrape s.t. smooth, cut s.t. lightly, trim s.t.** láalshum VTI1B; **cut s.t. thickly** kohpakúshum VTI1B; **cut splints, cut splints of wood for baskets** pòháhkweew VAI; **cut the last of s.t. animate, cut s.t. animate off at the end** póhkwsheew VTA; **cut the last of s.t., cut s.t. off at the end** póhkwshum VTI1B; **cut things** look=shíikeew VAI; **cut things** *(of something string-like)* paxkshíikeew VAI; **cut things up and make a mess, make a mess while cutting** aniisk=shíikeew VAI; **cut things, cut grass** tŭmushíikeew VAI; **cut weeds** *(with a scythe)*, **cut with a scythe** tŭmask=híikeew VAI; **cut wood** manáxeew VAI; **finish cutting s.t.** kíish'shum VTI1B; **finish cutting s.t. animate** kíish'=sheew VTA; **finish cutting things** kiish'shíikeew VAI; **get one's hair cut** moonzháasuw VAI; **hit and cut s.o.** tashakihtéeheew VTA; **saw s.t., cut and sever s.t.** tŭmúshum VTI1B; **saw timber, cut logs** tŭmushháhkweew VAI; **start cutting s.t.** alúmshum VTI1A; **start cutting s.t. animate** alúmsheew VTA; **start cutting things** alumshíi=keew VAI; **stop cutting s.t. animate, cease cutting s.t. animate** éhkw=sheew VTA; **stop cutting s.t., cease**

**cutting s.t.** éhkwshum VTI1B; **be cut short** *(diminutive)* chahkwshaashíi=shuw VII; **be cut thick** kohpakusháa=suw VII, kohpakusháasuw VAI; **stop cutting things, cease cutting things** ehkwshíikeew VAI; **trim trees, cut underbrush** mahkháhkweew VAI.

**cut around** VT **cut s.t. animate around the edge** wiiwŭnúsheew VTA; **cut s.t. around the edge** wiiwŭnúshum VTI1B.

**cut closely** VT **cut s.t. animate closely** *(as whiskers)* chíikwsheew VTA; **cut s.t. animate closely** shíikwsheew VTA; **cut s.t. closely** chíikwshum VTI1B; **cut s.t. closely** shíikwshum VTI1A.

**cut down** VT **chop s.t. down, chop s.t. off, cut s.t. down, cut s.t. off** tŭmáh=am VTI1A; **chop s.t. animate down, chop s.t. animate off, cut s.t. animate down, cut s.t. animate off** tŭmáheew VTA; **chop with an ax, cut down trees, trim trees** tŭmaháh=kweew VAI; **cut down trees** tŭmáh=kweew VAI; **cut s.t. animate down** kawúsheew VTA; **cut s.t. down** ka=wúshum VTI1B; **be cut down, be knocked over, be broken off** tŭmáh=ookw VAI **The tree was knocked over, broken off.** 'Tŭmáhookw míhtukw.'

**cut hair** VT **cut s.o.'s hair** móonzheew VTA.

**cut off** ADJ **have a bobbed tail, have a cut-off tail** *(diminutive)* chŭmoochŭ=yéeshuw VAI.

**cut off** VT **break s.o.'s neck, sever s.o. at the neck, break s.o. at the neck, cut s.o. off at the neck** tŭmiikwée=heew VTA; **chop s.t. animate down, chop s.t. animate off, cut s.t. animate down, cut s.t. animate off** tŭmáheew VTA; **cut a piece off s.t.** kwashúshum VTI1B; **cut a piece off s.t. animate** kwashúsheew VTA; **cut a piece off s.t. animate, cut s.t. animate off** máhksheew VTA; **cut a piece off s.t., cut s.t. off** máhkshum VTI1B; **cut s.t. animate off, cut a limb off s.t. animate** *(of trees)* tŭmáhkw=sheew VTA; **cut s.t. animate off, cut a piece off s.t. animate** pŭláksheew VTA; **chop s.t. down, chop s.t. off, cut s.t. down, cut s.t. off** tŭmáham VTI1A; **cut s.t. off** *(of something wooden)* tŭmáhkwshum VTI1B; **cut s.t. off, cut a piece off s.t.** pŭlákshum VTI1B; **cut the last of s.t., cut s.t. off at the end** póhkwshum VTI1B; **have a cut-off leg, have one's leg severed** tŭmukáateew VAI; **hit and sever s.t. animate, cut s.t. animate off** tŭmih=téeheew VTA; **hit and sever s.t., cut s.t. off** tŭmihtéeham VTI1A; **be cut off** *(of trees)* tŭmáhkwsuw VAI; **be cut off, be severed** tŭmahkwsháasuw VII, tŭmáhkwat VII.

**cut out** VT **cut out a pattern** ktushíi=keew VAI; **cut s.t. animate out** ktúsh=eew VTA; **cut s.t. out of something** ktúshum VTI1B.

**cut through** VT **cut through s.t.** shaap=wshéeshum VTI1B, **cut through s.t. animate** éesh'sheew VTA; **cut through s.t. animate, cut and break s.t. animate, cut s.t. animate** *(of something string-like)* páxksheew VTA; **cut through s.t., cut and break s.t., cut s.t.** *(of something string-like)* páxk=shum VTI1B.

**cut up** VT **cut s.t. animate up, cut s.t. animate into pieces** píiksheew VTA; **cut s.t. up for s.o.** piikshúmaweew VTAO; **cut s.t. up, cut s.t. into pieces** píikshum VTI1B; **cut things up** meht=shíikeew VAI; **cut things up** *(of animate objects)* paxkshúweew VAI; **dice s.t. animate, cut s.t. animate up into small pieces, chop s.t. animate, crack s.t. animate** píikheew VTA; **dice s.t., cut s.t. up into small pieces, chop s.t. up, crack s.t.** píikham VTI1A; **saw up all of s.t. animate, cut up all of s.t. animate** méhtsheew VTA; **saw**

**up all of s.t., cut up all of s.t.** méht=shum VTI1B.

**cute** ADJ **be cute looking** weewŭlii=náakwsuw VAI.

**cutter** N kátul NA *type of carriage;* **use a cutter** kàtŭláhŭmeew VAI.

**cycle by** VI **go by s.t., drive by s.t., fly by s.t., cycle by s.t.** loowíhleew VAIO; **go by, drive by, fly by, cycle by** loowíhleew VAI.

# D

**damage** VT **damage s.t., make s.t. lame** kwŭlúkwŭnum VTI1B **I sprained my foot.** 'Ngwulkwúnŭmun nzíit.'

**damn!** IJ kwàtalákay PC *considered impolite.*

**damp** ADJ **be damp, be wet** skapíixiin VAI, skapíixun VII; **be damp, be wet, be soft** wtákeew VII **My washing's still damp.** 'Wtákeew íiyaach kee=shiixtàwáaniil.'; **be damp, be wet, be soft** wtáksuw VAI; **get damp, become soft from dampness** wtakíixun VII, wtakíixiin VAI; **sweat, be damp from heat, be wet from heat** skapachásuw VAI, skapacháteew VII.

**dampen** VT **dampen s.o., dampen s.t. animate** skapháaleew VTA; **dampen s.t.** skapháatoow VTI2.

**dampness** N **be soft from dampness** wtákpeew VII, wtákpeew VAI **The papers are softened from being in water.** 'Pambíilak wtakpéewak.'

**dance** N **do a fast dance** akutakúkeew VAI, kàktákkeew VAI; **take part in a dance** wíitkeew VAI; **waltz around, do a round dance** apaamiikwsíhleew VAI.

**dance** VI **dance, be dancing** kúndkeew VAI; **come back from dancing, return from dancing** áapkeew VAI; **dance far apart** wahlŭmukéewak VAI *usually plural;* **dance in a certain manner, dance in a certain direction** lúkeew VAI; **dance slowly** sháhwkeew VAI; **finish dancing, be finished dancing** kíishkeew VAI; **go to dance** mawúkeew VAI; **make a shuffling noise while dancing** shóhwkeew VAI.

**dance with** VT **dance with s.o.** niish=kéemeew, wiitkéemeew VTA.

**danger** N **be in danger** nxáawapuw VAI.

**dangerous** ADJ **be in a frightening condition, be in a dangerous condition** kxwaawíixiin VAI, kxwaawíixun VII; **do dangerous work, work regardless of the consequences or risks** laalxawalóhkeew VAI; **lie in a dangerous place** laalxawíixiin VAI, laal=xawíixun VII; **look dangerous, look scary** kxwaawiináakwat VII, kxwaa=wiináakwsuw VAI; **place s.o. recklessly, place s.o. in a dangerous spot, place s.o. regardless of the consequences or risks** laalxawíixŭ=meew VTA; **place s.t. recklessly, put s.t. in a dangerous spot, place s.t. regardless of the consequences or risks** laalxawíixtoow VTI2.

**dark** ADJ **be dark** páhkŭnum VII **Because it was so dark.** 'Éelkih-páhkŭnung.'; **be dark-coloured, be a blackish colour, have a black tinge to it** nzukŭléexiin VAI, nzukŭléexun VII; **be extra dark out, be awfully dark** spwiingwéewii-páhkŭnum VII; **get dark** *(rapidly)* pahkŭnumwíh=leew VII **The light went out and it got dark quickly.** 'Wchiimáhteew pahkŭnumwíhleew.'; **have a dirty leg, have a dark leg** niiskkáateew VAI; **have dark eyes** nzukaalakíin=gweew VAI; **look dark, be dark-looking** nzukaapamúkwat VII, nzukaapa=múkwsuw VAI.

**daughter** N **my daughter** ndáanus NAD; **be s.o.'s daughter, have s.o. as a**

daughter wtáansuw VAIO; **have a daughter** wtáansuw VAI.
**daughter-in-law** N **my daughter-in-law** nxúm NAD.
**dawn** N **be dawn** wáapan VII **It's daylight now.** 'Méhch wáapan.', **Tomorrow.** 'Waapánge.'; **be the break of day, get to be daylight** *(just before dawn)* kshiixáapan VII.
**day** N **be a certain hour of the day** *(with number preverb)* kŭlákuw VII **At ten o'clock.** 'Wíimbat txú-kŭlakíi= ke.', **You'll come at four o'clock.** 'Néew-kŭlakíike-uch kúnj kpá.'; **be a certain kind of weather, be a certain kind of day** láhkameew VII **What's the weather like?** 'Thá láhkameew?'; **be a cold day** tháhkameew VII; **be a hot day** kshuláandeew VII, kshutee= wáhkameew VII; **be a nice day** wŭ= láhkameew VII; **be a wet day** skapee= wáhkameew VII; **be five days** naala= nookwŭnákat VII **Five days ago** 'Naalanookwŭnákate.'; **be gone for five days** naalanookwŭnáhkeew VAI; **be gone for four days** neewookwŭ= náhkeew VAI; **be gone for many nights, be gone for many days** xweelookwŭnáhkeew VAI; **be gone for several days** keexookwŭnáhkeew VAI; **be gone for so many days** txoo= kwŭnáhkeew VAI *usually with number particle* **I was gone for six days.** 'Ngwútaash ndundxookwŭnáhke.'; **be gone for three days** nxookwŭ= náhkeew VAI; **be gone for two days** niishookwŭnáhkeew VAI; **be many nights, be many days** xweelookwŭ= nákat VII; **be one day** ngwutáhkameew VII **I'll come in a day.** 'Ngwutahka= méeke náh mbá.'; **be the break of day, be clearing** *(of the sky)* alúmu-waaxéhleew VII; **be three days** nxoo= kwŭnákat VII **Three days ago.** 'Nxoo= kwŭnákate.'; **be two days** niishoo= kwŭnákat VII **He went there two days ago.** 'Niishookwŭnákate náh éew.', **He's going there in two days.** 'Niishookwŭnakáhke náh éew.'; **be two days** niisháhkameew VII; **clock, hour of the day** kŭlák NA **You will come at four o'clock.** 'Néew-kŭlák-uch kúnj kpá.'; **five days** naalanóo= kwŭnii PC; **four days** neewóokwŭnii PC; **half a day** pasáhkameew PC; **one day** ngwutóokwŭnii PC; **shine, be shining out** *(of the weather)*, **be a sunny day** waasŭláandeew VII; **so many days** txóokwŭnii PC *usually with number particle* **Six days.** 'Ngwútaash txóokwŭnii.'; **three days, for three days** nxóokwŭnii PC; **two days** niishóokwŭnii PC.
**daylight** N **be daylight coming, be daylight** peetáapan VII; **be the break of day, get to be daylight** *(just before dawn)* kshiixáapan VII; **be bright out** *(at night)*, **be daylight** waaxée= yeew VII **It gets bright out** 'Alúmu-waaxéeyeew.', **There's a new moon.** 'Wúsku-waaxéeyeew.'; **see daylight, live to daylight** waapanáheew VAI.
**daytime** N **during the daytime** kiish= kwŭnúwii PC **I'll cook during the daytime.** 'Kiishkwŭnúwii ápih nát= pwi.'
**dead** ADJ **die, be dead** ehkwáawsuw VAI; **to death, dead, permanently, for good** aapchii- PN **Woman who died of old age.** 'Áapchii-kihtóxkwees.'; **to death, dead, permanently, for good** aapchii- PV **The peaches are really overripe.** 'Piilkúshak áapchii-atúsŭwak.'; **to death, dead, permanently, for good** aapchu- PV *informal* **I lost it for good.** 'Ndáapchu-aníh= toon.', **He bled to death.** 'Áapchu-mohkwíixiin.'
**deaf** ADJ **be deaf** akéepxweew VAI.
**deal** N **tell the truth, make a deal** wŭláamweew VAI.
**death** N mbuwáakan NI; **be driven to**

**one's death, be tormented to death** aapchiinalúkwsuw VAI; **beat s.o. to death** pŭlupihtéeheew VTA; **bleed to death** aaptupéhleew VAI; **drink oneself to death** aapchíisŭmuw VAI; **drive s.o. to death, work s.o. to death, work s.o. very hard** aapchíi=naleew VTA; **fall to one's death** aap=tihtéexiin VAI; **freeze to death** aap=táchuw VAI; **grieve oneself to death, die of grief, be grieving** aapteelún=dam VOTI1; **scare s.o. to death** aap=tahpáaheew VTA; **starve, starve to death** shawaláamuw VAI; **to death** aaptii- PN **Woman who died of old age.** 'Áaptii-kihtóxkwees.'; **to death, dead, permanently, for good** aapchii- PN **Woman who died of old age.** 'Áapchii-kihtóxkwees.'; **to death, dead, permanently, for good** aapchii- PV **The peaches are really overripe.** 'Piilkúshak áapchii-atúsŭwak.'; **to death, dead, permanently, for good** aapchu- PV *informal* **I lost it for good.** 'Ndáapchu-aníhtoon.', **He bled to death.** 'Áapchu-mohkwíixiin.'; **work oneself to death** aaptalóhkeew VAI **He went to prison for life.** 'Mawí-aaptalóhkeew.'

**decay** VI **decay, go bad, spoil** machíh=leew VII; **run badly** *(especially of vehicles)*, **decay, go bad, spoil** machíh=leew VAI; **decayed wood** aláxakw NI.

**deceptive** ADJ **look deceptive, look misleading** pahchoolŭweewiináakwsuw VAI.

**decision** N **come to a difficult decision** àhweelúndam VOTI1.

**deed** N **be a bad worker, do bad deeds** amatalóhkeew VAI.

**deep** ADJ **be big, be deep** *(of holes)* xwushéeyeew VII; **be deep** *(of pockets)* kwŭnushéesuw VAI; **be deep** *(of bodies of water)* kwŭnushéeyeew VII; **be a deep hole** kwŭnáalakat VII; **be deep enough** *(of holes)* teepáalakat VII; **be deep mud** kwŭnasíiskŭwat VII; **be deep snow** xwáhteew VII; **be deep water** kwŭnupéekat VII, kwŭnúpeew VII; **be deep water, be a lot of water** xwupéekat VII; **be high water, be deep water, be a flood, be flooding** xwahkwíixun VII; **have a deep voice** xwaalakaxóoneew VAI; **make a big hole, make a deep hole** kwŭnáal=heew VAI.

**deer** N ató NA, atóh NA; **kill a deer** nih=latóhweew VAI.

**defecate** VI másktuw VAI; **be constipated, be unable to defecate** aalŭwásk=tuw VAI, pwaawásktuw VAI; **beat s.o. until they defecate** masktihtéeheew VTA; **defecate a large amount, go to the bathroom a lot** amangásktuw VAI, xwásktuw VAI; **defecate in s.t., defecate on s.t.** maskchíhtam VTI1A; **defecate while in motion** maskchíh=leew VAI; **defecate while sitting** masktápuw VAI; **defecate while sleeping** masktóngwaam VAI; **defecate while walking** masktóoxweew VAI; **finish defecating, be finished defecating** kiishásktuw VAI.

**defend** VT **defend s.o. in a fight** ihkáa=leew VTA; **take s.o.'s side in an argument, speak on s.o.'s behalf in an argument, defend s.o.** ihkáameew VTA.

**deficient** ADJ **be deficient, be lacking, be short of something, be not quite enough of something, fall short** noondéexiin VAI, noondéexun VII.

**deformed** ADJ **have a deformed hip, have one hip higher than the other, have a lopsided hip** waakhóotŭyeew VAI.

**Delaware** N **Indian woman, Delaware woman** lunaapéexkweew NA; **Indian, Delaware Indian** lunáapeew NA; **be an Indian, be a Delaware Indian** lunaapéewuw VAI; **speak Delaware, speak a native language** hulŭníixsuw

VAI; **speaking an Indian language, the Delaware language** hulŭniix=suwáakan NI.

**Delaware Indian** N **Delaware Indian, Munsee Delaware Indian** múnsiiw NA.

**deliberately** ADV **deliberately, on purpose** áhweel PC **I hit him on purpose.** 'Áhweel mbákamaaw.', **He did it on purpose.** 'Áhweel wtulŭnúmun.'

**delicate** ADJ **be fragile, be delicate** póoxpeew VII; **be fragile, be delicate** *(s.t. animate)*, **be delicate in health** póoxpsuw VAI.

**dent** VT **dent s.t.** *(using the foot or body)*, **kick and dent s.t.** kwŭlapíh=kam VTI1A; **dent s.t.** *(using a tool or instrument)* kwŭlápham VTI1A; **dent s.t.** *(using the hands)* kwŭlápŭnum VTI1A; **dent s.t. animate** *(using the foot or body)*, **kick and dent s.t. animate** kwŭlapíhkaweew VTA; **dent s.t. animate** *(using a tool or instrument)* kwŭlápheew VTA; **dent s.t. animate** *(using the hands)* kwŭlápŭneew VTA; **hit and dent s.o., hit and dent s.t. animate** *(as the body of a car)* kwŭ=lapihtéexŭmeew VTA; **hit and dent s.t.** kwŭlapihtéextoow VTI2; **hit and dent s.t.** *(using a tool or instrument)* kwŭlapihtéeham VTI1A; **hit and dent s.t. animate** kwŭlapihtéeheew VTA; **be dented** kwŭlápeew VII, kwŭlápsuw VAI.

**dentures** N **wear dentures, wear false teeth** wiipiithámeew VAI.

**deny** VT **deny s.t.** pasúweew VAIO.

**depend on** VT **rely on s.o., depend on s.o., need s.o.'s help** nahkáaleew VTA; **rely on s.t., depend on s.t.** nahkáa=tum VTI1A.

**depth** N **be a certain depth, be a certain length** *(of holes)* sahkáalakat VII **It is the same depth (of a hole).** 'Ngwúteel sahkáalakat.'

**derogatory** ADJ **mildly derogatory expression** xéetiis PC.

**descend** VI **come down, descend, get out of a vehicle** níixiiw VAI-S.

**desolate** ADJ **feel oneself to be at a loss, feel desolate** *(having no place to go or to live)* kwiilaweelúnzuw VAI.

**destination** N **walk directly to one's destination, go directly to one's destination, follow a good path in life** shaaxkóoxweew VAI.

**destroy** VT **destroy all of s.o., kill all of s.o., get rid of all of s.o.** weemíiheew VTA *object usually plural.*

**detach** VT **detach s.t. animate, knock s.t. animate off** *(using a tool or instrument)* máhkheew VTA; **detach s.t. animate, pull s.t. animate off, take s.t. animate away, remove s.t. animate** *(using the hands)* máhkŭneew VTA; **detach s.t., knock s.t. off** máhkham VTI1A; **detach s.t., pull s.t. off, take s.t. away, remove s.t.** *(using the hands)* máhkŭnum VTI1B; **fall off, come off, become detached** mahkíhleew VAI, mahkíhleew VII; **hit and knock s.t. animate off, hit and detach s.t. animate** mahkihtéeheew VTA; **hit and knock s.t. off, hit and detach s.t.** mahkihtéehum VTI1B; **hit s.t. and knock it off, hit and detach s.t.** mahkihtéextoow VTI2; **hit s.t. animate and knock it off, hit and detach s.t. animate** mahkihtéexŭmeew VTA; **knock s.t. animate off, cause s.t. animate to be knocked off, detach s.t. animate** mahkíixŭmeew VTA; **knock s.t. off, cause s.t. to be knocked off, detach s.t.** mahkíixtoow VTI2; **be knocked off, be hit and detached** mahkihtéexiin VAI, mahkih=téexun VII.

**devil** N matántoow NA.

**diabetes** N **get diabetes, develop diabetes, have diabetes** shookŭlíhleew VAI.

**diagonal** ADJ **crawl sideways, crawl on the diagonal** piimíikwsuw VAI; **tilt**

**s.o., tip s.o., cause s.o. to be on the diagonal, bend s.o.** *(using the hands)* píimŭneew VTA; **tilt s.t., tip s.t., cause s.t. to be on the diagonal, bend s.t.** *(using the hands)* píimŭnum VTI 1B.

**dialect** N **speak a certain language, speak a certain dialect** líixsuw VAI **He speaks another language or dialect.** 'Palíi ayulíixsuw.'

**diaper** N **diaper, napkin** ahpcháawan NI; **change s.o.'s diaper, make s.o. be dry** peengwíixŭmeew VTA; **wear a diaper** ahpchaawanáhŭmeew VAI, shaapwaalhóosuw VAI.

**diarrhea** N **have diarrhea** shaapwíh=leew VAI; **have diarrhea, have stomach flu** watéeneew VAI.

**dice** VT **dice s.t. animate, cut s.t. animate up into small pieces, chop s.t. animate, crack s.t. animate** píikheew VTA; **dice s.t., cut s.t. up into small pieces, chop s.t. up, crack s.t.** píik=ham VTI 1A.

**die** VI maníhleew VAI, éhkwi-pŭmáaw=suw VAI, éhkwu-pŭmáawsuw VAI; **grieve oneself to death, die of grief, be grieving** aapteelúndam VOTI 1; **be a man who died of old age** aaptihlóo=suw VAI **I'm just about dying of old age.** 'Péexoot ndaaptihlóosi.'; **be a woman who died of old age** áapchii-kihtoxkwéesuw VAI; **be condemned to die for evil deeds, die deservedly, be thought incapable** kundeelŭmúk=wsuw VAI; **be in a hurry** *(for s.o. to do something)*, **be in a hurry for s.o. to die** shawáaleew VTA, shàhwáaleew VTA **I'm in a hurry for him to go to town.** 'Nzhahwáalaaw ootéeneeng wtáan.'; **condemn s.o., want s.o. to die, think s.o. incapable of doing something** kundéelŭmeew VTA; **die from s.t.** mbuwáatam VTI 1A; **die in one's sleep, die while sleeping** aap=tóngwaam VAI; **die in pain** aaptàw=éendam VOTI 1; **die, be dead** eh=kwáawsuw VAI; **fall and die, be beaten to death, get hit and die** pŭlupih=téexiin VAI.

**difference** N **be able to tell the difference between people, 'make strange'** *(of babies)* chihchpiináasuw VAI, chpiináasuw VAI.

**different** ADJ **be a room, be a divided room, be different rooms, be another room** *(in a dwelling)* chpún=deew VII; **find that s.o. looks different** chpíinaweew VTA; **find that s.t. looks different, s.t. looks different to someone** chpíinam VTI 1A; **look different** chehchpiinaakwsúwak VAI *usually plural;* **sound odd, sound different, sound strange** maashih=táakwsuw VAI, maashihtáakwat VII.

**difficult** ADJ **be difficult, be hard** áhwat VII; **come to a difficult decision** àh=weelúndam VOTI 1; **do reluctantly, be reluctant about doing something, be difficult to do something, be hard to do something** mihka PC **I didn't want to go to work (but I did).** 'Míhka nŭmáw-alóhke.', **It's hard for me to get up.** 'Míhka mbáskwi.'; **find s.t. difficult, find s.t. difficult to do** àhweelúndam VTI 1A; **very, intense, hard, difficult** ahwi- PV **It has a lot of salt on it.** 'Áhwi-shŭwaháasuw.'; **very, intense, hard, difficult** ahwu- PV *informal* **He has a hard time, he has bad luck.** 'Áhwu-líinam.', **He is getting enormously big.** 'Áhwu-wulíikuw.'

**difficulty** N **have difficulty while walking, have difficulty in travelling, be hard for one to travel** àhwóoxweew VAI.

**dig** VT **dig a hole** wáalheew VAI.

**dig out** VT **dig s.o out, pry s.o out, remove s.o.** *(using a tool or instrument)* kchiikwáaleew VTA; **dig s.t. out, pry s.t. out, remove s.t.** *(using a tool or instrument)* kchiikwáatam VTI 1A.

**dig up** VT **dig s.o. up** móonheew VTA; **dig s.o. up, dig s.t. animate up** páanheew VTA; **dig s.t. up** móonham VTI1; **dig s.t. up** páanham VTI1A **I dug it up where he is.** 'Mbaanhámun éepiit.'; **dig things up** moonhíikeew VAI; **dig up potatoes** moonhíhpŭneew VAI.

**dimension** N **measure the dimensions of s.t.** kwsáham VTI1A.

**dinner** N **have dinner** ndúnaluw VAI.

**dip for** VT **scoop things up, dip** *(for water)* anz'híikeew VAI; **scoop things, dip** *(for water)* anzŭníikeew VAI, án=zŭnum VOTI1.

**dipper** N **dipper, cup with handle** páyund NA; **scoop, dipper, something used to dip for water** anz'híikan NI.

**direction** N **because, in a certain manner, in a certain direction** eel- PV *followed by verb in conjunct order* **Now it must be because he had overcome the medicine.** 'Nál xéet ná kwáy éel- wchápihk -aluwíhkang.', **Because you picked him up you'll always find lots of things (to hunt).** 'Kwáy éel-náatŭnat ngúmee-uch xwéelu kwéek kŭmóxkam.'; **because, in a certain manner, in a certain direction** eeli- PV *followed by verb in conjunct order* **She wanted to kill him because he had cracked the eggs.** 'Kwáta-nihláawal éeli- wáhwal -pwáhkhang.'; **direction** wúndakw PC **Where does he live?** 'Tá wúndakw wíikiin?', **You crawled the other way.** 'Kíi palíi wúndakw ktulíikwsi.'; **do something to s.o. in a certain manner, do something to s.o. in a certain direction** *(using the foot or body)* líhkaweew VTA; **do something to s.t. in a certain manner, do something to s.t. in a certain direction** *(using the foot or body)* líhkam VTI1A **I shoved it to the side.** 'Pálii ndulíh=kamun.'; **face in a certain direction, face in a certain manner** lohkwée=xiin VAI, lohkwéexun VII; **face in the wrong direction, face the wrong way** chanohkwéexiin VAI, chanoh=kwéexun VII; **in a certain manner, in a certain direction** li- PV **I waited until he came in.** 'Mbéehaaw wtúli-piinjíikeen.', **Then he crawled inside the house.** 'Nál wtúlu- wiikwáhmung -piinjíikwsiin.'; **in a certain manner, in a certain direction** lu- PV *informal* **I looked around for the medicine, I looked for it everywhere.** 'Nál há mbápaa-kwíilamun wchápihk, wéemu táa ndúlu-kwíilamun.', **Then I went outside and I threw it as far as I could.** 'Nál kwáchŭmung ndáan táa ndúlu-aseesahkáaheen.'; **look in a certain direction, look in a certain manner** liingwéexiin VAI **I don't know where he's looking.** 'Máh nŭweewiiháawu tá eeliingwéexiit.'; **make s.o. look in a certain direction, make s.o. face in a certain direction** liingwéexŭmeew VTA **I put the doll facing over there.** 'Yéelak nduliingwéexŭmaaw naaníitus.'; **roll s.o. in a certain direction, roll s.o. in a certain manner** liinjkwéeneew VTA; **roll s.t. in a certain direction, roll s.t. in a certain manner** luchée=num VTI1B; **roll s.t. in a certain manner, roll s.t. in a certain direction** liinjkwéenum VTI1A; **shine a light in a certain direction, shine a light in a certain manner** laasŭléenŭmeew VAI; **shine in a certain direction** *(of the sun)* láandeew VII; **shine in this direction, shine here** *(of lights)* pee=táasŭleew VAI, peetáasŭleew VII; **shine s.t. in a certain direction, shine s.t. in a certain manner** *(of lights)* laa=sŭléenum VTI1A, laasŭléenŭmeew VAIO **I shone the lantern over there.** 'Yeelak ndulaasŭléenŭmaan waasŭ=leeníikan.'; **swim in this direction,**

**swim here, swim this way** peetáa=shŭweew VAI; **turn s.o. to face in a certain direction, turn s.o. to face in a certain manner** lohkwéexŭ=meew VTA; **turn s.o. to face in the wrong direction, turn s.o. to face the wrong way** chanohkwéexŭmeew VTA; **turn s.t. to face in a certain direction, turn s.t. to face in a certain manner** lohkwéextoow VTI2 **I faced it towards the front.** 'Shayéemung ndulohkwéextoon.'; **turn s.t. to face in the wrong direction, turn s.t. to face the wrong way** chanohkwéex=toow VTI2; **use s.t. to come here, use s.t. to come in this direction** peeta=wéeheew VAIO.

**directly** ADV **walk directly to one's destination, go directly to one's destination, follow a good path in life** shaaxkóoxweew VAI.

**dirt** N **have dirt on it, be sandy** ahkŭ=yóowuw VII; **throw powder on s.o., throw dust on s.o., throw sand on s.o., throw dirt on s.o.** ponghwáa=leew VTA.

**dirty** ADJ **be dirty** níiskeew VII, níisk=suw VAI; **be dirty looking, look dirty** niiskiináakwat VII, niiskiináakwsuw VAI; **be dirty water** niiskpéekat VII; **dirty cat** niiskapóoshiish NA; **dirty dog** níiskxum NA; **dirty s.o., make s.o. dirty** niiskíiheew VTA; **dirty s.t., make s.t. dirty** niiskíhtoow VTI2; **dirty water** níiskpuy NI; **have a dirty ear, have dirty ears** niiskihtawákeew VAI; **have a dirty face** niiskchàlíin=gweew VAI; **have a dirty foot** niisk=síiteew VAI; **have a dirty hand** niis=kŭnáxkeew VAI; **have a dirty head** niiskáandpeew VAI; **have a dirty house** niiskíikeew VAI; **have a dirty knee** niiskiiktúkweew VAI; **have a dirty leg, have a dark leg** niiskkáa=teew VAI; **have a dirty mouth** niisk=tóoneew VAI; **have a dirty nose** niisk=cháaleew VAI; **have dirty fingernails** aniiskíhkasheew VAI; **have dirty hair** niiskaalóhkweew VAI; **have dirty hair, have a dirty head** niiskóh=kweew VAI; **have dirty hands** aniis=kŭnáxkeew VAI; **have dirty knees** aniiskiiktúkweew VAI; **make s.o. dirty** *(using the foot or body)*, **step on s.o. and make them dirty** niis=kíhkaweew VTA; **make s.t. dirty** *(using the foot or body)*, **step on s.t. and make it dirty** niiskíhkam VTI1A; **talk a lot, gossip, talk dirty** niisktóon=heew VAI; **talk dirty** niiskaachíimuw VAI; **think that s.o. is dirty** niiskée=lŭmeew VTA; **think that s.t. is dirty** niiskeelúndam VTI1A; **touch and dirty s.o., make s.o. dirty** *(using the hands)* níiskŭneew VTA; **touch and dirty s.t., make s.t. dirty** *(using the hands)* níiskŭnum VTI1A; **wear dirty clothes** aníiskakuw VAI; **be a 'dirty' picker, pick only the most accessible fruits or berries, pick only the most accessible products** aníiskii-paxkŭníi=keew VAI.

**disagree with** VT **disagree with s.o., find fault with s.o.** chaníimeew VTA.

**disappear** VI **disappear, crawl out of sight** wchíikwsuw VAI; **disappear, go out of sight, shrink** wchíhleew VII **His head disappeared out of sight.** 'Wíil wchíhleew.'; **disappear, go out of sight, shrink** wchíhleew VAI **He was looking out the window, then he disappeared, he's hiding.** 'Ee=heeshandéekan lí któhkweew, nál táa wtúlu-wchíhlaan, káatapuw.'

**disappoint** VT **make s.o. tired, tire s.o. out, disappoint s.o.** shiiwiilawée=heew VTA.

**disbelieve** VT **disbelieve s.o.** palustáw=eew VTA; **disbelieve s.t.** palústam VTI1A **I didn't believe what I heard.** 'Kwéek mbúndam, mbalsútam.'; **don't believe s.o., disbelieve s.o.**

maxksútaweew VTA; **don't believe s.t., disbelieve s.t.** maxksútam VTI1A.
**disc** N **be discing, use a disc** *(of farming equipment)* piikshííkeew VAI.
**discontented** ADJ **be discontented** mun=daweelúndam VOTI1; **be discontented with s.o. over their actions** múnda=wameew VTA.
**discourage** VT **be annoyed, be discouraged** chaneelúndam VOTI1.
**discuss** VT **be finished being discussed** kiishakunootáasuw VII.
**discussion** N **take part in a discussion** wiitaachíimuw VAI.
**disease** N **have a certain disease, have a disease in a certain place** líineew VAI **I wonder what disease I have.** 'Kwéek éet há ndulíine.', **I have a sore stomach.** 'Ndáyung ndúnda-líine.'; **have a cough, have a coughing disease** xwukwíineew VAI; **transmit an infectious disease to s.o.** mshíiheew VTA.
**disembark** VI **disembark, get out of a vehicle** kóhpiiw VAI-S.
**dish** N wŭláakanus NI; **big dish** xwach=íinjuw NI; **dry the dishes** peen=gwahkhwíikeew VAI, peengwiikwáa=keew VAI; **gather the dishes** maa=weehíinjŭweew VAI, maaweenjŭ=weextíikeew VAI; **wash the dishes** kshiixíinjŭweew VAI; **wooden cup, wooden dish** xwusíinjuw NI.
**dishcloth** N kshiixiinjŭwáakan NI.
**dishpan** N éhunda-kshiixíinjŭweeng VII.
**dislike** VT **hate s.o., dislike s.o.** shiin=gíinaweew VTA; **hate s.t., dislike s.t.** shiingíinam VTI1A; **dislike listening to s.o., dislike the sound of s.o., dislike hearing about s.o.** shiingsúta=weew VTA; **dislike listening to s.t., dislike the sound of s.t.** shiingsútam VTI1A; **dislike s.t.** shiingáatam VTI1A; **dislike the looks of s.o.** machíinaweew VTA; **dislike the looks of s.t.** machíinam VTI1B; **be hateful, dislike people** shiingiináasuw VAI; **dislike it where one is, dislike it where one stays** shíingapuw VAIO; **dislike where one is** shíingapuw VAI.
**dismantle** VT **collapse s.t., tear s.t. down, dismantle s.t.** *(using the hands)* mŭlákwŭnum VTI1B; **pull s.t. animate apart, dismantle s.t. animate** lookhéewaleew VTA; **pull s.t. apart, dismantle s.t.** lookhéewatoow VTI2.
**dismiss** VT **dismiss s.o., fire s.o.** sèk=háaleew VTA.
**disobey** VT **disobey, refuse to listen, be stubborn** achiingíiwsuw VAI.
**disorganized** ADJ **have disorganized colours, have mixed up colours** pàpŭlakaapamúkwat VII, pàpŭlakaa=pamúkwsuw VAI.
**display** VT **display s.t. of importance, show s.t. of importance, display s.t.** *(of one's feelings)*, **show s.t.** *(of one's feelings)* pŭnoondíhkeew VAIO **You showed that you didn't love her.** 'Kpunoondíhkeen máh ktahwaaláa=wi.'; **uncover s.o., expose s.o., display s.o., cause s.o. to be exposed** mihchíixŭmeew VTA.
**dispose of** VT **get rid of s.t., completely dispose of s.t., sell all of s.t.** weema=lóhkeew VAIO **I gave away all of my belongings.** 'Nŭweemalóhkeen neh=láatamaan.'
**disrupt** VT **butt in, disrupt the conversation** ìhŭlutóonheew VAI.
**dissatisfied with** VT **blame s.o., be dissatisfied with s.o.'s actions** mandóo=meew VTA.
**distance** N **throw s.t. a certain distance** sahkáaheew VAIO **I threw it far.** 'Wáhlu nzahkáaheen.'; **walk so far, go so far, go a certain distance** sahkóoxweew VAI **He went very far.** 'Móxa wáhlu sahkóoxweew.'; **way over there, over there a considerable distance** yóolak PR.

**distaste** N **have a look of distaste on one's face, turn one's nose up at something** niiskcheengwéexiin VAI.

**divide** VT **be a room, be a divided room, be different rooms, be another room** *(in a dwelling)* chpún=deew VII.

**dizzy** ADJ **be dizzy** kiiwaníindkweew VAI; **get dizzy all of a sudden** kiiwa=niindkwéhleew VAI.

**do** VT **do s.t., hand s.t. in a certain direction, hand s.t. in a certain manner** lúnum VTI1B **Hand it here!** 'Yó lúnih!', **Why did you do that?** 'Kwéek há nú kóonju-lúnŭmun?'; **be easy to do, be easy** *(to read, to understand)* aapŭwíixiin VAI; **cook s.t. animate done, cook s.t. animate to completion** kíish'seew VTA; **cook s.t. done, cook s.t. to completion** kíish'=sum VTI1B; **find s.o. easy** *(to do something with)* aapŭwéelŭmeew VTA **I find him easy to teach.** 'Ndaapŭ=wéelŭmaaw ndakehkíimaan.', **I find him easy to play with.** 'Ndaapŭwée=lŭmaaw nŭmeelawusóomaan.'; **find s.t. easy to do, think s.t. easy to do** aapŭweelúndam VTI1A **I don't think anything of going to town.** 'Ndaa=pŭweelúndamun ootéeneeng ndáan.', **I find it easy to go to sleep.** 'Ndaa=pŭweelúndamun nŭmáw-kawí.'; **have an overwhelming amount of work to do** laawalóhkeew VAI; **know how to do s.t.** nihtáhtoow VTI2; **let s.t. go, give s.t. up, give up doing s.t., give up making s.t.** pooníhtoow VTI2; **like to do something with s.o.** wiingáa=leew VTA *requires complement in subordinative mode* **I like to play with him.** 'Nŭwiingáalaaw nŭmeeláwíi=haan.'; **make it easy for someone to do s.t., fix s.t. so it would be easy** *(to do something)* aapŭwíixtoow VTI2; **be done cooking, be finished cooking** *(of cooks)* kiishatúpuw VAI; **be done cooking** kíish'suw VAI; **be done talking, say all one has to say, run out of things to say** mehtaaptóoneew VAI.

**do to** VT **do something to s.o. in a certain manner, do something to s.o. in a certain direction** *(using the foot or body)* líhkaweew VTA; **do something to s.t. in a certain manner, do something to s.t. in a certain direction** *(using the foot or body)* líhkam VTI1A **I shoved it to the side.** 'Pálii ndulíh=kamun.'

**do up** VT **button s.t. up, do s.t. up tightly, make a down payment on s.t.** kŭláhkhwam VTI1A.

**doctor** N ndáaktul NA; **be treated by a doctor** ndaaktulhámeew VAI.

**dodge** VT **shield oneself, dodge from something** tàtapásuw VAI.

**dog** N mwáakaneew NA; **my dog, my horse, my close pet** *(of dogs and horses)* ndálŭmoonz NAD; **bad dog** mataakanáxum NA, matáxum NA; **big dog** xwátxum NA; **dirty dog** níiskxum NA; **doghouse** mwaakaneewíikaan NI; **female dog, female of animal species** oxkwéexum NA; **kill a dog, beat a dog** nihlaakanáxŭmweew VAI; **look for a dog** ndawxúmweew VAI; **old dog** xúwxum NA; **young dog** wúsk=xum NA.

**dog excrement** N mwaakanéewchuy NI.

**doll** N naaníitus NA; **big doll** xwataaníi=tus NA.

**dollar** N ndálaas NI *singular only, usually with number prenoun* **It costs one dollar.** 'Ngwút-ndálaas láawa=tuw.', **It costs six dollars.** 'Ngwút=aash txú-ndálaas láawatuw.'

**dominate** VT **overcome s.o., dominate s.o.** *(especially one's spouse)* aluwíh=kaweew VTA.

**don't** VI chíi PC **Don't help him!** 'Chíi wiichŭmáawu!', **Don't go to sleep!** 'Chíi kawíiwi!'; **don't** chíile PC **Don't go that way!** 'Chíile náh áawu!', **Don't eat those strawberries!** 'Chíilu níil wteehíimal miichíi=wu!'

**donkey** N kweekwáanxaash NA.

**door** N kpáhoon NI; **stick placed across the door to indicate that no one is at home** nootíikees NI.

**doorstep** N **doorstep, threshold of house** uskwáandu PC.

**double** ADJ **be double, be in two layers** *(of something sheet-like)* niishéeksuw VAI; **be double, lie double, be in layers** pihtawíixiin VAI, pihtawíixun VII **Two-story houses.** 'Niishéeli pihta=wíixŭnool wiikwáhmal.'; **double, doubled, one over the other** pihtawii- PV **I papered over the other wallpaper.** 'Mbíhtawii-pambiilhíike.'; **be double, be in two layers** niishéekat VII; **be in layers, be double** pihta=wúsuw VAI, píhtaweew VII **It is in two layers.** 'Níishu-píhtawe.', **It's in three layers.** 'Nxéeli píhtaweew.'; **grow double** pihtawíikuw VAI, pihta=wíikun VII; **make s.t. animate be double, cause s.t. animate to be double, lay s.t. animate in a layer on top of something else** pihtawíi=xŭmeew VTA; **make s.t. be double, cause s.t. to be double, lay s.t. in a layer on top of something else** pih=tawíixtoow VTI2; **sit doubled over, sit doubled up** paxkawohkwéepuw VAI, paxkawápuw VAI; **be bent over, be doubled up** tamáksuw VAI.

**doughnut** N shalapwáanush NI.

**dove** N moowíhleesh NA; **pigeon, mourning dove** míimiiw NA.

**down** ADV **be placed, be put down** ahtáasuw VII; **fall down** pŭnihtéexiin VAI **He fell out of bed.** 'Apíineeng wúnj-pŭnihtéexiin.'; **fall down off of something** pŭníhleew VII; **flow down** *(of liquids)* pŭnaapŭwéhleew VII; **go down** *(of water)* pŭnahkwíixun VII; **go down, fall down, slide down** *(of curtains, of pants)* chiixíhleew VII; **hang down** pŭnaapéhleew VII; **lay s.o. down** shungíixŭmeew VTA; **lay s.t. down** shungíixtoow VTI2; **lie down** shungíixiin VAI; **spill, fall down, come down** *(of water)* sook=péhleew VII.

**downhill** ADV **go downhill** púmbiiw VAI-S; **go downhill, fall downhill, slide downhill** pumbíhleew VAI; **run downhill** niixahtakíhleew VAI; **slide downhill, slide down a hill** chii=xiikwsíhleew VAI.

**downwards** ADV **crawl downwards** niixíikwsuw VAI.

**drag** VT **drag s.o. by, drag s.o. along** pŭmutaachíhleew VTA; **drag s.t. by, drag s.t. along** pŭmutáachiind VTI3; **drag s.o. in a certain direction, drag s.o. in a certain manner** lutaachíhleew VTA; **drag s.o. to here, drag s.t. animate to here, drag s.o. towards the speaker, drag s.t. animate towards the speaker** peettaa=chíhleew VTA; **drag s.o. up** usptaa=chíhleew VTA; **drag s.t. in a certain direction, drag s.t. in a certain manner** lutaachíindam VTI1A; **drag s.t. to here, drag s.t. towards the speaker** peettaachíindam VTI1A, peettáachiind VTI3; **go after and drag s.o., go after and drag s.t. animate** naattaachíhleew VTA; **go after and drag s.t., fetch and drag s.t.** naat=taachíindam VTI1A; **pull and drag s.o., pull and drag s.t. animate** wtut=aachíhleew VTA; **pull and drag s.t.** wtutaachíindam VTI1A; **be dragged in a certain manner, be dragged in a certain direction** lutaachíhleew VAI.

**drain** VT **drain s.t.** síhlatoow VTI2; **drain s.t. animate** síhlaleew VTA; **be drained** *(especially of wells)* siihŭnáasuw VII.

**draw** VT **draw a circle around a picture of s.o., draw a circle on a picture of s.o., circle a picture of s.o.**

wiiwŭnéekheew VTA; **draw a circle around s.t., draw a circle on s.t., circle s.t.** wiiwŭnéekham VTI1A; **draw a circle around things, circle things** wiiwŭneekhíikeew VAI; **take a photograph of s.o., draw a picture of s.o., make a tracing of s.o.** ktéekheew VTA; **take photographs, make a drawing, draw things** kteekhíikeew VAI.

**drawing** N **take photographs, make a drawing, draw things** kteekhíikeew VAI.

**dream** N **dream about s.o., have a dream about s.o.** namongwáaleew VTA; **have a dream** lóngwaam VAI **I dreamt that I climbed up.** 'Ndulón=gwaam wáhkwung ndulakóosi.'; **dream about s.t., have a dream about s.t.** namongwáatam VTI1A; **have a bad dream** chiipóngwaam VAI; **have a bad dream** matóngwaam VAI; **have a good dream** wŭlóngwaam VAI **I always have good dreams.** 'Ngúmee nŭwaawŭlóngwaam.'; **have an odd dream** maashóngwaam VAI; **wake after a bad dream, wake up screaming, have a nightmare** akii=wóngxwiin VAI.

**dream about** VT **dream about s.o., have a dream about s.o.** namon=gwáaleew VTA; **dream about s.t.** lóngwaam VTI3, namongwáatam VTI1A.

**drench** VT **be soaking wet, be drenched, be limp from water** piisŭlúpeew VII, piisŭlúpeew VAI.

**dress** N **dress, coat** weendakwíiwan NI; **have a short dress on, wear a short dress** chahkhooshíishuw VAI; **old dress** xuweendakwíiwan NI; **short dress** chahkweenjakwíiwanush NI; **silk dress** silkeendakwíiwan NI; **wear a long dress, have a long dress on** kwŭnahóosuw VAI; **wear a sheer dress, wear a transparent dress** shiikaláhoosuw VAI; **winter dress** loowaneendakwíiwan NI; **wrinkled dress** wchuleendakwíiwan NI.

**dress** VI **get dressed, get ready** wéech=puw VAI; **get dressed, get ready, be ready, be dressed** kiishéechpuw VAI; **be badly dressed** matákuw VAI; **dress haphazardly, dress hurriedly, throw on one's clothes** pàpŭlakéechpuw VAI; **dress in a certain manner** lákuw VAI; **dress in a hurry** akaa=wéechpuw VAI; **dress plainly, be dressed plainly** kahkanákuw VAI; **dress raggedly, wear ragged clothing** piikwshákuw VAI; **be fancy looking** *(s.t. animate)*, **be dressed up fancily** wiilawiináakwsuw VAI **He's dressed up fancy.** 'Móxa wiilawii=náakwsuw.'; **look like one could run fast, look smartly dressed, look frisky while going by** kshihleewii=náakwsuw VAI.

**dress** VT **buy s.o. clothes to wear, get s.o. clothes to wear, dress s.o.** a=kwúneew VTA; **dress s.o.** weechpóo=leew VTA; **dress s.o. nicely, put bedcovers on s.o.** wŭlakwunáheew VTA; **dress s.o., get s.o. ready** weechpún=eew VTA.

**dress up** VI **be brightly coloured, be dressed up** wŭluléexiin VAI.

**drink** N **give a drink to s.o.** mŭnáheew VTA; **have a drink of something cold** thíisŭmuw VAI; **sap, Kool-Aid, soft drink, sweet drink** shookŭláapoow NI; **something to drink, a drink** méhmuneeng VII **Give me a drink.** 'Méhmŭnéeng míiliil.'; **take a big drink, take a lot of liquid, drink a lot** *(including non-alcoholic beverages)* xwíisŭmuw VAI; **take a strong drink** *(including non-alcoholic beverages)* àhwíisŭmuw VAI.

**drink** VI mŭnéew VAI **I never drink.** 'Máhta nŭmiimŭneewíiwi.'; **drink**

often, drink a lot** eewachíisŭmuw VAI; **drink one's fill, be full from drinking** kiispáapŭweew VAI; **drink oneself to death** aapchíisŭmuw VAI; **drink too much** wsaamíisŭmuw VAI; **drink until one urinates** shàshkíisŭ=muw VAI; **give s.o. something bad to drink** machiisŭmóoleew VTA; **have enough to drink** teepíisŭmuw VAI **Did you have enough to drink?** 'Méhch kteepíisŭmwi?'; **have plenty to drink** wŭyakíisŭmuw VAI; **like to drink** wiingíisŭmuw VAI; **stop drinking** ehkwíisŭmuw VAI **You should quit drinking.** 'Kóolu- áa -ehkwíi=sŭmwi.'; **be crazy from drinking, be silly from drinking** kpucheewíisŭ=muw VAI.

**drink** VT **drink s.t.** mŭnéew VAIO.

**drinking** N mŭneewáakan NI **Drinking will kill you.** 'Mŭneewáakan-uch kŭníhlkwun.'; **hotel, drinking establishment, bootlegger's place** sook=hupeesíikaan NI.

**drip** VI **drip, be dripping** pángpeew VII **It's really dripping.** 'Kíhchu-páng=pe.'; **drip, be dripping** pángpeew VAI.

**drive** VI **drive by, drive along** pŭmuch=éhleew VAI; **drive across** aashŭwuch=éhleew VAI; **drive ahead, drive in the lead, drive first** shayeewchéhleew VAI; **drive and make a loud noise, make a rattling noise while driving** *(of wagon wheels)* tiiwchéhleew VAI; **drive back, drive across** *(the river)* kwaxkchéhleew VAI; **drive backwards** ashahkchéhleew VAI; **drive close by** peexŭwuchéhleew VAI; **drive crookedly** pàptukchéhleew VAI; **drive fast, drive quickly** kshuchéhleew VAI; **drive from a certain place, drive for a certain reason** wundchéhleew VAI **They were driving from Chatham.** 'Chétum wundchehléewak.'; **drive from a certain place, drive from there** wunjchéhleew VAI **They were driving from Munceytown.** 'Naláhii wunjchehléewak.'; **drive here and there, drive about, drive around** apaamchéhleew VAI; **drive in a certain manner, drive in a certain direction** luchéhleew VAI; **drive in a circle, drive around something** wiiwŭnuchéhleew VAI; **drive in this direction, drive here, come here driving, drive toward the speaker** peech'chéhleew VA peetchéhleew VAI; **drive quietly** kwiishkwchéhleew VAI **He drives quietly.** 'Móxa kwiishk=wchéhle.'; **drive recklessly, go regardless of the consequences or risks** laalxawíhleew VAI; **drive slowly** ashahwchéhleew VAI; **drive slowly** *(diminutive)* chkawchehléeshuw VAI; **drive through the water** kamukw=chéhleew VAI; **drive up** uspchéhleew VAI; **fall sideways, drive crookedly** piimchéhleew VAI; **fly by, fly along, go by, go along, drive by, drive along, pedal by, pedal along** pŭ=míhleew VAI; **fly in various directions, drive in various directions, go in various directions, fly, drive** msíhleew VAI; **go across, drive across, pedal across, fly across** aa=shŭwíhleew VAI; **go by s.t., drive by s.t., fly by s.t., cycle by s.t.** loowíh=leew VAIO; **go by, drive by, fly by, cycle by** loowíhleew VAI; **straighten out, go straight**, **go quickly in the right direction, drive correctly** mayaawíhleew VAI; **turn around, turn around while in motion, turn around while driving, flip over** kwŭlupíhleew VAI; **drive a buggy** mbakiiháameew VAI.

**drive** VT **drive a car, use a car** kaal=háameew VAI, ahtamoombiilháameew VAI; **drive s.o. to death, work s.o. to**

**death, work s.o. very hard** aapchíi=naleew VTA; **drive s.t. animate, pilot s.t. animate** pŭmushíhkaweew VTA **The horses are being driven.** 'Pŭ=mushihkawáawak nehnayóongsak.'

**drive away** VI alumchéhleew VAI.

**drive away with** VT **drive away with s.o.** alumchéhlaleew VTA; **drive away with s.t.** alumchéhlatoow VTI2.

**drive in** VT **pound s.t. animate in, drive s.t. animate in** kunjchihtéeheew VTA; **pound s.t. in, drive s.t. in** kunjchih=téeham VTI1A; **turn s.t., screw s.t., wind s.t., drive s.t. in** *(of screws)* tùpáhkhwam VTI1A.

**drive inside** VI **go inside, fly inside, drive inside, fall inside** piinjíhleew VAI.

**drive inside** VT **chase s.o. inside, send s.o. inside, drive s.o. inside** *(of animals)* piindshíhkaweew VTA; **take s.o. inside, chase s.o. inside, send s.o. inside, drive s.o. inside** *(of animals)* piindshíiheew VTA.

**drive into** VT **chase s.o. into the water, drive s.o. into the water** kamukw=shíiheew VTA.

**driveway** N **be a flat road, be a flat driveway** pàkatéexun VII.

**drool** VI pŭliisóohŭweew VAI.

**drop** VI **have s.t. drop and break off, have s.t. drop and be severed** tŭ=míixtoow VTI2; **land, drop, arrive, arrive at a position by falling** matéexiin VAI **I fell on top of the box.** 'Níi mbákshung wáxkiich nŭmatée=xiin.', **The ball landed over there.** 'Yéelak matéexiin néenaxkw.'; **land, drop, arrive, arrive at a position by falling** matéexun VII **Where the road goes.** 'Éeli-matéexung.'

**drop** VT **crack s.t. animate, drop and crack s.t. animate, break s.t. animate in half** pasíixŭmeew VTA; **crack s.t., drop and crack s.t., break s.t. in half** pasíixtoow VTI2; **drop and break s.t.** lookíixtoow VTI2; **drop and break s.t. animate** lookíixŭ=meew VTA; **drop and break s.t. animate, wreck s.t. animate** lookihtée=xŭmeew VTA; **drop and break s.t., wreck s.t.** lookihtéextoow VTI2; **drop and chip s.t.** kwashihtéextoow VTI2; **drop and chip s.t. animate** kwashih=téexŭmeew VTA; **drop food from one's mouth, have food fall out of one's mouth, miss one's mouth while eating** palándam VOTI1; **drop s.o.** palúneew VTA; **drop s.o. and make them shatter, hit s.o. and make them shatter** sehtéexŭmeew VTA; **drop s.o. and sever their neck** tŭmiikwéexŭmeew VTA; **drop s.t.** palúnum VTI1B **He dropped it in the snow.** 'Pàlŭnúmun lí kóonung.'; **drop s.t. and make it shatter, hit s.t. and make it shatter** sehtéextoow VTI2; **drop s.t. and split it in two** pasih=téextoow VTI2; **drop s.t. animate and split it in two** pasihtéexŭmeew VTA; **drop s.t. animate from one's mouth, have s.t. animate fall out of one's mouth, miss one's mouth with s.t. animate** *(of food)* paláméew VTA; **drop s.t. animate so that it makes a sharp noise** chàhwihtéexŭmeew VTA; **drop s.t. from one's mouth, have s.t. fall out of one's mouth, miss one's mouth with s.t.** palándam VTI1A; **drop s.t. so that it makes a sharp noise** chàhwihtéextoow VTI2, chàhwíixtoow VTI2; **fall and make a sharp noise, make a sharp noise when dropped** chàhwíixiin VAI, chàhwíixun VII; **throw s.o. down with a thud, drop s.o. so that they make a thud** pòhwíixŭmeew VTA; **throw s.t. down with a thud, drop s.t. so**

**that it makes a thud** pòhwíixtoow VTI2; **throw something through a hole, drop s.t. in a hole** pkwáaheew VAIO.

**droppings** N **cat excrement, cat droppings** pooshíish'chuy NI; **chicken droppings, chicken excrement** kii=kiipsúchuy NI; **cow droppings, cow excrement** kóoychuy NI; **horse droppings, horse excrement** nehnayoon=gsúchuy NI.

**drops** N **bathe one's eyes, put drops in one's eyes** sookhíingweew VAI.

**drown** VI **drown** aapsúpeew VAI, aap=túpeew VAI.

**drown** VT **drown s.o.** aapsúpaleew VTA.

**drum** N pòhwŭníikan NI; **beat a drum, play a drum** pòhwŭníikeew VAI, **drum, be drumming** pòhámeew VAI; **beat a drum, play a drum, beat** *(on a black ash log, so that strips of wood will come off)* pòhwŭnúmeew VAI.

**drum** VI **drum, be drumming** pòhámeew VAI.

**drunk** ADJ **be drunk, be a drunk** mee=néetuw VAI; **be drunk and unpleasant, do bad things while drunk, drink poison** *(especially to induce miscarriage)* machíisŭmuw VAI; **be very drunk** waníisŭmuw VAI; **drunken person, a drunk** méeneet NA.

**drunk** N **be drunk, be a drunk** mee=néetuw VAI; **drunken person, a drunk** méeneet NA.

**dry** ADJ **be dry, be dried out** *(by heat)* káahsuw VAI, káahteew VII; **be dry** *(after being wet)* péengwat VII **My washing is dry.** 'Péengwatool kee=shiixtàwáaniil.'; **be dry** *(after being wet)* péengwun VII; **be dry ground** kaahahkéeyeew VII, peengwahkée=yeew VII; **be dry weather** káahkeew VII; **be dried, dry out** peengwíhleew VII; **be boiled dry** sihkpéesuw VAI; **boil down, boil dry** ihkpéeteew VII, ihkpéesuw VAI; **boil dry** sihkpatíi=keew VAI, sihkpeewchásuw VAI, sihk=peewcháteew VII; **change s.o.'s diaper, make s.o. be dry** peengwíixŭ=meew VTA; **run dry** *(of an amount of water)* sihkpéhleew VII.

**dry** VT **dry s.o.** *(with a towel held in the hand)* kaahiikwáaleew VTA; **dry s.o.** *(with a towel)*, **wipe s.o. off** *(with a towel)* peengwiikwáaleew VTA; **dry s.o., dry s.t. animate** *(by heat)* péengwseew VTA; **dry s.o., wring s.o. out** péengwŭneew VTA; **dry s.t. animate out** *(by heat)* káahseew VTA; **dry s.t. out** *(by heat)* káahsum VTI1B; **dry s.t.** peengwáhkhwam VTI1A; **dry s.t.** *(with a towel)*, **wipe s.t. off** *(with a towel)* peengwíikwam VTI1A; **dry s.t.** *(by heat)* péengwsum VTI1B; **dry s.t., wring s.t. out** *(using the hands)* péengwŭnum VTI1B; **dried** peengwii- PN **Dried stone.** 'Péengwii-asún.'; **be dried** *(by heat)* kaahsáasuw VII, kaahsáasuw VAI; **be dried by heat** *(after being wet)* péengwsuw VAI, péengwteew VII; **be dried by the wind, be dried out by the wind** péengxookw VAI, péengxwun VII; **be dried, dry out** peengwíhleew VII; **dried apple** kaaháapŭlush NA; **dried-out bread** káahapwaan NI; **dry the dishes** peengwahkhwíikeew VAI, peengwiikwáakeew VAI; **piece of dried wood** káahxakw NI, péeng=xwakw NI.

**dryer** N **clothes dryer** peengwsíikan NI.

**duck** N wshíhweew NA.

**dull** ADJ **be a dull colour** mataapamúk=wat VII, mataapamúkwsuw VAI; **be dull, have a dull edge, have a dull point** matalóosuw VAI, matalóoyeew VII; **make s.t. dull** *(using a tool or instrument)* matalóoham VTI1A.

**dumpling** N chooskŭnapwáanush NI.
**during** PREP **during the daytime** kiish=kwŭnúwii PC **I'll cook during the daytime.** 'Kiishkwŭnúwii ápih nát=pwi.'; **during the fall, during the autumn** takwaakwŭnúwii PC; **during the winter** loowanúwii PC.
**dust** N póngw NI; **throw powder on s.o., throw dust on s.o., throw sand on s.o., throw dirt on s.o.** pong=hwáaleew VTA.
**dustbath** N **powder oneself, give one-self a dustbath** ponghwúnzuw VAI.
**dusty** ADJ **be dusty** pongóohuw VAI, pongóowuw VII, póngwsuw VAI.
**dwell** VI **dwell there, live there** wíikuw VAI **My house.** 'Wíikŭyaan.', **Your house.** 'Wíikŭyan.'
**dye** VT **dye s.t., dye s.t. a certain colour** lúchasum VTI1B **I dyed my hair.** 'Nii=láxkal ndulchásŭmun.'; **dye s.t. ani-mate a certain colour** lúchaseew VTA; **be burnt black, be dyed black** nzuk=chásuw VAI, nzukcháteew VII; **be dyed red, turn red, be red from heat, be browned** *(of meat)* maxkcháteew VII; **be dyed red, turn red, burn red, be red from heat, get a sunburn, be browned** maxkchásuw VAI; **blacken s.t.** *(by heat)*, **dye s.t. black** nzuk=chásum VTI1B; **dye s.o. green** askask=wcháseew VTA; **dye s.t. animate brown, dye s.t. animate grey** wii=pongwcháseew VTA; **dye s.t. animate red, brown s.t. animate** maxkchás=eew VTA; **dye s.t. animate white, heat s.t. animate up and whiten it** *(when washing clothes)* waapcháseew VTA; **dye s.t. animate yellow, dye s.t. animate brown** wiisaawcháseew VTA; **dye s.t. brown, dye s.t. grey** wiipong=wchásum VTI1B; **dye s.t. green** as=kaskwchásum VTI1B; **dye s.t. red, brown s.t.** *(of meat)* maxkchásum VTI1B; **dye s.t. white, heat s.t. up and whiten it** *(when washing clothes)* waapchásum VTI1B; **dye s.t. yellow, dye s.t. brown** wiisaawchásum VTI1B; **scorch s.t. animate, blacken s.t. ani-mate** *(by heat)*, **dye s.t. animate** nzukcháseew VTA.

# E

**each other** PR **be related to each other** laangóondŭwak VAI *usually plural;* **bite each other** sahsakándŭwak VAI, sakandawéewak VAI; **love each other** àhwaaltúwak VAI *usually plural;* **sleep with each other, sleep together** wihpéendŭwak VAI *usually plural;* **work together, help each other** takwundaméewak VAI.
**ear** N **my ear** níhtawak NID; **cover one's ears, have one's ears covered** kpax=éexiin VAI, kpoxwéexiin VAI; **cover s.o.'s ears** *(using the hands)* kpaxée=neew VTA, kpoxwéeneew VTA; **cover s.o.'s ears** kpaxéexŭmeew VTA; **have a big ear** mángxeew VAI; **have a clean ear** piilihtawákeew VAI, píil=xeew VAI; **have a dirty ear, have dirty ears** niiskihtawákeew VAI; **have a long ear** kwŭnihtawákeew VAI, kwŭnáxeew VAI; **have big ears** a=mángxeew VAI; **have long ears** a=kwáanxeew VAI; **have one's ears standing up** niipawaxéexiin VAI; **have one's ears lying in a certain manner, have one's ears lying in a certain direction** laxéexiin VAI **His ears are hanging down to the ground.** 'Áhkiing làxéexiin.'; **raise one's ears, have one's ears raised** uspxéexiin VAI; **slap s.o. across the face** *(close to the ears)*, **slap s.o. across the ears** paakxehtéeheew VTA; **wash one's ears** kshiixihtawákeew

VAI; **wash people's ears** kshiixihta=wakeeníikeew VAI; **wash s.o.'s ears** kshiixihtawakéeneew VTA.

**earache** N **have an earache** wihtawak=íineew VAI.

**early** ADJ **early, easily** aapwi- PV **I came early.** 'Ndáapwi-pá.'; **early, easily** aapwu- PV *informal* **My grandmother was sick early on, she had rheumatism.** 'Áapwu- nóohum -wiinamál=suw, lumtiisíineew.', **You cry easily.** 'Ktáapwu-lpákw.'; **early, easily** aapŭwu- PV *informal* **I got up early.** 'Ndáapŭwu-áamwi.', **He blushes easily** 'Ayáapŭwu-maxkchàlíin=gweew.'; **early, easily** áapwi PC **I came early.** 'Áapwi mbáam.', **He's coming back from working soon.** 'Áapwi aapalóhkeew.'; **early, easily** áapwu PC *informal* **Did you go to sleep early?** 'Áapwu há kíi káwi?', **I went to work early.** 'Áapwu nŭ=mawalóhke.'; **early in the morning** kihtayapáayu PC; **more, more than, early** aluwii- PV **Early afternoon.** 'Alúwii-laawahkwéewŭnii.'; **more, more than, early** alúwii PC.

**earn** VT **earn money, earn a wage** pŭnáham VOTI1; **earn s.t.** pŭnáham VTI1A.

**earnest** ADJ **be in earnest, be serious** *(about something)*, **get up the nerve** *(to do something)* kihteelúndam VOTI1 **I'm serious about going there.** 'Ngihteelúndam náh ndá.', **I got up the nerve to tell him to go home.** 'Ngihteelúndam, ndúlaa máachiil.'

**earring** N sakaxeehóonay NI, sakaxée=hoon NI, skaxeehóonay NI; **wear earrings** sakaxeehoonhámeew VAI, skax=éehuw VAI.

**earth** N **land, earth** áhkuy NI; **be brown earth, be grey earth** wiipongwah=kéeyeew VII; **be level earth** shaax=kahkéexun VII.

**easily** ADV **early, easily** aapwi- PV **I came early.** 'Ndáapwi-pá.'; **early, easily** aapwu- PV *informal* **My grandmother was sick early on, she had rheumatism.** 'Áapwu- nóohum -wii=namálsuw, lumtiisíineew.', **You cry easily.** 'Ktáapwu-lpákw.'; **early, easily** aapŭwu- PV *informal* **I got up early.** 'Ndáapŭwu-áamwi.', **He blushes easily** 'Ayáapŭwu-maxk=chàlíingweew.'; **early, easily** áapwi PC **I came early.** 'Áapwi mbáam.', **He's coming back from working soon.** 'Áapwi aapalóhkeew.'; **early, easily** áapwu PC *informal* **Did you go to sleep early?** 'Áapwu há kíi káwi?', **I went to work early.** 'Áapwu nŭ=mawalóhke.'; **get angry very easily** ayaapŭwanóongsuw VAI; **get cold easily** ayáhwachuw VAI; **scare easily, be easy to scare** aapŭwahpáasuw VAI.

**Easter** N **celebrate Easter, be Easter** *(indefinite subject)* íishtaliin VAI, íisŭliin VAI.

**easy** ADJ **be easy** *(to do)* aapŭwíixun VII, áapŭwat VII; **be easy to do, be easy** *(to read, to understand)* aapŭwíixiin VAI; **find s.o. easy** *(to do something with)* aapŭwéelŭmeew VTA **I find him easy to teach.** 'Ndaapŭwéelŭmaaw ndakehkíimaan.', **I find him easy to play with.** 'Ndaapŭwéelŭmaaw nŭ=meelawusóomaan.'; **find s.t. easy to do, think s.t. easy to do** aapŭwee=lúndam VTI1A **I don't think anything of going to town.** 'Ndaapŭweelún=damun ootéeneeng ndáan.', **I find it easy to go to sleep.** 'Ndaapŭwee=lúndamun nŭmáw-kawí.'; **get an easy job, have an easy job** aapŭwal=óhkeew VAI; **make it easy for someone to do s.t., fix s.t. so it would be easy** *(to do something)* aapŭwíixtoow VTI2; **make s.t. animate so that it would be easy, fix s.t. animate so**

**that it would be easy** *(for someone to do something)* aapŭwíixŭmeew VTA **I made it so that the window would be easy for me to open.** 'Ndaapŭ= wíixŭmaaw eeheeshandéekan wéenj-káng-tawúnak.'; **scare easily, be easy to scare** aapŭwahpáasuw VAI.

**eat** VI míitsuw VAI **I'll eat later.** 'Ápih nŭmíitsi.'; **be full from eating** kíis= puw VAI; **eat a lot** mangaléetŭyeew VAI; **eat an awful lot, overeat** chii= palóosuw VAI *considered impolite;* **eat like a pig** achiipíilatoow VAI; **glutton, someone who eats a lot, someone who never gets full** máaleew NA; **have one's eyes bigger than one's belly, take more than one can eat** mangshéengweew VAI; **have plenty to eat, have an abundance of food** wŭyakíipuw VAI.

**eat** VT **eat s.t.** míichuw VTI3 **They didn't have anything to eat.** 'Kwíila-kwéek -míichŭwak.'; **eat s.t. animate** mhwéew VTA **I ate that apple already.** 'Méhch áa ngáta-mhwáaw ná áapŭ= lush.'; **be glad to eat s.t.** *(not having had it for some time)* payahkwándam VTI1A; **be glad to eat s.t. animate** *(not having had it for some time)* payáhkwameew VTA; **be tired of eating s.t.** peekándam VTI1A; **be tired of eating s.t. animate** péekameew VTA; **eat greasy food** shamuchéepuw VAI **I ate too much greasy food.** 'Noosáa= mi-shamuchéepwi.'; **eat s.o. with something** náxpameew VTA; **eat s.t. alone, eat s.t. with nothing else** mooshándam VTI1A **Don't eat it alone, eat it with bread.** 'Chíi mooshandamóowi, náxpu-míichiil apwáan.'; **eat s.t. animate alone, eat s.t. animate with nothing else** móo= shameew VTA; **eat s.t. animate bare, strip s.t. animate to the bone** chíi= kwameew VTA; **eat s.t. animate by accident** páhtameew VTA, píhtameew VTA; **eat s.t. animate raw** áskameew VTA; **eat s.t. bare, strip s.t. to the bone** chiikwándam VTI1A **The horse ate the grass to the ground.** 'Neh= nayóongus wchiikwándamun mii= xáskwal.'; **eat s.t. by accident** pah= tándam VTI1A, pihtándam VTI1A; **eat s.t. raw** askándam VTI1A; **eat s.t. with something** naxpándam VTI1A; **eat supper** sápaluw VAI; **leave scraps of s.t. animate behind, don't eat all of s.t. animate** *(of food)* píiwameew VTA; **leave scraps of s.t. behind** *(of food)*, **don't eat all of s.t.** piiwándam VTI1A **I left a little bit.** 'Chángiish mbiiwándamun.'; **only eat some of s.t. animate, have a piece of s.t. animate to eat, only eat some of s.t. animate on one's plate** mshámeew VTA; **only eat some of s.t., have a piece of s.t. to eat, only eat part of s.t. on one's plate** mshándam VTI1A.

**eat up** VT **eat s.t. animate up** ktámweew VTA **I ate him up long ago.** 'Ngih= ktámwa.'; **eat s.t. up** ktáam VTI3.

**eat with** VT **eat with s.o.** wihpóomeew VTA; **eat with s.o., stay with s.o.** wiitapóomeew VTA.

**edge** N **at the edge of something** wsháyee PC **He's walking at the edge of the water.** 'Wsháyee mbíing pŭ= músuw.'; **at the edge of something** wsháyii PC **I put the book at the edge of the table.** 'Pámbiil wsháyii eehundaxpóonung ndáhlaaw.'; **at the edge of something** *(diminutive)* wsháyiish PC **I sleep at the edge.** 'Wsháyiish ngáwi.'; **at the edge of the bed** wshayapíineeng PC; **be dull, have a dull edge, have a dull point** matalóosuw VAI, matalóoyeew VII; **be sewn along the edges, be sewn up** paxkawiikwáasuw VII; **cut s.t. around the edge** wiiwŭnúshum VTI1B; **edge of the hill** wshayaawún= ge PC; **lake, edge of water** wsháype

PC **I went out to the lake.** 'Wsháype nóom.'; **sew around the edge of s.t., turn up and sew s.t.** paxkawíikwam VTI 1 A; **sew around the edges** wiiwŭ=niikwáakeew VAI; **sew around the edges of s.t.** wiiwŭníikwam VTI 1 A; **sew around the edges of s.t. animate** wiiwŭniikwáaleew VTA; **sew around the edges, put a hem on** paxkawii=kwáakeew VAI; **sew s.t. animate up, sew around the edge of s.t. animate** paxkawiikwáaleew VTA.

**Edward** N étŭwat NA.

**egg** N wáhwal NI; **hide eggs** *(of chickens)* kaatáhwheew VAI; **lay an egg** wáhw=heew VAI; **little egg** *(diminutive)* changáhwalush NI; **set s.o. on eggs** *(of chickens)* kxahwéexŭmeew VTA.

**eight** N xáash PC **Eighteen.** 'Xáash txaaníhka.'

**either** CJ **either, any** akwáawu PC **I want anything.** 'Akwáawu kwéekw ngatáatam.', **I can go anywhere.** 'Akwáawu táa ndá.'

**elbow** N **my elbow** níiskwan NAD, níis=kwan NID; **wash one's elbows** kshii=xíiskwaneew VAI.

**elderberry** N asanakóonzhuy NA.

**elderly** ADJ **look old, look like an elderly person** kihkeesŭwiináakwsuw VAI.

**eleven** N ngwutaaníhka PC.

**Eli** N iiláyush NA.

**Elizabeth** N líshpet NA.

**elm** N **American elm** wŭlaakanaamíin=zhuy NA, wŭlaakanahóonzhuy NA.

**else** ADJ **eat s.t. animate alone, eat s.t. animate with nothing else** móosha=meew VTA; **mistake s.o. for someone else** pahchíinaweew VTA; **mistake s.t. for something else** pahchíinam VTI 1 A; **eat s.t. alone, eat s.t. with nothing else** mooshándam VTI 1 A **Don't eat it alone, eat it with bread.** 'Chíi mooshandamóowi, náxpu-míichiil apwáan.'

**elsewhere** ADV **elsewhere, somewhere else** palii- PV **I put it elsewhere.** 'Mbálii-áhtoon.', **He went the other way.** 'Palíi-lóoxwe.'; **elsewhere, somewhere else** palu- PV *informal* **I said it in a hurry.** 'Mbálu-íin.'; **elsewhere, somewhere else** palí PC *informal* **Take the stone off the table.** 'Palí lúnih nú asún wúnju-eehundax=póonung.'; **elsewhere, somewhere else** palíi PC **Drive somewhere else!** 'Palíi luchéhlaal!', **Go away!** 'Palíi áal!'; **elsewhere, somewhere else** palíiwi PC **They stood him somewhere else.** 'Palíiwi íin wŭniipalaa=wáawal.'; **stand over, stand somewhere else, stand elsewhere** palii=káapawuw VAI.

**Emerson** N émshun NA *man's name.*

**emphatic particle** N **also, emphatic** kwŭlúp PC **I went that way, and also he went the other way.** 'Níi nú wúndakw ndá, kwŭlúp néeka yéelak wúndakw éew.', **He thinks he's a real angel ('He thinks he has wings').** 'Kwŭlúp liitéeheew wŭlón=gwanuw.'; **emphatic** alán PC **I don't care.** 'Alán ná.', **I'd better not.** 'Alán áa máh há.'; **emphatic** táa PC **I don't know why he brought it.** 'Táa níik éet kwéekw wéenj-péetaakw.', **I looked everywhere for it.** 'Wéemu táa ndúlu-kwíilamun.'; áayee PC **Let's go to town today while I'm able to walk.** 'Ootéeneeng áa kwáy ktáhna kwáy kíishkwihk áayee má ngíish-pumúsiin.', **Please help me.** 'Áayee má kŭwíichŭmi.'; **emphatic** áng PC **Sometimes I mistake him for someone else.** 'Mbahchíinawaa áng táas.', **He couldn't even talk to my mother.** 'Ách áng wtayáalu-kihkŭlooláawal ngúkal.'; **emphatic, should** xáa PC **You should try to save your money.** 'Káta- xáa -keeshéetsiin kshulpúl=um.', **I wish he'd go home** 'Táas xáa máachiiw.'; **indeed, emphatic** áx PC **I told you she was going to have a child.** 'Ktúlul áx amiimúnzal katákxánuw.'; **long ago, until, emphatic** kúnj PC **You will come at four o'clock.** 'Néew-kŭlák-uch kúnj kpá.', **He came a while ago.** 'Kúnj wéeti péew.'; **maybe, emphatic** xéet PC **That's not the one.** 'Máh xéet ná.', **I wonder if he's there yet.** 'Wách xéet náh péew.'; **one time, emphatic** táas PC **My late grandmother told me.** 'Noohŭmáya táas ndúkw.'; **question marker, emphatic** há PC **This is where he used to work.** 'Nún há wtihúnda-alóhkeen.', **Do you think so?** 'Ktíit há?'

**empty** ADJ **be empty** aláxan VII, aláxsuw VAI; **be an empty room** alaxúndeew VII; **be an empty town, be no one in town** alaxootéenayuw VII.

**empty** VT **empty s.t.** *(using the hands)* aláxŭnum VTI1B; **empty s.t. animate** *(using the hands)* aláxŭneew VTA; **throw s.t. and empty it out, empty s.t. out** alaxáaheew VAIO.

**empty handed** ADJ **be empty handed** mooshŭlúnjeew VAI; **go empty handed, go bare handed, don't take anything** *(especially to a gathering)* mooshŭlunjéhleew VAI.

**empty headed** ADJ **be empty headed, be stupid** kpáandpeew VAI.

**encourage** VT **encourage s.o.** kiihíi=meew VTA.

**end** N **be at the end of a row, be at the end of a line, be at the end of something** wihkwáameew VII **It is a little ways to the end of it.** 'Péexwiish wihkwáameew.', **We've come to the end now.** 'Méhch kwáy éenda-wih=kwaámeek kpáhna.'; **be the end of the road** wihkwatéexun VII; **come to an end, be the end of something** wíhkweew VII; **cut the last of s.t., cut s.t. off at the end** póhkwshum VTI1B; **the end of the road** wihkwáanay NI.

**English** N **English person** eenglúsh=maan NA; **speak English** shihshŭ=wánakuw VAI.

**enjoy** VT **enjoy one's food** wiingchée=puw VAI; **enjoy playing, have fun while playing** wiingeelawúsuw VAI; **like to listen, enjoy listening, enjoy hearing something** wiingxéexiin VAI **This one likes to listen.** 'Wiingxée=xiin há wá.'

**enough** ADJ **enough, sufficiently** teep- PV *informal* **It's not cooked enough.** 'Máh téep-kiishtéewi.', **Do you have enough?** 'Ktéep-kxáni?'; **enough, sufficiently** teepu- PV *informal* **It is big enough.** 'Téepu-lukíhkwun.', **It's time you got a haircut.** 'Méhch áa ktéepu-moonzháasi.'; **be enough** teepéelook VAI *usually plural,* tee=péeltool VII *usually plural;* **have enough of s.t.** teepíhlatoow VTI2; **have enough of s.t. animate** teepíh=laleew VTA; **be deep enough** *(of holes)* teepáalakat VII; **be deficient, be lacking, be short of something, be not quite enough of something** *(s.t. animate)*, **fall short** noondéexiin VAI, noondéexun VII; **be not enough of something** noondaawíixun VII; **charge a fair price for s.t.** teepaa=watóoheew VAIO; **have enough to drink** teepíisŭmuw VAI **Did you have enough to drink?** 'Méhch kteepíi=sŭmwi?'

**enter** VI **go inside quickly, run inside, enter a dwelling running** piinjiikéh=leew VAI.

**envious** ADJ **be jealous, be envious** akaxeelúnzuw VAI; **be jealous of s.o.'s achievements, be jealous of s.o.'s possessions, be envious of s.o.** kxéelŭmeew VTA.

**Ephraim** N íipŭleesh NA.

**epilepsy** N **be afflicted with epilepsy, have epilepsy** wihwchiipíisuw VAI.

**epileptic** ADJ **have a fit, have a seizure, have an epileptic seizure** wchiipíi=suw VAI.

**erratic** ADJ **go crookedly, fly crookedly, fly on an erratic course** pàptukíh=leew VAI.

**erroneously** ADV **misunderstand s.o., mishear s.o., hear s.o. erroneously, don't hear s.o. correctly** chanus=táweew VTA; **misunderstand s.t., mishear s.t., hear s.t. erroneously, don't hear s.t. correctly** chanústam VTI1A.

**error** N **by accident, in error** pahchi- PV **I cut him by accident.** 'Mbáhchi-tŭmúshaaw.'; **by accident, in error** pahchu- PV *informal* **He said it by accident.** 'Páhchu- kwéek -úw.', **I stepped on it by accident.** 'Mbáhchu-ahpalíhkeen.'; **by mistake, in error** chanu- PV *informal* **You said it wrong.** 'Kchánu-íin.'

**escape** VI póolŭweew VAI; **run away to here, escape to here** peetshíimuw VAI.

**escape from** VT **escape from s.o.** póo=leew VTA.

**establishment** N **hotel, drinking establishment, bootlegger's place** sook=hupeesíikaan NI.

**Ethel** N éshŭlush NA.

**Evelyn** N éflin NA.

**even** ADJ **be even ground, be smooth ground** wŭlahkéeyeew VII; **be even, be in order, lie correctly** mayaawíi=xun VII; **be level, be on level, be even, be on even, be even with something** tpuskŭwíixun VII.

**even** ADV kách PC **What, again?** 'Kách wáak?', **I've already made the bread.** 'Nál kách apwáan noolíh=toon.'; **even** ách PC **Not even half of it.** 'Ách máh pasíi.', **Even the coat he was wearing had a long tail behind.** 'Ách nú kóotum eewéeheet kwuníi-shkwúnayeew wtéeng.'; **even** áhch PC **I'll see him anyway.** 'Áhch-uch wáak néewaaw.', **He didn't even go there.** 'Áhch máh náh éewu.'

**evening** N **be a certain kind of evening** láakuw VII **It's a cold evening.** 'Thíi-láakuw.'; **be a cool evening** thíi-láakuw VII; **be evening** wŭláakuw VII **I'll go this evening.** 'Wulaakwíike-uch náh mbá.', **He came to visit last evening.** 'Peetootéewuw weelaa=kwíike'; **during the evening** wŭlaa=kwŭnúwii PC **I walk around in the evenings.** 'Wŭlaakwŭnúwii áng nŭmáw-paapŭmúsi.'

**evenly** ADV **be pretty, be evenly shaped, be nicely shaped** wŭluchéesuw VAI, wŭluchéeyeew VII; **fit s.t. level, fit s.t. evenly** tpuskŭwíixtoow VTI2 **My hat is on evenly.** 'Ndupuskŭwíixtoon ndaakongwéepuy.'

**event** N **miss an event, miss a regular event** palíhleew VAI.

**eventually** ADV **later, eventually** aa=yáaxkwu PC **I went later.** 'Aayáax=kwu náh ndá.', **We'll be leaving eventually.** 'Aayáaxkwu-ch ktalŭ=musíhna.'

**everlasting** ADJ **forever, everlasting** hálŭmii PC **I went away eventually.** 'Hálŭmii ndalŭmúsi.'

**every** ADJ éesh PC **Every once in a while.** 'Éesh tá lúkih.'; **every** héesh PC **Everytime I go there.** 'Héesh náh ayáan.', **Every evening my father told me: "Fetch the cows from the other side of the road."** 'Héesh wŭláakwiik nóox ndukw: "Naatkóo=yeel awasiixkanáwe."'

**evil** ADJ **be condemned to die for evil deeds, die deservedly, be thought incapable** kundeelŭmúkwsuw VAI; **have evil thoughts, have bad thoughts** *(as if without regret)* chii=piitéeheew VAI; **do evil** matalóhkeew VAI; **evil** matalohkeewáakan NI.

**exact** ADJ **speak the exact truth** shaax=

kaaptóoneew VAI.

**excessively** ADV **too much, excessively** wsaa- PV **It's too long.** 'Wsáa-kwŭnéew.', **The bat's too heavy.** 'Wsáa-laanzhíhkan pakandíikan.'; **too much, excessively** wsaami- PV **He is too lazy.** 'Wsáami-kihtamún=eew.', **It's too big, the hole is too deep.** 'Wsáami-xwushéeyeew.'; **too much, excessively** wsaamu- PV *informal* **Right away they told their son, "Don't marry her, she runs around too much."** 'Sháa wtulaawáawal kwiissùwáawal, "Chíi takwapŭwaa=láahan, wsáamu-mihmsahtakíhle."', **Your cane is too short.** 'Wsáamu-chahkwéeshuw ktaláawan.'

**exchange** VT **exchange s.t. animate, return s.t. animate, give s.t. animate back** *(after borrowing it)* aashŭwún=eew VTA; **exchange s.t., give s.t. back, return s.t.** *(after borrowing it)* aashŭwúnum VTI1B.

**exciting** ADJ **tell a tall tale, tell an exciting story, brag** kaanzhaachíimuw VAI; **tell s.o. a tall tale, tell s.o. an exciting story** kaanzhaachŭmóhka=weew VTA.

**excrement** N mwíichtuy NI, móoy NI; **be covered in excrement** móoyuw VAI; **black excrement** nzúkchuy NI; **cat excrement, cat droppings** poo=shíish'chuy NI; **chicken droppings, chicken excrement** kiikiipsúchuy NI; **cow droppings, cow excrement** kóoychuy NI; **dog excrement** mwaa=kanéewchuy NI; **have excrement on one's backside** mwíitŭyeew VAI; **horse droppings, horse excrement** nehnayoongsúchuy NI; **walk with excrement on one's backside** *(indicating a certain attitude)* mwiitŭyéew=xeew VAI.

**exhausted** ADJ **be tired out, be exhausted** shawíhleew VAI.

**expectant** ADJ **be hopeful, be expectant, want help** nahkéewsuw VAI.

**expensive** ADJ **be expensive** xwáawatuw VII, xwáawatuw VAI; **be expensive, cost a lot** amangaawatúwal VII *usually plural.*

**experience** N **take s.o. through something, take s.o. through an experience** eeshóoxwaleew VTA.

**experience** VT **go through s.t., experience s.t.** eeshóoxweew VAIO.

**explain** VT **explain s.t.** mihtakunóotum VTI1B; **explain s.t. to s.o.** mihtakun=ootŭmáweew VTAO; **expose s.t. for s.o., explain s.t. to s.o.** mihchiixtáw=eew VTAO; **uncover s.t., expose s.t., explain s.t.** mihchíixtoow VTI2.

**explode** VI **explode, blow up, burst** *(from heat, s.t. animate)* pwáhksuw VAI, pwáhkteew VII; **make s.t. animate explode, make s.t. animate blow up** *(from heat)* pwáhkseew VTA; **make s.t. explode, make s.t. blow up** *(from heat)* pwáhksum VTI1B.

**expose** VT **uncover s.o., expose s.o.** mihchíhlaleew VTA; **uncover s.o., expose s.o., display s.o., cause s.o. to be exposed** mihchíixŭmeew VTA; **uncover s.t., expose s.t.** mihchíhlatoow VTI2; **uncover s.t., expose s.t., explain s.t.** mihchíixtoow VTI2; **expose s.t. for s.o., explain s.t. to s.o.** mih=chiixtáweew VTAO; **lie down uncovered, lie down exposed, lie down in the open** mihchíixiin VAI; **be exposed, be in the open** mihchíixun VII; **be found out, be exposed** mihchíh=leew VAI; **be uncovered, be exposed to view** mihchiixtáasuw VII, mih=chiixtáasuw VAI; **have bare hands, have bare arms, have exposed hands, have exposed arms** mihtŭ=náxkeew VAI; **have bare hands, have exposed hands** mihtŭlúnjeew VAI; **have bare hands, have no gloves on, have one's hands exposed, have one's hands showing** mihtŭlunjée=

xiin VAI; **have one's arms exposed, have bare arms, have one's hands exposed, have bare hands** mihtŭ=naxkéexiin VAI; **have one's back exposed, have one's back showing** mihtpoxkwanéexiin VAI; **have one's backside exposed, have one's backside sticking out** mihchiitŭyéexiin VAI; **have one's foot exposed, have one's feet showing** mihtsiitéexiin VAI; **have one's head exposed, have one's head out in the open** mihtaandpée=xiin VAI; **have one's legs showing, have one's legs exposed, have bare legs** mihtkaatéexiin VAI; **have one's teeth exposed** mihtaniikéexiin VAI; **walk by with one's backside exposed** mooshakiitŭyéewxeew VAI.

**expression** N **have an expression on one's face indicating that one is about to cry** ooshawutoonéhleew VAI.

**extend** VT **add on to s.t. animate, extend s.t. animate** aaníhkhweew VTA; **add on to s.t., extend s.t.** aaníhk=hwam VTI 1 A.

**extent** N **certain amount, certain extent** eelkih- PV *followed by verb in conjunct order* **It's getting close to when I want to leave.** 'Peexŭwíhle éelkih-katá-alumsúyaan.', **It's time to eat.** 'Éelkih-miitsáhtiing.'; lúkih PC **I go there to visit once in a while.** 'Héesh táa lúkih náh ndulootéewi.', **Some time ago.** 'Táa lúkih.'; **extent, volume, amount** lukíhkwi PC **Later on.** 'Táa lukíhkwi.', **How much does the table weigh?** 'Tá lukíhkwi póon=dakat eehundáxpwiing?'

**extinguish** VT **put s.t. animate out, extinguish s.t. animate** *(of fires)* wchii=mahtéeheew VTA; **put s.t. out, extinguish s.t.** *(of fires)* wchiimahtéeham VTI 1 A **Last night someone turned off the lights at my place.** 'Piiskéeku awéen oochiimahtéehŭmun wíikŭ=yaan.'; **go out, be extinguished** *(of fires)* ahtéhleew VII.

**extra** ADJ **be extra dark out, be awfully dark** spwiingwéewii-páhkŭnum VII; **carry s.t. extra, carry s.t. in addition** naxpasánuw VAIO; **have (extra) clothes in layers, have on more clothes than someone else** pihta=wákuw VAI **I am covered in three layers, I am dressed in three layers.** 'Nxú mbihtawákwi.'; **wear an extra shirt** pihtawahéembteew VAI.

**extreme** ADJ **extreme pain, suffering** aweendamuwáakan NI.

**extremely** ADV **be extremely lazy** lax=kalákayeew VAI *considered impolite,* laxktúyeew VAI; **very, extremely, intensely** shihshíikaanzh PC **A great big snake.** 'Shihshíikaanzh lúkih xwáchu-áxkook.', **I got really wet.** 'Shihshíi=kaanzh lúkih níiskpe.'; **very, extremely, intensely** shíikaanzh PC **She really made me mad.** 'Shíikaanzh lúkih nŭwiiníihukw.', **It really runs well.** 'Shíikaanzh lúkih wŭlíhleew.'

**eye** N **my eye, my face** nuskíinjukw NID; **bathe one's eyes, put drops in one's eyes** sookhíingweew VAI; **be big eyed** *(after seeing something unusual)*, **lie with one's eyes open** *(especially if one cannot sleep)* amangaalakiin=gwéexiin VAI; **be cross-eyed** piima=teelíingweew VAI; **be struck in the eye, brush against something which goes into the eye** laapsheengwéexiin VAI; **graze s.o.'s eye** laapsheengwée=heew VTA; **have a black eye** nzuk=shéengweew VAI; **have a sty in one's eye** wtohwaníingweew VAI; **have big eyes** amangaalakíingweew VAI, man=gateelíingweew VAI; **have dark eyes** nzukaalakíingweew VAI; **have green eyes** askaskwaalakíingweew VAI; **have grey eyes** wiipongwaalakíingweew VAI; **have infected eyes, have pus in one's eyes, have 'sleep' in one's eyes** mŭleelíingweew VAI; **have light-**

**coloured eyes**, **have grey eyes** waa=xeelíingweew VAI; **have nice eyes** weewŭlaalakíingweew VAI; **have one eye** ngwutíingweew VAI; **have one's eye's half closed** spwiingwéexiin VAI; **have one's eyes bigger than one's belly, take more than one can eat** mangshéengweew VAI; **have one's eyes closed** sohpwiingwéexiin VAI; **have one's eyes closed, close one's eyes** sohpwíingweew VAI; **have one's eyes open** aapakiingwéexiin VAI; **have one's eyes open** *(especially of a dead person)* toongiingwéexiin VAI; **have one's eyes open, have big eyes** xwaalakiingwéexiin VAI; **have one's eyes sticking out, look out, peek out** ktiingwéexiin VAI; **have one's eyes swollen shut** samwusheengwéexiin VAI, samwushéengweew VAI; **have one's eyes wide open, have big eyes** xwaapakiingwéexiin VAI; **have pulled-down eyes** taaxksheengwéexiin VAI; **have pus in one's eyes, have infected eyes** mŭluyeelíingweew VAI; **have red eyes, blush, have a red face** maxkshéengweew VAI; **have round ('button') eyes** kŭnoopaalakíin=gweew VAI; **have shiny eyes** *(especially in the dark)* waaseeliingwée=xiin VAI; **have small eyes** *(as if closed)* spwíingweew VAI; **have something in one's eye** psúm VOTI1; **have sore eyes** wuskiinjkwíineew VAI; **have tears in one's eyes** akeexpéengweew VAI; **open one's eyes** aapakíingweew VAI; **pull one's eyes down, have one's eyes pulled down** taaxkshéengweew VAI; **pull s.o.'s eye down, hold s.o.'s eye open** taaxksheengwéeneew VTA; **scratch one's eyes, have itchy eyes** kshiipaalakíingweew VAI; **see the whites of someone's eyes** waapee=liingwéexiin VAI; **sit with shining eyes** *(especially in the dark)* waasee=liingohkwéepuw VAI; **stick one's finger in s.o.'s eye** laapsheengwéeneew VTA.

**eyebrow** N maamaaliingwáawan NI, maamáawan NI; **eyebrows** maamaa=líingwal NI *usually plural.*

**eyeglasses** N **eyeglasses, glasses** wus=kiinjkwahíikanal NI *usually plural;* **wear eyeglasses, wear glasses** wus=kiinjkwáhŭmeew VAI.

**eyelash** N miixiingwáawan NA.

**eyesight** N **have poor eyesight, have a hard time seeing** matatawáapuw VAI **You might have a hard time seeing.** 'Kŭmatatawáapi éet.'; **see a long way, have good eyesight** wŭlatawáapuw VAI.

# F

**face** N **my eye**, **my face** nuskíinjukw NID; **bump one's face against something** paakiingwéexiin VAI; **have a big face** xwíingweew VAI; **have a clean face** piilchàlíingweew VAI; **have a cold face** thíingweew VAI; **have a dirty face** niiskchàlíingweew VAI; **have a hairy face** wiixŭwíingweew VAI; **have a long face** kwŭníingweew VAI; **have a look of distaste on one's face, turn one's nose up at something** niiskcheengwéexiin VAI; **have a red face** maxkchàlíingweew VAI, maxkshéengweew VAI, maxkíin=gweew VAI; **have a scabby face, have scabs on one's face** mŭkuychàlíin=geew·VAI; **have a scratch on one's face** kchaxkíingweew VAI; **have a straight face, have a sober face, have a poker face** shaaxkiingwéexiin VAI; **have a strange look on one's face**, **have a guilty look on one's face, look guilty of something** maashiingwéexiin VAI; **have a swollen face** paaschàlíingweew VAI; **have**

**a swollen face, have one's face swell up** makwíingweew VAI, paasíingweew VAI; **have a wrinkled face** pihpiis=chàlíingweew VAI; **have a wrinkled face** pihpiisŭlíingweew VAI; **have a wrinkled face, have a contorted face** wchulíingweew VAI; **have an expression on one's face indicating that one is about to cry** ooshawut=oonéhleew VAI; **have an odd face, have a strange face** maashíingweew VAI; **have one's face wrinkled, have one's face contorted, pout, be in a temper, be discontented** *(as if about to cry)* wchuliingwéexiin VAI; **have pimples on one's face** pimpŭlíin=gweew VAI; **have red eyes, blush, have a red face** maxkshéengweew VAI; **hit and flatten one's face against something** pàkiingwehtéexiin VAI; **hit one's face hard against something** pwàhwsheengwéexiin VAI; **lie with one's face sticking out, lie with one's face showing, have one's face showing** kchiingwéexiin VAI; **make a face, have an unpleasant face** chiipiin=gwéexiin VAI; **make faces, act up, act out of the ordinary** achíipŭnum VOTI1; **scratch an itch on s.o.'s face for them** kshiipiingwáaleew VTA, kshiipiingwéeneew VTA; **scratch one's face, have an itchy face** kshiipíin=gweew VAI; **scratch s.o. on the face** siisiingwáaleew VTA; **show one's face** *(quickly)* kchiingwéhleew VAI; **slap s.o. across the face** *(close to the ears)*, **slap s.o. across the ears** paak=xehtéeheew VTA; **slap s.o. in the face** *(loud enough to be heard)* pwàhwiin=gwéeheew VTA, pwàhwsheengwée=heew VTA, pwàhwsúmaweew VTA; **smile, have a smile on one's face** kaakŭluksuwiingwéexiin VAI; **wash one's face** ksíingweew VAI; **wash s.o.'s face** ksiingwéeneew VTA; **act oddly, act strangely, make faces** amáashŭnum VOTI1.

**face** VI **face in a certain direction, face in a certain manner** lohkwéexiin VAI, lohkwéexun VII; **face in the wrong direction, face the wrong way** cha=nohkwéexiin VAI, chanohkwéexun VII; **make s.o. look in a certain direction, make s.o. face in a certain direction** liingwéexŭmeew VTA **I put the doll facing over there.** 'Yéelak nduliingwéexŭmaaw naaníitus.'; **turn s.o. to face in a certain direction, turn s.o. to face in a certain manner** lohkwéexŭmeew VTA; **turn s.o. to face in the wrong direction, turn s.o. to face the wrong way** chanoh=kwéexŭmeew VTA; **turn s.t. to face in a certain direction, turn s.t. to face in a certain manner** lohkwéextoow VTI2 **I faced it towards the front.** 'Shayéemung ndulohkwéextoon.'; **turn s.t. to face in the wrong direction, turn s.t. to face the wrong way** chanohkwéextoow VTI2.

**fade** VI **wash s.t. and make it fade, make s.t. fade by washing it** kaas=pátoow VTI2; **be faded** *(by sun or heat)* kaaschásuw VAI, kaascháteew VII; **be faded** *(by heat)* kaasxásuw VAI, kaasxáteew VII; **be faded** *(of colours)* kaasíhleew VAI, kaasíhleew VII; **be faded from washing** kaaspáteew VII.

**faint** VI **be overheated, be overcome with heat, faint from the heat** aap=túsuw VAI; **faint** ngwutíhleew VAI.

**fair** ADJ **be a fair price**teepáawatuw VAI, teepáawatuw VII; **charge a fair price for s.t.** teepaawatóoheew VAIO.

**fair** N **be a fair going on** *(indefinite subject)* féeliin VAI.

**fall** N **be fall, be autumn** takwáakuw VII **I'm going there next fall.** 'Takwaa=kíike náh ndá.', **I went there last fall.** 'Takwáakuw náh ndá.'; **during the fall, during the autumn** takwaa=kwŭnúwii PC.

**fall** VI **fall and break off, be severed** tŭmíixun VII; **fall and bump** *(against something)*, **bump into an object** paakihtéexiin VAI **I bumped into the fence.** 'Meenáxkung mbaakihtée= xiin.'; **fall and bump** *(against something)*, **bump into an object** paa= kihtéexun VII **It bumped into my leg.** 'Paakihtéexun níhkaat.', **The door banged against something.** 'Paa= kihtéexun kpáhoon.'; **fall and bump against s.t.** *(with something)* paakih= téextoow VTI2 **He bumped his leg against something.** 'Wíhkaat paakihtéextoon.'; **fall and bump into s.o., fall and bump s.o.** *(with something)* paakihtéexŭmeew VTA; **fall and burst open, lie broken** lookchéexiin VAI, lookchéexun VII; **fall and die, be beaten to death, get hit and die** pŭlupihtéexiin VAI; **fall and get chipped** kwashihtéexiin VAI; **fall and get crushed** shkwihtéexiin VAI; **fall and get knocked out** ngwutihtéexiin VAI; **fall and get shaken up, be hit and get shaken up** wŭyamoxkihtéexiin VAI; **fall and make a loud noise** tii= wíixiin VAI, tiiwíixun VII; **fall and make a noise, fall and make a dull noise, fall with a thud** pwàhwíixun VII, pòhwíixun VII; **fall and make a noise, fall and make a dull noise, fall with a thud, fall down hard, fall flat on one's face** pwàhwíixiin VAI; **fall and make a sharp noise when dropped** chàhwíixiin VAI, chàhwíixun VII; **fall and shatter** sehtéexiin VAI, sehtéexun VII; **fall and split in two** pasihtéexun VII; **fall down** pŭnihtée= xiin VAI **He fell out of bed.** 'Apíineeng wúnj-pŭnihtéexiin.'; **fall due to be being weak, fall due to being limp** piisŭlihtéexiin VAI; **fall forward** achiichkwalehtéexiin VAI; **fall head first** achiichkwalíhleew VAI; **fall in a certain manner, fall in a certain direction** lihtéexiin VAI **He fell out of place.** 'Palíi-lihtéexiin.', **I fell this way and that way.** 'Nŭmúsu-lihtée= xiin.'; **fall in a certain manner, fall in a certain direction** lihtéexun VII **It fell to the front.** 'Shayéemung lih= téexun.'; **fall in sitting, miss one's seat** palapíhleew VAI; **fall in the water, get soaked, get immersed** ka= mukwíhleew VAI; **fall into water** chooxpwíhleew VAI; **fall on one's backside while sitting** pŭniitŭyée= puw VAI; **fall on one's behind** *(especially when squatting down)* aamoo= tŭyéhleew VAI; **fall on one's stomach, land on one's stomach, fall flat, fall face down** pàkchehtéexiin VAI; **fall on top of something, lie on top of something** waxkiitihtéexiin VAI, waxkii= tihtéexun VII; **fall out of bed while sleeping** pŭnóngwaam VAI, pŭnóng= xwiin VAI; **fall through an opening** pkwíhleew VAI, pkwíhleew VII; **fall through the ice** pkwaskwíhleew VAI; **fall to one's death** aaptihtéexiin VAI; **fall upside down** aaloolihtéexiin VAI, aaloolihtéexun VII; **fall while sitting, sit down hard** lŭmatapihtéexiin VAI; **fall with a thud** pòhwíixiin VAI; **be injured, get hurt, fall and get injured** kshihtéexiin VAI; **crack, fall and crack, fall and get chipped** kwashihtéexun VII; **fall all over, bounce around, get hit about** msih= téexiin VAI; **go down, fall down, slide down** *(of curtains, of pants)* chiixíh= leew VII; **go downhill, fall downhill, slide downhill** pumbíhleew VAI; **go through, fall through** eeshíhleew VII, eeshíhleew VAI **I went through the ice.** 'Móhkamiing ndeeshíhla.'; **have a cracked head, have a cut on one's head, fall and crack one's head, fall and cut one's head** pasaandpéexiin VAI; **hit and injure s.o., injuring s.o. by making them fall** kshihtéexŭ=

meew VTA; **hit s.o. and knock them over, hit s.o. and make them fall backwards** aamihtéeheew VTA; **hit s.t. and knock it over, hit s.t. and make it fall backwards** aamihtée=ham VTI1A; **kneel, fall on one's knees** níishii-takwíixiin VAI; **land, drop, arrive, arrive at a position by falling** matéexiin VAI **I fell on top of the box.** 'Níi mbákshung wáxkiich nŭmatée=xiin.', **The ball landed over there.** 'Yéelak matéexiin néenaxkw.'; **land, drop, arrive, arrive at a position by falling** matéexun VII **Where the road goes.** 'Éeli-matéexung.'; **lie upside down, turn upside down, fall upside down** aapoochkwíhleew VAI; **make s.o. fall backwards** aamihtée=xŭmeew VTA; **make s.t. fall backwards** aamihtéextoow VTI2; **miss one's seat while sitting down, fall while sitting** palápuw VAI; **rub against something and fall, brush up against something and fall** laalihtéexiin VAI; **be about to fall, be placed so as to fall** lxawíixiin VAI, lxawíixun VII; **spill, fall down, come down** *(of water)* sookpéhleew VII; **fall upside down** aapoochkwàlíhleew VAI.

**fall apart** VI **fall apart in cooking, boil down, be cooked down** shkwúcha=suw VAI, shkwúchateew VII; **fall to pieces, fall apart** *(in cooking)* piik=chásuw VAI, piikchéesuw VAI, piik=cháteew VII.

**fall back** VI **rebound off something, bounce back and fall, fall back** *(s.t. animate)*, **be a foul ball** *(baseball)* kwaxkwíixiin VAI.

**fall backwards** VI aapamíhleew VAI, aamihtéexiin VAI, aamihtéexun VII.

**fall down** VI kawíhleew VAI; **fall down and make a noise** pwàhwihtéexiin VAI; **fall down off of something** pŭ=níhleew VII, pŭníhleew VAI; **make s.o. fall down, knock s.o. down** *(using the foot or body)* kawíhkaweew VTA.

**fall off** VI **be knocked off, fall off** mah=kíixiin VAI, mahkíixun VII; **fall off** *(as fruits from a tree or bush)* pawíhleew VAI; **fall off** *(as a leaf)*, **shed** *(as hair)* pawíhleew VII; **fall off, come off, become detached** mahkíhleew VII, mahkíhleew VAI.

**fall out** VI **fall out in chunks, be a chunk falling out, have a chip fall out, have a chunk fall out, break off** kwàkwashíhleew VAI, kwàkwashíh=leew VII; **fall out, run out, come out** kchíhleew VAI, kchíhleew VII; **have one's hair fall out** moonaalohkwéh=leew VAI.

**fall out of** VT **drop food from one's mouth, have food fall out of one's mouth, miss one's mouth while eating** palándam VOTI1; **drop s.t. animate from one's mouth, have s.t. animate fall out of one's mouth, miss one's mouth with s.t. animate** *(of food)* palámeew VTA; **drop s.t. from one's mouth, have s.t. fall out of one's mouth, miss one's mouth with s.t.** paléndam VTI1A.

**fall over** VI **fall over, be knocked down, be knocked over** aamíhleew VAI, aamíhleew VII; **get uprooted and fall over** *(of trees)* moonáhkhookw VAI.

**fall sideways** VI piimihtéexiin VAI, pii=mihtéexun VII; **fall sideways, drive crookedly** piimchéhleew VAI.

**fall to pieces** VI **be burnt up, fall to pieces, be in pieces after being cooked** shkwúteew VII, shkwútsuw VAI; **fall to pieces, fall apart** *(in cooking)* piikchásuw VAI, piikcháteew VII, piik=chéesuw VAI; **go to pieces, fall to pieces** piikíhleew VII, piikíhleew VAI.

**fall underneath** VT **fall underneath something, lie underneath something** alaamihtéexiin VAI, alaamih=téexun VII, eekwihtéexiin VAI, ee=

kwihtéexun VII.

**fall upon** VT **step upon s.o., fall upon s.o., sit upon s.o.** ahpíhkaweew VTA; **step upon s.t., fall upon s.t., sit upon s.t.** ahpíhkam VTI1A.

**false** ADJ **wear dentures, wear false teeth** wiipiithámeew VAI.

**false face mask** N **mask, false face mask, scarecrow, someone dressed up with a false face** msíingw NA.

**family** N **be by oneself, be on one's own, be the only one in a family** nxoohóowuw VAI; **be the last of one's family** wihkwáhleew VAI; **be the last of one's family, be last of one's lineage** wehkwáhleew VAI; **have a bunch of kids, have a big family** mŭlee=kóonzheew VAI; **marry and add on to one's family, take on relatives** aandshiilúndam VOTI1; **marry into a certain family** lushiilúndam VAI; **marry into a certain family** lushii=lúngeew VAI **It serves him right for marrying into that family.** 'Kách káa wáak ná wtulshiilúngeen.'

**fan** N lehleewhíikan NI.

**fan** VT **fan oneself** lehleewhúnzuw VAI.

**fancy** ADJ **be fancy looking** wiilawii=náakwat, wiilawiináakwsuw VAI **He's dressed up fancy.** 'Móxa wiilawii=náakwsuw.'; **fancy** wiilawii- PN **A fancy car.** 'Wíilawii-káal.'; **act fancily** wiilawíiyayuw VAI; **fancy chair** wiilawáhpapoon NI; **fancy hat** wiila=waakongwéepuy NI; **have a fancy walk, walk fancily** wiilawóoxweew VAI; **sound fancy** wiilawihtáakwat VII, wiilawihtáakwsuw VAI.

**far** ADV wáhli PC **He hit it a long way to the fence, and it went over the fence.** 'Wáhli laháhkweew méenaxk, paalíhleew meenáxkung lí.'; **far** wáhlu PC *informal* **It is far away.** 'Wáhlu áhteew.', **He lives far away.** 'Wáhlu wíikuw.'; **be far apart** *(of trees)* awahlŭmahkwsúwak VAI *usually plural;* **be far apart** awahlŭ=mahtéewal VII *usually plural,* wahlŭ=mahtéewal VII *usually plural;* **be far away** wáhlŭmat VII; **dance far apart** wahlŭmukéewak VAI *usually plural;* **live far apart** wahlŭmiikéewak VAI *usually plural;* **sit far apart** awahlŭ=mohkwéepŭwak VAI *usually plural;* **sit far apart, be far apart, be far away** wahlŭmápŭwak VAI; **sound far away** laawihtáakwat VII, laawih=táakwsuw VAI, wahlŭmihtáakwat VII, wahlŭmihtáakwsuw VAI; **stand far apart** wahlŭmiikaapawúwak VAI *usually plural;* **throw s.t. as far as one can** seesahkáaheew VAIO **Then I went outside and I threw it as far as I could.** 'Nál kwáchŭmung ndáan táa ndúlu-aseesahkáaheen.'; **walk so far, go so far, go a certain distance** sahkóoxweew VAI **He went very far.** 'Móxa wáhlu sahkóoxweew.'

**farm** VI **be a farmer, farm** fáamŭluw VAI.

**farm** VT **be worked at, be farmed, be worked** *(of fields)* alohkehtáasuw VII.

**farmer** N fáamŭl NA; **be a farmer, farm** fáamŭluw VAI.

**fart** N póoktuw VAI **He wants to fart.** 'Katá-póoktuw.'; **smell like a fart** pooktiimáakwsuw VAI; **fart while sitting down** pooktohkwéepuw VAI; **fart while sleeping** pooktóngwaam VAI.

**farther** ADJ **throw s.t. over, throw s.t. farther than intended** paaláaheew VAIO **I threw it over the house.** 'Mbaaláaheen wiikwáhmung.'

**fast** ADJ **fast, quickly** kshi- PV **I can dance fast.** 'Níi áa ngíish-kshí-kúndka.'; **fast, quickly** kshu- PV *informal* **The time is going quickly.** 'Kshú-kŭlákuw.', **It's snowing a lot.** 'Kshú-wíineew.'; **quick, fast** akuta=ku- PV **I went away fast.** 'Ngaktáku-alúmsi.'; **do a fast dance** akutakúk=eew VAI, kàktákkeew VAI; **drive fast,**

**drive quickly** kshuchéhleew VAI; **go fast** *(in or on a vehicle or bicycle)* pàpxoowíhleew VAI; **lead a fast life** ktakáawsuw VAI; **look like one could run fast, look smartly dressed, look frisky while going by** kshihleewii= náakwsuw VAI; **make s.o. go fast** kshushíhkaweew VTA; **run fast** kihtaaméhleew VAI, kshahtakíhleew VAI; **run fast, run quickly, fly quickly, go quickly** kshíhleew VAI; **speak quickly, talk fast** akushaaptóonheew VAI; **start off fast, start off running** *(especially when running in a race)* ktakíixiin VAI; **swim fast** pàpxoowaa= shŭwíhleew VAI; **walk fast, walk quickly** kshóoxweew VAI; **work fast** kshalóhkeew VAI.

**fasten** VT **fasten s.t. onto something, stick s.t. onto something** kŭlamóo= toow VTI2 **I stuck it onto the door.** 'Kpahóonung ngulamóotoon.'; **fasten something onto s.o.** kŭlamóoleew VTA; **fasten things, button things, hook things up** kŭlahkhwíikeew VAI; **sew s.t. animate tightly, sew s.t. animate down, fasten s.t. animate down by sewing it** kŭliikwáaleew VTA; **sew s.t. tightly, sew s.t. down, fasten s.t. down by sewing** kŭlíikwam VTI1A.

**fat** ADJ **be fat** wíisuw VAI; **fat man** wii= sŭwatéelŭnuw NA; **fat woman** wiisŭ= wóxkweew NA.

**father** N **my father** nóox NAD; **have a father** wtóoxuw VAI; **have s.o. as a father, think of s.o. as one's father** wtóoxuw VAIO **He is my uncle but I think of him as my father.** 'Wán há nzhíis shúkw nootóoxwiin.'; **my paternal aunt, my father's sister, my cross-aunt** nŭmiilíhtaakw NAD; **my uncle, my father's brother, parallel uncle** nóoxwush NAD.

**father-in-law** N **my father-in-law** nzhiilíhloos NAD.

**fatten** VT **fatten s.o., fatten s.t.** wiisóo= heew VAIO.

**fatty** ADJ **be fatty** *(of meat)* wiisóowuw VII.

**fault** N **disagree with s.o., find fault with s.o.** chaníimeew VTA.

**feast** N takwiipwáakan NI; **hold a feast** takwíipuw VAI; **hold a feast for s.o.** takwiipóoleew VTA.

**feather** N míikwan NA; **have feathers, have feathers on** miikwanóowuw VAI **I'm all covered in feathers.** 'Wéemu táa ndúlu-miikwanóowiin.'; **have no feathers on one's backside** moosha= kíitŭyeew VAI *usually of birds;* **white feather** waapíikwan NA.

**feed** VT **feed s.o.** xámeew VTA; **feed s.t. to s.o.** xámeew VTAO **I fed her the potatoes.** 'Ndáxamaan óhpŭnal.', **I fed him the meat.** 'Wŭyóos ndáxa= maan.'; **feed people** xángeew VAI; **feed s.o. by hand** shahkamóoleew VTA; **suck s.o., feed at s.o.'s breast, nurse from s.o.** noonáaleew VTA.

**feel** VI **be at a loss, don't know which way to turn, feel one has no place to go, not know where one will stay** kwiilaweelúndam VOTI1; **be restless, be bothered, feel restless** sàkwa= málsuw VAI; **be tired of feeling a certain way, be tired of living** peekah= téenamuw VAI; **do strange things to s.o., do things that make s.o. feel strange** maashiilawéeheew VTA; **feel 'smart,' feel lively** ktakamálsuw VAI; **feel angry about one's illness, feel odd, feel angry** manoongamálsuw VAI; **feel as if one would like to rest** alaaxiimwahtéenamuw VAI; **feel ashamed** miixaneelúndam VOTI1; **feel better** liiwamálsuw VAI; **feel better** miingasawamálsuw VAI; **feel cross, feel angry** manoongeelúndam VOTI1; **feel lazy** laxkamálsuw VAI; **feel like a White person** shŭwanakwamalúsuw VAI; **feel nauseous, feel sick to one's stomach** wŭyakaskíilaweew VAI; **feel**

peaceful nalawamálsuw VAI; **feel poorly, feel low** ktumaakamálsuw VAI; **feel rough** kaaxkamámkwat VII, kaaxkamamkwúsuw VAI; **feel sad, be sad, be in a bad mood** mateelúndam VOTI1; **feel sick, feel like vomiting** wŭyakaskíhleew VAI; **feel that one is White, think that one is White** waapamálsuw VAI; **feel tired, feel restless** *(especially when sick)* shii=wamálsuw VAI; **feel unwell, be sick** matamalúsuw VAI; **feel weak** piisŭ=lamalúsuw VAI, shawamalúsuw VAI; **feel well** wŭlamalúsuw VAI; **find that s.o. feels better, find that s.o. feels good, feel comfortable with s.o.** wŭlámameew VTA; **find that s.t. feels better, find that s.t. feels good** wŭ=lamándam VTI1A **My hand feels better.** 'Noolamándamun náxk.', **My shoes feel good.** 'Mahksúnal noola=mandamúnal.'; **have s.t. that feels rough** kaaxkamándam VTI1A **My throat feels rough.** 'Ngaaxkamán=damun ngwundáakan.'; **make people feel strange** maashiilawéhtoow VAI; **make s.o. feel ashamed** miixanée=lŭmeew VTA; **make s.o. feel good** wŭliilawéeheew VTA; **talk to s.o. and make them feel good** wŭliilawée=meew VTA; **the way one looks makes someone feel like vomiting** mŭlam=andamuwiináakwsuw VAI.

**feel** VT **feel a certain way, have a certain physical sensation** lamalúsuw VAI **He thinks he's so good ('has wings')** 'Làmalúsuw wŭlóngwa=nuw.', **How do you feel?** 'Thá há ktulamálsi?'; **feel for s.o., feel s.o.** *(using the hands)* mihkwchéeneew VTA; **feel for s.t., feel s.t.** *(using the hands)* mihkwchéenum VTI1B; **feel numb, have a sensation of numbness** pihkwamálsuw VAI; **feel oneself to be at a loss, feel desolate** *(having no place to go or to live)* kwiilawee=lúnzuw VAI; **feel s.o.** *(using the hands)* kwàkwtuchéeneew VTA; **feel s.t.** *(using the hands)* kwàkwtuchéenum VTI1B; **feel s.t. as a sensation in one's body** làmándam VTI1A; **feel s.t. as an ache, feel s.t. as a pain, feel s.t. as a soreness in one's body** amándam VTI1A; **feel sorry for oneself** ktum=aakeelúnzuw VAI; **feel the sensation that s.o. makes, feel the sensation of s.o.** amámeew VTA; **grieve, feel grief** ooshawamalúsuw VAI; **grieve, feel grief, be sad** ooshaweelúndam VOTI1; **have s.t. animate that feels rough** kaaxkamámeew VTA **My knee feels rough.** 'Ngaaxkamámaaw ngútkuw.'; **rape s.o. in secret, feel s.o. secretly** kíimŭneew VTA.

**feel for** VT **feel for s.o., feel s.o.** *(using the hands)* mihkwchéeneew VTA; **feel for s.t., feel s.t.** *(using the hands)* mihkwchéenum VTI1B; **grope around for things, feel around for things** kwtucheeníikeew VAI, kwàkwchee=níikeew VAI; **grope for s.o., feel for s.o.** *(using the hands)* kwtúneew VTA; **grope for s.t., feel for s.t.** *(using the hands)* kwtúnum VTI1B.

**feeling** N **feeling, sensation, feeling in a sore body part** amandamuwáakan NI; **have a bad thought, think bad thoughts, have bad feelings** chii=pahtéenamuw VAI; **have a strange feeling** maasheelúndam VOTI1; **have s.t. hurt** *(of one's feelings)* kshamán=dam VTI1A **He said something and really hurt my feelings.** 'Néeka kwéek úw, móxa ngushamándamun.'; **show one's feelings to s.o.** pŭnoon=dŭláweew VTA.

**feel sorry for** VT **feel sorry for s.o.** ktumaakéelŭmeew VTA.

**fell** VT **fell trees, knock trees down** kawaháhkweew VAI.

**female** N **female dog, female of animal species** oxkwéexum NA; **hen, female**

**bird** oxkwéhleew NA; **my female cousin** ndaangwsóxkweew NAD.

**fence** N méenaxk NI; **inside the fence** alaameenáxke PC; **make a fence** meenáxkheew VAI; **outside the fence** kwachŭmeenáxke PC; **the other side of the fence** awaseenáxke PC.

**fence rail** N meenáxkaaxkw NI.

**fencepost** N **post, fencepost** póosht NI.

**fetch** VT **go after s.o., fetch s.o.** náaleew VTA; **go after s.t., fetch s.t.** náatum VTI1B; **go after s.t. for s.o., fetch s.t. for s.o.** naatamáweew VTAO; **be fetched** *(especially the body of a deceased person)* naaláasuw VAI; **be gone after, be brought, be fetched** naatáasuw VII; **crawl to fetch s.o., crawl after s.o.** naachíikwsuw VAIO; **fetch s.o.** *(using something held in the hand)* naachiikwáaleew VTA; **fetch s.t.** *(using something held in the hand)* naachíikwam VTI1A; **fetch water, go after water, go to get liquor** naat=húpeew VAI; **fetch wood, go after wood** naatxákweew VAI; **go after and carry s.t., fetch and carry s.t.** naa=tasánuw VAIO; **go after and drag s.t., fetch and drag s.t.** naattaachíindam VTI1A; **go after food, fetch food** naa=chiichŭwáakaneew VAI; **go after something to fetch it, go after something to take it** naathéewasuw VAI; **go and fetch a load** naachŭwáleew VAI; **go to fetch a load of s.t., fetch and carry a load of something on one's back** naachŭwáleew VAIO; **run to fetch s.o., fetch s.o.** naachíipheew VTA; **run to fetch s.t., fetch s.t.** naa=chiipáhtoow VTI2.

**fever** N **have a fever** kshuléexiin VAI; **have measles, have scarlet fever, turn red** maxkíhleew VAI.

**few** ADJ **not very often, a few times** táatxun PC **I drank my medicine a few times.** 'Táatxun noochapíhkum nŭmúneen.', **I didn't go to town very often.** 'Ootéeneeng táatxun ndá.'

**fib** N **tell a fib, tell lies** maxkáaheew VAI.

**fidget** VI **fidget, sit in various ways** msú-lápuw VAI; **shift around while sitting, fidget** kwàkwchúkwapuw VAI.

**field** N ahkiiháakan NI; **work in a tobacco field, work picking tobacco** kwshahtéewheew VAI.

**fifteen** N naalanaaníhka PC.

**fifty** N naalaniináxke PC.

**fight** N **challenge s.o. to a fight** ndóo=naleew VTA; **defend s.o. in a fight** ihkáaleew VTA; **fight vigourously, have a big fight** kihtatáhkeew VAI; **participate, take part, take part in a game, take part in a fight** wii=chóohŭweew VAI.

**fight** VI matáhkeew VAI; **be tired of fighting** peekatáhkeew VAI; **fight for a certain length of time, fight until now** sahkatáhkeew VAI; **fight vigourously, have a big fight** kihtatáhkeew VAI; **go and fight** mawatáhkeew VAI; **like to fight** wiingatáhkeew VAI; **want to fight, want to compete** katoonáa=suw VAI.

**fight** VT **want to fight s.o., want to kill s.o., want to compete with s.o.** ka=tóonaleew VTA; **fight with s.o.** ma=tahkháaleew VTA.

**fighting** N **join in the fighting** wiita=táhkeew VAI.

**figure** N **be in terrible shape, have a terrible figure, have a terrible shape, be in a bad shape** chiipáhk=wsuw VAI; **have a slender figure, have a slight build, be slim** lum=báhkwsuw VAI; **have a trim shape, have a good shape, have a good figure** wŭláhkwsuw VAI.

**file** N **file, sharpening stone, grindstone** kiinhíikan NI.

**fill** VT **fill s.t.** wchuwíixtoow VTI2; **fill s.t. animate** wchuwíixŭmeew VTA; **fill s.t with liquid** wchuwáapŭweew

VAIO; **fill s.t. level to the top** *(of liquids)* tpuskŭwúpeew VAIO; **fill s.t. to the brim with water** tpuskhwúpeew VAIO; **measure the size of s.o, measure the height of s.o., measure s.t. animate out, fill s.t. animate to the brim** *(as a pail)* tpúskhweew VTA; **plug things up, caulk things, fill in chinks** kpaskhíikeew VAI.

**fill up** VI **fill s.t. animate up** wchupáh=leew VTA; **fill s.t. animate up** *(with non-liquid)* wchuwáhleew VTA; **fill s.t. up** *(with non-liquid)* wchuwáh=toow VTI2; **fill s.t. up with water, fill s.t. up with liquid** wchúwpeew VAIO; **fill up with liquid** wchuwpéhleew VAI, wchuwpéhleew VII.

**finally** ADV **reluctantly, (do) reluctantly, finally** péhkiik PC **I went there reluctantly.** 'Péhkiik náh ndá.', **I wrote to him and he finally answered me.** 'Mbeeteekhámawaa, péhkiik nax=kóomukw.'

**find** VT **find s.o., find s.t. animate** móxkaweew VTA; **find s.t.** móxkam VTI1A; **be found out, be exposed** mihchíhleew VAI; **find s.o. useful, find s.t. animate useful, be useful to s.o.** laapéemeew VTA **He's useful to me.** 'Ndulaapéemaaw.', **I'm useful to him.** 'Ndulaapéemukw.'

**find easy** VT **find s.t. easy to do, think s.t. easy to do** aapŭweelúndam VTI1A **I don't think anything of going to town.** 'Ndaapŭweelúndamun ootée=neeng ndáan.', **I find it easy to go to sleep.** 'Ndaapŭweelúndamun nŭmáwkawí.'; **find s.o. easy** *(to do something with)* aapŭwéelŭmeew VTA **I find him easy to teach.** 'Ndaapŭ=wéelŭmaaw ndakehkíimaan.', **I find him easy to play with.** 'Ndaapŭwée=lŭmaaw nŭmeelawusóomaan.'

**find fault with** VT **disagree with s.o., find fault with s.o.** chaníimeew VTA.

**fine** ADJ **fine grained** wŭlaamii- PN **Fine sand.** 'Wŭláamii-léekuw.'; **be fine in grain, be fine grained** *(of flour, of sand)* wŭláamat VII; **be fine rain, be misty rain** awáhŭlaan VII; **fine comb** máanzakwus NA, máasakwus NA; **have fine hair, have nice hair, have good hair** wŭlaalóhkweew VAI; **have thin hair, have fine hair** shiikalaa=lóhkweew VAI.

**finely** ADV **cut s.t. animate finely** wŭ=láamsheew VTA; **cut s.t. finely** wŭ=láamshum VTI1B.

**finger** N **my finger** náxkush NID; **my pointing finger** ndalochíikan NID, nduloohíikan NID; **have forked fingers** lxawŭlunjéesuw VAI, lxawŭlun=jéeyeew VII *as of a fork;* **little finger** changŭlunjáawanush NI; **middle finger** leeláawŭlunj NI; **pick s.t. up with one's fingers, use one's fingers to pick s.t. up** kwàkwtákwŭnum VTI1B; **pick things up with one's fingers, use one's hands to pick things up** kwàkwtakwŭníikee VAI; **spread one's fingers apart, have one's fingers spread apart** sayaaxkŭlunjéexiin VAI; **stick one's finger in s.o.'s eye** laap=sheengwéeneew VTA.

**fingernail** N **my fingernail** níhkash NAD; **have clean fingernails** apiilíhka=sheew VAI; **have dirty fingernails** aniiskíhkasheew VAI; **have long fingernails** akwaaníhkasheew VAI.

**finish** VI **be finished an activity** ehkoo=haawatúwak VAI *usually plural;* **make s.t. animate, finish making s.t. animate, be finished making s.t. animate** kiishíiheew VTA; **make s.t., finish making s.t., be finished making s.t.** kiishíhtoow VTI2 **I've finished making it.** 'Méhch ngiishíhtoon.'; **stop before one finishes** *(doing something)* pohkwii- PV **I quit making bread.** 'Mbóhkwii-apwáanhe.', **I quit looking at it.** 'Mbóhkwii-punámun.'; **stop before one finishes** *(doing some-*

*thing)* pohkwu- PV *informal* **He stopped while eating.** 'Póhkwu-míitsuw.'

**finish** VT **finish making s.t.** kiishíix=toow VTI2; **make s.t. animate, finish making s.t. animate, be finished making s.t. animate** kiishíiheew VTA; **finish cutting s.t.** kíish'shum VTI1B; **finish cutting s.t. animate** kíish'=sheew VTA; **finish cutting things** kiish'shíikeew VAI; **be done cooking, be finished cooking** *(of cooks)* kii=shatúpuw VAI; **be finished being discussed** kiishakunootáasuw VII; **be done cooking, be finished cooking** kiish'suw, kíishteew VII; **be finished planting** kiishahkkíiheew VAI; **be finished, be already placed there** kii=sháhteew VII; **finish building a house** kiishíikheew VAI; **finish dancing, be finished dancing** kíishkeew VAI; **finish defecating, be finished defecating** kiishásktuw VAI; **finish one's chores, be finished one's chores, get through one's chores** kiishanáakw=suw VAI; **finish packing a load on one's back, be finished packing a load on one's back, be already packed** kiishŭwálheew VAI; **finish packing up, be finished packing up** kiishas=kŭneextíikeew VAI; **finish putting s.o. down, finish putting s.o. there** kii=sháhleew VTA; **finish putting s.t. there** kiisháhtoow VTI2; **finish running, be through running** kiishaa=méhleew VAI; **finish setting the table, be finished setting the table** kiishii=njŭweextíikeew VAI; **finish sewing, finish sewing things** kiishiikwáa=keew VAI; **finish speaking, be finished speaking** kiishaaptóoneew VAI; **finish talking** kiishtóonheew VAI; **finish talking about s.t.** kiishakunóo=tum VTI1B; **finish tying s.o., finish harnessing s.o.** kiishambíileew VTA; **finish tying s.t. up** kiishámbtoow VTI2; **judge s.o., finish talking about s.o.** kiishakuníimeew VTA.

**fire** N túndeew NI; **be gone out, go out quickly** *(of fires)* wchiimahtéhleew VII; **go out** *(of fires)*, **be burnt up** *(in a fire)* wchiimáhteew VII; **have a good fire** wŭlulawásuw VAI; **have one's fire go out** wchiimahtawásuw VAI; **light a fire for s.o., make a fire for s.o.** tundeewháweew VTA; **light s.t. animate, set s.t. animate on fire** náxkwseew VTA; **light s.t., set s.t. on fire** náxkwsum VTI1B; **make a fire** tundéewheew VAI; **put s.t. animate out, extinguish s.t. animate** *(of fires)* wchiimahtéeheew VTA; **put s.t. out, extinguish s.t.** *(of fires)* wchiimah=téeham VTI1A **Last night someone turned off the lights at my place.** 'Piiskéeku awéen oochiimahtéehŭ=mun wíikŭyaan.'; **put wood on the fire** póonxeew VAI **I put in too much green wood.** 'Noosáamu- askxákwal -póonxe.'; **set s.t. on fire for s.o.** naxkwsúmaweew VTAO; **set things on fire, set a fire** naxkwsíikeew VAI; **turn s.t. animate down** *(of lights, of sources of fire)* wtuléeneew VTA; **turn s.t. down** *(of flames, of sources of fire)* wtuléenum VTI1B.

**fire** VT **dismiss s.o., fire s.o.** sèkháaleew VTA.

**firmly** ADV **be tied firmly** maskanam=bíisuw VAI, maskanambíisuw VII; **hold s.o. firmly** maskanúneew VTA; **hold s.t. animate firmly** *(in the mouth, with the mouth)* kŭlámeew VTA; **hold s.t. firmly** *(in the mouth, with the mouth)* kŭlándam VTI1A; **hold s.t. firmly** maskanúnum VTI1B; **tie s.o. firmly** maskanambíileew VTA; **tie s.t. firmly** maskanámbtoow VTI2.

**first** ADJ shayee- PV **I eat before, I eat ahead of the others.** 'Nzháyee-míitsi.', **He took his coat off first.** 'Néeka shayée-ktuniikóote.'; **first** shayéewi PC; **fall head first** achiich=

kwalíhleew VAI; **be in the lead, go first, fly first, run first, drive first, proceed first, go ahead, run ahead** shayéhleew VAI **The little one came in first.** 'Cheengshíishiit éel-péechi-shayéhlaat.'; **drive ahead, drive in the lead, drive first** shayeewchéh=leew VAI; **be first, be first in line, be first in a competition** shayéexiin VAI.

**fish** N namées NA; **big fish** xwátameekw NA; **fishing net** akwaaníikan NA; **pike fish** kiinhóhkwus NA; **small fish** changaméeshush NA.

**fish** VI **be fishing, fish** namées'heew VAI; **fish with a line** weendáameew VAI; **fish with a net** akwáanŭmeew VAI.

**fishworm** N wéechiis NA.

**fist** N ptukwŭlunjeewáakan NI, ptúkwŭ=lunj NI; **have one's hand clenched in a fist** ptukwŭlunjéexiin VAI, ptukwŭ=lúnjeew VAI; **make a fist** ptukwŭlunj=hámeew VAI.

**fit** N **be a tight fit** maskaníixiin VAI, maskaníixun VII; **be loose, be a loose fit** *(of clothes)* piisŭlíixun VII.

**fit** N **have a fit, have a seizure, have an epileptic seizure** wchiipíisuw VAI.

**fit** VI **fit** *(into something)*, **'it fits'** tée=pamuw VII **My foot fits into the shoe.** 'Nzíit téepamuw mahksúnung.'

**fit** VT **fit s.t.** *(of clothing)*, **'it fits'** tee=píhkam VTI1A **It fits me.** 'Ndeepíh=kamun.', **The shoe fits me.** 'Ndee=píhkamun máhksun.'; **fit s.t. animate** *(of clothing)*, **'it fits'** teepíhkaweew VTA **They fit me.** 'Ndeepihkawáa=wak.', **The mitt fits him.** 'Wteepih=kawáawal wándal.'; **find s.t. animate too small, find that s.t. animate doesn't fit, be too small for s.t. animate** *(of clothing)* wŭlíhkaweew VTA **They are too small, they don't fit me.** 'Noolihkawáawak.', **My mitt doesn't fit.** 'Noolíhkawaaw nŭwánd.'; **find s.t. too small, find that s.t. doesn't fit, be too small for s.t.** *(of clothing)* wŭlíhkam VTI1A **It's too small for me, it doesn't fit me.** 'Noolíhka=mun.', **My shirt doesn't fit.** 'Noo=líhkamun ndahéembut.'; **fit s.t. level, fit s.t. evenly** tpuskŭwíixtoow VTI2 **My hat is on evenly.** 'Ndupuskŭ=wíixtoon ndaakongwéepuy.'

**five** N náalan PC; **be five** naalanúnool VII *usually plural;* **be five days** naala=nookwŭnákat VII **Five days ago** 'Naalanookwŭnákate.'; **be five of them sitting there, be five of them there** naalanápŭwak VAI; **be five of them there** naalanahtéewal VII *usually plural;* **be five pairs, be in five pairs** naalanéelook VAI *usually plural,* naalanéeltool VII *usually plural;* **be five pieces** *(of something string-like)* naalanáhtakat VII; **be five, be five of them** naalanúwak VAI *usually plural;* **be gone for five days** naalanookwŭ=náhkeew VAI; **be in five layers** *(of something sheet-like)* naalaneekíixiin VAI, naalaneekíixun VII; **five** naalanu- PV **It's in five slices.** 'Náalanu-pan=géeyeew.'; **five** naalanu- PN **I worked there for five months.** 'Náalanu-kíishooxkw náh ndúnda-làlóhke.'; **five** naalii- PV; **five** naalu- PV *informal* **It's in five slices.** 'Náalu-pangée=yeew.'; **five** naalu- PN **He weighs five pounds.** 'Náalu-póond txú-poonda=kúsuw.'; **five days** naalanóokwŭnii PC; **five hundred** naalanaapóxku PC; **five times** náalanun PC; **five, in fives** naalanéeli PC **They're stacked in fives.** 'Naalanéeli pihtawíixŭnool.'; **have five pages** *(of something sheet-like)* naalanaapéeksuw VAI *usually of pieces of paper;* **take five steps** naalanalíhkeew VAI; **walk in fives, be in groups of five** naalanatxooxwée=wak VAI *usually plural.*

**fix** VT **fix s.t. animate, repair s.t. animate, put s.o. to bed** wŭlíixŭmeew VTA; **fix s.t., repair s.t.** wŭlíixtoow

VTI2; **fix s.t. for s.o.** wŭliixtáweew VTAO; **fix things** wŭliixtáasuw VAI; **get s.t. fixed** wŭliixtáakeew VAIO; **be fixed, be repaired** wŭliixtáasuw VII; **fix s.o. up, grab s.o., grasp s.o.** wŭlúneew VTA **I grabbed the dog by the back of the neck.** 'Nóolŭnaaw mwáakaneew wtéeng oxkweekán= ganung.'

**flag** N maxkeewehlatíikan NI.

**flap** VI **be hungry, have the sole of one's shoe come off and flap around** katóopuw VAI.

**flat** ADJ **be flat** pákeew VII, páksuw VAI, pàkchéesuw, pàkchéeyeew VII; **flat** pàkii- PN **Flat-bottomed boat.** 'Pákíi-amóxool.'; **go flat** pàkíhleew VII; **be a flat road, be a flat driveway** pàka= téexun VII; **have a flat backside** pàkíitŭyeew VAI; **have a flat head** *(of blow adders)*, **have one's head go flat** *(when blowing)* pàkaandpéhleew VAI; **have a flat head** pàkáandpeew VAI; **have a flat nose** pàkcháaleew VAI; **lie sprawled, lie spread out, lie flat** toongchéexiin VAI, toongchéexun VII.

**flatten** VT **flatten s.o.** pàkchéeheew VTA; **flatten s.o.** *(using the hands)* pàk= chéeneew VTA; **flatten s.o.** *(using the foot or body)* pàkchéhkaweew VTA, pàkíhkaweew VTA; **flatten s.o., flatten s. t. animate** *(using the hands)* pákŭneew VTA; **flatten s.o., flatten s.t. animate** *(using a tool or instrument)* pákheew VTA; **flatten s.t.** *(using a tool or instrument)* pákham VTI1A; **flatten s.t.** pákŭnum VTI1B; **flatten s.t.** pàkchéehum VTI1B; **flatten s.t.** *(using the foot or body)* pàkchéhkam VTI1A, pàkíhkam VTI1A; **flatten s.t., straighten s.t.** *(using the hands)* pàkchéenum VTI1B; **hit and flatten one's face against something** pàk= iingwehtéexiin VAI; **hit and flatten one's nose against something** pàk= chaalehtéexiin VAI; **hit and flatten s.o., hit and flatten s.t. animate** pàkihtéeheew VTA; **hit and flatten s.t.** pàkihtéehum VTI1B; **smash s.t. animate, squash s.t. animate, flatten s.t. animate** shkwihtéeheew VTA; **smash s.t., squash s.t., flatten s.t.** shkwihtéeham VTI1A.

**flax** N **flax plant, wild hemp** áhlap NA, áhlapiis NA.

**flea** N apíikw NA.

**flee** VI **run away from a certain place, flee from a certain place** wundshíi= muw VAI **He's running away from the house.** 'Wiikwáhmung wundshíi= muw.'; **run away from s.o., flee from s.o.** wshíimeew VTA; **run away inside the house, flee inside the house** piindshíimuw VAI; **run away, flee** alumshíimuw VAI; **run away, flee** wshíimuw VAI.

**flip over** VI aaloolíhleew VAI, aaloolíh= leew VII; **turn around, turn around while in motion, turn around while driving, flip over** kwŭlupíhleew VAI.

**flip over** VT **flip s.o., flip s.t. over** kwŭ= lupáaheew VAIO.

**float** VI **float away** alumáathookw VAI, alumáathun VII; **float by, float along** pŭmáathookw VAI **He floated right by here.** 'Yú pùmaathóokwun.'; **float by, float along** pŭmáhookw VAI, pŭmáaphookw VAI; **float here and there, float about, float around** apaamáathookw VAI, apaamáathun VII; **float here, float in this direction** peetáathookw VAI, peetáathun VII; **float, float by, float along** pŭmáat= hun VII, pŭmáhan VII; **float, paddle by, paddle along, paddle a water-craft** pŭmáham VOTI1 **The duck is paddling by.** 'Wshíhwe pŭmáham.'; **go by in a boat, go along in a boat, float by in a boat, float along in a boat** pŭmáatham VAI; **swim away, float away** alumáashŭwihl VAI, alum=

aashŭwíhleew VAI.

**flood** N **be a flood, be a lot of water lying around** kaanzhahkwíixun VII; **be high water, be deep water, be a flood, be flooding** xwahkwíixun VII.

**floor** N **be in contact with the ground, be in contact with the floor** mshíi=xiin VAI, mshíixun VII; **have one's foot touching down on a surface, have one's foot touching on the floor** mshusiitéexiin VAI; **scrub the floor** kshiixiikwáhmeew VAI.

**flour** N lohkhámun NI; **porridge made from water and flour rubbed together** wshaaxsáapaan NI.

**flow** VI **be water flowing, have water form** *(as on sour milk)* mbuyíhleew VII; **be water flowing, flow** *(of water)* nanpuyíhleew VII; **flow by, flow along** *(of water)* pŭmaapŭwéhleew VII; **flow down** *(of liquids)* pŭnaapŭ=wéhleew VII; **go over, flow over** paa=líhleew VII, paalíhleew VAI.

**flower** N peepáxkwŭleesh NA, pehpáx=kwŭleesh NA; **sunflower** wáaxaweew NA; **be in full bloom** *(of flowers)* wŭluléewuw VAI; **have flowers on it** peepaxkwŭleesh'háasuw VAI, peepax=kwŭleesh'háasuw VII.

**flu** N **have diarrhea, have stomach flu** watéeneew VAI.

**fly** N oochéew NA, óocheewees NA; **kill a fly** nihloochéeweew VAI.

**fly** VI **fly by, fly along, go by, go along, drive by, drive along, pedal by, pedal along** pŭmíhleew VAI; **fly away, go away, pedal away** alumíhleew VAI; **come here flying, fly towards the speaker** peechíhleew VAI; **be in the lead, go first, fly first, run first, drive first, proceed first, go ahead, run ahead** shayéhleew VAI **The little one came in first.** 'Cheengshíishiit éel-péechi-shayéhlaat.'; **go by s.t., drive by s.t., fly by s.t., cycle by s.t.** loowíhleew VAIO; **go by, drive by, fly by, cycle by** loowíhleew VAI; **fly in various directions, drive in various directions, go in various directions, fly, drive** msíhleew VAI; **get close, approach, fly close by, go close by** peexŭwíhleew VII, peexŭwíhleew VAI; **go across, drive across, pedal across, fly across** aashŭwíhleew VAI; **go back and forth, ride back and forth, fly back and forth** wŭyakíh=leew VAI **The cars are going back and forth.** 'Káalak wŭyakihléewak.'; **go crookedly, fly crookedly, fly on an erratic course** pàptukíhleew VAI; **go home, drive home, fly home, pedal home** aapaachíhleew VAI; **go in a certain manner, go in a certain direction, fly in a certain manner, fly in a certain direction, proceed in a certain manner, proceed in a certain direction** líhleew VAI **You fell in the water but your head is sticking out.** 'Mbíing ktulíhla shùkéhla ksaakaandpéexiin.'; **go straight, fly straight** shaaxkíhleew VAI; **run fast, run quickly, fly quickly, go quickly** kshíhleew VAI.

**fly back** VI **fly back, go back** kwaxkíh=leew VAI.

**fly inside** VI **go inside, fly inside, drive inside, fall inside** piinjíhleew VAI.

**foam** N píhteew NI.

**foamy** ADJ **be a foamy liquid** pihtee=wáapŭweew VII.

**fog** N **be fog** awán VII, awánuw VII.

**foggy** ADJ **be foggy, be misty** awaníixun VII.

**fold** VT **fold s.o., fold s.t. animate** *(using the hands)* paxkawúneew VTA; **fold s.t.** *(using the hands)* paxka=wúnum VTI1B; **fold s.t.** *(of something sheet-like)* wŭléekŭnum VTI1B; **fold s.t. animate** *(of something sheet-like)* wŭléekŭneew VTA; **fold s.t. animate carelessly** machéekŭneew VTA; **fold s.t. carelessly** machéekŭnum VTI1B;

**fold one's arms, have one's arms folded** paxkawiinaxkéesuw VAI, paxkawiinaxkéexiin VAI; **sit with one's legs folded, sit hunched over** ptukohkwéepuw VAI; **sit with one's legs folded, sit hunched over** ptúk=wapuw VAI.

**follow** VT **follow s.o.** náawaleew VTA; **follow s.t., follow along with s.t., follow s.t.** *(of religions)* naawalóotam VTI1A; **follow and come behind s.o., come behind s.o., come from behind s.o.** wtéhkaweew VTA; **follow people** naawáhkeew VAI **He likes to follow people.** 'Wíhwiing-naawáh=keew.'; **like to follow people** shkwunéesuw VAI; **walk directly to one's destination, go directly to one's destination, follow a good path in life** shaaxkóoxweew VAI.

**fond** ADJ **be fond of men, like all the men, be 'boy-crazy'** wiingiilŭnúw=eew VAI.

**food** N miichŭwáakan NI; **eat greasy food** shamuchéepuw VAI **I ate too much greasy food.** 'Noosáami-shamuchéepwi.'; **enjoy one's food** wiingchéepuw VAI; **go after food, fetch food** naachiichŭwáakaneew VAI; **have lots of food, have an abundance of food** wŭyakiichŭwáaka=neew VAI; **have plenty to eat, have an abundance of food** wŭyakíipuw VAI.

**foolish** ADJ **be silly, be foolish** kpúch=eew VAI; **talk foolishly** kpucheew=tóonheew VAI.

**foot** N **my foot** nzíit NID; **get one's foot snagged, have one's foot snagged** laapsiitéhleew VAI; **have a dirty foot** niisksíiteew VAI; **have a scabby foot, have scabs on one's foot** mŭkuy=síiteew VAI; **have a short foot** chahk=wshiichéeshuw VAI; **have a sore foot** kiihiitsíiteew VAI; **have big feet** a=mangsíiteew VA, xwusíiteew VAI; **have clean feet** piilsíiteew VAI; **have cold feet** saasiitéepookw VAI, thusíiteew VAI; **have forked feet** lxawsiitéesuw VAI, lxawsiitéeyeew VII; **have hot feet** kshusiitéexiin VAI; **have one's feet brushing against a surface, have one's feet contacting a surface** chasksiitéexiin VAI; **have one's feet here, have one's feet sticking this way** peetsiitéexiin VAI **He can't get his feet there.** 'Áalu- náh -peetsii=téexiin.'; **have one's feet in the water, soak one's feet** chooxpwsiitée=xiin VAI; **have one's feet lying the length of something** sahksiitéexiin VAI **His feet are at the edge of the bed.** 'Wsháyee apíineeng sahksiitée=xiin.'; **have one's feet sinking into a substance** *(of mud, of snow, of sand, of grain)* akwaanamwíhleew VAI; **have one's feet up on something** poxkwsiitéexiin VAI; **have one's foot exposed, have one's feet showing** mihtsiitéexiin VAI; **have one's foot sticking out** saaksíiteew VAI; **have one's foot touching down on a surface, have one's foot touching on the floor** mshusiitéexiin VAI; **have one's feet swell up, have swollen feet** makwusíiteew VAI; **have swollen feet** paassíiteew VAI; **have tired feet** shiiwsiitéexiin VAI; **have warm feet** kiishŭwusiitéexiin VAI, kiishŭwusíi=teew VAI; **have warm feet** *(inside one's shoes)* kshuteewsiitéexiin VAI; **have wet feet** skapsíiteew VAI; **have wide feet** paansíiteew VAI; **jump to one's feet** niipawáakchehl VAI; **make a noise while shuffling one's feet** shòhwsiitéexiin VAI; **make noise with one's feet** pwàhwsiitéexiin VAI; **put one's feet up, sit with one's feet upon something** poxkwsiitéepuw VAI; **put one's feet upon something** poxkwsíiteew VAI; **scratch one's feet, have itchy feet** kshiipsíiteew VAI;

**soak one's feet in the water** kamuk=wsíiteew VAI; **soak one's feet in the water, have one's feet in the water** kamukwsiitéexiin VAI; **sole of the foot** aláamsiit PC; **stamp with one's feet, keep time with one's feet** pòhwsii=téexiin VAI; **stick one's feet out, have one's feet sticking out** ktusiitéexiin VAI, saaksiitéexiin VAI; **take a step, put one's foot in something, put one's foot on something** alíhkeew VAI **I put my foot on the ice and I slipped.** 'Ndalíhke móhkamiing, nooshàaxihla.', **He put his foot in the water.** 'Mbíing alíhkeew.'; **wash one's feet** kshiixsíiteew VAI; **wash s.o.'s feet** kshusiitéeneew VTA, kshiix=siitéeneew VTA; **wipe one's feet** kaas=siitéexiin VAI.

**for good** ADV **for good, permanently** wchiimwii- PV **You shut it for good.** 'Koochíimwii-kpáhŭmun.', **I lost it for good.** 'Noochíimwii-aníhtoon.'; **go away for good, stay away for good** wchiimwáhkeew VAI; **stay away for good** wchíimapuw VAI.

**force** N **rob people, take things from people by force** shihkwihtáasuw VAI; **take s.t. from s.o. by force, force s.o. to do s.t.** shihkwíhtaweew VTAO.

**force** VT **take s.t. from s.o. by force, force s.o. to do s.t.** shihkwíhtaweew VTAO.

**forehead** N **forehead, top of head** laa=wáandpe PC; **middle of the forehead** laawaaxkaláwe PC.

**foreigner** N aweenáhkeew NA.

**forest** N **forest, in the bush** kóhpii PC **There are lots of good roads in the bush.** 'Wéemi talí wŭlatéexun kóhpii.', **They went in the bush.** 'Kóhpii éewak.'; **be a lot of thick trees, be a lot of dense trees, be a dense forest** spwihtkwíhkeew VII.

**forever** ADV **forever, everlasting** hálŭ=mii PC **I went away eventually.** 'Hálŭmii ndalŭmúsi.'

**forget** VI wanúsuw VAI **He always forgets.** 'Ngúmee wahwanúsiin.'

**forget** VT **forget s.o., forget s.t.** wanús=uw VAIO **Don't forget your lunch.** 'Chíi wanusíiwu kŭniimáawan.'

**forgive** VT **forgive s.o.** pooneelunda=máweew VTA; **forgive people** poo=neelundáasuw VAI, pooneelundáasuw VII.

**forgiveness** N pooneelundamuwáakan NI.

**fork** N lehlxawalóoyeek NI.

**forked** ADJ **be forked** lxáweew VII, lxáwsuw VAI; **have forked feet** lxaw=siitéesuw VAI, lxawsiitéeyeew VII; **have forked fingers** lxawŭlunjéesuw VAI, lxawŭlunjéeyeew VII *as of a fork;* **be a forked tree** lxawáhkwsuw VAI.

**former** ADJ **my former friend** mbaak=chóosum NAD.

**fortune teller** N kwehkwsáapiis NA.

**forty** N neewiináxke PC.

**forward** ADV **fall forward** achiichkwàl=ehtéexiin VAI.

**foul** ADJ **talk terribly, talk badly, use foul language** chiiptóonheew VAI.

**foul ball** N **rebound off something, bounce back and fall, fall back** *(s.t. animate)*, **be a foul ball** *(baseball)* kwaxkwíixiin VAI.

**four** N néewa PC **He weighs four pounds.** 'Néewa poondakúsuw.'; **be four of them, be four** néewŭwak VAI *usually plural,* néewŭnool VII *usually plural;* **be four pairs, be four sets** neewée=look VAI *usually plural,* neewéeltool VII *usually plural;* **be four pieces** *(of something string-like)* neewáhtakat VII; **be gone for four days** neewoo=kwŭnáhkeew VAI; **be in four layers** *(of something sheet-like)* neeweekíi=xiin VAI, neeweekíixun VII; **four** neew- PV **It's four o'clock.** 'Néew-kŭlák=uw.'; **four** neew- PN **I worked there for four months.** 'Néew-kíishooxkw náh ndúnda-làlóhke.'; **four days** neewóokwŭnii PC; **four hundred** neewaapóxku PC; **four, in fours** nee=wéeli PC **They're stacked in fours.** 'Neewéeli pihtawíixŭnool.'; **have four pages** *(of something sheet-like)* neewaapéeksuw VAI *usually of pieces of paper;* **take four steps** neewalíh=keew VAI; **walk in groups of four** neewataxooxwéewak VAI *usually plural.*

**Four Corners** N **be a crossroads, the Four Corners** *(main intersection near band office at Moraviantown, Ontario)* aashŭwatéexun VII **I'm going to the Four Corners.** 'Aashŭ=watéexun numáw-níipawi.'

**fourteen** N neewaaníhka PC.

**fowl** N **guinea fowl** pókhwiit NA; **rooster, male fowl** lunŭwéhleew NA.

**fox** N xwáalŭwees NA.

**fragile** ADJ **be fragile, be delicate** póoxpeew VII; **be fragile, be delicate** *(s.t. animate)*, **be delicate in health** póoxpsuw VAI.

**frame** N **frame house, board house** pasiikaaxkwíikaan NI.

**free** ADJ **be free, be unmarried, have no attachments** nihlaapéewuw VAI; **set s.o. free** nihlaapeewháaleew VTA; **set s.o. free, make s.o. free** nihlaaw=sooháaleew VTA; **set s.o. free, make s.o. free** nihlaawsóoheew VAIO.

**free** VT **free s.o.** nihlaapéewheew VAIO; **let go of s.o., give s.o. up, let s.o. go, free s.o.** póonŭneew VTA.

**freeze** VI kŭláchuw VAI, kulátun VII; **freeze to death** aaptáchuw VAI.

**Frenchman** N pŭlánzhŭmaan NA.

**fresh** ADJ **fresh grass, green grass** wuskiixáskwal NI *usually plural.*

**Friday** N **be Friday** fráyteew VII **I'm going to visit him on Friday.** 'Nŭ=máw-ooteewáalaaw éenda-fraytéeke.'

**friend** N **my friend** njóos NAD **My friend (vocative).** 'Njó.'; **be friends** *(with each other)* wchoosúndŭwak VAI *usually plural;* **be s.o.'s friend, be friends with s.o.** wchóosŭmeew VTA; **my former friend** mbaakchóosum NAD; **my no-good friend** numatchóo=sum NAD.

**friends with** VT **be friends with s.o.** wŭlaangóomeew VTA.

**friendship** N wŭlaangoondŭwáakan NI.

**frighten** VT **frighten s.o., scare s.o.** wíishaleew VTA; **frighten people, scare people** wiishalúweew VAI.

**frightened of** VT **be frightened of s.t., be nervous about s.t.** kwíhtam VTI 1A.

**frightening** ADJ **be in a frightening condition, be in a dangerous condition** kxwaawíixiin VAI, kxwaawíixun VII.

**frightful** ADJ **frightful, terrible** achiipi- PV **I think bad thoughts.** 'Njachíipi-liitéeha.'; **frightful, terrible** achiipu- PV *informal* **Some people have bad underarm perspiration** 'Áalund awéen achíipu-ashiilóngwane.'; **frightful, terrible** chiipii- PV **It is thundering loudly.** 'Chíipii-pehtáh=kuw.'; **frightful, terrible** chiipu- PV *informal* **Something terrible happened.** 'Chíipu-léew.'; **look terrible, be terrible looking, have a frightful appearance** chiipiináakwat VII, chii=piináakwsuw VAI.

**frog** N chkwál NA.

**from** PREP **from a certain place, for a certain reason** wunj- PV *informal* **I ran down from the top of the hill** 'Waxkiitáawung nóonj-niixahtakíh=la.', **My head was sticking out of the water.** 'Mbíing nóonj-saakoh=kwéexiin.'; **from a certain place, for a certain reason** wunji- PV **I came out of the house.** 'Wiikwáhmung nóonji-kchíim.'; **place, reason** wunju- PN *informal* **Off the table.** 'Wúnju-eehundaxpóonung.', **They didn't play cards for money any more.**

'Máh njíhnal shkuphameewíiwak wúnju-shúlpul.'

**front** N **be at the front, be in the lead** shayéexun VII; **in the lead, in front** shayéemung PC **My front tooth.** 'Shayéemung níipiit éhteek.', **She changed her seat to the front.** 'Shayéemung lú áandapuw.'; **in the lead, in front** shéemung PC **It fell forward, it went to the front.** 'Shéemung líhle.'; **put s.o. in the front, put s.o. in the lead** shayée=xŭmeew VTA; **put s.t. in the front, put s.t. in the lead** shayéextoow VTI2; **walk in the lead, walk in front, go ahead, walk ahead** sha=yéewxeew VAI **He likes to be ahead.** 'Wíhwiing-shayéewxeew.', **He always likes to go ahead.** 'Wíhwiing-shàshayéewxeew.'

**frost** N **be frost** tóhpun VII.

**frozen** ADJ **be frozen together** takwátun VII; **be covered, have a lid, be frozen over** kpátun VII; **be frozen ground** kŭlatŭnahkéeyeew VII.

**fruit** N **be a 'dirty' picker, pick only the most accessible fruits or berries, pick only the most accessible products** aníiskii-paxkŭníikeew VAI.

**fry** VI **cook by frying** *(of cooks)* salásŭ=meew VAI.

**fry** VT **fry s.t.** salásŭm VTI1B; **fry s.t. animate** saláseew VTA.

**fry bread** N salápwaan NI.

**frying pan** N pán NA.

**full** ADJ **be full** wchuwíixiin VAI, wchuwíixun VII; **be full** *(with non-liquid)* wchuwáhteew VII, wchúwapuw VAI; **be full of water, be full of liquids** wchúwpeew VAI, wchúwpeew VII **The creeks are full of water.** 'Shii=póosh'shal weewchuwpéewal.'; **be full to the brim, be level with the top** *(of non-liquids)* tpuskŭwáhteew VII; **overflow, be filled over the top** paaláhteew VII; **overflow, be full over the top** páalapuw VAI; **be round** *(s.t. animate)*, **be full** *(of the moon)* ptúkwsuw VAI; **be full from eating** kíispuw VAI; **drink one's fill, be full from drinking** kiispáapŭweew VAI; **overeat, be full to the bursting point** kiispwulóosuw VAI.

**fully** ADV **be ready, be ripe, be fully grown** teepíikun VII, teepíikuw VAI.

**fun** N **enjoy playing, have fun while playing** wiingeelawúsuw VAI; **have a good time, have fun** wiingáawsuw VAI; **have fun, get into things in a playful way** kpucheewháasuw VAI; **make fun of people** wehweemwáa=lŭweew VAI; **make fun of s.o.** weh=wéemwaaleew VTA.

**funeral** N **be a funeral going on** kwtawúndiin VAI *indefinite subject only;* **have one's funeral** kwtawŭníi=keew VAI; **have one's funeral** kwtáw=ŭnaaw VTA *indefinite subject only.*

**fur** N **be bare, be lacking in fur, be lacking in hair** mooshakúsuw VAI; **be bare, be lacking in fur, be lacking in hair; be lean** *(of meat)* móosha=keew VII.

# G

**game** N **participate, take part, take part in a game, take part in a fight** wiichóohŭweew VAI; **play a certain game, play at a certain game** leela=wúsuw VAI **He's playing at different things.** 'Músu- kwéek -leelawúsiin.', **What are you playing?** 'Kwéek ktuleelawúsi?'

**gang up on** VT **gang up on s.o.** tputoo=haaléewak VTA *subject usually plural.*

**garden** N wchupahkiiháakan NI.

**garter** N kihkaatéepuy NI.

**garter snake** N maamaaláxkook NA.

**gas** N **have a swollen stomach, be**

**bloated, have gas** paasatáyeew VAI.

**gate** N taweenaxkŭníikan NI, tehtawee=naxkŭníikan NI; **open the gate for s.o.** taweenáxkŭneew VTA.

**gather** VT **gather s.o. up** maawéeheew VTA; **gather s.o. up** *(using the hands)* maawéeneew VTA *object usually plural;* **gather s.t.** *(using the hands)* maawéenum VTI1B; **gather s.t. up** maawéehum VTI1B; **gather the dishes** maaweehíinjŭwcew VAI; **gather things up** maawhúnzuw VAI; **gather things, rake things up** maawee=kwáakeew VAI; **gather together, meet** maawehléewak VAI *usually plural;* **gather up and take a load of s.t. away** alumhéewatoow VTI2, alumée=watoow VTI2; **gather up and take away a load of s.t. animate** alum=héewaleew VTA, aluméewaleew VTA; **gather up the dishes** maaweenjŭ=weextíikeew VAI; **gather wood chips** wsheexakwáheew VAI; **make kindling, gather kindling** wŭlaxakwáh=eew VAI.

**gathering** N **speak** *(especially in public),* **speak at a meeting, speak at a gathering** aaptóoneew VAI **Now he's speaking (as of a baby starting to talk)** 'Kwáy méhch aaptóone.'

**gear** N **harness tug, harness gear** wtuníikan NI.

**get** VT **get s.o., buy s.o., keep s.o., have s.o.** ayúweew VTA; **get s.t., buy s.t., keep s.t., have s.t.** ayúm VTI1B; **get s.o. from a certain place** óhleew VTA **I don't know where I got him.** 'Táa néek éet wéhlak.'; **get s.t. from a certain place, get s.t. from somewhere** wúnd VTI3 **I got it in Chatham.** 'Chétum nóondun.'; **get s.t. animate cheaply, buy s.t. animate cheaply** aapŭwíiheew VTA; **get s.t. cheap, pay a little for s.t.** aapŭ=walóhkeew VAIO; **get s.t. cheaply, buy s.t. cheaply** aapŭwíhtoow VTI2 **Get it as cheaply as you can.** 'Kángu-uch lúkih -aapŭwíhtawan.'; **go to get a load** *(of one's belongings)* naathéewasuw VAI; **go to get a load of s.o.** naathéewaleew VTA; **go to get a load of s.t.** naathéewatoow VTI2; **reach out one's hand to get s.t.** naachiináxkeew VAIO.

**get along with** VT **be hard to get along with** machiitéeheew VAI.

**get credit** VI **get credit, be given credit, 'get trusted'** lahtkwéehaaw VTA *usually with indefinite subject.*

**get on** VI **get on board a vehicle** póo=siiw VAI-S.

**get out** VI **disembark, get out of a vehicle** kóhpiiw VAI-S.

**get out of** VT **come down, descend, get out of a vehicle** níixiiw VAI-S.

**get ready** VT **get s.o. ready** kehtéexŭ=meew VTA.

**get through** VI **go through, pass through, get through** éeshiiw VAI-S; **go through s.t., pass through s.t., get through s.t.** éeshiiw VAIO **I went across his property.** 'Ndéeshiin wtootéeneeng.'

**get up** VI **get up from lying down** áamwiiw VAI-S; **get up from sitting** pasúkwiiw VAI-S; **get up in a hurry** pasukwiipáhtoow VAI; **get up quickly from lying down** aamwiipáhtoow VAI; **hit s.o. and make them get up** aa=mwihtéeheew VTA; **make s.o. get up from lying down** aamwihkshíh=kaweew VTA.

**get up** VT **talk to s.o. to get them up from lying down, holler at s.o. to get them up from lying down** aa=mwihkíimeew VTA.

**ghost** N chíipay NA.

**gift** N miiltuwáakan NI.

**girl** N oxkwéesus NA.

**girl-crazy** ADJ **like women, be 'girl-crazy'** wiingoxkwéeweew VAI.

**give** VT **give s.t. to s.o.** míileew VTAO **I**

**gave him the money.** 'Shúlpul nŭ=míilaan.'; **give s.o. away to people, give s.t. away to people** míilŭweew VAIO; **be given** *(especially something from heaven)* miilkwúsuw VAI; **do good for s.o., give s.o. luck** wŭlíi=hukw VTA *inanimate subject only* **The medicine did me good.** 'Noolíih=kwun wchápihk.', **It did me good to get out of the house.** 'Noolíihkwun wiikwáhmung wúnj-kchúyaan.'; **give a drink to s.o.** mŭnáheew VTA; **give s.o. a swollen head, hit s.o. and give them a lump on the head** ma=kwaandpéeheew VTA; **give s.o. something bad to drink** machiisŭmóo=leew VTA; **hit s.o. and give them a lump on the head** makwaandpehtée=heew VTA.

**give a ride** VT **give s.o. a ride** poosóo=leew VTA.

**give away** VT **give s.t. away** méek VAIO **She often gives away some money.** 'Éewachu-méek shúlpul.'

**give back** VT **exchange s.t. animate, return s.t. animate, give s.t. animate back** *(after borrowing it)* aashŭwún=eew VTA; **exchange s.t., give s.t. back, return s.t.** *(after borrowing it)* aashŭ=wúnum VTI1B.

**give credit** VT **get credit, be given credit, 'get trusted'** lahtkwéehaaw VTA *usually with indefinite subject.*

**give up** VI laaweelúndam VOTI1, laa=weelúnzuw VAI.

**give up** VT **give s.t. up, let go of s.t., let s.t. go** *(of debts)* pooneelúndam VTI1A; **leave s.o. alone, have nothing to with s.o., let s.o. go, give up on s.o., break up with s.o., give up making s.t. animate** pooníiheew VTA; **let go of s.o., give s.o. up, let s.o. go, free s.o.** póonŭneew VTA; **let go of s.t., give s.t. up** póonŭnum VTI1B; **let s.t. go, give s.t. up, give up doing s.t., give up making s.t.** pooníhtoow VTI2.

**give up on** VT **give up on s.o.** laawiila=wéeheew VTA, laawéelŭmeew VTA; **give up on s.o., let go of s.o.** *(especially of someone who has died)* poo=néelŭmeew VTA; **give up over s.t.** laaweelúndam VTI1A.

**glad** ADJ **be glad about s.t., be happy about s.t.** wŭleelúndam VTI1A; **be glad about something** payahkwu- PV **I'm glad I left.** 'Mbayáhkwu-alúm=si.', **I'm glad I went home.** 'Mbay=áhko-péech-máachi.'; **be glad to eat s.t.** *(not having had it for some time)* payahkwándam VTI1A; **be glad to eat s.t. animate** *(not having had it for some time)* payáhkwameew VTA; **be glad to go** wiingóoxweew VAI **We were so glad to go.** 'Móxa nŭwiin=gooxwéhna.'; **be glad to hear s.o., be glad to listen to s.o.** payahkw=sútaweew VTA; **be glad to hear s.t., be glad to listen to s.t.** payahkwsút=am VTI1A; **be glad to see s.o.** payah=kwíinaweew VTA; **be glad to see s.t.** payahkwíinam VTI1A; **be glad to see someone** payahkwiinúakwsuw VAI; **be glad, be happy** wiingeelúndam VAI; **be glad, be happy** wŭleelúndam VOTI1; **be glad about s.t., be happy about s.t.** wiingeelúndam VTI1A.

**glasses** N **eyeglasses, glasses** wuskiinj=kwahíikanal NI *usually plural;* **wear eyeglasses, wear glasses** wuskiinj=kwáhŭmeew VAI.

**glimpse** N **be a glimpse of someone seen while going by** laashíhleew VAI **He was going so fast that one only saw a glimpse of him.** 'Éelkih-kshíhlaat shùkéhla laashíhleew.'

**glove** N **leather glove** xáyii-wánd NA.

**glue** VT **glue s.t. animate together, paste s.t. animate** psakwpéhlaleew VTA; **glue s.t. together, paste s.t.** psakwpéhlatoow VTI2; **glue s.t., stick s.t. together** psákwŭnum VTI1B; **paste s.o. together, glue s.o. together**

psakwpáleew VTA *object usually plural;* **paste s.t. together, glue s.t. together** psakwpátoow VTI2 *object usually plural* **I glued the pieces of wood together.** 'Mbusakwupatóonal xwúsal.'

**glutton** N **glutton, someone who eats a lot, someone who never gets full** máaleew NA; **be a glutton, be greedy at the table** maaléewuw VAI.

**go** VI éew VAI **Go away!** 'Yéelak áal!', **Come here!** 'Yóh áal!'; **go** *(to do)*, **go** *(and do)* mawii- PV **He attends school.** 'Mawíi-shkóoluw.'; **go** *(to do)*, **go** *(and do)* maw- PV **He's gone to work.** 'Alúmsuw há wá máwalóhke.', **When I got there I wanted to eat at noontime before I went to the funeral.** 'Náh peeyayáane ngátamíitsi laawahkwéewŭnii iiyéeskwa máw-kwtawŭniikéewaan.'; **go** *(to do)*, **go** *(and do)* mawi- PV **If it doesn't rain I'll go to the ball game.** 'Máhta sookŭlaanóokwe nŭmáwi-ch-pŭnámun éenda-neenaxkhwátiing.'; **go** *(to do)*, **go** *(and do)* mawu- PV *informal* **I spent the spring in town.** 'Nŭmáwu-siikwanámwi ootée=neeng.', **I went to put my legs in the water.** 'Nŭmáwu-kamukwkáate.'; **be a glimpse of someone seen while going by** laashíhleew VAI **He was going so fast that one only saw a glimpse of him.** 'Éelkih-kshíhlaat shùkéhla laashíhleew.'; **be all gone, everybody is gone** weemooltúwak VAI; **be glad to go** wiingóoxweew VAI **We were so glad to go.** 'Móxa nŭwiingooxwéhna.'; **be gone a certain length of time** sahkáhkeew VAI **He was gone for two months.** 'Níish-kíishooxkw sahkáhkeew.', **How long has he been gone?** 'Thá sahkáhke?'; **be gone for five days** naalanookwŭnáhkeew VAI; **be gone for four days** neewookwŭnáhkeew VAI; **be gone for many nights, be gone for many days** xweelookwŭ=náhkeew VAI; **be gone for several days** keexookwŭnáhkeew VAI; **be gone for so many days** txookwŭ=náhkeew VAI *usually with number particle* **I was gone for six days.** 'Ngwútaash ndundxookwŭnáhke.'; **be gone for so many weeks** kundŭ=weewŭnáhkeew VAI *usually with number preverb* **He was gone for two weeks.** 'Níish-kundŭweewŭnáh=keew.', **You were gone for four weeks.** 'Kŭnéewu-kunduweewŭnáh=ke.'; **be gone for three days** nxoo=kwŭnáhkeew VAI; **be gone for two days** niishookwŭnáhkeew VAI; **be gone overnight** ngwutookwŭnáh=keew VAI; **be unwilling to go, be reluctant to go** shiingóoxweew VAI; **fly in various directions, drive in various directions, go in various directions, fly, drive** msíhleew VAI; **get close, approach, fly close by, go close by** peexŭwíhleew VII, peexŭ=wíhleew VAI; **go across the water** kwáxkakeew VAI; **go all over, roam with no purpose in mind, throw one's backside about as one goes** msiitŭyéewxeew VAI; **go along** *(with others)* wiitóoxweew VAI; **go and fight** mawatáhkeew VAI; **go and urinate** mawíisheew VAI; **go back and forth, ride back and forth, fly back and forth** wŭyakíhleew VAI **The cars are going back and forth.** 'Káalak wŭyakihléewak.'; **go by in a boat, go along in a boat, float by in a boat, float along in a boat** pŭmáatham VAI; **go by oneself** nxóoxweew VAI; **go crookedly, fly crookedly, fly on an erratic course** pàptukíhleew VAI; **go downhill** púmbiiw VAI-S; **go downhill, fall downhill, slide downhill** pumbíhleew VAI; **go fast** *(in or on a vehicle or bicycle)* pàpxoowíhleew

VAI; **go here and there crying, go about crying** apaaméewtam VOTI1; **go home, drive home, fly home, pedal home** aapaachíhleew VAI; **go in a certain direction, go in a certain manner** liitŭyéhleew VAI **You went far.** 'Wáhlu ktuliitŭyéhla.', **He went here and there.** 'Msú-liitŭyéhleew.'; **go in a certain manner, go in a certain direction, fly in a certain manner, fly in a certain direction, proceed in a certain manner, proceed in a certain direction** líhleew VAI **You fell in the water but your head is sticking out.** 'Mbíing ktulíhla shùkéhla ksaakaandpéexiin.'; **go in a circle, go around, roll in a circle** wiiwŭníhleew VII, wiiwŭníhleew VAI; **go out** któoxweew VAI; **go out of sight** waníhleew VAI; **go over, flow over** paalíhleew VAI, paalíhleew VII; **go slowly** wàwtamiitŭyéhleew VAI; **go straight, fly straight** shaaxkíhleew VAI; **go through s.t., experience s.t.** eeshóoxweew VAIO; **go to dance** ma=wúkeew VAI; **go to get a load** *(of one's belongings)* naathéewasuw VAI; **go to get a load of s.o.** naathéewaleew VTA; **go to get a load of s.t.** naathéewa=toow VTI2; **go to work, go and work** mawalóhkeew VAI; **go up, climb up** uspakóosuw VAI; **go up, come up, start to come up** uspíhleew VAI, us=píhleew VII; **go uphill** kwtákwteew VAI; **go uphill** *(on a road)* uspaawún=geew VAI; **go with one's tail in a certain direction, go with one's tail in a certain manner** laalŭwéhleew VAI; **lift s.o. up, make s.o. go up** *(using the hands)* úspŭneew VTA; **lift s.t. up, make s.t. go up** *(using the hands)* úspŭnum VTI1B; **make s.o. go fast** kshushíhkaweew VTA; **make s.o. go overboard** *(romantically)* kshuwóo=leew VTA; **move on, go from one place to another** aandóoxweew VAI; **run in a certain manner, run in a certain direction, go in a certain manner, go in a certain direction** shíhleew VAI **He was running close by.** 'Náhnalii shíhleew.'; **stop going, stop working** *(of machines)* ehkwíh=leew VII; **stop going, stop working** ehkwíhleew VAI; **walk so far, go so far, go a certain distance** sahkóo=xweew VAI **He went very far.** 'Móxa wáhlu sahkóoxweew.'

**go across** VI **go across, drive across, pedal across, fly across** aashŭwíh=leew VAI; **go across, take a shortcut** kaxkéeweew VAI.

**go after** VT **go after s.o., fetch s.o.** náa=leew VTA; **go after s.t., fetch s.t.** náa=tum VTI1B; **go after s.t. for s.o., fetch s.t. for s.o.** naatamáweew VTAO; **go after and carry s.t., fetch and carry s.t.** naatasánuw VAIO; **go after and drag s.o., go after and drag s.t. animate** naattaachíhleew VTA; **go after and drag s.t., fetch and drag s.t.** naattaachíindam VTI1A; **be gone after, be brought, be fetched** naatáasuw VII; **fetch water, go after water**, **go to get liquor** naathúpeew VAI; **fetch wood, go after wood** naatxákweew VAI; **go after food, fetch food** naa=chiichŭwáakaneew VAI; **go after something to fetch it, go after something to take it** naathéewasuw VAI.

**go along** VI **go along, accompany** wíi=teew VAI.

**go around** VI **go around, rotate, spin** tùpíhleew VAI; **hit s.o. and make them go around, hit s.o. and make them spin around** tùpihtéeheew VTA; **hit s.t. and make it go around, hit s.t. and make it spin around** tùpih=téeham VTI1A.

**go away** VI **fly away, go away, pedal away** alumíhleew VAI; **go away crying** aluméewtam VOTI1; **go away for good, stay away for good** wchii=

mwáhkeew VAI; **go away with things** alumŭwaléhleew VAI.

**go back** VI **fly back, go back** kwaxkíh=leew VAI.

**go by** VI **be rain going by** lóowŭlaan VII; **bring a load of s.t., go by with a load of s.t., haul a load of s.t.** éewa=toow VTI2 **I hauled a load of hay.** 'Ndéewato miixáskwal.'; **fly by, fly along, go by, go along, drive by, drive along, pedal by, pedal along** pŭmíhleew VAI; **go by s.t., drive by s.t., fly by s.t., cycle by s.t.** loowíh=leew VAIO; **go by, drive by, fly by, cycle by** loowíhleew VAI; **roar, go by roaring** tamongwíhleew VAI, tamon=gwíhleew VII.

**go down** VI síhleew VII *of the water level;* **recede, go down** ahkwíhleew VII *of the water level.*

**go home** VI máachiiw VAI-S.

**go inside** VI **go inside quickly, run inside, enter a dwelling running** piin=jiikéhleew VAI; **go inside, fly inside, drive inside, fall inside** piinjíhleew VAI.

**go off** VI **leave, go off** alúmsuw VAI.

**go out** VI **come out, go out, go to the bathroom** kchíiw VAI-S **I came out of the house.** 'Wiikwáhmung nóonj-kchíim.'

**go out** VI **be gone out, go out quickly** *(of fires)* wchiimahtéhleew VII; **go out** *(of fires)*, **be burnt up** *(in a fire)* wchiimáhteew VII; **go out, be extinguished** *(of fires)* ahtéhleew VII; **have one's fire go out** wchiimahtawásuw VAI.

**go straight** VI **straighten out, go straight**, **go quickly in the right direction, drive correctly** mayaawíh=leew VAI.

**go through** VI **go through s.t., pass through s.t., get through s.t.** éeshiiw VAIO **I went across his property.** 'Ndéeshiin wtootéeneeng.'; **go through, fall through** eeshíhleew VII, eeshíhleew VAI **I went through the ice.** 'Móhkamiing ndeeshíhla.'; **go through, pass through, get through** éeshiiw VAI-S.

**go to pieces** VI **go to pieces, fall to pieces** piikíhleew VII, piikíhleew VAI.

**go with** VT **accompany s.o., go with s.o.** wiichéeweew VTA **She liked to go around with any man at all.** 'Wíh=wiing- wéemu awéeniil lúnŭwal -wiicheewáawal.'

**God** N pahtamáwaas NA; **be God** pahta=mawáasuw VAI; **think that one is God** pahtamaweelúnzuw VAI.

**gone** ADJ **be all gone** txíhleew VAI, txíh=leew VII **The fish are all gone.** 'Txih=léewak naméesak.'; **be all gone, be used up** weemíhleew VII.

**good** ADJ **be pretty, be good, be nice** wŭlúsuw VAI, wŭlút VII; **nice, good** pshihki- PN **A good man.** 'Pshíhki-lúnuw.'; **nice, good** pshihku- PN *informal* **A nice horse.** 'Pshíhku-neh=nayóongus.', **A nice dog.** 'Pshíhku-mwáakaneew.'; **nice, good** pshihku- PV *informal* **He has a nice disposition.** 'Pshíhku-únd.'; **nice, good** wŭli- PV **He has a nice tail.** 'Wŭlí-shkwún=ayeew.'; **nice, good** wŭlu- PV *informal* **We had two horses, and one was very nice.** 'Níishŭwak nehnayóong=sak ngaxaníhna, mayáawsuw móxa wúlu-únd.', **He supported that girl well and treated her well, but this girl would always leave.** 'Óolu-tapaaláawal yóol oxkwéessal wáak oolaliiháawal, shúkw wá oxkwéesus ngúmee alúmsuw.'; **be correct, be good** wŭlíixun VII **Your hat looks good on you.** 'Ktaakongwéepuy wŭ=líixun.'; **be a good cook** nihtaawa=túpuw VAI; **be a good pitcher** níhtaa-píchuw VAI; **be a good road, be a good path** wŭlatéexun VII; **be a good singer** nihtaawaláamuw VAI; **be a**

**good speaker** *(also of a child learning how to speak)*, **be good at speaking, be good at public speaking** nihtaawaaptóoneew VAI; **be clear water, be good water** wŭlupéekat VII; **be good grass** wŭláskat VII; **be good shade, give good shade** wŭlahka=chíhteew VII; **be good, be straight, be a good strand of thread, be fine** *(of something stringlike)* wŭláhtakat VII; **be happy, be in good spirits** wŭlahtéenamuw VAI; **be in a nice place, be well seated, have a good home** *(of an adopted child or a person in heaven)* wŭlápuw VAI; **be nice, be good, be pleasant, be good-natured** wŭliitéeheew VAI; **be praised, have a good name** wŭlakŭniim=kwúsuw VAI; **do good for s.o., give s.o. luck** wŭlíihukw VTA *inanimate subject only* **The medicine did me good.** 'Noolíihkwun wchápihk.', **It did me good to get out of the house.** 'Noolíihkwun wiikwáhmung wúnj-kchúyaan.'; **do good work** wŭlalóh=keew VAI; **feel in good humour, want to laugh** kŭlukeelúndam VOTI1; **find that s.o. feels better, find that s.o. feels good, feel comfortable with s.o.** wŭlámameew VTA; **find that s.t. feels better, find that s.t. feels good** wŭlamándam VTI1A **My hand feels better.** 'Noolamándamun náxk.', **My shoes feel good.** 'Mahksúnal noola=mandamúnal.'; **give a good account of onself, tell a favourable story** wŭ=laachíimuw VAI; **good medicine** wŭ=laapasíhkan NI; **have a good dream** wŭlóngwaam VAI **I always have good dreams.** 'Ngúmee nŭwaawŭlón=gwaam.'; **have a good fire** wŭlula=wásuw VAI; **have a good head on one's shoulders** wŭláandpeew VAI; **have a good time, have fun** wiin=gáawsuw VAI; **have a trim shape, have a good shape, have a good figure** wŭláhkwsuw VAI; **have fine hair, have nice hair, have good hair** wŭ=laalóhkweew VAI; **have good teeth** awulaníikeew VAI; **look good, be nice looking, have a nice appearance** wŭliináakwat VII, wŭliináakwsuw VAI; **make a good road, make a good path, have a good road, have a good path** wŭlatéexteew VAI; **make good tracks** wŭléelham VOTI1; **make s.o. feel good** wŭliilawéeheew VTA; **say good things about s.o., praise s.o.** wŭlakŭníimeew VTA; **say good things, preach** wŭlaaptóoneew VAI; **say something good about s.o.** wŭlaaptoonáaleew VTA; **see a long way, have good eyesight** wŭlata=wáapuw VAI; **shoot skillfully, be a good shot** nihtaawayáxkham VOTI1; **smell good, be good smelling, have a good smell** wiingiimáakwat VII, wiingiimáakwsuw VAI; **sound good, sound nice** wŭlihtáakwat VII, wŭlih=táakwsuw VAI; **take good aim** *(with a gun)*, **throw well** wŭláaheew VAI; **talk to s.o. and make them feel good** wŭliilawéemeew VTA; **talk well, say good things** awulaaptóoneew VAI; **taste good** wíingan VII **It tastes better.** 'Míingasa wíingan.'; **taste good** wíingul VAI, wŭliipóokwat VII, wŭlii=póokwsuw VAI; **think that s.o. is handy, find s.o. handy, be helpful towards s.o., be good for s.o.** wŭ=laapéemeew VTA; **treat s.o. well, be good to s.o.** wŭlú-líiheew VTA; **write well, have good handwriting** awul=eekhíikeew VAI.

**good** N **be too smart for one's own good** machíi-lpwéew VAI.

**good for nothing** ADJ **bad man, good for nothing man, man of poor character** matahéapeew NA; **bad woman, good for nothing woman, woman of poor character** matahóxkweew NA; **be a bad person, be a good for no-**

thing person matahaapéewuw VAI; **be a bad woman, be a good for nothing woman, be a woman of poor character** matahoxkwéewuw VAI.

**good-natured** ADJ **be nice, be good, be pleasant, be good-natured** wŭliitée=heew VAI.

**goodness!** IJ kwáachund PC **Then my mother said, "Goodness, I wouldn't have believed if it hadn't happened."** 'Nál ngúk úw, "Kwáachund, máh noolsutamóowun shúkw sháxkiiléew."'; **goodness!** kaanjchéena PC, kaanzhchéenaakw PC **My goodness, I can't say it.** 'Kaanzhchéenaakw ndáalu-íin.'

**goose** N waapsuwíhleew NA.

**gooseberry** N keekíingŭlush NA.

**gosh!** IJ **shoot! gosh! silly question! shame on you!** kéesan PC, kéesand PC.

**gossip** N **know all the news, hear everything, hear all the gossip** wih=wéewsuw VAI; **talk a lot, gossip, talk dirty** niisktóonheew VAI.

**grab** VT **grab s.o.** alíipheew VTA, nax=píhleew VTA; **grab s.t.** naxpíhtoow VTI2, náxpŭnum VTI1B, wŭlúnum VTI1B **I could go and grab the wood.** 'Ngíish- áa -wŭlúnŭmun xwús.'; **fix s.o. up, grab s.o., grasp s.o.** wŭlún=eew VTA **I grabbed the dog by the back of the neck.** 'Nóolŭnaaw mwáakaneew wtéeng oxkweekánga=nung.'; **grab a handful of s.t. animate** anzíipheew VTA; **grab s.o. by the hand, tug at s.o, pull on s.o.** sakúneew VTA; **grab s.o. by the leg, pull on s.o.'s leg** sakukaatéeneew VTA; **grab s.o. in a hurry** tàhwíip=heew VTA; **grab s.o.'s leg** sakukaa=téeheew VTA; **grab s.t. by the hand, tug and pull on s.t.** sakúnum VTI1B; **grab s.t. in a hurry** tàhwiipáhtoow VTI2; **grab s.t. in a hurry, grab s.t. quickly, grab a handful of s.t.** an=ziipáhtoow VTI2 **Grab the money and let's go to town.** 'Ánziipáhtool shúlpul ootéeneeng áatookw.'; **grab s.t., seize and take s.t. along** nax=píhleew VAIO.

**grace** N **say grace** keenáamuw VAI.

**grain** N **fine grained** wŭlaamii- PN **Fine sand.** 'Wŭláamii-léekuw.'; **thresh grain** pakáhŭmeew VAI; **be fine in grain, be fine grained** *(of flour, of sand)* wŭláamat VII.

**grandchild** N **my grandchild** nóoxwiis NAD; **have a grandchild** wtooxwíi=suw VAI; **have s.o. as a grandchild, be s.o.'s grandchild** wtooxwíisuw VAIO, **my great-grandchild** ndaat=xóoxwiis NAD; **have great-grandchildren** taatxooxwíisuw VAI.

**grandfather** N **my grandfather** nŭ=moxóomus NAD.

**grandmother** N **my grandmother** nóohum NAD.

**grape** N **grape, raisin** wíisakiim NI.

**grasp** VT **fix s.o. up, grab s.o., grasp s.o.** wŭlúneew VTA **I grabbed the dog by the back of the neck.** 'Nóolŭ=naaw mwáakaneew wtéeng oxkwee=kánganung.'

**grass** N míixaskwal NI *usually plural;* **be good grass** wŭláskat VII; **be long grass** kwŭnaskwéeyeew VII, kwŭnás=kwat VII; **be short grass** chahkwas=kwéeyeew VII, chahkwiixáskwat VII; **be the middle of the grass** laawas=kwíhkeew VII; **be wet grass** skapáskat VII, skapáskwat VII; **cut things, cut grass** tŭmushíikeew VAI; **fresh grass, green grass** wuskiixáskwal NI *usually plural,* askíixaskwal NI *usually plural;* **old grass, weeds** xuwáskwal NI *usually plural,* xuwiixáskwal NI *usually plural;* **short grass** chahkwii=xáskwal NI; **sweetgrass** wiingíimaskw NI.

**grasshopper** N waakchéhlashiish NA.

**grave** N machíiyay NI.

**graze** VT **graze s.o.'s eye** laapsheen=gwéeheew VTA; **hit and graze s.o. with an object** laalihtéeheew VTA.

**grease** N pŭmúy NI; **oil for greasing** shamuníikan NI, shamuníiwu-káanoos NA; **put grease on s.o., put grease on s.t. animate** shamúneew VTA; **put grease on s.t.** shamúnum VTI1B.

**grease** VT **grease a buggy** shamaatpùn=íikaneew VAI.

**greasy** ADJ **be greasy** shaméew VII, sha=músuw VAI; **eat greasy food** sha=muchéepuw VAI **I ate too much greasy food.** 'Noosáami-shamuchée=pwi.'; **greasy pig** shamóoshkoosh NA; **greasy wagon** shamaatpùníikan NA; **have a greasy mouth** shamutóoneew VAI; **have greasy hair** shamóhkweew VAI; **have greasy hands** shamunáx=keew VAI.

**great** ADJ **great, wonderful, amazing** kaanzhu- PV **Something wonderful happened.** 'Káanzhu-léew.'; **be a great noise, be a big rumour, be a great report of an activity** *(especially of a story that gets modified or exaggerated)* kaanzhihtáakwat VII; **brag, say great things** *(especially when making a speech)* akaanzhaap=tóoneew VAI; **make a great noise** kaanzhihtáakwsuw VAI; **tell a great story** kihtaachíimuw VAI.

**great-grandchild** N **my great-grandchild** ndaatxóoxwiis NAD; **have great-grandchildren** taatxooxwíisuw VAI.

**greedy** ADJ **be a glutton, be greedy at the table** maaléewuw VAI.

**green** ADJ **be green** askáskweew VII, as=káskwsuw VAI; **be a greenish colour, have a green tinge to it** askaskwŭ=léexiin VAI, askaskwŭléexun VII; **be green in colour, be green-coloured** askaskwaapamúkwat VII, askaskwaa=pamúkwsuw VAI; **dye s.o. green** as=kaskwcháseew VTA; **dye s.t. green** askaskwchásum VTI1B; **fresh grass, green grass** wuskiixáskwal NI *usually plural;* **green** askaskwii- PV **I painted it green** 'Ndaskáskwii-shóohŭmun.'; **green bean** káshayeem NI; **green corn** askxáskwiim NI; **green grass** askíixaskwal NI *usually plural;* **green onion** askiinóonzhuy NA; **green snake** askaskwáxkook NA; **green wood** áskxakw NI; **have green eyes** askas=kwaalakíingweew VAI; **turn green** askaskwíhleew VII; **turn green** as=kaskwíhleew VAI; **green thread** as=kaskwáhtakw NI; **new corn, green corn** wuskxáskwiim NI.

**grey** ADJ **be brown, be grey** wiipón=gweew VII, wiipóngwsuw VAI; **brown, grey** wiipongwii- PV **I painted it brown, grey.** 'Nŭwiipóngwii-shóo=hŭmun.'; **be brown coloured, be grey coloured** wiipongwaapamúkwat VII, wiipongwaapamúkwsuw VAI; **be a brownish colour, have a brown tinge to it, be a greyish colour, have a grey tinge to it** wiipongwŭléexiin VAI, wiipongwŭléexun VII; **be brown earth, be grey earth** wiipongwah=kéeyeew VII, wiipongwáhtakw NI; **dye s.t. animate brown, dye s.t. animate grey** wiipongwcháseew VTA; **dye s.t. brown, dye s.t. grey** wiipongwchás=um VTI1B; **have a grey beard, have a white beard** waapihtóonayeew VAI; **have grey eyes, have brown eyes** wiipongwaalakíingweew VAI; **have grey hair** waapáandpeew VAI; **have light-coloured eyes, have grey eyes** waaxeelíingweew VAI; **turn brown, turn grey** wiipongwíhleew VAI, wii=pongwíhleew VII.

**grief** N **be out of one's mind with grief** wanahkwateelúndam VOTI1; **grieve oneself to death, die of grief, be grieving** aapteelúndam VOTI1; **grieve, feel grief** ooshawamalúsuw VAI; **grieve, feel grief, be sad** ooshawee=lúndam VOTI1; **make sounds of grief,**

**sound full of grief** *(especially of singing)* ooshawihtáakwsuw VAI.

**grieve** VI ooshawahtéenamuw VAI; **be sad, be grieving** shiiweelún=dam VOTI1; **grieve oneself to death, die of grief, be grieving** aapteelún=dam VOTI1; **grieve, feel grief** oosha=wamalúsuw VAI; **grieve, feel grief, be sad** ooshaweelúndam VOTI1; **look sad, look to be grieving** ooshawii=náakwsuw VAI.

**grind** VT **crush s.t., pound s.t., grind s.t.** shkwáham VTI1A; **pound things, grind things** shkwahíikeew VAI.

**grinder** N **crank, handle for turning, hand grinder** tùpŭníikan NI; **mill, grinder** shkwahíikan NI.

**grindstone** N **file, sharpening stone, grindstone** kiinhíikan NI.

**groan** VI **grunt, groan** múndam VOTI1.

**groceries** N kŭlooshliihiiwáakanal NI *usually plural.*

**grocery** N **grocery peddler** kŭlooshlíi=lŭnuw NA; **grocery store** kŭlooshlii=híikaan NI.

**groove** N **have grooves** *(usually of wooden objects)* kàkatíhkeew VII; **make grooves in s.t.** kàkatihkíhtoow VTI2.

**grope** VI **grope around, feel around for things** kwàkwcheeníikeew VAI.

**grope for** VT **grope around for things, feel around for things** kwtuchee=níikeew VAI; **grope for s.o., feel for s.o.** *(using the hands)* kwtúneew VTA; **grope for s.t., feel for s.t.** *(using the hands)* kwtúnum VTI1B.

**ground** N **be a hole in the ground** waa=lahkéeyeew VII; **be bloody ground** mohkwahkéeyeew VII; **be cold ground** thahkéeyeew VII; **be dry ground** kaahahkéeyeew VII, peen=gwahkéeyeew VII; **be even ground, be smooth ground** wŭlahkéeyeew VII; **be frozen ground** kŭlatŭnahkée=yeew VII; **be hard ground** maska=nahkéeyeew VII; **touch, make contact, be in contact with the ground, be in contact with the floor** mshíi=xiin VAI, mshíixun VII; **be level ground** shaaxkahkéeyeew VII; **be slippery ground** wshaaxahkéeyeew VII; **be snowy ground, be snow on the ground** koonahkéeyeew VII; **be soft ground** wtakahkéeyeew VII; **be stony ground** asunahkéeyeew VII; **be uneven ground, be crooked ground** piimahkéeyeew VII; **be wet ground** skapahkéeyeew VII; **land, land on the ground, alight** awáhleew VAI **I landed over there.** 'Yéelak ndúlu-awáh=la.'; **pit, hole in ground** *(especially for storing vegetables in winter)* wáalakw NI.

**groundhog** N moonáhkeew NA.

**group** N **be in a group of people crowded close together, make one's way through the crowd** kàkchúkamuw VAI; **be many of them standing** *(in a group)* xweeliikaapawúwak VAI *usually plural;* **group together** màm=shihléewak VAI *usually plural;* **in groups of so many** txéeli PC **They're stacked in sixes.** 'Ngwútaash txéeli pihtawíixŭnool.', **They are in eight pairs.** 'Xáash txéelook.'; **walk in fives, be in groups of five** naalanat=xooxwéewak VAI *usually plural;* **walk in groups of four** neewataxooxwée=wak VAI *usually plural;* **walk in groups of two** niishataxooxwéewak VAI *usually plural.*

**grouse** N pahpáhkuw NA.

**grow** VI **grow, be growing** alumíikun VII, alumíikuw VAI; **be grown, be through growing** kiishíikun VII; **be ready, be ripe, be fully grown** tee=píikun VII, teepíikuw VAI; **grow apart** chàchpíikŭwak VAI *usually plural,* chàchpíikŭnool VII *usually plural;* **grow badly** machíikun VII, machíi=kuw VAI; **grow close together** kchuk=íikŭwak VAI *usually plural,* spwíikŭ=

wak VAI *usually plural,* spwíikŭnool VII *usually plural;* **grow crookedly, grow sideways** pŭmiichíikuw VAI, pŭmiichíikun VII **My tooth came up crooked.** 'Pŭmiichíikun níipiit.'; **grow crookedly** waakíikun VII, waa=kíikuw VAI; **grow double** pihtawíikun VII, pihtawíikuw VAI; **grow from a certain source, grow for a certain reason** wunjíikun VII, wunjíikuw VAI; **grow in a certain place, grow in a certain manner** líikuw VAI; **grow mixed in with others** kohlawíikun VII, kohlawíikuw VAI; **grow quickly** kshíikun VII, kshíikuw VAI; **grow together** takwíikŭnool VII *usually plural,* takwíikŭwak VAI *usually plural;* **grow too much, be overgrown** wsaamíikun VII, wsaamíikun VAI; **grow unevenly, grow crookedly, come up crooked** piimíikun VII, pii=míikuw VAI; **grow up with s.o.** nax=píikuw VAIO; **grow well** wŭlíikun VII; **grow big, grow well** wŭlíikuw VAI; **multiply, grow as a bunch, grow close together** mŭléekuw VAI **It's really multiplied.** 'Móxa mŭléekuw.'; **start to grow** noochíikuw VAI **He was slow to start growing, he's growing now.** 'Áawiis noochíikuw, méhch alumíikuw.'; **stop growing** ehkwíi=kuw VAI, ehkwíikun VII.

**growl** VI níingiiw VAI-S.

**growl at** VT **growl at s.o.** niingíhtaweew VTA.

**grown-up** ADJ **be grown-up, be an adult** kihkŭwawéenuw VAI.

**grub** N **white grub** móoxwees NA.

**grunt** VI **grunt, groan** múndam VOTI 1.

**guess** VI **do reluctantly, I guess I'll do** *(something)* káa PC **I guess I'll go to bed.** 'Sháxkii káa nŭmáw-kawí.', **I'll walk (rather than riding).** 'Káa mbúmsi.'

**guilty** ADJ **have a strange look on one's face, have a guilty look on one's face, look guilty of something** maa=shiingwéexiin VAI.

**guinea fowl** N pókhwiit NA.

**gulp down** VT **gulp things down, be hungry for things** akwéendameew VAI **I'm really hungry for something.** 'Móxa ngwakwéendama.'

**gum** N **gum, pitch** pkúw NA.

**gums** N wŭyoosŭniikáawan NI.

**gun** N **gun, rifle** payaxkhíikan NI; **shoot off a gun** payaxkhóotam VOTI 1.

**guts** N **guts, intestines, innards** wŭlák=shuy NI.

# H

**habitually** ADV **habitually, lots, dirty** aniisku- PV **He loves to sleep, he sleeps easily, he sleeps lots.** 'Aníisku-kawíiw.', **He washes the dishes and leaves them dirty.** 'Aníisku-kshii=xíinjŭwe.'

**hair** N **my hair on head** níilaxk NID; **body hair** wiixéekan NI; **be bare, be lacking in fur, be lacking in hair** mooshakúsuw VAI; **be bare, be lacking in fur, be lacking in hair, be lean** *(of meat)* móoshakeew VII; **comb one's (own) hair** wŭlíikwameew VAI; **comb s.o.'s hair** wŭliikwamáweew VTA; **comb s.o.'s hair for them** chiix=hámaweew VTAO; **cut people's hair** móonzhŭweew VAI; **cut s.o.'s hair** móonzheew VTA; **get one's hair cut** moonzháasuw VAI; **have black hair** nzukaalóhkweew VAI; **have brown hair** wiipongwaalóhkweew VAI; **have curly hair** wchupŭlaalóhkweew VAI, wchupŭláandpeew VAI; **have dirty hair** niiskaalóhkweew VAI; **have dirty hair, have a dirty head** niiskóhkweew VAI; **have fine hair, have nice hair, have good hair** wŭlaalóhkweew VAI; **have greasy hair** shamóhkweew VAI;

**have grey hair** waapáandpeew VAI; **have long hair** kaanzhaalóhkweew VAI, kwŭnaalóhkweew VAI; **have long hair** *(especially of non-humans)* kwŭnawéesuw VAI; **have messy hair** piikwsháandpeew VAI, sayaandpéexiin VAI; **have neat hair, have plastered-down hair** wŭlawéexteew VAI; **have one's hair blowing about** sayaand=péhleew VAI; **have one's hair fall out** moonaalohkwéhleew VAI; **have red hair** maxkaalóhkweew VAI; **have short hair** chahkwaalóhkweew VAI; **have straight hair** shaaxkaalóh=kweew VAI; **have tangled hair, have matted hair, have messy hair** piikwshaalóhkweew VAI; **have terrible looking hair** chiipaalóhkweew VAI; **have thick hair** kohpakaalóh=kweew VAI; **have thin hair, have fine hair** shiikalaalóhkweew VAI; **have wet hair** skapáandpeew VAI; **have white hair** waapóhkweew VAI; **part one's hair, have one's hair parted** pasaaxcháneew VAI; **part s.o.'s hair** pasaaxchánaweew VTA; **pull s.o.'s hair, pull on s.o.'s hair** sakiindpée=neew VTA; **tie something around s.t., 'put s.t. up'** *(of someone's hair)* wiiwŭnámbtoow VTI2; **turn s.t. up and tie it** *(of a horse's tail, of a person's hair)*, **do s.t. up in a bun** *(of someone's hair)* wiimbámbtoow VTI2; **wash one's hair** kshiixóhkweew VAI.

**hair pin** N wíilaxkii-píinj NI, wíilaxkii-píinj NA.

**hairy** ADJ **be hairy** wiixeekanóowuw VII, wiixeekanóowuw VAI, wiixŭwús=uw VAI **The dog is furry.** 'Mwáaka=neew wiixŭwúsuw.'; **be hairy** wíixŭ=weew VII; **have a hairy face** wiixŭ=wíingweew VAI.

**half** N pasíi PC **It's four-thirty.** 'Néew-kŭlák wáak pasíi.'; **be cracked, be split in two, be in half** pasúsuw VAI; **crack s.t. animate, drop and crack s.t. animate, break s.t. animate in half** pasíixŭmeew VTA; **crack s.t., drop and crack s.t., break s.t. in half** pasíixtoow VTI2; **cut s.t. animate in two, cut s.t. animate in half, split s.t. animate in two by cutting it** pasúsheew VTA; **cut s.t. in two, cut s.t. in half, split s.t. in two by cutting it** pasúshum VTI1B; **half a day** pasáhkameew PC; **have one's eye's half closed** spwiingwéexiin VAI.

**hammer** N hámul NA.

**hand** N **my hand, my arm** náxk NID; **break s.o.'s arm, break s.o.'s hand** kaxkŭnaxkéeheew VTA, kaxkŭnax=kéexŭmeew VTA; **bump one's hand against something** paakŭnaxkéexiin VAI; **close one's hand(s) tightly** mas=kaniilúnjeew VAI; **feed s.o. by hand** shahkamóoleew VTA; **grab s.o. by the hand, tug at s.o, pull on s.o.** sakún=eew VTA; **grab s.t. by the hand, tug and pull on s.t.** sakúnum VTI1B; **hand s.t. to s.o.** lunŭmáweew VTAO; **have a broken arm, have a broken hand** kaxkŭnaxkéexiin VAI, kaxkŭnáxkeew VAI; **have a cold hand** thunáxkeew VAI; **have a dirty hand** niiskŭnáx=keew VAI; **have a scabby hand, have scabs on one's hand, have a scabby arm, have scabs on one's arm** mŭ=kuyŭnáxkeew VAI; **have a scratch on one's arm, have a scratch on one's hand** kchaxkŭnáxkeew VAI; **have a sore arm, have a sore hand** kiihii=tŭnáxkeew VAI; **have a sprained hand** chiilŭnaxkéexiin VAI. chiilŭ=náxkeew VAI; **have a swollen hand** paasŭnáxkeew VAI; **have a tired hand** shiiwŭnaxkéexiin VAI; **have bare hands, have bare arms, have exposed hands, have exposed arms** mihtŭnáxkeew VAI; **have bare hands, have exposed hands** mihtŭlúnjeew VAI; **have bare hands, have no gloves on, have one's hands exposed, have**

**one's hands showing** mihtŭlunjée=xiin VAI; **have clean hands** piilŭnáx=keew VAI; **have cold hands** saasŭlun=jéepookw VAI; **have dirty hands** aniiskŭnáxkeew VAI; **have greasy hands** shamunáxkeew VAI; **have one hand** ngwutŭnáxkeew VAI; **have one's arms exposed, have bare arms, have one's hands exposed, have bare hands** mihtŭnaxkéexiin VAI; **have one's hand clenched in a fist** ptukwŭlunjéexiin VAI; **have one's hand clenched in a fist** ptukwŭlún=jeew VAI; **have one's hand(s) closed tightly** maskaniilunjéexiin VAI; **have one's hand(s) in water, soak one's hand(s) in water** kamukwŭnaxkée=xiin VAI; **have one's hand(s) sticking out** sakunaxkéexiin VAI; **have one's hands barely touching a surface** mshiinaxkéexiin VAI **He almost fell but he was just hanging on by his fingers.** 'Wéenaa pŭníhleew shùkéhla mshiinaxkéexiin.'; **have one's hands open, have one's hands wide open** aapiilunjéexiin VAI, aapŭlunjéexiin VAI; **have one's hands straight out** a=shaaxkùnáxkeew VAI; **have one's hands in a certain position** liináx=keew VAI **I had my hands in my pockets.** 'Nzheewandíikanung ndul=iináxke.'; **have rough hands, have chapped hands** kaaxkŭnáxkeew VAI; **have soft hands** wtakŭnáxkeew VAI; **have swollen hands** amakwŭnáx=keew VAI; **have wrinkled hands** apii=sŭlunáxkeew VAI. pihpiisŭlunáxkee VAI; **hold s.o.'s hand** sakáhkwŭneew VTA; **open up one's hand, open up one's hands** aapŭlúnjeew VAI, aapii=lúnjeew VAI; **palm of the hand** aláa=mŭlunj PC; **pick things up with one's fingers, use one's hands to pick things up** kwàkwtakwŭníikee VAI; **raise one's hand** uspiináxkeew VAI; **reach out one's hand to get s.o.** naachiinaxkéeneew VTA; **reach out one's hand to get s.t.** naachiináx=keew VAIO; **rub s.t.** *(using the hands)*, **run one's hand over s.t.** láalŭnum VTI1B; **shake hands with s.o., hold hands with s.o.** sakiinaxkéeneew VTA; **soak one's hand(s) in water, immerse one's hand(s) in water** kamukwŭnáxkeew VAI; **stick one's hand out straight, have one's hand(s) out straight** shaaxkùnax=kéexiin VAI; **stick one's hand out, have one's hand sticking out** kchii=naxkéexiin VAI, saakŭnaxkéexiin VAI; **stretch one's hand out, have one's hand stretched out** shiipŭnaxkéexiin VAI; **stretch one's hands out** shiipŭ=náxkeew VAI; **use one hand** ngwut=oonáxkeew VAI, ngwutoonáxkwiiw VAI-S, ngwutŭnaxkéexiin VAI; **wash one's hands** ksiilúnjeew VAI.

**hand** VT **hand s.o. in a certain direction, hand s.o. in a certain manner** lúneew VTA **I lifted him upstairs.** 'Wáhkwung ndúlŭnaaw.'; **do s.t., hand s.t. in a certain direction, hand s.t. in a certain manner** lúnum VTI1B **Hand it here!** 'Yó lúnih!', **Why did you do that?** 'Kwéek há nú kóonju-lúnŭmun?'; **hand s.t. to s.o.** peetŭnúmaweew VTAO.

**hand saw** N **saw, hand saw** tŭmushah=kwáakan NI.

**handful** N **grab a handful of s.t. animate** anzíipheew VTA; **take a handful of s.t. animate, scoop s.t. animate up** *(using the hands)* ánzŭneew VTA; **take a handful of s.t., scoop s.t. up** *(using the hands)* ánzŭnum VTI1B.

**handkerchief** N **handkerchief, shawl** héengchiis NI.

**handle** N **ax-handle** wsíitahkw NI; **crank, handle for turning, hand grinder** tùpŭníikan NI; **dipper, cup with handle** páyund NA.

**handle** VT **be hard to handle, don't**

obey the rules, be 'out of hand' wŭyakáawsuw VAI.

**handwriting** N **write well, have good handwriting** awuleekhíikeew VAI.

**handy** ADJ **be handy, be helpful** wŭlaa=péewuw VAI; **be handy, be helpful, be useful** wŭlaapéenzuw VAI; **think that s.o. is handy, find s.o. handy, be helpful towards s.o., be good for s.o.** wŭlaapéemeew VTA; **think that s.t. is handy, find s.t. handy, think that s.t. is useful, find s.t. useful** wŭlaapéendam VTI1A **My medicine is good for me.** 'Noolaapéendamun noochapíhkum.'

**hang** VI **hang, be hanging** wéhleew VII **My coat is hanging up.** 'Wéhleew ngóotum.'; **hang, be hanging** wéh=leew VAI **The picture is hanging up.** 'Wéhleew píkchul.'; **hang from a certain place, hang for a certain reason** wundaapéhleew VAI, wundaa=péhleew VII; **hang closed, be closed** kpaapéhleew VII; **hang crookedly** piimaapéhleew VII, piimaapéhleew VAI; **hang in a certain direction, hang in a certain manner** laapéh=leew VII; **hang loosely, hang limply, hang wrinkled** piisŭlaapéhleew VII; **hang open, be open** tawaapéhleew VII; **hang out** ktaapéhleew VII, ktaa=péhleew VAI **My mitts are hanging out.** 'Ktaapehléewak nŭwándŭmak.'; **hang over something** laapaapéhleew VAI, laapaapéhleew VII; **hang over something, be put over something** laapíixiin VAI, laapíixun VII; **hang there** talámŭwak VAI *usually plural* **They're hanging all over.** 'Wéemi táa talámŭwak.', **The apples are hanging there bunched together.** 'Talámŭwak aapŭlúshak ngwúteel talí.'; **hang upside down** aapooch=kwàlaapéhleew VII; **have one's head hanging in a certain manner, have one's head hanging in a certain direction** lohkwéexiin VAI; **hang upside down** aapoochkwàlaapéhleew VAI.

**hang** VT **hang s.o. upside down, hang s.t. animate upside down** aapooch=kwalaapéhlaleew VTA; **hang s.t. animate in the open** mihtaapéhlaleew VTA; **hang s.t. from a certain place, hang s.t. for a certain reason** wun=daapéhlatoow VTI2 **I hung it over there.** 'Yéelak noondaapéhlatoon.'; **hang s.t. in the open** mihtaapéhla=toow VTI2; **hang s.t. over something** laapaapéhlatoow VTI2; **hang s.o. up, hang s.t. animate up** wéhlaleew VTA; **hang s.t. up** wéhlatoow VTI2; **hang s.t. upside down** aapoochkwàlaa=péhlatoow VTI2.

**hang down** VI **hang down** pŭnaapéh=leew VAI, pŭnaapéhleew VII, saakaa=péhleew VII, saakaapéhleew VAI; **hang down a long way** kwŭnaapéhleew VII; **have one's head hanging down** achihtawohkwéexiin VAI; **hang s.o. down** pŭnaapéhlaleew VTA; **hang s.t. down** pŭnaapéhlatoow VTI2.

**hang over** VT **hang over something, lie over something** paalíixiin VAI, paalíi=xun VII; **hang s.t. animate over something** paalaapéhlaleew VTA; **hang s.t. over something** paalaapéhlatoow VTI2.

**hangover** N **have a hangover** paalaa=péhleew VAI.

**Hanna** N hánaas NA.

**happen** VI **be, happen** léew VII **It's true.** 'Léew nú kwáy.'; **have something lucky happen** *(to oneself)* nhíinaakw VAIO.

**happy** ADJ **be glad, be happy** wiingee=lúndam VAI, wŭleelúndam VOTI1; **be glad about s.t., be happy about s.t.** wŭleelúndam VTI1A; **be happy about s.t., be glad about s.t.** wiingeelún=dam VTI1A; **be happy, be in good spirits** wŭlahtéenamuw VAI; **tell**

**something to s.o. and make them happy** wiingiilawéemeew VTA.

**hard** ADJ **be a restless person, be an active person, be hard to handle** séeksuw VAI; **be difficult, be hard** áhwat VII; **be hard ground** maska=nahkéeyeew VII; **be hard to get along with** machiitéeheew VAI; **be hard to handle, don't obey the rules, be 'out of hand'** wŭyakáawsuw VAI; **be strong, be hard** *(to eat, s.t. animate)* maskanúsuw VAI; **be strong, be hard** máskaneew VII; **bite s.o., bite s.o. hard** akúshameew VTA; **bite s.t., bite s.t. hard** akushándam VTI1A; **do reluctantly, be reluctant about doing something, be difficult to do something, be hard to do something** mihka PC **I didn't want to go to work (but I did).** 'Míhka nŭmáw-alóhke.', **It's hard for me to get up.** 'Míhka mbáskwi.'; **drive s.o. to death, work s.o. to death, work s.o. very hard** aapchíinaleew VTA; **have difficulty while walking, have difficulty in travelling, be hard for one to travel** àhwóoxweew VAI; **hit one's face hard against something** pwàhwsheen=gwéexiin VAI; **hit s.o. too much, hit s.o. too hard** wsaamihtéeheew VTA; **rain hard, rain heavily** kshíilaan VII; **throw s.t. hard** ksháaheew VAIO; **very, intense, hard, difficult** ahwi- PV **It has a lot of salt on it.** 'Áhwi-shŭwaháasuw.'; **very, intense, hard, difficult** ahwu- PV *informal* **He has a hard time, he has bad luck.** 'Áhwu-líinam.', **He is getting enormously big.** 'Áhwu-wulíikuw.'; **walk badly, have a hard time walking** amatóo=xweew VAI; **work hard** àhwalóhkeew VAI.

**hard maple** N **hard maple tree** asun=aamíinzhuy NA.

**hardly** ADV **hardly, not at all** msúchee PC **That's not so; no way.** 'Msúchee máh nú léewi.', **When he got to my mother's he told her, "Now I'm not going to talk to her anymore and I don't want her at all."** 'Peeyáatu ngúkung wtuláawal, "Kwáy máh há njíhnal ngihkihkŭlooláawu, wáak ngataaláawu msúchee."'; **not very, hardly at all** mánheel PC *followed by negative verb* **He hardly ever works.** 'Mánheel iiyalohkéewi.', **It's not a very nice day.** 'Mánheel wŭlahka=méewi.'; **seldom, hardly, very little, a scant amount** máamchiish PC **I seldom work.** 'Máamchiish ndalóhke.', **There's hardly any left over.** 'Máamchiish aluwíhleew.'

**harness** N wiiwŭlaháakanal NI *usually plural;* **harness tug, harness gear** wtuníikan NI; **finish tying s.o., finish harnessing s.o.** kiishambíileew VTA; **put a harness on** wŭlambtíikeew VAI.

**harp** N **Jew's harp** tŭlúmb NI; **play Jew's harp** tŭlumbhámeew VAI.

**harsh** ADJ **speak quickly, speak in a harsh tone, speak in a sharp tone, say harsh things, say sharp things** kshaaptóoneew VAI.

**hat** N aakongwéepuy NI; **fancy hat** wii=lawaakongwéepuy NI; **have a pointed hat** chpwaakongwéepŭyeew VAI; **pointed hat** chpwaakongwéepuy NI; **wear a hat** aakongweepíisuw VAI.

**hatch** VI **hatch** pwahkháweew VAI *of chicks.*

**hate** VT **hate s.o., dislike s.o.** shiingíi=naweew VTA; **hate s.t., dislike s.t.** shiingíinam VTI1A; **hate people** shiin=gáalŭweew VAI.

**hateful** ADJ **be hateful, dislike people** shiingiináasuw VAI.

**haul** VT **bring a load of s.t., go by with a load of s.t., haul a load of s.t.** ée=watoow VTI2 **I hauled a load of hay.** 'Ndéewato miixáskwal.'

**have** VI **have to** asku- PV *informal* **That's the reason why I was good at riding**

**a horse, because I had to fetch the cows.** 'Nún há nóonj-níhtaa-póxka=piin éel-ásku-naatkóoyayaan.'; **have to, must** ayáskii PC **I have to feed him by hand.** 'Ayáskii nzhashahka=móolaaw.'; **have to, must** ayásku PC *informal* **I have to leave right away.** 'Ayásku ndalŭmúsi.', **He always has to say something.** 'Ayásku ngúmee kwéek úw.'; **have to, must** ásk PC *informal* **He must be there.** 'Ásk éct náh apúw.'; **have to, must** áskii PC **I had to wait for them.** 'Áskii mbee=háawak.', **You had to tie it.** 'Áskii kùlámbtoon.'

**have** VT **get s.o., buy s.o., keep s.o., have s.o.** ayúweew VTA; **get s.t., buy s.t., keep s.t., have s.t.** ayúm VTI1B; **have enough of s.t.** teepíhlatoow VTI2; **have enough of s.t. animate** teepíhlaleew VTA; **have s.t., have s.t. animate** kxánuw VAIO **I have some money.** 'Ngáxani shúlpul.', **I've got the gun.** 'Níi ngáxaniin payaxkhíi=kan.'

**have on** VT **have s.t. animate on inside out** *(of clothing)* aapoochíhkaweew VTA.

**hawk** N **chicken hawk** nehnihliikíip=sheet NA; **hawk, large bird** awéhleew NA.

**hay** N **hay rake, collection plate in church** maaweeníikan NI; **pile hay up** mshamootíikeew VAI; **rake things up, rake hay** maaweeníikeew VAI.

**haystack** N shték NI.

**hazelnut** N kéhtaam NI.

**he** PR **he, him, she, her** néeka PR **It's his/her turn.** 'Néeka áashtee.'

**head** N **my head** níil NID, niilushtíikan NID *rare;* **bang s.o.'s head against something** paakaandpéexŭmeew VTA; **be bare headed** mihtáandpeew VAI; **be red headed** maxkáandpeew VAI; **bug species with nodding head** tàtamakohkwehláashiit NA, tàtamak=ohkwéhlaash NA; **bump one's head** paakaandpéexiin VAI; **cock one's head, turn one's head, look to the side** piimóhkweew VAI; **crack one's head** pwahkaandpéexiin VAI; **fall head first** achiichkwàlíhleew VAI; **forehead, top of head** laawáandpe PC; **get hit on the head with a maul, have a bump on the head** mookŭ=laandpéexiin VAI; **give s.o. a swollen head, hit s.o. and give them a lump on the head** makwaandpéeheew VTA; **have a big head** xwáandpeew VAI; **have a bloody head** mohkwáand=peew VAI; **have a cracked head, have a cut on one's head, fall and crack one's head, fall and cut one's head** pasaandpéexiin VAI; **have a cracked head, have a cut on one's head** pasáandpeew VAI; **have a dirty head** niiskáandpeew VAI; **have a flat head** *(of blow adders)*, **have one's head go flat** *(when blowing)* pàkaandpéhleew VAI; **have a flat head** pàkáandpeew VAI; **have a good head on one's shoulders** wŭláandpeew VAI; **have a long head** kwŭnáandpeew VAI; **have a lump on one's head, have a bump on one's head** wchihkwáandpeew VAI; **have a scabby head, have scabs on one's head** mŭkuyáandpeew VAI; **have a swollen head, have a bump on one's head** makwáandpeew VAI; **have a swollen head, have one's head swell up** paasáandpeew VAI; **have dirty hair, have a dirty head** niiskóhkweew VAI; **have one's head exposed, have one's head out in the open** mihtaandpéexiin VAI; **have one's head hanging down** achihtawoh=kwéexiin VAI; **have one's head lying the length of something** sahkaand=péexiin VAI **His head was by the door.** 'Kíixkii kpahóonung sahkaand=péexiin.'; **have one's head shaking** *(involuntarily)* nungohkwéhleew VAI;

**have one's head sticking out** saa=káandpeew VAI **I didn't see him but his head was sticking out.** 'Máh neewáawi shúkw péech-saakáand=peew.'; **have one's head sticking out, lie with one's head sticking out, stick one's head out** saakaand=péexiin VAI; **have one's heads together** kchukaandpeexíinook VAI *usually plural;* **have one's head hanging in a certain manner, have one's head hanging in a certain direction** loh=kwéexiin VAI; **have something tied around one's head** kŭlaandpeepíi=suw VAI; **have something wrapped around one's head, wrap one's head up** kpaandpeepíisuw VAI; **hit s.o. and give them a lump on the head** makwaandpehtéeheew VTA; **hit s.o. on the head** chàhwaandpéeheew VTA, paakaandpéeheew VTA; **lie with one's head sticking out, have one's head sticking out** saakohkwéexiin VAI **My head was sticking out of the water** 'Mbíing nóonj-saakohkwée=xiin.', **I was covered up but my head was sticking out.** 'Nŭmuta=kwaháasi shùkéhla nzaakohkwée=xiin.'; **lift up one's head** uspoh=kwéhleew VAI; **look sideways, turn one's head** pŭmiitóhkweew VAI; **my hair on head** níilaxk NID; **nod one's head** tàtamakohkwaandpéhleew VAI, tamakohkwéhleew VAI; **pig's head** kooshkooshaándup NI; **raise one's head, look up** uspóhkweew VAI; **rub s.o. on the head, pet s.o. on the head** siikwaandpéeneew VTA; **scratch one's head, have an itchy head** kshiipáandpeew VAI; **shake one's head** kwàkwtukohkwaandpéhleew VAI, kwàkwtukohkwéhleew VAI; **shake one's head, move one's head back and forth** kwàkwchukohkwéhleew VAI; **stick one's head out, have one's head sticking out** ktaandpéexiin VAI; **top of head** waxkáandpe PC; **turn one's head, look back** kwŭlupóh=kweew VAI.

**headache** N **have a headache** wiilíi=neew VAI.

**heal** VT **cure s.o., heal s.o.** kiikéeheew VTA; **be cured, be healed** kíikeew VAI.

**health** N **be fragile, be delicate** *(s.t. animate)*, **be delicate in health** póoxp=suw VAI.

**heap** N **put s.t. animate in a heap, heap s.t. animate up** mshamóoleew VTA *object usually plural;* **put s.t. in a heap, heap s.t. up** mshamóotoow VTI2 *object usually plural.*

**heap up** VT **put s.t. animate in a heap, heap s.t. animate up** mshamóoleew VTA *object usually plural;* **put s.t. in a heap, heap s.t. up** mshamóotoow VTI2 *object usually plural;* **be bunched up, be heaped up** mshámŭwak VAI *usually plural,* màmshámuw VII; mshámŭwal VII *usually plural.*

**hear** VI **make s.o. hear** pundamóoheew VAIO.

**hear** VT **hear s.o.** púndaweew VTA; **hear s.t.** púndam VTI1A **You didn't hear it correctly.** 'Máh kóolu-pundamóo=wun.'; **be glad to hear s.o., be glad to listen to s.o.** payahkwsútaweew VTA; **be glad to hear s.t., be glad to listen to s.t.** payahkwsútam VTI1A; **be heard** pundáakwat VII, pundáakwsuw VAI; **hear incorrectly** chanáxeew VAI; **hear s.o. from a certain direction, hear s.o. for a certain reason** wund=sútaweew VTA; **hear s.o., hear s.o. in a certain manner, hear s.o. in a certain direction** lustáweew VTA **I heard him and he sings terribly.** 'Ndulsút=awaaw amataláamuw.'; **hear s.t. from a certain place, hear s.t. for a certain reason** wundsútam VTI1A **I heard it from the forest.** 'Kóhpii noondsútamun.'; **hear s.t., hear s.t. in a certain manner, hear s.t. in a certain direction lústam VTI1A **I heard that you weren't well.** 'Ndul=sútamun máh koolamalsíiwi.', **What did you hear?** 'Kwéek há ktulsúta=mun?'; **know the news, hear the news, know what's going on** wéew=suw VAI; **like to listen, enjoy listening, enjoy hearing something** wiingxéexiin VAI **This one likes to listen.** 'Wiingxéexiin há wá.'; **misunderstand s.o., mishear s.o., hear s.o. erroneously, don't hear s.o. correctly** chanustáweew VTA; **misunderstand s.t., mishear s.t., hear s.t. erroneously, don't hear s.t. correctly** chanústam VTI1A.

**hear about** VT **dislike listening to s.o., dislike the sound of s.o., dislike hearing about s.o.** shiingsútaweew VTA; **dislike listening to s.t., dislike the sound of s.t.** shiingsútam VTI1A.

**heart** N **my heart** ndéeh NAD; **have heart trouble** wteehíineew VAI.

**heartwood** N **heartwood of tree, spine** wíimb NI.

**heat** N **be damp from the heat, be wet from the heat** skapacháteew VII; **sweat, be damp from heat, be wet from heat** skapachásuw VAI; **be dried** *(by heat)* kaahsáasuw VII; **be dried** *(by heat, s.t. animate)* kaahsáasuw VAI; **be dried by heat** *(after being wet)* péengwsuw VAI, péengwteew VII; **be overheated, be overcome with heat, faint from the heat** aaptúsuw VAI.

**heat** VT **heat s.t. animate up** kiishŭ=wúseew VTA; **heat s.t. animate up, warm s.t. animate up** kshúseew VTA; **heat s.t. up** kiishŭwúsum VTI1A; **heat s.t. up, warm s.t. up** kshúsum VTI1B; **heat s.t. up** *(of water)* kiishŭwaapŭ=wéesum VTI1A; **heat s.t. up** *(of water)* kiishŭwúpatoow VTI2; **dye s.t. animate white, heat s.t. animate up and whiten it** *(when washing clothes)* waapcháseew VTA; **dye s.t. white, heat s.t. up and whiten it** *(when washing clothes)* waapchásum VTI1B; **boil over, overflow** *(from being heated)* paalchásuw VAI, paalcháteew VII.

**heaven** N awasáhkameew PC.

**heavily** ADV **breathe heavily** leexéew=suw VAI; **rain hard, rain heavily** kshíilaan VII.

**heavy** ADJ **be heavy in weight** laan=zhíhkan VII, laanzhíhksuw VAI; **carry a heavy load on one's back** laanzhih=kŭwáleew VAI; **have a heavy beard** kaanzhihtóonayeew VAI.

**heel** N **my heel** nángwan NAD, nángwan NID; **have one's heel sticking out, stick one's heel out** saakangwanée=xiin VAI.

**height** N **be a certain height** sahkáh=kwat VII **How tall is the house?** 'Tá sahkáhkwat wíikwahm?'; **be a certain height** sahkáhkwsuw VAI **I wonder how tall he is.** 'Táa éet thá wsahkáhkwsiin.', **How tall is he?** 'Thá wsahkáhkwsiin?'; **measure the size of s.o, measure the height of s.o., measure s.t. animate out, fill s.t. animate to the brim** *(as a pail)* tpúskhweew VTA; **measure the size of s.t., measure the height of s.t., measure s.t. out** tpúskhwam VTI1A.

**hell** N matantoowíineeng PC **You'll go to hell.** 'Matantoowíineeng-uch kpáam.'

**help** N **be hopeful, be expectant, want help** nahkéewsuw VAI; **being hopeful, hopefulness, wanting help** nahkeew=suwáakan NI; **rely on s.o., depend on s.o., need s.o.'s help** nahkáaleew VTA.

**help** VT **help s.o.** wíichŭmeew VTA **I want to help you.** 'Káta-wíichŭmul.'; **help with s.t.** *(of a project)*, **second s.t.** *(of a motion at a meeting)* wii=chúndam VTI1A; **help people, help out** wiichkúneew VAI; **work together, help each other** takwundaméewak VAI.

**helpful** ADJ **be helpful, be handy** wŭ=laapéewuw VAI; **be helpful, be handy, be useful** wŭlaapéenzuw VAI; **think that s.o. is handy, find s.o. handy, be helpful towards s.o., be good for s.o.** wŭlaapéemeew VTA.

**hem** N **put a hem on s.t.** aapíikwam VTI1A; **sew around the edges, put a hem on** paxkawiikwáakeew VAI.

**hemorrhage** VI **be hemorrhaging** kaanzhpéhleew VAI.

**hemp** N **flax plant, wild hemp** áhlap NA, áhlapiis NA.

**hen** N **hen, female bird** oxkwéhleew NA.

**Henry** N héenŭliis NA.

**her** PR **he, him, she, her** néeka PR **It's his/her turn.** 'Néeka áashtee.'

**here** ADV **about, around, here and there** apaamu- PV **I fell about by myself.** 'Nxóo mbapáamu-kawíhla.'; **about, around, here and there** papaa- PV **I keep falling about by myself.** 'Nxóo há mbápaa-kàkawíh=laan.', **She lived with her husband for a while, then she left him, and then she went looking for my uncle.** 'Náakeesh wiitaawsoomáawal wiita=weemáachiil, nál wáak pàkíilaan, nál wáak nzhíisal pápaa-kwíilawaan.'; **swim here and there, swim about** apaamáashŭweew VAI; **here, there, in a certain place** talí PC **It's icy in the water.** 'Mohkamúyuw talí mbíing.', **He saw ghosts in a coffin.** 'Chíipayal néeweew kúshtung talí.'; **here, there, in a certain place** talú PC **It rains heavily here.** 'Akushíilaan yóon talú.', **He got stuck in the snow.** 'Kóonung talú kŭláhkweew.'; **here, there, thus, so** lí PC **He spat on the ground.** 'Áhkiing lí súkwiiw', **He went around the road.** 'Wiiwŭnóo=xwe lí áaneeng.'; **here, there, thus, so** líi PC **The roads are muddy everywhere.** 'Wéemu asiiskŭwatéexun táa líi.'; **here, there, thus, so** lú PC *informal* **They crawled to here.** 'Yó lú peechiikwsúwak.', **They moved to the United States.** 'Xwanzhíikanung lú ngatahkéewak.'; **here, to here, towards the speaker** peech- PV **Soon he called me back, "I didn't find them. They're not here."** 'Méhch=xiish láapii mbéech-lúkw, "Máhta nŭmoxkamóowŭnal. Máhta yóh ahteewíiwal."', **She would leave for several days, and when my uncle came (to visit) if she came with him he couldn't do anything.** 'Àhalúm=suw kehkeexookwŭnáhke, wáak áng nzhíis péeyaat péech-wiicheewáatu, wŭlú áng kéhla áalu- kwéek -lúnum.'; **here, to here, towards the speaker** peechi- PV **He's coming here to cheat me.** 'Ngáta-péechi-pahpahchóo=lukw.', **I came inside.** 'Mbéech-piinjíike.'; **here, to here, towards the speaker** peechu- PV *informal* **He answered me.** 'Mbéechu-naxkóo=mukw.', **I came walking.** 'Mbéechu-pŭmúsi.'; **be rain coming in this direction** péetŭlaan VII; **be there, be here** apúw VAI **There he is.** 'Ná éepiit.'; **bring s.o. here in a hurry** peechíipheew VTA; **bring s.t. here in a hurry** peechiipáhtoow VTI2; **come, come here** peeyéewuw VII **Something good is coming** 'Peeyéewuw wúlu-léek.'; **come, come here** pee=yéeyuw VII **The cold weather is here.** 'Peeyéeyuw téeheek.', **The sickness is coming.** 'Peeyéeyuw wiinamal=suwáakan.'; **float here and there, float about, float around** apaamáat=hookw VAI, apaamáathun VII; **float here, float in this direction** peetáat=hookw VAI, peetáathun VII; **here** yóh PC **Pass it here.** 'Yóh lúnih!', **Come here!** 'Yóh áal!'; **shine in this direction, shine here** *(of lights)* peetáasŭ=leew VAI, peetáasŭleew VII; **swim in**

**this direction, swim here, swim this way** peetáashŭweew VAI; **this** *(inanimate)*, **here** yú PR *used in inanimate 'where' questions* **This teacup.** 'Yú tiihíinjuw.', **Where is it?** 'Thá yú?'; **use s.t. to come here, use s.t. to come in this direction** peetawéeheew VAIO.

**here!** IJ **here! here it is! take it!** máh PC.

**heron** N káaxkw NA.

**hesitate** VT **hesitate about s.t.** shàh=wáapeew VAIO.

**hiccup** VI pwahpwaawíikwham VOTI1.

**hide** N **hide, skin** xáy NA.

**hide** VI **hide, hide sitting down** káata=puw VAI, kaatohkwéepuw VAI; **hide, hide out of sight** wanohtáasuw VAI; **hide, lie hidden, be hidden** kaachíi=xiin VAI, kaachíixun VII.

**hide** VT **put s.o. away, hide s.o., put s.t. animate away, hide s.t. animate** káaleew VTA; **put s.t. away, hide s.t.** káatoow VTI2; **put s.t. animate away, put s.o. away, hide s.o.** kaatáhleew VTA; **put s.t. away, hide s.t.** kaatáh=toow VTI2; **hide s.o.** *(using the hands)* káatŭneew VTA; **hide s.t.** *(using the hands)* káatŭnum VTI1B; **hide s.o. in a hurry** kaachíipheew VTA; **hide s.o., put s.o. away** kaachíixŭmeew VTA; **hide s.t. in a hurry** kaachiipáhtoow VTI2; **hide s.t. while carrying it** kaa=tasánuw VAIO; **hide s.t., put s.t. away** kaachíixtoow VTI2; **be hidden, lie placed out of sight** kaatáhteew VII; **hide eggs** *(of chickens)* kaatáhwheew VAI; **hide, lie hidden, be hidden** kaa=chíixiin VAI, kaachíixun VII.

**hide from** VT **hide from s.o.** kaatapóo=meew VTA; **hide from s.o.** *(especially to keep the doors locked while at home)* wanóhtaweew VTA.

**hide-and-seek** N **play hide-and-seek** kaateelawúsuw VAI, kahkáatapuw VAI.

**high** ADJ **be high, be tall** kwŭnáhkwat VII; **be high water** kihtahkwíixun VII; **be high water, be deep water, be a flood, be flooding** xwahkwíixun VII; **be piled high** kihtshámuw VAI, kiht=shámuw VII, tohpshámuw VAI, tohp=shámuw VII; **in the middle of the high weeds** laawáskwe PC **He's walking in the middle of the high weeds.** 'Laawáskwe pŭmúsuw.', **I was sticking out of the weeds up to my neck.** 'Laawáskwe nóonj-saakxoonéexiin.'; **make a big pile of s.t., pile s.t. high** mangshamóotoow VTI2; **pile s.t. high, pile up many of s.t.** xwushamóotoow VTI2; **pile up a lot of s.t. animate, pile s.t. animate up high** tohpsham=óoleew VTA; **pile up a lot of s.t., pile s.t. up high** tohpshamóotoow VTI2.

**high pitched** ADJ **have a soft voice, have a high pitched voice** *(diminutive)* changaalakaxoonéeshuw VAI.

**higher** ADJ **have a deformed hip, have one hip higher than the other, have a lopsided hip** waakhóotŭyeew VAI.

**highly** ADV **think a lot of s.o., think highly of s.o., have a high regard for s.o.** kaanzhéelŭmeew VTA, xwée=lŭmeew VTA; **think a lot of s.t., think highly of s.t., have a high regard for s.t.** kaanzheelúndam VTI1A, xweelún=dam VTI1A; **think well of oneself, think highly of oneself** wŭleelúnzuw VAI.

**hill** N **be a hill, be a mound** pòwah=kéeyeew VII; **be a steep hill** àhwaa=wúngeew VII; **be in a mound, be in a hill** wŭlámkweew VII; **bottom of a hill** alaamaawúnge PC; **edge of the hill** wshayaawúnge PC; **mountain, hill** amangaawúnge PC; **pile s.t. animate up, build a hill around s.t. animate** *(of potatoes)* wŭlamkwiixŭ=méewak VTA *object usually plural;* **slide downhill, slide down a hill** chiixiikwsíhleew VAI; **slope down** *(of the ground)*, **be a hill** pumbahkée=

yeew VII **I walked to the hill.** 'Éenda-pumbahkéeyeek ndúlu-pŭmúsi.'; **top of the hill** waxkiitáawung PC.

**hilly** ADJ **be hilly, be mountainous** amangaawangéeyayeew VII **I live near the mountains.** 'Níi kíixkii nŭwíiki éenda-amangaawangée=yayeek.'

**him** PR **he, him, she, her** néeka PR **It's his/her turn.** 'Néeka áashtee.'

**hint at** VT **make remarks to s.o., make 'digs' at s.o., hint at something to s.o., be reluctant to say something outright to s.o.** maashiilatáweew VTA.

**hip** N **my hip** nzóokan NID; **be lame in the hip** kwŭlukwiitŭyéhleew VAI; **have a deformed hip, have one hip higher than the other, have a lop-sided hip** waakhóotŭyeew VAI; **walk with a limp, walk with one hip higher than the other** piimiitŭyéew=xeew VAI.

**hire** VT **hire s.o.** alóoleew VTA.

**hit** VT **hit s.o.** pakámeew VTA; **hit s.t.** pakándam VTI1A; **almost hit s.o., 'nick' s.o.** chaskihtéeheew VTA; **always hit s.o.** ngumeewihtéeheew VTA; **be hit** aláhookw VAI; **be hit and get bent** waakihtéexiin VAI; **be hit, be trapped, be hit by a car** kŭláhookw VAI; **be knocked off, be hit and detached** mahkihtéexiin VAI, mahkih=téexun VII; **be thrown upwards, hit something and bounce, bounce** uspihtéexiin VAI; **be unable to hit s.o.** *(using a tool or instrument)* pwáaw=heew VTA; **be unable to hit s.t.** *(using a tool or instrument)* pwáawham VTI1A; **cut s.t. by accident** páhtshum VTI1B; **drop s.o. and make them shatter, hit s.o. and make them shatter** sehtéexŭmeew VTA; **drop s.t. and make it shatter, hit s.t. and make it shatter** sehtéextoow VTI2; **fall all over, bounce around, get hit about** msihtéexiin VAI; **fall and die, be beaten to death, get hit and die** pŭlupihtéexiin VAI; **fall and get shaken up, be hit and get shaken up** wŭyamoxkihtéexiin VAI; **get hit by accident** páhthookw VAI; **get hit on the head with a maul, have a bump on the head** mookŭlaandpéexiin VAI; **have the covering of something be hit and knocked off, have the skin of something be hit and knocked off** pŭlakihteeháasuw VAI; **hit all of s.o.** weemihtéeheew VTA *object usually plural;* **hit all of s.t.** weemihtée=ham VTI1A *object usually plural* **I chopped down all of the bushes.** 'Nŭweemihteehŭmúnal mihtkwúsal.'; **hit and bend s.t.** waakihtéeham VTI1A; **hit and bend s.t. animate** waakih=téeheew VTA; **hit and bend s.t. animate, hit s.t. animate and cause it to become bent** waakihtéexŭmeew VTA; **hit and bend s.t., hit s.t. and cause it to become bent** waakih=téextoow VTI2; **hit and break s.o.** kaxkihtéeheew VTA; **hit and break s.o.'s neck** tŭmiikwehtéeheew VTA; **hit and break s.t.** kaxkihtéeham VTI1A; **hit and break s.t.** lookihtée=ham VTI1A; **hit and break s.t. animate** lookihtéeheew VTA; **hit and crack s.o., hit and crack s.t. animate** pwahkihtéeheew VTA; **hit and crack s.t.** pwahkihtéeham VTI1A; **hit and crush s.o.** shkwihtéexŭmeew VTA; **hit and cut s.o.** tashakihtéeheew VTA; **hit and dent s.o., hit and dent s.t. animate** *(as the body of a car)* kwŭlapihtéexŭmeew VTA; **hit and dent s.t.** *(using a tool or instrument)* kwŭlapihtéeham VTI1A; **hit and dent s.t.** kwŭlapihtéextoow VTI2; **dent s.t.** *(using a tool or instrument)* kwŭláp=ham VTI1A; **hit and dent s.t. animate** kwŭlapihtéeheew VTA; **hit and flatten one's face against something** pàk=iingwehtéexiin VAI; **hit and flatten**

**one's nose against something** pàk=chaalehtéexiin VAI; **hit and flatten s.o., hit and flatten s.t. animate** pàkihtéeheew VTA; **hit and flatten s.t.** pàkihtéehum VTI1B; **hit and get bent** waakihtéexun VII; **hit and graze s.o. with an object** laalihtéeheew VTA; **hit and injure s.o.** kshihtéeheew VTA; **hit and injure s.o., injuring s.o. by making them fall** kshihtéexŭmeew VTA; **hit and injure s.t.** kshihtéextoow VTI2 **I injured my foot.** 'Ngushih=téextoon nzíit.'; **hit and knock s.t. animate off, hit and detach s.t. animate** mahkihtéeheew VTA; **hit and knock s.t. off, hit and detach s.t.** mahkihtéehum VTI1B; **hit and sever s.t. animate, cut s.t. animate off** tŭmihtéeheew VTA; **hit and sever s.t., cut s.t. off** tŭmihtéeham VTI1A; **hit and split s.t.** pasihtéeham VTI1A; **hit and straighten s.o., hit and straighten s.t. animate** shaaxkihtéeheew VTA; **hit and straighten s.t.** shaaxkihtée=ham VTI1A; **hit and turn s.o. upside down, hit and invert s.o.** aaloolih=téexŭmeew VTA; **hit and turn s.t. upside down, hit and invert s.t.** aaloo=lihtéextoow VTI2; **hit one's face hard against something** pwàhwsheen=gwéexiin VAI; **hit s.o. and give them a lump on the head** makwaandpeh=téeheew VTA; **hit s.o. and knock the covering off them, hit s.o. and knock the skin off them** pŭlakihtée=heew VTA; **hit s.o. and knock them down** kawihtéeheew VTA; **hit s.o. and knock them down, hit s.o. and knock them off, hit s.o. and knock them over** pŭnihtéeheew VTA; **hit s.o. and knock them over, hit s.o. and make them fall backwards** aamih=téeheew VTA; **hit s.o. and knock them sideways** piimihtéeheew VTA; **hit s.o. and make a hole in them** pkwihtéeheew VTA; **hit s.o. and make them cry** chaangihtéeheew VTA; **hit s.o. and make them get up** aamwih=téeheew VTA; **hit s.o. and make them go around, hit s.o. and make them spin around** tùpihtéeheew VTA; **hit s.o. and send them away** alumihtée=heew VTA; **hit s.o. and shatter them** sehtéeheew VTA; **hit s.o. and startle them** salaxkihtéeheew VTA; **hit s.o. anew, hit s.o. another time** aandih=téeheew VTA; **hit s.o. by accident** pahtihtéeheew VTA; **hit s.o. by accident** páhtheew VTA; **hit s.o. on the head** chàhwaandpéeheew VTA, paa=kaandpéeheew VTA; **hit s.o. so that they make a sharp noise** chàhwih=téeheew VTA; **hit s.o. too much, hit s.o. too hard** wsaamihtéeheew VTA; **hit s.o. with a maul** *(on the head)* mookŭlihtéeheew VTA **I'm going to hit him with a maul.** 'Ápih nŭmoo=kŭlihtéeha.'; **hit s.t. again** aandihtée=ham VTI1A; **hit s.t. and knock it down, knock s.t. down by hitting it** kawihtéeham VTI1A; **hit s.t. and knock it off, hit and detach s.t.** mahkihtéextoow VTI2; **hit s.t. and knock it over, hit s.t. and make it fall backwards** aamihtéeham VTI1A; **hit s.t. and knock it sideways** pii=mihtéehum VTI1B; **hit s.t. and make a hole in it** pkwihtéeham VTI1A; **hit s.t. and make it go around, hit s.t. and make it spin around** tùpihtée=ham VTI1A; **hit s.t. animate and knock it off, hit and detach s.t. animate** mahkihtéexŭmeew VTA; **hit s.t. by accident** pahtihtéeham VTI1A; **hit s.t. by accident** páhtham VTI1A; **hit s.t. over something** *(farther than intended)* paalháhkweew VAIO; **hit something in a certain manner, hit something in a certain direction** laháh=kweew VAI **I hit it a long way.** 'Wáhli nduláhkwe.'; **hit together** takwihtee=xíinook VAI *usually plural,* takwih=

téexŭnool VII *usually plural;* **knock s.o. around, knock s.o. all over, bounce s.o., hit s.o. various ways** msihtéeheew VTA; **knock s.t. around, bounce s.t., hit s.t. various ways** msihtéehum VTI1B; **miss at hitting s.o., miss at hitting s.t. animate** palihtéeheew VTA; **miss at hitting s.t.** palihtéeham VTI1A; **miss hitting s.o., miss hitting s.t. animate** *(using a tool or instrument)* paláheew VTA; **miss hitting s.t.** *(using a tool or instrument)* paláham VTI1A; **nail s.t. together, hit s.t. and join it together** takwihtéehum VTI1B; **pound and make a noise, hit and make a noise** *(on wood, on solid objects)* tiiwháh=kweew VAI; **retaliate by hitting s.o., hit s.o. in return** kwaxkihtéeheew VTA; **split s.t. animate by forceful contact, split s.t. animate by shot, split s.t. animate with a projectile** pasúlaweew VTA; **split s.t. by forceful contact, split s.t. by shot, split s.t. by hitting it with a projectile** pasúl=am VTI1A; **touch s.o., make contact with s.o., run into s.o., hit s.o.** aláh=eew VTA; **touch s.t., run into s.t., drive into s.t., make contact with s.t. forcefully, hit s.t.** aláham VTI1A **I ran into it.** 'Ná ndalhámun.'

**hit over** VT **hit s.t. animate a long way over, knock s.t. animate way over something** *(using a tool or instrument)* páalheew VTA; **hit s.t. animate over** *(farther than intended)* paalih=téeheew VTA; **hit s.t. way over something, knock s.t. way over something** *(using a tool or instrument)*, **knock s.t. over something** páalham VTI1A.

**hoe** N akwiipŭláawan NI, takwiipŭláa=wan NI.

**hoe** VI **be hoeing, hoe things** moonask=híikeew VAI, moonáskham VOTI1.

**hoe** VT **hoe s.t.** moonáskham VTI1A.

**hold** VT **hold s.o., hold on to s.o., hold on tightly to s.o., carry s.o.** *(using the hands)* kŭlúneew VTA; **hold s.t., hold onto s.t., hold on tightly to s.t., carry s.t.** *(using the hands)* kŭlúnum VTI1B; **hold s.o. firmly** maskanúneew VTA; **hold s.o. tightly** máskŭneew VTA; **hold s.o. tightly around the waist, have one's arms around s.t. animate** kaskatéeneew VTA; **hold s.o. upside down** *(using the hands)* aapooch=kwálŭneew VTA; **hold s.o.'s hand** sa=káhkwŭneew VTA; **hold s.t. animate firmly** *(in the mouth, with the mouth)* kŭlámeew VTA; **hold s.t. firmly** *(in the mouth, with the mouth)* kŭlándam VTI1A; **hold s.t. firmly** maskanúnum VTI1B; **hold s.t. shut** samwúnum VTI1B; **hold s.t. tightly, have one's arms around s.t.** kaskatéenum VTI1B; **hold s.t. upside down** *(using the hands)* aapoochkwálŭnum VTI1B.

**hold a feast** VI **hold a feast for s.o.** takwiipóoleew VTA.

**hold down** VT **hold s.o. down** *(using the foot or body)*, **step on s.o. and hold them down, sit on s.o. and hold them down** kŭlíhkaweew VTA; **hold s.t. down** *(using the foot or body)*, **step on s.t. and hold it down, sit on s.t. and hold it down** kŭlíhkam VTI1A; **pull s.o.'s eye down, hold s.o.'s eye open** taaxksheengwéeneew VTA.

**hold hands with** VT **shake hands with s.o., hold hands with s.o.** sakiinax=kéeneew VTA.

**hole** N **pit, hole in ground** *(especially for storing vegetables in winter)* wáalakw NI; **be a certain depth, be a certain length** *(of holes)* sahkáalakat VII **It is the same depth (of a hole).** 'Ngwúteel sahkáalakat.'; **be a deep hole** kwŭnáalakat VII; **be a hole in the ground** waalahkéeyeew VII; **be a hole through something** eesh'shée=suw VAI **The window has a hole in it.** 'Eesh'shéesuw eeheeshandéekan.';

**be a hole through something** eesh'=shéeyeew VII **I've got a hole in my shoe.** 'Eesh'shéeyeew nŭmáhksun.'; **be a hole through something** shaap=wshéeyeew VII; **have a hole, have a hollow, be concave** wáaleew VII, wáalsuw VAI; **button hole** kŭnoopáa=lakw NI; **cut a hole in s.o.** pkwúsheew VTA; **cut a hole in s.t.** pkwúshum VTI1B; **cut holes in things** pkwushíi=keew VAI; **dig a hole** wáalheew VAI; **have a hole in it** pkwushéesuw VAI, waalakéeyeew VII; **have a hole in one's leg** pkwukáateew VAI; **have a hole in the sole of something** *(of shoes or boots)* pkwusiitéeyeew VII; **have a hole made in it** pkwuchee=náasuw VII; **have a hole, be a hole** pkwát VII, waalshéeyeew VII, pkwushéeyeew VII; **have a hole, have holes** pkwúsuw VAI **The paper has holes in it.** 'Pámbiil pkwúsuw.'; **hit s.o. and make a hole in them** pkwihtéeheew VTA; **hit s.t. and make a hole in it** pkwihtéeham VTI1A; **insert s.t. in a hole, make a hole in s.t.** *(using the hands)* pkwúnum VTI1B; **jump through a hole** pkwáakchehl VAI; **look through a hole, look through an opening, look through something** pkóhkweew VAI; **make a big hole, make a deep hole** kwŭ=náalheew VAI; **make a hole in s.o., make a hole in s.t. animate** pkwún=eew VTA; **make a hole in s.t.** *(using a tool or instrument)* pkwáham VTI1A; **make a hole in s.t.** *(using the foot or body)* pkwíhkam VTI1A; **make a hole in s.t.** ptukwchéenum VTI1B; **make a hole in s.t. animate** *(using a tool or instrument)* pkwáheew VTA; **make a hole in s.t. animate by forceful contact, make a hole in s.t. animate with an instrument, make a hole in s.t. animate with a projectile** pkwúlaweew VTA; **make a hole in s.t. by forceful contact, make a hole in s.t. with an instrument, make a hole in s.t. with a projectile** pkwúl=am VTI1A; **make a hole in s.t., open s.t. up** pkwuchéenum VTI1B; **open s.t. animate up, operate on s.o.** *(as a doctor)*, **make a hole in s.o., take the insides out of s.o.** pkwuchéeneew VTA **He had an operation.** 'Pkwuch=éenaaw.'; **step on s.o. and make a hole in them** pkwíhkaweew VTA; **throw something through a hole, drop s.t. in a hole** pkwáaheew VAIO.

**holler** VI **bawl, holler, make noise** *(of vocal sounds)* sáangweew VAI **The frogs are bawling.** 'Chkwálak saangwéewak.'; **yell, holler** kaan=zhaláamuw VAI.

**holler at** VT **talk to s.o. to get them up from lying down, holler at s.o. to get them up from lying down** aa=mwihkíimeew VTA.

**hollow** ADJ **be hollow** sh'xiikwshéesuw VAI, sh'xiikwshéeyeew VII, sh'xíi=kweew VII, sh'xíikwsuw VAI, sh'xíi=kwun VII; **have a hole, have a hollow, be concave** wáaleew VII; wáalsuw VAI.

**hollow out** VT **hollow s.t. animate out** sh'xiikwáaleew VTA.

**home** N **be in a nice place, be well seated, have a good home** *(of an adopted child or a person in heaven)* wŭlápuw VAI; **go home** máachiiw VAI-S; **go home, drive home, fly home, pedal home** aapaachíhleew VAI; **return home** aapáachiiw VAI-S; **run home** maachahtakíhleew VAI, maa=tahtakíhleew VAI; **run s.o. home** maachíipheew VTA; **run s.t. home, take s.t. back** *(especially of borrowed items)* maachiipáhtoow VTI2; **send s.o. home** maatshíhkaweew VTA; **stay at home alone** nootíikeew VAI; **stick placed across the door to indicate that no one is at home** nootíi=kees NI; **take s.o. home** *(to their* *place)* máachaleew VTA; **take s.t. home** *(to where it belongs)* máacha=toow VTI2.

**homely** ADJ **be homely, be ugly** matus=íisuw VAI; **look homely** lunŭwíixteew VAI.

**honest** ADJ **be honest** shaaxkaapéewuw VAI.

**hook** N **catch s.t. animate with a hook** ptáheew VTA **I caught two pickerel.** 'Níishŭwak waasíingwak mbutháa=wak.'; **lifter, hook, something to lift with** uspŭníikan NI; **pothook** óhkwaan NA.

**hook up** VT **fasten things, button things, hook things up** kŭlahkhwíi=keew VAI; **hook s.o. up, hook up s.t. animate** *(as a belt)*, **trap s.t. animate** kŭláhkhweew VTA.

**hooked up** VT **be buttoned, be hooked up** kŭlahkhwáasuw VII.

**hopeful** ADJ **be hopeful** *(especially as one hopes to go to heaven)* nahkee=weelúndam VOTI1; **be hopeful, be expectant, want help** nahkéewsuw VAI; **being hopeful, hopefulness, wanting help** nahkeewsuwáakan NI.

**hopefulness** N **being hopeful, hopefulness, wanting help** nahkeewsuwáa=kan NI.

**hopeless** ADJ **find that s.o. appears hopeless, regret seeing s.o.** laawíi=naweew VTA; **find that s.t. appears hopeless** laawíinam VTI1B; **look hopeless, look overwhelming, appear to be hopeless** laawcheenáakwsuw VAI **He's hopeless, he's never getting dressed.** 'Laawcheenáakwsuw máh kiikiisheechpíiwi.'; **look overwhelming, look hopeless, appear to be hopeless** laawiinánakwsuw VAI, laa=wiináakwat VII.

**horn** N pootaatíikan NA; **antler, horn** wiiláawan NI.

**horrified** ADJ **be horrified about something, think something to be terrible** chiipeelúndam VAI.

**horse** N nehnayóongus NA; **my dog, my horse, my close pet** *(of dogs and horses)* ndálŭmoonz NAD; **bit for horse's bridle** kehkŭlúndang NI; **horse droppings, horse excrement** nehnayoongsúchuy NI; **horse rider** pehpóxkapiis NA; **horse's bridle** laaptoonéepuy NI; **look for horses** ndawehnayóongseew VAI; **young horse** wuskehnayóongus NA.

**horseback** N **come here riding on horseback, ride towards the speaker** peethóomeew VAI; **go crookedly while riding on horseback** pàptuk=hóomeew VAI; **pass by s.o. on horseback, pass by s.t. on horseback** loowhóomeew VAIO; **ride away on horseback** alumhóomeew VAI; **ride by on horseback, ride along on horseback** pŭmahóomeew VAI; **ride on horseback with s.o.** wiithóomeew VTA.

**hot** ADJ **be a hot day** kshuláandeew VII, kshuteewáhkameew VII; **be a hot room, be warm in the house** kshut=eewiikamíikat VII; **be hot** kshúteew VII; **be hot water** kshupéeteew VII, kshuteewáapŭweew VII; **be hot, be sweating** kshúsuw VAI; **get hot** *(all of a sudden)* kshutéhleew VAI, pehtchás=uw VAI **She has hot flashes.** 'Pehpeh=tchásuw.'; **have hot feet** kshusiitée=xiin VAI.

**hotel** N **hotel, drinking establishment, bootlegger's place** sookhupeesíikaan NI.

**hour** N **be a certain hour of the day** *(with number preverb)* kŭlákuw VII **At ten o'clock.** 'Wíimbat txú-kŭlakíi=ke.', **You'll come at four o'clock.** 'Néew-kŭlakíike-uch kúnj kpá.'; **clock, hour of the day** kŭlák NA **You will come at four o'clock.** 'Néew-kŭlák-uch kúnj kpá.'

**house** N wíikwahm NI **My house, where**

**I live.** 'Wíikŭuyaan.', **His house, where he lives.** 'Wíikiit.'; **be a hot room, be warm in the house** kshut=eewiikamíikat VII; **be cold, be cool** *(of houses, of rooms)* thiikamíikat VII; **be the corner** *(of the house)* siingii=kamíikat VII; **big houses** amangachii=káanal NI *usually plural;* **brick house** maxkasuníikaan NI; **build a house** wíikheew VAI; **chicken house** kiikiip=shíikaan NI; **doghouse** mwaakanee=wíikaan NI; **doorstep, threshold of house** uskwáandu PC; **finish building a house** kiishíikheew VAI; **frame house, board house** pasiikaaxkwíi=kaan NI; **have a big house** xwachíi=keew VAI, xwíikeew VAI; **have a clean house** piilíikeew VAI; **have a dirty house** niiskíikeew VAI; **have a house that's leaning** piimíikeew VAI; **have a warm house** kiishŭwíikeew VAI; **house that leans** piimíikaan NI; **house with a pointed roof** chpwíikaan NI; **inside a house** alaamiikwáhmung PC, alaamíikaan NI; **log house** apanzhíi=kaan NI; **new house** wuskíikaan NI; **old house** xuwíikaan NI; **on the other side of the house** awasáaku PC **The box is on the other side of the house.** 'Mbáksh awasáaku áhte.'; **run away inside the house, flee inside the house** piindshíimuw VAI; **small house** changiikáanush NI; **stone house** asuníikaan NI; **the top of the roof, the top of the house** waxkíitaakw PC **The top of the roof leaks.** 'Waxkíi=taakw wunjíikuw.'; **trade houses** aashŭwiikéewak VAI *usually plural;* **warm house** kiishŭwíikaan NI; **white house** waapíikaan NI.

**how** ADV **how** *(question word)* thá PC **Where is the man?** 'Thá wá ná lúnuw?'; **how** tá PC **Where is he going?** 'Tá éew?', **Where does he live?** 'Tá wúndakw wíikiin?'

**hug** VT **hug s.o. around the neck** kih=koxkwéeneew VTA.

**humour** N **feel in good humour, want to laugh** kŭlukeelúndam VOTI1.

**humpbacked** ADJ **be humpbacked** waakpóxkwaneew VAI.

**hunch over** VI **be hunched over** waak=poxkwanéexiin VAI; **bend over, be hunched over, be bent over** ahtée=xiin VAI; **sit bent over, sit hunched over** ahteewohkwéepuw VAI; **sit hunched over** waakpoxkwanéepuw VAI; **sit with one's legs folded, sit hunched over** ptukohkwéepuw VAI, ptúkwapuw VAI.

**hundred** N **five hundred** naalanaapóx=ku PC; **four hundred** neewaapóxku PC; **one hundred** ngwutaapóxku PC; **so many hundred** txaapóxke PC *with number particles to form numbers 600-900* **Six hundred.** 'Ngwútaash txaapóxke.'; **three hundred** nxaa=póxku PC.

**hungry** ADJ **be hungry, have the sole of one's shoe come off and flap around** katóopuw VAI; **gulp things down, be hungry for things** akwéendameew VAI **I'm really hungry for something.** 'Móxa ngwakwéendama.'

**hungry for** VT **be hungry for s.t.** ka=tóotam VTI1A; **be hungry for s.t. animate** katóopweew VTA; **gulp things down, be hungry for things** akwéen=dameew VAI **I'm really hungry for something.** 'Móxa ngwakwéenda=ma.'

**hunt** VI aláwiiw VAI-S; **come back from hunting** aapaláwiiw VAI-S.

**hurriedly** ADV **dress haphazardly, dress hurriedly, throw on one's clothes** pàpŭlakéechpuw VAI.

**hurry** N **be in a hurry** shaweelúndam VOTI1; **be in a hurry** *(for s.o. to do something)*, **be in a hurry for s.o. to die** shawáaleew VTA, shàhwáaleew VTA **I'm in a hurry for him to go to town.** 'Nzhahwáalaaw ootéeneeng wtáan.'; **bring s.o. here in a hurry** peechíipheew VTA; **bring s.t. here in a hurry** peechiipáhtoow VTI2; **dress in a hurry** akaawéechpuw VAI; **get up in a hurry** pasukwiipáhtoow VAI; **grab s.o. in a hurry** tàhwíipheew VTA; **grab s.t. in a hurry** tàhwiipáh=toow VTI2; **grab s.t. in a hurry, grab s.t. quickly, grab a handful of s.t.** anziipáhtoow VTI2 **Grab the money and let's go to town.** 'Ánziipáhtool shúlpul ootéeneeng áatookw.'; **hide s.o. in a hurry** kaachíipheew VTA; **hide s.t. in a hurry** kaachiipáhtoow VTI2; **in a hurry** wáhleesh PC **Chop wood in a hurry!** 'Wáhleesh manáx=eel!'; **run away in a hurry** kihtshíi=muw VAI; **say something in a hurry, leave something out of a story, don't tell the whole story** pàpalaachíimuw VAI; **take s.o. across in a hurry** aa=shŭwíipheew VTA; **take s.o. away in a hurry** alumíipheew VTA; **take s.o. through in a hurry** eeshíipheew VTA; **take s.t. across in a hurry** aashŭwii=páhtoow VTI2; **take s.t. away in a hurry** alumiipáhtoow VTI2; **take s.t. through in a hurry** eeshiipáhtoow VTI2.

**hurry** VI **hurry by with s.t., hurry along with s.t.** pŭmiipáhtoow VTI2; **hurry inside** piinjiipáhtoow VAI; **hurry inside with s.o.** piinjíipheew VTA; **hurry inside with s.t.** piinjii=páhtoow VAIO; **hurry out with s.o.** kchíipheew VTA; **hurry out with s.t.** kchiipáhtoow VTI2; **hurry, hurry up** akaawíhlatoow VOTI2 **I'm hurrying as fast as I can.** 'Kéeng- lúkih -akaawihlatáwaan.'; **take s.o. by in a hurry, take s.o. along in a hurry** pŭmíipheew VTA.

**hurry up!** IJ **hurry up!, in a hurry** akáawee PC **He left in a hurry.** 'Née=ka akáawee alúmsuw.'; **hurry up!, in a hurry** akáawii PC.

**hurt** VT **be injured, get hurt** kshihtée=xun VII **My foot got hurt.** 'Kshihtée=xun nzíit.'; **be injured, get hurt, fall and get injured** kshihtéexiin VAI; **be sore in s.t.** *(of body parts)*, **hurt s.t.** wiinamándam VTI1A **His foot is sore.** 'Wiinamándamun wsíit.'; **be sore in s.t. animate** *(of body parts)*, **hurt s.t. animate** wiinamámeew VTA **I hurt my little knee.** 'Nguchkóohush nŭ=wiinamámaaw.'; **have s.t. hurt** *(of one's feelings)* kshamándam VTI1A **He said something and really hurt my feelings.** 'Néeka kwéek úw, móxa ngushamándamun.'

**husband** N **my wife, my husband, my spouse** wiitawéemak VTA **His wife, her husband, his or her spouse.** 'Wiitaweemáachiil.', **Your wife, your husband, your spouse.** 'Wiita=wéemat.'

**husk** N **corn husk mat** wtéeskwii-ehahpalíhkeeng NI, wtéeskw NI.

**husk** VT **husk corn** pxwiináskweew VAI.

**hymn** N loonzŭweewáakan NI; **sing a hymn** lóonzŭweew VAI.

# I

**I** PR **I, me** níi PR **That's what I said.** 'Nún há níi nzíin.', **It's my turn.** 'Níi áashtee.'

**ice** N móhkamuy NA; **be raining ice** mohkamíilaan VII; **fall through the ice** pkwaskwíhleew VAI.

**icy** ADJ **be icy** mohkamúyuw VII.

**ill** ADJ **be mentally ill** kpucheewíineew VAI.

**illness** N **feel angry about one's illness, feel odd, feel angry** manoongamál=suw VAI; **have an illness in a certain part of one's body** talíineew VAI **His leg is sore.** 'Wihkáatung talíineew.'; **recover from an illness** kiikéhleew

VAI.

**imitate** VT **imitate someone's behaviour** mongíisuw VAI; **imitate the way s.o. talks, imitate s.o.'s speech** naa=naxpŭlóhtaweew VTA.

**immediately** ADV **right away, immediately** sháa PC **Okay, I'll look for them right away.** 'Yó, kwáy sháa ngwiilamúnal.', **My mother told my grandmother and my grandfather right away.** 'Sháa ngúk wtúlaan nóohŭmal wáak nŭmoxóomsal.'; **right away, immediately** sháawu PC **I didn't recognize you right away.** 'Máh sháawu kŭnunoolóowu.', **You'll have to plant right away.** 'Ayásku-ch sháawu ktahkíiheem.'

**immerse** VT **fall in the water, get soaked, get immersed** kamukwíhleew VAI; **lie immersed in the water, lie soaking in the water** kamukwíixiin VAI, kamukwíixun VII; **soak one's hand(s) in water, immerse one's hand(s) in water** kamukwŭnáxkeew VAI.

**important** ADJ **important person** káanzhaween PR; **look important** kaanzhiináakwat VII, kaanzhiináakw=suw VAI.

**improperly** ADV **speak improperly, pronounce words incorrectly** amat=aaptóoneew VAI.

**improved** ADJ **better condition, improved condition, better state, improved state** míingasa PC **It's better now, it shuts well (of a door).** 'Míingasa kwáy wŭlú-kpíhle.', **It's good that you came early.** 'Míingasa ktáapwi-pá.'

**in addition** ADV **carry s.t. extra, carry s.t. in addition** naxpasánuw VAIO; **take s.t. along as well, take s.t. along in addition** naxpóoxweew VAIO.

**in the way** ADV **be in the way** kàkpíi=xun VII.

**in turn** N **one after the other, in turn, every other one** eháashtee PC **They took turns eating** 'Eháashtee miit=súwak.', **I went from one place to another (and then back).** 'Eháashtee ndá.'

**incapable** ADJ **be condemned to die for evil deeds, die deservedly, be thought incapable** kundeelŭmúkw=suw VAI; **condemn s.o., want s.o. to die, think s.o. incapable of doing something** kundéelŭmeew VTA.

**inchworm** N kwehkwsahíikeet VAI.

**incorrectly** ADV **cut s.t. animate incorrectly** matúsheew VTA; **cut s.t. incorrectly** matúshum VTI1B; **hear incorrectly** chanáxeew VAI; **speak improperly, pronounce words incorrectly** amataaptóoneew VAI.

**indeed** ADV **indeed, emphatic** áx PC **I told you she was going to have a child.** 'Ktúlul áx amiimúnzal katá-kxánuw.'; **indeed, yes** píish PC **I told him but he still forgot.** 'Píish ndúl=aan shukéhla wánsiin.', **You should hire him.** 'Píish áa ná káta-alóo=laaw.'; **really, indeed, that's right, well** wŭlú PC **I didn't see him.** 'Wŭlú máh neewáawi.', **I can't understand him.** 'Wulú ndáalu-nóhtawaaw.'

**independent** ADJ **be independent** àh=waapéenzuw VAI; **be independent, be smart, be alive, be strong** *(especially a sick person who gets up because he or she is feeling better)* àhwaapée=wuw VAI.

**Indian** N **Christian Indian, Moravian convert** kéendŭwees NA; **Delaware Indian, Munsee Delaware Indian** múnsiiw NA; **Indian agent** échun NA **I'm going to the agent's.** 'Échŭnung ndá.'; **Indian woman, Delaware woman** lunaapéexkweew NA; **Indian, Delaware Indian** lunáapeew NA; **Ojibwe Indian** wshíipŭweew NA; **Oneida Indian** méengweew NA; **bad**

**Indian** matulŭnáapeew NA **That's where that bad Indian comes from.** 'Nún há oonjíiyayiin ná matulŭnáa= pe.'; **be an Indian, be a Delaware Indian** lunaapéewuw VAI; **speaking an Indian language, the Delaware language** hulŭniixsuwáakan NI.

**Indian bread** N lúnapwaan NI.

**industrious** ADJ **be smart, be industrious, like to work** lihlpúneew VAI.

**inexpensive** ADJ **be cheap, be inexpensive** aapŭwáawatuw VAI, aapŭwáawa= tuw VII.

**infected** ADJ **be infected, have pus in it** mŭliiháasuw VAI, mŭliiháasuw VII; **have infected eyes, have pus in one's eyes, have 'sleep' in one's eyes** mŭ= leelíingweew VAI, mŭluyeelíingweew VAI.

**infectious** ADJ **transmit an infectious disease to s.o.** mshíiheew VTA.

**inferior** ADJ **think oneself inferior** noondayeelúnzuw VAI.

**influence** VT **bewitch s.o., use medicine to influence s.o.** mŭtáanheew VTA.

**information** N **mistakenly reveal some information, 'let the cat out of the bag'** pahtaaptóoneew VAI.

**inherit** VT **inherit s.t.** *(especially characteristics of personality)*, **live with s.t.** naxpáawsuw VAIO.

**inheritance** N **want a share of an inheritance** *(especially someone who is not a member of the immediate family)* katá-waapéenzuw VAI.

**injure** VT **be injured, get hurt** kshih= téexun VII **My foot got hurt.** 'Kshih= téexun nzíit.'; **be injured, get hurt, fall and get injured** kshihtéexiin VAI; **bite and injure s.o.** kshámeew VTA; **bite s.t. and injure it** kshándam VTI1A; **hit and injure s.o.** kshihtéeheew VTA; **hit and injure s.o., injuring s.o. by making them fall** kshihtéexŭmeew VTA; **hit and injure s.t.** kshihtéex= toow VTI2 **I injured my foot.** 'Ngush= ihtéextoon nzíit.'; **injure s.o.** *(using the foot or body)*, **kick and injure s.o., sit on and injure s.o.** kshíhka= weew VTA; **injure s.o.** *(with an instrument)* kshúlaweew VTA; **injure s.o.** kshúneew VTA **It is tight on me.** 'Ngushŭnúkwun.'; **injure s.t.** *(using the foot or body)*, **kick and injure s.t., sit on and injure s.t.** kshíhkam VTI1A; **injure s.t.** kshíixtoow VTI2; **injure s.t.** *(using the hands)* kshúnum VTI1B; **make a cutting remark to s.o., talk so as to injure s.o.** kshaap= toonáaleew VTA.

**innards** N **guts, intestines, innards** wŭlákshuy NI.

**insect** N **insect, bug** axkóokus NA.

**insert** VT **insert s.t. in a hole, make a hole in s.t.** *(using the hands)* pkwún= um VTI1B; **insert s.t., put s.t. inside** píindham VTI1A.

**inside** ADV **be put on, be put inside** piindŭnáasuw VII **The boards were put inside the house.** 'Pasíikaaxkw piindŭnáasuw wíikwahm.'; **be the inside angle of a corner** póocheew VII **Go stand the broom in the corner.** 'Eénda-póocheek máw-níipatool chiikhíikan.'; **bring wood inside** piindxákweew VAI; **chase s.o. inside, send s.o. inside, drive s.o. inside** *(of animals)* piindshíhkaweew VTA; **come inside** piinjíikeew VAI **He came in.** 'Péech-piinjíikeew.'; **crawl inside** piinjíikwsuw VAI **Then he crawled into the house.** 'Nál wtúlu- wii= kwáhmung -piinjíikwsiin.'; **go inside quickly, run inside, enter a dwelling running** piinjiikéhleew VAI; **go inside, fly inside, drive inside, fall inside** piinjíhleew VAI; **have a lining inside** alaamháasuw VII; **hurry inside with s.o.** piinjíipheew VTA; **hurry inside with s.t.** piinjiipáhtoow VAIO; **insert s.t., put s.t. inside** píindham

VTI1A; **inside** aláamii PC **I looked inside the cup.** 'Aláamii tiihíinjuw ndulóhkween.'; **inside a house** alaa=miikwáhmung PC; **inside my body** ndalaamhákeeng NID; **inside the fence** alaameenáxke PC; **inside the house** alaamíikaan NI; **inside the stomach** aláamatay PC **Inside the stomach.** 'Alaamatáye.'; **jump inside** piindáakchehl VAI; **lie inside, lie inside something** piindáameew VAI, piindáameew VII **He was listening from the other room. ('His ears were lying inside here.')** 'Wihta=wákal péech-piindaaméewal.'; **put s.o. inside** píindŭneew VTA; **put s.t. in, put s.t. inside** piinjíhlatoow VTI2; **put s.t. inside** píindŭnum VTI1B; **run away inside the house, flee inside the house** piindshíimuw VAI; **run inside** piindahtakíhleew VAI; **rush inside, hurry inside** piinjiipáhtoow VAI; **take s.o. inside, take s.t. animate inside, bring s.o. inside** piindóoxwa=leew VTA; **take s.o. inside, take s.t. animate inside, take a load of s.t. animate inside** piindhéewaleew VTA; **take s.t. inside, bring s.t. inside** piindóoxwatoow VTI2; **take s.t. inside, take a load of s.t. inside** piind=héewatoow VTI2.

**inside out** ADV **be on inside out, be upside down** aapoochíixiin VAI, aapoo=chíixun VII; **have s.t. animate on inside out** *(of clothing)* aapoochíhka=weew VTA; **have s.t. on inside out, put s.t. on inside out** *(of clothing)* aapoochíhkam VTI1A; **put s.t. animate on wrong side out, put s.t. animate on inside out, put s.o. upside down** aapoochíixŭmeew VTA; **turn s.t. animate inside out** *(using the hands)* aapóotŭneew VTA; **turn s.t. inside out** *(using the hands)* aapóo=tŭnum VTI1B; **turn s.t. inside out, turn s.t. upside down** aapoochkwàl=íixtoow VTI2; **wear s.t. inside out** aapootawéeheew VAIO.

**insides** N **operate** *(of doctors)*, **take out the insides of things** pkwucheeníi=keew VAI; **press the insides out of s.o., squeeze the insides out of s.o.** sŭluskihtéeheew VTA; **press the insides out of s.t., squeeze the insides out of s.t.** sŭluskihtéeham VTI1A.

**instead** ADV **instead, next, then** áashtee PC **I'll go there instead.** 'Áashtee-uch yéelak ndá.', **I'll use this instead, I'll wear this instead.** 'Áashtee-uch yóon ndawéeheen.'

**instrument** N **musical instrument** apíikwan NI.

**insult** VT **think poorly of s.o., insult s.o., abuse s.o.** *(including physical abuse)* matéelŭmeew VTA.

**intend** VI **want to, intend** kata- PV **It's going to rain.** 'Katá-sóokŭlaan.', **I want to talk to him.** 'Ngáta-kihkŭ=lóolaaw.'

**intense** ADJ **very, intense, hard, difficult** ahwi- PV **It has a lot of salt on it.** 'Áhwi-shŭwaháasuw.'; **very, intense, hard, difficult** ahwu- PV *informal* **He has a hard time, he has bad luck.** 'Áhwu-líinam.', **He is getting enormously big.** 'Áhwu-wulíikuw.'

**intensely** ADV **very, extremely, intensely** shihshíikaanzh PC **A great big snake.** 'Shihshíikaanzh lúkih xwáchu-áxkook.', **I got really wet.** 'Shihshíi=kaanzh lúkih níiskpe.'; **very, extremely, intensely** shíikaanzh PC **She really made me mad.** 'Shíikaanzh lúkih nŭwiiníihukw.', **It really runs well.** 'Shíikaanzh lúkih wŭlíhleew.'; **very, intensely** kihkihchu- PV *informal* **The little one was really crying.** 'Kihkíhchu-lpákshuw.'

**intently** ADV **listen, listen intently** aap=xéexiin VAI.

**intermittently** ADV **rain on and off, rain intermittently** pehpéhtŭlaan VII.

**interpret** VI **add on to a story, interpret** aanihkwaachíimuw VAI.
**interrupt** VT **bother s.o., interrupt s.o.** lxawóoleew VTA; **bother people, interrupt people** lxawóolŭweew VAI.
**intertwine** VI **have one's arms together, have one's arms intertwined** laapii=naxkéexiin VAI.
**intestines** N **guts, intestines, innards** wŭlákshuy NI.
**invert** VT **hit and turn s.o. upside down, hit and invert s.o.** aaloolihtéexŭ=meew VTA; **hit and turn s.t. upside down, hit and invert s.t.** aaloolih=téextoow VTI2.
**iron** N **clothes iron** chiingaalsíikan NI, shaaxkùtsíikan NI.
**iron** VT **iron s.t.** *(of clothing)* shaaxkút=sum VTI1B; **iron s.t. animate** *(of clothing)* shaaxkútseew VTA.
**iron kettle** N **iron kettle with legs** wehkáathoos NA, wihkaathóosus NA, wihkáathoos NA.
**irritable** ADJ **be worried, be upset, be irritable, be restless** sákwsuw VAI.
**irritating** ADJ **make an irritating noise, make an annoying noise** níiskŭweew VAI, níiskŭweew VII.
**Isaac** N áyshuk NA.
**island** N mŭnáhan NI.
**isolated** ADJ **be apart, be isolated, be separated from other people** chpúsuw VAI.
**itch** N **scratch an itch** kshiipŭníikeew VAI; **scratch an itch on s.o.'s face for them** kshiipiingwáaleew VTA, kshii=piingwéeneew VTA; **scratch s.o.'s itch** kshíipŭneew VTA.
**itchy** ADJ **be itchy** kshíipeew VII; **be itchy, scratch oneself** kshíipsuw VAI; **scratch one's back, have an itchy back** kshiippóxkwaneew VAI; **scratch one's eyes, have itchy eyes** kshiipaa=lakíingweew VAI; **scratch one's face, have an itchy face** kshiipíingweew VAI; **scratch one's feet, have itchy feet** kshiipsíiteew VAI; **scratch one's head, have an itchy head** kshii=páandpeew VAI; **scratch one's leg, have an itchy leg** kshiipkáateew VAI; **scratch s.t., scratch s.t. that is itchy** kshíipŭnum VTI1B.
**ivy** N **poison ivy** lehlóosŭweek NI.

# J

**jacket** N **jacket, corset, vest** chékut NI; **wear a jacket** chèkùthámeew VAI.
**Jacobina** N njékpiin NA *woman's name.*
**jail** N kpahootíikaan NI; **be in jail, be shut in, be shut out** kpaháasuw VAI; **pry s.o. out** *(using a tool or instrument)*, **bail s.o. out of jail** ktáhk=hweew VTA.
**jar** N **bottle, jar** eeheeshaapamúkwahk NA, eeheesháapamukw NA.
**jaw** N **my jaw** ndawambíikan NID.
**jay** N **blue jay** tíitiis NA.
**jealous** ADJ **be jealous** manáasuw VAI; **be jealous, be envious** akaxeelúnzuw VAI; **be jealous of people, be envious of people** kxeelúngeew VAI; **be jealous of s.o.** manáaleew VTA; **be jealous of s.o.'s achievements, be jealous of s.o.'s possessions, be envious of s.o.** kxéelŭmeew VTA.
**Jew's harp** N tŭlúmp NI; **play Jew's harp** tŭlumphámeew VAI.
**jewellery** N **wear something around the neck, wear a scarf, wear jewellery** wiilawahkwéelŭnuw VAI.
**job** N **get an easy job, have an easy job** aapŭwalóhkeew VAI.
**John** N nján NA.
**join** VI **come together, join together** takwíhleew VII, takwihléewak VAI *usually plural.*
**join** VT **be in the army, join the army**

sóochŭluw VAI; **join in the fighting** wiitatáhkeew VAI; **lay s.o. together, join s.o. together** takwíixŭmeew VTA *object usually plural;* **lay s.t. together, join s.t. together** takwíixtoow VTI2 *object usually plural;* **nail s.t. together, hit s.t. and join it together** takwihtéehum VTI1B.

**joint** N **bend at a joint** tamakíhleew VAI, tamakíhleew VII, tamákeew VII; **press down on s.o., push down on s.o., bend s.o. at a joint** *(using the hands)* tamákŭneew VTA; **press down on s.t., push down on s.t., bend s.t. at a joint** *(using the hands)* tamákŭnum VTI1B.

**judge** VT **judge s.o., finish talking about s.o.** kiishakuníimeew VTA.

**Julia** N njóoliish NA; **nickname for person named Julia** njík NA.

**jump** N **take a big start in a competition, take a jump in a competition, take a leap in a competition, get a running start** wundaaméhleew VAI.

**jump** VI **be startled, be surprised, jump** ktakíhleew VAI; **jump about** msáakchehl VAI; **jump away** alum=áakchehl VAI; **jump down** pŭnáak=chehl VAI; **jump from a certain place, jump for a certain reason** wundáakchehl VAI **I jumped from far away.** 'Wáhlu noondáakchehl.'; **jump here and there, jump about, jump around** apaamáakchehl VAI; **jump in the water** chooxpwáakchehl VAI, kamukwáakchehl VAI, láakchehl VAI; **jump inside** piindáakchehl VAI; **jump on board** poosáakchehl VAI; **jump out** ktáakchehl VAI; **jump through a hole** pkwáakchehl VAI; **jump to a new location** aandáak=chehl VAI; **jump to one's feet** niipa=wáakchehl VAI; **jump up, jump upwards** uspáakchehl VAI; **surprise s.o., startle s.o., make s.o. jump** ktakíh=laleew VTA.

**jump over** VT **jump over s.o., jump over s.t.** *(farther than intended)* paalaakchéhleew VAIO; **jump over s.t., jump over s.o.** *(farther than intended)* paaláakchehl VAIO.

# K

**keep** VT **get s.o., buy s.o., keep s.o., have s.o.** ayúweew VTA; **get s.t., buy s.t., keep s.t., have s.t.** ayúm VTI1B; **have s.o. for a pet, keep s.o. as a pet** wtalŭmóonzuw VAIO; **have s.o. for a pet, keep s.o. as a pet, make a pet out of s.o.** alumóonzuw VAIO **He made a pet out of the cat.** 'Wtalŭ=moonzíinal pooshíishal.'; **keep s.t. in mind** kŭleelúndam VTI1A; **put s.t. animate away, keep s.t. animate** wŭláhleew VTA.

**keep time** VI **stamp with one's feet, keep time with one's feet** pòhwsii=téexiin VAI.

**kettle** N **kettle, pot** hóosus NA; **iron kettle with legs** wehkáathoos NA, wih=kaathóosus NA, wihkáathoos NA; **tea kettle** tíihoos NA.

**key** N tawiikwáakan NA.

**kick** VT **kick s.o.** pasuchéhkaweew VTA **He really kicked him about.** 'Kwíh=chu-paapasuchehkawáawal.'; **kick s.t.** pasuchéhkam VTI1A; **dent s.t.** *(using the foot or body)*, **kick and dent s.t.** kwŭlapíhkam VTI1A; **dent s.t. animate** *(using the foot or body)*, **kick and dent s.t. animate** kwŭlapíhka=weew VTA; **injure s.o.** *(using the foot or body)*, **kick and injure s.o., sit on and injure s.o.** kshíhkaweew VTA; **injure s.t.** *(using the foot or body)*, **kick and injure s.t., sit on and injure s.t.** kshíhkam VTI1A; **kick s.o.**

**and give them a swollen leg, kick s.o. and give them a bump on the leg, sit on s.o. and give them a swollen leg, sit on s.o. and give them a bump on the leg** makwukaatéhka=weew VTA; **kick s.o. by accident** pahchíhkaweew VTA; **make s.o. cry** *(using the foot or body)*, **kick s.o. and make them cry** chaangíhka=weew VTA; **nudge s.o., kick s.o., poke s.o.** *(to get his or her attention)* kiixkíhkaweew VTA.

**kick out** VT **kick out one's legs, stretch out one's legs, maneuver** *(of trains)* shándham VOTI1.

**kid** N **have a bunch of kids, have a big family** mŭleekóonzheew VAI.

**kidney bean** N maxkaaláxkwsiit NI.

**kill** VT **kill s.o., beat s.o. up** níhleew VTA; **kill s.t.** níhtoow VTI2 **What did you kill?** 'Kwéek kŭníhto?'; **kill s.o. for s.o.** nihtamáweew VTAO; **murder, kill people** níhlŭweew VAI; **be killed** nihlkwúsuw VAI; **be killed in an accident** mamúkw VAI; **destroy all of s.o., kill all of s.o., get rid of all of s.o.** weemíiheew VTA *object usually plural;* **kill a bear** nihliimáxkweew VAI, nihláxkweew VAI; **kill a bird** nihla=wehleeshóosheew VAI; **kill a chicken** nihliikíipsheew VAI; **kill a deer** nihla=tóhweew VAI; **kill a dog, beat a dog** nihlaakanáxŭmweew VAI; **kill a fly** nihloochéeweew VAI; **kill a louse** nihlawiilpíisheew VAI; **kill a snake** nihlaxkóokeew VAI; **kill an animal, beat an animal** nihlxúmweew VAI; **want to fight s.o., want to kill s.o., want to compete with s.o.** katóona=leew VTA.

**kindling** N **kindling, piece of kindling** wŭláxakw NI; **make kindling of s.t.** wŭlaxakwáheew VAIO **I want to make kindling of them.** 'Ngáta-wŭlaxa=kwahéenal.'; **make kindling, gather kindling** wŭlaxakwáheew VAI.

**kiss** VT **kiss s.o.** waangóomeew VTA.

**kitten** ADJ cháng-póoshiish NA.

**Kleenex** N **little bit of paper, Kleenex** pambíilush NA.

**knee** N **my knee** ngútko NAD, ngútkuw NAD; **have a dirty knee** niiskiiktúk=weew VAI; **have a swollen knee** paa=siiktúkweew VAI; **have an sore knee** kiihiichiiktúkweew VAI; **have clean knees** piiliiktúkweew VAI, **have dirty knees** aniiskiiktúkweew VAI; **kneel, fall on one's knees** níishii-takwíixiin VAI; **sit on one's knees** níishii-ta=kwápuw VAI; **wash one's knees** kshiixiiktúkweew VAI.

**kneel** VI **kneel down** niishíitakuw VAI; **kneel to s.o.** niishiitakwíhtaweew VTA.

**knife** N paxkshíikan NI; **big knife**, **the United States** xwanzhíikan NI, xwat=anzhíikan NI; **butcher's knife** mboch=ŭlanzhíikan NI; **long knife** kwŭnan=zhíikan NI; **sharp knife** kiinanzhíikan NI.

**knock** VI **knock, rap** *(on a door)* pòh=íikeew VAI.

**knock** VT **get bounced loose, get knocked loose** lxakwihtéexun VII

**knock around** VT **knock s.o. around, knock s.o. all over, bounce s.o., hit s.o. various ways** msihtéeheew VTA; **knock s.t. around, bounce s.t., hit s.t. various ways** msihtéehum VTI1B.

**knock down** VT **fell trees, knock trees down** kawaháhkweew VAI; **hit s.o. and knock them down** kawihtée=heew VTA; **hit s.o. and knock them down, hit s.o. and knock them off, hit s.o. and knock them over** pŭnih=téeheew VTA; **hit s.t. and knock it down, knock s.t. down by hitting it** kawihtéeham VTI1A; **knock s.o. down and make them cry** chaangihtéexŭ=meew VTA; **knock s.o. down, knock s.o. over** *(with a stick, with a car, with a bicycle, with a gunshot)* aa=

mŭláweew VTA; **knock s.o. down, knock s.o. over, knock s.o. off something** *(using the foot or body)* pŭníh=kaweew VTA **I knocked him off the bed.** 'Mbuníhkawaaw wúnj-apíi=neeng.'; **knock s.t. down** *(using the foot or body)* kawíhkam VTI1A; **knock s.t. down from something, knock s.t. off** pŭnihtéeham VTI1A; **knock s.t. down, knock s.t. over** *(using the foot or body)* pŭníhkam VTI1A; **knock s.t. down, knock s.t. over** *(with a stick, with a car, with a bicycle, with a gunshot)* áamŭlam VTI1A; **make s.o. fall down, knock s.o. down** *(using the foot or body)* kawíhkaweew VTA; **trap s.o., trap s.t. animate, knock a tree down on s.o.** kŭláheew VTA; **fall backwards, be knocked over, be knocked down** aamihtéexiin VAI; **fall over, be knocked down, be knocked over** aamíhleew VAI, aamíhleew VII.

**knock off** VT **detach s.t. animate, knock s.t. animate off** *(using a tool or instrument)* máhkheew VTA; **detach s.t., knock s.t. off** máhkham VTI1A; **have the covering of something be hit and knocked off, have the skin of something be hit and knocked off** pŭlakihteeháasuw VAI; **hit and knock s.t. animate off, hit and detach s.t. animate** mahkihtée=heew VTA; **hit and knock s.t. off, hit and detach s.t.** mahkihtéehum VTI1B; **hit s.o. and knock the covering off them, hit s.o. and knock the skin off them** pŭlakihtéeheew VTA; **hit s.o. and knock them down, hit s.o. and knock them off, hit s.o. and knock them over** pŭnihtéeheew VTA; **hit s.t. and knock it off, hit and detach s.t.** mahkihtéextoow VTI2; **hit s.t. animate and knock it off, hit and detach s.t. animate** mahkihtéexŭmeew VTA; **knock s.o. down, knock s.o. over, knock s.o. off something** *(using the foot or body)* pŭníhkaweew VTA **I knocked him off the bed.** 'Mbuníhkawaaw wúnj-apíineeng.'; **knock s.t. animate off, cause s.t. animate to be knocked off, detach s.t. animate** mahkíixŭmeew VTA; **knock s.t. down from something, knock s.t. off** pŭnihtéeham VTI1A; **knock s.t. off, cause s.t. to be knocked off, detach s.t.** mahkíix=toow VTI2; **be knocked off, be hit and detached** mahkihtéexiin VAI, mahkihtéexun VII; **be knocked off, fall off** mahkíixiin VAI, mahkíixun VII.

**knock on** VT **knock on s.t.** *(especially of drums)*, **tap on s.t.** póham VTI1A.

**knock out** VT **knock s.o.'s tooth out** aamaniikéexŭmeew VTA; **fall and get knocked out** ngwutihtéexiin VAI; **have a tooth knocked out** aamanii=kéexiin VAI, ktaniikehtéexiin VAI.

**knock over** VT **knock s.o. over, push s.o. over, bend s.o. over, tilt s.o. over** *(using the hands)* áamŭneew VTA; **knock s.o. over, tip s.o. over** *(using the foot or body)* aamíhkaweew VTA; **knock s.t. animate over** *(of wood, using a tool or instrument)* aamáhk=hweew VTA; **knock s.t. down, knock s.t. over** *(with a stick, with a car, with a bicycle, with a gunshot)* áamŭlam VTI1A; **knock s.t. over** *(using a tool or instrument)* aamáhkhwam VTI1A; **knock s.t. over, push s.t. over, bend s.t. over, tilt s.t. over** *(using the hands)* áamŭnum VTI1B; **knock s.t. over, tip s.t. over** *(using the foot or body)* aamíhkam VTI1A; **tip something over, tip something backwards, knock something over, knock something over backwards** aamáaheew VAIO; **be cut down, be knocked over, be broken off** tŭmáh=ookw VAI **The tree was knocked over, broken off.** 'Tŭmáhookw míh=tukw.'; **be knocked over by the**

**wind, be blown over by the wind** kawáxookw VAI, kawáxun VII; **cut and knock over s.t. animate** áam=sheew VTA; **cut and knock s.t. over** áamshum VTI1B; **fall backwards, be knocked over, be knocked down** aamihtéexiin VAI; **fall over, be knocked down, be knocked over** aamíh=leew VAI, aamíhleew VII; **hit s.o. and knock them down, hit s.o. and knock them off, hit s.o. and knock them over** pŭnihtéeheew VTA; **hit s.o. and knock them over, hit s.o. and make them fall backwards** aamih=téeheew VTA; **hit s.t. and knock it over, hit s.t. and make it fall backwards** aamihtéeham VTI1A; **hit s.t. animate a long way over, knock s.t. animate way over something** *(using a tool or instrument)* páalheew VTA; **hit s.t. way over something, knock s.t. way over something** *(using a tool or instrument)*, **knock s.t. over something** páalham VTI1A; **knock s.o. down, knock s.o. over** *(with a stick, with a car, with a bicycle, with a gunshot)* aamŭláweew VTA; **knock s.o. down, knock s.o. over, knock s.o. off something** *(using the foot or body)* pŭníhkaweew VTA **I knocked him off the bed.** 'Mbuníhkawaaw wúnj-apíineeng.'

**knock sideways** VT **hit s.o. and knock them sideways** piimihtéeheew VTA; **hit s.t. and knock it sideways** pii=mihtéehum VTI1B; **knock s.o. sideways, knock s.t. crooked** *(by shot, by physical contact, with a projectile)* piimŭláweew VTA; **knock s.t. sideways, knock s.t. crooked** *(by shot, by physical contact, with a projectile)* píimŭlam VTI1A.

**knock through** VT **knock s.t. through** *(with a stick)* éeshŭlam VTI1A.

**knot** N **be tied up in a knot, be tied in a knot** wchiimambíisuw VAI, wchii=mambíisuw VAI; **have a knot** *(s.t. animate)*, **have a lump, have a bump** wchíhkwsuw VAI; **tie s.o. in a knot** wchiimambíileew VTA; **tie s.t. in a knot** wchiimámbtoow VTI2.

**know** VT **know s.o.** weewíiheew VTA; **know s.t.** weewíhtoow VTI2; **be nosy, want to know things** katá-wéewsuw VAI, kíhkata-wéewsuw VAI; **know all the news, hear everything, hear all the gossip** wihwéewsuw VAI; **know how to do s.t.** nihtáhtoow VTI2; **know the news, hear the news, know what's going on** wéewsuw VAI; **skillfully, know how to** *(do something)* nihtaa- PV **He watches everything.** 'Wŭníhtaa- wéemi kwéek -saakíh=toon.', **He's a good preacher.** 'Níh=taa-pŭmutóonheew.'; **be at a loss, don't know which way to turn, feel one has no place to go, not know where one will stay** kwiilaweelún=dam VOTI1.

**Kool-Aid** N **sap, Kool-Aid, soft drink, sweet drink** shookŭláapoow NI.

# L

**lace** N **lace curtain, transparent curtain** shehshíikaleek NI.

**lace** VT **sew things, be sewing, lace things, thread things** laaphíikeew VAI.

**lace up** VT **lace s.t. up, thread s.t.** láapham VTI1A.

**lack** VI **be deficient, be lacking, be short of something, be not quite enough of something, fall short** noondéexiin VAI, noondéexun VII; **be short, be lacking** noondéeyeew VII.

**lack** VT **be short of s.t., lack s.t.** liiwíh=lateew VAIO **He ran short of paper.** 'Liiwíhlateew pambíilal.', **I'm short a little bit.** 'Liiwíhlata chángiish.';

lack a commodity, run out of something txíhlateew VAI; **lack s.t. animate** *(of commodities)* noondéexŭ=meew VTA **I have not quite enough paper.** 'Noondéexŭma pambíilak.'; **lack s.t., lack sufficiently of s.t.** *(to cover something, to reach something)* noondéextoow VTI2; **lacking** kwiila- PV **I have nothing to do.** 'Ngwíila-kwéek -lúnum.', **I didn't have anything to feed them.** 'Ngwíila- kwéek -xamáawak.'; **run short of s.t., be lacking s.t.** *(a commodity)* noondéh=leew VAIO **I ran short of the paper.** 'Noondéhlaan pámbiil.'; **run short of s.t., lack s.t.** liiwíhleew VAIO **He ran out of boards.** 'Liiwíhleew pasii=káaxkwal.'; **be bare, be lacking in fur, be lacking in hair** mooshakúsuw VAI.

**lacrosse** N **lacrosse stick** niimcheehŭ=máakan NI; **play lacrosse** niimchée=hŭmeew VAI.

**ladder** N sakeehíikan NA.

**lake** N mbíisus NI **I went swimming in the lake.** 'Níi ndahíixŭmwi mbíissung talí.'; **lake, edge of water** wsháype PC **I went out to the lake.** 'Wsháype nóom.'

**lamb's quarters** N waxkanúsak NA *usually plural.*

**lame** ADJ **limp, be lame** kiihiitalíhkeew VAI; **be lame, have a sprain** kwŭluk=wíixiin VAI, kwŭlukwíixun VII; **be lame, walk with a limp** kwŭlukwíh=leew VAI; **be lame in the hip** kwŭ=lukwiitŭyéhleew VAI; **damage s.t., make s.t. lame** kwŭlúkwŭnum VTI1B **I sprained my foot.** 'Ngwulkwún=ŭmun nzíit.'; **have a sore leg, have a lame leg** wihkaatíineew VAI.

**lamp** N **light, lamp** waasŭleeníikan NA; **turn s.t. animate down** *(of lamps)* ahkwŭléeneew VTA; **turn s.t. animate down** *(of lamps)* áhkwŭneew VTA.

**land** N **land, earth** áhkuy NI; **town, land** ootéenay NI; **barren land on which nothing grows** lunáhkuy NI; **collectively held land, land that belongs to the band** tputaawáhkuy NI; **have a lot of land** kihtootéenayuw VAI, xwat=ootéenayuw VAI; **have a lot of land** xwáhkŭyeew VAI.

**land** VI **land, drop, arrive, arrive at a position by falling** matéexiin VAI **I fell on top of the box.** 'Níi mbák=shung wáxkiich nŭmatéexiin.', **The ball landed over there.** 'Yéelak ma=téexiin néenaxkw.'; **land, drop, arrive, arrive at a position by falling** matéexun VII **Where the road goes.** 'Éeli-matéexung.'; **land, land on the ground, alight** awáhleew VAI **I landed over there.** 'Yéelak ndúlu-awáh=la.'

**land on** VT **fall on one's stomach, land on one's stomach, fall flat, fall face down** pàkchehtéexiin VAI.

**language** N **speak Delaware, speak a native language** hulŭníixsuw VAI; **speak a certain language, speak a certain dialect** líixsuw VAI **He speaks another language or dialect.** 'Palíi ayulíixsuw.'; **speaking an Indian language, the Delaware language** hulŭniixsuwáakan NI; **talk terribly, talk badly, use foul language** chiip=tóonheew VAI; **use bad language, curse, swear** matutóonheew VAI; **use bad language, tell a lie, perjure oneself** mataaptóoneew VAI.

**lantern** N liindawáakan NA, niindawáa=kan NA; **carry a lantern** níindaweew VAI.

**lap** VT **rub one's mouth on s.o., lap s.o., lick s.o.** síisameew VTA.

**large** ADJ **be a large room** xwúndeew VII; **be a lot of water, be a large amount of water** xwáapŭweew VII; **defecate a large amount, go to the bathroom a lot** amangásktuw VAI, xwásktuw VAI; **have large rooms** *(of* *buildings)* amangúndeew VII; **hawk, large bird** awéhleew NA; **large piece of timber** kihtapánzhuy NI.

**last** ADJ **be the last of one's family** wihkwáhleew VAI; **be the last of one's family, be last of one's lineage** wehkwáhleew VAI; **cut the last of s.t. animate, cut s.t. animate off at the end** póhkwsheew VTA; **cut the last of s.t., cut s.t. off at the end** póhkwshum VTI1B; **take all of s.t. animate, take the last piece of s.t. animate** póh=kwŭneew VTA; **take all of s.t., take the last piece of s.t., quit while doing s.t.** póhkwŭnum VTI1B.

**late** ADV áawiis PC **He came late.** 'Áa=wiis péew.'; **oversleep, sleep late, sleep in** wsaamóngwaam VAI, eelón=gwaam VAI; **come too late** mehtxih=káasuw VAI.

**later** ADV **later, eventually** aayáaxkwu PC **I went later.** 'Aayáaxkwu náh ndá.', **We'll be leaving eventually.** 'Aayáaxkwu-ch ktalŭmusíhna.'

**laugh** VI kŭlúksuw VAI, akulkúsuw VAI; **feel in good humour, want to laugh** kŭlukeelúndam VOTI1; **laugh a lot, laugh out loud** amángu-láatam VOTI1, mángu-láatam VOTI1; **make s.o. laugh** kŭlukíiheew VTA.

**lay** VT **lay an egg** wáhwheew VAI; **lay s.o. to soak in the water** kamukwíi=xŭmeew VTA; **lay s.t. to soak in the water** kamukwíixtoow VTI2; **lay s.t. straight** shaaxkíixtoow VTI2; **make s.t. animate be double, cause s.t. animate to be double, lay s.t. animate in a layer on top of something else** pihtawíixŭmeew VTA; **make s.t. be double, cause s.t. to be double, lay s.t. in a layer on top of something else** pihtawíixtoow VTI2; **straighten s.o., lay s.o. straight** shaaxkíixŭmeew VTA; **straighten s.t., lay s.t. straight** shaaxkíixtoow VTI2.

**lay down** VT **lay s.o. down** shungíixŭ=meew VTA; **lay s.o. down and spread them out** shiipchéexŭmeew VTA; **lay s.t. down** shungíixtoow VTI2; **lay s.t. down spread open** shiipchéextoow VTI2.

**lay out** VT **stretch s.o. out, lay s.o. out** shiipíixŭmeew VTA; **stretch s.t. out, lay s.t. out** shiipíixtoow VTI2.

**lay together** VT **lay s.o. together, join s.o. together** takwíixŭmeew VTA *object usually plural;* **lay s.t. together, join s.t. together** takwíixtoow VTI2 *object usually plural.*

**layer** N **be double, be in two layers** *(of something sheet-like)* niishéekat VII, niishéeksuw VAI; **be double, lie double, be in layers** pihtawíixiin VAI, pihtawíixun VII **Two-story houses.** 'Niishéeli pihtawíixŭnool wiikwáh=mal.'; **be in five layers** *(of something sheet-like)* naalaneekíixiin VAI, naala=neekíixun VII; **be in four layers** *(of something sheet-like)* neeweekíixiin VAI, neeweekíixun VII; **be in layers, be double** pihtawúsuw VAI, píhta=weew VII **It is in two layers.** 'Níishu-píhtawe.', **It's in three layers.** 'Nxée=li píhtaweew.'; **be in one layer** *(of something sheet-like)* ngwuteekíixiin VAI **Buy two-ply toilet paper, don't buy one-ply.** 'Kŭmáhlawaa-uch niisheekíixiit wiikwáhmshii-pámbiil, chíi mahlawáahan ngwuteekíixiit.'; **be in one layer** *(of something sheet-like)* ngwuteekíixun VII; **be in so many layers** *(of something sheet-like)* txeekíixiin VAI *usually with number particle* **It is in six layers.** 'Ngwútaash txeekíixiin.'; **be in three layers** *(of something sheet-like)* nxeekíixiin VAI, nxeekíixun VII; **be in two layers** *(of something sheet-like)* niisheekíixiin VAI, niisheekíixun VII; **be so many layers** *(of something sheet-like)* txeekíixun VII *usually with number particle* **It is in eight layers.**

'Xáash txeekíixun.'; **have (extra) clothes in layers, have on more clothes than someone else** pihta=wákuw VAI **I am covered in three layers, I am dressed in three layers.** 'Nxú mbihtawákwi.'; **make s.t. animate be double, cause s.t. animate to be double, lay s.t. animate in a layer on top of something else** pih=tawíixŭmeew VTA; **make s.t. be double, cause s.t. to be double, lay s.t. in a layer on top of something else** pihtawíixtoow VTI2; **take the covering off s.t. animate, take the outer layer off s.t. animate, remove the shell from s.t. animate** pŭlákŭneew VTA; **take the covering off s.t., take the outer layer off s.t., remove the shell from s.t.** pŭlákŭnum VTI1A; **wear more than one pair of shoes, wear more than one layer of footwear, wear overshoes** pihtawahk=súneew VAI.

**Lazarus** N léeshŭlush NA.

**lazy** ADJ **be lazy** kihtamúneew VAI; **be extremely lazy** laxkalákayeew VAI *considered impolite,* laxktúyeew VAI *considered impolite;* **feel lazy** lax=kamálsuw VAI.

**lead** N **be at the front, be in the lead** shayéexun VII; **be in the lead, go first, fly first, run first, drive first, proceed first, go ahead, run ahead** shayéhleew VAI **The little one came in first.** 'Cheengshíishiit éel-péechi-shayéhlaat.'; **crawl ahead, crawl in the lead** shayeewíikwsuw VAI; **drive ahead, drive in the lead, drive first** shayeewchéhleew VAI; **in the lead, in front** shayéemung PC **My front tooth.** 'Shayéemung níipiit éhteek.', **She changed her seat to the front.** 'Sha=yéemung lú áandapuw.'; **in the lead, in front** shéemung PC **It fell forward, it went to the front.** 'Shéemung líhle.'; **put s.o. in the front, put s.o. in the lead** shayéexŭmeew VTA; **put s.t. in the front, put s.t. in the lead** shayéextoow VTI2; **walk in the lead, walk in front, go ahead, walk ahead** shayéewxeew VAI **He likes to be ahead.** 'Wíhwiing-shayéewxeew.', **He always likes to go ahead.** 'Wíh=wiing-shàshayéewxeew.'

**lead** VI **run ahead, be leading in a race** shayeewaaméhleew VAI, shayeewah=takíhleew VAI; **lead a fast life** ktak=áawsuw VAI; **lead an odd life, lead a strange life** maanjŭwáawsuw VAI; **lead an unsettled life, lead a restless life** sàkwáawsuw VAI.

**lead** VT **lead s.o. along with a string, lead s.o. by with a string, lead s.o. along by the reins, lead s.o. by by the reins** *(of horses)* pŭmaapéeneew VTA; **lead s.o. by the arm, take s.o. by the arm, be arm in arm with s.o.** laapiinaxkéeneew VTA, laapiináxkeew VAIO; **lead s.o. in a certain direction with a string, lead s.o. in a certain manner with a string, lead s.o. in a certain direction by the reins, lead s.o. in a certain manner by the reins, put the reins on s.o.** *(of horses)* laapéeneew VTA.

**leader** N **be chief, be the leader** kíhka=yuw VAI; **leader, person in position of authority** líilŭnuw NA.

**leaf** N waníipakw NI; **have leaves on it** waníipakuw VAI.

**leak** VI wúndpeew VII, wunjíikun VII, wunjíikuw VAI; wunjíikuw VII **The teakettle is leaking.** 'Tíihoos wunjíi=kuw.'; **leak** wúndpeew VAI **The pail is leaking.** 'Wúndpeew wsháphoos.'; **leak badly** niiskpéhleew VII **There's a bad leak from the stovepipe.** 'Ehŭliingwáhteek wúnj-niiskpéh=leew.'

**lean** ADJ **be bare, be lacking in fur, be lacking in hair, be lean** *(of meat)* móoshakeew VII; **lean meat** moo=

shéewakw NI.

**lean** VI **be lopsided, be uneven, lean to one side** piimchéesuw VAI; **have a house that's leaning** piimíikeew VAI; **house that leans** piimíikaan NI; **lean** *(against something)* aapchíixiin VAI, aapchíixun VII; **lean over, lean to one side** *(s.t. animate)*, **be crooked, lean** piimíixiin VAI **You drove around the Four Corners too fast and you were leaning.** 'Koosáamu-kshú-wiiwŭníh=laan éenda-aashŭwatéexung, kwŭlúp kpiimíixiin.'; **lean over, lean to one side, be on crooked** piimíixun VII; **lean over, sit crookedly, lie crookedly** piimchéexiin VAI; **lean to one side** piimíhleew VAI, **lean to one side** píimsuw VAI.

**lean** VT **lean s.o. to one side, lean s.t. animate to one side** piimíixŭmeew VTA; **lean s.o., lean s.t. animate** *(against something)* aapchíixŭmeew VTA; **lean s.t.** *(against something)* aapchíixtoow VTI2; **lean s.t. to one side, put s.t. on crooked** piimíixtoow VTI2.

**lean back** VI aamchéexiin VAI; **lean back while sitting** aamchéepuw VAI.

**lean-to** N pihtawíikaan NI *addition to house.*

**leather** N **leather bag** xayiinóotay NI; **leather coat** xáyii-kóot NI; **leather glove** xáyii-wánd NA; **leather shoe** xayáhksun NI; **leather shoelace** xáyii-aníixan NI.

**leave** VI **leave, go off** alúmsuw VAI; **leave running, run away, start to run** alumahtakíhleew VAI; **regret that s.o. leaves** loosóomeew VTA; **wait to take off, wait to leave, be ready for action** kehtéexiin VAI.

**leave** VT **leave crooked tracks** pàptuk=éelham VOTI1; **leave s.o., leave s.o. behind alone, leave s.o. behind and lonely** mayaníixkaleew VTA.

**leave alone** VT **leave s.o. alone, have nothing to with s.o., let s.o. go, give up on s.o., break up with s.o., give up making s.t. animate** pooníiheew VTA; **leave s.o. alone, leave s.o. behind** *(at home, in a competition)*, **leave everyone behind** weemíixka=leew VTA **We were left behind (by the deceased).** 'Nŭweemiixkalukéh=na.'

**leave behind** VT **leave s.o. behind** ngáleew VTA; **leave s.t. animate behind on one's plate** *(of food)* shíh=kwameew VTA; **leave s.t. behind** ngátum VTI1B; **leave s.t. behind on one's plate** *(of food)* shihkwándam VTI1A; **leave scraps of s.t. animate behind, don't eat all of s.t. animate** *(of food)* píiwameew VTA; **leave scraps of s.t. behind** *(of food)*, **don't eat all of s.t.** piiwándam VTI1A **I left a little bit.** 'Chángiish mbiiwándamun.'

**leave open** VT **leave s.t. animate open** tawíixŭmeew VTA, toongchéexŭmeew VTA; **leave s.t. animate wide open** tawushéexŭmeew VTA; **leave s.t. open** tawíixtoow VTI2; **leave s.t. open** *(as a door)* toongchéextoow VTI2; **leave s.t. wide open** tawushéextoow VTI2.

**leave out** VT **leave out part of the story while talking** pàpŭlakaachíimuw VAI; **leave out words when one speaks** pohpohkwíixsuw VAI; **say something in a hurry, leave something out of a story, don't tell the whole story** pàpalaachíimuw VAI.

**leave undone** VT **leave s.o. undone, unhitch s.o.** kchaxkíixŭmeew VTA; **leave s.t. undone, unhitch s.t.** kchaxkíix=toow VTI2.

**left over** ADJ **be left over** piiwíhleew VII; **be left over, be one of the survivors** piiwíixiin VAI; **be some left over, be left over** aluwíhlateew VAI, aluwíhla=teew VII; **be left over, be some left over** aluwíhleew VII, aluwíhleew VAI **There's some fish left over.** 'Aluw=

íhleew namées.'; **have s.o. left over, have s.o. unused** píiwŭneew VTA; **have s.o. remaining, have s.o. left over** piiwíiheew VTA; **have s.t. left over, have s.t. unused** píiwŭnum VTI1B; **have s.t. remaining, have s.t. left over** piiwíhtoow VTI2.

**left-handed** ADJ **be left-handed** mŭlán=jiiw VAI-S, mŭnánjiiw VAI-S.

**leg** N **my leg** níhkaat NID; **be spread out, have one's legs open** toongíixiin VAI; **break s.o.'s leg** kaxkkaatéeheew VTA; **break s.o.'s leg** *(using the foot or body)*, **step on and break s.o.'s leg** kaxkkaatéhkaweew VTA; **bump one's leg against something** paakkaatée=xiin VAI; **cross one's legs** aashŭwiix=kéexiin VAI; **give s.o. a swollen leg, give s.o. a bump on their leg** ma=kwukaatéeheew VTA; **grab s.o. by the leg, pull on s.o.'s leg** sakukaatéeneew VTA; **grab s.o.'s leg** sakukaatéeheew VTA; **have a big leg, have big legs** xwukáateew VAI; **have a broken leg** kaxkkáateew VAI; **have a cut-off leg, have one's leg severed** tŭmukáateew VAI; **have a dirty leg, have a dark leg** niiskkáateew VAI; **have a hole in one's leg** pkwukáateew VAI; **have a scabby leg, have scabs on one's leg** mŭkuykáateew VAI; **have a sore leg** kiihiitkáateew VAI; **have a sore leg, have a lame leg** wihkaatíineew VAI; **have a stiff leg** chiingaalkáateew VAI; **have a swollen leg, have a bump on one's leg** makwukáateew VAI; **have a swollen leg, have one's leg swell up** paaskáateew VAI; **have big legs** a=mangkáateew VAI; **have crooked legs** piimkaatéeyeew VII; **have long legs** akwaankáateew VAI, akwaankaatée=yeew VII; **have one leg** ngwutkáateew VAI; **have one's legs crossed** aashŭ=wukaatéexiin VAI; **have one's legs in the water** kamukwkaatéexiin VAI; **have one's legs shaking, be afraid** nungkaatéhleew VAI; **have one's legs showing, have one's legs exposed, have bare legs** mihtkaatéexiin VAI; **have one's legs spread apart** toong=kaatéexiin VAI; **have one's legs together** takwukaatéexiin VAI; **have short legs** *(diminutive)* achahkwkaa=cheeyéeshuw VII; **have small legs** *(diminutive)* achangkaachéeshuw VAI; **iron kettle with legs** wehkáathoos NA, wihkaathóosus NA, wihkáathoos NA; **kick out one's legs, stretch out one's legs, maneuver** *(of trains)* shándham VOTI1; **kick s.o. and give them a swollen leg, kick s.o. and give them a bump on the leg, sit on s.o. and give them a swollen leg, sit on s.o. and give them a bump on the leg** makwukaatéhkaweew VTA; **put one's leg up, raise one's legs** uspkáateew VAI; **raise one's legs up, have one's legs raised up** uspkaa=téexiin VAI; **scratch one's leg, have an itchy leg** kshiipkáateew VAI; **sit with legs open, sit with one's legs spread apart** toongohkwéepuw VAI; **sit with one's legs folded, sit hunched over** ptukohkwéepuw VAI, ptúk=wapuw VAI; **sit with one's legs open, sit with one's legs spread apart** tóongapuw VAI; **sit with one's legs up, raise one's legs while sitting** uspkaatéepuw VAI, uspkaatéewapuw VAI; **soak one's legs in the water, put one's legs in the water** kamukw=káateew VAI; **stand lopsided, stand with one leg higher than the other** piimiitŭyéexiin VAI; **stand with one's legs open, stand with one's legs spread apart** toongiikáapawuw VAI; **use one leg** ngwutkaatéexiin VAI; **wash one's legs** kshiixkáateew VAI; **wash s.o.'s legs** kshiixkaatéeneew VTA.

**lend** VT **lend s.t. to s.o.** ndumíiheew VTAO; **lend s.t., lend s.t. animate**

ndumíihŭweew VAIO; **lend things, lend things to people** ndumíihŭ=weew VAI.

**length** N **a certain length** *(of time, measurement)* sahkii- PV; **a certain length** *(of time, measurement)* sahku PC *informal* **He lived with her for a long time, and she really dominated my uncle for a long time.** 'Kwúnii-wiitaawsoomáawal, tá sáhku shíi=kaanzh lúkih wtalŭwihkawáawal nzhíisal.'; **a certain length** *(of time, measurement)* sahku- PV *informal* **I've been working since this morning.** 'Séhku-wáapang ndalóhke.', **I waited for him until two o'clock.** 'Mbéehaaw sáhku-níish-kŭlakíike.'; **a certain length** *(of time, measurement)* sáhkii PC **For nine months.** 'Sáhkii nóoli kíishooxkw.'; **be a certain depth, be a certain length** *(of holes)* sahkáalakat VII **It is the same depth (of a hole).** 'Ngwúteel sah=káalakat.'; **be a certain length** *(of rooms)* sahkúndeew VII **He was pacing back and forth in the room.** 'Asahkóoxweew sehkúndeek.'; **be a certain length** sáhkeew VII **How long is the board?** 'Thá sáhkeew pasíi=kaaxkw?', **The length of the house.** 'Séhkeek wíikwahm.'; **be a certain length** sáhksuw VAI **How long is the snake?** 'Thá wsáhksiin ná áxkook?'; **be gone a certain length of time** sahkáhkeew VAI **He was gone for two months.** 'Níish-kíishooxkw sahkáh=keew.', **How long has he been gone?** 'Thá sahkáhke?'; **fight for a certain length of time, fight until now** sah=katáhkeew VAI; **have one's feet lying the length of something** sahk̍siitée=xiin VAI **His feet are at the edge of the bed.** 'Wsháyee apíineeng sahk=siitéexiin.'; **have one's head lying the length of something** sahkaand=péexiin VAI **His head was by the door.** 'Kíixkii kpahóonung sah=kaandpéexiin.'; **live a certain length of time** sahkáawsuw VAI **If I live until springtime.** 'Siikwángu sahkaaw=s̍uyáane.'

**lengthen** VT **add on to s.t., lengthen s.t., make s.t. longer** aanihkwíhtoow VTI2; **add on to s.t. animate, lengthen s.t. animate, make s.t. animate longer** aanihkwíiheew VTA.

**less** ADJ **less** *(than someone or something else)* nóondaa PC **I weigh less.** 'Nóondaa ndúndxu-poondakúsi.', **He's smaller.** 'Nóondaa lúkiil.'

**let** VT **let s.o.** *(do something)* léelŭmeew VTA *followed by verbal complement in the subordinative* **I let him eat some candy.** 'Nduléelŭmaaw shookŭlúshal míichiin.'

**let go** VT **give s.t. up, let go of s.t., let s.t. go** *(of debts)* pooneelúndam VTI1A; **give up on s.o., let go of s.o.** *(especially of someone who has died)* poo=néelŭmeew VTA; **leave s.o. alone, have nothing to with s.o., let s.o. go, give up on s.o., break up with s.o., give up making s.t. animate** pooníi=heew VTA; **let go of s.o., give s.o. up, let s.o. go, free s.o.** póonŭneew VTA; **let go of s.o., let go of s.t.** poonáa=heew VAIO; **let go of s.t., give s.t. up** póonŭnum VTI1B; **let s.t. go, give s.t. up, give up doing s.t., give up making s.t.** pooníhtoow VTI2.

**let out** VT **let out a cry** sŭláamuw VAI.

**let's** VI **let's go** háaw há PC; **let's, I'd better, we'd better** yóhkwa PC **Let's leave.** 'Yóhkwa alumsíitookw.', **I'd better go to sleep.** 'Yóhkwa nŭ=máwu-kawíin.'

**lethargically** ADV **walk limply, walk lethargically** apiisŭlóoxweew VAI.

**letter** N létul NA; **book, paper, letter** pámbiil NA **Old books.** 'Xúwii-pambíilak.'; **write a letter, write a letter to here** peeteekhíikeew VAI;

**write, write a letter** leekhíikeew VAI.
**lettuce** N shŭláash NI.
**level** ADJ **be full to the brim, be level with the top** *(of non-liquids)* tpuskŭ=wáhteew VII; **be level earth** shaax=kahkéexun VII; **be level ground** shaaxkahkéeyeew VII; **be level with the top** *(of non-liquids)* tpuskŭwáp=uw VAI; **be level, be on level, be even, be on even, be even with something** tpuskŭwíixun VII; **contain liquid level with the top** *(of containers)*, **be level with the top of a container** *(of liquids)* tpuskŭwáapŭweew VII; **contain liquid level with the top, be liquid level to the top of container** tpuskŭwúpeew VAI, tpuskŭwúpeew VII; **fill s.t. level to the top** *(of liquids)* tpuskŭwúpeew VAIO; **fit s.t. level, fit s.t. evenly** tpuskŭwíixtoow VTI2 **My hat is on evenly.** 'Ndupus=kŭwíixtoon ndaakongwéepuy.'; **make s.t. level with the top of a container** *(of liquids)* tpuskŭwáapŭweew VAIO; **place s.t. animate level with the top of container** tpuskŭwáhleew VTA; **place s.t. level with the top of container** tpuskŭwáhtoow VTI2.
**level** N **catch up to s.o., overtake s.o., catch up to s.o.'s level** matáleew VTA.
**liar** N **be a liar, tell a lie** maxkalákayeew VAI *considered impolite.*
**lice** N **give s.o. lice, give s.o. bugs** nax=kwáaleew VTA.
**lick** VT **lick s.o., lick s.t. animate** sáa=pameew VTA; **lick s.o., rub s.o. with the mouth** síikwameew VTA; **lick s.o., rub, nuzzle s.o. with mouth** láala=meew VTA; **lick s.o., wipe s.t. animate with the mouth** káasameew VTA; **lick s.t.** laalándam VTI1B, saapándam VTI1A; **lick s.t., rub on s.t. with the mouth** siikwándam VTI1A; **lick s.t., wipe s.t. with the mouth** kaasándam VTI1A; **rub one's mouth on s.o., lap s.o., lick s.o.** síisameew VTA; **rub one's mouth on s.t, lick s.t.** siisán=dam VTI1A.
**lid** N **be covered, have a lid, be frozen over** kpátun VII; **open s.t. animate, take the lid off s.t. animate** *(as the cover of a pail)* áapŭneew VTA.
**lie** N **tell a lie** kŭlóoneew VAI, akulóo=neew VAI, maxktúyeew VAI; **tell a fib, tell lies** maxkáaheew VAI; **tell s.o. a lie** kŭloonéeheew VTA; **use bad language, tell a lie, perjure oneself** mataaptóoneew VAI.
**lie** VI **be a liar, tell a lie** maxkalákayeew VAI *considered impolite.*
**lie** VI **be close together, lie close together** takwiixíinook VAI *usually plural,* takwíixŭnool VII *usually plural;* **be curled up, lie curled up** ptukwíi=xiin VAI, ptukwíixun VII, wihwiimbíi=xun VII; **be double, lie double, be in layers** pihtawíixiin VAI, pihtawíixun VII **Two-story houses.** 'Niishéeli pih=tawíixŭnool wiikwáhmal.' **be even, be in order, lie correctly** mayaawíi=xun VII; **be hidden, lie placed out of sight** kaatáhteew VII; **be in a line, be lined up, be in a line there, lie there in a line** pŭmáameew VAI **He was lying across the length of the house.** 'Pumáameen séhkeek wíikwahm.', **The snake was lying on the road.** 'Áxkook pŭmáameew áaneeng.'; **be in a line, be lined up, lie** pŭmáameew VII **The rope is lying straight.** 'Pee=máameek ptukwáhtakw.', **There's a road over there.** 'Áanaay yéelak pŭmáameew.'; **be in order, lie correctly, be lined up straight** *(s.t. animate)*, **be the main one, be the top person** mayaawíixiin VAI; **be many of them lying together** xweelaangwée=wak VAI *usually plural;* **be scattered, lie scattered** sayéexŭnool VII *usually plural* **Your dishes are scattered.** 'Sayéexŭnool koolaakanúsal.'; **be tired of lying in bed** peekiikanáaxiin

VAI; **be twisted, be at an angle, lie at an angle, be lopsided, lie on its side, be misaligned** *(of a misbuttoned shirt)* piimoxkwíixun VII; **fall and burst open, lie broken** lookchéexiin VAI, lookchéexun VII; **fall on top of something, lie on top of something** waxkiitihtéexiin VAI, waxkiitihtéexun VII; **hang over something, lie over something** paalíixiin VAI, paalíixun VII; **have one's back in a certain direction, lie with one's back in a certain direction** lupoxkwanéexiin VAI **She had her back turned yesterday.** 'Wuláakwu ná lupoxkwanéexiin.'; **have one's feet lying the length of something** sahksiitéexiin VAI **His feet are at the edge of the bed.** 'Wsháyee apíineeng sahksiitéexiin.'; **have one's head lying the length of something** sahkaandpéexiin VAI **His head was by the door.** 'Kíixkii kpahóonung sah=kaandpéexiin.'; **have one's head sticking out, lie with one's head sticking out, stick one's head out** saakaandpéexiin VAI; **have one's ears lying in a certain manner, have one's ears lying in a certain direction** laxéexiin VAI **His ears are hanging down to the ground.** 'Áhkiing làx=éexiin.'; **hide, lie hidden, lie hiding** kaachíixiin VAI; **lean over, sit crookedly, lie crookedly** piimchéexiin VAI; **lie close together** kchukaangwéewak VAI *usually plural;* **lie close together, be close together, lie close to something** psakwiixíinook VAI *usually plural,* psakwíixun VII **The chair is up against the door.** 'Psakwíixun áhpa=poon kpahóonung.'; **lie crookedly** piimáangweew VAI, pàptukíixiin VAI, pàptukíixun VII; **lie crookedly, lie sideways, lie on it's side** pŭmiichíi=xiin VAI, pŭmiichíixun VII; **lie crosswise, be twisted, be at an angle, lie at an angle, be lopsided** piimox=kwíixiin VAI; **lie down** shungíixiin VAI; **lie down, be in bed, lie in bed** wŭ=líixiin VAI **I'm going to lie down, I'm going to sleep.** 'Kwáy nŭmáwi-wulíixiin, nŭmáw-kawí.'; **lie immersed in the water, lie soaking in the water** kamukwíixiin VAI, kamukwíi=xun VII; **lie in a certain manner** luchéewuw VAI **He twists and turns.** 'Músu-luchéewiin.'; **lie in a certain manner, lie in a certain direction** líixiin VAI, líixun VII **Table cloth.** 'Ee=hundaxpóonung ehŭlíixung.'; **lie in a dangerous place** laalxawíixiin VAI, laalxawíixun VII; **lie in a pitiful state, lie in a sickly state** ktumaakíixiin VAI; **lie in threes** nxaangwéewak VAI *usually plural;* **lie inside, lie inside something** piindáameew VAI, piin=dáameew VII **He was listening from the other room. ('His ears were lying inside here.')** 'Wihtawákal péech-piindaaméewal.'; **lie naked** sheexka=láangweew VAI; **lie on one's back** waasatéexiin VAI; **lie on one's side** shàwéexiin VAI; **lie on one's stomach** aalaanjkwéexiin VAI, pàkatéexiin VAI, waalatéexiin VAI; **lie on top of something** waxkiitáangweew VAI; **lie scattered, be scattered** sayeexíinook VAI *usually plural* **The papers are scattered.** 'Sayeexíinook pambíilak.'; **lie sprawled, lie spread out, lie flat** toongchéexiin VAI, toongchéexun VII; **lie spread out** shiipchéexiin VAI, shiipchéexun VII; **lie still** kŭlamíixun VII; **lie still, lie quietly** kŭlamíixiin VAI **The snake is still.** 'Áxkook kŭ=lamíixiin.'; **lie straight** shaaxkíixiin VAI, shaaxkíixun VII; **lie stretched out, be stretched out** shiipíixiin VAI, shiipíixun VII; **lie together** takwaan=gwéewak VAI *usually plural;* **lie uncovered** paaxkéexiin VAI, paaxkéexun VII; **lie underneath something** alaa=míixiin VAI, alaamíixun VII; **lie upside**

**down** aapoochkwàlíixiin VAI, aa=poochkwàlíixun VII; **lie upside down, come to rest in an upside down position** aapoochkwàlihtéexiin VAI, aapoochkwàlihtéexun VII; **lie upside down, turn upside down, fall upside down** aapoochkwíhleew VAI; **lie with one's face sticking out, lie with one's face showing, have one's face showing** kchiingwéexiin VAI; **lie with one's head sticking out, have one's head sticking out** saakohkwéexiin VAI **My head was sticking out of the water** 'Mbíing nóonj-saakohkwée=xiin.', **I was covered up but my head was sticking out.** 'Nŭmutakwaháasi shùkéhla nzaakohkwéexiin.'; **lie, recline** shungíixun VII; **be a flood, be a lot of water lying around** kaanzhah=kwíixun VII; **be big eyed** *(after seeing something unusual)*, **lie with one's eyes open** *(especially if one cannot sleep)* amangaalakiingwéexiin VAI.

**lie down** VI **get up from lying down** áamwiiw VAI-S; **get up quickly from lying down** aamwiipáhtoow VAI; **hit s.o. and make them get up from lying down** aamwihtéeheew VTA; **lie down uncovered, lie down exposed, lie down in the open** mihchíixiin VAI; **lie down, be in bed, lie in bed** wŭ=líixiin VAI **I'm going to lie down, I'm going to sleep.** 'Kwáy nŭmáwi-wulíixiin, nŭmáw-kawí.'; **make s.o. get up from lying down** aamwihk=shíhkaweew VTA; **move about while lying down** kwàkwchukwíixiin VAI; **talk to s.o. to get them up from lying down, holler at s.o. to get them up from lying down** aamwihkíimeew VTA; **turn over while lying down** kwŭlupíixiin VAI.

**life** N **be an old woman, undergo menopause, undergo change of life** kihtoxkwéesuw VAI; **be an unbeliever, don't believe in a Christian way of life, lead a quiet life** nala=wáawsuw VAI; **lead a bad life, be a sinner** matáawsuw VAI; **lead a fast life** ktakáawsuw VAI; **lead a pitiful life, lead a not very good life** ktum=aakáawsuw VAI; **lead a sad life** oo=shawáawsuw VAI; **lead an odd life, lead a strange life** maanjŭwáawsuw VAI; **lead an unsettled life, lead a restless life** sàkwáawsuw VAI; **life** pŭmaawsuwáakan NI; **live a long life, live for a long time** kwŭnáawsuw VAI **Maybe you'll live a long life.** 'Táas áa kwùnáawsi.'

**lift** VT **lift s.o. up, lift s.t. animate up** uspíixŭmeew VTA; **lift s.o. up, make s.o. go up** *(using the hands)* úspŭneew VTA; **lift s.t. up** uspíixtoow VTI2; **lift s.t. up, make s.t. go up** *(using the hands)* úspŭnum VTI1B; **lift up one's head** uspohkwéhleew VAI; **open s.t., lift s.t. off** *(as the cover of a box or coffin)* áapŭnum VTI1B; **raise s.t. animate up, lift s.t. animate up** *(using a tool or instrument)* uspáhkhweew VTA; **raise s.t. up, lift s.t. up** *(using a tool or instrument)* uspáhkhwam VTI1A; **be unable to lift s.o.** pwáawŭ=neew VTA; **be unable to lift s.t.** pwáawŭnum VTI1A.

**lifter** N **lifter, hook, something to lift with** uspŭníikan NI.

**light** ADJ **be light in weight** láangan VII, láangsuw VAI; **be light in weight** *(diminutive)* laangánzhuw VII; **be light snow, be powdery snow** leexéesuw VAI; **be lightweight looking, look light in weight** laangiináakwat VII, laangiináakwsuw VAI; **have light-coloured eyes, have grey eyes** waaxee=língweew VAI; **be light in colour, be a whitish colour, have a white tinge to it** waapŭléexiin VAI, waapŭléexun VII.

**light** N **light, lamp** waasŭleeníikan NA; **be bright light** wŭláasŭleew VII; **be**

**wasted light** niiskáasŭleew VII **The light was left on overnight.** 'Ngwút=ii-tpóhkwe niiskáasŭle.'; **shine a light in a certain direction, shine a light in a certain manner** laasŭlée=nŭmeew VAI; **shine, be light, be a light on** wáasŭleew VII **Are you home? ('Is your house shining?').** 'Kíi wíikŭyan wáasŭleew?'; **sight, seeing the light** neemwáakan NI; **turn on the light** waasŭléenŭmeew VAI; **turn s.t. animate down** *(of lights, of sources of fire)* wtuléeneew VTA; **turn s.t. down** *(of flames, of sources of fire)* wtuléenum VTI1B.

**light** VT **light a fire for s.o., make a fire for s.o.** tundeewháweew VTA; **light s.t. animate, set s.t. animate on fire** náxkwseew VTA; **light s.t., set s.t. on fire** náxkwsum VTI1B.

**lightly** ADV **touch s.o. lightly** *(using the hands)* cháskŭneew VTA; **touch s.t. lightly** *(using the hands)* cháskŭnum VTI1B.

**lightning** N **be lightning** saapŭléhleew VII, wahwaasŭléhleew VII; **be struck by lightning** payáxkhaaw VTA *indefinite subject only* **I was struck by lightning.** 'Mbayaxkhóoke.'

**lightweight** ADJ **be lightweight looking, look light in weight** laangiináa=kwat VII, laangiináakwsuw VAI.

**like** ADV **like, resembling** máash PC **Also it looks sharp, his nose.** 'Kwŭlúp máash kíineew wihkíiwan.', **He looks like a White person.** 'Máash shŭwanakwiináakwsuw.'

**like** VI **as one likes, as one wishes** léh=lapiit VAI *usually only in conjunct order* **He can do what he wants.** 'Léh=lapiit lúnum.', **She's a widow, she can go where she likes.** 'Shiikóowuw léhlapiit-uch kwáy éew.'

**like** VT **like the look of s.o.** wiingíina=weew VTA; **like the look of s.t.** wiin=gíinam VTI1A; **like the looks of s.o., admire s.o.** wŭlíinaweew VTA; **like the looks of s.t., admire s.t.** wŭlíinam VTI1A; **like the smell of s.o.** wiingii=máaleew VTA; **like the smell of s.t.** wiingiimáatam VTI1A; **like the sound of s.o., like the sound of s.t. animate, like to listen to s.o.** wiingsútaweew VTA; **like the sound of s.t., like to listen to s.t.** wiingsútam VTI1A **They (inanimate) sound good to me.** 'Nŭwiingsutamúnal.'; **like the taste of s.t.** wiingándam VTI1A **He didn't like the taste of it.** 'Máh wiinganda=móowun.'; **like the taste of s.t. animate** wíingameew VTA; **like to** wih=wiing- PV **He likes to follow people.** 'Wíhwiing-naawáhkeew.', **He likes to talk.** 'Wíhwiing- kwéek -úw'; **like to** wiingu- PV *informal* **I'd like to go with you (plural).** 'Níi áa kŭwíingu-wiicheewŭlóhmwa.', **I'm glad to see you.** 'Kŭwíingu-néewul.'; **like s.t.** wiingáatam VTI1A **I like to eat.** 'Nŭ=wiingáatamun nŭmíitsiin.'; **like s.t., be stingy about s.t.** àhwáatam VTI1A; **like to do something with s.o.** wiin=gáaleew VTA *requires complement in subordinative mode* **I like to play with him.** 'Nŭwiingáalaaw nŭmeela=wíihaan.'; **like to drink** wiingíisŭ=muw VAI; **like to fight** wiingatáhkeew VAI; **like to follow people** shkwunée=suw VAI; **like to listen, enjoy listening, enjoy hearing something** wiingxéexiin VAI **This one likes to listen.** 'Wiingxéexiin há wá.'; **like to stare** ayahwhiingwéexiin VAI; **like to wade in the water** wihwiingaashóo=keew VAI; **like to work** wiingalóh=keew VAI; **like water** wiingáapŭweew VAI; **be fond of men, like all the men, be 'boy-crazy'** wiingiilŭnúweew VAI; **be smart, be industrious, like to work** lihlpúneew VAI; **feel as if one would like to rest** alaaxiimwahtée=namuw VAI; **like it where one is** wíin=

gapuw VAI; **like looking at things, enjoy the view** wiingatawáapuw VAI; **like women, be 'girl-crazy'** wiin=goxkwéeweew VAI.

**limb** N **my branch, my limb** ndóhwan NID; **cut s.t. animate off, cut a limb off s.t. animate** *(of trees)* tŭmáhk=wsheew VTA.

**limp** ADJ **be limp, be wrinkled** píisŭleew VII **My dress is wrinkled.** 'Píisŭleew nŭweendakwíiwan.'; **be limp, be weak, be a weakling** piisŭlúsuw VAI; **be soaking wet, be drenched, be limp from water** piisŭlúpeew VAI, piisŭlúpeew VII; **fall due to be being weak, fall due to being limp** piisŭ=lihtéexiin VAI.

**limp** N **be lame, walk with a limp** kwŭlukwíhleew VAI; **walk with a limp, walk with one hip higher than the other** piimiitŭyéewxeew VAI.

**limp** VI **limp, be lame** kiihiitalíhkeew VAI.

**limply** ADV **hang loosely, hang limply, hang wrinkled** piisŭlaapéhleew VII; **walk limply** piisŭlóoxweew VAI; **walk limply, walk lethargically** apiisŭ=lóoxweew VAI.

**line** N **fish with a line** weendáameew VAI.

**line** N **be at the end of a row, be at the end of a line, be at the end of something** wihkwáameew VII **It is a little ways to the end of it.** 'Péexwiish wihkwáameew.', **We've come to the end now.** 'Méhch kwáy éenda-wihkwaámeek kpáhna.'; **be first, be first in line, be first in a competition** shayéexiin VAI; **be in a line in a certain manner, be a line in a certain direction** láameew VAI **The cars are in a line over there.** 'Yéelak laaméewak káalak.', **A big snake was lying on the timbers the length of the house.** 'Xwáchu-áxkook wtuláameen apánzhŭyung séhkeek wíikwahm.'; **be in a line in a certain manner, be in a line in a certain direction** láameew VII **The fence is in a line over there.** 'Yéelak láameew méenaxk.'; **be in a line, be lined up, be in a line there, lie there in a line** pŭmáameew VAI **He was lying across the length of the house.** 'Pumáameen séhkeek wíikwahm.', **The snake was lying on the road.** 'Áxkook pŭmáa=meew áaneeng.'; **be in a line, be lined up, lie** pŭmáameew VII **The rope is lying straight.** 'Peemáameek ptukwáhtakw.', **There's a road over there.** 'Áanaay yéelak pŭmáameew.'; **be in a straight line, be in a row** wŭlaaméewak VAI *usually plural,* wŭlaaméewal VII *usually plural;* **be in a straight row, be in a straight line** shaaxkáameew VII **What I planted is in a straight row.** 'Shaaxkáameew ehkíihayaan.'; **be lined up, be in a line, line up** wŭlaameexíinook VAI *usually plural,* wŭlaaméexŭnool VII *usually plural;* **be long, be in a long line** kwŭnáameew VII **There is a long row of corn.** 'Xwáskwiim kwŭnáa=me.'; **be long, be in a long line** kwŭnáameew VAI **The snake is long.** 'Áxkook kwŭnáame.'; **be marked in a straight line** shaaxkeekháasuw VII, shaaxkeekháasuw VAI; **have spots on it, have a line of spots on it, be marked with spots** sàsàpeekháasuw VII, sàsàpeekháasuw VAI; **make a mark on s.o. in a straight line, mark s.o. in a straight line** shaaxkéekheew VTA; **make a straight line of things, write in a straight line** shaaxkeek=híikeew VAI; **put spots on s.o., make a line of spots on s.o., mark spots on s.o.** sàsàpéekheew VTA; **put spots on s.t., make a line of spots on s.t., mark s.t. with spots** sàsàpéekham VTI1A.

**line up** VT **line s.o. up, line s.t. animate up** wŭlaaméexŭmeew VTA *object usually plural;* **line s.t. up** wŭlaaméex=toow VTI2 *object usually plural;* **be in a line, be lined up, be in a line there, lie there in a line** pŭmáameew VAI **He was lying across the length of the house.** 'Pumáameen séhkeek wíikwahm.', **The snake was lying on the road.** 'Áxkook pŭmáameew áaneeng.'; **be in a line, be lined up, lie** pŭmáameew VII **The rope is lying straight.** 'Peemáameek ptukwáh=takw.', **There's a road over there.** 'Áanaay yéelak pŭmáameew.'; **be lined up, be in a line, line up, be in a straight line** wŭlaameexíinook VAI *usually plural,* wŭlaaméexŭnool VII *usually plural.*

**lining** N **lining** *(of coats, of quilts)* pih=tawiikwáakan NI; **have a lining inside** alaamháasuw VII; **make a lining for s.t.** pihtawíikwam VTI1A; **make a lining in s.t. animate** pihtawiikwáaleew VTA.

**link** VT **have one's arms linked** laapii=naxkeeniikéewak VAI *usually plural.*

**lip** N shéetoon NI; **close one's lips tightly, have one's lips tightly closed** samwutoonéexiin VAI; **close one's mouth tightly, have one's mouth closed, have one's lips pursed, pout** spwutoonéexiin VAI; **have an odd twist to one's mouth, have an odd twist to one's lips** *(indicating a certain attitude)* maashtoonéexiin VAI; **have one's lips sticking out, pout** niixsheetóonayeew VAI; **have one's lips sticking out, stick one's lips out** sheetoonéexiin VAI; **have red lips** amaxksheetóoneew VAI, maxkshee=tóoneew VAI; **have rough lips** kaaxk=sheetóoneew VAI; **have thick lips** aa=poosktóoneew VAI; **purse one's lips, have one's mouth in a pout, have one's mouth sticking out pointed** chpwutoonéexiin VAI; **sit with one's lips sticking out** sheetoonohkwéepuw VAI; **stick one's lips up, have one's lips sticking out** uspsheetóonayeew VAI.

**liquid** N **be a foamy liquid** pihteewáa=pŭweew VII; **be clear liquid** wŭláa=pŭweew VII; **be full of water, be full of liquids** wchúwpeew VII **The creeks are full of water.** 'Shiipóosh'shal weewchuwpéewal.'; **be full of water, be full of liquids** wchúwpeew VAI; **be mixed together in a liquid** takwaa=pŭwehléewal VII; **be red coloured liquid** maxkáapŭweew VII; **be thick** *(of liquids)* tahtakáapŭweew VII; **break up bread in milk, break bread into liquid, break crackers into liquid** piikŭnúmeew VAI; **contain liquid level with the top** *(of containers),* **be level with the top of a container** *(of liquids)* tpuskŭwáapŭweew VII; **contain liquid level with the top, be liquid level to the top of container** tpuskŭwúpeew VAI, tpuskŭwúpeew VII; **fill s.t with liquid** wchuwáapŭ=weew VAIO; **fill s.t. up with water, fill s.t. up with liquid** wchúwpeew VAIO; **fill up with liquid** wchuwpéhleew VII, wchuwpéhleew VAI; **pour out a liquid** sookpéenŭmeew VAI; **soak s.t. in liquid** sookhupátoow VTI2; **soften s.t.** *(with liquid)* wtakíixtoow VTI2; **take a big drink, take a lot of liquid, drink a lot** *(including non-alcoholic beverages)* xwíisŭmuw VAI.

**liquor** N **fetch water, go after water, go to get liquor** naathúpeew VAI.

**listen** VI **disobey, refuse to listen, be stubborn** achiingíiwsuw VAI; **like to listen, enjoy listening, enjoy hearing something** wiingxéexiin VAI **This one likes to listen.** 'Wiingxéexiin há wá.'; **listen** kŭlaxéexiin VAI; **listen, listen intently** aapxéexiin VAI.

**listen to** VT **listen to s.o.** kŭlustáweew

VTA; **listen to s.t.** kŭlústam VTI1A; **be glad to hear s.o., be glad to listen to s.o.** payahkwsútaweew VTA; VT **be glad to hear s.t., be glad to listen to s.t.** payahkwsútam VTI1A; **be tired of listening to s.o.** peeksútaweew VTA; **be tired of listening to s.t.** peeksútam VTI1A; **dislike listening to s.o., dislike the sound of s.o., dislike hearing about s.o.** shiingsútaweew VTA; **dislike listening to s.t., dislike the sound of s.t.** shiingsútam VTI1A; **like the sound of s.o., like the sound of s.t. animate, like to listen to s.o.** wiingsútaweew VTA.

**little** ADJ **a little while** náakeesh PC **After a while he'll jump up in a hurry.** 'Náakeesh-uch shúkw nál-uch pas=kwiipáhtoon.', **Wait for a while, don't get married right away.** 'Náa=keesh-uch kpéesi, chíi sháa takwapŭ=waaláahan.'; **seldom, hardly, very little, a scant amount** máamchiish PC **I seldom work.** 'Máamchiish ndal=óhke.', **There's hardly any left over.** 'Máamchiish aluwíhleew.'; **some, a little bit, a small amount** tangii- PV **Can you speak a little Delaware now?** 'Méhch há kíish-tángii-hulŭ=níixsi?'; **some, a little bit, a small amount** tángii PC **There's a bit of bread there.** 'Tángii nú yéelak áhte apwáan.', **Do you want to eat a little bit?** 'Tángii káta-míitsi?'; **some, a small amount, a little bit** changíi=wiish PC **I don't drink but I drink a little bit.** 'Máhta níi nŭmunéewi changíiwiish shúkw nŭmúne.'; **some, a small amount, a little bit** chángiish PC **There's just a little frost.** 'Chán=giish shúkw tóhpun.', **I left a little bit of the food.** 'Chángiish mbiiwán=damun.'; **very little, not a lot** cháach=xiish PC **I slept very little.** 'Cháach=xiish ngáwi.', **I didn't work a lot.** 'Cháachxiish ndalóhke.'; **feel lowly, think little** *(of oneself)* tangeelúndam VOTI1; **get s.t. cheap, pay a little for s.t.** aapŭwalóhkeew VAIO; **little bit of paper, Kleenex** pambíilush NA; **little egg** *(diminutive)* changáhwalush NI; **little finger** changŭlunjáawanush NI; **little old man** changihlóoshush NA; **little round Mary** pchúkwu-meelíi=shush NA.

**little person** N weemachéekaniish NA.

**live** VI **live, be alive, be living** pŭmáaw=suw VAI; **be separated from one's spouse, live apart** chpooxwéewak VAI *usually plural;* **be tired of feeling a certain way, be tired of living** peekahtéenamuw VAI; **be tired of living** peekáawsuw VAI; **dwell there, live there** wíikuw VAI **My house.** 'Wíikŭyaan.', **Your house.** 'Wíikŭ=yan.'; **live a certain length of time** sahkáawsuw VAI **If I live until springtime.** 'Siikwángu sahkaawsuyáane.'; **live a long life, live for a long time** kwŭnáawsuw VAI **Maybe you'll live a long life.** 'Táas áa kwŭnáawsi.'; **live alone, be on one's own** nxoohálŭ=nuw VAI; **live common-law** matápuw VAI; **live far apart** wahlŭmiikéewak VAI *usually plural;* **live from s.o., live from s.t.** wundáawsuw VAIO **He lives from his wife's money.** 'Oondáaw=siin mùshúshŭmal wshulpúlum.', **I live from what I earn.** 'Noondáaw=siin peenhámaan.'; **live in a certain manner** láawsuw VAI; **live in a shanty** shentiihámeew VAI; **live in town** ooteenayápuw VAI; **live near s.o., live close to s.o.** peexŭwiikáaleew VTA; **live there** taláawsuw VAI; **live to a certain age, live until now** peetáaw=suw VAI **I've lived to the age where I can't go anywhere.** 'Náh mbeetáaw=si éenda-áalu- tá -ayáan.'; **live together in threes, stay together in threes** nxiilŭnúwak VAI *usually plural;* **live until morning** *(of a sick per-*

*son)* waapanáaxiin VAI; **live until morning** waapanámuw VAI; **live until springtime, survive until springtime** siikwanámuw VAI; **live until summer, survive until summer** niipŭnámuw VAI; **live until winter, survive until winter** loowanámuw VAI; **live well** wŭláawsuw VAI; **make s.o. live, revive s.o.** laawsooháaleew VTA; **make s.o. live, revive s.o.** laaw=sóoheew VAIO; **make s.o. live, save s.o., give s.o. a reason to live** pŭ=maawsooháaleew VTA; **see daylight, live to daylight** waapanáheew VAI; **stay there quietly, be there quietly, live there quietly** naláwapuw VAI.

**live with** VT **inherit s.t.** *(especially characteristics of personality)*, **live with s.t.** naxpáawsuw VAIO; **live with s.o.** wiitaawsóomeew VTA.

**lively** ADJ **feel 'smart,' feel lively** ktak=amálsuw VAI.

**liver** N xwíhk NA.

**load** N **bring a load of s.t., go by with a load of s.t., haul a load of s.t.** ée=watoow VTI2 **I hauled a load of hay.** 'Ndéewato miixáskwal.'; **carry a big load** tohphéewasuw VAI; **carry a heavy load on one's back** laanzhih=kŭwáleew VAI; **carry a load on one's back** pŭmúwaleew VAI; **cart away a load** *(of one's belongings)* alumhée=wasuw VAI; **finish packing a load on one's back, be finished packing a load on one's back, be already packed** kiishŭwálheew VAI; **gather up and take away a load of s.t.** alumhéewatoow VTI2, aluméewatoow VTI2; **gather up and take away a load of s.t. animate** alumhéewaleew VTA, aluméewaleew VTA; **go to fetch a load** naachŭwáleew VAI; **go to fetch a load of s.t., fetch and carry a load of something on one's back** naachŭ=wáleew VAIO; **go to get a load** *(of one's belongings)* naathéewasuw VAI; **go to get a load of s.o.** naathéewaleew VTA; **go to get a load of s.t.** naathéewa=toow VTI2; **take s.o. inside, take s.t. animate inside, take a load of s.t. animate inside** piindhéewaleew VTA; **take s.t. inside, take a load of s.t. inside** piindhéewatoow VTI2.

**location** N **jump to a new location** aandáakchehl VAI.

**lock** N wchiimhíikan NA.

**lock** VT **lock s.t.** wchíimham VTI1A; **lock s.t. animate** wchíimheew VTA.

**log** N sáalaak NI; **cut logs** saaláakheew VAI; **log house** apanzhíikaan NI; **stable, log stable** shtépul NI; **saw timber, cut logs** tŭmusháhkweew VAI.

**lonely** ADJ **be lonely** maamayaníilŭnuw VAI, mayaníilŭnuw VAI; **leave s.o., leave s.o. behind alone, leave s.o. behind and lonely** mayaníixkaleew VTA.

**long** ADJ **be long** kwŭneew VII, kwŭ=nóosuw VAI; **be long** akwaansúwak VAI *usually plural,* akwaanéewal VII *usually plural;* **be long** *(diminutive)* akwaanéeshŭwal VII *usually plural;* **be long** *(of something string-like)* kwŭnahtakúsuw VAI, kwŭnáhtakat VII; **be long grass** kwŭnaskwéeyeew VII, kwŭnáskwat VII; **be long in shape, have a long shape** kwŭnuchéesuw VAI, kwŭnuchéeyayeew VII; **be long, be in a long line** kwŭnáameew VII **There is a long row of corn.** 'Xwás=kwiim kwŭnáame.'; **be long, be in a long line** kwŭnáameew VAI **The snake is long.** 'Áxkook kwŭnáame.'; **climb up a long flight of stairs** kwŭnakóo=suw VAI; **give long shade** kwŭnahka=chihtéexiin VAI, kwŭnahkachihtéexun VII, kwŭnahkachíhteew VII; **hang down a long way** kwŭnaapéhleew VII; **have a long arm, reach a long way** kwŭniináxkeew VAI; **have a long beard, have long whiskers** kwŭnih=tóonayeew VAI; **have a long ear** kwŭ=

nihtawákeew VAI, kwŭnáxeew VAI; **have a long face** kwŭníingweew VAI; **have a long head** kwŭnáandpeew VAI; **have a long neck** kwŭnaxóoneew VAI; **have a long nose** kwŭnucháaleew VAI; **have a long shape, have a long body** kwŭnoochéeyeew VII **And it was short, it was wrapped around in a bundle, and it was a rectangular little thing.** 'Kéhla wáak chah=kwéeshuw, tàtùpháasuw, kwŭnoo=cheeyéeshuw.'; **have a long shape, have a long body** kwŭnuchéeyeew VII; **have a long tail** kwŭnáalŭweew VAI; **have long arms** akwaanŭnáx=keew VAI; **have long breasts, have long udders** *(of a cow)* akwaaníila=neew VAI; **have long ears** akwáan=xeew VAI; **have long fingernails** akwaaníhkasheew VAI; **have long hair** kaanzhaalóhkweew VAI, kwŭ=naalóhkweew VAI; **have long hair** *(especially of non-humans)* kwŭnaw=éesuw VAI; **have long legs** akwaan=kaatéeyeew VII, akwaankáateew VAI; **have long sleeves** akwaanŭnaxkée=yeew VII *especially of shirts or coats,* kwŭnunaxkamáyeew VII; **have long teeth** akwaananíikeew VAI; **live a long life, live for a long time** kwŭ=náawsuw VAI **Maybe you'll live a long life.** 'Táas áa kwùnáawsi.'; **long** kwŭnii- PN **Overcoat** 'Kwŭníi-kóot.'; **long** kwŭnii- PV **He lived with her for a long time.** 'Kwúnii-wiitaaw=soomáawal.', **I cooked the apples too long.** 'Nóosaa-kwŭníi-ndupwíinak aapŭlúshak.'; **long knife** kwŭnan=zhíikan NI; **long piece of wood** kwŭ=náxakw NI; **long sleeves** kwŭnunax=kamáyal NI *usually plural;* **see a long way, have good eyesight** wŭlata=wáapuw VAI; **take a long time to say one's words** akwaaníixsuw VAI; **take long steps** akwaanalíhkeew VAI; **be away a long time** kwŭnáhkeew VAI; **think s.t. to be a long time** kwŭnee=lúndam VTI1A **I think it's taking a long time for evening to come.** 'Níi ngwuneelúndamun nál ápih wŭláa=kuw.', **I think that it's a long time until the end of the service.** 'Níi ngwuneelúndamun nál-uch éhkwu-maawéewiin.'; **wear a coat with a long tail** kwŭníi-shkwúnayii-koot=hámeew VAI; **wear a long coat, have a long coat on** kwŭníi-koothámeew VAI; **wear a long dress, have a long dress on** kwŭnahóosuw VAI; **wear something that has a long tail** kwŭníi-shkwúnayeew VAI *usually of coats.*

**long ago** ADV kéenj PC **Back in the good old days.** 'Kéenj táa éenda-wŭlú-léek.', **Long ago.** 'Kéenj táa.'; **long ago** láawate PC **What happened years ago.** 'Láawate áayleek.'**long ago, until, emphatic** kúnj PC **You will come at four o'clock.** 'Néew-kŭlák-uch kúnj kpá.', **He came a while ago.** 'Kúnj wéeti péew.'

**longer** ADJ **add on to s.t., lengthen s.t., make s.t. longer** aanihkwíhtoow VTI2; **add on to s.t. animate, lengthen s.t. animate, make s.t. animate longer** aanihkwíiheew VTA; **no longer require s.o.'s services** ehkwalóoleew VTA.

**look** N **have a look of distaste on one's face, turn one's nose up at something** niiskcheengwéexiin VAI; **have a strange look on one's face, have a guilty look on one's face, look guilty of something** maashiingwéexiin VAI; **like the look of s.o.** wiingíinaweew VTA; **like the look of s.t.** wiingíinam VTI1A.

**look** VI **cock one's head, turn one's head, look to the side** piimóhkweew VAI; **like looking at things, enjoy the view** wiingatawáapuw VAI; **look around searching, look around** *(in* *expectation of someone or something)* ndawáapuw VAI; **look from a certain place, look for a certain reason** wundhiingwéexiin VAI; **look from a certain place, look from there** wun=datawáapuw VAI **I looked from the house.** 'Wiikwáhmung noondataw=áapi.'; **look here and there, look about, look around** apaamohkwéh=leew VAI, apaamóhkweew VAI; **look in a certain direction, look in a certain manner** lóhkweew VAI, lahiingwée=xiin VAI **He's looking out the window.** 'Eeheeshandéekanung lahiingwée=xiin.'; **look in a certain direction, look in a certain manner** liingwée=xiin VAI **I don't know where he's looking.** 'Máh nŭweewiiháawu tá eeliingwéexiit.'; **look in a mirror** pehpŭnáwsuw VAI; **look in this direction, look over here** peethiingwée=xiin VAI; **look sideways, turn one's head** pŭmiitóhkweew VAI; **look straight ahead** shaaxkóhkweew VAI; **make s.o. look in a certain direction, make s.o. face in a certain direction** liingwéexŭmeew VTA **I put the doll facing over there.** 'Yéelak nduliingwéexŭmaaw naaníitus.'

**look** VI **appear to be close by, look to be close by** peexŭwiináakwat VII, peexŭwiináakwsuw VAI; **be clean looking, have a clean appearance** piiliináakwat VII, piiliináakwsuw VAI; **be cold looking, look cold** thiináa=kwat VII, thiináakwsuw VAI; **be cute looking** weewŭliináakwsuw VAI; **be dirty looking, look dirty** niiskiináa=kwat VII, niiskiináakwsuw VAI; **be fancy looking** wiilawiináakwat VII; **be fancy looking, be dressed up fancily** wiilawiináakwsuw VAI **He's dressed up fancy.** 'Móxa wiilawii=náakwsuw.'; **be lightweight looking, look light in weight** laangiináakwat VII, laangiináakwsuw VAI; **be plain looking, have a plain appearance** kahkaniináakwat VII, kahkaniináakw=suw VAI; **be strong-looking** maska=niináakwat VII, maskaniináakwsuw VAI; **find that s.o. looks different** chpíinaweew VTA; **find that s.t. looks different, s.t. looks different to someone** chpíinam VTI1A; **have terrible looking hair** chiipalóhkweew VAI; **look better** *(than before)* miin=gasawiináakwsuw VAI; **look big** xwachiináakwat VII, xwachiináakw=suw VAI; **look cold** takwachŭwii=náakwsuw VAI; **look dangerous, look scary** kxwaawiináakwat VII, kxwaa=wiináakwsuw VAI; **look dark, be dark-looking** nzukaapamúkwat VII, nzukaapamúkwsuw VAI; **look deceptive, look misleading** pahchoolŭ=weewiináakwsuw VAI; **look different** chehchpiinaakwsúwak VAI *usually plural;* **look good, be nice looking, have a nice appearance** wŭliináa=kwat VII, wŭliináakwsuw VAI; **look homely** lunŭwíixteew VAI; **look hopeless, look overwhelming, appear to be hopeless** laawcheenáakwsuw VAI **He's hopeless, he's never getting dressed.** 'Laawcheenáakwsuw máh kiikiisheechpíiwi.'; **look overwhelming, look hopeless, appear to be hopeless** laawiináakwsuw VAI, laa=wiináakwat VII; **look important** kaanzhiináakwat VII, kaanzhiináakw=suw VAI; **look like an adult woman** oxkweewiináakwsuw VAI; **look like an old woman** kihtoxkweesŭwii=náakwsuw VAI; **look like a White person** shŭwanakwiináakwsuw VAI; **look like one could run fast, look smartly dressed, look frisky while going by** kshihleewiináakwsuw VAI; **look new, look young** wuskiináakwat VII, wuskiináakwsuw VAI; **look not very nice** lunŭwiináakwat VII, lunŭ=wiináakwsuw VAI **My car doesn't**

**look very nice.** 'Lunŭwiináakwsuw ngáalum.'; **look old, be old-looking, look older than one's age** kihkŭwii=náakwsuw VAI; **look old, look like an elderly person** kihkeesŭwiináakw=suw VAI; **look sad, look to be grieving** ooshawiináakwsuw VAI; **look shameful** miixaniináakwat VII, miixaniináakwsuw VAI; **look strange, have an odd appearance** maashii=náakwat VII, maashiináakwsuw VAI; **look terrible, be terrible looking, have a frightful appearance** chiipii=náakwat VII; chiipiináakwsuw VAI; **look the same, look alike** eeyŭlii=naakwsúwak VAI *usually plural;* **look troubled** sàkwiináakwat VII, sàkwii=náakwsuw VAI; **look weak** shawii=náakwat, shawiináakwsuw VAI; **the way one looks makes someone feel like throwing up, the way one looks makes someone feel like vomiting** wŭyakaskeelŭmuwiináakwsuw VAI, mŭlamandamuwiináakwsuw VAI.

**look after** VT **take care of s.o., look after s.o., tend to a responsibility with regard to s.o.** lxawéelŭmeew VTA **You should take care of your car, don't drive it needlessly.** 'Káta-lxawéelŭ=maa ktahtamoombíilum, chíi amaya=kaweehéehan.'; **take care of s.t., look after s.t., tend to a responsibility with regard to s.t.** lxaweelúndam VTI1B **Take care of the food (said of an empty refrigerator).** 'Katá-lxaweelúndah miichŭwáakan.'

**look at** VT **look at s.o., look at s.t. animate** pŭnáweew VTA; **look at s.t.** pŭnám VTI1A; **look at s.t. in a certain manner, look at s.t. in a certain direction** lóhkweew VAIO; **be tired of looking at s.o., find s.o. tiresome to look at** peekíinaweew VTA; **be tired of looking at s.t., find s.t. tiresome to look at** peekíinam VTI1A; **look at s.o. angrily** manoongáapameew VTA.

**look back** VI **turn one's head, look back** kwŭlupóhkweew VAI.

**look beyond** VI **look past, look beyond** loowatawáapuw VAI.

**look beyond** VT **look past s.t., look beyond s.t.** loowatawáapuw VAIO.

**look for** VT **look around searching for s.o., look out to see s.o., look out for s.o.** ndawáapameew VTA; **look around searching for s.t., look out to see s.t., look out for s.t.** ndawaa=pándam VTI1A; **look for s.o., search for s.o.** *(especially in vain)* kwíila=weew VTA; **look for s.t., search for s.t.** *(especially in vain)* kwíilam VTI1A **I won't be able to find it.** 'Ápih ngwihkwíilamun.'; **look for a cat** ndawapooshíisheew VAI; **look for a cow, look for cows** ndawakóoyeew VAI; **look for a dog** ndawxúmweew VAI; **look for a man** noochiilŭnúw=eew VAI; **look for a woman** nootox=kwéeweew VAI; **look for horses** ndawehnayóongseew VAI.

**look on** VI pŭnáasuw VAI **Lots of people watched the baseball game.** 'Xwée=look lúnŭwak pŭnáasŭwak éenda-neenaxkhwátiing.'

**look out** VI któhkweew VAI, ktohkwée=xiin VAI **He was looking out from the door.** 'Ktohkwéexiin wúnj-kpahóonung.'; **have one's eyes sticking out, look out, peek out** ktiin=gwéexiin VAI.

**look out for** VT **watch out for s.o., be wary of what may happen to s.o.** nxaawéelŭmeew VTA.

**look out from** VT **look out from an opening** pkwahiingwéexiin VAI.

**look over** VT **look over s.t., look over s.o., look past s.t., look past s.o.** paalatawáapuw VAIO; **peek over, look over something** paalhiingwéexiin VAI.

**look past** VI **look past, look beyond** loowatawáapuw VAI; **look over s.t.,**

**look over s.o., look past s.t., look past s.o.** paalatawáapuw VAIO; **look past s.t., look beyond s.t.** loowa=tawáapuw VAIO.

**look through** VT **look through** eesha=tawáapuw VAI; **look through a hole, look through an opening, look through something** pkóhkweew VAI; **look through something, see through something** eeshatawáapuw VAIO.

**look up** VI **raise one's head, look up** uspóhkweew VAI.

**looks** N **dislike the looks of s.o.** ma=chíinaweew VTA; **dislike the looks of s.t.** machíinam VTI1B; **like the looks of s.o., admire s.o.** wŭlíinaweew VTA; **like the looks of s.t., admire s.t.** wŭlíinam VTI1A.

**loose** ADJ **be loose, be a loose fit** *(of clothes)* piisŭlíixun VII; **be loose, do not adhere tightly** *(of lids, of bolts)* lxakwíixun VII; **get bounced loose, get knocked loose** lxakwihtéexun VII; **get loose** lxakwíhleew VII; **get loose** lxíhleew VAI **He wants to get loose.** 'Katá-lxíhle.'; **get loose** lxíhleew VII.

**loosely** ADV **be tied loosely** lxakwam=bíisuw VII, lxakwambíisuw VAI; **hang loosely, hang limply, hang wrinkled** piisŭlaapéhleew VII.

**loosen** VT **loosen s.t.** lxákwŭnum VTI1B; **loosen s.t. animate** lxákwŭneew VTA.

**lopsided** ADJ **be crooked, be lopsided, be uneven** píimeew VII **Your cane is crooked.** 'Ktaláawan píimeew.'; **be lopsided, be uneven** piimchéeyeew VII, piimchéesuw VAI; **be twisted, be at an angle, lie at an angle, be lopsided, lie on its side, be misaligned** *(of a misbuttoned shirt)* piimoxkwíi=xun VII; **cut s.t. animate lopsided, cut s.t. animate unevenly** píimsheew VTA; **cut s.t. lopsided, cut s.t. unevenly** píimshum VTI1B; **have a crooked mouth, have a lopsided mouth** piimtoonéexiin VAI; **stand lopsided, stand with one leg higher than the other** piimiitŭyéexiin VAI.

**lose** VT **lose s.o., lose s.t. animate** a=náheew VTA; **lose s.t.** aníhtoow VTI2; **be lost** anáhookw VAI, awáaniiw VAI-S, aníhteew VII.

**loss** N **be at a loss, don't know which way to turn, feel one has no place to go, not know where one will stay** kwiilaweelúndam VOTI1; **feel oneself to be at a loss, feel desolate** *(having no place to go or to live)* kwiilawee=lúnzuw VAI.

**lot** N **a lot, lots** tohpi- PV **Take a deep breath.** 'Tóhpi-léexeel!'; **a lot, lots** tohpu- PV *informal* **He had too much to drink.** 'Tóhpu-mŭnéew.', **I swallowed too much.** 'Ndóhpu-kwún=dam.'; **be a flood, be a lot of water lying around** kaanzhahkwíixun VII; **be a lot of Oneidas, Oneida Town, Ontario** meengweewíhkeew VII; **be a lot of bushes** mihtkwunzíhkeew VII **Where there are a lot of bushes.** 'Éenda-mihtkwunzíhkeek.'; **be a lot of people** kihtéelook VAI *usually plural;* **be a lot of smoke** *(from a chimney),* **be smoky** kaanzhiingwáhteew VII; **be a lot of thick trees, be a lot of dense trees, be a dense forest** spwihtkwíhkeew VII; **be a lot of thistles** kaawunzhíhkeew VII; **be a lot of trees** mihtkwíhkeew VII; **be a lot of water** xwéelpeew VII; **be a lot of water** *(as in a puddle or ditch)* xwúp=eew VII; **be a lot of water, be a large amount of water** xwáapŭweew VII; **be a lot of weeds** kaanzháskweew VII; **be a lot of weeds, be a lot of grass** miixaskwíhkeew VII; **be deep water, be a lot of water** xwupéekat VII; **be expensive, cost a lot** aman=gaawatúwal VII *usually plural;* **charge a lot** amangaawatóoheew VAI **You charge too much.** 'Kóosaa-aman=

gaawatóohe.'; **charge a lot for s.t.** xwaawatóoheew VAIO; **defecate a large amount, go to the bathroom a lot** amangásktuw VAI, xwásktuw VAI; **do a lot of work, work a lot** toh=palóhkeew VAI; **drink often, drink a lot** eewachíisŭmuw VAI; **eat a lot** mangaléetŭyeew VAI; **eat an awful lot, overeat** chiipŭlóosuw VAI *considered impolite;* **glutton, someone who eats a lot, someone who never gets full** máaleew NA; **habitually, lots, dirty** aniisku- PV **He loves to sleep, he sleeps easily, he sleeps lots.** 'Aníisku-kawíiw.', **He washes the dishes and leaves them dirty.** 'Aníisku-kshiixíinjŭwe.'; **have a lot of children** sŭluskóonzheew VAI; **have a lot of land** kihtootéenayuw VAI; **have a lot of land** xwatootéenayuw VAI, xwáhkŭyeew VAI; **have lots of food, have an abundance of food** wŭyakiichŭwáakaneew VAI; **laugh a lot, laugh out loud** amángu-láatam VOTI1; **laugh a lot, laugh out loud** mángu-láatam VOTI1; **make a lot of noise** shòhwŭnáakwsuw VAI **The mouse was making a lot of noise somewhere.** 'Aapíikwus táa wtúnda-shòhwŭnáakwsiin.'; **make a lot of noise, make a big noise** amángŭ=weew VII; **make a lot of noise, make a big noise** amángŭweew VAI; **make a lot of smoke** kaanzhiingwahtawás=uw VAI; **make a lot of smoke, make a lot of smoke with things** kaanzhiin=gwahteeníikeew VAI; **make a lot of tracks** kaanzhéelham VAI; **make a lot of tracks, make many tracks** xwéelham VOTI1; **make noise, make a lot of noise** káanzhŭweew VAI, káanzhŭweew VII; **pay a lot** xween=híikeew VAI; **pay a lot for s.t., pay too much for s.t.** xwalóhkeew VAIO; **pay a lot for s.t., pay too much for s.t.** xwulóhkeew VAIO; **pile up a lot of s.t.** xweelshamóotoow VTI2 *object usually plural;* **pile up a lot of s.t. animate** xweelshamóoleew VTA *object usually plural;* **pile up a lot of s.t. animate, pile s.t. animate up high** tohpshamóoleew VTA; **pile up a lot of s.t., pile s.t. up high** tohp=shamóotoow VTI2; **plant many things, plant lots, plant a large amount** amangahkíiheew VAI; **pound on wood a lot** kaanzh'háhkweew VAI; **swim often, swim a lot** wŭyakaashŭwíhleew VAI; **take a big drink, take a lot of liquid, drink a lot** *(including non-alcoholic beverages)* xwíisŭmuw VAI; **talk a lot** niisktuyéemuw VAI, kaan=zhíixsuw VAI, kaanzhtóonheew VAI; **talk a lot, gossip, talk dirty** niisk=tóonheew VAI; **talk lots to s.o., talk too much to s.o.** paakweenztoon=háaleew VTA; **talk lots, make noise** paakwéenzuw VAI; **think a lot of s.o., think highly of s.o., have a high regard for s.o.** xwéelŭmeew VTA; **think a lot of s.t., think highly of s.t., have a high regard for s.t.** kaanzheelún=dam VTI1A; xweelúndam VTI1A; **urinate a lot** amangíisheew VAI; **urinate a lot** xwíisheew VAI; **very little, not a lot** cháachxiish PC **I slept very little.** 'Cháachxiish ngáwi.', **I didn't work a lot.** 'Cháachxiish ndalóhke.'; **very, many, a lot** xwéeli PC **You'll find lots of things.** 'Xwéeli kwéek kŭmóx=kam.', **He always found plenty, it is said.** 'Xwéeli íin ngúmee kwéek móxkam.'; **very, many, a lot** xwéelu PC *informal* **She told her, "Look in the cup! He left me a lot of money."** 'Wtuláawal, "Pŭnáh nú tiihíinjuw! Nùkatúmaakw xwéelu shúlpul."', **Now because you picked him up you'll always find lots of things.** 'Kwáy éel-náatŭnat ngúmee-uch xwéelu kwéek kŭmóxkam.'

**loud** ADJ **drive and make a loud noise,**

**make a rattling noise while driving** *(of wagon wheels)* tiiwchéhleew VAI; **fall and make a loud noise** tiiwíixiin VAI, tiiwíixun VII; **laugh a lot, laugh out loud** amángu-láatam VOTI1, mángu-láatam VOTI1; **play loud music** amangapíikweew VAI, niiskapíi=kweew VAI; **sing out loud** amanga=láamuw VAI; **sound loud, sound terrible** chiipihtáakwat VII, chiipih=táakwsuw VAI; **talk in a loud voice, talk loudly** amangíixsuw VAI; **throw s.o. down hard so as to make a loud noise, set s.o. down hard so as to make a loud noise** tiiwíixŭmeew VTA; **throw s.t down hard so as to make a loud noise, set s.t down hard so as to make a loud noise** tiiwíixtoow VTI2; **walk and make a loud noise** tiiwóoxweew VAI.

**loudly** ADV **talk in a loud voice, talk loudly** amangíixsuw VAI; **talk loudly** amangaaptóoneew VAI, mangaaptóo=neew VAI, mangíixsuw VAI, xwíixsuw VAI.

**louse** N awíilpiish NA; **kill a louse** nihlawiilpíisheew VAI.

**lousy** ADJ **be lousy** awiilpíishuw VAI.

**love** VT **love s.o.** àhwáaleew VTA; **love each other** àhwaaltúwak VAI *usually plural;* **be loved** àhwaalkwúsuw VAI, àhwaatáasuw VII.

**loving** N **loving** àhwaaltuwáakan NI.

**low** ADJ **have a low price** tangáawatuw VII; **feel poorly, feel low** ktumaaka=málsuw VAI; **make a soft sound, make a low sound** kwíishkwŭweew VII; **make a soft sound, make a low sound, say in a soft voice, say in a low voice** kwíishkwŭweew VAI; **talk in a low voice, talk in a soft voice** *(diminutive)* achangiixshíishuw VAI.

**lower** VT **lower s.o., take s.o. down** níixŭneew VTA; **lower s.t., take s.t. down** níixŭnum VTI1B; **lower the price of s.t.** tangaawatóoheew VAIO; **pull s.t. down, lower s.t.** *(using the hands)* chíixŭnum VTI1B.

**lowly** ADJ **feel lowly, think little** *(of oneself)* tangeelúndam VOTI1.

**luck** N **do good for s.o., give s.o. luck** wŭlíihukw VTA *inanimate subject only* **The medicine did me good.** 'Noo=líihkwun wchápihk.', **It did me good to get out of the house.** 'Noolíih=kwun wiikwáhmung wúnj-kchúyaan.'

**lucky** ADJ **be lucky** làkíihuw VAI, nhíi=naakw VAI; **have something lucky happen** *(to oneself)* nhíinaakw VAIO.

**lump** N **get a lump, get a bump** wchih=kwíhleew VAI, wchihkwíhleew VII; **have a knot, have a lump, have a bump** wchíhkwsuw VAI; **have a lump on one's head, have a bump on one's head** wchihkwáandpeew VAI; **have lumps protruding from a surface** *(of food cooking)* pòwcháteew VII; **hit s.o. and give them a lump on the head** makwaandpehtéeheew VTA; **stick up in a lump** pòwíixiin VAI, pòwíixun VII.

**lumpy** ADJ **be lumpy in shape, be out of shape** matuchéesuw VAI, matuch=éeyeew VII.

**lunch** N **my lunch** niimáawan NID; **make lunch** niimaawanáheew VAI; **take one's lunch along** níimaaw VAI-S.

**lung** N wáhpan NA.

**lye** VT **lye corn** pxwásŭmeew VAI.

# M

**machine** N **machine, piece of machinery** múshiin NI **My machine won't run.** 'Aalŭwíhle nŭmushíinum.'; **washing machine** kehkshiixtíikan NI, kehkshiixtíikeeng VII.

**mad** ADJ **make people mad** awiiníh=toow VOTI2.

**maggot** N óhkw NA; **be maggots** oh=

kóowuw VII **Because there are maggots.** 'Éeli-ohkóowiik.'

**main** ADJ **be in order, lie correctly, be lined up straight** *(s.t. animate)*, **be the main one, be the top person** mayaawíixiin VAI.

**make** N **be a certain nationality, be a certain breed, be a certain make, have a certain characteristic** lah=kéewuw VAI **Other races.** 'Palíi eelahkeewíhtiit.'

**make** VT **make s.o.** *(do something)* líiheew VTA *followed by verbal complement in the subordinative* **I made him clean house.** 'Ndulíihaan piila=lóhkeen.', **He made me cut firewood.** 'Ndulíihkwun nŭmánxeen.'; **make s.t.** wŭlíhtoow VTI2 **They made lots of fence rails.** 'Kíhchi- meenax=káaxkwal -wulihtóowak.'; **make s.t. animate** wŭlíiheew VTA; **make s.t. animate from something, make s.t. animate for a certain reason** wun=jíiheew VTA; **make s.t. animate, finish making s.t. animate, be finished making s.t. animate** kiishíiheew VTA; **make s.t. from something, make s.t. for a certain reason** wunjíhtoow VTI2; **make s.t., finish making s.t., be finished making s.t.** kiishíhtoow VTI2 **I've finished making it.** 'Méhch ngiishíhtoon.'; **make s.t. for s.o.** wŭlíhtaweew VTAO.

**make fun of** VT **make fun of people** wehweemwáalŭweew VAI; **make fun of s.o.** wehwéemwaaleew VTA.

**make up** VT **make up one's mind** kii=sheelúndam VOTI1, kiishiitéeheew VAI; **be certain about s.o., have one's mind made up about s.o.** mayaa=wéelŭmeew VTA; **be certain, be sure, have one's mind made up** mayaa=weelúndam VOTI1 **Now I'm sure that Lyle's not coming home.** 'Kwáy nŭmayaaweelúndam máh há péewu Lyle.', **I'm sure that it's going to rain.** 'Nŭmayaaweelúndam katá-sóokŭlaan.'

**make up with** VT **make up with s.o., apologize to s.o.** mehmeendawám=eew VTA.

**makeup** N **put on makeup** shoohúnzuw VAI.

**male** N **adult male, adult man** kihkŭ=wíilunuw NA, kíhkwu-lúnuw NA; **male animal** lunŭwéexum NA; **my male cousin** ndáangwus NAD; **rooster, male fowl** lunŭwéhleew NA.

**man** N lúnuw NA; **White man** shŭwán=akw NA; **adult male, adult man** kihkŭwíilunuw NA, kíhkwu-lúnuw NA; **bad man, good for nothing man, man of poor character** matahàa=peew NA; **be a Black man** neeskàl=éenguw VAI; **be a man who died of old age** aaptihlóosuw VAI **I'm just about dying of old age.** 'Péexoot ndaaptihlóosi.'; **be a proud man, be arrogant, have an attitude, think that one knows more than anyone else** lunŭweelúnzuw VAI; **be an old man** mihlóossuw VAI; **be fond of men, like all the men, be 'boy-crazy'** wiingiilŭnúweew VAI; **fat man** wiisŭ=watéelŭnuw NA; **fighting man, soldier** matahkeewíilŭnuw NA; **little old man** changihlóoshush NA; **look for a man** noochiilŭnúweew VAI; **old man** mihlóosus NA, xuwihlóosus NA; **rotten old man** akwaakwalihlóosus NA, alihlóosus NA; **young man** wuskíilŭ=nuw NA; **'wolf,' man who chases after women** chíixkw NA.

**manner** N **because, in a certain manner, in a certain direction** eel- PV *followed by verb in conjunct order* **Now it must be because he had overcome the medicine.** 'Nál xéet ná kwáy éel- wchápihk -aluwíhkang.', **Because you picked him up you'll always find lots of things (to hunt).** 'Kwáy éel-náatŭnat ngúmee-uch xwéelu kwéek kŭmóxkam.'; **because, in a certain manner, in a certain direction** eeli- PV *followed by verb in conjunct order* **She wanted to kill him because he had cracked the eggs.** 'Kwáta-nihláawal éeli- wáhwal -pwáhkhang.'; **in a certain manner, in a certain direction** li- PV **I waited until he came in.** 'Mbéehaaw wtúli-piinjíikeen.', **Then he crawled inside the house.** 'Nál wtúlu- wiikwáhmung -piinjíikwsiin.'; **in a certain manner, in a certain direction** lu- PV *informal* **I looked around for the medicine, I looked for it everywhere.** 'Nál há mbápaa-kwíilamun wchápihk, wéemu táa ndúlu-kwíilamun.', **Then I went outside and I threw it as far as I could.** 'Nál kwáchŭmung ndáan táa ndúlu-aseesahkáaheen.'

**many** ADJ **very, many, a lot** xwéeli PC **You'll find lots of things.** 'Xwéeli kwéek kŭmóxkam.', **He always found plenty, it is said.** 'Xwéeli íin ngúmee kwéek móxkam.'; **very, many, a lot** xwéelu PC *informal* **She told her, "Look in the cup! He left me a lot of money."** 'Wtuláawal, "Pŭnáh nú tiihíinjuw! Nùkatúmaakw xwéelu shúlpul."', **Now because you picked him up you'll always find lots of things.** 'Kwáy éel-náatŭnat ngúmee-uch xwéelu kwéek kŭmóx=kam.'; **be gone for many nights, be gone for many days** xweelookwŭ=náhkeew VAI; **be many** xwéeltool VII *usually plural;* **be many nights, be many days** xweelookwŭnákat VII; **be many of them** xwéelook VAI *usually plural* **Many of them came out.** 'Xwéelook kchooltúwak.'; **be many of them lying together** xweelaan=gwéewak VAI *usually plural;* **be many of them standing** *(in a group)* xwee=liikaapawúwak VAI *usually plural;* **be many roads** xweelatéexun VII; **have many children** xweelóonzheew VAI; **have many cows** xweelkóoyeew VAI; **have many pages** *(of books)* xwee=laapéeksuw VAI; **make a lot of tracks, make many tracks** xwéelham VOTI1; **many times** xwéelun PC **I went to town several times.** 'Xwéelun oo=téeneeng nóom.'; **pile s.t. high, pile up many of s.t.** xwushamóotoow VTI2.

**maple** N **hard maple tree** asunaamíin=zhuy NA.

**marble** N máapŭlush NA *children's toy;* **play marbles** maapŭlusheelawúsuw VAI.

**Margaret** N máakŭlut NA.

**mark** N **be marked black, have a black mark, have a black stripe** nzukeek=háasuw VII, nzukeekháasuw VAI; **be scraped, have a scrape mark on it** síixiin VAI, síixun VII; **make a mark on s.o. in a straight line, mark s.o. in a straight line** shaaxkéekheew VTA; **make a mark on s.o., make a mark on s.t. animate, write on s.t. animate** wŭléekheew VTA **I'm writing a letter.** 'Nooléekha pámbiil.'; **make a mark on s.t. in a straight line, mark s.t. in a straight line** shaaxkéekham VTI1A; **make marks here and there, make streaks all over** *(on paper)* apaameekhíikeew VAI; **mark s.t.** *(using a tool or instrument),* **make a mark on s.t.** *(using a tool or instrument)* káskham VTI1A; **mark s.t. animate, make a sign on s.t. animate, make a mark on s.t. animate** *(using a tool or instrument)* kíhkheew VTA; **put a mark on s.t. animate** *(using a tool or instrument)* káskheew VTA; **scrape s.o., make a scrape mark on s.o.** síixŭmeew VTA; **scrape s.t., make a scrape mark on s.t.** síixtoow VTI2.

**mark** VT **make a mark on s.t. in a straight line, mark s.t. in a straight**

**line** shaaxkéekham VTI1A; **mark s.t.** *(using a tool or instrument),* **make a mark on s.t.** *(using a tool or instrument)* káskham VTI1A; **mark s.t., make a sign on s.t., put one's name on clothes, mark the perimeters of s.t.** *(using a tool or instrument)* kíhk=ham VTI1A; **mark s.t.animate, make a sign on s.t. animate, make a mark on s.t. animate** *(using a tool or instrument)* kíhkheew VTA; **put spots on s.o., make a line of spots on s.o., mark spots on s.o.** sàsàpéekheew VTA; **put spots on s.t., make a line of spots on s.t., mark s.t. with spots** sàsàpéekham VTI1A; **be marked** kihkháasuw VII, kihkháasuw VAI; **be marked black, have a black mark, have a black stripe** nzukeekháasuw VII, nzukeekháasuw VAI; **be marked in a straight line** shaaxkeekháasuw VII, shaaxkeekháasuw VAI; **be marked red, have red stripes** maxkeekháa=suw VII, maxkeekháasuw VAI; **be marked, be trimmed, be pruned** *(of trees)* laalsháasuw VAI; **have spots on it, have a line of spots on it, be marked with spots** sàsàpeekháasuw VII, sàsàpeekháasuw VAI.

**marry** VI **marry and add on to one's family, take on relatives** aandshii=lúndam VOTI1.

**marry** VT **marry s.o.** takwapŭwáaleew VTA, wiitawéemeew VTA; **get married** takwápuw VAI **I want to get married.** 'Ngáta-takwápi.'; **get married** wii=tawéengeew VAI; **marry into a certain family** lushiilúndam VAI; **marry into a certain family** lushiilúngeew VAI **It serves him right for marrying into that family.** 'Kách káa wáak ná wtulshiilúngeen.'

**Mary** N méeliis NA; **little round Mary** pchúkwu-meelíishush NA.

**mash** VT **pound s.t. animate, mash s.t. animate** shàshkwáheew VTA.

**mask** N **mask, false face mask, scarecrow, someone dressed up with a false face** msíingw NA.

**mat** N **corn husk mat** wtéeskwii-ehah=palíhkeeng NI, wtéeskw NI.

**material** N **bandage, wrapping paper, material used for wrapping** wiix=kweeptíikan NI; **bedding material** anaanzŭwahíikan NI; **be transparent, be thin** *(of material)* shiikalúsuw VAI shíikaleew VII.

**matted** ADJ **have tangled hair, have matted hair, have messy hair** piik=wshaalóhkweew VAI.

**maul** N móokul NA; **get hit on the head with a maul, have a bump on the head** mookŭlaandpéexiin VAI; **hit s.o. with a maul** *(on the head)* mookŭ=lihtéeheew VTA **I'm going to hit him with a maul.** 'Ápih nŭmookŭlihtée=ha.'; **maul** móokul NA.

**maybe** ADV **maybe** téet PC **I have an itchy head, maybe I'm lousy.** 'Ngushiipáandpa, téet ndawiilpíishi.', **I'm weak, maybe I'm hungry.** 'Nzháwsi, téet ngatóopwi.'; **maybe** éet PC **Maybe it's going to rain.** 'Píht éet katá-sóokŭlaan.', **That must be it.** 'Nún éet há.'; **maybe, emphatic** xéet PC **That's not the one.** 'Máh xéet ná.', **I wonder if he's there yet.** 'Wách xéet náh péew.'; **maybe, perhaps** píht PC **Maybe it will snow.** 'Píht éet katá-wíineew.', **You might be able to sleep.** 'Píht áa kíish- áa -kawíim.'

**me** PR **I, me** níi PR **That's what I said.** 'Nún há níi nzíin.', **It's my turn.** 'Níi áashtee.'

**measles** N **get measles, get chicken pox, come out in blotches, come out in spots** saakpéhleew VAI; **have measles, have scarlet fever, turn red** maxkíhleew VAI.

**measure** VT **measure s.o.** kwsáheew VTA; **measure the dimensions of s.t.**

kwsáham VTI1A; **measure the size of s.o, measure the height of s.o., measure s.t. animate out, fill s.t. animate to the brim** *(as a pail)* tpúskhweew VTA; **measure the size of s.t., measure the height of s.t., measure s.t. out** tpúskhwam VTI1A; **measure things** kwsahíikeew VAI; **measure things** tpuskhíikeew VAI.

**measurement** N **a certain length** *(of time, measurement)* sahkii- PV; **a certain length** *(of time, measurement)* sahku PC *informal* **He lived with her for a long time, and she really dominated my uncle for a long time.** 'Kwúnii-wiitaawsoomáawal, tá sáhku shíikaanzh lúkih wtalŭwihkawáawal nzhíisal.'; **a certain length** *(of time, measurement)* sahku- PV *informal* **I've been working since this morning.** 'Séhku-wáapang ndalóhke.', **I waited for him until two o'clock.** 'Mbéehaaw sáhku-níish-kŭlakíike.'; **a certain length** *(of time, measurement)* sáhkii PC **For nine months.** 'Sáhkii nóoli kíishooxkw.'; **be short** *(of a measurement)* liiwíhleew VAI **The paper wasn't long enough.** 'Liiwíhleew pámbiil.'; **be short** *(of a measurement)* liiwíhleew VII **The cloth wasn't long enough.** 'Liiwíh=leew wshapakwíiwan.'; **be short** *(of a measurement)* liiwíixun VII **The boards are not long enough.** 'Pasii=káaxkwal liiwíixŭnool.'

**measuring stick** N **something used for measuring, ruler, measuring tape, measuring stick** tpuskhíikan NI.

**meat** N wŭyóos NI; **cold meat** théewakw NI; **lean meat** mooshéewakw NI; **raw meat, unsalted meat** askéewakw NI.

**medicine** N **medicine** wchápihk NI; **bewitch s.o., use medicine to influence s.o.** mŭtáanheew VTA; **good medicine** wŭlaapasíhkan NI.

**meet** VI **gather together, meet** maa=wehléewak VAI *usually plural.*

**meet** VT **meet s.o.** ngíiskaweew VTA; **meet s.t.** ngíiskam VTI1A; **miss s.o., miss meeting s.o.** mehtxíhkaweew VTA.

**meeting** N **'testify' at a religious meeting, 'testify' in church** pasukwtóon=heew VAI; **speak** *(especially in public)*, **speak at a meeting, speak at a gathering** aaptóoneew VAI **Now he's speaking (as of a baby starting to talk)** 'Kwáy méhch aaptóone.'; **speak** *(especially in public)*, **speak at a meeting, speak at a gathering** aap=tóoneew VAI.

**Melbourne** N **Melbourne, Ontario** mílalung PC **Every time they go to Melbourne, it's raining.** 'Héesh-mílalung -áhtiit, sóokŭlaan.'

**melt** VI lungíhleew VAI, lungíhleew VII, lúngsuw VAI, lúngteew VII.

**melt** VT **melt s.t.** lúngsum VTI1A; **melt s.t. animate** lúngseew VTA; **be melted** *(by heat)* lungsáasuw VII, lungsáasuw VAI.

**memorize** VT **memorize s.t.** shash=kwakíindam VTI1A.

**memory** N **say things from memory, recite from memory** shàshkwak=íinzuw VAI.

**menopause** N **be an old woman, undergo menopause, undergo change of life** kihtoxkwéesuw VAI.

**mentally** ADV **be mentally ill** kpuchee=wíineew VAI.

**mention** VT **name s.o., mention s.o. by name, call s.o. by name** wíhleew VTA **I call him by that name.** 'Ndáaylu-wíhlaaw.'; **name s.t., mention s.t. by name, call s.t. by name** wíindam VTI1A; **be named, be mentioned** wiindáasuw VII; **be named, be mentioned by name** wihlkwúsuw VAI.

**mermaid** N wehwtúnŭwees NA.

**mess** N **cut things up and make a mess, make a mess while cutting**

aniiskshíikeew VAI; **make a mess, do a messy job, do dirty work, do unsatisfactory work** niiskalóhkeew VAI.

**messily** ADV **write messily** niiskeekhíi= keew VAI **I'm writing all over.** 'Wéemi táa ndúlu-niiskeekhíike.'

**messy** ADJ **have a ragged beard, have a messy beard** piikwshihtóonayeew VAI; **have messy hair** piikwsháand= peew VAI, sayaandpéexiin VAI; **have messy writing** amateckhíikeew VAI; **have tangled hair, have matted hair, have messy hair** piikwshaalóh= kweew VAI; **make a mess, do a messy job, do dirty work, do unsatisfactory work** niiskalóhkeew VAI.

**metal** N **make a noise on metal, hit something metallic that makes noise** taliinghwáhkweew VAI.

**Methodist minister** N mehttusíiwu-pehpŭmutóonhees NA.

**middle** ADJ **in the middle** leeláawii PC **When I had gone half way.** 'Éenda-leeláawii -payáane.'; **in the middle** léelaa PC **I'm sitting in the middle.** 'Léelaa lùmatápi.', **He's walking in the middle.** 'Léelaa pŭmúsuw.'; **be big and round, be big around the middle, be big in girth** xwáhkwsuw VAI; **be the middle of the grass** laa= waskwíhkeew VII; **in the middle of the high weeds** laawáskwe PC **He's walking in the middle of the high weeds.** 'Laawáskwe pŭmúsuw.', **I was sticking out of the weeds up to my neck.** 'Laawáskwe nóonj-saak= xoonéexiin.'; **middle** laawii- PV; **middle finger** leeláawŭlunj NI; **middle of the forehead** laawaaxkaláwe PC; **middle of the town, middle of the village** laawootéenay PC **It's there in the middle of town.** 'Laawootéenay áhte.'; **be the middle of a room** laawúndeew VII.

**midnight** N **be midnight** láawii-tpíhkat VII.

**might** VI awúyee PC **I might slip.** 'Awúyee nooshanzhíhla.', **I might drink too much.** 'Awúyee noosaa= mwíisŭmwi.'; **might** *(undeclared intention)* táas PC **I might go to town.** 'Táas-uch ootéeneeng ndá.', **I might go to church.** 'Táas-uch nŭmáw-maawéewi.'; **might** *(undeclared intention)* táasa PC **I might buy it.** 'Táasa áa nŭmáhlamun.', **I might go to town.** 'Táasa áa ootéeneeng ndá.'; **might, future** ápih PC **I'll be back.** 'Ápih láapii mbáam.', **The owl might hear you.** 'Ápih kóokhoos kpún= daakw.'

**mild** ADJ **be a warm night, be a mild night** wtákanii-tpíhkat VII; **be warm out, be mild out** wtákaneew VII; **mild** wtakanii- PV **Because it is a mild evening.** 'Éelii-wtákanii-láakwiik.', **It's a warm night.** 'Wtákanii-tpíhkat.'

**milk** N mŭlúk NI; **be milking, milk an animal** siiníikeew VAI; **buttermilk, sour milk** shŭwíi-mŭlúk NI; **milk s.o.** síineew VTA.

**milk snake** N mŭlukáxkook NA.

**mill** N **mill, grinder** shkwahíikan NI.

**mind** N **be certain about s.o., have one's mind made up about s.o.** mayaa= wéelŭmeew VTA; **be certain, be sure, have one's mind made up** mayaa= weelúndam VOTI1 **Now I'm sure that Lyle's not coming home.** 'Kwáy nŭmayaaweelúndam máh há péewu Lyle.', **I'm sure that it's going to rain.** 'Nŭmayaaweelúndam katá-sóokŭlaan.'; **be out of one's mind** wanáatam VAI; **be out of one's mind with grief** wanahkwateelúndam VOTI1; **be out of one's mind, be unconscious** wanahkwatéhleew VAI; **have a calm mind** kŭlameelúndam VOTI1; **have a peaceful mind, have a calm mind** kŭlamahtéenamuw VAI; **keep s.t. in mind** kŭleelúndam VTI1A; **make up one's mind** kiisheelúndam VOTI1;

**make up one's mind** kiishiitéeheew VAI; **remind s.o., bring something to s.o.'s mind** mihkóomeew VTA.

**minister** N **Anglican minister** eeng=lushmaaníiwu-pehpŭmutóonhees NA; **Methodist minister** mehttusíiwu-pehpŭmutóonhees NA.

**mink** N wiiníingwus NA.

**mirror** N pehpŭnáwus NA; **look in a mirror** pehpŭnáwsuw VAI.

**miscarriage** N **have a miscarriage** shkwáteew VAI.

**mishear** VT **misunderstand s.o., mishear s.o., hear s.o. erroneously, don't hear s.o. correctly** chanus=táweew VTA; **misunderstand s.t., mishear s.t., hear s.t. erroneously, don't hear s.t. correctly** chanústam VTI1A.

**misleading** ADJ **look deceptive, look misleading** pahchoolŭweewiináakw=suw VAI.

**miss** VT **come too late, miss an opportunity, miss one's chance** mehtxíh=keew VAI **The service was over when I arrived, I came too late.** 'Kíishi-maawéewiin náh peeyayáane, nŭ=mehtxíhke.'; **drop food from one's mouth, have food fall out of one's mouth, miss one's mouth while eating** palándam VOTI1; **drop s.t. animate from one's mouth, have s.t. animate fall out of one's mouth, miss one's mouth with s.t. animate** *(of food)* palámeew VTA; **drop s.t. from one's mouth, have s.t. fall out of one's mouth, miss one's mouth with s.t.** palándam VTI1A; **fall in sitting, miss one's seat** palapíhleew VAI; **miss an event, miss a regular event** palíhleew VAI; **miss at hitting s.o., miss at hitting s.t. animate** palihtée=heew VTA; **miss at hitting s.t.** palih=téeham VTI1A; **miss hitting s.o., miss hitting s.t. animate** *(using a tool or instrument)* paláheew VTA; **miss hitting s.t.** *(using a tool or instrument)* paláham VTI1A; **miss one's seat while sitting down, fall while sitting** pa=lápuw VAI; **miss s.o.** kwiilóomeew VTA; **miss s.o., miss meeting s.o.** mehtxíhkaweew VTA; **miss stepping on s.o., miss stepping on s.t. animate** palíhkaweew VTA; **miss stepping on s.t.** palíhkam VTI1A.

**missing** ADJ **be chipped, have a chip missing, have a chunk missing** kwashát VII, kwashúsuw VAI.

**mistake** N **by mistake, in error** chanu- PV *informal* **You said it wrong.** 'Kchánu-íin.'; **make a mistake in doing s.t.** palíhtoow VTI2 **I made a mistake in making the cake.** 'Mbal=íhtoon shookŭlápwaan.'; **make a mistake in putting s.t. animate on, put s.t. animate on wrongly** chaníixŭ=meew VTA; **make a mistake in putting s.t. on, put s.t. on wrongly** cha=níixtoow VTI2; **make a mistake in sewing s.t. animate, sew s.t. animate wrongly, sew s.t. animate in the wrong place** chaniikwáaleew VTA; **make a mistake in sewing s.t., sew s.t. wrongly, sew s.t. in the wrong place** chaníikwam VTI1A; **make a mistake in writing** chaneekhíikeew VAI; **mistakenly reveal some information, 'let the cat out of the bag'** pahtaaptóoneew VAI; **pick s.o. up by mistake, touch s.o. by mistake** páh=tŭneew VTA; **pick s.t. up by mistake, touch s.t. by mistake** páhtŭnum VTI1B.

**mistake for** VT **mistake s.o. for someone else** pahchíinaweew VTA; **mistake s.t. for something else** pahchíinam VTI1A.

**misty** ADJ **be fine rain, be misty rain** awáhŭlaan VII; **be foggy, be misty** awaníixun VII.

**misunderstand** VT **misunderstand s.o., mishear s.o., hear s.o. erroneously, don't hear s.o. correctly** chanustáw=

eew VTA; **misunderstand s.t., mishear s.t., hear s.t. erroneously, don't hear s.t. correctly** chanústam VTI1A.

**mitt** N wánd NA; **make mitts** wándheew VAI; **put on one's mitts** piindŭnii=wándeew VAI.

**mix** VT **mix s.o. in with others** kohla=wíixŭmeew VTA; **mix s.t. in with others** kohlawíixtoow VTI2; **mix s.t. in with something** kohlawáaheew VAIO; **be mixed in with others** kohlawíi=xiin VAI, kohlawíixun VII; **be mixed together in a liquid** takwaapŭweh=léewal VII; **get mixed in** *(with something)* kohlawíhleew VAI **He got mixed in with the crowd.** 'Kohlawíhleew éenda-xwéelung.'; **get mixed in** *(with something)* kohlawíhleew VII; **grow mixed in with other** kohlawíikuw VAI, kohlawíikun VII; **mixed, mixed in** *(with something)* kóhla PC **You're part Indian.** 'Kíi kóhla kŭlunaapée=wi.', **There's some water mixed in with the vinegar.** 'Shŭwáapoow kóhla mbúy náh áhteew.'

**mixed up** ADJ **be mixed up, be confused** chàchanaandpéhleew VAI; **have disorganized colours, have mixed up colours** pàpŭlakaapamúkwat VII, pàpŭ=lakaapamúkwsuw VAI.

**moan** VI múndaweew VAI.

**moccasin** N shoopéekal NI *usually plural.*

**Mohawk** N chkáhaaw NA.

**moisture** N **swell from moisture, swell in moisture** páaspeew VII **The wood is swollen from dampness.** 'Xwús páaspeew.'

**molasses** N **syrup, molasses** mŭlée=shiish NI.

**Molly** N máaliish NA.

**moment** N **see s.o. briefly, see s.o. for a moment** laashíinaweew VTA; **see s.t. briefly, see s.t. for a moment** laa=shíinam VTI1A; **touch s.t. briefly, touch s.t. for a moment** láashu-lúnum VTI1A.

**Monday** N **be Monday** mándeew VII **It's not Monday.** 'Píish máhta mandée=wu.', **I went there last Monday.** 'Éenda-mandéeke náh nóom.'

**money** N shúlpul NI; **be broke, have spent all one's money** pohkwíhleew VAI; **bet, play for money** ahtíikeew VAI; **earn money, earn a wage** pŭ=náham VOTI1; **have money** wshulpúl=ŭmuw VAI; **make a contribution, put money in the collection plate** maa=wéewapuw VAI, máawapuw VAI.

**monkey** N móngiis NA.

**mood** N **feel sad, be sad, be in a bad mood** mateelúndam VOTI1.

**moon** N niipáahum NA; **be new** *(especially of babies)*, **be a new moon** wúskapuw VAI; **be round** *(s.t. animate)*, **be full** *(of the moon)* ptúkw=suw VAI.

**moonlight** N **be moonlight** wŭleeláh=kameew VII.

**moose** N móos NA.

**Moraviantown** N **Moraviantown, Ontario** náahii PC *'downstream.'*

**more** ADJ **more** hálŭwii PC **I speak badly.** 'Hálŭwii njachíipsi.'; **more** njíhnal PC **Do you want to know some more?** 'Njíhnal kwéek káta-weewíhto?', **I don't go with her anymore.** 'Kwáy máh há njíhnal nŭwiicheewáawu.'; **more, more than, early** aluwii- PV **Early afternoon.** 'Alúwii-laawah=kwéewŭnii.'; **more, more than, early** alúwii PC.

**morning** N **in the morning** ayapáawŭ=nii PC, ayapáayu PC **I got up first in the morning before he did.** 'Mbúm=ŭnaa ayapáayu níi nzháye-áamwi.'; **in the morning** nayapáawunii PC **I'll see you in the morning.** 'Nayapáa=wŭnii-uch kŭnéewul.'; **be an unpleasant morning** matáapan VII; **early in the morning** kihtayapáayu PC; **live until morning** *(of a sick per-*

*son)* waapanáaxiin VAI; **live until morning** waapanámuw VAI.

**mortar** N takwaháakan NI.

**mosquito** N sakíimeew NA.

**most** ADJ **alone, on its own, the most, the best** *(of something)* nxoo- PV **He's the tallest.** 'Wŭnáxoo-kwŭnáhk=wsiin.', **I'm the best cook.** 'Náxoo-nihtaawatúpwiin.'

**moth** N póngwush NA, wtohwaníingwus NA.

**mother my mother** ngúk NAD **Mother (vocative)** 'Ngúkaa.', **Mother (vocative)** 'Ngúkaash.'; **have a mother** kwúkuw VAI; **have s.o. as a mother** kwúkuw VAIO **She is my mother.** 'Nóokkiin.', **She is his mother.** 'Ookkíinal.'; **my paternal uncle, my mother's brother, my cross-uncle** nzhíis NAD.

**mother-in-law** N **my mother-in-law** nzúkwiis NAD.

**motion** N **be put through** *(of a motion at a meeting, of business)* eeshoo=xwatáasuw VII; **push s.t., shove s.t.** *(using the hands)*, **move s.t.** *(of motions at a meeting)* kunjchúnum VTI1B.

**motion** N **be constantly in motion, be constantly in operation** ngumee=wíhleew VAI **My hammer's going all the time.** 'Ndahámŭlum ngumee=wíhleew.'; **be constantly in motion, be constantly in operation** ngumee=wíhleew VII; **defecate while in motion** maskchíhleew VAI; **push s.t., shove s.t.** *(using the hands)*, **move s.t.** *(of motions at a meeting)* kunj=chúnum VTI1B; **turn around, turn around while in motion, turn around while driving, flip over** kwŭlupíhleew VAI; **urinate while in motion, urinate while walking** shkíhleew VAI.

**mouldy** ADJ **be mouldy** kwáakwalul VAI, kwáakwalut VII.

**mound** N **be a hill, be a mound** pòw=ahkéeyeew VII, wŭlámkweew VII; **make a mound of things** wŭlam=kwihtáasuw VAI; **make s.t. into a pile, make s.t. into a mound** wŭlam=kwáaheew VAIO; **pile s.t. animate up, make s.t. animate into mounds** wŭ=lamkwaaháaleew VTA; **pile s.t. up, make s.t. into a mound** wŭlam=kwáham VTI1A; **pile s.t. up, make s.t. into mounds** wŭlamkwaaháatoow VTI2; **pile things up, make mounds, make things into mounds** *(as when hilling potatoes)* wŭlamkwahíikeew VAI.

**mountain** N **be a mountain** kwŭnaa=wúngeew VII **I walked to the mountain.** 'Ndúlu-pumúsi éenda-kwŭnaa=wúngeek.'; **mountain, hill** aman=gaawúnge PC.

**mountainous** ADJ **be hilly, be mountainous** amangaawangéeyayeew VII **I live near the mountains.** 'Níi kíixkii nŭwíiki éenda-amangaawangéeya=yeek.'

**mourning dove** N **pigeon, mourning dove** míimiiw NA.

**mouse** N aapíikwus NA.

**mouth** N **my mouth** ndóon NID; **bump one's mouth** paaktoonéexiin VAI; **close one's mouth tightly, have one's mouth closed, have one's lips pursed, pout** spwutoonéexiin VAI; **drop food from one's mouth, have food fall out of one's mouth, miss one's mouth while eating** palándam VOTI1; **drop s.t. animate from one's mouth, have s.t. animate fall out of one's mouth, miss one's mouth with s.t. animate** *(of food)* palámeew VTA; **drop s.t. from one's mouth, have s.t. fall out of one's mouth, miss one's mouth with s.t.** palándam VTI1A; **have a big mouth** xwutóo=neew VAI; **have a black mouth** nzuk=tóoneew VAI; **have a crooked mouth, have a lopsided mouth** piimtoonée=

xiin VAI; **have a dirty mouth** niisk=tóoneew VAI; **have a greasy mouth** shamutóoneew VAI; **have a scabby mouth, have scabs on one's mouth** mŭkuytóoneew VAI; **have a swollen mouth, have a bump on one's mouth** makwutóoneew VAI; **have a wide mouth** paantoonháasuw VAI; **have an odd twist to one's mouth, have an odd twist to one's lips** *(indicating a certain attitude)* maashtoonéexiin VAI; **have one's mouth open** toongtoo=néexiin VAI; **have something wrong with the shape of one's mouth, be always saying bad things about people**, **have a sore mouth** matutóo=neew VAI; **lick s.o., rub s.o. with the mouth** síikwameew VTA; **lick s.o., rub, nuzzle s.o. with mouth** láala=meew VTA; **lick s.o., wipe s.t. animate with the mouth** káasameew VTA; **lick s.t., rub on s.t. with the mouth** sii=kwándam VTI1A; **lick s.t., wipe s.t. with the mouth** kaasándam VTI1A; **pout, close one's mouth** spwutóo=neew VAI; **purse one's lips, have one's mouth in a pout, have one's mouth sticking out pointed** chpwutoonée=xiin VAI; **rub one's mouth on s.o., lap s.o., lick s.o.** síisameew VTA; **rub one's mouth on s.t, lick s.t.** siisán=dam VTI1A.

**move** VI kwchúkwiiw VAI-S; **move, stir** kwàkwchúkuw VAI **He's moving. Maybe he's alive.** 'Kwàkwchúkuw. Pŭmáawsuw éet.'; **move, stir, shake** kwchukwíhleew VAI, kwchúkwihl VAI; **be rapidly moving water** kshupéh=leew VII; **be slow-moving** alaawíiya=yuw VAI; **be unable to work, be unable to move, be unable to run, be out of order** aalŭwíhleew VII, aalŭ=wíhleew VAI; **crawl around, move around** msiikwsíhleew VAI; **make noise while moving** *(of water)* chàchxuwaapŭwéhleew VII; **move about while lying down** kwàkw=chukwíixiin VAI; **move around, stir** wàwŭyamoxkchéhleew VAI; **move on, go from one place to another** aan=dóoxweew VAI; **move, move one's residence** ngatáhkeew VAI; **shake s.t. back and forth, move s.t. back and forth, wave s.t. back and forth, rock s.t. back and forth** kwàkw=chukwáaheew VAIO; **shake, move, be thrown about** kwàkwchukwíhleew VII, kwàkwchukwíhleew VAI.

**move** VT **move s.o.** *(using the foot or body)* kwchukwíhkaweew VTA; **move s.o.** kwchúkwŭneew VTA; **move s.o. from one place to another** aandóo=xwaleew VTA; **move s.t.** *(using the foot or body)* kwchukwíhkam VTI1A; **move s.t.** kwchúkwŭnum VTI1; **move s.t. animate in a certain direction, move s.t. animate in a certain manner** *(using something held in the hand)* liikwáaleew VTA **He moved him to the back.** 'Wtéeng wtulii=kwaaláawal.'; **move s.t. from one place to another** aandóoxwatoow VTI2; **move s.t. in a certain direction, move s.t. in a certain manner** *(using something held in the hand)* líikwam VTI1A **I moved it to the front.** 'Shayéemung ndulíikwamun.', **Move it over there!** 'Yéelak líi=kwah!'; **push s.t., shove s.t.** *(using the hands)*, **move s.t.** *(of motions at a meeting)* kunjchúnum VTI1B; **be moved back and forth, be shaken back and forth** kwàkwchúkhookw VAI.

**mud** N asíiskuw NI; **be deep mud** kwŭ=nasíiskŭwat VII; **be stuck in mud** kŭ=lasíiskŭweew VAI; **pack mud on things** *(as between logs of a house)*, **pack plaster on things** asiiskŭwah=íikeew VAI; **pack mud onto s.t.** *(as of houses)*, **put plaster onto s.t.** asiis=kŭwáham VTI1A **I put mud/plaster**

**on the house.** 'Ndasiiskŭwáhŭmun wíikwahm.'

**muddy** ADJ **be a muddy road** asiiskŭ=watéexun VII; **be muddy water** asiis=kŭwáapŭweew VII; **have muddy shoes** asiiskŭwahksúneew VAI; **muddy clothes** asíiskŭwii-éhakwiing NI; **muddy shoe** asiiskŭwáhksun NI.

**multiple** N **multiple of twenty** *(in counting)* txiináxke PC *with number particle for numbers 60-90* **Eighty.** 'Xáash txiináxke.'

**multiply** VI **multiply, grow as a bunch, grow close together** mŭléekuw VAI **It's really multiplied.** 'Móxa mŭlée=kuw.'

**Munceytown** N **Munceytown, Ontario** naláhii PC *'upstream'* **I walked to Munceytown.** 'Náh naláhii ndúlupŭmúsiim.'

**Munro** N múnŭlo NA *man's name.*

**Munsee** N **Delaware Indian, Munsee Delaware Indian** múnsiiw NA.

**murder** VI **murder, kill people** níhlŭweew VAI.

**muscle** N wchéht NA.

**music** N **play loud music** niiskapíi=kweew VAI, amangapíikweew VAI.

**musical instrument** N apíikwan NI; **clarinet, wooden musical instrument** xwusapíikwan NI; **play a musical instrument** apíikweew VAI.

**musician** N ehapíikwees NA.

**muskmelon** N shpánzhpeekw NI.

**muskrat** N **muskrat** xwáskwus NA; **muskrat, Little Muskrat** *(nickname)* xwáshkwshush NA.

**must** VI **have to, must** ayáskii PC **I have to feed him by hand.** 'Ayáskii nzhashahkamóolaaw.'; **have to, must** ayásku PC *informal* **I have to leave right away.** 'Ayásku ndalŭmúsi.', **He always has to say something.** 'Ayásku ngúmee kwéek úw.'; **have to, must** ásk PC *informal* **He must be there.** 'Ásk éet náh apúw.'; **have to, must** áskii PC **I had to wait for them.** 'Áskii mbeeháawak.', **You had to tie it.** 'Áskii kùlámbtoon.'; **must be** sháxk PC *informal* **It must be cracked.** 'Sháxk éet pasát.', **He must be part white.** 'Sháxk éet shaashŭ=wánakuw.'; **must be** sháxkii PC **I guess I'll have to go.** 'Sháxkii ayásku náh ndá.'

**mustache** N **have a beard, have a mustache, have whiskers** wihtóonayuw VAI; **have a black beard, have a black mustache** nzukihtóonayeew VAI; **have a nice beard, have a nice mustache** wŭlihtóonayeew VAI; **have a small beard, have a small mustache** changihchoonayéeshuw VAI.

**mute** N **a mute, a person who can't talk** kéeptoon NA, kpútoon NA; **be mute, be unable to talk** kputóoneew VAI, akeeptóoneew VAI.

**mutter** VI **mutter, talk under one's breath** mŭnumohktóonheew VAI.

**mutton** N meemeekshéewakw NI.

# N

**nail** N mŭkóos NA.

**nail** VT **crucify s.o., nail s.o. up, nail s.o. down** psakwihtéeheew VTA **He was crucified.** 'Psakwihtéehaa.'; **nail s.t. together, hit s.t. and join it together** takwihtéehum VTI1B.

**naked** ADJ **be naked** sheexkalúsuw VAI; **get naked** sheexkalíhleew VAI; **lie naked** sheexkaláangweew VAI; **run naked** sheexkalaaméhleew VAI; **run naked, run bare** mooshakaaméhleew VAI *especially of animals with missing fur;* **sit naked** sheexkalohkwéepuw VAI; **sleep naked** sheexkalóngwaam VAI, shéexkalii-kawíiw VAI; **stand naked** sheexkaliikáapawuw VAI.

**name** N shiinzŭwáakan NI; **be named,**

be mentioned by name wihlkwúsuw VAI; **be praised, have a good name** wŭlakŭniimkwúsuw VAI; **call s.o. by a certain name** shiinzŭwáaleew VTA; **have a certain name, be named** shínzuw VAI, shiindáasuw VII; **name s.o., mention s.o. by name, call s.o. by name** wíhleew VTA **I call him by that name.** 'Ndáaylu-wíhlaaw.'; **name s.t., mention s.t. by name, call s.t. by name** wíindam VTI1A.

**name** VT **name s.o., mention s.o. by name, call s.o. by name** wíhleew VTA **I call him by that name.** 'Ndáaylu-wíhlaaw.'; **name s.t., mention s.t. by name, call s.t. by name** wíindam VTI1A; **be named, be mentioned** wiindáasuw VII; **be named, be mentioned by name** wihlkwúsuw VAI.

**nap** N **take a nap** niimaawanáhŭmeew VAI.

**napkin** N **diaper, napkin** ahpcháawan NI.

**narrow** ADJ **be narrow** wíipaweew VII **The river is narrow.** 'Wiipawée=shuw nú síipuw.'; **narrow shoe** wiipawáhksun NI.

**nationality** N **be a certain nationality, be a certain breed, be a certain make, have a certain characteristic** lahkéewuw VAI **Other races.** 'Palíi eelahkeewíhtiit.'; **have a certain characteristic** *(of people)*, **be a certain type of person** laapéewuw VAI **He's good for nothing.** 'Máh kwéek laapeewíiwu.'

**native** N **speak Delaware, speak a native language** hulŭníixsuw VAI.

**nauseous** ADJ **feel nauseous, feel sick to one's stomach** wŭyakaskíilaweew VAI; **make s.o. nauseous, make s.o. throw up, make s.o. vomit** wŭyakas=kíileew VTA.

**navel** N **my navel** mbooshíishum NAD **He's nosy (because) he lost his umbilical cord.** 'Wíhwiing sh'xeehíi=keew, pooshíishŭmal anaháate.', **You're nosy ('you've lost your navel').** 'Kpooshíishum ktánhaaw.'

**near** ADV **be near, be soon** péexŭwat VII **It will rain soon.** 'Péexŭwat sóokŭ=laan.'; **live near s.o., live close to s.o.** peexŭwiikáaleew VTA; **near** kíixkii PC **Near the house.** 'Kíixkii wiikwáh=mung.', **I lived near the mountains.** 'Níi kíixkii nŭwíiki eénda-amangaa=wungéeyayeek.'; **near** kíixku PC *informal* **He flew close by.** 'Kíixku peechíhle.'; **near to, close by, nearly** péexwiish PC **He has a little ways to the end (of the road).** 'Péexwiish wihkwáameew.', **I'm not going far.** 'Péexwiish náh ndá.'

**nearly** ADV **almost, nearly** wéenaa PC **He almost froze to death.** 'Wéenaa kŭláchuw.', **He nearly got scared to death.** 'Wéenaa aaptahpáasuw.'; **near to, close by, nearly** péexwiish PC **He has a little ways to the end (of the road).** 'Péexwiish wihkwáa=meew.', **I'm not going far.** 'Pée=xwiish náh ndá.'; **soon, nearly** pée=xoot PC **I'm almost sleeping.** 'Pée=xoot ngáwiim.', **It must be going to rain pretty soon.** 'Péexoot éet sóo=kŭlaan.'

**neat** N **have neat hair, have plastered-down hair** wŭlawéexteew VAI.

**neatly** ADV **be piled up neatly, be piled up nicely, be piled up properly** *(of something wood- or stick-like)* wŭ=lahkweexíinook VAI *usually plural*, wŭlahkwéexŭnool VII *usually plural*.

**neck** N oxkweekángan NI **That's right! ('You bet your neck!').** 'Ktahtíike koxkweekánganum!'; **my back of neck** nihtángan NID; **break s.o.'s neck** kaxkxoonéeheew VTA; **break s.o.'s neck** *(using the hands)* kaxk=xoonéeneew VTA, *(using the hands)* tŭmiikwéeneew VTA; **break s.o.'s neck, sever s.o. at the neck, break**

**s.o. at the neck, cut s.o. off at the neck** tŭmiikwéeheew VTA; **drop s.o. and sever their neck** tŭmiikwéexŭ=meew VTA; **have a broken neck** tŭmiikwéexiin VAI; **have a long neck** kwŭnaxóoneew VAI; **have a stiff neck** chiingaalxoonéexiin VAI, chiingaal=xóoneew VAI; **have a swollen neck, have one's neck swell up** paasxóo=neew VAI; **have something around one's neck** wahkwéelŭnuw VAI; **hit and break s.o.'s neck** tŭmiikweh=téeheew VTA; **hug s.o. around the neck** kihkoxkwéeneew VTA; **stick one's neck out, have one's neck sticking out** saakxoonéexiin VAI; **wear s.t. around one's neck** wah=kwéelŭnuw VAIO **She's got beads around her neck.** 'Wahkwéelŭnuw maanzháapŭyal.'; **wear something around the neck, wear a scarf, wear jewellery** wiilawahkwéelŭnuw VAI.

**necklace** N **wear a necklace** laapxoo=néexiin VAI, laapxóoneew VAI.

**necktie** N **scarf, collar, necktie, horse's collar** wehwahkwéelŭniing NI.

**need** VT **want s.t., need s.t.** katáatam VTI1A; **be wanted, be needed** kataal=kwúsuw VAI, katáalkwat VII; **rely on s.o., depend on s.o., need s.o.'s help** nahkáaleew VTA.

**needle** N ambiilaméekwaan NA.

**negative** ADJ **no, not, negative** máh PC **It's not cooked enough.** 'Máh téep-kiishtéewi.', **He has no parents.** 'Máh kihkeesíiwi.'; **no, not, negative** máhta PC **It's not raining here.** 'Yóh máhta lí sookŭlaanóowi.', **I don't kill birds anymore.** 'Máhta níi njíhnal nihlaawíiwak awehleeshóoshak.'

**nerve** N **be in earnest, be serious** *(about something)*, **get up the nerve** *(to do something)* kihteelúndam VOTI1 **I'm serious about going there.** 'Ngihteelúndam náh ndá.', **I got up the nerve to tell him to go home.** 'Ngihteelúndam, ndúlaa máachiil.'

**nervous** ADJ **be afraid, be nervous** nahtáachuw VAI; VT **be frightened of s.t., be nervous about s.t.** kwíhtam VTI1A.

**nest** N wshíixay NI; **make a nest** wshii=xayáheew VAI.

**net** N **fishing net** akwaaníikan NA; **fish with a net** akwáanŭmeew VAI.

**nettle** N laalamúwees NA, lehlóosiing NI, lehlóosŭweeng NI.

**never** ADV wíixka PC **He never came.** 'Máhta wíixka péewi.', **I never went there.** 'Máh wíixka náh noomóowi.'

**new** ADJ **new, young** wuskii- PN **A new book.** 'Wúskii-pámbiil.'; **be new** *(especially of babies)*, **be a new moon** wúskapuw VAI; **be new, be young** wúsksuw VAI, wúskun VII; **have new shoes** wuskahksúneew VAI; **jump to a new location** aandáakchehl VAI; **look new, look young** wuskiináakwat VII, wuskiináakwsuw VAI; **new chair** wuskáhpapoon NI; **new cloth** wusk=shapakwíiwan NI; **new corn, green corn** wuskxáskwiim NI; **new house** wuskíikaan NI; **new potato** wuskíh=pun NA; **new shoe** wuskáhksun NI; **wear new clothes** wúskakuw VAI; **young pig, new pig** wuskóoshkoosh NA.

**New Year's Day** N néwiyaal PC **Happy New Year!** 'Néwiyaal!'; **celebrate New Year's day** newiyáaliin VAI *indefinite subject only*.

**news** N **bring news to here from s.o., bring news to s.o.** peetaachŭmóhka=weew VTA; **bring news, spread the word** peetaachíimuw VAI; **know all the news, hear everything, hear all the gossip** wihwéewsuw VAI; **know the news, hear the news, know what's going on** wéewsuw VAI.

**newspaper** N noospépul NA.

**next** ADJ **instead, next, then** áashtee PC **I'll go there instead.** 'Áashtee-uch yéelak ndá.', **I'll use this instead, I'll wear this instead.** 'Áashtee-uch yóon ndawéeheen.'

**nice** ADJ **nice, good** pshihki- PN **A good man.** 'Pshíhki-lúnuw.'; **nice, good** pshihku- PN *informal* **A nice horse.** 'Pshíhku-nehnayóongus.', **A nice dog.** 'Pshíhku-mwáakaneew.'; **nice, good** pshihku- PV *informal* **He has a nice disposition.** 'Pshíhku-únd.'; **nice, good** wŭli- PV **He has a nice tail.** 'Wŭlí-shkwúnayeew.'; **nice, good** wŭlu- PV *informal* **We had two horses, and one was very nice.** 'Níishŭwak nehnayóongsak ngaxa=níhna, mayáawsuw móxa wúlu-und.', **He supported that girl well and treated her well, but this girl would always leave.** 'Óolu-tapaaláawal yóol oxkwéessal wáak oolaliiháawal, shúkw wá oxkwéesus ngúmee alúm=suw.'; **be a nice day** wŭláhkameew VII; **be a nice person** pshíhku-awée=nuw VAI; **be a nice wind** wŭláxun VII; **be in a nice place, be well seated, have a good home** *(of an adopted child or a person in heaven)* wŭlápuw VAI; **be nice, be good, be pleasant, be good-natured** wŭliitéeheew VAI; **be pretty, be good, be nice** wŭlúsuw VAI, wŭlút VII; **have a nice beard, have a nice mustache** wŭlihtóona=yeew VAI; **have a nice smell** *(of something cooking)* wiingiimasúmeew VAI, wiingíimateew VII; **have fine hair, have nice hair, have good hair** wŭlaalóhkweew VAI; **have nice eyes** weewŭlaalakíingweew VAI; **look good, be nice looking, have a nice appearance** wŭliináakwat VII, wŭliináakw=suw VAI; **look not very nice** lunŭwii=náakwat VII, lunŭwiináakwsuw VAI **My car doesn't look very nice.** 'Lun=ŭwiináakwsuw ngáalum.'; **sound good, sound nice** wŭlihtáakwat VII, wŭlihtáakwsuw VAI.

**nicely** ADV **be nicely browned** wŭlúch=asuw VAI, wŭlúchateew VII; **be pretty, be evenly shaped, be nicely shaped** wŭluchéesuw VAI, wŭluchéeyeew VII; **cut a pattern, cut things nicely** wŭlushíikeew VAI; **cut s.t. animate nicely, cut s.t. animate in a pattern** wŭlúsheew VTA; **cut s.t. nicely, cut s.t. in a pattern** wŭlúshum VTI1B; **dress s.o. nicely, put bedcovers on s.o.** wŭlakwunáheew VTA.

**nick** VT **almost hit s.o., 'nick' s.o.** chaskihtéeheew VTA.

**nickname** N píipush NA *man's nickname;* pshúm NA *nickname;* njík NA *nickname for person named Julia.*

**night** N **be night** píiskeew VII **I went there last night.** 'Piiskéeke náh ndá.', **I'll go there tonight.** 'Piiskéeke-uch náh ndá.'; **get to be night** piiskéh=leew VII; **night, at night** piiskéewŭnii PC **Just at night.** 'Piiskéewŭnii áng shúkw.' **be a cold night** thíi-tpíhkat VII; **be a warm night, be a mild night** wtákanii-tpíhkat VII; **be gone for many nights, be gone for many days** xweelookwŭnáhkeew VAI; **be gone overnight** ngwutookwŭnáh=keew VAI; **be many nights, be many days** xweelookwŭnákat VII.

**nighthawk** N píishkw NA.

**nightmare** N **wake after a bad dream, wake up screaming, have a nightmare** akiiwóngxwiin VAI.

**nine** N nóolii PC **Nineteen.** 'Nóoli txaa=níhka.'

**nipple** N **my breast, my nipple** noo=náakan NID.

**no** ADV **no longer require s.o.'s services** ehkwalóoleew VTA; **no, not, negative** máh PC **It's not cooked enough.** 'Máh téep-kiishtéewi.', **He has no parents.** 'Máh kihkeesíiwi.'; **no, not, negative** máhta PC **It's not raining here.** 'Yóh máhta lí sookŭlaanóowi.', **I don't kill birds anymore.** 'Máhta níi njíhnal nihlaawíiwak awehlee=shóoshak.'

**no one** PR **be an empty town, be no one in town** alaxootéenayuw VII.

**no-good** ADJ **my no-good friend** nŭ=matchóosum NAD.

**nod** VI **bug species with nodding head** tàtamakohkwehláashiit NA, tàtamak=ohkwéhlaash NA; **nod one's head** tamakohkwéhleew VAI, tàtamakoh=kwaandpéhleew VAI; **nod s.t.** *(of one's head)* àhahtéhtoow VTI2.

**noise** N **bawl, holler, make noise** *(of vocal sounds)* sáangweew VAI **The frogs are bawling.** 'Chkwálak saangwéewak.'; **be a great noise, be a big rumour, be a great report of an activity** *(especially of a story that gets modified or exaggerated)* kaan=zhihtáakwat VII; **cluck, make a noise like a chicken** kwŭlukhwámeew VAI; **drive and make a loud noise, make a rattling noise while driving** *(of wagon wheels)* tiiwchéhleew VAI; **drop s.t. animate so that it makes a sharp noise** chàhwihtéexŭmeew VTA; **drop s.t. so that it makes a sharp noise** chàhwihtéextoow VTI2; **drop s.t. so that it makes a sharp noise** chàh=wíixtoow VTI2; **fall and make a loud noise** tiiwíixiin VAI, tiiwíixun VII; **fall and make a noise, fall and make a dull noise, fall with a thud** pòh=wíixun VII, pwàhwíixun VII; **fall and make a noise, fall and make a dull noise, fall with a thud, fall down hard, fall flat on one's face** pwàh=wíixiin VAI; **fall and make a sharp noise when dropped** chàhwíixiin VAI, chàhwíixun VII; **fall down and make a noise** pwàhwihtéexiin VAI; **hit s.o. so that they make a sharp noise** chàhwihtéeheew VTA; **make a certain kind of noise** lúweew VAI **I'm making all kinds of noise.** 'Wéemi táa ndayŭlúween.'; **make a great noise** kaanzhihtáakwsuw VAI; **make a lot of noise** shòhwŭnáakwsuw VAI **The mouse was making a lot of noise somewhere.** 'Aapíikwus táa wtúnda-shòhwŭnáakwsiin.'; **make a lot of noise, make a big noise** amángŭ=weew VII; **make a lot of noise, make a big noise** amángŭweew VAI; **make a noise** kunjíimuw VAI; **make a noise like an animal, make a crowing noise** akeenjíimuw VAI; **make a noise on metal, hit something metallic that makes noise** taliinghwáhkweew VAI; **make a noise while shuffling one's feet** shòhwsiitéexiin VAI; **make a shuffling noise while dancing** shóhwkeew VAI; **make an irritating noise, make an annoying noise** níiskŭweew VII, níiskŭweew VAI; **make noise** *(of water)* chàchxúweew VII **My belly is making noise.** 'Ndáy chàch=xúweew.'; **make noise** kòhŭnáakw=suw VAI; **make noise** *(once)* ngwuta=láamuw VAI; **make noise** shóhweew VAI *usually of non-humans* **The birds are making noise.** 'Shohwéewak awehleeshóoshak.'; **make noise in a certain place** talúweew VAI **He's making noise close by.** 'Péexwiish talúweew.'; **make noise while moving** *(of water)* chàchxuwaapŭwéh=leew VII; **make noise with one's feet** pwàhwsiitéexiin VAI; **make noise, make a lot of noise** káanzhŭweew VAI, káanzhŭweew VII; **make s.t. make noise** *(especially when blowing a horn)* kaanzhŭwéhtoow VTI2; **noise** paakwáakan NI **They're awfully noisy.** 'Móxa paakwáakan.'; **pound and make a noise, hit and make a noise** *(on wood, on solid objects)* tiiwháhkweew VAI; **ring a bell, make a ringing noise** *(on metal)* taliing=hwíikeew VAI; **ring, make a ringing noise, make a tinny noise** taliin=gwihtéexun VII; **start to make noise**

nóotŭweew VAI; **talk lots, make noise** paakwéenzuw VAI; **throw s.o. down hard so as to make a loud noise, set s.o. down hard so as to make a loud noise** tiiwíixŭmeew VTA; **throw s.t down hard so as to make a loud noise, set s.t down hard so as to make a loud noise** tiiwíixtoow VTI2; **walk and make a loud noise** tiiwóo=xweew VAI.

**noisy** ADJ **be noisy** niiskihtáakwat VII, niiskihtáakwsuw VAI.

**nominate** VT **nominate s.o. for an office, nominate s.o. for a position** kiishíimeew VTA.

**noontime** N laawahkwéewŭni PC **It's almost noon.** 'Péexoot laawahkwée=wŭni.'; **be noontime** laawáhkweew VII.

**north** N loowanéewung PC; **be a north wind** loowanáxun VII.

**nose** N **my nose** nihkíiwan NID; **blow one's nose** saníikuw VAI; **break s.o.'s nose** kaxkchaaléeheew VTA; **bump one's nose against something** paak=chaaléexiin VAI; **have a big nose** xwucháaleew VAI; **have a bloody nose** mohkwcháaleew VAI, mŭkíhtaneew VAI; **have a broken nose** kaxkcháa=leew VAI; **have a dirty nose** niisk=cháaleew VAI; **have a flat nose** pàk=cháaleew VAI; **have a long nose** kwŭ=nucháaleew VAI; **have a red nose** maxkcháaleew VAI; **have a runny nose** niiskŭlaníikameew VAI, sihtaníi=neew VAI; **have a scabby nose, have scabs on one's nose** mŭkuycháaleew VAI; **have a small nose** *(diminutive)* changchaaléeshuw VAI; **have a swollen nose, have a bump on one's nose** makwucháaleew VAI; **have a swollen nose, have one's nose swell up** paascháaleew VAI; **have one's nose broken, have a broken nose** kaxk=chaaléexiin VAI; **hit and flatten one's nose against something** pàkchaaleh=téexiin VAI; **stick one's nose out, have one's nose sticking out** ktuch=aaléexiin VAI; **wipe one's nose** kaas=cháaleew VAI.

**nosy** ADJ **be nosy, want to know things** katá-wéewsuw VAI, kíhkata-wéewsuw VAI.

**not** **no, not, negative** máh PC **It's not cooked enough.** 'Máh téep-kiishtée=wi.', **He has no parents.** 'Máh kih=keesíiwi.'; **no, not, negative** máhta PC **It's not raining here.** 'Yóh máhta lí sookŭlaanóowi.', **I don't kill birds anymore.** 'Máhta níi njíhnal nihlaa=wíiwak awehleeshóoshak.'; **not very often, a few times** táatxun PC **I drank my medicine a few times.** 'Táatxun noochapíhkum nŭmúneen.', **I didn't go to town very often.** 'Ootéeneeng táatxun ndá.'; **not very, hardly at all** mánheel PC *followed by negative verb* **He hardly ever works.** 'Mánheel iiyalohkéewi.', **It's not a very nice day.** 'Mánheel wŭlahkaméewi.'; **not yet** éeskwa PC *followed by negative verb* **I didn't get a letter yet.** 'Éeskwa létul nŭmushŭnáawi.', **I didn't eat yet.** 'Éeskwa nŭmiitsíiwi.'; ADV **be deficient, be lacking, be short of something, be not quite enough of something, fall short** noondéexiin VAI, noondéexun VII; **be not enough of something** noondaawíixun VII; **don't** chíi PC **Don't help him!** 'Chíi wiichŭmáawu!', **Don't go to sleep!** 'Chíi kawíiwi!'; **don't** chíile PC **Don't go that way!** 'Chíile náh áawu!', **Don't eat those strawberries!** 'Chíilu níil wteehíimal miichíiwu!'; **look not very nice** lunŭwiináakwat VII, lunŭ=wiináakwsuw VAI **My car doesn't look very nice.** 'Lunŭwiináakwsuw ngáalum.'; **very little, not a lot** cháachxiish PC **I slept very little.** 'Cháachxiish ngáwi.', **I didn't work a lot.** 'Cháachxiish ndalóhke.'

**not at all** ADV **hardly, not at all** msúchee PC **That's not so; no way.** 'Msúchee máh nú léewi.', **When he got to my mother's he told her, "Now I'm not going to talk to her anymore and I don't want her at all."** 'Peeyáatu ngúkung wtuláawal, "Kwáy máh há njíhnal ngihkihkŭlooláawu, wáak ngataaláawu msúchee."'

**nothing** N **eat s.t. alone, eat s.t. with nothing else** mooshándam VTI1A **Don't eat it alone, eat it with bread.** 'Chíi mooshandamóowi, náxpumíichiil apwáan.'; **eat s.t. animate alone, eat s.t. animate with nothing else** móoshameew VTA.

**notify** VT **notify s.o.** amáameew VTA **I was notified.** 'Ndamáamkee.'

**now** ADV kwáy PC **Go to sleep right away (you plural)!** 'Kwáy sháawu kawíikw!', **I'm going there today.** 'Kwáy kíishkwihk ápih náh ndáan.'; **now** méhch PC **He's returned from working.** 'Méhch aapalóhkeew.', **Have you washed your face yet?** 'Méhch há kùsíingwe?'; **live to a certain age, live until now** peetáawsuw VAI **I've lived to the age where I can't go anywhere.** 'Náh mbeetáaw=si éenda-áalu- tá -ayáan.'

**nudge** VT **nudge s.o., kick s.o., poke s.o.** *(to get his or her attention)* kiix=kíhkaweew VTA; **poke s.o., nudge s.o.** *(to get his or her attention)* kíixkŭ=neew VTA.

**nuisance** N **be a nuisance** sàkwaxk=túyeew VAI.

**numb** ADJ **be numb** pihkŭwúsuw VAI **My knee is numb.** 'Pihkŭwúsuw ngútko.'; **be numb** píhkeew VII **My hand is numb.** 'Náxk píhkeew.'; **be numb** píhksuw VAI **I'm half numb (of someone who had a stroke).** 'Pasíi mbíhksi.'; **be numb** píhkŭ=weew VII; **feel numb, have a sensation of numbness** pihkwamálsuw VAI; **get numb** pihkwíhleew VAI; **get numb** pihkŭwíhleew VAI, pihkŭwíh=leew VII.

**numbness** N **feel numb, have a sensation of numbness** pihkwamálsuw VAI.

**nurse** VI **nurse** *(of a child)* noonóosuw VAI.

**nurse** VT **nurse a baby** nohláawasuw VAI; **nurse s.o.** nóhleew VTA; **suck s.o., feed at s.o.'s breast, nurse from s.o.** noonáaleew VTA.

**nut** N **chestnut** wáapiim NI; **crack nuts** pakásŭmeew VAI; **hazelnut** kéhtaam NI.

**nuzzle** VT **lick s.o., rub, nuzzle s.o. with mouth** láalameew VTA.

# O

**o.k.** N **o.k, all right** yó PC.

**oatmeal** N **cornmeal mush, oatmeal** nzáapaan NI.

**obey** VI awulsútam VOTI1.

**obey** VT **be hard to handle, don't obey the rules, be 'out of hand'** wŭyak=áawsuw VAI.

**ocean** N **ocean, sea, salt water** shŭ=wánpuy NI.

**odd** ADJ **do odd things** maanjŭwúnum VOTI1; **feel angry about one's illness, feel odd, feel angry** manoongamál=suw VAI; **have an odd dream** maa=shóngwaam VAI; **have an odd face, have a strange face** maashíingweew VAI; **have an odd twist to one's mouth, have an odd twist to one's lips** *(indicating a certain attitude)* maashtoonéexiin VAI; **lead an odd life, lead a strange life** maanjŭ=wáawsuw VAI; **look strange, have an odd appearance** maashiináakwat VII, maashiináakwsuw VAI; **odd person, bad person, person who does bad things** chíipaween PR; **odd person,**

**strange person** maanjŭwáween PR; **sound odd, sound different, sound strange** maashihtáakwat VII, maa=shihtáakwsuw VAI.

**oddly** ADV **act oddly, act strangely, make faces** amáashŭnum VOTI1; **talk oddly** maamaashíixsuw VAI, maash=tóonheew VAI.

**odds and ends** N **old things, odds and ends** machéewayal NI *usually plural.*

**office** N **nominate s.o. for an office, nominate s.o. for a position** kiishíi=meew VTA.

**often** ADV **always, often** yáanee PC **I fall down a lot.** 'Yáanee ngakawíhla.', **He visits here often.** 'Yáanee pee=tootéewuw.'; **often** eewachu- PV **I eat often.** 'Ndéewachu-míitsi.', **He goes to the doctor often.** 'Éewachu-ndaaktúlung -éew.'; **often** wŭyaku- PV *informal* **I don't see him often.** 'Máh nóoyaku-neewáawu.', **They fly by often.** 'Wŭyáku-pŭmihléewak.'; **drink often, drink a lot** eewachíisŭ=muw VAI; **run often** eewatahtakíhleew VAI; **sing often** eewataláamuw VAI; **swim often, swim a lot** wŭyakaa=shŭwíhleew VAI; **urinate often** eewa=chíisheew VAI; **walk often** eewatóo=xweew VAI.

**oil** N **coal oil** káanoos NA; **oil can** kaa=noosiilamóokan NA; **oil for greasing** shamuníikan NI, shamúníiwu-káanoos NA.

**Ojibwe** N **Ojibwe Indian** wshíipŭweew NA; **Ojibwe woman** wshiipŭwéex=kweew NA; **speak Ojibwe** wihwshii=pŭwéewuw VAI.

**old** ADJ **be old, be worn out** xuwíiya=yuw VAI, xuwíiyayuw VII; **look old, be old-looking, look older than one's age** kihkŭwiináakwsuw VAI; **look old, look like an elderly person** kihkee=sŭwiináakwsuw VAI; **old** xuwii- PN **Old books.** 'Xúwii-pambíilak.', **Old chicken.** 'Xúwii-kiikíipush.'; **old** xúwii PC **Old clothing.** 'Xúwii éhakwiing.'; **old** xúwu PC *informal* **He wears old things.** 'Xúwu kwée=kwiil awéehe.'; **be a man who died of old age** aaptihlóosuw VAI **I'm just about dying of old age.** 'Péexoot ndaaptihlóosi.'; **be a woman who died of old age** áapchii-kihtoxkwée=suw VAI; **be an old man** mihlóossuw VAI; **be an old woman, undergo menopause, undergo change of life** kihtoxkwéesuw VAI; **be old, get old** kihkéesuw VAI; **little old man** chan=gihlóoshush NA; **look like an old woman** kihtoxkweesŭwiináakwsuw VAI; **old chair** xuwáhpapoon NI; **old dog** xúwxum NA; **old dress** xuween=dakwíiwan NI; **old grass, weeds** xuwáskwal NI *usually plural,* xuwii=xáskwal NI *usually plural;* **old house** xuwíikaan NI; **old man** mihlóosus NA, xuwihlóosus NA; **old person** kíhkees NA; **old pig** xuwóoshkoosh NA; **old shoe** xuwáhksun NI; **old things, odds and ends** machéewayal NI *usually plural;* **old tree** xuwíhtukw NA, xúw=ahkw NA; **old woman** kihtóxkwees NA; **rotten old man** akwaakwalihlóo=sus NA, alihlóosus NA.

**older** ADJ **be older than s.o.** kihkayúm=eew VTA, kíhkayuw VAIO; **older single woman** kihkóxkweew NA.

**older brother** N **my older brother** nxánz NAD.

**older sister** N **my older sister** nŭmíis NAD.

**Olive** N àlífush NA *woman's name.*

**Oliver** N áalful NA *man's name.*

**Olivia** N lúpŭyaan NA, lúpŭyeen NA *woman's name.*

**once** ADV **once, one time** ngwutun- PV **She went there one time.** 'Wŭnúk=wtun- náh -áan.', **All of a sudden one time he came, and he told my mother, "We want to get married."** 'Wíixkwii wŭnúkwtun-páan, wtuláa=

wal ngúkal, "Ngáta-takwapíhna."'; **once, one time** ngwútun PC **I only bet once.** 'Ngwútun shúkw ndahtíike.'

**one** ADJ mayáat PC **One knife.** 'Mayáat paxkshiíkan.'; **one** ngwut- PV **It's in one piece.** 'Ngwút-pangéeyeew.', **One slice.** 'Néekwtu-pangéesiit.'; **one** ngwut- PN **I worked there for one month.** 'Ngwút-kíishooxkw náh ndúnda-làlóhke.'; **one** ngwúti PC; **once, one time** ngwutun- PV **She went there one time.** 'Wŭnúkwtun-náh -áan.', **All of a sudden one time he came, and he told my mother, "We want to get married."** 'Wíix=kwii wŭnúkwtun-páan, wtuláawal ngúkal, "Ngáta-takwapíhna."'; **once, one time** ngwútun PC **I only bet once.** 'Ngwútun shúkw ndahtíike.'; **one after the other, in turn, every other one** eháashtee PC **They took turns eating** 'Eháashtee miitsúwak.', **I went from one place to another (and then back).** 'Eháashtee ndá.'; **be by oneself, be on one's own, be the only one in a family** nxoohóowuw VAI; **be gone overnight** ngwutookwŭnáh=keew VAI; **be in one layer** *(of something sheet-like)* ngwuteekíixiin VAI **Buy two-ply toilet paper, don't buy one-ply.** 'Kŭmáhlawaa-uch niishee=kíixiit wiikwáhmshii-pámbiil, chíi mahlawáahan ngwuteekíixiit.'; **be in one layer** *(of something sheet-like)* ngwuteekíixun VII; **be one day** ngwut=áhkameew VII **I'll come in a day.** 'Ngwutahkaméeke náh mbá.'; **be one page, be one sheet** ngwutéekat VII; **be one piece** *(of something string-like)* ngwutáhtakat VII; **be one, be one of them** mayáawsuw VAI **There is one horse.** 'Mayáawsuw nehnayóon=gus.'; **be whole, all in one piece** msuchéeyeew VII, msuchéesuw VAI **The apples are whole.** 'Msuchéesŭ=wak aapŭlúshak.'; **have one eye** ngwutíingweew VAI; **have one hand** ngwutŭnáxkeew VAI; **have one leg** ngwutkáateew VAI; **have one page** *(of something sheet-like)* ngwutaapéek=suw VAI *usually of pieces of paper;* **on one side** yáawii PC **You have a short arm on one side.** 'Yáawii kchah=kwŭnaxkáashi.', **I just planted on one side.** 'Yáawii shúkw ndundalah=kíihe.'; **one day** ngwutóokwŭnii PC; **one hundred** ngwutaapóxku PC; **one time, emphatic** táas PC **My late grandmother told me.** 'Noohŭmáya táas ndúkw.'; **take one step** ngwuta=líhkeew VAI; **use one hand** ngwutoo=náxkeew VAI, ngwutoonáxkwiiw VAI-S, ngwutŭnaxkéexiin VAI; **use one leg** ngwutkaatéexiin VAI.

**Oneida** N **Oneida Indian** méengweew NA; **Oneida woman** meengwéex=kweew NA; **be a lot of Oneidas, Oneida Town, Ontario** meengwee=wíhkeew VII; **speak Oneida** meh=meengwéewuw VAI.

**oneself** PR **by oneself** níhlii PC **You hit yourself.** 'Níhlii kpákamaaw khák=ay.', **I got dressed by myself.** 'Níhlii nŭwéechpii.'

**onion** N wiinóonzhuy NA; **green onion** askiinóonzhuy NA.

**only** ADJ **but, only** shúkw PC **They were laughing, saying all sorts of things to me, and touching me, but I didn't understand them.** 'Akulkúsŭwak, wéemu kwéek ndukwŭnéewa, wáak ngihkiixkŭnúkook, shúkw msúchee máh nùnohtawaawíiwak.', **But he's in my way.** 'Shúkw kàkpíixiin.'; **be by oneself, be on one's own, be the only one in a family** nxoohóowuw VAI; **only** shùkéhla PC **I told him but he still forgot.** 'Píish ndúlaan shùk=éhla wánsiin.', **He only drinks tea.** 'Shùkéhla mŭnéew tíi.'; **only eat some of s.t. animate, have a piece of s.t. animate to eat, only eat some of**

**s.t. animate on one's plate** msһám=eew VTA; **only eat some of s.t., have a piece of s.t. to eat, only eat part of s.t. on one's plate** mshándam VTI1A.

**onto** PREP **sew something onto s.t.** ah=píikwam VTI1A; **sew something onto s.t. animate** ahpiikwáaleew VTA.

**open** ADJ **be big eyed** *(after seeing something unusual)*, **lie with one's eyes open** *(especially if one cannot sleep)* amangaalakiingwéexiin VAI; **be open** tawíixiin VAI, tawíixun VII **His door is open.** 'Taatawíixun kwúphoon.'; **be blown open by the wind** tawáxookw VAI, tawáxun VII **The door was blown open by the wind.** 'Tawáxun kpáh=oon.'; **be spread out, be open** *(as sole of shoe flapping)*, **be open, be apart** *(as a shirt)* toongíixun VII; **be spread out, have one's legs open** toongíixiin VAI; **come open, open up** *(as a shoe with sole flapping)* aapíh=leew VII; **hang open, be open** tawaa=péhleew VII; **have an open sore, be skinned, be peeled off** *(of bedsores, of blisters)* pxwíisksuw VAI; **have one's eyes open** aapakiingwéexiin VAI; **have one's eyes open** *(especially of a dead person)* toongiingwéexiin VAI; **have one's eyes open, have big eyes** xwaalakiingwéexiin VAI, xwaa=pakiingwéexiin VAI; **have one's hands open, have one's hands wide open** aapiilunjéexiin VAI, aapŭlunjéexiin VAI; **have one's mouth open** toong=toonéexiin VAI; **leave s.t. animate wide open** tawushéexŭmeew VTA; **leave s.t. animate wide open** tawíi=xŭmeew VTA, toongchéexŭmeew VTA; **leave s.t. open** tawíixtoow VTI2; **leave s.t. open** *(as a door)* toongchéextoow VTI2; **leave s.t. wide open** tawush=éextoow VTI2; **open up** *(as a flower)* aapíhleew VAI; **open up, come open** toongíhleew VII; **sit with one's legs open, sit with one's legs spread apart** toongohkwéepuw VAI, tóon=gapuw VAI; **stand with one's legs open, stand with one's legs spread apart** toongiikáapawuw VAI; **be exposed, be in the open** mihchíixun VII.

**open** N **hang s.t. animate in the open** mihtaapéhlaleew VTA; **hang s.t. in the open** mihtaapéhlatoow VTI2; **have one's head exposed, have one's head out in the open** mihtaandpée=xiin VAI; **in the open** míhchii PC **I hung the mitts in the open.** 'Míhchii wándak nŭwehlaláawak.'; **lie down uncovered, lie down exposed, lie down in the open** mihchíixiin VAI.

**open** VT **open s.t.** *(using the hands)* tawúnum VTI1B; **open s.t. animate** tawúneew VTA; **open s.t. animate, take the lid off s.t. animate** *(as the cover of a pail)* áapŭneew VTA; **open s.t., lift s.t. off** *(as the cover of a box or coffin)* áapŭnum VTI1B; **open one's eyes** aapakíingweew VAI; **open one's hand** aapŭlúnjeew VAI; **open the gate for s.o.** taweenáxkŭneew VTA.

**open up** VI **open up, come open** *(as a shoe with sole flapping)* aapíhleew VII; **open up, come open** *(as a flower)* aapíhleew VAI; **open up, come open** toongíhleew VII.

**open up** VT **make a hole in s.t., open s.t. up** pkwuchéenum VTI1B; **open s.t. animate up, operate on s.o.** *(as a doctor)*, **make a hole in s.o., take the insides out of s.o.** pkwuchéeneew VTA **He had an operation.** 'Pkwuch=éenaaw.'; **open up one's hand, open up one's hands** aapiilúnjeew VAI; **turn s.t. animate over, open s.t. animate up** *(of something sheet-like)* aapéekŭneew VTA *usually of pieces of paper.*

**opening** N **crawl through an opening** pkwíikwsuw VAI; **fall through an opening** pkwíhleew VAI, pkwíhleew VII; **look out from an opening**

pkwahiingwéexiin VAI; **look through a hole, look through an opening, look through something** pkóhkweew VAI.

**operate** VI **operate** *(of doctors)*, **take out the insides of things** pkwuchee=níikeew VAI.

**operate on** VT **open s.t. animate up, operate on s.o.** *(as a doctor)*, **make a hole in s.o., take the insides out of s.o.** pkwuchéeneew VTA **He had an operation.** 'Pkwuchéenaaw.'

**operation** N **be constantly in motion, be constantly in operation** ngumee=wíhleew VAI **My hammer's going all the time.** 'Ndahámŭlum ngumee=wíhleew.'; **be constantly in motion, be constantly in operation** ngumee=wíhleew VII.

**opinion** N **think s.o. to be smart, have a high opinion of s.o., think s.o. competent** kshéelŭmeew VTA.

**opportunity** N **come too late, miss an opportunity, miss one's chance** mehtxíhkeew VAI **The service was over when I arrived, I came too late.** 'Kíishi-maawéewiin náh peeya=yáane, nemehtxíhke.'

**orange** ADJ **turn reddish-brown, turn yellow, turn orange** *(by heat)* wii=saawxásuw VAI.

**orange** N áalunj NA.

**orchard** N **work in an apple orchard** aapŭlúsh'heew VAI.

**order** N **be even, be in order, lie correctly** mayaawíixun VII; **be in order, lie correctly, be lined up straight** *(s.t. animate)*, **be the main one, be the top person** mayaawíixiin VAI.

**ordinary** ADJ **plain, ordinary** kahkanii- PN **Broth, plain soup.** 'Káhkanii-kshíiteew.'; **plain, ordinary** lunii- PN **Any kind of fish.** 'Lúnii-namées.'

**orphan** N **be an orphan** shiikwíineew VAI.

**other** ADJ **on the other side of the house** awasáaku PC **The box is on the other side of the house.** 'Mbáksh awasáa=ku áhte.'; **the other side of something** awásii PC **I put it over there on the other side.** 'Yéelak awásii ndáh=toon.', **On the other side of the door.** 'Awásii kpahóonung.'; **the other side of the fence** awaseenáxke PC; **the other side of the river** káamung PC; **the other side of the road** awas=iixkanáwe PC.

**other** N **be mixed in with others** koh=lawíixiin VAI, kohlawíixun VII; **grow mixed in with others** kohlawíikun VII, kohlawíikuw VAI; **mix s.o. in with others** kohlawíixŭmeew VTA; **mix s.t. in with others** kohlawíixtoow VTI2; **one after the other, in turn, every other one** eháashtee PC **They took turns eating** 'Eháashtee miitsúwak.', **I went from one place to another (and then back).** 'Eháashtee ndá.'; **other, the other** *(inanimate)* ktákan PR; **other, the other** *(animate)* ktákan PR **My mother was the oldest, then there was my uncle, and then another girl.** 'Níi ngúk wunáxoo-kíh=kayiin, nál há wá nzhíis, nál wáak ktákan oxkwéesus.'

**ouch!** IJ awíi PC; **ouch!** àhwalákay PC *considered impolite.*

**out** ADV **go out** któoxweew VAI; **come out** *(of water)* ktupéhleew VII; **go out of sight** waníhleew VAI; **hang out** ktaapéhleew VII, ktaapéhleew VAI **My mitts are hanging out.** 'Ktaapehlée=wak nŭwándŭmak.'; **have one's arms out** ktunaxkéexiin VAI, ktunŭnaxkée=xiin VAI; **have one's slip sticking out** ktahóosuw VAI; **hide, hide out of sight** wanohtáasuw VAI; **hurry out with s.o.** kchíipheew VTA; **hurry out with s.t.** kchiipáhtoow VTI2; **run out of sight** wanahtakíhleew VAI; **run outside, run out** ktahtakíhleew VAI; **be out of one's mind** wanáatam VAI;

**go out** *(of fires)*, **be burnt up** *(in a fire)* wchiimáhteew VII; **be out of one's mind with grief** wanahkwateelún=dam VOTI1; **be out of one's mind, be unconscious** wanahkwatéhleew VAI.

**out loud** ADV **laugh a lot, laugh out loud** amángu-láatam VOTI1; **sing out loud** amangaláamuw VAI.

**outhouse** N **outhouse, toilet** wiikwáh=mush NI.

**outside** ADJ **be the outside angle of a corner** síingeew VII **The corner of the house.** 'Éenda-síingeek wíi=kwahm.'; **be the outside angle of a corner** síingsuw VAI; **outside** kwách=ŭmung PC **So they were lying there, outside, just where the car tracks are.** 'Nál há yóol sheengiixúngiil, kwáchumung, wúlu náh ahtamóombil pehpŭmíhlaat.'; **run outside, run out** ktahtakíhleew VAI.

**outside** PREP **outside the fence** kwach=ŭmeenáxke PC.

**over** ADV **be bent, be bent over, be curved** wáaksuw VAI; **be covered over with water** wanúpeew VAI, wanúpeew VII; **be hunched over** waakpoxkwanéexiin VAI; **boil over** *(of one's cooking)*, **have one's cooking boil over** paalchásŭmeew VAI; **bury s.o., cover s.o. over** psúndheew VTA **He was covered up, buried.** 'Psúndhaaw.'; **climb over** paalakóo=suw VAI; **cover s.o. over with water, cover s.t. animate over with water** wanúpaleew VTA; **cover s.t. over with water** wanúpatoow VTI2; **go over, flow over** paalíhleew VII, paalíhleew VAI; **hit s.t. animate over** *(farther than intended)* paalihtéeheew VTA; **hit s.t. way over something, knock s.t. way over something** *(using a tool or instrument)*, **knock s.t. over something** páalham VTI1A; **over there** yéelak PR **I put it over there on the other side.** 'Yéelak awási ndáhtoon.'; **boil over, overflow** *(from being heated)* paalchásuw VAI, paalcháteew VII; **put s.o. over something, put s.o. on something, put s.o. around something** laapíixŭmeew VTA; **put s.t. over something, put s.t. on something, put s.t. around something** laapíixtoow VTI2; **repeat, say something over** laapíixsuw VAI; **sit hunched over** waakpoxkwanéepuw VAI; **throw s.t. over, throw s.t. farther than intended** paaláaheew VAIO **I threw it over the house.** 'Mbaaláa=heen wiikwáhmung.'; **walk bent over, walk stooped over** waakóo=xweew VAI.

**over** PREP **double, doubled, one over the other** pihtawii- PV **I papered over the other wallpaper.** 'Mbíhta=wii-pambiilhíike.'; **hang over something** laapaapéhleew VAI; **hang over something** laapaapéhleew VII; **hang over something, be put over something** laapíixiin VAI, laapíixun VII; **hang over something, lie over something** paalíixiin VAI; **hang s.t. over something** laapaapéhlatoow VTI2, paalaapéhlatoow VTI2; **hit s.t. animate a long way over, knock s.t. animate way over something** *(using a tool or instrument)* páalheew VTA; **hit s.t. over something** *(farther than intended)* paalháhkweew VAIO; **jump over s.o., jump over s.t.** *(farther than intended)* paalaakchéhleew VAIO; **jump over s.t., jump over s.o.** *(farther than intended)* paaláakchehl VAIO; **look over s.t., look over s.o., look past s.t., look past s.o.** paala=tawáapuw VAIO; **make s.t. over something** paalíhtoow VTI2; **peek over, look over something** paalhiingwée=xiin VAI; **pile s.t. over something** *(of something wood- or stick-like)* paa=lahkwéextoow VTI2; **put s.o. over the top of something** *(using the hands)* páalŭneew VTA; **put s.t. animate over something** paalíixŭmeew VTA; **put s.t. over something, make s.t. overlap** paalíixtoow VTI2; **put s.t. over the top of something** *(using the hands)* páalŭnum VTI1A; **step over s.o., step over s.t. animate** paalíhka=weew VTA; **step over s.t.** paalíhkam VTI1A; **step over s.t., step over s.o.** paalalíhkeew VAIO.

**overboard** ADV **make s.o. go overboard** *(romantically)* kshuwóoleew VTA.

**overcome** VT **overcome s.o., dominate s.o.** *(especially one's spouse)* aluwíh=kaweew VTA; **overcome s.t.** aluwíh=kam VTI1A; **overcome s.t., get the better of s.t.** pŭmunóotam VTI1A; **overcome s.t., get the better of s.t.** pŭmúnum VTI1A; **be overheated, be overcome with heat, faint from the heat** aaptúsuw VAI.

**overcook** VT **overcook s.o., overheat s.o.** wsaamcháseew VTA; **overcook s.t., overheat s.t.** wsaamchásum VTI1B; **be overcooked, be overheated** wsaamchásuw VAI.

**overeat** VI **eat an awful lot, overeat** chiipŭlóosuw VAI *considered impolite;* **overeat** wsaamŭlóosuw VAI; **overeat to the point of being sick** aaptulóo=
suw VAI; **overeat, be full to the bursting point** kiispwulóosuw VAI.

**overfill** VT **overfill s.t.** paaláhtoow VTI2; **overfill s.t., make s.t. overflow** páal=peew VAIO; **overfill s.t. animate** paa=láhleew VTA.

**overflow** VI **overfill s.t., make s.t. overflow** páalpeew VAIO; **overflow** *(of heated liquid, of radiator, of container that boils over)* paalpáteew VII; **overflow** *(of containers)* páalpeew VII, páalpeew VAI; **overflow, be filled over the top** paaláhteew VII; **overflow, be full over the top** páalapuw VAI; **boil over, overflow** *(from being heated)* paalchásuw VAI, paalcháteew VII.

**overgrown** ADJ **go to seed, be overgrown** *(of plants)* aapchíikuw VAI; **go to seed, be overgrown** aapchíikun VII; **grow too much, be overgrown** wsaamíikuw VAI, wsaamíikun VII.

**overheat** VT **overcook s.o., overheat s.o.** wsaamcháseew VTA; **overcook s.t., overheat s.t.** wsaamchásum VTI1B; **be overcooked, be overheated** wsaamchásuw VAI; **be overheated, be overcome with heat, faint from the heat** aaptúsuw VAI.

**overlap** VI **put s.t. over something, make s.t. overlap** paalíixtoow VTI2.

**overnight** ADJ **stay out overnight** ngwútii-tpohkweewáhkeew VAI; **stay overnight** mawíikeew VAI.

**overshoe** N **rubber overshoe** làpŭláh=ksun NI, pihtawáhksun NI; **wear more than one pair of shoes, wear more than one layer of footwear, wear overshoes** pihtawahksúneew VAI.

**oversleep** VI **oversleep, sleep late, sleep in** wsaamóngwaam VAI; eelóngwaam VAI.

**overtake** VT **catch up to s.o., overtake s.o., catch up to s.o.'s level** matáleew VTA.

**overwhelming** ADJ **have an overwhelming amount of work to do** laawa=lóhkeew VAI; **look overwhelming, look hopeless, appear to be hopeless** laawcheenáakwsuw VAI **He's hopeless, he's never getting dressed.** 'Laawcheenáakwsuw máh kiikii=sheechpíiwi.'; **look overwhelming, look hopeless, appear to be hopeless** laawiináakwsuw VAI, laawiináa=kwat VII.

**owe** VT **owe s.t. to people** kŭlunŭmáa=suw VAIO **He owes a lot of money.** 'Kŭlunŭmáasuw xwéelu shúlpul.'; **owe to s.o.** kŭlunŭmáweew VTA.

**owl** N kóokhoos NA; **screech owl** kxah=wéemwiish NA.
**own** N **live alone, be on one's own** nxoohaálŭnuw VAI.
**own** VT **own s.o.** nihláaleew VTA; **own s.t.** nihláatam VTI1A.
**ox** N áakshun NA.

# P

**pace** VI **pace back and forth** asahkóo=xweew VAI.
**pack** N **carry s.t. away in a pack or bundle** alumŭwáleew VAIO; **carry s.t. away, carry s.t. away in a pack** alumŭwaléhleew VAIO; **pack** nehna=yoondíikan NI.
**pack** VT **finish packing a load on one's back, be finished packing a load on one's back, be already packed** kii=shŭwálheew VAI; **pack up one's things, be packing up** wŭlaskŭneex=tíikeew VAI.
**pack mud on** VT **pack mud on things** *(as between logs of a house)*, **pack plaster on things** asiiskŭwahíikeew VAI; **pack mud onto s.t.** *(as of houses)*, **put plaster onto s.t.** asiiskŭwáham VTI1A **I put mud/plaster on the house.** 'Ndasiiskŭwáhŭmun wíi=kwahm.'
**pack up** VI **finish packing up, be finished packing up** kiishaskŭneex=tíikeew VAI.
**paddle** VI **float, paddle by, paddle along, paddle a watercraft** pŭmáh=am VOTI1 **The duck is paddling by.** 'Wshíhwe pŭmáham.'; **paddle away, row away** alúmham VOTI1; **paddle here and there, paddle about** apáamham VOTI1; **paddle in a certain manner, paddle in a certain direction** láham VOTI1; **paddle this way in the water** peethámeew VAI; **row across the water, paddle across the water** kwaxkhámeew VAI; **row this way, come here paddling, paddle towards the speaker** péetham VOTI1.
**page** N **be one page, be one sheet** ngwutéekat VII; **have five pages** *(of something sheet-like)* naalanaapéek=suw VAI *usually of pieces of paper;* **have four pages** *(of something sheet-like)* neewaapéeksuw VAI *usually of pieces of paper;* **have many pages** *(of books)* xweelaapéeksuw VAI; **have one page** *(of something sheet-like)* ngwutaapéeksuw VAI *usually of pieces of paper;* **have three pages** *(of something sheet-like)* nxaapéeksuw VAI *usually of pieces of paper;* **have two pages** *(of something sheet-like)* nii=shaapéeksuw VAI *usually of pieces of paper.*
**pail** N wsháphoos NA.
**pain** N **be in pain, suffer** awéendam VOTI1; **die in pain** aaptàwéendam VOTI1; **extreme pain, suffering** aweendamuwáakan NI; **feel s.t. as an ache, feel s.t. as a pain, feel s.t. as a soreness in one's body** amándam VTI1A; **get sore, hurt, have a pain, have a sharp pain, have a brief pain** wiisakíhleew VII, wiisakíhleew VAI **My knee had a sharp pain.** 'Ngútko wiisakíhleew.'
**paint** N **paint, paint brush** shoohíikan NI, shehshoohíikeeng NI.
**paint** VT **paint s.o., rub s.o., rub on s.o.** shóoheew VTA; **paint s.t., rub s.t. on, rub s.t.** shóoham VTI1A; **paint things, be painting** shoohíikeew VAI; **be painted** shooháasuw VAI, shooháasuw VII.
**paint brush** N **paint brush** wéhwunj-shoohíikeeng NI.
**pair** N **be five pairs, be in five pairs** naalanéelook VAI *usually plural,* naa=

lanéeltool VII *usually plural;* **be four pairs, be four sets** neewéelook VAI *usually plural,* neewéeltool VII *usually plural;* **be so many, be so many pairs** txéeltool VII *usually plural; usually with number particle* **They are in six pairs.** 'Ngwútaash txéel= tool.'; **be so many of them, be so many of them in pairs** txéelook VAI *usually plural; usually with number particle* **They are in eight pairs.** 'Xáash txéelook.'; **be three of them, be three in number, be in three pairs** nxéeltool VII *usually plural,* nxéelook VAI *usually plural;* **be two pairs, be two sets** niishéelook VAI, niishéeltool VII *usually plural;* **walk in twos, walk as a pair** niishoo= xwéewak VAI *usually plural;* **wear more than one pair of pants** pihta= wiipŭlóokeew VAI; **wear more than one pair of socks** pihtawashíikaneew VAI.

**pale** ADJ **be pale, turn pale** waaptíhk= suw VAI; **turn pale** waaptihkíhleew VAI.

**palm** N **palm of the hand** aláamŭlunj PC.

**pan** N **frying pan** pán NA; **tin pan** wshaphoosíinjuw NI.

**pan bread** N pánapwaan NI.

**pancake** N pánkook NA.

**pants** N pŭlóok NI; **change one's pants** aashŭwiipŭlóokeew VAI; **take off one's pants** ktuniipŭlóokeew VAI; **wear more than one pair of pants** pihtawiipŭlóokeew VAI.

**paper** N **book, paper, letter** pámbiil NA **Old books.** 'Xúwii-pambíilak.'; **bandage, wrapping paper, material used for wrapping** wiixkweeptíikan NI; **little bit of paper, Kleenex** pam= bíilush NA.

**paper bag** N pambiiliinóotay NI.

**park** VI **be at the side of the road, park at the side of the road** paxkée= xiin VAI.

**part** ADJ **be part Black** naaneeskàléen= guw VAI; **be part White** shaashŭwán= akuw VAI **He must be part White.** 'Sháxk éet shaashŭwánakuw.'; **part Black person** paseeskáleengw NA.

**part** N **take part in a discussion** wii= taachíimuw VAI.

**part hair** VT **part one's hair, have one's hair parted** pasaaxcháneew VAI; **part s.o.'s hair** pasaaxchánaweew VTA.

**participate** VI **participate, take part, take part in a game, take part in a fight** wiichóohŭweew VAI.

**partridge** N pahpáhkuw NA.

**pass by** VI lóowiiw VAI-S **I passed by there.** 'Náh mbúmu-lóowi.'

**pass by** VT **pass by s.o. on horseback, pass by s.t. on horseback** loowhóo= meew VAIO; **pass by s.t.** *(one's destination)* lóowham VTI1A; **pass by s.t.** lóowiiw VAIO.

**pass through** VT **go through s.t., pass through s.t., get through s.t.** éeshiiw VAIO **I went across his property.** 'Ndéeshiin wtootéeneeng.'; **go through, pass through, get through** éeshiiw VAI-S.

**past** ADV **look past, look beyond** loo= watawáapuw VAI.

**past** PREP **look over s.t., look over s.o., look past s.t., look past s.o.** paala= tawáapuw VAIO; **look past s.t., look beyond s.t.** loowatawáapuw VAIO.

**paste** VT **glue s.t. animate together, paste s.t. animate** psakwpéhlaleew VTA; **glue s.t. together, paste s.t.** psakwpéhlatoow VTI2; **paste s.o. together, glue s.o. together** psakwpál= eew VTA *object usually plural;* **paste s.t. together, glue s.t. together** psakwpátoow VTI2 *object usually plural* **I glued the pieces of wood together.** 'Mbusakwupatóonal xwúsal.'

**patch** N **be patched, have patches** pxanghwáasuw VII, pxanghwáasuw

VAI.

**patch** VT **patch s.t.** pxánghwam VTI 1 A; **patch s.t. animate** pxánghweew VTA; **patch things** pxanghwíikeew VAI; **be patched, have patches** pxanghwáa=suw VII, pxanghwáasuw VAI.

**path** N **be a good road, be a good path** wŭlatéexun VII; **be a road or path going in a certain direction, be a certain kind of road or path** latée=xun VII **There's a road going to the bush.** 'Kóhpii làtéexun.'; **be a sandy road, be a sandy path** leekŭwatée=xun VII; **make a good road, make a good path, have a good road, have a good path** wŭlatéexteew VAI.

**pattern** N **cut a pattern, cut things nicely** wŭlushíikeew VAI; **cut out a pattern** ktushíikeew VAI; **cut s.t. animate nicely, cut s.t. animate in a pattern** wŭlúsheew VTA; **cut s.t. nicely, cut s.t. in a pattern** wŭlúshum VTI 1 B.

**pay** VT **pay a lot** xweenhíikeew VAI; **pay s.o.** eenháweew VTA; **pay s.o. back** kwaxkeenháweew VTA **pay s.t.** een=híikeew VAIO **I paid what I owe.** 'Ndeenhíikeen keelŭnumáasŭyaan.'

**pay for** VT **get s.t. cheap, pay a little for s.t.** aapŭwalóhkeew VAIO; **pay a certain amount for s.t.** leenhíikeew VAIO **I paid two dollars for it.** 'Níish ndálaas nduleenhíikeen.'; **pay a certain amount for s.t.** lulóhkeew VAIO **I paid two dollars for it.** 'Níish ndálaas ndulŭlóhkeen.', **How much did he pay for it?** 'Kéexu wtulŭlóhkeen?'; **pay a lot for s.t., pay too much for s.t.** xwalóhkeew VAIO, xwulóhkeew VAIO; **pay for s.o., pay to s.o.** een=heelxáweew VTA; **pay s.o. for s.t.** eenheelxáweew VTAO.

**pay to** VT **pay for s.o., pay to s.o.** een=heelxáweew VTA.

**payment** N **button s.t. up, do s.t. up tightly, make a down payment on s.t.** kŭláhkhwam VTI 1 A.

**pea** N ptukwaaláxkwsiit NI.

**peaceful** ADJ **feel peaceful** nalawamál=suw VAI; **have a peaceful mind, have a calm mind** kŭlamahtéenamuw VAI.

**peacefully** ADV **peacefully, quietly, contentedly** naláwii PC **He lives there quietly.** 'Naláwii wíikuw.'; **peacefully, quietly, contentedly** aayaláwii PC **He's sitting quietly.** 'Aayaláwii laalŭmátapuw.', **They're playing quietly.** 'Aayaláwii meela=wúsŭwak.'

**peach** N píilkush NA, píilakush NA.

**peacock** N **peacock, peahen** páaw NA.

**peahen** N **peacock, peahen** páaw NA.

**pear** N wŭlamookanáapŭlush NA, wŭ=namongáapŭlush NA.

**pedal** VI **fly away, go away, pedal away** alumíhleew VAI; **fly by, fly along, go by, go along, drive by, drive along, pedal by, pedal along** pŭmíhleew VAI; **go home, drive home, fly home, pedal home** aapaachíhleew VAI.

**peddle** VI **peddle, go about selling** naahóosuw VAI.

**peddler** N mehmshúwaleesh NA, neh=naahóosiit VAI; **grocery peddler** kŭ=looshlíilŭnuw NA.

**peek** VI **peek over, look over something** paalhiingwéexiin VAI.

**peek out** VI **peek out, peep out** ktoh=kwéhleew VAI; **have one's eyes sticking out, look out, peek out** ktiin=gwéexiin VAI; **look out, peek out** ktohkwéexiin VAI **He was looking out from the door.** 'Ktohkwéexiin wúnj-kpahóonung.'

**peel** VI **peel, be peeled** pxwíixun VII **My skin is peeling.** 'Ndáxay pxwíixun.'

**peel** VT **peel s.t. animate** pxwásheew VTA; **be skinned, be peeled off** *(of bedsores, of blisters)* pxwíiskeew VII; **have an open sore, be skinned, be peeled off** *(of bedsores, of blisters)* pxwíisksuw VAI; **peel apples** pxwaa=

pŭlúsheew VAI, pxwashaapŭlúsheew VAI; **peel potatoes** pxwashíhpŭneew VAI; **peel, be peeled** pxwíixiin VAI, pxwíixun VII **My skin is peeling.** 'Ndáxay pxwíixun.'

**peep out** VI **peek out, peep out** ktoh=kwéhleew VAI.

**pencil** N pénsul NI.

**pepper** N pépul NI.

**pepper shaker** N pèpŭlíinjuw NI.

**perch** VI **perch upon something** poxkwchéepuw VAI.

**perhaps** ADV **maybe, perhaps** píht PC **Maybe it will snow.** 'Píht éet katá-wíineew.', **You might be able to sleep.** 'Píht áa kíish- áa -kawíim.'

**perimeter** N **mark s.t., make a sign on s.t., put one's name on clothes, mark the perimeters of s.t.** *(using a tool or instrument)* kíhkham VTI1A.

**perjure** VT **use bad language, tell a lie, perjure oneself** mataaptóoneew VAI.

**permanently** ADV **for good, permanently** wchiimwii- PV **You shut it for good.** 'Koochíimwii-kpáhŭmun.', **I lost it for good.** 'Noochíimwii-aníhtoon.'; **to death, dead, permanently, for good** aapchii- PN **Woman who died of old age.** 'Áapchii-kihtóxkwees.'; **to death, dead, permanently, for good** aapchii- PV **The peaches are really overripe.** 'Piil=kúshak áapchii-atúsŭwak.'; **to death, dead, permanently, for good** aapchu- PV *informal* **I lost it for good.** 'Ndáap=chu-aníhtoon.', **He bled to death.** 'Áapchu-mohkwíixiin.'

**person** N **Black person** neeskáleengw NA; **English person** eenglúshmaan NA; **Scottish person** skáchmaan NA; **mute, a person who can't talk** kéeptoon NA, kpútoon NA; **bad person** mataakanáween PR, matálakay NA *considered impolite;* **be a White person** shŭwánakuw VAI; **be a bad person, be a good for nothing person** matahaapéewuw VAI; **be a crabby person** manoongchéetŭyeew VAI; **be a nice person** pshíhku-awéenuw VAI; **be a restless person, be an active person** seekawéenuw VAI; **be a restless person, be an active person, be hard to handle** séeksuw VAI; **become White, act like a White person** shŭwanakwíhleew VAI; **bothersome person, worry-wart** sàkwáxktiis NA; **bothersome person, worry-wart** sàkwáxktuy NA; **feel like a White person** shŭwanakwamalúsuw VAI; **have a certain characteristic** *(of people),* **be a certain type of person** laapéewuw VAI **He's good for nothing.** 'Máh kwéek laapeewíiwu.'; **important person** káanzhaween PR; **leader, person in position of authority** líilŭnuw NA; **little person** weemachéekaniish NA; **look like a White person** shŭwanakwiináakw=suw VAI; **look old, look like an elderly person** kihkeesŭwiináakwsuw VAI; **odd person, bad person, person who does bad things** chíipaween PR; **odd person, strange person** maan=jŭwáween PR; **old person** kíhkees NA; **part Black person** paseeskáleengw NA; **person who is never satisfied** mehmúndawees NA; **restless person, active person** séekaween PR; **shy person, 'backwards' person** cheh=chíipsiit NA; **strange person** máasha=ween PR; **think of oneself as a White person** shŭwanakweelúnzuw VAI; **who, someone, a person** awéen PR **Who could that be now?** 'Awéen éet há ná kwáy?', **Who's he going with?** 'Awéeniil há wiichéewe?'

**perspire** VI **perspire from one's armpits** ashiilóngwaneew VAI.

**pet** N **have s.o. for a pet, keep s.o. as a pet** wtalŭmóonzuw VAIO; **have s.o. for a pet, keep s.o. as a pet, make a pet out of s.o.** alumóonzuw VAIO **He**

**made a pet out of the cat.** 'Wtalŭ=moonzíinal pooshíishal.'; **my dog, my horse, my close pet** *(of dogs and horses)* ndálŭmoonz NAD.

**pet** VT **rub s.o. on the head, pet s.o. on the head** siikwaandpéeneew VTA; **rub s.o., brush up against s.t. animate, pet s.o., caress s.o.** *(using the hands)* láalŭneew VTA; **rub s.o., pet s.o.** *(using the hands)* síikwŭneew VTA.

**petticoat** N **slip, petticoat** akóotay NI.

**pheasant** N laaweewiikíipush NA.

**Phillipine** N pŭlúpiin NA *woman's name.*

**Phoebe** N fíipii NA *woman's name.*

**photograph** N **take a photograph of s.o., draw a picture of s.o., make a tracing of s.o.** ktéekheew VTA; **take a photograph of s.t., draw a picture of s.t., make a tracing of s.t.** ktéek=ham VTI1A; **take photographs, make a drawing, draw things** kteekhíikeew VAI.

**physical** ADJ **feel a certain way, have a certain physical sensation** lamalús=uw VAI **He thinks he's so good ('has wings')** 'Làmalúsuw wŭlóngwa=nuw.', **How do you feel?** 'Thá há ktulamálsi?'

**pick** VT **break s.t. animate, break s.t. animate off, pick s.t. animate** páx=kŭneew VTA **I picked some apples.** 'Aapŭlúshak mbáxkŭna.'; **break s.t., break s.t. off** *(of strings, using the hands)*, **pick s.t.** páxkŭnum VTI1B; **pick apples** makunhaapŭlúsheew VAI; **pick apples** *(off the tree)* paxkŭnaa=pŭlúsheew VAI; **pick berries** makóh=puw VAI; **pick cherries** *(off the stems)* paxkŭniichèlíiseew VAI; **pick cherries, work in a cherry orchard** cheelíis'=heew VAI, chèlíis'heew VAI; **pick potatoes** makunhíhpŭneew VAI; **pick s.o. up** *(using the hands)*, **pick s.t. animate** *(off trees)* makúneew VTA; **pick s.t.** *(of fruits)* makóhpuw VAIO **I picked his strawberries.** 'Nŭmak=ohpwíinal ooteehíimal.'; **pick things** paxkŭníikeew VAI; **pull beans, pick beans** moonaalaxkwsíiteew VAI; **work in a tobacco field, work picking tobacco** kwshahtéewheew VAI.

**pick up** VT **pick s.o. up** náatŭneew VTA; **pick s.t. up** náatŭnum VTI1B, náx=kwŭnum VTI1A; **pick s.o. up** *(using the hands)*, **pick s.t. animate** *(off trees)* makúneew VTA; **pick s.o. up by mistake, touch s.o. by mistake** páh=tŭneew VTA; **pick s.t. animate up** *(off the ground)* makúnheew VTA **I picked up some apples.** 'Nŭmakŭnáha aa=pŭlúshak.'; **pick s.t. up** *(using a tool or instrument)* makúnham VTI1A; **pick s.t. up by mistake, touch s.t. by mistake** páhtŭnum VTI1B; **pick s.t. up with one's fingers, use one's fingers to pick s.t. up** kwàkwtákwŭnum VTI1B; **pick things up with one's fingers, use one's hands to pick things up** kwàkwtakwŭníikee VAI.

**picker** N **be a 'dirty' picker, pick only the most accessible fruits or berries, pick only the most accessible products** aníiskii-paxkŭníikeew VAI.

**pickerel** N wáasiingw NA.

**pickle** N **make brine pickles** shŭwíi-kòkòmsháheew VAI.

**picture** N píkchul NA; **have one's picture taken** kteekháasuw VAI; **take a photograph of s.o., draw a picture of s.o., make a tracing of s.o.** ktéek=heew VTA; **take a photograph of s.t., draw a picture of s.t., make a tracing of s.t.** ktéekham VTI1A.

**pie** N páy NA.

**piece** N **be broken into pieces** piikih=téexun VII; **be burnt up, fall to pieces, be in pieces after being cooked** shkwúteew VII, shkwútsuw VAI; **be five pieces** *(of something string-like)* naalanáhtakat VII; **be four pieces** *(of something string-like)* neewáhtakat VII; **be in pieces, be in slices** pangée=

suw VAI *usually with number particle* **It's in three slices.** 'Nxú pangée=suw.', **It's in several pieces.** 'Kéexu pangéesuw.'; **be in pieces, be in slices** pangéeyeew VII *usually with number particle* **It's in four slices.** 'Néew-pangéeyeew.', **It's in big pieces** 'Amángu-pangéeyeew.'; **be one piece** *(of something string-like)* ngwutáhtakat VII; **be so many pieces** *(of something string-like)* txáhtakat VII **Six pieces of string.** 'Ngwútaash txáhtakat.'; **be two pieces** *(of something string-like)* niisháhtakat VII; **be whole, be all in one piece** msuchée=suw VAI **The apples are whole.** 'Msuchéesŭwak aapŭlúshak.'; **break a piece off s.t. animate, break a chunk off s.t. animate** *(using the hands)* kwashúneew VTA; **break a piece off s.t., break a chunk off s.t.** *(using the hands)* kwashúnum VTI1B; **crumble s.t. animate, break s.t. animate up into pieces, shred s.t. animate** *(using the hands)* píikŭneew VTA; **crumble s.t., break s.t. up into pieces, shred s.t.** *(using the hands)* píikŭnum VTI1B; **cut a piece off s.t.** kwashúshum VTI1B; **cut a piece off s.t. animate** kwashúsheew VTA; **cut a piece off s.t. animate, cut s.t. animate off** máhksheew VTA; **cut a piece off s.t., cut s.t. off** máhkshum VTI1B; **cut s.t. animate in pieces, cut s.t. animate in slices** pangéesheew VTA **I cut him in two pieces.** 'Níisha mbangéeshaaw.'; **cut s.t. animate off, cut a piece off s.t. animate** pŭ=láksheew VTA; **cut s.t. animate up, cut s.t. animate into pieces** píiksheew VTA; **cut s.t. in pieces, cut s.t. in slices** pangéeshum VTI1A **I cut it in two pieces.** 'Níisha mbangéeshŭ=mun.'; **cut s.t. off, cut a piece off s.t.** pŭlákshum VTI1B; **cut s.t. up, cut s.t. into pieces** píikshum VTI1B; **long piece of wood** kwŭnáxakw NI; **only eat some of s.t. animate, have a piece of s.t. animate to eat, only eat some of s.t. animate on one's plate** mshámeew VTA; **only eat some of s.t., have a piece of s.t. to eat, only eat part of s.t. on one's plate** mshándam VTI1A; **piece of dried wood** péeng=xwakw NI; **short piece of rope, short piece of string** chahkwáamanush NI; **shred things, break things into pieces** piikŭníikeew VAI; **take all of s.t. animate, take the last piece of s.t. animate** póhkwŭneew VTA; **take all of s.t., take the last piece of s.t., quit while doing s.t.** póhkwŭnum VTI1B; **take s.t. animate apart to pieces** piikhéewaleew VTA; **take s.t. apart to pieces** piikhéewatoow VTI2.

**pig** N kóoshkoosh NA; **bad pig** matóosh=koosh NA; **big pig** xwatóoshkoosh NA; **eat like a pig** achiipíilatoow VAI; **greasy pig** shamóoshkoosh NA; **old pig** xuwóoshkoosh NA; **young pig, new pig** wuskóoshkoosh NA.

**pig's head** N kooshkooshháandup NI.

**pigeon** N míimiish NA; **pigeon, mourning dove** míimiiw NA.

**pike fish** N kiinhóhkwus NA.

**pile** N **be a big pile** *(as of hay)* amang=shámuw VII; **make a big pile of s.t., pile s.t. high** mangshamóotoow VTI2; **make s.t. into a pile, make s.t. into a mound** wŭlamkwáaheew VAIO.

**pile** VT **be piled high** kihtshámuw VAI, kihtshámuw VII, tohpshámuw VAI, tohpshámuw VII; **pile s.t. high, pile up many of s.t.** xwushamóotoow VTI2; **pile things up, make mounds, make things into mounds** *(as when hilling potatoes)* wŭlamkwahíikeew VAI.

**pile over** VT **pile s.t. over something** *(of something wood- or stick-like)* paalahkwéextoow VTI2.

**pile up** VT **be piled up** wŭlamkwiixíi=

nook VAI *object usually plural* **The apples are piled up.** 'Wŭlamkwii=xíinook aapŭlúshak.'; **be piled up** wŭlamkwíixŭnool VII *usually plural* **The grass is piled up.** 'Wŭlamkwíi=xŭnool miixáskwal.'; **be piled up neatly, be piled up nicely, be piled up properly** *(of something wood- or stick-like)* wŭlahkweexíinook VAI *usually plural,* wŭlahkwéexŭnool VII *usually plural;* **pile hay up** mshamootíi=keew VAI; **pile s.t. animate up, build a hill around s.t. animate** *(of potatoes)* wŭlamkwíixŭmeew VTA *object usually plural;* **pile s.t. animate up, make s.t. animate into mounds** wŭ=lamkwaaháaleew VTA; **pile s.t. high, pile up many of s.t.** xwushamóotoow VTI2; **pile s.t. up** màmshamóotoow VTI2, wŭlamkwiixtóowal VTI2 *object usually plural;* **pile s.t. up, make s.t. in a mound** wŭlamkwáham VTI1A; **pile s.t. up, make s.t. into mounds** wŭlamkwaaháatoow VTI2; **pile up a lot of s.t.** xweelshamóotoow VTI2 *object usually plural;* **pile up a lot of s.t. animate** xweelshamóoleew VTA *object usually plural;* **pile up a lot of s.t. animate, pile s.t. animate up high** tohpshamóoleew VTA; **pile up a lot of s.t., pile s.t. up high** tohp=shamóotoow VTI2; **pile up wood, pile things up** *(of something wood- or stick-like)* wŭlahkweextíikeew VAI; **store s.t. animate, pile s.t. animate up** *(of something wood- or stick-like)* wŭlahkwéexŭmeew VTA *object usually plural;* **store s.t., pile s.t. up** *(of something wood- or stick-like)* wŭ=lahkwéextoow VTI2 *object usually plural.*

**pill** N kwehkwundáasiik NI.

**pillow** N **pillow, cushion** mŭlihkáawan NI, mŭlihkáawan NA; **use a pillow** mŭlihkóosuw VAI.

**pilot** VT **drive s.t. animate, pilot s.t. animate** pŭmushíhkaweew VTA **The horses are being driven.** 'Pŭmush=ihkawáawak nehnayóongsak.'

**pimple** N **have pimples on one's face** pimpŭlíingweew VAI.

**pin** N píinj NA; **clothes pin** kŭlahkhwíi=kan NI; **hair pin** wíilaxkii-píinj NI, wíilaxkii-píinj NA.

**pincers** N takwundíikan NI.

**pins and needles** N **be a tingling sensation, have pins and needles** *(of body parts)* wchiipiisóowuw VII **I went to the doctor because my arm was numb.** 'Ndaaktúlung ndáam éelu-náxk -wchiipiisóowiik.'

**pipe** N **pipe** *(for smoking)* matásun NA; **smoke a pipe, smoke tobacco** óh=pweew VAI; **chimney pipe** ehŭliin=gwáhteek NI.

**pit** N **pit, hole in ground** *(especially for storing vegetables in winter)* wáa=lakw NI.

**pitch** N **gum, pitch** pkúw NA.

**pitcher** N pehpíchiis NA *baseball;* **be a good pitcher** níhtaa-píchuw VAI.

**pitiable** ADJ **be poor, feel poorly, be pitiable** ktumáaksuw VAI.

**pitiful** ADJ **lead a pitiful life, lead a not very good life** ktumaakáawsuw VAI; **lie in a pitiful state, lie in a sickly state** ktumaakíixiin VAI.

**place** N **from a certain place, for a certain reason** wunj- PV *informal* **I ran down from the top of the hill** 'Wax=kiitáawung nóonj-niixahtakíhla.', **My head was sticking out of the water.** 'Mbíing nóonj-saakohkwéexiin.'; **from a certain place, for a certain reason** wunju- PV *informal* **Why did you do that?** 'Kwéek há nú kóonju-lúnŭmun?', **He got off the horse.** 'Nehnayóongsung wúnju-níixiiw.'; **have an illness in a certain part of one's body** talíineew VAI **His leg is sore.** 'Wihkáatung talíineew.'; **here, there, in a certain place** talí PC **It's**

**icy in the water.** 'Mohkamúyuw talí mbíing.', **He saw ghosts in a coffin.** 'Chíipayal néeweew kúshtung talí.'; **place, reason** wunj- PN *informal* **They didn't cut them off the big trees.** 'Máh mahkshaawíiwal wúnj-xwacháhkwung.', **I crawled down from the tree.** 'Njiixíikwsi wúnj-míhtkwung.'; **place, reason** wunju- PN *informal* **Off the table.** 'Wúnju-eehundaxpóonung.', **They didn't play cards for money any more.** 'Máh njíhnal shkuphameewíiwak wúnju-shúlpul.'; **here, there, in a certain place** talú PC **It rains heavily here.** 'Akushfíilaan yóon talú.', **He got stuck in the snow.** 'Kóonung talú kŭláhkweew.'; **urinate in a new place** aanjíisheew VAI; **variously, various places** msu- PV *informal* **It lies all over.** 'Msú-líixun.', **But they were always fighting, and this girl would always go all over, she was always going away.** 'Shúkw ngúmee màma=tahkéewak, wáak wá oxkwéesus ngúmee músu-áan, àhalúmsuw.'; **be a road that comes from a certain place** wundatéexun VII **The road leads from the forest.** 'Kóhpii wun=datéexun.'; **be in a nice place, be well seated, have a good home** *(of an adopted child or a person in heaven)* wŭlápuw VAI; **change one's place while sitting** áandapuw VAI; **come from a certain place** *(quickly)* wun=jíhleew VAI; **drive from a certain place, drive from there** wunjchéh=leew VAI **They were driving from Munceytown.** 'Naláhii wunjcheh=léewak.'; **jump from a certain place, jump for a certain reason** wun=dáakchehl VAI **I jumped from far away.** 'Wáhlu noondáakchehl.'; **lie in a dangerous place** laalxawíixiin VAI, laalxawíixun VII; **make a mistake in sewing s.t. animate, sew s.t. animate wrongly, sew s.t. animate in the wrong place** chaniikwáaleew VTA; **make a mistake in sewing s.t., sew s.t. wrongly, sew s.t. in the wrong place** chaníikwam VTI1A; **move on, go from one place to another** aan=dóoxweew VAI; **move s.o. from one place to another** aandóoxwaleew VTA; **move s.t. from one place to another** aandóoxwatoow VTI2; **sew at the wrong place** chaniikwáakeew VAI; **shine from a certain place, shine for a certain reason** *(of lamps)* wundáasŭleew VAI; **shine from a certain place, shine for a certain reason** wundáasŭleew VII; **take s.o.'s place** láapapuw VAIO; **talk from a certain place, talk for a certain reason, holler from a certain place, holler for a certain reason, call from a certain place, call for a certain reason** *(especially on the telephone)* wundaaptóoneew VAI **I talked from far away.** 'Wáhlu noon=daaptóone.'

**place** VT **place s.o. apart, place s.t. animate apart** chpáhleew VTA *object usually plural;* **place s.o. correctly, make s.o. be correctly arranged, straighten s.o. up, arrange s.o. correctly** mayaawíixŭmeew VTA; **place s.o. on top** *(of something)* poxkwáh=leew VTA; **place s.o. recklessly, place s.o. in a dangerous spot, place s.o. regardless of the consequences or risks** laalxawíixŭmeew VTA; **place s.t. animate level with the top of container** tpuskŭwáhleew VTA; **place s.t. apart, set s.t. aside** chpáhtoow VTI2 *object usually plural;* **place s.t. correctly, make s.t. be correctly arranged, straighten s.t. up** mayaa=wíixtoow VTI2; **place s.t. level with the top of container** tpuskŭwáhtoow VTI2; **place s.t. on top** *(of something)* poxkwáhtoow VTI2; **place s.t. reck-**

**lessly, put s.t. in a dangerous spot, place s.t. regardless of the consequences or risks** laalxawíixtoow VTI2; **be about to fall, be placed so as to fall** lxawíixiin VAI, lxawíixun VII; **be finished, be already placed there** kiisháhteew VII; **be placed around something, be placed all around something** wiiwŭniixíinook VAI, wii=wŭníixŭnool VII *usually plural;* **be placed, be put down** ahtáasuw VII.

**plain** ADJ **plain, ordinary** kahkanii- PN **Broth, plain soup.** 'Káhkanii-kshíi=teew.'; **plain, ordinary** lunii- PN **Any kind of fish.** 'Lúnii-namées.'; **be a plain colour, be plain coloured** kah=kanaapamúkwat VII, kahkanaapa=múkwsuw VAI; **be plain looking, have a plain appearance** kahkanii=náakwat VII kahkaniináakwsuw VAI; **dress plainly, be dressed plainly** kahkanákuw VAI; **have a plain taste** kahkaniipóokwat VII, kahkaniipóok=wsuw VAI.

**plainly** ADV **dress plainly, be dressed plainly** kahkanákuw VAI.

**plant** VI **be planting** ahkíiheew VAI; **be reluctant to plant** shiingahkíiheew VAI; **replant, put in new plants** laa=pahkíiheew VAI.

**plant** VT **plant s.t.** ahkíiheew VAIO **I planted a walnut tree.** 'Ptukwii=míinzhuy ndahkíihe.'; **be finished planting** kiishahkíiheew VAI; **come back from planting** aapahkíiheew VAI; **plant many things, plant lots, plant a large amount** amangahkíi=heew VAI; **plant things in a certain place, plant things there** talahkíi=heew VAI.

**plantain** N aanayaapasíhkan NI.

**plaster** N **pack mud on things** *(as between logs of a house),* **pack plaster on things** asiiskŭwahíikeew VAI; **pack mud onto s.t.** *(as of houses),* **put plaster onto s.t.** asiiskŭwáham VTI1A **I put mud/plaster on the house.** 'Ndasiiskŭwáhŭmun wíikwahm.'

**plaster** VT **have neat hair, have plastered-down hair** wŭlawéexteew VAI.

**plate** N pàkíinjuw NI.

**play** VI meelawúsuw VAI; **be tired of playing** laxkeelawúsuw VAI; **enjoy playing, have fun while playing** wiingeelawúsuw VAI; **play for a cause, play for a certain reason** *(especially to gamble)* wundeelawúsuw VAI **I played for money.** 'Noondeelawúsi shúlpul.', **I played for marbles.** 'Noondeelawúsi máapŭlush.'; **play in a certain place, play there** taleela=wúsuw VAI **He's playing outside.** 'Kwáchŭmung taleelawúsuw.'; **play together** niisheelawúsŭwak VAI *usually plural.*

**play** VT **beat a drum, play a drum** pòhwŭníikeew VAI; **beat a drum, play a drum, beat** *(on a black ash log, so that strips of wood will come off)* pòhwŭnúmeew VAI; **play Jew's harp** tŭlumphámeew VAI; **play a certain game, play at a certain game** leelawúsuw VAI **He's playing at different things.** 'Músu- kwéek -leela=wúsiin.', **What are you playing?** 'Kwéek ktuleelawúsi?'; **play a musical instrument** apíikweew VAI; **play ball** neenáxkuw VAI; **play cards** shkuphámeew VAI; **play checkers** koonjcháashuw VAI; **play hide-and-seek** kaateelawúsuw VAI, kahkáata=puw VAI; **play lacrosse** niimchéehŭ=meew VAI; **play loud music** amanga=píikweew VAI, niiskapíikweew VAI; **play marbles** maapŭlusheelawúsuw VAI; **play tag** maaléewuw VAI, tahtáh=wŭneew VAI; **play the violin** pŭyool=hámeew VAI.

**play for** VT **bet, play for money** ahtíi=keew VAI.

**play with** VT **play with s.o.** meelawus=óomeew VTA, meelawíiheew VTA;

**play with s.t.** meelawíhtoow VTI2.

**player** N **ball player** nehneenáxkwiis NA.

**playful** ADJ **have fun, get into things in a playful way** kpucheewháasuw VAI.

**pleasant** ADJ **be nice, be good, be pleasant, be good-natured** wŭlii= téeheew VAI.

**plenty** ADJ **be in abundance, be plenty** wŭyaksúwak VAI *usually plural,* wŭ= yákat VII; **have plenty to drink** wŭ= yakíisŭmuw VAI; **have plenty to eat, have an abundance of food** wŭyak= íipuw VAI; **have plenty of apples** wŭyakaapŭlúsheew VAI; **have plenty of clothes** wŭyákakuw VAI.

**pliers** N shkwundíikan NI.

**plow** N laapeexíikan NI; **use a plow, plow things, be plowing** laapeexíi= keew VAI.

**plow** VT **plow s.t.** laapéextoow VTI2; **use a plow, plow things, be plowing** laapeexíikeew VAI.

**plug** N **plug, cork** kpaskhíikan NI, kpas= kŭníikan NI.

**plug** VT **can s.t. animate, put s.t. animate in cans, block s.o., plug s.t. animate, fill in the cracks of s.t. animate, winterize s.t. animate** *(especially of windows)* kpáskheew VTA; **plug things up, caulk things, fill in chinks** kpaskhíikeew VAI.

**plum** N pwáhkamaash NA, pwáhkamaash NI.

**pocket** N sheewandíikan NA; **have pockets, have pockets on it** wsheewan= diikanaháasuw VII.

**point** N **be dull, have a dull edge, have a dull point** matalóosuw VAI, matal= óoyeew VII; **have a sharp point, be sharp and pointed** kiinalóosuw VAI, kiinalóowŭyeew VII; **cut s.t. and make a point on it, cut a point on s.t.** chpwúshum VTI1B; **cut s.t. and make a point on it, cut a point on s.t.** chpwúshum VTI1B; **cut s.t. animate and make a point on it, cut a point on s.t. animate** chpwúsheew VTA.

**point at** VT **point at s.o.** lóoheew VTA; **point at s.t.** lóoham VTI1B.

**pointed** ADJ **be pointed** chpwéew VII, chpwúsuw VAI; **have a pointed hat** chpwaakongwéepŭyeew VAI; **house with a pointed roof** chpwíikaan NI; **pointed hat** chpwaakongwéepuy NI; **purse one's lips, have one's mouth in a pout, have one's mouth sticking out pointed** chpwutoonéexiin VAI.

**pointing finger** N **my pointing finger** ndaloohíikan NID, nduloohíikan NID.

**poison** N mataapasíhkan NI; **be drunk and unpleasant, do bad things while drunk, drink poison** *(especially to induce miscarriage)* machíi= sŭmuw VAI.

**poison ivy** N lehlóosŭweek NI.

**poke** VT **nudge s.o., kick s.o., poke s.o.** *(to get his or her attention)* kiixkíh= kaweew VTA, kíixkŭneew VTA; **sew s.t. animate straight, poke s.o. straight, straighten s.o. out** *(with a tool)* shaaxkiikwáaleew VTA; **sew s.t. straight, poke s.t. straight, straighten s.t.** *(with a tool)* shaaxkíikwam VTI1A.

**pole** N **pole, something used for pushing** kunjchahíikan NI.

**policeman** N tehtàhwŭníikees NA.

**polish** VT **shine things, polish things** waasŭleextíikeew VAI.

**pond** N **swamp, pond** máskeekw NI.

**poor** ADJ **be poor** ashóokuw VAI; **bad man, good for nothing man, man of poor character** matahápeew NA; **bad woman, good for nothing woman, woman of poor character** ma= tahóxkweew NA; **be a bad woman, be a good for nothing woman, be a woman of poor character** matahox= kwéewuw VAI; **be poor, feel poorly, be pitiable** ktumáaksuw VAI; **have**

**poor eyesight, have a hard time seeing** matatawáapuw VAI **You might have a hard time seeing.** 'Kŭmata=tawáapi éet.'; **read badly, be a poor reader** amatakíinzuw VAI.

**poorly** ADV **be poor, feel poorly, be pitiable** ktumáaksuw VAI; **feel poorly, feel low** ktumaakamálsuw VAI.

**poplar tree** N paawsúwahkw NA.

**pork** N kooshkooshéewakw NI; **salt pork** shŭwéewakw NI.

**porridge** N **porridge made from water and flour rubbed together** wshaax=sáapaan NI.

**position** N **be up, be in a raised position** uspíixiin VAI, uspíixun VII; **have one's hands in a certain position** liináxkeew VAI **I had my hands in my pockets.** 'Nzheewandíikanung nduliináxke.'; **lie upside down, come to rest in an upside down position** aapoochkwàlihtéexiin VAI, aapooch=kwàlihtéexun VII.

**post** N **post, fencepost** póosht NI.

**pot** N **kettle, pot** hóosus NA; **clay pot** asiiskŭwahóosus NA, asiiskŭwáhoos NA; **tea pot** tíipat NA.

**potato** N óhpun NA; **big potato** xwach=íhpun NA; **dig up potatoes** moonhíh=pŭneew VAI; **new potato** wuskíhpun NA; **peel potatoes** pxwashíhpŭneew VAI; **pick potatoes** makunhíhpŭneew VAI; **raw potato** askíhpun NA; **scrape potatoes** kahkhíhpŭneew VAI.

**Potawatomi** N pooteewáatamiiw NA; **speak Potawatomi** pooteewaata=míixsuw VAI.

**pothook** N óhkwaan NA.

**pound** N póond NI *singular only, usually with number prenoun* **He weighs two pounds.** 'Níish-poond txu-poonda=kúsuw.', **He weighs six pounds.** 'Ngwútaash txú-poondakúsuw.'

**pound** VT **pound s.t., crush s.t., grind s.t.** shkwáham VTI1A; **pound and make a noise, hit and make a noise** *(on wood, on solid objects)* tiiwháh=kweew VAI; **pound on wood a lot** kaanzh'háhkweew VAI; **pound s.o., crush s.o., grind s.o.** *(using a tool or instrument)* shkwáheew VTA; **pound s.t. animate, mash s.t. animate** shàshkwáheew VTA; **pound s.t. animate in, drive s.t. animate in** kunj=chihtéeheew VTA; **pound s.t. in, drive s.t. in** kunjchihtéeham VTI1A; **pound things, grind things** shkwahíikeew VAI.

**pour away** VT **spill s.t, pour s.t. away** sookáaheew VAIO; **spill s.t. animate out, pour s.t. animate away** sóok=heew VTA **I got the potatoes out (of a container).** 'Nzookháawak óhpŭ=nak.'; **spill s.t., pour s.t. away** sóok=ham VTI1A.

**pour out** VT **pour out a liquid** sook=péenŭmeew VAI; **spill s.t. animate, pour s.t. animate out** sookáhlaleew VTA; **spill s.t., pour s.t. out** sookáh=latoow VTI2.

**pout** VI **have one's face wrinkled, have one's face contorted, pout, be in a temper, be discontented** *(as if about to cry)* wchuliingwéexiin VAI; **have one's lips sticking out, pout** niix=sheetóonayeew VAI; **pout** pòhwtoo=néexiin VAI; **pout, close one's mouth** spwutóoneew VAI; **purse one's lips, have one's mouth in a pout, have one's mouth sticking out pointed** chpwutoonéexiin VAI.

**powder** N **throw powder on s.o., throw dust on s.o., throw sand on s.o., throw dirt on s.o.** ponghwáaleew VTA.

**powder** VT **powder oneself, give oneself a dustbath** ponghwúnzuw VAI.

**powdery** ADJ **be light snow, be powdery snow** leexéesuw VAI.

**practice** VT **practice running** akwee=taaméhleew VAI; **practice shooting** akweetaxkhíikeew VAI; **practice sing-**

**ing** akweetaláamuw VAI; **practice throwing** akweetáaheew VAI.

**praise** VT **be praised, have a good name** wŭlakŭniimkwúsuw VAI; **say good things about s.o., praise s.o.** wŭlakŭníimeew VTA.

**pray** VI pahtamáweew VAI; **pray to s.o.** pahtamáweew VTA; **pray to s.o., pray for s.o.** pahtamaweelxáweew VTA.

**preach** VI pŭmutóonheew VAI; **say good things, preach** wŭlaaptóoneew VAI.

**preach to** VT **preach to s.o.** pŭmutoon=háaleew VTA.

**preacher** N pehpŭmutóonhees NA.

**prefer** VT **prefer s.o. to someone else, think more of s.o. than of someone else, think s.o. better than someone else** aluwéelŭmeew VTA; **prefer s.t. to s.t. else, think more of s.t. than of something else, think s.t. better than something else, want to do s.t. first** aluweelúndam VTI 1A.

**presence** N **sense s.o.'s presence, sense the presence of s.o.** namáaleew VTA; **sense s.t.'s presence, sense the presence of s.t.** namáatam VTI 1A **I feel that it's going to rain.** 'Nàmáatamun katá-sóokŭlaan.'

**preserve** VT **salt s.t. animate, put salt on s.t. animate, preserve s.t. animate in salt** shŭwáheew VTA; **salt s.t., put salt on s.t., preserve s.t. in salt** shŭwáham VTI 1A.

**press** VT **press down on s.o., push down on s.o., bend s.o. at a joint** *(using the hands)* tamákŭneew VTA; **press down on s.t., push down on s.t., bend s.t. at a joint** *(using the hands)* tamákŭnum VTI 1B; **press s.o., squeeze s.o.** *(using the hands)* sŭlúskŭneew VTA; **press s.t., squeeze s.t.** *(using the hands)* sŭlúskŭnum VTI 1B; **press the insides out of s.o., squeeze the insides out of s.o.** sŭluskihtéeheew VTA; **press the insides out of s.t., squeeze the insides out of s.t.** sŭluskihtéeham VTI 1A.

**preterite particle** N má PC **If you had told me, I would have stayed.** 'Lúy=ane áa má, nál áa yú ntápiin.', **If he had gone home, I would have gone with him.** 'Maachíite áa má, nŭwii=chéewaaw áa.'

**pretty** ADJ **be pretty, be evenly shaped, be nicely shaped** wŭluchéesuw VAI, wŭluchéeyeew VII; **be pretty, be good, be nice** wŭlúsuw VAI; **be pretty, be good, be nice** wŭlúsuw VAI, wŭlút VII.

**price** N **be a fair price** teepáawatuw VAI, teepáawatuw VII; **charge a certain price for s.t.** laawatóoheew VAIO; **charge a fair price for s.t.** teepaa=watóoheew VAIO; **have a low price** tangáawatuw VII; **lower the price of s.t.** tangaawatóoheew VAIO; **raise the price of s.t.** uspaawatóoheew VAIO.

**priest** N **Catholic priest** keeslukíiwi-pehpŭmutóonhees NA.

**proceed** VI **go in a certain manner, go in a certain direction, fly in a certain manner, fly in a certain direction, proceed in a certain manner, proceed in a certain direction** líh=leew VAI **You fell in the water but your head is sticking out.** 'Mbíing ktulíhla shùkéhla ksaakaandpéexiin.'

**product** N **be a 'dirty' picker, pick only the most accessible fruits or berries, pick only the most accessible products** aníiskii-paxkŭníikeew VAI.

**projectile** N **make a hole in s.t. animate by forceful contact, make a hole in s.t. animate with an instrument, make a hole in s.t. animate with a projectile** pkwúlaweew VTA; **make a hole in s.t. by forceful contact, make a hole in s.t. with an instrument, make a hole in s.t. with a projectile** pkwúlam VTI 1A; **split s.t. animate by forceful contact, split s.t. animate by shot, split s.t. animate with a**

**projectile** pasúlaweew VTA; **split s.t. by forceful contact, split s.t. by shot, split s.t. by hitting it with a projectile** pasúlam VTI1A.
**pronounce** VT **speak improperly, pronounce words incorrectly** amataap=tóoneew VAI.
**properly** ADV **be piled up neatly, be piled up nicely, be piled up properly** *(of something wood- or stick-like)* wŭlahkweexíinook VAI *usually plural,* wŭlahkwéexŭnool VII *usually plural;* **put a harness on s.o., tie s.o up properly, tie s.o. up well** wŭlam=bíileew VTA; **read skillfully, be able to read properly** nihtaawakíinzuw VAI; **tie s.t. up properly, tie s.t. up well** wŭlámbtoow VTI2 **You bandaged it up where he got hurt.** 'Koo=lámbtoon éenda-kshihteexíinge.'
**protect** VT **be protected from the wind, be away from the wind** aakawáxun VII.
**protrude** VI **have lumps protruding from a surface** *(of food cooking)* pòwcháteew VII.
**proud** ADJ **be a proud man, be arrogant, have an attitude, think that one knows more than anyone else** lunŭweelúnzuw VAI; **be proud** xwee=lúnzuw VAI; **be proud of s.o.** niipa=wéelŭmeew VTA; **be proud of s.t.** niipaweelúndam VTI1A.
**prune** VT **be marked, be trimmed, be pruned** *(of trees)* laalsháasuw VAI.
**pry out** VT **dig s.o out, pry s.o out, remove s.o.** *(using a tool or instrument)* kchiikwáaleew VTA; **dig s.t. out, pry s.t. out, remove s.t.** *(using a tool or instrument)* kchiikwáatam VTI1A; **pry s.o. out** *(using a tool or instrument),* **bail s.o. out of jail** ktáhkhweew VTA; **pry s.t. out of wood** *(using a tool or instrument)* ktáhkhwam VTI1A.
**public** N **be a good speaker** *(also of a child learning how to speak),* **be good at speaking, be good at public speaking** nihtaawaaptóoneew VAI.
**puddle** N **be a big puddle** amangpee=kíixun VII; **be water in a puddle** kxupéexun VII.
**pull** VT **pull s.o., pull at s.o.** wtúneew VTA **He kept pulling at me.** 'Nŭ=wawtúnukw.'; **pull s.t., pull at s.t.** wtúnum VTI1B **I want to pull it.** 'Ngáta-wtúnŭmun.'; **pull and drag s.o., pull and drag s.t. animate** wtutaachíhleew VTA; **pull and drag s.t.** wtutaachíindam VTI1A; **pull s.o.'s hair, pull on s.o.'s hair** sakiindpée=neew VTA; **pull things** wtuníikeew VAI.
**pull apart** VT **pull s.t. animate apart, dismantle s.t. animate** lookhéewa=leew VTA; **pull s.t. apart, dismantle s.t.** lookhéewatoow VTI2.
**pull down** VT **pull s.t. down** taaxkshée=num VTI1B; **pull s.t. down, lower s.t.** *(using the hands)* chíixŭnum VTI1B; **pull s.o.'s eye down, hold s.o.'s eye open** taaxksheengwéeneew VTA; **have pulled-down eyes** taaxksheengwée=xiin VAI; **pull one's eyes down, have one's eyes pulled down** taaxkshéen=gweew VAI.
**pull off** VT **detach s.t. animate, pull s.t. animate off, take s.t. animate away, remove s.t. animate** *(using the hands)* máhkŭneew VTA; **detach s.t., pull s.t. off, take s.t. away, remove s.t.** *(using the hands)* máhkŭnum VTI1B; **pull s.t. animate off, take s.t. animate off, take s.t. animate out** *(using the hands)* ktúneew VTA; **pull s.t. off, take s.t. off, take s.t. out** *(using the hands)* ktúnum VTI1B.
**pull on** VT **grab s.o. by the hand, tug at s.o, pull on s.o.** sakúneew VTA; **grab s.o. by the leg, pull on s.o.'s leg** sakukaatéeneew VTA; **grab s.t. by the hand, tug and pull on s.t.** sa=kúnum VTI1B; **pull s.o.'s hair, pull on**

**s.o.'s hair** sakiindpéeneew VTA.

**pull out** VT **pull s.t. animate out** *(using the hands)* móonŭneew VTA; **pull s.t. out** *(using the hands)* móonŭnum VTI1B.

**pumpkin** N máhkahkw NI.

**puppy** N changxúmwush NA.

**purpose** N **deliberately, on purpose** áhweel PC **I hit him on purpose.** 'Áhweel mbákamaaw.', **He did it on purpose.** 'Áhweel wtulŭnúmun.'

**purse** N shulpùliinóotay NI.

**pus** N mŭlúy NI; **be infected, have pus in it** mŭliiháasuw VAI, mŭliiháasuw VII; **be pus-filled, be pussy** mŭluy=óowuw VAI, mŭluyóowuw VII; **have infected eyes, have pus in one's eyes, have 'sleep' in one's eyes** mŭ=leelíingweew VAI; **have pus in one's eyes, have infected eyes** mŭluyee=líingweew VAI.

**push** VT **push s.o.** *(using the foot or body)* kunjchíhkaweew VTA; **push s.o., push s.t. over, shove s.o. over, shove s.t. over** kundáaheew VAIO; **push s.o., shove s.o.** kunjchaaháa=leew VTA; **push s.o., shove s.o.** *(using the hands)* kunjchúneew VTA **He pushed the baby buggy.** 'Kwunj=chunáawal chaachpùniikanúshal.'; **push s.t.** *(using the foot or body)* kunjchíhkam VTI1A; **push s.t., shove s.t.** kunjcháaheew VAIO; **push s.t., shove s.t.** *(using the hands)*, **move s.t.** *(of motions at a meeting)* kunj=chúnum VTI1B; **push things** *(using the hands)* kunjchuníikeew VAI.

**push down** VT **push s.o. down, shove s.o. down** kundaaháaleew VTA.

**push on** VT **press down on s.o., push down on s.o., bend s.o. at a joint** *(using the hands)* tamákŭneew VTA; **press down on s.t., push down on s.t., bend s.t. at a joint** *(using the hands)* tamákŭnum VTI1B.

**push over** VT **knock s.o. over, push s.o. over, bend s.o. over, tilt s.o. over** *(using the hands)* áamŭneew VTA; **knock s.t. over, push s.t. over, bend s.t. over, tilt s.t. over** *(using the hands)* áamŭnum VTI1B; **push s.o., push s.t. over, shove s.o. over, shove s.t. over** kundáaheew VAIO.

**put** VT **bunch s.o. up together, put s.o. in a bunch** mŭníixŭmeew VTA *object usually plural;* **bunch s.t. up together, put s.t. together in a bunch** mŭníixtoow VTI2 *object usually plural;* **can s.t. animate, put s.t. animate in cans** kéenheew VTA; **can s.t., put s.t. in cans** kéenham VTI1A; **can things, put things in cans** keenhíi=keew VAI; **finish putting s.o. down, finish putting s.o. there** kiisháhleew VTA; **finish putting s.t. there** kii=sháhtoow VTI2; **fix s.t. animate, repair s.t. animate, put s.o. to bed** wŭlíixŭmeew VTA; **hang over something, be put over something** laa=píixun VII; **put a mark on s.t. animate** *(using a tool or instrument)* káskheew VTA; **put s.o. in the front, put s.o. in the lead** shayéexŭmeew VTA; **put s.o. upside down** aaloolíi=xŭmeew VTA; **put s.o. upside down** *(using the hands)* aalóolŭneew VTA; **put s.t. in the front, put s.t. in the lead** shayéextoow VTI2; **put s.t. on wrong side out, put s.t. upside down** aapoochíixtoow VTI2; **put s.t. upside down** aaloolíixtoow VTI2; **put s.t. upside down** *(using the hands)* aalóolŭnum VTI1B; **soak one's legs in the water, put one's legs in the water** kamukwkáateew VAI.

**put around** VT **put s.t. animate around something, put s.t. animate all around something** wiiwŭníixŭmeew VTA *object usually plural;* **put s.t. around something, put s.t. all around something** wiiwŭníixtoow VTI2 *object usually plural.*

**put away** VT **put s.o. away, hide s.o., put s.t. animate away, hide s.t. animate** káaleew VTA; **put s.t. animate away, keep s.t. animate** wŭláhleew VTA; **put s.t. animate away, put s.o. away, hide s.o.** kaatáhleew VTA; **put s.t. away, hide s.t.** kaatáhtoow VTI2; **put s.t. away, hide s.t.** káatoow VTI2; **put s.t. away, store s.t.** wŭláhtoow VTI2 **I want to put it away.** 'Ngátawŭláhtoon.'; **be stored, be put away** wŭlahtáasuw VII; **hide s.o., put s.o. away** kaachíixŭmeew VTA; **hide s.t., put s.t. away** kaachíixtoow VTI2; **put things away, store things, be buried** wŭlahtáasuw VAI.

**put down** VT **put s.o. down, put s.t. animate down** áhleew VTA; **put s.t. down** áhtoow VTI2; **be placed, be put down** ahtáasuw VII; **finish putting s.o. down, finish putting s.o. there** kiisháhleew VTA.

**put in** VT **bottle s.t., put s.t. in cans, block s.t.** kpáskham VTI1A; **can s.t. animate, put s.t. animate in cans, block s.o., plug s.t. animate, fill in the cracks of s.t. animate, winterize s.t. animate** *(especially of windows)* kpáskheew VTA; **make a contribution, put money in the collection plate** máawapuw VAI; **put s.o. in the water** chóoxpwŭneew VTA; **put s.t. in the water** chóoxpwŭnum VTI1A; **put s.t. in, put s.t. inside** piinjíhlatoow VTI2; **take a step, put one's foot in something, put one's foot on something** alíhkeew VAI **I put my foot on the ice and I slipped.** 'Ndalíhke móhkamiing, noosháaxihla.', **He put his foot in the water.** 'Mbíing alíh=keew.'; **bathe one's eyes, put drops in one's eyes** sookhíingweew VAI.

**put in a heap** VT **put s.t. animate in a heap, heap s.t. animate up** msham=óoleew VTA *object usually plural;* **put s.t. in a heap, heap s.t. up** msham=óotoow VTI2 *object usually plural.*

**put inside** VT **put s.o. inside** píindŭ=neew VTA; **put s.t. inside** píindŭnum VTI1B; **insert s.t., put s.t. inside** píindham VTI1A; **be put on, be put inside** piindŭnáasuw VII **The boards were put inside the house.** 'Pasíi=kaaxkw piindŭnáasuw wíikwahm.'

**put on** VT **put s.t. animate on wrong side out, put s.t. animate on inside out, put s.o. upside down** aapoo=chíixŭmeew VTA; **put s.t. animate on wrong side out, put s.t. animate on inside out, put s.o. upside down** aapoochíixŭmeew VTA; **put s.t. animate on wrongly** *(of clothing)*, **put on the wrong one of s.t. animate** chaníhkaweew VTA; **put s.t. animate on wrongly** *(of clothing)*, **put on the wrong one of s.t. animate** chaníhka=weew VTA; **put s.t. on** *(of clothing)* píind VTI3 **I put my pants on.** 'Mbíindun mbulóokum.'; **put s.t. on for s.o.** *(of clothing)* píindaweew VTAO; **put s.t. on wrong side out, put s.t. upside down** aapoochíixtoow VTI2; **put s.t. on wrongly** *(of clothing)*, **put on the wrong one of s.t.** chaníhkam VTI1A; **put s.t. on wrongly, put on the wrong one of s.t.** *(of clothing)* chanawéeheew VAIO; **be put on, be put inside** piindŭnáasuw VII **The boards were put inside the house.** 'Pasíikaaxkw piindŭnáasuw wíikwahm.'; **crucify s.o., put s.o. on the cross** aashtehtéeheew VTA; **dress s.o. nicely, put bedcovers on s.o.** wŭlakwunáheew VTA; **have s.t. on inside out, put s.t. on inside out** *(of clothing)* aapoochíhkam VTI1A; **lean s.t. to one side, put s.t. on crooked** piimíixtoow VTI2; **make a mistake in putting s.t. animate on, put s.t. animate on wrongly** chaníixŭmeew VTA; **make a mistake in putting s.t. on, put s.t. on wrongly** chaníixtoow

VTI2; **put a collar on s.o., put a scarf on s.o.** wahkwéelŭneew VTA; **put a harness on** wŭlambtíikeew VAI; **put a harness on s.o., tie s.o up properly, tie s.o. up well** wŭlambíileew VTA; **put a hem on s.t.** aapíikwam VTI1A; **put bedcovers on s.o.** akwúnheew VTA; **put blinders on s.o.** *(especially of horses)* kpiingwéexŭmeew VTA; **put blueing on s.t. animate** oolihk=páleew VTA; **put butter on s.t.** pootŭ=láham VTI1A; **put butter on s.t. animate** *(using a tool or instrument)* pootŭláheew VTA; **put grease on s.o., put grease on s.t. animate** shamún=eew VTA; **put grease on s.t.** shamún=um VTI1B; **put on makeup** shoohún=zuw VAI; **put on one's mitts** piindŭ=niiwándeew VAI; **put on one's shirt** piindhéembteew VAI; **put on one's shoes** piindŭnahksúneew VAI; **put on one's socks** piindashíikaneew VAI; **put s.o. on to boil** chóoskŭneew VTA; **put shingles on a roof** apaháhkeew VAI; **put shoes on s.o.** *(especially of horses)* mahksunháaleew VTA; **put shoes on s.o.** piindŭnahksunéeneew VTA; **put spots on s.o., make a line of spots on s.o., mark spots on s.o.** sàsàpéekheew VTA; **put spots on s.t., make a line of spots on s.t., mark s.t. with spots** sàsàpéekham VTI1A; **put starch on s.t.** *(of clothing)* chiin=gaalchásum VTI1B; **put sugar on s.o., put sugar on s.t. animate** shookŭ=laaháaleew VTA; **put sugar on s.t.** shookŭláham VTI1A; **put wood on the fire** póonxeew VAI **I put in too much green wood.** 'Noosáamu- askxákwal -póonxe.'; **salt s.t. animate, put salt on s.t. animate, preserve s.t. animate in salt** shŭwáheew VTA; **salt s.t., put salt on s.t., preserve s.t. in salt** shŭwáham VTI1A; **take a step, put one's foot in something, put one's foot on something** alíhkeew VAI **I put my foot on the ice and I slipped.** 'Ndalíhke móhkamiing, noosháaxih=la.', **He put his foot in the water.** 'Mbíing alíhkeew.'

**put out** VT **put s.t. animate out, extinguish s.t. animate** *(of fires)* wchii=mahtéeheew VTA; **put s.t. out** *(of fires)* ahtéeham VTI1A; **put s.t. out, extinguish s.t.** *(of fires)* wchiimah=téeham VTI1A **Last night someone turned off the lights at my place.** 'Piiskéeku awéen oochiimahtéehŭ=mun wíikŭyaan.'

**put over** VT **put s.o. over something, put s.o. on something, put s.o. around something** laapíixŭmeew VTA; **put s.o. over the top of something** *(using the hands)* páalŭneew VTA; **put s.t. animate over something** paalíixŭmeew VTA; **put s.t. over something, make s.t. overlap** paalíixtoow VTI2; **put s.t. over something, put s.t. on something, put s.t. around something** laapíixtoow VTI2; **put s.t. over the top of something** *(using the hands)* páalŭnum VTI1A.

**put through** VT **be put through** *(of a motion at a meeting, of business)* eeshooxwatáasuw VII.

**put together** VT **put s.o. close together, put s.t. animate close together, stick s.o. up against something** psakwíi=xŭmeew VTA *object usually plural;* **put s.t. animate together** *(using the hands)* takwúneew VTA; **put s.t. close together, stick s.t. up against something** psakwíixtoow VTI2; **put s.t. together** *(using the hands)* takwúnum VTI1B.

**put underneath** VT **put s.o. underneath** alaamíixŭmeew VTA; **put s.o. underneath something** eekwíixŭmeew VTA; **put s.t. underneath** alaamíixtoow VTI2; **put s.t. underneath something** eekwíixtoow VTI2.

**put up** VT **put one's feet up, sit with**

**one's feet upon something** poxkw=siitéepuw VAI; **put one's leg up, raise one's legs** uspkáateew VAI; **put up wallpaper** pambiilhíikeew VAI; **tie something around s.t., 'put s.t. up'** *(of someone's hair)* wiiwŭnámbtoow VTI2.

**put upon** VT **put one's feet upon something** poxkwsíiteew VAI.

# Q

**quail** N pohpóokwush NA.

**quarrel** VI **argue, quarrel** pŭmiinee=híikeew VAI.

**quarrel with** VT **argue with s.o., quarrel with s.o.** pŭmiinéeheew VTA.

**question marker** N **question marker, emphatic** há PC **This is where he used to work.** 'Nún há wtihúnda-alóhkeen.', **Do you think so?** 'Ktíit há?'

**question word** N **how** *(question word)* thá PC **Where is the man?** 'Thá wá ná lúnuw?'; **how** tá PC **Where is he going?** 'Tá éew?', **Where does he live?** 'Tá wúndakw wíikiin?'

**quick** ADJ **quick, fast** akutaku- PV **I went away fast.** 'Ngaktáku-alúmsi.'

**quickly** ADV **fast, quickly** kshi- PV **I can dance fast.** 'Níi áa ngíish-kshí-kúndka.'; **fast, quickly** kshu- PV *informal* **The time is going quickly.** 'Kshú-kŭlákuw.', **It's snowing a lot.** 'Kshú-wíineew.'; **be gone out, go out quickly** *(of fires)* wchiimahtéh=leew VII; **break s.t.** *(quickly)* lookíh=latoow VTI2; **break s.t. animate** *(quickly)* lookíhlaleew VTA; **carry something away quickly** alumasan=íhleew VAIO; **crawl quickly** kshiikw=síhleew VAI, kshíikwsuw VAI; **drive fast, drive quickly** kshuchéhleew VAI; **get up quickly from lying down** aamwiipáhtoow VAI; **go quickly using a cane** kshalaawhúnzuw VAI; **grab s.t. in a hurry, grab s.t. quickly, grab a handful of s.t.** anziipáhtoow VTI2 **Grab the money and let's go to town.** 'Ánziipáhtool shúlpul ootée=neeng áatookw.'; **grow quickly** kshíikun VII, kshíikuw VAI; **read quickly** akushakíinzuw VAI; **run away quickly** kshushíimuw VAI; **run fast, run quickly, fly quickly, go quickly** kshíhleew VAI; **run sort of quickly, run at half-speed** kaak=shaaméhleew VAI **He was trotting by because he's nosy.** 'Móxa kaakshaa=méhleew kíhkata-wéewsuw.'; **speak quickly, speak in a harsh tone, speak in a sharp tone, say harsh things, say sharp things** kshaap=tóoneew VAI; **speak quickly, talk fast** akushaaptóonheew VAI; **swim quickly** kshaashŭwíhleew VAI; **talk quickly** akushíixsuw VAI; **walk fast, walk quickly** kshóoxweew VAI, akushóo=xweew VAI, akutakóoxweew VAI; **write quickly** akusheekhíikeew VAI.

**quiet** ADJ **be an unbeliever, don't believe in a Christian way of life, lead a quiet life** nalawáawsuw VAI; **be silent, keep quiet** chihtamwúsuw VAI; **sit quietly, be quiet** kŭlámapuw VAI.

**quietly** ADV **drive quietly** kwiishk=wchéhleew VAI **He drives quietly.** 'Móxa kwiishkwchéhle.'; **lie still, lie quietly** kŭlamíixiin VAI **The snake is still.** 'Áxkook kŭlamíixiin.'; **peacefully, quietly, contentedly** naláwii PC **He lives there quietly.** 'Naláwii wíikuw.'; **quietly, peacefully, contentedly** aayaláwii PC **He's sitting quietly.** 'Aayaláwii laalŭmátapuw.', **They're playing quietly.** 'Aayaláwii meelawúsŭwak.'; **run quietly** kwiishkwíhleew VAI *especially of vehicles;* **run quietly** kwiishkwíhleew VII *usually of motors;* **sit quietly**

kŭlamohkwéepuw VAI; **sit quietly, be quiet** kŭlámapuw VAI; **stay there quietly, be there quietly, live there quietly** naláwapuw VAI.

**quilt** N pàpxangakwíiwan NI.

**quit** VI **stop urinating, cease urinating, quit urinating** ehkwíisheew VAI; **stop working, break off working, quit before one is done** *(without necessarily having completed a task)* poh=kwalóhkeew VAI.

# R

**rabbit** N móoshkiingw NA; mooshkíin=gwus NA.

**raccoon** N éespan NA.

**race** N **beat s.o. in a race, beat s.o. in a competition** méelameew VTA; **race, take part in a race** meemeelanda=wéewak VAI *usually plural;* **run ahead, be leading in a race** shayee=waaméhleew VAI, shayeewahtakíh=leew VAI.

**race** VI **race, take part in a race** mee=meelandawéewak VAI *usually plural.*

**racket** N **make a racket, make a nonoral sound** kòhíikeew VAI.

**rag** N **cloth, cotton, rag** wshapakwíi=wan NI.

**rage** N **be very angry, go into a rage** kihtanóongsuw VAI.

**ragged** ADJ **be ragged, be bushy** píik=wsheew VII, piikwshúsuw VAI; **dress raggedly, wear ragged clothing** piikwshákuw VAI; **have a ragged beard, have a messy beard** piikw=shihtóonayeew VAI.

**rail** N **fence rail** meenáxkaaxkw NI.

**railroad** N **railroad, railroad track** nzukasunáanay NI.

**rain** N **be fine rain, be misty rain** awáhŭlaan VII; **be rain coming in this direction** péetŭlaan VII; **be rain going by** lóowŭlaan VII; **be sprinkling rain** pàpsákŭlaan VII, sahsáa=pŭlaan VII.

**rain** VI **rain, be raining** sóokŭlaan VII **If it rains I'll stay at home.** 'Katá-ch sookŭláange wíikŭyaan-uch ndápi.'; **be raining ice** mohkamíilaan VII; **be unable to rain** aalŭwúlaan VII; **begin raining** alúmŭlaan VII; **rain hard, rain heavily** kshíilaan VII; **rain on and off, rain intermittently** peh=péhtŭlaan VII; **rain steadily** *(diminutive)* chkawŭláanzhuw VII; **stop raining** éhkwŭlaan VII.

**raise** VT **raise s.t. animate up, lift s.t. animate up** *(using a tool or instrument)* uspáhkhweew VTA; **raise s.t. up, lift s.t. up** *(using a tool or instrument)* uspáhkhwam VTI1A; **be up, be in a raised position** uspíixiin VAI, uspíixun VII; **get s.o. into sitting position, raise s.o., raise s.o. in bed** *(from lying down)* aamwíhkŭneew VTA; **put one's leg up, raise one's legs** uspkáateew VAI; **raise one's ears, have one's ears raised** uspxéexiin VAI; **raise one's hand** uspiináxkeew VAI; **raise one's head, look up** us=póhkweew VAI; **raise one's legs up, have one's legs raised up** uspkaa=téexiin VAI; **raise s.o., be through with planting s.t. animate** kiishíi=kŭneew VTA; **raise s.t.** *(of crops)* kiishíikŭnum VTI1B; **raise the price of s.t.** uspaawatóoheew VAIO; **sit with one's legs up, raise one's legs while sitting** uspkaatéepuw VAI, uspkaatée=wapuw VAI.

**raisin** N **grape, raisin** wíisakiim NI.

**rake** N lxeekwáakan NI; **hay rake, collection plate in church** maaweeníi=kan NI.

**rake** VT **rake s.t. up** maawéekwam VTI1A *object usually plural;* **gather things, rake things up** maawee=kwáakeew VAI; **rake s.t.** lxéekwam

VTI 1 A; **rake things up, rake hay** maaweeníikeew VAI; **rake things, be raking** lxeekwáakeew VAI.

**rap** VI **knock, rap** *(on a door)* pòhíi=keew VAI.

**rape** VT **rape s.o.** msúneew VTA **She was raped.** 'Msúnaaw.'; **rape s.o. in secret, feel s.o. secretly** kíimŭneew VTA.

**rapidly** ADV **be rapidly moving water** kshupéhleew VII.

**rare** ADJ **undercook s.t., cook s.t. raw, cook s.t. rare** askatúpuw VAIO.

**raspberry** N lehlookíhlaash NA.

**rat** N xwataapíikwus NA.

**rattle** N **rattle** shòhwŭníikan NI; **use a rattle, make a rattling sound** shòh=wŭníikeew VAI, shòhwŭnúmeew VAI.

**rattle** VI **drive and make a loud noise, make a rattling noise while driving** *(of wagon wheels)* tiiwchéhleew VAI.

**rattlesnake** N wiishalúwees NA, wiisha=lúweew NA.

**raw** ADJ **be raw** áskun VII, ásksuw VAI; **eat s.t. animate raw** áskameew VTA; **eat s.t. raw** askándam VTI 1 A; **raw** askii- PN **Raw meat.** 'Áskii-wŭyóos.'; **raw meat, unsalted meat** askéewakw NI; **raw potato** askíhpun NA; **undercook s.t. animate, cook s.t. animate raw** askcháseew VTA; **undercook s.t., cook s.t. raw** askchásum VTI 1 B; **undercook s.t., cook s.t. raw, cook s.t. rare** askatúpuw VAIO.

**reach** VI **have a long arm, reach a long way** kwŭniináxkeew VAI; **reach across** aashŭwiináxkeew VAI; **reach out one's hand to get s.o.** naachii=naxkéeneew VTA; **reach out one's hand to get s.t.** naachiináxkeew VAIO.

**read** VI **read, count** akíinzuw VAI; **read badly, be a poor reader** amatakíin=zuw VAI; **read quickly** akushakíinzuw VAI; **read skillfully, be able to read properly** nihtaawakíinzuw VAI; **read slowly** ashahwakíinzuw VAI.

**read** VT **count s.t., read s.t.** akíindam VTI 1 A; **count s.t. animate, read s.t. animate** akíimeew VTA; **read s.t. animate correctly** wŭlakíimeew VTA; **read s.t. correctly** wŭlakíindam VTI 1 A.

**read to** VT **read s.t. to s.o.** akiinda=máweew VTAO; VT **read to s.o.** akiin=zŭwóoleew VTA.

**ready** ADJ **be ready to use, be all set** kiishíixiin VAI, kiishíixun VII **My bed is made.** 'Kiishíixun ndapíinay.'; **be ready, be ripe, be fully grown** tee=píikun VII, teepíikuw VAI; **dress s.o., get s.o. ready** weechpúneew VTA; **get dressed, get ready** wéechpuw VAI; **get dressed, get ready, be ready, be dressed** kiishéechpuw VAI; **get s.o. ready** kiishíixŭmeew VTA; **wait to take off, wait to leave, be ready for action** kehtéexiin VAI.

**ready-made** ADJ **be ready-made** kii=shihtáawanuw VII.

**real** ADJ **true, real** mayáawii PC **His real name.** 'Mayáawii eeshíinziit.', **The main road.** 'Mayáawii áanay.'

**really** ADV kéhla PC **For sure he's not well.** 'Wúlu kéhla máh wŭlamalusíi=wu.', **We'll wait for a while.** 'Kéhla-uch mbeesíhna-uch náake.'; **really, indeed, that's right, well** wŭlú PC **I didn't see him.** 'Wŭlú máh neewáa=wi.', **I can't understand him.** 'Wulú ndáalu-nóhtawaaw.'; **really, indeed, that's right, well** wŭlé PC **Are you sleepy?' 'That's right!** 'Kàkawóng=xwiin? Wŭlé!'

**reason** N **from a certain place, for a certain reason** wunj- PV *informal* **I ran down from the top of the hill** 'Waxkiitáawung nóonj-niixahtakíh=la.', **My head was sticking out of the water.** 'Mbíing nóonj-saakoh=kwéexiin.'; **from a certain place, for a certain reason** wunji- PV **I came out of the house.** 'Wiikwáhmung nóonji-kchíim.'; **from a certain place, for a certain reason** wunju- PV *informal* **Why did you do that?** 'Kwéek há nú kóonju-lúnŭmun?', **He got off the horse.** 'Nehnayóongsung wúnju-níixiiw.'; **place, reason** wunj- PN *informal* **They didn't cut them off the big trees.** 'Máh mahkshaa=wíiwal wúnj-xwacháhkwung.', **I crawled down from the tree.** 'Njii=xíikwsi wúnj-míhtkwung.'; **place, reason** wunju- PN *informal* **Off the table.** 'Wúnju-eehundaxpóonung.', **They didn't play cards for money any more.** 'Máh njíhnal shkupham=eewíiwak wúnju-shúlpul.'; **grow from a certain source, grow for a certain reason** wunjíikun VII, wunjíi=kuw VAI; **jump from a certain place, jump for a certain reason** wun=dáakchehl VAI **I jumped from far away.** 'Wáhlu noondáakchehl.'; **make s.o. live, save s.o., give s.o. a reason to live** pŭmaawsoohááleew VTA; **make s.t. animate from something, make s.t. animate for a certain reason** wunjíiheew VTA; **make s.t. from something, make s.t. for a certain reason** wunjíhtoow VTI2; **shine from a certain place, shine for a certain reason** *(of lamps)* wun=dáasŭleew VAI, wundáasŭleew VII; **talk from a certain place, talk for a certain reason, holler from a certain place, holler for a certain reason, call from a certain place, call for a certain reason** *(especially on the telephone)* wundaaptóoneew VAI **I talked from far away.** 'Wáhlu noon=daaptóone.'

**Rebecca** N lúpkaash NA.

**rebound** VI **rebound off something, bounce back and fall, fall back** *(s.t. animate)*, **be a foul ball** *(baseball)* kwaxkwíixiin VAI.

**recede** VI **recede, go down** *(of water level)* ahkwíhleew VII.

**receive** VT **receive s.o., receive s.t. animate** mshúneew VTA; **receive s.t.** mshúnum VTI1B.

**recently** ADV kunjóoka PC **I saw Dianne recently.** 'Kunjóoka Dianne néewaaw.', **I fixed my car recently.** 'Kunjóoka noolíixŭmaaw ngáalum.'

**recite** VT **say things from memory, recite from memory** shàshkwakíinzuw VAI.

**recklessly** ADV **drive recklessly, go regardless of the consequences or risks** laalxawíhleew VAI; **place s.o. recklessly, place s.o. in a dangerous spot, place s.o. regardless of the consequences or risks** laalxawíixŭ=meew VTA; **place s.t. recklessly, put s.t. in a dangerous spot, place s.t. regardless of the consequences or risks** laalxawíixtoow VTI2.

**recline** VI **lie, recline** shungíixun VII.

**recognize** VT **recognize s.o.** náweew VTA; **recognize s.t.** nám VTI1B; **recognize the taste of s.t.** mihkóhptam VTI1A; **recognize the taste of s.t. animate** mihkohptámweew VTA.

**recover** VI **recover from an illness** kii=kéhleew VAI.

**red** ADJ **be red** máxkeew VII, máxksuw VAI; **red** maxkii- PV **I painted it red.** 'Nŭmáxkii-shóohŭmun.'; **red** maxkii- PN **Red shoelace** 'Máxkii-aníixan.'; **red thread** maxkáhtakw NI; **be a reddish colour, have a red tinge to it** maxkŭléexiin VAI, maxkŭléexun VII; **be dyed red, turn red, be red from heat, be browned** *(of meat)* maxk=cháteew VII; **be dyed red, turn red, burn red** *(s.t. animate)*, **be red from heat, get a sunburn, be browned** maxkchásuw VAI; **be marked red, have red stripes** maxkeekháasuw VII, maxkeekháasuw VAI; **be red coloured** maxkaapamúkwat VII, maxkaapa=múkwsuw VAI; **be red coloured liq-**

uid maxkáapŭweew VII; **be red headed** maxkáandpeew VAI; **be red with cold** máxkachuw VAI, máxkatun VII; **dye s.t. animate red, brown s.t. animate** maxkcháseew VTA; **dye s.t. red, brown s.t.** *(of meat)* maxkchásum VTI1B; **have a red face** maxkchàlíin=gweew VAI, maxkshéengweew VAI, maxkíingweew VAI; **have a red nose** maxkcháaleew VAI; **have measles, have scarlet fever, turn red** max=kíhleew VAI; **have red bricks on it** *(of houses)* maxkasunháasuw VII; **have red eyes, blush, have a red face** maxkshéengweew VAI; **have red hair** maxkaalóhkweew VAI; **have red lips** amaxksheetóoneew VAI, maxkshee=tóoneew VAI; **turn red** maxkíhleew VII; **turn reddish-brown, turn yellow** *(by heat)*, **be a ripened colour** *(of grain ready to harvest)* wiisaaw=xáteew VII; **turn reddish-brown, turn yellow, turn orange** *(by heat)* wiisaawxásuw VAI; **red squirrel** wii=saawaníikwus NA.

**red-headed woodpecker** N meemax=kóhkwees NA.

**reduce** VT **be crushed down, get reduced in cooking** shkwíhleew VAI.

**refuse** VT **unwillingly, refuse to do** shiing- PV *informal* **He wouldn't milk the cow.** 'Shíing-siiníikeew.', **They didn't want to leave.** 'Shíing-alumsúwak.'; **unwillingly, refuse to do** shiingi- PV **He wouldn't let them (do something).** 'Wshíingi-leelŭ=máawal.', **He wouldn't go with me.** 'Nzhíingi-wiichéewukw.'; **unwillingly, refuse to do** shiingu- PV *informal* **He wouldn't get in.** 'Shíingu-póo=siiw.', **He wouldn't eat** 'Shíingu-míitsuw.'; **disobey, refuse to listen, be stubborn** achiingíiwsuw VAI; **be balky, refuse to do something** mbaakíihuw VAI.

**regard** N **think a lot of s.o., think highly of s.o., have a high regard for s.o.** kaanzhéelŭmeew VTA, xwée=lŭmeew VTA; **think a lot of s.t., think highly of s.t., have a high regard for s.t.** kaanzheelúndam VTI1A, xweelún=dam VTI1A.

**regardless** ADV **anyway, regardless, go ahead and do something** téexii PC **I just went ahead and cooked, but no one came.** 'Téexii nátpwiin máh awéen péewi.', **They went ahead and lived together.** 'Téexii ngwúteel apúwak.'; **do dangerous work, work regardless of the consequences or risks** laalxawalóhkeew VAI; **drive recklessly, go regardless of the consequences or risks** laalxawíhleew VAI.

**regret** VT **regret that s.o. leaves** loo=sóomeew VTA; **find that s.o. appears hopeless, regret seeing s.o.** laawíi=naweew VTA.

**reins** N sakahtakuníikanal NI *usually plural;* **lead s.o. along with a string, lead s.o. by with a string, lead s.o. along by the reins, lead s.o. by by the reins** *(of horses)* pŭmaapéeneew VTA; **lead s.o. in a certain direction with a string, lead s.o. in a certain manner with a string, lead s.o. in a certain direction by the reins, lead s.o. in a certain manner by the reins, put the reins on s.o.** *(of horses)* laa=péeneew VTA.

**related to** VT **be related to s.o.** laan=góomeew VTA; **be related to s.o. as well** naxpaangóomeew VTA; **be closely related to s.o., want to be related to s.o.** àhwaangóomeew VTA; **be related to each other** laangóondŭwak VAI *usually plural.*

**relative** N **marry and add on to one's family, take on relatives** aandshii=lúndam VOTI1.

**relax** VI **walk slowly, walk in a relaxed fashion** wàwtamóoxweew VAI.

**relieve** VT **be relieved** laangíhleew VAI.

**religious** ADJ **'testify' at a religious meeting, 'testify' in church** pasuk=wtóonheew VAI.

**reluctant** ADJ **be reluctant** shiingee=lúndam VOTI1; **be reluctant to plant** shiingahkíiheew VAI; **be unwilling to go, be reluctant to go** shiingóoxweew VAI; **do reluctantly, be reluctant about doing something, be difficult to do something, be hard to do something** mihka PC **I didn't want to go to work (but I did).** 'Míhka nŭmáw-alóhke.', **It's hard for me to get up.** 'Míhka mbáskwi.'; **make remarks to people, make 'digs' at people, be reluctant to come out and say things to people** maashiila=táasuw VAI; **make remarks to s.o., make 'digs' at s.o., hint at something to s.o., be reluctant to say something outright to s.o.** maashii=latáweew VTA.

**reluctantly** ADV **do reluctantly, I guess I'll do** *(something)* káa PC **I guess I'll go to bed.** 'Sháxkii káa nŭmáw-kawí.', **I'll walk (rather than riding).** 'Káa mbúmsi.'; **do reluctantly, be reluctant about doing something, be difficult to do something, be hard to do something** mihka PC **I didn't want to go to work (but I did).** 'Míhka nŭmáw-alóhke.', **It's hard for me to get up.** 'Míhka mbáskwi.'; **reluctantly** alíike PC **I ate the fried bread reluctantly.** 'Alíike salápwaan numíichiin.', **I went to church reluctantly.** 'Alíike nŭmáw-maawéewi.'; **reluctantly, (do) reluctantly, finally** péhkiik PC **I went there reluctantly.** 'Péhkiik náh ndá.', **I wrote to him and he finally answered me.** 'Mbee=teekhámawaa, péhkiik naxkóomukw.'

**rely on** VT **rely on s.o., depend on s.o., need s.o.'s help** nahkáaleew VTA; **rely on s.t., depend on s.t.** nahkáatum VTI1A.

**remain** VI **have s.o. remaining, have s.o. left over** piiwíiheew VTA; **have s.t. remaining, have s.t. left over** piiwíhtoow VTI2.

**remark** N **make a cutting remark to s.o., talk so as to injure s.o.** kshaap=toonáaleew VTA; **make remarks to people, make 'digs' at people, be reluctant to come out and say things to people** maashiilatáasuw VAI; **make remarks to s.o., make 'digs' at s.o., hint at something to s.o., be reluctant to say something outright to s.o.** maashiilatáweew VTA.

**remember** VT **think about s.o., remember s.o.** msháaleew VTA **Someone must be thinking about you.** 'Awéen éet kŭmusháalukw.'; **think about s.t., remember s.t.** msháatam VTI1A.

**remind** VT **remind s.o., bring something to s.o.'s mind** mihkóomeew VTA.

**remove** VT **detach s.t. animate, pull s.t. animate off, take s.t. animate away, remove s.t. animate** *(using the hands)* máhkŭneew VTA; **detach s.t., pull s.t. off, take s.t. away, remove s.t.** *(using the hands)* máhkŭnum VTI1B; **dig s.o out, pry s.o out, remove s.o.** *(using a tool or instrument)* kchiikwáaleew VTA; **dig s.t. out, pry s.t. out, remove s.t.** *(using a tool or instrument)* kchiikwáatam VTI1A; **have one's cataracts removed** pŭ=lakiingwáalaaw VTA *indefinite subject only;* **remove s.o.'s cataracts** pŭlak=iingwéeneew VTA; **skin s.t. animate, remove the covering from s.t. animate** pxwíineew VTA; **skin s.t., remove the covering from s.t., shell s.t.** *(of corn)* pxwíinam VTI1A; **take s.o. along, remove s.o.** alumóoxwa=leew VTA; **take s.t. along, remove s.t.** alumóoxwatoow VTI2; **unload s.o.,**

**take s.o. out of the water, take s.o. out of a vehicle, remove s.o.** kóhpŭ=neew VTA **I took the potatoes off (the stove).** 'Ngohpŭnáawak óhpŭnak.'; **wear s.t. animate out by washing it, wash s.t. animate away, remove s.t. animate by washing, wash s.t. animate completely, wash s.t. animate right out** mehtapáleew VTA **I washed away where the writing was.** 'Nŭ=mehtapálaaw éenda-leekháasiit.'; **wear s.t. out by washing it, wash s.t. completely, wash s.t. right out, wash s.t. away, remove s.t. by washing** mehtapátoow VTI2.

**repair** VT **fix s.t. animate, repair s.t. animate, put s.o. to bed** wŭlíixŭ=meew VTA; **fix s.t., repair s.t.** wŭlíix=toow VTI2; **be fixed, be repaired** wŭliixtáasuw VII.

**repeat** VT **repeat, say something over** laapíixsuw VAI.

**replace** VT **replace s.o., replace s.t. animate** laapáhleew VTA; **replace s.t.** laapáhtoow VTI2; **replace s.t. for s.o.** laapáhtaweew VTAO.

**replant** VI **replant, put in new plants** laapahkíiheew VAI.

**report** N **be a great noise, be a big rumour, be a great report of an activity** *(especially of a story that gets modified or exaggerated)* kaanzhih=táakwat VII.

**reprimand** VT **reprimand s.o., chew s.o. out** nahpŭnáleew VTA.

**require** VT **no longer require s.o.'s services** ehkwalóoleew VTA.

**resemble** VT **like, resembling** máash PC **Also it looks sharp, his nose.** 'Kwŭ=lúp máash kíineew wihkíiwan.', **He looks like a White person.** 'Máash shŭwanakwiináakwsuw.'

**residence** N **move, move one's residence** ngatáhkeew VAI.

**respect** VT **think well of s.o., respect s.o.** wŭlíi-pŭnáweew VTA.

**responsibility** N **take care of s.o., look after s.o., tend to a responsibility with regard to s.o.** lxawéelŭmeew VTA **You should take care of your car, don't drive it needlessly.** 'Káta-lxawéelŭmaa ktahtamoombíilum, chíi amayakaweehéehan.'; **take care of s.t., look after s.t., tend to a responsibility with regard to s.t.** lxawee=lúndam VTI1B **Take care of the food (said of an empty refrigerator).** 'Katá-lxaweelúndah miichŭwáakan.'

**rest** N **rest, resting** *(especially after death)* alaaxiimŭwáakan NI; **rest, take a rest** alaaxíimuw VAI.

**rest** VI **rest, take a rest** alaaxíimuw VAI; **feel as if one would like to rest** alaaxiimwahtéenamuw VAI.

**restless** ADJ **be a restless person, be an active person** seekawéenuw VAI, séeksuw VAI; **be restless, be bothered, feel restless** sàkwamálsuw VAI; **be worried, be upset, be irritable, be restless** sákwsuw VAI; **feel tired, feel restless** *(especially when sick)* shiiwamálsuw VAI; **lead an unsettled life, lead a restless life** sàkwáawsuw VAI; **restless person, active person** séekaween PR.

**Resurrection** N aamwiiwáakan NI.

**retaliate** VI **retaliate by hitting s.o., hit s.o. in return** kwaxkihtéeheew VTA.

**return** N **retaliate by hitting s.o., hit s.o. in return** kwaxkihtéeheew VTA.

**return** VI **back, return** kwaxku- PV *informal* **I gave it back.** 'Ngwáxku-méekun.'; **come back from dancing, return from dancing** áapkeew VAI; **return from** *(doing something)* aapi- PV **I came back from the funeral.** 'Ndáapi-kwtawŭníike.'; **return from** *(doing something)* aapu- PV *informal* **He comes back from cutting wood.** 'Áapu-manáxe.'; **return home** aa=páachiiw VAI-S; **return, come back** kwáxkiiw VAI-S **I'm back.** 'Méhch wáak mbéech-kwáxki.'

**return** VT **exchange s.t. animate, return s.t. animate, give s.t. animate back** *(after borrowing it)* aashŭwún=eew VTA; **exchange s.t., give s.t. back, return s.t.** *(after borrowing it)* aashŭwúnum VTI1B; **return s.o., bring s.o. back** kwaxkóoxwaleew VTA; **return s.t., bring s.t. back** kwaxkóo=xwatoow VTI2; **turn s.t. animate back** *(of clocks, using the hands)*, **return s.o.** kwáxkŭneew VTA; **turn s.t. back** *(using the hands)*, **return s.t.** kwáxkŭnum VTI1B.

**reunite** VI **get together again, reunite** laapíilŭnuw VAI.

**reveal** VT **tell about s.t., reveal s.t.** kchíhlatoow VTI2 **You told about what happened (and weren't supposed to).** 'Kùchíhlatoon kwéek éeleek.'

**revive** VT **make s.o. live, revive s.o.** laawsoohá aleew VTA, laawsóoheew VAIO.

**rheumatism** N **have rheumatism** lum=tiisíineew VAI.

**rhubarb** N shŭwáskw NI.

**ribbon** N síluk NI; **have ribbons on it** silkaháasuw VII; **wear a ribbon** sìl=káhŭmeew VAI.

**rice** N pehpáasteek NI.

**rich** ADJ **be rich** pawálsuw VAI; **make s.o. rich** pawalsóoheew VAIO.

**rid of** VT **destroy all of s.o., kill all of s.o., get rid of all of s.o.** weemíiheew VTA *object usually plural.*

**ride** VI **come here riding on horseback, ride towards the speaker** peethóo=meew VAI; **go back and forth, ride back and forth, fly back and forth** wŭyakíhleew VAI **The cars are going back and forth.** 'Káalak wŭyakih=léewak.'; **go crookedly while riding on horseback** pàptukhóomeew VAI; **ride away on horseback** alumhóo=meew VAI; **ride by on horseback, ride along on horseback** pŭmahóo=meew VAI; **ride on horseback with s.o.** wiithóomeew VTA.

**rider** N **horse rider** pehpóxkapiis NA.

**rifle** N **gun, rifle** payaxkhíikan NI.

**right away** ADV **right away, immediately** sháa PC **Okay, I'll look for them right away.** 'Yó, kwáy sháa ngwiilamúnal.', **My mother told my grandmother and my grandfather right away.** 'Sháa ngúk wtúlaan nóohŭmal wáak nŭmoxóomsal.'; **right away, immediately** sháawu PC **I didn't recognize you right away.** 'Máh sháawu kŭnunoolóowu.', **You'll have to plant right away.** 'Ayásku-ch sháawu ktahkíiheem.'

**right-handed** ADJ **be right-handed** mayaawŭnáxkeew VAI.

**ring** N tíhtŭyaak NI, tíhtŭyaak NA; **wear a ring** tihtŭyaakhámeew VAI.

**ring** VI **ring a bell, make a ringing noise** *(on metal)* taliinghwíikeew VAI; **ring, be ringing** taliingwíixiin VAI, taliingwíixun VII, talíingweew VII; **ring, make a ringing noise, make a tinny noise** taliingwihtéexun VII, ta=liingwihtéexun VII.

**ring** VT **ring a bell, make a ringing noise** *(on metal)* taliinghwíikeew VAI; **ring a bell** taliingwŭnúmeew VAI.

**rinse** VT **rinse s.t. animate, rinse s.t. animate out** kshiixpéhlaleew VTA; **rinse s.t., rinse s.t. out** kshiixpéhla=toow VTI2; **rinse, rinse things** kshiixpehlatíikeew VAI.

**rip** VT **be ripped, be torn** tashakíhleew VII, tashakíhleew VAI.

**ripe** ADJ **be ready, be ripe, be fully grown** teepíikun VII, teepíikuw VAI; **be ripe** atíhteew VII **Only pick the ripe ones.** 'Shùkéhla eetihtéekiil ayíh.'; **be ripe** atúsuw VAI; **turn reddish-brown, turn yellow** *(by heat)*, **be a ripened colour** *(of grain ready to harvest)* wiisaawxáteew VII.

**rise** VI páasteew VII; **rise** *(of yeast)* paa=sawíixun VII.

**risk** N **be a bad risk for credit, be a 'poor pay'** màmateenhíikeew VAI; **do dangerous work, work regardless of the consequences or risks** laal=xawalóhkeew VAI; **drive recklessly, go regardless of the consequences or risks** laalxawíhleew VAI; **place s.o. recklessly, place s.o. in a dangerous spot, place s.o. regardless of the consequences or risks** laalxaw=íixŭmeew VTA; **place s.t. recklessly, put s.t. in a dangerous spot, place s.t. regardless of the consequences or risks** laalxawíixtoow VTI2.

**river** N síipuw NI; **along the bank, down by the river, close to the river** yáa=pee PC **I walked along the shore.** 'Yáapee mbúmsi.'; **big river** kihtsíi=puw NI; **over across the river** kaa=mŭnúwiing PC; **the other side of the river** káamung PC.

**road** N áanay NI; **be a crooked road** piimatéexun VII, pàptukatéexun VII; **be a flat road, be a flat driveway** pàk=atéexun VII; **be a good road, be a good path** wŭlatéexun VII; **be a muddy road** asiiskŭwatéexun VII; **be a road or path going in a certain direction, be a certain kind of road or path** latéexun VII **There's a road going to the bush.** 'Kóhpii làtéexun.'; **be a road that comes from a certain place** wundatéexun VII **The road leads from the forest.** 'Kóhpii wundatée=xun.'; **be a sandy road, be a sandy path** leekŭwatéexun VII; **be a straight road** shaaxkàtéexun VII; **be a wide road** paanatéexun VII; **be a winding road** waakatéexun VII; **be at the side of the road, park at the side of the road** paxkéexiin VAI; **be many roads** xweelatéexun VII; **be the end of the road** wihkwatéexun VII; **be the start of a road** alumatéexun VII; **make a good road, make a good path, have a good road, have a good path** wŭ=latéexteew VAI; **straight road** shaax=káanay NI; **the end of the road** wih=kwáanay NI; **the other side of the road** awasiixkanáwe PC; **walk crookedly, walk on a crooked road** pàp=tukóoxweew VAI.

**roam** VI **go all over, roam with no purpose in mind, throw one's backside about as one goes** msiitŭyéewxeew VAI; **roam with no purpose in mind, throw one's behind about as one goes** msiitŭyéhleew VAI.

**roar** VI **roar, go by roaring** tamon=gwíhleew VII; **roar, go by roaring, run well** tamongwíhleew VAI.

**roast** VI **roast, be roasting** *(of foods)* apóosuw VAI.

**roast** VT **roast s.t.** apóosuw VAIO.

**rob** VT **rob people, take things from people by force** shihkwihtáasuw VAI.

**robin** N chiishkóhkoosh NA.

**rock** N **stone, rock** asún NI.

**rock** VT **rock oneself, be rocking** nee=neemíhleew VAI; **shake s.o. back and forth, move s.o. back and forth, wave s.o. back and forth, rock s.o. back and forth** kwàkwchukwaaháa=leew VTA.

**rocking chair** N neeneemáhpapoon NI.

**roll** VI **roll, roll around** tùpchéhleew VAI, tùpchéhleew VII; **roll around, roll in a circle** wiiwŭniinjkwéhleew VAI; **roll away** alumiinjkwéhleew VAI; **roll over, roll around, roll along** tùpiinjkwéhleew VAI, tùpiinjkwéhleew VII; **roll over onto one's stomach** pàkatéhleew VAI; **go in a circle, go around, roll in a circle** wiiwŭníh=leew VII; **roll by, roll along** pŭmiinj=kwéhleew VAI, pŭmiinjkwéhleew VII; **roll here, roll towards the speaker** peechiinjkwéhleew VAI **He's rolling this way (of a fat person).** 'Méhch wáak peechiinjkwéhleew.'; **roll in a**

**certain manner, roll in a certain direction** liinjkwéhleew VAI, liinjkwéh=leew VII; **roll straight** wŭliinjkwéh=leew VAI, wŭliinjkwéhleew VII.

**roll** VT **roll s.o. around in a circle** wii=wŭniinjkwéhlaleew VTA; **roll s.o. in a certain direction, roll s.o. in a certain manner** liinjkwéeneew VTA; **roll s.t around** tùpiinjkweeyáaheew VAIO; **roll s.t. around in a circle** wiiwŭ=niinjkwéhlatoow VTI2; **roll s.t. away** alumiinjkweeyáaheew VAIO; **roll s.t. by, roll s.t. along** pŭmiinjkweeyáa=heew VAIO; **roll s.t. in a certain direction, roll s.t. in a certain manner** luchéenum VTI1B, liinjkweeyáaheew VAIO; **roll s.t. in a certain manner, roll s.t. in a certain direction** liinj=kwéenum VTI1A; **roll s.t. to here, roll s.t. towards the speaker** peechiinj=kweeyáaheew VAIO; **spread s.t. out, roll s.t. out** *(using a tool or instrument)* shiipáhkhwam VTI1A.

**roll up** VT **roll s.t. animate up** *(using the hands)* ptúkwŭneew VTA; **roll s.t. up** *(using the hands)* ptúkwŭnum VTI1B; **wrap s.t. animate around something, roll s.o. up, tie s.o. up** túpheew VTA; **wrap s.t. around something, roll s.t. up** túpham VTI1A; **be rolled up, be tied up** tùpháasuw VII, tùpháasuw VAI.

**roller** N **use a roller** shiipahkhwíikeew VAI.

**roof** N apahahkáakan NI; **house with a pointed roof** chpwíikaan NI; **put shingles on a roof** apaháhkeew VAI; **the top of the roof, the top of the house** waxkíitaakw PC **The top of the roof leaks.** 'Waxkíitaakw wunjíi=kuw.'

**room** N **be a certain length** *(of rooms)* sahkúndeew VII **He was pacing back and forth in the room.** 'Asahkóo=xweew sehkúndeek.'; **be a hot room, be warm in the house** kshuteewii=kamíikat VII; **be a large room** xwún=deew VII; **be a room, be a divided room, be different rooms, be another room** *(in a dwelling)* chpún=deew VII; **be a warm room** kiishŭ=wiikamíikat VII, kiishŭwúndeew VII; **be an empty room** alaxúndeew VII; **be the middle of a room** laawún=deew VII; **have large rooms** *(of buildings)* amangúndeew VII.

**rooster** N **rooster, male fowl** lunŭwéh=leew NA.

**root** N wchapíhkxakw NI; **root cellar** ahkŭyáalakw NI.

**rope** N ptukwáhtakw NI; **rope, piece of rope** áaman NI; **short piece of rope, short piece of string** chahkwáama=nush NI.

**Rosie** N lóoshiin NA.

**rot** VI **rot, be rotten** alúl VAI, alút VII.

**rotate** VI **go around, rotate, spin** tùp=íhleew VII, tùpíhleew VAI.

**rotten** ADJ **rot, be rotten** alúl VAI, alút VII; **rotten old man** akwaakwalih=lóosus NA, alihlóosus NA; **smell rotten, have a rotten smell** aliimáakwat VII, aliimáakwsuw VAI; **taste rotten, have a rotten taste** aliipóokwat VII, aliipóokwsuw VAI.

**rough** ADJ **be rough, be coarse** kaaxka=shúsuw VAI, káaxkasheew VII; **be rough** káaxksuw VAI; **feel rough** kaaxkamamkwúsuw VAI, kaaxka=mámkwat VII; **have rough hands, have chapped hands** kaaxkŭnáx=keew VAI; **have rough lips** kaaxk=sheetóoneew VAI; **have s.t. animate that feels rough** kaaxkamámeew VTA **My knee feels rough.** 'Ngaaxka=mámaaw ngútkuw.'; **have s.t. that feels rough** kaaxkamándam VTI1A **My throat feels rough.** 'Ngaaxka=mándamun ngwundáakan.'; **rough, coarse** kaaxkashii- PN **Coarse flour.** 'Káaxkashii-lohkhámun.', **Coarse cloth.** 'Káaxkashii-wshapakwíiwan.';

taste rough kaaxkiipóokwsuw VAI.

**round** ADJ **be round** ptúkweew VII; **be round** *(s.t. animate)*, **be full** *(of the moon)* ptúkwsuw VAI; **be big and round, be big around the middle, be big in girth** xwáhkwsuw VAI; **be round in shape** ptukwchéesuw VAI, ptukwchéeyeew VII; **cut s.t. animate in a round shape** ptúkwsheew VTA; **cut s.t. in a round shape** ptúkwshum VTI1B; **have round ('button') eyes** kŭnoopaalakíingweew VAI; **have round shoulders** ptukwpoxkwanée=xiin VAI; **little round Mary** pchúkwu-meelíishush NA; **round table** ptuk=weehundáxpoon NI.

**row** N **be at the end of a row, be at the end of a line, be at the end of something** wihkwáameew VII **It is a little ways to the end of it.** 'Péexwiish wihkwáameew.', **We've come to the end now.** 'Méhch kwáy éenda-wih=kwaámeek kpáhna.'; **be in a straight line, be in a row** wŭlaaméewak VAI *usually plural,* wŭlaaméewal VII *usually plural;* **be in a straight row, be in a straight line** shaaxkáameew VII **What I planted is in a straight row.** 'Shaaxkáameew ehkíihayaan.'; **stand in rows, stand several deep** pihta=wiikaapawúwak VAI *usually plural.*

**row** VI **paddle away, row away** alúm=ham VOTI1; **row across the water, paddle across the water** kwaxk=hámeew VAI; **row this way, come here paddling, paddle towards the speaker** péetham VOTI1.

**rub** VT **rub s.o., brush up against s.t. animate, pet s.o., caress s.o.** *(using the hands)* láalŭneew VTA; **rub s.o., pet s.o.** *(using the hands)* síikwŭneew VTA; **rub s.t.** *(using the hands)*, **run one's hand over s.t.** láalŭnum VTI1B; **rub s.t.** *(using the hands)* síikwŭnum VTI1B; **brush s.t., rub s.t.** *(using a tool or instrument)* láalham VTI1A; **rub s.t. animate** *(using a tool or instrument)* síikhweew VTA; **lick s.o., rub s.o. with the mouth** síikwameew VTA; **lick s.o., rub, nuzzle s.o. with mouth** láalameew VTA; **paint s.o., rub s.o., rub on s.o.** shóoheew VTA; **paint s.t., rub s.t. on, rub s.t.** shóo=ham VTI1A; **rub one's mouth on s.o., lap s.o., lick s.o.** síisameew VTA; **rub one's mouth on s.t, lick s.t.** siisán=dam VTI1A; **rub s.o. on the head, pet s.o. on the head** siikwaandpéeneew VTA; **rub s.t.** *(of clothes on a washboard)* síikhwam VTI1A.

**rub against** VT **rub against something and fall, brush up against something and fall** laalihtéexiin VAI; **rub against something, rub up against something** siikwíixiin VAI, siikwíixun VII.

**rub on** VT **lick s.t., rub on s.t. with the mouth** siikwándam VTI1A; **paint s.o., rub s.o., rub on s.o.** shóoheew VTA; **paint s.t., rub s.t. on, rub s.t.** shóo=ham VTI1A.

**rubber** N **rubber overshoe** làpŭláhksun NI, pihtawáhksun NI.

**rug** N **carpet, rug** ehahpalíhkeeng VII.

**rule** N aaptoonáakan NI; **be hard to handle, don't obey the rules, be 'out of hand'** wŭyakáawsuw VAI; **voice** *(especially of the Lord).*

**ruler** N **something used for measuring, ruler, measuring tape, measuring stick** tpuskhíikan NI.

**run** VI **run by, run along** pŭmahtakíh=leew VAI; **run close by** peexŭwaa=méhleew VAI; **run downhill** niixah=takíhleew VAI; **run fast** kihtaaméh=leew VAI, kshahtakíhleew VAI; **run fast, run quickly, fly quickly, go quickly** kshíhleew VAI; **run here and there, run about, run around** apaa=mahtakíhleew VAI; **run here, run in this direction, come here running** peetaaméhleew VAI, peetahtakíhleew

VAI; **run home** maachahtakíhleew VAI; **run in a certain manner, run in a certain direction** laaméhleew VAI **He's running towards the forest.** 'Kóhpii laaméhleew.'; **run in a certain manner, run in a certain direction** lahtakíhleew VAI **I'm going to the bathroom.** 'Wiikwáhmshung ndulahtakíhla.'; **run in a certain manner, run in a certain direction, go in a certain manner, go in a certain direction** shíhleew VAI **He was running close by.** 'Náhnalii shíh=leew.'; **run in a circle, run around something** wiiwŭnahtakíhleew VAI; **run naked** sheexkalaaméhleew VAI; **run naked, run bare** mooshakaa=méhleew VAI *especially of animals with missing fur;* **run often** eewatah=takíhleew VAI; **run out of sight** wa=nahtakíhleew VAI; **run outside, run out** ktahtakíhleew VAI; **run quietly** kwiishkwíhleew VAI *especially of vehicles;* **run quietly** kwiishkwíhleew VII *usually of motors;* **run secretly, run in secret** kiimahtakíhleew VAI; **run silently, whisper, run well** kwiishkwihtáakwat VII, kwiishkwih=táakwsuw VAI; **run slowly** ashahwah=takíhleew VAI, chkawahchakihlée=shuw VAI; **run sort of quickly, run at half-speed** kaakshaaméhleew VAI **He was trotting by because he's nosy.** 'Móxa kaakshaaméhleew kíhkata-wéewsuw.'; **run to fetch s.o., fetch s.o.** naachíipheew VTA; **run to fetch s.t., fetch s.t.** naachiipáhtoow VTI2; **run well** wŭlíhleew VAI, wŭlíhleew VII; **run zigzag** pàptukahtakíhleew VAI; **start off fast, start off running** *(especially when running in a race)* ktakíixiin VAI; **take off, run with one's tail up** aapaalŭwéhleew VAI **I just took off all of a sudden.** 'Wíix=kwii ndaapaalŭwéhla.', **I'm running off into town.** 'Ndaapaalŭwéhla oo=téeneeng ndá.'; **walk by, walk along; run** *(of equipment)* pŭmúsuw VAI; **be tired from running, be tired of running** shiiwaaméhleew VAI; **be unable to work, be unable to move, be unable to run, be out of order** aalŭ=wíhleew VII, aalŭwíhleew VAI; **finish running, be through running** kii=shaaméhleew VAI; **leave running, run away, start to run** alumahtakíhleew VAI; **look like one could run fast, look smartly dressed, look frisky while going by** kshihleewiináakw=suw VAI; **practice running** akweetaa=méhleew VAI; **run across** aashtéhleew VAI; **run ahead, be leading in a race** shayeewaaméhleew VAI, shayeewah=takíhleew VAI; **run all over** msahta=kíhleew VAI; **run as well, run with** wiitaaméhleew VAI; **run backwards** ashahkcheewahtakíhleew VAI; **run badly** *(especially of vehicles)*, **decay, go bad, spoil** machíhleew VAI.

**run across** VI **run across** *(the road)* aashŭwahtakíhleew VAI.

**run around** VI **run around, run wild, run all over** wŭyakahtakíhleew VAI.

**run away** VI **run away, flee** alumshíi=muw VAI, wshíimuw VAI; **run away crookedly** pàptukshíimuw VAI; **run away from a certain place, flee from a certain place** wundshíimuw VAI **He's running away from the house.** 'Wiikwáhmung wundshíi=muw.'; **run away in a certain direction, flee in a certain direction** lushíimuw VAI **He's running towards the house.** 'Wiikwáhmung lushíi=muw.'; **run away in a hurry** kiht=shíimuw VAI; **run away inside the house, flee inside the house** piind=shíimuw VAI; **run away quickly** kshushíimuw VAI; **run away to here, escape to here** peetshíimuw VAI.

**run down** VT **criticize s.o., abuse s.o. verbally, 'run s.o. down'** akusha=kuníimeew VTA, akushíimeew VTA.

**run from** VT **run away from s.o., flee from s.o.** wshíimeew VTA.

**run home** VI maatahtakíhleew VAI, **run s.o. home** maachíipheew VTA; **run s.t. home, take s.t. back** *(especially of borrowed items)* maachiipáhtoow VTI2.

**run inside** VI piindahtakíhleew VAI; **go inside quickly, run inside, enter a dwelling running** piinjiikéhleew VAI.

**run into** VT **run into s.o., make physical contact with s.o.** alíhkaweew VTA; **run into s.t., make physical contact with s.t.** alíhkam VTI1A; **touch s.o., make contact with s.o., run into s.o., hit s.o.** aláheew VTA; **touch s.t., run into s.t., drive into s.t., make contact with s.t. forcefully, hit s.t.** aláham VTI1A **I ran into it.** 'Ná ndal=hámun.'

**run out** VI **fall out, run out, come out** kchíhleew VAI, kchíhleew VII.

**run out of** VT **be done talking, say all one has to say, run out of things to say** mehtaaptóoneew VAI; **lack a commodity, run out of something** txíh=lateew VAI; **run out of s.t.** wihkwiitŭ=yéhleew VAIO *considered impolite;* **run out of s.t.** wihkwíhleew VAIO, pohkwíhleew VAIO **He ran out of meat.** 'Pohkwíhlaan wŭyóos.'

**run over** VT **run over s.o.** *(especially in a car)* káxkheew VTA; **break s.t., run over s.t.** káxkham VTI1A; **get run over, be broken off** káxkhookw VAI.

**run short** VI **run short of s.t., be lacking s.t.** *(a commodity)* noondéhleew VAIO **I ran short of the paper.** 'Noondéhlaan pámbiil.'

**run wild** VI **run around, run wild, run all over** wŭyakahtakíhleew VAI.

**runaround** ADJ **run around, be the 'runaround' type** mihmsahtakíhleew VAI.

**runaway** N pehpóolŭwees NA.

**runny** ADJ **have a runny nose** niiskŭ=laníikameew VAI, sihtaníineew VAI.

**Russell** N láshŭlush NA.

**rust** VI máxkalul VAI, máxkalut VII.

# S

**sad** ADJ **be sad** matahtéenamuw VAI; **be sad, be grieving** shiiweelúndam VOTI1; **feel sad, be sad, be in a bad mood** mateelúndam VOTI1; **grieve, feel grief, be sad** ooshaweelúndam VOTI1; **lead a sad life** ooshawáawsuw VAI; **look sad, look to be grieving** ooshawiináakwsuw VAI; **be sad about s.t., be sorry about s.t.** shiiweelún=dam VTI1A.

**saddle** N **cushion, saddle** eháhpapiing NI.

**sail** VT **sail a boat, use a boat** amox=oolhámeew VAI, amoxóolham VOTI1.

**saliva** N **spit, saliva** sùkwiináakan NI.

**salt** N shíiwang NI; **ocean, sea, salt water** shŭwánpuy NI; **salt shaker** shii=wangíinjuw NI; **salt water** shiiwan=gáapoow NI.

**salt** VT **salt s.t. animate, put salt on s.t. animate, preserve s.t. animate in salt** shŭwáheew VTA; **salt s.t., put salt on s.t., preserve s.t. in salt** shŭwáham VTI1A; **be salted** shŭwaháasuw VAI, shŭwaháasuw VII **It doesn't have enough salt.** 'Máh téep-shŭwaháa=siiwu.'

**salt pork** N shŭwéewakw NI.

**salty** ADJ **be salty, be sour** shŭwán VII, shŭwúl VAI.

**same** ADJ **look the same, look alike** eeyŭliinaakwsúwak VAI *usually plural;* **the same** ngwúteel PC **In one**

**place.** 'Ngwúteel talí.', **They stay in the same place; they live together.** 'Ngwúteel apúwak.'

**sand** N léekuw NI **He fell into the sand.** 'Leekóohung lú kawíhleew.', **You need a little bit of sand in the pail.** 'Wshaphóosh'shung ktúnda-katáatam leekóohush.'

**sandy** ADJ **be a sandy road, be a sandy path** leekŭwatéexun VII; **have dirt on it, be sandy** ahkŭyóowuw VII.

**sane** ADJ **be sane** wŭleewáatam VOTI1.

**sap** N **sap, Kool-Aid, soft drink, sweet drink** shookŭláapoow NI.

**Sarah** N shéeliish NA.

**satisfied with** VT **be satisfied with s.o.** teepéelŭmeew VTA; **be satisfied with s.t.** teepeelúndam VTI1A **I'm satisfied with the way I live.** 'Ndeepeelúnda=mun weendaawsúyaan.'

**satisfy** VT **be satisfied** teepeelúndam VOTI1, teepiilaweehkwúsuw VAI, tee=piitéeheew VAI; **make s.o. content, satisfy s.o.** teepiilawéeheew VTA **He/she satisfies me.** 'Ndeepiilawée=haaw.'; **person who is never satisfied** mehmúndawees NA.

**Saturday** N **be Saturday** sátateew VII, sátteew VII **I went to town last Saturday.** 'Ootéeneeng ndá éenda-sàttéeke.'

**saucer** N shungawíinjuw NI.

**sauerkraut** N shŭwíi-képuch NI.

**sausage** N piindhíikanush NA; **baloney, sausage** piindhíikan NA.

**save** VI **save, be thrifty** keeshéetsuw VAI.

**save** VT **save s.t.** *(of money)*, **be thrifty about s.t.** keeshéetsuw VAIO **I'm thrifty about my car.** 'Ngeeshéetsiin ndahtamoombíilum.'; **make s.o. live, save s.o., give s.o. a reason to live** pŭmaawsoohááleew VTA.

**saw** N **saw, hand saw** tŭmushahkwáa=kan NI.

**saw** VT **saw s.t., cut and sever s.t.** tŭ=múshum VTI1B; **saw timber, cut logs** tŭmusháhkweew VAI.

**saw up** VT **saw up all of s.t. animate, cut up all of s.t. animate** méhtsheew VTA; **saw up all of s.t., cut up all of s.t.** méhtshum VTI1B.

**say** VT **say, say so** úw VAI **That's what I'd say.** 'Nún ná há níi nzíin.'; **say s.t.** úw VAIO **I can't say it.** 'Máh ngíish-íiwun.'; **brag, say great things** *(especially when making a speech)* akaanzhaaptóoneew VAI; **be done talking, say all one has to say, run out of things to say** mehtaap=tóoneew VAI; **be shamed by what someone says** miixaniimkwúsuw VAI; **have something wrong with the shape of one's mouth, be always saying bad things about people, have a sore mouth** matutóoneew VAI; **make a soft sound, make a low sound, say in a soft voice, say in a low voice** kwíishkwŭweew VAI; **make remarks to people, make 'digs' at people, be reluctant to come out and say things to people** maashiila=táasuw VAI; **make remarks to s.o., make 'digs' at s.o., hint at something to s.o., be reluctant to say something outright to s.o.** maashii=latáweew VTA; **make s.o. ashamed by speech, say shameful things to s.o.** miixaníimeew VTA; **repeat, say something over** laapíixsuw VAI; **say good things, preach** wŭlaaptóoneew VAI; **say grace** keenáamuw VAI; **say something good about s.o.** wŭlaaptoo=náaleew VTA; **say something in a hurry, leave something out of a story, don't tell the whole story** pàpalaachíimuw VAI; **say the wrong thing** chanutóonheew VAI; **say things from memory, recite from memory** shàshkwakíinzuw VAI; **speak quickly, speak in a harsh tone, speak in a sharp tone, say harsh things, say**

**sharp things** kshaaptóoneew VAI; **take a long time to say one's words** akwaaníixsuw VAI; **talk well, say good things** awulaaptóoneew VAI.

**say about** VT **say good things about s.o., praise s.o.** wŭlakŭníimeew VTA.

**say to** VT **say to s.o., tell s.o.** léew VTA.

**scab** N mŭkúy NI; **have a scabby nose, have scabs on one's nose** mŭkuy=cháaleew VAI.

**scabby** ADJ **have a scab, have scabs** mŭkúysuw VAI; **have a scabby behind** mŭkíitŭyeew VAI; **have a scabby face, have scabs on one's face** mŭ=kuychàlíingeew VAI; **have a scabby foot, have scabs on one's foot** mŭ=kuysíiteew VAI; **have a scabby hand, have scabs on one's hand, have a scabby arm, have scabs on one's arm** mŭkuyŭnáxkeew VAI; **have a scabby head, have scabs on one's head** mŭkuyáandpeew VAI; **have a scabby leg, have scabs on one's leg** mŭkuykáateew VAI; **have a scabby mouth, have scabs on one's mouth** mŭkuytóoneew VAI; **have a scabby nose, have scabs on one's nose** mŭ=kuycháaleew VAI; **have scabs** mŭkúy=uw VAI.

**scales** N **measuring scales** poondhíikan NI.

**scarce** ADJ **be scarce** ndáwat VII, ndáw=suw VAI.

**scare** VT **frighten s.o., scare s.o.** wíi=shaleew VTA; **be afraid, be scared** wiisháasuw VAI; **scare s.o. to death** aaptahpáaheew VTA; **frighten people, scare people** wiishalúweew VAI; **scare easily, be easy to scare** aapŭ=wahpáasuw VAI.

**scarecrow** N **mask, false face mask, scarecrow, someone dressed up with a false face** msíingw NA.

**scarf** N **put a collar on s.o., put a scarf on s.o.** wahkwéelŭneew VTA; **scarf, collar, necktie, horse's collar** weh=wahkwéelŭniing NI; **wear something around the neck, wear a scarf, wear jewellery** wiilawahkwéelŭnuw VAI.

**scarlet fever** ADJ **have measles, have scarlet fever, turn red** maxkíhleew VAI.

**scary** ADJ **look dangerous, look scary** kxwaawiináakwat VII, kxwaawii=náakwsuw VAI.

**scatter** VT **scatter s.o.** sàsehshíhkaweew VTA *object usually plural;* **scatter s.t., throw s.t. about** seeyéeheew VAIO; **sow s.t.** *(of seeds),* **scatter s.t.** sàsée=ham VTI1A; **be scattered, lie scattered** sayéexŭnool VII *usually plural* **Your dishes are scattered.** 'Sayéexŭnool koolaakanúsal.'; **lie scattered, be scattered** sayeexíinook VAI *usually plural* **The papers are scattered.** 'Sayeexíinook pambíilak.'

**school** N **attend school** shkóoluw VAI; **teach school** shkoolháalŭweew VAI.

**schoolteacher** N shehshkoolháalŭwees NA; N **woman schoolteacher** shehsh=koolhaalŭweesóxkweew NA.

**scissors** N takwalooníikan NI.

**scold** VT **scold s.o.** laxkáameew VTA; **scold people** laxkáangeew VAI.

**scoop** N **scoop, dipper, something used to dip for water** anz'híikan NI.

**scoop** VT **scoop s.t. animate up** *(with something held in the hand)* anzii=kwáaleew VTA; **scoop s.t. animate up** *(using a tool or instrument)* ánz'heew VTA; **scoop s.t. up** *(with something held in the hand)* anzíikwam VTI1A; **scoop s.t. up** *(using a tool or instrument)* ánz'ham VTI1A; **scoop things up, dip** *(for water)* anz'híikeew VAI; **scoop things, dip** *(for water)* anzŭ=níikeew VAI; **scoop things, dip** *(for water)* ánzŭnum VOTI1; **take a handful of s.t., scoop s.t. up** *(using the hands)* ánzŭnum VTI1B; **take a handful of s.t. animate, scoop s.t. ani-**

**mate up** *(using the hands)* ánzŭneew VTA.

**scorch** VT **scorch s.t. animate, blacken s.t. animate** *(by heat)*, **dye s.t. animate** nzukcháseew VTA.

**Scottish person** ADJ skáchmaan NA.

**scrape** N **be scraped, have a scrape mark on it** síixiin VAI, síixun VII.

**scrape** VT **cut s.t. animate smoothly, scrape s.t. animate smooth, cut s.t. animate lightly, trim s.t. animate** láalsheew VTA; **cut s.t. smoothly, scrape s.t. smooth, cut s.t. lightly, trim s.t.** láalshum VTI1B; **scrape potatoes** kahkhíhpŭneew VAI; **scrape s.o., make a scrape mark on s.o.** síixŭmeew VTA; **scrape s.o., scrape s.t. animate** *(using a tool or instrument)* káhkheew VTA; **scrape s.t.** kahkíikwam VTI1A; **scrape s.t.** *(using a tool or instrument)* káhkham VTI1A; **scrape s.t. animate off** *(using something held in the hand)* mahkiikwáa=leew VTA; **scrape s.t. off** *(using something held in the hand)* mahkíikwam VTI1A; **scrape s.t., make a scrape mark on s.t.** síixtoow VTI2; **be scraped, have a scrape mark on it** síixiin VAI, síixun VII.

**scraper** N kahkhíikan NI.

**scraps** N **leave scraps of s.t. animate behind, don't eat all of s.t. animate** *(of food)* píiwameew VTA; **leave scraps of s.t. behind** *(of food)*, **don't eat all of s.t.** piiwándam VTI1A **I left a little bit.** 'Chángiish mbiiwándamun.'

**scratch** N **be scratched, have a scratch** kcháxkeew VII; **have a scratch on one's arm, have a scratch on one's hand** kchaxkŭnáxkeew VAI; **have a scratch on one's face** kchaxkíin=gweew VAI.

**scratch** VT **scratch s.o., claw s.o.** *(using the hands)* síisŭneew VTA; **scratch s.t., claw s.t.** *(using the hands)* síisŭ=num VTI1B; **scratch s.t., scratch s.t. that is itchy** kshíipŭnum VTI1B; **scratch things** siisŭníikeew VAI; **be itchy, scratch oneself** kshíipsuw VAI; **be scratched, get scratched** kchax=kíixiin VAI, kchaxkíixun VII, kcháx=keew VII; **scratch s.o.'s itch** kshíipŭ=neew VTA; **scratch an itch** kshiipŭ=níikeew VAI; **scratch an itch on s.o.'s face for them** kshiipiingwáaleew VTA, kshiipiingwéeneew VTA; **scratch one's back, have an itchy back** kshiippóxkwaneew VAI; **scratch one's eyes, have itchy eyes** kshiipaalakíin=gweew VAI; **scratch one's face, have an itchy face** kshiipíingweew VAI; **scratch one's feet, have itchy feet** kshiipsíiteew VAI; **scratch one's head, have an itchy head** kshii=páandpeew VAI; **scratch one's leg, have an itchy leg** kshiipkáateew VAI; **scratch s.o. on the face** siisiingwáa=leew VTA; **scratch s.o.'s back** kshiip=poxkwanéeneew VTA.

**screech owl** N kxahwéemwiish NA.

**screen window** N shiikaleeheeshan=déekan NA.

**screw** VT **turn s.t., screw s.t., wind s.t., drive s.t. in** *(of screws)* tùpáhkhwam VTI1A.

**scrub** VT **scrub the floor** kshiixiikwá=hmeew VAI.

**scythe** N tŭmaskhíikan NI; **cut weeds** *(with a scythe)*, **cut with a scythe** tŭmaskhíikeew VAI.

**sea** N **ocean, sea, salt water** shŭwánpuy NI; **sea shell, snail** chiikwaláleesh NA.

**search** VI **look around searching, look around** *(in expectation of someone or something)* ndawáapuw VAI; **search, snoop, be snooping** sh'xeehíikeew VAI.

**search** VT **search s.o.** sh'xéeheew VTA; **search s.t.** sh'xéeham VTI1A.

**search for** VT **look around searching for s.o., look out to see s.o., look out for s.o.** ndawáapameew VTA; **look**

**around searching for s.t., look out to see s.t., look out for s.t.** ndawaapándam VTI1A; **look for s.o., search for s.o.** *(especially in vain)* kwíilaweew VTA; **look for s.t., search for s.t.** *(especially in vain)* kwíilam VTI1A **I won't be able to find it.** 'Ápih ngwihkwíilamun.'

**seat** N **change seats, sit somewhere else** aandapíhleew VAI; **miss one's seat while sitting down, fall while sitting** palapíhleew VAI, palápuw VAI.

**secret** ADJ **secretly** kiimii- PV **He's hovering around him.** 'Kwíimii-wii=cheewáawal.'; **secretly** kíimii PC **I sneaked a glance to the side.** 'Kíimii mbiimóhkwe.'; **sneak around crawling, crawl secretly** kiimíikwsuw VAI.

**securely** ADV **tie s.o. to something, tie s.o. securely to something** kŭlam=bíileew VTA; **tie s.t. to something, tie s.t. securely to something** kŭlámb=toow VTI2; **run secretly, run in secret** kiimahtakíhleew VAI; **rape s.o. in secret, feel s.o. secretly** kíimŭneew VTA.

**see** VI **see a long way, have good eyesight** wŭlatawáapuw VAI; **see in a certain manner, see in a certain direction** latawáapuw VAI.

**see** VT **see s.o.** néeweew VTA; **see s.t.** néem VTI 3; **be a glimpse of someone seen while going by** laashíhleew VAI **He was going so fast that one only saw a glimpse of him.** 'Éelkih-kshíhlaat shùkéhla laashíhleew.'; **be coloured in a certain manner, be seen in a certain manner** laapamúk=wat VII **It can be seen through.** 'Éeshu-laapamúkwat.'; **be coloured in a certain manner** *(s.t. animate)*, **be seen in a certain manner** laapa=múkwsuw VAI; **be glad to see s.o.** payahkwíinaweew VTA; **be glad to see s.t.** payahkwíinam VTI1A; **be glad to see someone** payahkwiináakwsuw VAI; **have poor eyesight, have a hard time seeing** matatawáapuw VAI **You might have a hard time seeing.** 'Kŭmatatawáapi éet.'; **look around searching for s.o., look out to see s.o., look out for s.o.** ndawáapameew VTA; **look around searching for s.t., look out to see s.t., look out for s.t.** ndawaapándam VTI1A; **see daylight, live to daylight** waapanáheew VAI; **see s.o. briefly, see s.o. for a moment** laashíinaweew VTA; **see s.o. in a certain place** talatawáapameew VTA **I saw him in the house.** 'Wiikwáh=mung ndundalatawáapamaaw.'; **see s.t. briefly, see s.t. for a moment** laashíinam VTI1A; **see s.t. in a certain place** talatawaapándam VTI1A **I saw it in the house.** 'Wiikwáhmung ndun=dalatawaapándamun.'; **see something in a certain place** talatawáapuw VAI **He saw it in the forest.** 'Kóhpii talatawáapuw.'; **see strange things** maashatawáapuw VAI; **see the whites of someone's eyes** waapeeliingwée=xiin VAI; **look through something, see through something** eeshatawáa=puw VAIO.

**seed** N wáxkaniim NI; **go to seed, be overgrown** *(of plants)* aapchíikuw VAI; **go to seed, be overgrown** aap=chíikun VII.

**seize** VT **grab s.t., seize and take s.t. along** naxpíhleew VAIO.

**seizure** N **have a fit, have a seizure, have an epileptic seizure** wchiipíi=suw VAI.

**seldom** ADV **seldom, hardly, very little, a scant amount** máamchiish PC **I seldom work.** 'Máamchiish ndalóhke.', **There's hardly any left over.** 'Máamchiish aluwíhleew.'

**self** N **myself** *(in reflexive expressions)* nhákay NAD **I burned myself.** 'Lóo=saaw nhákay.', **He shot himself.** 'Níhlii pàyaxkháawal hwákayal.'

**sell** VI **peddle, go about selling** naa=hóosuw VAI.

**sell** VT **sell s.t.** mahlamáakeew VAIO; **sell s.t. to s.o., try to sell s.t. to s.o.** naa=hóosaweew VTAO **He sold me some strawberries.** 'Naahóosaakw wtee=híimal.'; VT **sell to s.o.** naahoosíhta=weew VTA; **come here to sell things, come here selling things** peetaahóo=suw VAI; **get rid of s.t., completely dispose of s.t., sell all of s.t.** weema=lóhkeew VAIO **I gave away all of my belongings.** 'Nŭweemalóhkeen neh=láatamaan.'

**send** VT **send s.o. away** alumshíhka=weew VTA, alumshíiheew VTA; **send s.o. home** maatshíhkaweew VTA; **send s.o. to bed** kawushíhkaweew VTA; **chase s.o. inside, send s.o. inside, drive s.o. inside** *(of animals)* piind=shíhkaweew VTA; **hit s.o. and send them away** alumihtéeheew VTA; , **take s.o. inside, chase s.o. inside, send s.o. inside, drive s.o. inside** *(of animals)* piindshíiheew VTA; **send s.o. out** ktushíhkaweew VTA.

**sensation** N **be a tingling sensation, have pins and needles** *(of body parts)* wchiipiisóowuw VII **I went to the doctor because my arm was numb.** 'Ndaaktúlung ndáam éelu-náxk -wchiipiisóowiik.'; **be strong** *(of a sensation)* áhwan VII; **feel a certain way, have a certain physical sensation** lamalúsuw VAI **He thinks he's so good ('has wings')** 'Làma=lúsuw wŭlóngwanuw.', **How do you feel?** 'Thá há ktulamálsi?'; **feel numb, have a sensation of numbness** pih=kwamálsuw VAI; **feel s.t. as a sensation in one's body** làmándam VTI1A; **feel the sensation that s.o. makes, feel the sensation of s.o.** amámeew VTA; **feeling, sensation, feeling in a sore body part** amandamuwáakan NI.

**sense** VT **sense s.o.'s presence, sense the presence of s.o.** namáaleew VTA; **sense s.t.'s presence, sense the presence of s.t.** namáatam VTI1A **I feel that it's going to rain.** 'Nàmáatamun katá-sóokŭlaan.'

**senses** N **regain consciousness, come to one's senses, sober up** taaxpéh=leew VAI **I came to all of a sudden.** 'Wíixkwii méhch ndaaxpéhla.', **I just came to.** 'Lúkih ndaaxpéhlaan.'

**separate** VT **separate s.o., sort s.o.** chpíixŭmeew VTA *object usually plural;* **separate s.t. animate, sort s.t. animate** *(using the hands)* chpúneew VTA; **separate s.t., sort s.o.** chpíix=toow VTI2 *object usually plural;* **separate s.t., sort s.t.** *(using the hands)* chpúnum VTI1B; **be apart, be isolated, be separated from other people** chpúsuw VAI; **be apart, be separated** chpiixíinook VAI *usually plural,* chpíixŭnool VII *usually plural;* **be apart, be separated by birth or location** chpápŭwak VAI *usually plural;* **be separated from one's spouse** machíilŭnuw VAI; **be separated from one's spouse, live apart** chpooxwée=wak VAI *usually plural.*

**serious** ADJ **be in earnest, be serious** *(about something)*, **get up the nerve** *(to do something)* kihteelúndam VOTI1 **I'm serious about going there.** 'Ngihteelúndam náh ndá.', **I got up the nerve to tell him to go home.** 'Ngihteelúndam, ndúlaa máachiil.'

**servant** N **servant, worker** alohkáakan NA.

**service** N **attend church, attend a service** maawéewuw VAI.

**set** ADJ **be ready to use, be all set** kii=shíixiin VAI, kiishíixun VII **My bed is made.** 'Kiishíixun ndapíinay.'

**set** N **be four pairs, be four sets** nee=wéelook VAI *usually plural,* neewéel=tool VII *usually plural;* **be three pairs, be three sets, be three of them, be**

three in number nxéelook VAI *usually plural;* **be two pairs, be two sets** niishéelook VAI, niishéeltool VII *usually plural.*

**set** VI **set** *(as a chicken on eggs)* kxah= wéexiin VAI.

**set** VT **set s.o. on eggs** *(of chickens)* kxahwéexŭmeew VTA; **set the table** wŭliinjŭweextíikeew VAI; **place s.t. apart, set s.t. aside** chpáhtoow VTI2 *object usually plural;* **finish setting the table, be finished setting the table** kiishiinjŭweextíikeew VAI.

**set down** VT **set s.o. down** lŭmatáhleew VTA; **set s.t. down** lŭmatáhtoow VTI2; **throw s.o. down hard so as to make a loud noise, set s.o. down hard so as to make a loud noise** tiiwíixŭ= meew VTA; **throw s.t down hard so as to make a loud noise, set s.t down hard so as to make a loud noise** tiiwíixtoow VTI2.

**set free** VT **set s.o. free** nihlaapeewháa= leew VTA, nihlaawsoohaáleew VTA.

**set on fire** VT **light s.t. animate, set s.t. animate on fire** náxkwseew VTA; **light s.t., set s.t. on fire** náxkwsum VTI1B; **set s.t. on fire for s.o.** naxk= wsúmaweew VTAO; **set things on fire, set a fire** naxkwsíikeew VAI.

**seven** N níishaash PC.

**sever** VT **break s.o., sever s.o.** *(using the hands)* tŭmúneew VTA; **break s.t., sever s.t.** *(using the hands)* tŭmúnum VTI1B; **cut s.t. animate, cut and sever s.t. animate** tŭmúsheew VTA; **have s.t. drop and break off, have s.t. drop and be severed** tŭmíixtoow VTI2; **hit and sever s.t. animate, cut s.t. animate off** tŭmihtéeheew VTA; **hit and sever s.t., cut s.t. off** tŭmih= téeham VTI1A; **saw s.t., cut and sever s.t.** tŭmúshum VTI1B; **be blown over by the wind, be broken off by the wind, be severed by the wind** tŭ= máxookw VAI, tŭmáxun VII; **be cut off, be severed** tŭmahkwsháasuw VII, tŭmáhkwat VII; **drop s.o. and sever their neck** tŭmiikwéexŭmeew VTA; **fall and break off, be severed** tŭ= míixun VII; **have a cut-off leg, have one's leg severed** tŭmukáateew VAI; **break s.o.'s neck, sever s.o. at the neck, break s.o. at the neck, cut s.o. off at the neck** tŭmiikwéeheew VTA.

**several** ADJ **several** keexéeli PC **It is several different colours.** 'Keexéeli laapamúkwat.'; **stand in rows, stand several deep** pihtawiikaapawúwak VAI *usually plural;* **several times** kéexun PC **He came alone several times.** 'Kéexun áng páan nxóoxwe.'; **be gone for several days** keexoo= kwŭnáhkeew VAI.

**sew** VI oxkwáakeew VAI; **be tired of sewing** peekiikwáakeew VAI; **sew around the edges** wiiwŭniikwáa= keew VAI; **sew around the edges, put a hem on** paxkawiikwáakeew VAI; **sew at the wrong place** chaniikwáa= keew VAI; **sew badly** amachiikwáa= keew VAI.

**sew** VT **sew s.t.** óxkwam VTI1; **sew s.t. animate** oxkwáaleew VTA; **be sewn** oxkwáasuw VII; **be sewn along the edges, be sewn up** paxkawiikwáasuw VII; **be sewn shut** samwiikwáasuw VII, samwiikwáasuw VAI; **be tightly sewn** kŭliikwáasuw VII; **finish sewing, finish sewing things** kiishii= kwáakeew VAI; **make a mistake in sewing s.t. animate, sew s.t. animate wrongly, sew s.t. animate in the wrong place** chaniikwáaleew VTA; **make a mistake in sewing s.t., sew s.t. wrongly, sew s.t. in the wrong place** chaníikwam VTI1A; **sew around the edge of s.t., turn up and sew s.t.** paxkawíikwam VTI1A; **sew around the edges of s.t.** wiiwŭníi= kwam VTI1A; **sew around the edges of s.t. animate** wiiwŭniikwáaleew

VTA; **sew s.o. closed** spwiikwáaleew VTA; **sew s.t. animate crookedly** pàptukiikwáaleew VTA, waakiikwáa=leew VTA; **sew s.t. animate straight, poke s.o. straight, straighten s.o. out** *(with a tool)* shaaxkiikwáaleew VTA; **sew s.t. animate tightly, sew s.t. animate down, fasten s.t. animate down by sewing it** kŭliikwáaleew VTA; **sew s.t. animate shut** *(of an opening)* samwiikwáaleew VTA; **sew s.t. animate together** takwiikwáa=leew VTA; **sew s.t. animate up, sew around the edge of s.t. animate** paxkawiikwáaleew VTA; **sew s.t. closed** spwíikwam VTI1A; **sew s.t. crookedly** pàptukíikwam VTI1A, waakíikwam VTI1A; **sew s.t. shut** *(of an opening)* samwíikwam VTI1A; **sew s.t. straight, poke s.t. straight, straighten s.t.** *(with a tool)* shaaxkíi=kwam VTI1A; **sew s.t. tightly, sew s.t. down, fasten s.t. down by sewing** kŭlíikwam VTI1A; **sew s.t. together** takwíikwam VTI1; **sew something onto s.t.** ahpíikwam VTI1A; **sew something onto s.t. animate** ahpiikwáa=leew VTA; **sew things closed** spwii=kwáakeew VAI; **sew things crookedly** pàptukiikwáakeew VAI, waakiikwáa=keew VAI; **sew things straight, straighten things** *(with a tool)* shaaxkiikwáakeew VAI; **sew things, be sewing, lace things, thread things** laaphíikeew VAI; **sew things together** takwiikwáakeew VAI.

**shade** N **be good shade, give good shade** wŭlahkachíhteew VII; **be in the shade** ahkachihtéexiin VAI **He's sitting in the shade.** 'Ahkachihtéexiin apúw.'; **be in the shade** ahkachihtéexun VII **He's sitting where there's shade.** 'Éenda-ahkchihtéexung laalŭmáta=puw.'; **be shade** ahkachíhteew VII **He's sitting in the shade.** 'Éenda-ahkachíhteek lŭmátapuw.', **It's shady by the house.** 'Pŭmíichii wiikwáh=mung talí ahkachíhteew.'; **give long shade** kwŭnahkachihtéexiin VAI, kwŭnahkachihtéexun VII, kwŭnahka=chíhteew VII.

**shake** VI **have one's head shaking** *(involuntarily)* nungohkwéhleew VAI; **have one's legs shaking, be afraid** nungkaatéhleew VAI; **have one's stomach shaking** nungatayéhleew VAI; **move, stir, shake** kwchukwíh=leew VAI, kwchúkwihl VAI; **shake** nungíhleew VII, nungíhleew VAI; **shake, move, be thrown about** kwàkwchukwíhleew VII, kwàkw=chukwíhleew VAI.

**shake** VT **shake and stir s.t., agitate s.t.** wŭyamoxkíhtoow VTI2; **shake s.o. back and forth, move s.o. back and forth, wave s.o. back and forth, rock s.o. back and forth** kwàkw=chukwaaháaleew VTA; **shake s.t.** apawáaheew VAIO, **s.t.** kwchukwáa=heew VAIO; **shake s.t. back and forth, move s.t. back and forth, wave s.t. back and forth, rock s.t. back and forth** kwàkwchukwáaheew VAIO; **shake s.t., shake s.t. out** pa=wáaheew VAIO; **shake back and forth, sway back and forth** apawíhleew VII, apawíhleew VAI; **shake one's head** kwàkwtukohkwaandpéhleew VAI, kwàkwtukohkwéhleew VAI; **shake one's head, move one's head back and forth** kwàkwchukohkwéhleew VAI; **be blown back and forth by the wind, be shaken by the wind** apáw=xookw VAI, apáwxun VII; **be moved back and forth, be shaken back and forth** kwàkwchúkhookw VAI.

**shake hands with** VT **shake hands with s.o., hold hands with s.o.** sakiinax=kéeneew VTA.

**shake up** VT **shake s.t. up** wŭyamox=káaheew VAIO; **fall and get shaken up, be hit and get shaken up** wŭ=

yamoxkihtéexiin VAI; **get shaken up** wŭyamoxkíhleew VII.

**shaker** N **pepper shaker** pèpŭlíinjuw NI; **salt shaker** shiiwangíinjuw NI.

**shallow** ADJ **be shallow water** chaach=xupeekachúshuw VII, taatxupéekat VII.

**shame** IJ shée PC **For shame! You dropped it!** 'Shée! Kpalŭnúmun.'

**shame** N miixanusŭwáakan NI.

**shame** VT **be shamed by what someone says** miixaniimkwúsuw VAI.

**shameful** ADJ **look shameful** miixanii=náakwat VII, miixaniináakwsuw VAI.

**shanty** N shéntii NI; **live in a shanty** shentiihámeew VAI.

**shape** N **be a certain shape** luchéesuw VAI, luchéeyeew VII **What shape is it?** 'Tá luchéeyeew?'; **be big, have a big shape** xwuchéesuw VAI **The tree is big.** 'Xwuchéesuw míhtukw.'; **be in terrible shape, have a terrible figure, have a terrible shape, be in a bad shape** chiipáhkwsuw VAI; **be long in shape, have a long shape** kwŭnuchéesuw VAI, kwŭnuchéeya=yeew VII; **be lumpy in shape, be out of shape** matuchéesuw VAI, matuch=éeyeew VII; **be round in shape** ptukwchéesuw VAI, ptukwchéeyeew VII; **be pretty, be evenly shaped, be nicely shaped** wŭluchéesuw VAI. wŭ=luchéeyeew VII; **cut s.t. animate in a round shape** ptúkwsheew VTA; **cut s.t. in a round shape** ptúkwshum VTI1B; **have a bent shape, be bent, be curved** waakchéesuw VAI, waak=chéeyeew VII **Your cane is bent.** 'Waakchéeyeew ktaláawan.'; **have a long shape, have a long body** kwŭ=noochéeyeew VII **And it was short, it was wrapped around in a bundle, and it was a rectangular little thing.** 'Kéhla wáak chahkwéeshuw, tàtùp=háasuw, kwŭnoocheeyéeshuw.'; **have a long shape, have a long body** kwŭnuchéeyeew VII; **have a square shape** hàshawuchéesuw VAI, hàsha=wuchéeyeew VII; **have a trim shape, have a good shape, have a good figure** wŭláhkwsuw VAI.

**share** N **want a share of an inheritance** *(especially someone who is not a member of the immediate family)* katá-waapéenzuw VAI.

**sharp** ADJ **be sharp** kíineew VII, kíinsuw VAI; **have a sharp point, be sharp and pointed** kiinalóosuw VAI, kiina=lóowŭyeew VII; **have sharp teeth** akiinaníikeew VAI; **sharp** kiinii- PN **A sharp knife.** 'Kíinii-paxkshíikan.', **A sharp axe.** 'Kíinii-tŭmahíikan.'; **sharp knife** kiinanzhíikan NI; **hit s.o. so that they make a sharp noise** chàhwihtéeheew VTA; **drop s.t. animate so that it makes a sharp noise** chàhwihtéexŭmeew VTA; **drop s.t. so that it makes a sharp noise** chàh=wihtéextoow VTI2; **drop s.t. so that it makes a sharp noise** chàhwíixtoow VTI2; **fall and make a sharp noise when dropped** chàhwíixiin VAI; **get sore, hurt, have a pain, have a sharp pain, have a brief pain** wiisakíhleew VII, wiisakíhleew VAI **My knee had a sharp pain.** 'Ngútko wiisakíhleew.'

**sharpen** VT **sharpen s.t.** kíinham VTI1A; **sharpen s.t. animate** kíinheew VTA; **cut s.t. and sharpen it, sharpen s.t. by cutting** kíinshum VTI1B.

**sharpening stone** N **file, sharpening stone, grindstone** kiinhíikan NI.

**shatter** VI **drop s.o. and make them shatter, hit s.o. and make them shatter** sehtéexŭmeew VTA; **drop s.t. and make it shatter, hit s.t. and make it shatter** sehtéextoow VTI2; **fall and shatter** sehtéexiin VAI, seh=téexun VII; **splatter, shatter, splash, scatter** séhleew VII; **hit s.o. and shatter them** sehtéeheew VTA.

**shave** VI moonzhihtóonayeew VAI, móonzhuw VAI.

**shawl** N **handkerchief, shawl** héeng=chiis NI.
**she** PR **he, him, she, her** néeka PR **It's his/her turn.** 'Néeka áashtee.'
**shed** N **cow shed, cow barn** kooyíikaan NI.
**sheep** N meeméekush NA.
**sheer** ADJ **wear a sheer dress, wear a transparent dress** shiikalahóosuw VAI.
**sheet** N anáanzoon NI.
**shell** N wshákay NI; **sea shell, snail** chiikwaláleesh NA; **skin s.t., remove the covering from s.t., shell s.t.** *(of corn)* pxwíinam VTI1A; **take the covering off s.t. animate, take the outer layer off s.t. animate, remove the shell from s.t. animate** pŭlákŭ=neew VTA; **take the covering off s.t., take the outer layer off s.t., remove the shell from s.t.** pŭlákŭnum VTI1A.
**shell** VT **shell corn** pawiingweehíikeew VAI.
**shield** VT **shield oneself, dodge from something** tàtapásuw VAI.
**shift** VI **shift around while sitting, fidget** kwàkwchúkwapuw VAI.
**shin** N **my shin** nihkáxkwan NID; **have bare shins** *(of a woman not wearing stockings)* amehchkáxkwaneew VAI.
**shine** VI **shine** *(of the sun)*, **be shiny** waasŭléexiin VAI; **shine** *(of the sun)* wŭláandeew VII; **shine brightly, be brilliant** *(especially light)*, **wear bright colours** saapŭléexiin VAI; **shine brightly, be brilliant, be brightly coloured** *(especially light)* saapŭlée=xun VII; **shine from a certain place, shine for a certain reason** *(of lamps)* wundáasŭleew VAI, wundáasŭleew VII; **shine going away** *(of lights)* alumáa=sŭleew VAI, alumáasŭleew VII; **shine in a certain direction** *(of the sun)* láandeew VII; **shine in this direction, shine here** peetáasŭleew VAI, peetáa=sŭleew VII; **shine s.t. animate, make s.t. animate shine** waasŭléexŭmeew VTA; **shine s.t., make s.t. shine** waasŭléextoow VTI2; **shine, be light, be a light on** wáasŭleew VII **Are you home? ('Is your house shining?').** 'Kíi wíikŭyan wáasŭleew?'; **shine, be shining out** *(of the weather)*, **be a sunny day** waasŭláandeew VII; **shine, be shiny** waasŭléexun VII; **shining star** waasaláangweew NA; **sit with shining eyes** *(especially in the dark)* waaseeliingohkwéepuw VAI.
**shine** VT **shine s.t. animate, make s.t. animate shine** waasŭléexŭmeew VTA; **shine s.t. in a certain direction, shine s.t. in a certain manner** *(of lights)* laasŭléenum VTI1A, laasŭlée=nŭmeew VAIO **I shone the lantern over there.** 'Yeelak ndulaasŭléenŭ=maan waasŭleeníikan.'; **shine s.t., make s.t. shine** waasŭléextoow VTI2; **shine things, polish things** waasŭ=leextíikeew VAI; **shine a light in a certain direction, shine a light in a certain manner** laasŭléenŭmeew VAI.
**shiner** N wshaphóosameekw NA *fish species.*
**shingle** N **be covered in shingles** *(of a house)* apahahkáasuw VII; **put shingles on a roof** apaháhkeew VAI.
**shiny** ADJ **shine** *(of the sun)*, **be shiny** waasŭléexiin VAI; **shine, be shiny** waasŭléexun VII; **have shiny eyes** *(especially in the dark)* waaseeliin=gwéexiin VAI; **have shiny shoes** waa=sŭlahksúneew VAI; **be shiny bald, be completely bald** waaxamóhkweew VAI.
**shirt** N héembut NI; **change one's shirt** aandhéembteew VAI, aashŭwahéemb=teew VAI; **have a wrinkled shirt** wchulhéembteew VAI; **put on one's shirt** piindhéembteew VAI; **wear a shirt** heembtáhŭmeew VAI; **wear a white shirt, have a white shirt on** waaphéembteew VAI; **wear an extra**

**shirt** pihtawahéembteew VAI.
**shiver** VI **shiver from the cold** núnga=chuw VAI.
**shocked** ADJ **be surprised, be shocked, be startled** salaxkíhleew VAI.
**shoe** N máhksun NI; **be hungry, have the sole of one's shoe come off and flap around** katóopuw VAI; **button shoe** kŭnoopáhksun NI; **have bad shoes** achiipahksúneew VAI; **have big shoes** amangahksúneew VAI; **have clean shoes** piilahksúneew VAI; **have muddy shoes** asiiskŭwahksúneew VAI; **have new shoes** wuskahksúneew VAI; **have shiny shoes** waasŭlahksún=eew VAI; **have wet shoes** skapahk=súneew VAI; **leather shoe** xayáhksun NI; **muddy shoe** asiiskŭwáhksun NI; **narrow shoe** wiipawáhksun NI; **new shoe** wuskáhksun NI; **old shoe** xuw=áhksun NI; **put on one's shoes** piin=dŭnahksúneew VAI; **put shoes on s.o.** *(especially of horses)* mahksunháa=leew VTA; **put shoes on s.o.** piindŭ=nahksunéeneew VTA; **take off one's shoes** ktunahksúneew VAI; **trade shoes, change one's shoes** aashŭ=wahksúneew VAI; **wear more than one pair of shoes, wear more than one layer of footwear, wear over-shoes** pihtawahksúneew VAI; **wet shoe** skapáhksun NI; **wide shoe** paanáhk=sun NI.
**shoe tack** N mahksúnii-mŭkóos NA.
**shoelace** N aníixan NA, aníixan NI; **leather shoelace** xáyii-aníixan NI.
**shoot** VI payaxkhíikeew VAI, payáxkham VOTI1; **shoot s.o.** payáxkheew VTA; **shoot s.t., shoot at s.t.** payáxkham VTI1A; payaxkhóotam VTI1A; **practice shooting** akweetaxkhíikeew VAI; **shoot badly, be a bad shot** amata=yáxkham VOTI1; **shoot off a gun** pa=yaxkhóotam VOTI1; **shoot skillfully, be a good shot** nihtaawayáxkham VOTI1.
**shoot!** IJ **shoot! gosh! silly question! shame on you!** kéesan PC, kéesand PC.
**shop** VI **shop, go shopping** mahla=mwúsuw VAI.
**shorebird** N **yellow legs, shorebird** yehyaapéhlaash NA.
**short** ADJ **short** chahkwii- PN **Short laces.** 'Cháhkwii-aníixanal.'; **be short** *(diminutive)* chahkwahkwshíi=shuw VAI, chahkwéeshuw VII; **be cut short** *(diminutive)* chahkwshaashíi=shuw VII; **be short grass** chahkwas=kwéeyeew VII, chahkwiixáskwat VII; **cut s.t. animate short** cháhkwsheew VTA **I cut the window (glass) short.** 'Njáhkwshaaw eeheeshandéekan.'; **cut s.t. short** cháhkwshum VTI1B; **have a short arm** *(diminutive)* chah=kwŭnaxkéeshuw VAI; **have a short dress on, wear a short dress** chahk=hooshíishuw VAI; **have a short foot** chahkwshiichéeshuw VAI; **have short arms** *(diminutive)* achahkwŭnaxkée=shuw VAI; **have short hair** chah=kwaalóhkweew VAI; **have short legs** *(diminutive)* achahkwkaacheeyée=shuw VII; **have short sleeves** *(diminutive)* chahkwŭnaxkeeyéeshuw VII; **have short sleeves** chahkwŭnaxkée=yeew VII; **make s.t. short, shorten s.t.** chahkwihchóoshuw VTI2; **run short of s.t., lack s.t.** liiwíhleew VAIO **He ran out of boards.** 'Liiwíhleew pasiikáaxkwal.'; **short apron** peh=pŭlakíixtaang VII; **short dress** chah=kweenjakwíiwanush NI; **short grass** chahkwiixáskwal NI; **short piece of rope, short piece of string** chah=kwáamanush NI; **short table** chah=kweehundáxpoon NI; **take short steps** *(diminutive)* achahkwalihkehléeshuw VAI; **take short steps** *(diminutive)* achahkwalihkéeshuw VAI; **be short** *(of a measurement)* liiwíhleew VAI **The paper wasn't long enough.** 'Liiwíhleew pámbiil.'; **be short** *(of a*

*measurement)* liiwíhleew VII **The cloth wasn't long enough.** 'Liiwíh=leew wshapakwíiwan.'; **be short** *(of a measurement)* liiwíixun VII **The boards are not long enough.** 'Pasii=káaxkwal liiwíixŭnool.'; **be short of s.t., lack s.t.** liiwíhlateew VAIO **He ran short of paper.** 'Liiwíhlateew pambíilal.', **I'm short a little bit.** 'Liiwíhlata chángiish.'; **be short, be lacking** noondéeyeew VII.

**shortchange** VT **cheat s.o., shortchange s.o.** piimŭnúmaweew VTA.

**shortcut** N **go across, take a shortcut** kaxkéeweew VAI.

**shorten** VT **make s.t. short, shorten s.t.** *(diminutive)* chahkwihchóoshuw VTI2.

**shortly** ADV **shortly, in a while, in a little while, soon, as soon as** méhchxiish PC **I'd slap him in the face.** 'Méhch=xiish áa mbwahwsúmawa.', **I'll be done cooking in a little while.** 'Méhchxiish-uch ngiishatúpwi.'; **shortly, in a while, in a little while, soon, as soon as** méhtxii PC **As soon as I got through eating.** 'Méhtxii ngíish-míitsiin.', **He will come in a while.** 'Mehtxíiwu-ch páan.'

**shot** N **shoot badly, be a bad shot** a=matayáxkham VOTI1; **shoot skillfully, be a good shot** nihtaawayáxkham VOTI1; **split s.t. animate by forceful contact, split s.t. animate by shot, split s.t. animate with a projectile** pasúlaweew VTA; **split s.t. by forceful contact, split s.t. by shot, split s.t. by hitting it with a projectile** pa=súlam VTI1A.

**should** VI **emphatic, should** xáa PC **You should try to save your money.** 'Káta- xáa -keeshéetsiin kshulpúl=um.', **I wish he'd go home** 'Táas xáa máachiiw.'; **should, would, can, could** áa PC **We (inclusive) should hide.** 'Kiilóona áa kaatapíhna.', **I'd really like to go with you (plural).** 'Píish áa móxa kŭwíingu-wiichee=wŭlóhmwa.'

**shoulder** N **my shoulder** ndúkuy NAD, ndúkuy NID; **have a good head on one's shoulders** wŭláandpeew VAI; **have round shoulders** ptukwpox=kwanéexiin VAI.

**shove** VT **push s.o., shove s.o.** kunj=chaahháaleew VTA; **push s.o., shove s.o.** *(using the hands)* kunjchúneew VTA **He pushed the baby buggy.** 'Kwunjchunáawal chaachpùniika=núshal.'; **push s.t., shove s.t.** kunj=cháaheew VAIO; **push s.t., shove s.t.** *(using the hands)*, **move s.t.** *(of motions at a meeting)* kunjchúnum VTI1B, **push s.o. down, shove s.o. down** kundaahháaleew VTA; **push s.o., push s.t. over, shove s.o. over, shove s.t. over** kundáaheew VAIO.

**shovel** N **playing card, shovel** shkúp NA.

**show** VI **have bare hands, have no gloves on, have one's hands exposed, have one's hands showing** mihtŭlunjéexiin VAI; **have one's back exposed, have one's back showing** mihtpoxkwanéexiin VAI; **have one's foot exposed, have one's feet showing** mihtsiitéexiin VAI; **have one's legs showing, have one's legs exposed, have bare legs** mihtkaatéexiin VAI; **lie with one's face sticking out, lie with one's face showing, have one's face showing** kchiingwéexiin VAI.

**show** VT **show s.o., show s.t.** loohŭ=máasuw VAIO; **show s.t. to s.o.** loo=hŭmáweew VTAO; **display s.t. of importance, show s.t. of importance, display s.t.** *(of one's feelings)*, **show s.t.** *(of one's feelings)* pŭnoondíh=keew VAIO **You showed that you didn't love her.** 'Kpunoondíhkeen máh ktahwaaláawi.'; **show one's face** *(quickly)* kchiingwéhleew VAI; **show one's feelings to s.o.** pŭnoondŭláw=

eew VTA.

**show off** VI kshiilawéhtoow VOTI2.

**shred** VT **crumble s.t. animate, break s.t. animate up into pieces, shred s.t. animate** *(using the hands)* píikŭ=neew VTA; **crumble s.t., break s.t. up into pieces, shred s.t.** *(using the hands)* píikŭnum VTI1B; **shred things, break things into pieces** piikŭníi=keew VAI; **be shredded, be torn up** píikat VII, píiksuw VAI.

**shriek** VI **shriek, be shrill** sàsaláxkŭ=weew VAI.

**shrill** ADJ **shriek, be shrill** sàsaláxkŭ=weew VAI.

**shrink** VI **disappear, go out of sight, shrink** wchíhleew VII **His head disappeared out of sight.** 'Wíil wchíh=leew.'; **disappear, go out of sight** *(s.t. animate)*, **shrink** wchíhleew VAI **He was looking out the window, then he disappeared, he's hiding.** 'Eeheeshandéekan lí któhkweew, nál táa wtúlu-wchíhlaan, káatapuw.'; **shrink** *(in water)* wtúpeew VII, wtúp=eew VAI.

**shrink** VT **shrink s.t.** *(in water)* wtúpa=toow VTI2; **shrink s.t. animate, shrink s.o.** *(in water)* wtúpaleew VTA; **get weak, get shrivelled** piisŭlíhleew VAI; **shrivelled apple** piisuláapŭlush NA.

**shrub** N **shrub, bush** míhchkwshush NI.

**shuffle** VT **make a noise while shuffling one's feet** shòhwsiitéexiin VAI; **make a shuffling noise while dancing** shóhwkeew VAI.

**shut** ADJ **be sewn shut** samwiikwáasuw VII, samwiikwáasuw VAI; **have one's eyes swollen shut** samwusheen=gwéexiin VAI, samwushéengweew VAI; **hold s.t. shut** samwúnum VTI1B; **sew s.t. animate shut** *(of an opening)* samwiikwáaleew VTA; **sew s.t. shut** *(of an opening)* samwíikwam VTI1A; **slam s.t. shut** *(of windows, of doors)* kpáaheew VAIO; **tie s.t. shut** sa=mwámbtoow VTI2.

**shut** VT **be blown shut by the wind, be shut in by the wind, be shut out by the wind** kpáxookw VAI, kpáxun VII; **be closed, be shut in, be shut out** kpaháasuw VII; **be in jail, be shut in, be shut out** kpaháasuw VAI; **shut s.t. out, shut s.t. in, close s.t.** kpáham VTI1A; **shut s.o. out, shut s.o. in, close s.t. animate** kpáheew VTA; **close things up, shut things in, shut things out** kpahíikeew VAI.

**shy** ADJ **act shy** apwaalíiyayuw VAI; **be shy** *(of animals)*, **be stingy** áhwsuw VAI; **be shy, be 'backwards'** achíip=suw VAI; **shy person, 'backwards' person** chehchíipsiit NA.

**sick** ADJ **be sick** wiinamálsuw VAI; **be very sick** àhwamálsuw VAI; **feel nauseous, feel sick to one's stomach** wŭyakaskíilaweew VAI; **feel sick, feel like vomiting** wŭyakaskíhleew VAI; **feel unwell, be sick** matamalúsuw VAI; **overeat to the point of being sick** aaptulóosuw VAI.

**sickly** ADV **lie in a pitiful state, lie in a sickly state** ktumaakíixiin VAI.

**side** N **be at the side of the road, park at the side of the road** paxkéexiin VAI; **be lopsided, be uneven, lean to one side** piimchéesuw VAI; **cock one's head, turn one's head, look to the side** piimóhkweew VAI; **lean over, lean to one side** *(s.t. animate)*, **be crooked, lean** piimíixiin VAI **You drove around the Four Corners too fast and you were leaning.** 'Koo=sáamu-kshú-wiiwŭníhlaan éenda-aashŭwatéexung, kwŭlúp kpiimíi=xiin.'; **lean over, lean to one side, be on crooked** piimíixun VII; **lean s.o. to one side, lean s.t. animate to one side** piimíixŭmeew VTA; **lean s.t. to one side, put s.t. on crooked** pii=míixtoow VTI2; **lean to one side** pii=

míhleew VAI, piimíhleew VII; **lean to one side** píimsuw VAI; **lie crookedly, lie sideways, lie on it's side** pŭmii=chíixiin VAI, pŭmiichíixun VII; **lie on one's side** shàwéexiin VAI; **on both sides of something** weewúndakwii PC **They live on both sides of the road.** 'Weewúndakwii áaneeng wíikŭwak.', **They're walking on both sides (of you).** 'Weewúndakwii pŭmúsŭwak.'; **on one side** yáawii PC **You have a short arm on one side.** 'Yáawii kchahkwŭnaxkáashi.', **I just planted on one side.** 'Yáawii shúkw ndunda=lahkíihe.'; **on the other side of the house** awasáaku PC **The box is on the other side of the house.** 'Mbáksh awasáaku áhte.'; **the other side of something** awásii PC **I put it over there on the other side.** 'Yéelak awásii ndáhtoon.', **On the other side of the door.** 'Awásii kpahóonung.'; **the other side of the river** káamung PC; **the other side of the road** awas=iixkanáwe PC; **turn over from one side to the other, turn over in bed** kwŭlupatéexiin VAI.

**sideways** ADJ **hit s.o. and knock them sideways** piimihtéeheew VTA; **hit s.t. and knock it sideways** piimihtéehum VTI1B; **crawl sideways, crawl on the diagonal** piimíikwsuw VAI; **fall sideways** piimihtéexiin VAI, piimihtéexun VII; **fall sideways, drive crookedly** piimchéhleew VAI; **grow crookedly, grow sideways** pŭmiichíikun VII **My tooth came up crooked.** 'Pŭmiichíi=kun níipiit.'; **grow crookedly, grow sideways** pŭmiichíikuw VAI; **knock s.o. sideways, knock s.t. crooked** *(by shot, by physical contact, with a projectile)* piimŭláweew VTA; **knock s.t. sideways, knock s.t. crooked** *(by shot, by physical contact, with a projectile)* píimŭlam VTI1A; **lie crookedly, lie sideways, lie on it's side** pŭmiichíixiin VAI, pŭmiichíixun VII; **look sideways, turn one's head** pŭ=miitóhkweew VAI; **sit sideways** pŭ=miitohkwéepuw VAI, pŭmíitapuw VAI; **slip, slip sideways** wshanzhíhleew VAI; **stand sideways, stand beside someone** pŭmiichiikáapawuw VAI; **walk sideways** pŭmich'chéewxeew VAI, pŭmiitchéewxeew VAI.

**sieve** N sihkpeeníikan NI.

**sift** VT **sift s.t.** pawúnum VTI1B; **sift things** pawuníikeew VAI; **sift things, be sifting** pàhŭníikeew VAI; **be sifted** pawunáasuw VII.

**sifter** N pawuníikan NI, pàhŭníikan NI.

**sight** N **be hidden, lie placed out of sight** kaatáhteew VII; **climb out of sight** kaatakóosuw VAI; **disappear, crawl out of sight** wchíikwsuw VAI; **disappear, go out of sight, shrink** wchíhleew VII **His head disappeared out of sight.** 'Wíil wchíhleew.'; **disappear, go out of sight** *(s.t. animate)*, **shrink** wc̣híhleew VAI **He was looking out the window, then he disappeared, he's hiding.** 'Eeheeshundée=kan lí któhkweew, nál táa wtúlu=wchíhlaan, káatapuw.'; **go out of sight** waníhleew VAI; **hide, hide out of sight** wanohtáasuw VAI; **run out of sight** wanahtakíhleew VAI; **sight, seeing the light** neemwáakan NI.

**sign** N **mark s.t., make a sign on s.t., put one's name on clothes, mark the perimeters of s.t.** *(using a tool or instrument)* kíhkham VTI1A; **mark s.t. animate, make a sign on s.t. animate, make a mark on s.t. animate** *(using a tool or instrument)* kíhkheew VTA.

**silent** ADJ **be silent, keep quiet** chihta=mwúsuw VAI.

**silently** ADV **run silently, whisper, run well** kwiishkwihtáakwat VAI, kwiish=kwihtáakwsuw VII.

**silk** N **silk dress** silkeendakwíiwan NI.

**silly** ADJ **be silly** paseewáatam VOTI1; **be silly, be foolish** kpúcheew VAI; **become silly, become crazy** kpuchéh= leew VAI, **be crazy from drinking, be silly from drinking** kpucheewíisŭ= muw VAI.

**sin** N mataawsuwáakan NI.

**sing** VI naxkóohŭmeew VAI; **be tired of singing** shiiwaláamuw VAI; **come here singing, come in this direction singing** peetaláamuw VAI; **practice singing** akweetaláamuw VAI; **sing a hymn** lóonzŭweew VAI; **sing along** wiitaláamuw VAI; **sing badly** amata= láamuw VAI; **sing often** eewataláa= muw VAI; **sing out loud** amangaláa= muw VAI; **sing together** niishaláa= muw VAI; **sing when not wanted, sing and get on someone's nerves, cry, wail** niiskaláamuw VAI; **start off singing** *(especially in church)*, **burst out crowing** *(of roosters)* kundaláa= muw VAI; **start singing** alumaláamuw VAI.

**sing to** VT **sing to s.o.** naxkóoheew VTA.

**singer** N **be a good singer** nihtaawa= láamuw VAI.

**single** ADJ **older single woman** kihkóx= kweew NA.

**sink** VI **have one's feet sinking into a substance** *(of mud, of snow, of sand, of grain)* akwaanamwíhleew VAI; **sink, sink down in the water** kwtawíhleew VII, kwtawíhleew VAI.

**sink** VT **sink s.t.** kwtáwŭnum VTI1B.

**sinner** N **lead a bad life, be a sinner** matáawsuw VAI.

**sister** N **my sister** nŭwíitkoxkw NAD; **my older sister** nŭmíis NAD; **my paternal aunt, my father's sister, my cross-aunt** nŭmiilíhtaakw NAD; **my sister** *(man speaking)* ndoxkwéehum NAD; **my younger brother, my younger sister, my younger sibling** nxíisŭmus NAD.

**sister-in-law** N **my sister-in-law** *(woman speaking)* nalíhkan NAD; **my sister-in-law** *(man speaking)*, **my brother-in-law** *(woman speaking)* níilum NAD.

**sit** VI **sit down** lŭmátapuw VAI; **sit there** lŭmatáhteew VII **It sits on top.** 'Wáx= kiich lŭmatáhteew.'; **sit upon something** poxkwáhteew VII; **sit alone** nxohkwéepuw VAI; **sit astride something, sit straddling something** póxkapuw VAI, póxkwapuw VAI; **sit back** áamapuw VAI; **sit bent over** waakohkwéepuw VAI; **sit bent over, sit hunched over** ahteewohkwéepuw VAI; **sit close together** kchukapúwak VAI *usually plural,* kchukohkwéepŭ= wak VAI *usually plural,* psakohkwée= pŭwak VAI *usually plural,* psakwa= púwak VAI *usually plural;* **sit crookedly** piimohkwéepuw VAI, píimapuw VAI; **sit doubled over, sit doubled up** paxkawohkwéepuw VAI, paxkawápuw VAI; **sit far apart** awahlŭmohkwée= pŭwak VAI *usually plural;* **sit far apart, be far apart, be far away** wahlŭmápŭwak VAI; **sit hunched over** waakpoxkwanéepuw VAI; **sit in a certain manner, sit in a certain direction** lápuw VAI **She's sitting in the back.** 'Wtéeng lápuw.'; **sit in a circle** wiiwŭnohkwéepŭwak VAI *usually plural;* **sit in threes** nxohkwée= pŭwak VAI *usually plural;* **sit in twos** niishohkwéepŭwak VAI *usually plural;* **sit naked** sheexkalohkwéepuw VAI; **sit on one's backside in a certain manner, sit on one's backside in a certain direction** liitŭyéepuw VAI **He slid to the front (of the chair).** 'Shayéemung liitŭyéepuw.', **He's sitting this way and that way.** 'Msú-liitŭyéepuw.'; **sit on one's knees** níishii-takwápuw VAI; **sit quietly** kŭlamohkwéepuw VAI, kŭláma= puw VAI; **sit sideways** pŭmiitohkwée= puw VAI, pŭmíitapuw VAI; **sit straight**

shaaxkohkwéepuw VAI; **sit the wrong way** chanohkwéepuw VAI; **sit upon something, sit astride** poxkohkwée=puw VAI; **sit with one's legs open, sit with one's legs spread apart** tóon=gapuw VAI, toongohkwéepuw VAI; **sit with one's backside barely touching a surface, sit on the edge of something** mshiitŭyéepuw VAI; **sit with one's legs folded, sit hunched over** ptukohkwéepuw VAI, ptúkwa=puw VAI; **sit with one's legs up, raise one's legs while sitting** uspkaatée=puw VAI, uspkaatéewapuw VAI; **sit with one's lips sticking out** sheetoo=nohkwéepuw VAI; **sit with shining eyes** *(especially in the dark)* waasee=liingohkwéepuw VAI; **be five of them sitting there, be five of them there** naalanápŭwak VAI; **be three of them sitting there** nxápŭwak VAI *usually plural;* **be tired of sitting** shiiwoh=kwéepuw VAI, shíiwapuw VAI; **be tired of sitting on one's backside, have a sore backside from sitting down** shiiwiitŭyéepuw VAI; **change one's place while sitting** áandapuw VAI; **change seats, sit somewhere else** aandapíhleew VAI; **defecate while sitting** masktápuw VAI; **fall in sitting, miss one's seat** palapíhleew VAI; **fall on one's backside while sitting** pŭ=niitŭyéepuw VAI; **fall while sitting, sit down hard** lŭmatapihtéexiin VAI; **fart while sitting down** pooktohkwéepuw VAI; **fidget, sit in various ways** msú=lápuw VAI; **get s.o. into sitting position, raise s.o., raise s.o. in bed** *(from lying down)* aamwíhkŭneew VTA; **get up from sitting** pasúkwiiw VAI-S; **hide, hide sitting down** kaatohkwée=puw VAI, káatapuw VAI; **lean back while sitting** aamchéepuw VAI; **lean over, sit crookedly, lie crookedly** piimchéexiin VAI; **miss one's seat while sitting down, fall while sitting** palápuw VAI; **put one's feet up, sit with one's feet upon something** poxkwsiitéepuw VAI; **shift around while sitting, fidget** kwàkwchúkwa=puw VAI; **turn around while sitting** kwŭlúpapuw VAI; **urinate while sitting** shkohkwéepuw VAI, shkápuw VAI.

**sit on** VT **hold s.o. down** *(using the foot or body)*, **step on s.o. and hold them down, sit on s.o. and hold them down** kŭlíhkaweew VTA; **hold s.t. down** *(using the foot or body)*, **step on s.t. and hold it down, sit on s.t. and hold it down** kŭlíhkam VTI1A; **injure s.o.** *(using the foot or body)*, **kick and injure s.o., sit on and injure s.o.** kshíhkaweew VTA; **injure s.t.** *(using the foot or body)*, **kick and injure s.t., sit on and injure s.t.** kshíhkam VTI1A.

**sit upon** VT **sit upon something** áhpa=puw VAIO; **sit upon something, sit astride** poxkohkwéepuw VAI; **step upon s.o., fall upon s.o., sit upon s.o.** ahpíhkaweew VTA; **step upon s.t., fall upon s.t., sit upon s.t.** ahpíhkam VTI1A.

**sit with** VT **sit with s.o.** niishapóomeew VTA.

**six** N ngwútaash PC **Ninety-six.** 'Nóolii txiináxku wáak ngwútaash.'

**Six Nations** N **Six Nations, Ontario** shŭwéeka PC.

**size** N **be a certain size** lukíhkwun VII **The chair is smaller (than something else).** 'Nóondaa lukíhkwun áhpapoon.'; **be a certain size** lúkiil VAI **He is smaller than someone else.** 'Nóondaa lúkiil.'; **measure the size of s.o, measure the height of s.o., measure s.t. animate out, fill s.t. animate to the brim** *(as a pail)* tpúskhweew VTA; **measure the size of s.t., measure the height of s.t., measure s.t. out** tpúskhwam VTI1A.

**skate** N chéehakwaak NA.

**skate** VI **skate, be skating** cheeha=kwáakuw VAI.

**skillfully** ADV **skillfully, know how to** *(do something)* nihtaa- PV **He watches everything.** 'Wŭníhtaa- wéemi kwéek -saakíhtoon.', **He's a good preacher.** 'Níhtaa-pŭmutóonheew.'; **read skillfully, be able to read properly** nih=taawakíinzuw VAI; **shoot skillfully, be a good shot** nihtaawayáxkham VOTI1.

**skin** N **hide, skin** xáy NA; **have the covering of something be hit and knocked off, have the skin of something be hit and knocked off** pŭlak=ihteeháasuw VAI; **hit s.o. and knock the covering off them, hit s.o. and knock the skin off them** pŭlakihtée=heew VTA.

**skin** VT **skin s.t.** *(especially of body parts)* pxwíiskham VTI1A; **skin s.t. animate, remove the covering from s.t. animate** pxwíineew VTA; **skin s.t., remove the covering from s.t., shell s.t.** *(of corn)* pxwíinam VTI1A; **be skinned, peeled off** *(of bedsores, of blisters)* pxwíiskeew VII; **have an open sore, be skinned, be peeled off** *(of bedsores, of blisters)* pxwíisksuw VAI.

**skinny** ADJ **be thin, be skinny** waxka=núsŭw VAI.

**skunk** N shkáakwus NA.

**slam** VT **slam s.t. shut** *(of windows, of doors)* kpáaheew VAIO.

**slap** VT **slap s.o.** *(loud enough to be heard)* pwàhwihtéeheew VTA; **slap s.o. across the face** *(close to the ears)*, **slap s.o. across the ears** paak=xehtéeheew VTA; **slap s.o. in the face** *(loud enough to be heard)* pwàhwiin=gwéeheew VTA, pwàhwsheengwée=heew VTA, pwàhwsúmaweew VTA.

**sled** N shŭléet NA.

**sleep** VI kawíiw VAI-S **I slept very little last night.** 'Máamchiish ngáwi piis=kéeke.'; **defecate while sleeping** masktóngwaam VAI; **die in one's sleep, die while sleeping** aaptón=gwaam VAI; **fall out of bed while sleeping** pŭnóngxwiin VAI; **fart while sleeping** pooktóngwaam VAI; **oversleep, sleep late, sleep in** wsaamón=gwaam VAI; eelóngwaam VAI; **put s.o. to sleep** kawóoheew VAIO; **sleep naked** sheexkalóngwaam VAI, shéexkalii-kawíiw VAI; **sleep with each other, sleep together** wihpéendŭwak VAI *usually plural;* **sleep with s.o.** wih=péemeew VTA; **sleep with someone, sleep as well** wiitóngwaam VAI; **urinate while sleeping** shkíingwaam VAI.

**sleepy** ADJ **be sleepy** akawóngxwiin VAI.

**sleeting** VI **be sleeting** wsháaxŭlaan VII.

**sleeve** N **my sleeve** náxkamay NID; **have long sleeves** akwaanŭnaxkéeyeew VII *especially of shirts or coats;* **have long sleeves** kwŭnunaxkamáyeew VII; **have short sleeves** *(diminutive)* chahkwŭnaxkeeyéeshuw VII; **have short sleeves** chahkwŭnaxkéeyeew VII; **long sleeves** kwŭnunaxkamáyal NI *usually plural.*

**sleigh** N chaacháshkwshush NA, shŭlée=chush NA, táataskw NA.

**slender** ADJ **have a slender figure, have a slight build, be slim** lumbáhkwsuw VAI.

**slice** N **be in pieces, be in slices** pan=géesuw VAI *usually with number particle* **It's in three slices.** 'Nxú pan=géesuw.', **It's in several pieces.** 'Kéexu pangéesuw.'; **be in pieces, be in slices** pangéeyeew VII *usually with number particle* **It's in four slices.** 'Néew-pangéeyeew.', **It's in big pieces** 'Amángu-pangéeyeew.'; **cut s.t. animate in pieces, cut s.t. animate in slices** pangéesheew VTA **I cut him in two pieces.** 'Níisha mban=géeshaaw.'; **cut s.t. in pieces, cut s.t. in slices** pangéeshum VTI1A **I cut it in two pieces.** 'Níisha mbangéeshŭ=

mun.'

**slice** VT **slice s.t. animate thinly** wsháp=sheew VTA; **slice s.t. thinly** wsháp=shum VTI1B; **be sliced thin** wshap=sháasuw VAI, wshapsháasuw VII.

**slide** VI **slide down** *(of curtains)* chiixa=kwíhleew VII; **slide down** chiixíhleew VAI; **slide down on something** *(from roof, from snow pile)*, **slide down** *(of windows)* chiixakwíhleew VAI; **slide down, slide off** laalakwíhleew VAI; **slide downhill, slide down a hill** chiixiikwsíhleew VAI; **slide in a certain manner, slide in a certain direction** liikwsíhleew VAI; **go down, fall down, slide down** *(of curtains, of pants)* chiixíhleew VII; **go downhill, fall downhill, slide downhill** pum=bíhleew VAI.

**slight** ADJ **have a slight build, be slim** laangáhkwsuw VAI; **have a slender figure, have a slight build, be slim** lumbáhkwsuw VAI.

**slim** ADJ **have a slight build, be slim** laangáhkwsuw VAI.

**slip** N **slip, petticoat** akóotay NI; **have one's slip sticking out** ktahóosuw VAI; **have one's slip sticking out** saakhóosuw VAI.

**slip** VI wshaaxíhleew VAI; **slip, slip sideways** wshanzhíhleew VAI.

**slippery** ADJ **be slippery** wsháaxan VII, wsháaxsuw VAI; **be slippery ground** wshaaxahkéeyeew VII.

**sliver** N palalíikaaxkw NI.

**slope down** VI **slope down** *(of the ground)*, **be a hill** pumbahkéeyeew VII **I walked to the hill.** 'Éenda-pumbahkéeyeek ndúlu-pŭmúsi.'

**slow** ADJ shahwi- PV **I can dance slow.** 'Níi áa ngíish-sháhwi-kúndka.'; **be slow-moving** alaawíiyayuw VAI.

**slowly** ADV malóoniish PC **Dianne got up slowly.** 'Malóoniish pasúkwiiw Dianne.'; **slowly** chkáwiish PC **Say it slowly!** 'Chkáwiish íil!'; **crawl slowly** ashahwíikwsuw VAI, chkawiikw=shíishuw VAI; **dance slowly** sháhw=keew VAI; **drive slowly** ashahwchéh=leew VAI, chkawchehléeshuw VAI *diminutive;* **go slowly** wàwtamiitŭyéh=leew VAI *considered impolite;* **kind of slowly, somewhat slowly** maama=lóoniish PC **He's walking kind of slowly.** 'Maamalóoniish pumúsuw.', **He woke up slowly.** 'Maamalóoniish tóhkiiw.'; **read slowly** ashahwakíin=zuw VAI; **run slowly** ashahwahtakíh=leew VAI, chkawahchakihléeshuw VAI; **swim slowly** ashahwaashŭwíhleew VAI, chkawaashŭwihléeshuw VAI *diminutive;* **talk slowly** ashahwíixsuw VAI; **walk slowly** *(diminutive)* chkaw=ooxwéeshuw VAI; **walk slowly, be a slow walker** ashahwóoxweew VAI; **walk slowly, walk in a relaxed fashion** wàwtamóoxweew VAI; **work slowly** shàhwalóhkeew VAI; **work slowly, work to to suit oneself** wàw=támsuw VAI; **write slowly** ashah=weekhíikeew VAI.

**small** ADJ **small** changii- PN **A little pie.** 'Chángii-páyush.'; **small** changu- PN *informal* **A little gate.** 'Chángu-chaweenaxkŭníikanush.'; **small** changu- PV *informal* **It's in small pieces.** 'Chángu-pangeeyéeshuw.'; **some, a little bit, a small amount** tangii- PV **Can you speak a little Delaware now?** 'Méhch há kíish-tángii-hulŭníixsi?'; **some, a little bit, a small amount** tángii PC **There's a bit of bread there.** 'Tángii nú yéelak áhte apwáan.', **Do you want to eat a little bit?** 'Tángii káta-míitsi?'; **find s.t. animate too small, find that s.t. animate doesn't fit, be too small for s.t. animate** *(of clothing)* wŭlíhka=weew VTA **They are too small, they don't fit me.** 'Noolihkawáawak.', **My mitt doesn't fit.** 'Noolíhkawaaw nŭwánd.'; **find s.t. too small, find**

that s.t. doesn't fit, be too small for s.t. *(of clothing)* wŭlíhkam VTI1A **It's too small for me, it doesn't fit me.** 'Noolíhkamun.', **My shirt doesn't fit.** 'Noolíhkamun ndahéembut.'; **have a small beard, have a small mustache** changihchoonayéeshuw VAI; **have a small nose** *(diminutive)* changchaaléeshuw VAI; **have small eyes** *(as if closed)* spwíingweew VAI; **have small legs** *(diminutive)* achang=kaachéeshuw VAI; **small fish** changa=méeshush NA; **small house** changii=káanush NI; **small snake** changax=kóokush NA; **small tree** *(diminutive)* changáhkwush NA; **small tree** chan=gíhchkwush NA.

**small amount** N **some, a small amount, a little bit** changíiwiish PC **I don't drink but I drink a little bit.** 'Máhta níi nŭmunéewi changíiwiish shúkw nŭmúne.'; **some, a small amount, a little bit** chángiish PC **There's just a little frost.** 'Chángiish shúkw tóh=pun.', **I left a little bit of the food.** 'Chángiish mbiiwándamun.'

**smallpox** N **have smallpox** pwahkpéh=leew VAI.

**smart** ADJ **be clever, be smart** lpwéew VAI; **be independent, be smart, be alive, be strong** *(especially a sick person who gets up because he or she is feeling better)* àhwaapéewuw VAI; **be smart, be industrious, like to work** lihlpúneew VAI; **be too smart for one's own good** machíi-lpwéew VAI; **feel 'smart,' feel lively** ktaka=málsuw VAI; **think s.o. to be smart, have a high opinion of s.o., think s.o. competent** kshéelŭmeew VTA.

**smash** VT **smash s.t. animate, squash s.t. animate, flatten s.t. animate** shkwihtéeheew VTA; **smash s.t., squash s.t., flatten s.t.** shkwihtéeham VTI1A.

**smell** N **have a bad smell, stink** ma=chiimáakwat VII, machiimáakwsuw VAI; **have a burning smell, smell as if it is burning** *(of something cooking)* machíimasuw VAI, machíimateew VII; **have a nice smell** *(of something cooking)* wiingiimasúmeew VAI, wiingíimateew VII; **have a strange smell, smell strange** maashiimáa=kwat VII, maashiimáakwsuw VAI; **like the smell of s.o.** wiingiimáaleew VTA; **like the smell of s.t.** wiingiimáatam VTI1A; **make an unpleasant smell** *(of one's cooking)* machiimatásŭmeew VAI; **smell good, be good smelling, have a good smell** wiingiimáakwat VII, wiingiimáakwsuw VAI; **smell rotten, have a rotten smell** aliimáakwat VII, aliimáakwsuw VAI; **smell strong, have a strong smell** àhwiimáakwat VII, àhwiimáakwsuw VAI.

**smell** VI **have a burning smell, smell as if it is burning** *(of something cooking)* machíimasuw VAI, machíimateew VII; **have a strange smell, smell strange** maashiimáakwat VII, maa=shiimáakwsuw VAI; **smell good, be good smelling, have a good smell** wiingiimáakwat VII, wiingiimáakw=suw VAI; **smell like a fart** pooktii=máakwsuw VAI; **smell rotten, have a rotten smell** aliimáakwat VII, alii=máakwsuw VAI; **smell strong, have a strong smell** àhwiimáakwat VII, àhwiimáakwsuw VAI.

**smell** VT **smell s.o., smell s.t. animate** *(involuntarily)* mŭláaweew VTA; **smell s.t.** *(involuntarily)* mŭláam VTI3; **smell s.o.** kwchiimáaleew VTA; **smell s.t.** kwchiimáatam VTI1A.

**smile** N **smile, have a smile on one's face** kaakŭluksuwiingwéexiin VAI.

**smile** VI kaakŭlúksuw VAI; **smile, have a smile on one's face** kaakŭluksuwiin=gwéexiin VAI.

**smile at** VT **smile at s.o.** kŭluksíhta=weew VTA.

**smock** N shmák NI; **wear a smock** shmakhámeew VAI.

**smoke** N **be a lot of smoke** *(from a chimney)*, **be smoky** kaanzhiingwáh=teew VII; **make a lot of smoke** kaan=zhiingwahtawásuw VAI; **make a lot of smoke, make a lot of smoke with things** kaanzhiingwahteeníikeew VAI; **make a lot of smoke, smoke, be smoking** kwaalxéesuw VAI; **make smoke** kwaalxeeníikeew VAI, kwaal=xéenŭmeew VAI.

**smoke** VI **be smoky, smoke** kwáalxeew VII; **make a lot of smoke, smoke, be smoking** kwaalxéesuw VAI.

**smoke** VT **smoke s.t.** *(of tobacco)* óh=pweew VAI **I smoked a cigar.** 'Ndóh=pwa shíkaash.'; **be smoked** ohpwáa=suw VII; **smoke a pipe, smoke tobacco** óhpweew VAI.

**smoky** ADJ **be a lot of smoke** *(from a chimney)*, **be smoky** kaanzhiingwáh=teew VII; **be smoky, smoke** kwáal=xeew VII.

**smooth** ADJ **be even ground, be smooth ground** wŭlahkéeyeew VII.

**smoothly** ADV **cut s.t. animate smoothly, scrape s.t. animate smooth, cut s.t. animate lightly, trim s.t. animate** láalsheew VTA; **cut s.t. smoothly, scrape s.t. smooth, cut s.t. lightly, trim s.t.** láalshum VTI1B.

**snagged** ADJ **get one's foot snagged, have one's foot snagged** laapsiitéh=leew VAI.

**snail** N **sea shell, snail** chiikwaláleesh NA.

**Snake** N shŭnék NA *family name.*

**snake** N áxkook NA; **big snake** xwatáx=kook NA; **garter snake** maamaaláx=kook NA; **green snake** askaskwáx=kook NA; **kill a snake** nihlaxkóokeew VAI; **milk snake** mŭlukáxkook NA; **rattlesnake** wiishalúwees NA, wii=shalúweew NA; **small snake** chan=gaxkóokush NA.

**sneak** VI **sneak around crawling, crawl secretly** kiimíikwsuw VAI.

**sneeze** VI eekwsháamuw VAI.

**snoop** VI **search, snoop, be snooping** sh'xeehíikeew VAI.

**snore** VI kwaaxkwsóngwaam VAI.

**snow** N kóon NA; **be snowing** wíineew VII **When it was snowing.** 'Éenda-wiinéeke.'; **be covered in snow, have snow on oneself** koonóowuw VAI **I'm all covered in snow.** 'Wéemu táa ndúlu-koonóowiin.'; **be deep snow** xwáhteew VII; **be light snow, be powdery snow** leexéesuw VAI; **make tracks in the snow** koonéelham VAI.

**snowy** ADJ **be snowy** kóonuw VAI, kóo=nuw VII; **be snowy ground, be snow on the ground** koonahkéeyeew VII.

**so** ADV **I think so** ndíit PC **You think so.** 'Ktíit.', **Do you think so?** 'Ktíit há?'; **here, there, thus, so** lí PC **He spat on the ground.** 'Áhkiing lí súkwiiw', **He went around the road.** 'Wiiwŭ=nóoxwe lí áaneeng.'; **here, there, thus, so** líi PC **The roads are muddy everywhere.** 'Wéemu asiiskŭwatée=xun táa líi.'; **here, there, thus, so** lú PC *informal* **They crawled to here.** 'Yó lú peechiikwsúwak.', **They moved to the United States.** 'Xwan=zhíikanung lú ngatahkéewak.'

**so many** ADV **so many, so many times** txu- PN *informal* **Nine months.** 'Nóolii txú-kíishooxkw.'; **so many, so many times** txii- PV **When he was fourteen years old.** 'Éenda- neewaa=níhka -txíi-katúnge.', **He is fifteen years old.** 'Naalanaaníhka txíi-katúm.'; **so many, so many times** txu- PV *informal* **Fourteen years old.** 'Neewaaníhka txú-katúngu.', **I was gone for six weeks.** 'Ngwútaash ndúndxu-kundŭweewŭnáhke.'; **be gone for so many days** txookwŭ=náhkeew VAI *usually with number particle* **I was gone for six days.**

'Ngwútaash ndundxookwŭnáhke.'; **be gone for so many weeks** kundŭ=weewŭnáhkeew VAI *usually with number preverb* **He was gone for two weeks.** 'Nı́ish-kundŭweewŭnáh=keew.', **You were gone for four weeks.** 'Kŭnéewu-kunduweewŭnáh=ke.'; **be in so many layers** *(of something sheet-like)* txeekı́ixiin VAI *usually with number particle* **It is in six layers.** 'Ngwútaash txeekı́ixiin.'; **be many** xwéeltool VII *usually plural;* **be so many, be so many pairs** txéeltool VII *usually plural; usually with number particle* **They are in six pairs.** 'Ngwútaash txéeltool.'; **be so many** txúwak VAI *usually plural; usually with number particle* **There are six men.** 'Ngwútaash txúwak lúnŭwak.', **There were almost one hundred of them.** 'Wéenaa ngwutaapóxke txúw=ak.'; **be so many layers** *(of something sheet-like)* txeekı́ixun VII *usually with number particle* **It is in eight layers.** 'Xáash txeekı́ixun.'; **be so many of them** txúnool VII *usually plural; usually with number particle* **There are six knives.** 'Ngwútaash txúnool paxkshı́ikanal.'; **be so many of them there** txápŭwak VAI *usually plural; usually with number particle* **There's six of them there.** 'Ngwút=aash txápŭwak.'; **be so many of them walking** txatxooxwéewak VAI *usually plural; usually with number particle* **We were walking in sixes.** 'Ngwút=aash ktundxatxooxwéhna'; **be so many of them, be so many of them in pairs** txéelook VAI *usually plural; usually with number particle* **They are in eight pairs.** 'Xáash txéelook.'; **be so many pieces** *(of something string-like)* txáhtakat VII **Six pieces of string.** 'Ngwútaash txáhtakat.'; **be so many there, be so many of them there** txahtéewal VII *usually plural; usually with number particle* **There are seven of them there.** 'Nı́ishaash txahtéewal.'; **be so many years of age** *(with number preverb)* katúm VAI **He is fifteen years old.** 'Naalanaa=nı́hka txı́i-katúm.'; **be so many years of age** *(with number preverb)* txú-katúm VAI **I'm ten years old.** 'Wı́im=bat ndúndxii-katúm.'; **in groups of so many** txéeli PC **They're stacked in sixes.** 'Ngwútaash txéeli pihtawı́ixŭ=nool.', **They are in eight pairs.** 'Xáash txéelook.'; **so many days** txóokwŭnii PC *usually with number particle* **Six days.** 'Ngwútaash txóokwŭnii.'; **so many hundred** txaapóxke PC *with number particles to form numbers 600-900* **Six hundred.** 'Ngwútaash txaapóxke.'; **so many times** txaanı́hka PC *with number particles to form numbers 16-19* **Seventeen.** 'Nı́ishaash txaanı́hka.', **Sixteen.** 'Ngwútaash txaanı́hka.'; **so many times** txún PC **Eight times.** 'Xáash txún.'; **take so many steps** txalı́hkeew VAI **He took six steps.** 'Ngwútaash txalı́hkeew.'

**soak** VI **be soaking wet** akwanóopeew VAI; **be soaking wet, be drenched, be limp from water** piisŭlúpeew VII, piisŭlúpeew VAI; **have one's hand(s) in water, soak one's hand(s) in water** kamukwŭnaxkéexiin VAI; **lay s.o. to soak in the water** kamukwı́ixŭ=meew VTA; **lie immersed in the water, lie soaking in the water** kamuk=wı́ixiin VAI, kamukwı́ixun VII; **lay s.t. to soak in the water** kamukwı́ixtoow VTI2; **soak in the water** kamukhwáa=suw VAI, kamukhwáasuw VII.

**soak** VT **soak s.o.** sookpáleew VTA; **soak s.t.** sookpátoow VTI2; **soak s.o. in water** *(using the hands)* kamúkwŭneew VTA; **soak s.o., soak s.t. animate** kamúkhweew VTA; **soak s.t. in liquid** sookhúpatoow VTI2; **soak s.t. in the**

**water** kamúkhwam VTI1A; **soak s.t. in water** *(using the hands)* kamúk=wŭnum VTI1B; **soak things** sookpatíi=keew VAI; **be soaked through** éesh=peew VAI, éeshpeew VII; **fall in the water, get soaked, get immersed** kamukwíhleew VAI; **soak one's feet, have one's feet in the water** choox=pwsiitéexiin VAI; **soak one's feet in the water** kamukwsíiteew VAI, ka=mukwsiitéexiin VAI; **soak one's hand(s) in water, immerse one's hand(s) in water** kamukwŭnáxkeew VAI; **soak one's legs in the water, put one's legs in the water** kamukw=káateew VAI.

**sober** ADJ **have a straight face, have a sober face, have a poker face** shaax=kiingwéexiin VAI; **regain consciousness, come to one's senses, sober up** taaxpéhleew VAI **I came to all of a sudden.** 'Wíixkwii méhch ndaax=péhla.', **I just came to.** 'Lúkih ndaaxpéhlaan.'

**sock** N ashíikan NI; **change one's socks** aashŭwashíikaneew VAI; **put on one's socks** piindashíikaneew VAI; **take off one's socks** ktunashíikaneew VAI; **wear more than one pair of socks** pihtawashíikaneew VAI.

**soda** N **baking soda** sótii NI.

**soft** ADJ **be damp, be wet, be soft** wtákeew VII **My washing's still damp.** 'Wtákeew íiyaach keeshiix=tàwáaniil.'; **be damp, be wet, be soft** wtáksuw VAI; **be soft from dampness** wtákpeew VAI, wtákpeew VII **The papers are softened from being in water.** 'Pambíilak wtakpéewak.'; **be soft ground** wtakahkéeyeew VII; **get damp, become soft from dampness** wtakíixiin VAI; **have soft hands** wtakŭnáxkeew VAI; **have a soft voice, have a high pitched voice** *(diminutive)* changaalakaxoonéeshuw VAI; **make a soft sound, make a low sound** kwíishkwŭweew VII; **make a soft sound, make a low sound, say in a soft voice, say in a low voice** kwíishkwŭweew VAI; **talk in a low voice, talk in a soft voice** *(diminutive)* achangiixshíishuw VAI.

**soft drink** N **sap, Kool-Aid, soft drink, sweet drink** shookŭláapoow NI.

**soften** VT **soften s.o. in water** wtak=páleew VTA; **soften s.t.** *(with liquid)* wtakíixtoow VTI2; **soften s.t. animate** wtákŭneew VTA; **soften s.t. in water** wtakpátoow VTI2.

**soldier** N sóochul NA, **fighting man, soldier** matahkeewíilŭnuw NA.

**sole** N **sole of the foot** aláamsiit PC; **be hungry, have the sole of one's shoe come off and flap around** katóopuw VAI; **have a hole in the sole of something** *(of shoes or boots)* pkwusiitée=yeew VII.

**some** ADJ áalund PC **Some people.** 'Áalund awéen.'; **some, a little bit, a small amount** tangii- PV **Can you speak a little Delaware now?** 'Méhch há kíish-tángii-hulŭníixsi?'; **some, a little bit, a small amount** tángii PC **There's a bit of bread there.** 'Tángii nú yéelak áhte apwáan.', **Do you want to eat a little bit?** 'Tángii káta-míitsi?'; **some, a small amount, a little bit** changíiwiish PC **I don't drink but I drink a little bit.** 'Máhta níi nŭmunéewi changíiwiish shúkw nŭmúne.'; **some, a small amount, a little bit** chángiish PC **There's just a little frost.** 'Chángiish shúkw tóh=pun.', **I left a little bit of the food.** 'Chángiish mbiiwándamun.'; **be some left over, be left over** aluwíh=lateew VAI, aluwíhlateew VII; **be left over, be some left over** aluwíhleew VII, aluwíhleew VAI **There's some fish left over.** 'Aluwíhleew namées.'; **only eat some of s.t. animate, have a piece of s.t. animate to eat, only**

**eat some of s.t. animate on one's plate** mshámeew VTA; **only eat some of s.t., have a piece of s.t. to eat, only eat part of s.t. on one's plate** mshándam VTI1A.

**someone** N **who, someone, a person** awéen PR **Who could that be now?** 'Awéen éet há ná kwáy?', **Who's he going with?** 'Awéeniil há wiichée=we?'

**somersault** N **do a somersault** aapooch=kwalhóosuw VAI.

**something** PR **something, what, thing** kwéek PR **He likes to talk** 'Wíhwiing-kwéek -úw.' **What did you say?** 'Kwéek ksí?'; **something, what, thing** kwéekw PR **He wears old things.** 'Xúwu-kwéekwiil awéehe.', **Why are you mad at me?** 'Kwéekw há kóonj-mataangóomi?'

**sometimes** ADV táhtaas PC **Sometimes I like the taste of it.** 'Táhtaas áng nŭ=wiingándamun.'

**somewhere** ADV **elsewhere, somewhere else** palii- PV **I put it elsewhere.** 'Mbálii-áhtoon.', **He went the other way.** 'Palíi-lóoxwe.'; **elsewhere, somewhere else** palu- PV *informal* **I said it in a hurry.** 'Mbálu-íin.'; **elsewhere, somewhere else** palí PC *informal* **Take the stone off the table.** 'Palí lúnih nú asún wúnju-eehundax=póonung.'; **elsewhere, somewhere else** palíi PC **Drive somewhere else!** 'Palíi luchéhlaal!', **Go away!** 'Palíi áal!'; **elsewhere, somewhere else** palíiwi PC **They stood him somewhere else.** 'Palíiwi íin wŭniipalaa=wáawal.'; **stand over, stand somewhere else, stand elsewhere** palii=káapawuw VAI; **change seats, sit somewhere else** aandapíhleew VAI.

**son** N **my son** ngwíisus NAD; **have a son** kwíissuw VAI.

**soon** ADV **soon, nearly** péexoot PC **I'm almost sleeping.** 'Péexoot ngáwiim.', **It must be going to rain pretty soon.** 'Péexoot éet sóokŭlaan.'; **be near, be soon** péexŭwat VII **It will rain soon.** 'Péexŭwat sóokŭlaan.'; **shortly, in a while, in a little while, soon, as soon as** méhchxiish PC **I'd slap him in the face.** 'Méhchxiish áa mbwahwsúmawa.', **I'll be done cooking in a little while.** 'Méhch=xiish-uch ngiishatúpwi.'; **shortly, in a while, in a little while, soon, as soon as** méhtxii PC **As soon as I got through eating.** 'Méhtxii ngíish-míitsiin.', **He will come in a while.** 'Mehtxíiwu-ch páan.'

**sore** ADJ **be sore in s.t.** *(of body parts)*, **hurt s.t.** wiinamándam VTI1A **His foot is sore.** 'Wiinamándamun wsíit.'; **be sore in s.t. animate** *(of body parts)*, **hurt s.t. animate** wiinamámeew VTA **I hurt my little knee.** 'Nguchkóo=hush nŭwiinamámaaw.'; **be sore, be tender, sting** *(of sores)* wiisakúsuw VAI, wíisakeew VII; **be sore, be tender, ache** *(of body parts)* kiihíicheew VII, kiihíitsuw VAI; **feeling, sensation, feeling in a sore body part** amanda=muwáakan NI; **get sore, hurt, have a pain, have a sharp pain, have a brief pain** wiisakíhleew VII, wiisa=kíhleew VAI **My knee had a sharp pain.** 'Ngútko wiisakíhleew.'; **have a backache, have a sore back** waa=wiikaníineew VAI; **have a sore arm, have a sore hand** kiihiitŭnáxkeew VAI; **have a sore foot** kiihiitsíiteew VAI; **have a sore leg** kiihiitkáateew VAI; **have a sore leg, have a lame leg** wihkaatíineew VAI; **have a sore throat** kwundaakaníineew VAI; **have a tired backside, have a sore backside** shiiwaasíitŭyeew VAI; **have an sore knee** kiihiichiiktúkweew VAI; **have something wrong with the shape of one's mouth, be always saying bad things about people, have a sore**

mouth matutóoneew VAI; **have sore eyes** wuskiinjkwíineew VAI.

**sore** N **have an open sore, be skinned, be peeled off** *(of bedsores, of blisters)* pxwíisksuw VAI.

**sorry** ADJ **be sad about s.t., be sorry about s.t.** shiiweelúndam VTI1A; **be sorry** alakweelúndam VOTI1; **be sorry about s.t.** alakweelúndam VTI1A; **feel sorry for oneself** ktumaakeelúnzuw VAI; **feel sorry for s.o.** ktumaakéelŭ=meew VTA.

**sort** VT **separate s.o., sort s.o.** chpíixŭ=meew VTA *object usually* plural; **separate s.t., sort s.t.** *(using the hands)* chpúnum VTI1B; **separate s.t. animate, sort s.t. animate** *(using the hands)* chpúneew VTA; **separate s.t., sort s.o.** chpíixtoow VTI2 *object usually plural;* **sort s.t. animate, sort s.t. animate out** chpahéewaleew VTA *object usually plural;* **sort s.t., sort s.t. out** chpahéewatoow VTI2 *object usually plural.*

**sound** N **have a certain sound, make a certain sound** lihtáakwsuw VAI **The car sounds like it's going to break down.** 'Káal lihtáakwsuw alúmulookíhleew.'; **like the sound of s.o., like the sound of s.t. animate, like to listen to s.o.** wiingsútaweew VTA; **like the sound of s.t., like to listen to s.t.** wiingsútam VTI1A **They (inanimate) sound good to me.** 'Nŭwiing=sutamúnal.'; **dislike listening to s.o., dislike the sound of s.o., dislike hearing about s.o.** shiingsútaweew VTA; **dislike listening to s.t., dislike the sound of s.t.** shiingsútam VTI1A; **make a racket, make a non-oral sound** kòhíikeew VAI; **creak, squeak, make a creaking sound, make a squeaking sound** kíiskŭweew VAI, kíiskŭweew VII; **make a soft sound, make a low sound** kwíishkwŭweew VII; **make a soft sound, make a low sound, say in a soft voice, say in a low voice** kwíishkwŭweew VAI; **make sounds of grief, sound full of grief** *(especially of singing)* ooshawih=táakwsuw VAI; **use a rattle, make a rattling sound** shòhwŭníikeew VAI, shòhwŭnúmeew VAI.

**sound** VI **find that s.o. sounds awful** chiipsútaweew VTA; **find that s.t. sounds awful** chiipsútam VTI1A; **make sounds of grief, sound full of grief** *(especially of singing)* oosha=wihtáakwsuw VAI; **sound angry, be angry-sounding** manoongihtáakw=suw VAI; **sound close by** peexŭwih=táakwat VII, peexŭwihtáakwsuw VAI; **sound fancy** wiilawihtáakwat VII, wiilawihtáakwsuw VAI; **sound far away** laawihtáakwat VII, laawih=táakwsuw VAI, wahlŭmihtáakwat VII, wahlŭmihtáakwsuw VAI; **sound good, sound nice** wŭlihtáakwat VII, wŭlih=táakwsuw VAI; **sound loud, sound terrible** chiipihtáakwat VII, chiipih=táakwsuw VAI; **sound odd, sound different, sound strange** maashihtáa=kwat VII, maashihtáakwsuw VAI; **sound weak** piisŭlihtáakwat VII, piisŭlihtáakwsuw VAI.

**soup** N kshíiteew NI; **corn soup** kaa=háhkwteew NI; **make soup** kshii=téewheew VAI.

**sour** ADJ shŭwii- PN **Brine pickle.** 'Shŭwíi-kòkómush.'; **be angry, be frustrated, be discouraged, be annoyed, be put-out, be bitter, be sour** *(of foods)* láxksuw VAI; **be bitter, taste bitter, taste sour, taste strong** láxkun VII; **be salty, be sour** shŭwán VII, shŭwúl VAI; **be sour, turn sour, spoil** shŭwálul VAI **They are too sour.** 'Wsáami-shŭwálŭlook.'; **be sour, turn sour, spoil** shŭwálut VII; **buttermilk, sour milk** shŭwíi-mŭlúk NI; **find that s.t. animate has a sour taste** láxkameew VTA; **find that s.t.**

**has a sour taste** laxkándam VTI1A; **have a bitter taste, have a sour taste** laxkiipóokwat VII, laxkiipóokwsuw VAI, laxkiipóokwun VII; **taste sour, have a sour taste** shŭwiipóokwan VII, shŭwiipóokwat VII, shŭwiipóokwsuw VAI.

**source** N **grow from a certain source, grow for a certain reason** wunjíi=kuw VAI; **grow from a certain source, grow for a certain reason** wunjíikun VII.

**south** N shaawanéewung PC **The wind is from the south.** 'Shaawanéewung wúndxun.'; **south, in the south** siikwanéewung PC.

**sow** VT **sow s.t.** *(of seeds)*, **scatter s.t.** sàséeham VTI1A.

**spank** VT **spank s.o., give s.o. a spanking** paakaasiitŭyéeheew VTA.

**spanking** N **spank s.o., give s.o. a spanking** paakaasiitŭyéeheew VTA.

**speak** VI **speak Delaware, speak a native language** hulŭníixsuw VAI; **speak Oneida** mehmeengwéewuw VAI; **speak Potawatomi** pooteewaata=míixsuw VAI; **speak English** shihshŭ=wánakuw VAI; **speak Ojibwe** wih=wshiipŭwéewuw VAI; **speak Unami** wihwŭnaamíiwuw VAI; **speak a certain language, speak a certain dialect** líixsuw VAI **He speaks another language or dialect.** 'Palíi ayulíix=suw.'; **be unable to speak** aalaap=tóoneew VAI; **finish speaking, be finished speaking** kiishaaptóoneew VAI; **leave out words when one speaks** pohpohkwíixsuw VAI; **speak** *(especially in public)*, **speak at a meeting, speak at a gathering** aaptóoneew VAI **Now he's speaking (as of a baby starting to talk)** 'Kwáy méhch aap=tóone.'; **speak** *(especially in public)*, **speak at a meeting, speak at a gathering** aaptóoneew VAI; **speak improperly, pronounce words incorrectly** amataaptóoneew VAI; **speak in a certain manner** lutóonheew VAI **He likes to stick his noise in.** 'Wíh=wiing- ná -lutóonheew.', **I speak slowly.** 'Maamalóoniish ndultóon=he.'; **speak loudly** xwíixsuw VAI; **speak quickly, speak in a harsh tone, speak in a sharp tone, say harsh things, say sharp things** kshaaptóoneew VAI; **speak quickly, talk fast** akushaaptóonheew VAI; **speak the exact truth** shaaxkaap=tóoneew VAI; **speak well** wŭlíixsuw VAI; **speak with s.o.** *(especially on the telephone)* aaptoonáaleew VTA; **start to speak** alumtóonheew VAI; **take s.o.'s side in an argument, speak on s.o.'s behalf in an argument, defend s.o.** ihkáameew VTA.

**speaker** N **be a good speaker** *(also of a child learning how to speak)*, **be good at speaking, be good at public speaking** nihtaawaaptóoneew VAI.

**spear** N **sword, spear** tangamíikan NI, tangamíikan NA, tangandíikan NI.

**speech** N **imitate the way s.o. talks, imitate s.o.'s speech** naanaxpŭlóh=taweew VTA; **make a speech** kihtaap=tóoneew VAI; **make s.o. ashamed by speech, say shameful things to s.o.** miixaníimeew VTA.

**speed** N **run sort of quickly, run at half-speed** kaakshaaméhleew VAI **He was trotting by because he's nosy.** 'Móxa kaakshaaméhleew kíhkata-wéewsuw.'

**spend all of** VT **be broke, have spent all one's money** pohkwíhleew VAI.

**spider** N meexalapóotiis NA.

**spill** VI **spill, fall down, come down** *(of water)* sookpéhleew VII.

**spill** VT **spill s.t. animate out, pour s.t. animate away** sóokheew VTA **I got the potatoes out (of a container).** 'Nzookháawak óhpŭnak.'; **spill s.t. animate, pour s.t. animate out**

sookáhlaleew VTA; **spill s.t., pour s.t. away** sóokham VTI1A; **spill s.t., pour s.t. out** sookáhlatoow VTI2; **spill s.t, pour s.t. away** sookáaheew VAIO; **spill s.t.** *(while using a tool)* paalíikwam VTI1A; **spill out, spill, be spilt** soo= káhleew VAI, sookáhleew VII.

**spin** VI **go around, rotate, spin** tùpíh= leew VAI, tùpíhleew VII; **hit s.o. and make them go around, hit s.o. and make them spin around** tùpihtée= heew VTA; **hit s.t. and make it go around, hit s.t. and make it spin around** tùpihtéeham VTI1A.

**spin** VT **spin and throw s.t., throw and spin s.t., twirl s.t. around** tùpáaheew VAIO **A good pitcher throws the ball with a spin to it.** 'Néhtaa-píchiit wtupaahéenal áng neenáxkwal.'; **be blown around by the wind, be spun around by the wind** túpxookw VAI, túpxun VII.

**spine** N **heartwood of tree, spine** wíimb NI.

**spirit** N manútoow NA.

**spirits** N **be happy, be in good spirits** wŭlahtéenamuw VAI.

**spit** N **spit, saliva** sùkwiináakan NI.

**spit** VI súkwiiw VAI.

**spit at** VT **spit at s.o.** sùkhwáaleew VTA.

**splash** VI **splatter, shatter, splash, scatter** séhleew VII.

**splatter** VI **splatter, shatter, splash, scatter** séhleew VII.

**splint** N **cut splints, cut splints of wood for baskets** pòháhkweew VAI.

**split** VT **split s.t. animate** *(using a tool or instrument)* pasáheew VTA; **split s.t.** *(using a tool or instrument)* pa= sáham VTI1A; **split s.t. animate** *(using the foot or body)* pasíhkaweew VTA; **split s.t.** *(using the foot or body)* pasíhkam VTI1A; **split s.t. animate by forceful contact, split s.t. animate by shot, split s.t. animate with a projectile** pasúlaweew VTA; **split s.t. by forceful contact, split s.t. by shot, split s.t. by hitting it with a projectile** pasúlam VTI1A; **split wood** pasaháhkweew VAI; **tear s.t. animate, split s.t. animate in two** pasúneew VTA; **tear s.t., split s.t. in two** pasún= um VTI1B; **be cracked, be split in two, be in half** pasát VII **It must be cracked.** 'Sháxk éet pasát.'; **be cracked, be split in two, be in half** pasúsuw VAI; **cut s.t. animate in two, cut s.t. animate in half, split s.t. animate in two by cutting it** pa= súsheew VTA; **cut s.t. in two, cut s.t. in half, split s.t. in two by cutting it** pasúshum VTI1B; **drop s.t. and split it in two** pasihtéextoow VTI2; **drop s.t. animate and split it in two** pasih= téexŭmeew VTA; **fall and split in two** pasihtéexun VII; **hit and split s.t.** pa= sihtéeham VTI1A; **split in two** pasíh= leew VAI, pasíhleew VII.

**spoil** VI **be sour, turn sour, spoil** shŭ= wálul VAI **They are too sour.** 'Wsáa= mi-shŭwálŭlook.'; **be sour, turn sour, spoil** shŭwálut VII; **decay, go bad, spoil** machíhleew VII; **run badly** *(especially of vehicles)*, **decay, go bad, spoil** machíhleew VAI.

**spoil** VT **spoil s.o.** machíiheew VTA; **spoil s.t., use up all of s.t., use up all of s.t. unwisely** machíhtoow VTI2 **I spent all of my money.** 'Nŭmachíh= toon wéemi nzhulpúlum.'

**spoon** N eemhwáanus NA; **tablespoon** xwateemhwáanus NA, tiiheemhwáa= nus NA.

**spot** N **get measles, get chicken pox, come out in blotches, come out in spots** saakpéhleew VAI; **have spots on it, have a line of spots on it, be marked with spots** sàsàpeekháasuw VII, sàsàpeekháasuw VAI; **put spots on s.o., make a line of spots on s.o., mark spots on s.o.** sàsàpéekheew VTA; **put spots on s.t., make a line of**

spots on s.t., mark s.t. with spots sàsàpéekham VTI1A; **see black, see things, see spots** *(especially after being sick)* mahmaashatawáapuw VAI.

**spotted** ADJ **be spotted** pàpsákeew VII, pàpsáksuw VAI, sàsápeew VII, sàsáp=suw VAI.

**spouse** N **my wife, my husband, my spouse** wiitawéemak VTA **His wife, her husband, his or her spouse.** 'Wiitaweemáachiil.', **Your wife, your husband, your spouse.** 'Wiita=wéemat.'; **be separated from one's spouse** machíilŭnuw VAI; **be separated from one's spouse, live apart** chpooxwéewak VAI *usually plural.*

**spout** N **have a chipped spout** kwa=shutóoneew VAI.

**sprain** N **be lame, have a sprain** kwŭ=lukwíixiin VAI, kwŭlukwíixun VII; **have a sprain** *(of body parts)* chii=líhleew VAI **I sprained my ankles.** 'Njiilíhla nihkáxkwanal.'; **have a sprain** chiilíixiin VAI.

**sprain** VT **sprain s.t.** *(of body parts)* chíilŭnum VTI1B; **sprain s.t. animate** *(of body parts)* chíilŭneew VTA; **have a sprained hand** chiilŭnaxkéexiin VAI, chiilŭnáxkeew VAI.

**sprawl** VI **lie sprawled, lie spread out, lie flat** toongchéexiin VAI, toongchée=xun VII.

**spray** VT **sprinkle s.o. with water, spray s.o. with water** sookalúnda=weew VTA; **sprinkle s.t. with water, spray s.t. with water** sookalúndam VTI1A.

**spread apart** VT **have one's legs spread apart** toongkaatéexiin VAI; **sit with legs open, sit with one's legs spread apart** toongohkwéepuw VAI, tóonga=puw VAI; **spread one's fingers apart, have one's fingers spread apart** sayaaxkŭlunjéexiin VAI; **spread one's toes apart, have one's toes spread apart** sayaaxksiitéexiin VAI; **stand with one's legs open, stand with one's legs spread apart** toongiikáa=pawuw VAI.

**spread open** VI **lay s.t. down spread open** shiipchéextoow VTI2.

**spread out** VI **stretch, spread, spread out** shiipíhleew VII.

**spread out** VT **spread s.o. out** shíip=heew VTA; **spread s.t. out** shíipham VTI1A; **spread s.t. out, roll s.t. out** *(using a tool or instrument)* shii=páhkhwam VTI1A; **be spread out** shiipháasuw VII; **be spread out** shiip=háasuw VAI; **be spread out, be open** *(as sole of shoe flapping)*, **be open, be apart** *(as a shirt)* toongíixun VII; **be spread out, have one's legs open** toongíixiin VAI; **lay s.o. down and spread them out** shiipchéexŭmeew VTA; **lie sprawled, lie spread out, lie flat** toongchéexiin VAI, toongchéexun VII; **lie spread out** shiipchéexiin VAI, shiipchéexun VII.

**spring** N **be spring** síikwan VII **I want to go there next spring.** 'Siikwánge ngáta- náh -á.', **I went there last spring.** 'Síikwane náh nóom.'; **during springtime, happen during springtime** siikwanúwii PC; **live until springtime, survive until springtime** siikwanámuw VAI.

**spring well** N **spring well, cold water** thupéekw NI.

**sprinkle** VI **be sprinkling rain** pàpsák=ŭlaan VII, sahsáapŭlaan VII.

**sprinkle** VT **sprinkle s.o. with water, spray s.o. with water** sookalúnda=weew VTA; **sprinkle s.t. with water, spray s.t. with water** sookalúndam VTI1A; **sprinkle things with water** sookalundíikeew VAI.

**sprout** VI **sprout, come up** *(of plants)* saakíikuw VAI, saakíikun VII; **sprout, come up** *(out of the ground)* sáakuw VAI, sáakun VII.

**square** ADJ **be square** hàshawéesuw VAI,

hàshawéeyeew VII; **cut s.t. and make it square, cut s.t. square** ashawée=shum VTI1B; **cut s.t. animate and make it square, cut s.t. animate square** ashawéesheew VTA; **have a square shape** hàshawuchéesuw VAI, hàshawuchéeyeew VII.

**squash** VT **crush s.o., squash s.o.** *(using the foot or body)* shkwíhkaweew VTA; **crush s.t., squash s.t.** *(using the foot or body)* shkwíhkam VTI1A; **smash s.t. animate, squash s.t. animate, flatten s.t. animate** shkwih=téeheew VTA; **smash s.t., squash s.t., flatten s.t.** shkwihtéeham VTI1A.

**squat** VI **be squatting, squat** weewee=tŭyéepuw VAI.

**squeak** VI **squeak, creak** kwíiskweew VII; kwíiskwsuw VAI; **squeak, creak, make a creaking sound, make a squeaking sound** kíiskŭweew VII; kíiskŭweew VAI.

**squeeze** VT **press s.o., squeeze s.o.** *(using the hands)* sŭlúskŭneew VTA; **press s.t., squeeze s.t.** *(using the hands)* sŭlúskŭnum VTI1B; **press the insides out of s.o., squeeze the insides out of s.o.** sŭluskihtéeheew VTA; **press the insides out of s.t., squeeze the insides out of s.t.** sŭluskihtéeham VTI1A; **squeeze s.t.** shkwúnum VTI1B; **squeeze s.t. animate** shkwúneew VTA.

**squirm** VI **wriggle, squirm** wiimbíh=leew VAI.

**squirrel** N **black squirrel** psakwŭlún=jeew NA; **red squirrel** wiisaawaníi=kwus NA.

**stab** VT **stab s.o.** tángameew VTA.

**stable** N **stable, log stable** shtépul NI.

**stagger** VI cheemíhleew VAI.

**stairs** N **climb up a long flight of stairs** kwŭnakóosuw VAI.

**stamp** VT **stamp with one's feet, keep time with one's feet** pòhwsiitéexiin VAI.

**stand** VI níipawuw VAI, níipateew VII; **be many of them standing** *(in a group)* xweeliikaapawúwak VAI *usually plural;* **be tired of standing** shiiwiikáa=pawuw VAI; **stand between something** teetawiikáapawuw VAI; **stand bunched together** mŭniikaapawúw=ak VAI *usually plural;* **stand close together** kchukiikaapawúwak VAI *usually plural;* **stand far apart** wahlŭ=miikaapawúwak VAI *usually plural;* **stand in a bunch, be bunched up standing together** kohpakiikaapa=wúwak VAI *usually plural;* **stand in a certain manner, stand in a certain direction** liikáapawuw VAI **He's standing out of the way.** 'Palíi lii=káapawuw.', **He's fidgeting as he stands.** 'Músu-liikáapawiin.'; **stand in a circle** wiiwŭniikaapawúwak VAI *usually plural;* **stand in rows, stand several deep** pihtawiikaapawúwak VAI *usually plural;* **stand in the way** kpiikáapawuw VAI; **stand in threes, be three standing there** nxiikaapa=wúwak VAI *usually plural;* **stand lopsided, stand with one leg higher than the other** piimiitŭyéexiin VAI; **stand naked** sheexkaliikáapawuw VAI; **stand over, stand somewhere else, stand elsewhere** paliikáapawuw VAI; **stand sideways, stand beside someone** pŭmiichiikáapawuw VAI; **stand straight** shaaxkiikáapawuw VAI **You know how to stand straight.** 'Kŭníhtaa-shaaxkiikáapawi.'; **stand with one's legs open, stand with one's legs spread apart** toongiikáa=pawuw VAI; **turn around while standing** kwŭlupiikáapawuw VAI.

**stand up** VI **have one's ears standing up** niipawaxéexiin VAI.

**stand up** VT **stand s.o. up, stand s.t. animate up** níipaleew VTA; **stand s.t. up** níipatoow VTI2; **stand things up** niipatíikeew VAI.

**stand upon** VT **stand upon something** poxkwiikáapawuw VAI.

**star** N aláangweew NA, aláangweesh NA; **shining star** waasaláangweew NA.

**starch** N **put starch on s.t.** *(of clothing)* chiingaalchásum VTI1B.

**stare** VI kaanzh'hiingwéexiin VAI; **like to stare** ayahwhiingwéexiin VAI.

**start** N **be the start of a road** aluma=téexun VII; **take a big start in a competition, take a jump in a competition, take a leap in a competition, get a running start** wundaaméhleew VAI.

**start** VI **start to** nooch- PV *informal* **He's starting to yawn.** 'Nóoch-tohtoongtóone.', **He was angry for a while, and then as soon as the baby was born he started to go with her (the woman) again.** 'Náakeesh shúkw manóongsuw, nál wáak méh=txii amíimunz wtulkíilun nál wáak wŭnóoch-wiichéewaan.'; **start to** noochi- PV **He's starting to walk.** 'Nóochi-apáamsuw.', **I'm starting to walk.** 'Nóochi-apáamsi.'; **start to** noochu- PV *informal* **Now he's starting to play ball.** 'Kwáy íin nóochu-neenáxkuw.'; **go up, come up, start to come up** uspíhleew VAI; **leave running, run away, start to run** alum=ahtakíhleew VAI; **start cutting s.t.** alúmshum VTI1A; **start cutting s.t. animate** alúmsheew VTA; **start cutting things** alumshíikeew VAI; **start off fast, start off running** *(especially when running in a race)* ktakíixiin VAI; **start off singing** *(especially in church)*, **burst out crowing** *(of roosters)* kundaláamuw VAI; **start singing** alumaláamuw VAI; **start to crawl** noochíikwsuw VAI; **start to grow** noochíikuw VAI **He was slow to start growing, he's growing now.** 'Áawiis noochíikuw, méhch alumíikuw.'; **start to make noise** nóotŭweew VAI; **start to speak** alumtóonheew VAI, noottóonheew VAI; **start up** *(of fires, of furnaces)* naxkwtéhleew VII; **start working** nootalóhkeew VAI.

**startle** VT **hit s.o. and startle them** salaxkihtéeheew VTA; **surprise s.o., startle s.o., make s.o. jump** ktakíh=laleew VTA; **be startled, be surprised, jump** ktakíhleew VAI; **be startled, be surprised, be shocked** sa=laxkíhleew VAI.

**starve** VI **starve, starve to death** sha=waláamuw VAI.

**state** N **better condition, improved condition, better state, improved state** míingasa PC **It's better now, it shuts well (of a door).** 'Míingasa kwáy wŭlú-kpíhle.', **It's good that you came early.** 'Míingasa ktáapwi-pá.'

**stay** VI **stay at home alone** nootíikeew VAI; **stay overnight** mawíikeew VAI; **stay there quietly, be there quietly, live there quietly** naláwapuw VAI; **be at a loss, don't know which way to turn, feel one has no place to go, not know where one will stay** kwii=laweelúndam VOTI1; **begin to stay there, begin to stay here** nóotapuw VAI; **dislike it where one is, dislike it where one stays** shíingapuw VAIO; **live together in threes, stay together in threes** nxiilŭnúwak VAI *usually plural.*

**stay away** VI **go away for good, stay away for good** wchiimwáhkeew VAI; **stay away for good** wchíimapuw VAI.

**stay out** VI **stay out overnight** ngwútii-tpohkweewáhkeew VAI.

**stay with** VT **eat with s.o., stay with s.o.** wiitapóomeew VTA.

**steadily** ADV **rain steadily** *(diminutive)* chkawŭláanzhuw VII.

**steal** VI kŭmóotkeew VAI; **steal s.t.** kŭmóotkeew VAIO.

**steal from** VT **steal s.t. from s.o.**

kŭmóotŭmeew VTAO.

**steep** ADJ **be a steep hill** àhwaawún=geew VII.

**step** N **take a step, put one's foot in something, put one's foot on something** alíhkeew VAI **I put my foot on the ice and I slipped.** 'Ndalíhke móhkamiing, nooshάaxihla.', **He put his foot in the water.** 'Mbíing alíh=keew.'; **take five steps** naalanalíh=keew VAI; **take four steps** neewalíh=keew VAI; **take long steps** akwaana=líhkeew VAI; **take one step** ngwuta=líhkeew VAI; **take short steps** *(diminutive)* achahkwalihkehléeshuw VAI; **take so many steps** txalíhkeew VAI **He took six steps.** 'Ngwútaash txalíhkeew.'; **take two steps** niisha=líhkeew VAI.

**step on** VT **break s.o.'s leg** *(using the foot or body)*, **step on and break s.o.'s leg** kaxkkaatéhkaweew VTA; **break s.t.** *(using the foot or body)*, **step on and break s.t.** kaxkíhkam VTI **I stepped on his leg and broke it.** 'Ngaxkíhkamun wíhkaat.'; **break s.t. animate** *(using the foot or body)*, **step on and break s.t. animate** kax=kíhkaweew VTA; **hold s.o. down** *(using the foot or body)*, **step on s.o. and hold them down, sit on s.o. and hold them down** kŭlíhkaweew VTA; **hold s.t. down** *(using the foot or body)*, **step on s.t. and hold it down, sit on s.t. and hold it down** kŭlíhkam VTI1A; **make s.o. dirty** *(using the foot or body)*, **step on s.o. and make them dirty** niiskíhkaweew VTA; **make s.t. dirty** *(using the foot or body)*, **step on s.t. and make it dirty** niis=kíhkam VTI1A; **miss stepping on s.o., miss stepping on s.t. animate** palíh=kaweew VTA; **miss stepping on s.t.** palíhkam VTI1A; **step on and bend s.t.** *(of a pedal)* tamakíhkam VTI1A; **step on s.o. and make a hole in them** pkwíhkaweew VTA.

**step over** VT **step over s.o., step over s.t. animate** paalíhkaweew VTA; **step over s.t.** paalíhkam VTI1A; **step over s.t., step over s.o.** paalalíhkeew VAIO.

**step upon** VT **step upon s.o.** ahpchéh=kaweew VTA; **step upon s.o., fall upon s.o., sit upon s.o.** ahpíhkaweew VTA; **step upon s.t.** ahpalihkéhleew VAIO; **step upon s.t., fall upon s.t., sit upon s.t.** ahpíhkam VTI1A; **step upon s.t., step upon s.o.** ahpalíhkeew VAIO.

**stepchild** N **my stepchild** nohkwtóomus NAD.

**stepfather** N **my stepfather** nŭmóxoom NAD.

**stepmother** N **my stepmother** nóohŭ=mus NAD.

**stick** N míhtkwus NI; **stick placed across the door to indicate that no one is at home** nootíikees NI; **stirring stick** eewaxkhíikan NI, wŭyamoxk=híikan NI; **lacrosse stick** niimcheehŭ=máakan NI; **something used for measuring, ruler, measuring tape, measuring stick** tpuskhíikan NI.

**stick** VI **have one's feet here, have one's feet sticking this way** peetsiitéexiin VAI **He can't get his feet there.** 'Áalu-náh -peetsiitéexiin.'; **fasten s.t. onto something, stick s.t. onto something** kŭlamóotoow VTI2 **I stuck it onto the door.** 'Kpahóonung ngulamóotoon.'; **glue s.t., stick s.t. together** psákwŭ=num VTI1B; **stick one's finger in s.o.'s eye** laapsheengwéeneew VTA; **put s.o. close together, put s.t. animate close together, stick s.o. up against something** psakwíixŭmeew VTA *object usually plural.*

**stick into** VT **stick into something a certain manner, stick into something in a certain direction** lamwíh=leew VAI **A pin went into my arm.** 'Píinj làmwíhleew náxkung.'; **stick into something in a certain manner,**

**stick into something a certain direction** lamwíhleew VII **A sliver went in my hand.** 'Palalíikaaxkw làmwíh=le náxkung.'; **stick s.t. animate into something in a certain manner, stick s.t. animate into something in a certain direction, stick s.t. animate into something** làmóoleew VTA; **stick s.t. into something in a certain manner, stick s.t. into something in a certain direction, stick s.t. into something** làmóotoow VTI2 **I stuck the wood in the box.** 'Mbáksung ndulamóotoon xwúsal.'

**stick out** VI ktámuw VAI **He's sticking out the door.** 'Uskwáande wúnj-ktámuw.'; **stick out** ktámuw VII; **stick out** saakíhleew VII **Your sweater was sticking out.** 'Saakíhleew ksuwétŭ=lum.'; **stick out** saakíixiin VAI, saa=kíixun VII **His tail is sticking out.** 'Wshúkwŭnay saakíixun.'; **stick out, stick out over the top** ktáskaneew VAI **Your navel's sticking out.** 'Kpoo=shíishum péech-ktáskaneew.', **The potatoes are sticking up out of the pail.** 'Óhpŭnak wshaphóosung wúnj-ktaskanéewak.'; **stick out, stick out over the top** ktáskaneew VII; **have one's backside exposed, have one's backside sticking out** mihchiitŭyée=xiin VAI; **have one's eyes sticking out, look out, peek out** ktiingwée=xiin VAI; **have one's foot sticking out** saaksíiteew VAI; **have one's hand(s) sticking out** sakunaxkéexiin VAI; **have one's head sticking out** saakáand=peew VAI **I didn't see him but his head was sticking out.** 'Máh nee=wáawi shúkw péech-saakáandpeew.'; **have one's head sticking out, lie with one's head sticking out, stick one's head out** saakaandpéexiin VAI; **have one's heel sticking out, stick one's heel out** saakangwanéexiin VAI; **have one's lips sticking out, pout** niixsheetóonayeew VAI; **have one's lips sticking out, stick one's lips out** sheetoonéexiin VAI; **have one's slip sticking out** ktahóosuw VAI, saak=hóosuw VAI; **have one's tongue sticking out** saapiilanuwéexiin VAI; **lie with one's face sticking out, lie with one's face showing, have one's face showing** kchiingwéexiin VAI; **lie with one's head sticking out, have one's head sticking out** saakohkwéexiin VAI **My head was sticking out of the water** 'Mbíing nóonj-saakohkwée=xiin.', **I was covered up but my head was sticking out.** 'Nŭmutakwaháasi shùkéhla nzaakohkwéexiin.'; **sit with one's lips sticking out** sheetoonoh=kwéepuw VAI; **stick one's backside out, have one's backside sticking out** saakiitŭyéexiin VAI, uspootŭyée=xiin VAI; **stick one's belly out, have one's belly sticking out** saakatayée=xiin VAI; **stick one's feet out, have one's feet sticking out** ktusiitéexiin VAI, saaksiitéexiin VAI; **stick one's hand out, have one's hand sticking out** kchiinaxkéexiin VAI, saakŭnax=kéexiin VAI; **stick one's head out, have one's head sticking out** ktaandpéexiin VAI; **stick one's lips up, have one's lips sticking out** uspsheetóonayeew VAI; **stick one's neck out, have one's neck sticking out** saakxoonéexiin VAI; **stick one's nose out, have one's nose sticking out** ktuchaaléexiin VAI; **walk bent over with one's behind sticking out** waakhootŭyéewxeew VAI; **walk with one's belly sticking out, have one's belly sticking out as one walks** saakatayéewxeew VAI.

**stick out** VT **stick s.t. out** saakíixtoow VTI2; **stick s.t. out** sáakŭnum VTI1B; **have one's head sticking out, lie with one's head sticking out, stick one's head out** saakaandpéexiin VAI;

**have one's lips sticking out, stick one's lips out** sheetoonéexiin VAI; **stick one's backside out, have one's backside sticking out** saakiitŭyée=xiin VAI, uspootŭyéexiin VAI, siingii=tŭyéexiin VAI; **stick one's belly out, have one's belly sticking out** saaka=tayéexiin VAI; **stick one's feet out, have one's feet sticking out** ktusii=téexiin VAI; **stick one's hand out straight, have one's hand(s) out straight** shaaxkùnaxkéexiin VAI; **stick one's hand out, have one's hand sticking out** kchiinaxkéexiin VAI, saakŭnaxkéexiin VAI; **stick one's head out, have one's head sticking out** ktaandpéexiin VAI; **stick one's neck out, have one's neck sticking out** saakxoonéexiin VAI; **stick one's tongue out at s.o.** saapiilanuwéhta=weew VTA; **stick out one's tongue** saapiilanúweew VAI.

**sticky** ADJ **be sticky** psákweew VII, psákwsuw VAI, pàpsákuw VAI; **sticky** psakwii- PN **Sticky paper.** 'Psákwii-pámbiil.'

**stiff** ADJ **be stiff** chiingáaleew VII, chiin=gáalsuw VAI; **have a stiff leg** chiin=gaalkáateew VAI; **have a stiff neck** chiingaalxoonéexiin VAI, chiingaal=xóoneew VAI.

**still** ADJ **be still water** kŭlampéekat VII, kŭlampéexun VII; **lie still** kŭlamíixiin VAI, kŭlamíixun VII **The snake is still.** 'Áxkook kŭlamíixiin.'

**still** ADV **still, yet** íiyaach PC **I'm still working.** 'Íiyaach ndalóhke.', **You're still sweating.** 'Íiyaach kúsh'si.'

**sting** VI **be sore, be tender**, **sting** *(of sores)* wiisakúsuw VAI.

**sting** VT **sting s.o.** sáapheew VTA'.

**stingy** ADJ **be shy** *(of animals)*, **be stingy** áhwsuw VAI; **like s.t., be stingy about s.t.** àhwáatam VTI1A.

**stink** VI **have a bad smell, stink** ma=chiimáakwat VII, machiimáakwsuw VAI.

**stir** VI **move around, stir** wàwŭyamox=kchéhleew VAI; **move, stir** kwàkw=chúkuw VAI **He's moving. Maybe he's alive.** 'Kwàkwchúkuw. Pŭ=máawsuw éet.'; **move, stir, shake** kwchukwíhleew VAI, kwchúkwihl VAI.

**stir** VT **stir s.t.** wŭyamóxkham VTI1A; **stir s.t.** *(using the hands)* wŭyamóx=kŭnum VTI1B; **stir s.t. animate** wŭ=yamóxkheew VTA; **stir things** eewax=khíikeew VAI; **stir things** wŭyamoxk=híikeew VAI, wŭyamóxkham VOTI1; **be stirred, be stirred up** wŭyamoxk=háasuw VAI, wŭyamoxkháasuw VII **It's stirred up now.** 'Méhch wŭyamoxk=háasuw.'; **shake and stir s.t., agitate s.t.** wŭyamoxkíhtoow VTI2.

**stirring stick** N eewaxkhíikan NI, wŭ=yamoxkhíikan NI.

**stomach** N **my stomach** natáy NID, nzheemóotay NID; **fall on one's stomach, land on one's stomach, fall flat, fall face down** pàkchehtéexiin VAI; **feel nauseous, feel sick to one's stomach** wŭyakaskíilaweew VAI; **have a swollen stomach, be bloated, have gas** paasatáyeew VAI; **have an upset stomach** *(especially from morning sickness)* machíilaweew VAI; **have diarrhea, have stomach flu** watéeneew VAI; **have one's stomach shaking** nungatayéhleew VAI; **inside the stomach** aláamatay PC **Inside the stomach.** 'Alaamatáye.'; **lie on one's stomach** aalaanjkwéexiin VAI, pàka=téexiin VAI, waalatéexiin VAI; **roll over onto one's stomach** pàkatéhleew VAI.

**stone** N **stone, rock** asún NI; **stone house** asuníikaan NI; **file, sharpening stone, grindstone** kiinhíikan NI.

**Stonefish** N asúnameekw NA *family name.*

**stony** ADJ **be stony ground** asunahkée=yeew VII.

**stood up** VT **be stood up** niipatáasuw

VAI.

**stoop** VI **walk bent over, walk stooped over** waakóoxweew VAI.

**stop** VI **stop, cease** ehkwi- PV **I couldn't see him.** 'Ndéhkwi-néewa.'; **stop, cease** ehkwu- PV *informal* **He quit breathing.** 'Éhkwu-léexeew.', **The service is over.** 'Éhkwu-maawée=wiin.'; **stop before one finishes** *(doing something)* pohkwii- PV **I quit making bread.** 'Mbóhkwii-apwáan=he.', **I quit looking at it.** 'Mbóhkwii-punámun.'; **stop before one finishes** *(doing something)* pohkwu- PV *informal* **He stopped while eating.** 'Póhkwu-míitsuw.'; **stop** ngíhleew VAI; **stop burning** ehkwchásuw VAI, ehkwcháteew VII; **stop burning, cease burning** éhkwsuw VAI, éhkw=teew VII; **stop cutting s.t. animate, cease cutting s.t. animate** éhkw=sheew VTA; **stop cutting s.t., cease cutting s.t.** éhkwshum VTI1B; **stop cutting things, cease cutting things** ehkwshíikeew VAI; **stop drinking** ehkwíisŭmuw VAI **You should quit drinking.** 'Kóolu- áa -ehkwíisŭ=mwi.'; **stop going, stop working** *(of machines)* ehkwíhleew VII; **stop going, stop working** ehkwíhleew VAI; **stop growing** ehkwíikun VII, ehkwíi=kuw VAI; **stop raining** éhkwŭlaan VII; **stop talking, cease talking** ehk=wtóonheew VAI; **stop urinating, cease urinating, quit urinating** eh=kwíisheew VAI; **stop working, break off working, quit before one is done** *(without necessarily having completed a task)* pohkwalóhkeew VAI.

**stop** VT **stop s.o.** ngúneew VTA; **stop s.t.** ngúnum VTI1B; **stop s.o.** *(with an elongated object)*, **bunt a ball** *(in baseball)* ngiikwáaleew VTA **I bunted the ball.** 'Nàkiikwáalaaw áng née=naxkw.'; **be stopped, stop** ngíixiin VAI.

**store** N koopmaaníikaan NI; **grocery store** kŭlooshliihíikaan NI.

**store** VT **put s.t. away, store s.t.** wŭláh=toow VTI2 **I want to put it away.** 'Ngáta-wŭláhtoon.'; **store s.t. animate, pile s.t. animate up** *(of something wood- or stick-like)* wŭlah=kwéexŭmeew VTA *object usually plural;* **store s.t., pile s.t. up** *(of something wood- or stick-like)* wŭlah=kwéextoow VTI2 *object usually plural;* **put things away, store things, be buried** wŭlahtáasuw VAI; **be stored, be put away** wŭlahtáasuw VII.

**storekeeper** N kóopmaan NA.

**story** N **add on to a story, interpret** aanihkwaachíimuw VAI; **give a good account of onself, tell a favourable story** wŭlaachíimuw VAI; **leave out part of the story while talking** pàp=ŭlakaachíimuw VAI; **say something in a hurry, leave something out of a story, don't tell the whole story** pàpalaachíimuw VAI; **tell a great story** kihtaachíimuw VAI; **tell a story** laachíimuw VAI; **tell a tall tale, tell an exciting story, brag** kaanzhaa=chíimuw VAI; **tell s.o. a story** laachŭ=móhkaweew VTA; **tell s.o. a tall tale, tell s.o. an exciting story** kaanzhaa=chŭmóhkaweew VTA.

**stove** N kehkshúteek NI.

**straddle** VT **sit astride something, sit straddling something** póxkapuw VAI, póxkwapuw VAI.

**straight** ADJ **be a straight road** shaax=kàtéexun VII; **be good, be straight, be a good strand of thread, be fine** *(of something stringlike)* wŭláhtakat VII; **be in a straight line, be in a row** wŭlaaméewak VAI *usually plural,* wŭlaaméewal VII *usually plural;* **be in a straight row, be in a straight line** shaaxkáameew VII **What I planted is in a straight row.** 'Shaaxkáameew ehkíihayaan.'; **be in order, lie correctly, be lined up straight** *(s.t. animate)*, **be the main one, be the top person** mayaawíixiin VAI; **be lined up, be in a straight line** wŭlaamée=xŭnool VII *usually plural;* **be marked in a straight line** shaaxkeekháasuw VII, shaaxkeekháasuw VAI; **be straight** *(of something string-like)* shaaxkáh=takat VII, shaaxkahtakúsuw VAI; **be straight** sháaxkat VII, sháaxkeew VII, shaaxkúsuw VAI; **climb straight up** kundakóosuw VAI; **go straight** shaax=kíhleew VII, shaaxkíhleew VAI; **have a straight face, have a sober face, have a poker face** shaaxkiingwéexiin VAI; **have one's hands straight out** ashaaxkùnáxkeew VAI; **have straight hair** shaaxkaalóhkweew VAI; **have straight teeth** ashaaxkàníikeew VAI; **straighten s.t., lay s.t. straight** shaaxkíixtoow VTI2; **lie straight** shaaxkíixiin VAI, shaaxkíixun VII; **look straight ahead** shaaxkóhkweew VAI; **make a mark on s.o. in a straight line, mark s.o. in a straight line** shaaxkéekheew VTA; **make a straight line of things, write in a straight line** shaaxkeekhíikeew VAI; **roll straight** wŭliinjkwéhleew VAI, wŭ=liinjkwéhleew VII; **sew s.t. animate straight, poke s.o. straight, straighten s.o. out** *(with a tool)* shaaxkii=kwáaleew VTA; **sew s.t. straight, poke s.t. straight, straighten s.t.** *(with a tool)* shaaxkíikwam VTI1A; **sew things straight, straighten things** *(with a tool)* shaaxkiikwáa=keew VAI; **sit straight** shaaxkoh=kwéepuw VAI; **stand straight** shaax=kiikáapawuw VAI **You know how to stand straight.** 'Kŭníhtaa-shaaxkii=káapawi.'; **stick one's hand out straight, have one's hand(s) out straight** shaaxkùnaxkéexiin VAI; **straight road** shaaxkáanay NI; **straighten s.o., lay s.o. straight** shaaxkíixŭmeew VTA.

**straighten** VT **straighten s.o.** *(using the hands)* shaaxkúneew VTA; **straighten s.o. out** mayáawŭneew VTA; **straighten s.o., lay s.o. straight** shaaxkíi=xŭmeew VTA; **straighten s.o., straighten s.o. out** *(using the foot or body)* shaaxkíhkaweew VTA; **straighten s.t.** shaaxkíhtoow VTI2; **straighten s.t.** *(using the hands)* shaaxkúnum VTI1B; **straighten s.t. out** mayáawŭ=num VTI1B; **straighten s.t., straighten s.t. out** *(using the foot or body)* shaaxkíhkam VTI1A; **flatten s.t., straighten s.t.** *(using the hands)* pàkchéenum VTI1B; **hit and straighten s.o., hit and straighten s.t. animate** shaaxkihtéeheew VTA; **hit and straighten s.t.** shaaxkihtéeham VTI1A; **place s.o. correctly, make s.o. be correctly arranged, straighten s.o. up, arrange s.o. correctly** mayaa=wíixŭmeew VTA; **place s.t. correctly, make s.t. be correctly arranged, straighten s.t. up** mayaawíixtoow VTI2; **sew s.t. straight, poke s.t. straight, straighten s.t.** *(with a tool)* shaaxkíikwam VTI1A; **sew s.t. animate straight, poke s.o. straight, straighten s.o. out** *(with a tool)* shaaxkiikwáaleew VTA; **sew things straight, straighten things** *(with a tool)* shaaxkiikwáakeew VAI.

**straighten out** VI **straighten out, go straight, go quickly in the right direction, drive correctly** mayaawíh=leew VAI.

**strain** VT **strain s.t.** sihkpéenum VTI1B; **strain s.t. animate** sihkpéeneew VTA; **strain things** sihkpeeníikeew VAI.

**strange** ADJ **strange person** máasha=ween PR; **do strange things to s.o., do things that make s.o. feel strange** maashiilawéeheew VTA; **have a strange feeling** maasheelúndam

VOTI1; **have a strange look on one's face, have a guilty look on one's face, look guilty of something** maa=shiingwéexiin VAI; **have a strange smell, smell strange** maashiimáa=kwat VII, maashiimáakwsuw VAI; **have an odd face, have a strange face** maashíingweew VAI; **lead an odd life, lead a strange life** maanjŭwáawsuw VAI; **look strange, have an odd appearance** maashiináakwat VII, maa=shiináakwsuw VAI; **make people feel strange** maashiilawéhtoow VAI; **odd person, strange person** maanjŭ=wáween PR; **see strange things** maashatawáapuw VAI; **sound odd, sound different, sound strange** maa=shihtáakwat VII, maashihtáakwsuw VAI; **be able to tell the difference between people, 'make strange'** *(of babies)* chihchpiináasuw VAI, chpii=náasuw VAI.

**strangely** ADV **act oddly, act strangely, make faces** amáashŭnum VOTI1; **act strangely** amaashíiyayuw VAI.

**strangle** VT **choke s.o., strangle s.o.** kchiixkwéeneew VTA.

**strawberry** N wtéehiim NI.

**streak** N **make marks here and there, make streaks all over** *(on paper)* apaameekhíikeew VAI.

**strength** N maskanusŭwáakan NI.

**stretch** VI **stretch, be stretching** shiip=chéewuw VAI; **stretch, spread, spread out** shiipíhleew VII; **stretch, stretched** shiipii- PV **I stretched it out and tacked it down.** 'Nzhíipii-kŭlahk=hwámun.'; **stretch, stretched** shiipii- PV **I stretched it out and tacked it down.** 'Nzhíipii-kŭlahkhwámun.'

**stretch** VT **stretch s.t.** *(using the hands)* shíipŭnum VTI1B; **stretch s.t. animate** *(using the hands)* shíipŭneew VTA.

**stretch out** VT **stretch s.o. out, lay s.o. out** shiipíixŭmeew VTA; **stretch s.t. out, lay s.t. out** shiipíixtoow VTI2; **be stretched out** shiipchéesuw VAI; **be stretched out** shiipáameew VAI, shii=páameew VII; **be stretched out** shii=pŭnáasuw VAI, shiipŭnáasuw VII; **kick out one's legs, stretch out one's legs, maneuver** *(of trains)* shándham VOTI1; **lie spread out** shiipchéexiin VAI, shiipchéexun VII; **lie stretched out, be stretched out** shiipíixiin VAI, shiipíixun VII; **stretch one's hand out, have one's hand stretched out** shiipŭnaxkéexiin VAI; **stretch one's hands out** shiipŭnáxkeew VAI; **stretch out one's arm** shiipiináxkeew VAI.

**strike** VT **be struck by lightning** pa=yáxkhaaw VTA *indefinite subject only* **I was struck by lightning.** 'Mbay=axkhóoke.'; **be struck in the eye, brush against something which goes into the eye** laapsheengwéexiin VAI.

**strike out** VI méhtham VOTI1 *baseball.*

**string** N koopmaanáhtakw NI, koxptíi=kan NI; **be string in a certain manner, be string in a certain direction** láhtakat VII; **black thread, black string** nzukáhtakw NI; **blue thread, blue string** oolihkáhtakw NI; **lead s.o. along with a string, lead s.o. by with a string, lead s.o. along by the reins, lead s.o. by by the reins** *(of horses)* pŭmaapéeneew VTA; **lead s.o. in a certain direction with a string, lead s.o. in a certain manner with a string, lead s.o. in a certain direction by the reins, lead s.o. in a certain manner by the reins, put the reins on s.o.** *(of horses)* laapéeneew VTA; **short piece of rope, short piece of string** chahkwáamanush NI.

**strip** VT **eat s.t. animate bare, strip s.t. animate to the bone** chíikwameew VTA; **eat s.t. bare, strip s.t. to the bone** chiikwándam VTI1A **The horse ate the grass to the ground.** 'Neh=nayóongus wchiikwándamun mii=

xáskwal.'; **be bare, be stripped bare** chíikweew VII **The forest is bare.** 'Chíikweew kóhpii.'; **be bare, be stripped bare** chíikwsuw VAI **The tree is bare.** 'Chíikwsuw míhtukw.'

**stripe** N **be marked black, have a black mark, have a black stripe** nzukeek=háasuw VAI, nzukeekháasuw VII; **be marked red, have red stripes** max=keekháasuw VII, maxkeekháasuw VAI.

**striped** ADJ **be striped** maamáaleew VII, maamáalsuw VAI.

**strong** ADJ **be strong** *(of a sensation)* áhwan VII; **be strong willed, be strong in character**, **be brave** maskaniitée=heew VAI **He's not brave yet (usually said of a young person).** 'Éeskwa néeka maskaniiteehéewu.'; **be strong, be hard** máskaneew VII; **be strong, be hard** *(to eat, s.t. animate)* maska=núsuw VAI; **be strong-looking** mas=kaniináakwat VII, maskaniináakwsuw VAI; **be a strong wind** *(especially of tornados)* kíhtxun VII; **be bitter, taste bitter, taste sour, taste strong** láx=kun VII; **be independent, be smart, be alive**, **be strong** *(especially a sick person who gets up because he or she is feeling better)* àhwaapéewuw VAI; **smell strong, have a strong smell** àhwiimáakwat VII, àhwiimáakwsuw VAI; **take a strong drink** *(including non-alcoholic beverages)* àhwíisŭ=muw VAI; **taste strong, be strong in taste** àhwiipóokwat VII, àhwiipóokw=suw VAI.

**strong-willed** ADJ **be strong willed, be strong in character**, **be brave** mas=kaniitéeheew VAI **He's not brave yet (usually said of a young person).** 'Éeskwa néeka maskaniiteehéewu.'

**stub one's toe** VI paaksiitéexiin VAI; **trip, stub one's toe** pasusiitéexiin VAI.

**stubborn** ADJ **be balky, be stubborn** acheexáakwsuw VAI; **disobey, refuse to listen, be stubborn** achiingíiwsuw VAI.

**stuck** ADJ **be stuck** *(with a thorn, with a sliver, with a thistle)* moxkawúsuw VAI; **be stuck in mud** kŭlasíiskŭweew VAI; **be stuck on, be stuck together** psákwamuw VII, psákwamuw VAI; **be stuck onto something** kŭlámuw VAI; **be stuck together** takwámŭwak VAI *usually plural,* takwámŭwal VII *usually plural;* **be stuck, get stuck, be trapped** kŭláhkweew VAI, kŭláhkweew VII **My shoe is stuck.** 'Kŭláhkweew nŭmáhksun.'

**stump** N **tree stump** wíhkwanahkw NI.

**stupid** ADJ **be empty headed, be stupid** kpáandpeew VAI.

**sturdy** ADJ **be sturdy looking, be strong looking** maskaniináakwsuw VAI.

**stutter** VI nahnakúweew VAI, nànakíix=suw VAI.

**sty** N **have a sty in one's eye** wtohwa=níingweew VAI.

**subsequently** ADV **then, subsequently** nál PC **Then I left again.** 'Nál wáak ndalŭmúsiin.', **Then he crawled inside the house.** 'Nál wtúlu- wii=kwáhmung -piinjíikwsiin.'

**substance** N **have one's feet sinking into a substance** *(of mud, of snow, of sand, of grain)* akwaanamwíhleew VAI.

**suck** VT **suck s.o., feed at s.o.'s breast, nurse from s.o.** noonáaleew VTA.

**sudden** ADJ **all of a sudden** wíixkwii PC **All of a sudden they started talking about him.** 'Wíixkwii wtakŭniimaa=wáawal.', **His car stopped all of a sudden.** 'Kwáalŭmal wíixkwii ngíh=leew.'; **get dizzy all of a sudden** kiiwaniindkwéhleew VAI.

**suffer** VI **be in pain, suffer** awéendam VOTI1.

**suffering** N **extreme pain, suffering** aweendamuwáakan NI.

**sufficiently** ADV **enough, sufficiently** teep- PV *informal* **It's not cooked**

**enough.** 'Máh téep-kiishtéewi.', **Do you have enough?** 'Ktéep-kxáni?'; **enough, sufficiently** teepu- PV *informal* **It is big enough.** 'Téepu-lukíh=kwun.', **It's time you got a haircut.** 'Méhch áa ktéepu-moonzháasi.'; **lack s.t., lack sufficiently of s.t.** *(to cover something, to reach something)* noondéextoow VTI2.

**sugar** N shóokul NI; **have sugar on it, have sugar in it** shookŭlaháasuw VAI, shookŭlaháasuw VII; **put sugar on s.o., put sugar on s.t. animate** shoo=kŭlaaháaleew VTA; **put sugar on s.t.** shookŭláham VTI1A; **sugar bowl** shookŭlíinjuw NI.

**summer** N **be summer** níipun VII **Last summer.** 'Níipŭne.', **Next summer.** 'Niipúnge.'; **live until summer, survive until summer** niipŭnámuw VAI.

**summon** VT **call s.o., summon s.o.** wunjíimeew VTA.

**sun** N kíishooxkw NA, kíishŭwoxkw NA; **be the sun coming through** eeshŭ=láandeew VII; **be the sun coming up** ktanaxkíhleew VII **East, where the sun comes up.** 'Éhunda-ktanaxkíh=laak.'; **shine in a certain direction** *(of the sun)* láandeew VII.

**Sunday** N **Sunday, week** *(with number prefix)* kúndŭween PC **One week.** 'Ngwút-kúndŭween.', **Two weeks.** 'Níish-kúndŭween.'; **be Sunday, be a week** kúndŭween VII **I went to church last Sunday.** 'Keendŭwéenge ndáap-maawéewi.', **I go to church on Sunday.** 'Kundŭwéenge nŭmáw-maawéewi.'

**sunflower** N wáaxaweew NA.

**sunny** ADJ **become sunny** wŭlaandéh=leew VII; **shine, be shining out** *(of the weather)*, **be a sunny day** waasŭ=láandeew VII.

**sunset** N **be sunset** wsíhkaan VII, wsíh=kaaw VII-S **It was starting to be sunset.** 'Alúmu-wsíhkaan.'

**supper** N **eat supper** sápaluw VAI.

**sure** ADJ **be certain, be sure, have one's mind made up** mayaawee=lúndam VOTI1 **Now I'm sure that Lyle's not coming home.** 'Kwáy nŭmayaaweelúndam máh há péewu Lyle.', **I'm sure that it's going to rain.** 'Nŭmayaaweelúndam katá-sóokŭlaan.'

**surface** N **have lumps protruding from a surface** *(of food cooking)* pòwchát=eew VII; **have one's feet brushing against a surface, have one's feet contacting a surface** chasksiitéexiin VAI; **have one's foot touching down on a surface, have one's foot touching on the floor** mshusiitéexiin VAI; **have one's hands barely touching a surface** mshiinaxkéexiin VAI **He almost fell but he was just hanging on by his fingers.** 'Wéenaa pŭníhleew shùkéhla mshiinaxkéexiin.'; **sit with one's backside barely touching a surface, sit on the edge of something** mshiitŭyéepuw VAI.

**surprise** VT **surprise s.o.** kaanzhiila=wéeheew VTA; **surprise s.o., startle s.o., make s.o. jump** ktakíhlaleew VTA; **be startled, be surprised, jump** ktakíhleew VAI; **be surprised** kaan=zheelúndam VOTI1; **be surprised, be shocked, be startled** salaxkíhleew VAI.

**surround** VT **surround s.o.** wiiwŭnih=kawéewak VTA *subject usually plural;* **surround s.t.** wiiwŭníhkamook VTI1A *subject usually plural.*

**survive** VI **live until springtime, survive until springtime** siikwanámuw VAI; **live until summer, survive until summer** niipŭnámuw VAI; **live until winter, survive until winter** loowa=námuw VAI.

**survivor** N **be left over, be one of the survivors** piiwíixiin VAI.

**suspenders** N **braces, suspenders**

ngélsak NA *usually plural.*

**swallow** VT **swallow s.t.** kwúndam VTI 1 A; **swallow s.t. animate** kwíhleew VTA; **be swallowed** kwundáasuw VII.

**swamp** N **swamp, pond** máskeekw NI.

**sway** VI **shake back and forth, sway back and forth** apawíhleew VII, apawíhleew VAI.

**swear** VI kaakŭlóhkeew VAI; **use bad language, curse, swear** matutóon=heew VAI.

**swear at** VT **swear at s.o.** kŭlóoleew VTA, kaakŭlóoleew VTA, amáchu-leew VTA **He swore at me and that's the reason I got mad.** 'Nŭmámachu-lúkw, noondanóongsiin.'

**sweat** VI **be hot, be sweating** kshúsuw VAI; **sweat, be damp from heat, be wet from heat** skapachásuw VAI.

**sweater** N sŭwétul NI.

**sweep** VT **sweep s.t.** chíikham VTI 1 A; **sweep things** chiikhíikeew VAI.

**sweet** ADJ **have a sweet taste, be sweet in taste** shookŭliipóokwan VII, shoo=kŭliipóokwat VII, shookŭliipóokwsuw VAI.

**sweet flag** N péepakang NI **I chewed the sweet flag.** 'Nzhashkwándamun pée=pakang.'

**sweetgrass** N wiingíimaskw NI.

**swell** VI **have s.t. swell up** makwíisiin VAIO **His mouth swelled up.** 'Màk=wíisiin wtóon.', **My shoulder swelled up.** 'Nŭmakwíisiin ndúkuy.'; **swell up** páasiiw VAI-S **My knee swelled up.** 'Páasiiw ngútko.'; **swell up** páasiiw VII-S; **have a swollen face, have one's face swell up** makwíin=gweew VAI, paasíingweew VAI; **have a swollen head, have one's head swell up** paasáandpeew VAI; **have a swollen leg, have one's leg swell up** paas=káateew VAI; **have a swollen neck, have one's neck swell up** paasxóo=neew VAI; **have a swollen nose, have one's nose swell up** paascháaleew VAI; **swell from moisture, swell in moisture** páaspeew VII **The wood is swollen from dampness.** 'Xwús páaspeew.'

**swim** VI pŭmáashŭwihl VAI, pŭmaashŭ=wíhleew VAI, pŭmáashŭwiiw VAI-S; **swim across** kwaxkaashŭwíhleew VAI; **swim away** alumáashŭweew VAI, alumaashŭwíhleew VAI, alumáashŭ=wihl VAI; **swim backwards** ashahk=cheewaashŭwíhleew VAI; **swim fast** pàpxoowaashŭwíhleew VAI; **swim here and there, swim about** apaa=maashŭwíhleew VAI, apaamáashŭ=weew VAI, apaamáashŭwihl VAI; **swim in a certain direction, swim in a certain manner** laashŭwíhleew VAI; **swim in a circle, swim around something** wiiwŭnaashŭwíhleew VAI; **swim in this direction, swim here, swim this way** peetáashŭweew VAI, peetaashŭwíhleew VAI **Before he got across to the other side.** 'Eéskwa káamung peetaashŭwíhlaakw.'; **swim often, swim a lot** wŭyakaashŭwíh=leew VAI; **swim quickly** kshaashŭ=wíhleew VAI; **swim slowly** ashahwaa=shŭwíhleew VAI, chkawaashŭwih=léeshuw VAI; **swim zigzag** pàptukaa=shŭwíhleew VAI; **swim, be in swimming, be in the water, take a bath** thíixŭmuw VAI.

**swing** N weewehkáasoon NI.

**swing** VI **swing, be swinging** weeweh=káasuw VAI.

**swollen** ADJ **give s.o. a swollen head, hit s.o. and give them a lump on the head** makwaandpéeheew VTA; **give s.o. a swollen leg, give s.o. a bump on their leg** makwukaatéeheew VTA; **have a swollen face** paaschàlíin=gweew VAI; **have a swollen face, have one's face swell up** makwíin=gweew VAI, paasíingweew VAI; **have a swollen hand** paasŭnáxkeew VAI; **have a swollen head, have a bump**

on one's head makwáandpeew VAI; **have a swollen head, have one's head swell up** paasáandpeew VAI; **have a swollen knee** paasiiktúkweew VAI; **have a swollen leg, have a bump on one's leg** makwukáateew VAI; **have a swollen leg, have one's leg swell up** paaskáateew VAI; **have a swollen mouth, have a bump on one's mouth** makwutóoneew VAI; **have a swollen neck, have one's neck swell up** paasxóoneew VAI; **have a swollen nose, have a bump on one's nose** makwucháaleew VAI; **have a swollen nose, have one's nose swell up** paascháaleew VAI; **have a swollen stomach, be bloated, have gas** paa=satáyeew VAI; **have a swollen udder, have a swollen breast** paasíilaneew VAI; **have one's eyes swollen shut** samwusheengwéexiin VAI, samwush=éengweew VAI; **have one's feet swell up, have swollen feet** makwusíiteew VAI; **have swollen feet** paassíiteew VAI; **have swollen hands** amakwŭ=náxkeew VAI; **kick s.o. and give them a swollen leg, kick s.o. and give them a bump on the leg, sit on s.o. and give them a swollen leg, sit on s.o. and give them a bump on the leg** makwukaatéhkaweew VTA.

**sword** N **sword, spear** tangamíikan NI, tangamíikan NA, tangandíikan NI.

**Sylvia** N shílpaa NA.

**syrup** N **syrup, molasses** mŭléeshiish NI.

# T

**table** N eehundáxpoon NI, eehundáx=pwiing VII; **finish setting the table, be finished setting the table** kii=shiinjŭweextíikeew VAI; **on top of the table** waxkiiteehundaxpóone PC; **round table** ptukweehundáxpoon NI; **set the table** wŭliinjŭweextíikeew VAI; **short table** chahkweehundáx=poon NI.

**tablespoon** N xwateemhwáanus NA.

**tack** N **shoe tack** mahksúnii-mŭkóos NA.

**tacks** N téksak NA *usually plural.*

**tag** N **play tag** maaléewuw VAI, tahtáh=wŭneew VAI.

**tail** N **my tail** nzhúkwŭnay NID; **go with one's tail in a certain direction, go with one's tail in a certain manner** laalŭwéhleew VAI; **have a bobbed tail, have a cut-off tail** *(diminutive)* chŭmoochŭyéeshuw VAI; **have a long tail** kwŭnáalŭweew VAI; **have one's tail up** uspaalŭwéexiin VAI; **take off, run with one's tail up** aapaalŭwéh=leew VAI **I just took off all of a sudden.** 'Wíixkwii ndaapaalŭwéhla.', **I'm running off into town.** 'Ndaa=paalŭwéhla ootéeneeng ndá.'; **wag one's tail** kwàkwchukwaalŭwéhleew VAI; **wear a coat with a long tail** kwŭníi-shkwúnayii-koothámeew VAI; **wear something that has a long tail** kwŭníi-shkwúnayeew VAI *usually of coats.*

**take** VT **go after something to fetch it, go after something to take it** naat=héewasuw VAI; **take s.o. away in a hurry** alumíipheew VTA; **take s.o. through in a hurry** eeshíipheew VTA; **take s.o. through something, take s.o. through an experience** eeshóo=xwaleew VTA; **take s.o.'s place** láa=papuw VAIO; **take s.t. across in a hurry** aashŭwiipáhtoow VTI2; **take s.t. away in a hurry** alumiipáhtoow VTI2; **take s.t. through in a hurry** eeshiipáhtoow VTI2; **take s.t. through something** *(of a matter of business)* eeshóoxwatoow VTI2; **lead s.o. by the arm, take s.o. by the arm, be arm in arm with s.o.** laapiinaxkéeneew VTA, laapiináxkeew VAIO; **take a nap**

niimaawanáhŭmeew VAI; **take five steps** naalanalíhkeew VAI; **take four steps** neewalíhkeew VAI; **take one step** ngwutalíhkeew VAI; **take one's time** saasiingtuyéewuw VAI **You know how to take your time.** 'Kŭníhtaa-saasiingtuyéewi.'; **take one's lunch along** níimaaw VAI-S; **take s.o. across in a hurry** aashŭwíipheew VTA; **take short steps** *(diminutive)* achahkwa=lihkehléeshuw VAI, achahkwalihkée=shuw VAI; **take so many steps** txalíh=keew VAI **He took six steps.** 'Ngwút=aash txalíhkeew.'; **take two steps** niishalíhkeew VAI; **take up the collection** *(in church)* maawéenŭmeew VAI; **go empty handed, go bare handed, don't take anything** *(especially to a gathering)* mooshŭlunjéhleew VAI; **have one's eyes bigger than one's belly, take more than one can eat** mangshéengweew VAI; **have one's picture taken** kteekháasuw VAI.

**take a bite of** VT **take a bite out of s.o.** kwasháameew VTA; **take a bite out of s.t.** kwashándam VTI1A.

**take a handful of** VT **take a handful of s.t. animate, scoop s.t. animate up** *(using the hands)* ánzŭneew VTA; **take a handful of s.t., scoop s.t. up** *(using the hands)* ánzŭnum VTI1B.

**take a photograph of** VT **take a photograph of s.o., draw a picture of s.o., make a tracing of s.o.** ktéekheew VTA; **take a photograph of s.t., draw a picture of s.t., make a tracing of s.t.** ktéekham VTI1A.

**take all of** VT **take all of s.t. animate, take the last piece of s.t. animate** póhkwŭneew VTA; **take all of s.t., take the last piece of s.t., quit while doing s.t.** póhkwŭnum VTI1B.

**take along** VT **bring s.o. along as well, take s.o. along as well** naxpóoxwa=leew VTA; **bring s.o., take s.o. along** lóoxwaleew VTA; **bring s.t. along as well, take s.t. along as well** naxpóo=xwatoow VTI2; **bring s.t., take s.t. along** lóoxwatoow VTI2 **What shall I bring?** 'Kwéekw-uch há ndulóoxwa=to?'; **grab s.t., seize and take s.t. along** naxpíhleew VAIO; **take s.o. along, remove s.o.** alumóoxwaleew VTA; **take s.t. along as well, take s.t. along in addition** naxpóoxweew VAIO; **take s.t. along, carry s.t.** wŭ=lásanuw VAIO **I carried the groceries.** 'Noolasániin kŭlooshliihiiwáakanal.'; **take s.t. along, remove s.t.** alumóo=xwatoow VTI2.

**take apart** VT **take s.t. animate apart to pieces** piikhéewaleew VTA; **take s.t. animate apart, take s.o. apart** *(using a tool or instrument)* chpáhk=hweew VTA; **take s.t. apart** *(using a tool or instrument)* chpáhkhwam VTI1A; **take s.t. apart to pieces** piik=héewatoow VTI2.

**take away** VT **take away from s.o.** chíi=kŭneew VTA; **take s.t. away from s.o.** chíikŭneew VTAO; **gather up and take away a load of s.t.** alumhéewa=toow VTI2, aluméewatoow VTI2; **gather up and take away a load of s.t. animate** alumhéewaleew VTA, aluméewaleew VTA; **be taken away** *(especially to heaven)* naatŭnúkwsuw VAI; **being taken away** naatŭnukw=suwáakan NI; **detach s.t. animate, pull s.t. animate off, take s.t. animate away, remove s.t. animate** *(using the hands)* máhkŭneew VTA; **detach s.t., pull s.t. off, take s.t. away, remove s.t.** *(using the hands)* máh=kŭnum VTI1B.

**take back** VT **run s.t. home, take s.t. back** *(especially of borrowed items)* maachiipáhtoow VTI2.

**take care of** VT **take care of a child, babysit** noocháawsuw VAI; **take care of s.o.'s child for them** noochaaw=sáweew VTA; **take care of s.o., look**

**after s.o., tend to a responsibility with regard to s.o.** lxawéelŭmeew VTA **You should take care of your car, don't drive it needlessly.** 'Káta-lxawéelŭmaa ktahtamoombíilum, chíi amayakaweehéehan.'; **take care of s.t., look after s.t., tend to a responsibility with regard to s.t.** lxawee=lúndam VTI1B **Take care of the food (said of an empty refrigerator).** 'Katá-lxaweelúndah miichŭwáakan.'

**take down** VT **lower s.o., take s.o. down** níixŭneew VTA; **lower s.t., take s.t. down** níixŭnum VTI1B.

**take from** VT **rob people, take things from people by force** shihkwihtáa=suw VAI; **take s.t. from s.o. by force, force s.o. to do s.t.** shihkwíhtaweew VTAO.

**take home** VT **take s.o. home** *(to their place)* máachaleew VTA; **take s.t. home** *(to where it belongs)* máacha=toow VTI2.

**take inside** VT **take s.o. inside, chase s.o. inside, send s.o. inside, drive s.o. inside** *(of animals)* piindshíiheew VTA; **take s.o. inside, take s.t. animate inside, bring s.o. inside** piin=dóoxwaleew VTA; **take s.o. inside, take s.t. animate inside, take a load of s.t. animate inside** piindhéewa=leew VTA; **take s.t. inside, bring s.t. inside** piindóoxwatoow VTI2; **take s.t. inside, take a load of s.t. inside** piindhéewatoow VTI2.

**take off** VI **take off, run with one's tail up** aapaalŭwéhleew VAI **I just took off all of a sudden.** 'Wíixkwii ndaa=paalŭwéhla.', **I'm running off into town.** 'Ndaapaalŭwéhla ootéeneeng ndá.'; **wait to take off, wait to leave, be ready for action** kehtéexiin VAI.

**take off** VT **take s.o.'s clothes off for s.o., take s.t. out for s.o.** ktunŭmáw=eew VTAO; **take the covering off s.t. animate, take the outer layer off s.t. animate, remove the shell from s.t. animate** pŭlákŭneew VTA; **take the covering off s.t., take the outer layer off s.t., remove the shell from s.t.** pŭlákŭnum VTI1A; **take the covers off oneself** paaxkeehúnzuw VAI; **undress s.o., take off all of s.o.'s clothes** sheexkalúneew VTA **She's just going to undress me again.** 'Kách wáak ápih shúkw nzheexka=lúnukw.'; **get undressed, take off one's clothes** ktunéechpuw VAI; **open s.t. animate, take the lid off s.t. animate** *(as the cover of a pail)* áapŭ=neew VTA; **pull s.t. animate off, take s.t. animate off, take s.t. animate out** *(using the hands)* ktúneew VTA; **pull s.t. off, take s.t. off, take s.t. out** *(using the hands)* ktúnum VTI1B; **take off one's pants** ktuniipŭlóokeew VAI; **take off one's shoes** ktunahksúneew VAI; **take off one's socks** ktunashíi=kaneew VAI; **take the bridle off s.o.** ktohkwéeneew VTA.

**take out** VT **open s.t. animate up, operate on s.o.** *(as a doctor)*, **make a hole in s.o., take the insides out of s.o.** pkwuchéeneew VTA **He had an operation.** 'Pkwuchéenaaw.'; **operate** *(of doctors)*, **take out the insides of things** pkwucheeníikeew VAI; **pull s.t. animate off, take s.t. animate off, take s.t. animate out** *(using the hands)* ktúneew VTA; **pull s.t. off, take s.t. off, take s.t. out** *(using the hands)* ktúnum VTI1B; **take all of s.t. animate out** shíikwŭneew VTA; **take all of s.t. out** *(of something)* shíi=kwŭnum VTI1A; **take s.o.'s clothes off for s.o., take s.t. out for s.o.** ktunŭ=máweew VTAO; **unload s.o., take s.o. out of the water, take s.o. out of a vehicle, remove s.o.** kóhpŭneew VTA **I took the potatoes off (the stove).** 'Ngohpŭnáawak óhpŭnak.'; **unload s.t., take s.t. out of the water, take**

**s.t. out of a vehicle** kóhpŭnum VTI1B.

**take part** VI **race, take part in a race** meemeelandawéewak VAI *usually plural;* **participate, take part, take part in a game, take part in a fight** wiichóohŭweew VAI; **take part in a conversation, butt into a conversation** wiittóonheew VAI; **take part in a dance** wíitkeew VAI.

**tale** N **tell s.o. a tall tale, tell s.o. an exciting story** kaanzhaachŭmóhka=weew VTA.

**talk** VI **start to talk** noottóonheew VAI; **stop talking, cease talking** ehkw=tóonheew VAI; **mute, a person who can't talk** kéeptoon NA, kpútoon NA; **be always talking** ngumeewtóon=heew VAI; **be done talking, say all one has to say, run out of things to say** mehtaaptóoneew VAI; **be mute, be unable to talk** kputóoneew VAI, akeeptóoneew VAI; **finish talking** kiishtóonheew VAI; **imitate the way s.o. talks, imitate s.o.'s speech** naa=naxpŭlóhtaweew VTA; **leave out part of the story while talking** pàpŭlak=aachíimuw VAI; **mutter, talk under one's breath** mŭnumohktóonheew VAI; **speak quickly, talk fast** akush=aaptóonheew VAI; **talk a lot** niisk=tuyéemuw VAI *considered impolite;* **talk a lot, brag** kaanzhíixsuw VAI; **talk a lot, gossip, talk dirty** niisk=tóonheew VAI; **talk by oneself** naan=xootóonheew VAI; **talk dirty** niiskaa=chíimuw VAI; **talk foolishly** kpuch=eewtóonheew VAI; **talk from a certain place, talk for a certain reason, holler from a certain place, holler for a certain reason, call from a certain place, call for a certain reason** *(especially on the telephone)* wundaaptóoneew VAI **I talked from far away.** 'Wáhlu noondaaptóone.'; **talk in a loud voice, talk loudly** amangíixsuw VAI; **talk in a low voice, talk in a soft voice** *(diminutive)* achangiixshíishuw VAI; **talk lots** kaanzhtóonheew VAI; **talk lots, make noise** paakwéenzuw VAI; **talk loudly** amangaaptóoneew VAI, mangaap=tóoneew VAI, mangíixsuw VAI, aman=gíixsuw VAI; **talk oddly** maamaa=shíixsuw VAI, maashtóonheew VAI; **talk quickly** akushíixsuw VAI; **talk slowly** ashahwíixsuw VAI; **talk terribly, talk badly, use foul language** chiiptóonheew VAI; **talk well, say good things** awulaaptóoneew VAI.

**talk about** VT **talk about s.o.** akuníi=meew VTA; **talk about s.t.** akunóotam VTI1A; **talk about things, talk about people** akuníingeew VAI; **finish talking about s.t.** kiishakunóotum VTI1B; **judge s.o., finish talking about s.o.** kiishakuníimeew VTA; **talk badly about s.o.** mataachŭmóhkaweew VTA; **talk badly about s.o.** matakŭníi=meew VTA.

**talk back to** VT **talk back to s.o.** aloh=táameew VTA, alóhtaweew VTA.

**talk to** VT **talk to s.o.** kihkŭlóoleew VTA; **make a cutting remark to s.o., talk so as to injure s.o.** kshaaptoonáaleew VTA; **talk lots to s.o., talk too much to s.o.** paakweenztoonháaleew VTA; **talk to oneself** nxootóonheew VAI; **talk to s.o. and make them cry** chaangtoonháaleew VTA, chaangíi=meew VTA; **talk to s.o. and make them feel good** wŭliilawéemeew VTA; **talk to s.o. to get them up from lying down, holler at s.o. to get them up from lying down** aamwihkíi=meew VTA.

**tall** ADJ **be high, be tall** kwŭnáhkwat VII; **be long** *(of something wood- or stick-like)*, **be tall** *(of a person)* kwŭ=náhkwsuw VAI.

**tanned** ADJ **be tanned** nzukxásuw VAI.

**tangled** ADJ **have tangled hair, have matted hair, have messy hair**

piikwshaalóhkweew VAI.

**tap on** VT **knock on s.t.** *(especially of drums)*, **tap on s.t.** póham VTI1A.

**tap trees** VI wiis'háhkweew VAI.

**tassel** N **have tassels** *(of corn)* wihtóo=nayuw VII.

**taste** N **be bitter in taste** tíhtpan VII; **find that s.t. animate has a sour taste** láxkameew VTA; **find that s.t. has a sour taste** laxkándam VTI1A; **have a bitter taste, have a sour taste** laxkiipóokwat VII, laxkiipóokwsuw VAI, laxkiipóokwun VII; **have a not very good taste** lunŭwiipóokwat VII, lunŭwiipóokwsuw VAI; **have a plain taste** kahkaniipóokwat VII, kahkanii=póokwsuw VAI; **have a sweet taste, be sweet in taste** shookŭliipóokwan VII, shookŭliipóokwat VII, shookŭlii=póokwsuw VAI; **have an unpleasant taste, taste bad** machiipóokwsuw VAI, machiipóokwan VII, machiipóo=kwat VII; **like the taste of s.t.** wiin=gándam VTI1A **He didn't like the taste of it.** 'Máh wiingandamóo=wun.'; **like the taste of s.t. animate** wíingameew VTA; **recognize the taste of s.t.** mihkóhptam VTI1A; **recognize the taste of s.t. animate** mihkohp=támweew VTA; **taste rotten, have a rotten taste** aliipóokwat VII, alii=póokwsuw VAI; **taste sour, have a sour taste** shŭwiipóokwan VII, shŭ=wiipóokwat VII; shŭwiipóokwsuw VAI; **taste strong, be strong in taste** àh=wiipóokwat VII àhwiipóokwsuw VAI.

**taste** VI **be bitter, taste bitter, taste sour, taste strong** láxkun VII; **have an unpleasant taste, taste bad** ma=chiipóokwsuw VAI, machiipóokwan VII, machiipóokwat VII; **taste awful** mataxeepóokwat VII; **taste good** wíingan VII **It tastes better.** 'Míin=gasa wíingan.'; **taste good** wíingul VAI; **taste good** wŭliipóokwat VII, wŭliipóokwsuw VAI; **taste rotten, have a rotten taste** aliipóokwat VII, aliipóokwsuw VAI; **taste rough** kaax=kiipóokwsuw VAI; **taste sour, have a sour taste** shŭwiipóokwan VII, shŭ=wiipóokwat VII, shŭwiipóokwsuw VAI; **taste strong, be strong in taste** àh=wiipóokwat VII, àhwiipóokwsuw VAI.

**taste** VT **taste s.t.** kwtándam VTI1A; **taste s.t. animate** kwtámeew VTA.

**tea** N tíi NI.

**tea kettle** N tíihoos NA.

**tea pot** N tíipat NA.

**tea towel** N kaasahkhwíikan NI, peen=gwahkhwíikan NI, peengwiikwáakan NI.

**teach** VT **teach s.o.** akehkíimeew VTA; **teach s.o. a certain way** làkehkíi=meew VTA; **teach people** akehkíin=geew VAI; **teach school** shkoolháa=lŭweew VAI.

**teacup** N tiihíinjuw NI.

**tear** VT **tear s.t.** *(using the hands)* ta=shákŭnum VTI1B; **tear s.t. animate** *(using the hands)* tashákŭneew VTA; **tear s.t. animate, split s.t. animate in two** pasúneew VTA; **tear s.t., split s.t. in two** pasúnum VTI1B; **be ripped, be torn** tashakíhleew VAI, tashakíh=leew VII; **collapse s.t., tear s.t. down, dismantle s.t.** *(using the hands)* mŭlákwŭnum VTI1B; **be shredded, be torn up** píikat VII, píiksuw VAI.

**tears** N **have tears in one's eyes** akeex=péengweew VAI.

**tease** VI akayíhksuw VAI; **tease people** akayihkíihŭweew VAI; **tease s.o.** akayihkíiheew VTA.

**teaspoon** N tiiheemhwáanus NA.

**tell** VT **tell a story** laachíimuw VAI; **tell s.o. a story** laachŭmóhkaweew VTA; **tell a great story** kihtaachíimuw VAI; **betray s.o., tell on s.o., betray s.o.'s confidence** kchíhlaleew VTA; **tell about s.t., reveal s.t.** kchíhlatoow VTI2 **You told about what happened (and weren't supposed to).** 'Kùch=

íhlatoon kwéek éeleek.'; **be able to tell the difference between people, 'make strange'** *(of babies)* chih=chpiináasuw VAI, chpiináasuw VAI; **be a liar, tell a lie** maxkalákayeew VAI *considered impolite;* **give a good account of onself, tell a favourable story** wŭlaachíimuw VAI; **say to s.o., tell s.o.** léew VTA; **tell a fib, tell lies** maxkáaheew VAI; **tell a lie** akulóo=neew VAI, kŭlóoneew VAI, maxktúy=eew VAI *considered impolite;* **tell a tall tale, tell an exciting story, brag** kaanzhaachíimuw VAI; **tell s.o. a lie** kŭloonéeheew VTA; **tell s.o. a tall tale, tell s.o. an exciting story** kaan=zhaachŭmóhkaweew VTA; **tell s.o. about something** laachiimóoleew VTA; **tell something to s.o. and make them happy** wiingiilawéemeew VTA; **tell the truth** shaaxkaachíimuw VAI; **tell the truth, make a deal** wŭláa=mweew VAI.

**ten** N wíimbat PC **Ten o'clock.** 'Wíimbat txú-kŭlakíike.'

**tender** ADJ **be sore, be tender, sting** *(of sores)* wiisakúsuw VAI; **be sore, be tender, sting** *(of a sore)* wíisakeew VII; **be sore, be tender, ache** *(of body parts)* kiihíicheew VII; **be sore, be tender, ache** kiihíitsuw VAI.

**tent** N wshapakwiiwaníikaan NI.

**terrible** ADJ **be horrified about something, think something to be terrible** chiipeelúndam VAI; **be in terrible shape, have a terrible figure, have a terrible shape, be in a bad shape** chiipáhkwsuw VAI; **frightful, terrible** achiipi- PV **I think bad thoughts.** 'Njachíipi-liitéeha.'; **frightful, terrible** achiipu- PV *informal* **Some people have bad underarm perspiration** 'Áalund awéen achíipu-ashii=lóngwane.'; **frightful, terrible** chiipii- PV **It is thundering loudly.** 'Chíipii-pehtáhkuw.'; **frightful, terrible** chiipu- PV *informal* **Something terrible happened.** 'Chíipu-léew.'; **have terrible looking hair** chiipaa=lóhkweew VAI; **look terrible, be terrible looking, have a frightful appearance** chiipiináakwat VII, chiipii=náakwsuw VAI; **sound loud, sound terrible** chiipihtáakwat VII, chiipih=táakwsuw VAI.

**test** VT **try s.t. animate out, test s.t. animate** kwchíhlaleew VTA; **try s.t. out, test s.t.** kwchíhlatoow VTI2.

**testify** VI **'testify' at a religious meeting, 'testify' in church** pasukwtóon=heew VAI.

**Thamesville** N **Thamesville, Ontario** témbul NI **He lives in Thamesville.** 'Témbul wíiku̧w.'

**than** CJ **less** *(than someone or something else)* nóondaa PC **I weigh less.** 'Nóondaa ndúndxu-poondakúsi.', **He's smaller.** 'Nóondaa lúkiil.'; **more, more than, early** aluwii- PV **Early afternoon.** 'Alúwii-laawah=kwéewŭnii.'; **more, more than, early** alúwii PC; **prefer s.o. to someone else, think more of s.o. than of someone else, think s.o. better than someone else** aluwéelŭmeew VTA; **prefer s.t. to s.t. else, think more of s.t. than of something else, think s.t. better than something else, want to do s.t. first** aluweelúndam VTI1A; **be older than s.o.** kihkayúmeew VTA, kíhkayuw VAIO; **think oneself better than s.o. else** aluweelúnzuw VAIO; **be a proud man, be arrogant, have an attitude, think that one knows more than anyone else** lunŭweelúnzuw VAI; **be arrogant, have an attitude, think oneself better than others, to put on airs** *(of women)* leetíisuw VAI, ox=kweeweelúnzuw VAI; **beat s.o. in a competition, best s.o., do better than s.o.** pŭmúneew VTA; **have (extra) clothes in layers, have on more**

clothes than someone else pihta=wákuw VAI **I am covered in three layers, I am dressed in three layers.** 'Nxú mbihtawákwi.'; **have a deformed hip, have one hip higher than the other, have a lopsided hip** waakhóotŭyeew VAI; **throw s.t. over, throw s.t. farther than intended** paaláaheew VAIO **I threw it over the house.** 'Mbaaláaheen wiikwáh=mung.'; **wear more than one coat** pihtawiikóoteew VAI; **wear more than one pair of pants** pihtawiipŭlóokeew VAI; **wear more than one pair of socks** pihtawashíikaneew VAI.

**thank you** IJ anúshiik PC.

**that** ADV **that** *(animate)*, **emphatic** ná PR **Grab him by the ear.** 'Ná alíipah wihtawákung', **That's me.** 'Ná há níi.'; **that** *(animate emphatic)* nán PR **All he does is drive around.** 'Nán há shúkw apaamchéhle.'; **that** *(animate)* néen PR; **that** *(inanimate)* nú PR **That's the reason why the children were (born) far apart.** 'Nú óonj-tóhpu-chpapiinéewa amiimúnzak.', **Did you see it?** 'Kŭnéemun há nú?'; **that** *(inanimate emphatic)* nún PR **That must be it.** 'Nún éet há.', **That's what I should do.** 'Nún áa ndulŭnúmun.'; **that, those** *(animate obviative)* níil PR.

**them** PR **they, them** neekŭmáawa PR.

**then** ADV **instead, next, then** áashtee PC **I'll go there instead.** 'Áashtee-uch yéelak ndá.', **I'll use this instead, I'll wear this instead.** 'Áashtee-uch yóon ndawéeheen.'; **then, subsequently** nál PC **Then I left again.** 'Nál wáak ndalŭmúsiin.', **Then he crawled inside the house.** 'Nál wtúlu- wiikwáhmung -piinjíikwsiin.'

**there** ADV **about, around, here and there** apaamu- PV **I fell about by myself.** 'Nxóo mbapáamu-kawíhla.'; **here, there, in a certain place** talí PC **It's icy in the water.** 'Móhkamuyuw talí mbíing.', **He saw ghosts in a coffin.** 'Chíipayal néeweew kúshtung talí.'; **here, there, thus, so** lí PC **He spat on the ground.** 'Áhkiing lí súkwiiw', **He went around the road.** 'Wiiwŭnóoxwe lí áaneeng.'; **here, there, thus, so** líi PC **The roads are muddy everywhere.** 'Wéemu asiis=kŭwatéexun táa líi.'; **here, there, thus, so** lú PC *informal* **They crawled to here.** 'Yó lú peechiikwsúwak.', **They moved to the United States.** 'Xwanzhíikanung lú ngatahkéewak.'; **over there** yéelak PR **I put it over there on the other side.** 'Yéelak awási ndáhtoon.'; **sit there** lŭmatáh=teew VII **It sits on top.** 'Wáxkiich lŭmatáhteew.'; **there** náh PC **Maybe he's there.** 'Téet náh apúw.', **There were women in the house.** 'Ox=kwéewak náh apúwak wiikwáh=mung.'; **here, there, in a certain place** talú PC **It rains heavily here.** 'Akushíilaan yóon talú.', **He got stuck in the snow.** 'Kóonung talú kŭláhkweew.'; **way over there, over there a considerable distance** yóo=lak PR; **be there** áhteew VII; **be there together** takwahtéewal VII *usually plural;* **be there, be here** apúw VAI **There he is.** 'Ná éepiit.'; **finish putting s.o. down, finish putting s.o. there** kiisháhleew VTA; **finish putting s.t. there** kiisháhtoow VTI2; **be finished, be already placed there** kiisháhteew VII.

**these** ADV **these** *(animate)* yóok PR; **these** *(inanimate)* yóol PR; **this, these** *(animate obviative)* yóol PR.

**they** PR **they, them** neekumáawa PR; **they, them** neekáawa PR; **they, them** neekáawa PR.

**thick** ADJ **be thick** kohpakúsuw VAI, kóhpakan VII; **be thick** *(of liquids)* tahtakáapŭweew VII; **be thick in con-**

**sistency** táhtakan VII; **thick** kohpakii- PN **A thick towel.** 'Kóhpakii-kehkaa=siingwéehiin.'; **thick** kohpaku- PV *informal* **It's in thick pieces.** 'Kóhpaku-pangéeyeew.'; **thick in consistency** tahtakii- PN **Thick milk.** 'Táhtakii-mŭlúk.'; **be a lot of thick trees, be a lot of dense trees, be a dense forest** spwihtkwíhkeew VII; **be cut thick** kohpakusháasuw VAI, kohpakusháa=suw VII; **be thick** *(of books or papers)* kohpakaapéeksuw VAI; **have thick hair** kohpakaalóhkweew VAI; **have thick lips** aapoosktóoneew VAI; **thick thread, yarn** kohpakáhtakw NI.

**thickly** ADV **cut s.t. animate thickly** kohpakúsheew VTA; **cut s.t. thickly** kohpakúshum VTI1B.

**thief** N **be a thief** mataapéewuw VAI.

**thigh** N **my thigh** mbwáam NID.

**thimble** N éhwiis NA.

**thimbleberry** N akwaaníilŭnus NA.

**thin** ADJ **be thin** *(as cake that didn't rise, slice of bread, meat, board)* wshápan VII; **be thin** wshápsuw VAI; **be thin, be skinny** waxkanúsŭw VAI; **thin** wshapiiwu- PN *informal* **Thin towel.** 'Wshapíiwu-kehkaasiingwée=hiin.'; **thin** wshapu- PV *informal* **It's in thin pieces.** 'Wshápu-pangée=yeew.'; **be transparent, be thin** *(of material)* shiikalúsuw VAI, shíikaleew VII; **be sliced thin** wshapsháasuw VAI, wshapsháasuw VII; **have thin hair, have fine hair** shiikalaalóhkweew VAI; **slice s.t. animate thinly** wsháp=sheew VTA; **slice s.t. thinly** wsháp=shum VTI1B.

**thing** N **something, what, thing** kwéek PR **He likes to talk** 'Wíhwiing- kwéek -úw.' **What did you say?** 'Kwéek ksí?; **something, what, thing** kwéekw PR **He wears old things.** 'Xúwu-kwéekwiil awéehe.', **Why are you mad at me?** 'Kwéekw há kóonj-mataangóomi?'

**think** VI liitéeheew VAI **We (inclusive) agree, we think the same.** 'Ngwúteel ktiiteeháhna.', **They agree, they think the same.** 'Ngwúteel liiteehéewak.'; **think** pŭnaweelúndam VOTI1; **think about s.t., think about s.t. in a certain manner** leelúndam VTI1A **After a while I didn't think anything of riding a horse.** 'Aayáakwu máh kwéek nduleelundamóowun nehna=yóongus mbóxkapiin.'; **think, think in a certain manner** leelúndam VOTI1 **We (inclusive) think alike.** 'Ngwút=eel ktuleelundamóhna.'; **I think so** ndíit PC **You think so.** 'Ktíit.', **Do you think so?** 'Ktíit há?'; **be horrified about something, think something to be terrible** chiipeelúndam VAI; **feel lowly, think little** *(of oneself)* tangeelúndam VOTI1; **feel that one is White, think that one is White** waapamálsuw VAI; **think badly of oneself** mateelúnzuw VAI; **think oneself better than s.o. else** aluweelún=zuw VAIO; **think oneself inferior** noondayeelúnzuw VAI; **think s.o. to be smart, have a high opinion of s.o., think s.o. competent** kshéelŭ=meew VTA; **think s.t. to be a long time** kwŭneelúndam VTI1A **I think it's taking a long time for evening to come.** 'Níi ngwuneelúndamun nál ápih wŭláakuw.', **I think that it's a long time until the end of the service.** 'Níi ngwuneelúndamun nál-uch éhkwu-maawéewiin.'; **think that one is God** pahtamaweelúnzuw VAI; **think that s.o. is dirty** niiskéelŭmeew VTA; **think that s.t. is dirty** niiskeelúndam VTI1A.

**think** VT **have a bad thought, think bad thoughts, have bad feelings** chiipahtéenamuw VAI; **think oneself better than s.o.** aluweelunzíhtaweew VTA; **think s.o. to be close** peexŭ=wéelŭmeew VTA; **think s.t. to be close**

peexŭweelúndam VTI1A; **think that s.o. is handy, find s.o. handy, be helpful towards s.o., be good for s.o.** wŭlaapéemeew VTA; **think well of oneself, think highly of oneself** wŭleelúnzuw VAI; **think well of s.o., respect s.o.** wŭlíi-pŭnáweew VTA.

**think about** VT **think about s.o.** pŭ=naweélŭmeew VTA; **think about s.o., remember s.o.** msháaleew VTA **Someone must be thinking about you.** 'Awéen éet kŭmusháalukw.'; **think about s.t.** pŭnaweelúndam VTI1A; **think about s.t., remember s.t.** msháatam VTI1A.

**think of** VT **think a lot of s.o., think highly of s.o., have a high regard for s.o.** kaanzhéelŭmeew VTA; xwée=lŭmeew VTA; **think a lot of s.t., think highly of s.t., have a high regard for s.t.** kaanzheelúndam VTI1A, xweelún=dam VTI1A; **be well thought of** kaan=zheelŭmúkwsuw VAI, xweelŭmúkw=suw VAI; **think of oneself as a White person** shŭwanakweelúnzuw VAI; **think poorly of s.o., insult s.o., abuse s.o.** *(including physical abuse)* matéelŭmeew VTA; **prefer s.o. to someone else, think more of s.o. than of someone else, think s.o. better than someone else** aluwéelŭ=meew VTA; **prefer s.t. to s.t. else, think more of s.t. than of something else, think s.t. better than something else, want to do s.t. first** aluweelúndam VTI1A.

**thirsty** ADJ **be thirsty** katóosŭmuw VAI.

**thirteen** N nxaaníhka PC.

**thirty** N nxiináxke PC.

**this** ADV **this** *(animate)* wá PR *used in animate 'where' questions* **But they always fought, and this girl was always going all over, she would frequently go away.** 'Shúkw ngúmee màmatahkéewak, wáak wá oxkwée=sus ngúmee músu-áan, àhalúmsuw.', **Where is the man?** 'Tá wá ná lúnuw?'; **this** *(animate, emphatic)* wán PR **It's me.** 'Wán há níi.'; **this** *(inanimate emphatic)* yóon PR **Let's go this way.** 'Yóon lí áatookw.', **This one's too hot also.** 'Yóon wáak wsáamu-kshúteew.'; **this** *(inanimate)*, **here** yú PR *used in inanimate 'where' questions* **This teacup.** 'Yú tiihíin=juw.', **Where is it?** 'Thá yú?'; **this, these** *(animate obviative)* yóol PR.

**thistle** N káawunzh NA; **thistle bush** kaawúnzhahkw NA; **be a lot of thistles** kaawunzhíhkeew VII.

**those** ADV **those** *(animate)* néek PR, níik PR; **those** *(inanimate)* níil PR; **that, those** *(animate obviative)* níil PR.

**thought** N **have a bad thought, think bad thoughts, have bad feelings** chiipahtéenamuw VAI; **have evil thoughts, have bad thoughts** *(as if without regret)* chiipiitéeheew VAI.

**thousand** N táwsun NI *singular only, with number particle or prenoun* **He's sleeping for a thousand years.** 'Kawíiw ngwúti táwsun txú-katúne.', **Two thousand.** 'Níish-táwsun.'

**thread** N piimŭnáhtaan NI, piimŭnáh=takw NI; **be big, be coarse** *(of something stringlike)* xwáhtakat VII; **be good, be straight, be a good strand of thread, be fine** *(of something stringlike)* wŭláhtakat VII; **black thread, black string** nzukáhtakw NI; **blue thread, blue string** oolihkáh=takw NI; **brown thread, grey thread** wiipongwáhtakw NI; **green thread** askaskwáhtakw NI; **lace s.t. up, thread s.t.** láapham VTI1A; **red thread** max=káhtakw NI; **thick thread, yarn** koh=pakáhtakw NI; **white thread** waa=páhtakw NI; **yellow thread** wiisaa=wáhtakw NI.

**thread** VT **sew things, be sewing, lace things, thread things** laaphíikeew VAI; **thread s.t. animate** *(of needles)* láapheew VTA.

**three** N nxáh PC **My grandfather and my grandmother had three children.** 'Nîi nŭmoxóomus wáak nóo=hum kxánŭwak nxáh amiimúnzal.'; **three** nxu- PV **It's three o'clock.** 'Nxú-kŭlákuw.', **Three pieces.** 'Néexu-pangéeyeek.'; **three** nxu- PN **It cost three dollars.** 'Nxú-ndálaas láawatuw.'; **three** nxú PC **I am covered in three layers, I am dressed in three layers.** 'Nxú mbihtawákwi.', **It is in three pieces.** 'Nxú pangée=suw.'; **be gone for three days** nxoo=kwŭnáhkeew VAI; **three hundred** nxaapóxku PC; **three times** nxún PC; **three, in threes** nxéeli PC **The boxes are stacked in threes.** 'Nxéeli pih=tawíixŭnool mbáksal.'; **be in three layers** *(of something sheet-like)* nxee=kíixiin VAI, nxeekíixun VII; **be three** *(of something string-like)* nxáhtakat VII; **be three days** nxookwŭnákat VII **Three days ago.** 'Nxookwŭnákate.'; **be three of them** nxíiwak VAI-S; **be three of them sitting there** nxápŭ=wak VAI *usually plural;* **be three of them there** nxahtéewal VII *usually plural;* **be three of them, be three in number** nxúnool VII *usually plural;* **be three of them, be three in number, be in three pairs** nxéeltool VII *usually plural,* nxéelook VAI *usually plural;* **be tied in threes** nxambíisŭ=wak VAI *usually plural,* nxambíisŭwal VII; **have three pages** *(of something sheet-like)* nxaapéeksuw VAI *usually of pieces of paper;* **lie in threes** nxaangwéewak VAI *usually plural;* **live together in threes, stay together in threes** nxiilŭnúwak VAI *usually plural;* **sit in threes** nxohkwéepŭwak VAI *usually plural;* **stand in threes, be three standing there** nxiikaapa=wúwak VAI *usually plural;* **three days, for three days** nxóokwŭnii PC; **tie s.o. in threes** nxambíileew VTA *object usually plural;* **tie s.t. in threes** nxámbtoow VTI2 *object usually plural;* **walk in threes** nxat=xooxwéewak VAI *usually plural.*

**thresh** VT **thresh grain** pakáhŭmeew VAI.

**threshing barn** N **barn, threshing barn** pakahíikan NI.

**threshold** N **doorstep, threshold of house** uskwáandu PC.

**thrifty** ADJ **be thrifty** keeshéewsuw VAI; **save s.t.** *(of money),* **be thrifty about s.t.** keeshéetsuw VAIO **I'm thrifty about my car.** 'Ngeeshéetsiin ndah=tamoombíilum.'; **save, be thrifty** keeshéetsuw VAI.

**throat** N kwundáakan NI; **have a sore throat** kwundaakaníineew VAI.

**through** ADV eeshii- PV **I see through him (as of a window).** 'Ndéeshii-néewaaw.'; **through** eeshu- PV *informal* **It can be seen through.** 'Éeshu-laapamúkwat.'; **go through, fall through** eeshíhleew VAI **I went through the ice.** 'Móhkamiing ndeeshíhla.'; **go through, fall through** eeshíhleew VII; **go through, pass through, get through** éeshiiw VAI-S; **knock s.t. through** *(with a stick)* éeshŭlam VTI1A; **look through** eeshatawáapuw VAI; **be soaked through** éeshpeew VAI, éeshpeew VII; **be the sun coming through** eeshŭ=láandeew VII; **be through being angry** ehkwanóongsuw VAI; **crawl through** *(a space)* eeshíikwsuw VAI; **cut through s.t. animate, cut and break s.t. animate, cut s.t. animate** *(of something string-like)* páxksheew VTA; **finish running, be through running** kiishaaméhleew VAI.

**through** PREP **be a hole through something** eesh'shéesuw VAI **The window has a hole in it.** 'Eesh'shéesuw eeheeshandéekan.'; **be a hole through**

**something** eesh'shéeyeew VII **I've got a hole in my shoe.** 'Eesh'shée=yeew nŭmáhksun.'; **be a hole through something** shaapwshéeyeew VII; **be put through** *(of a motion at a meeting, of business)* eeshooxwatáasuw VII; **crawl through an opening** pkwíi=kwsuw VAI; **cut through s.t.** shaapw=shéeshum VTI1B; **cut through s.t.** éesh'shum VTI1B; PREP **cut through s.t. animate** éesh'sheew VTA; **cut through s.t., cut and break s.t., cut s.t.** *(of something string-like)* páxk=shum VTI1B; **drive through the water** kamukwchéhleew VAI; **fall through an opening** pkwíhleew VAI, pkwíh=leew VII; **fall through the ice** pkwas=kwíhleew VAI; **go through s.t., experience s.t.** eeshóoxweew VAIO; **go through s.t., pass through s.t., get through s.t.** éeshiiw VAIO **I went across his property.** 'Ndéeshiin wtootéeneeng.'; **jump through a hole** pkwáakchehl VAI; **look through something, see through something** eeshatawáapuw VAIO; **take s.o. through in a hurry** eeshíipheew VTA; **take s.o. through something, take s.o. through an experience** eeshóo=xwaleew VTA; **take s.t. through in a hurry** eeshiipáhtoow VTI2; **take s.t. through something** *(of a matter of business)* eeshóoxwatoow VTI2; **throw something through a hole, drop s.t. in a hole** pkwáaheew VAIO.

**throw** VI **practice throwing** akweetáa=heew VAI; **take good aim** *(with a gun)*, **throw well** wŭláaheew VAI; **throw well** nihtaawáaheew VAI.

**throw** VT **throw s.t., throw s.t. in a certain direction, throw s.t. in a certain manner** láaheew VAIO; **spin and throw s.t., throw and spin s.t., twirl s.t. around** tùpáaheew VAIO **A good pitcher throws the ball with a spin to it.** 'Néhtaa-píchiit wtupaahéenal áng neenáxkwal.'; **throw s.o. and make them cry** chaangaaháaleew VTA; **throw s.o. and make them cry** chaangáaheew VAIO; **throw s.o. in the water, throw s.t. in the water** chooxpwáaheew VAIO; **throw s.t. a certain distance** sahkáaheew VAIO **I threw it far.** 'Wáhlu nzahkáaheen.'; **throw s.t. and empty it out, empty s.t. out** alaxáaheew VAIO; **throw s.t. as far as one can** seesahkáaheew VAIO **Then I went outside and I threw it as far as I could.** 'Nál kwáchŭmung ndáan táa ndúlu-asee=sahkáaheen.'; **throw s.t. hard** ksháa=heew VAIO; **throw s.t. in the water** kamukwáaheew VAIO; **throw s.t. to s.o., knock s.t. to s.o.** *(using a tool or instrument)* lahŭmáweew VTAO; **throw s.t. upside down** aalooláaheew VAIO; **throw s.t. upside down** aapooch=kwàláaheew VAIO; **throw s.t., throw s.t. off** alumáaheew VAIO; **throw the cover off s.o., throw the cover off s.t.** paaxkeeyáaheew VAIO; **be thrown upwards, hit something and bounce, bounce** uspihtéexiin VAI.

**throw about** VT **scatter s.t., throw s.t. about** seeyéeheew VAIO; **shake, move, be thrown about** kwàkw=chukwíhleew VII, kwàkwchukwíh=leew VAI.

**throw away** VT **throw s.o. away, throw s.t. animate away** pakíileew VTA; **throw s.t. away** pakíitoow VTI2.

**throw down** VT **throw s.o. down** ka=waaháaleew VTA; **throw s.o. down hard so as to make a loud noise, set s.o. down hard so as to make a loud noise** tiiwíixŭmeew VTA; **throw s.o. down with a thud, drop s.o. so that they make a thud** pòhwíixŭmeew VTA; **throw s.o. down, throw s.o. in** pŭnaaháaleew VTA; **throw s.o. down, throw s.t. down** kawáaheew VAIO; **throw s.t down hard so as to make**

**a loud noise, set s.t down hard so as to make a loud noise** tiiwíixtoow VTI2; **throw something out** ktáaheew VAIO; **throw s.t. down with a thud, drop s.t. so that it makes a thud** pòhwíixtoow VTI2; **throw s.t. down, throw s.t. in** pŭnáaheew VAIO; **throw s.t. over, throw s.t. farther than intended** paaláaheew VAIO **I threw it over the house.** 'Mbaaláaheen wii= kwáhmung.'

**throw in** VT **throw s.o. down, throw s.o. in** pŭnaaháaleew VTA; **throw s.t. down, throw s.t. in** pŭnáaheew VAIO.

**throw off** VT **throw s.o. off, unload s.o.** kohpaaháaleew VTA; **throw s.t. off, unload s.t.** kohpáaheew VAIO; **throw s.t., throw s.t. off** alumáaheew VAIO.

**throw on** VT **throw powder on s.o., throw dust on s.o., throw sand on s.o., throw dirt on s.o.** ponghwáa= leew VTA; **dress haphazardly, dress hurriedly, throw on one's clothes** pàpŭlakéechpuw VAI.

**throw through** VT **throw something through a hole, drop s.t. in a hole** pkwáaheew VAIO.

**throw up** VI **throw up, vomit** mŭlándam VOTI1; **feel sick, feel like throwing up, feel like vomiting** wŭyakaskíh= leew VAI; **make s.o. nauseous, make s.o. throw up, make s.o. vomit** wŭ= yakaskíileew VTA; **the way one looks makes someone feel like throwing up, the way one looks makes someone feel like vomiting** mŭlamanda= muwiináakwsuw VAI, wŭyakaskeelŭ= muwiináakwsuw VAI.

**thud** N **fall and make a noise, fall and make a dull noise, fall with a thud** pwàhwíixun VII, pòhwíixun VII; **fall and make a noise, fall and make a dull noise, fall with a thud, fall down hard, fall flat on one's face** pwàhwíixiin VAI, pòhwíixiin VAI; **throw s.o. down with a thud, drop s.o. so that they make a thud** pòh= wíixŭmeew VTA; **throw s.t. down with a thud, drop s.t. so that it makes a thud** pòhwíixtoow VTI2.

**thumb** N moxŭlunjáawan NI; **my thumb** nŭmoxohkwéewŭlunj NID.

**thunder** VI **thunder, be thundering** pehtáhkuw VII, pehpehtáhkuw VII.

**thunderstorm** N **be a thunderstorm** akaanzháhkuw VII; **be a bad thunderstorm** akaanzháhkweew VII.

**tickle** VT **tickle s.o.** akeelxákŭneew VTA.

**ticklish** ADJ **be ticklish** akeelxáksuw VAI.

**tie** VT **tie s.o. firmly** maskanambíileew VTA; **tie s.o. in a knot** wchiimambíi= leew VTA; **tie s.o. in threes** nxambíi= leew VTA *object usually plural;* **tie s.o. to something, tie s.o. securely to something** kŭlambíileew VTA; **tie s.t. firmly** maskanámbtoow VTI2; **tie s.t. in a knot** wchiimámbtoow VTI2; **tie s.t. in threes** nxámbtoow VTI2 *object usually plural;* **tie s.t. shut** sa= mwámbtoow VTI2; **tie s.t. to something, tie s.t. securely to something** kŭlámbtoow VTI2; **turn s.t. up and tie it** *(of a horse's tail, of a person's hair),* **do s.t. up in a bun** *(of someone's hair)* wiimbámbtoow VTI2; **be tied firmly** maskanambíisuw VII, maskanambíisuw VAI; **be tied from a certain place, be tied for a certain reason** wundambíisuw VAI, wundam= bíisuw VII **The dog is tied to the post** 'Mwáakanew wundambíisuw póos= tung.'; **be tied in threes** nxambíisŭ= wak VAI *usually plural,* nxambíisŭwal VII; **be tied loosely** lxakwambíisuw VAI, lxakwambíisuw VII; **finish tying s.o., finish harnessing s.o.** kiisham= bíileew VTA.

**tie across** VT **tie s.t. across** aashŭ= wámbtoow VTI2.

**tie around** VT **tie something around s.o.** wiiwŭnambíileew VTA; **tie some-**

**thing around s.t., 'put s.t. up'** *(of someone's hair)* wiiwŭnámbtoow VTI2; **have something tied around one's head** kŭlaandpeepíisuw VAI.

**tie together** VT **tie s.o. together** ta=kwambíileew VTA *object usually plural;* **tie s.t. together** takwámbtoow VTI2 *object usually plural;* **be tied together** takwambíisŭwak VAI *usually plural,* takwambíisŭwal VII *usually plural.*

**tie up** VT **tie s.o. up** koxpíileew VTA; **tie s.o. up** tùpambíileew VTA; **tie s.t. up** kóxptoow VTI2; **tie s.t. up properly, tie s.t. up well** wŭlámbtoow VTI2 **You bandaged it up where he got hurt.** 'Koolámbtoon éenda-kshihteexíin=ge.'; **wrap s.t. animate around something, roll s.o. up, tie s.o. up** túpheew VTA; **wrap s.t. around, tie s.t. up** tùpámbtoow VTI2; **be rolled up, be tied up** tùpháasuw VAI, tùp=háasuw VII; **be tied up** koxpiilkwús=uw VAI, koxptáasuw VII, koxpíisuw VAI, kŭlambíisuw VAI, tùpambíisuw VAI, tùpambíisuw VII; **be tied up in a knot, be tied in a knot** wchiimam=bíisuw VAI, wchiimambíisuw VII; **finish tying s.t. up** kiishámbtoow VTI2; **put a harness on s.o., tie s.o up properly, tie s.o. up well** wŭlambíi=leew VTA.

**tight** ADJ **be a tight fit** maskaníixiin VAI, maskaníixun VII; **have a tight backside, have a tight ass** kpaasíitŭyeew VAI.

**tighten** VT **tighten s.t.** maskaníixtoow VTI2; **tighten s.t. animate, make s.t. animate tight** maskaníixŭmeew VTA.

**tightly** ADV **be tightly sewn** kŭliikwáa=suw VII; **button s.t. up, do s.t. up tightly, make a down payment on s.t.** kŭláhkhwam VTI1A; **close one's hand(s) tightly** maskaniilúnjeew VAI; **close one's lips tightly, have one's lips tightly closed** samwutoonéexiin VAI; **close one's mouth tightly, have one's mouth closed, have one's lips pursed, pout** spwutoonéexiin VAI; **have one's hand(s) closed tightly** maskaniilunjéexiin VAI; **hold s.o. tightly** máskŭneew VTA; **hold s.o., hold on to s.o., hold on tightly to s.o., carry s.o.** *(using the hands)* kŭlúneew VTA; **hold s.t. tightly, have one's arms around s.t.** kaskatéenum VTI1B; **hold s.t., hold onto s.t., hold on tightly to s.t., carry s.t.** *(using the hands)* kŭlúnum VTI1B; **sew s.t. animate tightly, sew s.t. animate down, fasten s.t. animate down by sewing it** kŭliikwáaleew VTA; **sew s.t. tightly, sew s.t. down, fasten s.t. down by sewing** kŭlíikwam VTI1A.

**tilt** VT **tilt s.o., tip s.o., cause s.o. to be on the diagonal, bend s.o.** *(using the hands)* píimŭneew VTA; **tilt s.t., tip s.t., cause s.t. to be on the diagonal, bend s.t.** *(using the hands)* píimŭnum VTI1B.

**tilt over** VT **knock s.o. over, push s.o. over, bend s.o. over, tilt s.o. over** *(using the hands)* áamŭneew VTA; **knock s.t. over, push s.t. over, bend s.t. over, tilt s.t. over** *(using the hands)* áamŭnum VTI1B.

**timber** N apánzhuy NI; **large piece of timber** kihtapánzhuy NI; **saw timber, cut logs** tŭmusháhkweew VAI.

**time** N **a certain length** *(of time, measurement)* sahkii- PV; **certain length** *(of time, measurement)* sahku PC *informal* **He lived with her for a long time, and she really dominated my uncle for a long time.** 'Kwúnii-wiitaawsoomáawal, tá sáhku shíi=kaanzh lúkih wtalŭwihkawáawal nzhíisal.'; **a certain length** *(of time, measurement)* sahku- PV *informal* **I've been working since this morning.** 'Séhku-wáapang ndalóhke.', **I waited for him until two o'clock.**

'Mbéehaaw sáhku-níish-kŭlakíike.'; **once, one time** ngwutun- PV **She went there one time.** 'Wŭnúkwtun-náh -áan.', **All of a sudden one time he came, and he told my mother, "We want to get married."** 'Wíix=kwii wŭnúkwtun-páan, wtuláawal ngúkal, "Ngáta-takwapíhna."'; **once, one time** ngwútun PC **I only bet once.** 'Ngwútun shúkw ndahtíike.'; **one time, emphatic** táas PC **My late grandmother told me.** 'Noohŭmáya táas ndúkw.'; **some time ago** chíingu PC **I went to town some time ago.** 'Chíingu ootéeneeng nóom.', **I talked to the clever one recently.** 'Chíingu léepwaat ngihkŭlóolaaw.'; **be away a long time** kwŭnáhkeew VAI; **be gone a certain length of time** sahkáhkeew VAI **He was gone for two months.** 'Níish-kíishooxkw sahkáh=keew.', **How long has he been gone?** 'Thá sahkáhke?'; **every time** héesh PC **Everytime I go there.** 'Héesh náh ayáan.', **Every evening my father told me: "Fetch the cows from the other side of the road."** 'Héesh wŭláakwiik nóox ndukw: "Naatkóo=yeel awasiixkanáwe."'; **fight for a certain length of time, fight until now** sahkatáhkeew VAI; **have a good time, have fun** wiingáawsuw VAI; **live a certain length of time** sahkáawsuw VAI **If I live until springtime.** 'Sii=kwángu sahkaawsuyáane.'; **live a long life, live for a long time** kwŭ=náawsuw VAI **Maybe you'll live a long life.** 'Táas áa kwùnáawsi.'; **stamp with one's feet, keep time with one's feet** pòhwsiitéexiin VAI; **take a long time to say one's words** akwaaníixsuw VAI; **take one's time** saasiingtuyéewuw VAI **You know how to take your time.** 'Kŭníhtaa-saa=siingtuyéewi.'; **think s.t. to be a long time** kwŭneelúndam VTI1A **I think it's taking a long time for evening to come.** 'Níi ngwuneelúndamun nál ápih wŭláakuw.', **I think that it's a long time until the end of the service.** 'Níi ngwuneelúndamun nál-uch éhkwu-maawéewiin.'

**times** N **five times** náalanun PC; **many times** xwéelun PC **I went to town several times.** 'Xwéelun ootéeneeng nóom.'; **not very often, a few times** táatxun PC **I drank my medicine a few times.** 'Táatxun noochapíhkum nŭmúneen.', **I didn't go to town very often.** 'Ootéeneeng táatxun ndá.'; **several times** kéexun PC **He came alone several times.** 'Kéexun áng páan nxóoxwe.'; **so many times** txaaníhka PC *with number particles to form numbers 16-19* **Seventeen.** 'Níishaash txaaníhka.', **Sixteen.** 'Ngwútaash txaaníhka.'; **so many times** txún PC **Eight times.** 'Xáash txún.'; **so many, so many times** txu- PV *informal* **Fourteen years old.** 'Neewaaníhka txú-katúngu.', **I was gone for six weeks.** 'Ngwútaash ndúndxu-kundŭweewŭnáhke.'; **three times** nxún PC; **two times** níishun PC.

**tin pan** N wshaphoosíinjuw NI.

**tinge** N **be a blueish colour, have a blue tinge to it** oolihkŭléexiin VAI, oolihkŭléexun VII; **be a brownish colour, have a brown tinge to it, be a greyish colour, have a grey tinge to it** wiipongwŭléexiin VAI, wiipon=gwŭléexun VII; **be a greenish colour, have a green tinge to it** askaskwŭ=léexiin VAI, askaskwŭléexun VII; **be a reddish colour, have a red tinge to it** maxkŭléexiin VAI, maxkŭléexun VII; **be a yellowish colour, have a yellow tinge to it** wiisaawŭléexiin VAI, wii=saawŭléexun VII; **be dark-coloured, be a blackish colour, have a black tinge to it** nzukŭléexiin VAI, nzukŭ=léexun VII; **be light in colour, be a**

**whitish colour, have a white tinge to it** waapŭléexiin VAI, waapŭléexun VII.

**tingle** VI **be a tingling sensation, have pins and needles** *(of body parts)* wchiipiisóowuw VII **I went to the doctor because my arm was numb.** 'Ndaaktúlung ndáam éelu- náxk -wchiipiisóowiik.'

**tinny** ADJ **ring, make a ringing noise, make a tinny noise** taliingwihtéexun VII.

**tip** VT **tilt s.o., tip s.o., cause s.o. to be on the diagonal, bend s.o.** *(using the hands)* píimŭneew VTA; **tilt s.t., tip s.t., cause s.t. to be on the diagonal, bend s.t.** *(using the hands)* píimŭnum VTI1B.

**tip backwards** VT **tip something over, tip something backwards, knock something over, knock something over backwards** aamáaheew VAIO.

**tip over** VT **knock s.o. over, tip s.o. over** *(using the foot or body)* aamíh=kaweew VTA; **knock s.t. over, tip s.t. over** *(using the foot or body)* aamíh=kam VTI1A; **tip something over, tip something backwards, knock something over, knock something over backwards** aamáaheew VAIO.

**tiptoe** VI kihkiimalíhkeew VAI.

**tire out** VT **make s.o. tired, tire s.o. out, disappoint s.o.** shiiwiilawée=heew VTA.

**tired** ADJ **be tired** shiiwasánuw VAI; **be tired from running, be tired of running** shiiwaaméhleew VAI; **be tired from walking** shiiwóoxweew VAI; **be tired of crawling** shiiwíikwsuw VAI; **be tired of singing** shiiwaláamuw VAI; **be tired of sitting** shíiwapuw VAI, shiiwohkwéepuw VAI; **be tired of sitting on one's backside, have a sore backside from sitting down** shiiwii=tŭyéepuw VAI; **be tired of standing** shiiwiikáapawuw VAI; **feel tired, feel restless** *(especially when sick)* shii=wamálsuw VAI; **have a tired backside, have a sore backside** shiiwaa=síitŭyeew VAI; **have a tired hand** shiiwŭnaxkéexiin VAI; **have tired feet** shiiwsiitéexiin VAI; **make s.o. tired, tire s.o. out, disappoint s.o.** shiiwii=lawéeheew VTA.

**tired of** VT **tired of, be tired of** shiiwu- PV *informal* **I'm tired of waiting.** 'Nzhíiwu-péesi.', **I'm tired of waiting for him.** 'Nzhíiwu-péehaaw.'; **(be) tired of** peeku- PV *informal* **He is tired of lying down.** 'Péeku-shungíixiin.'; **be tired of eating s.t.** peekándam VTI1A; **be tired of eating s.t. animate** péekameew VTA; **be tired of feeling a certain way, be tired of living** peekahtéenamuw VAI; **be tired of fighting** peekatáhkeew VAI; **be tired of listening to s.o.** peeksútaweew VTA; **be tired of listening to s.t.** peeksútam VTI1A; **be tired of living** peekáawsuw VAI; **be tired of looking at s.o., find s.o. tiresome to look at** peekíinaweew VTA; **be tired of looking at s.t., find s.t. tiresome to look at** peekíinam VTI1A; **be tired of lying in bed** peekiikanáaxiin VAI; **be tired of playing** laxkeelawúsuw VAI; **be tired of s.o., find s.o. tiresome** peekiilawéeheew VTA; **be tired of sewing** peekiikwáakeew VAI; **be tired of working** peekalóhkeew VAI; **be tired of writing** peekeekhíikeew VAI.

**tired out** ADJ **be tired out, be exhausted** shawíhleew VAI.

**tiresome** ADJ **be tired of looking at s.o., find s.o. tiresome to look at** peekíi=naweew VTA; **be tired of looking at s.t., find s.t. tiresome to look at** pee=kíinam VTI1A; **be tired of s.o., find s.o. tiresome** peekiilawéeheew VTA.

**toad** N káaxkashii-chkwál NA.

**tobacco** N kwsháhteew NI; **tobacco, what one smokes** ehóhpwaang VII;

**chew tobacco** cháahuw VAI; **work in a tobacco field, work picking tobacco** kwshahtéewheew VAI.

**today** ADV kíishkwihk PC **Today.** 'Kwáy kíishkwihk.'

**toe** N **my toe** nzhíichush NID; **my big toe** nŭmoxwsiitáawan NID, nŭmoxoh=kwéewsiit NID; **spread one's toes apart, have one's toes spread apart** sayaaxksiitéexiin VAI; **stub one's toe** paaksiitéexiin VAI; **trip, stub one's toe** pasusiitéexiin VAI.

**together** ADV **be bunched up together** mŭniixíinook VAI *usually plural,* mŭ=níixŭnool VII *usually plural;* **be close together** kchukáhteew VII; **be close together, lie close together** takwii=xíinook VAI *usually plural,* takwíixŭ=nool VII *usually plural;* **be frozen together** takwátun VII; **be in a group of people crowded close together, make one's way through the crowd** kàkchúkamuw VAI; **be many of them lying together** xweelaangwéewak VAI *usually plural;* **be mixed together in a liquid** takwaapŭwehléewal VII; **be stuck on, be stuck together** psák=wamuw VAI, psákwamuw VII; **be stuck together** takwámŭwak VAI *usually plural,* takwámŭwal VII *usually plural;* **be there together** takwahtéewal VII *usually plural;* **be tied together** takwambíisŭwak VAI *usually plural,* takwambíisŭwal VII *usually plural;* **bunch s.o. up together, put s.o. in a bunch** mŭníixŭmeew VTA *object usually plural;* **bunch s.t. up together, put s.t. together in a bunch** mŭníix=toow VTI2 *object usually plural;* **come together, join together** takwíhleew VII, takwihléewak VAI *usually plural;* **gather together, meet** maawehlée=wak VAI *usually plural;* **get together again, reunite** laapíilŭnuw VAI; **glue s.t. animate together, paste s.t. animate** psakwpéhlaleew VTA; **glue s.t. together, paste s.t.** psakwpéhlatoow VTI2; **glue s.t., stick s.t. together** psákwŭnum VTI1B; **group together** màmshihléewak VAI *usually plural;* **grow close together** kchukíikŭwak VAI *usually plural,* spwíikŭwak VAI *usually plural,* spwíikŭnool VII *usually plural;* **grow together** takwíikŭ=wak VAI *usually plural.* takwíikŭnool VII *usually plural;* **have one's arms together, have one's arms intertwined** laapiinaxkéexiin VAI; **have one's heads together** kchukaand=peexíinook VAI *usually plural;* **have one's legs together** takwukaatéexiin VAI; **hit together** takwihteexíinook VAI *usually plural,* takwihtéexŭnool VII *usually plural;* **lay s.o. together, join s.o. together** takwíixŭmeew VTA *object usually plural;* **lay s.t. together, join s.t. together** takwíixtoow VTI2 *object usually plural;* **lie close together** kchukaangwéewak VAI *usually plural;* **lie close together, be close together, lie close to something** psakwiixíinook VAI *usually plural,* psakwíixun VII **The chair is up against the door.** 'Psakwíixun áh=papoon kpahóonung.'; **lie together** takwaangwéewak VAI *usually plural;* **live together in threes, stay together in threes** nxiilŭnúwak VAI *usually plural;* **multiply, grow as a bunch, grow close together** mŭléekuw VAI **It's really multiplied.** 'Móxa mŭlée=kuw.'; **nail s.t. together, hit s.t. and join it together** takwihtéehum VTI1B; **paste s.o. together, glue s.o. together** psakwpáleew VTA *object usually plural;* **paste s.t. together, glue s.t. together** psakwpátoow VTI2 *object usually plural* **I glued the pieces of wood together.** 'Mbusakwupatóonal xwúsal.'; **play together** niisheela=wúsŭwak VAI *usually plural;* **put s.o. close together, put s.t. animate close**

**together, stick s.o. up against something** psakwíixŭmeew VTA *object usually plural;* **put s.t. animate together** *(using the hands)* takwúneew VTA; **put s.t. close together, stick s.t. up against something** psakwíixtoow VTI2; **put s.t. together** *(using the hands)* takwúnum VTI1B; **sew s.t. animate together** takwiikwáaleew VTA; **sew s.t. together** takwíikwam VTI1; **sew things together** takwiikwáakeew VAI; **sing together** niishaláamuw VAI; **sit close together** kchukapúwak VAI *usually plural;* **sit close together** kchukohkwéepŭwak VAI *usually plural;* **sit close together** psakohkwée=pŭwak VAI *usually plural,* psakwa=púwak VAI *usually plural;* **sleep with each other, sleep together** wihpéen=dŭwak VAI *usually plural;* **stand bunched together** mŭniikaapawúw=ak VAI *usually plural;* **stand close together** kchukiikaapawúwak VAI *usually plural;* **stand in a bunch, be bunched up standing together** koh=pakiikaapawúwak VAI *usually plural;* **tie s.o. together** takwambíileew VTA *object usually plural;* **tie s.t. together** takwámbtoow VTI2 *object usually plural;* **work together, help each other** takwundaméewak VAI.

**toilet** N **outhouse, toilet** wiikwáhmush NI.

**tomato** N tùmétoos NA.

**tongue** N **my tongue** níilanuw NID; **have one's tongue sticking out** saapiila=nuwéexiin VAI; **stick one's tongue out at s.o.** saapiilanuwéhtaweew VTA; **stick out one's tongue** saapiilanúw=eew VAI.

**too** ADV **be here too, be present** wíita=puw VAI; **be too smart for one's own good** machíi-lpwéew VAI; **come too late** mehtxihkáasuw VAI; **come too late, miss an opportunity, miss one's chance** mehtxíhkeew VAI **The service was over when I arrived, I came too late.** 'Kíishi-maawéewiin náh peeyayáane, nemehtxíhke.'; **find s.t. animate too small, find that s.t. animate doesn't fit, be too small for s.t. animate** *(of clothing)* wŭlíhka=weew VTA **They are too small, they don't fit me.** 'Noolihkawáawak.', **My mitt doesn't fit.** 'Noolíhkawaaw nŭwánd.'; **find s.t. too small, find that s.t. doesn't fit, be too small for s.t.** *(of clothing)* wŭlíhkam VTI1A **It's too small for me, it doesn't fit me.** 'Noolíhkamun.', **My shirt doesn't fit.** 'Noolíhkamun ndahéembut.'

**too bad** ADV **too bad** *(that it happened)* alákwe PC.

**too much, excessively** wsaa- PV **It's too long.** 'Wsáa-kwŭnéew.', **The bat's too heavy.** 'Wsáa-laanzhíhkan pa=kandíikan.'; **too much, excessively** wsaami- PV **He is too lazy.** 'Wsáami-kihtamúneew.', **It's too big, the hole is too deep.** 'Wsáami-xwushée=yeew.'; **too much, excessively** wsaa=mu- PV *informal* **Right away they told their son, "Don't marry her, she runs around too much."** 'Sháa wtulaawáawal kwiissùwáawal, "Chíi takwapŭwaaláahan, wsáamu-mih=msahtakíhle."', **Your cane is too short.** 'Wsáamu-chahkwéeshuw ktaláawan.'; **drink too much** wsaa=míisŭmuw VAI; **grow too much, be overgrown** wsaamíikun VII, wsaa=míikun VAI; **be too much of something** wsaamíixun VII; **pay a lot for s.t., pay too much for s.t.** xwulóh=keew VAIO, xwalóhkeew VAIO. **talk lots to s.o., talk too much to s.o.** paakweenztoonháaleew VTA; **walk too much** wsaamóoxweew VAI; **hit s.o. too much, hit s.o. too hard** wsaamihtéeheew VTA.

**tooth** N **my tooth** níipiit NID; **wear dentures, wear false teeth** wiipiithám=

eew VAI; **be toothless, have no teeth** mooshaníikeew VAI; **have teeth** wii=píituw VAI; **brush one's teeth** kshii=xaníikeew VAI; **have a broken tooth** kaxkaniikéexiin VAI; **have a broken tooth** lookaníikeew VAI; **have a chipped tooth, have a chip off one's tooth** kwashaníikeew VAI; **have a crooked tooth** piimaníikeew VAI; **have a tooth knocked out** aamanii=kéexiin VAI; **have a tooth knocked out** ktaniikehtéexiin VAI; **have bad teeth** amataníikeew VAI; **have clean teeth** apiilaníikeew VAI, apiimaní=ikeew VAI; **have crooked teeth** pii=moxkwaníikeew VAI; **have good teeth** awulaníikeew VAI; **have long teeth** akwaananíikeew VAI; **have one's teeth exposed** mihtaniikéexiin VAI; **have sharp teeth** akiinaníikeew VAI; **have straight teeth** ashaaxkàníikeew VAI; **knock s.o.'s tooth out** aamanii=kéexŭmeew VTA.

**toothless** ADJ **be toothless, have no teeth** mooshaníikeew VAI.

**top** N **above, on top of** waxkíichi PC **On top of the timbers.** 'Waxkíichi apánzhŭyung.'; **above, on top of** wáxkiich PC *informal* **I fell on top of the box.** 'Níi mbákshung wáxkiich nŭmatéexiin.', **I put something on top of the table.** 'Wáxkiich eehun=dáxpwiing kwéek ndáhtoon.'; **be full to the brim, be level with the top** *(of non-liquids)* tpuskŭwáhteew VII, tpuskŭwápuw VAI; **contain liquid level with the top** *(of containers)*, **be level with the top of a container** *(of liquids)* tpuskŭwáapŭweew VII; **contain liquid level with the top, be liquid level to the top of container** tpuskŭwúpeew VAI, tpuskŭwúpeew VII; **fall on top of something, lie on top of something** waxkiitihtéexiin VAI, waxkiitihtéexun VII; **fill s.t. level to the top** *(of liquids)* tpuskŭwúpeew VAIO; **forehead, top of head** laa=wáandpe PC; **lie on top of something** waxkiitáangweew VAI; **make s.t. level with the top of a container** *(of liquids)* tpuskŭwáapŭweew VAIO; **on top of the bed** waxkiitapíinaye PC **I was lying on top of the bed.** 'Nzhungíi=xiin waxkiitapíinaye.'; **on top of the table** waxkiiteehundaxpóone PC; **place s.o. on top** *(of something)* poxkwáhleew VTA; **place s.t. animate level with the top of container** tpuskŭwáhleew VTA; **place s.t. level with the top of container** tpuskŭ=wáhtoow VTI2; **place s.t. on top** *(of something)* poxkwáhtoow VTI2; **stick out, stick out over the top** ktáska=neew VAI **Your navel's sticking out.** 'Kpooshíishum péech-ktáskaneew.', **The potatoes are sticking up out of the pail.** 'Óhpŭnak wshaphóosung wúnj-ktaskanéewak.'; **stick out, stick out over the top** ktáskaneew VII; **the top of the roof, the top of the house** waxkíitaakw PC **The top of the roof leaks.** 'Waxkíitaakw wunjíikuw.'; **top of head** waxkáandpe PC; **top of the hill** waxkiitáawung PC.

**tormented** ADJ **be driven to one's death, be tormented to death** aapchiina=lúkwsuw VAI.

**touch** VI **touch, make contact** mshíixiin VAI, mshíixun VII **It's hanging down and it almost touches (the floor).** 'Pŭnaapéhleew wéenaa mshíixun.', **My feet are touching the floor.** 'Mshíixŭnool nzíital áhkiing.'

**touch** VT **touch s.o.** alúneew VTA; **touch s.t.** alúnum VTI1B; **touch s.o. lightly** *(using the hands)* cháskŭneew VTA; **touch s.t. lightly** *(using the hands)* cháskŭnum VTI1B; **touch s.o., make contact with s.o., run into s.o., hit s.o.** aláheew VTA; **touch s.t., run into s.t., drive into s.t., make contact with s.t. forcefully, hit s.t.** aláham

VTI1A **I ran into it.** 'Ná ndalhámun.'; **touch s.t. briefly, touch s.t. for a moment** láashu-lúnum VTI1A; **have one's foot touching down on a surface, have one's foot touching on the floor** mshusiitéexiin VAI; **have one's hands barely touching a surface** mshiinaxkéexiin VAI **He almost fell but he was just hanging on by his fingers.** 'Wéenaa pŭníhleew shùkéhla mshiinaxkéexiin.'; **pick s.o. up by mistake, touch s.o. by mistake** páhtŭneew VTA; **pick s.t. up by mistake, touch s.t. by mistake** páh=tŭnum VTI1B; **sit with one's backside barely touching a surface, sit on the edge of something** mshiitŭyéepuw VAI; **touch and dirty s.o., make s.o. dirty** *(using the hands)* níiskŭneew VTA; **touch and dirty s.t., make s.t. dirty** *(using the hands)* níiskŭnum VTI1A.

**towards** PREP **here, to here, towards the speaker** peech- PV **Soon he called me back, "I didn't find them. They're not here."** 'Méhchxiish láapii mbéech-lúkw, "Máhta nŭmox=kamóowŭnal. Máhta yóh ahteewíi=wal."', **She would leave for several days, and when my uncle came (to visit) if she came with him he couldn't do anything.** 'Àhalúmsuw kehkeexookwŭnáhke, wáak áng nzhíis péeyaat péech-wiicheewáatu, wŭlú áng kéhla áalu- kwéek -lúnum.'; **here, to here, towards the speaker** peechi- PV **He's coming here to cheat me.** 'Ngáta-péechi-pahpahchóolukw.', **I came inside.** 'Mbéech-piinjíike.'; **here, to here, towards the speaker** peechu- PV *informal* **He answered me.** 'Mbéechu-naxkóomukw.', **I came walking.** 'Mbéechu-pŭmúsi.'

**towel** N kehkaasiingweehíikan NI, keh=kaasiingwéehoon NI, kehkaasíin=gweeng VAI; **tea towel** kaasahkhwíi=kan NI, peengwahkhwíikan NI, peen=gwiikwáakan NI.

**town** N **town, land** ootéenay NI; **big town, city** kihtootéenay NI, xwatoo=téenay NI; **live in town** ooteenayápuw VAI; **be an empty town, be no one in town** alaxootéenayuw VII; **middle of the town, middle of the village** laa=wootéenay PC **It's there in the middle of town.** 'Laawootéenay áhte.'

**toy** N mehmeelawihtáasiik NI.

**track** N **leave crooked tracks** pàptuk=éelham VOTI1; **make a lot of tracks** kaanzhéelham VAI, xwéelham VOTI1; **make good tracks** wŭléelham VOTI1; **make tracks coming this way, make tracks coming towards the speaker** peetéelham VAI; **make tracks in a certain direction, make tracks in a certain manner** léelham VOTI1 **He's making tracks the other way.** 'Yée=lak léelham.'; **make tracks in the snow** koonéelham VAI; **railroad, railroad track** nzukasunáanay NI.

**trade** VT **trade chairs, change chairs** aashŭwahpapoonéewak VAI *usually plural,* aashŭwahpapóonheew VAI; **trade houses** aashŭwiikéewak VAI *usually plural;* **trade shoes, change one's shoes** aashŭwahksúneew VAI.

**trade with** VT **trade with s.o.** aashŭ=walóoleew VTA.

**train** N tundeewaatpùníikan NI; **kick out one's legs, stretch out one's legs, maneuver** *(of trains)* shándham VOTI1.

**train car** N **car, train car** káal NA.

**transmit to** VT **transmit an infectious disease to s.o.** mshíiheew VTA.

**transparent** ADJ **be transparent, be thin** *(of material)* shiikalúsuw VAI, shíikaleew VII; **lace curtain, transparent curtain** shehshíikaleek NI; **wear a sheer dress, wear a transparent dress** shiikalahóosuw VAI.

**transplant** VT **transplant s.t.** aanjiikáa=patoow VTI2; **transplant s.t. animate**

aanjiikáapaleew VTA.

**trap** N kŭlahíikan NI.

**trap** VT **hook s.o. up, hook up s.t. animate** *(as a belt),* **trap s.t. animate** kŭláhkhweew VTA; **trap s.o., trap s.t. animate, knock a tree down on s.o.** kŭláheew VTA; **trap things, be trapping** kŭlahíikeew VAI; **be hit, be trapped, be hit by a car** kŭláhookw VAI; **be stuck, get stuck, be trapped** kŭ=láhkweew VII **My shoe is stuck.** 'Kŭ=láhkweew nŭmáhksun.'; **be stuck, get stuck, be trapped** kŭláhkweew VAI.

**travel** VI **have difficulty while walking, have difficulty in travelling, be hard for one to travel** àhwóoxweew VAI; **travel all over** *(mode of transportation unspecified)* msahkéewxeew VAI; **travel all over, travel around** msóo=xweew VAI.

**treat** VT **treat s.o. in a certain manner** lacháaheew VTA; **treat s.o. well** wŭ=lacháaheew VTA; **treat s.o. well, be good to s.o.** wŭlú-líiheew VTA; **treat s.o. badly** matacháaheew VTA; **be treated by a doctor** ndaaktulhámeew VAI; **be treated in a certain manner** líinam VOTI1 **I'm well treated.** 'Nóo=lu-líinam.', **I have a hard time, I have bad luck.** 'Ndáhwu-líinam.'; **be treated well** wŭlú-líinam VOTI1.

**tree** N míhtukw NA; **tree stump** wíh=kwanahkw NI; **apple tree** aapŭlúsh=ahkw NA; **be a forked tree** lxawáhk=wsuw VAI; **be a lot of thick trees, be a lot of dense trees, be a dense forest** spwihtkwíhkeew VII; **be a lot of trees** mihtkwíhkeew VII; **big tree** xwáchahkw NA; **cedar tree** shún=dahkw NA; **chop down a tree** aam=háhkweew VAI; **chop with an ax, cut down trees, trim trees** tŭmaháh=kweew VAI; **cut down trees** tŭmáh=kweew VAI; **fell trees, knock trees down** kawaháhkweew VAI; **hard maple tree** asunaamíinzhuy NA; **heartwood of tree, spine** wíimb NI; **old tree** xuwíhtukw NA, xúwahkw NA; **small tree** *(diminutive)* changáh=kwush NA, changíhchkwush NA; **tap trees** wiis'háhkweew VAI; **trap s.o., trap s.t. animate, knock a tree down on s.o.** kŭláheew VTA; **trim trees, cut underbrush** mahkháh=kweew VAI; **walnut tree** ptukwii=míinzhuy NA; **young tree** wuskíhtukw NA.

**trenchmouth** N **have trenchmouth** alutóoneew VAI.

**trim** ADJ **have a trim shape, have a good shape, have a good figure** wŭláhkwsuw VAI.

**trim** VT **cut s.t. animate smoothly, scrape s.t. animate smooth, cut s.t. animate lightly, trim s.t. animate** láalsheew VTA; **cut s.t. smoothly, scrape s.t. smooth, cut s.t. lightly, trim s.t.** láalshum VTI1B; **trim trees, cut underbrush** mahkháhkweew VAI; **be marked, be trimmed, be pruned** *(of trees)* laalsháasuw VAI; **be trimmed** laalsháasuw VII.

**trip** VT **trip s.o.** laapsiitéhkaweew VTA, pasusiitéhkaweew VTA; **trip, stub one's toe** pasusiitéexiin VAI.

**trot** VI lumbíhleew VAI *especially of horses.*

**trouble** N **have heart trouble** wteehíi=neew VAI.

**troubled** ADJ **look troubled** sàkwiináa=kwat VII, sàkwiináakwsuw VAI.

**trough** N kwŭníinjuw NI.

**true** ADJ **true, real** mayáawii PC **His real name.** 'Mayáawii eeshíinziit.', **The main road.** 'Mayáawii áanay.'

**trunk** N **chest, trunk, small box, casket, coffin** kúsht NI; **container, trunk** ehahtíikeeng VII.

**truth** N wŭlaamweewáakan NI; **speak the exact truth** shaaxkaaptóoneew VAI; **tell the truth** shaaxkaachíimuw

VAI; **tell the truth, make a deal** wŭ=láamweew VAI.

**try** VI **try to** *(do)*, **try and** *(do)* kwchi- PV **Try to fix it!** 'Kwchí-wŭlíixtool!'; **try to** *do*, **try and** *(do)* kwchu- PV *informal* **I'm trying to think about it.** 'Ngwúchu-msháatamun', **He tried to leave.** 'Kwchú-alúmsuw.'; **try to (do), try and (do)** akweechi- PV **I'm trying to fix it.** 'Ngwakwéechi-wŭlíixtoon.'

**try on** VT **try s.t. animate on** *(of clothing)* kwchíhkaweew VTA; **try s.t. on** *(of clothing)* aanjíhkam VTI1A, kwchíhkam VTI1A.

**try out** VT **try s.t. animate out, test s.t. animate** kwchíhlaleew VTA; **try s.t. out, test s.t.** kwchíhlatoow VTI2.

**tub** N éemul NA.

**tug** N **harness tug, harness gear** wtun=íikan NI.

**tug at** VT **grab s.o. by the hand, tug at s.o, pull on s.o.** sakúneew VTA; **grab s.t. by the hand, tug at and pull on s.t.** sakúnum VTI1B.

**tunnel** N **be a tunnel** tàtùpáalakat VII.

**turkey** N pŭléew NA, **turkey feather** pŭléewii-míikwan NA.

**turn** VI **lie upside down, turn upside down, fall upside down** aapooch=kwíhleew VAI; **turn** *(of something sheet-like)* aapeekíhleew VAI *usually of pieces of paper,* aapéeksuw VAI *usually of pieces of paper;* **turn** *(off the road)* paxkéhleew VAI; **turn yellow, turn brown** wiisaawíhleew VII; **turn yellow, turn brown** wiisaawíh=leew VAI.

**turn** VT **turn s.t., screw s.t., wind s.t., drive s.t. in** *(of screws)* tùpáhkhwam VTI1A; **twist and turn s.t., turn s.t. up** *(of hair)* wíimbŭnum VTI1B; **turn** *(off the road)* páxkeew VAI **This is where you turn (off).** 'Yóon-uch ktúnda-páxkeen.'; **turn a crank, crank things, turn things around** tùpŭníikeew VAI; **turn one's head, look back** kwŭlupóhkweew VAI; **turn s.o. to face in a certain direction, turn s.o. to face in a certain manner** lohkwéexŭmeew VTA; **turn s.o. to face in the wrong direction, turn s.o. to face the wrong way** chanoh=kwéexŭmeew VTA; **turn s.t. to face in a certain direction, turn s.t. to face in a certain manner** lohkwéextoow VTI2 **I faced it towards the front.** 'Shayéemung ndulohkwéextoon.'; **be turned** *(of something sheet-like)* aapeekŭnáasuw VAI *usually of pieces of paper;* **be turned by the wind, be blown by the wind** *(of something sheet-like)* aapéekxookw VAI *usually of pieces of paper;* **cock one's head, turn one's head, look to the side** piimóhkweew VAI; **have a look of distaste on one's face, turn one's nose up at something** niiskcheen=gwéexiin VAI; **look sideways, turn one's head** pŭmiitóhkweew VAI; **turn s.t. to face in the wrong direction, turn s.t. to face the wrong way** chanohkwéextoow VTI2.

**turn around** VI kwŭlúpiiw VAI-S; **turn around while crawling** kwŭlupíikw=suw VAI; **turn around while sitting** kwŭlúpapuw VAI; **turn around while standing** kwŭlupiikáapawuw VAI; **turn around, turn around while in motion, turn around while driving, flip over** kwŭlupíhleew VAI.

**turn around** VT **turn s.o. around, crank s.t. animate** *(using the hands)* túpŭ=neew VTA; **turn s.o. around, turn s.o. over** tùpíixŭmeew VTA; **turn s.o. over, turn s.o. around** *(using the foot or body)* kwŭlupíhkaweew VTA; **turn s.o. over, turn s.o. around** *(using the hands)* kwŭlúpŭneew VTA; **turn s.t. around, crank s.t.** *(using the hands)* túpŭnum VTI1B; **turn s.t. around, turn s.t. over** tùpíixtoow VTI2; **turn**

s.t. over, turn s.t. around *(using the foot or body)* kwŭlupíhkam VTI1A; **turn s.t. over, turn s.t. around** *(using the hands)* kwŭlúpŭnum VTI1B; **turn a crank, crank things, turn things around** tùpŭníikeew VAI.

**turn back** VT **turn s.t. animate back** *(of clocks, using the hands)*, **return s.o.** kwáxkŭneew VTA; **turn s.t. back** *(using the hands)*, **return s.t.** kwáx=kŭnum VTI1B.

**turn down** VT **turn s.t. animate down** *(of lights or sources of heat)* ahkwŭ=léeneew VTA, áhkwŭneew VTA; ahtee=háaleew VTA, wtuléeneew VTA; **turn s.t. down** *(of lights or sources of heat)* ahkwŭléenum VTI1B, áhkwŭnum VTI1B, wtuléenum VTI1B.

**turn inside out** VT **turn s.t. inside out, turn s.t. upside down** aapoochkwàl=íixtoow VTI2; **turn s.t. animate inside out** *(using the hands)* aapóotŭ=neew VTA; **turn s.t. inside out** *(using the hands)* aapóotŭnum VTI1B.

**turn on** VT **turn on the light** waasŭlée=nŭmeew VAI.

**turn over** VI tùpíixiin VAI; **turn over from one side to the other, turn over in bed** kwŭlupatéexiin VAI; **turn over while lying down** kwŭlupíixiin VAI; **upset, turn over** kooxkáaweew VAI, kooxkáaweew VII.

**turn over** VT **turn s.o. around, turn s.o. over** tùpíixŭmeew VTA; **turn s.o. over, turn s.o. around** *(using the foot or body)* kwŭlupíhkaweew VTA; **turn s.o. over, turn s.o. around** *(using the hands)* kwŭlúpŭneew VTA; **turn s.t. animate over, open s.t. animate up** *(of something sheet-like)* aapéekŭ=neew VTA *usually of pieces of paper;* **turn s.t. around, turn s.t. over** tùp=íixtoow VTI2; **turn s.t. over, turn s.t. around** *(using the foot or body)* kwŭlupíhkam VTI1A; **turn s.t. over, turn s.t. around** *(using the hands)* kwŭlúpŭnum VTI1B.

**turn up** VT **sew around the edge of s.t., turn up and sew s.t.** paxkawíikwam VTI1A; **turn s.t. animate up** *(of lanterns, of flames)* uspŭléeneew VTA; **turn s.t. up** *(as a stove)* uspŭléenum VTI1B; **turn s.t. up and tie it** *(of a horse's tail, of a person's hair)*, **do s.t. up in a bun** *(of someone's hair)* wiimbámbtoow VTI2; **twist and turn s.t., turn s.t. up** *(of hair)* wíimbŭnum VTI1B.

**turn upside down** VT **hit and turn s.o. upside down, hit and invert s.o.** aaloolihtéexŭmeew VTA; **hit and turn s.t. upside down, hit and invert s.t.** aaloolihtéextoow VTI2; **turn s.o. upside down** aapoochkwàlíixŭmeew VTA.

**turnip** N pehpéetkweek NA.

**turtle** N takwáx NA.

**twelve** N niishaaníhka PC.

**twenty** N takw̩iináxke PC; **multiple of twenty** *(in counting)* txiináxke PC *with number particle for numbers 60-90* **Eighty.** 'Xáash txiináxke.'

**twin** N kapées NA; **be twins** kapéesŭwak VAI *usually plural.*

**twirl** VT **spin and throw s.t., throw and spin s.t., twirl s.t. around** tùpáaheew VAIO **A good pitcher throws the ball with a spin to it.** 'Néhtaa-píchiit wtupaahéenal áng neenáxkwal.'

**twist** N **have an odd twist to one's mouth, have an odd twist to one's lips** *(indicating a certain attitude)* maashtoonéexiin VAI.

**twist** VT **twist and turn s.t., turn s.t. up** *(of hair)* wíimbŭnum VTI1B; **be twisted** *(especially of iron)* piimóxkweew VII; **be twisted, be at an angle, lie at an angle, be lopsided, lie on its side, be misaligned** *(of a misbuttoned shirt)* piimoxkwíixun VII; **lie cross-**

**wise, be twisted, be at an angle, lie at an angle, be lopsided** piimox=kwíixiin VAI.

**two** N nísha PC; **two** niish- PV **You are using two canes.** 'Kŭníish-alaaw=húnzi.'; **two** niish- PN **I worked there for two months.** 'Níish-kíishooxkw náh ndúnda-làlóhke.', **He weighs two pounds.** 'Níish-póond txú-poonda=kúsuw.'; **two** niishu- PV **It's in two pieces.** 'Níishu-pangéeyeew.'; **two** níishii PC **I sewed them in twos.** 'Níishii ndoxkwamúnal.'; **be cracked, be split in two, be in half** pasát VII **It must be cracked.** 'Sháxk éet pasát.'; **be double, be in two layers** niishéekat VII, niishéeksuw VAI; **be gone for two days** niishookwŭnáh=keew VAI; **be in two layers** *(of something sheet-like)* niisheekíixiin VAI, niisheekíixun VII; **be two days** nii=shookwŭnákat VII **He went there two days ago.** 'Niishookwŭnákate náh éew.', **He's going there in two days.** 'Niishookwŭnakáhke náh éew.'; **be two days** niisháhkameew VII; **be two of them** níishŭwak VAI, níishŭnool VII *usually plural;* **be two pairs, be two sets** niishéelook VAI, niishéeltool VII *usually plural;* **be two pieces** *(of something string-like)* niisháhtakat VII; **cut s.t. in two, cut s.t. in half, split s.t. in two by cutting it** pasúsh=um VTI1B; **have two pages** *(of something sheet-like)* niishaapéeksuw VAI *usually of pieces of paper;* **have two wives** pihpíhtawi-takwápuw VAI; **sit in twos** niishohkwéepŭwak VAI *usually plural;* **take two steps** niishalíh=keew VAI; **two days** niishóokwŭnii PC; **two times** níishun PC; **two, in twos** niishéeli PC **They're stacked in twos.** 'Niishéeli pihtawíixŭnool.', **I saw two fires.** 'Níi néem niishéeli éenda-náxkwteek.'; **walk in groups of two** niishataxooxwéewak VAI *usually plural;* **walk in twos, walk as a pair** niishooxwéewak VAI *usually plural.*

**type** N **run around, be the 'runaround' type** mihmsahtakíhleew VAI.

# U

**udder** N **have a swollen udder, have a swollen breast** paasíilaneew VAI; **have big breasts, have big udders** *(of a cow)* xwíilaneew VAI; **have long breasts, have long udders** *(of a cow)* akwaaníilaneew VAI.

**ugly** ADJ **be homely, be ugly** matusíisuw VAI.

**umbrella** N ahkchíikŭloos NA.

**unable** ADJ **unable to** pwaawii- PV **He can't push it.** 'Pwáawii-kunjchúnŭ=mun.', **I can't pull it.** 'Mbwáawii-wtúnŭmun.'; **unable, be unable, be unable to** *(do something)* aalu- PV *informal* **I can't eat.** 'Ndáalu-míitsi.', **I couldn't sleep.** 'Ndáalu-kawíim.'; **unable, unable to, be unable to** *(do something)* aali- PV **He is unable to speak Delaware.** 'Áali-hulŭníix=suw.'; **be unable to bite s.o.** pwáa=wameew VTA; **be unable to bite s.t.** pwaawándam VTI1A; **be unable to cut s.o.** pwáawsheew VTA; **be unable to cut s.t.** pwáawshum VTI1A; **be unable to hit s.o.** *(using a tool or instrument)* pwáawheew VTA; **be unable to hit s.t.** *(using a tool or instrument)* pwáawham VTI1A; **be unable to lift s.o.** pwáawŭneew VTA; **be unable to lift s.t.** pwáawŭnum VTI1A; **be constipated, be unable to defecate** aalŭwásktuw VAI, pwaawásktuw VAI; **be mute, be unable to talk** kputóo=neew VAI, akeeptóoneew VAI; **be unable to rain** aalŭwúlaan VII; **be un-**

**able to speak** aalaaptóoneew VAI; **be unable to urinate** aalŭwíisheew VAI; **be unable to work, be unable to move, be unable to run, be out of order** aalŭwíhleew VAI, aalŭwíhleew VII.

**unafraid** ADJ **be content, be unworried about anything, be unafraid** nalaw=áhkeew VAI.

**Unami** N **speak Unami** wihwŭnaamíi=wuw VAI.

**unbeliever** N **be an unbeliever, don't believe in a Christian way of life, lead a quiet life** nalawáawsuw VAI.

**uncle** N **my uncle, my mother's brother, my cross-uncle** nzhíis NAD; **my uncle, my father's brother, parallel uncle** nóoxwush NAD.

**unconscious** ADJ **be out of one's mind, be unconscious** wanahkwatéhleew VAI.

**uncover** VT **uncover s.o.** *(using the hands)* paaxkéeneew VTA; **uncover s.o., expose s.o.** mihchíhlaleew VTA; **uncover s.o., expose s.o., display s.o., cause s.o. to be exposed** mih=chíixŭmeew VTA; **uncover s.t.** *(using the hands)* paaxkéenum VTI1B; **uncover s.t., expose s.t.** mihchíhlatoow VTI2; **uncover s.t., expose s.t., explain s.t.** mihchíixtoow VTI2; **be uncovered, be exposed to view** mih=chiixtáasuw VAI, mihchiixtáasuw VII; **lie down uncovered, lie down exposed, lie down in the open** mih=chíixiin VAI; **lie uncovered** paaxkée=xiin VAI, paaxkéexun VII.

**underbrush** N **clear away underbrush, be underbrushing** piilháhkweew VAI; **trim trees, cut underbrush** mahk=háhkweew VAI.

**underclothes** N ehaláamakwiing NI.

**undercook** VT **undercook s.t., cook s.t. raw** askchásum VTI1B; **undercook s.t., cook s.t. raw, cook s.t. rare** askatúpuw VAIO; **undercook s.t. animate, cook s.t. animate raw** ask=cháseew VTA; **be undercooked** aska=túpuw VAI **The fish is undercooked.** 'Askatúpuw namées.'; **be undercooked** askatúpuw VII **The meat is undercooked.** 'Askatúpuw wúyoos.'; **be undercooked** askchéepuw VAI.

**underneath** PREP **underneath** éekwii PC **He killed him from under the water.** 'Éekwii mbíng óonju-nihláawal.', **I put it underneath.** 'Éekwii ndáh=toon.'; **fall underneath something, lie underneath something** eekwih=téexiin VAI, alaamíixiin VAI, alaamih=téexiin VAI, alaamíixun VII; **put s.o. underneath something** eekwíixŭ=meew VTA; **put s.t. underneath something** alaamíixtoow VTI2; **put s.t. underneath something** eekwíixtoow VTI2; **wear s.t. underneath something else** eekwawéeheew VAIO.

**undershirt** N **wear an undershirt** alaamheembtáhŭmeew VAI.

**understand** VI nohtáasuw VAI, nóhta=meew VAI.

**understand** VT **understand s.o.** nóhta=weew VTA; **understand s.t.** nóhtam VTI1A; **be understood** nohtáakwat VII, nohtáakwsuw VAI.

**undo** VT **unfasten s.o, unhook s.o., undo s.o.** kcháxkŭneew VTA; **unfasten s.t., unhook s.t., undo s.t.** kcháxkŭnum VTI1B; **be undone** *(of items of clothing)* kchaxkíixiin VAI, kchaxkíixun VII; **be undone, be unhooked** kchaxkŭnaháasuw VII; **come undone** kcháxkihl VAI, kchaxkíhleew VAI; **have an item of clothing undone** *(especially fly of pants)* kchax=kíixteew VAI; **leave s.o. undone, unhitch s.o.** kchaxkíixŭmeew VTA; **leave s.t. undone, unhitch s.t.** kchaxkíix=toow VTI2.

**undress** VT **undress s.o.** ktuneechpóo=leew VTA, sheexkalúneew VTA **She's just going to undress me again.**

'Kách wáak ápih shúkw nzheexka= lúnukw.'; **get undressed, take off one's clothes** ktunéechpuw VAI.
**uneven** ADJ **be lopsided, be uneven** piimchéeyeew VII, piimchéesuw VAI; **be uneven ground, be crooked ground** piimahkéeyeew VII.
**unevenly** ADV **cut s.t. animate lopsided, cut s.t. animate unevenly** píimsheew VTA; **cut s.t. lopsided, cut s.t. unevenly** píimshum VTI1B; **grow unevenly, grow crookedly, come up crooked** piimíikuw VAI; **grow unevenly, grow crookedly, come up crooked** piimíi= kun VII.
**unfasten** VT **unfasten s.o, unhook s.o., undo s.o.** kcháxkŭneew VTA; **unfasten s.t., unhook s.t., undo s.t.** kcháxkŭnum VTI1B.
**unhappy** ADJ **make s.o. unhappy** ma= tahteenamoohháaleew VTA, matahtee= namóoheew VAIO.
**unhitch** VT **leave s.o. undone, unhitch s.o.** kchaxkíixŭmeew VTA; **leave s.t. undone, unhitch s.t.** kchaxkíixtoow VTI2.
**unhook** VT **unfasten s.o, unhook s.o., undo s.o.** kcháxkŭneew VTA; **unfasten s.t., unhook s.t., undo s.t.** kcháxkŭnum VTI1B; **be undone, be unhooked** kchaxkŭnaháasuw VII.
**United States** N **big knife, the United States** xwanzhíikan NI, xwatanzhíi= kan NI.
**unload** VT **throw s.o. off, unload s.o.** kohpaaháaleew VTA; **throw s.t. off, unload s.t.** kohpáaheew VAIO; **unload s.o., take s.o. out of the water, take s.o. out of a vehicle, remove s.o.** kóhpŭneew VTA **I took the potatoes off (the stove).** 'Ngohpŭnáawak óhpŭnak.'; **unload s.t., take s.t. out of the water, take s.t. out of a vehicle** kóhpŭnum VTI1B.
**unlock** VT **unlock s.t.** tawíikwam VTI1A, tawíikwŭnum VTI1B; **unlock s.t. animate** tawiikwáaleew VTA; **be unlocked** tawiikwáasuw VAI, tawii= kwáasuw VII.
**unmarried** ADJ **be free, be unmarried, have no attachments** nihlaapéewuw VAI; **unmarried adult woman** kih= kaapéexkweew NA.
**unpleasant** ADJ **be an unpleasant morning** matáapan VII; **be drunk and unpleasant, do bad things while drunk, drink poison** *(especially to induce miscarriage)* machíisŭmuw VAI; **be unpleasant weather** níiskŭlaan VII; **have an unpleasant taste, taste bad** machiipóokwsuw VAI, machiipóo= kwan VII, machiipóokwat VII; **make a face, have an unpleasant face** chii= piingwéexiin VAI; **make an unpleasant smell** *(of one's cooking)* machii= matásŭmeew VAI.
**unripe** ADJ **be raw, be unripe** áskun VII.
**unsalted** ADJ **raw meat, unsalted meat** askéewakw NI.
**unsatisfactory** ADJ **make a mess, do a messy job, do dirty work, do unsatisfactory work** niiskalóhkeew VAI.
**unsettled** ADJ **lead an unsettled life, lead a restless life** sàkwáawsuw VAI.
**untie** VT **untie s.o., untie s.t. animate** lxúneew VTA; **untie s.t.** lxúnum VTI1B.
**until** ADV **long ago, until, emphatic** kúnj PC **You will come at four o'clock.** 'Néew-kŭlák-uch kúnj kpá.', **He came a while ago.** 'Kúnj wéeti péew.'
**unused** ADJ **have s.o. left over, have s.o. unused** píiwŭneew VTA; **have s.t. left over, have s.t. unused** píiwŭnum VTI1B.
**unwell** ADV **feel unwell, be sick** ma= tamalúsuw VAI.
**unwilling** ADJ **be unwilling to go, be reluctant to go** shiingóoxweew VAI; **be unwilling to work** shiingalóh= keew VAI.
**unwillingly** ADV **unwillingly, refuse to**

**do** shiing- PV *informal* **He wouldn't milk the cow.** 'Shíing-siiniikeew.', **They didn't want to leave.** 'Shíing-alumsúwak.'; **unwillingly, refuse to do** shiingi- PV **He wouldn't let them (do something).** 'Wshíingi-leelŭ=máawal.', **He wouldn't go with me.** 'Nzhíingi-wiichéewukw.'; **unwillingly, refuse to do** shiingu- PV *informal* **He wouldn't get in.** 'Shíingu-póosiiw.', **He wouldn't eat** 'Shíingu-míitsuw.'

**unwisely** ADV **spoil s.t., use up all of s.t., use up all of s.t. unwisely** ma=chíhtoow VTI2 **I spent all of my money.** 'Nŭmachíhtoon wéemi nzhulpúlum.'

**unworried** ADJ **be content, be unworried about anything, be unafraid** nalawáhkeew VAI.

**up** ADV **up, upwards, upstairs** wáh=kwung PC **I dreamt I climbed up.** 'Ndulóngwaam wáhkwung ndula=kóosi.'; **be thrown upwards, hit something and bounce, bounce** uspihtéexiin VAI; **be up, be in a raised position** uspíixiin VAI, uspíi=xun VII; **crawl up** uspíikwsuw VAI; **drag s.o. up** usptaachíhleew VTA; **drive up** uspchéhleew VAI; **go up, climb up** uspakóosuw VAI; **go up, come up, start to come up** uspíhleew VAI, uspíhleew VII; **have one's tail up** uspaalŭwéexiin VAI; **jump up, jump upwards** uspáakchehl VAI; **lift s.o. up, lift s.t. animate up** uspíixŭmeew VTA; **lift s.o. up, make s.o. go up** *(using the hands)* úspŭneew VTA; **lift s.t. up** uspíixtoow VTI2; **lift s.t. up, make s.t. go up** *(using the hands)* úspŭnum VTI1B; **lift up one's head** uspoh=kwéhleew VAI; **put one's leg up, raise one's legs** uspkáateew VAI; **raise one's head, look up** uspóh=kweew VAI; **raise one's legs up, have one's legs raised up** uspkaatéexiin VAI; **raise s.t. up, lift s.t. up** *(using a tool or instrument)* uspáhkhwam VTI1A; **sit with one's legs up, raise one's legs while sitting** uspkaatée=puw VAI, uspkaatéewapuw VAI; **stick one's lips up, have one's lips sticking out** uspsheetóonayeew VAI.

**uphill** ADV **go uphill** kwtákwteew VAI; **go uphill** *(on a road)* uspaawúngeew VAI.

**uprooted** ADJ **be uprooted** *(especially of trees)* móonhookw VAI; **be uprooted by the wind** móonxookw VAI; **get uprooted and fall over** *(of trees)* moonáhkhookw VAI.

**upset** ADJ **be worried, be upset, be irritable, be restless** sákwsuw VAI; **have an upset stomach** *(especially from morning sickness)* machíilaweew VAI.

**upset** VI **upset** *(of boats)* kooxkáhleew VII; **upset, turn over** kooxkáaweew VII, kooxkáaweew VAI.

**upside down** ADV **be on inside out, be upside down** aapoochíixiin VAI, aa=poochíixun VII; **fall upside down** aa=loolihtéexiin VAI, aaloolihtéexun VII; **fall upside down** aapoochkwàlíhleew VAI; **hang s.o. upside down, hang s.t. animate upside down** aapoochkwàl=aapéhlaleew VTA; **hang s.t. upside down** aapoochkwàlaapéhlatoow VTI2; **hang upside down** aapoochkwàlaa=péhleew VII; **hang upside down** aa=poochkwàlaapéhleew VAI; **hit and turn s.o. upside down, hit and invert s.o.** aaloolihtéexŭmeew VTA; **hit and turn s.t. upside down, hit and invert s.t.** aaloolihtéextoow VTI2; **hold s.o. upside down** *(using the hands)* aapoochkwálŭneew VTA; **hold s.t. upside down** *(using the hands)* aapoochkwálŭnum VTI1B; **lie upside down** aapoochkwàlíixiin VAI, aa=poochkwàlíixun VII; **lie upside down, come to rest in an upside down position** aapoochkwàlihtéexiin VAI, aapoochkwàlihtéexun VII; **lie upside down, turn upside down, fall upside down** aapoochkwíhleew VAI; **put s.o. upside down** aaloolíixŭmeew VTA; **put s.o. upside down** *(using the hands)* aalóolŭneew VTA; **put s.t. on wrong side out, put s.t. upside down** aapoochíixtoow VTI2; **put s.t. upside down** aaloolíixtoow VTI2; **put s.t. upside down** *(using the hands)* aalóolŭnum VTI1B; **throw s.t. upside down** aalooláaheew VAIO, aapooch=kwàláaheew VAIO; **turn s.o. upside down** aapoochkwàlíixŭmeew VTA; **turn s.t. inside out, turn s.t. upside down** aapoochkwàlíixtoow VTI2.

**upstairs** ADV **up, upwards, upstairs** wáhkwung PC **I dreamt I climbed up.** 'Ndulóngwaam wáhkwung ndul=akóosi.'

**upwards** ADV **up, upwards, upstairs** wáhkwung PC **I dreamt I climbed up.** 'Ndulóngwaam wáhkwung ndul=akóosi.'

**urge on** VT **urge s.o. on** kunjchíimeew VTA *especially to horses.*

**urinate** VI shkíiw VAI-S; **be unable to urinate** aalŭwíisheew VAI; **drink until one urinates** shàshkíisŭmuw VAI; **go and urinate** mawíisheew VAI; **stop urinating, cease urinating, quit urinating** ehkwíisheew VAI; **urinate a lot** amangíisheew VAI, xwíisheew VAI; **urinate in a new place** aanjíisheew VAI; **urinate in this direction, urinate to here** peechíisheew VAI; **urinate often** eewachíisheew VAI; **urinate while in motion, urinate while walking** shkíhleew VAI; **urinate while sitting** shkohkwéepuw VAI, shkápuw VAI; **urinate while sleeping** shkíin=gwaam VAI.

**urine** N shkíiwan NI.

**use** N **it's no use** aláw PC **There's no use in you calling me.** 'Aláw há yú koonjíimi.', **There's no use in my eating, I'm not hungry.** 'Aláw nŭmíitsi, máh ngatoopwíiwi.'

**use** VT **use s.t., wear s.t.** awéeheew VAIO; **use s.t. to come here, use s.t. to come in this direction** peetawée=heew VAIO; **use s.t. with something else** ahpawéeheew VOTI; **use s.t. with something, wear s.t. with something** naxpawéeheew VAIO; **be ready to use, be all set** kiishíixiin VAI, kii=shíixun VII **My bed is made.** 'Kii=shíixun ndapíinay.'; **drive a car, use a car** kaalhámeew VAI, ahtamoom=biilhámeew VAI; **go quickly using a cane** kshalaawhúnzuw VAI; **sail a boat, use a boat** amoxóolham VOTI1; **use a cane** alaawhúnzuw VAI; **use a plow, plow things, be plowing** laa=peexíikeew VAI; **use a roller** shii=pahkhwíikeew VAI; **use a wagon** taatpùniikanáhŭmeew VAI, xwataat=pùniikanáhŭmeew VAI; **use a washboard** siikhwíikeew VAI; **use blueing** oolihkpatíikeew VAI; **use one hand** ngwutoonáxkeew VAI, ngwutoonáx=kwiiw VAI-S, ngwutŭnaxkéexiin VAI; **use one leg** ngwutkaatéexiin VAI.

**use up** VT **use s.t. up** pohkwíhlatoow VTI2; **use s.t. up, use up all of s.t.** weemawéeheew VAIO; **use s.t. up, use up all of s.t., spend all of it** *(of money)* weemíhlatoow VTI2; **use up all of s.t. animate** weemíhlaleew VTA; **be all gone, be used up** weemíhleew VII; **spoil s.t., use up all of s.t., use up all of s.t. unwisely** machíhtoow VTI2 **I spent all of my money.** 'Nŭmachíh=toon wéemi nzhulpúlum.'

**useful** ADJ **be helpful, be handy, be useful** wŭlaapéenzuw VAI; **find s.o. useful** wŭlíhlaleew VTA; **find s.o. useful, find s.t. animate useful, be useful to s.o.** laapéemeew VTA **He's useful to me.** 'Ndulaapéemaaw.', **I'm useful to him.** 'Ndulaapéemukw.'; **find s.t. useful, be useful to s.o.**

laapéendam VTI1A; **find s.t. useful** wŭlíhlatoow VTI2; **make oneself useful, be useful** laapéenzuw VAI **You should make yourself useful.** 'Kátaxáa -laapéenzi.', **Ira's useful now that he's older.** 'Ira kwáy laapéen=zuw éel-alúwi-xwukíiluk.'; **think that s.t. is handy, find s.t. handy, think that s.t. is useful, find s.t. useful** wŭlaapéendam VTI1A **My medicine is good for me.** 'Noolaapéenda=mun noochapíhkum.'

# V

**value** N **have a certain value, cost a certain amount** láawatuw VII, láawa=tuw VAI.

**various** ADJ **variously, various places** msu- PV *informal* **It lies all over.** 'Msú-líixun.', **But they were always fighting, and this girl would always go all over, she was always going away.** 'Shúkw ngúmee màmatahkée=wak, wáak wá oxkwéesus ngúmee músu-áan, àhalúmsuw.'; **fidget, sit in various ways** msú-lápuw VAI; **fly in various directions, drive in various directions, go in various directions, fly, drive** msíhleew VAI; **knock s.t. around, bounce s.t., hit s.t. various ways** msihtéehum VTI1B; **write in various places, write all over** msee=khíikeew VAI.

**vehicle** N **come down, descend, get out of a vehicle** níixiiw VAI-S; **disembark, get out of a vehicle** kóhpiiw VAI-S; **get on board a vehicle** póosiiw VAI-S; **unload s.t., take s.t. out of the water, take s.t. out of a vehicle** kóh=pŭnum VTI1B.

**very** ADV **big, very** kihchi- PV **There is a heavy frost.** 'Kíhchi-tóhpun.', **They are praying hard.** 'Kíhchi-pahta=máweewak.'; **big, very** kihchu- PV *informal* **They're painting them.** 'Kwíhchu-shoohŭmúnal.', **Everybody is cutting cordwood** 'Kíhchu-kaatxakhwátiin.'; **not very often, a few times** táatxun PC **I drank my medicine a few times.** 'Táatxun noochapíhkum nŭmúneen.', **I didn't go to town very often.** 'Ootéeneeng táatxun ndá.'; **not very, hardly at all** mánheel PC *followed by negative verb* **He hardly ever works.** 'Mánheel iiyalohkéewi.', **It's not a very nice day.** 'Mánheel wŭlahkaméewi.'; **very** móxa PC **He looks very young.** 'Móxa wuskiináakwsuw.', **It's much too big.** 'Móxa wsáamu-xwukíh=kwun.'; **very little, not a lot** cháach=xiish PC **I slept very little.** 'Cháach=xiish ngáwi.', **I didn't work a lot.** 'Cháachxiish ndalóhke.'; **very, extremely, intensely** shihshíikaanzh PC **A great big snake.** 'Shihshíikaanzh lúkih xwáchu-áxkook.', **I got really wet.** 'Shihshíikaanzh lúkih níiskpe.'; **very, extremely, intensely** shíi=kaanzh PC **She really made me mad.** 'Shíikaanzh lúkih nŭwiiníihukw.', **It really runs well.** 'Shíikaanzh lúkih wŭlíhleew.'; **very, intense, hard, difficult** ahwi- PV **It has a lot of salt on it.** 'Áhwi-shŭwaháasuw.'; **very, intense, hard, difficult** ahwu- PV *informal* **He has a hard time, he has bad luck.** 'Áhwu-líinam.', **He is getting enormously big.** 'Áhwu-wulíikuw.'; **very, intensely** kihkihchu- PV *informal* **The little one was really crying.** 'Kihkíhchu-lpákshuw.'; **very, many, a lot** xwéeli PC **You'll find lots of things.** 'Xwéeli kwéek kŭmóxkam.', **He always found plenty, it is said.** 'Xwéeli íin ngúmee kwéek móxkam.'; **very, many, a lot** xwéelu PC *informal* **She told her, "Look in the cup! He left me a lot of money."** 'Wtuláawal,

"Pŭnáh nú tiihíinjuw! Nùkatúmaakw xwéelu shúlpul."', **Now because you picked him up you'll always find lots of things.** 'Kwáy éel-náatŭnat ngúmee-uch xwéelu kwéek kŭmóx=kam.'; **be very angry, go into a rage** kihtanóongsuw VAI; **be very drunk** waníisŭmuw VAI; **be very sick** àhwa=málsuw VAI; **get angry very easily** ayaapŭwanóongsuw VAI; **look not very nice** lunŭwiináakwat VII, lunŭ=wiináakwsuw VAI **My car doesn't look very nice.** 'Lunŭwiináakwsuw ngáalum.'

**vest** N **jacket, corset, vest** chékut NI.

**view** N **like looking at things, enjoy the view** wiingatawáapuw VAI.

**vigorously** ADV **fight vigourously, have a big fight** kihtatáhkeew VAI.

**village** N **middle of the town, middle of the village** laawootéenay PC **It's there in the middle of town.** 'Laa=wootéenay áhte.'

**vinegar** N shŭwáapoow NI.

**violin** N pŭyóol NI; **play the violin** pŭ=yoolhámeew VAI.

**visible** ADJ **be visible, be born** míhta=puw VAI; **be visible from here** pee=taapamúkwat VII, peetaapamúkwsuw VAI.

**visit** VI ootéewuw VAI; **come here to visit, come here visiting** peetootée=wuw VAI; **visit a certain place** loo=téewuw VAI; **visit s.o.** ooteewáaleew VTA, wtáxeew VTA.

**voice** N **voice** *(especially of the Lord)*, **rule** aaptoonáakan NI; **have a deep voice** xwaalakaxóoneew VAI; **have a soft voice, have a high pitched voice** *(diminutive)* changaalakaxoonéeshuw VAI; **talk in a loud voice, talk loudly** amangíixsuw VAI; **talk in a low voice, talk in a soft voice** *(diminutive)* achangiixshíishuw VAI.

**volume** N **extent, volume, amount** lukíhkwi PC **Later on.** 'Táa lukíh=kwi.', **How much does the table weigh?** 'Tá lukíhkwi póondakat eehundáxpwiing?'

**vomit** VI **throw up, vomit** mŭlándam VOTI1; **feel sick, feel like throwing up, feel like vomiting** wŭyakaskíh=leew VAI; **make s.o. nauseous, make s.o. throw up, make s.o. vomit** wŭ=yakaskíileew VTA; **the way one looks makes someone feel like throwing up, the way one looks makes some-one feel like vomiting** mŭlamanda=muwiináakwsuw VAI, wŭyakaskeelŭ=muwiináakwsuw VAI.

**vote** VI **vote, cast a vote** nvóotuw VAI **He's going to vote.** 'Máw-nvóotuw.'

**vote for** VT **vote for s.o.** nvootíhtaweew VTA.

# W

**wade** VI **wade in the water** pŭmaa=shóokeew VAI; **like to wade in the water** wihwiingaashóokeew VAI; **wade here and there in the water, wade around in the water, wade across** apaamaashóokeew VAI.

**wag** VT **wag one's tail** kwàkwchuk=waalŭwéhleew VAI.

**wage** N **earn money, earn a wage** pŭ=náham VOTI1.

**wagon** N taatpùníikan NA, xwataatpùn=íikan NA, xwataatpùníikan NI; **greasy wagon** shamaatpùníikan NA; **use a wagon** taatpùniikanáhŭmeew VAI, xwataatpùniikanáhŭmeew VAI.

**wail** VI **sing when not wanted, sing and get on someone's nerves, cry, wail** niiskaláamuw VAI.

**waist** N **hold s.o. tightly around the waist, have one's arms around s.t. animate** kaskatéeneew VTA.

**wait** VI **wait for s.o.** péeheew VTA; **wait for s.t.** péhtoow VTI2; **wait, be wait-**

ing péesuw VAI **I've been waiting for a long time.** 'Méhch ngwúnii-péesi.'; **wait to take off, wait to leave, be ready for action** kehtéexiin VAI.

**wake** N **be a wake going on** waaphátiin VAI *usually indefinite subject only* **There's going to be a wake.** 'Katá-waaphátiin.'

**wake up** VI tóhkiiw VAI-S, tohkíhleew VAI; **wake after a bad dream, wake up screaming, have a nightmare** akiiwóngxwiin VAI.

**wake up** VT **wake s.o. up** tohkíiheew VTA; **wake s.o. up** *(using the hands)* tóhkŭneew VTA; **wake s.o. up by calling to them** tohkíimeew VTA **Anything can wake you up.** 'Akwáawu kwéek áa ktohkíimkwun.'

**walk** N **have a fancy walk, walk fancily** wiilawóoxweew VAI.

**walk** VI **walk by, walk along; run** *(of equipment)* pŭmúsuw VAI; **be lame, walk with a limp** kwŭlukwíhleew VAI; **be so many of them walking** txatxooxwéewak VAI *usually plural; usually with number particle* **We were walking in sixes.** 'Ngwútaash ktundxatxooxwéhna'; **be tired from walking** shiiwóoxweew VAI; **defecate while walking** masktóoxweew VAI; **have a fancy walk, walk fancily** wiilawóoxweew VAI; **have difficulty while walking, have difficulty in travelling, be hard for one to travel** àhwóoxweew VAI; **urinate while in motion, urinate while walking** shkíhleew VAI; **walk across** aashŭ=wóoxweew VAI; **walk across the water** aashŭwaakchóoxwee VAI; **walk and make a loud noise** tiiwóoxweew VAI; **walk around something** wiiwŭ=nóoxweew VAI; **walk backward** ashahkchéewxeew VAI; **walk badly, have a hard time walking** amatóo=xweew VAI; **walk barefoot** mee=meexksiitéewxeew VAI; **walk bent over with one's behind sticking out** waakhootŭyéewxeew VAI; **walk bent over, walk stooped over** waakóo=xweew VAI; **walk by with one's backside exposed** mooshakiitŭ=yéewxeew VAI; **walk close by** peexŭ=wóoxweew VAI; **walk crookedly, walk on a crooked road** pàptukóo=xweew VAI; **walk directly to one's destination, go directly to one's destination, follow a good path in life** shaaxkóoxweew VAI; **walk fast, walk quickly** akushóoxweew VAI, akutakóoxweew VAI, kshóoxweew VAI; **walk here and there, walk about** apáamsuw VAI; **walk in a certain manner, walk in a certain direction** lóoxweew VAI; **walk in fives, be in groups of five** naalanatxoo=xwéewak VAI *usually plural;* **walk in groups of four** neewataxooxwéewak VAI *usually plural;* **walk in groups of two** niishataxooxwéewak VAI *usually plural;* **walk in the lead, walk in front, go ahead, walk ahead** sha=yéewxeew VAI **He likes to be ahead.** 'Wíhwiing-shayéewxeew.', **He always likes to go ahead.** 'Wíhwiing-shàshayéewxeew.'; **walk in the water** aashóokeew VAI, laashóokeew VAI; **walk in threes** nxatxooxwéewak VAI *usually plural;* **walk in twos, walk as a pair** niishooxwéewak VAI *usually plural;* **walk limply** piisŭlóoxweew VAI, apiisŭlóoxweew VAI; **walk often** eewatóoxweew VAI; **walk sideways** pŭmiich'chéewxeew VAI, pŭmiit=chéewxeew VAI; **walk slowly** *(diminutive)* chkawooxwéeshuw VAI; **walk slowly, be a slow walker** ashahwóo=xweew VAI; **walk slowly, walk in a relaxed fashion** wàwtamóoxweew VAI; **walk so far, go so far, go a certain distance** sahkóoxweew VAI **He went very far.** 'Móxa wáhlu sah=kóoxweew.'; **walk too much** wsaa=

móoxweew VAI; **walk with a limp, walk with one hip higher than the other** piimiitŭyéewxeew VAI; **walk with excrement on one's backside** *(indicating a certain attitude)* mwii=tŭyéewxeew VAI; **walk with one's belly sticking out, have one's belly sticking out as one walks** saaka=tayéewxeew VAI.

**Walker** N wáakul NA *man's name.*

**wallpaper** N **put up wallpaper** pam=biilhíikeew VAI.

**walnut** N ptukwíim NI; **walnut tree** ptukwiimíinzhuy NA.

**Walpole Island** N **Walpole Island, Ontario** wáalpool NI **I'm going to Walpole Island.** 'Waalpóolung ndá.'

**waltz** VI **waltz around, do a round dance** apaamiikwsíhleew VAI.

**want** VT **want s.o.** katáaleew VTA; **want s.t., need s.t.** katáatam VTI1A; **want to, intend** kata- PV **It's going to rain.** 'Katá-sóokŭlaan.', **I want to talk to him.** 'Ngáta-kihkŭlóolaaw.'; **be closely related to s.o., want to be related to s.o.** àhwaangóomeew VTA; **be hopeful, be expectant, want help** nahkéewsuw VAI; **be nosy, want to know things** katá-wéewsuw VAI, kíhkata-wéewsuw VAI; **be wanted, be needed** kataalkwúsuw VAI, katáalkwat VII; **being hopeful, hopefulness, wanting help** nahkeewsuwáakan NI; **condemn s.o., want s.o. to die, think s.o. incapable of doing something** kundéelŭmeew VTA; **feel in good humour, want to laugh** kŭlukeelúndam VOTI1; **want a share of an inheritance** *(especially someone who is not a member of the immediate family)* katá-waapéenzuw VAI; **want to fight s.o., want to kill s.o., want to compete with s.o.** katóonaleew VTA; **want to fight, want to compete** katoonáa=suw VAI.

**warm** ADJ **warm** kiishŭwii- PN **Warm house.** 'Kíishŭwii-wíikwahm.'; **be a warm night, be a mild night** wtáka=nii-tpíhkat VII; **be a warm room** kii=shŭwiikamíikat VII, kiishŭwúndeew VII; **be warm** *(of temperatures)* kíi=shŭweew VII; **be warm out, be mild out** wtákaneew VII; **be warm water** kiishŭwáapŭweew VII; **get warm** kiishŭwíhleew VAI, kiishŭwíhleew VII; **have a warm house** kiishŭwíikeew VAI; **have warm feet** kiishŭwusii=téexiin VAI, kiishŭwusíiteew VAI; **have warm feet** *(inside one's shoes)* kshuteewsiitéexiin VAI; **warm house** kiishŭwíikaan NI; **warm water** kii=shŭwúpuy NI.

**warm oneself** VT awásuw VAI.

**warm up** VT **heat s.t. animate up, warm s.t. animate up** kshúseew VTA; **heat s.t. up, warm s.t. up** kshúsum VTI1B.

**wart** N sahsanákwtiis NA.

**wary** ADJ **be afraid of s.o., be wary of s.o.** kxwéew VTA; **be wary of s.t.** nxáatam VTI1A; **watch for s.o., watch out for s.o., be wary of s.o.** nxáaleew VTA; **watch out for s.o., be wary of what may happen to s.o.** nxaawée=lŭmeew VTA; **watch out, be wary** nxáasuw VAI **Look out! It'll cut you!** 'Nxáasiil! Ktumshóokwun-uch.'

**wash** VT **wash s.o.** kshíixŭmeew VTA **I washed your car.** 'Ngushíixŭmaaw káalum.'; **wash s.t.** kshíixtoow VTI2; **wash the dishes** kshiixíinjŭweew VAI; **wash things, do the washing** kshiix=tíikeew VAI; **wash oneself** kshiixhún=zuw VAI, kshíixsuw VAI; **be washed** kshiixtáasuw VII; **wash one's ears** kshiixihtawákeew VAI; **wash one's elbows** kshiixíiskwaneew VAI; **wash one's face** ksíingweew VAI; **wash one's hair** kshiixóhkweew VAI; **wash one's hands** ksiilúnjeew VAI; **wash one's knees** kshiixiiktúkweew VAI; **wash one's legs** kshiixkáateew VAI;

**wash one's feet** kshiixsíiteew VAI; **wash people's ears** kshiixihtawak=eeníikeew VAI; **wash s.o.'s ears** kshii=xihtawakéeneew VTA; **wash s.o.'s face** ksiingwéeneew VTA; **wash s.o.'s feet** kshusiitéeneew VTA; **wash s.o.'s legs** kshiixkaatéeneew VTA; **wash s.o.'s feet** kshiixsiitéeneew VTA; **wash s.t. and make it fade, make s.t. fade by washing it** kaaspátoow VTI2; **be faded from washing** kaaspáteew VII; **wear s.t. animate out by washing it, wash s.t. animate away, remove s.t. animate by washing, wash s.t. animate completely, wash s.t. animate right out** mehtapáleew VTA **I washed away where the writing was.** 'Nŭ=mehtapálaaw éenda-leekháasiit.'; **wear s.t. out by washing it, wash s.t. completely, wash s.t. right out, wash s.t. away, remove s.t. by washing** mehtapátoow VTI2.

**washboard** N siikhwíikan NI; **use a washboard** siikhwíikeew VAI.

**washing machine** N kehkshiixtíikan NI, kehkshiixtíikeeng VII.

**waste** VT **waste s.t.** mayakíhtoow VTI2, amayakíhtoow VTI2, mayakawéeheew VAIO **He's using the car for no good reason.** 'Màmayakaweehéenal ahta=moombíilal.'; **waste s.t. animate** amayakíiheew VTA; **be wasted light** niiskáasŭleew VII **The light was left on overnight.** 'Ngwútii-tpóhkwe niiskáasŭle.'

**wasteful** ADJ **be wasteful** amayakúsuw VAI, mayáksuw VAI.

**watch** N wách NA.

**watch** VI **watch for s.o., watch out for s.o., be wary of s.o.** nxáaleew VTA; **watch s.o., watch for s.o., watch out for s.o.** saakíiheew VTA; **watch s.t., watch for s.t., watch out for s.t.** saakíhtoow VTI2 **He watches everything.** 'Wŭníhtaa- wéemi kwéek -saakíhtoon.'; **watch out, be wary** nxáasuw VAI **Look out! It'll cut you!** 'Nxáasiil! Ktumshóokwun-uch.'

**water** N mbúy NI; **ocean, sea, salt water** shŭwánpuy NI; **salt water** shii=wangáapoow NI; **scoop, dipper, something used to dip for water** anz'híikan NI; **spring well, cold water** thupéekw NI; **add water to s.t.** *(to make a drink or medicine)* wŭlupée=num VTI1B **I want to make a drink.** 'Ngáta-wŭlupéenŭmun.'; **be a flood, be a lot of water lying around** kaanzhahkwíixun VII; **be a lot of water** xwéelpeew VII; **be a lot of water** *(as in a puddle or ditch)* xwúpeew VII; **be a lot of water, be a large amount of water** xwáapŭweew VII; **be clear water, be good water** wŭ=lupéekat VII; **be cold water** thupéekat VII, tháapŭweew VII; **be covered over with water** wanúpeew VAI, wanúpeew VII; **be covered with water** psúnd=peew VII, psúndpeew VAI; **be deep water** kwŭnupéekat VII, kwŭnúpeew VII, xwupéekat VII; **be dirty water** niiskpéekat VII; **be full of water, be full of liquids** wchúwpeew VII **The creeks are full of water.** 'Shii=póosh'shal weewchuwpéewal.'; **be full of water, be full of liquids** wchúwpeew VAI; **be high water** kihtahkwíixun VII; **be high water, be deep water, be a flood, be flooding** xwahkwíixun VII; **be hot water** kshupéeteew VII, kshuteewáapŭweew VII; **be muddy water** asiiskŭwáapŭ=weew VII; **be rapidly moving water** kshupéhleew VII; **be shallow water** chaachxupeekachúshuw VII, taatxup=éekat VII; **be still water** kŭlampéekat VII, kŭlampéexun VII; **be warm water** kiishŭwáapŭweew VII; **be water flowing, have water form** *(as on sour milk)* mbuyíhleew VII; **be water in a puddle** kxupéexun VII; **be water flowing, flow** *(of water)* nanpuyíhleew

VII; **be weak from being in the water** shawúpeew VAI; **bring water in this direction, bring water towards the speaker** peethúpeew VAI; **chase s.o. into the water** chooxpwshíiheew VTA; **chase s.o. into the water, drive s.o. into the water** kamukwshíiheew VTA; **chase s.o. out of the water** chooxpwshíhkaweew VTA; **cold water** thúpuy NI; **come out** *(of water)* ktup=éhleew VII; **cover s.o. over with water, cover s.t. animate over with water** wanúpaleew VTA; **cover s.t. over with water** wanúpatoow VTI2; **cover s.t. with water** psúndpeew VAIO; **dirty water** níiskpuy NI; **drive through the water** kamukwchéhleew VAI; **fall in the water, get soaked, get immersed** kamukwíhleew VAI; **fall into water** chooxpwíhleew VAI; **fetch water, go after water, go to get liquor** naat=húpeew VAI; **fill s.t. to the brim with water** tpuskhwúpeew VAIO; **fill s.t. up with water, fill s.t. up with liquid** wchúwpeew VAIO; **flow by, flow along** *(of water)* pŭmaapŭwéhleew VII; **go across the water** kwáxkakeew VAI; **have one's feet in the water, soak one's feet** chooxpwsiitéexiin VAI; **have one's hand(s) in water, soak one's hand(s) in water** kamukwŭ=naxkéexiin VAI; **have one's legs in the water** kamukwkaatéexiin VAI; **heat s.t. up** *(of water)* kiishŭwaapŭ=wéesum VTI1A; **heat s.t. up** *(of water)* kiishŭwúpatoow VTI2; **jump in the water** chooxpwáakchehl VAI, kamuk=wáakchehl VAI, láakchehl VAI; **lake, edge of water** wsháype PC **I went out to the lake.** 'Wsháype nóom.'; **lay s.o. to soak in the water** kamukwíi=xŭmeew VTA; **lay s.t. to soak in the water** kamukwíixtoow VTI2; **lie immersed in the water, lie soaking in the water** kamukwíixiin VAI, kamuk=wíixun VII; **like to wade in the water** wihwiingaashóokeew VAI; **like water** wiingáapŭweew VAI; **paddle this way in the water** peethámeew VAI; **porridge made from water and flour rubbed together** wshaaxsáapaan NI; **put s.o. in the water** chóoxpwŭneew VTA; **put s.t. in the water** chóoxpwŭ=num VTI1A; **row across the water, paddle across the water** kwaxk=hámeew VAI; **run dry** *(of an amount of water)* sihkpéhleew VII; **shrink** *(in water)* wtúpeew VAI; **shrink s.t.** *(in water)* wtúpatoow VTI2; **shrink s.t. animate, shrink s.o.** *(in water)* wtúpaleew VTA; **sink, sink down in the water** kwtawíhleew VII, kwtaw=íhleew VAI; **soak in the water** ka=mukhwáasuw VAI, kamukhwáasuw VII; **soak one's feet in the water** kamukwsíiteew VAI; **soak one's feet in the water, have one's feet in the water** kamukwsiitéexiin VAI; **soak one's hand(s) in water, immerse one's hand(s) in water** kamukwŭ=náxkeew VAI; **soak one's legs in the water, put one's legs in the water** kamukwkáateew VAI; **soak s.o. in water** *(using the hands)* kamúkwŭneew VTA; **soak s.t. in the water** kamúk=hwam VTI1A; **soak s.t. in water** *(using the hands)* kamúkwŭnum VTI1B; **soften s.o. in water** wtakpáleew VTA; **soften s.t. in water** wtakpátoow VTI2; **spill, fall down, come down** *(of water)* sookpéhleew VII; **sprinkle s.o. with water, spray s.o. with water** sookalúndaweew VTA; **sprinkle s.t. with water, spray s.t. with water** sookalúndam VTI1A; **sprinkle things with water** sookalundíikeew VAI; **swim, be in swimming, be in the water, take a bath** thíixŭmuw VAI; **throw s.o. in the water, throw s.t. in the water** chooxpwáaheew VAIO; **throw s.t. in the water** kamukwáa=heew VAIO; **unload s.t., take s.t. out**

**of the water, take s.t. out of a vehicle** kóhpŭnum VTI1B; **wade here and there in the water, wade around in the water, wade across** apaamaa=shóokeew VAI; **wade in the water** pŭmaashóokeew VAI; **walk across the water** aashŭwaakchóoxwee VAI; **walk in the water** aashóokeew VAI, laa=shóokeew VAI; **warm water** kiishŭ=wúpuy NI.

**watermelon** N waatŭlamóokan NI.

**wave** VI **be waving, wave** tíhtpuw VAI; **shake s.t. back and forth, move s.t. back and forth, wave s.t. back and forth, rock s.t. back and forth** kwàkwchukwáaheew VAIO; **shake s.o. back and forth, move s.o. back and forth, wave s.o. back and forth, rock s.o. back and forth** kwàkw=chukwaaháaleew VTA; **wave at people, wave for people** tihtpihtáasuw VAI; **wave to s.o., wave at s.o.** tih=tpíhtaweew VTA.

**way** ADV **way over there, over there a considerable distance** yóolak PR.

**way** N **be in the way** kpíixiin VAI, kpíi=xun VII, kàkpíixiin VAI, kàkpíixun VII; **face in the wrong direction, face the wrong way** chanohkwéexiin VAI, chanohkwéexun VII; **hang down a long way** kwŭnaapéhleew VII; **have a long arm, reach a long way** kwŭnii=náxkeew VAI, kwŭniináxkeew VAI; **have fun, get into things in a playful way** kpucheewháasuw VAI; **sit the wrong way** chanohkwéepuw VAI; **stand in the way** kpiikáapawuw VAI.

**we** PR kiilóona PR *inclusive;* niilóona PR *exclusive.*

**weak** ADJ **be limp, be weak, be a weakling** piisŭlúsuw VAI; **be weak** shawéew VII **My hand is weak.** 'Shawéew náxk.'; **be weak** shawúsuw VAI; **be weak from being in the water** shawúpeew VAI; **fall due to be being weak, fall due to being limp** piisŭ=lihtéexiin VAI; **feel weak** piisŭlama=lúsuw VAI; **feel weak** shawamalúsuw VAI; **get weak, get shrivelled** piisŭ=líhleew VAI; **look weak** shawiináa=kwat VII, shawiináakwsuw VAI; **sound weak** piisŭlihtáakwat VII, piisŭlih=táakwsuw VAI.

**weakling** N **crybaby, weakling, coward** míikwul NA; **be a crybaby, be a weakling, be a coward** míikwŭluw VAI; **be limp, be weak, be a weakling** piisŭlúsuw VAI.

**wear** VT **use s.t., wear s.t.** awéeheew VAIO; **wear s.t.** akúw VAIO **My clothing.** 'Eekwŭyáaniil.', **His/her clothing.** 'Eekwíichiil.'; **wear s.t. around one's neck** wahkwéelŭnuw VAIO **She's got beads around her neck.** 'Wahkwéelŭnuw maanzháapŭyal.'; **wear s.t. inside out** aapootawéeheew VAIO; **wear s.t. underneath something else** eekwawéeheew VAIO; **wear something around the neck, wear a scarf, wear jewellery** wiilawah=kwéelŭnuw VAI; **wear something that has a long tail** kwŭníi-shkwún=ayeew VAI *usually of coats;* **wear new clothes** wúskakuw VAI; **be brightly coloured, wear bright colours** ktak=ŭléexiin VAI; **buy s.o. clothes to wear, get s.o. clothes to wear, dress s.o.** akwúneew VTA; **dress raggedly, wear ragged clothing** piikwshákuw VAI; **have a short dress on, wear a short dress** chahkhooshíishuw VAI; **shine brightly, be brilliant** *(especially light),* **wear bright colours** saapŭ=léexiin VAI; **use s.t. with something, wear s.t. with something** naxpawée=heew VAIO; **wear a black coat** nzúkii-koothámeew VAI; **wear a blouse** weesthámeew VAI, weysthámeew VAI; **wear a coat** koothámeew VAI; **wear a coat with a long tail** kwŭníi-shkwúnayii-koothámeew VAI; **wear a diaper** ahpchaawanáhŭmeew VAI, shaapwaalhóosuw VAI; **wear a hat** aakongweepíisuw VAI; **wear a jacket** chèkùthámeew VAI; **wear a long coat, have a long coat on** kwŭníi-koot=hámeew VAI; **wear a long dress, have a long dress on** kwŭnahóosuw VAI; **wear a necklace** laapxoonéexiin VAI, laapxóoneew VAI; **wear a ribbon** sìlkáhŭmeew VAI; **wear a ring** tihtŭ=yaakhámeew VAI; **wear a sheer dress, wear a transparent dress** shiikalah=óosuw VAI; **wear a shirt** heembtáhŭ=meew VAI; **wear a smock** shmak=hámeew VAI; **wear a white shirt, have a white shirt on** waaphéemb=teew VAI; **wear an extra shirt** pihta=wahéembteew VAI; **wear an undershirt** alaamheembtáhŭmeew VAI; **wear clean clothes** apíilakuw VAI; **wear dentures, wear false teeth** wiipiit=hámeew VAI; **wear earrings** sakaxee=hoonhámeew VAI, skaxéehuw VAI; **wear eyeglasses, wear glasses** wus=kiinjkwáhŭmeew VAI; **wear more than one coat** pihtawiikóoteew VAI; **wear more than one pair of pants** pihtawiipŭlóokeew VAI; **wear more than one pair of shoes, wear more than one layer of footwear, wear overshoes** pihtawahksúneew VAI; **wear more than one pair of socks** pihtawashíikaneew VAI.

**wear out** VI **wear out** mehchíhleew VII, mehchíhleew VAI.

**wear out** VT **wear s.t. out** mehchíhkam VTI1A; **wear s.t. out** *(of clothing)* mehsíhkam VTI1A; **wear s.t. out** mehtawéeheew VAIO; **wear s.t. animate out** mehchíhkaweew VTA; **wear s.t. animate out** *(of clothing)* meh=síhkaweew VTA; **wear s.t. animate out by washing it, wash s.t. animate away, remove s.t. animate by washing, wash s.t. animate completely, wash s.t. animate right out** mehta=páleew VTA **I washed away where the writing was.** 'Nŭmehtapálaaw éenda-leekháasiit.'; **wear s.t. out by washing it, wash s.t. completely, wash s.t. right out, wash s.t. away, remove s.t. by washing** mehtapát=oow VTI2; **be old, be worn out** xuw=íiyayuw VAI; **be old, be worn out** xuwíiyayuw VII.

**weasel** N manuchooxúmwush NA.

**weather** N **be a certain kind of weather, be a certain kind of day** láhka=meew VII **What's the weather like?** 'Thá láhkameew?'; **be bad weather** matáhkameew VII; **be dry weather** káahkeew VII; **be unpleasant weather** níiskŭlaan VII.

**Wednesday** N **be Wednesday** wéenzh=teew VII **She's going there on Wednesday.** 'Wéenzhteek náh éew.', **I went there last Wednesday.** 'Éenda-weenzhtéeke náh nóom.'; **be Wednesday** wéenzteew VII.

**weed** N machiixáskwal NI *usually plural,* matáskwal NI *usually plural;* **old grass, weeds** xuwáskwal NI *usually plural,* xuwiixáskwal NI *usually plural;* **be a lot of weeds** kaanzhás=kweew VII; **be a lot of weeds, be a lot of grass** miixaskwíhkeew VII; **cut weeds** *(with a scythe),* **cut with a scythe** tŭmaskhíikeew VAI; **in the middle of the high weeds** laawáskwe PC **He's walking in the middle of the high weeds.** 'Laawáskwe pŭmúsuw.', **I was sticking out of the weeds up to my neck.** 'Laawáskwe nóonj-saakxoonéexiin.'

**week** N **Sunday, week** *(with number prefix)* kúndŭween PC **One week.** 'Ngwút-kúndŭween.', **Two weeks.** 'Níish-kúndŭween.'; **be Sunday, be a week** kúndŭween VII **I went to church last Sunday.** 'Keendŭwéenge ndáap-maawéewi.', **I go to church on Sunday.** 'Kundŭwéenge nŭmáw-maawéewi.'; **be gone for so many**

**weeks** kundŭweewŭnáhkeew VAI *usually with number preverb* **He was gone for two weeks.** 'Níish-kundŭ=weewŭnáhkeew.', **You were gone for four weeks.** 'Kŭnéewu-kundŭwee=wŭnáhke.'

**weigh** VT **weigh a certain amount, have a certain weight** poondakúsuw VAI *usually with number particle* **They weigh four pounds.** 'Néewa poon=dakúsŭwak.'; **weigh a certain amount, have a certain weight** póondakat VII *usually with number particle* **How much does it weigh?** 'Kéexu póondakat?', **It weighs two pounds.** 'Níishu póondakat.'; **weigh s.o.** póondheew VTA; **weigh s.o., weigh s.t.** póondheew VAIO; **weigh s.t.** póondham VTI1A; **weigh things** poondhíikeew VAI; **be weighed** poondháasuw VAI, poondháasuw VII.

**weight** N **be heavy in weight** laanzhíh=kan VII, laanzhíhksuw VAI; **be light in weight** láangan VII, láangsuw VAI; **be lightweight looking, look light in weight** laangiináakwat VII, laangii=náakwsuw VAI; **weigh a certain amount, have a certain weight** poondakúsuw VAI *usually with number particle* **They weigh four pounds.** 'Néewa poondakúsŭwak.'; **weigh a certain amount, have a certain weight** póondakat VII *usually with number particle* **How much does it weigh?** 'Kéexu póondakat?', **It weighs two pounds.** 'Níishu póon=dakat.'

**well** ADV **be treated well** wŭlú-líinam VOTI1; **be well thought of** kaanzhee=lŭmúkwsuw VAI, xweelŭmúkwsuw VAI; **burn well** wíingŭleew VII, wŭlúl=eew VAI, wŭlúleew VII; **feel well** wŭ=lamalúsuw VAI; **grow big, grow well** wŭlíikuw VAI; **grow well** wŭlíikun VII; **live well** wŭláawsuw VAI; **put a harness on s.o., tie s.o up properly, tie s.o. up well** wŭlambíileew VTA; **run silently, whisper, run well** kwiish=kwihtáakwat VII, kwiishkwihtáakw=suw VAI; **run well** wŭlíhleew VAI, wŭlíhleew VII; **speak well** wŭlíixsuw VAI; **take good aim** *(with a gun)*, **throw well** wŭláaheew VAI; **talk well, say good things** awulaaptóoneew VAI; **think well of oneself, think highly of oneself** wŭleelúnzuw VAI; **think well of s.o., respect s.o.** wŭlíi-pŭ=náweew VTA; **throw well** nihtaawáa=heew VAI; **tie s.t. up properly, tie s.t. up well** wŭlámbtoow VTI2 **You bandaged it up where he got hurt.** 'Koolámbtoon éenda-kshihteexíin=ge.'; **treat s.o. well** wŭlacháaheew VTA; **treat s.o. well, be good to s.o.** wŭlú-líiheew VTA; **work well, do one's work correctly** nihtaawalóh=keew VAI; **write well, have good handwriting** awuleekhíikeew VAI.

**well** IJ **really, indeed, that's right, well** wŭlú PC **I didn't see him.** 'Wŭlú máh neewáawi.', **I can't understand him.** 'Wulú ndáalu-nóhtawaaw.'; **really, indeed, that's right, well** wŭlé PC **Are you sleepy?' 'That's right!** 'Kàkawóngxwiin? Wŭlé!'

**well** N sháakpuy NI; **spring well, cold water** thupéekw NI.

**well sweep** N ehanz'híikan NI.

**west** N éenda-wsíhkaang VII *where the sun sets.*

**wet** ADJ **be wet** skápeew VII, skápsuw VAI; **get wet** niiskpáteew VII, nísk=peew VAI, nískpeew VII; **sweat, be damp from heat, be wet from heat** skapachásuw VAI; **be damp from heat, be wet from heat** skapachát=eew VII; **be damp, be wet** skapíixiin VAI, skapíixun VII; **be damp, be wet, be soft** wtákeew VII **My washing's still damp.** 'Wtákeew íiyaach kee=shiixtàwáaniil.'; **be damp, be wet, be soft** wtáksuw VAI; **be soaking wet**

akwanóopeew VAI; **be soaking wet, be drenched, be limp from water** piisŭlúpeew VII, piisŭlúpeew VAI; **be somewhat wet** sàskápeew VII; **be wet grass** skapáskat VII, skapáskwat VII; **be wet ground** skapahkéeyeew VII; **get s.o. wet, make s.o. wet** niiskpál=eew VTA; **get s.t. wet, make s.t. wet** niiskpátoow VTI2; **have wet feet** skapsíiteew VAI; **have wet hair** skap=áandpeew VAI; **have wet shoes** skap=ahksúneew VAI; **wet shoe** skapáhksun NI; **be a wet day** skapeewáhkameew VII.

**what** PR **something, what, thing** kwéek PR **He likes to talk** 'Wíhwiing- kwéek -úw.' **What did you say?** 'Kwéek ksí?'; **something, what, thing** kwéekw PR **He wears old things.** 'Xúwu-kwéekwiil awéehe.', **Why are you mad at me?** 'Kwéekw há kóonj-mataangóomi?'

**when** PR **when** eenda- PV *followed by verb in conjunct order* **When my uncle was a young man he used to go with a girl.** 'Éenda- nzhiis -wuskii=lŭnuwíite, wihwiichéeweew ox=kwéessal.', **Right away when he felt for it he thought right away, "Now this must be it."** 'Sháa éenda-mihk=wchéenungu sháa liitéehe, "Yóon éet kwáy."'

**where** PR **where** eenda- PV *followed by verb in conjunct order* **He told his older brother, "Hang the lantern at the end of the creek so I'll know where to stop."** 'Xwánzal wtuláawal, "Liindawáakan-uch náh kŭwéhlalaan éenda-wíhkweek shiipóoshush wéenj-uch -weewíhtawaan táa neekíhla=yaan."', **Then they lived together in the forest where my uncle worked.** 'Nál ngwúteel wíikŭwak tá kóhpii nzhíis éenda-làlóhkeet.'

**while** CJ neeli- PV *followed by verb in conjunct order* **While she's alive.** 'Néeli-pŭmáawsiit.'; **while** weetŭmu- PV *followed by verb in the conjunct order* **While I was stoking the fire.** 'Wéetŭmu-poonxáyaan.', **I came while he was working.** 'Náh mbá wéetŭmu-alóhkeet.'

**while** N **a little while** náakeesh PC **After a while he'll jump up in a hurry.** 'Náakeesh-uch shúkw nál-uch pas=kwiipáhtoon.', **Wait for a while, don't get married right away.** 'Náakeesh-uch kpéesi, chíi sháa takwapŭwaaláahan.'; **for a while, after a while** náakee PC **I'm going to sleep for a while.** 'Náakee ngáwi.', **I stopped for a while and visited.** 'Náake nàkíhlaan ndootéewi.'; **in a while** naakaayéeke VII *usually only in conjunct order* **I'll come in a little while.** 'Naakaayéeke ápih náh mbá.', **We'll eat in a while.** 'Naakaayéeke ápih kŭmiitsíhna.'; **in a while** wéetu PC **I'm leaving soon.** 'Ápih wéetu ndalŭmúsi.'; **shortly, in a while, in a little while, soon, as soon as** méhch=xiish PC **I'd slap him in the face.** 'Méhchxiish áa mbwahwsúmawa.', **I'll be done cooking in a little while.** 'Méhchxiish-uch ngiishatúpwi.'; **shortly, in a while, in a little while, soon, as soon as** méȟtxii PC **As soon as I got through eating.** 'Méhtxii ngíish-míitsiin.', **He will come in a while.** 'Mehtxíiwu-ch páan.'

**whip** N shŭwíip NI.

**whip** VT **whip s.o.** seexeekawihtéeheew VTA, seexeekawíiheew VTA; **whip people** seexeekawíihŭweew VAI.

**whipporwhill** N wèkóoliis NA.

**whiskers** N **my beard, my whiskers** nihtóonay NAD; **beard, whiskers** nŭwihtóonay NAD; **black beard, black whiskers** nzukihtóonay NI; **have a beard, have a mustache, have whiskers** wihtóonayuw VAI; **have a long beard, have long whisk-**

**ers** kwŭnihtóonayeew VAI.

**whiskey** N wúshkii NI.

**whisper** VI kwiishkwtóonheew VAI; **run silently, whisper, run well** kwiish=kwihtáakwat VII, kwiishkwihtáakw=suw VAI.

**whistle** N pootaatíikanush NA.

**whistle** VI shíipŭweew VAI.

**whistle at** VT **whistle at s.o.** shiipŭ=wámeew VTA.

**White** ADJ **White man** shŭwánakw NA; **White woman** shŭwanakóxkweew NA; **be a White person** shŭwánakuw VAI; **be part White** shaashŭwánakuw VAI **He must be part White.** 'Sháxk éet shaashŭwánakuw.'; **become White, act like a White person** shŭwanakwíhleew VAI; **feel like a White person** shŭwanakwamalúsuw VAI; **feel that one is White, think that one is White** waapamálsuw VAI; **look like a White person** shŭwana=kwiináakwsuw VAI; **think of oneself as a White person** shŭwanakwee=lúnzuw VAI.

**white** ADJ **be white** wáapeew VII, wáap=suw VAI; **white** waapii- PN **White snow.** 'Wáapii-kóon.', **White shoe-lace.** 'Wáapii-aníixan.'; **white** waapii-PV **I painted it white.** 'Nŭwáapii-shóohŭmun.'; **white** waapu- PV *informal* **He feels that he is White.** 'Wáapu-làmalúsuw.', **It has white dots.** 'Awáapu-sàsápe'; **be light in colour** *(s.t. animate)*, **be a whitish colour, have a white tinge to it** waa=pŭléexiin VAI, waapŭléexun VII; **be white** waapaapamúkwat VII; **dye s.t. animate white, heat s.t. animate up and whiten it** *(when washing clothes)* waapcháseew VTA; **dye s.t. white, heat s.t. up and whiten it** *(when washing clothes)* waapchásum VTI1B; **have a grey beard, have a white beard** waapihtóonayeew VAI; **have white hair** waapóhkweew VAI; **turn white** waapíhleew VII; **wear a white shirt, have a white shirt on** waap=héembteew VAI; **white beard** waa=pihtóonay NI; **white bread, baker's bread** shŭwánakwii-apwáan NI, wáa=papwaan NI; **white feather** waapíi=kwan NA; **white grub** móoxwees NA; **white house** waapíikaan NI; **white thread** waapáhtakw NI.

**white bean** N waapaaláxkwsiit NI.

**whiten** VT **dye s.t. animate white, heat s.t. animate up and whiten it** *(when washing clothes)* waapcháseew VTA; **dye s.t. white, heat s.t. up and whiten it** *(when washing clothes)* waapchásum VTI1B.

**whites** N **see the whites of someone's eyes** waapeeliingwéexiin VAI.

**who** PR **who, someone, a person** awéen PR **Who could that be now?** 'Awéen éet há ná kwáy?', **Who's he going with?** 'Awéeniil há wiichéewe?'

**whole** ADJ **whole** msuchee- PV **I cooked them whole.** 'Nŭmúschee-ndapwíi=nak.'; **whole** msucheewu- PV **I boiled them whole.** 'Nŭmuschéewu-sah=kaláawak.'**be whole, all in one piece** msuchéeyeew VII; **be whole, be all in one piece** msuchéesuw VAI **The ap-ples are whole.** 'Msuchéesŭwak aapŭlúshak.'

**whoop** VI paapaakalóohuw VAI, pahpaa=kaláamuw VAI.

**whooping cough** N **have whooping cough** aapchíhleew VAI, àhaapchíh=leew VAI.

**wide** ADJ **be wide** akáameew VII, akáam=suw VAI, páaneew VII, wiipawúsuw VAI; **be a wide road** paanatéexun VII; **have a wide blade** paanalóowŭyeew VII; **have a wide mouth** paantoon=háasuw VAI; **have one's eyes wide open, have big eyes** xwaapakiin=gwéexiin VAI; **have one's hands open, have one's hands wide open** aapiilunjéexiin VAI, aapŭlunjéexiin

VAI; **have wide feet** paansíiteew VAI; **leave s.t. wide open** tawushéextoow VTI2; **wide shoe** paanáhksun NI.

**widow** N shiikóxkweew NA.

**widowed** ADJ **be widowed, be a widower** shiikóowuw VAI.

**widower** N **be widowed, be a widower** shiikóowuw VAI.

**wife** N **my wife** nŭmushúshum NAD; **my wife, my husband, my spouse** wii=taweemak VTA **His wife, her husband, his or her spouse.** 'Wiitawee=máachiil.', **Your wife, your husband, your spouse.** 'Wiitawéemat.'; **have two wives** pihpíhtawi-takwápuw VAI.

**wild** ADJ laaweewii- PN **Wild food.** 'Laawéewii-miichŭwáakan.'; **run around, run wild, run all over** wŭ=yakahtakíhleew VAI.

**wildcat** N **bobcat, wildcat** laaweewa=póoshiish NA.

**wilt** VI **be wilted** shawíipasuw VAI, sha=wíipateew VII.

**win** VI pŭmohkáasuw VAI.

**wind** N **be windy, be blowing** *(of the wind)* ksháxun VII; **be a cold wind** tháxun VII; **be a nice wind** wŭláxun VII; **be a north wind** loowanáxun VII; **be a strong wind** *(especially of tornados)* kíhtxun VII; **be blown along by the wind, be blown by by the wind** pŭmáxookw VAI, pŭmáxun VII; **be blown around by the wind, be spun around by the wind** túpxookw VAI, túpxun VII; **be blown back and forth by the wind** kwàkwchúkxookw VAI, kwàkwchúkxwun VII; **be blown back and forth by the wind, be shaken by the wind** apáwxookw VAI, apáwxun VII; **be blown in this direction by the wind, be blown here by the wind** péetxookw VAI; **be blown open by the wind,** tawáxookw VAI, tawáxun VII **The door was blown open by the wind.** 'Tawáxun kpáh=oon.'; **be blown over by the wind** áamxookw VAI, áamxun VII; **be blown over by the wind, be broken off by the wind, be severed by the wind** tŭmáxookw VAI, tŭmáxun VII; **be blown shut by the wind, be shut in by the wind, be shut out by the wind** kpáxookw VAI, kpáxun VII; **be collapsed by the wind** mŭlákwxun VII; **be dried by the wind, be dried out by the wind** péengxookw VAI, péengxwun VII; **be knocked over by the wind, be blown over by the wind** kawáxookw VAI, kawáxun VII; **be protected from the wind, be away from the wind** aakawáxun VII; **be turned by the wind, be blown by the wind** *(of something sheet-like)* aapéekxookw VAI *usually of pieces of paper;* **be uprooted by the wind** móonxookw VAI; **blow away in the wind, be blown away by the wind** alúmxookw VAI, alúmxun VII.

**wind** VT **turn s.t., screw s.t., wind s.t., drive s.t. in** *(of screws)* tùpáhkhwam VTI1A; **wind s.t. animate** *(as a clock)*, **crank s.t. animate** *(as a car)* tùp=áhkhweew VTA.

**winding** ADJ **be a winding road** waa=katéexun VII; **be crooked, be winding** pàptúkeew VII **The river is winding.** 'Pàptúkeew nú síipuw.'

**window** N eeheeshandéekan NA, eehee=shándeek NA; **screen window** shii=kaleeheeshandéekan NA.

**windy** ADJ **be windy, be blowing** *(of the wind)* ksháxun VII.

**wine** N wáyun NI **People are drinking wine.** 'Wáyun mŭnáhtiin.'

**wing** N **my wing, my armpit** lóngwan NID.

**wink** VI nànkwutíingweew VAI, **be winking** ngwutiingwéhleew VAI.

**wink at** VT **wink at s.o.** ngwutiingwéh=taweew VTA.

**winter** N **be winter** lóowan VII **I went there last winter.** 'Náh nóom lóo=

wanu.'; **during the winter** loowa=núwii PC; **live until winter, survive until winter** loowanámuw VAI; **winter dress** loowaneendakwíiwan NI.

**wipe** VT **wipe s.o. clean** *(with something held in the hand)* piiliikwáaleew VTA; **wipe s.t. clean** *(with something held in the hand)* piilíikwam VTI1A; **lick s.o., wipe s.t. animate with the mouth** káasameew VTA; **lick s.t., wipe s.t. with the mouth** kaasándam VTI1A; **wipe one's feet** kaassiitéexiin VAI; **wipe one's nose** kaascháaleew VAI; **cloth for wiping** kaas'híikan NI.

**wipe off** VT **dry s.o.** *(with a towel)*, **wipe s.o. off** *(with a towel)* peengwiikwáa=leew VTA; **dry s.t.** *(with a towel)*, **wipe s.t. off** *(with a towel)* peengwíi=kwam VTI1A; **wipe s.o. off** kaasii=kwáaleew VTA; **wipe s.o. off, wipe s.t. animate off** káas'heew VTA; **wipe s.t. off** kaasíikwam VTI1A; **wipe s.t. off** káas'ham VTI1A.

**wish** VI **as one likes, as one wishes** léhlapiit VAI *usually only in conjunct order* **He can do what he wants.** 'Léhlapiit lúnum.', **She's a widow, she can go where she likes.** 'Shii=kóowuw léhlapiit-uch kwáy éew.'

**witch** N kiimóoxweew NA; **try to be a witch** kaakiimooxwéewuw VAI.

**with** PREP **in addition, with something else** naxpii- PV **He ate it with something else.** 'Wŭnáxpii-míichiin.'; **use s.t. with something, wear s.t. with something** naxpawéeheew VAIO; **with, accompanying** wiichii- PV **I went to the service with someone.** 'Nŭwíi=chii-maawéewi.'; **eat s.o. with something** náxpameew VTA; **eat s.t. with something** naxpándam VTI1A.

**wolf** N wíixcheew NA; **'wolf,' man who chases after women** chíixkw NA.

**woman** N oxkwéew NA; **young woman** wuskóxkweew NA; **Indian woman, Delaware woman** lunaapéexkweew NA; **Ojibwe woman** wshiipŭwéex=kweew NA; **Oneida woman** meen=gwéexkweew NA; **White woman** shŭwanakóxkweew NA; **adult woman** kíhkwu-óxkweew NA; **woman schoolteacher** shehshkoolhaalŭweesóx=kweew NA; **bad woman, good for nothing woman, woman of poor character** matahóxkweew NA; **be a bad woman, be a good for nothing woman, be a woman of poor character** matahoxkwéewuw VAI; **be a woman who died of old age** áapchii-kihtoxkwéesuw VAI; **be an old woman, undergo menopause, undergo change of life** kihtoxkwéesuw VAI; **fat woman** wiisŭwóxkweew NA; **like women, be 'girl-crazy'** wiingox=kwéeweew VAI; **look for a woman** nootoxkwéeweew VAI; **look like an adult woman** oxkweewiináakwsuw VAI; **look like an old woman** kihtox=kweesŭwiináakwsuw VAI; **old woman** kihtóxkwees NA; **older single woman** kihkóxkweew NA; **unmarried adult woman** kihkaapéexkweew NA; **'wolf,' man who chases after women** chíixkw NA.

**wonder** VI **I wonder** wách PC **I wonder if he left.** 'Wách xéet néeka alúm=suw.', **I wonder if he's well.** 'Wách xéet wŭlamalúsuw.'; **I wonder** wéech PC **I wonder if he's going to town.** 'Wéech xéet lí ootéeneeng katá-éew.', **Would that be it?** 'Wéech xéet nú?'

**wonderful** ADJ **great, wonderful, amazing** kaanzhu- PV **Something wonderful happened.** 'Káanzhu-léew.'

**wood** N **wood, piece of wood** xwús NI; **cord wood** káatxakw NI; **decayed wood** aláxakw NI; **green wood** ásk=xakw NI; **long piece of wood** kwŭ=náxakw NI; **piece of dried wood** káahxakw NI, péengxwakw NI; **wooden cup, wooden dish** xwusíinjuw NI;

**be piled up neatly, be piled up nicely, be piled up properly** *(of something wood- or stick-like)* wŭlah=kweexíinook VAI *usually plural,* wŭ=lahkwéexŭnool VII *usually plural;* **bring wood inside** piindxákweew VAI; **chop up wood** piikháhkweew VAI; **come back from cutting wood** aapanáxeew VAI; **cut cordwood** kaat=xákhweew VAI; **cut splints, cut splints of wood for baskets** pòháhkweew VAI; **cut wood** manáxeew VAI; **fetch wood, go after wood** naatxákweew VAI; **pile s.t. over something** *(of something wood- or stick-like)* paa=lahkwéextoow VTI2; **pile up wood, pile things up** *(of something wood- or stick-like)* wŭlahkweextíikeew VAI; **pound on wood a lot** kaanzh'háh=kweew VAI; **put wood on the fire** póonxeew VAI **I put in too much green wood.** 'Noosáamu- askxákwal -póonxe.'; **split wood** pasaháhkweew VAI; **store s.t. animate, pile s.t. animate up** *(of something wood- or stick-like)* wŭlahkwéexŭmeew VTA *object usually plural;* **store s.t., pile s.t. up** *(of something wood- or stick-like)* wŭlahkwéextoow VTI2 *object usually plural.*

**wood chip** N wshéexakw NI; **gather wood chips** wsheexakwáheew VAI.

**woodpecker** N **red-headed woodpecker** meemaxkóhkwees NA.

**woodtick** N ashíikw NA.

**word** N **bring news, spread the word** peetaachíimuw VAI; **leave out words when one speaks** pohpohkwíixsuw VAI; **take a long time to say one's words** akwaaníixsuw VAI.

**work** N **do a lot of work, work a lot** tohpalóhkeew VAI; **do good work** wŭlalóhkeew VAI; **have an overwhelming amount of work to do** laawalóhkeew VAI; **make a mess, do a messy job, do dirty work, do unsatisfactory work** niiskalóhkeew VAI; **work well, do one's work correctly** nihtaawalóhkeew VAI.

**work** VI alóhkeew VAI; **work hard** àh=walóhkeew VAI; **work in a certain manner, work in a certain place, be engaged in a certain activity** lalóh=keew VAI **I've go nothing to do.** 'Ngwíila- kwéek -làlóhke.', **What are you doing?** 'Kwéek ktulalóh=ke?'; **work in a certain place, work there** talalóhkeew VAI; **work in a tobacco field, work picking tobacco** kwshahtéewheew VAI; **work in an apple orchard** aapŭlúsh'heew VAI; **work slowly** shàhwalóhkeew VAI; **work slowly, work to to suit oneself** wàwtámsuw VAI; **work together, help each other** takwundaméewak VAI; **work well, do one's work correctly** nihtaawalóhkeew VAI; **work all over** msalóhkeew VAI; **work along with others, work with others** wiitalóh=keew VAI; **work fast** kshalóhkeew VAI; **work oneself to death** aaptalóhkeew VAI **He went to prison for life.** 'Mawí-aaptalóhkeew.'; **be a bad worker, do bad deeds** amatalóhkeew VAI; **be smart, be industrious, like to work** lihlpúneew VAI; **be tired of working** peekalóhkeew VAI; **be unable to work, be unable to move, be unable to run, be out of order** aa=lŭwíhleew VII; **be unable to work, be unable to move, be unable to run, be out of order** aalŭwíhleew VAI; **be unwilling to work** shiingalóhkeew VAI; **be worked at, be farmed, be worked** *(of fields)* alohkehtáasuw VII; **come back from working** aapalóh=keew VAI; **do a lot of work, work a lot** tohpalóhkeew VAI; **do dangerous work, work regardless of the consequences or risks** laalxawalóhkeew VAI; **drive s.o. to death, work s.o. to death, work s.o. very hard** aapchíi=

naleew VTA; **go to work, go and work** mawalóhkeew VAI; **like to work** wiingalóhkeew VAI; **pick cherries, work in a cherry orchard** cheelíis'=heew VAI, chèlíis'heew VAI; **start working** nootalóhkeew VAI; **stop going, stop working** *(of machines)* eh=kwíhleew VII; **stop going, stop working** ehkwíhleew VAI; **stop working, break off working, quit before one is done** *(without necessarily having completed a task)* pohkwalóhkeew VAI.

**work at** VT **work at s.t.** alohkéhtam VTI1A.

**work for** VT **work for s.o.** alohkéhta=weew VTA.

**work with** VT **work with s.o.** niisha=lohkéemeew VTA.

**worker** N **servant, worker** alohkáakan NA.

**worm** N **fishworm** wéechiis NA.

**worry** VI **worry about s.o.** sàkwéelŭ=meew VTA, sàkwíiheew VTA; **worry about s.t.** sàkweelúndam VTI1A; **worry s.o., make s.o. worried** sàk=wiilawéeheew VTA; **be worried** sàk=wahtéenamuw VAI, sàkweelúndam VOTI1; **be worried, be upset, be irritable, be restless** sákwsuw VAI.

**worry-wart** N **bothersome person, worry-wart** sàkwáxktiis NA, sàkwáx=ktuy NA.

**worse** ADJ **change, take a turn for the worse, have one's medical condition worsen** aanjíhleew VAI; **make s.o.'s condition worse** máatŭneew VTA; **make s.t. worse** máatŭnum VTI1B.

**would** VI **should, would, can, could** áa PC **We (inclusive) should hide.** 'Kii=lóona áa kaatapíhna.', **I'd really like to go with you (plural).** 'Píish áa móxa kŭwíingu-wiicheewŭlóhmwa.'

**wrap** VT **wrap s.o. up** tùpháaleew VTA, wiixkweepíileew VTA; **wrap s.t. up** wiixkwéeptoow VTI2; **wrap s.t. animate around something, roll s.o. up, tie s.o. up** túpheew VTA; **wrap s.t. around something, roll s.t. up** túp=ham VTI1A; **wrap s.t. around, tie s.t. up** tùpámbtoow VTI2; **be wrapped up** wiixkweepíisuw VAI, wiixkweepíisuw VII; **have something wrapped around one's head, wrap one's head up** kpaandpeepíisuw VAI.

**wrapping paper** N **bandage, wrapping paper, material used for wrapping** wiixkweeptíikan NI.

**wreck** VT **drop and break s.t. animate, wreck s.t. animate** lookihtéexŭmeew VTA; **drop and break s.t., wreck s.t.** lookihtéextoow VTI2.

**wrestle** VI kwchiináhkeew VAI.

**wrestle** VT **wrestle s.o.** kwchíinaleew VTA.

**wrestler** N kwehkwchiináhkees NA.

**wriggle** VI wiimbíhleew VAI, wihwiimb=chéhleew VAI; **wriggle, go crookedly** pàptukiikwsíhleew VAI.

**wring out** VT **dry s.o., wring s.o. out** péengwŭneew VTA; **dry s.t., wring s.t. out** *(using the hands)* péengwŭ=num VTI1B.

**wrinkled** ADJ **be wrinkled** wchúleew VII **The clothes are wrinkled.** 'Wchul=éewal ehakwíingiil.'; **be wrinkled** wchúlsuw VAI **The mitts are wrinkled.** 'Wándak wchulsúwak.'; **be wrinkled, be bunched up** wchupŭ=lúsuw VAI; **be limp, be wrinkled** píisŭleew VII **My dress is wrinkled.** 'Píisŭleew nŭweendakwíiwan.'; **hang loosely, hang limply, hang wrinkled** piisŭlaapéhleew VII; **have a wrinkled face** pihpiischàlíingweew VAI, pihpii=sŭlíingweew VAI; **have a wrinkled face, have a contorted face** wchul=íingweew VAI; **have a wrinkled face, have a contorted face, pout, be in a temper, be discontented** *(as if about to cry)* wchuliingwéexiin VAI; **have a**

**wrinkled shirt** wchulhéembteew VAI; **have wrinkled hands** apiisŭlunáx= keew VAI, pihpiisŭlunáxkee VAI; **wrinkled dress** wchuleendakwíiwan NI.

**write** VI **write, write a letter** leekhíi= keew VAI; **write a letter, write a letter to here** peeteekhíikeew VAI; **write in various places, write all over** mseekhíikeew VAI; **write messily** niiskeekhíikeew VAI **I'm writing all over.** 'Wéemi táa ndúlu-niiskeek= híike.'; **write quickly** akusheekhíi= keew VAI; **write slowly** ashahweek= híikeew VAI; **write well, have good handwriting** awuleekhíikeew VAI; **be tired of writing** peekeekhíikeew VAI; **make a mistake in writing** chaneek= híikeew VAI; **be marked in a straight line, be written in a straight line** shaaxkeekháasuw VAI; **be written crookedly** pàptukeekháasuw VII; **make a straight line of things, write in a straight line** shaaxkeekhíikeew VAI.

**write** VT **write s.t. down** wŭléekham VTI1A; **write to s.o.** leekhámaweew VTA, peeteekhámaweew VTA; **write on s. t. animate** léekheew VTA; **write on s.t., write s.t. down** léekham VTI1A; **make a mark on s.o., make a mark on s.t. animate, write on s.t. animate** wŭléekheew VTA **I'm writing a letter.** 'Nooléekha pámbiil.'

**writing** N **have messy writing** amat= eekhíikeew VAI.

**wrong** ADJ **face in the wrong direction, face the wrong way** chanohkwéexiin VAI, chanohkwéexun VII; **have something wrong with the shape of one's mouth, be always saying bad things about people, have a sore mouth** matutóoneew VAI; **make a mistake in sewing s.t. animate, sew s.t. animate wrongly, sew s.t. animate in the wrong place** chaniikwáaleew VTA; **make a mistake in sewing s.t., sew s.t. wrongly, sew s.t. in the wrong place** chaníikwam VTI1A; **put s.t. animate on wrong side out, put s.t. animate on inside out, put s.o. upside down** aapoochíixŭmeew VTA; **put s.t. animate on wrongly** *(of clothing)*, **put on the wrong one of s.t. animate** chaníhkaweew VTA; **put s.t. on wrong side out, put s.t. upside down** aapoochíixtoow VTI2; **put s.t. on wrongly** *(of clothing)*, **put on the wrong one of s.t.** chaníhkam VTI1A; **put s.t. on wrongly, put on the wrong one of s.t.** *(of clothing)* chanawéeheew VAIO; **say the wrong thing** chanutóonheew VAI; **sew at the wrong place** chaniikwáakeew VAI; **sit the wrong way** chanohkwéepuw VAI; **turn s.o. to face in the wrong direction, turn s.o. to face the wrong way** chanohkwéexŭmeew VTA; **turn s.t. to face in the wrong direction, turn s.t. to face the wrong way** chanohkwéextoow VTI2.

**wrongly** ADV **make a mistake in putting s.t. animate on, put s.t. animate on wrongly** chaníixŭmeew VTA; **make a mistake in putting s.t. on, put s.t. on wrongly** chaníixtoow VTI2; **put s.t. animate on wrongly** *(of clothing)*, **put on the wrong one of s.t. animate** chaníhkaweew VTA; **put s.t. on wrongly** *(of clothing)*, **put on the wrong one of s.t.** chaníhkam VTI1A; **put s.t. on wrongly, put on the wrong one of s.t.** *(of clothing)* chanawéeheew VAIO.

# Y

**Yankee** N **Yankee, American** yángiis NA, yéengiis NA.

**yarn** N ashiikanáhtakw NI; **thick thread, yarn** kohpakáhtakw NI.

**yawn** VI tohtoongtóoneew VAI.
**year** N **be a year** katún VII **This year.** 'Kwáy kéetung.', **Next year.** 'Láapii katúnge.'; **be so many years of age** *(with number preverb)* katúm VAI **He is fifteen years old.** 'Naalanaaníhka txíi-katúm.'; **be so many years of age** *(with number preverb)* txú-katúm VAI **I'm ten years old.** 'Wíimbat ndúndxii-katúm.'
**yeast** N paasawiixíikan NI.
**yell** VI **yell, holler** kaanzhaláamuw VAI.
**yell at** VT **yell at s.o.** kaanzhalaamwíh=taweew VTA.
**yellow** ADJ **be yellow** wiisáaweew VII, wiisáawsuw VAI; **yellow** wiisaawii- PV **I painted them yellow.** 'Nŭwiisáawii-shoohŭmúnal.'; **yellow** wiisaawii- PN **Yellow beans.** 'Wiisáawii-maalaxk=wsíital.', **Yellow green beans.** 'Wii=sáawii-kàshayéemal.'; **be yellow coloured** wiisaawaapamúkwat VII, wii=saawaapamúkwsuw VAI; **be a yellowish colour, have a yellow tinge to it** wiisaawŭléexiin VAI, wiisaawŭléexun VII; **dye s.t. animate yellow, dye s.t. animate brown** wiisaawcháseew VTA; **dye s.t. yellow, dye s.t. brown** wiisaawchásum VTI1B; **turn reddish-brown, turn yellow** *(by heat)*, **be a ripened colour** *(of grain ready to harvest)* wiisaawxáteew VII; **turn reddish-brown, turn yellow, turn orange** *(by heat)* wiisaawxásuw VAI; **turn yellow, turn brown** wiisaawíh=leew VAI, wiisaawíhleew VII; **yellow bean** wiisáawii-maaláxkwsiit NI; **yellow thread** wiisaawáhtakw NI.
**yellow legs** N **yellow legs, shorebird** yehyaapéhlaash NA.
**yes** ADV **indeed, yes** píish PC **I told him but he still forgot.** 'Píish ndúlaan shukéhla wánsiin.', **You should hire him.** 'Píish áa ná káta-alóolaaw.'
**yesterday** N wŭláakwe PC **I bought some soup yesterday.** 'Wuláakwe nŭmáhlam kshíiteew.'
**yet** ADV **not yet** éeskwa PC *followed by negative verb* **I didn't get a letter yet.** 'Éeskwa létul nŭmushŭnáawi.', **I didn't eat yet.** 'Éeskwa nŭmiitsíi=wi.'; **still, yet** íiyaach PC **I'm still working.** 'Íiyaach ndalóhke.', **You're still sweating.** 'Íiyaach kúsh'si.'
**you** PR **you** kíi PR **It's your turn.** 'Kíi áashtee.'; **you** *(plural)* kiilóowa PR.
**young** ADJ **be new, be young** wúsksuw VAI, wúskun VII; **look new, look young** wuskiináakwat VII, wuskii=náakwsuw VAI; **new, young** wuskii- PN **A new book.** 'Wúskii-pámbiil.'; **young dog** wúskxum NA; **young horse** wuskehnayóongus NA; **young man** wuskíilŭnuw NA; **young pig, new pig** wuskóoshkoosh NA; **young tree** wuskíhtukw NA; **young woman** wuskóxkweew NA.
**younger** ADJ **my younger brother, my younger sister, my younger sibling** nxíisŭmus NAD.

# Z

**zigzag** ADJ **crawl zigzag** pàptukíikwsuw VAI; **run zigzag** pàptukahtakíhleew VAI; **swim zigzag** pàptukaashŭwíh=leew VAI.

# Bibliography


Anonymous. 1847. *Morning and evening prayers, the administration of the sacraments, and other rites and ceremonies of the church. According to the use of the United Church of England and Ireland.* London: Society for Promoting Christian Knowledge.

Baraga, Frederic. 1878. *A dictionary of the Otchipwe language, explained in English. A new edition by a missionary of the Oblates. Part I, English-Otchipwe. Part II, Otchipwe-English.* Montreal: Beauchemin and Valois.

Brinton, Daniel. 1888. Lenâpé conversations. *Journal of American Folklore* 1: 37-43.

Brinton, Daniel, and Albert Seqaqkind Anthony. 1888. *A Lenâpé-English dictionary.* Philadelphia: Historical Society of Pennsylvania.

Frantz, Donald G., and Norma Jean Russell. 1989. *Blackfoot dictionary of stems, roots, and affixes.* Toronto: University of Toronto Press.

Goddard, Ives. 1973. Delaware kinship terminology (with comparative notes). *Studies in Linguistics* 23: 39-56.

Goddard, Ives. 1974a. The Delaware language, past and present. In *A Delaware Indian symposium,* ed. Herbert C. Kraft. 103-10. Anthropological Series 4. Harrisburg: Pennsylvania Historical and Museum Commission.

Goddard, Ives. 1974b. Dutch loanwords in Delaware. In *A Delaware Indian symposium,* ed. Herbert C. Kraft, 153-60. Harrisburg: The Pennsylvania Historical and Museum Commission.

Goddard, Ives. 1978. Delaware. In *Handbook of North American Indians,* ed. Bruce Trigger, 212-39. Volume 15. Northeast. Washington, D.C.: Smithsonian Institution.

Goddard, Ives. 1979. *Delaware verbal morphology: A descriptive and comparative study.* Outstanding Dissertations in Linguistics. New York: Garland.

Goddard, Ives. 1982. The historical phonology of Munsee. *International Journal of American Linguistics* 48(1): 16-48.

Harrington, Mark R. 1908. Vestiges of material culture among the Canadian Delawares. *American Anthropologist* 10: 408-18.

Hewitt, J.N.B. 1896. Cosmologic legend. Text collected from John Armstrong at Cattaraugus, New York. October 8, 1896. National Anthropological Archives, manuscript 15. Smithsonian Institution, Washington.

Leavitt, Robert M., and David A. Francis, eds. 1984. *Kolusuwakonol: Peskoto-*

*muhkati-Wolastoqewi naka Ikolisomani Latuwewakon / Philip S. Lesourd's English and Passamaquoddy-Maliseet dictionary.* Fredericton, N.B.: University of New Brunswick.

Michelson, Truman. 1912. Notes and texts collected in Kansas. National Anthropological Archives, manuscript 2776. Smithsonian Institution, Washington.

Michelson, Truman. 1922. Notes collected at Moraviantown and Six Nations, Ontario. National Anthropological Archives, manuscript 1635. Smithsonian Institution, Washington.

Nichols, John D., and Earl Nyholm. 1979. *Ojibwewi-ikidowinan: An Ojibwe word resource book.* Occasional Publications in Minnesota Anthropology. St. Paul: Minnesota Archaeological Society.

Piggott, Glyne L., and Ann Grafstein. 1983. *An Ojibwa lexicon.* National Museum of Man Mercury Series, Canadian Ethnology Service, paper 90. Ottawa: National Museums of Canada.

Prince, John Dynely. 1900. Notes on the modern Minsi-Delaware. *American Journal of Philology* 21: 295-302.

Prince, John Dynely. 1902. A modern Delaware tale. *Proceedings of the American Philosophical Society* 41: 20-34.

Rhodes, Richard A. 1985. *Eastern Ojibwa-Chippewa-Ottawa dictionary.* Trends in Linguistics, documentation 3. Berlin: Mouton Publishers.

Speck, Frank. 1946. Bird nomenclature and song interpretation of the Canadian Delaware: An essay in ethno-ornithology. *Journal of the Washington Academy of Sciences* 36: 249-58.

Speck, Frank, and Jesse Moses. 1945. The last performance of the bear sacrifice ceremony. In *The celestial bear comes down to earth.* Ed. Frank Speck. Reading Public Museum and Art Gallery, Scientific Publications, no. 7, 60-2. Reading, Pennsylvania.

Wampum, John B., and H.C. Hogg. 1887. *Morning and evening prayer, the administration of the sacraments, and certain other rites and ceremonies of the Church of England; together with hymns.* London: Society for Promoting Christian Knowledge.

Zeisberger, David. 1887. *Zeisberger's Indian dictionary: English, German, Iroquois — the Onondaga, and Algonquian —the Delaware.* Ed. Ebenezer N. Horsford. Cambridge, Massachusetts: John Wilson.